New Dictionary of Scientific Biography

Published by special arrangement with the American Council of Learned Societies

The American Council of Learned Societies, organized in 1919 for the purpose of advancing the study of the humanities and of the humanistic aspects of the social sciences, is a nonprofit federation comprising thirty-three national scholarly groups. The Council represents the humanities in the United States in the International Union of Academies, provides fellowships and grants-in-aid, supports research-and-planning conferences and symposia, and sponsers special projects and scholarly publications.

MEMBER ORGANIZATIONS

American Philosophical Society, 1743
American Academy of Arts and Sciences, 1780
American Antiquarian Society, 1812
American Oriental Society, 1842
American Numismatic Society, 1858
American Philological Association, 1869
Archaeological Institute of America, 1879
Society of Biblical Literature, 1880
Modern Language Association of America, 1883
American Historical Association, 1884
American Economic Association, 1885
American Folklore Society, 1888
American Society of Church History, 1888
American Dialect Society, 1889
American Psychological Association, 1892
Association of American Law Schools, 1900
American Philosophical Association, 1900
American Schools of Oriental Research, 1900
American Anthropological Association, 1902
American Political Science Association, 1903
Bibliographical Society of America, 1904
Association of American Geographers, 1904
Hispanic Society of America, 1904
American Sociological Association, 1905
American Society of International Law, 1906
Organization of American Historians, 1907
American Academy of Religion, 1909
College Forum of the National Council of Teachers of English, 1911
Society for the Advancement of Scandinavian Study, 1911
College Art Association, 1912
National Communication Association, 1914
History of Science Society, 1924
Linguistic Society of America, 1924
Medieval Academy of America, 1925
American Association for the History of Medicine, 1925
American Musicological Society, 1934
Economic History Association, 1940

Society of Architectural Historians, 1940
Association for Asian Studies, 1941
American Society for Aesthetics, 1942
American Association for the Advancement of Slavic Studies, 1948
American Studies Association, 1950
Metaphysical Society of America, 1950
North American Conference on British Studies, 1950
American Society of Comparative Law, 1951
Renaissance Society of America, 1954
Society for Ethnomusicology, 1955
Society for French Historical Studies, 1956
International Center of Medieval Art, 1956
American Society for Legal History, 1956
American Society for Theatre Research, 1956
African Studies Association, 1957
Society for the History of Technology, 1958
Society for Cinema and Media Studies, 1959
American Comparative Literature Association, 1960
Law and Society Association, 1964
Middle East Studies Association of North America, 1966
Latin American Studies Association, 1966
Association for the Advancement of Baltic Studies, 1968
American Society for Eighteenth Century Studies, 1969
Association for Jewish Studies, 1969
Sixteenth Century Society and Conference, 1970
Society for American Music, 1975
Dictionary Society of North America, 1975
German Studies Association, 1976
American Society for Environmental History, 1976
Society for Music Theory, 1977
National Council on Public History, 1979
Society of Dance History Scholars, 1979

New Dictionary of Scientific Biography

VOLUME 7
TAMMES–ZYGMUND

Noretta Koertge
EDITOR IN CHIEF

CHARLES SCRIBNER'S SONS
An imprint of Thomson Gale, a part of The Thomson Corporation

THOMSON

GALE

Detroit • New York • San Francisco • New Haven, Conn. • Waterville, Maine • London

New Dictionary of Scientific Biography
Noretta Koertge

LIBRARY OF CONGRESS CATALOGING-IN-PUBLICATION DATA

New dictionary of scientific biography / Noretta Koertge, editor in chief.
    p. cm.
    Includes bibliographical references and index.
    ISBN 978-0-684-31320-7 (set : alk. paper)—ISBN 978-0-684-31321-4 (vol. 1 : alk. paper)—ISBN 978-0-684-31322-1 (vol. 2 : alk. paper)—ISBN 978-0-684-31323-8 (vol. 3 : alk. paper)—ISBN 978-0-684-31324-5 (vol. 4 : alk. paper)—ISBN 978-0-684-31325-2 (vol. 5 : alk. paper)—ISBN 978-0-684-31326-9 (vol. 6 : alk. paper)—ISBN 978-0-684-31327-6 (vol. 7 : alk. paper)—ISBN 978-0-684-31328-3 (vol. 8 : alk. paper)
    1. Scientists—Biography—Dictionaries. I. Koertge, Noretta.

Q141.N45 2008
509.2'2—dc22
[B]

2007031384

Editorial Board

T

TAMMES, JANTINA (*b*. Groningen, The Netherlands, 23 June 1871; *d*. Groningen, The Netherlands, 20 September 1947), *genetics, botany*.

Tammes demonstrated that the heredity of continuous characters can be explained within the framework of Mendelian genetics. Because she interpreted her experimental data more in probabilistic terms than others who were publishing on this topic around 1910, her work was the most convincing. In 1919 she became the first person in The Netherlands to occupy a chair in genetics. In addition, she was the second female professor in the country.

Early Years. Jantina, or Tine, Tammes was born in 1871 into a lower-middle-class family. In 1883 she entered a secondary school for girls. She later took private lessons in mathematics, physics, and chemistry, and in 1890 she enrolled at the University of Groningen, becoming one of only eleven women students. She was allowed to follow the lectures and practical courses, but her secondary-school diploma did not allow her to take the academic examinations. In 1892 she obtained a teacher's certificate in physics, chemistry, and cosmography and later, in 1897, one in botany, zoology, mineralogy, and geology. After a few years of teaching, she became, in 1897, the assistant of the professor of botany Jan Willem Moll and worked in the Botanical Laboratory in Groningen.

Moll used his friendship with Hugo De Vries to foster Tammes's scientific development. De Vries stimulated her emerging interest in evolution and heredity, and through Moll's mediation Tammes worked for a couple of months in De Vries's laboratory. However, this visit did not result in an appointment as assistant in the phytopathological laboratory in Amsterdam, because, according to De Vries, "a lady cannot be required to inspect the fields in all weathers" (Stamhuis, 1995, p. 501).

Because she had not taken an academic degree, Tammes could not obtain a doctorate. Moll, however, thought that her publication "Die Periodicität morphologischer Erscheinungen bei den Pflanzen" (The periodicity of morphological phenomena in plants) had the qualities of a doctoral dissertation, and he made various efforts—all unsuccessful at the time—to procure for her both an honorary doctorate and a position. The obstacles were, officially, her weak constitution (in the case of jobs at the Agricultural Experiment Station in Wageningen and the Deep-Sea Research Station in Den Helder but also in the case of a prestigious scholarship in the Dutch East Indies), and unofficially, her need to care for her aging parents. Her innate diffidence and fear of failure may also have played a role.

Mendel's Law for Continuous Characters. After 1899 she continued her research at the Botanical Laboratory in Groningen in an unpaid position. In 1903 she began research into cultivated flax. Moll managed to arrange that a prize contest, dedicated to the study of flax, was organized by the Hollandsche Maatschappij der Wetenschappen (Holland Society of Sciences) at Haarlem, and in May 1907 Tammes duly won the prize. The jury's assessment of her work was extremely positive. The report was published in the Society's proceedings under the title "Der Flachsstengel: Eine statistisch-anatomische Monographie" (The flax stalk: A statistical-anatomical monograph).

In the following years Tammes began to hybridize flax varieties. On the basis of this work she proved more convincingly than others, including the Swede Herman Nilsson-Ehle and the American E. M. East, that the heredity of continuous characters could be explained within the framework of Mendelian genetics by the multiple-factor hypothesis. Tammes's conclusion was more persuasive because she made well-argued claims concerning the number of hereditary factors that contributed to the values of the continuous characters involved. She was able to draw these conclusions because she interpreted her experimental data in more probabilistic terms than others who were publishing on this topic around 1910. Her work was, however, undervalued by her contemporaries as well as by historians, and her case can therefore be considered an example of the so-called "Matilda effect," the systematic undervaluation of the scientific achievements of women.

Professorship. In 1910 Moll recommended Tammes for an honorary doctorate at the University of Groningen, and she received the honorary degree in 1911. Earlier, Moll had proposed her appointment as an extraordinary professor in the theory of heredity and variability. His argument in support of a new chair in heredity was based on the rapid expansion of the field and its potential significance for agriculture. He also argued that in the Botanical Laboratory there was already available (as he said) "a person qualified in all respects," who moreover would probably be willing to accept the "not well-paid job of an Extraordinary Professor" (Stamhuis, 1995 p. 505). Although the university accepted Moll's proposal, the Minister of Internal Affairs did not approve the appointment, stating that the establishment of the new professorship did not seem an urgent matter.

In April 1912, as Moll's eyesight was deteriorating, Tammes began to supervise the practical courses in botany for students at the University of Groningen. In 1917 Moll's successor started a new campaign to get Tammes appointed as professor. This campaign resulted in her appointment in 1919 as extraordinary professor in variability and heredity. Tammes became the first person in The Netherlands to occupy a chair in genetics. She was also the second female professor in the country and the first at the University of Groningen. After her appointment she attended genetics conferences, visited other genetic institutions, developed relationships with other geneticists, and exchanged students, mainly with German institutions. Eight students gained their doctorate under her guidance. She was editor of *Genetica* from 1932 to 1943.

In her inaugural address as professor Tammes expressed her skepticism about the growing eugenic movement and its proposals to improve the human race.

She felt that not enough was known about the genetic constitution of humans to provide a scientific basis for eugenics. She expected more from improvement of the social and economic conditions in society. This, however, did not prevent her from being a member of the Nederlandsche Eugenetische Federatie (Dutch Eugenic Federation). Although Tammes cannot be characterized a feminist, she stood at the start of *Magna Pete*, the female student organization in Groningen, and was a member of the Dutch branch of the International Federation of University Women (IFUW). She retired in 1937 at the age of sixty-six and died in 1947.

BIBLIOGRAPHY

A bibliography of Tammes's publications appears in Genetica *22 (1941): 6–8. Seven of Tammes's articles are reprinted in the issue as well.*

WORKS BY TAMMES

"Die Periodicität Morphologischer Erscheinungen bei den Pflanzen." *Verhandelingen. Koninklijke Akademie van Wetenschappen te Amsterdam*, 2nd sec., 9, no. 5 (1903): 1–148.

"On the Influence of Nutrition on the Fluctuating Variability of Some Plants." *Proceedings of the Section of Science of the Koninklijke Akademie van Wetenschappen* 7 (1904): 398–411. Reprinted in *Genetica* 22 (1941): 9–24.

"Der Flachsstengel. Eine Statistisch-Anatomische Monographie." *Natuurkundige Verhandelingen Hollandsche Maatschappij van Wetenschappen* 3, vol. I. 4. Haarlem (1907): 1-285.

"Das Verhalten Fluktuierend Variierender Merkmale bei der Bastardierung." *Recueil des Travaux Botaniques Néerlandais* 8 (1911): 201–288. Reprinted in *Genetica* 22 (1941): 25–88

"Some Correlation Phenomena in Hybrids." *Proceedings of the Section of Science of the Koninklijke Akademie van Wetenschappen te Amsterdam* 15 (1912): 1004–1014. Reprinted in *Genetica* 22 (1941): 91–102.

"Die genotypische Zusammensetzung einiger Varietäten derselben Art und ihr genetischer Zusammenhang." *Recueil des Travaux Botaniques Néerlandais* 12 (1915): 217–277. Reprinted in *Genetica* 22 (1941): 115–161.

De Leer der Erffactoren en hare Toepassing op den Mensch. Inaugural address. Groningen: Wolters, 1919.

OTHER SOURCES

Jaarboek der Rijksuniversiteit te Groningen 1948. Groningen, Wolters, 1948. See pp. 62–63.

Schiemann, Elisabeth. "Tine Tammes zum Gedächtnis." *Die Züchter. Zeitschrift für theoretische und angewandte Genetik* 19, no. 7 (1949): 181–184.

Stamhuis, Ida H. "Statistiek en Waarschijnlijkheidsrekening in het Werk van Tine Tammes (1871–1947)." *Gewina* 15 (1992): 195–207.

———. "A Female Contribution to Early Genetics ... Tine Tammes and Mendel's Laws for Continuous Characters." *Journal of the History of Biology* 28 (1995): 495–531.

Westerdijk, Johanna. *Mededeelingen van de Nederlandsche Vereeniging van Vrouwen met Academische Opleiding* 8 (July 1937): 12–13; *ibidem* 14 (March 1948): 2–3.

Wilde, Inge de. *'Nieuwe Deelgenoten in de Wetenschap'. Vrouwelijke Studenten en Docenten aan de Rijksuniversiteit Groningen, 1871–1919.* Assen: Van Gorcum, 1998.

Ida H. Stamhuis

TANSLEY, SIR ARTHUR GEORGE

(*b.* London, England, 15 August 1871; *d.* Grantchester, England, 25 November 1955), *ecology, psychology.*

A man of twin professional preoccupations, Tansley was the most eminent British ecologist of his generation as well as an important early twentieth-century popularizer of Freudian psychoanalysis. His networking zeal led to the creation of several key organizations, including the British Ecological Society (BES), the world's first national society of its kind, and the Nature Conservancy, of which he was the first chairman. Tansley was an influential editor and also worked to clarify both psychological and ecological terminology. In 1935, he introduced a central and still relevant concept—the "ecosystem."

Early Influences. Tansley was the only son and youngest child of Amelia Lawrence and George Tansley. George had a lucrative business organizing society functions, and, after early retirement, he devoted his full energies to voluntary teaching at the Working Man's College, where his real enthusiasm lay. Arthur became enthralled by field botany as a young teenager due in part to the example set by the masters at his preparatory school at Worthing who were avid field naturalists. His botanical library began to grow at this time and included Edwin Lee's *Botany of the Malvern Hills* and J. G. Baker's *Elementary Lessons in Botanical Geography.* From the age of fifteen, Arthur was educated (poorly, he judged) at Highgate School and, seeking better instruction, his father enrolled him in science classes at University College, London (UCL) in 1889. Here the botanist Francis Wall Oliver aroused Tansley's interest in ferns and bryophytes and would later share Tansley's excitement for the new subject of ecology. In 1890 Tansley entered Trinity College, Cambridge, where he studied botany, physiology, zoology, and geology and, as he recalled, took part in the "usual interminable discussions on the universe—on philosophy, psychology, religion, politics, art and sex" (Cameron, 1999, p. 6). An early extracurricular interest in psychology appears to have manifested in his character study and counsel of his friend, Bertrand Russell, with whom he worked on a student journal, *The Cambridge Observer.* During his final

year at Trinity, he assisted Oliver in teaching and research at UCL. Despite the challenges of this employment in addition to his Cambridge studies, he obtained a double first in the Natural Sciences Tripos in 1893–1894.

Tansley continued in the botany department at UCL for the next twelve years working closely with Oliver. Tansley taught himself German during this period and thus could read the 1896 German translation of Eugenius Warming's *Plantesamfund* and A. F. W. Schimper's 1898 *Pflanzen-Geographie auf Physiologischer Grundlage.* Tansley held that these books were foundational for plant ecology as they developed concepts of plant communities and detailed relations between plants, soils, and climates. An admirer of Herbert Spencer's scientific philosophy, Tansley also aided the elderly scholar by overseeing the sections on plant morphology and physiology in the revised 1899 edition of Spencer's *The Principles of Biology.* In 1900–1901 Tansley traveled to Ceylon, the Malaya Peninsula, and North Africa in the company of paleobotanist William Henry Lang. Tansley maintained a diary during this time, describing human, animal, and plant activity with insight and humor. He also corresponded with his former student, co-author, and future wife, Edith Chick. Edith was the daughter of a lace merchant, Samuel Chick, and her six well-educated sisters included Harriet Chick, a nutritionist who was later appointed a Dame in the Order of the British Empire (DBE) for her achievements. Tansley married Edith in 1903 and they had three daughters, Katharine, Margaret, and Helen, who were to become a physiologist, an architect, and an economist, respectively.

Plant Geography and the New Ecology. In 1906, Tansley returned to Cambridge on his appointment to a university lectureship in botany. His family took up residence at Grove Cottage in the nearby village of Grantchester. Tansley had by this time already demonstrated one of his key attributes: his gift for organizing and leading scientific enterprises, acting as catalyst in a group of like-minded enthusiasts. He was now editor of a botanical journal, *The New Phytologist,* begun in 1902 and funded by his private income. Besides providing, as he hoped, a "medium of easy communication" and discussion on all matters of botanical research and teaching, Tansley was able to recruit leading authors able to stimulate and direct research in the new areas of plant physiology, ecology, and genetics (Godwin, 1985, p. 2). Already a fellow of the Linnean Society, Tansley was pivotal in wedding the activities of naturalist societies to the interests of professional botanists in the national survey projects of the British Vegetation Committee, which he co-founded in 1904.

As the scope of this necessarily collaborative phytogeographical activity was broadened to include botanists from outside Britain, Tansley organized the first International Phytogeographical Excursion (IPE). Tansley indicated in *The New Phytologist* that his initiative attempted to redress the confusing situation in which "Workers in different countries use different names for the same thing and the same name for different things" (1911, p. 273). The main split was between continental plant sociology and Anglo-American plant ecology. The continental approach emphasized floristic composition with "association" as the central unit. The Americans and the British emphasized the dynamic nature of vegetation, the study of the process of vegetational change known as "plant succession," and the "formation" as the fundamental unit of analysis of which the "association" is only a stage in development. In order to create some consensus concerning the concepts and language of ecological plant geography, Tansley brought together leading plant geographers and other botanical experts from Europe and North America to explore together the vegetation of a particular host country. It was held first in the British Isles and the group (eleven distinguished guests from foreign countries and a varying number of regional experts) traveled for four weeks in the month of August 1911, ending up in Portsmouth for the meeting of the British Association.

The American ecologist Henry Chandler Cowles, who would host the second IPE in America in 1913, declared the IPE a great success, noting in *The Botanical Gazette* that "The chief result of this excursion has been to internationalize for all time the subject of plant geography, and to divest it of the provincialism which has hitherto too greatly characterized it" (1912, p. 348). To acquaint the non-British scientists with local vegetation, of which they knew virtually nothing, Tansley edited *Types of British Vegetation* (1911) for the IPE. The book was the first systematic description of British vegetation, and immediately found a larger home market besides the invited foreign botanists who received advance copies. Contributors included established scholars as well as emerging botanical workers such as Marietta Pallis, who had completed new research on the Norfolk Broads vegetation. The IPE became a thriving twentieth-century institution (the last excursion was held in Poland in 1991), meeting every two to four years in a different country, with its headquarters at the Geobotanical Institute of the Swiss Federal Institute of Technology in Zürich.

In 1913 the British Vegetation Committee became the British Ecological Society, the world's first ecological organization. Tansley was its first president and also acted as editor of the new society's *Journal of Ecology* from 1917 to 1938. In 1915, he was elected fellow of the Royal Society; this was an important honor for him, and in later years he would always add the letters "FRS" to his signature. Early proponents of ecology such as Tansley and the

American plant ecologists Cowles and Frederic Edward Clements were particularly attuned to the *dynamic* aspects of vegetation. This was in sharp contrast to static morphology and "descriptive" botany, with its emphasis on species lists. Clements, another member of the 1911 IPE, argued that the plant formation was a "complex organism" that developed progressively toward a single end point, the "climatic climax." His method stressed the compatibility of physiology and ecology, for he believed the structure and functions of the "complex organism" could be examined in the same way that physiology approached the individual organism. Tansley initially supported Clements's successional approach to vegetation as a shared endeavor, but over the next two decades would increasingly voice discomfort with Clements's choice of terminology, the organismic analogy and belief in the monoclimax.

Clementsian ecology emphasized that natural vegetation, progressing toward normal climax, existed in isolation from humans. Tansley asserted that in a country where humans have so extensively modified the vegetation, most of what the ecologist could study was seminatural. The country Tansley had in mind was his beloved England, and he had another name for these touched landscapes: "anthropogenic nature," which meant nature produced by man. The term recognized that the distinctive vegetation of the English countryside that he and his colleagues were working to survey, such as the fens, moors, heaths, and woodlands, often depended as much on the intervening hand of human beings as so-called "nature." From 1908 on, Tansley had begun to recognize and inspire the first research on biotic effects, those factors due to organisms, and when directly or indirectly due to human activity give rise to communities of semi-natural vegetation. In 1916, after Tansley was wounded in World War I, his research student Ernest Pickworth Farrow returned to Cambridge to complete one of these early studies, an investigation of biotic successions associated with rabbit attacks on the vegetation of Breckland. Another student, Alexander Stuart Watt, examined the effects of grazing on English woodlands. Unlike Clements, Tansley wanted to speak of many kinds of vegetation climaxes, including anthropogenic climaxes caused by fire, grazing, or by mowing. Such an appreciation of polyclimax implied that the semi-natural and disturbed or tended vegetation was to be given as much attention and value as the so-called "natural."

Eager to promote and properly teach the new ecology, Tansley used his editorial authority to agitate for change in university botany courses. The 1917 so-called "Manifesto" in *The New Phytologist* (signed by Tansley and Oliver amongst others) pleaded for a vitalized and practical curriculum, to be based on plant physiology and ecology alongside, rather than subordinate to, the currently dominant morphology. Tansley's ideas for reform were denounced as "Botanical Bolshevism" by Frederick Bower, the Regius Professor of botany at Glasgow, and had a similarly chilly reception in the Cambridge Botany School. As he complained to Clements in 1918, "Reactionary forces are pretty strong here, and it will be a hard struggle to get anything progressive done" (Golley, 1993, p. 208). An additional source of frustration may have been Tansley's ultimately unsuccessful attempt, beginning in late 1917, to create a Scientific Research Association for the promotion of pure research (an initiative supported by leading psychologists as well as ecologists). The SRA was dissolved in December 1919, the same month Tansley learned that his bid for the Sherardian Chair of botany at Oxford was unsuccessful.

Psychoanalysis and the New Psychology. However, even before 1917, Tansley was looking elsewhere than English botany schools or even the international ecology movement for intellectual direction. Tansley had been aware of developments in psychopathology before the war, but, by his own account, his knowledge owed more to conversation than careful study. His own former student Bernard Hart, who worked as a doctor in asylums near London, would often entertain Tansley and discuss with him the new discoveries. Hart's interests were in the psychology of insanity, the title of his phenomenally successful short book first published in 1912. Tansley would mention Sigmund Freud in his botany lectures and even shared proofs of Hart's book with undergraduates in his classes. Appreciative students included Pickworth Farrow, who would himself later publish work in both ecology and psychoanalysis and correspond with Freud. Another was E. Margaret Hume, a pioneer in the field of nutrition research. When war broke out and Tansley began service in London as a clerk in the Ministry of Munitions, his self-taught German now allowed him to read Freud's published works.

Tansley's crisis in career direction—botany or psychoanalysis?—began to develop at this time and culminated ten years later, when, at the age of fifty-five and having attained the pinnacle of a scientist in early twentieth-century Britain, he was hopelessly torn as to whether he should become a professional psychoanalyst or retain a central position in his chosen field of botany. As Tansley related, the instigating event was a dream. Occurring sometime around 1916, the dream and his own analysis of it impressed him so deeply that he resolved to read Freud's work, beginning with the *Traumdeutung*, and the *Drei Abhandlungen zur Sexualtheorie*, a book he found particularly exciting. In 1953, when asked to record for the Sigmund Freud Archives (later sited at the Library of Congress), his memories of his relationship with Freud and psychoanalysis, he wrote: "My interest in the whole subject was now thoroughly aroused, and after a good deal

of thought I determined to write my own picture of it as it shaped itself in my mind" (Cameron and Forrester, 1999, p. 69). This "picture" was *The New Psychology and Its Relation to Life*, a book Tansley published in June 1920. It was reprinted ten times in four years, in the first three years selling more than ten thousand copies in the United Kingdom, more than four thousand in the same period in the United States, and was translated into Swedish and German.

Tansley had caught the postwar wave of enthusiasm for Freudianism and produced one of the most celebrated surveys of the "new psychology" to date. It was an attempt, he said, to capture for the general reader the "biological" view of the mind with the concepts taken from the work of "the great modern psychopathologists, Professor Freud and Dr. [Carl Gustav] Jung" (p. 6). Tansley stressed the immense influence of the doctrine of evolution that was shaping the study of animals and plants, but also investigations into the human mind. In this book Tansley, without attributing it to himself, offered a somewhat censored version of his own dream as a good example of dreams about sexual relations: "the man with a rifle surrounded by savages and unable to break through them is a true poetic symbol of the man in conflict with the herd, which separates him from the object of desire" (p. 131). This dream, Tansley's submission to the Freud Archives made clear, was one of the major turning points in his life; as he interpreted it, he, a married man, had fallen in love with a student. But this conflict seemed to be supplanted by another: from the dream came his interest in psychoanalysis, a serious new rival for his long-time beloved, ecology (Cameron and Forrester, 1999, p. 89).

The bestseller received generally admiring reviews from leading commentators in several countries, including Ernest Jones, Freud's "lieutenant" in England. It acquired a diverse readership, becoming, for instance, a textbook for the Psychological Section of the Croydon Natural History Society. In October 1920, Tansley was invited to speak before the British Society for the Study of Sex Psychology on one of his book's themes, "Freud's theory of sex from a biological point of view." On the whole, Tansley was disconcerted by the response to his book. Not only did it instigate critical correspondence with eminent figures, including old Cambridge colleagues from his undergraduate days, psychologist William McDougall and physician Walter Langdon-Brown, but he received many letters from strangers wanting expert help. Feeling he could not give adequate answers without further knowledge of psychoanalysis, Tansley asked Jones for an introduction to Freud so that he could undergo analysis. Freud, Jones, and others had already begun to follow Tansley's psychoanalytic progress with some interest and Freud arranged for Tansley to spend three months in Vienna, from the end of March to June 1922. Lodgings for Tansley were obtained in the house of the recently deceased famous botanist Julius Wiesner (whose lectures on plant physiology were familiar to Freud himself). In a letter to Jones, dated 6 April 1922, Freud wrote, "Tansley started analysis last Saturday. I find a charming man in him, a nice type of the English scientist. It might be a gain to win him over to our science at the loss of botany" (Cameron, 1999, p. 4).

Both Freud and Tansley seem to have agreed that the three months of analysis that ended in June 1922 was incomplete. Though intent on returning to Freud, it is probable that Tansley's duties kept him in Cambridge during the academic year 1922–1923. After his return to England, Tansley played a major role in a symposium on the relations of complex and sentiment for the July 1922 meeting of the British Psychological Society. In contrast to the positions taken by W. H. R. Rivers and Alexander Shand (whose language of "sentiments" was the home-grown English competitor with the vocabulary of "complexes"), Tansley argued that "complex" was a key connecting term for normal and abnormal psychology and should not be limited to the latter field. As he stressed here and later in a 1923 letter to Clements outlining his view of the central issues in the field of psychology: "The question of the applicability of Freudian method to the 'normal' mind is doubtless the crucial question." Along with the notion that all energy, both physical and psychical, tended towards a state of equilibrium, this focus on "normal" and "abnormal" provided conceptual links for his thinking in both psychology and ecology. As he explained to Clements, "The limiting conception of 'normality' is an abstraction—never seen in concrete form. We use the word 'normal' in practice to cover quite large deviations from a theoretic balanced mean, just as we do with species."

Despite his increasing involvement with psychology, Tansley founded the Cambridge Ecology Club in 1921 and published substantial works in botany, including *Elements of Plant Biology* in 1922, based on the lecture course he gave to first-year medical students, and *Practical Plant Ecology* in 1923, the key book of his generation for introducing plant ecology into schools. He also produced a co-edited volume *Aims and Methods in the Study of Vegetation* in 1926, which was based on a successional point of view and intended for practical use throughout the British Empire. In addition, he was president of the Botanical Section, British Association for the Advancement of Science in 1923, and spent part of the summer months doing research at Wicken Fen near Cambridge. This was a site of special scientific interest for Tansley and his young colleague Harry Godwin where their research on the effects of crop-taking was providing evidence for *plagioseres* (Tansley's term), deflections from the natural develop-

ment from waterlogged grounds to fen, the normal hydrosere.

But as Tansley commented to Clements, the "double pull" of psychology and ecology was "a considerable strain." In the late spring of 1923, Tansley made his decision and resigned from the Cambridge Botany School. His future seemed open as he wrote to Clements that summer, "if, as is quite possible, I become more and more absorbed in psychological research I may gradually drop plant ecology from sheer lack of time" (12 July 1923, Frederic E. Clements Papers, University of Wyoming). Tansley moved to Vienna with his wife and daughters in September of 1923; analysis with Freud resumed in late December, following Freud's operation for mouth cancer. After returning to London in May 1924, at which time Tansley was elected an associate member of the British Psychoanalytic Society, Tansley attended the Eighth International Psychoanalytic Congress in Salzburg. On Freud's recommendation, he took on a psychoanalytic case, to acquaint himself fully with the discipline, and on 7 October 1925, he was elected to full membership of the Society.

Tansley quickly developed psychoanalytic communities in at least two different milieus, both informal: one within Cambridge, a psychoanalytic discussion group consisting of physician John Rickman, Freud translator James Strachey, geophysicist Harold Jeffreys, medical student Lionel Penrose, and philosopher Frank Ramsey; and another connected with the field sciences, including Pickworth Farrow, Godwin and C. C. Fagg. Throughout the summer of 1925, Tansley also led a public polemic defending psychoanalysis in *The Nation* and *The Athenæum*. However, as the year passed, Tansley may have judged that as a non-medical biologist, his opportunities were beginning to appear limited in psychoanalytical circles. The international psychoanalytic movement was rapidly moving toward a system of education committees that marked the beginning of more strictly hierarchical institutions devoted to training professional and frequently medically qualified psychoanalysts. At the same time, Tansley's ecological work continued to be held in high regard, and in 1926, he accepted an invitation to re-apply for the Sherardian Chair of botany at Oxford. In Godwin's later judgment, the years 1923 to 1927 had been for Tansley years "in the wilderness so far at least as his relations to botanical science were concerned and especially those with British botanists. ... Not until the end of 1926 did he complete what Freud had forecast for him, 'the return to the mother subject,' ... He was elected in January 1927. Indecision was abandoned" (1957, p. 236).

Return to the Mother Subject. Tansley took up the post in October 1927, together with a fellowship at Magdalen College, although he continued to maintain his home in

Grantchester. He set to work modernizing teaching and research in botany at Oxford and promoting ecology as a practical pursuit with obvious utility for agriculture and forestry throughout the British Empire. Tansley remained a stalwart defender of psychoanalysis, publicly and in more private Oxford circles such as the Magdalen College Philosophy Club, and left a number of unpublished psychoanalytic papers, including an incomplete manuscript titled "The Historical Foundations of Psychoanalysis." Tansley continued to correspond with Freud and Freudian circles, but his main work of the 1930s was in the discipline of botany—and productive of a concept of central importance to its future development : the "ecosystem."

The concept emerged in a debate in the *Journal of Ecology* with Clements's South African disciple John Phillips, who was advocating Clementsian organismic concepts as well as the holistic philosophy of South Africa's elder statesman, General Jan Christiaan Smuts. In his 1935 article, "The Use and Abuse of Vegetational Concepts and Terms," Tansley contended that the organismal analogy for vegetation had been pushed too far, and in place of Clements's "complex organism" offered the term "ecosystem" (first suggested to him by his young Oxford colleague Arthur Roy Clapham) as the fundamental unit of ecological study. The ecosystem was an interacting, interdependent and dynamic system of organic and inorganic components, tending toward stable equilibrium. Vegetation succession was an instance in the universal process moving in the direction of integration and stability (climax), and ecosystems varied in their ability to resist forces of disintegration. The influences on Tansley's thinking have been detailed in terms of physics, psychoanalysis, politics, and philosophy. With the term *ecosystem* Tansley was addressing the profound question at the heart of his dispute with Clements and Phillips, "Is man part of nature or not?" (Tansley, 1935, p. 303).

Clements had come to agree that humans could be understood as part of biotic communities, but maintained what Tansley saw as an artificial distinction between low-impact tribal groups and destructive "modern" man. The term *ecosystem* would integrate the work on anthropogenic nature: within it the human was to be regarded as the most powerful biotic factor, "which increasingly upsets the equilibrium of preexisting ecosystems and eventually destroys them, at the same time forming new ones of a very different nature" (p. 303). For Tansley there was no difference in functional or moral terms between natural and man-made ecosystems. "We cannot confine ourselves to the so-called 'natural' entities and ignore the processes and expressions of vegetation now so abundantly provided us by the activities of man" (p. 304). The concept not only addressed past disputes but also suggested future research directions, such as the integration of plant and animal studies and a recognition of the myriad organic and inor-

Arthur Tansley. *Tansley in 1949 holding a fen orchid, in Newbridge Fen, County Wicklow, Ireland, during a meeting of the International Phytogeographical Excursion.* **COURTESY OF THE DEPARTMENT OF PLANT SCIENCES, UNIVERSITY OF CAMBRIDGE, U.K.**

ganic factors that constituted and affected a particular study area.

During the 1930s Tansley worked on expanding and revising his 1911 *Types*. In 1931, he handed over ownership and editorship of *The New Phytologist,* and in 1938, he finally gave up editing of the *Journal of Ecology,* one year after his retirement from Oxford. Eventually completed in 1939, *The British Islands and Their Vegetation,* his magnum opus, was a finely illustrated survey of more than 900 pages, culminating the phase of ecology that he had initiated. As the first major book to employ the ecosystem concept, it showed vegetational communities to be the result of the interacting processes of plants, climates, and soils in a dynamic landscape alive with human and animal activities. Summarizing the work of a generation of researchers that he had so vigorously promoted, the book instantly became the standard reference, and in 1941 it was awarded the Linnean Gold Medal.

Contributions to Nature Conservation, Mind, and Life. There is little to suggest that Tansley saw ecology as an environmentalist alternative to mainstream science. Yet he did much in his time to advocate for landscape conservation. This was in contrast to a "hands-off" preservationist approach, which he understood as irresponsible and naive. For Tansley, intervention over the long term had largely created nature as it existed in England. Since 1914 he had been a member of the Society for the Promotion of Nature Reserves: in his experience, a rigid preservation of a nature reserve in its so-called natural state with no management such as cutting was simply a fast way to eradicate desirable species.

In 1942 he took a guiding role in the planning of postwar nature conservation which led to the foundation of the Nature Conservancy in 1949, of which he was the first chairman. To help achieve this success, Tansley had published a semi-popular publication in 1945, *Our Heritage of Wild Nature: A Plea for Nature Conservation.* Within the conservancy, Tansley's ideas about the need for intervention in plant communities not only helped to establish the ecologist's authority and a network of reserves after the war, but were also compatible with progressive, postwar planning intentions. With significant government backing, the nature reserve was recast as an element of state responsibility with the ecologist as its expert manager.

In addition to this activity, Tansley was heavily involved (as president from 1947 to 1953) in the Council for the Promotion of Field Studies (later the Field Studies Council), a voluntary organization which maintained resident field centers in locations of ecological and geological significance (such as Flatford Mill in Suffolk) where student interests in nature could be stimulated. To this effort he also contributed a volume entitled *Oaks and Oak Woods* (1952), designed with the users of the field centers in mind. Such an interest in decentralized education and the nurturing of "scientific curiosity" resonated with his active joint leadership (with John Baker and Michael Polanyi) of the Society for Freedom in Science, an organization which, from 1940, fought strongly against the central planning of scientific research. In this, yet another of the new organizations that he had helped to found over his lifetime, Tansley brought to bear his views on psychology in a pamphlet, "The Psychological Connexion of Two Basic Principles of the SFS."

In 1942 he was asked to deliver the Herbert Spencer Lecture to the University of Oxford in which he spoke upon "The Values of Science to Humanity." In 1944 he was made an honorary fellow of Trinity College, Cambridge, and three years later he became an honorary member of the British Ecological Society. Tansley received his knighthood in 1950. In 1952, the year before he resigned from his chairmanship of the Nature Conservancy due to increasing deafness, Tansley completed his final book,

Mind and Life: An Essay in Simplification. True to its title, it was an overarching synthesis of the twin preoccupations of his professional career. Although it did not receive the acclaim of *The New Psychology*, the book was an eloquent testament to his concern with the place of the man in relation to nature and the place of nature within man. Employing the hydraulic metaphor, Tansley argued once again that all life, including mental life, was dominated by the need of the organism to discharge energy, thus aiming toward a stable state. Tansley carried the nineteenth-century concept of "equilibrium" into both his ecology and psychology, but he was modern (and more Freudian) in emphasizing the many factors of instability which ensure that this state of balance is rarely, if ever, attained.

Godwin related that Tansley, when asked at an Oxford gathering "to name the man who, since the birth of Christ, would prove to have had the most lasting influence upon the world, he unhesitatingly chose Freud" (1977, p. 25). In 1941, Tansley had provided the Royal Society with an obituary for Freud and Godwin perceptively noted that nearly all of the gifts that Tansley described in Freud were ones that he "unconsciously acknowledged" as attributes they held in common: "full of attractive ironic humour and with a very pungent wit" and "free from illusions about human nature" (Godwin, 1977, p. 25).

Tansley enjoyed fine living: wine lists sometimes followed species lists in his field notebooks. In appearance, Tansley was tall and slender: in photographs, he seems rarely to conceal the webbed fingers of his left hand and in later years, is often posed smoking a pipe. A memorial to Tansley is inscribed on a sarsen stone overlooking one of his favorite places in England, the magnificent yew wood of Kingley Vale in Sussex: "In the midst of this Nature Reserve which he brought into being this stone calls to memory Sir Arthur George Tansley, F.R.S., who during a long lifetime strove with success to widen the knowledge, to deepen the love and to safeguard the heritage of nature in the British Islands."

Tansley's papers are in several archives. The Plant Sciences Library of the University of Cambridge includes some of Tansley's correspondence and papers; the Archives of the British Psychoanalytical Society includes some correspondence; the Sigmund Freud Papers of the Library of Congress includes some of his papers; the American Heritage Center of the University of Wyoming includes some correspondence; the Natural History Museum (London) houses some correspondence and papers; the British Library houses some correspondence; the Bertrand Russell Archives at the University of McMaster includes some correspondence; the Royal Society houses some correspondence and papers; and the Bodleian Library of Oxford University includes correspondence.

BIBLIOGRAPHY

WORKS BY TANSLEY

"The Problems of Ecology." *New Phytologist* 3, no. 8 (1904): 191–200.

"The International Phytogeographical Excursion in the British Isles." *New Phytologist* 10 (1911): 271–291.

As editor. *Types of British Vegetation.* Cambridge, U.K.: Cambridge University Press, 1911.

With Frederick F. Blackman, Vernon H. Blackman, Frederick Keeble, and Francis W. Oliver. "The Reconstruction of Elementary Botanical Teaching." *New Phytologist,* 16 (10, 1917): 241–252.

"The Classification of Vegetation and the Concept of Development." *Journal of Ecology* 8, no. 2 (1920): 118–149.

The New Psychology and Its Relation to Life. London: Allen and Unwin, 1920.

Elements of Plant Biology. London: Allen and Unwin, 1922.

"The Relations of Complex and Sentiment Symposium." *British Journal of Psychology* 13 (1922): 113–122.

"Studies of the Vegetation of the English Chalk: II. Early Stages of Redevelopment of Woody Vegetation on Chalk Grassland." *Journal of Ecology* 10 (1922): 177–223.

Practical Plant Ecology: A Guide for Beginners in Field Study of Vegetation. London: Allen and Unwin, 1923.

"Some Aspects of the Present Position of Botany." Presidential Address to the British Association, Botanical Section, Liverpool. *Reports of the British Association for the Advancement of Science* (1923): 227–246.

As editor, with Thomas F. Chipp. *Aims and Methods in the Study of Vegetation.* London: Whitefriars Press, 1926.

The Future Development and Functions of the Oxford Department of Botany. Oxford, U.K.: Clarendon Press, 1927.

With Harry Godwin. "The Vegetation of Wicken Fen." In *The Natural History of Wicken Fen Part V,* edited by Stanley Gardiner. Cambridge, U.K.: Bowes & Bowes, 1929.

"The Use and Abuse of Vegetational Concepts and Terms." *Ecology* 16, no. 3 (1935): 284–307.

"British Ecology during the Past Quarter-Century: The Plant Community and the Ecosystem." *Journal of Ecology* 27, no. 2 (1939): 513–530.

The British Islands and their Vegetation. Cambridge, U.K.: Cambridge University Press, 1939.

"Sigmund Freud, 1856–1939." *Obituary Notices of Fellows of the Royal Society* 3, no. 9 (1939–1941): 246–275.

The Values of Science to Humanity. London: Allen and Unwin, 1942.

Our Heritage of Wild Nature: A Plea for Organized Nature Conservation. Cambridge, U.K.: Cambridge University Press, 1945.

With John R. Baker. "The Course of the Controversy on Freedom in Science." *Nature* (London) 158 (1946): 574–576.

"The Early History of Modern Plant Ecology in Britain." *Journal of Ecology* 35 (1947): 130–7.

Britain's Green Mantle: Past, Present, and Future. London: Allen and Unwin, 1949.

Mind and Life: An Essay in Simplification. London: Allen and Unwin, 1952.

Oaks and Oak Woods. London: Methuen, 1952.

"The Psychological Connexion of Two Basic Principles of the SFS." *Society for Freedom in Science,* Occasional Pamphlet no. 12, 1952.

"What is Ecology?" Reprint. *Biological Journal of the Linnean Society* 32 (1987): 5–16.

OTHER SOURCES

Anker, Peder J. *Imperial Ecology: Environmental Order in the British Empire, 1895–1945.* Cambridge, MA: Harvard University Press, 2001.

———. "The Context of Ecosystem Theory." *Ecosystems* 5 (2002): 611–613. A philosophical contextualization of Tansley's 1932 paper "The Temporal Genetic Series as a Means of Approach to Philosophy," which is also reprinted published for the first time here.

Armstrong, Patrick H. "Arthur George Tansley, 1871–1955." *Geographers: Biobibliographical Studies* 13 (1991): 93–100.

Bocking, Stephen. *Ecologists and Environmental Politics.* New Haven, CT: Yale University Press, 1997.

Boney, Arthur D. "The 'Tansley Manifesto' Affair." *New Phytologist* 118 (1991): 3–21.

Cameron, Laura. "Histories of Disturbance." *Radical History Review* 74 (1999): 2–24.

———. "A Nice Type of the English Scientist: Tansley and Freud." *History Workshop Journal* 48 (Autumn 1999): 65–100.

———. "Tansley's Psychoanalytic Network: An Episode Out of the Early History of Psychoanalysis in England." *Psychoanalysis and History* 2, no. 2 (2000): 189–256.

Dagg, Joachim L. "Arthur G. Tansley's 'New Psychology' and Its Relation to Ecology." *Web Ecology* 7 (2007): 27–34.

Forrester, John, and Laura Cameron. "'A Cure with a Defect': A Previously Unpublished Letter by Freud Concerning 'Anna O.'" *International Journal of Psychoanalysis* 80 (October 1999): 929–942. Considers the text of a letter from Freud addressed probably to Tansley.

Hope-Simpson, John F. "Sir Arthur Tansley." In *Oxford Dictionary of National Biography.* Oxford, U.K.: Oxford University Press, 2004. Available from http://www.oxforddnb.com.

Godwin, Harry. "Arthur George Tansley, 1871–1955." *Biographical Memoirs of Fellows of the Royal Society* 3 (1957): 227–46.

———. "Sir Arthur George Tansley, FRS, 1871–1955." *Journal of Ecology* 46 (1958): 1–8.

———. "Sir Arthur Tansley: The Man and His Subject." (First Tansley Lecture.) *Journal of Ecology* 65 (1977): 1–26.

———. "Early Development of the New Phytologist." *New Phytologist* 100 (1985): 1–4.

Golley, Frank Benjamin. *A History of the Ecosystem Concept in Ecology.* New Haven, CT: Yale University Press, 1993.

Hagen, Joel. *An Entangled Bank: The Origins of Ecosystem Ecology.* New Brunswick, NJ: Rutgers University Press, 1992.

Sheail, John. *Seventy-five Years in Ecology: The British Ecological Society.* Oxford, U.K.: Blackwell Scientific Publications, 1987.

Laura Jean Cameron

TARSKI, ALFRED

(*b.* Warsaw, Poland, 14 January 1901; *d.* Berkeley, California, 27 October 1983), *mathematical logic, model theory, set theory, algebra, formal semantics.* For the original article on Tarski see *DSB,* vol. 18, Supplement II.

Tarski and Kurt Gödel are considered the leading figures in the development of mathematical logic and its applications during the twentieth century. Tarski's name continues to be linked with contemporary research in set theory, decision problems, and axiomatic geometry, as well as the metamathematical study of semantical concepts, especially definitions of truth for formalized languages. Through his students and his students' students, Tarski's influence extends far into mathematical linguistics, database theory, and theoretical computer science. Recent biographical research affords new information about significant events in Tarski's life, both in Europe and later in America, and the milieu in which they transpired.

Early Work in Europe. At the Warsaw University when Tarski matriculated in 1918, mathematics, with the other exact sciences, was in the School of Philosophy. After first enrolling in biology, Tarski turned to mathematics under the tutelage of Stefan Mazurkiewicz, chair of the Mathematics Department in Warsaw, and Wacław Sierpiński, set theorist and topologist, and, shortly thereafter, the topologist Kazimierz Kuratowski. He took courses and seminars in logic and philosophy with the philosopher-logicians Stanisław Leśniewski and Jan Łukasiewicz. In the dedication to the collection *Logic, Semantics, Metamathematics* of Tarski's early papers, in both the first and the second editions, Tarski acknowledged the Warsaw philosopher Tadeusz Kotarbiński as a teacher. In 1924, the year in which Tarski was awarded his PhD, he changed his name from Teitelbaum or Tajtelbaum to Tarski and converted to Catholicism. The name change may have been a career move expressive of Polish nationalism and a response to growing anti-Semitism; it was encouraged by Łukasiewicz and Leśniewski. Tarski's work toward the degree was carried out under the supervision of Leśniewski. His PhD diploma mentions examinations in mathematics, philosophy, and Polish philology.

Despite the name change, Tarski's career suffered from the anti-Semitism increasingly evident in Poland and central Europe in the 1930s. He lost his first teaching post, at the Polish Pedagogical Institute of Warsaw, because his female charges complained that their mathematics teacher was Jewish. It also appears that, in 1937, he was denied a professorial post in Poznań because of his religious background.

Between 1928 and 1930, Tarski competed with the logician Leon Chwistek for a professorial post in logic in the Faculty of Mathematics and Natural Sciences at L'viv. It seems that Tarski was sorely disappointed when the position went to Chwistek, who had received a letter of recommendation from Bertrand Russell. Later, Russell would give Tarski warm and enthusiastic support when the latter was searching for a permanent post in the United States.

The significance of Tarski's work on metamathematics and semantics for the Vienna Circle, and especially for Rudolf Carnap, a leading member of the circle, should not be underestimated. Tarski visited Vienna in 1930 and again in 1935; his conversations there with Carnap were major stimuli for the development of the latter's theory of pure syntax and, later, his adoption of a semantical viewpoint. During the 1935 visit, Tarski's presentation of his semantical theory of truth also exerted tremendous influence on the thinking of the Austrian philosopher Karl Popper. During the First International Unity of Science Congress, at the Sorbonne in September 1935, Tarski spoke on his theory of truth and on his study of logical consequence; the conferees were not uniformly enthusiastic in their reception of the new ideas. Also in 1935, Tarski received a grant from the Rockefeller Foundation for research in Vienna and Paris.

Later Work in America. On 11 August 1939, Tarski sailed to New York on the *Piłsudski* in order to attend the Fifth International Congress on the Unity of Science, organized by Willard Van Orman Quine, the noted Harvard University philosopher and logician. While on a visitor's visa in the United States, Tarski also gave a series of lectures. He had brought with him to America only a small suitcase filled with summer clothes. The invasion of Poland and the outbreak of World War II made it impossible for him to return to his homeland. His wife Maria and two children Jan and Ina were to remain in Poland throughout the war; the family would be reunited after a separation period of seven years. Starting in January 1942, Tarski took up a Guggenheim Fellowship at the Institute for Advanced Study in Princeton.

Tarski was instrumental in establishing at the University of California at Berkeley the renowned program in logic and the methodology of science. The proposal for a PhD in that area was approved in May 1957. Tarski was famous as an organizer and promoter of international conventions and congresses, among them the First

Alfred Tarski. *Alfred Tarski, 1968.* MATHEMATISCHES FORSCHUNGSINSTITUT OBERWOLFACH. REPRODUCED BY PERMISSION.

International Congress for Logic, Methodology, and Philosophy of Science, held at Stanford, California, in August 1960. In 1978 Tarski received the honorary degree Doctor Honoris Causa from the Université d'Aix-Marseille II.

Continuing Influence. In mathematical logic and analytical philosophy, scholarly interest in definitions of truth and notions of logical consequence, both areas in which Tarski did work of the highest significance, continues to be keen. Tarski's student Richard Montague extended his teacher's ideas on formal semantics to natural languages. Dana Scott, another Tarski student, brought Tarski's work on topological models into nonclassical analysis by constructing interpretations for the intuitionistic theory of real numbers. Scott also devised formal semantics for computer programming languages, and calculi of functions and arguments.

SUPPLEMENTARY BIBLIOGRAPHY

WORKS BY TARSKI

With Steven Givant. *A Formalization of Set Theory without Variables.* Colloquium Publications vol. 41. Providence, RI: American Mathematical Society, 1987.

———. "Tarski's System of Geometry." *Bulletin of Symbolic Logic* 5 (1999): 175–214.

OTHER SOURCES

Feferman, Anita Burdman. "How the Unity of Science Saved Alfred Tarski." In *Alfred Tarski and the Vienna Circle,* edited by Jan Woleński and Eckehart Köhler. Dordrecht, Netherlands: Kluwer, 1999.

———, and Solomon Feferman. *Alfred Tarski: Life and Logic.* Cambridge, U.K.: Cambridge University Press, 2004. A fine and fascinating biography of Tarski.

Feferman, Solomon. "Tarski and Gödel between the Lines." In *Alfred Tarski and the Vienna Circle,* edited by Jan Woleński and Eckehart Köhler. Dordrecht, Netherlands: Kluwer, 1999.

Givant, Steven. "A Portrait of Alfred Tarski." *Mathematical Intelligencer* 13, no. 3 (1991): 16–32.

Woleński, Jan, and Eckehart Köhler, eds. *Alfred Tarski and the Vienna Circle.* Dordrecht, Netherlands: Kluwer, 1999. An important collection for biographical information.

Charles McCarty

TATUM, EDWARD LAWRIE (*b.* Boulder, Colorado, 14 December 1909; *d.* New York City, 5 November 1975), *biochemistry, embryology, physiology, genetics, microorganisms.*

Tatum was an American-born biologist who together with George Beadle received the 1958 Nobel Prize in Physiology or Medicine "for their discovery that genes act by regulating definite chemical events." Tatum worked primarily within biochemistry, studying the nutrition and genetics of microorganisms and of *Drosophila.* He was a seminal figure in the development of physiological genetics, made fundamental contributions to understanding biochemical processes and their relation to gene action, and was a pioneer in the use of microorganisms as genetic models. He also was one of the first to experimentally demonstrate the importance of "sex" in bacteria.

Early Years. Edward Lawrie Tatum was the son of Arthur Lawrie Tatum, a pharmacologist, and Mabel Webb Tatum. Carla Harriman was his stepmother. The elder Tatum held a variety of positions, including one at the University of Chicago from 1918 to 1928, and moving from there to the Madison Wisconsin where he had been appointed as a professor of pharmacology at the University of Wisconsin Medical School. Edward Tatum attended the University of Chicago for two years, then transferred to the University of Wisconsin, receiving his BA in chemistry in 1931, MS in microbiology in 1932, and PhD in biochemistry in 1934. Tatum's undergraduate work focused on the growth of bacteria. He continued to work on *Clostridium septicum* in his graduate work, studying the effects of an aspartic acid derivative on its growth. This substance was later shown to be asparagines. His PhD in biochemistry concerned nutrition and metabolism of bacteria, work he carried out under the direction of Edwin Broun Fred and William Harold Peterson. He identified vitamin B1, or thiamine, as one of the required growth factors for microorganisms. (Before this time, the need for B vitamins was underappreciated.) After receiving his PhD he married June Alton on 28 June 1934; the couple would have two daughters, Margaret and Barbara, before divorcing in 1956.

Edward L. Tatum. © BETTMANN/CORBIS.

Tatum stayed at Wisconsin from 1934 to 1937, though visiting during 1935 at the University of Utrecht in Holland. At Utrecht he worked with Fritz Kögl, who had himself recognized the importance of biotin, and with Nils Fries. Tatum worked on identifying growth factors in staphylocci, though he was apparently unsatisfied with the results.

At the University of Wisconsin, together with H. G. Wood, Esmond E. Snell, and Peterson, Tatum worked on factors affecting the growth of bacteria, indicating that thiamine was crucial. They showed that vitamins were critical to the growth of a variety of bacterial species. For comparative biochemistry, it was an illustration of the conservation of biochemical processes across diverse species. This suggested that insofar as biologists were interested in metabolism, the simplest method might be to attack problems of growth in microorganisms. That was a theme to which Tatum returned throughout his career.

Work on *Drosophila.* When Beadle moved to Stanford University from Harvard University in 1937, he invited Tatum to join him working on *Drosophila.* Tatum was a research associate with Beadle's group from 1937 through 1941 and an assistant professor from 1941 to 1945. The Rockefeller Foundation supported this work as one of the ventures into molecular biology. They worked on the genetics underlying eye color in *Drosophila*, and subsequently on *Neurospora crassa*. It was this work that ultimately earned Tatum and Beadle the 1958 Nobel Prize, which was shared with Joshua Lederberg.

This research was intended to follow up on the work that had been initiated by Beadle and Boris Ephrussi at California Institute of Technology and subsequently in Paris. Beadle and Ephrussi had shown that there were "hormones" involved in the synthesis of eye pigment in *Drosophila*, and that their contributions to the synthesis of eye pigment are not independent. Tatum's training as a chemist made him an ideal choice for Beadle. The idea was that a biochemist might be able to identify the specific substances involved. Jobs were scarce during the Depression, and Tatum accepted Beadle's offer. Tatum brought substantial expertise in microbiology and biochemisty. Beadle brought a deep understanding of classical Mendelian genetics.

From 1937 through 1941 Tatum focused on extracting precursors to pigments from *Drosophila* larvae. Ephrussi and Simon Chevais had reported that normal eye color could be restored in mutant flies when provided with tryptophan. Tatum showed that a bacterial contaminant actually was the source of the hormone, which again, in his mind, confirmed the functional equivalence of growth factors in bacteria and animals. After visiting Caltech and learning some additional techniques from Arie J. Haagen-Smit, Tatum returned to the problem of identifying the hormones involved in *Drosophila* eye colors, isolating one of them, the v+ hormone in a crystalline state, and identifying it as kynurenine. Tatum was preceded in this discovery by Adolf Butenand. That experience encouraged Beadle and Tatum to look for another model organism that might prove to be more tractable.

Work on *Neurospora*. They turned to *Neurospora*, a bread mold. Tatum knew from previous work that biotin (another B vitamin) was required if *Neurospora* was to be cultivated on inorganic media. They set about to investigate its nutritional requirements, recognizing that genes must control the biosynthetic processes in nutrition and, furthermore, that these processes would exhibit considerable complexity at the genetic or physiological level. Their plan was to reveal the underlying genetic complexity by investigating the nutritional requirements of mutant strains.

As an experimental organism *Neurospora* offered a number of distinct advantages. They knew that *Neurospora* could be grown on a variety of well-understood media. It requires only biotin as a supplement to a medium otherwise, including only inorganic salts and sugars. This means that *Neurospora* is capable of synthesizing most of what is necessary for growth. In addition to having such simple nutritional requirements, since *Neurospora* is haploid in its vegetative phase, there is no masking of the effects of mutant genes. The genes will be expressed, and a gene that is inactivated by mutation will have the effect of disabling any pathway of which it is a constituent. Finally, *Neurospora* can reproduce either sexually or asexually. Asexual reproduction allows for a sizable culture of genetically identical individuals whose nutritional requirements can be experimentally determined.

Early in 1941 Beadle and Tatum set about to x-ray *Neurospora* in order to induce mutations and identify them. This work depended crucially on Wilhelm Röntgen's work with x-rays and on Hermann Muller's demonstration that x-rays induced mutations in *Drosophila*. From a technical standpoint, the important fact was that they could induce mutations and did not have to wait for natural spontaneous mutations to occur. They assumed that mutations would have the effect of selectively inactivating the genes and eliminate the intermediate reactions they control. After irradiating the organisms, and allowing meiosis to take place, Beadle and Tatum were able to obtain a host of genetically homogeneous spores. Having grown them all on amply supplemented mediums, they transferred samples to a medium having the minimal amount of supplements required for the growth of non-mutant strains. Any strains that could grow on more generous mediums but not on the minimal medium had to be incapable of synthesizing some product that normal, wild-type, strains could synthesize. By then transferring the mutant strains to a variety of alternately supplemented mediums, they were able to identify the specific products that the organisms could not synthesize. As a result, they could also reconstruct the biosynthetic pathways in the original wild-type organisms.

Once they began to work with *Neurospora* it took Beadle and Tatum only five months to find the first three nutritional mutants. Isolate 299 was the first identifiable mutant, requiring pyridoxine for normal synthesis. The other two required para-aminobenzoic acid and thiamine. (Subsequently they identified a large number of mutants, literally cataloging hundreds of mutants.) The mutants behaved properly from a Mendelian standpoint, suggesting it had an identifiable location on the chromosomes. They concluded that their assumption that genes control enzymatic reactions must be correct. In May 1941 Beadle and Tatum sent their report to the *Proceedings of the National Academy of Sciences*. Their first studies of *Neurospora* were published that year. The key conclusion was straightforward: "A single gene may be considered to be concerned with the primary control of a specific chemical reaction" (Tatum and Beadle, 1942, p. 240). As a consequence, "the gene and enzyme specificities are of the same order" (Beadle and Tatum, 1941b, pp. 499–500).

Different mutants responded to different nutritional supplements. There are, for example, at least four mutant strains of *Neurospora* that are deficient in thiamine. The first two strains would grow with a wide variety of supplements, which means the mutations must have blocked the initial stages of the pathway; other intermediate compounds were available for the organism to complete the synthesis. The third strain required thiamine, indicating that the metabolic block must have occurred somewhere prior to the synthesis of thiamine. The fourth strain would not grow on a pyrimidine supplement, but it would if offered thiamine or a precursor to thiamine, so the block must occur between those two steps. The differences can be summarized as follows:

thi-1. Growth with any of the pathway intermediates.

thi-2. Growth with any of the pathway intermediates.

thi-3. Growth only when supplemented with thiamine.

thi-4. Growth if supplemented by either thiamine or its precursor.

It was also possible to conduct "crosses" of the strains, using a methodology analogous to that developed by Beadle and Ephrussi in *Drosophila*. Beadle and Ephrussi transplanted imaginal disks (which develop into eyes) onto genetically distinct larvae. This allowed them to assess the substances produced by the different strains. Beadle and Tatum could do something quite similar with *Neurospora* strains. When strains of *thi-1* and *thi-2* were grown in close proximity, it was found that the resulting hybrid cells (heterokaryons) containing both nuclei did *not* require complex nutritional supplements. Since the heterokaryon could once again grow on a minimal medium, without nutritional supplements, these two mutations had to affect different genes.

The key contributions of this work were to the study of gene action and the development of a variety of experimental techniques. The reports on this work suggested there were varying degrees of genetic control for enzymes affecting growth. They wrote in one of their first papers that "genes control or regulate specific reactions in the cell system either by acting directly as enzymes or by determining the specificities of enzymes" (Beadle and Tatum, 1941, p. 499). They were not yet decided on whether enzymes are produced by genes or whether genes might themselves be enzymes. (At this point, it is worth remembering, proteins were prime candidates for being genes, and nucleic acids were thought to be secondary.)

One very important practical consequence of their work with *Neurospora* and subsequently with mutants in *Acetobacter* and *Escherichia coli* was that it promoted bacteria as useful resources for genetic analysis. Another practical consequence was the introduction of induced mutations as a standard technique. The centerpiece of the program is what came to be seen as the one gene–one enzyme hypothesis: Each gene controls the production of a specific enzyme, and the function of that enzyme is determined by the genetic structure. Since their earliest announcements, the hypothesis has been modified to a one gene–one protein principle and then to one gene–one polypeptide, recognizing that not all gene products are enzymes and that proteins are often complexes of polypeptides. Still, the thought that genes and enzymes are "of the same order of specificity" was foundational for biochemical genetics.

Many of the principles they deployed have become standard views in biochemistry:

1. All biochemical processes are under genetic control;

2. these processes can be described as a series of steps;

3. each step is a reaction that is controlled by a single gene;

4. mutation in any of these genes inhibits the capacity of the organism to carry out just one reaction. These simple assumptions have a variety of important consequences:

5. Mutations sometimes result in altered proteins;

6. those alterations can render to the products either enzymatically inactive, or modify the activity;

7. this can include changes relevant not only to enzymatic properties but also, for example, to stability of the molecules.

Overall, Beadle and Tatum developed a methodology for exploring the impact of genes on the physiology of cells and promoted the one gene–one enzyme theory committed to the idea that chromosomal genes control the synthesis of proteins and thereby influence development. Along with the establishment of *Neurospora* as a model organism within genetics, they more generally promoted the place of bacteria in genetic research.

Bacterial Sex. For a variety of reasons, many involving university politics, Tatum's position at Stanford became tenuous. He was, after all, trained as a chemist and occupying a position in a Biology Department. Tatum moved briefly to Washington University in St. Louis and in 1945 landed a position at Yale University. (Shortly thereafter, Beadle left Stanford for Caltech.) Tatum's task at Yale was to develop the microbiology program.

Joshua Lederberg, who had been at the Columbia University Medical School, worked with Tatum starting in 1946 before moving to Wisconsin. In a series of important papers they showed that there was recombination between mutant strains of *E. coli*. This is sometimes thought of as bacterial sex. Tatum had already developed mutant strains of *E. coli*, using techniques similar to those deployed in the *Neurospora* work with Beadle. Tatum used these same techniques of inducing mutations, applying them to bacteria. By facilitating bacterial sex Lederberg and Tatum showed that bacterial genetics was not significantly different from the genetics of higher organisms and that they could be fruitful organisms for genetic study.

Once again, Tatum's strong biochemical orientation meant that he did not get the level of support that he thought was necessary at Yale. So in 1948 Douglas Whitaker enticed Tatum to return to Stanford. The academic leadership at Stanford put considerable energy into the development of scientific fields. Tatum encouraged not only the development of biochemistry but also the development of a curriculum in the medical school. In 1956 he was appointed head of the newly formed Department of Biochemistry. For personal reasons, with the dissolution of his marriage, he found it desirable to leave Stanford, moving to the Rockefeller Institute and marrying Viola Kanter in New York City on 16 December 1956.

Later Years. At the Rockefeller Institute, Tatum again found himself occupied with institutional affairs. He devoted a significant amount of time to national science policy, encouraging fellowship support for young scientists. He also served as chairman of the board for the Cold Spring Harbor Biological Laboratory. In terms of research, he continued to work on *Neurospora*, studying the effects of various changes on their morphology.

Tatum's Nobel Prize in 1958 added to his list of honors, which included election to the National Academy of Sciences (1952), the Remsen Award from the American Chemical Society (1953), presidency of the Harvey Society (1964–1965), and numerous honorary degrees.

His wife Viola died of cancer on 21 April 1974. He married Elsie Bergland later that year, but Tatum's own health was already compromised. He died on 7 November 1975 from heart failure, no doubt promoted by chronic emphysema.

BIBLIOGRAPHY

WORKS BY TATUM

"Studies in the Biochemistry of Microorganisms." PhD diss., University of Wisconsin, 1934.

With George W. Beadle. "Development of Eye Colors in Drosophila: Some Properties of the Hormones Involved." *Journal of General Physiology* 22 (1938): 239–253.

"Development of Eye Colors in Drosophila: Bacterial Synthesis of v+ Hormone." *Proceedings of the National Academy of Sciences USA* 25 (1939): 486–490.

"Nutritional Requirements of *Drosophila melanogaster*." *Proceedings of the National Academy of Sciences USA* 25 (1939): 490–497.

With George W. Beadle. "Experimental Control of Development and Differentiation." *American Naturalist* 75 (1941): 107–116.

With George W. Beadle. "Genetic Control of Biochemical Reactions in Neurospora." *Proceedings of the National Academy of Sciences USA* 27 (1941): 499–506.

With George W. Beadle. "Vitamin B Requirements of *Drosophila melanogaster*." *Proceedings of the National Academy of Sciences USA* 27 (1941): 193–197.

With George W. Beadle. "Genetic Control of Biochemical Reactions in Neurospora: An 'Aminobenzoicless' Mutant." *Proceedings of the National Academy of Sciences USA* 28 (1942): 234–243.

With Norman H. Horowitz, David Bonner, Hershel K. Mitchell, et al. "Genetic Control of Biochemical Reactions in Neurospora." *American Naturalist* 79 (1945): 304–317.

With Joshua Lederberg. "Gene Recombination in *Escherichia coli*." *Nature* 158 (1946): 558.

"Induced Biochemical Mutations in Bacteria." *Cold Spring Harbor Symposia in Quantitative Biology* 11 (1946): 278–284.

With Joshua Lederberg. "Novel Genotypes in Mixed Cultures of Biochemical Mutants of Bacteria." *Cold Spring Harbor Symposia in Quantitative Biology* 11 (1946): 113–114.

"A Case History in Biological Research." *Science* 129 (1959): 1711–1715. Also in *Les prix Nobel en 1958*, edited by Göran Liljestrand. Stockholm: Nobel Foundation, 1959.

"Perspectives from Physiological Genetics." In *The Control of Human Heredity and Evolution*, edited by Tracy M. Sonneborn. New York: Macmillan, 1965.

OTHER SOURCES

Kay, Lilly E. "Selling Pure Science in Wartime: The Biochemical Genetics of G. W. Beadle." *Journal of the History of Biology* 22 (1989): 73–101.

Lederberg, Joshua. "Genetic Recombination in Bacteria: A Discovery Account." *Annual Review of Genetics* 21 (1987): 23–46.

———. "Edward Lawrie Tatum." *Biographical Memoirs, National Academy of Sciences* 59 (1990): 356–386.

Robert C. Richardson

TEICHERT, CURT (*b.* Königsberg, Prussia, 8 May 1905; *d.* Arlington, Virginia, 10 May 1996), *geology, paleozoic stratigraphy and paleontology, Cephalopoda, ancient and modern reefs, correlation and sedimentation.*

Teichert made significant contributions to knowledge of a variety of fossil organisms, particularly cephalopods.

The best-known current examples of this class of Mollusca are the squid and octopus. The modern chambered Nautilus, which Teichert also studied, is the only living, shelled cephalopod. In older times, particularly in the Paleozoic, the ancestors of Nautilus were abundant and diverse forms, having a long fossil record. Along with his contributions to paleontology, Teichert was prominent in correlation, the matching of beds of the same age in different locations. As a result of his later activities on several continents, he was a master of worldwide correlation of sedimentary rocks.

Early Life and Career. Teichert received his PhD in 1928 from Albertus Magnus University in Königsberg, having studied also in the universities of Munich and Freiberg. In later years he recalled that in high school a teacher directed his attention to Alfred Wegener's book on continental drift, which initiated his interest in geology. This was an era of rampant inflation in Germany, such that any available money was spent first thing in the morning, for by afternoon it was worthless. Notwithstanding desperate poverty, Teichert was able to complete his thesis on Silurian-age rocks in Estonia. This became the first of his more than 325 publications. In December of the year he completed his degree, he married Gertrude Kaufmann, daughter of a physics professor at the university. Until her death in 1993, Trude was his constant companion, helpmate, and inspiration.

Teichert was an assistant at Freiburg from 1927 to 1929 and in 1930 received a Rockefeller Fellowship, which enabled him to come to the National Museum of Natural History in Washington, D.C., where in 1930–1931 he honed his knowledge of early cephalopods. After that year abroad, he joined a Danish expedition to East Greenland, spending fifteen months there, including a winter, in 1931–1932. He was one of the few members of the expedition previously to have been on skis, though sketching while seated on a moving dogsled was a new experience.

In 1933 Teichert returned to a Germany under Nazi control. Because Trude was Jewish, Teichert was told by university authorities to divorce her. Rather than obeying, he and Trude left abruptly for Copenhagen in 1933. They arrived with no money and no prospects. Fortunately, he received a tiny stipend to study Greenland fossils, and they were able to survive in poverty for the next four years.

Research in Australia. Teichert started afresh on another continent in 1937. A Carnegie Foundation fellowship program paid the salary of displaced scholars for several years, enabling the University of Western Australia, in Perth, to employ him. He was virtually the only paleontologist in thousands of square miles of unstudied fossilif-

erous rock. One immediate result was a special paper of the Geological Society of America on a peculiar Permian fossil. With the outbreak of World War II in 1939, he and Trude were briefly interned; authorities offered them the opportunity to return to Germany as an exchange for Australians and seemed surprised when they refused. Later in the war, he investigated reefs at the behest of military officials. During 1940 and 1941 he was also a consultant to Caltex Oil, searching for favorable localities in western Australia.

Teichert moved eastward in Australia in 1945 to the position of assistant chief geologist of the Department of Mines in the state of Victoria. From 1947 to 1952 he was a senior lecturer at the University of Melbourne. Teichert also did some consulting work for Standard Vacuum Oil. More significantly, he served as a consultant to the Australian Bureau of Mines, traveling widely to investigate sedimentary basins. During this period he examined rocks of every age as far back as Cambrian. Earlier, in 1949, Raymond C. Moore of the University of Kansas asked him to organize the Cephalopoda volume for the *Treatise on Invertebrate Paleontology* (1953–1981). A Fulbright Fellowship and a fifty-university lecture tour in 1951–1952 allowed him to meet many of the potential authors for portions of this volume.

In the American West. During 1952 Teichert moved to another continent, beginning work in December at the New Mexico School of Mines in Socorro. He investigated the rocks of the Devonian age in that state, and his manuscript on the subject was published by the U.S. Geological Survey (USGS). Early in 1954 he formally joined the USGS to set up a laboratory at the Denver Federal Center to enhance the mission of the Fuels Branch. As an example of Teichert's dedication and style, he toured, along with two others, branch facilities in sixteen states within six weeks and produced a sixty-two-page report outlining the scope and projects for the new laboratory. He found the time in 1958 to briefly slip back into German academia as a guest professor at the universities of Bonn, Freiberg, and Göttingen.

Program Work in Pakistan. The Denver laboratory was so successful that, in 1961, Teichert was asked to transfer to Quetta, Pakistan, where an Agency for International Development-USGS program was helping to expand the Geological Survey of Pakistan and develop a minerals and exploration program. The program in which he was involved included training on the outcrop through a detailed investigation of the Permian-Triassic boundary in the Salt Range. He led development of a National Stratigraphic Code for Pakistan. In turn, that led to stratigraphic correlations among the Central Treaty Organization countries of Pakistan, Iran, and Turkey.

Kansas and New York. At the end of the Pakistan assignment in 1964, Teichert once more returned to academia, this time as Regents' Distinguished Professor at the University of Kansas. In addition to academic duties, during this interval he edited seven volumes of the *Treatise on Invertebrate Paleontology*. That effort necessitated visits to authors in Europe and South America.

In 1975, at age seventy, Teichert officially retired from the University of Kansas, though he taught there for another two years. During 1977 he moved to New York State to become an adjunct professor at the University of Rochester, where he continued his research for another eight years. As president of the International Palaeontological Association, he may have been the first western invertebrate paleontologist to visit the People's Republic of China. In addition to the intangible benefits of this contact, a direct result was a significant monograph on Late Cambrian cephalopods.

His wife died in 1993, and in 1995 he moved to Arlington, Virginia, not far from the National Museum of Natural History in Washington, D.C., where he had studied six decades earlier. Although he rearranged his scientific library, failing health finally stilled his prolific pen.

Among his many honors were the David Syme Prize from the University of Melbourne (1950), the Raymond C. Moore Medal of the Society for Sedimentary Geology (1982), and the Paleontological Society Medal (1984). Eight different countries were represented among the nineteen scientific or cultural organizations with which he was associated.

BIBLIOGRAPHY

The manuscript of Curt Teichert's autobiography is at the Paleontological Research Institute at Ithaca, New York. A list of Teichert publications may be found in C. E. Brett, Wolfgang Struve, and E. L. Yochelson, Curt Teichert Festschrift, *Senckenbergiana Lethaea, vol. 69 (Frankfurt am Main, 1988).*

WORKS BY TEICHERT

A New Ordovician Fauna from Washington Land, North Greenland. Copenhagen: C.A. Reitzel, 1937.

Permian Crinoid Calceolispongia. New York: Geological Society of America, 1949.

Devonian Rocks and Paleogeography of Central Arizona. Washington, DC: U.S. Government Printing Office, 1965.

With Claude Spinosa. *Cretaceous and Tertiary Rhyncholites from the Western Atlantic Ocean and from Mississippi.* Lawrence: University of Kansas Paleontological Institute, 1971.

OTHER SOURCES

Brett, C. E., Wolfgang Struve, and E. L. Yochelson. *Curt Teichert Festschrift.* Senckenbergiana Lethaea, vol. 69. Frankfurt am Main, Germany, 1988.

Crick, Rex E., and George D. Stanley Jr. "Curt Teichert, May 8, 1905–May 10, 1996." *Journal of Paleontology* 71, no. 4 (July 1997): 750–752.

Reinemund, J. A. "Memorial to Curt Teichert 1905–1996." *Geological Society of America, Memorials* 28 (1997): 39–42.

Ellis Yochelson

TEISSERENC DE BORT, LÉON PHILIPPE
(*b.* Paris, France, 6 November 1855; *d.* Cannes, France, 8 January 1913), *meteorology, aerology.*

Teisserenc de Bort is famous in meteorology for his discovery of the stratosphere, "the most surprising discovery in the whole history of meteorology" (Shaw, 1926, p. 225), but also for his works on dynamic meteorology (the science that attempts to explain atmospheric motions), on the classification of clouds, and on the general circulation of the atmosphere.

He was born to a prominent and wealthy family, never got married, and devoted his fortune to atmospheric research. Suffering from poor health, he was taught at home by a private tutor who gave him his taste for sciences. For the same reason he made several long stays in Grasse, in the hinterland of Cannes, France, where he started meteorological observations that were sent for publication to the Société météorologique de France (French Meteorological Society). He joined the staff of the newly created Bureau central météorologique (BCM) in 1898 and became the chief of its general meteorology department the following year. When his father died, in 1892, he was left with a substantial income and he requested a long-term leave from BCM, which was granted, in order to devote his free time to the exploration of the atmosphere. After 1904, his poor health prevented him from traveling to foreign countries to attend meetings or participate in the scientific cruises or experiments he co-organized.

The BCM Years. At BCM Teisserenc de Bort made extensive studies concerning the distribution of temperature and pressure at the surface of Earth. In 1879 he established the empirical "law" of isanomals (an isanomal is a line joining the points where the difference between a meteorological parameter and its zonal mean is constant), which relates the anomaly of the monthly mean temperature relative to its zonal mean, to the mean surface pressure: the minima (respectively maxima) of thermal isanomals are associated with pressure maxima (resp. minima). In 1886 he also introduced the concept of *centre d'action* (center of action) seasonal or permanent, in order to explain the character of seasons, mainly winters, He identified five of these centers of action, the most popular being the anticyclones of the Azores and Siberia, and the Icelandic low, which explain the cold and warm winters in Western Europe.

Concerning the general circulation of the atmosphere, he drew mean isobars at the mean sea level and also in altitude including the 4,000-meter level, the elevation of the Pike's Peak, Colorado, observatory. He also made a tentative sketch of how the cloud distribution would be seen from space for both hemispheres.

After his years at the BCM, during which he mainly conducted theoretical research, Teisserenc de Bort shifted to problems associated with the design and construction of kites, balloons, and instruments specially built for his researches. In his observatory were developed very interesting devices concerning practically all the technological aspects of these activities, for instance insulating the thermometer from the unwanted influence of the sounding device. His work in this area attracted in Trappes a lot of foreign scientists such as Richard Assmann and Arthur Berson in 1899.

The Dynamic Meteorology Observatory. In 1896 Teisserenc de Bort founded the Observatoire de météorologie dynamique (Dynamic Meteorology Observatory) in Trappes (not far from Versailles, in the western suburbs of Paris) in order to participate in the International Cloud Year (ICY). One of the goals of the ICY was to measure the altitude and displacement of clouds to have a global view of the atmospheric circulation. For this purpose, Teisserenc de Bort installed two photographic theodolites 1,300 meters apart and connected by telephone. Later he also used also this device to measure the altitude of his sounding balloons and compare it with the one computed using the barometric formula, the validity of which was disputed; he proved that it was a reasonable estimate of the altitude, the barometer being slightly delayed during the ascent and the descent.

Under the auspices of the International Meteorological Organization (IMO), Teisserenc de Bort participated in the ICY in 1896–1897, serving together with Hugo Hildebrand Hildebrandsson and Albert Riggenbach on a committee charged with the publication of an international cloud atlas. Teisserenc de Bort eventually financed the project because the IMO had provided no funds for the publication.

After the conclusion of the ICY in 1897, Teisserenc de Bort started the vertical exploration of the atmosphere using kites, following the ideas of his friend Abbott

Lawrence Rotch, the director of the Blue Hill Observatory, near Boston, whom he had met in Paris in 1896 during the International Meteorological Conference. At the observatory Teisserenc de Bort installed a workshop in order to build kites, a laboratory for building and calibrating meteorological instruments, and a rotating electrical winch to operate the kites. He invented a line of kites connected by piano wires with diameters decreasing with altitude, a device that was also adopted by the other meteorological observatories, and which allowed his instruments to reach their highest altitude of 5,250 meters in 1901.

In 1898 he started exploring the atmosphere with sounding balloons, a technique devised a few years before by Gustave Hermite and Georges Besançon (1892), and also adopted by Assmann in Germany and Hugo Hergesell in Strasbourg (then in Germany). Teisserenc de Bort used the same kind of instruments as on his kites, but contrary to what his colleagues did, he launched his instruments with lacquered paper balloons (the others, Assmann and Hergesell for instance, used gold beater skin or silk, much heavier), filled with hydrogen produced by the reaction of sulfuric acid on iron filings, and launched from a rotating shelter. The rotating shelter was necessary to launch the delicate paper balloons in the direction of the wind, while the use of hydrogen, instead of town gas (a gas produced from coal and distributed by pipes to houses and buildings for heating, lighting and cooking) was mandatory to reach higher altitudes. Although this technique did not allow Teisserenc de Bort's balloons to reach altitudes higher than 20 kilometers, as Assmann had, it was much cheaper and allowed him to perform a very large number of launches compared to his rivals and friends.

Similar to the results of Hermite and Besançon, but unlike Assmann and Hergesell, Teisserenc de Bort found a layer of increasing temperature above 10 kilometers during his very first launches in April 1898. It is not known what he thought about his finding, but it is known that he corrected his measurements of temperature when the temperature increased in the upper atmosphere in order to preserve the same vertical gradient of temperature as under that layer because at that time meteorologists thought the temperature of the high atmosphere always had to decrease with height (arguments in favor of this opinion have been summarized by Ohring, 1964, p. 12) and that the horizontal heterogeneities of temperature generated by the ground disappeared at high altitude, where temperature has to be constant on a constant altitude surface. From the beginning, Teisserenc de Bort launched his sounding balloons during the night in order to avoid solar radiation affecting the temperature measurements. Teisserenc de Bort must have been unsure about the performance of his instruments, so he decided to multiply the launches in order to verify his conclusions:

for instance he launched three balloons during the same night. From 1898 to 1902, he alluded only once to this problem during a conference in 1899 when he also explained the large temporal variations of temperature he had measured in the high atmosphere.

The Discovery of the Stratosphere. When he finally decided to publish his findings in 1902, he had launched 236 sounding balloons above 11 kilometers, whereas at the same period Assmann in Berlin had only launched 20. In his paper to the Academie des sciences, Teisserenc de Bort reported that the temperature ceased to decrease in a layer he called the isothermal layer. He was aware that in the isothermal layer temperature increased, but he was unable to explain why. In his report he also presented a climatology of the altitude of the base of this layer that is higher in anticyclonic areas than in cyclonic areas. Assmann had reached the same conclusion concerning the existence of what he called the "upper inversion," and published his results a few days later than Teisserenc de Bort. The two men corresponded and Assmann visited the Trappes Observatory in 1899.

While Hildebrandsson and Teisserenc de Bort were preparing the international cloud atlas, they were also designing a very interesting two-volume book, *Les bases de la météorologie dynamique* (The basis of dynamical meteorology), which was published, chapter by chapter, between 1898 and 1907, one of the most beautiful books concerning meteorology because it contains a lot of old documents, mainly maps at their original size—a valuable source of information on the history of meteorology.

Exploration of the Polar and Tropical Atmospheres. Even before the publication of the discovery of what is now called the stratosphere, Teisserenc de Bort decided to extend the geographical area of his researches, in order to give a universal range to his upper-air measurements. In 1900 he organized a field experiment in Saint Petersburg and Moscow, Russia, headed by Alfred de Quervain, a Swiss geophysicist who later explored Greenland.

Teisserenc de Bort also cofinanced the establishment in 1902 of a meteorological observatory in Hald, Denmark, with his colleagues Hildebrandsson (Sweden) and Adam Paulsen (Denmark) and the help of Eleuthère Mascart, the head of BCM. Their kites and sounding balloons launched at the observatory were complemented by launches by the Danish navy in the Baltic sea.

With Rotch, Teisserenc de Bort cofinanced in 1905 and 1906 cruises on his ship *Otaria,* bought to investigate the existence of (westerly) antitrade winds. Hergesell had denied their existence above Tenerife Island in 1905, but observations by kites and balloons confirmed their existence over a large area including Tenerife. The two men

also extended their soundings to the equatorial Atlantic, even in the Southern Hemisphere, in the Saint Helena anticyclone where they found stratospheric temperatures much colder than in temperate latitudes at the same altitude.

With his friend Hildebrandsson, Teisserenc de Bort also organized a three-year (1907–1909) expedition to investigate the arctic atmosphere in Kiruna, Lapland. The results were published by his collaborator M. Maurice after his death. The main result of all these expeditions was that the altitude of the base of the isothermal layer is higher in tropical than in arctic or temperate regions, and that at the same altitude this layer is colder in the tropical latitudes than in the others.

Teisserenc de Bort not only discovered the stratosphere but also coined the words *stratosphere* (sphere of layers) and *troposphere* (sphere of turning) in 1908. He thought that no vertical motion took place in the stratosphere, in opposition to what occurs in the troposphere where vertical motions are responsible for the existence of the vertical gradient of temperature. The word *tropopause* was coined later by William Henry Dines (1910).

After his death in 1913, the Dynamic Meteorology Observatory was donated by his heiress, his niece Hermine Teisserenc de Bort, to the French army, after first being refused by the French Academy of Sciences. Into the twenty-first century the observatory continues to exist, belonging to Météo-France, the French meteorological service, and still launches balloons carrying radiosondes not unlike those that were first invented at the observatory in 1929 by Robert Bureau.

BIBLIOGRAPHY

The correspondence between Hildebrandsson and Teisserenc de Bort is available both at the Uppsala observatory (Sweden) and at Météo-France (Paris).

WORKS BY TEISSERENC DE BORT

With Hugo Hildebrand Hildebrandsson and Albert Riggenbach. *Atlas international des nuages* [International cloud atlas]. Paris: Gauthier-Villars, 1896.

With Hugo Hildebrand Hildebrandsson. *Les bases de la météorologie dynamique: historique—État de nos connaissances.* 2 vols. Paris: Gauthier-Villars, 1898–1907.

"Résultats sommaires des ascensions de trois ballons-sondes exécutées à Trappes." *Comptes rendus de l'Académie des sciences* 133 (13 June 1898): 1754–1755.

"Variations de la température de l'air libre, dans la zone comprise entre 8 et 15 kilomètres d'altitude." *Comptes rendus de l'Académie des sciences* 134 (28 April 1902): 987–989.

Notice sur les travaux scientifiques de M. Léon Teisserenc de Bort. Paris: Imprimerie générale Lahure, 1906. Analysis of his own works with an extensive bibliography. A five-page supplement to the notice was published in 1909.

OTHER SOURCES

Hann, Julius von. *Lehrbuch der Meteorologie.* Leipzig: C. H. Tauchnitz, 1901.

Hoinka, Klaus P. "The Tropauose: Discovery, Definition and Demarcation." *Meteorologische Zeitschrift neue Folge* 6 (1997): 281–303.

Ohring, George. "A Most Surprising Discovery." *Bulletin of the American Meteorological Society* 45 (1964): 12–14.

Rochas, Michel. "L'atlas international des nuages." *La Météorologie* 15 (1996): 35–42.

———. "Il y a un siècle. Le contexte scientifique de la surprenante découverte de la stratosphère." *La Météorologie* 37 (2002): 57–69.

Shaw, Napier. *Manual of Meteorology,* vol. 1, *Meteorology in History.* Cambridge, U.K.: Cambridge University Press, 1926.

Michel Rochas

Edward Teller. © ROGER RESSMEYER/CORBIS.

TELLER, EDWARD (*b.* Budapest, Hungary, 15 January 1908; *d.* Palo Alto, California, 9 September 2003), *theoretical physics, fusion, science policy.*

Though an accomplished theoretical physicist, Teller is best known for his early contributions to the development of the hydrogen bomb and his unwavering defense of nuclear weapons. His support of weapons and opposition to test bans, along with his advocacy of projects such as the Strategic Defense Initiative, made him both one of the most controversial physicists of the twentieth century and one of the most politically influential.

Early Years. Teller was born into a Hungarian-Jewish family the son of Max Teller, a lawyer, and the former Ilona Deutsch, a pianist. Turbulent politics entered Edward's life early. At the age of eleven, he witnessed the rise to power of Hungarian Communists, many of whom were Jewish, and the proclamation on 21 March 1919 of a Hungarian Soviet Republic. Although brief, the Communist rule inspired a strongly anti-Semitic reaction, the "white terror," resulting in the execution of approximately five thousand people, most of whom were Jewish, and the displacement of tens of thousands more. Although Edward stayed in Hungary during this period, his father told him that he would have to emigrate when he was older.

Education. Even as a young child Edward displayed extraordinary mathematical ability and as a teenager he saw this as his ticket out of what he believed to be a doomed Hungarian society. In 1926 he relocated to southwestern Germany, enrolling in the Technical Insti-

tute at Karlsruhe. Although he desired to study mathematics, he initially chose chemistry as a compromise with his father, who feared that math offered limited career prospects. The focus on chemistry was short-lived, as Teller quickly resumed his studies in mathematics in addition to chemistry. During his second year at Karlsruhe Teller was introduced to quantum mechanics. Upon obtaining the approval of his father, he left Karlsruhe and chemistry for good in April 1928. Within a few weeks Edward enrolled in the University of Munich to study under Arnold Sommerfeld, whose students had included future Nobel laureates Werner Heisenberg, Wolfgang Pauli, and Hans Bethe. In spite of Sommerfeld's reputation as a great teacher Teller did not enjoy the experience and by the fall of 1928 he began studying under Heisenberg at the University of Leipzig.

Enjoying this experience, Teller turned to what became his doctoral research project—calculating the energy states of the hydrogen molecular ion, two hydrogen nuclei and one electron, beyond its ground state. Upon receiving his doctorate in January 1930, Teller assumed a postdoctoral position as Heisenberg's assistant, which he maintained until that fall when he became an assistant to a physical chemist in Göttingen, the historic center of German math and physics. Teller would later remark that being a young scientist in Germany was the most satisfying period of his life.

This satisfying period was short, as Teller witnessed Adolf Hitler's rise to power and knew that he would have to relocate again. In February 1934 he married Augusta Maria "Mici" Harkanyi, a marriage that would last more than fifty years. That same year he and his new bride arrived at Niels Bohr's Institute for Theoretical Physics in Copenhagen. While in Denmark Teller became acquainted with the young Russian physicist and fellow political émigré, George Gamow. Gamow soon left the institute after obtaining a position on the faculty at George Washington University in Washington, D.C. In 1935 Teller followed Gamow to the university and relocated to the United States. He remained in America for the rest of his life, becoming a citizen in 1941. Though he had left Europe, the specter of increasing totalitarianism followed him across the Atlantic, as both his parents and sister remained there.

Dawn of the Atomic Age. Teller first began to consider the possibilities of a hydrogen weapon in late 1941 when, during a brief period at Columbia University, he met with Nobel laureate Enrico Fermi. Fermi had proposed that a fission explosion might create conditions close enough to what occurs within stars to induce the fusion of heavy hydrogen or deuterium nuclei, which, unlike standard hydrogen nuclei that contain only one proton, feature both a proton and a neutron. Though Teller was initially skeptical, he quickly established himself as the leading proponent of fusion weapons. During a 1942 meeting of top physicists at the University of California at Berkeley called by J. Robert Oppenheimer to discuss the potential development of fission weapons, Teller suggested that the prospect of building a hydrogen weapon, a "Super," be explored as well.

In early 1943, by which time he had joined the faculty at the University of Chicago, Edward, along with his wife and their six-week-old son Paul, moved to Los Alamos, New Mexico, to join the collection of scientists and engineers working on the Manhattan Project. While working under Bethe, head of the theoretical division at Los Alamos (with whom Teller had been close friends throughout the 1930s, dating back to his time as a student in Germany), Teller came into conflict with both his immediate supervisor, Bethe, and Oppenheimer, the head of the project, over what he perceived to be the lack of attention paid to the question of developing the Super. This tension culminated in his being removed from the theoretical division during the war and allowed to devote himself full time to the question of fusion.

Development of the H-Bomb. In February 1946 Teller left Los Alamos and returned to Chicago where his second child, Susan Wendy, was born on 31 August. In spite of the move back to Illinois, his attention remained focused on the development of fusion weapons and throughout the postwar years he continued to work on the technical challenges presented by them, returning to New Mexico periodically until November 1951 to consult with scientists still working there. Nevertheless, because numerous leading figures in the physics community opposed his goal of hydrogen weapons, Teller found it difficult to attract scientists to the lab that had been the center of the Manhattan Project.

His call for a hydrogen weapons program did, however, receive considerable support from military and political figures, especially in the wake of the Soviet Union's successful detonation of an atomic bomb in summer 1949. This increased support culminated in the January 1950 announcement by President Harry Truman that the United States would "continue its work on all forms of atomic weapons, including the so-called hydrogen or super bomb."

Unlike the atomic bombs detonated over Hiroshima and Nagasaki, Japan, which release energy when heavy elements such as uranium and plutonium undergo fission, hydrogen weapons function when, under intense heat and pressure, hydrogen isotopes—deuterium (one proton and one neutron) and tritium (one proton and two neutrons)—experience fusion. The energy released by fusion, the same process that occurs in the Sun, is orders of magnitude larger than that of fission, with some weapons more than two thousand times as powerful as the one dropped on Hiroshima. In addition to being far more efficient in terms of energy yield, hydrogen weapons, unlike fusion bombs, have no theoretical strength limit. The strength of the bomb can continue to increase as long as additional deuterium is added.

Fusion weapons are also quite different from fission bombs in terms of theoretical complexity. Although numerous scientists almost immediately recognized the potential military application of fission upon hearing of it in early 1939, the feasibility of fusion weapons was far less certain in the years immediately after World War II. Whereas many scientists were hesitant to work on fusion weapons due to ethical concerns, another aspect of the bomb that made many hesitant was a technical one: by the late 1940s it had become clear that the standard model of the Super, in which the detonation of a fission weapon would produce sufficient heat and energy to ignite a fusion reaction, was not feasible. The shock waves

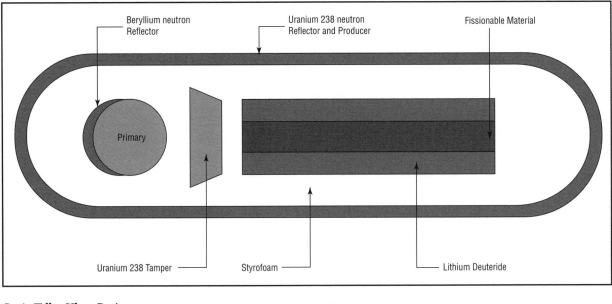

Beryllium neutron Reflector

Uranium 238 neutron Reflector and Producer

Fissionable Material

Primary

Uranium 238 Tamper

Styrofoam

Lithium Deuteride

Basic Teller-Ulam Design.

produced by the A-bomb would propagate too slowly to permit assembly of the thermonuclear stage before the bomb blew itself apart. The question of how to ignite the hydrogen weapon continued to be a grave technical obstacle until early in 1951.

In March 1951 Stanislaw Ulam, a young Polish mathematician, came to Teller with a new approach. Together the men developed what became known as the Teller-Ulam design. This design broke up the fusion process into stages where the primary stage, resembling the classical Super, featured the detonation of an atomic bomb. The difference was that, unlike the previous model, which relied on heat and shock waves to trigger fusion, the Teller-Ulam approach made use of the radiation produced in the primary stage. In order to take advantage of this they introduced a material, polystyrene or styrofoam, which captured the high energy of gamma-ray radiation.

In bombs of this design, the styrofoam is placed around cylinders containing the fuel, a compound of lithium and deuterium known as lithium deuteride, which powers the thermonuclear or secondary stage of the reaction. As the radiation is absorbed, each cylinder is subject to intense compression at almost the same moment, which in turn compresses the lithium deuteride. In addition to compression, the lithium is bombarded by neutrons that are reflected back after being released by both the fission reaction and additional Uranium-238 placed around the weapon. As a result of the compressed lithium deuteride core being bombarded with neutrons, tritium, a hydrogen isotope featuring two neutrons, is formed and the fusion process begins when the newly produced tritium fuses with the deuterium from the original fuel.

After development of the Teller-Ulam design it became clear that the creation of fusion weapons was technically feasible. Any doubt about their possibility came to an end on 31 October 1952 when the United States detonated its first thermonuclear device, "Mike," on Enewetak Atoll in the South Pacific. The device, while far too large to be a deliverable weapon, had a yield equivalent to approximately 10.4 megatons of TNT, or more than 500 times the yield of the bomb dropped on Hiroshima.

Teller and the Oppenheimer Hearing. Teller's position and continuous advocacy of hydrogen weapons, which he saw as the best response to the increasing threat posed by the Soviet Union, resulted in a number of conflicts with other physicists that often led to the dissolution of longtime friendships. Teller was not alone among physicists in calling for the development of fusion weapons; other notable advocates of a hydrogen program included Nobel laureate (1939) Ernest Lawrence, future Nobel laureate (1968) Luis Alvarez, and John Wheeler, whose 1939 *Physical Review* paper with Bohr on fission was one of the foundational works in the field. Teller, however, was the program's most active advocate and the scientist most closely associated with it. As he attempted to marshal the resources necessary to pursue hydrogen weapons in a way comparable to the Manhattan Project, a number of physicists, many of whom had worked on the Manhattan Project in one capacity or another, made their opposition to this new program clear. These scientists included thenpresident of Harvard University James Conant, Enrico Fermi, I. I. Rabi, and former Los Alamos director Oppenheimer.

Whereas Teller's position on weapons put him into conflict with any number of scientists, it was his conflict with Oppenheimer that had the most profound effect on Teller and his relationships to other physicists. This conflict, which first emerged at Los Alamos, intensified in the postwar years. Teller found few takers in his effort to have scientists return to Los Alamos and continue work on fusion weapons. Although there were a number of reasons for declining, not the least of which was the uncertainty over whether or not fusion weapons were technically feasible, Teller attributed much of the hesitancy to Oppenheimer's influence over the physics community and his failure to support the hydrogen program. The clearest expression of this opposition came on 30 October 1949 when a blue-ribbon panel of scientists led by Oppenheimer and known as the General Advisory Committee (GAC) to the Atomic Energy Commission (AEC) issued a report to President Truman that advised against developing fusion bombs. In an addendum to the report Fermi and Rabi stated, "By its very nature it [a fusion bomb] cannot be confined to a military objective but becomes a weapon … of genocide…. It is necessarily an evil thing considered in any light."

Whereas Teller and Oppenheimer had been in conflict over the issue of fusion weapons since their days together at Los Alamos, it was Teller's testimony at Oppenheimer's 1954 AEC security hearing, testimony that many physicists saw simply as retaliation for Oppenheimer's failure to support fully a fusion program, which proved to be a defining event in Teller's often tumultuous relationship with other elite physicists. The hearing concerned the question of whether or not Oppenheimer should be stripped of security clearance. Although Teller made it clear during his testimony that he did not believe Oppenheimer had ever been disloyal, he also stated, "In a great number of cases I have seen Dr. Oppenheimer act … in a way which for me was exceedingly hard to understand. I thoroughly disagreed with him in [*sic*] numerous issues and his actions frankly appeared to me confused and complicated. To this extent I feel that I would like to see the vital interests of this country in hands which I understand better, and therefore trust more. In this very limited sense I would like to express a feeling that I would feel personally more secure if public matters would rest in other hands" (U.S. Energy Commission, 1971, p. 710).

Once the transcript of the hearing was made public shortly after its conclusion, a number of physicists who read his testimony felt that Teller had betrayed Oppenheimer, and what were already difficult relationships were stretched to the breaking point. The situation deteriorated to the point where, according to lifelong friend Wheeler, some physicists would literally turn their backs on Teller when he entered a room.

Teller as Policy Advisor. Though Teller's advocacy of nuclear weapons put him at odds with many in the scientific community, it also provided him with powerful allies in the military and government who shared Teller's vision of sophisticated, often then-unrealized, technology playing a major role in defense. Whereas he never achieved the same high profile as Oppenheimer once had, Teller maintained an important voice on issues of science and defense in numerous administrations up to and including that of Ronald Reagan.

Teller's first important political victory came with President Truman's decision in January 1950 that the United States would pursue a full-scale hydrogen bomb program. A second and perhaps more telling victory came with the creation of a second weapons laboratory in Livermore, California, just east of Berkeley. Although physicists at Berkeley such as Lawrence and Alvarez sought to be involved in responding to the Soviet atomic detonation in the summer of 1949, the establishment of the Lawrence Livermore Laboratory in 1952 resulted primarily from Teller's efforts. In successfully campaigning for a second lab he showed great aptitude for marshaling political resources and for building upon networks of sympathetic government and military officials.

While working at Los Alamos in the late 1940s Teller became involved in a protracted conflict with Norris Bradbury—the director of Los Alamos from October 1945, when he took over from Oppenheimer, to 1970—over the best way to pursue a hydrogen weapons program. The conflict reached a head in the summer of 1951, just months after the Teller-Ulam breakthrough, when Teller decided that a second and independent lab was necessary to pursue fully the new design. Shortly thereafter, Teller's influence in political and military circles began to show. Under pressure to do so, the GAC reviewed the matter and, with only one dissenting vote, argued against building a second lab on the grounds that it would divert resources and manpower from Los Alamos. The series of events that followed suggested that in many important ways Teller had already supplanted Oppenheimer as the most powerful scientific voice in Washington, even prior to the latter's security hearing. Undaunted by the GAC report, Teller solicited and found great support within the U.S. Air Force. Moving their way up the chain of command Teller's views were fully supported by Secretary of the Air Force Thomas Finletter. As the military became more active in directly sponsoring nuclear research, the AEC came under increasing pressure to form a second lab. The desired result was achieved in June 1952 when the AEC approved a laboratory at Livermore, where weapons work included conducting diagnostic experiments during weapons tests. The new lab officially opened its doors in September 1952.

While continuing to work on hydrogen weapons Teller again took on the role of de facto policy advisor in 1957, when the question of atmospheric testing arose. After almost a decade of exploding atomic weapons in the atmosphere, the fallout began to settle and a growing number of nations were concerned about the potential health consequences. The pressure to move away from atmospheric testing increased when Albert Schweitzer, the 1952 Nobel Peace Prize winner, called for a ban on weapons tests. In that same year Congressional hearings focused public concern on the cancer hazard posed by exposure to radiation. Finally, Linus Pauling, the 1954 Nobel Prize winner in chemistry, obtained nine thousand signatures from concerned scientists around the world who supported a test ban. The public concern resonated with President Dwight D. Eisenhower, who was himself concerned by the buildup of nuclear weapons. By 19 June 1957 a moratorium seemed likely when, shortly after the Russians proposed a two- to three-year ban, the president announced that he "would be perfectly delighted to make some satisfactory arrangement for temporary suspension of tests."

Teller, along with his close ally and AEC chairman, Lewis Strauss, strongly opposed any freeze. On 21 June 1957 Teller and two other AEC physicists met with the president to argue for the continuation of tests on the grounds that such tests would help in the development of clean bombs, that is, bombs free of radioactive fallout, which Teller suggested would be realized within six or seven years. In spite of his earlier statement and the growing global support for a test ban, Eisenhower deferred to Teller and the AEC consultants in the belief that "the real peaceful use of atomic science depends on their developing clean weapons," giving no weight to Teller's suggestion that such weapons still did not exist. Though he was successful in dissuading Eisenhower, Teller's ability to forestall an atmospheric ban was compromised with the 1960 election of Democrat John F. Kennedy. In a pattern that would persist throughout his life, Teller found a less receptive audience in the Democratic administration and on 5 August 1963 the United States, USSR, and United Kingdom signed the Limited Test Ban Treaty, which prohibited atmospheric testing.

Though Teller continued to give his input on issues relating to science and defense throughout the Cold War, emphasizing the need for futuristic technology, he found his most receptive audience in the Reagan administration. It was in this period that the nuclear freeze movement gained support with its claim that the continued stockpiling of weapons was unnecessary, given the large arsenals already in existence. In response to these arms-control advocates Teller suggested to government officials that nuclear weapons research could be presented as necessary for defense and funded under the rubric of a defensive

shield. He was able to convince politicians of the feasibility of a laser defense system known as the Strategic Defense Initiative, but referred to by critics as "Star Wars," a system of satellites firing x-ray lasers at incoming missiles. Teller's critics became increasingly vocal as, despite the tens of billions of dollars committed to the project, the promised technology never came to be.

In addition to his university appointments at George Washington University and Chicago, Teller was appointed professor of physics at the University of California at Berkeley and associate director of Livermore Lab in 1953. He became director of the lab in 1958 before resigning in 1960 to become professor of physics at large for the University of California. In 1975 he was named director emeritus of Livermore. He was a Fellow of the American Academy of Arts and Sciences, the American Association for the Advancement of Science, and the American Nuclear Society. Among the honors he received were the Albert Einstein Award, the Enrico Fermi Award, and the National Medal of Science. He was also named as part of the group of U.S. scientists who were *Time* magazine's People of the Year in 1960. He was awarded the Presidential Medal of Freedom, the nation's highest civilian award, by President George W. Bush in July 2003, less than two months before his death.

BIBLIOGRAPHY

Teller's archival collection, The Papers of Edward Teller, *1946–2003, is held at the Hoover Institution on War, Revolution and Peace; Archives; Stanford University, Stanford, CA 94305.*

WORKS BY TELLER

"The Rate of Selective Thermonuclear Reactions." *Physical Review* 53, no. 7 (April 1938): 608–609.

"On the Polar Vibrations of Alkali Halides." *Physical Review* 59, no. 8 (April 1941): 673–676.

With Allen Brown. *The Legacy of Hiroshima.* Garden City, NY: Doubleday, 1962.

With Wilson K. Talley and Gary H. Higgins. *The Constructive Uses of Nuclear Explosives.* New York: McGraw-Hill, 1968.

Better a Shield Than a Sword: Perspectives on Defense and Technology. New York: Free Press/Macmillan, 1987.

With Judith Shoolery. *Memoirs: A Twentieth-Century Journey in Science and Politics.* Cambridge, MA: Perseus, 2001.

OTHER SOURCES

Galison, Peter, and Barton Berstein. "In Any Light: Scientists and the Decision to Build the Superbomb, 1952–1954." *Historical Studies in the Physical Sciences* 19, no. 2 (1989): 267–347.

Herken, Gregg. *Brotherhood of the Bomb: The Tangled Lives and Loyalties of Robert Oppenheimer, Ernest Lawrence, and Edward Teller.* New York: Holt, 2002.

O'Neill, Dan. *The Firecracker Boys*. New York: St. Martin's Press, 1994.

Phodes, Richard. *Dark Sun: The Making of the Hydrogen Bomb*. New York: Simon & Schuster, 1995.

U.S. Atomic Energy Commission. *In the Matter of J. Robert Oppenheimer: Transcript of Hearing before Personnel Security Board and Texts of Principal Documents and Letters*. Foreword by Philip M. Stern. Cambridge, MA: MIT Press, 1971.

York, Herbert F. *The Advisors: Oppenheimer, Teller, and the Superbomb*. Stanford, CA: Stanford University Press, 1989.

Shawn Mullet

TERMAN, LEWIS MADISON (*b.* Franklin, Indiana, 15 January 1877; *d.* Palo Alto, California, 21 December 1956), *psychology, education, mental testing, human sexuality.*

Terman was one of the leaders in the development of psychological tests that measured individual and group differences. He played a major role in establishing the use of intelligence and achievement tests in American schools. His most noteworthy research dealt with the intellectually gifted.

Early Life and Professional Training. Lewis M. Terman was born and raised on a farm in central Indiana, the twelfth of James William and Martha's fourteen children. He went to a one-room school, completing the eighth grade when he was twelve. He was determined to continue his education, but with no high school near his home, the only avenue open for higher education was teacher training at a normal college. Terman was fifteen before his parents were able to pay for his education; he then enrolled at Central Normal College in Danville, Indiana. At seventeen, with basic teacher preparation achieved, he obtained his first teaching position and four years later he became a high school principal. Over a six-year period, he earned three undergraduate degrees at the normal college. During his teacher training, he met fellow student Anna Belle Minton (no relation to this author), whom he married in 1899.

With aspirations beyond school teaching, Terman entered Indiana University in 1901, earning a master's degree in psychology in two years. With the encouragement of his Indiana mentor Ernest H. Lindley, he proceeded to doctoral studies in 1903 at Clark University under the direction of G. Stanley Hall, one of the early leaders in American psychology. For his dissertation, Terman conducted an experimental study of mental tests, comparing the performance of a "bright" and a "dull" group of ten- to thirteen-year-old boys. Because Hall did

not approve of mental tests, Edmund C. Sanford supervised his dissertation, and Terman obtained his PhD in 1905. Hall, however, influenced Terman's thinking about the nature of intelligence. Consistent with Hall's evolutionary perspective on individual and group differences, Terman assumed that mental tests measured native ability.

While studying at Clark, Terman became ill with tuberculosis. Although he made a successful recovery, he decided to seek employment in a warm climate. With his graduate work completed, he accepted a position as a high school principal in San Bernardino, California. A year later, he was able to attain more intellectually challenging work, teaching child study and pedagogy at the Los Angeles State Normal School. In 1910 he received an appointment at prestigious Stanford University's education department. He spent the rest of his career at Stanford, becoming head of the psychology department in 1922, a position he held until his retirement in 1942.

Mental Test Pioneer. The move to Stanford in 1910 coincided with Terman's full recovery from tuberculosis, and he was thus able to take on a more active academic workload. He resumed his earlier research in mental testing and began to work with Alfred Binet's 1908 scale, the first widely accepted measure of intelligence. Henry H. Goddard had published translations from the French of Binet's original 1905 scale and the subsequent 1908 revision. Terman's first tentative revision of the Binet appeared in 1912 and with the assistance of a team of graduate students, the final version—the "Stanford-Binet"—was published in 1916. An innovative feature of the Stanford-Binet was the inclusion of a total score in the form of an "Intelligence Quotient" or IQ—that is, the ratio between mental and chronological ages—a concept first introduced by the German psychologist William Stern, but not previously used in mental tests. The mental age represented test performance based on age norms. While there were several competitive versions, Terman's revision of the Binet utilized the largest standardized sample and by the 1920s became the most widely used individually administered intelligence test.

With the publication of the Stanford-Binet, Terman became a highly visible figure in the American mental testing movement. Reflecting his reputation, he was invited in 1917 to serve on a committee that had been assembled at the Vineland Training School for the mentally retarded in New Jersey to develop mental tests for the U.S. Army. The United States had entered World War I and Robert M. Yerkes, the president of the American Psychological Association, organized the psychologists' contribution to the war effort. Yerkes chaired the testing committee, and the membership was made up of the leading psychologists in the mental testing field. Terman brought with him a new group-administered version of the Stanford-Binet that had been developed by his graduate student, Arthur S. Otis. The Otis test served as the basis for the construction of the army group tests (the Alpha and Beta examinations). While serious questions have been raised about the significance of the psychologists' contribution to the war, it is clear that the war provided an enormous boost for the mental testing movement. Approximately 1.75 million men were tested, and on this basis, recommendations were made with regard to job placements or immediate discharge from the army. The major weakness of the army testing program was the psychologists' failure to incorporate the impact of cultural differences on tested intelligence. Thus, the lower IQ scores earned by foreign-born and poor native-born soldiers were interpreted as reflecting low levels of native ability rather than other factors such as limited acculturation and schooling. Terman, like the other members of the army testing committee, adhered to the assumption that mental abilities were primarily a product of heredity.

Mass Testing in the Schools. After the war, Terman seized upon the contribution of the army tests to military efficiency and predicted that they would soon be universally used in the schools. To achieve this goal, Terman and the other psychologists who constructed the army tests adapted them for school-age children. The resulting "National Intelligence Tests" for grades three to eight were published in 1920. Terman became an advocate for the use of intelligence tests as a means of reorganizing schools so that pupils could be classified into homogeneous ability groups. He worked closely with the National Education Association, which in 1918 had opted for a differentiated curriculum—a policy aimed at bringing order out of the chaos of a burgeoning population of schoolchildren, swelled by large numbers of recent immigrants. Thus, during the 1920s, intelligence testing and the tracking system of ability grouping became common practice in schools and Terman played a central role in fostering these programs.

Terman was also a leader in the development of standardized group achievement tests, which measured school learning. With a team of Stanford colleagues, he produced the first achievement test battery—the Stanford Achievement Test. Terman viewed the widespread adoption of tests in the schools as a reflection of how testing could benefit American society. It was to be a major means of achieving his vision of a meritocracy within the American democratic ideal—a social order based on ranked levels of native ability. As a measure of native ability, intelligence tests could identify children who were cognitively gifted and therefore had the potential to emerge as leaders of society. Once these children were identified, it was the responsibility of the schools to devote the necessary time and effort to cultivate their intellectual talent.

The Study of the Gifted. To fulfill his meritocratic goals and supported by a research grant from the Commonwealth Fund of New York, Terman launched a longitudinal study of gifted children in 1921. This was an innovative project because it was the first investigation to use a large sample of subjects who were followed over the course of several years. The criterion for categorizing gifted children was an IQ of at least 135, which constituted the highest 1 percent of the distribution of IQ scores. With a pool of more than a quarter-million schoolchildren in California public schools, Terman and his research team selected elementary and secondary schools in urban areas. To further the efficiency of the selection process, the researchers relied on teacher nominations of the "brightest" pupils in their classes. The resulting sample of approximately 1,500 gifted children thus turned out to be largely white and middle-class. Terman, however, did not appear to be sensitive to the bias inherent in teacher nominations, because he attributed race and class differences primarily to heredity.

In an effort to dispel the popular notion that gifted children were underdeveloped in nonintellectual areas, Terman included medical and physical assessments, as well as measures of personality, character, and interests. The gifted sample was compared with a control group of California schoolchildren of comparable age. In the first of a series of monographs on the gifted study, the major finding was that gifted children excelled in measures of academic achievement when matched with age for control children. The composite portrait of the gifted children also revealed that they were emotionally as well as intellectually mature.

Based on these initial findings, Terman strongly advocated a differentiated school curriculum that would place gifted children in special classrooms where they could accelerate academically according to their ability rather than their age. With additional research funding, Terman followed up his gifted sample for a period of thirty-five years. At midlife, as reported in a 1959 monograph, the intellectual level of the gifted group continued to be within the upper 1 percent of the general population, and their occupational achievement was well above the average of college graduates. Furthermore, as earlier reports had demonstrated, they showed few signs of such serious problems as insanity, delinquency, or alcoholism. The midlife report also included some striking gender differences. Whereas the men as a group had attained a high level of career success, few women had comparable levels of career achievement. As Terman noted, career opportunities for women were restricted by gender-role conformity and job discrimination.

Terman's involvement with the gifted study entailed more than data collection and research reports. Particularly after he retired from teaching in 1942, he devoted himself to the interests of gifted children by promoting special education for the gifted and, through contacts with journalists, disseminated the results of the gifted study in newspapers and magazines. He also popularized his work by making guest appearances on the radio show "The Quiz Kids." His appearance in 1947 coincided with the publication of the twenty-five year follow-up. By utilizing the public media, Terman aimed to eradicate the public's negative stereotype of gifted children as maladjusted. In his work with the gifted, Terman experienced particular satisfaction with the personal contacts he was able to establish with some of the research participants. He maintained correspondence with many of them over the years and in some instances received them as guests in his own home. Thus, for a number of the gifted children who "grew up" and came to be labeled as "Termites," he was a benevolent father figure and psychological counselor. By the early 1950s, with plans under way for the continuation of the gifted follow-up, Terman appointed Stanford colleague Robert R. Sears (who also happened to be a member of the gifted sample) to succeed him as research director. The gifted sample was thus followed up through late adulthood.

The Testing Debates. As one of the leading advocates of intelligence testing, Terman was often challenged by critics of the testing movement. These challenges began in the early 1920s when the results of the army testing became widely known. The influential journalist Walter Lippmann wrote a series of highly critical articles about the army tests in the *New Republic*. Lippmann singled out Terman because of his development of the Stanford-Binet and asserted that there was no foundation to support the assumption made by Terman and the other army psychologists that the tests measured innate ability. It should be noted that Lippmann did not simply rely on persuasive argument in challenging Terman: he specifically drew attention to what he believed were faulty interpretations of the data. Terman was enraged by Lippmann's attack. Despite the technical sophistication of many of the criticisms, Terman in his published reply in the *New Republic* recommended that Lippmann, as a layman, should stay out of issues he was not informed about. In fact, Terman was quite evasive in responding to the points Lippmann raised, such as an environmental interpretation of the correlation between tested intelligence and social class.

During the 1920s Terman also engaged in a series of published debates about testing with psychologist William

C. Bagley, another critic of the hereditarian view of intelligence. In an effort to resolve matters, Terman took on the task of chairing a committee that organized an edited book on the nature-nurture controversy. In this monograph, published in 1928, leading advocates on each side of the issue marshaled evidence and arguments, but as in previous exchanges, nothing was resolved.

In 1940 Terman was once again drawn into the nature-nurture debate, this time challenged by a team of environmental advocates at the University of Iowa led by George D. Stoddard. In a series of studies, the Iowa researchers reported that mental growth, as reflected by increases in IQ scores, was facilitated by school experience at both the preschool and elementary school levels. Their major conclusion was that IQ scores could be raised if children were exposed to environmentally stimulating conditions. Stoddard therefore argued that because of environmental influences intelligence tests should not be used to make long-term predictions; in essence, attacking the widespread use of intelligence tests in the schools as a means of sorting students into ability tracks. Terman viewed Stoddard's position as a threat to his career objective of establishing a meritocracy based on IQ differences. The 1940 debate, as in the past, led to an impasse. Intelligence testing in the schools continued to be common practice. It would not be until the 1960s, as a consequence of the civil rights movement, that mass testing was seriously challenged. Terman did modify his position to some extent. In the 1930s, mindful of the racial propaganda of Nazi Germany, he resigned his long-standing membership in the American Eugenics Society. After World War II, although he still held to his democratic ideal of a meritocracy, he no longer supported a hereditarian explanation of race differences, and he acknowledged that among the gifted, home environment was related to degree of success.

Studies of Gender and Marital Adjustment. Terman's interest in the study of individual and group differences extended beyond mental abilities and achievement. As a result of his research on the gifted, he became interested in measuring nonintellectual differences. By examining emotional and motivational characteristics, he sought to demonstrate that the gifted had well-adjusted and well-rounded personalities. To gain insight into this facet of human differences, he proceeded to measure gender identity, which was viewed as a composite of emotional and motivational traits that differentiated the sexes. By the 1910s psychologists had begun to study sex differences in motor, sensory, and intellectual abilities, but after a decade of inconclusive research results there was a shift of interest towards exploring broader concepts, such as the notions of masculinity and femininity. Terman tapped into this trend by identifying masculine and feminine interests from a questionnaire filled out by the gifted sample regarding their preferences for various play activities, games, and amusements. The initial survey conducted in 1922 revealed that the gifted and control children did not differ in gender orientation as derived from their activity preferences. In 1925 Terman was awarded a National Research Council grant to study sex differences and with his former student, Catharine Cox Miles, constructed a masculinity-femininity (M-F) test, the first measure of its kind. The final version, published in 1936 and labeled the "Attitude-Interest Analysis Test" to disguise its purpose, was based on normative samples of male and female groups ranging in age from early adolescence to late adulthood, although the core of the sample was high school juniors and college sophomores. The test consisted of approximately 450 multiple choice items that assessed preferences for a variety of activities and interests, as well as responses to emotionally-laden situations that might arouse feelings of anger or fear.

In an effort to validate the M-F test, Terman had the opportunity to collect test protocols from a group of male homosexuals in San Francisco who were motivated to volunteer for a team of scientists interested in studying them. As he expected, the results revealed that male homosexuals had high feminine scores. He thus concluded that marked deviations from gender-appropriate behaviors and norms were psychologically unhealthy because such deviation had the potential to lead to homosexuality. Even if this "maladjustment" did not develop, other problems could arise. Referring to those individuals with cross-gender identities in their 1936 monograph, "Sex and Personality: Studies in Masculinity and Femininity," Terman and Miles opined, "One would like to know whether fewer of them marry, and whether a larger proportion of these marriages are unhappy" (p. 46). Underscoring this point, they commented that "aggressive and independent" females could very well be at a disadvantage in the "marriage market" (p. 452). They also expressed the concern that too much competition between the sexes would not be socially desirable. In essence, the authors supported the conventional patriarchal relationship between the sexes. (It is not clear the extent to which Catharine Cox Miles concurred with this position, because Terman acknowledged prime responsibility for the conclusions in their book.)

Terman's conclusions on gender identity were based on the standardized norms he generated from his M-F test. The test represented the gender norms of the 1930s, but Terman was insensitive to the cultural and historical limits of his measure. He chose to emphasize the need to raise and train girls and boys so that they would conform to the existing gender norms that bolstered a clear distinction between the sexes. Consistent with his vision of a social order ranked by native ability, Terman professed

that sex differences also had to follow a prescribed ranking. Paralleling the need to cultivate ability differences to meet the needs of an increasingly urban and industrialized society, he also stressed the necessity of ensuring compatible sex roles in times of social change. Many social scientists during the interwar era, mindful of the feminist challenge, preached the need for compatibility rather than conflict between the sexes.

Terman's interest in gender identity and sex differences expanded to the study of marital adjustment. His attraction to exploring marriage was part of a growing trend among social scientists in the 1920s and 1930s to study and hence claim expertise on issues affecting families, including childrearing, sexuality, and marriage. In 1934 Terman conducted a large-scale survey of several hundred married and divorced couples in the San Francisco area. His major conclusion was that personality and social background factors were more influential than sexual compatibility in predicting marital happiness. This finding was contrary to previous studies that had argued that sexual compatibility was the key to marital success. Terman noted that this discrepancy was due to the fact that previous studies had neglected to consider psychological factors because they had been carried out by physicians and social workers. For Terman, this indicated the importance of psychologists being involved in the study of marital relations and human sexuality. In his study, Terman stressed that the key to marital adjustment was the extent to which each spouse accepted the other's needs and feelings and did not push to get his or her own way. To emphasize this argument, he noted that happily married women could be characterized as being cooperative and accepting of their prescribed subordinate roles. Terman's conventional views of gender carried over from his gender identity study to his marital research.

Terman's Contributions and Legacy. Terman's seminal contributions to the development of psychological testing and the study of the intellectually gifted ensure his position as one of the pioneers of American psychology. More than any of the other advocates of the testing movement, he was successful in devising a wide variety of methods assessing individual and group differences. His interest in the gifted led him to go far beyond the measurement of ability. As a result, he was in the forefront of developing indices of school achievement, gender identity, interests, marital adjustment, and sexual behavior. Aside from these personal accomplishments, Terman has left us with an unfulfilled legacy. What he wanted to achieve with his psychological tests and identification of the intellectually gifted was a more socially just and democratic society. A considerable part of Terman's project, however, has had an unintended dehumanizing effect. For racial and ethnic minorities and lower-class individuals, his differential educational system based on IQ scores served as a barrier for personal growth and social advancement. His views on gender and homosexuality worked against the creation of a more pluralistic society. What Terman failed to understand was the intricate way in which scientific knowledge reflects social power. By uncritically accepting the power inequities of the American social order of his day, he produced scientific knowledge and technology that functioned to perpetuate the status quo.

BIBLIOGRAPHY

The major archival resource is the Lewis M. Terman papers at the Stanford University Archives, Stanford University Libraries. A complete bibliography of Terman's publications is included in Minton, cited below.

WORKS BY TERMAN

The Measurement of Intelligence. Boston: Houghton-Mifflin, 1916.

The Stanford Revision and Extension of the Binet-Simon Scale for Measuring Intelligence. Boston: Houghton-Mifflin, 1917.

The Intelligence of School Children. Boston: Houghton-Mifflin, 1919.

Genetic Studies of Genius, Vol. 1, *Mental and Physical Traits of a Thousand Gifted Children.* Stanford, CA: Stanford University Press, 1925. The first in a series of monographs on the study of the gifted.

"Trails to Psychology." In *A History of Psychology in Autobiography*, edited by Carl A. Murchison. Worcester, MA: Clark University Press, 1932. Terman's autobiographical chapter.

With Catharine Cox Miles. *Sex and Personality: Studies in Masculinity and Femininity.* New York: McGraw-Hill, 1936.

With Maud A. Merrill. *Measuring Intelligence.* Boston: Houghton-Mifflin, 1937.

Psychological Factors in Marital Happiness. New York: McGraw-Hill, 1938.

With Melita H. Oden. *Genetic Studies of Genius*, Vol. 4: *The Gifted Child Grows Up: Twenty-Five Years of Follow-Up of a Superior Group.* Stanford, CA: Stanford University Press, 1947.

With Melita H. Oden. *Genetic Studies of Genius*, Vol. 5: *The Gifted Child at Mid-Life: Thirty-Five Years of Follow-Up of the Superior Child.* Stanford, CA: Stanford University Press, 1959.

With Robert R. Sears, Lee J. Cronbach, and Pauline S. Sears. "Terman Life-Cycle Study of Children with High Ability, 1922–1991." Available from www.ciser.cornell.edu. Final report of the study of the gifted.

OTHER SOURCES

Chapman, Paul Davis. *Schools as Sorters: Lewis M. Terman, Applied Psychology, and the Intelligence Testing Movement, 1890–1930.* New York: New York University Press, 1988.

Fancher, Raymond E. *The Intelligence Men: Makers of the IQ Controversy.* New York: W. W. Norton, 1985.

Gould, Stephen Jay. *The Mismeasure of Man.* New York: W. W. Norton, 1981. Includes a critical analysis of the mental testing movement.

Kimmel, Michael. *Manhood in America: A Cultural History.* New York: Free Press, 1996. Includes a critical analysis of Terman's study of masculinity-femininity.

Minton, Henry L. *Lewis M. Terman: Pioneer in Psychological Testing.* New York: New York University Press, 1988. Includes a complete bibliography of Terman's publications.

Samelson, Franz. "Putting Psychology on the Map: Ideology and Intelligence Testing." In *Psychology in Social Context*, edited by Alan R. Buss. New York: Irvington, 1979.

Seagoe, May V. *Terman and the Gifted.* Los Altos, CA: Kaufmann, 1975.

Zenderland, Leila. *Measuring Minds: Henry Herbert Goddard and the Origins of American Intelligence Testing.* Cambridge, U.K.: Cambridge University Press, 1998.

Henry L. Minton

TEUTONICUS, A.
SEE **Albertus Magnus, Saint**.

THARP, MARIE
(*b.* Ypsilanti, Michigan, 30 July 1920; *d.* Nyack, New York, 23 August 2006), *cartography, sea-floor mapping, oceanography.*

One of the most influential cartographers of the mid-twentieth century, Tharp created the first physiographic maps of the seafloor. These maps, made in collaboration with the geologist Bruce Heezen, were the first to reveal the detailed topography and multi-dimensional geographical landscape of the ocean bottom; they became significant evidence for the emerging theory of plate tectonics in the late 1960s. A research associate at Columbia University's Lamont Geological Observatory for the first part of the career, Tharp worked as an independent researcher after the late 1960s.

Early Years. Marie Tharp was born in Ypsilanti, Michigan, the daughter of William Edgar Tharp, a soil surveyor for the federal Bureau of Chemistry and Soils, and Bertha Louise (Newton) Tharp, a teacher of German and Latin. Her father's work caused the family to move frequently, and Tharp attended more than twenty different public schools in six states and the District of Columbia. After her father's retirement in 1931, the family settled on a farm in Bell Fountain, Ohio, where Tharp graduated from high school. She subsequently enrolled in the University of Ohio.

Tharp had not decided on a major when she started college. Her father insisted that she pick a subject that she liked and that would offer her a way to earn her own living. While at Ohio, Tharp changed her major every semester, and might have decided to become a teacher had her mother not died before she graduated. She received her bachelor's degree in English and music in 1943.

While she was finishing her degree at Ohio, Tharp happened upon a brochure from the University of Michigan's geology program encouraging young women to apply for graduate training to prepare for positions in the petroleum industry. With classrooms empty of men during the war years, Michigan—which had never allowed women into its geology program—was trying to fill seats. Tharp jumped at the chance, graduated with a master's degree in 1944, and went to work for Standlind Oil and Gas Company in Tulsa, Oklahoma, as a junior geologist. Upon her arrival, she discovered that women were not allowed to do field work, and so Tharp was stuck in an office coordinating maps and data for her male colleagues. During this time, she took enough courses at the University of Tulsa to earn a second bachelor's degree in mathematics in 1948.

East to Columbia University. Four years in Tulsa left Tharp eager for a new challenge that would include research. She headed east to Columbia University and found a position as a research assistant to geology graduate student Bruce Heezen. Heezen worked under the direction of the eminent geophysicist W. Maurice Ewing. He became her close professional collaborator and the two worked together as a creative couple, a relationship that continued almost thirty years until Heezen's death in 1977.

Her initial task at Columbia involved compiling oceanic bathymetry data. Prior to World War II, only widely scattered measurements had been made in the deep oceans, principally by government-sponsored expeditions such as those conducted by the British *HMS Challenger* (1872–1876) and the German *Meteor* (1925–1927). Although these expeditions had revealed certain large-scale features, including an extended rise called the Mid-Atlantic Ridge, the general characteristics of the seafloor remained largely unknown.

Interest in the oceans increased during and after World War II, owing to military concerns with understanding the ocean environment for anti-submarine warfare. By the early 1950s Heezen (now a junior PhD associate of Ewing at Columbia's new Lamont Geological Observatory) and his colleagues began gathering wide-ranging data on the ocean floor, including its elevation. Tharp's role at Lamont expanded to include assessing the reliability of past and contemporary depth measurements and interpreting the geographic landscapes they began to reveal. In the process Tharp made one of her most important discoveries: a rift valley bisecting the Mid-Atlantic Ridge that was structurally similar to the Great Rift Valley in Africa. Initially Heezen refused to accept this find, but relented after noticing that seismological records of undersea earthquake epicenters correlated with the mid-Atlantic rift valley. As precise measurements extended across Earth's oceans, Heezen, Tharp, and Ewing also discovered that the Mid-Atlantic Ridge was part of a 40,000 mile long world-encircling ridge system, the largest tectonic feature on Earth's surface and a significant geological finding.

Seafloor Cartography. In 1952 Heezen sought to make a detailed map of the North Atlantic seafloor, aware that existing maps were coarse and provided limited insight into distinct geographical provinces and landforms (including abyssal plains and mountain ridges) that depth soundings were revealing. He and Tharp decided against making a contour map in favor of a physiographic one, portraying physical features from an oblique perspective with scale and position carefully controlled. They did this for several reasons: beyond providing a realistic bird's eye view, a physiographic map enabled them to circumvent navy classification policies because it did not provide precise depth data. By 1957, with support from telecommunications companies then laying the first transatlantic undersea telephone lines, Heezen and Tharp completed their pioneering detailed physiographic map of the North Atlantic Ocean seafloor, one of the most significant new maps of the twentieth century.

In the 1960s and 1970s Heezen and Tharp extended their mapping project to all the world's oceans. Drawing on her artistic and drafting skills to create individual ocean basin maps, Tharp worked with Heezen and also the Austrian artist Heinrich Berann to produce the 1977 "World Ocean Floor" panorama, a widely circulated iconic map that depicted what was then known about seafloor topography. While these maps stimulated geophysical and oceanographic research—Heezen used the North Atlantic map to support the expanding Earth concept—the mapping project also exacerbated tensions between Heezen and Ewing involving publication credit and priority. In the late 1960s Ewing barred Tharp, who unlike Heezen did not occupy a tenured position, from working at Lamont, causing her to shift her mapping work to her nearby home.

Awards and Later Career. Tharp gained her first opportunity to go to sea in 1965 on a research cruise Heezen organized on Duke University's *R/V Eastward* (at Lamont, Ewing still prohibited women from working at sea).

Largely invisible as a researcher early in her career, Tharp gained recognition for her geographic insights and cartographic skills later in life. She received awards from the Geography and Map Division of the Library of Congress and Woods Hole Oceanographic Institution, as well as the first annual Lamont-Doherty Earth Observatory Heritage Award in 2001. Four years later, Lamont created the Marie Tharp Visiting Fellowship program to aid promising women researchers.

After Heezen's death, Tharp remained a professional map-maker, selling copies of the Heezen-Tharp seafloor maps from her research office-home in Nyack, New York, overlooking the Hudson River. Largely unfazed by the intense professional rivalry between Heezen and Ewing, Tharp was regarded by Lamont colleagues as intensely focused, wholly devoted to Heezen, and largely unconcerned with fashion or worldly pursuits. Tharp died of cancer in Nyack, New York, in August 2006.

BIBLIOGRAPHY

A collection of transcribed oral history interviews with Tharp resides at the Niels Bohr Library of the American Institute of Physics in College Park, Maryland. Her map collection is held at the Geography and Map Division of the U.S. Library of Congress.

WORKS BY THARP

With Bruce C. Heezen. "Physiographic Diagram of the North Atlantic." *Geological Society of America Bulletin* 67 (1956): 1704.

With Bruce C. Heezen and Maurice Ewing. *The Floors of the Ocean.* Geological Society of America Special Paper 65. New York: Geological Society of America, 1959.

With Bruce C. Heezen. "Tectonic Fabric of the Atlantic and Indian Oceans and Continental Drift." *Philosophical Transactions of the Royal Society of London. Series A, Mathematical and Physical Sciences* 258, no. 1088 (1965): 90–106.

With Bruce C. Heezen. "Physiography of the Indian Ocean." *Philosophical Transactions of the Royal Society of London, Series A: Mathematical and Physical Sciences* 259 (1966): 137–149.

With Henry Frankel. "Mappers of the Deep: How Two Geologists Plotted the Mid-Atlantic Ridge and Made a Discovery that Revolutionized the Earth Sciences." *Natural History* 95, no. 10 (1986): 49–62.

OTHER SOURCES

Barton, Cathy. "Marie Tharp, Oceanographic Cartographer, and Her Contributions to the Revolution in the Earth Sciences." In *The Earth Inside and Out: Some Major Contributions to Geology in the Twentieth Century,* edited by David R. Oldroyd. London: Geological Society, 2002.

Doel, Ronald E., Tanya J. Levin, and Mason K. Marker. "Extending Modern Cartography to the Ocean Depths; Military Patronage, Cold War Priorities, and the Heezen-

Tharp Mapping Project, 1952–1959." *Journal of Historical Geography* 32 (2006): 605–626.

Ronald E. Doel
Kristine C. Harper

THEORELL, AXEL HUGO THEODOR
(*b.* Linköping, Sweden, 6 July 1903, *d.* Stockholm, Sweden, 15 August 1982), *chemistry, biochemistry, structural chemistry, physical chemistry.*

Theorell was awarded the Nobel Prize for Physiology or Medicine in 1955 for his discoveries concerning the nature and mode of action of oxidation enzymes. Enzymes are the workhorses of the never-ending process of chemical transformations that characterizes the world of living organisms. In this maelstrom of chemical reactions, the substrates are supplied in an activated form that makes them ready for further processing. A crucial role in their activation is played by so-called coenzymes and prosthetic groups. Theorell made major discoveries regarding the molecular structure of enzymes, coenzymes acting as activation groups and substrates, and the mechanisms of the interactions between them. His elucidation of spatial structures of molecules greatly contributed to closing the gap between biochemistry and subcellular morphology, which had persisted until the 1960s.

Family Life and Professional Career. Axel Hugo Theodor Theorell was born on 6 July 1903, the son of Thure Theorell, surgeon-major to the First Life Grenadiers, who practiced medicine in Linköping, and his wife Armida Bill. Hugo Theorell, often known as Theo, had two sisters. At the age of three, he suffered a severe poliomyelitis infection, which left his left leg permanently paralyzed. He later underwent a muscle transplant, which allowed him to walk with relative ease. Perhaps it was because of his disability that he developed strong arms and shoulders, giving him a muscular appearance.

Theo was educated at a state-run secondary school in Linköping for nine years, passing his matriculation exam there on 23 May 1921. In September 1921 he started studying medicine at the Karolinska Institute in Stockholm, where he graduated with a bachelor of medicine in 1924. In 1930 he obtained his MD degree, having written a thesis on the lipids of blood plasma, and was appointed lecturer in physiological chemistry at the Karolinska Institute. Theorell started to work under Einar Hammarsten, who at the time was only thirty-five. One year after obtaining his doctorate, Theo moved to the institute led by The Svedberg at Uppsala University in Sweden, where he was appointed associate professor of

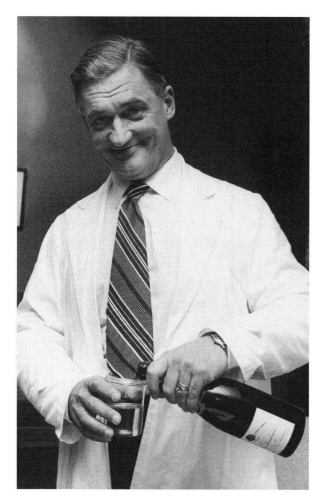

A. Hugo T. Theorell. *Theorell upon learning he has been awarded the 1955 Nobel Peace Prize.* AP IMAGES.

medical and physiological chemistry in 1932. In 1933 a Rockefeller Foundation fellowship enabled him to go to Berlin-Dahlem to work with the biochemist and cell physiologist Otto Warburg.

It was through his interest in music that he met his future wife, harpsichordist Elin Margit Elisabeth Alenius, whom he married on 5 June 1931. They had a daughter Eva Kristina, who died of tuberculosis in 1935, shortly after the family had returned to Sweden from Berlin-Dahlem, and later had three sons. His great interest in music is apparent from the fact that he became a member of the Swedish Royal Academy of Music, as well as chairman of the Stockholm Symphony Society.

Upon his return to Sweden, Theorell once again took up a post at the Karolinska Institute, and in 1936 he was appointed head of the newly established Biochemical Department of the Nobel Medical Institute. This institute, which was officially opened in 1937, was located at the Karolinska Institute, which also took care of its

administrative affairs. It was not until 1947 that the Nobel Medical Institute got its own building on the outskirts of Stockholm. The institute's staff had no teaching duties, which suited Theorell, as he was not particularly interested in teaching. He was, however, a gifted speaker with a good command of several languages, and he was an inspired raconteur of humorous anecdotes. He continued to head the Biochemical Department until 1970.

During World War II, Sweden remained neutral, but became relatively isolated, and Theorell's laboratory had very few guest researchers from abroad. Immediately after the war, however, a stream of prominent foreign biochemists came to work there for shorter or longer periods. Those among the postdoctoral students and guest researchers who worked under Theorell's supervision were usually encouraged by him to publish their results without including Theorell as a coauthor. It was Hugo Theorell's combination of creative imagination, critical accuracy, and technical skills that made him such an outstanding researcher and research supervisor.

The "Yellow Enzyme." In the 1930s, biochemists were taking an avid interest in oxidation and reduction reactions in living organisms. Warburg had studied the process of respiration in cells and the role of a catalytic iron compound in this process in the 1920s. He had called this enzyme *Atmungsferment* and had studied the effects of carbon monoxide and light on the respiratory process, research for which he was awarded the Nobel Prize for Physiology or Medicine in 1931, and more laboratories started to investigate biological oxidation-reduction reactions. The latter support the transduction of energy and the transformation of metabolites. In general, the enzymes which catalyze biological oxidation-reduction are organized in systems of enzymes, which function as a terminal respiratory chain, that is, a group of enzymes that transfers reducing equivalents to O_2.

In the respiratory chain, oxidation takes place through a series of cytochromes, which receive and process the activated hydrogen atoms from the substrate. What makes the respiratory chain such an excellent research model is that the redox status of the cytochromes can be followed spectroscopically. At Cambridge, David Keilin was doing outstanding research in this field. Within the cytochrome system, it is molecules such as pyridine nucleotides and flavoproteins that are involved in the oxidation reactions, that is, in the transfer of hydrogen atoms. Many specific steps in the redox reactions could be followed experimentally as the oxidized state had different physico-chemical properties than the reduced state. Warburg's laboratory was to become world-famous for this type of cell physiology research; its status is reflected by the number of Nobel Prizes won by Warburg's pupils:

Otto F. Meyerhof in 1922, Hans A. Krebs in 1953, and Hugo Theorell in 1955.

Warburg found a so-called yellow enzyme, whose color faded upon reduction and returned upon oxidation. In view of this enzyme's remarkable properties, several prominent researchers started studying it, including its discoverer Warburg at Berlin, Richard Kuhn at Heidelberg, and Paul Karrer at Zürich. It turned out that a prosthetic group—a yellow pigment—acted as the hydrogen carrier. The pigment was isolated and was referred to as lactoflavin, riboflavin, or vitamin B$_2$. The phenomenon of the reversible redox reactions occurred only when it was bound to the high molecular weight protein part of the enzyme.

The receipt of a Rockefeller Foundation grant in 1933 allowed Theorell to work at Warburg's laboratory in Berlin-Dahlem for eighteen months. He spent this time researching the yellow enzyme's redox reactions in more detail. As part of his dissertation research, he had developed an electrophoresis machine to separate various lipid components, some time before Arne Tiselius developed a similar machine. When he left for Berlin, he took two of his electrophoresis machines with him, one for analytical and one for preparative uses, and used them to study and isolate the yellow enzyme.

Using electrophoresis at pH 4.2–4.5, Theorell was able to remove polysaccharide contaminants from Warburg's yellow enzyme preparation. Studies with Svedberg's centrifuge at Uppsala subsequently revealed that the purified product was a protein with a molecular weight of 75,000. This was the first time that anyone had been able to separate an active enzyme into components—a protein and a prosthetic group—that were pure. Individually they were inactive, but when combined, the full enzymatic activity was produced. The protein and the prosthetic group—or coenzyme—were obtained in stoichiometric proportions. In Theorell's electrophoresis machine, the flavin moved to the anode, making it unlikely that it was only neutral flavin. He was later able to show that it was actually lactoflavin phosphoric acid ester, in which the pigment was bound to the protein via phosphoric acid. The coenzyme was eventually named FMN (flavin mononucleotide).

Theorell's chemical and physical examinations of the yellow enzyme put him at the forefront of research into vitamins, coenzymes, and prosthetic groups. This was a very fruitful research area, as was evident from the Nobel Prizes for Chemistry that were awarded to Walter N. Haworth and Paul Karrer in 1937 and to Richard Kuhn in 1938 for their work on vitamins, carotenes, and flavins. These awards were, however, mostly based on studies of the chemical structure of the compounds involved, rather than the interaction between protein and coenzyme. In

the years after his return to Sweden, Theorell focused on the specific chemical interactions between heme as a coenzyme and proteins, as in cytochrome *c*. Painstaking research revealed that the heme component was bound to the protein by two cysteine-S bridges and that the iron atom in the heme was bound to a histidine in the protein.

The fact that Theorell received the Nobel Prize for Physiology or Medicine in 1955, twenty years after his pioneering work on the yellow enzyme at Warburg's laboratory, allows two conclusions. The first is that this concerned a different type of work from the straightforward chemical characterization of biologically active compounds by Haworth, Karrer, and Kuhn: Theorell's work was concerned with physiology, the chemistry of dynamic processes. The second is that Theorell's use of new physico-chemical techniques—in combination with comparative studies—meant a revolutionary new experimental approach. In Warburg's letter of recommendation to the Nobel Committee, the German cell physiologist wrote that the separating and reuniting of protein and coenzyme continued to provide the foundation for the study of enzyme action: "immer sind es die Experimente Theorells, auf denen das Gebäude man kann fast sagen der modernen Biochemie ruht" (Werner, 1991, p. 266).

One year before Theorell was awarded his Nobel Prize, Linus Pauling had delivered his 1954 Nobel Lecture. In this lecture, he presented newly developed three-dimensional chemical models, in which the nature of the bonds, possible hydrogen bridges, and steric hindrance determined the hypothetical molecular structures. Pauling had made a gift of these models to Theorell, and they featured for the second time in a Nobel lecture when Theorell accepted his prize in 1955. The meccano-type models allowed Theorell to discard a number of steric molecular configurations for cytochrome *c* as improbable on the basis of the distances between the atoms and the valence angles. He ended up with twenty alternatives, one of which had the highest probability. It was this option that he displayed at the Nobel ceremony. The model featured an alpha helix, which Pauling had proved to be a stable protein configuration. The presence of alpha helices was confirmed by x-ray crystallography but instead of being left-handed as suggested by Theorell in his Nobel Lecture, it was later shown to be right-handed (Dalziel, 1983, p. 596).

From Chemistry to Physiology. The strength of the bonds between the prosthetic group and the protein differs between enzymes. Cytochrome *c* is an example of an enzyme with an immobile prosthetic group that remains bound even if the protein is denatured. The yellow enzyme is a conjugated protein with a coenzyme that can be dissociated but is then nonfunctional, whereas liver alcohol dehydrogenase has a coenzyme that remains functional after dissociation. These differences offer opportunities for comparative studies into the mode of action of enzymes and the involvement of coenzymes. The key concept in Theorell's views was that the wide variety of properties of, for instance, various iron-containing enzymes had to be caused by the way in which the iron is bound to the protein.

As a result, Theorell's research program was based on studying enzymes within a particular category, and involved isolating, purifying, and characterizing as many different enzymes from such a category as possible, after which comparative studies provided insights into their physiology. He focused mainly on enzymes having iron porphyrins as coenzymes, a category that includes a wide range of enzymes, such as hemoglobin, cytochromes, catalases, and peroxidases. After cytochrome *c* had been discovered by Keilin, Theorell was the one to purify and characterize it as a heme protein with a molecular weight of 13,000. The enzymes were isolated using standard procedures from biochemistry, such as fractionated precipitation with ammonium sulfate, further differentiation using a range of pH values, and denaturation of the byproducts. Of course, Theorell also applied methods from physical chemistry, such as electrophoresis, and he used ultracentrifugation to check the purity of the enzymes and determine their molecular weights. The fact that Svedberg and Tiselius—the world's most renowned experts on ultracentrifugation—were working at Uppsala was obviously very helpful.

The comparative studies showed in how many different ways enzymes can use coenzymes. Inspired by his own love of music, Theorell used a musical metaphor for the relation between enzyme and coenzyme. In his words, protein entities control the prosthetic groups "etwa wie ein Virtuose sein Instrument beherrscht" (Theorell, 1944, p. 96). While the enzyme is able to play the same melody on different instruments, the iron in the coenzyme is limited by the expressive opportunities offered by the instrument. All this, Theorell stated, highlights the delicate differentiation of enzymes and proteins in biology.

This field obviously yielded a wide-ranging research program, which used rather laborious methods, so it is not surprising that Theorell's laboratory employed about twenty permanent staff, including technicians and mechanics. The research also required great experimental dexterity, and in this respect Theorell was able to rely on the valuable assistance of Åke Åkeson; it is not unusual to find that behind a great chemical researcher there is a great technician. The postwar period saw the arrival of a whole series of guest researchers, who were made very welcome, notwithstanding the somewhat primitive working conditions at the Karolinska Institute because of deprivation during the war and overcrowding of laboratory space. The researchers visiting Theorell's lab shortly after the war included top names such as Britton Chance, Ralph Holman, Christian Anfinsen (winner of the 1972 Nobel Prize for Chemistry), and J. M. Buchanan from the United States; Christian de Duve (winner of the 1974 Nobel Prize for Medicine) from Belgium; Andreas Maehley from Switzerland; and Elèmer Mihalyi from Hungary.

In 1947 the Nobel Medical Institute moved into new premises at Solnavägen on the outskirts of Stockholm. The new laboratory occupied three floors; its equipment has been cofinanced by the Rockefeller Foundation and the U.S. National Institutes of Health. Four years later, a further wing was added: the Wallenberg Foundation Laboratory for Physiological Chemistry, as well as a wing with guest accommodations. From the second half of the 1940s, many new instruments were acquired, including reliable photoelectric quartz spectrophotometers (such as the Beckman DU instrument), which removed the need to use complex methods based on Warburg manometers. In 1956 a new technique to purify proteins, ion-exchange chromatography, became available.

The Fourth Dimension of Biochemistry. Successful biochemical research is determined to a considerable extent by a felicitous choice of experimental model. After the war, Theorell's staff took up the subject of alcohol dehydrogenase, or ADH, while continuing their work on heme-based enzymes. The enzyme ADH had first been crystallized from yeast in 1937. In 1948 Theorell succeeded in crystallizing it also from horse liver, and subsequently by x-ray diffraction studies. The enzyme has a specific coenzyme, NAD^+, which is reduced to NADH. These reduction-oxidation processes are accompanied by many changes in light absorption and fluorescence, allowing them to be followed and analyzed with the right instruments.

Theorell and his staff started elaborate studies on the enzyme's kinetics, equilibriums, reaction mechanisms with various substrates and inhibitors, and so on. They found that the formation of the complex of enzyme and coenzyme and the ensuing reactions led to changes in the conformation of the enzymatic protein. These phenomena attracted great interest among biochemical researchers in the 1950s and 1960s. Various names were coined for them, such as "conformational adaptability," "rack mechanism," "induced fit," and finally "allosteric effects," the name that stuck. From his work on ADH, Theorell drew the important conclusion that biological macromolecules possessed an extra dimension. Proteins are not just the three-dimensional static structures that are found by x-ray diffraction studies; a macromolecule's conformation also depends on its environment and can change in time.

Theorell concluded that active enzymes "have, as 'a fourth dimension,' their conformational adaptability" (Theorell, 1967, p. 40).

The results of Theorell's studies of ADH kinetics were later applied in quantitative assessment of blood alcohol levels. The ADH method proved more sensitive than previous techniques, and was also highly specific for ethanol, so there was no interference from other alcohols. Hence, forensic chemists in Sweden and Germany adopted an ADH-based method.

Executive Positions. In 1967 Hugo Theorell was elected president of the Swedish Academy of Science. In addition, he was president of the International Union of Biochemistry from 1967 to 1973. An important achievement was the building of the Wenner-Gren Center in Stockholm. Axel Wenner-Gren, owner of companies such as Electrolux, had already founded the Wenner-Gren Foundation for the Support of Scientific Research in 1937. In 1954 Swedish scientists approached Wenner-Gren with the proposal to establish a center for scientific conferences. The center was opened in 1961, and Theorell was president of its board until 1976. A Wenner-Gren symposium was held there in Theorell's honor in 1970, on the occasion of his retirement.

In 1971, while Theorell was chairman of the board of the Wenner-Gren Foundation, a case of fraud at the foundation came to light. Several members of the foundation, including Theorell, were indicted for fraudulent administration but only the executive director was found guilty (Theorell's case was dismissed because of his ill health). This affair came as a great shock to Theorell, as his complete confidence in his staff had been shaken. In 1981 he suffered a severe case of bronchitis, which hospitalized him for weeks. He died in the summer of 1982.

BIBLIOGRAPHY

A complete bibliography of Hugo Theorell's publications is included in Dalziel's biography.

WORKS BY THEORELL

"Über die Wirkungsgruppe des Gelben Ferments." *Biochemische Zeitschrift* 275 (1934): 37–38. Translated and reprinted in Herman M. Kalckar, *Biological Phosphorylations: Development of Concepts.* Englewood Cliffs, NJ: Prentice-Hall, 1969.

"Ein neuer Kataphoreseapparat für Untersuchungszwecke." *Biochemische Zeitschrift* 275 (1935): 2–10.

"Das gelbe Oxydationsferment." *Biochemische Zeitschrift* 278 (1935): 263–290.

"Konstitution und Wirkung einiger Häminproteide." In *Zur Chemie, Physiologie und Pathologie des Eiweisses: Eine Vortragsreihe veranstaltet von der Berner Biochemischen Vereinigung, 1943*, edited by R. Signer et al. Bern: Verlag Paul Haupt, 1944.

"Nobel Lecture, December 12, 1955: The Nature and Mode of Action of Oxidation Enzymes." *Nobel Lectures Including Presentation Speeches and Laureates' Biographies: Physiology or Medicine, 1942–1962.* Amsterdam: Elsevier Publishing, 1964.

"Function and Structure of Liver Alcohol Dehydrogenase." *Harvey Lectures 1965–1966* 61 (1967): 17–41. An honorary lecture delivered at the end of Theorell's career, reflecting his lifelong interest in the chemistry and structural chemistry of enzymes.

"My Life with Proteins and Prosthetic Groups." In *Proteolysis and Physiological Regulation: Miami Winter Symposia Volume 11*, edited by Douglas W. Ribbons and Keith Brew. New York: Academic Press, 1976.

Växlande Vindar. Stockholm: Natur och Kultur, 1977. Biographical memoir.

OTHER SOURCES

Beinert, Helmut, and Peter Hemmerich. "Flavins and Flavoproteins." In *The Encyclopedia of Biochemistry*, edited by Roger J. Williams and Edwin M. Lansford Jr. New York: Reinhold, 1967. A concise and accurate overview of the chemistry and biological significance of flavins (including their role as coenzymes).

Buchanan, John Machlin. "A Backward Glance." In *Selected Topics in the History of Biochemistry: Personal Recollections II, Comprehensive Biochemistry.* Vol. 36, edited by Giorgio Semenza. Amsterdam: Elsevier Science Publishers, 1986.

Dalziel, K. "Axel Hugo Theodor Theorell, 6 July 1903–15 August 1982." *Biographical Memoirs of Fellows of the Royal Society* 29 (1983): 583–621.

Szent-Györgyi, Albert, et al. "Papers Dedicated to Hugo Theorell on His 60th Birthday, 6 July 1963, Copenhagen, 1963." *Acta Chemica Scandinavica* 17, supp. 1 (1963): 1–352.

Werner, Petra, ed. *Ein Genie irrt seltener … Otto Heinrich Warburg: Ein Lebensbild in Dokumenten.* Berlin: Akademie Verlag, 1991. Includes correspondence between Hugo Theorell, Otto Warburg, and others.

Ton Van Helvoort

THIENEMANN, AUGUST FRIEDRICH (*b.* Gotha, Germany, 7 September 1882; *d.* Plön, Germany, 22 April 1960), *limnology.*

Thienemann was Europe's leading limnologist (freshwater ecologist), being a productive author, director of a research institute, university professor, and editor of a leading scientific journal. He documented the life histories of aquatic insects, classified lakes according to their physico-chemical characterics and their biological productivity, promoted fish production, and by comparing northern European and tropical Indonesian lakes shed light on climatic influences on lake life.

Early Life and Career. August was the eldest of Carl Friedrich Thienemann and Emilie Noack Thienemann's six children. His father and grandfather were prosperous book publishers and bookshop owners in Gotha. August could have followed in their footsteps. However, he developed an early love of nature and was an excellent student, and he attended the University of Greifswald, where he majored in zoology, with a strong interest in aquatic insects. He also spent semesters at the universities in Innsbruck and Heidelberg (1903–1904), before receiving his PhD degree in 1905 from Greifswald.

He joined the faculty of the University of Greifswald for two years and then joined the Zoological Institute of the University of Münster in the Department for Fisheries and Waste Water for ten years. In the latter position he became involved in practical measures to promote fish production. In 1911 he married Siri Jönsson, who was Swedish, and they had two sons and three daughters. In 1914, he was called into the German Army as it mobilized for World War I. He was soon wounded in battle and was subsequently released from service.

In 1916, Professor Otto Zacharias, founder of the Hydrobiologische Anstalt at Plön, died, and in 1917 it became affiliated with the Kaiser Wilhelm Gesellschaft (later Max Planck Gesellschaft) and Thienemann became its director. Simultaneously, he joined the faculty of the University of Kiel and in 1924 became professor of hydrobiology. He was an excellent manager and a productive limnologist, publishing 460 works, including seven books (a limnology textbook, three brief popularizations of limnology, two lengthy monographs, and an autobiography). He remained director at Plön for forty years, retiring in 1957. He was also editor of *Archiv für Hydrobiologie* for more than forty years.

In April 1921, August and Siri Thienemann traveled to Sweden to attend her father's funeral, and afterward they visited Einar Christian Leonard Naumann at the University of Lund, where he taught limnology and botany. The two limnologists had corresponded but had not previously met. Thienemann had a calm, friendly temperament, while Naumann was volatile and impulsive, but they quickly established a close working relationship.

Naumann, who was nine years younger than Thienemann, suggested that they establish an international society. Thienemann liked the idea, and they later developed a plan in their correspondence. Thienemann suggested using the term *hydrobiology* in the name of their organization, but Naumann preferred *limnology*, which emphasized the environment, and he prevailed. In January 1922 they sent a prospectus to over 100 colleagues, stressing the need for international cooperation to solve both practical and theoretical questions and asked for comments. There were 101 favorable responses, though eight declined to join (two for political and six for personal reasons). A Foundation Assembly was held at the University of Kiel, 3–5 August 1922, and Thienemann published the plans in *Archiv für Hydrobiologie* (1922). Coming less than four years after World War I, no one from France and only one from England joined then, but 188 joined from twenty-three countries. The Internationale Vereinigung für Limnologie (later called Societas Internationalis Limnologiae) had three goals: (1) embrace limnologists of all countries; (2) combine theoretical and applied aspects of freshwater research; and (3) bring together limnologists working in hydrographical and biological fields. Thienemann suggested that the society publish an annual yearbook of its proceedings (*Verhandlungen*), with lists of members and limnological research centers, and possibly reviews of current literature from different countries. The first volume of the *Verhandlungen* had 414 pages. Thienemann was elected chairman of the society and served until August 1939. Naumann was very active in it until he died in 1934, aged forty-three. In 1925 Thienemann and Naumann also started a monograph series, *Die Binnengewässer,* and Thienemann edited twenty of its volumes (writing three of them). At the society's fiftieth anniversary in 1972, there were over 2,000 members from about sixty countries. Thienemann also developed an early interest in the history of biology and limnology, which he expressed in obituaries of limnologists published the *Archiv für Hydrobiologie,* the longest being on Naumann (1938).

Theoretical Concepts. Also in 1921 both Thienemann and Naumann published their separate research on the biological types of lakes. Their researches were complementary and became the foundation of "Seetypenlehre" (relating physico-chemical characteristics of lakes to their biological productivity), a dominant focus for limnological research. Naumann introduced into limnology the concepts of oligotrophy (little organic productivity) and eutrophy (much organic productivity); C. A. Weber (1907) had coined the terms to distinguish different peat bogs. Thienemann adopted these terms for clear lakes, and in 1925 he coined the term *dystrophy* (brown-water lakes with low lime content and high humus content) for oligotrophic humic lakes. In the same year H. Järnefelt coined the term *mixotrophy* (with phytoplankton absorbing organic nutrients from water) for eutrophic humic (with organic substances in a colloidal state) lakes. Thienemann's studies of hypolimnon (deepest layer) fauna showed that species composition and populations depended on the oxygen content of the deepest layer of water. The Naumann-Thienemann lake classification was developed from the study of temperate lakes.

In 1928 and 1929 Thienemann was joined by Austrian limnologist Franz Ruttner and German zoologist H.

J. Feuerborn on an expedition to the Sunda Islands (Java, Sumatra, and Bali). They worked in the field for ten months, collected numerous animals, and later, with the help of more than one hundred specialists, described eleven hundred new species. Their important results were published in eleven supplementary volumes of *Archiv für Hydrobiologie,* 1931–1958. These findings led to a better understanding of variations in lake productivity in relation to climate. Thienemann was so fascinated by this experience that he devoted 132 pages of his autobiography to it.

The American zoologist Stephen A. Forbes wrote an influential essay in 1887, "The Lake as a Microcosm," that attempted to explain the dynamic equilibrium of life in a lake. It appeared in an Illinois journal unlikely to reach Germany, and there is no evidence Thienemann saw it. Nevertheless, Thienemann used the same word, *microcosm,* to describe life in a lake, and he used the superorganism metaphor to describe the interacting species. His lake researches from the 1920s to 1950s led to three important ecological generalizations, the first two in the 1920s:

1. The more variable the biotope (=environmental) conditions in a locality, the greater is the number of species in the biocenosis (=biotic community).

2. The more biotope conditions deviate from the optimal for most species, the smaller the number of species are found there, but the greater the number of individuals which represent those species.

3. The longer a locality has remained in the same condition, the richer and more stable is its biocenosis.

In 1926 Thienemann first used the concepts of producers, consumers, and reducers to organize his biological data, and in 1931 he published a pioneering article on biological productivity. Raymond L. Lindeman, in his epoch-making article, "The Trophic-Dynamic Aspect of Ecology" (1942), was partly indebted to three of Thienemann's papers. He cited Thienemann (1926) on the cycling of nutrients in water, and Lindeman's diagram of the lacustrine system is similar to one in Thienemann's paper.

During World War II, Thienemann remained active in limnological research, and he published about fifty scientific articles, which, however, found a smaller readership due to the war. Afterward he became alarmed at the decline in Europe's environment. In 1955 he developed a six-point program that he continually preached for the rest of his life: the public should be informed about changes in supply and quality of natural waters; when changes are necessary, consult limnologists; water laws must be enforced; a river system should be managed in its entire length, regardless of administrative boundaries; hydroengineers must be taught ecological thinking; and theoretical water research is the basis of practice and needs increased support. Thienemann began planning a larger modern building for the Hydrobiologischen Anstalt of the Max Planck Gesellschaft in Plön before World War II, but the war delayed its implementation until 1961, after he had died.

BIBLIOGRAPHY

WORKS BY THIENEMANN

Die Binnengewässer Mitteleuropas: Eine Limnologische Einführung. Stuttgart, Germany: Verlag Schweizerbart, 1925.

"Der Nahrungskreislauf Im Wasser." *Verhandlungen Der Deutschen Zoologischen Gesellschaft* 31 (1926): 29-79.

Verbreitungsgeschichte Der Süsswassertierwelt Europas. Die Binnengewässer, Band XVIII. Stuttgart, Germany: Verlag Schweizerbart, 1950.

Chironomus: Leben, Verbreitung Und Wirtschaftliche Bedeutung Der Chironomiden. Die Binnengewässer, Band XX. Stuttgart, Germany: Verlag Schweizerbart, 1954.

Erinnerungen und Tagebuchblätter eines Biologen: Ein Leben im Dienste der Limnologie. Stuttgart, Germany, 1959. A 500-page autobiography, which contains his complete bibliography and the best guide to his publications.

OTHER SOURCES

Elster, Hans-Joachim. "History of Limnology." *Mitteilungen Internationale Vereinigung für theoretische und angewandte Limnologie* 20 (1974): 7-30.

Golley, Frank B. *A History of the Ecosystem Concept in Ecology: More than the Sum of the Parts.* New Haven, CT: Yale University Press, 1993. Discusses Thienemann's contributions to developing the concept.

Lindeman, Raymond L. "The Trophic-Dynamic Aspect of Ecology." *Ecology* 23 (1942) 399-418.

Macfadyen, Anyan. "The Meaning of Productivity in Biological Systems." *Journal of Animal Ecology* 17 (1949): 75-80. Evaluated Thienemann's contribution to productivity studies.

McIntosh, Robert P. *The Background of Ecology: Concept and Theory.* Cambridge, U.K.: Cambridge University Press, 1985.

Ohle, Waldemar. "August Thienemann 1882-1960: Sein Werk und Vermächtnis." *Archiv für Hydrobiologie* 57 (1961): 1-12. Obituary.

Overbeck, Jürgen. "70 Jahre Seetypenlehre: Gedenktafel für August Thienemann." *Naturwissenschaftliche Rundschau* 38 (1985): 58-60. Acknowledges the continuing influence of Thienemann's work.

Rodhe, Wilhelm. "Crystallization of Eutrophication Concepts in Northern Europe." In *Eutrophication: Causes, Consequences, Correctives.* Proceedings of International Symposium on Eutrophication, University of Wisconsin, 1967. Washington, DC: National Academy of Sciences, 1969. Discusses Thienemann's role in developing a lake classification.

———. "The International Association of Limnology: Creation and Functions." *Mitteilungen Internationale Vereinigung für theoretische und angewandte Limnologie* 20 (1974): 44–70. Both this and the president's lecture describe Thienemann's role in its founding.

———. "Limnology Turns to Warm Lakes." *Archiv für Hydrobiologie* 73 (1974): 537–546. On the history of the Sunda Expedition of 1928–1929.

———. "President's Lecture: The SIL Founders and Our Fundament." *Verhandlungen der Internationalen Vereinigung für theoretische und angewandte Limnologie* 19 (1975): 16–25.

Steleanu, Adrian. *Geschichte der Limnologie und ihrer Grundlagen.* Frankfurt am Main, Germany: Haag + Herchen, 1989.

Frank N. Egerton

THOMAS OF BRADWARDINE
SEE **Bradwardine, Thomas**.

THORNTHWAITE,   CHARLES
WARREN (*b.* Pinconning, Michigan, 7 March 1899; *d.* Arlington, Virginia, 11 June 1963), *geography, climatology.*

Thornthwaite changed the course of climatology in the twentieth century and influenced the development of the modern field of climatology. He devised the eponomous Thornthwaite climate classification system by modifying and enhancing the famous Köppen climate system. Thornthwaite was the founder of the field of applied climatology. He advocated the study of microclimates, or topoclimatology, and his water budget model has been used by hydrologists throughout the world.

Early Years. The Thornthwaite family name came originally from Cumberland County in the Lake District in northwestern England. Thornthwaite's parents, Ernest and Mildred Thornthwaite, lived on a farm near Pinconning in central Michigan. All four of their children were born on the farm; Charles Warren Thornthwaite was the eldest. The Thornthwaites, like many of the other enterprising settlers in Michigan, placed a high value on education. There was no high school in Pinconning, so Thornthwaite went to live in Mount Pleasant in order to attend high school. He worked as a janitor of the Methodist church and lived in a room in the church.

After graduating from high school in 1918, Thornthwaite was inducted into the Army Cadet Corps. World War I ended shortly thereafter and the corps was disbanded, so he enrolled at Central Michigan Normal School (now Central Michigan University) in Mount

Pleasant, intending to become a schoolteacher. Thornthwaite was able to get financial assistance from the Student's Army Training Corps. While in college, he met his future wife, Denzil Slentz, as well as John Leighly, who became an important figure in Thornthwaite's life and work. Leighly had come to Central Michigan to obtain his high school teaching certificate. The two men met during a school break, when both were members of a crew that unloaded lumber from boxcars; they formed a lifelong friendship.

Thornthwaite enjoyed music and mathematics and sang in the college chorus. One of his professors introduced him to grand opera, which remained as one of Thornthwaite's passions. Thornthwaite graduated in 1922 and obtained a job teaching science at the high school in Owosso, Michigan. He took courses in the summers of 1923 and 1924 at the University of Michigan. In 1924 Thornthwaite and his college friend Leighly drove to California in a Model T Ford. This in itself was a geographic adventure! Upon arrival, both men entered the University of California at Berkeley to pursue graduate work with the distinguished geographer Carl Sauer. Sauer, who was fluent in German, encouraged both Thornthwaite and Leighly to read German and to become acquainted with German scientists such as climatologist Wladimir Köppen. At Berkeley, Sauer taught an introductory course in physical geography. He rejected the popular geographic concepts of Ellen Churchill Semple (the first female geographer who stated that man is a product of Earth's surface, and that the choices people made in response to the environment were predetermined) and was known for his work in cultural geography. The department attracted many distinguished visiting geographers.

Thornthwaite and Slentz were married in California in 1925. Because money was a problem for the new couple, Thornthwaite started to do some part-time work for the Kentucky Geological Survey. Because Thornthwaite needed to be in Kentucky and Sauer was interested in the geography of the area, Sauer suggested that Thornthwaite conduct his doctoral research on the city of Louisville. Thornthwaite finished his course work at Berkeley in 1927 and was awarded his doctoral degree in 1930 with a dissertation titled "Louisville, Kentucky: A Study in Urban Geography."

The Climate Classification System. Thornthwaite was hired as a professor of geography at the University of Oklahoma in Norman in 1927. At that time, geography was classified in the "mathematical and natural sciences" group of the College of Arts and Sciences. Thornthwaite taught four or five courses each semester at the University of Oklahoma until the spring of 1934. He also continued to work part time for the Kentucky Geological Survey through 1930. His first article on meteorology; "The Polar Front in the Interpretation and Prediction of Oklahoma Weather" was published in 1929 in the *Proceedings of the Oklahoma Academy of Science.* This work was done in an era before the U.S. Weather Bureau had adopted the Bergen school methods of analysis, which presented new methods of forecasting, including the inclusion of air mass and frontal analysis.

The first article by Thornthwaite that attracted worldwide attention was his work on climate classification, "The Climates of North America according to a New Classification," published in 1931. Thornthwaite was very familiar with the widely used Köppen system and had studied it extensively at Berkeley. Köppen had developed the first numerical classification of climate based on actual observations of temperature and precipitation that also described the general relationships of vegetation and soils to climate. Thornthwaite pointed out that Köppen did not consider his classification system a finished product due to the omission of a moisture effectiveness factor. For example, in the Köppen system, equal amounts of annual rainfall produce forest vegetation in Siberia and desert plants in Africa. Thornthwaite also pointed out that Köppen had no category for a subhumid climate. It was this fact more than any other that prompted Thornthwaite to recognize the work that needed to be done. In his 1931 article, Thornthwaite observed that the "effective" temperature and precipitation were more accurate climate descriptors than were actual measurements of temperature and precipitation.

Thornthwaite used the term *effective temperature* to relate the rate of plant growth to temperature and the term *effective precipitation* to indicate that plant growth was not only dependent on the amount of precipitation but also on the amount of water lost by evaporation and transpiration. He calculated effective precipitation from measurements of precipitation and evaporation published in the U.S. Weather Bureau Bulletin to obtain a "P-E index," which provided a relationship between precipitation and evaporation for any location where the data was available. Thornthwaite also derived a "T-E index," expressing the empirical relationship between temperature and evaporation. Köppen approved of Thornthwaite's attempts to design a more complete foundation for the classification of climate. Subsequently, Thornthwaite began to apply the new classification system globally. He acquired climate data from four thousand stations from around the globe, applied his classification system, and produced a world map indicating the various climates. This very complicated map was not included in the commonly used climate classification system.

Soil Conservation. In 1934 Thornthwaite resigned from the University of Oklahoma and started to work with the Study of Population Distribution of the University of Pennsylvania. The opportunity to work on this study in Washington, D.C., with the University of Pennsylvania allowed him to leave Oklahoma, where he may have had some working tension with one of his colleagues. His work *Internal Migration in the United States,* published in 1934, was an intensive study of population and migration of American-born white and black populations, complete with maps. His work at the University of Pennsylvania also resulted in a collaborative publication on migration and economic opportunity in the Great Plains, his only published work on this topic.

In July 1935 Thornthwaite, on the recommendation of Sauer, became the director of the new Climatic and Physiographic Research Section of the Soil Conservation Service, Department of Agriculture. Thornthwaite moved to Arlington, Virginia, with his wife and three daughters. During his time he was involved in several projects, including the establishment of a climatic research center in western Oklahoma and involvement with the Polacca Wash project in Arizona. Through the establishment of the climatic research center, two hundred weather stations were established in an area of about 1,800 square miles (about 4,600 sq. km). The fact that Thornthwaite recommended such a dense network of climatic stations is an indication that as early as 1935 he realized the importance of mesoscale meteorology. The Polacca Wash project yielded important scientific results. His monograph "Climate and Accelerated Erosion in the Arid and Semiarid Southwest, with Special Reference to the Polacca Wash Drainage Basin, Arizona," with C. F. Stewart Sharpe and Earl F. Dosch, appeared in 1942, summing up the principal findings concerning the rate of gully erosion and rainfall frequency and intensity in a dry climate.

Most importantly, Thornthwaite's work with the Soil Conservation Service heightened his interest in the relationship between precipitation and evaporation and the loss of water from land surfaces to air by evaporation and transpiration. The central idea behind this revision was evapotranspiration, which was a new term in climatology at that time. His interpretation and concept of evapotranspiration and the hydrologic cycle was presented in "An Approach toward a Rational Classification of Climate," published in 1948 in the *Geographical Review.* This paper introduced a new approach to climate classification, but also presented fundamental ideas on water storage in the soil and evapotranspiration. The paper was also exceptional in its portrayal of the hydrologic cycle applied to the United States.

Seabrook and the Institute for Climatic Research. Thornthwaite decided to move to Seabrook Farms in New Jersey as an irrigation consultant in 1946. Seabrook Farms was at the time a leading producer of frozen vegetables. His decision was based on the decreasing interest in the Soil Conservation Service and his conversations with John Seabrook, the general manager of the farms. Upon his arrival, he stood in the factory yard, surrounded by trucks filled with shelled peas. He noted that the factory was operating at full capacity, yet the trucks in the yard seemed to be fixed in place. Trucks stood there in the sun for hours, and he recognized that this delay would not improve the freshness of the peas. He launched a major research project to study the "pea problem." He arrived at a system that involved variable harvest times, which was successfully implemented in 1947. After the success of this operation, the system was expanded to include all crops grown at Seabrook Farms. Thornthwaite transformed his information on planting and harvest dates of the various crops to a growth-unit slide rule that he called a "crop meter." He became particularly interested in agricultural climatology and conducted a variety of studies in this area that included daily plant readings.

Thornthwaite also worked on obtaining a mathematical expression for the variation of temperature, moisture, and wind with height to learn about turbulence near the ground. He utilized crop duster planes and the smoke puffer, a device that would shoot a puff of smoke into the air so that its duration of visibility could be a direct measurement of the turbulence structure of the lower layer of the atmosphere. This instrument helped him study and clarify some of the complexities in the understanding of atmospheric turbulence. The disposal of industrially polluted effluent by means of spray irrigation, which was pioneered by Thornthwaite at Seabrook Farms and is possibly the largest system ever installed for an industry, provided a radically different solution to a complex problem of growing importance to industry. Thornthwaite was very happy and productive at Seabrook Farms from 1946 to 1952. The results of his work were described in both farm publications and scientific journals.

C. W. Thornthwaite Associates. Thornthwaite's growing reputation led to the establishment of his own consulting firm, C. W. Thornthwaite Associates, a partnership with his brother-in-law, Floyd Slentz, in the early 1950s. In addition to the various consulting activities, Thornthwaite was involved with the design and construction of instruments in the company's Laboratory of Climatology. During this time, five patents were issued to Thornthwaite for several improvements and modifications to instruments. A patent issued to him in 1941 (before the establishment of his consulting firm) was for improvements to an instrument that showed changes in the moisture concentration

of a gas over time. This led to the ability to measure small changes in the dew point of the air. Another patent was for modifications to the dew point recorder and indicator in 1942. Three of the other patents were not officially issued until 1965 and 1966, after his death.

Other Activities. Thornthwaite chaired the American Geophysical Union's committee on climatology in 1947 and 1948. He was elected the first president of the Commission for Climatology at the first congress of the World Meteorological Organization in 1951 and served a second term until January 1957. He was concerned about the creation of a world climate atlas. Thornthwaite felt that there was a growing interest in a global climate atlas among other technical commissions and regional associations. He started to build support, especially with the Food and Agriculture Organization and UNESCO. Even though he was able to obtain support for only one small set of water budget maps, he nevertheless was satisfied that climatology had taken steps in developing independently from meteorology (ironically, the field of climate dynamics was just emerging in the work of Guy S. Callendar and Gilbert Plass, among others).

In 1952 Thornthwaite was honored by the Association of American Geographers with its Outstanding Achievement Award. He served on a number of committees, including the Geography Advisory Committee to the Office of Naval Research of the National Research Council. His most significant publication of this period, "Topoclimatology," was published in 1954. This paper had a considerable impact on climatology because it concluded that the study of climatology had to include the understanding and mapping of elements of Earth's surface that affect the heat and water cycle, namely, topography, albedo, vegetation, and surface roughness. Thornthwaite was awarded the prestigious Cullum Geographical Medal of the American Geographical Society in 1959 in New York City.

Last Years. In the 1960s Thornthwaite was involved in the development of microclimatic instruments. He was chosen as the honorary president of the Association of the American Geographers from 1960 to 1961. During 1961 he began experiencing severe back pains, which interfered with his work schedule and increased during the last few months of his wife's battle with cancer in 1962. He established a memorial scholarship for her at Central Michigan University. In 1963 he was awarded an honorary doctorate from his alma mater in recognition of his contributions to the fields of climatology and geography. He was unable to attend the ceremony, which took place nine days before his death, also from cancer, on 11 June 1963.

BIBLIOGRAPHY

WORKS BY THORNTHWAITE

"The Polar Front in the Interpretation and Prediction of Oklahoma Weather." *Proceedings of the Oklahoma Academy of Science* 9 (1929): 93–99.

"The Climates of North America according to a New Classification." *Geographical Review* 21 (1931): 635–655.

Internal Migration in the United States. Philadelphia: University of Pennsylvania Press, 1934.

With Carter Goodrich, Bushrod W. Allin, et al. *Migration and Economic Opportunity.* Philadelphia: University of Pennsylvania Press, 1936.

With C. F. Stewart Sharpe and Earl F. Dosch. "Climate and Accelerated Erosion in the Arid and Semiarid Southwest, with Special Reference to the Polacca Wash Drainage Basin, Arizona." U.S. Dept. of Agriculture, *Technical Bulletin,* no. 808, 1942.

"An Approach toward a Rational Classification of Climate." *Geographical Review* 38 (1948): 55–94.

"Topoclimatology." *Proceedings of the Toronto Meteorological Conference 1953.* London: Royal Meteorological Society, 1954, pp. 227–232.

OTHER SOURCES

Hare, F. Kenneth. "Charles Warren Thornthwaite, 1899–1963." *Geographical Review* 53, no. 4 (1963): 595–597.

Leighly, John. "Charles Warren Thornthwaite, March 7, 1899–June 11, 1963." *Annals of the Association of American Geographers* 54 (1964): 615–621.

Mather, John R., and Marie Sanderson. *The Genius of C. Warren Thornthwaite.* Norman and London: University of Oklahoma Press, 1996.

Wheeler, James O., and Stanley D. Brunn. "An Urban Geographer before His Time: C. Warren Thornthwaite's 1930 Doctoral Dissertation." *Progress in Human Geography* 26, no. 4 (2002): 463–486.

Sepideh Yalda

THORPE, WILLIAM HOMAN (*b.* Hastings, Sussex, United Kingdom, 1 April 1902; *d.* Woodwalton Fen, Cambridgeshire, United Kingdom, 7 April 1986), *entomology, ethology, science and religion, antireductionism, animal welfare.*

Thorpe played a major role in establishing ethology as a branch of academic biology in the English-speaking world after World War II. His ethological career was effectively his second, having made his reputation with diverse studies at Cambridge in entomology, on the strength of which he was elected a Fellow of the Royal Society in 1951. His discipline-building achievements on ethology's behalf included the founding at Cambridge of an ornithological field station, where, alongside other research into the natural behavior of birds, he launched an enduring experimental project on the interplay of instinct and learning in song acquisition. Later decades saw him emerge as one of the leading voices against modern biology's reductionist spirit, a theme he addressed in its scientific but also philosophical and, as a Quaker, religious dimensions. His several sides combined to political effect in his efforts to conserve natural sites and to safeguard animals from suffering.

From Entomology to Ethology. There was no tradition of farming in Thorpe's family when he entered Jesus College, Cambridge, in 1921 to study agriculture. The son of an accountant, "Bill" (as he was always known) was raised in the southern English coastal towns of Hastings and Weston-super-Mare, where he came to share his parents' pleasure in the outdoors and devotion to their Congregationalist faith. Like music, another lifelong passion dating from his childhood, natural history (especially birdwatching) became a pastime that suited a religiously minded and rather solitary boy. These tendencies combined with frequently poor health to make for an indifferent school career. Initially planning to make his way as a naturalist or farmer without the benefit of university training, he changed his mind on learning of the opportunities opening up in economic entomology. Taking advice, he decided on the Cambridge degree in agriculture as the best route, staying on for an entomologically focused Diploma year, then for a PhD (1929).

After a few years at the Farnham Royal Parasite Laboratory (part of the Imperial Institute of Entomology), Thorpe returned to Cambridge in 1932, taking up positions as a university lecturer in entomology and a tutor and Fellow of Jesus College. Already his main preoccupations as a research entomologist, engaged equally in theory, experiment, and field observation, had emerged. There was, first of all, an interest in the natural and artificial production of new biological "races," and ultimately of new species, as different preferences for different kinds of food stabilized within a species. An example from Thorpe's early research was the apparent differentiation of the ermine moth into biologically—though not (yet) structurally—distinct groups that fed and laid their eggs on different kinds of trees, apple or hawthorn. A second interest was in the role of parasites in controlling agriculturally destructive insects like ermine moths. A third interest was in figuring out the details of parasite respiration.

These related inquiries merged in the mid-1930s in a study of what Thorpe called "olfactory conditioning." Having shown that a parasite had an inherited tendency to prefer a certain moth host, and that the parasite identified the larvae of this host by smell, Thorpe contaminated the larvae of a usually ignored kind of moth with the smell of the normal host to see whether he could induce the parasite to adopt the new host for egg laying. The experiment proved successful, with the parasite offspring, accustomed from birth to the smell of the new host, going on to have a weakened preference for the old host as egg-laying adults. For a time, Thorpe entertained the possibility that these host-preference studies might prove supportive of the "Lamarckian" doctrine of the inheritance of acquired characters. Although he eventually decided that they did not, animal learning—for decades the domain of the psychologists—came increasingly to dominate his research. Discovering the work of the Austrian zoologist Konrad Lorenz, who under the banner of "ethology" was refashioning learning, and with it instinct, as zoological topics, confirmed Thorpe in his new direction.

Establishing Ethology in Britain. After World War II, Thorpe committed himself to a new science, ethology, as well as a new religion, Quakerism. In neither case was there dramatic conversion. He had been attending meetings of the Society of Friends since his Farnham Royal days. When the war came, he registered, on the Quaker model, as a conscientious objector, though he made himself useful as an expert in eliminating the agricultural pests that threatened Britain's ability to feed itself. His turn toward ethology, and toward the study of the instinctive and learned behaviors of birds—Lorenz's favored organisms—was similarly an extension of gradual. For all that the immediate postwar period saw Thorpe energetically proselytizing for ethology, he was also immersed in his most innovative research thus far on the respiratory physiology of insects. By the early 1950s, however, the disciplinary change was complete: a remarkable, midlife transformation in someone who, as his new status as a Fellow of the Royal Society demonstrated, had already made his mark.

Thorpe had much to offer ethology, particularly with respect to its institutional development. A science with a small but expanding institutional life in continental Europe before the war, ethology, like war-torn Europe itself, needed reconstruction. Niko Tinbergen, the Dutch zoologist commonly regarded as ethology's co-founder, was attempting this at the University of Leiden. Lorenz, however, who had been captured by the Russians and interred as a prisoner of war, had no institutional base in Austria when he finally returned there in 1948. Rumors—not without a certain basis—that Lorenz had had a Nazi past were not yet widespread. At least they do not appear to have been an issue for Thorpe as he sought to give ethology a new home in Britain. As with most complex undertakings, the motivations underpinning this one were mixed and mostly obscure. Whatever ambitions, scientific or spiritual, gave Thorpe his sense of mission, what is

undoubted is that he admired Lorenz's prewar papers deeply, especially those on the kind of instinct-constrained learning that Lorenz's translators called "imprinting," and which Thorpe had retrospectively recognized as at work in his moth parasites.

Orchestrating ethology's return engaged him on several fronts. During the war he joined the Institute for the Study of Animal Behaviour, whose members and *Bulletin* sought to promote just the sort of naturalistic, objective studies the ethologists prized. After the war's end, he began corresponding with Tinbergen, accepting Tinbergen's invitation to be an editor of Tinbergen's new journal for ethological research, *Behaviour*. When the news came in 1948 that Lorenz was alive and back home near Vienna, Thorpe made the journey, exploiting some personal connections to arrange some emergency research funding for Lorenz. Working again with Tinbergen, Thorpe began planning a conference that, as a meeting in Cambridge in 1949 and subsequently in its published proceedings, would do much to publicize ethological aims, methods, theories, and personalities. None of the personalities came larger than Lorenz's; and one of the meeting's many successes was the reunion at Thorpe's Cambridge home between Lorenz and Tinbergen.

Although not everyone in Cambridge zoology was as impressed with ethology as was Thorpe, he managed the following year to start an ornithological field station on four acres of woods and meadows recently acquired by the university in the nearby village of Madingley. There was talk for a time of hiring Lorenz as curator. The position ultimately went to Robert Hinde, who, fresh from doctoral studies with Tinbergen at Oxford, was soon at work setting up, stocking, and maintaining the aviaries that became the mainstay of the station's research. Between them, the Lorenz-inspired Thorpe and the Tinbergen-inspired Hinde trained generations of Cambridge graduate students in ethology. Acutely aware of differences between psychological and ethological approaches, the two men nevertheless reached out to psychological colleagues, in Thorpe's case most notably in his extraordinary synthesis of studies in both traditions, *Learning and Instinct in Animals* (1956), and in a famous seminar series run with the Cambridge psychologist Oliver Zangwill.

Experiments in Song Learning. Like his embrace of ethology more generally, Thorpe's turn toward bird behavior, and in particular song acquisition in the chaffinch, had its roots in his pre-ethological work. As a student in the 1920s he had been an avid bird-watcher, cofounding the Cambridge Bird Club and even publishing ornithological papers. Chaffinches were and are plentiful in Cambridge, indeed throughout Britain. What most likely drew them to Thorpe's attention in the 1930s, however, was well-known research suggesting that chaffinches exhibited behavior patterns that—as in the moths he was then studying—could be transmitted stably from one generation to the next without being entirely genetically fixed. The behavior patterns in question were song versions or "dialects," whose maintenance in separate areas of a region of Russia was thought to arise from chaffinches having learned the dialects sung around them as juveniles and then returning to their birthplaces for mating. Here instinct and experience seemed to mix in just the ways that Lorenz had made central to ethologists' concerns.

After the war, as Thorpe developed his plans for an experimental study of song learning in the chaffinch, he became aware of a new technology apparently custom-made for his purposes. Fitting onto a desktop, the sound spectrograph, or Sonagraph to use its commercial name, produced visual displays showing the distribution of frequencies and intensities making up a complex sound. Although invented at Bell Laboratories as a secret wartime project (enabling, for instance, the identification at a distance of different vessels by their underwater acoustics), the device was publicized at war's end as a boon for the deaf, helping them to read incoming telephone calls and reply with speech improved through spectrograph-aided education. Almost incidentally, the paper introducing the spectrograph included bird-song spectrograms, made to test how well it handled rapid changes of pitch. Among the ornithologists who saw the potential was Thorpe, who, in the early 1950s, made use of a British military spectrograph before acquiring his own.

His 1954 paper in *Nature,* "The Process of Song-Learning in the Chaffinch as Studied by Means of the Sound Spectrograph," gave notice to the scientific community that Cambridge was now home to a novel research program on the interaction of learning and instinct. The basic experimental method was straightforward. With spectrographic snapshots of the songs of normally raised local chaffinches serving to define "normal" song, Thorpe and the station's first graduate student, Peter Marler, systematically varied the conditions under which birds were raised in order to see—literally, thanks to the spectrograph—how the adult songs of these birds came to differ from normal song, and so how sensitive the song acquisition process was to changes in experience. To take the simplest example, individuals reared in acoustic isolation almost from birth were found to sing crude but still chaffinchlike songs. These experiments appeared to reveal the species' innate song, before experience elaborated and refined it.

Courtesy of the engineering prowess of Bell Labs and its military and commercial agenda, a whole new class of animal behaviors—vocalizations—was now open to quantitatively robust ethological investigation. Between them,

Thorpe and Marler exploited the new opportunities to the fullest. Before leaving Madingley in 1957 for the University of California at Berkeley, where he went on to develop the song-learning paradigm using a local species, the white-crowned sparrow, Marler published classic papers on, for instance, the relationship between the biological function of bird calls and their spectrographically revealed acoustic structures (ethological doctrine of the day had it that signal structures were arbitrary). Thorpe summarized Marler's conclusions and much else in a compact 1961 book, *Bird-Song: The Biology of Vocal Communication and Expression in Birds.* It would be his last major contribution to a research lineage that, first under Marler at Berkeley and the Rockefeller University, then under Marler's former students at Rockefeller and elsewhere, continues to yield textbook-altering research.

Antireductionism. Animal behavior is no more intrinsically "reductionist" or "holist" than any other area of biology. It is nevertheless true that, from the later nineteenth century, an emphasis on the (especially purposeful) activity of animals and its evolutionary importance has often appealed to those wishing, for one reason or another, to strike a blow against the idea that science has revealed life to be mechanism all the way down and all the way up. The spiritually questing Thorpe belongs firmly in this tradition. His early work on biological races and the emergence of new feeding habits grew out of sympathetic interest in one of the great antimechanical themes of modern biology, the inheritance of acquired characters. Among animal psychologists, where learning through trial and error defined the mechanical extreme, dissenters tend to concentrate on problems whose solutions demand that animals perceive and act on relationships. Alongside his song research, such "insight" learning in birds became one of Thorpe's major ethological preoccupations.

After 1961, as Thorpe entered his sixties, he continued with his experimental research. There was, however, a noticeable shifting in ambition, as he turned increasingly from the business of doing animal behavior biology, for an audience of scientific peers, to the business of reflecting on it for the benefit of the general public. Two lecture-series-turned-books, *Biology and the Nature of Man* (1962) and *Science, Man, and Morals* (1965), brought into the open the largely implicit antireductionist thrust of his previous work, as well as the all but invisible Christian imperatives to which it answered. Exhibiting humankind as the product of an evolutionary process regularly transcending mere mechanism, Thorpe engaged his considerable synthetic talents to ranging over immense tracts of biology, psychology, philosophy, and theology. With such performances, it is little wonder that when the man of letters Arthur Koestler organized a soon-famous 1968 symposium on the life sciences "beyond reductionism," he secured Thorpe's participation.

The culmination of Thorpe's efforts along these lines was *Animal Nature and Human Nature* (1974), a long tome born of his lectures in the distinguished natural-theological Gifford series at St. Andrews between 1969—the year of his formal retirement from the Chair of Ethology created for him three years previously—and 1971. Old-fashioned in spirit but up to date in its materials, the book built toward its uplifting vision of evolutionary progress by way of everything from the difference between life and nonlife to man as a religious animal. There was, however, a new challenge to be faced: a popular reductionist tract on biology, *Chance and Necessity* (1971), by the French molecular geneticist Jacques Monod. No less unsettling from Thorpe's perspective was the emergence of a new "sociobiology," bent not just on reducing animal social behavior to genetic mechanisms but on bypassing ethology in doing so. Responding to these developments led Thorpe to write his final books, respectively, *Purpose in a World of Chance* (1978) and the valedictory *The Origins and Rise of Ethology* (1979). He died peacefully in a nursing home in 1986.

Legacies. What, aside from the song-learning research tradition, endures of Thorpe's achievements? His articles and books are not much read nowadays; and ethology as an identifiable discipline did not long survive in the sociobiological era. But the ethological attitude remains a live option, not least because several of the institutions that Thorpe helped establish still flourish, notably the Madingley station, long since grown into a subdepartment of animal behavior at Cambridge. Perhaps the legacy touching the most people, however, lies with what Thorpe once, in the Quaker journal *Friend* (he was a frequent contributor), called "Man's Responsibilities To and For Nature." In his view, evolution's gifts to humankind brought with them a duty of care. No mere thinker on this matter, he campaigned energetically for decades on behalf of the conservation of wildlife areas and—with rather more delayed success—animal welfare in laboratories and factory farms. Rarely have science and religion reconciled so beneficently.

BIBLIOGRAPHY

The papers of William Homan Thorpe are maintained at the, Department of Manuscripts and University Archives, Cambridge University Library, Cambridge, U.K. A very full bibliography of Thorpe's writings can be found in Robert Hinde's obituary notice (see below).

WORKS BY THORPE

"Biological Races in *Hyponomeuta padella* L." *Journal of the Linnaean Society (Zoology)* 36 (1929): 621–634.

"Biological Races in Insects and Allied Groups." *Biological Reviews of the Cambridge Philosophical Society* 5 (1930): 177–212.

"The Natural Control of *Hyponomeuta padellus,* L." *Proceedings of the Entomological Society of London* 5 (1930): 28–30.

"Experiments upon Respiration in the Larvae of Certain Parasitic Hymenoptera." *Proceedings of the Royal Society of London (B)* 109 (1932): 450–471.

With F. G. W. Jones. "Olfactory Conditioning in a Parasitic Insect and Its Relation to the Problem of Host Selection." *Proceedings of the Royal Society of London (B)* (1937): 56–81.

"Ecology and the Future of Systematics." In *The New Systematics,* edited by Julian Huxley. London: Oxford University Press, 1940.

"Types of Learning in Insects and Other Arthropods." Parts 1, 2, and 3. *British Journal of Psychology* 33 (1942–1943): 220–235; 34 (1943–1944): 20–31, 66–76. The first of several synthetic surveys of animal learning.

"A Type of Insight Learning in Birds." *British Birds* 37 (1943): 29–31.

"The Modern Concept of Instinctive Behaviour." *Bulletin of Animal Behaviour* 7 (1948): 2–12. An early "promotional" piece for Lorenzian ethology.

"The Process of Song-Learning in the Chaffinch as Studied by Means of the Sound Spectrograph." *Nature* 173 (1954): 465–469.

Learning and Instinct in Animals. London: Methuen, 1956; 2nd ed., 1963.

Bird-Song: The Biology of Vocal Communication and Expression in Birds. London: Cambridge University Press, 1961.

With O. L. Zangwill, eds. *Current Problems in Animal Behaviour.* Cambridge, U.K.: Cambridge University Press, 1961.

Biology and the Nature of Man. London: Oxford University Press, 1962.

Science, Man, and Morals. London: Methuen, 1965.

"Retrospect." In *Beyond Reductionism: New Perspectives in the Life Sciences—The Alpbach Symposium 1968,* edited by Arthur Koestler and J. R. Smythies. London: Hutchinson, 1969.

"Welfare of Domestic Animals." *Nature* 224 (4 October 1969): 18–20. A plea for Parliament to act in full on the report of the important Brambell Committee, of which Thorpe was a member.

"Man's Responsibility To and For Nature." Parts 1, 2, and 3. *Friend* (28 January, 4 February, and 11 February 1972): 100–102, 129–131, 161–162.

Animal Nature and Human Nature. London: Methuen, 1974.

Purpose in a World of Chance: A Biologist's View. Oxford: Oxford University Press, 1978.

The Origins and Rise of Ethology: The Science of the Natural Behaviour of Animals. London: Heinemann Educational, 1979. A still-useful chronicle interleaved with personal impressions.

OTHER SOURCES

Bidder, Anna M. "William Thorpe." *Friend* (16 May 1986): 621–622. A remembrance of Thorpe as Quaker biologist.

Boakes, Robert. *From Darwin to Behaviourism: Psychology and the Minds of Animals*. Cambridge, U.K.: Cambridge University Press, 1984. An excellent introduction to animal psychology as Thorpe came to know it, including insight learning.

Burkhardt, Richard W., Jr. *Patterns of Behaviour: Konrad Lorenz, Niko Tinbergen, and the Founding of Ethology*. Chicago: University of Chicago Press, 2005. An outstanding history of ethology, with much of interest on Thorpe, some of it based on interviews.

Durant, John R. "The Making of Ethology: The Association for the Study of Animal Behaviour, 1936–1986." *Animal Behaviour* 34 (1986): 1601–1616. An invaluable study of this organization and Thorpe's role in particular.

Gillispie, Neal C. "The Interface of Natural Theology and Science in the Ethology of W. H. Thorpe." *Journal of the History of Biology* 23 (1990): 1–38. The most extensive discussion of this topic currently available.

Hall-Craggs, Joan. "William Homan Thorpe 1902–1986." *Ibis* 129 (1987): 564–569.

Hinde, Robert A. "William Homan Thorpe, 1902–1986." *Biographical Memoirs of Fellows of the Royal Society* 33 (1987): 620–639. The fullest of the obituary notices, with excellent summaries of Thorpe's scientific writings.

Marler, Peter. "Science and Birdsong: The Good Old Days." In *Nature's Music: The Science of Birdsong*, edited by Peter Marler and Hans Slabbekorn. Boston: Elsevier, 2004. A concise and authoritative overview of the research program Thorpe began; includes a CD with Thorpe's own chaffinch recordings.

Wilson, David A. H. "Animal Psychology and Ethology in Britain and the Emergence of Professional Concern for the Concept of Ethical Cost." *Studies in History and Philosophy of Biological and Biomedical Sciences* 33 (2002): 235–261. A pioneering article, placing Thorpe's animal welfare activities in context.

Gregory Radick

THUDICHUM, JOHANN LUDWIG WILHELM

(*b.* Büdingen, Hesse-Darmstadt, Germany, 27 August 1829; *d.* London, United Kingdom, 7 September 1901), *chemistry, neurochemistry, otolaryngology, public health, oenology.*

Over a period of sixteen years, Thudichum labored at the chemical study of the human and animal brain, in the time he could spare from his medical practice. He is now regarded as the most significant nineteenth-century contributor to our knowledge of the chemistry of the brain. In addition, he made pioneer contributions to chemical pathology, surgery, war medicine, and public health, demonstrating a most unusual versatility.

The Thudichum family originated in Württemberg, but moved to Hesse in 1778. Ludwig, the oldest of six children, received a classical education under the tutelage of his father, Georg, a Lutheran pastor and Greek scholar of wide interests. In 1847 Ludwig was accepted for studies in medicine at the University of Giessen, but took part of his medical studies in Heidelberg. Among his teachers was the brilliant chemist Justus Liebig, and in Heidelberg he encountered Theodor Bischoff, Robert Wilhelm Bunsen, and Jacob Henle.

After a fruitful postgraduate year in Liebig's laboratory, he opened a medical practice in Giessen (1852). On learning of a new post in pathology at the university he applied for it, but was rejected; his brief participation in the 1848 Revolution probably spoke against him. It is also possible that his service as a volunteer assistant surgeon in the army of Schleswig-Holstein in 1850 and 1851 made him suspect in the eyes of the Prussian authorities. His disenchantment with his prospects in Germany prompted him to emigrate to England in 1853. He settled in London, where his betrothed, Charlotte Dupré, a distant cousin, was now living. He married her in 1854. The couple had eight children, one of whom died at an early age.

Thudichum rapidly established himself in London, gaining membership in the Royal College of Surgeons in 1855; he also secured a teaching post ("natural philosophy") at a now-defunct medical school, a hospital appointment, and membership in the Royal College of Physicians in 1860. In 1859 he became a British citizen. During this period he published a well received *Treatise on the Pathology of Urine*. A few years later he published a book on gallstones.

His accomplishments in medical practice, his published works, his participation in the defense at the trial of an unjustly accused doctor, and especially his interest in chemical pathology brought him to the attention of John Simon, then medical officer of the Privy Council, who appointed him as a consultant. Thudichum's initial assignment was to survey the meat markets of London, with special attention to parasitic diseases affecting humans. He spent eight months in this work, finally delivering an extensive document on parasitology, published in a government "Blue Book."

His next task was to study cholera and typhus, epidemic diseases that periodically recurred in the country, with special concern for chemical changes in the brain that might explain how that organ was affected. He recognized that he first needed information about the normal brain. He conducted his research sometimes at St. Thomas's Hospital, where Simon had recommended him for an appointment, and sometimes in his private laboratory. He reported his work in chemical journals, and as supplements to Simon's annual reports to the Privy Council. His first document on the chemistry of the brain, including a history of previous studies of the subject, appeared in 1874. His research on phospholipids was particularly noteworthy. Thudichum was a prolific writer and published on many other subjects as well: otolaryngology, public health, the coca of Peru, oenology (study of wine), cookery, and diverse medical problems.

Thudichum was involved in some scientific controversies that pitted him against powerful adversaries. The most significant dispute concerned the nature of *protagon*, an extract that the German pharmacologist Oscar Liebreich had obtained from brain, and which he considered to be a unitary, high-molecular-weight substance. Thudichum showed that it was actually a mixture of lipids by characterizing its components. Although his stance was principled and generally correct in these various disputes, Thudichum's career was affected adversely by the criticisms, for after Simon's retirement he was pressured to terminate his government-sponsored work. He finally published his treatise on the chemistry of the brain, based upon his own studies, in 1884; it was quickly translated into Russian, the first of many translations. It was reprinted twice in the twentieth century. Thudichum brought the work up to date shortly before his death in 1901.

Having completed his work on brain, he now concentrated on his medical specialty. In otorhinolaryngology his name is preserved in the "Thudichum nasal speculum," an instrument that he invented.

During the Franco-Prussian War Thudichum raised money to establish, with Simon's help, a military hospital in 1870 at Bingen, Germany, where care was provided for the injured and ill of both sides of the conflict. The epidemiological success of this venture demonstrated the value of the principles of public health long advocated by Simon.

Thudichum was aided in his research by a successive number of assistants, the best known of these being James Alfred Wanklyn, Charles Thomas Kingzett, and Henry Wilson Hake, all of whom eventually made their mark in British scientific life. Lacking an academic post, Thudichum was not able to maintain a long-lasting cadre of research personnel that could develop into a "school." As a result, his work did not get the attention it deserved, and was neglected or forgotten.

Otto Rosenheim, a lecturer on chemical physiology at King's College, London, began to investigate the history of protagon in 1907, and was especially impressed with the work of Thudichum on the subject. He became interested in discovering who that writer was, eventually achieving posthumous recognition for him. A 1932 paper by the medical historian Karl Sudhoff about Thudichum also helped in the rehabilitation of this "Hessian savant," with a reassessment of his important researches. Both Rosenheim and Sudhoff regarded Thudichum as the first British biochemist. In the late 1920s Irvine H. Page,

another trailblazing investigator of brain chemistry, also drew attention to Thudichum's pioneer work. Further, the American biochemist David Drabkin, while working on the urinary pigment urobilin, became interested in Thudichum, who had much earlier conducted prize-winning research on that subject, and Drabkin became a prime authority on the man and his work.

Thudichum's interest in the brain has led to his being eulogized as "chemist of the brain" but it is important to recognize his wide interests that fall under the broader rubric of public health: his parasite studies, writings on health in towns and countryside, his promulgation of the Turkish bath as a health measure, his lecturing on the germ theory of disease, and his interest in measures to improve the nutrition of the people.

Fifty years after his graduation Thudichum was honored by the University of Giessen with ceremonial renewal of his diploma. In it he was described as "a most celebrated exponent of the art of Medicine and Chemistry." A fortnight later he died of a cerebral hemorrhage. He was cremated, his papers were burned (by his request), and his library distributed.

BIBLIOGRAPHY

WORKS BY THUDICHUM

A Treatise on the Pathology of Urine. London: John Churchill, 1858.

With August Dupré. *A Treatise on the Origin, Nature and Varieties of Wine.* London: Macmillan, 1872.

A Treatise on the Chemical Constitution of the Brain. London: Baillière, Tindall & Cox, 1884. Reprinted with a historical introduction by D. L. Drabkin. Hamden, CT: Archon Books, 1962. Also reprinted in Birmingham Classics of Neurology and Neurosurgery, Birmingham, Alabama, 1990.

Grundzüge der anatomischen und klinischen Chemie. Berlin: A. Hirschwald, 1886.

The Spirit of Cookery: A Popular Treatise on the History, Science, Practice and Ethical and Medical Import of the Culinary Art, with a Dictionary of Culinary Terms. London: F. Warne, 1895.

The Progress of Medical Chemistry, Comprising Its Application to Physiology, Pathology, and the Practice of Medicine. London: Baillière, Tindall & Cox, 1896.

Die chemische Konstitution des Gehirns des Menschen und der Tiere. Tübingen, Germany: F. Pietzcker, 1901.

OTHER SOURCES

Breathnach, Caoimhghin S. "Johann Ludwig Wilhelm Thudichum 1829–1901: Bane of the *Protagonisers.*" *History of Psychiatry* 12 (2001): 37–62.

Chatagnon, C., and P.-A. Chatagnon. "L'étude chimique des constituents du tissu cerebral au cours du XIXe siècle. Un pionnier en Grande-Bretagne J. L. W. Thudichum (1828–1901)[*sic*]." *Annales médico-psychologiques* 116 (1958): 267–282.

Drabkin, David L. *Thudichum: Chemist of the Brain.* Philadelphia: University of Pennsylvania Press, 1958. Includes annotated bibliography of J. L. W. Thudichum's papers and books.

MacLean, Hugh, and Ida Smedley MacLean. *Lecithin and Allied Substances: The Lipins.* 2nd ed. London: Longmans, Green, 1927. For the protagon controversy.

Schulte, Bento. "Johann Ludwig Wilhelm Thudichum (1829–1901): Protagonist and 'Anti-protagonist' of Brain Chemistry." In *De novis inventis: Essays in the History of Medicine in Honour of Daniel de Moulin,* edited by A. H. M. Kerkhoff, Antoine M. Luyendijk-Elshout, and M. J. D. Poulissen. Amsterdam: APA-Holland University Press, 1984.

Sourkes, Theodore L. "How Thudichum Came to Study the Brain." *Journal of the History of the Neurosciences* 2 (1993): 107–119. This paper contains a detailed list of Thudichum's appendices to the Annual Reports of the Medical Officer to the Privy Council (1858–1870; 1874–1877) and to the Local Government Board (1874–1876).

———. "The Protagon Phoenix." *Journal of the History of the Neurosciences* 4 (1995): 37–62.

———. *The Life and Work of J. L. W. Thudichum, 1829–1901.* Montreal: Osler Library, McGill University, 2003. Appendix 4 contains a list of currently known surviving Thudichum correspondence.

Sudhoff, K. "Ludwig Thudichum (1829–1901). Rettung eines hessischen Gelehrten aus Liebigs Schule." *Nachrichten der Giessener Hochschulgesellschaft* 9 (1932): 33–45.

Theodore L. Sourkes

TIMOCHARIS (*fl.* c. 300 BCE, Alexandria), *astronomy.*

Timocharis is the earliest Greek astronomer who is known to have made and recorded large numbers of scientific observations of the heavenly bodies. No writings by him are extant, and his work has survived chiefly in the form of observations and measurements reported in Ptolemy's *Almagest* (second century CE). According to Ptolemy, Hipparchus (second century BCE) also exploited Timocharis's observations in his investigations of precession.

Among the observations of Timocharis that Hipparchus used in his lost book, *On the Displacement of the Solsticial and Equinoctial Points,* were lunar eclipses, but Ptolemy does not preserve their dates or any other details. He does, however, cite the reports of four occultations or near passages of fixed stars by the Moon, which Timocharis observed between 295 and 283 BCE in Alexandria. Timocharis recorded not only the dates but the times of night to a precision of about half an hour, as well as which part of the Moon's rim passed over or closest to the star in question. The dates are expressed in the Callippic calen-

dar, which was a schematic lunisolar calendar counting years in seventy-six-year cycles, and also in the Egyptian calendar. If this was an original feature of the reports, Timocharis was the earliest attested user of the Callippic calendar, which remained in use among astronomers until the first century CE. Ptolemy preserves one other pair of dated observation reports by Timocharis, pertaining to the passage of Venus by a fixed star in 272 BCE. There is no information about the original purpose of any of these observations.

As well as observations of the Moon and planets on specific dates, Timocharis made measurements of the positions of fixed stars, again being the first Greek known to have done so. Ptolemy gives a list of twelve undated declinations of stars attributed to him, together with six more attributed to Aristyllus, whom Ptolemy apparently regarded as Timocharis's contemporary and associate. As transmitted, the declinations are expressed in degrees and fractions of a degree, and they would be—by more than a century—the earliest instances of degrees in a Greek source if one could be confident that the numbers represented the form in which Timocharis originally reported them. Both Timocharis's and Aristyllus's declinations are reasonably accurate, presuming they were observed in the first decades of the third century, but they do not provide an adequate statistical basis for more precise dating.

BIBLIOGRAPHY

Britton, John Phillips. *Models and Precision: The Quality of Ptolemy's Observations and Parameters.* New York: Garland, 1992. Astronomical analysis of the observation reports.

Goldstein, Bernard R., and Alan C. Bowen. "On Early Hellenistic Astronomy: Timocharis and the First Callippic Calendar." *Centaurus* 32 (1989): 272–293.

———. "The Introduction of Dated Observations and Precise Measurement in Greek Astronomy." *Archive for History of Exact Sciences* 43 (1991): 93–132.

Maeyama, Yasukatsu. "Ancient Stellar Observations: Timocharis, Aristyllus, Hipparchus, Ptolemy—the Dates and Accuracies." *Centaurus* 27 (1984): 280–310.

Toomer, Gerald J., trans. *Ptolemy's Almagest.* Princeton, NJ: Princeton University Press, 1998. Ptolemy's references to Timocharis are in Book VII, 1–3, and Book X, 4.

Alexander Jones

TINBERGEN, NIKOLAAS (NIKO) (*b.* The Hague, Netherlands, 15 April 1907; *d.* Oxford, United Kingdom, 21 December 1988), *ethology, animal behavior, natural history, popularization of science, filming.*

Tinbergen was, with Konrad Lorenz, one of the two main founders of the science of ethology, or biological study of animal behavior, and for this he received the Nobel Prize. Tinbergen approached animal behavior studies experimentally in the field, and advocated a rigorous separation of causal, functional, developmental, and evolutionary analysis—known as "Tinbergen's four why's." He began as a bird-watcher and field-worker with insects in the Netherlands, was interned as a hostage during the German occupation during World War II, and after the war moved to Oxford in England. He established a group of students, many of whom became well known in their field, and brought the science of animal behavior to a wide public. He was a brilliant communicator as well as a natural field biologist, and gained international recognition with his photography and several behavior films. In later life he focused his studies on childhood autism.

Early Life in Holland Born and bred in the Netherlands, Niko moved to England in later years, but he had the good fortune to grow up in a country with an extremely rich natural history, and in a family with strong academic interests and background. His father Dirk Cornelis Tinbergen was a grammar school teacher of Dutch language in The Hague, and a respected scholar of medieval Dutch. He had a PhD and was the author of several books, including a widely used Dutch grammar. He was also keen on drawing as a hobby, a passion that Niko acquired from him. Dirk Cornelis was a hardworking, very organized person, intellectually stimulating, full of humor and joie de vivre, as well as a devoted father and family man, often taking his family on country walks and holiday trips.

Niko's mother Jeanette was also a schoolteacher. She was more mathematical than her husband, but keen on literature, and spoke French, English, and German as well as Dutch. She was the heart of the family, a warm and impulsive person. They lived in a rather bourgeois street of terraced houses (Bentinckstraat, The Hague): simple, thrifty and rather austere, and the work ethic dominated.

There were five children. The eldest was Jan, who in academic achievement stood out above the others from a very early age. He became a physicist, later turned to economics, and ended up with the 1969 Nobel Prize in Economics, twenty honorary doctorates, a knighthood, and many other honors. He was very hardworking, even as a young boy, and whereas Niko larked about as a boy and just scraped through his school exams, Jan worked. In later life, Jan was the man of meticulous quantification, whereas Niko watched birds and had broad ideas. The two brothers were never particularly close.

Of the other siblings, Niko's older sister Jakomien and younger brother Dik did not follow prominent aca-demic careers; she became a teacher and head of languages in a grammar school, and Dik an engineer and later director of Public Energy in The Hague. For Niko the closest sibling was his brother Luuk, eight years his junior. Niko was in awe of him; he thought Luuk the most intelligent in the family, a keen naturalist and artist. When Niko was in his twenties he did many natural history projects on birds jointly with Luuk. Luuk later became a professor in Groningen University and a prominent ecologist, but he suffered from depression and took his own life at the age of thirty-nine.

Although the example of his parents and the interests of his siblings must have facilitated Tinbergen's career as a natural historian, scientist, and writer, his development was not instigated by his family. Niko mapped out his own course, encouraged but not guided by his parents. As a boy, his life was about roaming around in the Dutch countryside, watching little creatures, walking, and messing about with nature, identifying birds, and bringing oiled birds home from the beach and cleaning them.

At his government grammar school in The Hague he did not do particularly well, except at sports (he even briefly played on the Dutch national hockey team). But in his spare time he became a fanatic teenage naturalist, encouraged by his biology master Dr. Abraham Schier-beek. What probably largely predetermined Tinbergen's career as a biologist was his involvement in a youth organization, the Nederlandse Jeugdbond voor Natuurstudie (NJN; Dutch Youth League for Nature Study).

Spurred on by his NJN friends, his brother, his parents, and his schoolteacher, by the age of sixteen Tinbergen had produced his first publications, in popular natural history magazines, and he had made a significant start with wildlife photography, which in the 1920s was a new development. Yet he was somewhat suspicious of academia, and at the end of his school years he could not see a career in biology, a subject he saw dominated by morphology and taxonomy. He had a flair for languages, with an excellent command of Dutch and good working knowledge of German, French, and English, but he disliked any of these subjects in the disciplined, formalized context of school. He was full of doubts.

At the end of school in 1925, his parents persuaded him to take a "working holiday" at a biological field station on the Baltic Sea, the bird migration station (Vogelwarte) directed by Johannes Thienemann in the Kurische Nehrung, in East Prussia (now in Kaliningrad, part of Russia). He spent most of his time there with photography rather than science, yet when he returned he immediately enrolled for a five-year degree course in biology at the University of Leiden, close to The Hague.

Later, Tinbergen wrote: "I started my studies in Leiden at the tail end of a period of the most narrow-minded, purely 'homology-hunting' phase of comparative anatomy, taught by old professors" (Tinbergen, 1989, p. 438). For him, biology in the university consisted of lists of facts and dry comparisons, contemplated in endless lectures in stuffy rooms. But outside with his friends, he could study birds in their nests and insects on bright flowers, along beaches and drifting skies. He spent a minimum of time on course work, was absent as often as he could be, just making sure he would pass, while all the time doing exciting extracurricular projects in order to keep sane. The undergraduate study itself had little impact on him, but his activities away from university all the more.

His extracurricular activities during his student years brought him in contact with several people who had a long-lasting influence on him. They included Gerard Tijmstra, a maverick who at the time was a math teacher as well as an ornithologist, and who induced Tinbergen to start serious observations on gulls. There was Jan Verwey, who lectured in zoology at Leiden, and who was very much a field man and bird-watcher; he produced some of the first analyses of bird behavior (herons), drawing attention to their "ritualized movements" and "behavior out of context." He later became director of the Dutch marine institute. Verwey and Tinbergen clicked, and spent many hours on bird observations together. There was A. F. J. (Frits) Portielje, a supervisor at the Amsterdam zoo, a keen observer of animals in captivity, also of gulls (he wrote a seminal paper on their behavior), and in Holland a widely known popularizer of things natural.

Tinbergen, as an undergraduate, watched and wrote about the behavior of herring gulls, terns, several raptors and owls, about migration and bird territories, and about shells and birds on the beaches, all in Dutch natural history magazines (*Levende Natuur, Ardea, Amoeba, Meidoorn, Wandelaar,* and others). In 1930, jointly with three friends, he published his first book *Vogeleiland* (Bird island), a natural history description of an area, De Beer near Rotterdam; he was the main author, but the authors' names came in alphabetical order. In 1929, through the NJN, he met his later wife, Elisabeth (Lies) Rutten, the sister of one of his coauthors of *Vogeleiland.* In the last of his undergraduate years, 1930, Tinbergen did his first small, serious scientific study (though still largely descriptive), on the courtship behavior of common terns, published the following year in German—without any involvement of his university teachers.

Despite further doubts about an academic career, after graduating Tinbergen accepted a job as research assistant in the Zoology Department in Leiden, under Cornelis Jakob van der Klaauw. In this department Hildebrand Boschma was one of Tinbergen's main contacts, specializing in taxonomy and physiology of invertebrates, not himself interested in zoological fieldwork, but

accepting that such studies provided additional strength to the department. He encouraged Tinbergen and the two would maintain a regular contact and correspondence for decades after. Tinbergen had decided on a PhD project on a species of digger wasp, the bee wolf *Philanthus triangulum,* to be supervised by Boschma. He had been intrigued by these insects in a dune area in the center of the Netherlands, Hulshorst, where his parents had a holiday cottage, and he had previously done a small undergraduate project on them.

The bee wolf is one of the larger solitary wasps, yellow and black. In sandy dune country the female digs a tunnel about half a meter deep, with a few chambers at the end that she supplies with dead honeybees, several per chamber. She lays one egg in each chamber, and the larva feeds on the bees. When the female returns to the nest with a dead bee, she somehow finds the inconspicuous entrance to her nest, and Tinbergen investigated, among other things, what recognition criteria she used to find the right place. He designed elegant field experiments to address this, experiments that would become classics in later years. For instance, he surrounded the nest entrance with a 30-centimeter circle of pine cones before the bee left for a hunting trip, then moved the circle over a short distance after the bee had left, and observed the effect when the insect returned (confusion). He did this also using other objects, some flat, some tall and farther away from the nest, and he investigated the role of scent (absent). Similarly, he investigated the hunting behavior of the wasps, how they catch their honeybees (and only honeybees), and the important role of scent in recognizing honeybees.

Tinbergen's PhD thesis, "Über die Orientierung des Bienenwolfes" (On the orientation of the bee wolf), was twenty-nine pages long, in German, and published in 1932 in *Zeitschrift für Vergleichende Physiologie* (Journal of comparative physiology). It was one of the shortest theses ever in this field, generally judged at the time to be a good paper, but nothing outstanding. It was one of the beginnings of field experimental studies of animal behavior, but years later Tinbergen was still amazed that he got away with it. The reason for its perfunctory quality was that Tinbergen had been selected as one of the participants in a one-year expedition to Greenland, and had to shorten his project; he became doctor of philosophy on 12 April 1932, got married to Lies Rutten on 14 April, and left for Greenland a few weeks later.

One of the remarkable aspects of Tinbergen's PhD work on bee wolves was the difference with contemporary experimental methods, which in the laboratory sought to study animals under conditions that were all controlled as much as possible. In contrast, Tinbergen studied animals in conditions that were "natural," and in which he attempted to change just one single variable. This was to characterize his later field-experimental work.

Greenland. In the context of the International Polar Year 1932–1933, the Tinbergens spent a year in Angmagssalik (now Tassiusaq), East Greenland. They stayed with Inuit, studied birds and the social life of sledge dogs, and collected a large number of Inuit utensils and objects d'art for the anthropological museum in The Hague. The Tinbergens' many field notes on sledge dogs never saw the light of day, but the behavior studies of the snow bunting *Plectrophonax nivalis* and of the red-necked phalarope *Phalaropus lobatus* produced interesting papers after their return to the Netherlands. For both studies Tinbergen focused on the defense of a territory around the nest; he included discussions of the concepts of territorial behavior and gave detailed descriptions of behavior during the breeding cycle. The phalarope, a small wading bird, was especially interesting to him, being unusual among birds in that the female is brightly colored and defends the area, whereas the male is drab, and incubates and takes care of the chicks. Niko's interest in territorial behavior was to be a main aspect of his future behavior studies, and this developed in Greenland.

More important than the immediate results of these Greenland field studies, however, was the effect of this interlude on Tinbergen himself. He gained confidence in his ability to carry out significant science under trying conditions, and in Holland he became an international scientist. Also, as an initially somewhat sentimental naturalist-conservationist, he became immersed in the Inuit culture of exploitation of animals and wildlife, and, staying most of his time there with the family of a shaman, he absorbed an Inuit view of animals as organisms just as plants are. He lost the notion of animals having sentiments; later this was to facilitate the concepts of animal behavior that he developed.

The Tinbergens returned from Greenland to Leiden in the fall of 1933, to his job as a research assistant to Van der Klaauw. He published a book in Dutch on his experiences, *Eskimoland* (1935), illustrated with many of his photographs, and a series of articles in popular natural history journals.

Development of Ethology in Leiden in 1930s. The subject of territorial defense by birds, which emerged in Tinbergen's studies in Greenland, made him aware of a need to underpin his fieldwork with a theoretical base and a clear phrasing of questions. As he wrote in a Dutch article, instead of what birds are fighting for, we should be asking "what drives birds to fight, what do they fight, and what is the effect of their fighting?" He began

to be involved with contemporary theories of animal psychology.

In the Netherlands at the time the leading student of animal behavior was Johan Bierens de Haan, who was to become an important force in Tinbergen's development. The two men exchanged a frequent, voluminous, and often personal and friendly correspondence over more than twenty years. Tinbergen's senior by twenty-four years, the animal psychologist Bierens de Haan was a lecturer at the University of Amsterdam and author of several books and papers. He saw animal instinct as having a clear purpose: It was innate and species-specific; it involved first of all an "awareness" followed by a "feeling," followed by a "striving." That, in turn, produced overt behavior, and according to him, a good animal observer would be able to recognize this chain of events by intuition. In response, Tinbergen urged that physiological phenomena be separated from psychological ones, and that science should be interested only in the former, as "subjective phenomena cannot be observed objectively in animals, it is idle either to claim or to deny their existence" (Tinbergen, 1951, p. 4).

The views of Bierens de Haan were broadly in line with those of the British psychologist William McDougall. Almost diametrically opposed to this were the views of the American John Broadus Watson, the man behind behaviorism, an approach that was equally an anathema to Tinbergen. Watson considered that all behavior was acquired, none was innate; every animal was a trained response machine and any behavior could be taught. Tinbergen was repulsed by the preoccupation of the behaviorists with white rats and monkeys in cages, pressing levers; later he said that behaviorism had given him a mental allergy to white rats from which he never fully recovered.

Another, different approach to animal behavior concentrated on its "directiveness." It was that of the English biologist Edward Stuart Russell, who assumed that "the objective aim or 'purpose' of an activity controls its detailed course" (e.g., animals mate *in order to* produce offspring). Tinbergen objected that this precluded any physiological explanation of behavior (1951, pp. 3–4).

What struck Tinbergen about all the animal behavior theorists was that none of them knew animals in their natural environment, none of them was a field biologist. But, at least initially, he had little alternative to offer. Later, he would refer to the

> haphazard, kaleidoscopic attempts at understanding animal behavior done by the future ethologists … made difficult rather than facilitated by the many early brands of psychology to which we turned for enlightenment, but which had disappointed us so bitterly. (Tinbergen, 1989, p. 440)

Nikolaas Tinbergen. *Nikolaas Tinbergen painting chicken eggs to resemble gull eggs for an experiment in camouflage.* **NINA LEEN/TIME LIFE PICTURES/GETTY IMAGES.**

In the Zoology Department at Leiden in the 1930s, Tinbergen was charged by Van der Klaauw with a lecture course in comparative anatomy, and with the organization of student courses in animal behavior. His lectures and field courses were highly popular, and resulted in several outstanding research projects by Tinbergen with his undergraduate students, also independent PhD projects, and publications that were important in the development of ethology.

At the site of his previous PhD work in central Holland, the dunes of Hulshorst, one set of joint projects employing Tinbergen's inductive approach (see below) was done, mostly with insects and all including a strong experimental element. This included extensions of his studies on *Philanthus*, including the PhD project of his student Gerard Baerends on the caterpillar-killing wasp *Ammophila* (Baerends was later to become a highly influential figure in Dutch zoology, and in animal behavior sciences), and research on the courtship behavior of a

butterfly, the grayling *Eumenis semele*. In all these projects, sequences of behavior patterns were dissected into separate components, and causal factors as well as subsequent effects of each component were determined through simple, but ingenious, experiments in the field. The students loved it, and the resulting clear publications, in both scientific journals and more popular magazines, made a large impact.

In a similar approach in the laboratory, Tinbergen and his students carried out projects on the breeding behavior of small fish in a more or less natural context in tanks, especially on the three-spined stickleback *Gasterosteus aculeatus*. These were to become critical in his assessment and development of the theoretical views then being promoted by Konrad Lorenz, the German scientist who was to be the main force in Tinbergen's further career in animal behavior.

The paths of Tinbergen and Lorenz crossed for the first time during a symposium on instinct held in Leiden, in 1936. Their characters were poles apart: Tinbergen the naturalist, gentle and self-deprecating, worrying, analyzing, and experimenting; Lorenz keeping animals at home, ebullient and brilliant, a philosophical mind, bubbling with ideas without testing or following them through. Nevertheless, the two hit it off immediately and became lifelong friends, despite many later controversies between them, and despite World War II that saw them passionately committed to opposite sides.

Lorenz had attracted Tinbergen's attention with his 1935 German-language paper "Der Kumpan in des Umwelt des Vogels," (The Companion in the Bird's World) which described how instincts function in the social life of birds. He treated behavior patterns as if they were organs that can be compared between species, arguing that each behavior pattern was "released" by a combination of species-specific stimuli in the environment, like a key that fitted a lock. He also referred to behavior as occurring in different functional contexts, such as breeding or fighting, though he did not propose an internal systematic arrangement of behaviors. Such ideas were music to Tinbergen's ears, and fitted in well with his experiments at that time on stickleback fish and insects. From his side, Lorenz found in Tinbergen's experiments the scientific testing of his own as yet unsubstantiated ideas.

Their single joint publication, much quoted afterward, came after Niko and family stayed with Konrad in his home Altenberg in Austria in the spring of 1937, and the two scientists experimented with Lorenz's greylag geese on the behavior of these birds when rolling a stray egg back into the nest. They described an "instinct action" with its specific releaser, and a separate direction component also with its own stimuli, jointly resulting in the egg being steered into the nest. Lorenz provided elaborate terminology and theory in the paper, Tinbergen the sections dealing with the experiments themselves.

Other classic experiments from that time in Altenberg involved cardboard models that were pulled overhead over young goslings and turkeys (later published in Tinbergen's *Study of Instinct* [1951]). The models resembled a bird of prey (short neck, long tail) when pulled in one direction, and a duck when pulled in the other. The goslings responded as the investigators expected, reinforcing the idea of a very simple set of stimuli that directs behavior. Later students have found it difficult, however, to repeat the results.

Much of Tinbergen's prewar approach to animal behavior is summarized in his "An Objectivistic Study of the Innate Behaviour of Animals," published in 1942. In this he argued that animal behavior has internal and external causes, and can be arranged in hierarchical fashion. For instance, environmental factors would cause a fish or a bird to be in "reproductive drive," then other stimuli would cause "subdrives" such as nest-building, courting, or fighting. Such stepwise organization schemes would apply to all behavior: There would be a hierarchy and such a hierarchy could be analyzed physiologically. Different drives (e.g., reproduction, aggression, predator-defense, feeding) would be mutually exclusive. All such behavior patterns would be inherited and innate, and he referred to them as "stereotyped movements" (later "fixed action patterns"), each set off by a release mechanism that was triggered by a specific stimulus.

Tinbergen's "Objectivistic Study" paper contained many definitions and categorizations, with long discussions of terms such as instinct reaction chains, reflexes, vacuum activities, intention movements, and substitute activities. His ideas of hierarchical organization went much further than those of Lorenz. The paper also singled out the importance of studying not merely the causal background of behavior, but also its function, especially in communication, that is, behavior that is designed to carry information for other animals. It contrasted sharply with the subjectivist approach of McDougall and Bierens de Haan, where the animals' feelings were paramount.

Tinbergen's contribution firmly showed ethology to be an exact science. By expressing the principles more clearly than Lorenz had ever done, Tinbergen became the mouthpiece of the new discipline in the English-speaking world. In the meantime, in 1939 he had been appointed as "lector" in Leiden (comparable to a present-day readership).

World War II. In May 1940 the Netherlands were overrun by the German forces. In 1941 most of the teaching staff of Leiden University resigned in protest against the treatment of their Jewish colleagues, and in 1942 many of them, including Tinbergen as well as many other of the most prominent figures in Dutch society (professors, cabinet ministers), were taken hostage by the Germans. They were to be the subject for reprisals after actions by the Dutch underground; in the end, some twenty of them were shot. The hostages were interned in a former training college for priests in Sint-Michielsgestel in the south of Holland.

Tinbergen was to spend two years in the hostage camp, in reasonable comfort but with the threat hanging over him. The inmates organized lectures, plays, and concerts, and there was considerable intellectual activity as well as political discussion. Tinbergen was able to write. One product of that time was a text in Dutch, *Inleiding tot de diersociologre* (Introduction to Animal sociology), published as a 184-page paperback after the war, in 1946. It was visually appealing, with many of his drawings, but it was never much of a success, having been written in a rather schoolmasterly style. There was a kaleidoscope of social behavior, with several arguments about behavior organization as in his previous publications. As an interesting kind of throwback, in places Tinbergen insisted that animals behave for the good of the species. Given the context in which it was written, it was not surprising that the author was not in top form. Another result of his hostage camp efforts was a series of handwritten and richly illustrated booklets about animals, for his children at home. Two of these were later published in English: *Kleew* (1947), about gulls, and *The Tale of John Stickle* (1954), about the behavior of sticklebacks.

After Tinbergen was finally released from the hostage camp in September 1944, he would spend seven more months under the German occupation, living with his family close to his field study sites near Hulshorst. Life in Leiden was too difficult in that period, known as the "hunger winter," with serious shortages.

Leiden after the War. After the war was over, rebuilding a research establishment took time, against a background of the problems of day-to-day living for a family with four children, in a shattered country. There was nothing to work with, not even notepaper, not even a bicycle to get around, and this in the face of a huge burden of lecturing to the flood of new students that followed the five years of war (for instance, Tinbergen had to lecture on animal morphology to some seven hundred medical students). He threw himself into the new, difficult life, and with missionary zeal even started a new journal for behavior studies, *Behaviour*, specifically to address his own young science.

In January 1947 he was appointed to a full professorship at Leiden, in experimental zoology. In his inaugural lecture, titled "Nature Is Stronger Than Nurture," and subtitled "In Praise of Fieldwork," Tinbergen outlined the aims and methods of ethology, the biological study of animal behavior. In the years following, he maintained a program of field research with his students just as in the 1930s, based in the same site Hulshorst, and also near the colonies of herring gulls on the Friesian island of Terschelling.

One set of (now well-known) field experiments there was aimed at the analysis of the pecking response gull chicks directed at their parents' bills (thus eliciting food regurgitation): which colors, bill shapes, and movements could make the chicks peck. It was published in *Behaviour* in 1950; it could be criticized in its methods, but the innovative approach opened new avenues in biology.

In 1946 Tinbergen had made a three-month lecture tour through the United States and Canada, organized by Ernst Mayr. In a set of six lectures at Columbia University he set out the approach to ethology that was to become the framework for his magnum opus, *The Study of Instinct,* which he wrote during 1947 and 1948, but published only in 1951. It was the major product of his postwar years in Leiden. It gave an outline of the entire structure of animal behavior, its internal and external mechanisms, its development, and its biological function and evolution. It provided order in the perceived chaos of behaving animals, with simple explanations and ideas about how to watch and study, with no jargon, and with easy-to-read graphs and pleasant natural drawings. Later much of the structure of behavior proposed here was dismantled again, but *The Study of Instinct* served its purpose. It was ethology's first real text, and it was critical for establishing the field's identity.

It begins by explaining how ethology relates to physiology, psychology, other biological sciences, behaviorism, and vitalism, outlining the questions that Tinbergen thought important. The following chapters describe the hierarchical organization of behavior and the role of external "releasing" stimuli, and of internal factors such as hormones and the central nervous system, in causing behavior. The last three chapters discuss the development of behavior in an individual's lifetime, including learning and conditioning, and discuss adaptation and evolution.

At the same time he was writing *The Study of Instinct,* Tinbergen published many scientific and popular papers. By any standards, he was highly successful in Leiden: professor at an unusually young age, many admiring students, renowned internationally, his major book about to burst onto the world scene, editor of the main international journal in his field, and able to travel as much as he liked. Yet in 1949 he abandoned his chair in Leiden for a job as demonstrator, well below the level of lecturer, in Oxford, England.

Reasons for his move were partly a missionary zeal to spread his ethology message in the English-speaking world, and partly that he had enough of the Netherlands, with its judgmental provincialism, its crowds, its choking rules and regulations, its celebration of financial gain, and the university where he had to spend too much time on administrative matters.

Oxford. Tinbergen was recruited to Oxford by the then-head of the Department of Zoology, Alister Hardy. He arrived in September 1949 with his family, Lies expecting their fifth child. It was a big upheaval, much greater than it would have been in the early twenty-first century, starting life in a quite different kind of society, in a foreign language, with children between four and fifteen going to local schools. But they were happy, and also, by the time Tinbergen started in the Department of Zoology his job had been upgraded to that of lecturer. He soon attracted a group of outstanding research students; there was an atmosphere of high spirits and tremendous enthusiasm.

In England Tinbergen again started behavioral fieldwork in gull colonies, initially in Norfolk, later on the Farne Islands and in Ravenglass, on the Irish Sea. With his students, he addressed by comparative and experimental methods the founding ideas of ethology as developed in the *Study of Instinct.* Among the products of this period were scores of popular articles, as well as theoretical papers (e.g., on "derived" activities, 1952) and several books. His postdoctoral student Esther Cullen's paradigmatic contribution (1957) showed the varied aspects of bird behavior that had evolved in response to environmental requirements, in her classical paper on the adaptiveness of the behavior of a cliff-nesting gull, the kittiwake. Although the research was largely Cullen's own initiative and work, it was always seen as a product of the Tinbergen group.

The *Study of Instinct* appeared in 1951, to excellent reviews all round; it established Tinbergen alongside of Lorenz as the leading scientist in this field. Although many of the underlying ideas had come from Lorenz, Tinbergen was perceived as responsible for ethology's scientific foundation. *The Study of Instinct* was soon followed by *Social Behaviour in Animals* (1953), which made little impact, and by *The Herring Gull's World* (1953), a detailed description of the behavior of the herring gull, and the book that Tinbergen himself was always most pleased with. There was the more popular *Bird Life* (1954), and *Curious Naturalists* (1958), in which he wrote about his fieldwork for a naturalist readership.

Niko Tinbergen attained great authority with his work in Oxford, and jointly with Konrad Lorenz in Germany, he was surrounded by the success of ethology. Then, out of the blue in 1953, came a potentially devastating criticism from Daniel Lehrman, a comparative psychologist based at Rutgers University in Newark. It was directed especially at Lorenz, but also at Tinbergen. Lehrman argued that there was no such thing as simply innate behavior. There was no evidence for a single causal background of similar behavior patterns in different species. There was no evidence for any underlying neurophysiological mechanisms, which in any case were likely to be different between species. Lehrman saw the simple behavioral models of Lorenz and Tinbergen as a danger to understanding.

Tinbergen invited Lehrman to Oxford, they argued, and later they were to become good friends. Tinbergen agreed with many of Lehrman's points, especially with the criticism that ethology made a clear distinction between innate and learned behavior (nature/nurture), and Tinbergen agreed that there had been much oversimplification. But he also made Lehrman see that he had rejected some useful aspects and methodologies of ethology. Lorenz was much more offended, and, unlike Tinbergen, saw nothing of value in Lehrman's critique. He later interacted with Lehrman at ethological meetings and other conferences, but he never fully appreciated Lehrman's objection that Lorenz's sharp distinction between innate and learned behavior stood in the way of a better understanding of how behavior develops in the individual.

In subsequent years, Tinbergen no longer focused on any of the causal relationships underlying animal behavior; he published one more long paper on the comparative behavior of gull species (1959), but after that his interest concentrated on what he saw as the functional and evolutionary significance of behavior, on the effects of behavior patterns on the animals' survival. These were topics that suited his talents best: the study of how behavior patterns contribute to the animals' survival in the world, in their natural habitat.

At Oxford University itself, Tinbergen remained somewhat of an outsider. His lectures were popular, but the social side of university life did not appeal to him, and his interests were academically rather narrow. He was a fellow of the ancient Merton College for some years, a college typical of Oxford's dreaming spires and full of ritual, but he resigned from that and instead moved to the more modern, down-to-earth Wolfson College. He had few friends in the university, and in general the Tinbergens rather kept to themselves.

But the research with his dynamic group of PhD students and collaborators continued vigorously in the late 1950s and the 1960s. He maintained intensive fieldwork, in which he actively participated himself. Especially in the large gull colonies of Ravenglass, on the Irish Sea, several innovative behavior studies were launched. One was a study of a simple behavior pattern of black-headed gulls, the removal of eggshells from their nests after eggs had hatched; this became a classic (1962). In elegant field experiments, Tinbergen analyzed the stimuli that induce the behavior (especially color and texture), and simultaneously (also experimentally) its biological function, that is, how this behavior contributes to the maintenance of camouflage of the nest.

In 1963 he published the paper that is considered to be his most significant contribution to ethology, "On Aims and Methods of Ethology," dedicated to Konrad Lorenz for his sixtieth birthday; its message became known as "Tinbergen's four whys." Tinbergen elaborated the approach that he took in *The Study of Instinct:* As a biological science, ethology deals with observable phenomena—the starting point is inductive. It is concerned with four different problems: that of causation, of effect (function, or survival value), of evolution, and of ontogeny (nature-nurture). Tinbergen reviewed these four aspects in detail, and the urgent need for experiments, and added a plea for what he saw as a continuing duty of ethology: the detailed observation and description of behavior.

During the 1960s Tinbergen's active involvement in fieldwork declined to almost a full stop. He still supervised students, still contributed several papers; there were further popular books (including a Time/Life book *Animal Behavior*, 1965) and many popular articles. However, his enthusiasm for carrying out research himself disappeared. It was replaced by his developing interest in moviemaking (which he had been doing on a small scale since the 1940s), which culminated in the television movie on the behavior of the herring gull, *Signals for Survival.* He spent several years filming it himself, in the huge bird colony on Walney Island, and edited it jointly with the experienced Hugh Falkus. It won the coveted Italia Prize for documentaries (1969).

Last Projects. Internationally, numerous distinctions came his way in the 1960s, including Fellowship of the Royal Society in 1962, at the age of fifty-five, honorary memberships of many societies, and invitations to lecture from all over the world. At Oxford his status was recognized rather belatedly, with a full professorship in 1966. He still had many students; he was ably assisted in their supervision (since the mid-1950s) by Michael Cullen, who, with a wide-ranging but severely critical and quantitative mind, was a perfect complement to Tinbergen. In Oxford Tinbergen was one of the instigators of the new undergraduate course in human sciences. He became closely involved in setting up and maintaining the Serengeti Research Institute in Tanzania, which he visited annually. But coincident with his declining interest in field studies, he struggled with health problems, especially with profound depressions that incapacitated him.

The main change in Tinbergen's interest was toward the application of ethology in studying the behavior of people, and toward human problems. Having suffered lifelong feelings of guilt about his lack of interest in the suffering of people, he followed Konrad Lorenz and his former student Desmond Morris in the use of knowledge acquired in the study of animals to understand ills of humanity such as aggression and warfare. His inaugural lecture in Oxford (1968), titled "On War and Peace in Animals and Man," was published in *Science* and created much discussion about whether comparisons of human and animal behavior were permissible. Tinbergen compared animal group territories with those of people and pointed out the malfunction of our "innate" appeasement gestures when long-range weapons were being used. He urged scientists not blithely to apply animal results to people (and he criticized Lorenz for this), but merely to use the methodology of ethology in the human context.

Tinbergen's wife Lies took an interest in the behavior of children, and she and Niko started an observational study on the unusual behavior of autistic children, which was to be his last project. It culminated in their 1983 book *"Autistic" Children: New Hope for a Cure*. The Tinbergens' research, papers, and lectures on childhood autism were controversial, as they drew profound conclusions on an emotional subject, with only anecdotal evidence as support. Using an ethological analysis, studying approach of and avoidance by children, the researchers concluded that defective parental behavior is the main cause of autism. Criticism was to be expected, and it was especially severe because of Niko Tinbergen's international standing as a behavioral scientist.

In 1973 Tinbergen, jointly with Lorenz and Karl von Frisch, was presented with the Nobel Prize for Physiology or Medicine "for their discoveries concerning organization and elicitation of individual and social behaviour patterns." A Nobel Prize for such a wide theme is unusual; more often, it is awarded for a single discovery. Von Frisch had, indeed, made such a single discovery, in the communication system of honeybees, but Lorenz and Tinbergen were awarded for their new approach. In his acceptance lecture, Tinbergen concentrated almost entirely on his autism studies, and on what he saw as an evaluation of the Alexander technique, an alternative and nonscientific technique to improve human body posture and movement. It drew much criticism.

In his retirement Tinbergen withdrew entirely from academia and science, and from moviemaking. He was close to his family, he corresponded warmly with many people but saw few friends, and was often severely depressed. He died of a stroke at the age of 81, on 21 December 1988.

Evaluation. The contribution of the bird-watcher who received the Nobel Prize was that of an innovator. He suggested the questions one should ask of the behavior of animals, both in the field methods used to study them, and in the experiments that change just one or two factors in the animals' environment rather than take them into totally controlled captivity. Tinbergen's contributions were all the more effective because he was a talented communicator, in many different ways.

Among students of animal behavior, Tinbergen is known for his "four whys": the why of causation, of ontogeny, of survival value, and of evolution; these were the questions he addressed by experiment and comparison. Where Lorenz had a wealth of ideas, Tinbergen analyzed and experimented, and sorted wheat from chaff. Tinbergen's first model of the hierarchical organization of behavior has been overtaken by others, but it was Tinbergen himself who initiated this process. From Lorenz's first vague suggestions, it was Tinbergen who articulated the system of a hierarchy of behavior patterns. In general, the ideas of both Lorenz and Tinbergen about causation of behavior have largely been discarded, but studies such as Tinbergen's first ventures into problems of survival value, of biological function, have developed and amplified hugely into what is now called behavioral ecology, whereas Lorenz, not being a field naturalist himself, had little to offer. Tinbergen's first, simple experiments caused others to formulate questions of optimal performance, and the concept of optimality has been a major foundation of behavioral ecology. In his study of the evolution of behavior of gulls, Tinbergen had a major stroke of luck in the work of his postdoctoral student Esther Cullen, by putting her to work on the kittiwake, which demonstrated so beautifully how adaptation to a particular niche had repercussions for a whole range of species-specific behaviors.

Tinbergen's experimental methodology was greeted enthusiastically at the time, but on close inspection many of his studies had failings that would not have passed a present-day reviewer, and his lack of quantification was criticized later, even by his own students (although partly this was the state of the science at the time). Some of the celebrated simplicity of the experiments caused flaws, among others because in the absence of blind tests there often was a subjective influence of the observer. But Tinbergen encouraged such critical rejection; his arguments made sense, and what mattered most were the ideas that he presented. It was Tinbergen's rational questioning approach to the behavior of animals in their natural environment for which he will be remembered.

Publications and Impact. Tinbergen published sixteen books, several translated into many languages, and some 360 scientific and popular papers. Of these, *The Study of*

Instinct was the best known, and continues to be widely quoted in the early twenty-first century. About two-thirds of his papers were popular articles, mostly in Dutch, about one-third in English. His single most important scientific paper, "On Aims and Methods of Ethology" (1963), is quoted even more often than *The Study of Instinct*. His most important movie, *Signals for Survival*, had a strong science content as well as beautiful imagery.

Apart from the Nobel Prize for Physiology or Medicine (1973), Tinbergen received many other rewards. He had chairs in Leiden and in Oxford, numerous visiting professorships in universities in many countries, and honorary doctorates in Edinburgh and Leicester. He was a Fellow of the Royal Society, a fellow first of Merton, then of Wolfson College in Oxford, a foreign member of the U.S. National Academy of Sciences and of the Royal Netherlands Academy of Sciences and Arts, a member of the German Academy of Natural Sciences, and an honorary member of the German Ornithological Society, an honorary fellow of the American Academy of Arts and Sciences and of the Royal College of Psychiatry. He also received distinguished awards from many other societies, especially the Swammerdam Medal of the Dutch Academy of Sciences and Arts and the Godman Salvin Medal of the British Ornithological Union, as well as others. He supervised some forty PhD students, several of whom became highly influential (Gerard Baerends, Desmond Morris, John Krebs, and Richard Dawkins, among others).

BIBLIOGRAPHY

Hans Kruuk's Niko's Nature, *cited below, includes a complete bibliography.*

WORKS BY TINBERGEN

With G. van Beusekom, F. P. J. Kooymans, and M. G. Rutten. *Het Vogeleiland* [Bird island]. Laren, Netherlands: A. G. Schoonderbeek, 1930.

"Zur Paarungsbiologie der Flussseeschwalbe (*Sterna h. hirundo* L.)" [On the biology of reproduction in the common tern]. *Ardea* 20 (1931): 1–18.

"Über die Orientierung des Bienenwolfes (*Philanthus triangulum* Fabr)" [On the orientation of the bee wolf]. *Zeitschrift für vergleichende Physiologie* 16 (1932): 305–334.

Eskimoland. Rotterdam: D. van Sijn & Zonen, 1935.

"Field Observations of East Greenland Birds. I. The Behaviour of the Red-Necked Phalarope (*Phalaropus lobatus* L.) in Spring." *Ardea* 24 (1935): 1–42.

"The Function of Sexual Fighting in Birds, and the Problem of the Origin of 'Territory.'" *Bird Banding* 7 (1936): 1–8.

With Konrad Lorenz. "Taxis und Instinkthandlung in der Eirollbewegung der Graugans, I" [Taxis and instinctive movement in the egg-rolling of the greylag goose]. *Zeitschrift für Tierpsychologie* 2 (1938): 1–29.

The Behavior of the Snow Bunting in Spring. Transactions of the Linnaean Society of New York 5. New York, 1939.

"Die Übersprungbewegung" [Displacement activities]. *Zeitschrift für Tierpsychologie* 4 (1940): 1–40.

"Ethologische Beobachtungen am Samtfalter, *Satyrus semele* L." [Ethological observations on the grayling butterfly]. *Journal für Ornithologie* 89 (1941): 132–144.

"An Objectivistic Study of the Innate Behaviour of Animals." *Bibliotheca Biotheoretica* 1 (1942): 39–98.

Inleiding tot de diersociologie [Introduction to animal sociology]. Gorinchem, Netherlands: Noorduijn, 1946.

Kleew: The Story of a Gull. New York: Oxford University Press, 1947.

De Natuur is sterker dan de leer, of de lof van het veldwerk [Nature is stronger than nurture: In praise of fieldwork]. Leiden: Luctor et Emergo, 1947. Leiden University inaugural lecture, 25 April 1947.

"The Hierarchical Organisation of Nervous Mechanisms Underlying Instinctive Behaviour." *Symposia of the Society for Experimental Biology* 4 (1950): 305–312.

With A. C. Perdeck. "On the Stimulus Situation Releasing the Begging Response in the Newly-Hatched Herring Gull Chick (*Larus argentatus argentatus* Pont)." *Behaviour* 3 (1950): 1–39.

The Study of Instinct. Oxford: Clarendon Press, 1951.

"The Curious Behavior of the Stickleback." *Scientific American* 193 (December 1952): 22–26.

"'Derived' Activities: Their Causation, Biological Significance, Origin and Emancipation during Evolution." *Quarterly Review of Biology* 27 (1952): 1–32.

"On the Significance of Territory in the Herring Gull." *Ibis* 94 (1952): 158–159.

"A Note on the Origin and Evolution of Threat Display." *Ibis* 94 (1952): 160–162.

The Herring Gull's World. London: Collins, 1953.

Social Behaviour in Animals. London: Methuen, 1953.

Bird Life. London: Oxford University Press, 1954.

The Tale of John Stickle. London: Methuen, 1954.

"On the Functions of Territory in Gulls." *Ibis* 98 (1956): 401–411.

Curious Naturalists. London: Country Life, 1958.

"Comparative Studies of the Behaviour of Gulls (Laridae): A Progress Report." *Behaviour* 15 (1959): 1–70.

With G. J. Broekhuysen, F. Feekes, J. C. W. Houghton, et al. "Egg Shell Removal by the Black-Headed Gull, *Larus ridibundus* L.: A Behaviour Component of Camouflage." *Behaviour* 19 (1962): 74–117.

"On Aims and Methods of Ethology." *Zeitschrift für Tierpsychologie* 20 (1963): 410–433. Facsimile reprinted in *Animal Biology* 55, no. 4 (2005): 297–321.

Animal Behavior. Life Nature Library. New York: Time Incorporated, 1965.

With Eric A. Ennion. *Tracks.* Oxford: Clarendon Press, 1967.

"On War and Peace in Animals and Man." *Science* 160 (1968): 1411–1418.

With Hugh Falkus and Eric A. Ennion. *Signals for Survival.* Oxford: Clarendon Press, 1970. Book based on the 1969 film of the same name. VHS version: McGraw-Hill, 1970.

The Animal in Its World: Explorations of an Ethologist, 1932–1972, vol. 1, *Field Studies.* London: George Allen & Unwin, 1972. A compilation of ten of Tinbergen's scientific papers on experimental fieldwork, including studies on bee wolf, grayling butterfly, black-headed gull, and fox.

The Animal in Its World: Explorations of an Ethologist, 1932–1972, vol. 2. *Laboratory Experiments and General Papers.* London: George Allen & Unwin, 1972. A compilation of eight of Tinbergen's scientific papers, on laboratory studies (of thrushes and sticklebacks) and ethological theory.

"The Croonian Lecture, 1972: Functional Ethology and the Human Sciences." *Proceedings of the Royal Society of London, Series B, Biological Sciences* 182 (1972): 385–410.

With Elisabeth A. Tinbergen. *Early Childhood Autism: An Ethological Approach.* Advances in Ethology, supplements to *Journal of Comparative Ethology* (*Zeitschrift für Tierpsychologie*) 10. Berlin: P. Parey, 1972.

"Ethology and Stress Diseases." In *Les Prix Nobel en 1973.* Stockholm: Norstedt, 1974, and *Science* 185 (1974): 20–27. Nobel Lecture. Available from http://nobelprize.org/nobel_prizes/medicine/laureates/1973/tinbergen-lecture.html.

With Elisabeth A. Tinbergen. *"Autistic" Children: New Hope for a Cure.* London: Allen and Unwin, 1983.

"Watching and Wondering." In *Studying Animal Behavior: Autobiographies of the Founders,* edited by Donald A. Dewsbury. Chicago: University of Chicago Press, 1989.

OTHER SOURCES

Burkhardt, Richard W. *Patterns of Behavior.* Chicago: University of Chicago Press, 2005.

Cullen, Esther. "Adaptations in the Kittiwake to Cliff-Nesting." *Ibis* 99 (1957): 275–302.

Kruuk, Hans. *Niko's Nature.* Oxford: Oxford University Press, 2003.

Lorenz, Konrad. "Der Kumpan in der Umwelt des Vogels: Der Artgenosse als auslösendes Moment sozialer Verhaltungsweisen" [The companion in the bird's world: Fellow members of the species as releasers of social behavior]. *Journal für Ornithologie* 83 (1935): 137–215, 289–413.

Röell, D. René. *The World of Instinct: Niko Tinbergen and the Rise of Ethology in the Netherlands (1920–1950).* Assen, Netherlands: Van Gorcum, 2000.

Hans Kruuk

TING, V. K.
SEE **Ding Wenjiang**.

TINSLEY, BEATRICE MURIEL HILL (*b.* Chester, United Kingdom, 27 January 1941; *d.* New Haven, Connecticut, 23 March 1981), *astronomy, cosmology, evolution of galaxies, education.*

Tinsley was one of the first to show that galaxies evolve with time. She was famed as a synthesizer, constructing models that gave new ways of measuring the universe and creating new pathways for cosmologists. Her work, including collaboration with colleagues and her inspiring teaching, was honored by the American Astronomical Society with the Beatrice M. Tinsley Prize, first awarded in 1986. It recognizes "an outstanding research contribution to astronomy or astrophysics, of an exceptionally creative or innovative character." The University of Texas in Austin endowed a chair in her name in 1985.

Origins. Beatrice Muriel Hill was born prematurely after an air raid in World War II, and was not expected to live. Her unusual zest for living was evident from early childhood, however. It was to be said of her that she did not waste a minute of her life, whether it be purposeful play, constructing and following fourteen-hour daily timetables during her school days, or teaching herself to use her left hand to work on scientific papers in the last few months of her life, when partially paralyzed by a brain tumor caused by cancer.

She was the middle of three daughters born to Edward and Jean Hill, née Morton. Her parents, both from prominent families, instilled in their children a knowledge of their forebears, and made it plain that great things were expected of them. Innovative chemists were featured in Jean Hill's family company, Morton Sundour Fabrics. Edward Hill came from a line of land and shipping owners. The great influence in their lives, hence their children's, was the interfaith religious movement begun by an American, Frank Buchman, and known as the Oxford Group (not to be confused with Anglicanism's Oxford Movement), later Moral Re-Armament. Adherents were to live by the "Four Absolutes": Absolute Love, Absolute Purity, Absolute Honesty, and Absolute Unselfishness.

Beatrice grew up with religious and philosophical discussions around the dinner table, the big questions of life, death and the universe. While always respecting her parents and seeking their approval, she came to disagree with many of their beliefs and their strict interpretation of the Absolutes. She sought other answers, and turned to science.

From babyhood Beatrice had been cared for by a nanny, as were her parents before her. The austerity of postwar England, and the fact that Edward Hill had not been able to settle to a career, made him look to new horizons. In 1946 the family migrated to New Zealand. There Edward Hill was ordained in the Church of England, although he resigned from parish work to become mayor of the city of New Plymouth in 1953. Left behind was this nanny, the substitute-mother. Beatrice was to say that "a black hole of grief" opened up in her. The nanny was later brought out from England, but a second and final separation in 1949 desolated the child. It was soon after this that Beatrice drew up a timetable for living in which all her waking hours were purposefully occupied.

She increasingly became a "good" daughter, trying to please her parents while not following their religious beliefs. She also came to believe they needed protection from the barbs of criticism directed at them in their public lives: protecting them from what they did not need to know. Thus her long letters home, to the end of her life, give only a partial picture of what she was thinking and doing. Nevertheless, these letters, selected by her father with a narrative framework and published as *My Daughter Beatrice,* give an unusual insight into the development of a cosmologist.

Education. Beatrice's childhood was filled with music, books, ponies, and exploration of nature. At high school she excelled in every subject although she was always by far the youngest in her class. She was expected to gain a university scholarship in languages, or possibly become a professional violinist. Instead she stood firm and persuaded her headmistress and parents that mathematics, physics, and chemistry were her subjects. Astronomy was her goal. Working largely by herself she won a top scholarship, and in 1958 enrolled in the sciences at the University of Canterbury in Christchurch.

The young Beatrice's attempts to become part of a greater whole, as well as to shield her parents from anxiety if she had boyfriends, had led to her becoming engaged to be married when she was still only sixteen, an engagement soon painlessly broken. She did marry the next man to ask her, Brian Tinsley, a well-regarded science student four years her senior who was specializing in spectroscopy. At twenty the first of her classmates to marry, Beatrice by then was recognized as one of the university's outstanding students. Other than by taking a similar scientific rather than narrowly religious view of life, the Tinsleys were not well matched, as Beatrice was later to write. For many years, however, she strove to be her ideal of a good wife, although she had to contort her own life in the process.

Her student life was enriched by playing the violin in an orchestra, belonging to a philosophical debating club, the Socratic Society, and doing volunteer community work. She also had the good fortune to be able to use what was only the second computer to be imported into New Zealand, thus becoming familiar with an essential tool early in her short career. Cosmology was the subject she wanted to pursue but was not then taught at Canter-

bury University. Instead she was advised to write her MSc thesis on "Analysis of the optical absorption spectrum of neodymium magnesium nitrate." She had to fit experimental data into a scheme of theoretical expression, a model to accommodate all the data published by other workers to that date. She graduated with top honors and won all available prizes.

To advance their careers, both Tinsleys needed to study abroad. Brian, working on his doctorate, accepted a research position at the Southwest Center for Advanced Studies, Dallas, Texas (which later became part of the University of Texas), where Beatrice was assured she could use her postgraduate scholarship. She discovered, however, that no relevant teaching was available, so studied astronomy on her own. As precious time was passing, she decided to begin the family they had planned. It was when she was told she could not conceive that Beatrice talked the University of Texas at Austin (UTA) into accepting her as a PhD student in 1964. This involved spending four days weekly in Austin, and commuting 400 miles.

She exceeded expectations, completing her preliminary work in four months instead of the usual two years, then gaining her PhD in only twenty-three months instead of the expected five years. Her achievement was the more remarkable because, while working on her thesis, she felt she should accede to her husband's request that they adopt a baby soon to be born to a member of his family. This was part of her concept of being a good wife, although they had earlier agreed they would not adopt until they both had suitable university positions away from Dallas.

As the leading astronomer Sandra Faber would later argue, although she had been drawn to astronomy by cosmology, she rapidly decided that the pursuit of cosmology called for a much better understanding of the development of galaxies. The key point was that if old galaxies were systematically different from young ones, then cosmological measurements that assumed they were the same were sure to be misleading. In her thesis Tinsley explored how galaxies change over time in color and luminosity as the stars within them age. She did this by developing computer models that employed both observational data and theoretical information on the evolution of stars. Although the basic idea was not original to her, Tinsley's analysis was much more detailed than anything that had been done before and she produced numerical simulations. Her paper based on her thesis, "Evolution of the Stars and Gas in Galaxies," broke wholly new scientific ground. Bold and wide-ranging, it foreshadowed her own future research, as even a casual reading of her more than one hundred published papers shows. It was to be said of her that, "with a degree of realism never achieved before," she tackled in masterly fashion the evolution of stellar

Beatrice Tinsley. COURTESY OF CHRISTINE COLE CATLEY.

populations in galaxies, and modeled the complex interplay between star formation, stellar evolution and the recycling of the interstellar medium (Faber, 1981, pp. 110–111). Tinsley contended that the evolution of galaxies would produce much more significant changes in the brightness of galaxies than the small changes calculated to result from different cosmological models. She also suggested that different histories of star formation might explain the different sorts of normal galaxies without assuming different ages.

Selecting this paper for the *Astrophysical Journal*'s 1999 centennial issue as one of the fifty-three seminal papers of the twentieth century, the *AJ*'s editor, Robert Kennicutt Jr., has said its most enduring result is its clear demonstration that galaxy evolution is an eminently observable phenomenon. Within a decade this new subject was to grow into one of the largest subfields in extragalactic astronomy. When the paper was first published in 1968, the very eminent astronomer Allan Sandage decried it. He contended that the universe was closed whereas Tinsley had argued that it was open. For some time Tinsley felt her work was not fully appreciated. Astronomers

such as Ivan King and Hyron Spinrad of the University of California at Berkeley, however, early showed an interest and recognition that came to her as "water in the desert," Tinsley was to say. In turn, throughout her life she responded to and encouraged young astronomers, this being a much-appreciated component of her teaching style.

Family and Work. True to Beatrice's belief that "the right family" was of two children, the Tinsleys adopted a second child in 1968. Whenever she could arrange child care, Beatrice continued studying on her own. There was still no prospect of work in Dallas but she presented papers at American Astronomical Society meetings at the University of Colorado at Boulder in 1970 and the University of Massachusetts at Amherst in 1971, with a grant from the National Science Foundation enabling her to pay for some child care and travel to meetings. Tinsley very much reemerged as a researcher in 1971 and 1972 and in these years she published eleven papers.

James Gunn of the California Institute of Technology (Caltech) arranged for a three-month appointment for her at Pasadena in 1972, the first professional opportunity of her life. With her children living with her, she felt fulfilled and energized. Richard Larson of Yale University and Sandra Faber of Lick Observatory joined Gunn at this time in being among the first to perceive her abilities. They were all to become lifelong friends and colleagues. In particular, when collaborating with Gunn and later with Larson, she enjoyed an intense intellectual relationship of the kind she had never before experienced.

Back as a housewife again in Dallas, Beatrice resumed working with Gunn on the first of many important collaborations, and on a research project with the Frenchman Jean Audouze. She also worked on a proposal for an astronomy department at the University of Texas at Dallas (UTD), with a program leading to a master's degree. This, she hoped, might give her a work opportunity as her husband was becoming adamant that he would not look for a post elsewhere; at UTD he was well respected and secure. Other centers began to vie for her, and in 1973 the University of Maryland offered a visiting lectureship for eighteen months. Beatrice was elated but her husband objected, saying her place was with him in Dallas—this although he would often be away himself during that time, to meetings and on spectroscopy work. He did agree to her taking the children for six months, and another period of creativity opened up for her. Having arranged child care, she continued to accept invitations to speak at other centers, including a part-time position as assistant professor at UTA.

The Tinsleys' marital relationship was becoming increasingly strained with Beatrice growing ever more frustrated at the lack of scientific opportunities that the marriage implied. They divorced in 1974 and while she had the children for all their holidays, for her the separation from them meant lifelong trauma.

Her mother had died and her father in New Zealand had remarried, but Beatrice still felt impelled to protect him from distress. Now her divorce devastated him. She could offer only a crumb of comfort in the fact that she had been awarded the Annie J. Cannon Prize in Astronomy. This prize, for outstanding research and promise by a postdoctoral woman researcher, is given to a North American female astronomer within five years of receiving her PhD in the year of the award.

Professional Life. At the beginning of 1975 Tinsley accepted a six-month appointment at Lick Observatory before taking up an assistant professorship at Yale. This was prefaced by the first of what became regular summer working visits to Cambridge, England, to the NATO Advanced Study Institute. Here she worked with some of the world leaders in her field. The eminent astronomer and cosmologist Fred Hoyle had been her childhood hero and his books had introduced her to cosmology; she took time away from Cambridge to give the scene-setting review of cosmology at his sixtieth birthday celebrations, held in Venice.

After her arrival at Yale in September 1975, the Yale astronomy department entered an outstanding period. She both unified and electrified the department by bringing together two of its strongest areas, stellar evolution and galactic studies, through outstandingly fruitful collaborations with Larson. Her years at Yale saw something of a shift in her research, as she now pressed the study of galaxies not just as the means to better test cosmological models but as a crucial subject in its own right, too. Responding to the ideas of various theorists, she also examined how the mergers of galaxies might affect their brightnesses.

To further the study of the evolution of galaxies, Tinsley and her colleagues at Yale organized what became known as the Yale International Conference on the Evolution of Galaxies and Stellar Populations. She invited the outstanding people in the field worldwide. Held on 19–21 May 1977, it became one of the most memorable conferences in the lifetimes of its participants and would become widely regarded as a sort of watershed, as it marked the maturing of a field that had previously been largely concerned with classification. As it would come to be remembered, nearly everyone came with the view that galaxies were individuals in the universe whose lives were entirely influenced by their own internal dynamics. Everyone left knowing that galaxies existed in a universe full of other galaxies, and that their interactions among themselves were every bit as important as their internal interac-

tions. Gunn was later to summarize: "It was the single most important galaxy conference in the history of the subject. There has been no other similar conference. There is no Beatrice" (Catley, 2006, p. 297; Gunn to author, September 2001). From the day the conference ended, Tinsley had three years and ten months to live.

Energized by the conference and the children's holidays with her, she embarked on many projects, using every minute. She continued with her own papers and existing collaborations, and played more chamber music with Larson and a new graduate student, Linda Stryker, who was to become a part-substitute for her much-loved sister, Rowena Hill, a professor of English in Venezuela. Her feminist views led her to sit on relevant Yale committees; she regretted abandoning her maiden name when she married, and counseled women students about this. Always much sought after as a teacher, in spite of the rapidity of her speech sounding like "a stream of dried peas on a windowpane," she invited a stream of "greats" in their fields to visit her department. Scientific ideas and possibilities seemed unlimited (Catley, 2006, p. 275). In the view of at least one of her collaborators, the Yale International Conference on the Evolution of Galaxies and Stellar Populations also marked Tinsley's emergence as a true insider in the astronomical community.

Illness. Then, in early 1978, melanoma was diagnosed in her left upper leg. An operation revealed only a fifty-fifty chance of survival. Larson, with whom she had a close relationship, became her mainstay. After initial devastation she realized she must help everyone to cope with her cancer. Her postgraduate students and her children became her first priority. She continued teaching and research as her doctors, realizing the kind of patient she was, fitted in her numerous treatments as much as possible around her scientific activities in New Haven, the wider United States, and abroad. In July 1978 she became a full professor with tenure.

Another change in her personal circumstances came about the next year. Her daughter Teresa had always been hyperactive. Brian Tinsley had married again, and now the Dallas family decided they could no longer cope. The child, aged eleven, was sent to New Haven to live with Beatrice, who by now was suffering extensively from her cancer's side effects. Larson was again her main support, becoming a virtual father to the child, and moving into her apartment to care for mother and daughter. Her son Alan came to visit and everyone rallied to help.

In November 1980 came what they had dreaded, a brain tumor. Beatrice was left partially paralyzed but she rallied and worked on. Her room in the Yale Infirmary became both a social and a work center, with a stream of students and colleagues. Her joy in scientific endeavor, whether her own or that of others, continued throughout her illness. She taught herself to print with her left hand and in this way, plus dictation, she finished several papers in the infirmary, composed testimonials for her students to be used after her death, and kept up a flow of responses to her wide-ranging correspondents.

Her last thoughts were of her children, as she told astronomer Audouze when he telephoned her from Paris just before she died on 23 March 1981, aged forty (Catley, 2006, pp. 402–403; Audouze to author, July 2001).

Faber, her close friend and colleague, was asked to put into the simplest possible words, for nonscientists attending her funeral, what Tinsley had done and would continue to do for astronomy. She said that Tinsley's thesis, together with the many increasingly detailed papers she wrote on this and other related subjects over the next fourteen years, had had a profound impact on the course of cosmological studies. The redshift-magnitude test and other similar observations of distant galaxies that for decades had been reckoned to be pivotal cosmological tools had now come to be viewed as even more fertile means for studying galactic evolution. Her work had thus been instrumental in opening up an active and ongoing new field of research.

"More than any other single individual over the last decade, she succeeded in illuminating and unifying the complex processes which together constitute galactic evolution," Faber wrote in *Physics Today* (1981, pp. 110–111). She went on to mention the many concepts that Tinsley either originated or played a significant role in developing, which included, among others, the evolution of matter via nucleosynthetic processes and the importance of the physics of highly evolved stars in understanding the integrated properties of galaxies. "Any one of these diverse topics would provide ample material for years of study," Faber concluded, "but Beatrice Tinsley was highly regarded for her intimate familiarity with all of them."

BIBLIOGRAPHY

WORKS BY TINSLEY

"Evolution of the Stars and Gas in Galaxies." *Astrophysical Journal* 151 (1968): 547–565.

"Galactic Evolution: Program and Initial Results." *Astronomy and Astrophysics* 20 (1972): 383–396.

"Stellar Evolution in Elliptical Galaxies." *Astrophysical Journal* 178 (1972): 319–336.

With J. Richard Gott, James E. Gunn, et al. "An Unbound Universe?" *Astrophysical Journal* 194 (1974): 543–553.

With James E. Gunn. "Evolutionary Synthesis of the Stellar Population in Elliptical Galaxies. I. Ingredients, Broad-Band Colors, and Infrared Features." *Astrophysical Journal* 203 (1976): 52–62.

With G. A. Shields. "Composition. Gradients Across Spiral Galaxies. II. The Stellar Mass Limit." *Astrophysical Journal* 203 (1976): 66–71.

With Jean Audouze. "Chemical Evolution of Galaxies." *Annual Review of Astronomy and Astrophysics* 14 (1976): 43–79.

With Richard B. Larson. "Star Formation Rates in Normal and Peculiar Galaxies." *Astrophysical Journal* 219 (1978): 46–59.

———. "Chemical Evolution and the Formation of Galactic Disks." *Astrophysical Journal* 221 (1978): 554–561.

"Evolutionary Synthesis of the Stellar Population in Elliptical Galaxies. II. Late M Giants and Composition Effects." *Astrophysical Journal* 222 (1978): 14–22.

With Curtis Struck-Marcell. "Star Formation Rates and Infrared Radiation." *Astrophysical Journal* 221 (1978): 562–566.

"Stellar Lifetimes and Abundance Ratios in Chemical Evolution." *Astrophysical Journal* 229 (1979): 1046–1056.

"Evolution of the Stars and Gas in Galaxies." *Fundamentals of Cosmic Physics* 5 (1980): 287–388.

"On the Interpretation of Galaxy Counts." *Astrophysical Journal* 241 (1980): 41–53.

With Chi-Chao Wu, Sandra M. Faber, et al. "The Ultraviolet Continua of the Nuclei of M31 and M81." *Astrophysical Journal* 237 (1980): 290–302.

With Richard B. Larson and C. Nelson Caldwell. "The Evolution of Disk Galaxies and the Origin of S0 Galaxies." *Astrophysical Journal* 237 (1980): 692–707.

With James E. Gunn and Linda L. Stryker. "Evolutionary Synthesis of the Stellar Population in Elliptical Galaxies. III. Detailed Optical Spectra." *Astrophysical Journal* 249 (1981): 48–67.

OTHER SOURCES

Catley, Christine Cole. *Bright Star: Beatrice Hill Tinsley, Astronomer.* Auckland, New Zealand: Cape Catley, 2006.

Eisberg, Joann. "Making a Science of Observational Cosmology: The Cautious Optimism of Beatrice Tinsley." *Journal for the History of Astronomy* 32 (2001): 263–278.

Faber, Sandra. "Beatrice Tinsley." *Physics Today* 34 (1981): 110–111.

Hill, Edward. *My Daughter Beatrice, a Personal Memoir of Dr. Beatrice Tinsley, Astronomer.* New York: American Physical Society, 1986.

Larson, Richard B., and Linda Stryker. "Obituary, Beatrice Muriel Hill Tinsley." *Quarterly Journal of the Royal Astronomical Society* 23 (1982): 162–165.

Overbye, Dennis. *Lonely Hearts of the Cosmos.* New York: HarperCollins, 1991.

Trimble, Virginia. "Beatrice M. Tinsley." In *Visit to a Small Universe.* New York: American Institute of Physics, 1992, pp. 285–293.

Christine Cole Catley

TINTANT, HENRI (*b.* Dreux, France 10 June 1918; *d.* Condrieu, France, 14 November 2003), *invertebrate paleontology, evolutionary biology, jurassic stratigraphy, biostratigraphy.*

Tintant was educated in Versailles where his father was a lawyer. In 1936 he took a degree course at La Sorbonne University in Paris where he graduated in botany, geology, and mineralogy. When war broke out, he served as artillery lieutenant from 1939 to 1941. In 1942 he obtained a Diplôme d'Études Supérieures on the Callovian of Southern Jura, a stratigraphic and paleontologic study. Tintant began his teaching career in 1942 as a geology assistant lecturer at the University of Montpellier. In 1944 he moved to Dijon University where, in 1968, he was appointed Chair of Paleontology. This position was specially created for him.

Tintant commented that his interest in geology came from looking at the pavement stones of the parade ground facing the palace of Versailles and from collecting shells from the Stampian Sands (Oligocene) along the banks of the Grand Canal in the palace park. Actually, it is through stratigraphy that he became interested in paleontology. These two disciplines remained his privileged fields of research for more than half a century.

Main Research: Ammonites. Tintant's primary studies concerned ammonites (fossil Mollusca, Cephalopoda), first in Languedoc (southern France), then in the Jura Mountains, and finally on the Burgundy plateaux. His precise knowledge of fossils used as time markers provided him with the accurate data essential for relative dating and correlation of sedimentary series. Establishing reliable successions of fossils enabled him to develop his views on biological evolution by supporting them with concrete examples. In late 1940s France, invertebrate paleontology was considered a minor discipline, auxiliary to stratigraphy. Tintant was soon convinced of several things: first, that fossils are reliable tools for stratigraphy only if they are accurately identified by pure and fundamental paleontology; next, that such paleontology is possible with ammonites although only their fossil shells or prints are available; and finally, that invertebrate paleontology has its proper value.

Fossils: Living Organisms. According to Tintant, a fossil is not only a piece of rock in the shape of an animal, a sample to be described, classified, and labeled. It once was a living thing belonging to a population and representative of an animal species. This species lived during a limited time interval. It multiplied in a given environment over a geographical area that varied in both space and time. For him, it was necessary to give up the typological concept of the fossil and subsequently of the species to adopt a modern view of this taxon, taking into account the most recent data and concepts of zoology, biology, genetics, and a statistical approach to fossil populations. Tintant's major contributions to paleontology essentially concerned the study of shells of fossil cephalopod populations, ammonites, and nautiloids. A modern concept of biological species involved sexual macroconch-microconch dimorphism, non-sexual, intraspecific polymorphism, and paleoecology (morphofunctional analysis in relation with environmental factors).

Quantifying the Variability. Tintant's approach aimed at quantifying intra-population and intra-specific variability by applying statistical methods to biometry. Tintant insisted on close cooperation with biologists and zoologists since fossils should be considered organisms which lived in the past. He also took into account epistemiological contributions on concepts, theories, and modalities of evolution (phyletic gradualism, anagenesis, and cladogenesis) and stressed the importance of the notions of geologic time and irreversibility of biological evolution.

Owing to his great knowledge of ammonites gained by working on the paleontological collections of the University of Dijon, the National History Museum in Paris, several museums and universities in Western Europe, and his own findings, he was able to determine stratigraphic data for many Jurassic formations previously described and sometimes misdated.

He carried out his research in many areas in France, especially in Burgundy, and in the rest of Europe. He provided his students and many colleagues with the relative time framework indispensable for other geologic studies on sedimentology and paleogeography. He frequently participated in specific programs with stratigraphers and field geologists in France, Spain, and Portugal. However, Tintant's stratigraphic investigations always went beyond the simple analysis of sedimentary series: He frequently discussed the biozone concept, trying to improve the precision and use of this outstanding biostratigraphic unit.

Stratigraphic Nomenclature. Tintant actively participated in working groups that discussed the foundations and uses of units of stratigraphic nomenclature, in the "Comité français de Stratigraphie" and with British and German colleagues at a European level. Early in his career he was appointed French member for the Jurassic in the International Stratigraphic Committee of the European Mesozoic.

For the Sinemurian, Tintant collaborated on the revision of the French stages and the selection of stratotypes with comments on the stage définition. Owing to his experience in stratigraphy and biostratigraphy, he was invited to participate in the Geologic Synthesis of the

Paris Basin and in the Geologic Synthesis of the South-East Basin in France.

Tintant's curiosity of mind led him to work in micropaleontology (evolutionary patterns in small benthic foraminifera), speleology (detrital sedimentation and stacking patterns in karstic cavities), and archeology (description of historic and prehistoric tomb furniture). This could give the impression that he did not focus on his main field of research, but he was a very hard worker with an outstanding memory and strong tenacity. He was therefore able to undertake several kinds of investigations at the same time in different domains. However, he took little care of administrative tasks, occasionally giving some anxiety to those who worked with him.

Evolution and Philosophy. Throughout his career, Tintant paid attention to the links between evolution and philosophy, more generally between science and philosophy. He particularly dealt with two topics. His first concern was the methodological foundations of evolutionary biology, and second, the inevitable metaphysical implications of all scientific investigations.

Because he was born in a Roman Catholic family environment, Tintant wanted to make his knowledge available to those interested in the relations between science and faith. He stressed the complementarity of respective approaches of science and faith. He personally witnessed the intellectual and spiritual enrichment which could be gained through these parallel approaches. Supported by remarkable friends, his considerations on "Creativity of Evolution" and "The Time of Evolution" bear evidence of the serenity and depth of mind his living faith brought to his teaching and scientific research career.

BIBLIOGRAPHY

WORKS BY TINTANT

With R. Mouterde. "Le Sinémurien de Semur." *Colloque sur le Lias français, Chambéry 1960.* C. R. Congrès Soc. Sav. Paris et Départ., Sect. Sci., Sous-sect. Géol. *Mémoires du Bureau de Recherches Geologiques et Minieres.* 4 (1961): 287–295.

With J. Sigal. *Principes de classification et de nomenclature stratigraphiques.* Paris: Comité Français de Stratigraphie, 1962.

"Les Kosmocératidés du Callovien inférieur et moyen d'Europe occidentale. Essai de Paléontologie quantitative." PhD diss., University of Dijon, 1963.

"La notion d'espèce en paléontologie." *Mises à jour scientifiques,* Gauthier-Villars édit. 1 (1965): 273–294.

"Principes et méthodes d'une paléontologie moderne." *Bulletin d'Information des Géologues du Bassin de Paris* 7 (1966): 9–19.

"L'espèce et le temps. Point de vue du paléontologiste." *Bulletin de la Société Zoologique de France* 94, no. 4 (1969a): 559–576.

"Les Nautiles à côtes du Jurassique." *Annales Paléont. Invertébré* 55, no. 1 (1969b): 53–96.

With Elie Cariou, Serge Elmi, Charles Mangold, et al. "La succession des faunes dans le Callovien français. Essais de corrélation à l'échelle de la zone." In *Colloque du Jurassique, Luxembourg 1967. Mémoires du Bureau de Recherches Geologiques et Minieres* 75 (1971): 665–695.

With Rene Mouterde, et al. "Les zones du Jurassique en France." *Compte rendue sommaire des. séances de la Société Géologique de France* 6 (1971): 1–27.

With R. Laffitte, et al. "Essai d'accord international sur les problèmes essentiels de la Stratigraphie" [Some international agreement on essential problems of stratigraphy]. *Compte rendue sommaire des séances de la Société Géologique de France* 13 (1972): 36–45.

"La conception biologique de l'espèce et son application en biostratigraphie." In *Colloques sur les tendances et méthodes en Stratigraphie,* vol. 1. Orsay, 1970. Also published in *Mémoires du Bureau de Recherches Geologiques et Minieres* 77 (1972): 77–87.

"Le polymorphisme intraspécifique en Paléontologie (exemples pris chez les Ammonites)." *Haliotis* 6 (1976): 49–69.

"L'évolution et le temps: les fossiles, chronomètre de l'histoire de la vie." In *Méthodologie comparée des Sciences. Évolution et histoire,* Colloque de Dijon, Novembre 1977; *Revue des questions scientifiques* 149, no. 1 (1978): 27–54.

With René Mouterde. "Sinémurien." In *Les étages français et leurs stratotypes,* 50–58. *Mémoires du Bureau de Recherches Geologiques et Minieres* 109 (1980).

"Problématique de l'espèce en Paléozoologie." In *T. III. Les problèmes de l'espèce dans le monde animal,* edited by C. Bocquet et. al. *Memoires Societe Zoologie Francais* 40 (1980): 321–372.

With Didier Marchand and René Mouterde. "Relations entre les milieux marins et l'évolution des Ammonoïdés: les radiations adaptatives du Lias." *Bulletin de la Société Géologique de France,* 7th ser., 24, no. 5–6 (1982): 951–961.

"Cent ans après Darwin, continuité ou discontinuité dans l'Évolution." In *Modalités, rythmes et mécanismes de l'Evolution biologique,* edited by J. Chaline. Paris: Colloques Internationaux du CNRS Dijon, 1983.

With René Mouterde. "Lias; Bordure Nord-Est du Massif Central." In *Synthèse géologique du Sud-Est de la France.* Vol. I: *Stratigraphie et Paléogéographie,* edited by S. Debrand-Passard. *Mémoires du Bureau de Recherches Geologiques et Minieres* 125 (1984).

L'évolution du concept d'espèce en biologie. Structure ou relation? Le même et l'autre. Recherche sur l'individualité dans les Sciences de la Vie. Paris: Editions CNRS, 1986a.

"La loi et l'événement. Deux aspects complémentaires des Sciences de la Terre." *Bulletin de la Société Géologique de France,* 8th ser., 10, no. 1(1986b): 185–190.

"La créativité de l'évolution." *Cahiers de l'Institut Catholique de Lyon, Série Sciences* 18 (1987): 95–116.

"Temps et expérimentation dans l'évolution de la vie." In *Le Temps et l'Espace,* 353–356. Actes 23ème Congrès de l'Association des Sociétés de Philosophie de Langue Française, Dijon, Août 1988. Paris: J. Vrin, 1990.

"Le temps de l'évolution." In *Temps du Monde, Temps de l'Homme, Temps de Dieu.* Groupe interdisciplinaire de la

Faculté des Sciences. *Cahiers de l'Institut Catholique de Lyon* 24 (1991): 61–81.

La stratigraphie à la recherche du temps. Geobios, Mém. Spéc. 17 (1994): 31–36.

With Charles Devillers. *L'évolution: contingences et contraintes.* *Cahiers de l'Institut Catholique de Lyon, Sér. Sciences* 8 (1996): 17.

With Charles Devillers. *Questions sur la théorie de l'évolution.* Paris: Presses universitaires de France, 1996.

Pierre Rat
Jacques Thierry

TITELBAUM-TARSKI, ALFRED

SEE **Tarski, Alfred**.

TODD, ALEXANDER ROBERTUS (BARON TODD)

(*b.* Glasgow, United Kingdom, 2 October 1907; *d.* Cambridge, United Kingdom, 10 January 1997), *chemistry, natural products, vitamins, plant pigments, synthesis, structure.*

Todd was an outstanding organic chemist of the twentieth century. He worked chiefly on the synthesis and structure of natural products, including plant pigments, penicillin, and vitamins. His studies on nucleosides and nucleotides led to a Nobel Prize in 1957.

Early Years. Alexander Robertus Todd was born at Cathcart, Glasgow, the elder son of Alexander Todd, a clerk with the Glasgow Subway Railway Company, later to become its cashier and secretary. His mother was Jane Lowrie. The parents were born within a mile of each other in Glasgow and were hardworking people with no education beyond elementary schooling. Yet they passionately believed in the value of education and sent Alexander to local schools until, having passed the Scottish "eleven-plus" examination, he entered Allan Glen's School in Glasgow, otherwise known as the Glasgow High School of Science.

A few years earlier Todd had received a gift of a home chemistry set, and it may have been this gift that started his interest in the subject. He did well at most subjects except art (which prompted the teacher of that subject to remark on his parents' sense of humor in giving him the initials A.R.T.). At Allan Glen's he much enjoyed chemical lessons, while the proximity of Baird and Tatlock, laboratory suppliers, enabled him to purchase chemicals and apparatus for further experiments at home.

In 1924 Todd entered Glasgow University to read chemistry. Here he enjoyed lectures from the two professors, G. G. Henderson and T. S. Patterson, though he greatly disliked the routine of inorganic quantitative analysis, at which he fared badly. In 1928, his final undergraduate year, he carried out a research project on the action of phosphorus pentachloride on ethyl tartrate, which led to his first publication. After graduating with first-class honors, Todd worked for a year with Patterson on optical rotatory dispersion, then a technique in its infancy and requiring formidable mathematical skills. Having been attracted to organic chemistry, and with Patterson's approval, he sought a move to Germany, where natural product studies flourished. In 1929 he migrated to Frankfurt, joining the school of Walther Borsche, a former pupil of Adolf Windaus in Göttingen.

The Frankfurt laboratories were very well equipped, and Todd was set to work in the field of bile acids. These are members of the steroid family that had been studied for about thirty years by Windaus and Heinrich Wieland, but Todd's results suggested that their accepted structure for the steroid nucleus was wrong. In this respect he was correct, though his own alternative of a 7-membered ring was also wrong. He was awarded his doctorate on the grounds chiefly of his experimental results. Todd's stay at Frankfurt had been pleasant and gave him a fluency in German that would later serve him well. He was there in the dying years of the Weimar Republic and saw street fighting between students on the extreme left or right of the political spectrum. He formed the view that disillusionment with parliamentary government opens the way for extremists. Many of the student body had right-wing political leanings that would later lead them to support the Nazi regime. Todd was horrified by the leadership vacuum that Adolf Hitler would eventually fill. His experience inclined him, years later, to say that if he had been a really good demagogue he could have had left-wing students in Cambridge goose-stepping in jackboots down King's Parade in six months!

Oxford. Seeking to further his experience of natural products, but in Britain, Todd applied to join the team at Oxford headed by Robert Robinson. He was successful and in 1931 entered the Dyson Perrins Laboratory and also Oriel College where (unlike Robinson) he found the collegiate system much to his liking. Robinson was then absorbed in work on anthocyanins (red and blue flower pigments). These are glucosides of anthocyanidins, which Robinson had already synthesized; the problem was to make the pigments themselves, especially where they were 3,5-diglucosides. For this they needed the 2-glucoside of phloroglucinaldehyde, and Todd came up with a strategy of treating the aldehyde with β-bromoacetyl glucose. All his efforts proved unavailing, but an accidental spillage into hot water of a gummy product caused the crystalline product to appear the next day on the walls of the discarded glass flask—a classic example of serendipity in chemical discovery. By 1932 he and Robinson had synthesized the pigments hirsutin, pelargonin, malvin, and cyanin. Further work at Oxford included some less successful forays into steroid chemistry and the synthesis of hexatriene. A picnic beside Lake Bala in North Wales led to an unexpected chemical inquiry. Noting the aphid infestation on some nearby foxgloves, and the deep coloration of the aphids, Todd began to investigate the constituents. However, the onset of war before the next aphid season meant that this topic had to be postponed for many years.

Todd had been funded for these Oxford years by an 1851 Senior Studentship (an award derived from the Great Exhibition in London), but this expired in 1934. At Robinson's suggestion he went to the Medical Chemistry Department at Edinburgh to work under George Barger on the recently isolated vitamin B_1 (thiamine), a substance necessary for avoidance of the disease beriberi, and present in rice hulls. Together with Franz Bergel (a refugee from Austria), Todd effected a synthesis of an isomer of thiamine on the basis of a formula generally agreed on but now shown to be wrong. Synthesis of an isomer of this product led to the true vitamin and thus to its correct structure, with a pyrimidine nucleus linked to a thiazole nucleus by a methylene group (see Fig. 1). The delay caused by the first synthesis meant that they lost the priority to a German and an American group. This piece of classical organic chemistry inevitably brought contacts with people in the medical and biochemical fields. Pharmacology was another allied subject, and because its laboratories were next door to those of medical chemistry, Todd found himself frequently there. Among the postdoctoral students he met was Alison Dale, daughter of the physiologist Sir Henry Dale. By the time Todd left Edinburgh they were engaged, and in January 1937 they married.

Lister Institute, London. Todd's next move came by invitation from the Lister Institute of Preventive Medicine in London. This followed John Masson Gulland's appointment to a chair in Nottingham in 1936. Robinson had supported Todd's appointment to the vacant readership,

but in view of his youth (he was then 28) he had been in the post several months before this was granted.

Todd's experience in vitamin research was appropriate for the Lister, which had for years worked in this area (the name *vitamine* was invented there). He immediately began work on vitamin E, a component of wheat germ oil and necessary for the reproductive processes in rats. This vitamin is a mixture of tocopherols, substituted benzopyrans. Todd and his colleagues isolated and also synthesised α- and β-tocopherols and established their biochemical importance. He also started work on several other natural products, including cannabis. He had not been long at the Lister before he became aware of further possible career moves, notably in North America. In the end these came to nothing because he was offered, and accepted, the position of Sir Samuel Hall Professor of Chemistry at the University of Manchester.

Manchester. Todd brought with him from London two outstanding women research chemists, Anni Jacob and Marguerite Steiger. His first work at Manchester was a continuation of topics begun elsewhere. The studies on cannabis had to stop when it became clear that existing techniques of separation as column chromatography were inadequate for the task. Another twenty years elapsed before Israeli workers were able to isolate the active principle. The work on vitamin E was brought to a successful conclusion. By now Todd's interest in vitamins was so great that he embarked on an ambitious program to investigate how vitamins worked. By this time it was clear that they participate with coenzymes, several of which contain nucleotides in which bases such as purines and pyrimidines are associated with sugars and phosphoric acid. Accordingly, he started on the synthesis of purines and pyrimidines and then of their glycosides. To complete the syntheses, a satisfactory technique for phosphorylation had to be devised. This was a highly ambitious enterprise and, given the demands of war work, it is hardly surprising that it was not completed in Todd's six years at Manchester.

Just after the declaration of World War II, the Todds' first child, Alexander Henry (Sandy), was born. They had a daughter, Helen, in 1941. Fear of inner-city bombing led them to move home from Withington to Wilmslow. Meanwhile, Todd had joined the Dyestuffs Division Research Panel, which (despite its name) was an Imperial Chemical Industries (ICI) organization promoting all kinds of chemical research, including synthetic drugs. He also found himself chairman of the Chemical Committee of the Ministry of Supply, responsible for the development and production of agents for chemical warfare. With two research students and an industrial chemist, he discovered a vastly improved method for the manufacture of diphenyl chlorarsine (a potential war gas).

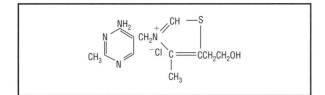

Figure 1. *Structure of B_1.*

Other activity associated with the war effort included participation in an Anglo-American project on penicillin. On his own admission, Todd was not very good at such cooperative efforts, especially those in which he did not have a strong personal interest. His chief success was to form a sulphoxide from penicillin, which demonstrated the lactam structure for the molecule and also paved the way for later syntheses of β-lactam antibiotics. Other topics "of national importance" included a study of the "hatching factor" of the potato eelworm, a parasite whose larvae hatch into worms that attach themselves to the roots of potatoes, causing "potato sickness." Their hatching is triggered by substances secreted by potato roots and also by tomatoes, which proved to be a more convenient source. Isolation proved to be impossible with the equipment available, and a further blow was the destruction of their tomato supply (in Cheshunt) by a flying bomb. Yet another abortive enterprise was a search for blood anticoagulants.

Despite such setbacks as these, the equipment in the Manchester laboratories was developed so fast that they became probably the best-equipped laboratories in Britain. Under Todd's guidance new items were developed by Ralph Gilson, the laboratory steward, and in some cases later became widely available. They included items such as evaporators, drying pistols, and electromagnetically stirred autoclaves.

Todd's Manchester days were much enjoyed, not least for the friendships formed. Some of these derived from communal efforts at nighttime fire-watching (locating fires started by incendiary bombs), which involved students and staff; he considered that this experience made the Manchester chemical school of those days into a tightly knit group and set up relationships of mutual trust and respect that endured for many years. One of those friendships was with Gilson and another was with Frank Stuart Spring. He stuck up a lively friendship with Arthur Lapworth, recently retired. James Kenner, from the Manchester College of Technology, and Patrick Maynard Stuart Blackett were abrasive individuals whose encounters he nevertheless enjoyed, though he distanced himself from Blackett's left-wing politics. However, the strongest links seem to have been with Michael Polanyi, the Hungarian-born chemist, sociologist, and philosopher.

These loyalties, combined with a supportive vice-chancellor in Sir John Stopford and a flourishing research school of about thirty chemists, made him reluctant to leave Manchester. An invitation in 1943 to take the chair of biochemistry at Cambridge was refused, partly for these considerations, partly because the Cambridge department was fragmented and ill-organized, and partly because Todd regarded himself as an organic chemist rather than a biochemist (later in life he saw the boundaries much less

sharply). However, moves continued in Cambridge to recruit him, and he was shortly invited to take the chair of organic chemistry that had, in fact, been founded as a chair of chemistry in 1702. Again he showed considerable resistance. Chemistry at Cambridge, like biochemistry, was in a fragmented condition. There were essentially two departments. The one he was invited to inherit, the Department of Organic and Theoretical Chemistry, was in a sadly run-down condition after years of neglect by the ailing professor Sir William J. Pope, whose death had triggered the new appointment. The other was the Department of Physical Chemistry, run by Ronald Norrish and likely to go its own way. A visit to the laboratories, then in Pembroke Street, showed them to be thoroughly unsatisfactory, with few facilities, in old buildings and with only gas lighting. Todd's reluctance was understandable.

Cambridge and Afterward. Todd eventually agreed to move to Cambridge, but stipulated many conditions. These included the removal from their wartime quarters of chemists from Queen Mary's College and St. Bartholomew's Hospital, and of the government's uranium research team; replacement of gas by electric lighting; appointment of Gilson, his own laboratory steward, and of B. Lythgoe (a Manchester lecturer working with Todd on nucleotides); and priority for a new university chemical laboratory on a different site. Perhaps surprisingly, all these conditions were accepted and, with many misgivings, Todd agreed to go to Cambridge, starting in October 1944. He chose a fellowship in Christ's College. The family quickly settled in, for it was familiar territory for Alison, who had studied at Newnham College, while her father and brother had been to Trinity. In 1946 a second daughter, Hilary, was born.

Many of his Manchester colleagues accompanied Todd to Cambridge, and at first they were the largest group in his department. These included Basil Lythgoe and James Baddiley. Years later, his Manchester research group formed the basis of a dining club formed in Cambridge (1971), named (at his suggestion) the Toddlers. John Edward Lennard-Jones was professor of theoretical chemistry. Seeing the dearth of modern inorganic chemistry at Cambridge, Todd was instrumental in recruiting Harry J. Eméleus in 1946, first as reader and soon afterward as professor of inorganic chemistry. Senior colleagues included the Cambridge chemists Frederick George Mann and Bernard Charles Saunders (authors of a best-selling textbook on practical organic chemistry), and Frederick Stanley Kipping and Peter "Pete" Maitland, following their demobilization from the armed forces.

With the end of the war, Todd was sent, with his friend and former colleague Bertie Kennedy Blount, to Germany in an attempt to revive science in the British

Zone of Occupation. Using Göttingen as a base, they visited Hamburg, Kiel, and Cologne. They also called at Frankfurt, though in the American Zone, and renewed old acquaintances in a town devastated by Allied bombing. In 1947 he was invited by Sir Henry Tizard to join his Advisory Council on Scientific Policy. Five years later he was invited by the lord president of the council, Lord Woolton, to succeed Tizard as chairman and to become Woolton's advisor in science. Under pressure, he agreed and remained until 1964, just before the Labour Party came to power. He regretted the council's restricted role under Labour, being mainly limited to advice on grants to research councils. He considered that the policy issues previously discussed were of greater value to the country, and under his chairmanship the money received by science increased tenfold.

In Cambridge the old laboratory had been greatly improved and library facilities much increased. The first major research effort was a resumption of the studies begun in Manchester on nucleosides and nucleotides (their phosphate esters). Contrary to popular wisdom, Todd proceeded to synthesize nucleotide coenzymes by traditional techniques of organic chemistry. By 1949 Todd and Baddiley had synthesised the nucleoside adenosine. With others he established the β-glycosidic nature of the linkage between sugar and the base. A new technique for phosphorylation using dibenzyl phosphorochloridate gave three nucleotide coenzymes based on adenine, AMP, ADP, and ATP (adenosine mono-, di- and triphosphates) (see Fig. 2). Their identity with the natural products was confirmed by their effects on muscle preparations. Reagents known as phosphoroamidates were found to react cleanly with other phosphates and so to convert (for example) AMP to ADP.

From this it was a natural step to examine further the mysterious molecules ribonucleic acid (RNA) and deoxyribonucleic acid (DNA). Again, classical methods were employed to work out the structures. Colleagues working on these topics included Daniel M. Brown and Roy Markham. In 1952 the 250th anniversary of the chair was celebrated; to mark it, the first papers about the general chemistry and structures of RNA and DNA were pub-

Alexander Todd. *Alexander Todd, Baron Trumpington.*
A. BARRINGTON BROWN/SCIENCE PHOTO LIBRARY.

lished. It turned out that the work in Todd's laboratory was of much value to James D. Watson, Francis Crick, and others in their formulation of the double-helical structure. By this time Todd's reputation was truly international. In 1954 he received a knighthood, and three years later was awarded the Nobel Prize for Chemistry for his work on nucleotides and nucleotide coenzymes.

Much other work was performed at Cambridge. The research begun on aphids before the war was resumed and the complicated structure of several pigments established. Vitamin B_{12}, known to combat pernicious anemia, had been isolated in 1948, but its structure was unknown and complex. Together with Alan Woodworth Johnson and others, Todd isolated a number of degradation products, which, in conjunction with the x-ray crystallographic analysis by Dorothy Hodgkin at Oxford, led to a complete solution of the problem (1955).

The promised new laboratory was not started until 1950, on its present site in Lensfield Road. The long delay was partly because it was to be a steel-framed structure, and steel was in short supply in the late 1940s. The organic laboratories were finished some six years later, and the building was officially opened on 6 November 1958 by Princess Margaret. The finest chemical laboratory in

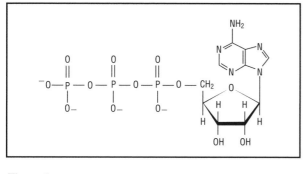

Figure 2.

Britain, it was very much Todd's creation, in terms of both modern equipment and of structure. A small wing was first built and then tested (almost to destruction) by his staff, with lessons learned then passed on to the architects. Refurbishment was not needed until the mid-1990s.

Todd was becoming increasingly involved in academic politics and foreign travel, his first visit to Southeast Asia being in 1958. In the late 1950s he attended meetings at the home of Winston Churchill about the foundation of a new college where science and technology were respected. This became Churchill College, with Todd as a trustee. From 1955 he served on the council of the International Union of Pure and Applied Chemistry, and from 1963 to 1965 was its president. By now he was a close friend of the American chemist Robert Burns Woodward, and together they would often attend conferences overseas. He was frequently invited abroad to receive honorary degrees. India, the United States, and (especially) Australia were among his favorite destinations.

In 1962 he was awarded a life peerage, with the title of Baron Todd of Trumpington, and took his seat on the cross-benches of the House of Lords. The next year he was appointed master of Christ's College, Cambridge. In 1965 he became the first chancellor of the University of Strathclyde and also chairman of the Royal Commission on Medical Education. Further demanding trips abroad, and extensive cigarette smoking, were beginning to take their toll, and in 1970 Todd suffered a massive heart attack. During his convalescence he attempted to teach himself Chinese. Taking warning from the episode, he resigned his chair the next year. He managed, however, to preside at the British Association in September 1970.

Other tasks however followed. Todd became chairman of the syndics of Cambridge University Press, then in the doldrums and in need of fresh ideas. These he supplied, and saw the press begin its rise to prosperity and success. He was also prevailed upon to become chairman of the managing trustees of the Nuffield Foundation in 1973. Then, in 1975, came an honor that he seems to have appreciated most: he became president of the Royal Society in 1942. His aims were to increase the influence of the society on government, to support research by funding further research posts, to relate more closely to technology, and to strengthen the society's international relations. In setting future trends in all these areas, he seems to have had considerable success during his five-year tenure. He received the Order of Merit in 1977. A few other appointments followed, but gradually he let go of committee work while maintaining former friendships and an interest in the progress of science in Britain. In 1987 his wife died; he survived for another ten years, in the care of his former secretary, Barbara Mann. His own death came on 10 January 1997 at a nursing home near Cambridge, from heart disease and pneumonia. He died a millionaire.

Alexander Todd was of striking appearance, over six feet six inches tall, with a strong Glaswegian accent. Even in the laboratory he dressed as a patrician, immaculate in a pin-striped suit, reflecting an awareness of how far he had traveled from his working-class origins. He did not like party politics, especially of the left, a tendency inherited from his father. Conservative by nature, he objected to student protests, and reacted strongly against the proposals of the Robbins Report of 1963 for extensive expansion of the universities. He believed this would lead to a diminution of standards and that the small number of very talented students would suffer. This was elitism, but in an academic rather than a social sense. Deemed arrogant by many, he possessed insatiable ambition and great tenacity. He had a fine sense of humor, which frequently surfaces in his well-written autobiography. He has been said to have had a "huge presence" in Cambridge, and his massive contribution to science policy, coupled with his immense achievements in organic chemistry and in biochemistry, make him one of the great men of twentieth-century science.

BIBLIOGRAPHY

Cambridge University Library maintains an archive of Todd's papers. The article by Brown and Kornberg cited below includes a bibliography of Todd's publications.

WORKS BY TODD

"Chemistry of Life." Interview. *Chemistry in Britain* 10, no. 6 (1974): 207–214.

A Time to Remember: The Autobiography of a Chemist. Cambridge, U.K.: Cambridge University Press, 1983.

OTHER SOURCES

Archer, Mary D., and Christopher D. Haley. *The 1702 Chair of Chemistry at Cambridge: Transformation and Change.* Cambridge, U.K.: Cambridge University Press, 2005.

Baddiley, James. "Lord Todd, 1907–1997." *Chemistry in Britain* 33, no. 4 (1997): 70.

Brown, Daniel M., and Hans Kornberg. *Biographical Memoirs of Fellows of the Royal Society* 46 (2000): 515–532.

Freemantle, M. "Cambridge Marks 300 Years of History." *Chemical & Engineering News* (12 August 2002): 39–43.

Colin Russell

TOUSCHEK, BRUNO (*b.* Vienna, Austria, 3 February 1921; *d.* Innsbruck, Austria, 25 May 1978), *theoretical particle physics, statistical mechanics, particle accelerators.*

Touschek is considered a pioneer in the field of matter–antimatter colliders. Both a theoretical physicist of elementary particles and an expert in accelerator problems, he also provided contributions to the fields of statistical mechanics, discrete symmetries, neutrino problems, and quantum electrodynamics.

Early Days and War Experience. Touschek was born in Vienna in 1921; he was the son of Franz Xaver Touschek, a staff officer in the Austrian Army who participated in World War I on the Italian front, and Camilla Weltmann. The epidemic Spanish flu in 1918 had left his mother in poor health, and Bruno only saw her in bed until her death in 1931.

In July 1934, after the assassination of the Christian-Socialist Engelbert Dollfuss by the National Socialists inspired by Adolf Hitler, the Nazis renewed Austria's latent anti-Semitism. Because Bruno's mother had been Jewish, he was banned from attending the Gymnasium in 1937, one year before the final state examination (the *Abitur*). He applied to take this *Abitur* as an external student at a different school, and passed the exam.

He then went to Rome for the school holiday and attended the first engineering university courses. But in the summer of 1938 he returned to Vienna. When, in September 1939, World War II began, Bruno's father refused to reenter active service; Bruno was very proud of this.

He decided to study physics and mathematics at the University in Vienna. He tried not to attract attention, but soon he was clearly the best student in the courses so that his origin was identified and in June 1940 he was expelled. Many outstanding professors helped him, among them Paul Urban and Edmund Hlawka, then Arnold Sommerfeld in Munich and Paul Harteck in Hamburg. Touschek moved to Hamburg and worked for a firm, Opta, originally Jewish property. In Hamburg, he studied betatrons and met Norwegian physicist Rolf Wideröe.

Unfortunately, the Gestapo noticed him and he was arrested at the beginning of 1945 because of his Jewish mother. Wideröe visited him frequently and bought him books, food, and cigarettes. He was taken with a group of prisoners from the Hamburg prison at the beginning of March 1945 and routed to a camp near Kiel; he had a high fever and collapsed in the ditch near the road. An SS officer shot at his head but only wounded him. During the rest of his life, Bruno told several slightly varied accounts of the events that immediately followed. To his Italian colleague Carlo Bernardini he recounted that some civilians realized he was not dead and brought him to a hospital. There he was treated but betrayed to the police. He then was transferred to the prison of Altona.

Post-War Positions. Freed by the English in June 1945, Touschek refused to accompany the troops as an interpreter. At the beginning of 1946, he reached Göttingen where he found physicists Ludwig Prandtl and Werner Heisenberg, among others. Touschek worked on the theory of the betatron, a machine that used magnetic induction to accelerate electrons in order to generate both high energy electrons and x-ray beams. This constituted his thesis work, and Touschek received the title of "Diplomphysiker" under the guidance of Richard Becker and Hans Kopfermann. He then began working with Heisenberg, writing a paper on double beta decay and a second one on the mathematics of the Schrödinger equation. Meanwhile, he was appointed as research worker at the Max Planck Institute in Göttingen. In February 1947, he moved to Glasgow where he started collaborating with Philip Dee and then with John Currie Gunn, who had formed a theoretical group there in 1949. In Glasgow, Touschek worked on nuclear physics with Ian Sneddon and on electron collisions, proton collisions, and meson production with Gunn and Edwin Power. He also published some work in field theory concerning bound states and divergences.

When Walter Thirring from Vienna reached Glasgow in 1950, Touschek immediately worked with him on "Bloch-Nordsieck method," a calculational technique in quantum electrodynamics (QED), which had been developed in 1937 to deal with the infrared divergence of the radiation spectrum: this problem was henceforth a leitmotif in Touschek's ideas. QED was the quantized theory of matter and energy which had replaced James Clerk Maxwell's classical theory of radiating electric charges.

Eventually, Touschek was drawn to Rome by the presence of his mother's sister Ada, who had married an Italian gentleman before World War II. His grandmother Josepha had also lived in Rome with her daughter Ada until the beginning of the war, at which time she returned to Vienna. She had been arrested by the Nazis in 1941, sent to the Theresienstadt concentration camp, and killed there. In Rome, Touschek was in contact with Bruno Ferretti, who, in 1948, had replaced Gian Carlo Wick at the University of Rome. In September 1952, Touschek was offered the possibility of remaining in Rome through a position at Italy's INFN (National Institute of Nuclear Physics), which he accepted. Touschek went back to Glasgow only to marry Elspeth Yonge, the daughter of a well-known zoologist in Edinburgh: they soon came to Rome where their sons Francis and Stefan were born (in 1958 and 1961).

Projects and Teaching. In a couple of years, before Ferretti's transfer to Bologna, Touschek illustrated his ideas to many young people: he was fascinated by neutrino physics and in some way speculated on the unification of weak and electromagnetic forces, anticipating some concepts of the later electroweak theory of S. Weinberg and A. Salam.

In 1950 and then again in 1952, the strong-focusing principle had been proposed for synchrotron-type particle accelerators—first by Nicholas Christophilos in an unpublished work and then independently by Ernest Courant, M. Stanley Livingston, and Hartland Snyder in a *Physical Review* article. In 1953 Touschek, along with Matthew Sands from Pasadena (California Institute of Technology) worked on practical stability problems. At almost the same time, he was collaborating with others on projects such as the decay of the so-called tau meson and a model for photoproduction of mesons. Following that work, Touschek collaborated in a large variety of fields: field theory and perturbative methods (particularly the Tamm-Dancoff method); discrete symmetries and time reversal; and conservation of leptonic number and γ_5 invariance. Touschek was very generous and stimulated continuous discussions in many different fields. Many of his ideas actually can be found in the papers of his pupils and colleagues.

Touschek was a very brilliant teacher: from 1953 to 1963 he gave advanced courses for postgraduates in the Physics Institute of the University of Rome, then he interrupted this activity to dedicate more time to his work at the Frascati Laboratories, 30 kilometers from Rome. He contributed many lectures both to the Scuola Normale Superiore in Pisa and to the Scuola Internazionale di Fisica in Varenna (where he directed some of the summer schools). He had many excellent pupils, among them Nicola Cabibbo, Francesco Calogero, Giovanni Gallavotti, and Paolo Di Vecchia. He also maintained close contacts with outstanding physicists like Wolfgang Pauli and Eduardo Caianiello, in addition to the Austrian colleagues he had met just after the end of the war. His university career in Italy was not easy because of the laws preventing foreigners from taking permanent positions: he refused to become an Italian citizen, and this caused some problems. He was nevertheless accepted as a member in the famous Italian Accademia dei Lincei. Meanwhile, he had many contacts with the Austrian goverment who wanted to restore Austrian research with the help of distinguished citizens working in other countries: Bruno Touschek and Victor Weisskopf among them. This project never went to a conclusion; still Touschek often dreamt about it.

Particle/Antiparticle Collisions. The turning point in Touschek's life came with a seminar he gave on 7 March 1960 at Frascati. He had already had a "strong feeling" about the physical importance of charged particle–antiparticle collisions in a single magnetic ring. The feel-

ing, as Cabibbo remembered, had originated during a seminar in Rome given by Stanford University physicist Wolfgang Panofsky. In that seminar, Panofsky was illustrating the tangent, double rings under construction by a Princeton-Stanford collaboration to explore electron-electron scattering at very high center-of-mass energies. Touschek already knew of the technical possibility of center-of-mass collisions in beam-beam configurations through his friend Wideröe. Wideröe had patented the idea in 1943 with an enlarged scope after Touschek expressed his disdain for the original patent application because—he often said later to his colleagues—one cannot patent trivial ideas. According to both Cabibbo and colleague Raul Gatto, Touschek made the comment at Panofsky's seminar that electron-positron physics might be much more interesting than electron-electron, because (in his picturesque language) this would "excite the vacuum" in a much cleaner initial state.

In the electron-electron scattering process, the two colliding electrons survive, possibly accompanied by photons. In electron-positron collisions, the initial particles can actually annihilate one another. They disappear in to pure electromagnetic energy, all of which is subsequently reconverted into new particles.

The Princeton-Stanford group did not immediately pursue the suggestion: nobody had seen a positron beam up to that time. Moreover, because of the extraordinary successes of Stanford physicist Robert Hofstadter on form factors, particularly the proton and neutron form factors, the Princeton-Stanford collaboration were interested in checking the reliability of Quantum Electrodynamics (QED), hoping to discover any possible structure possessed by what QED assumed to be "point" electrons; their machine was the appropriate instrument for this.

Therefore, Touschek decided to bring his idea to Frascati, where an excellent 1,100 MeV (megaelectron volt) electron synchrotron was just starting operations. Meanwhile, he alerted Frascati-ROME physicists Cabibbo and Gatto in order to get a panoramical view on the important processes to be studied by electron-positron annihilation. Cabibbo and Gatto quickly prepared a comprehensive paper on all possible outcomes of electron-positron annihilation; this paper was immediately called "the bible." In Touschek's seminar on 7 March 1960, he tried to convince the director of Frascati, Giorgio Salvini, to convert the synchrotron into a "collider," and, after Salvini's strong refusal, agreed try with a small prototype, AdA (from Anello di Accumulazione, Italian for "storage ring"—but also a nod to his beloved aunt Ada for those in the know). The prototype would study collisions of electrons and positrons of 250 MeV per beam.

In laboratories dedicated to high energy physics, two kind of specialists were cohabiting, experimental physicists and accelerator designers. Designers were planning quite sophisticated accelerator components and were mostly willing to build prototypes to test the adequateness of these components toward such goals as injection rate, stability of orbits and focusing, circulating currents, and so on. Physicists were afraid to waste time in realizing such sophisticated opportunities. The peculiarity of AdA was its conceptual simplicity, focusing on the main goal which was the experimental demonstration of the "luminosity formula," that is, of the actual complete overlap of the two opposite beams in the collision zone. The design did not attempt any of the sophisticated possibilities that "machine people" were suggesting at the time. Instead, at Frascati, the choice was made to plan two different rings, AdA as a simple demonstration device and a second, larger machine, Adone, as a "professional" machine. (Again, note the double entendre of the moniker: *Adone* in Italian means "large Ada" but it is also the Italian name for the Greeks' mythological Adonis.) Adone was approved in a rapid decision by the directors and presidents of the institutions involved (mainly the INFN, the CNEN [National Nuclear Energy Committee], and the LNF [Frascati National Laboratories]). Touschek also contributed to the design of Adone as a strong-focusing, separated-function (with bending, magnetic dipole sections plus separate, focusing, quadrupole magnets), single ring capable of storing 1.5 GeV (gigaelectron volt) beam of electrons and positrons (2×1.5 GeV following the present notation).

The design of AdA was quickly completed by the Frascati staff (including, besides Touschek, Carlo Bernardini, Gianfranco Corazza, and Giorgio Ghigo), the magnet was ordered, together with the radiofrequency cavity and the vacuum chamber—complete with ion pumps. The Frascati Labs were extremely cooperative so that by 27 February 1961, injection trials with AdA were already being attempted. Touschek was extremely excited, notwithstanding some difficulties in the injection procedure.

A linear accelerator was considered as an injector of both (1) electrons and (2) positrons produced at an efficient converter. The gamma ray beam of the main synchrotron at Frascati was too weak to meet the internal conversion performances needed for a reasonable positron or electron injection rate in AdA. Hence, the main improvement after the February 1961 trials was to accept the offer of the Orsay Labaratory in France to use their linear accelerator. Because the cleaning of the chamber had taken several months to reach the low presure of 10^{-9} torr, the ring, complete with the vacuum system still in operation, was transported across the Alps. Once it reached Paris the virtues of the Orsay Linac were appreciated immediately. A novel injection procedure was adopted, including a modulation of the radiofrequency amplitude during the now very short Linac pulse, and the

injection rate increased by no less than two orders of magnitude. Pierre Marin and François Lacoste from Orsay joined the Italian group which meanwhile had included Giuseppe Di Giugno and Ruggero Querzoli; then, Lacoste left and was replaced by Jacques Haïssinski. All together, the AdA staff was reasonably sized and Touschek, who abhorred large groups, was happy and satisfied.

At the beginning of 1963, the injection worked well, lifetimes of the beams were in the 10-hour range and a luminosity trial was in preparation. However, during a run at 195 MeV with a single beam injected, a saturation effect of the injection rate manifested itself. Interpolating the data, it was realized that the lifetime of a beam contained an unexpected correction term proportional to the particle number in that beam. Touschek found the mechanism of the phenomenon by spending some hours that same night working on it: he understood that there was a large momentum transfer from the radial to the longitudinal motion in a particle bunch due to the scattering of these particles within the same bunch. Since, the longitudinal motion had a much narrower stability region than the radial "betatron oscillations," many particles were lost when the density in the beam had reached a relevant value. Touschek had rapidly calculated the energy dependence, showing that it was luckily decreasing as $E^{-9/2}$. Because this effect could have been devastating for the operation of the larger machine, Adone, it was very reassuring to see that it would decrease so rapidly with energy. AdA was cured a few days later by inflating the beam with a rotated quadrupole magnet inserted ad hoc in a straight section of the machine, transferring momentum from the radial to the vertical betatron mode, which decreased the transverse beam density.

The discovered phenomenon was named the "Touschek effect." Though it meant that any particle-antiparticle annihilations in Ada would take place at a rate too low to record directly, a disappointment to be sure, it eventually helped in measuring luminosity by using a particular result, the beam-beam bremsstrahlung radiation, as a monitor reaction. The AdA exploitation ended in the autumn 1963; the magnet was brought back to Frascati and some time later was installed under a transparent protection in the grass, as in an open air museum. Touschek was extremely satisfied with this achievement: the feasibility of single ring electron-positron beams had been demonstrated, the luminosity formula checked, and some machine effects discovered.

Meanwhile, the ACO ring (2×550 MeV) had been constructed at Orsay, the VEPP II ring (2×700 MeV) at Novosibirsk, U.S.S.R., was nearly complete, the CEA electron-syncrotron at Harvard would be changed to a 2×2.5 GeV ring, the Stanford Linear Accelerator Center had begun to design a ring which would use its 20 GeV linear accelerator as an injector, and Adone had been approved and construction begun at Frascati under the direction of Fernando Amman. In any case, even with a minuscule luminosiy of $10^{24}/cm^2 s^1$. AdA was the first machine of the collider series to have registered actual collisions; the Princeton-Stanford's figure-eight configuration and VEPP 1 at Novosibirsk both electron-electron machines initiated a few years before AdA, went into operation some years later.

Touschek was very proud of the short time the staff had employed to complete the work. Moreover, everybody in high energy experimental physics was now convinced that future research activities in the field would require matter-antimatter colliders.

Final Years. In the years from 1964 (the end of the work with AdA) to 1978 (his death), Touschek worked and taught both in Italy and at CERN. He was highly celebrated and traveled around the world to talk about colliders. At the same time he collaborated, often with young students, on some very exotic theoretical possibilities: two-neutrino photon theory, relativistic reformulation of statistical mechanics, speculations on the possible "milestones" in high-energy physics, and reexamination of the classical Thirring effect on rotating frames in general relativity. Additional, very important work on radiative corrections for colliding beams experiments with Giulia Pancheri and E. Etim has since been known as the "discovery of the Bond factor" because of a numerical exponent B evaluated to be 0.07.

When the student "revolution" came, after 1968, Touschek no longer wanted to spend his hours at the university: a group of ignorant young protesters once called him "Nazi" and he did not want to reply, because he after all respected youth. Therefore, he retired to his home where he spent some time considering possible thresholds of high-energy physics: he sent a paper to *Physics Letters B* indicating his address as "Garvens, Roma, Piazza Indipendenza," the firm he had inherited from his beloved aunt Ada.

In those years, a scandal had developed in Italy: the "Ippolito case," following the "Mattei affaire." Felice Ippolito was the head of the Italian organization for nuclear energy; he was accused of having profited from his position for private interests. Edoardo Amaldi, the dean of Italian physicists, defended Ippolito against the politicians accusing him, discovering that an oil lobby was behind the attacks. The meetings of the group of scientists supporting Amaldi were held in Touschek's house. Touschek was quite upset by the situation, particularly when Ippolito was unjustly condemned for a ridiculous crime, "international embezzlement" (which did not exist in jurisprudence). Touschek decided to dedicate some time

to education in the schools and collaborated with the Accademia dei Lincei to improve scientific communication to the public. He gained many fans among teachers. His message to the teachers consisted in showing the importance of qualitative understanding of scientific problems.

For a time he considered the possibility of moving to CERN in Geneva. While visiting there, he was involved in the stochastic cooling of antiprotons with regards to the new proton-antiproton ring and wrote a Frascati prepent, his last work. His health was very poor: on 25 May 1978, Touschek died in the Medical Ward of the University Hospital, in Innsbruck, after a series of hepatic comas at the age of only 57. He had already suffered from such attacks since February 1977. Apart from his extremely brilliant scientific activity, he left a large number of vivid memories: his drawings (in the style of Egon Schiele), his quotations from the Viennese satirical literature (particularly Karl Kraus), his teaching abilities, his generosity with the young students, and his rigor with colleagues.

BIBLIOGRAPHY

An archive collection is maintained at the University of Rome at Sapienza, described in Le Carte Di Bruno Tousche, *edited by Giovanni Battimelli, Michelangelo Demaria, and Giovanni Paoloni. Rome: Facoltà di Scienze Matematiche, Fisiche e Naturali Università di Roma "La Sapienza," 1989. A complete bibliography is included in the Amaldi report, cited below.*

WORKS BY TOUSCHEK

With Ian N. Sneddon. "Nuclear Models." *Nature* 161 (1948): 61–63.

"Zur Theorie des doppelten Beta Zerfalls." *Zeitschrift für Physik* 125 (1948): 108–132.

With Walter E. Thirring. "A Covariant Formulation of the Bloch-Nordsieck Method." *Philosophical Magazine* 42 (1951): 244–249.

With Giacomo Morpurgo and Luigi Radicati. "On Time Reversal." *Nuovo Cimento* 12 (1954): 677–698.

With Wolfgang Pauli. "Report and Comment on F. Gürsey 'Group Structure of Elementary Particles.'" *Supplement Nuovo Cimento* 14 (1959): 205–211.

With Carlo Bernardini, Gianfranco Corazza, and Giorgio Ghigo. "The Frascati Storage Ring." *Nuovo Cimento* 18 (1960): 1293–1295.

With Jacques Haïssinski, Pierre Marin, and Ruggero Querzoli. "Measurement of the Rate of Interaction between Stored Electrons and Positrons." *Nuovo Cimento* 34 (1964): 1473–1493. Additional references are cited within the article.

With E. Etim and Giulia Pancheri. "The Infra-red Radiative Corrections for Colliding Beam (Electrons and Positrons) Experiments." *Nuovo Cimento* 51 (1967): 276–302

"Covariant Statistical Mechanics." *Nuovo Cimento* 58 (1968): 295–300.

"An Analysis of Stochastic Cooling." Rome: Laboratori Nazionali di Frascati Preprint, LNF-79/006.

OTHER SOURCES

Amaldi, Edoardo. *The Bruno Touschek Legacy.* Geneva: CERN, 1981. A complete bibliography can be found in this report.

Bernardini, Carlo. "AdA: The First Electron-Positron Collider." *Physics in Perspective* 6 (2004): 156–183.

Bonolis, L. "Bruno Touschek vs Machine Builders: AdA, the First Matter–Antimatter Collider." *La rivista del nuovo cimento* 28, no. 11 (2005): 1–60.

Cabibbo, Nicola. "E⁺E⁻ Physics—A View from Frascati in 1960's." In *ADONE, a Milestone on the Particle Way,* edited by Vincenzo Valente, 217–225. Frascati, Italy: Instituto Nazionale di Fisica Nucleare, Laboratori Physics Series viii, 1997.

Haïssinski, Jacques. "Experiences sur l'anneau de Collisions AdA." Thesis, Université de Paris. *Orsay,* Series A, 81 (1965).

Pellegrini, Claudio, and Andrew M. Sessler, eds. *The Development of Colliders.* New York: American Institute of Physics, 1995.

Rubbia, Carlo. "The Role of Bruno Touschek in Proton-Antiproton Collider Physics." In *Bruno Touschek Memorial Lectures, Frascati May 11, 1987,* edited by Mario Greco and Guilia Pancheri. Frascati, Italy: Istituto Nazionale di Fisica Nucleare.

Carlo Bernardini

TOUSEY, RICHARD

(*b.* Somerville, Massachusetts, 18 May 1908; *d.* Cheverly, Maryland, 15 April 1997), *vacuum ultraviolet techniques in photometry and spectroscopy, optics, solar physics, space science.*

Tousey, a laboratory spectroscopist and optical specialist who worked most of his career at the U.S. Naval Research Laboratory (NRL), led a team that was the first to successfully design, build, and fly a spectrograph on a captured German V-2 missile that produced a photographic record of the ultraviolet spectrum of the Sun, never before seen by humans. Tousey remained a central figure active in ultraviolet solar research with rockets, satellites, and human spacecraft throughout his career, and mentored several generations of space scientists.

Born in Somerville, Massachusetts, on 18 May 1908 to Adella Hill Tousey and Coleman Tousey, a dentist, Richard Tousey recalled being especially influenced by his early schooling at what was at first called the Harvard Cooperative Open-Air School and later the Shady Hill School. There he gained a deep fascination and appreciation for nature, which was enhanced by summers at a series of family homes on the Maine shore, where he was encouraged to learn to sail with his brother and sister. His

fascination continued through grade schools and was further stimulated by a family friend, John F. Cole, who introduced Tousey to his machine shop and extensive library and took an interest in the astronomical basis for navigation, which he shared with Tousey. Cole helped Tousey build a crystal receiver, learn Morse code, and then learn about vacuum-tube electronics.

Tousey entered Tufts University at age sixteen, the third generation in his family to do so, living at home and supported by his family. His interest in radio steered him into physics courses, but he was not committed to a career at first, ultimately taking a combined physics and mathematics curriculum. Graduating with highest honors in 1928, he entered Harvard University in physics, but still had not acquired any clear goals. He continued to explore options through contact with John Clark Slater and Theodore Lyman, and finally chose experimental physics under Lyman, because Lyman suggested a topic, the reflecting power of metals in the extreme ultraviolet, that encompassed Tousey's interests in solid-state physics gained under Slater.

Tousey was awarded the MA in 1929, taking courses under Friedrich Hund and Frederick A. Saunders, with whom he shared a strong interest in birding (both were members of the Nuthall Ornithological Club). The PhD came in 1933, and by then Tousey very much followed in Lyman's path, exploring a wide array of questions that required expertise in the vacuum ultraviolet. Tousey designed a vacuum spectrograph to study the optical characteristics of fluorite, a crystal that remains transparent deep into the ultraviolet and so can be useful for vacuum ultraviolet instrumentation. Throughout his graduate years, though his family continued to be prosperous, Tousey was largely supported by a series of substantial Harvard physics fellowships: the Whiting (1929–1931), the Tyndall (1931–1932), and the Bayard Cutting, which he won two years in a row, supported by Lyman. His 1936 thesis put him into contact with the machinist David Mann, head of the Physics Department shop, with whom he had a long fruitful collaboration. Tousey became especially adept at making his vacuum systems efficient and reliable, searching for leaks and handling humidity problems, though he recalls a certain amount of impatience working through the elaborate procedures Lyman had developed.

Tousey married Ruth Lowe in 1932. They met as undergraduates at Tufts, and shared interests in classical music, especially chamber ensembles, which they often entertained at their home.

After graduation Tousey stayed on in Lyman's laboratory as a tutor and laboratory researcher/instructor. He further developed his thesis for publication, mainly searching for refinements to methods in photographic photometry of the extreme ultraviolet centering on improving emulsion sensitivity using different fluorescing oils. His goal was to overcome the failure of photographic reciprocity and thereby improve the medium as an objective sensor of radiation.

Advised by Saunders that a tenured position at Harvard was unlikely, Tousey gained an appointment to a faculty position in the Tufts physics department in 1936, something that required, as he recalled in an interview, intervention by his father, who was friendly with John Cousens, president of Tufts. Cousens endowed a temporary research instructorship for Tousey, which put him somewhat at odds with other members of the physics department. Tousey participated in all the physics offerings, but research remained his top priority.

In 1941 Tousey was given a leave of absence from Tufts for war-related work at the NRL. He had known Edward O. Hulburt, research director at NRL, from summers boating at Bucks Harbor, Maine, where his grandfather owned extensive holdings. Hulburt had visited Tousey at Harvard, and this led Tousey to write, asking if a job was available. From this he received an excellent offer of employment, at a substantial raise.

Tousey moved his wife and daughter to Washington, D.C., in June 1941, anxious to get into war work. He found Hulburt's Optics Division a small, friendly, and collegial group, in contrast to Tousey's experience at Tufts, and during the war years Tousey contributed to many distinct problem areas the laboratory was concerned with, ranging from vision problems with binoculars and telescopes, to problems of night vision, creating optical camouflage, and developing means of infrared surveillance. The Bureau of Aeronautics had asked the NRL to explore the use of stars for daytime navigation from aircraft and Tousey took the lead in this area, acquainting himself with physiological optics and problems of visibility through haze and fog as well as techniques to assess sky brightness in the optical range. Tousey designed and built a periscopic telescope for aircraft that employed a prism to look at different parts of the sky. Advised by the Harvard astronomer Donald Menzel, Tousey carried his equipment to the High Altitude Observatory in Climax, Colorado, and through this came to know Walter Orr Roberts and other astronomers who were investigating relationships between solar activity and ionospheric characteristics. Tousey also carried his equipment on many aircraft, but out of this came an increased interest in the visibility of point sources in fields of extended brightness, which led to his participation in the Army-Navy Office of Scientific Research and Development (OSRD) Committee on Vision. Tousey also applied his knowledge of physiological optics to a study of the nighttime visibility of objects and limitations caused by dark adaptation and night

myopia. He also explored infrared visibility searching for secure methods of communication. And he continued earlier research on ultraviolet reflectance.

In late 1945, Hulburt casually asked Tousey if he might be interested in securing the spectrum of the Sun from a V-2 rocket. Hulburt had just attended a preliminary meeting of other NRL scientists with officers from the U.S. Army Ordnance department that was charged with testing and evaluating captured German V-2 missiles at White Sands, New Mexico. Army Ordnance invited both military and civilian groups to build a wide variety of instruments for flights on these missiles, for basic research related to improving guided missile technologies and a general understanding of the medium through which missiles traveled.

Tousey, intrigued, knew from the start that no laboratory spectrograph could possibly survive a rocket flight, and believed as well that photographic recording was the only way to gain reliable spectroscopic evidence in that day. Physical retrieval became a primary technical hurdle, as did devising a means of acquiring sunlight from a spinning and tumbling rocket. Starting in February 1946 he led a small group of engineers, physicists, and technicians to design a new and unique form of ultraviolet spectrograph. He replaced the classical entrance slit with a pair of tiny lithium fluoride beads barely a few millimeters in diameter. These beads could capture sunlight like ultrawide-angled lenses and the streaks formed by the moving solar image (caused by the tossing rocket) simulated the entrance slit of a proper spectrograph. Light from either bead was folded by mirrors and sent to a single Rowland grating that both focused and dispersed the sunlight onto specially sensitized 35-millimeter roll film. The film itself was carefully prepared to avoid static electrical damage from rolling over metal surfaces in a vacuum, and once exposed in a series of frames taken during flight, was wound into a thick-walled cassette of armor-piercing steel to improve the chances of physical recovery. The spectrograph was designed to fit into the conical nose cone, or warhead, of the missile. Because the army was already firing these missiles, lead time was very short, so Tousey contracted with Baird Associates of Cambridge, Massachusetts, to build six units. The first was flown in June and was never recovered, even after weeks of digging. German advisors suggested putting the spectrograph in a tail fin, and adding explosive charges to break apart the missile upon reentry. The tail section would then crash at subsonic speeds and increase the chance of recovery. A second flight on 10 October 1946 was completely successful. This was the twelfth American launch of a V-2. It rose to 173 kilometers in 227 seconds, and was successfully blown apart before landing. It took almost four days to find the spectrograph in the desert sands and retrieve the film cassette for processing back in Washington. Finally, between 18 and 21 October the film was processed and showed solar spectra to as far as 2,100 angstroms, far beyond the ultraviolet cutoff of Earth's atmosphere (at 2,900 angstroms). Moreover, the series of spectra obtained at different altitudes during the flight penetrated to different ultraviolet levels, which was interpreted as a record of passage through Earth's absorbing ozone layer. On 30 October 1946, the *Washington Post* hailed the detection on page 1.

Subsequent V-2 flights carried the remainder of the Baird instruments, while Tousey and his team planned modifications to improve the fidelity of the spectra. A second round of Baird instruments was also contracted, and flown through 1948. The first spectra were indeed very crude, and far below the quality hoped for by astrophysicists interested in composition studies of the solar atmosphere. They were fine for Tousey's and the NRL's purposes, mainly to demonstrate feasibility, point the way for technical improvements, and to explore the structure of Earth's ozone layer. But they did not penetrate as deeply as Tousey and his navy patrons hoped for: the goal was to reach the realm where solar radiation was believed to alter Earth's ionosphere, and hence to influence long-range communications capabilities. Reaching this region, it was hoped, would reveal the actual spectral mechanisms influencing the ionosphere, which would lead to predictive mechanisms of obvious tactical interest.

By 1949, Tousey's team was preparing far more efficient spectroscopic instruments for flights on new American-made vehicles, such as the navy's Viking and Aerobee sounding rockets. They continued to study near-ultraviolet ozone structure in detail, obtaining data that were widely regarded as definitive. But to reach the extreme ultraviolet region surrounding the Lyman alpha line (the first resonant line of hydrogen at 1,216 angstroms, named for Tousey's Harvard mentor) they sought out new means of detection and also promoted ways to increase exposure times during the short flight of a sounding rocket. Although still wedded to photographic technologies, Tousey teamed up with Kenichi Watanabe to explore using manganese-activated calcium sulfate phosphors and filters to reach the ultraviolet. At about the same time, a parallel NRL group effort headed by Herbert Friedman employed combinations of electronic halogen counters and filters. Both groups detected the Lyman alpha region but failed to explore its structure in detail. Tousey was convinced that only photography could do the job, and so parts of his team tried to develop gimballed servo-feedback systems that acted as homing devices, allowing the spectrograph to lock onto the Sun throughout the flight. Efforts to achieve this new level of sophistication at both the NRL and the Applied Physics Laboratory failed time and again in the late 1940s and early 1950s. Finally, a group headed by William Rense at

the University of Colorado was successful, with a lightweight biaxial pointing control carrying a grazing-incidence spectrograph developed for a series of air force Aerobee rockets. They first photographed the Lyman alpha line in December 1952, largely confirming the estimates made by the NRL groups.

Throughout the 1950s, Tousey's group continued to refine their techniques, pushing on several fronts. They worked to achieve both better spectral resolution and better ultraviolet penetration. The small Aerobees were the only launch vehicle available for sounding rocket flights, but they were adequate to carry clusters of stabilized instruments weighing in the range of 10 kilograms or so to well over 100 kilometers altitude, within budgets accessible to institutions such as the NRL. As a result, Tousey enjoyed little competition during this period beyond other groups at the NRL, and at the Air Force Cambridge Research Center based at Hanscomb Field, Massachusetts, where Watanabe had moved to develop systems based upon photoelectric and electronic technologies. Pointing controls were procured from the University of Colorado group, which had left academe to form a subsidiary to Ball Brothers Corporation in Boulder, Colorado. The NRL spectrographs now had proper slits, higher dispersion through echelle and doubly dispersing systems, greater resolution, and more sophisticated ways of eliminating stray visible light.

As a result, they were able to explore the fine structure in the region surrounding Lyman alpha, as well as record thousands of spectral features throughout the ultraviolet, both in absorption, and blueward of 2,000 angstroms, in emission, all the way down to 977 angstroms. They were also the first to create an ultraviolet spectroheliogram, an image of the full solar disk in the light of hydrogen at Lyman alpha. As they increased the sensitivity of their instruments, Tousey's group also started to make observations at night, mainly to assess ultraviolet airglow and other geocoronal phenomena.

One of the hallmarks of Tousey's career was persistence. As he noted in a 1967 review article, he continued to work to refine the ultraviolet solar line spectrum ever since obtaining the first one in 1946. An improved echelle design they adopted in 1952 did not work to their satisfaction until an Aerobee flight in 1961. Even so, the frustrations and challenges they faced, working within the NRL infrastructure, were nothing compared to those in the post-*Sputnik* National Aeronautics and Space Administration (NASA) era when both the pace and the possibilities for expanded activities grew immensely.

The NASA Era. Tousey was never particularly interested in leaving the NRL for NASA, as many of his group did. Rather he continued to concentrate on the local level, on

Richard Tousey. *Richard Tousey (right) and J. D. Purcell display a detailed photograph of the sun.* AP IMAGES.

instrument development, rather than institutional development on a national scale. His expertise was, of course, highly valued, especially by his former colleagues who were now NASA employees, and so his access to satellite berths was relatively unproblematic. This was certainly true for the various instrumented programs NASA developed, such as the Explorer series and the Orbiting Solar Observatory (OSO) series, but it became very complex

and frustrating in the programs where human spaceflight was the primary motivation.

During the 1960s, his team continued to fly instrumentation on Aerobees, and he was willing to provide instrumentation for human flights during the Gemini and Apollo programs, although he found this effort particularly frustrating, overcoming safety restrictions only to find that his airlock-based experiments were summarily canceled in favor of maximum egress access for the astronauts. Tousey had far more success in the OSO program, contributing extreme ultraviolet instrumentation for several flights in the 1960s and 1970s, as well as making one of the first attempts to fly a solar coronagraph, which had long been a dream not only of astronomers, but also of the air force and navy. The NRL white-light coronagraph, flown in 1965 on the second OSO, operated from February to November 1965. It used an external occulting disk to block out the bright solar image, rendering the faint outer atmosphere visible for some 1,000 orbits of the spacecraft and allowing for the first time a detailed record of structural changes in the outer atmosphere and their relation to other solar phenomena. His second flight of a coronagraph, on *OSO 7,* produced high-quality data for several years in the early 1970s.

Probably his largest involvement came with the human Skylab program starting in the late 1960s and lasting through the mid-1970s. He had been one of the primary experimenters on a canceled unmanned Advanced Orbiting Solar Observatory, and so was given first choices when those instruments were considered for a new post-Apollo program using surplus Apollo hardware. Among the eight major solar instruments on what was called the Apollo Telescope Mount for Skylab, Tousey was involved with at least four of them. He directed NRL teams to develop devices to maximize the use of long exposure times on the Skylab space station to gather extreme ultraviolet and soft x-ray spectral information that for the first time equaled ground-based visible studies in detail and resolution. His instruments worked in a broad wavelength range from the soft x-ray through the ultraviolet, employing a wide range of spectrograph and disperser designs, but typically using photographic recording, made possible because the film could be returned by the three crews working on the station. He also led the development of an instrument for recording television images of the Sun using an SEC Vidicon to allow onboard monitoring by the Skylab crews to focus in on interesting rapidly developing solar features. He was also involved in an extreme-ultraviolet double-dispersion photographic spectrograph, applying his experience with predisperser grating optics and using a photoelectric servo system to stabilize the solar image to better than to 1 second of arc at the limb. This instrument recorded 6,400 exposures. Tousey was also central in the NRL's extreme ultraviolet spectroheliograph, which employed a slitless Wadsworth grating spectrograph with photographic recording to record high-dispersion images of the solar chromosphere at 2 seconds of arc spatial resolution.

Tousey remained active into the early part of the shuttle era, planning instruments for flight. Although he was enormously inventive and productive, he and his team were sometimes criticized for concentrating so much on the production of data, and less on its analysis and interpretation. Tousey openly recognized this as a matter of personal choice throughout his career. In 1967, in his Henry Norris Russell Prize Lecture before the American Astronomical Society, he observed that "Interpretation of the results [by astronomers] does seem to the experimenters to have lagged, but I know, too, that the experimenters themselves have been slow in publishing completed results" (Tousey, 1967b, p. 251).

Tousey was elected a member of the National Academy of Sciences in 1960, and following that received many awards and honors from the academy, the Optical Society of America, the navy, the Royal Astronomical Society, and NASA. He retired in 1978, remaining active as a consultant. He died of pneumonia on 15 April 1997, at the age of eighty-eight.

BIBLIOGRAPHY

Tousey's professional papers between the 1940s and 1980s, but chiefly from the 1960s, are preserved in the National Air and Space Museum archives and include correspondence, speeches, minutes, and proceedings, photographs, prints, film, oral history transcripts, lantern slides, and glass plates.

WORKS BY TOUSEY

"An Apparatus for the Measurement of Reflecting Powers with Application to Fluorite at 1216 A." Unpublished PhD diss., Harvard University, 1936.

"Optical Constants of Fluorite in the Extreme Ultraviolet." *Physical Review* 50, no. 11 (1936): 1057–1066.

With William A. Baum, F. S. Johnson, J. J. Oberly, et al. "Solar Ultraviolet Spectrum to 88 Kilometers." *Physical Review* 70 (1946): 781–782.

With F. S. Johnson and J. D. Purcell. "Measurements of the Vertical Distribution of Atmospheric Ozone from Rockets." *Journal of Geophysical Research* 56 (1951): 583–594.

"Solar Spectroscopy in the Far Ultraviolet." *Journal of the Optical Society of America* 51 (1961): 384–395.

"The Spectrum of the Sun in the Extreme Ultraviolet." *Quarterly Journal of the Royal Astronomical Society* 5 (1964): 123–144.

"Highlights of Twenty Years of Optical Space Research." *Applied Optics* 6 (1967a): 2044–2070.

"Some Results of Twenty Years of Extreme Ultraviolet Solar Research." *Astrophysical Journal* 149 (1967b): 239–252. The AAS Henry Norris Russell Lecture.

With J.-D. F. Bartoe, J. D. Bohlin, G. E. Brueckner, et al. "A Preliminary Study of the Extreme Ultraviolet Spectroheliograms from Skylab." *Solar Physics* 33 (1973): 265–280.

With M. J. Koomen, C. R. Detwiler, G. E. Brueckner, et al. "White Light Coronagraph in *OSO-7.*" *Applied Optics* 14 (1975): 743–751.

"Interview with Dr. Richard Tousey" by David Compton. 20
April 1976. NASA History Office. Available from
http://history.nasa.gov/oralhistory/hqinventory.doc.

"Apollo Telescope Mount on Skylab: An Overview." *Applied
Optics* 16 (1977): 825–836.

"Richard Tousey Oral History" interview by David DeVorkin.
17 November 1981, and 8 January and 4 June 1982. Space
Astronomy Oral History Project, National Air and Space
Museum Archives.

"Solar Spectroscopy from Rowland to SOT." *Vistas in Astronomy*
29 (1986): 175–199.

With G. D. Sandlin, J.-D. F. Bartoe, G. E. Brueckner, et al.
"The High-Resolution Solar Spectrum, 1175–1710 Å."
Astrophysical Journal Supplement 61 (August 1986): 801–898.

OTHER SOURCES

Baum, William A. "Richard Tousey." *Biographical Memoirs,* vol.
81. Washington, DC: National Academy of Sciences, 2002.

Compton, W. David, and Charles D. Benson. *Living and
Working in Space: A History of Skylab.* Washington, DC:
National Aeronautics and Space Administration, 1983.

DeVorkin, David H. "Richard Tousey and His Beady-Eyed V-
2s." *Air & Space Smithsonian* 1 (June/July 1986): 86–94.

———. *Science with a Vengeance: How the Military Created the
US Space Sciences after World War II.* New York: Springer-
Verlag, 1992. Reprinted 1993, paperback study edition.

Friedman, Herbert, Nicholas J. Koomen, W. R. Hunter, et al.
"Richard Tousey 1908–1997: In Memoriam." *Optics &
Photonics News* 8 (July 1997): 9.

David H. DeVorkin

TRAILL, CATHARINE PARR
b. London, United Kingdom, 9 January 1802; *d.* Lakefield, Ontario, Canada, 28 August 1899), *botany, natural history, settler, author, conservationist.*

Traill, a nineteenth-century backwoods settler in Canada, was a well-known pioneering naturalist, author of two major books and several articles on botany, and the writer of immigrant and children's literature.

Background. Catharine Parr, the fifth daughter of Elizabeth Homer and Thomas Strickland, was educated at home and showed an early interest in science and literature. At a young age she learned to observe, collect, label, and classify plants and in her teens wrote and published stories and books for young readers. She married Thomas Traill in 1832; they emigrated to Canada and settled in the Peterborough district of what is now Ontario. Catharine Parr Traill brought with her a curiosity about the natural world and a keen observing eye for botany,

zoology, geology, and ecological processes. Her observations of nature, people, and social customs in her new environment became topics she explored in letters and in her published works.

Science Writers and Science in Canada. In early-nineteenth-century Europe, many women disseminated scientific knowledge in popular science books from which they earned an income. By contrast, in the 1830s, science writing was not yet an accepted occupation in sparsely settled Canada, a huge and varied geographical area insufficiently known by European and American naturalists. Catharine Parr Traill was the first naturalist and the first woman in this British colony to spend several decades studying nature. Prior to her studies, only native Canadians had a thorough environmental knowledge of any given area. European-trained explorers, naturalists, and military and survey personnel, all of them men, could only spend little time in the field and based their natural history studies on short-term observations. They focused on questions and problems defined by the European scientific community, sent collections to European naturalists, and published their findings in European journals.

In the early nineteenth century, the only scientific book on the botany of northern Canada was Frederick Pursh's *Flora Americae Septentrionalis* but this Latin work was only useful for specialists. Traill had no access to English-language works on science, there were no field guides to aid her, and she had no immediate colleagues with whom to exchange information. The mail service was slow, since road and railway networks were practically nonexistent. Thus she was effectively isolated from centers of learning and collections, such as universities, museums, and herbaria. She did have, however, considerable knowledge of botany and many years of field experience in England, was self-reliant, willing to learn about the medicinal and nutritional properties of plants from native women, and able to make systematic field observations around her new home. With her early training, inquiring mind, and fine observational skills, she soon built up a herbarium, kept nature journals, and, with time, developed a correspondence network. Better roads and railways enabled her, by the 1860s, to visit Kingston, Ottawa, and Toronto, and exchange ideas with male scientists, such as botany professor George Lawson and Dominion Naturalist John Macoun.

Science in the Backwoods. Traill's first Canadian book, *The Backwoods of Canada* (published in England in 1836), was based on letters she sent to her family. At the time there was need for books that explored life in a new settlement, provided practical advice for prospective settlers, and dealt with the physical and social environments of a recently colonized area. *Backwoods* did all this and also contained considerable information on natural history. Thus, it provided science lessons from the backwoods to English, Canadian, and American readers.

The popularity of *Backwoods* and *The Female Emigrant's Guide* (Toronto 1854), republished as *The Canadian Settler's Guide* (1855), made Catharine Parr Traill a household name among emigrants and the chief breadwinner of her large and struggling family. Her children's books, *Canadian Crusoes* (1852) and *Lady Mary and Her Nurse* (1856), added to her reputation as a writer. While the *Female Emigrant's Guide* was intended to be a practical "how-to" guide for prospective emigrant families, it incorporated references to applied science (food chemistry, mycology, and nutrition), and information about animal behavior and ecological relationships. The children's books (published first in England and republished in Canada) also contained considerable scientific information about plants, animals, geology, and climate as they dealt with living and surviving in the outdoors in a northern forest ecosystem.

Traill's long-term studies resulted in *Canadian Wild Flowers* (1868), the first Canadian botany book with an accessible text, written by Traill, and illustrated by her niece, Agnes FitzGibbon. From her lively readable descriptions, in which Traill used scientific terminology and mentioned her work with a powerful microscope in addition to fieldwork, it is evident that by this time she knew the work of European and North American male scientists. She referred to several systems of classification, and was not afraid to challenge the statements of American botanists. The book was well received and went through several editions.

Encouraged by its success she embarked on a more extensive volume, but given her age the work progressed slowly. By the time *Studies of Plant Life* appeared in 1885, botany had become institutionalized in Canada and there were other, dry, scientific books for the specialist. By contrast, Traill wrote for the general public and included descriptions and illustrations of the flowers, trees, shrubs, and ferns she had observed during half a century. Although *Studies* had fewer scientific terms than *Canadian Wild Flowers* or her botanical articles, she used scientific names and integrated nonwestern scientific information and practices. Additionally, she made strong statements about the disappearance of plants and animals and called for the preservation of fragile habitats.

Importance. Trained in the British natural history tradition, Traill became a pioneer of long-term botanical studies. Her accessible and popular plant books were the forerunners of modern field guides and, together with her articles on plants, provide important historical records of habitat destruction, changes in plant and animal life, ecological succession, and native environmental knowledge.

BIBLIOGRAPHY

WORKS BY TRAILL

The Young Emigrants; or, Picture of Life in Canada, Calculated to Amuse and Instruct the Minds of Youths. London: Harvey and Darton, 1826.

The Backwoods of Canada: Being Letters of the Wife of an Emigrant Officer, Illustrative of the Domestic Economy of British North America. London: Charles Knight, 1836.

Canadian Crusoes: Tale of the Rice Lake Plains, edited by Agnes Strickland. London: Arthur, Hall, Virtue, 1852.

The Female Emigrant's Guide, and Hints on Canadian Housekeeping. Toronto: Maclear, 1854. Reprinted as *The Canadian Settler's Guide.* Toronto: Old Countryman's Office, 1855.

Lady Mary and Her Nurse; or, A Peep into the Canadian Forest. London: Arthur, Hall, Virtue, 1856.

Canadian Wild Flowers. Montreal: John Lovell, 1868.

Studies of Plant Life in Canada; or, Gleanings from Forest, Lake and Plain. Ottawa: A. S. Woodburn, 1885.

Pearls and Pebbles; or, Notes of an Old Naturalist. Toronto: Briggs, 1894.

Cot and Cradle Stories, edited by Mary Agnes Fitzgibbon. Toronto: Briggs, 1895.

OTHER SOURCES

Ainley, Marianne Gosztonyi. "Last in the Field?: Canadian Women Natural Scientists, 1815–1965." In *Despite the Odds: Essays on Canadian Women and Science,* edited by M. G. Ainley. Montreal: Véhicule Press, 1990. Provides a history of women and science context for Traill's scientific contributions.

———. "Science in Canada's 'Backwoods': Catharine Parr Traill." In *Natural Eloquence: Women Reinscribe Science,* edited by Barbara T. Gates and Ann B. Shteir. Madison: University of Wisconsin Press, 1997. The most up-to-date study of Traill's scientific contributions by a historian of science.

Ballstadt, Carl A. "Catharine Parr Traill (1802–1899)." In *Canadian Writers and Their Works,* edited by Robert Lecker et al. Downsview, Ontario: ECW, 1983. Treats Traill mainly as a writer of emigrant literature.

Caitling, P. M., V. R. Caitling, and S. M. McKay-Kuja. "The Extent, Floristic Composition and Maintenance of the Rice Lake Plains, Ontario, Based on Historical Records." *Canadian Field-Naturalist* 106 (1992): 73–86. Recognizes the historical importance of Traill's botanical writings.

Cole, Jean M. "Catharine Parr Traill—Botanist." *Portraits: Peterborough Area Women Past and Present.* Peterborough, Ontario: Portrait Group, 1975.

MacCallum, Elizabeth. "Catharine Parr Traill, a Nineteenth-Century Ontario Naturalist." *Beaver* 360, no. 2 (Autumn 1975): 39–45.

Needler, G. H. "The Otonabee Trio of Women Naturalists: Mrs. Stewart, Mrs. Traill, Mrs. Moodie." *Canadian Field-Naturalist* 60 (1946): 97–101.

Peterman, Michael A. "'A Splendid Anachronism': The Record of Catharine Parr Traill's Struggles as an Amateur Botanist in Nineteenth-Century Canada." In *Re(dis)covering Our Foremothers: Nineteenth-Century Canadian Women Writers,* edited by Lorraine McMullen, 173–185. Ottawa: Carleton University Press, 1990. A literary scholar's attempt at evaluating Traill's scientific work that lacks the context of nineteenth-century Canadian science and women's history.

Pursh, Frederick. *Flora Americae Septentrionalis.* London: Printed for White, Cochrane, & Co., 1814.

Marianne Gosztonyi Ainley

TUCKER, ALBERT WILLIAM (*b.* Oshawa, Ontario, Canada, 28 November 1905; *d.* Hightstown, New Jersey, 25 January 1995), *mathematics, operations research.*

Tucker's name is in general associated with the mathematical disciplines of linear-nonlinear programming and game theory within operations research, and in particular with the duality theorem in linear programming, the Kuhn-Tucker conditions, and the Prisoner's Dilemma. In 1948 he became the leader of a university-based project on linear programming and game theory funded by the Office of Naval Research (ONR) and as such he was very influential in the early advancement of these fields. In 1994 his student John Forbes Nash received the Nobel Prize for his work on game theory and Tucker himself was awarded the John von Neumann Theory Prize in 1980 for his contributions to operations research.

Albert Tucker grew up in different small towns along the north coast of Lake Ontario. His special talent for mathematics was first recognized by his mathematics teacher in high school who informed Tucker's parents that he thought Tucker could have a career as an actuary. Tucker was awarded a provincial scholarship and began to study mathematics and physics at the University of Toronto in 1924 where his talent for mathematics was recognized for the second time. In 1928, Tucker received a bachelor degree and instead of pursuing further studies abroad he stayed at the University of Toronto for another year as a teaching assistant receiving a master's degree in 1929.

Tucker attended Princeton University for his doctoral studies. Some might have seen this as an odd choice at the time. According to Tucker several mathematicians tried to convince him to study in Europe or if he insisted on attending school in the United States he should choose the University of Chicago or Harvard University. Tucker was interested in geometry and had seen a catalog of graduate courses offered at Princeton, which in his opinion listed the most interesting courses. In the end Tucker was supported by Professor Chapelon and in 1929 Tucker began his graduate studies at Princeton. He received his PhD in 1932 with a thesis in topology written under the supervision of Professor Lefschetz.

From 1933 and until his retirement in 1974 Tucker held positions at the mathematics department at Princeton University. Once retired he organized Princeton's oral history project where he engaged in many of the oral history interviews with former Princeton mathematicians.

In 1938 he married Alice J. Curtiss. They had three children, a daughter who is an educator and two sons—both mathematicians. Tucker and Alice later divorced and in 1964 he married Mary F. Shaw.

ONR, Linear Programming, and Game Theory. Tucker's ONR project was a consequence of the huge military funding of science in the wake of the mobilization of scientists in the United States during World War II. The linear programming problem—to optimize a linear function subject to linear inequality constraints originated in the U.S. Air Force as a consequence of work done notably by George B. Dantzig during and after the war on the problem of calculating huge logistic planning programs.

One of the more well-known examples of linear programming problems is the transportation problem of determining how to ship amounts of a product between several centers of supply and markets in such a way that the total cost of transportation is minimized while the demands are satisfied.

The connection between linear programming and game theory was realized in the fall of 1947 by John von Neumann at the Institute for Advanced Study at Princeton University who, in his capacity as a consultant for the military, was contacted by Dantzig. The navy was interested in the possibilities of linear programming as an effective decision tool and decided to promote research in its mathematical theory and its relation to game theory. The result was the establishment of a separate logistic branch of the ONR's mathematics program. Tucker got involved in the project because he met Dantzig on one of Dantzig's visits to Princeton. The project began as a trial project in the summer of 1948 and continued with support from the ONR until 1972.

The Duality Theorem. The first group consisted of Tucker and two graduate students, Harold W. Kuhn and David Gale. They laid the theoretical foundation for linear programming in their first article "Linear Programming and the Theory of Games," which they presented at the first conference on linear programming in Chicago 1949. Among their main results was the first rigorous proof of the duality theorem, which states that for a linear maximizing/minimizing programming problem one can formulate another (dual) linear minimizing/maximizing programming problem on the same set of data. The original problem has a finite optimal solution if and only if the dual problem has a finite optimal solution and the optimal values are equal.

The Kuhn-Tucker Conditions. The linear programming problem did not originate in mathematics itself but in the context of solving a practical problem in the air force, but Tucker, Kuhn, and Gale's first work was purely theoretical. The duality result is interesting from a mathematical point of view and Tucker continued the work on the project trying to generalize the duality result for linear programming to nonlinear programming. This led to Tucker's famous paper coauthored with Kuhn (1951) in which they launched the mathematical theory of nonlinear programming.

Nonlinear programming is called for when some of the involved functions—either the function to be optimized or the constraints—are nonlinear. If in the transportation problem the location of the supply centers are not fixed but are to be determined so that the total distance weighted by the shipment from the supply centers is to be minimized, the problem turns into a nonlinear programming problem where both the shipments and the distances are to be determined.

Tucker took the Lagrangian multiplier method as the point of departure in the study of nonlinear programming problems because it exhibits the duality of linear programming in the following sense: To the linear programming problem

$$g(x) = \sum_{i=1}^{n} c_i x_i, \quad x = (x_1, \ldots, x_n), c_i \in \Re$$

where $x_1, \ldots, x_n$ are n real variables constrained by $m + n$ linear inequalities

$$f_h(x) = b_h - \sum_{i=1}^{n} a_{hi} x_i \geq 0,$$

$$x_i \geq 0, \quad h = 1, \ldots, m, \quad a_{hi}, b_h \in \Re$$

Kuhn and Tucker formed the corresponding Lagrangian function:

$$\phi(x, u) = g(x) + \sum_{h=1}^{m} u_h f_h(x), \quad u_h \in \Re$$

They realized that $x^0 = (x_1^0, \ldots, x_n^0)$ solves the linear programming problem if and only if there exists a vector $u^0 \in \Re^m$ with nonnegative components (multipliers) such that (x^0, u^0) is a saddlepoint for the Lagrangian. The vec-

tor u^0 then solves the dual problem. Following this approach for the nonlinear case Kuhn and Tucker proved that a necessary condition such that a point x^0 in $\Re^n$ solves a nonlinear programming problem is the existence of a point u^0 in $\Re^m$ such that (x^0, u^0) satisfy the necessary conditions for being a saddlepoint for the Lagrangian corresponding to the nonlinear programming problem. These necessary conditions later became known as the (Karush-) Kuhn-Tucker conditions and they constitute one of the main results in nonlinear programming.

ONR's way of funding science through university-based projects had the effect that ONR functioned as a mediating link between the interests of the military and peacetime research at the universities. A consequence of this is that ONR research, originally inspired by practical problems, could lead to highly theoretical results. The duality theorem in linear programming and the Kuhn-Tucker theorem in nonlinear programming are both such examples of theoretical results developed in the context of an ONR research project.

The Prisoner's Dilemma. Through Tucker's project Princeton became a main center for game theory in the postwar period. Tucker supervised PhD theses in game theory, the most famous being Nash's Nobel Prize–winning work on noncooperative games. Tucker himself is most famous for his interpretation—known as the Prisoner's Dilemma—of a payoff matrix for a two-person non-zero-sum game devised by Merrill Flood and Melvin Dresher at RAND in 1950: Two people are charged with a joint crime. If both confess they will be fined one unit each, if both deny they will both go clear. If one confesses and the other does not, the confessor will be rewarded with one unit the other will be fined two units. The game has a unique equilibrium point, the noncooperative solution of both confessing, but—and this is the dilemma—the prisoners are better off if they chose the nondominant strategy of denial. The prisoner's dilemma has played a significant role in social science.

The Influence on the Theory of Convexity. Tucker's project also initiated new research in the theory of convexity. In their joint nonlinear programming paper he and Kuhn proved that if the involved functions are concave and differentiable there will be complete equivalence between the saddle value problem for the corresponding Lagrangian function and the nonlinear programming problem suggesting that the theory of convex (concave) functions might be a promising tool in the theory of nonlinear programming. A convex (concave) function is a function whose graph curves upward (downward) so it has the property that a local minimum (maximum) will also be a global minimum (maximum). The new developments in the theory of convexity were primarily due to a series of lectures given by Werner Fenchel at Princeton University in the spring of 1951 during which Fenchel derived the first duality result for nonlinear programming. Tucker's project published the notes from these lectures in 1953 and they had a profound influence on the further development of the theory of convexity in the United States. This is another example where ONR research originally initiated by the need for solving practical logistic problems led to theoretical results and influenced developments in so-called pure mathematics.

BIBLIOGRAPHY

WORKS BY TUCKER

"A Two-Person Dilemma." Unpublished notes (May 1950), later published in *Readings in Games and Information*, edited by Eric Rasmusen. Oxford: Blackwell Publishers Ltd., 2001.

With Harold W. Kuhn, eds. *Contributions to the Theory of Games*. Annals of Mathematics Studies, no. 24. Princeton, NJ: Princeton University Press, 1950.

With David Gale and Harold W. Kuhn. "Linear Programming and the Theory of Games." In *Activity Analysis of Production and Allocation,* edited by T. C. Koopmans. New York: John Wiley and Sons, 1951.

With Harold W. Kuhn. "Nonlinear Programming." In *Proceedings of the Second Berkeley Symposium on Mathematical Statistics and Probability,* edited by J. Neyman. Berkeley: University of California Press, 1951.

———, eds. *Contributions to the Theory of Games,* vol. 2. Annals of Mathematics Studies, no. 28. Princeton, NJ: Princeton University Press, 1953.

———, eds. *Linear Inequalities and Related Systems*. Annals of Mathematics Studies, no. 38. Princeton, NJ: Princeton University Press, 1956.

With M. Dresher and P. Wolfe, eds. *Contributions to the Theory of Games,* vol. 3. Annals of Mathematics Studies, no. 39. Princeton, NJ: Princeton University Press, 1957.

With R. D. Luce, eds. *Contributions to the Theory of Games,* vol. 4. Annals of Mathematics Studies, no. 40. Princeton, NJ: Princeton University Press, 1959.

OTHER SOURCES

Albers, Donald J., and G. L. Alexanderson, eds. *Mathematical People: Profiles and Interviews*. Boston: Birkhäuser, 1985.

"A Guide to the Albert William Tucker Papers, 1946–1979," in Archives of American Mathematics, Center for American History, The University of Texas at Austin. Available from http://www.lib.utexas.edu/taro/utcah/00301/cah-00301.html. Consists of interviews with Albert W. Tucker from 1979 and reprints and photocopies of papers by and about Tucker and mathematics at Princeton University.

Kjeldsen, Tinne H. "The Emergence of Nonlinear Programming: Interactions between Practical Mathematics and Mathematics Proper." *Mathematical Intelligencer* 22 (Summer 2000): 50–54.

———. "A Contextualized Historical Analysis of the Kuhn-Tucker Theorem in Nonlinear Programming: The Impact of World War II." *Historia Mathematica* 27 (November 2000): 331–361.

———. "The Development of Nonlinear Programming in Post War USA: Origin, Motivation, and Expansion." In *The Way through Science and Philosophy: Essays in Honour of Stig Andur Pedersen,* edited by H. B. Andersen, F. V. Christiansen, K. F. Jørgensen, et al., 31–50. College Publications, 2006.

Kuhn, Harold W. "Nonlinear Programming: A Historical View." *SIAM-AMS Proceedings* 9 (1976): 1–26.

Nasar, Sylvia. "Obituary." *New York Times,* 27 January 1995.

Tinne Hoff Kjeldsen

TURING, ALAN MATHISON (*b.* London, England, 23 June 1912; *d.* Wilmslow, England, 7 June 1954), *mathematics, mathematical logic, computer technology.* For the original article on Turing see *DSB,* vol. 13.

It is perhaps not surprising that so many discussions of Turing's work have been confined to the esoteric realms of mathematics, logic, and philosophy given that his name is most often associated with a class of abstract machines within computability theory or in connection to a deliberately provocative test he proposed to determine whether a machine could think. However, as the significance of the computer looms ever larger, so too has general interest grown in Turing's work. In the time since van Rootselaar's original *DSB* entry, Turing scholarship has advanced to uncover the full extent of Turing's influence across a wide range of disciplines, including, mathematics, logic, cryptology, computer engineering (both hardware and software), artificial intelligence, cognitive science, philosophy, and biology. In addition, several biographies have since been published that bring to light many of the idiosyncratic qualities that defined Turing's life and research. While none of this scholarship alters the basic biographic contours presented by van Rootselaar, it does provide a richer context in which Turing's contributions can be seen to extend beyond mathematical logic or bold comments about thinking machines.

Entscheidungsproblem. One area where the scholarship has deepened concerns the publication date and significance of Turing's "On Computable Numbers, with an Application to the *Entscheidungsproblem*." Whereas the original *DSB* entry gives a publication date of 1937 and implies that the work was undertaken while Turing was at Princeton, more recent scholarship gives a date of 1936 (or sometimes as 1936–1937) and very clearly establishes that Turing had worked out his solution to the *Entscheidungsproblem* independently. Although the *Entscheidungsproblem* was at the time the outstanding problem of mathematical logic, the significance of Turing's independent solution lies not so much with any claim to priority (which is due to Alonzo Church), but, rather, the formal characterization Turing gave to intuitions about effective computation. Indeed, the fact that the unsolvability of the *Entscheidungsproblem* had a decapitating impact on David Hilbert's quest for a purely formal mathematics almost seems incidental as scholars have instead celebrated Turing's analysis of effective computation as the most influential among his contemporaries. Inspired by the human computer (i.e., the human engaged in computation), Turing described a notional machine that could read and write symbols along a segmented tape. The machine itself would be capable of assuming various internal states that, together with the input of a single symbol along the tape, could lead to a few primitive atomic actions. Based on the current state and the current symbol, each configuration specifies a change (or not) of symbol, a move right or left, and a next state. Working under some straightforward assumptions about the finite and discrete nature of the machine, Turing was able to demonstrate the wide range of numbers (equivalently, the wide class of functions) that could be computed and, moreover, able to specify a single machine, the universal machine, that would be capable of simulating the computations of any such machine. Turing's characterization has come to be seen as a more compelling account of what it means to be effective, mechanical, or algorithmic than any of the various extensionally equivalent formulations offered by his contemporaries.

Practical Computing. Scholarship has also deepened with respect to the contributions Turing made to the development of working electronic computers. Again, in terms of priority Turing misses out, as credit is most often given to John von Neumann for the first specification of the electronic stored-program computer. Nevertheless, scholars have continued to uncover Turing's contributions not just to developments in England but also to von Neumann's thinking. Scholars also point out that Turing's understanding of the significance of software was probably deeper than that of his contemporaries. While Turing's observations about computing might seem pedestrian by twenty-first-century standards, they are remarkable considering that Turing was anticipating practice which had yet to be fully realized in his time. In a similar spirit, some scholars have attributed to Turing the anticipation of so-called hypercomputers, machines capable of outstripping the bounds of computing as they are traditionally conceived. Although such attributions depend on a controversial reading of Turing's work, they have precipitated a lively debate

Alan Turing. *Alan Turing, 1951.* **LIFE MAGAZINE/TIME LIFE PICTURES/GETTY IMAGES.**

that touches on issues of mechanism, the limits of computation, and the proper interpretation of the Church-Turing thesis (roughly, the claim that the intuitive notion of effective computation can be identified with the class of functions computed by a Turing machine).

Turing scholarship has also broadened in several respects. First, some of Turing's less known works and other unpublished sources are receiving attention as possible antecedents to contemporary discussions of theoretical biology, "artificial life," machine learning, and connectionism. Second, as computers have become more powerful and the possibility of artificial intelligence becomes less remote in the popular imagination, Turing's once seemingly bold comments about machine intelligence have found a new audience. Of course, not all of the popular interest in machine intelligence and the mind's workings mentions, much less centers on, Turing, but enough of it does to breathe new life into the secondary literature. Finally, it is worth noting the great extent to which cognitive science in general has been shaped either directly by computational views of mind or in reaction to them. As the computational view of mind has come under increasing scrutiny, so too have more foundational questions about the nature of computing itself and the role it plays in our understanding of mind. Although these questions do not illuminate the historical Turing, they often invite the reexamination of the Turing machine and its role and significance in cognitive science.

Biographies of Turing emphasize his solitary tendencies and his unwillingness to conform to convention. It is often suggested that these are exactly the qualities that allowed Turing to bring such fresh perspective to difficult problems. It is also often suggested that these same qualities might have compounded the difficulties that ensued after Turing's arrest and "treatment" for homosexual behavior, then illegal in England. Considered a security risk, and subject to surveillance, Turing eventually committed suicide.

SUPPLEMENTARY BIBLIOGRAPHY

Several Web sites maintain Turing bibliographies along with online access to many primary and secondary sources. A good place to start is the Alan Turing Home Page (http://www.turing.org.uk/), maintained by the Turing biographer Andrew Hodges. Slightly less user friendly but containing digital facsimiles of many of Turing's unpublished works is the Turing Digital Archive (http://www.turingarchive.org/). Digital facsimiles of Turing's work are also available from the Turing Archive for the History of Computing (http://www.alanturing.net/).

WORKS BY TURING

The Undecidable: Basic Papers on Undecidable Propositions, Unsolvable Problems, and Computable Functions. Edited by Martin Davis. New York: Raven Press, 1965. Reprint, Mineola, NY: Dover, 2004. A collection of classic works of computability theory by Turing and his contemporaries.

Collected Works of A. M. Turing. Vol. 1, *Mechanical Intelligence,* edited by D. C. Ince. Vol. 2, *Pure Mathematics,* edited by J. L. Britton. Vol. 3, *Morphogenesis,* edited by P. T. Saunders. Vol. 4, *Mathematical Logic,* edited by R. O. Gandy and C. E. M. Yates. Amsterdam; New York: Elsevier Science, 1992, 2001.

The Essential Turing: Seminal Writings in Computing, Logic, Philosophy, Artificial Intelligence, and Artificial Life, plus the Secrets of Enigma. Edited by B. Jack Copeland. New York: Oxford University Press, 2004. A single volume that contains Turing's most influential work.

OTHER SOURCES

Herken, Rolf, ed. *The Universal Turing Machine: A Half-Century Survey.* Oxford: Oxford University Press, 1988. An excellent collection of commentaries on Turing's influence from the perspectives of leading mathematicians and logicians.

Hodges, Andrew. *Alan Turing: The Enigma.* New York: Simon & Schuster, 1983. Reprint, New York: Walker 2000. The authoritative biography of Turing.

———. *Turing: A Natural Philosopher.* London: Phoenix, 1997. A very concise, very accessible biography.

Leavitt, David. *The Man Who Knew Too Much: Alan Turing and the Invention of the Computer.* New York: Atlas Books, 2006. A good read, but occasionally misleading in its technical detail and presents some strained speculation about motives.

Scheutz, Matthias, ed. *Computationalism: New Directions.* Cambridge, MA: MIT Press, 2002. A book more about Turing's ideas than about Turing himself. A useful starting point into the vast secondary literature concerning computation, the philosophy of mind, and cognitive science.

Teuscher, Christof, ed. *Alan Turing: Life and Legacy of a Great Thinker.* Berlin: Springer, 2004. A wide-ranging collection of commentary on Turing.

Walter Warwick

TURNER, CHARLES HENRY (*b.* Cincinnati, Ohio, 3 February 1867; *d.* Chicago, Illinois, 14 February 1923), *zoology, invertebrate learning, education.*

Turner was the first African American scientist interested in the comparative analysis of behavior. He made fundamental contributions in the areas of vertebrate and invertebrate morphology, naturalistic observation, apparatus design, death feigning, and invertebrate learning. He was an early leader in the civil rights movement, contributing several seminal papers on race relations.

Life. Turner received the majority of his education in Cincinnati, Ohio. He attended Woodard High School and graduated valedictorian. Following his marriage to Leontine Troy in 1887, he earned both his BS and MS degrees in 1891 and 1892, respectively, under the direction of his mentor Clarence L. Herrick of the University of Cincinnati. Upon graduation, he held a number of appointments at various high schools in the southern United States and at Clark University in Atlanta, Georgia, before settling at Sumner High School in St. Louis, Missouri, in 1908, where he remained until his retirement precipitated by illness in 1922.

Turner earned his PhD in zoology, magna cum laude, at the University of Chicago in 1907. He died of myocarditis in the home of the younger of his two sons, Darwin Romanes Turner, a successful pharmacist in Chicago, Illinois. Turner's eldest son, Henry Owen Turner, assisted his younger brother in operating the pharmacy; there was also a daughter, Louisa Mae Turner. Turner's first wife, Leontine Troy, died in 1895, and in 1907 or 1908 (exact year not known) he married Lillian Porter.

During a career that spanned thirty-three years, Turner published at least seventy-one papers. This number compares favorably with his white male and female

Charles Henry Turner. *Portrait of Charles Henry Turner.*
COURTESY OF CHARLES ABRAMSON, TERRI SMALL-TURNER,
AND CHARLES HENRY TURNER II.

Morphology and Anatomy. Turner began his career by continuing a line of research begun by his mentor. He contributed original articles on the comparative anatomy of the pigeon brain, directly compared the brains of arthropods and annelids, and studied the mushroom bodies of crayfish. His work with pigeons is a fine example of the skills in dissection, histology, observation, drawing, and analysis that were to characterize his career. In addition to the morphological contributions, the pigeon work contains several unique contributions, including the description of a new tool to handle delicate tissue, the development of a new stain, and the suggestion that the compactness of the avian brain can be used as a taxonomic indicator. This work was even more remarkable because he did it while an undergraduate in 1891.

Insect Navigation. A second line of research attempted to answer the question of how insects navigate. There were several competing theories suggesting insects navigate by a homing instinct, tropism, limited learning ability, or higher intelligence. He designed an elaborate maze for ants, and using controls now known to be important in excluding alternative explanations (such as using heat filters with a light stimulus) and employing replicates of his observations, Turner demonstrated that ants navigate not by tropism or instinct but by using cues presented in the environment and by using higher intelligence. This work was also unique because it was among the first to investigate the influence of sex and age differences. Turner

peers and is made more remarkable because Turner had no formal laboratory resources, no access to research libraries, no undergraduate or graduate students, and no university appointment; most of his contributions were made as a high school science teacher. Turner's work was favorably recognized by leaders of the animal behavior movement and by leaders of the civil rights movement. In 1910, the French naturalist Victor Cornetz named the exploratory circling movements of ants "tournoiement de Turner" and in 1912 W. E. B. DuBois selected Turner as one of the *Crisis* magazine's "Men of the Month."

The Charles Henry Turner Open Air School for Crippled Children was established in St. Louis in 1925, and in 1954 the school became the Charles Henry Turner Middle Branch, which in 1999 became part of the Charles Henry Turner MEGA Magnet Middle School. In 1962, Turner-Tanner Hall was dedicated at Clark College in Atlanta and in 2002 the Animal Behavior Society created an annual Charles H. Turner Poster Session and Travel Award for undergraduates.

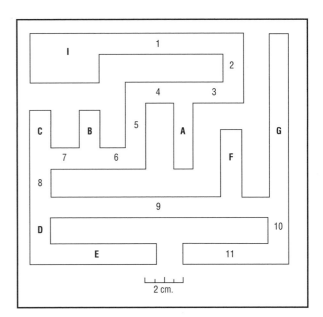

Figure 1. *Schematic diagram of a cockroach maze showing numerous passages and blind alleys.*

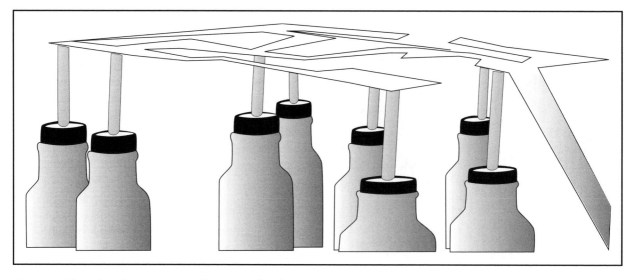

Figure 2. *The cockroach maze supported by a series of bottles.*

extended his navigation work to other invertebrates, including honey bees, wasps, and caterpillars.

His work on navigation suggested that insects possess "higher intelligence" or what we now call learning. Turner embarked on an ambitious research program investigating learning in a wide range of invertebrates. This required him to construct various apparatuses for both laboratory work and fieldwork. His major contributions include the first conclusive demonstrations that honeybees learn color and pattern discriminations, that cockroaches learn in a variety of situations, and that learning survives molting. Of particular interest are his experiments on the ability of moths to hear sound. The initial paper provided the first data that moths can hear and the second provided what might very well be the first demonstration of Pavlovian conditioning in an insect.

Other Interests. Another interest of Turner's was the ability of insects to play "possum." His results with ant lions, known colloquially as doodlebugs, indicated that such behavior is based not on learning but rather on what he termed "terror paralysis." These experiments were unique because of the many parameters that were investigated such as the relative duration of death feints, stimulus intensity, and hunger. The experiments also provided some of the earliest behavioral descriptions of ant lions. Behavioral description was a recurrent interest of Turner. He provided descriptions of a wide variety of invertebrates, including the microorganisms of Cincinnati, where he discovered a new species.

Turner maintained a lifelong interest in civil rights. His first paper on the topic appeared early in his career. In this, and other papers, he argued that prejudice can be studied through the science of comparative psychology and proposed that only through education can problems between the races be resolved.

BIBLIOGRAPHY

WORKS BY TURNER

"Morphology of the Avian Brain." *Journal of Comparative Neurology* 1 (1891): 39–93, 107–133, 265–286.

"Notes upon the Cladocera, Copepoda, Ostracoda and Rotifera of Cincinnati, with Descriptions of New Species." *Bulletin of the Scientific Laboratories of Denison University* 6, part 2 (1892): 57–74 and plates.

"Reason for Teaching Biology in Negro School." *Southwestern Christian Advocate* 32 (1897): 2.

"A Preliminary Paper on the Comparative Study of the Arthropod and Annelid Brain." *Zoological Bulletin* 2 (1899): 155–160.

"Will the Education of the Negro Solve the Race Problem." In *Twentieth Century Negro Literature: A Cyclopedia of Thought on the Vital Topics Relating to the American Negro,* edited by W. Culp. Naperville, IL: J. L. Nichols, 1902.

"The Homing of Ants: An Experimental Study of Ant Behavior." *Journal of Comparative Neurology and Psychology* 17 (1907): 367–434.

"Experiments on Color Vision of the Honey Bee." *Biological Bulletin* 19 (1910): 257–279.

"Experiments on Pattern-Vision of the Honey Bee." *Biological Bulletin* 21 (1911): 249–264.

"Behavior of the Common Roach (*Periplaneta orientalis* L.) on an Open Maze." *Biological Bulletin* 25 (1913): 348–365.

"An Experimental Study of the Auditory Powers of the Giant Silkworm Moths (Saturniidae)." *Biological Bulletin* 27 (1914): 325–332.

OTHER SOURCES

Abramson, C. I., L. D. Jackson, and C. L. Fuller, eds. *Selected Papers and Biography of Charles Henry Turner (1867–1923), Pioneer of Comparative Animal Behavior Studies.* Lewiston, NY: Edwin Mellen, 2003. Contains a wide range of Turner's papers, and bibliographic material from several sources including a chapter by Charles Henry Turner II.

"Charles Henry Turner: Contributions of a Forgotten African-American to Scientific Research." Available from http://psychology.okstate.edu/museum/turner/turnermain.html. This site contains a brief biography of Turner, a time line of significant events, a bibliography, and rare family photographs.

Ross, Michael Elsohn. *Bug Watching with Charles Henry Turner,* illustrated by Laurie A. Caple. Minneapolis, MN: Carolrhoda Books, 1997. This book is written for children and contains a nice biography and instructions on how to perform some of Turner's experiments.

Charles I. Abramson

AL-ṬŪSĪ, SHARAF AL-DĪN AL-MUẒAFFAR IBN MUḤAMMAD IBN AL-MUẒAFFAR

(*b.* Ṭūs [?], Iran; *d.* Iran, c. 1213–1214), *astronomy, mathematics.* For the original article on al-Ṭūsī, see *DSB,* vol. 13.

Al-Ṭūsī is best known for his mathematically impressive study of the conditions under which cubic equations have a positive real root and of numerical methods for finding a solution of such equations. He was, according to the thirteenth-century biographer Ibn Abī Usaibiʿa, "outstanding in geometry and the mathematical sciences, having no equal in his time." In 1986 Roshdi Rashed published *Oeuvres Mathématiques* (2 vols.), containing the extant mathematical works of Sharaf al-Dīn with an edited Arabic text and French translation and commentary. These works are his *Equations,* his *On the Construction of a Geometric Problem,* and his *On Two Lines that Approach Each Other but Do Not Meet* (a treatise on the asymptotes of the hyperbola).

Al-Ṭūsī's Solutions of Equations. Sharaf al-Dīn organized his treatment of the twenty-five possible cubic equations around whether the equation has a positive real root. (Since any cubic equation with real coefficients must have at least one real root, the discussion hinges on whether that root is positive.) Accordingly, the five cases in which there may be no root form the last group he discussed.

Sharaf al-Dīn brought new ideas even to the solution of quadratic equations. For example, in discussing the equation $ax + b = x^2$, he noted that making the substitution $x = X + a$ changes the equation to one of the form he

has previously explained, that is, $x^2 + ax = b$. This use of such substitutions served him well in a number of places, especially in the case of cubic equations.

From his description of the algorithms for solving the equations, it is clear that Sharaf al-Dīn assumed the reader would be doing the work on a *takht* (dust board), where one can conveniently write only a very few rows of numbers. The algorithms themselves are based on the idea that if $f(x) = c$ is a polynomial equation with root $a_n 10^n + b$, where b is a real number whose integer part is of order less than 10^n, then $f(a_n 10^n + x)$ has root b. The procedures then consist of finding $a_n 10^n$ and using the algorithms to calculate the coefficients of the latter polynomial.

Sharaf al-Dīn's method for finding $a_n 10^n$ succeeds (in most cases) because he was working with cubic equations. (The solutions in all cases are the same number, 321.) And, following his description of the algorithm, Sharaf al-Dīn justified in each case the positions of the coefficients as well as the algorithm he followed. These efforts to justify a wide class of numerical procedures show a new side of mathematics in medieval Islam. Sharaf al-Dīn, in his analysis of the equation $x^3 + c = ax^2$, showed first the obvious fact that if x is a real root then $x < a$, and he then showed that $x^2(a - x) = c$. He thought of c as representing a solid and showed that it is a rectangular parallelopiped with base x^2 and height $(a - c)$. He then showed that if $x = \frac{2}{3}a$, then the solid represented by $x^2(a - x)$ is as large as possible. Hence, he knew that if the equation has a solution, then c cannot exceed the maximum, $\frac{4}{27}a^3$. In the case where c is equal to the maximum, he knew, of course, that $x = \frac{2}{3}a$ is the unique root of the equation,

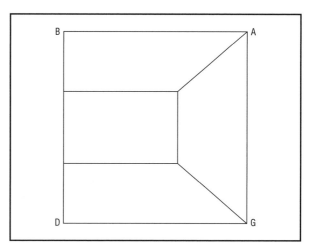

Figure 1. *Al-Ṭūsī's Dissection Problem.*

and when there are two roots, one in the interval $(0, \frac{2}{3}a)$ and one in the interval $(\frac{2}{3}a, a)$. His proof that the maximum value is attained when $x = 2a/3$ is an exercise in manipulation of volumes and areas that would be straightforward for a mathematician of Sharaf al-Dīn's caliber who had studied *Elements*, II.

How Sharaf al-Dīn discovered such conditions, however, is a subject on which historians have disagreed. The present writer inclines toward J. P. Hogendijk's suggestion that Sharaf al-Dīn arrived at the defining condition for the point where $f(x)$ obtained its maximum by assuming that x was such a point and then studying $f(x) - f(y)$ for y on either side of x to find a sufficient condition so that this difference is positive in both cases.

As it turns out, these two conditions force x to satisfy a quadratic equation that is equivalent (in modern terms) to setting the derivative, $f'(x)$, equal to 0. Other restorations of Sharaf al-Dīn's analysis of the equations appear in Rashed's *Oeuvres Mathématiques* and in Ali A. Daffa and John J. Stroyls's *Studies in the Exact Sciences in Medieval Islam* (1984).

Al-Ṭūsī's Linear Astrolabe. Sharaf al-Dīn was also the inventor of a linear astrolabe, a single rod with markings on it (sometimes called "the rod of al-Ṭūsī"). The rod represents the meridian of the planispheric astrolabe, and two threads attached to it, with movable beads on them, can be positioned at various points along the rod to serve in place of the rete (the top plate in the usual planispheric astrolabe, whose pointers indicate the position of certain prominent stars). The rod has a number of scales, one of which represents the intersections of the altitude circles with the meridian. Another represents the intersections with the meridian of concentric circles that are the stereographic projections of the circles containing the beginnings of the zodiacal signs. (See Figure 1.)

Sharaf al-Dīn's student, Kamāl al-Dīn Ibn Yūnus, improved his teacher's linear astrolabe, and Abū ʿAlī al-Marrākūshī wrote directions on how to use it. Although the instrument was known in al-Andalus (the Arab-controlled areas of the Iberian Peninsula), it was not, apparently, transmitted to the rest of Europe. Nor was it very popular in medieval Islam; Najm al-Dīn al-Misrī gave a very confused discussion of it in his *Treatise on Astronomical Instruments*.

Al-Ṭūsī on Geometrical Dissection. Sharaf al-Dīn's connection with the practical arts in Islam is witnessed by a problem that may have originated in his experience teaching the carpenter, Abū al-Faḍl, in Damascus, who, according to Ibn Abī Usaibiʿa, had become a devoted student of the writings of Euclid and Ptolemy. (Although the latter did not say so, the fact that Abū al-Faḍl had studied the works at the beginning and end of the standard curriculum of medieval Islamic instruction in the exact sciences

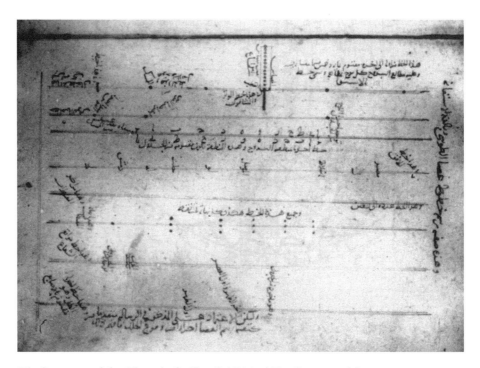

The linear astrolabe. *The scales for Sharaf al-Din's al-Ṭūsī linear astrolabe.* **ARCHIVES OF THE INSTITUTE FOR HISTORY OF SCIENCE, FRANKFURT UNIVERSITY.**

indicates that he would also have studied the intermediate works as well, such as Euclid's *Phenomena* and Theodosius's *Spherics*.)

The problem Sharaf al-Dīn addressed is that of dissecting a square ABGD of given side AB into one rectangle and three trapezia so that the areas have given ratios to each other. And he solved the problem for the case when the trapezea (beginning from the top and working clockwise in Figure 1) have the ratios 3, 5, and 2 to the rectangle.

The relevance of this kind of problem to problems that a craftsman would encounter in doing medieval Islamic tilings of plane surfaces is clear. That the solution would be of purely theoretical interest as well, however, is shown by Sharaf al-Dīn's requirement in the construction that a certain line segment be 3,024 times another segment.

In another short work, titled "On Two Lines that Never Meet," al-Ṭusi demonstrates that a hyperbola and its asymptotes, however far they are extended, never meet. This property was well-known to medieval Islamic geometers and al-Ṭusi's reasons for writing the treatise are unclear.

SUPPLEMENTARY BIBLIOGRAPHY

All three of Sharaf al-Dīn al-Ṭusī's extant mathematical works can be found in the Oeuvres Mathématiques, *edited and translated by Roshdi Rashed. No archive of his work exists; virtually no original manuscripts are extant, and the available medieval copies are spread across a number of libraries in the Islamic and western worlds.*

WORKS BY SHARAF AL-DĪN AL-ṬUSI

Oeuvres Mathématiques. 2 vols. Edited and translated by Roshdi Rashed. Paris: Belles Lettres, 1986.

OTHER SOURCES

Berggren, J. L. "Innovation and Tradition in Sharaf al-Dīn al-Ṭūsi's al-Muʿādalāt." *Journal of the American Oriental Society* 110, no. 2 (1990): 304–309.

Daffa, Ali A., and John J. Stroyls. *Studies in the Exact Sciences in Medieval Islam.* New York; Chichester, U.K.: Wiley, 1984.

Hogendijk, Jan P. "Sharaf al-Dīn al-Ṭūsi on the Number of Positive Roots of a Cubic Equation." *Historia Mathematica* 16, no. 1 (1989): 69–85.

King, David A. *In Synchrony with the Heavens: Studies in Astronomical Timekeeping and Instrumentation in Medieval Islamic Civilization.* Vol. 2. Leiden, Netherlands; Boston: Brill, 2005.

J. L. Berggren

TUTTE, WILLIAM (BILL) THOMAS

(*b.* Newmarket, United Kingdom, 14 May 1917, *d.* Waterloo, Ontario, Canada, 2 May 2002), *mathematics, graph theory, cryptography.*

Tutte will take his place in history for two reasons. First, as part of the famous code-breaking team at Bletchley Park, he made a significant individual contribution to the outcome of World War II. Second, he formulated and proved many of the theorems that form the foundations of graph theory. In both cases his achievements resulted from very deep insights into matters that, at first sight, might be thought simple. In 1930 Denes König, the author of the first book on graph theory, had mentioned two important outstanding problems: the conjecture of Tait and the extension of Petersen's theorem on factorization of graphs. Both problems, "and many others," were later settled by Tutte (Erdös, 1979, p. xxiii).

Graph theory has grown significantly in importance since that time, partly because of its links with advances in theoretical computer science. For that reason the name of Tutte is now recognized throughout the scientific community as the leading pioneer of an important branch of mathematics.

Origins. Tutte grew up in Chevely, a village near Newmarket, England, where his father was gardener at the Rutland Arms Hotel. He attended the village school until, at the age of eleven, he won a scholarship to the Cambridge and County High School. The school was 15 miles from his home, and the daily journey was difficult, but well worth the effort. He won many prizes, and in the school library he discovered W. W. Rouse Ball's book of *Mathematical Recreations and Essays*, in which he read about the five-color theorem and Petersen's theorem. Both these results were to figure largely in his life's work.

In 1935 he went to Trinity College, Cambridge, to read natural sciences. He specialized in chemistry, and was awarded a first-class honors degree. He also joined the Trinity Mathematical Society, where he met R. L. Brooks, C. A. B. Smith, and A. H. Stone. Together they worked on the problem of dividing a square into squares of different sizes. The story of their work on this problem has been told many times, including by Tutte himself in *Scientific American* (1958). Many important ideas arose first in this work. The ideas about spanning trees can be traced back to the electrical networks of Gustav Kirchhoff, but many of the algebraic results were new, as were the insights into planarity and duality.

Code Breaking. Tutte began research in chemistry, and produced two papers on his experimental results. His progress was interrupted when he was called up for national service in World War II, and after initial training he arrived at Bletchley Park, the British cryptographic headquarters, in 1941. At his eightieth birthday celebration in 1997 he felt able to talk informally about some of the details, and soon afterward he was persuaded to give a talk at the opening of the Center for Applied Cryptographic Research at the University of Waterloo. In this talk, "FISH and I" (2000), he tells how, others having failed, he was asked to work on the cipher system known at Bletchley as Tunny. This was one of the "Fish" codes used by the German High Command. He had an idea and, although not optimistic, he "thought it best to seem busy." So he copied out some cipher text onto sheets of squared paper, using chunks of various lengths, noticed certain patterns, and was able to infer the structure of the system. Indeed, he achieved a virtual reconstruction of an extremely complex machine using only scraps of information—an amazing feat that must rank as one of his greatest intellectual achievements.

Soon many people were helping to work out the implications of Tutte's discovery. This work continued throughout 1942 and 1943, with regular upgrading of the techniques to deal with improvements in the system. Eventually it became necessary to use a form of number-crunching statistical analysis, and Tutte saw how this could be done. He reported his ideas and, in his own words, "there were rapid developments." The outcome was that the famous Colossus computer was deployed on these problems.

At the end of the war, Trinity College elected Tutte to a research fellowship in mathematics. Although less prestigious in the public eye than the awards given to other civil servants, it was probably more appreciated by the recipient. Exactly how it came about is unclear. C. A. B. Smith recalled being stopped in the street by a fellow of Trinity, who said "we've just elected Tutte to a Fellowship but we don't know what he has done or where he lives" (Smith, 1979, pp. xix–xxi).

Graph Theory. The period at Trinity was a highly productive one. His PhD thesis on *An Algebraic Theory of Graphs* contained many seminal ideas, and these were published in papers that quickly established graph theory as a significant area of mathematics, with Tutte as its master builder. Among the papers that were published at that time, there are several classics. In a paper published in 1946 he disproved Tait's conjecture by constructing a planar cubic graph that has no Hamilton cycle. His paper on the symmetry of cubic graphs contains a truly unexpected bound on the order of a vertex-stabilizer, a fact that was to resurface twenty years later in the work of permutation-group theorists. Perhaps his most influential paper is the one on factorization of graphs, in which he obtains the canonical form of the basic result on this topic, with Petersen's theorem as a simple corollary.

Much later, in his book *Graph Theory as I Have Known It* (1998), he gave a fascinating account of how he arrived at some of these fundamental results. Perhaps not surprisingly, it was often by a process that offered an intellectual challenge rather than a guarantee of success. As well as graph theory, his thesis also contained important results about matroids, a subject that had been inaugurated by Hassler Whitney.

In 1948 he took up a teaching position at the University of Toronto. Here he continued to produce a stream of new ideas, including papers on aspects of the chromatic polynomial and its two-variable generalization, now known (justifiably) as the Tutte polynomial. Several famous conjectures, such as the conjecture that every bridgeless graph has a 5-flow, also appeared in print at this time.

In 1962 he was persuaded to move to the newly established University of Waterloo. By this time he had been appointed a Fellow of the Royal Society of Canada, and his eminence was being recognized internationally. The university created around him a world-famous Department of Combinatorics and Optimisation, which was instrumental in the foundation of the *Journal of Combinatorial Theory*.

By the 1970s the growth of air travel meant that Bill and his wife Dorothea, whom he had married in 1949, were able to travel extensively and they returned to England on several occasions. His work at this period centered on the enumeration of planar graphs, and specifically four-colorable planar graphs. There was a slight chance that the four-color conjecture could be settled "asymptotically," but he did not have great hopes for the method. He greeted the Appel-Haken resolution of the conjecture enthusiastically, agreeing that the strategy was sound, even if the calculations could not be checked by hand.

Retirement. He retired formally in 1985, but continued to be active in mathematics. In his quiet way he enjoyed the recognition that accompanied the growth in popularity and status of graph theory, the subject he had built. Outstanding mathematicians were attracted to work in this field, many of them inspired by Tutte's earlier results.

After Dorothea's death in 1994 he lived in England for a while. Since there were no children from the marriage Tutte did not settle in England, and eventually returned to his adopted home in Ontario. It was proper that his eightieth birthday should be marked by a celebration in Waterloo, where he was able to talk about his work to an audience that fully appreciated what he had achieved. Two years later he spoke about "The Coming of the Matroids" (1999), explaining how some of his work at Bletchley had helped him to understand the properties of linear dependence, and how this led to some of the fundamental theorems of matroid theory. In 2001 his eminence was recognized by the award of the Order of Canada, which he received with characteristic humor and humility.

At that time he was in good health, but in March 2002 he was diagnosed with lymphoma of the spleen, and he died in May, in his eighty-fifth year.

BIBLIOGRAPHY

WORKS BY TUTTE

"Squaring the Square." *Scientific American* (November 1958). Reprinted in *More Mathematical Puzzles and Diversions,* edited by M. Gardner. London: Penguin, 1961. Contains many interesting insights.

Selected Papers of W. T. Tutte. Edited by D. McCarthy and R. G. Stanton. St. Pierre, Manitoba, Canada: Charles Babbage Research Centre, 1979.

Graph Theory. Menlo Park, CA: Addison-Wesley, 1984. For mathematicians.

Graph Theory as I Have Known It. Oxford: Clarendon Press, 1998. The best account of his own work, written in simple terms.

"The Coming of the Matroids." In *Surveys in Combinatorics,* edited by J. D. Lamb and D. A. Preece. Cambridge, U.K.: Cambridge University Press, 1999. Describes the link between his wartime work and abstract mathematics.

"FISH and I." In *Coding Theory and Cryptology,* edited by D. Joyner. New York: Springer, 2000. Describes his work at Bletchley Park.

OTHER SOURCES

Erdős, P. "A Tribute." In *Graph Theory and Related Topics,* edited by J. A. Bondy and U. S. R. Murty. New York: Academic Press, 1979. An evaluation by one of the leading mathematicians of the twentieth century.

Smith, C. A. B. "Early Reminiscences." In *Graph Theory and Related Topics,* edited by J. A. Bondy and U. S. R. Murty. New York: Academic Press, 1979. Written by a lifelong friend.

Norman Biggs

TVERSKY, AMOS (*b.* Haifa, Israel, 16 March 1937; *d.* Stanford, California, 2 June 1996), *judgment and decision making, mathematical psychology, cognitive science.*

Tversky made profound and influential contributions to the study of human judgment and decision making and to the foundations of measurement. He published more articles in *Psychological Review,* the premier journal for theoretical psychology, founded more than a century before he died, than anyone else in the journal's history. In collaboration with his friend and colleague, Daniel Kahneman, he laid the foundations of new fields of research into heuristics and biases, behavioral decision theory, and judgment under uncertainty. Kahneman was awarded a Nobel Prize in Economics for this work in 2002 (jointly with the economist Vernon Smith), and he began his prize lecture by pointing out that the work for which he had earned the prize had been done in collaboration with Tversky, who had died several years earlier and was therefore ineligible to share it. The work of Tversky and Kahneman inspired subsequent generations of researchers in judgment and decision making and contributed significantly to the emergence of behavioral economics as a new field of research.

Early Life and Education. Tversky was born in Haifa, Israel, to parents who had emigrated from Poland via Russia to Israel, and he died of metastatic melanoma at age fifty-nine at his home in Stanford, California. His father, Yosef, originally trained in medicine, worked as a veterinarian, and his mother, Genia, was a social worker who also served in the Israeli parliament, the Knesset, from its establishment in 1948 until her death in 1964. Tversky served in the Israeli Defense Forces (IDF), rising to the rank of captain in a paratrooper unit, and he saw active service in three wars. He was wounded in 1956, not in combat but during a military exercise in front of the IDF general staff. In his role of platoon commander, Tversky sent one of his soldiers to place an explosive charge under a barbed wire fence in order to blast a hole in it. The soldier placed the charge, lit the fuse, and then lost his nerve, freezing to the spot. Tversky leapt from behind a rock where he was sheltering and managed to get the panic-stricken soldier away from the charge just before it exploded, being wounded in the process. For this act of bravery, Tversky was awarded Israel's highest military decoration.

Tversky graduated from the Hebrew University of Jerusalem with a bachelor of arts degree in 1961, majoring in philosophy and psychology, and he received a PhD degree from the University of Michigan in 1965. While studying for his doctorate, he met and married Barbara Gans, a fellow graduate student who later became a professor of cognitive psychology at Stanford University and with whom he had three children, Oren, Tal, and Dona. He taught at the Hebrew University of Jerusalem from 1966 to 1978 and then at Stanford University, where he was the first Davis-Brack Professor of Behavioral Sciences and principal investigator at the Stanford Center on Conflict and Negotiation. He spent leave periods at Harvard University, the Center for Advanced Studies in the Behavioral Sciences in Stanford, and the Oregon Research Institute. Tversky made frequent trips to Israel throughout his years in the United States, and from 1992 he was senior visiting professor of economics and psychology and permanent fellow of the Sackler Institute of Advanced Studies at Tel Aviv University. Although he tended to shun administrative work, he was in Stanford University's Faculty Senate from 1990 until his death and sat on the

Academic Council's advisory board to the president and provost.

Early Work. Tversky's early research was devoted to the study of individual choice behavior and the foundations of psychological measurement, preoccupations that were combined in his doctoral dissertation. His dissertation comprised a mathematical analysis of the necessary and sufficient conditions for the satisfaction of certain requirements of psychological measurement and an experimental test of expected utility theory. Expected utility theory is the theoretical foundation of orthodox decision theory, according to which decision makers choose options that maximize expected utility, a measure of the subjective desirability of outcomes or events. Tversky's doctoral dissertation, supervised by Clyde Coombs, earned him the Marquis Award from the University of Michigan.

Conjoint Measurement Theory. While working on his dissertation, Tversky met David H. Krantz, who joined the University of Michigan's faculty in 1964; this led to a fruitful collaboration on aspects of mathematical psychology, including conjoint measurement theory and multidimensional scaling. Conjoint measurement theory, introduced in 1964 by R. Duncan Luce and John W. Tukey, provides a mathematical method of constructing measurement scales for objects with multiple attributes—for example, houses that vary according to price, location, and number of rooms, or job applicants whose application forms reveal different strengths and weaknesses—in such a way that attributes are traded off against one another and the resultant value of each object is a suitable function of the scale values of its component attributes. In 1965 Luce invited Tversky and Krantz to join him and Patrick Suppes in coauthoring *The Foundations of Measurement,* which, when it was completed in 1990, became a major three-volume work. Among other things, this project presents a fully developed analysis of conjoint measurement that, because it provides a much-needed method of measuring and interpreting responses to multiattribute alternatives, has had an impact on commercial applications in market research and other areas.

Transitivity. Expected utility theory and other normative theories of choice require preferences to satisfy basic axioms, one of the most fundamental and compelling of which is transitivity. A decision maker who prefers *a* to *b* and *b* to *c* cannot, according to normative accounts, also prefer *c* to *a*—for example, a person who prefers tea to coffee and coffee to cocoa cannot prefer cocoa to tea without violating the consistency axiom. Intransitive preferences are considered a violation of rational choice. In "Intransitivity of Preferences" (1969), one of the most fre-

quently cited of Tversky's early publications, he reported on an experimental procedure that reliably induces people to violate the transitivity axiom. According to Tversky's interpretation of this phenomenon, people, when making decisions, often use approximation methods that work quite well but sometimes generate predictable errors. Such errors, in turn, can help us to understand how the decisions were made.

Theory of Similarity. The theory of similarity, known as the Contrast model, was presented by Tversky in "Features of Similarity" (1977) and elaborated by Tversky and Itamar Gati in "Studies of Similarity" (1978). This theory provided an explanation for a number of judgmental anomalies that had been observed by other researchers. In particular, it explained a remarkable asymmetry that had been noted in similarity judgments, wherein *a* may be judged as more similar to *b* than *b* is to *a*. For example, it seems more natural to claim that a son resembles his father than that a father resembles his son, and Tel Aviv is generally considered more similar to New York City than New York City is to Tel Aviv. These observations are inconsistent with the usual representation of similarity in terms of proximity of points in coordinate Euclidian space.

Tversky pointed out that our representations of stimuli are rich and complex, including attributes associated with appearance, function, relation to other objects, and further attributes inferred from general world knowledge. Objects or stimuli, he proposed, are represented by a collection of features, with some features necessarily attended to more than others, depending on the nature of the task. In his theory, each object *a* is denoted by a set *A* of features, and the similarity of *a* to *b*, denoted by $s(a, b)$, is a weighted linear function of three arguments, namely the features that *a* and *b* share in common, denoted by $A \cap B$, the distinctive features of *a*, denoted by $A - B$, and the distinctive features of *b*, denoted by $B - A$. Similarity increases with the measures of the common features and decreases with the measures of the distinctive features. The theory also includes a scale factor *f*, reflecting the salience or prominence of the various features and parameters allowing common or distinctive features to be weighted more or less heavily. Asymmetry of similarity can arise from one of the objects or stimuli (e.g., New York City) having more distinctive features than the other (Tel Aviv) or from a shift of attention, causing the person to focus on one of the stimuli as compared to the other, thus weighting its distinctive features more heavily than those of the referent. Hence, a toy train is quite similar to a real train, because most features of the toy train are included in the real train, but a real train is not as similar to a toy train, because many of its features are absent from a toy train. Tversky proved that, if the distinctive features of the subject are weighted more heavily than those of the referent, then $s(a, b) > s(b, a)$ if and only if $f(B - A) > f(A - B)$, which means that a appears more similar to b than b does to a if and only if the distinctive features of b are more salient than those of a, and this is generally the case when b is more prominent than a.

Elimination by Aspects. Another of Tversky's highly influential contributions was his article, "Elimination by Aspects" (1972). It describes a new theory of multiattribute decision making. According to the standard value-maximization model of multiattribute choice, a decision maker choosing between alternatives with multiple attributes forms a weighted average of each alternative's attribute values, the weights corresponding to perceived attribute importance, and then chooses the alternative with the highest average weighted value. But there are reasons to doubt that this model accurately reflects the behavior of decision makers with bounded rationality facing complex choices. Suppose a decision maker has to choose between two travel agencies a_1 and a_2 offering tours to two different destinations d_1 (Greece) and d_2 (South Africa). Agency a_1 offers only d_1, whereas agency a_2 offers both d_1 and d_2. There are three feasible combinations of travel agency and destination, a_1d_1, a_2d_1, and a_2d_2, and if the decision maker is equally attracted by Greece and South Africa and is also indifferent between the travel agencies, then each combination should have the same probability of being chosen, according to the standard value-maximization model. But it seems intuitively obvious that most people would choose first between the destinations and only then between the travel agencies, because destination is a more important attribute of a trip than travel agency. With this stipulation, although the decision maker is equally attracted to Greece and South Africa and is therefore equally likely to choose d_1 or d_2, the probabilities of choosing each of the three feasible combinations are $p(a_1d_1) = p(d_1)p(a_1) = 1/4$, $p(a_2d_1) = p(d_1)p(a_2) = 1/4$, and $p(a_2d_2) = p(d_2) = 1/2$. Thus, one of the agency-destination combinations is twice as likely to be chosen as either of the others.

This intuition is captured in Tversky's elimination by aspects (EBA) theory, according to which choice is reached through an iterated series of eliminations. At each iteration the decision maker selects an aspect (or attribute) whose probability of selection is proportional to its perceived importance, and eliminates all alternatives that fail to satisfy on that aspect. The decision maker then selects the next aspect and proceeds this way until all but one of the alternatives have been eliminated. This is a stochastic version of lexicographic choice; that is, it introduces a probabilistic element into a procedure where the decision maker first compares the alternatives on the most important attribute, then on the next most important attribute,

and so on until one alternative emerges as best (or else the set of attributes is exhausted without a definite preference emerging). In "Preference Trees" (1979), Tversky and Shmuel Sattath presented a revised version of EBA. Pretree, as the theory is also called, is more parsimonious than the general EBA model because it has fewer parameters. In essence, it is a restricted version of EBA that arranges subsets of similar alternatives in a hierarchical structure. Each alternative is represented as a collection of aspects and the entire ensemble of aspects is assumed to have a tree structure. At each stage, the decision maker selects an aspect (corresponding to a branch of the tree) and eliminates all the alternatives that do not belong on the selected branch; the process continues until a single alternative remains. Although lexicographic choice is not guaranteed to produce an optimal decision, experimental tests have tended to confirm the hypothesis that a process resembling EBA is characteristic of human multiattribute decision making.

Heuristics and Biases. From 1969 until the early 1980s, Tversky enjoyed an exceptionally fruitful collaboration with Daniel Kahneman, during which they initiated their influential research into heuristics and biases, prospect theory, and framing effects. Tversky was an owl, often working through the night, and Kahneman was a lark (a morning person), so their normal pattern of collaboration involved having lunch and working together through the afternoon. Heuristics, which Tversky and Kahneman illustrated through many clever vignettes, are rough-and-ready judgmental procedures or rules of thumb that are quick and useful but sometimes lead to systematic biases and errors. In 1971 Tversky and Kahneman published their first joint article, "Belief in the Law of Small Numbers." They showed that people tend to believe that the law of large numbers applies to small numbers as well or, in other words, that people expect even small samples to be representative of the populations from which they are drawn. Even researchers trained in statistics were shown to grossly overestimate the representativeness of small samples and to make other unwarranted inferences from data. This undermined the view widely accepted at the time that people are rather good intuitive statisticians.

A classic article, "Subjective Probability" (1972), naturally followed. In it, Kahneman and Tversky provided a theoretical interpretation of what looked like belief in the law of small numbers and laid the foundations of the heuristics and biases research program. For example, participants were asked to estimate probabilities, such as the probability that the average height of a group of people is over six feet. Participants produced almost identical estimates for group sizes of ten, one hundred, and one thousand, whereas in reality the probability that a sample average will be substantially higher than the population average is much greater for a small sample than a large one. This "sample size fallacy" is explained by the representativeness heuristic, in which people estimate the probability that something belongs to, or originates from, a particular class by the extent to which it is representative or typical of the class. This can lead to judgmental errors because perceived representativeness is insensitive to base rates and to sample sizes.

Next came the availability heuristic, according to which people judge the frequency or probability of an event by the ease with which instances of it come to mind. For example, one may assess the risk of heart attack among middle-aged people by recalling specific instances among one's acquaintances or through media exposure. Like other heuristics, availability provides a useful clue for assessing frequency or probability because it is usually easier to recall instances of classes that are big or frequent rather than instances of classes that are small and rare. Because availability is affected by factors other than frequency and probability, however, this heuristic, like other heuristics, can generate biased or incorrect judgment. For example, Tversky and Kahneman showed that when people are asked whether the English language contains more words beginning with the letter *k* or more words having the letter *k* in the third position, most find it easier to think of instances of the former rather than the latter, whereas in fact a typical long text contains twice as many words with *k* in the third position. In 1974 Tversky and Kahneman published a classic article, "Judgment under Uncertainty," that reviewed the basic findings. It brought heuristics and biases to the attention of a wide readership outside psychology, where the ideas were already well-known. In 1982 a book edited by Kahneman, Tversky, and Paul Slovic, *Judgment under Uncertainty: Heuristics and Biases,* collected a large number of relevant papers and brought the heuristics and biases research program to an ever-wider readership.

Prospect Theory. Kahneman and Tversky's "Prospect Theory," arguably their most important and influential joint work, appeared in 1979. It is an explicitly descriptive theory of risky choice, and it is built on a number of fundamental principles that have become the prominent alternative to expected utility theory in accounting for decision making in the real world. Prospect theory highlights several ways in which preferences tend to violate expected utility theory. Probabilities, according to prospect theory, are nonlinear, with very small probabilities often overweighted and moderate to high probabilities underweighted. Furthermore, people tend to evaluate outcomes as gains or losses relative to a current reference point or the status quo rather than in terms of final wealth, in contrast to expected utility theory, where outcomes are final states, irrespective of whether they were reached by gaining or losing. The theory is typically depicted by an S-shaped value function that assigns a subjective value to amounts gained or lost. The upper part of the function, representing gains, is concave, whereas the lower part, representing losses, is convex. This yields conflicting risk attitudes: risk aversion in the context of choices involving gains but risk seeking for losses.

Furthermore, the slope of the value function is steeper for losses than for corresponding gains, capturing the observation that a loss has greater subjective impact than an equivalent gain, which is known as "loss aversion." For example, most people will reject a fifty-fifty gamble in which they might lose twenty dollars unless they stand to win more than forty dollars. This discovery has profound implications not only for choice, but also for negotiation and the power of the status quo. One remarkable implication is the endowment effect, a phenomenon discovered by the economist Richard Thaler. The effect is illustrated by the owner of a bottle of vintage wine who refuses to sell it for two hundred dollars but would not pay more than one hundred dollars to replace it. The effect is explained by two principles of prospect theory: first, that the carriers of utility are not states (owning or not owning the wine), but gains or losses, and second, by loss aversion, the fact that losing an item in one's possession hurts more than obtaining that item is deemed worthwhile. In "Experiences of Collaborative Research" (2003), Kahneman expressed the view that the concept of loss aversion was the most useful contribution to the study of decision making made by his work with Tversky.

In "The Framing of Decisions and the Psychology of Choice" (1981), Tversky and Kahneman presented experimental data showing that 84 percent of a group of undergraduate students preferred a sure gain of $240 to a gamble involving a 25 percent chance of gaining $1,000 and a 75 percent chance of gaining nothing (risk aversion for gains), but 87 percent preferred a gamble involving a 75 percent chance of losing $1,000 and a 25 percent chance of losing nothing to a sure loss of $750 (risk seeking for losses). Combining these prospects, most respondents were expressing a preference for a portfolio containing a 25 percent chance of winning $240 and a 75 percent chance of losing $760 over a portfolio containing a 25 percent chance of winning $250 and a 75 percent chance of losing $750, contrary to the requirement of dominance. In "Advances in Prospect Theory" (1992), Tversky and Kahneman published an updated version of prospect theory called cumulative prospect theory, which was predicated on similar psychological principles but could be applied to more varied sets of alternatives.

Framing Effects. A framing effect occurs when people make different choices as a result of changes in the description, labeling, or presentation of options that do not logically alter the information available. In 1981 Tversky and Kahneman provided a classic example in "The Framing of Decisions and the Psychology of Choice." They invited participants to choose between two programs for combating a disease that was expected to kill 600 people. Participants in one group were told that program *A* would save 200 lives, whereas program *B* had a one-third probability of saving 600 lives and a two-thirds probability of saving no one; in this "gain" frame, 72 percent preferred *A* to *B*. Participants in a second group were told that under program *C*, 400 people would die, whereas under program *D* there was a one-third probability that no one would die and a two-thirds probability that all 600 would die; in this "loss" frame, 78 percent preferred *D* to *C*. As predicted, the majority of participants exhibited a risk-averse preference for *A* over *B* in the "gain" frame, but a risk-seeking preference for *D* over *C* in the "loss" frame. This is a framing effect, because the two frames presented different but logically equivalent descriptions of the same choice problem but elicited highly discrepant preferences. As suggested earlier, this effect is well explained by prospect theory, as are framing effects in the context of riskless choice.

Later Work. In the early 1990s, Tversky collaborated with Eldar Shafir and others in investigations of reason-based choice. People, they proposed, tend to look for compelling reasons when there are no obvious rules or evaluations to guide their decisions. This may be the standard method of decision making in legal contexts, for example. In "The Disjunction Effect in Choice under Uncertainty" (1992), Tversky and Shafir described an experiment in which they asked participants to assume they had just taken a tough qualifying examination. Members of one group were told they had passed the exam, others were told that they had failed, and those in a third group were told that they would learn the results the following day. Members of each group were invited to choose between buying a vacation in Hawaii immediately, not buying the vacation, or paying five dollars to retain the right to buy the vacation the following day. The majority of those who had purportedly passed or failed the examination chose to buy the vacation, but the majority of those who did not know the examination's outcome chose to retain the right to buy the vacation the following day, presumably because they did not have a compelling reason to buy it while the exam's outcome was unknown.

Tversky's last major contribution was support theory, developed in collaboration with Derek Koehler in an article titled "Support Theory" (1994). "Unpacking, Repacking, and Anchoring" (1997), an article by Yuval Rottenstreich and Tversky that elaborated support theory, was in press when Tversky died. Support theory was inspired by an observation reported in the literature that

the independently judged probabilities of an event and its complement generally sum to approximately one, but the judged probabilities of separate constituents of an inclusive event usually sum to more than the judged probability of that inclusive event. Tversky and Koehler showed that many descriptions of events are implicit disjunctions whose subjective probability is less than the sum of the components, once the former are unpacked. For example, when people are asked to judge the probability that a random person will die from an accident, judgments tend to be less than the sum of judgments of the separate possible causes—road traffic accidents, plane crashes, fire, drowning, and so on—that form part of the notion of an accident.

The basic elements in support theory are descriptions of events, called hypotheses. Descriptions are presented to participants for probabilistic judgment, and it is assumed that they are evaluated in terms of a mathematically defined "support function," s, which yields the judged support value $s(\alpha)$ for a description α. The theory assumes that different descriptions of the same event often produce different subjective probability estimates, and it explains this phenomenon in terms of subjective judgments of supporting evidence, which are eventually combined to yield judged support according to an equation specified in the theory. The process of evaluation is assumed to incorporate standard heuristics and therefore to be subject to the familiar biases. The theory explains the conjunction fallacy, a judgmental error identified and named by Tversky and Kahneman in "Extensional versus Intuitive Reasoning" (1983), according to which a conjunction of two or more attributes is judged to be more probable or likely than either attribute on its own. For example, Tversky and Kahneman presented undergraduate students with personality sketches of a hypothetical person called Linda (young, single, deeply concerned about social issues, and involved in antinuclear activity) and asked whether it was more probable that (a) Linda is a bank teller or that (b) Linda is a bank teller who is active in the feminist movement. Eighty-six percent of the students judged (b) to be more probable than (a). This is a fallacy, because the probability of a conjunction can never exceed the probability of either of its conjuncts. It is consistent with a reliance on the representativeness heuristic, because Linda appears more typical of a feminist bank teller than of a bank teller. The example also captures the aesthetic combination of compelling psychological intuition and insightful normative critique that characterized so much of Tversky's work.

Early in 1996, Amos Tversky was told that he had only months to live. Kahneman and Tversky began editing a book on decision making that would draw together the progress that had been made since they began working together on the topic more than twenty years earlier. That book, *Choices, Values, and Frames,* appeared in 2000, four years after Tversky's death. Tversky kept working until a few weeks before he died, and when he died he had twelve articles in press. An astonishing number of his papers continue to be considered both seminal and definitive.

Honors and Awards. Tversky's academic accomplishments were recognized with many honors and awards. Tversky was elected to the American Academy of Arts and Sciences in 1980, to the National Academy of Sciences in 1985, and to the Econometric Society in 1993. He shared with Daniel Kahneman the American Psychological Association's award for distinguished scientific contribution in 1982 and posthumously, in 2003, the University of Louisville Grawemeyer Award for Psychology. In 1984 he was awarded both a MacArthur Foundation Fellowship, given to "talented individuals who have shown extraordinary originality and dedication in their creative pursuits and a marked capacity for self-direction," and a Guggenheim Fellowship, awarded to "men and women who have already demonstrated exceptional capacity for productive scholarship or exceptional creative ability in the arts." He received the Warren Medal of the Society of Experimental Psychologists in 1995 and was awarded honorary doctorates by the University of Chicago, Yale University, the State University of New York at Buffalo, and the University of Göteborg in Sweden. The University of Chicago honorary degree citation in 1988 stated: "Through your extraordinary blend of inventive theory and creative experimentation, you have illuminated complex behavioral phenomena and influenced work by many other social scientists, who have been inspired by the combination of your substantive insights, rigorous modeling, and exacting use of experimental methods."

BIBLIOGRAPHY

WORKS BY TVERSKY

"Intransitivity of Preferences." *Psychological Review* 76 (1969): 31–48.

With Daniel Kahneman. "Belief in the Law of Small Numbers." *Psychological Bulletin* 76 (1971): 105–110.

With David H. Krantz, R. Duncan Luce, and Patrick Suppes. *Foundations of Measurement.* 3 vols. New York: Academic Press, 1971–1990.

"Elimination by Aspects: A Theory of Choice." *Psychological Review* 79 (1972): 281–299.

With Daniel Kahneman. "Subjective Probability: A Judgment of Representativeness." *Cognitive Psychology* 3 (1972): 430–454.

With Daniel Kahneman. "Judgment under Uncertainty: Heuristics and Biases." *Science* 185 (1974): 1124–1131.

"Features of Similarity." *Psychological Review* 84 (1977): 327–352.

With Itamar Gati. "Studies of Similarity." In *Cognition and Categorization,* edited by Eleanor Rosch and Barbara B. Lloyd. Hillsdale, NJ: Erlbaum, 1978.

With Shmuel Sattath. "Preference Trees." *Psychological Review* 86 (1979): 542–573. An updated version of the theory of elimination by aspects.

With Daniel Kahneman. "Prospect Theory: An Analysis of Decision under Risk." *Econometrica* 47 (1979): 263–291.

With Daniel Kahneman. "The Framing of Decisions and the Psychology of Choice." *Science* 211 (1981): 453–458.

With Daniel Kahneman and Paul Slovic, eds. *Judgment under Uncertainty: Heuristics and Biases.* Cambridge, U.K., and New York: Cambridge University Press, 1982.

With Daniel Kahneman. "Extensional versus Intuitive Reasoning: The Conjunction Fallacy in Probability Judgment." *Psychological Review* 90 (1983): 293–315.

With Daniel Kahneman. "Advances in Prospect Theory: Cumulative Representation of Uncertainty." *Journal of Risk and Uncertainty* 5 (1992): 297–323.

With Eldar Shafir. "The Disjunction Effect in Choice under Uncertainty." *Psychological Science* 3 (1992): 305–309.

With Derek J. Koehler. "Support Theory: A Nonextensional Representation of Subjective Probability." *Psychological Review* 101 (1994): 547–567.

With Yuval S. Rottenstreich. "Unpacking, Repacking, and Anchoring: Advances in Support Theory." *Psychological Review* 104 (1997): 406–415.

With Daniel Kahneman, eds. *Choices, Values, and Frames.* New York: Russell Sage Foundation, 2000; Cambridge, U.K. Cambridge University Press, 2000.

Preference, Belief, and Similarity: Selected Writings. Edited by Eldar Shafir. Cambridge, MA: MIT Press, 2003.

OTHER SOURCES

Evans, Jonathan St. B. T., and David E. Over. "The Contribution of Amos Tversky." *Thinking and Reasoning* 3 (1997): 1–8.

Gilovich, Thomas, Dale Griffin, and Daniel Kahneman, eds. *Heuristics and Biases: The Psychology of Intuitive Judgment.* Cambridge, U.K., and New York: Cambridge University Press, 2002.

Kahneman, Daniel. "Experiences of Collaborative Research." *American Psychologist* 58 (2003): 723–730.

———. "Maps of Bounded Rationality: A Perspective on Intuitive Judgment and Choice." In *Les Prix Nobel 2002: The Nobel Prizes 2002,* edited by Tore Frängsmyr. Stockholm: Nobel Foundation, 2003.

———, and Eldar Shafir. "Amos Tversky (1937–1996)." *American Psychologist* 53 (1998): 793–794.

Laibson, David, and Richard Zeckhauser. "Amos Tversky and the Ascent of Behavioral Economics." *Journal of Risk and Uncertainty* 16 (1998): 7–47.

McDermott, Rose. "The Psychological Ideas of Amos Tversky and Their Relevance for Political Science." *Journal of Theoretical Politics* 13 (2001): 5–33.

Shafir, Eldar, ed. "Belief and Decision: The Continuing Legacy of Amos Tversky." Special issue, *Cognitive Psychology* 38, no. 1 (1999).

———, ed. *Preference, Belief, and Similarity: The Selected Writings of Amos Tversky.* Cambridge, MA: MIT Press, 2004.

Andrew M. Colman
Eldar Shafir

U

UHLENBECK, GEORGE EUGENE

(*b.* Batavia, Java, Dutch East Indies [now Jakarta, Indonesia], 6 December 1900; *d.* Boulder, Colorado, 31 October 1988), *theoretical physics, statistical mechanics, nuclear and atomic physics.*

Uhlenbeck is perhaps most widely known for the discovery of electron spin, a discovery made jointly with Samuel Goudsmit when they were both graduate students at Leiden. In later years he did much important work in atomic structure, nuclear physics, and especially kinetic theory and statistical mechanics. Throughout his career he had a reputation as a superb lecturer and teacher.

Early Life and Education. Uhlenbeck was born into a military family in the Dutch East Indies. His father, Eugenius Marius Uhlenbeck, was a lieutenant colonel, while his mother, Anne Marie Beeger was the daughter of a major general. Of the four surviving children, George was the oldest son; he had an older sister Annie and two younger brothers Willem Jan and Eugenius Marius. In 1907 his father retired and, with the children's education in mind, the family moved permanently to the Netherlands. There they resided in The Hague, where Uhlenbeck attended elementary and high school. In high school he was influenced by his physics teacher, A. H. Borgesius, who encouraged him to read further in mathematics and physics. He was especially impressed by Hendrik A. Lorentz's textbook, *Beginselen der Natuurkunde* (Elements of physics; 2 vols., 1908–1909). In July 1918 Uhlenbeck obtained high marks in his final school examination. However, because his school studies had not included Latin and Greek, he could not enter a university; by law

entrance then required proficiency in those languages. Instead he entered the Technical University at Delft to study chemical engineering. Shortly afterward, the law was changed and he entered the University at Leiden in January 1919. There Uhlenbeck studied physics and mathematics under the professors Paul Ehrenfest, Heike Kamerlingh Onnes, and Johannes P. Kuenen, while the retired Lorentz came to lecture once per week. While still an undergraduate he studied Ludwig Boltzmann's *Vorlesungen über Gastheorie* (Lectures on gas theory; 2 vols, 1896–1898), which he found hard to understand until he discovered the article *Begriffliche Grundlagen* (Conceptual foundations; 1912) of Paul and Tatania Ehrenfest, which "was a revelation." These studies, together with his careful notes on Maxwell theory, so impressed his teachers that in his third and final year he was granted a state fellowship, sparing his parents the expense of tuition. In December 1920 he took his final examinations and became a graduate of Leiden. He then became a graduate student there.

Graduate Studies. As a graduate student Uhlenbeck at first supported himself by teaching part time at a high school in Leiden. He apparently disliked this work, but it gave him enough money to rent a room in Leiden while he continued his studies. He followed lectures by Paul Ehrenfest and was invited to attend the Wednesday evening colloquia, a Leiden tradition. Attendance was by invitation, and once invited, one was expected to continue attending.

Late in his second year of graduate studies, he heard from Ehrenfest of a teaching position in Rome. So it was that in September 1922 he took the post of tutor to a son of the Dutch ambassador to Italy, although he did not entirely neglect his studies. In September 1923 he received from Leiden the degree of doctorandus, roughly equivalent to a master's degree, or admission to a doctoral program in an American university. While in Rome he studied the Italian language, becoming sufficiently proficient to enable him to attend lectures in mathematics at the University of Rome. Upon his return to Leiden in the summer of 1923, Ehrenfest had asked him to contact Enrico Fermi, so it was that in the fall of 1923 that the two became acquainted. Together with other young Italian physicists, they organized a small Leiden-style colloquium. In this way Uhlenbeck and Fermi became close and longtime friends. It is said that it was Uhlenbeck who introduced Fermi, the native Roman, to the wonders of Roman art. Be that as it may, at about the same time Uhlenbeck became fascinated with art and art history, neglecting completely his studies of physics during his second year in Rome. His first published paper, which appeared in 1924, was on the topic of art. Only his contacts with Fermi and the other young physicists kept him from completely losing touch with physics.

In June 1925 Uhlenbeck returned to Leiden with the intention of studying art history. However, here his old nemesis, the classical languages, came back to haunt him. He began a serious study of Latin but was counseled by an uncle to continue his study of physics as "more practical." Accordingly, he contacted Ehrenfest, who agreed to take him on as a student. Thus began a relationship that had a profound and lasting influence. At first Uhlenbeck found the daily meetings to be exhausting and the emphasis on clarity as opposed to rigor frustrating, but he soon grew more comfortable. He wrote a paper on the wave equation in odd and even number of spatial dimensions, which was followed by a joint paper with Ehrenfest on the same topic.

Ehrenfest had suggested that he work with a fellow student, Goudsmit, who already was an expert on atomic spectra. The two of them wrote a paper on the spectrum of hydrogen, giving an improved interpretation involving half-integer quantum numbers. Then came their great discovery: electron spin. The quantum numbers they had assigned implied that the electron must have another degree of freedom; it must be rotating. With this idea everything fell into place. They published first a short note and then, at the encouragement of Niels Bohr, who visited Leiden shortly after their discovery, a longer paper that appeared in *Nature*. The origin of the spin-orbit interaction was apparently suggested by Albert Einstein, who also visited Leiden at the time and pointed out that in its rest frame, the electron sees an orbiting nucleus and hence a magnetic field. There remained an awkward factor of two in the spin precession rate. This was soon explained as a relativistic effect in an elegant paper by Llewellen H. Thomas. In their third and final paper on electron spin, Goudsmit and Uhlenbeck summarized

George Uhlenbeck. *George Uhlenbeck (left) with Samuel Goudsmit.* SPL/PHOTO RESEARCHERS, INC.

these results and gave what has become the accepted interpretation of electron spin and atomic spectra.

The discovery of electron spin was in the spirit of the old Bohr quantum mechanics. The new quantum mechanics had been born only a few months earlier with the appearance of Werner Heisenberg's first paper in July 1925. In common with most physicists of the time, Uhlenbeck found the new theory, with its mathematics of matrices, daunting. When in January 1926 Erwin Schrödinger's first paper on wave mechanics appeared, it came as a great relief: the mathematics of wave equations was much more familiar. In the spring of 1926 he studied assiduously Schrödinger's wave mechanics, becoming adept in the new quantum theory. Then Oskar Klein came to Leiden as a visitor, and he and Uhlenbeck had long discussions about the Klein-Gordon wave equation as well as Klein's ideas of unifying the Maxwell and Einstein equations through a five-dimensional wave equation. Uhlenbeck was much taken with the latter, writing a paper with Ehrenfest.

Since Uhlenbeck's study of Ludwig Boltzmann in his early student days, he had been fascinated with statistical physics, so when it came time to choose a thesis topic, it was in that field. The topic was the Boltzmann description of an ideal gas and its extension to the new Bose-Einstein and Fermi-Dirac statistics. Through his later writings and lectures, this material became familiar to a generation of physicists. In a brief passage in the thesis, he criticized Einstein's prediction of what came to be called the Bose-Einstein condensation. This presaged a lifelong interest in the problem of condensation: how does it come about that the equation of state shows a sharp discontinuity when a gas condenses to a liquid? It was another decade before it came to be recognized that the discontinuity occurs only in the thermodynamic limit in which the number of gas particles and the volume containing the gas each become infinite such that the ratio remains finite.

First Period at Michigan. Among the distractions at Leiden, writing the thesis was difficult. Therefore, Ehrenfest arranged a fellowship that allowed Uhlenbeck to spend two intensive months in the spring of 1927 at the Bohr Institute in Copenhagen, Denmark. There he did little but write his thesis. After finishing his dissertation he spent a month in Göttingen, Germany, where he met, among others, J. Robert Oppenheimer. He returned to Leiden with Oppenheimer, who was for a short time an assistant to Ehrenfest. After that things happened quickly. He and Goudsmit defended their theses on the same day, 7 July 1927. It had already been decided that they would go to Ann Arbor as instructors at the University of Michigan. That spring Walter Colby, a professor of theoretical physics at Michigan, had visited Europe seeking a candidate to replace Klein, who had returned to Europe after three years in Ann Arbor. Ehrenfest strongly urged him to consider making an offer to a pair of candidates, so they would have someone to talk to in the "wilderness." This he was able to do and Uhlenbeck and Goudsmit were both happy to accept, because it meant that they would be in a university and not have to teach in a high school. Then, on 23 August, Uhlenbeck married Else Ophorst, who had been a chemistry student at Leiden. In 1942 their son, Olke Cornelius, was born. He would go on to become a distinguished biochemist. On their arrival in New York, Oppenheimer met the newlyweds; the elegant apartment of Oppenheimer's parents especially impressed them. A short time later they arrived at Ann Arbor in time for the fall term.

Although at that time the United States had no rival of the European centers of theoretical physics, they found Ann Arbor to be not quite the wilderness they expected. Aside from Colby, there were two young theoretical physicists: Otto Laporte, a student of Arnold Sommerfeld who had arrived the year before, and David Dennison, who had received his PhD at Michigan under the direction of Colby and Klein and was returning after three years in Europe. Through these four young men, theoretical physics at Michigan rapidly grew in importance. There already existed a summer program of visiting lectures,

instituted in 1923 by Harrison M. Randall, chairman of the Physics Department, but it had remained modest and mostly of local interest. Under the influence of these younger men, and especially Uhlenbeck, this program changed quickly in character, becoming the Ann Arbor Summer Symposia in Theoretical Physics. These were internationally important events, unique in America, perhaps in the world, with distinguished rosters of lecturers. These summer schools continued until 1941, after which wartime conditions made them impracticable. They resumed after the war but were no longer unique and finally, after 1973, were discontinued.

The first notable work out of Michigan after the arrival of the young physicists was a study of rotational Brownian motion, published in 1929 jointly by Uhlenbeck and Goudsmit. In this work they explained observations by Walter Gerlach of the rotational motion of a tiny mirror fixed on a fine wire, showing how it was that for different pressures of the surrounding gas, the mean square displacement was the same while the displacement in time looked very different. This work presaged the classic paper by Uhlenbeck and Leonard Ornstein on the theory of Brownian motion, which appeared the following year. In that work Uhlenbeck and Ornstein initiated the modern description of Brownian motion, obtaining expressions at all times for the probability distributions for the positions and for the velocity. In doing this they made implicit use of what came to be called the Gaussian property of the Ornstein-Uhlenbeck process. Interestingly, although they obtained expressions for the moments of the joint distribution in position and velocity, they did not obtain either the joint probability distribution or the corresponding Fokker-Planck equation. This was remedied and more by a review article written by Uhlenbeck and Ming Chen Wang and published in 1945. This review article, which is still a standard reference in the field, summarized the theory of Brownian motion within the framework of the general theory of stochastic processes. It is a masterpiece of simplicity and clarity of exposition. These two articles—that with Ornstein and the review article with Wang—established Uhlenbeck as preeminent in the field.

Worth noting from those early days is a paper with Dennison, published in 1932, on the inversion spectrum of ammonia, in which the nitrogen atom makes a transition between equilibrium positions on either side of the plane of the three hydrogen atoms. What is interesting about this paper, aside from the fact that it was the first real application of the quantum mechanical double well problem, is that it sparked the birth of microwave spectroscopy, which resulted in the first direct measurement of the inversion transition. It was, however, ahead of its time, and microwave spectroscopy came into its own only after the World War II developments in radar.

The 1930s saw the rise of interest in nuclear physics, which was the topic of a Summer Symposium lecture in 1931 by Wolfgang Pauli and another in 1933 by Fermi. Inspired by these talks and related discussions, Uhlenbeck wrote, with his student Emil Konopinski, a pair of papers in 1935 on the theory of beta decay, proposing an alternative to the recently appeared Fermi theory involving gradients of the wave function. While at the time this Konopinski-Uhlenbeck theory seemed to give a better fit to the observed spectrum of electron energies, eventually improved techniques gave results supporting the subsequently-accepted Fermi theory. In 1941 Uhlenbeck and Konopinsky returned to the subject, offering a masterful discussion of the Fermi theory in its most general form, describing selection rules and energy distributions for allowed and forbidden transitions and arbitrarily charged nuclei.

Another contribution to nuclear physics appeared in a pair of papers written in 1950 with his student, David Falkoff. The subject was the angular correlation in successive nuclear radiations. Their work was important because it systematized the phenomena in great generality, forming a solid basis for the use of the method in determining the angular momentum and parity of excited states of nuclei.

Return to the Netherlands. In the fall of 1935 Uhlenbeck left Michigan to return to the Netherlands and take up the position of professor at the University of Utrecht. The position had become vacant after Hendrik Kramers, who had been a professor there, moved to Leiden upon the death of Ehrenfest. Soon after arriving, Uhlenbeck wrote a paper with Julian K. Knipp, a visiting fellow from Harvard University, in which they calculated the inner *bremsstrahlung* accompanying the beta decay of nuclei. At the time this was an important result, because it explained the faint radiation accompanying the decay of radium E.

While Uhlenbeck wrote a number of papers on topics in nuclear physics during his time at Utrecht, his most important work from that time is contained in a pair of papers, in 1937 and 1938, on the theory of condensation based on the thesis of his student, Boris Kahn. In his own thesis, Uhlenbeck had criticized Einstein's discussion of the Bose condensation, a criticism that at the time even Einstein considered serious. This changed rather dramatically at a 1937 conference in Amsterdam celebrating the one hundredth anniversary of the birth of the physicist Johannes Diderik van der Waals. There the subject of phase transitions was much discussed and Kramers made the important point that the associated sharp discontinuity could occur only in the thermodynamic limit. This Uhlenbeck realized at once, and in the papers with Kahn he not only accepted the Einstein theory but used it as a

model for a general theory of condensation. Kahn and Uhlenbeck's idea was that the phase transition is related to a singularity appearing in the equation of state when expressed in terms of the fugacity, this only in the thermodynamic limit. This Kahn-Uhlenbeck theory remained for a decade and a half the accepted description of the condensation phase transition, despite the fact that it was unable to account for the liquid state. This was remedied by Chen Ning Yang and Tsung-Dao Lee. They showed that if one studied the problem in the entire complex fugacity plane, one could arrive at a simple and correct description of the transition. In the meantime, Uhlenbeck continued to work on the condensation problem. Together with his students Robert J. Riddel and George W. Ford, as well as the mathematician Frank Harary, he embarked on a study of the mathematical theory of linear graphs, which can be used to classify the terms in the virial expansion of the equation of state. This work, which is summarized in a review article with Ford, has had an interest and application well beyond the problem that inspired it.

Uhlenbeck's interest in the condensation problem persisted. Some years later, in a beautiful series of three papers jointly with Mark Kac and Per C. Hemmer in 1963 and 1964, he discussed a one-dimensional fluid model in which the particle interaction has a hard core and a long-range exponential attraction. It had earlier been shown by Kac that in the thermodynamic limit this is an exactly soluble model. In the first of these papers, the three authors showed that in the further limit in which the range of the exponential becomes infinite while the strength goes to zero, one obtains an equation of state exactly of the well-known van der Waals form. Moreover, because theirs is an exact calculation involving the thermodynamic limit, they obtain the Maxwell equal area rule, which in the usual discussion of the van der Waals equation is obtained by an ad hoc argument. Thus, for this model the problem of condensation could be exactly solved, with an explicit description of the gas-liquid phase transition. In the following two papers they went on to obtain expressions for the two- and three-particle distribution functions and to discuss the critical behavior.

In the fall of 1938, while still a professor at Utrecht, Uhlenbeck was invited to spend a semester at Columbia University in New York. There he shared an office with Fermi, who had recently fled from Italy, and learned about the newly discovered nuclear fission. At the end of the year he returned to Utrecht, but only for a short time. In August 1939 he returned permanently to the United States, taking up again the position of professor at the University of Michigan. Shortly afterward, Adolf Hitler invaded Poland and World War II began.

Second Period at Michigan. Uhlenbeck was soon involved in war work and in 1943 moved to the Radiation Laboratory in Cambridge, Massachusetts, as the leader of a group doing theoretical work on wave guides and other radar-related topics. It was there that he formed his friendship with the mathematician Kac, which remained close and was a source of mutual inspiration until Kac's death in 1984. Some of the results of this war work are described in a book, *Threshold Signals* (1950), edited jointly with James Lawson.

In 1945 Uhlenbeck returned to Ann Arbor, taking up again his professorship at the University of Michigan. Not long after he began his long collaboration with C. S. Wang Chang, writing in all some eleven papers on topics in kinetic theory, ranging from sound propagation in rarefied gases to the thickness of shock waves. Although these appeared only in the form of reports of the Engineering Research Institute of the University of Michigan, they were widely circulated and achieved a kind of cult status. Later, about half of these reports were reprinted in *Studies in Statistical Mechanics* (Vol. 3, 1965).

In the mid-1950s Uhlenbeck embarked on a study of the kinetic theory of dense gases, with the goal of obtaining a density expansion of the transport coefficients (viscosity, heat conduction, etc.) analogous to the well-known virial expansion of the equation of state for a nonideal gas. Together with his student, Soon Tahk Choh, Uhlenbeck used a method first introduced by Nikolai Bogoliubov to obtain the Choh-Uhlenbeck equation, a generalized Boltzmann equation that includes the effects of three-particle collisions. They went on to construct the Chapman-Enskog solution of this equation, obtaining formal expressions for the corrections to the transport coefficients of first order in the density. This work was carried on by others, but the dream of a virial expansion of the kinetic coefficients came to an end with the discovery that the contributions to the generalized Boltzmann equation from four or more particle collisions are divergent. This was a great disappointment, but Uhlenbeck's efforts remain as an important contribution and catalyst to work on the deep question of the approach to equilibrium.

In the summer of 1960 Uhlenbeck delivered a series of lectures in Boulder, Colorado, at a summer school under the auspices of American Mathematical Society. Out of these came a book, *Lectures in Statistical Mechanics* (1963), jointly authored with George Ford, in which the general theme is the approach to equilibrium.

Rockefeller Years and Retirement. In 1961 Uhlenbeck left Michigan for the Rockefeller Institute for Medical Research (now Rockefeller University) in New York City, where he was named professor and member of the institute. His reasons for making the move were in part the

attraction of joining his old friends Ted Berlin and Kac, who went there at the same time. He and Berlin had long planned to write together a book on statistical mechanics. Another reason might have been the infectious enthusiasm of Detlev W. Bronk, the president of the institute, about plans for building a university. In any event, Uhlenbeck made the move and, in addition to the work with Hemmer and Kac as described above, he directed a number of students on problems of statistical physics and kinetic theory. Unfortunately, with the unexpected death of Berlin in 1962, the book was never written.

In 1971 Uhlenbeck retired from Rockefeller, but he remained active until 1985, when failing health led to a move first to Champagne-Urbana, where his son Olke was professor of microbiology at the University of Illinois, then in 1986 to Boulder when Olke was appointed professor at the University of Colorado. There he died of a stroke at age eighty-seven.

George Uhlenbeck was renowned as a teacher and lecturer. His talks, orderly and systematic, were models of clarity. In his later years he received many honors: Higgins Lecturer, Princeton University, 1954; Member of the U.S. National Academy of Sciences, 1955; Lorentz Professor, Leiden University, 1955; Henry Russel Lecturer, University of Michigan, 1956; Oersted Medal of the American Association of Physics Teachers, 1956; president of the American Physical Society, 1959; Van der Waals Professor, Amsterdam University, 1964; Planck Medal of the German Physical Society (with Samuel Goudsmit), 1965; Lorentz Medal of the Royal Dutch Academy of Sciences, 1970; National Medal of Science of the United States, 1977; commander, Order of Orange-Nassau, the Netherlands, 1977; Wolf Foundation of Israel Prize in physics, 1979.

BIBLIOGRAPHY

A collection of unpublished papers and letters is in the Bentley Historical Library of the University of Michigan, Ann Arbor, where a list of published works will also be found. Other collections are in the Rockefeller University Archives, Tarrytown, New York, and the Niels Bohr Library of the American Institute of Physics, College Park, Maryland.

WORKS BY UHLENBECK

With Samuel Goudsmit. "Spinning Electrons and the Structure of Spectra." *Nature* 117 (1926): 264–265. The key paper announcing the discovery of spin.

Over Statistische Methoden in de Theorie de Quanta. PhD diss., Leiden. The Hague: Martinus Nijhoff, 1927.

With Leonard S. Ornstein. "On the Theory of the Brownian Motion." *Physical Review* 36 (1930): 823–841.

With Boris Kahn. "On the Theory of Condensation." *Physica* 4 (1937) 1155–1156; 5 (1938): 399–416. Kahn's dissertation has been reprinted in *Studies in Statistical Mechanics,* edited by Jan de Boer and George E. Uhlenbeck, Vol. 3, Part C. Amsterdam: North-Holland, 1965.

With Ming Chen Wang. "On the Theory of Brownian Motion II." *Reviews of Modern Physics* 17 (1945): 323–342. This and the above composed the famous papers on Brownian motion. They are both reprinted in the "noise book": *Selected Papers on Noise and Stochastic Processes,* edited by Nelson Wax (New York: Dover, 1954).

With James L. Lawson, eds. *Threshold Signals.* New York: McGraw-Hill, 1950.

With George W. Ford. "The Theory of Linear Graphs with Applications to the Theory of the Virial Development of the Properties of Gases." In *Studies in Statistical Mechanics,* edited by Jan de Boer and George E. Uhlenbeck, Vol. 1, Part B. Amsterdam: North-Holland, 1962.

———. *Lectures in Statistical Mechanics.* Providence, RI: American Mathematical Society, 1963.

With Mark Kac and Per C. Hemmer. "On the van der Waals Theory of the Vapor-Liquid Equilibrium. I. Discussion of the Distribution Functions." *Journal of Mathematical Physics* 4 (1963): 216–228. The work on condensation in a one-dimensional gas model.

With Per C. Hemmer and Mark Kac. "On the van der Waals Theory of the Vapor-Liquid Equilibrium. II. Discussion of the Distribution Functions." *Journal of Mathematical Physics* 4 (1963): 229–247.

———. "On the van der Waals Theory of the Vapor-Liquid Equilibrium. III. Discussion of the Cricital Region." *Journal of Mathematical Physics* 5 (1964): 60–74.

OTHER SOURCES

Cohen, E. G. D. "George E. Uhlenbeck and Statistical Mechanics." *American Journal of Physics* 58 (1990): 618–625. A short biography of Uhlenbeck.

Pais, Abraham. "George Uhlenbeck." In his *The Genius of Science: A Portrait Gallery.* Oxford: Oxford University Press, 2000.

George W. Ford

UNSÖLD, ALBRECHT OTTO JO-HANNES (*b.* Bolheim, Württemberg, Germany, 20 April 1905; *d.* Kiel, Germany, 23 September 1995), *astrophysics, stellar atmosphere physics.*

German astrophysicist Unsöld, for the longest part of his career based at the University of Kiel, was among the first researchers applying the formalism of quantum mechanics to the physics of stellar atmospheres.

Early Life and Studies. Unsöld, son of a Protestant minister, attended primary and secondary school in Heidenheim, Württemberg. He developed an early interest in science because both his father and grandfather, a school

teacher in Stuttgart, were botany enthusiasts and his uncle, who owned a notable physical cabinet, conducted experiments in wireless telegraphy and on dynamos. After reading Arnold Sommerfeld's fairly technical textbook on quantum theory, *Atombau und Spektrallinien* (Atomic structure and spectral lines), which had then just appeared, the precocious fourteen-year old Albrecht wrote a letter to the prominent author, enclosing a manuscript of his own. (Transcription of these letters, also including Sommerfeld's very friendly response, have been published by Weidemann.)

After passing his school finals (*Abitur*), Unsöld started studying mathematics and physics at nearby Tübingen University, choosing astronomy as his minor. He attended courses by Alfred Landé, Friedrich Paschen, and Ernst Back, all of whom specialized in spectroscopy, but after three terms Unsöld changed to the University of Munich to study with Sommerfeld.

His first two papers on spectroscopic issues appeared in the prestigious *Zeitschrift für Physik* in 1925 and 1926. At twenty-one years of age, Unsöld submitted his PhD thesis titled "Contributions to the Quantum Mechanics of Atoms" to the University of Munich, receiving his doctoral degree summa cum laude in February 1927. (According to the interview with Owen Gingerich, Unsöld had actually been assigned the task of calculating the molecular hydrogen ion, but this subject turned out to be too difficult because of two essential singularities, so Unsöld calculated other things, such as the spectrum of helium [with exchange terms], the polarization of the atomic nucleus by an electron in highly excited quantum states, and the quadratic Stark effect.) His mentor and thesis supervisor, Arnold Sommerfeld, was a most gifted teacher and author of famous textbooks. Many pupils of the so-called Sommerfeld school (Eckert 1993, pp. 132f., 144f.) were major contributors to the semiclassical quantum theory and the new quantum mechanics of 1925 and 1926; Werner Heisenberg and Wolfgang Pauli were among their number. Consultations with Gregor Wentzel, then Sommerfeld's assistant, proved particularly helpful to the young Unsöld.

Unsöld's thesis was the first dealing explicitly with Erwin Schrödinger's version of quantum mechanics. It applied Schrödinger's wave mechanics to various problems in quantum chemistry, especially heteropolar chemical bonds. Subsequently as Sommerfeld's assistant, Unsöld continued to apply quantum mechanics to chemistry and crystal structure analysis.

Further Career. By 1927, Unsöld was convinced that theoretical astrophysics was the field most suited to him. "I thought, would it not be worthwhile just to try to understand how the Fraunhofer lines are produced?" he later told Owen Gingerich in an interview (1978, AIP transcript, p. 8f.). A colleague of Sommerfeld at Munich, Robert Emden, introduced him to the nascent field of theoretical astrophysics, in particular to the writings of Karl Schwarzschild. Emden, professor at the Munich Polytechnic, had pioneered the modeling of stars as hot gas balls. For the Sommerfeld Festschrift of 1928, Unsöld contributed a research paper on the influence of scattering on the Fraunhofer line profile, which followed up on techniques and ideas of Schwarzschild then still widely unknown to astronomers and physicists. But rather than conceiving this as a first step away from theoretical physics into astrophysics, Unsöld insisted on the continuity of his intellectual pursuits. When Gingerich asked how his colleagues had reacted to his shift in interest, he simply replied: "I have always remained a theoretical physicist."

Unsöld realized that in order to make any further progress, more precise observations of select spectrum line profiles were needed. Quite in line with this, and funded by the Notgemeinschaft der Deutschen Wissenschaft, Unsöld arranged for a research stay at the Einstein Tower telescope in Potsdam (cf. Hentschel, 1997, p. 98f.), where he worked with Erwin Finlay Freundlich, Hermann A. Brück, and Walter Grotrian and familiarized himself with the experimental techniques they used. With a fellowship from the International Education Board, he then went to the Mount Wilson Solar Observatory as guest researcher in 1928 and 1929. With the help of Charles Edward St. John and Harold Babcock (who prepared hypersensitized infrared photographic plates for him), Unsöld recorded chromospheric emission lines with the 150-foot tower telescope and investigated spectroheliograms. In California, Unsöld also met the elite of contemporary astrophysics, most notably Henry Norris Russell and Cecilia Payne-Gaposchkin, both pathbreaking theoreticians (cf. Unsöld, 1979; Haramundanis, 1996) On his way back, Unsöld visited Harvard University, where the twenty-four-year-old gave a talk on stellar spectra, with Harlow Shapley, Edward Arthur Milne, and Arthur Eddington sitting in the audience. Unsöld later recalled in an interview (1984, transcript p. 8f.), that his Harvard talk managed to convert everyone present to his point of view.

Unsöld and his listeners realized that stellar spectra held the key to understanding the physical conditions and processes in the interior of stars. It had been known since Gustav Kirchhoff and Robert Bunsen's discovery of qualitative spectrum analysis in 1859 that the presence (or absence) of characteristic lines in a stellar spectrum reliably indicates the presence (or absence) of specific chemical elements. But these qualitative features were not all that was encoded in spectrum lines. Quantitative information like the prevalence of an element in a star was correlated with the intensity of each line. Even finer characteristics of spectrum-line profiles could be explored

to learn more about a star's temperature, pressure, electron pressure, and variations of all these parameters at various depths of its atmosphere. But exactly how these inferences could be drawn was still under intense discussion at the time. Henry Norris Russell, for instance, declared that it was hardly to be doubted that the quantum theory, when properly applied, would clear up these questions. So the situation was perfect for Unsöld. As a student of Sommerfeld, he had obtained the best possible training in quantum theory. Even Russell, thus far the leading figure in applying astrophysics to quantum theory, wrote grudgingly to William Meggers at the Washington National Bureau of Standards: "I am rather inclined to leave the job for the present to Sommerfeld and his students, who are probably already deep into it" (quoted in DeVorkin and Kenat, p. 197). As a first step, Unsöld concentrated on sodium, which displays one of the most characteristic absorption lines in the solar spectrum, the Na D line. Combining Schwarzschild's transport equation with microphotometric data on the Na D line profile, Unsöld arrived at a first quantitative determination of the percentage of sodium in the solar photosphere.

Shortly after returning to Germany, Unsöld submitted his habilitation thesis (for certification as a university teacher) on the Balmer series of hydrogen to the University of Munich in 1929 (it was published in 1930). For eighteen months, Unsöld worked in Hamburg as assistant to Wilhelm Lenz and at the Bergedorf Observatory with his colleague and close friend, Walter Baade. During the great economic depression he was fortunately appointed *Ordinarius* for theoretical physics at the University of Kiel in September 1932 (thus becoming the youngest full professor on record in Germany). Unsöld pursued nearly the entire remainder of his career at Kiel as director of the Institute for Theoretical Physics and Observatory—a typical Unsöldian combination, quite unique among German universities with their strong tendency toward specialization. This professional arrangement was only dissolved in the 1990s when an independent Institute for Astronomy and Astrophysics was established.

In 1932, Unsöld developed the weight function method, which allows interpretation of the quantitative determinations of weak Fraunhofer line profiles and the wings of strong lines, provided one has a model of how the absorption changes with depth. Soon he would also study the influence of radiation damping (which broadens spectrum line profiles), Doppler shifts, electric fields, and varying pressure on the broadening of Fraunhofer lines in the solar spectrum. Unsöld also showed that the Doppler shifts were linked to convective currents in the solar atmosphere, particularly in the ionized hydrogen convection zone right under the solar photosphere. Using these techniques to analyze many other stellar spectra, Unsöld was later able to tabulate physical atmospheric parameters of the Sun and red giant stars as a function of depth and even to estimate the overall abundance of the lighter elements throughout the universe.

His textbook on the physics of stellar atmospheres, first published in 1938, quickly became a classic. Even though it was never translated, it was nevertheless widely used in foreign countries, as no other comparable summary of quantitative spectroscopy and its astrophysical applications existed. Further expanded editions appeared in 1955 and 1968 with a new subtitle, indicating special attention to the Sun. It is still used as a reliable reference work. Many of its sections open with historical introductions and the author's effort at lucidity and well-balanced acknowledgment of all contributors to the field is noticeable throughout the work. His own contributions are alluded to in the third person and are given rather less than their due.

Prior to World War II, Unsöld obtained a guest professorship at the Yerkes and McDonald Observatories, where he worked for six months in 1939 with Otto Struve on a coudé-spectrograph analysis of Tau Scorpii, a hot star of spectral type B0. The outcome of his quantitative study, the first detailed analysis of an early-type star other than the Sun, was an abundance of hydrogen (85%) and a surprisingly high percentage of the inert gas helium (nearly 15%), so rare on this planet. Furthermore, he was able to determine that this star had the very high surface temperature of 32,730 K. Unsöld could also specify its internal pressure, density and other physical characteristics. This study of Tau Scorpii became paradigmatic, setting the standard for similar work on other stars by Unsöld himself and by his pupils, who continued to refine and improve his techniques. Between about 1950 and 1970, many doctoral theses at the University of Kiel under Unsöld's guidance used his sophisticated model atmosphere techniques (*Feinanalyse*) to determine the chemical composition and physical conditions of various stars.

Shortly before the beginning of the war, Unsöld returned to the University of Kiel, where he built up a flourishing school of theoretical astrophysics, thus disseminating his extraordinary skill in mathematical physics combined with a sound intuition in interpreting experimental data. Many of his pupils (e.g., Bodo Baschek, Karl-Heinz Böhm, Erika Böhm-Vitense, Hartmut Holweger, Kurt Hunger, Dieter Reimers, Gerhard Traving, and Volker Weidemann) themselves became professors of astronomy or physics. Their teacher also established close ties with experimental physics, most notably with Walter Lochte-Holtgreven, who became *Ordinarius* for experimental physics after the war and specialized in plasma physics. Other of Unsöld's contacts included the nuclear physicists Heinrich Rausch von Traubenberg (who was fired by the Nazis and committed suicide in 1944);

August Eckardt and Rudolf Gebauer; and the applied physicist Werner Kroebel and his assistants Wolfgang Priester and Franz Dröge, who screened the Northern Hemisphere with a radio telescope he had built himself (see below). The collaboration on the reaction $Li^7 + H^1 = 2He^4$ was related to Unsöld's interest in the mechanism of nuclear energy production in stars (see his letter to Karl Hufbauer, 1978, and see Schönbeck, 2006, particularly on Rausch von Traubenberg's work with Unsöld).

Ties with the many centers for astrophysics outside Germany were also fostered. Particularly intense ones were established with the observatories in Utrecht and Edinburgh, where Unsöld's close friends Marcel Gilles Jozef Minnaert and Brück were directors. Unsöld and his pupils, also referred to as the "Kiel school," were frequent visitors at several observatories in the United States as well.

Journals, Editorships, Etc. The English-speaking world's leading periodical in this field since its inception was the *Astrophysical Journal* (appearing since 1895). In order to make room for high-class German contributions to the literature, it was decided to found the *Zeitschrift für Astrophysik* in 1930, to which Unsöld was a regular contributor. He subsequently became coeditor (from 1947 on) and after the death of Walter Grotrian was promoted to editor-in-chief in 1955 until the journal was merged with other European periodicals into *Astronomy and Astrophysics* in 1968. Unsöld also edited the more popularly oriented *Himmelswelt* from 1947 to 1950. According to Seaton (1997, p. 38), Unsöld ruled the *Zeitschrift für Astrophysik* with an iron hand, rejecting about one-third of the submitted papers out-of-hand ("I don't need a second opinion to recognize shoddy work"), accepting another third without qualification, and only sending the rest to referees. In his interview of 1984, Unsöld assured Harwit that this was ten times as fast as in other journals without any loss in quality.

Nazi Period. The rise of National Socialism was a heavy blow to Unsöld's internationally oriented research. Many members of the Sommerfeld school were either forced into exile or, like Hans Bethe, decided to leave Germany in order not to compromise with the new anti-Semitic rulers. Unsöld, however, decided to stay, partly because he felt that others needed the scarce jobs abroad more urgently, partly because he simply wanted to continue his own line of research and not give way to political pressure. When academic positions had to be refilled, he tried to uphold academic standards and not let party membership or other nonscientific criteria decide. But he deeply regretted the isolation and drastic deterioration of physics in Germany.

During the war, Unsöld was drafted as a meteorologist together with his friend Lochte-Holtgreven. He was stationed first at Kiel-Holtenau airport, then at nearby Travemünde, which meant he could continue some of his research on Tau Scorpii and other esoteric subjects under the cloak of "secret war research." Kiel observatory had been closed down in 1938 and most of its buildings were destroyed by the bombing that reduced about 85 percent of the city to rubble, but Unsöld managed to rescue the valuable old Schumacher library (Heinrich Christian Friedrich Schumacher's observatory in Altona had been moved to Kiel in 1873) by preemptively arranging for its removal into storage in a small town fifty kilometers north of Kiel.

Postwar Functions. After the fall of the Nazi regime, people such as Unsöld who had not compromised themselves by becoming members of the party, the university lecturers' league, the SA, the SS, or other affiliated Nazi organizations, were in high demand. Unsöld became the first dean of the philosophical faculty when the British Military Command allowed the University of Kiel to reopen in late November 1945. Conditions were extremely difficult then, as most buildings of the university had been destroyed, the faculty had shrunk drastically, and there was a dire scarcity of food, clothing, and housing. During this period under Allied occupation, Unsöld also served as a member of the local denazification committee, whose difficult task was to cleanse the personnel of former Nazis. By declining various calls to other universities, most notably to Munich, Unsöld managed to strengthen the local conditions for astronomical and astrophysical research in Kiel. A radio-astronomical observatory—initially with a dipole apparatus (built in 1952), later with a 7.5-meter dish—was operated on campus until 1975. In the following academic year Unsöld served as university president (*Rektor*), and in 1982 celebrated his fifty-year golden jubilee as university professor. The University of Kiel conferred upon him the distinction of honorary senator.

From 1949 until its dissolution in late 1951, Unsöld served as a member of the West German federal research council (Forschungsrat), initiated and presided over by Werner Heisenberg. Unsöld was also member of the senate of the German national research foundation (Deutsche Forschungsgemeinschaft) from 1954 to 1957. After his retirement in 1973, Unsöld remained active in research for another fifteen years. That Unsöld was also asked to serve as president of the Astronomische Gesellschaft in the immediate postwar period of 1947 to 1948 is also indicative of the unbroken trust in him by the international community. In 1988, the society elected him as its first honorary member. Unsöld was also a frequent speaker at conferences organized by the Interna-

tional Astronomical Union, but he recalled being shunned by French astronomers after 1945 (Gingerich interview, p. 23) and did not hold any offices there, although he took part in its structural reform in 1957 (see Blaauw, p. 209). He remained active long after his retirement at the age of sixty-seven.

Popularization and History of Science. Roughly a hundred years after the publication of Alexander von Humboldt's grand compendium *Kosmos*, Unsöld decided it was time to attempt another synthesis of the knowledge acquired in cosmology, astronomy, (astro)physics, chemistry, and allied sciences. He wrote *Der neue Kosmos* with the set purpose of making known to nonspecialists the major changes, revisions, and additions to the basic concepts of astrophysics. It went through six revised and expanded editions (the last four coedited by his pupil Bodo Baschek) and was also translated into English, Spanish, Italian, and Japanese.

As an aside, Unsöld's interest in the history of science in his later years should also be mentioned. In 1957, he wrote a short booklet about Max Planck; later he published a note interpreting Heinrich Hertz's principles of mechanics as foreshadowing elements of Einstein's thinking (see Unsöld, 1970, especially on geometrization and on the elimination of forces by constraining motion onto geodesics).

Unsöld's general view was that prior, much less known developments had prepared the way for revolutionary breakthroughs in the sciences, often occurring in more than one place at a time, Nicholas Cusa and the Copernican Revolution being other cases in point. An anthology of some of his semipopular papers and portraits of people he had met appeared in 1972. In his last book from 1981, Unsöld reflected on the evolution of cosmic, biological, and mental structures and sought a grand unifying view, thus building bridges across to other domains of knowledge.

International Functions and Honors. For his pathbreaking contributions to the theory of stellar atmospheres and quantitative spectral analysis, Unsöld obtained many honors, most notably the Bruce Medal of the Astronomical Society of the Pacific in 1956 and the Gold Medal of the London-based Royal Astronomical Society in 1957. The Royal Astronomical Society of Canada named him honorary member in 1956.

Unsöld's broad interest in more general issues of science is also reflected in his engagement for the Gesellschaft Deutscher Naturforscher und Ärzte and in his election as member of the Deutsche Akademie der Naturforscher Leopoldina in 1962, to whom it awarded its prestigious Cothenius Gold Medal for outstanding life work in 1973. Unsöld was also a member of the Göttingen and Bavarian academies of science, and of the International Academy of Astronautics. Honorary doctorates were conferred on him by the universities of Utrecht (1961), Edinburgh (1970), and Munich (1972). The University of Königsberg awarded him their Copernicus Prize as early as 1943.

He was quite averse to hagiography and undue deference, though—his harsh words about the idolization of genius on the occasion of the centenary of Einstein's birth in 1979 caused quite a stir in the scientific community and beyond (see Unsöld, 1980, and various letters to the editor in 1981; Unsöld's disgust about self-advertisement of scientists and the article from 1980 is also mentioned in the interview with Harwit [1984, transcript pp. 11f., 23f.]).

A Personal Note. Being a child of the province of Württemberg, Unsöld always retained a slight Swabian accent, which added a charming touch to his lectures. In 1934 he married the biologist Dr. Liselotte Kühnert (*d.* 1990), with whom he had four children. He was fond of music, played the first violin in the Kiel university orchestra as well as at private concerts, and also enjoyed watercolor painting. As one of his pupils, Volker Weidemann, said in his obituary, "Unsöld was a towering personality, a giant not only in physical stature."

BIBLIOGRAPHY

There are papers at the Unsöld Archive at the Institute for Astronomy & Astrophysics in Kiel. Unsöld's correspondence with Otto Struve is microfilmed and available at the American Institute of Physics (AIP) under call no. MI 78. The archive of the Deutsche Akademie der Naturforscher Leopoldina in Halle has a membership file on Unsöld. The Royal Astronomical Society in London and the Astronomical Society of the Pacific have files related to his prize awards. A select bibliography of some two dozen scanned articles authored by Unsöld and more useful historical articles are available from http://www.phys-astro.sonoma.edu/BruceMedalists/Unsold/UnsoldRefs.html.

WORKS BY UNSÖLD

"Beiträge zur Quantenmechanik der Atome." *Annalen der Physik,* 4th ser., 82 (1927): 355–393. PhD diss., University of Munich.

"Ueber die Balmerserie des Wasserstoffs im Sonnenspektrum." *Zeitschrift für Physik* 59 (1930): 353–377. Habilitation thesis from 1929.

Physik der Sternatmosphären [Physics of stellar atmospheres]. Berlin: Springer, 1938. 2nd rev. ed., 1955; 3rd ed., 1968.

"Die kosmische Häufigkeit der leichten Elemente." *Physikalische Zeitschrift* 41 (1940): 549–552.

"Quantitative Spektralanalyse des B0-Sternes τ Scorpii." *Zeitschrift für Astrophysik* 21 (1941): 1–21, 22–84, 229–248; 23 (1944): 75–97. Partly translated and commented on in *A Source Book in Astronomy and Astrophysics, 1900–1975,* edited by Kenneth R. Lang and Owen Gingerich. Cambridge, MA: Harvard University Press, 1979.

Der neue Kosmos. Berlin: Springer, 1967. 2nd ed. 1974, 3rd ed. 1981, 4th ed. 1988, 5th ed. 1991, 6th ed. 1999, 7th ed. 2002. Revised and expanded, since the 3rd edition together with B. Baschek). Also translated into English as *The New Cosmos.* New York: Springer, 1969. 2nd ed. 1977, 3rd ed. 1983, 4th ed. 1991, 5th ed. 2001.

"Heinrich Hertz. *Prinzipien der Mechanik*—Versuch einer historischen Erklärung." *Physikalische Blätter* 26 (1970): 337–342.

Sterne und Menschen. Aufsätze und Vorträge. Berlin: Springer, 1972.

Interview with Owen Gingerich. 1978. 2 cassettes, 27 pp. transcript. AIP. Call no. OH 500.

Autobiographical letter to Karl Hufbauer. 15 March 1978. AIP. Call no. MB31477.

"Introduction—A Fifty Years Retrospect." In *Les éléments et leur isotopes dans l'univers.* Université de Liège: Institut d'Astrophysique, 1979. Page 7 reviews the "explosive development of quantitative spectroscopy," starting with the contributions of Russell and Payne-Gaposchkin.

"Albert Einstein—Ein Jahr danach" [Albert Einstein—One year later]. *Physikalische Blätter* 36 (1980): 337–339.

Evolution kosmischer, biologischer und geistiger Strukturen. Stuttgart: Wissenschaftliche Verlagsgesellschaft, 1981.

"Unsöld on Einstein." *Nature* 291 (1981): 374. Letters by Unsöld and by Kal Kromphardt (editor of *Physikalische Blätter*), in response to "German Physicists in Row about Einstein." *Nature* 290 (1981): 535.

Letter to the Editor. *Physikalische Blätter* 37 (1981): 65, 229–230.

Interview with Martin Harwit. 24 February 1984. 2 cassettes and 30 pages transcript. AIP. Call no. OH 501.

OTHER SOURCES

Baschek, Bodo. "Nachruf: Albrecht Unsöld." *Mitteilungen der Astronomischen Gesellschaft* 79 (1996): 11–15. Abbreviated in *Physikalische Blätter* 52 (1996): 890–891.

Blaauw, Adriaan. *History of the IAU: The Birth and First Half-Century of the International Astronomical Union.* Dordrecht, Netherlands: Kluwer Academic Publishers, 1994.

Böhm, Karl-Heinz. "Albrecht Unsöld 60 Jahre." *Sterne und Weltraum* 4 (1965): 89.

DeVorkin, David, and R. Kenat. "Quantum Physics and the Stars." *Journal for the History of Astronomy* 14 (1983): 102–132, 180–222.

Eckert, Michael. *Die Atomphysiker: Eine Geschichte der theoretischen Physik am Beispiel der Sommerfeldschule.* Braunschweig: Vieweg, 1993.

Hentschel, Klaus. *The Einstein Tower: An Intertexture of Dynamic Construction, Relativity Theory, and Astronomy.* Stanford, CA: Stanford University Press, 1997.

Haramundanis, Katherine, ed. *Cecilia Payne-Gaposchkin: An Autobiography and Other Recollections.* 2nd ed. Cambridge, U.K.: Cambridge University Press, 1996. Page 179 gives an account of Unsöld's first meeting with Milne, with whom he had conducted a "spirited controversy on the printed page, no holds barred."

Jeffreys, Harold. "The President's Address on the Award of the Gold Medal." *Monthly Notices of the Royal Astronomical Society* 117 (1957): 344–346.

Kippenhahn, Rudolf. "Laudatio für Herrn Prof. Dr. Albrecht Unsöld anläßlich der Verleihung der Cothenius-Medaille." *Nova Acta Leopoldina* 42 (1974): 61–64.

Seaton, Mike. Obituary. *Astronomy and Astrophysics* 38 (1997): 37–38.

Schlüter, Arnulf. Obituary. *Jahrbuch der Bayerischen Akademie der Wissenschaften* 51 (1995): 285–287.

Schmidt-Schönbeck, Charlotte. *Dreihundert Jahre Physik und Astronomie an der Kieler Universitat.* Kiel: Hirt, 1965.

Sommerfeld, Arnold. *Atombau und Spektrallinien.* Braunschweig: Vieweg, 1919.

———. *Wissenschaftlicher Briefwechsel,* edited by Michael Eckert und Karl Märker. Berlin: Deutsches Museum, GNT-Verlag, 2004. Volume 2 publishes part of Unsöld's correspondence with Sommerfeld.

Voigt, Hans-Heinrich. "Zum 70. Geburtstag von Albrecht Unsöld." *Sterne und Weltraum* 14 (1970): 112–113.

Weidemann, Volker. "Albrecht Unsöld (1905–1995)." *Publications of the Astronomical Society of the Pacific* 108 (1996): 553–555.

Wilson, Olin C. "The Award of the Bruce Gold Medal to Dr. Albrecht Unsöld." *Publications of the Astronomical Society of the Pacific* 68 (1956): 89–91.

Wolfschmidt, Gudrun, ed. *Entwicklung der Astrophysik.* Nuncius Hamburgensis, 4. Norderstedt: books on demand, 2007. A series of papers honoring Unsöld's hundredth birthday in 2005. See contributions by Volker Weidemann, Bodo Baschek, and Charlotte Schönbeck. Unsöld's correspondence with Sommerfeld and with Lochte-Holtgreven is partly published in Weidemann's contribution.

Klaus Hentschel

V

VALENS, VETTIUS (*b.* Antioch, Syria, 8 February 120 CE [?]), *astrology.*

Life. Apart from the fact that Valens was born in Antioch scholars know very little about the life of the Greek astrologer. He seems to have published both his birth horoscope and his conception horoscope anonymously. The former dates from 8 February 120 CE and occurs twenty-one times throughout his work (David Pingree, 1986, pp. V and XIX; Otto Neugebauer and Henry Bartlett van Hoesen, 1959, pp. 116f.; Stephan Heilen: Hor. gr. 120.II.08), whereas the horoscope based on the date of his conception is cast for 13 May 119 CE, presumably back-dated from the birthdate (Val. 3,10,4: Pingree, 1986, p. V; Katrin Frommhold, 2004, pp. 110–118; Heilen: Hor. gr. 119.V.13). Valens was thus a slightly younger contemporary of Ptolemy (Neugebauer, 1954), whose works he knew and commented on (Alexander Jones, 1990). He states that in his youth he had to cope with avaricious teachers and furthermore mentions several journeys, especially to Egypt (Val. 4,11,4).

Work. Vettius Valens composed a comprehensive companion to astrology in Greek entitled Ἀνθολογίαι [anthologíai]. This textbook addressed a certain Markos (Val. 7,6,230. 9,1,1. 9,15,11; and Val. 4,11,11 ἀδελφέ [adelphé] "brother" could be metaphorical) and is divided into nine books. He wrote the bulk of his work from 152 to 162 CE, using earlier material in the earlier books and perhaps making a few additions in later years (Neugebauer, 1954).

The text has been corrupted and suddenly breaks off at the end of book nine. What survives is a recension from the fifth century. Apart from this, the book contains an unsystematic collection of various treatises that deal with the most important methods of astrology. The first three books provide an introduction to the topic: book one deals with the planets, the zodiac and the ascendant, book two with the geometrical aspects and the lots of heaven, and book three with chronocratories (rulership of certain units of time). From book four onwards, however, the items are put forward without any systematic order.

The last book focuses on katarchic horoscopy (interrogations about the most favorable beginning of an action)—a topic that was often dealt with at the end of a treatise (cf. Dorotheus and Hephaestio). It appears that the manual was not intended to be a literary unit (Komorowska, 2004, p. 413), but grew up continuously during the practical work. The state of the textual transmission is typical of literary productions intended for usage. As the author himself considered his books to be rather poor (ἰδιωτικωτέρας [idiōtikōterās]), he apologized bringing forward the weakness of his eyes and the death of a beloved pupil as an excuse (Val. 3,13,16).

Significance. Compared with the more theoretical and philosophical character of Ptolemy's *Apotelesmatika*, Valens's *Anthologiai* is a handbook of a practitioner who applied cruder astronomical techniques. Its enormous value consists in its transmission of a myriad of astrological methods employed by astrologers like Nechepso and Petosiris (Valens preserved some iambic fragments), Teucer of Babylon, Critodemus (from the Ὅρασις [Horasis]), Hipparchus, Hypsikles (Ἀναφορικός

[Anaphorikos]), Timaeus, Thrasyllus, and others. He claimed to have used the tables of Hipparchus, Sudines, Kidenas, Apollonius (?), and Apollinarius (Val. 9,11,10: Jones, 1990, pp.13–17). Valens explained in detail the complex *rule of Petosiris* for calculating the date of conception (Val. 2,21; Frommhold, 2004, pp. 88–130). Moreover, he transmitted the large amount of one-hundred twenty-three (or at least one-hundred twenty-one) horoscopes mainly cast between 140 and 173 CE for individuals who were born between 37 and 173 CE (Neugebauer and van Hoesen, 1959, passim; Pingree, 1986, pp. V–VII and the list on XVIII–XX, corrected by Heilen). The owner of the earliest horoscope, which probably was borrowed from a commentary on Critodemus, has been identified with Nero (Val. 5,7,20–5,7,35; Neugebauer and van Hoesen, 1959, p. 78f.; Pingree, 1986, p. VI; Heilen Hor.gr.37.XII.15; first identified by Benny Reece, 1969). The latest prediction concerns the year 184 CE (Val. 7,4,11–15), a later supplement the year 431 CE (Val. Add. I 16–37). The author compares different horoscopes to each other. Among these, to mention only one case, an inheritance quarrel of a couple: Whereas the husband succeeds in the first trial, his wife emerged victorious in the second (Val. 7,6,27–44). In an extreme case of synkrisis Valens juxtaposes six horoscopes (including his own) of individuals born between 118 and 133 CE. The *tertium comparationis* is their shared fate: They nearly drown when they shipwrecked during a sea storm in the spring of 154 CE (Val. 7,6,127–160). Valens did this in order to refute the traditional Carneadean argument that tried to disparage astrology by claiming that numerous individuals of different nativity can not perish in the same moment.

Intention and Method. Valens compiled his compendium for an initiated and advanced public, who would handle his work with caution, avoid misuse, and would not deliver it to non-authorized persons. To underline this, he invoked Heaven, the Zodiac, Sun and Moon, and the five Planets by oath (Val. 4,11,11; 7,1,1–4).

He would not create envy (φθόνος [phthónos]), but rather encouraged the adepts of the lore and engender willingness (Val. 3,10,19 προθυμία [prothymía]). He wanted to lead the students in an anagogical way "from the most tiny to greater things" (Val. 7,1,1 ἀπὸ τῶν ἐλαχίστων ἐπὶ τὰ μείζονα [apò tōn elachistōn epì tà meízona]) by inventing the image of a gradual ascension (διὰ βαθμῶν [dià bathmōn]) to a sanctuary.

Style. Valens boasted of his clear language, which he claimed to be different from the obscurity of many other writers. Although sometimes mysterious, he strove at clearness by putting forward evidence and by employing

comparisons (Otto Schönberger and Eberhard Knobloch, 2004, p. 360f.).

Several tables facilitate the use of his work. He cited some verses from Homer, the *Orphika* and *Cleanthes*. Because astrology was largely impregnated with stoic thought, he was an advocate of determinism: People are "soldiers of the Destiny" (Val. 5,6,9: στρατιῶται τῆς εἱμαρμένης [stratiōtai tēs heimarménēs]) and have to execute their pre-established parts (Val. 5,6,9–11).

Influence. The Ἀνθολογίαι [Anthologíai] have been used by Hephaestio of Thebes in the beginning of the fifth, by Rhetorius of Alexandria in the beginning of the seventh and by Theophilus of Edessa in the eighth centuries. Even in its unarranged form the Greek text became fragmentary at the latest in the seventh century. An intermediary, lost Pahlavī-version from the third century was translated into Arabic. Vettius Valens was highly esteemed by Arabian and Persian astrologers who drew several *epitomai* from his work. A large part of the fifth book has been compiled for the medieval *Liber Hermetis*. (Pingree, 1986, pp. 434–453: Appendix p. XX; synoptic edition by Simonetta Feraboli, 1994). Because of this high estimation several other works have been published under his name such as the "Useful Instruction" (CCAG IV [1903], p. 146 Χρῆσμα τεχνωθέν [Chrēsma technōthén]), "About the *paranatellonta* of each degree" (CCAG I [1898], p. 84,18. Περὶ τῶν παρανατελλόντων ἐκάστης μοίρας [Perì tōn paranatellóntōn hekástēs moíras]), and the "Judgment of Valens by Mahomet" (CCAG V 3 [1910] pp. 110-121: Κρίσις Οὐάλεντος διὰ τὸν Μουχοῦμετ [Krísis Valentos dià tòn Muchūmet]). Because of its practical character the work is more appreciated by modern believers than the *Tetrabiblos* of Ptolemy.

BIBLIOGRAPHY

WORKS BY VALENS

Auctores varii. *Catalogus codicum astrologorum Graecorum* (CCAG), vol. 1–12. Brussels: Henricus Lamertin, 1898–1953.

Kroll, Wilhelm. *Vettii Valentis* Anthologiarum *libri*, primum edidit Guilelmus (Wilhelm) Kroll. Berlin: Weidmann, 1908 (reprinted Dublin-Zürich 1973).

Pingree, David. *Vettii Valentis Antiocheni* Anthologiarum *libri novem*. Bibliotheca scriptorum Graecorum et Romanorum Teubneriana. Leipzig, Germany: Teubner, 1986.

Bara, Joëlle-Frédérique. *Vettius Valens d'Antioche, Anthologies, Livre I, Établissement, Traduction et Commentaire*, Études préliminaires aux religions orientales dans l'Empire romain. 111. Leiden, Germany: Brill, 1989. Not always reliable.

Feraboli, Simonetta. *Hermetis Trismegisti* De triginta sex decanis, Hermes Latinus IV 1 (Corpus Christianorum, Continuatio Mediaevalis, 144). Turnholti: Brepols, 1994. 4–15.

Schmidt, Robert. *Vettius Valens, The Anthology*, translated by Robert Schmidt, edited by Robert Hand, Project Hindsight, Greek Track. Berkeley Springs, WV: The Golden Hind Press, 1994ff. Also available from http://www.projecthindsight.com.

Schönberger, Otto, and Knobloch, Eberhard. *Vettius Valens, Blütenlese*, ins Deutsche übersetzt von Otto Schönberger und Eberhard Knobloch mit einem Nachwort von Eberhard Knobloch. Subsidia classica. 7. St. Katharinen, Germany: Scripta Mercaturae Verlag, 2004. According to St. Heilen, Mene 5 (2005), 373–381 unreliable.

OTHER SOURCES

Boer, Emilie. "Vettius Valens, der Astrologe" (No. 67). *Pauly's Realencyclopädie der classischen Altertumswissenschaft* 8A (1958): 1871–1873.

Cramer, Frederic Henry. *Astrology in Roman Law and Politics.* Memoirs of the American Philosophical Society. 37. Philadelphia: the American Philosophical Society, 1954 (reprinted Chicago 1996): 190f.

Gundel, Wilhelm and Hans Georg. *Astrologumena. Die astrologische Literatur in der Antike und ihre Geschichte.* Sudhoffs Archiv, Beiheft 6. Wiesbaden, Germany: Steiner, 1966: 216–221.

Frommhold, Katrin. *Bedeutung und Berechnung der Empfängnis in der Astrologie der Antike.* Orbis antiquus. 38. Münster, Germany: Aschendorff , 2004.

Heilen, Stephan. Hadrani genitura. *Die astrologischen Fragmente des Antigonos von Nikaia. Edition, Übersetzung und Kommentar.* Sammlung wissenschaftlicher Commentare, Berlin, Germany: olim Teubner, postea Bertelsmann, deinde Saur, deinde Thomson, Postremo de Gruyter (forthcoming).

Jones, Alexander. *Ptolemy's First Commentator.* Transactions of the American Philosophical Society. 80/7. Philadelphia: The American Philosophical Society, 1990: 13–17.

Komorowska, Joanna. *Vettius Valens of Antioch. An intellectual Monography*, Kraków, Poland: Księgarnia Akademicka. 2004.

Neugebauer, Otto. "The Chronology of Vettius Valens' Anthologiae." *Harvard Theological Review* 47 (1954): 65–67.

———, and Henry Bartlett van Hoesen.. *Greek Horoscopes.* Memoirs of the American Philosophical Society. 48. Philadelphia: The American Philosophical Society, 1959 (Addenda 1964, reprinted 1987): 116f.

Pingree, David. *The* Yavanajātaka *of Sphujidhvaja.* Harvard Oriental Series. 48,2. Cambridge, MA: Harvard University Press, 1978: II p. 444f..

Reece, Benny Ramon. "The date of Nero's death." *American Journal of Philology* 90 (1969): 72–74.

Riley, Mark. "A Survey of Vettius Valens." Available from http://www.csus.edu/indiv/r/rileymt/PDF_folder/Vettius Valens.PDF.

Warning, Guilelmus (Wilhelm). *De Vetti Valentis sermone*, Anklam, Germany: Poettcke, 1909.

Wolfgang Hübner

VALLOIS, HENRI VICTOR (*b.* Nancy, France, 11 April 1889; *d.* Paris, France, 26 August 1981) *anthropology, paleoanthropology, racial classifications, blood groups, hominid phylogeny, presapiens, Neanderthals.*

Vallois was a French anatomist and anthropologist whose publications carried on the French tradition of physical anthropology, defined as an attempt to describe and classify human varieties in space and time. From 1930 to 1970, Vallois held major institutional positions in his field. His main achievements in anthropology concerned the classifications of human races and the attempt to introduce blood groups into racial taxonomy. In palaeoanthropology he was one of the last and most persistent advocates of the now-rejected *presapiens* theory, which held that the *sapiens* lineage constituted a phylum distinct from Neandertals and coeval to them, which found its roots in early or middle Paleolithic Europe.

Early Years. Vallois was born in 1889 in Nancy (a city of Lorraine that remained French after the annexation of that department by Germany in 1871) to Jean-Baptiste Léon Marie Vallois and Marie Madeleine Jeanne Letellier. He was six and a half years old when in 1895 his father, an obstetrician, was sent to Montpellier after his agréga-tion (high-level academic teaching competition) to become a professor of medicine. In Montpellier the young man followed in the steps of his father. After his primary and secondary education, he became a student at the young age of sixteen, at the faculty of Science and then at the faculty of Medicine of Montpellier. He studied medicine under the direction of Paul Gilis, and comparative anatomy with Louis Vialleton, a renown specialist of vertebrate morphology, particularly of the comparative anatomy of the limbs. In 1914, while he worked as a preparator in the comparative anatomy laboratory of the University of Montpellier, Vallois undertook to write a doctoral dissertation in medicine on the anatomy of the limbs.

Functional Anatomy. Vallois then moved to Paris to concentrate on his work on anthology, especially on the articulation of the human knee, basing his research on human locomotion upon a comparative study, conducted at the Muséum d'histoire naturelle (Museum of Natural History), of humans and other primates. In this work, Vallois attributed the anatomical features observed in the knee not to phylogeny, but to functional differences linked with specific modes of locomotion; thus, he stated, it is bipedalism that makes the human knee unique among primates. Vallois's dissertation, published in 1914 as *Étude anatomique de l'articulation du genou chez les Primates* (Anatomical Study of the Articulation of the Primate Knee), is an authoritative, five-hundred-page volume, and several bone and ligament structures of the human knee are named after him.

During World War I, Vallois joined the army, where he served as a voluntary physician and received several medals and citations. In 1920, having passed his agrégation in anatomy, he was sent to the University of Toulouse where he obtained, at the young age of thirty-two, a chair in anatomy. There, he pursued his research on various human anatomical structures such as the diaphragmatic vertebra and the scapula. In 1926 he published a new edition of the volume of Poirier's *Treatise of Anatomy* devoted to arthrology (Vallois, 1926). By then Vallois had become a renowned specialist in arthrology, but his research was to take another orientation.

Raciology. Since his youth, Vallois had been interested in anthropology. From its foundation in 1859, anthropology, which was then in France a prominent discipline with its renowned institutions and journals, attracted wide attention from the public. Based on a positivist attempt to describe and hierarchically classify human diversity, the methods of physical anthropology aimed to evaluate in qualitative as well as quantitative terms the relationship of the frequency and fluctuation of anatomical data to racial types.

As early as 1912 Vallois became a member of the prestigious Société d'anthropologie de Paris, the establishment of which, in 1859 by Paul Broca, marked the institutional start of physical anthropology in France. Upon his arrival at the Muséum d'histoire naturelle in 1918, Vallois met the young Raoul Anthony, who nourished his interest in physical anthropology. Following in the footsteps of such masters as Paul Broca, Léonce-Pierre Manouvrier, Jean Louis Armand de Quatrefages, Marcellin Boule, Paul Topinard, and René Verneau, Vallois naturally concentrated on the typology and classification of human races. His knowledge of several languages—German (in which he was fluent), Italian, and English—in conjunction with his many travels through Asia, Africa, and America—provided invaluable aid in his exploration of human varieties.

Rejecting the polygenism then still accepted by some anthropologists, Vallois argued that all humans originated from a common stock. In *Les races humaines* (1944), he defined races as "natural human groups, showing a number of hereditary physical common features, whatever their language, habits or citizenship" (p. 6). These racial features are anatomical, physiological, and pathological, as well as psychological characteristics. Armed with this taxonomic framework, the anthropologist can distinguish

> great races [that] correspond to the fundamental divisions of mankind in our time. Their geographic localization is very marked. They have the

value of real subspecies. … Among the races *stricto sensu*, the existence of …local types, also called *subraces* (*Gautypen*), may often be revealed by detailed analysis. …They are modifications of racial types in a set environment—seaside regions, mountainous regions, desert regions—modifications which one may equate with those of mammals living in the same environment." (Vallois, 1953b, pp. 160–161)

Vallois's classification thus identified four great racial categories, the Australoid, the Leucoderm, the Melanoderm, and the Xanthoderm, divided into twenty-seven races, characterized by such features as size, skin color, appearance of the hair, and head shape. All of his professional life, Vallois strove hard to achieve a thorough scientific description of human races, studying the population of France and then of Portugal, the African pygmies, and the populations of Congo, Cameroon, Madagascar, and Central Africa, traveling the world in search of lesser-known races that still needed to be identified and described.

Vallois's great innovation was his attempt to introduce the serology of blood groups into the classification of human races and the understanding of their migrations. In his view the distribution of blood groups not only revealed genetic patterns but could also serve racial typologies; this could well be, he wrote in a 1953 article, "Race," the only novelty that genetics had yet brought to anthropology. However, he added, definitions of human races solely based on blood groups would still be partial and unsatisfactory if they rejected what he called "the study of the phenotype," that is, the descriptive classification of racial types. One can observe in the early twenty-first century that Vallois' innovation was not of great use: If the distribution of blood groups in the human species is indeed recognized to follow a Mendelian pattern, concepts and methods of population genetics in the early 2000s invalidate any attempt to connect blood groups with typological racial categories.

Using the category "race" had never been, and was not especially during the first half of the twentieth century, devoid of acute strong sociopolitical and practical implications. In his 1944 treatise, *Les races humaines*, Vallois warned the reader to beware of several misunderstandings of the "race" category. Race, he said, does not correspond to "political organizations" such as states or nations. Moreover, Vallois rejected the idea of "pure races." For example, he said, one should not speak of a "French race," for there are at least three races in France. Similarly, Aryans are not a "pure race," but a mixture of several, whose relationship with the Indo-European language is not clear. Also, he continued, races should not be mistaken for ethnic groups, linked by a common civilization and language:

From an anthropological point of view, *Jews* do not constitute a race. It is an ethnic group that, for more than 1500 years, was isolated in Palestine by its language, its religion and civilization, and was made out of two races: the anatolian race in its armenoid variety to the North, and the south oriental to the South. … Despite the dispersion of the Jews today, and their interbreeding with populations among which they lived, the features of both races generally persisted. The Armenoid type is particularly frequent among Askenazim. … The South oriental type is frequent among Sephardim. (1944, pp. 44–45)

Vallois is obviously being cautious here, but his definition of Jews as an "ethnic group" and his description of Jews' physical types are not meant particularly to deter anti-Semitism. As early as 1933–1934 another physician, René Martial, anticipating the Vichy regime policy of *épuration* (purification), had written about "the Jewish ethnic group" and proposed to trace its members through the determination of blood groups.

Vallois in Wartime France. Between 1937 and 1944 Vallois accumulated an impressive number of key positions within the institutions of French anthropology. He had already been, since 1930 (thanks to the protection of Marcellin Boule), one of the directors of the journal *L'anthopologie*, a crucial position in the field. In the ensuing years, Vallois split his time between Toulouse (where he secured in 1933 the establishment of an anthropology laboratory at the École pratique des hautes études, and Paris, becoming active in the capital within prominent institutions of the discipline. In 1937 he became the general secretary of the Société d'anthropologie de Paris and the director of its *Bulletins et mémoires*. In 1939, after Raoul Anthony's death, Vallois replaced him at the head of the Institut de paleontologie humaine, founded in 1910 by Albert Prince of Monaco. When the Vichy government fired the ethnologist Paul Rivet from Paris's Musée de l'Homme (Museum of Man) in 1941, Vallois took his place as a professor in ethnology and anthropology of modern and fossil humans of the Muséum d'histoire naturelle, and in the attached directorship of the Musée de l'homme.

At a time when many people were leaving Paris to go to southern France, which was free from German occupation, Vallois left Toulouse to settle in Paris. It is probably no coincidence that during these years he published his three major books on racial classifications: *Les races de l'empire français* (1939), *Anthropologie de la population française* (1943), and *Les races humaines* (1944), the latter of which went through many subsequent editions, well into the 1980s. Vallois remained, as has been seen, quite moderate and cautious in his racial descriptions, generally

refraining from explicit judgments on racial purity or hierarchies. But his typological perspective and his willingness to consider psychological features in determining race probably helped to convince the French authorities that he was a more acceptable director for the Musée de l'homme than Rivet, an opponent to Petain's policy and an activist in the Resistance. Vallois was in fact one of many French intellectuals who more or less acquiesced to the Vichy regime, but he never was suspected of collaboration; after Liberation, he was able to keep all the prestigious positions he had earned during the war and the Occupation, again replacing Rivet when he retired in 1951 after having retrieved his functions at the Musée de l'homme in 1945.

Personal ambition or opportunism are certainly insufficient to explain Vallois's scientific interest in human races. In the early 1950s a group of experts at the United Nations Educational, Scientific, and Cultural Organization (UNESCO) published several statements on racial prejudices and racialism, declaring that "race is less a biological fact than a social myth. The myth of race has created an enormous amount of human and social damage. In recent years it has taken a heavy toll in human lives and caused untold suffering" (1950, pp. 138–139), While this made scientific discourse on race hard to sustain any longer, Vallois continued his works on racial typologies. His embarrassed attempt in 1953 to review the debates of his time on the idea of race and on racial classifications reveals not only his poor talent for theory; it also brings to light the considerable amount of criticism that was by then directed against racialist endeavors such as his.

Palaeoanthropology. Vallois's scientific works explored yet another major field of anthropological research: the study of human fossils and the question of the origin and evolution of the hominid family. In the first decades of the twentieth century, the linear schemes of human evolution established by nineteenth century anthropologists such as Gabriel de Mortillet were strongly criticized by Marcellin Boule, who then became a major authority in the field. In Boule's view, several hominid lineages went back to the early Palaeolithic and subsequently *Presapiens* coexisted with the brutish Neanderthals, whom the more evolved *sapiens* eventually slaughtered to extinction. Boule's treatise, *Les Hommes fossils,* first published in 1921, became a cornerstone for the discipline of palaeoanthropology.

After Boule's death in 1942, Vallois undertook to produce a new version of *Les hommes fossiles.* Remaining faithful to Boule's ideas, his 1946 edition respected the letter and the ideas of his master, with Vallois taking the liberty only of adding a few chapters on recent paleontological finds from China, South Africa, and Palestine. Like Boule, Vallois accepted *Eoanthropus dawsoni* (Piltdown Man) as a valid taxon at a time when many anthropologists refused even to consider this problematical fossil, which was later identified as a fake. For Vallois, Piltdown Man was—along with the Swanscombe occipital found in England in 1936—a forerunner to modern humans, and the *presapiens* theory remained the basic framework for understanding the origin of modern humanity and the phylogenetic position of the Neanderthals.

In 1947 the discovery of a new hominid fossil in France was to provide, in Vallois's eyes, additional evidence for the relevance of this theory. A skull cap and several fragments of another skull were found in the Fontéchevade Cave at Charentes, in stratigraphic association with a lower Paleolithic industry, Tayacian. The antiquity of the fossil, on the one hand, and the (presumed) "human" structure of its frontal bone on the other—which was absent on the fossils but was reconstructed by Vallois from anatomical inference—provided in his view a definitive proof of the existence of a *presapiens* lineage since the early Palaeolithic:

> The interest of the Fontéchevade discovery is that it clarifies the problem. In contrast to earlier finds of human remains we have here, in effect, a specimen which is well dated and found in a stratigraphic context which allows of no dispute: *this is the first time that man, certainly not Neanderthal although earlier than Neanderthals, has been found in Europe under such conditions* [italics in original]. Now this type, as we have seen, taking all its characters together, aligns itself with the Piltdown-Swanscombe forms. This confirms in turn the correctness of associating these two fossils themselves. And above all, it provides definite proof of the existence, parallel to the Neanderthal phylum but independent of it, of a human line of development with an upright forehead lacking in a torus. (Vallois, 1949, pp. 357–358)

After the Piltdown fossil was revealed in 1955 to be a forgery, the Fontéchevade fragmentary skulls remained, along with the Swanscombe occipital, the only evidence likely to fuel the *presapiens* theory. Unfortunately, in both cases the structure of the frontal bone—on which the whole argument rested—remained totally hypothetical.

By the mid-twentieth century, the question of the relationship between *sapiens* and Neanderthals had become a major issue in paleanthropological debates. In Vallois's mind, the definitive proof for the coexistence of a *presapiens* lineage with the Neanderthal—and even the pre-Neanderthal—lineage was provided by another French find, a mandible found by Raoul Cammas in 1949 at Montmaurin in Haute-Garonne. For Vallois, the "primitive" features of the mandible allowed one to draw a single evolutionary line from the (early Paleolithic) Mauerjaw (from Germany) to the later Neanderthals via Montmaurin.

"The Montmaurin mandible," Vallois writes, "dating either from the Riss-Wurm, or possibly the Mindel-Riss, interglacial, is of Neandertaloid morphology in the main, but in certain points of detail is closer to the Mauer jaw. Smaller but at the same time more massive than the mandibles of the true Neanderthals, it doubtless belonged to an individual of the Preneanderthaloid type" (1956, p. 319).

Consequently, Vallois refused on the one hand to view Neanderthals as ancestral to modern humans—an idea which, first advocated by Thomas Henry Huxley and Gabriel de Mortillet, was reframed in the mid-twentieth century as the "Neanderthal phase theory" under the authority of such anthropologists as Aleš Hrdlička and Franz Weidenreich. On the other hand, Vallois also rejected the position of Francis Clark Howell, who in 1951 argued that a branch of the Neanderthals could have evolved into modern *Homo sapiens*. For Vallois, all Neanderthals form a coherent type and are much too primitive to have been ancestral to modern humans. *Presapiens,* he believed, originated in Asia and came to western Europe from the East, first sporadically, then massively, to annihilate the Neanderthals:

> Somewhere in the East, doubtless in Western Asia, and prior to the Würm, there must have existed *Presapiens* men who by gradual development became *sapiens* proper. … Under these circumstances one may suppose … that the Swanscombe and Fontéchevade men were emissaries of an Asiatic stock, coming into Europe during interglacial periods, which however were not able to maintain themselves here. … Reappearing with the second period of this glaciation, the descendants of the *presapiens* lost no time in taking a final revenge on their Mousterian conquerors. (1962, p. 495)

This scenario traces the common origin of both *presapiens* and pre-Neanderthals into the very deep past of the Pliocene era, at the very inception of the hominid family. Vallois's ideas were supported in England by Arthur Keith and his follower, Louis Leakey. Like them, Vallois believed that brain expansion was the motor of human evolution, and that no fossil skull could be defined as human if its endocranial capacity was below the cerebral "threshold," a minimal brain volume enabling engagement in genuine human thinking. For that reason, Vallois denied Australopithecines the status of hominids: "The Australopithecinae are a group of anthropoids in the process of evolving towards humanity, but which never crossed the 'threshold' to this condition and vanished without having become truly human. It cannot be denied that the fundamental human characteristic, that is the great development of the brain, the basis of all our psychological evolution, was never fulfilled in them" (Boule and Vallois, 1959, p. 231).

Above all, Vallois's position was faithful to the conception of evolution as parallel lines of descent inspired by neo-Lamarckism. This idea was advocated in evolutionary theories that flourished during the first decades of the twentieth century in Europe and the United States—for example, in the works of Henry Fairfield Osborn and Charles Deperet:

> It is now well established in fact that, in most vertebrates and notably in the mammals, the majority of groups branched out, almost from the moment of their origin, precociously provided with their essential characteristics, which proceeded to develop along parallel courses. This is called "bushlike" evolution, corresponding in general to the "adaptive radiation" of English-speaking authors. … An essential fact is the long parallel persistence of forms exhibiting very different degrees of evolution of which certain ones, were one not aware, might *a priori* be considered as descendant of others." (Vallois, 1962, p. 498)

Seldom did Vallois evoke Darwin. When he wrote about selection he referred, rather, to the neo-Lamarckian idea of environmental selection theorized by the French naturalist Lucien Cuénot.

In a Dying Tradition. Having had a successful career, Vallois retired from most of his academic and scientific responsibilities between 1961 and 1970. Over a period of forty years, he reigned over French anthropology; published more than four hundred scientific papers and thirty books; cumulated the posts of director of the Musée de l'Homme, director of the anthropology laboratory at the École des hautes études, director of the Institut de Paléontologie Humaine, and general secretary of the Société d'anthropologie de Paris; and was responsible for the three most prominent French journals in the field. In 1952 he was elected a member of the prestigious Académie de médecine. Many of his scientific papers and books were published in English and other foreign languages, making his works and ideas internationally accessible.

However, early twenty-first century anthropology disregards much of Vallois's ideas and writings. With regard to current science (and even, to some extent, to the science of his time), most of his ideas—his insistence on the importance of racial and typological classifications, his belief in the racial significance of blood groups, his reservations about the use of population genetics in anthropology, his support for the "*presapiens*" theory and the authenticity of the Piltdown fossil, his belief in the Asian origin of *Homo sapiens*, his statements on the phylogenetic

position of the Neanderthals and of the Australopithecines, and his neo-Lamarckian philosophy of evolution—appear obsolete, if not totally wrong.

The fate of Vallois's ideas and works parallels the fate of traditional physical anthropology in the twentieth century. Vallois never questioned the scientific framework of his masters' thinking, which he preserved unchanged and perpetuated until the end of his life. But by the time Vallois became a prominent authority in French anthropology, the field had undergone major changes. The validity of its traditional methods and concepts had been jeopardized on at least three levels: on scientific grounds, by new orientations in cultural anthropology and by the introduction of population genetics and later of molecular biology in the study of living and fossil humans; on institutional grounds, by the dominance of U.S. science in the fields of biological anthropology and palaeoanthropology; and last but not least, on social, political, and even ethical grounds, by the horrors of World War II, which appeared to the whole world as being in part an ultimate consequence of the "science of race" that had its roots in nineteenth-century physical anthropology.

A brilliant anatomist, a physician who was highly conscious of his scientific and institutional authority, a positivist attached to "facts" more than to ideas, Vallois wanted to embody the grand tradition of French physical anthropology, a discipline—and perhaps a whole world vision—that collapsed in the middle of the twentieth century. Vallois's career and works in anthropology sought to perpetuate, normalize, and institutionalize the frameworks of a decaying knowledge more than to open novel paths in scientific research. They belonged to a "normal" science (in the Kuhnian sense) at a time when it was deeply challenged in its sociological, institutional, conceptual, and methodological foundations.

BIBLIOGRAPHY

WORKS BY VALLOIS

Étude anatomique de l'articulation du genou chez les Primates. Montpellier, France: L'abeille, 1914.

Arthrologie. In *Traité d'anatomie humaine*, 4th. ed. Edited by P. Poirier and A. Charpy. Masson, Paris, 1926

Les races de l'empire français. Paris: La Presse MBdicale, 1940.

Anthropologie de la population française. Paris: Didier, 1943.

Les races humaines. Paris: Presses universitaires de France, 1944.

With Marcellin Boule. *Les hommes fossiles: Eléments de paléontologie humaine*, 3rd ed. Paris: Masson et Cie, 1946.

"The Fontéchevade Fossil Men." *American Journal of Anthropology* 7, no. 3 (September 1949): 339–362.

With Hallam L. Movius, eds. *Catalogue des hommes fossiles.* Nineteenth International Geological Congress, Algiers, 1952. Mâcon, France: Protat Frères, 1953a.

"Race." In *Anthropology Today*, edited by Alfred L. Kroeber. Chicago: University of Chicago, 1953b.

"Neanderthals and Praesapiens." *Journal of the Royal Anthropological Institute of Great Britain and Ireland* 84, nos. 1–2 (January–December 1954): 111–130.

"The Pre-mousterian Human Mandible from Montmaurin." *American Journal of Physical Anthropology* 14 (1956): 319–323.

With Marcellin Boule. "Australopithecines." In *Human Evolution: Readings in Physical Anthropology*, edited by Noel Korn and Harry Reece Smith. New York: Holt, 1959.

"The Origin of *Homo sapiens*." In *Ideas on Human Evolution: Selected Essays, 1949–1961*, edited by William Howells. Cambridge, MA: Harvard University Press, 1962.

OTHER SOURCES

Bocquet-Appel, Jean-Pierre. "Interview de Henri Victor Vallois, le 15 février 1981." *Bulletins et mémoires de la Société d'anthropologie de Paris* 8, nos. 1–2 (1996): 81–103.

Cohen, Claudine. *L'Homme des origines*. Paris: Seuil, 1999. See chapter 2, "'Seuils' de l'humanité," and chapter 6, "La notion de race en histoire des sciences."

Delmas, André. "Eloge d'Henri Vallois." *Bulletin de l'Académie nationale de médecine* 66, no. 3 (March 1982): 303–312.

Hublin, Jean-Jacques. "Vallois, Henri Victor (1889–1981)." In *History of Physical Anthropology*, edited by Frank Spencer. Vol. 2. New York: Garland Publishing, 1997.

UNESCO. "The Race Question," July 18th, 1950; published in *Man* 50 (October 1950): 138–139. Written by a group of experts under the direction of Ashley Montagu.

Claudine Cohen

VAN ALLEN, JAMES A. (*b.* 7 September 1914, Mount Pleasant, Iowa; *d.* 9 August 2006, Iowa City, Iowa), *Earth and planetary physics; geophysics; the space sciences; magnetospheric physics.*

Van Allen, trained as a nuclear physicist, became a central figure in the study of the upper atmosphere, near-Earth space environment, and the solar system using balloons, sounding rockets, satellites, and planetary probes. He will be chiefly remembered for his discovery of belts of trapped charged particles around the Earth in 1958, and for his leadership in mentoring and advocating the space sciences in the second half of the twentieth century.

Early Life. Born the second of four sons to Alfred Morris and Alma Olney Van Allen, a general purpose lawyer and a former normal school teacher, Van Allen grew up in the small (3,000 population) town of Mount Pleasant, Iowa, in a house built by his paternal grandfather in 1865. His mother had come from a farming family and was of Methodist background, but converted to Presbyterianism upon marriage. His father was an elder in the local church and served as sometime mayor of the town.

Van Allen attended public school and took his first science course as a senior in high school, and enjoyed it greatly along with plane and solid geometry. Upon graduation as high school valedictorian, he followed his older brother to Iowa Wesleyan College, their small hometown college, and lived at home. Through the early and mid-1930s, Van Allen's father's law practice more than insulated the family from the Depression. In fact he prospered, prudently purchasing several farms and managing them on a weekly basis, asking his sons to accompany him in his management circuit. Among the many projects Van Allen and his older brother George engaged in as teenagers, Van Allen recalled building a Tesla Coil from plans published in *Popular Mechanics*.

College Years. Van Allen's experience in his high school science laboratory carried through to college, stimulating an interest in physics, especially mechanics. His interest was solidified when he came into contact with physicist Thomas Poulter. Poulter made Van Allen his laboratory assistant early on. As a result, Van Allen helped to prepare Poulter's instruments for the Second Byrd Antarctic Expedition, which occurred a year after the second International Polar Year. Poulter, who had trained in physical chemistry at the University of Chicago, was interested in a broad range of geophysical problems, including meteoritics, terrestrial magnetism, and seismology.

Poulter had borrowed a field magnetometer from the Carnegie Institution of Washington's Department of Terrestrial Magnetism (DTM). Van Allen's job was to calibrate it and learn its characteristics and help Poulter learn to operate it. Van Allen accordingly set up a small magnetic observatory on campus and measured the declination of the magnetic needle as well as the total field strength, learning methods from a standard text by Sidney Chapman and Julius Bartels. This turned out to be Van Allen's first scientific contribution, because DTM did not have such data for his locale. Van Allen extended his work, making a magnetic survey of the county using a theodolite to determine the location of each station. He also assisted Poulter and astronomer Charles Clayton Wylie setting up a series of visual observing stations to determine meteor orbits and radiants. Van Allen recalls that this work was of great influence on his subsequent career, especially in his own expeditional work, "doing scientific measurements on a geophysical level" (Oral History Interviews [hereafter OHI], 1981, p. 49).

Van Allen graduated in the spring of 1935. Although his parents suggested other possible career paths, such as dentistry, Van Allen was won over by Poulter and by physics, attending graduate school at the University of Iowa, where his father and brother had also attended.

The University of Iowa's Physics Department, Van Allen recalled, had about twenty graduate students, about half as many as had been in his graduating class at Iowa Wesleyan. Edward P. T. Tyndall was his advisor and directed his first research project growing single crystals of zinc and measuring their mechanical properties, which was in fact his first real test at devising and operating very delicate equipment. This work led to his master's thesis.

Van Allen now enjoyed access to a broader range of expertise, as well as a full professional library, and began reading the journals. At Iowa Wesleyan he had been a lone wolf, but now he was part of a competitive and active pack of students and he felt the pressure to perform. His life was a single trek between his dormitory room in the Quadrangle and the physics laboratories. Classical physics came readily, but quantum theory and relativity were sufficiently challenging to keep him confined to more familiar experimentation and, as he regarded it, processes that could be directly observed and measured.

Upon completing his master's thesis, Van Allen switched advisors from Tyndall to Alexander Ellett to take part in Ellett's project to build a Cockcroft-Walton generator and enter the new realm of experimental nuclear physics. He recalls being fascinated by physicist Hans Bethe's announcement of his mechanism for energy production in stars, and with Ellett and another student Van Allen engaged in determining hydrogen and deuterium interaction cross-sections, which resulted in a paper with Ellett and Donald Bayley, a postdoctoral student, and finally his 1939 thesis. Experimentation remained Van Allen's forte; when he attempted to rationalize Bethe's theory and results in a graduate student colloquium, Van Allen recalled, he was "ripped to shreds" (OHI, 1981, pp. 63–64).

Department of Terrestrial Magnetism (1939–1942). In the spring of 1939, as he neared the end of his thesis work, Van Allen began thinking about what he would do after graduation. By the summer he had three options: one was to join Poulter, who had moved to the Armour Research Foundation in Chicago. He also had met a recruiter from Raytheon who was looking for physicists. Through Ellett, Van Allen was invited to DTM to continue his thesis studies along similar lines: developing and refining ways to count and evaluate particle interactions and new particles arising from proton scattering and deuteron-deuteron reactions.

Van Allen became part of a small group led by Norman P. Heydenberg, another of Ellett's graduates who was now responsible for one of the van de Graaff machines. Van Allen worked on a wide range of projects and enjoyed

them immensely, finding the collegiality and the facilities superior to any prior situation. Gregory Breit visited frequently and lectured, collaborating with Merle Tuve, and from these informal arrangements Van Allen began to appreciate far greater horizons in high-energy physics. He began working on determining the photo-disintegration cross section of deuterium and from these successes moved into a wider range of elementary particle experiments, all informed and stimulated by the informal yet exciting atmosphere of the place, under the general direction of Breit and Tuve.

Nuclear physics and fission studies were certainly the most important fields for Van Allen at the time, but he was also keenly aware of the DTM's strong geophysical traditions. DTM was then directed by John Fleming, who was a dominant figure in geomagnetism and atmospheric electricity, but more influential for Van Allen were people such as Harry Vestine, Scott Forbush, and Julius Bartels, who liked to take contemplative walks with junior staff through the local forests of Rock Creek Park, discussing broad issues ranging from geomagnetism and magnetic storms to statistical analysis. These mentors and other prominent geophysicists who visited from time to time helped to make Van Allen sensitive to opportunities lying at the disciplinary borderlands between experimental nuclear physics and geophysical phenomena, ranging from earth currents and atmospheric electricity to the magnetic field of the Earth. DTM's very existence and nature fostered such thinking.

War Work (1942–1946). Van Allen's two-year fellowship was coming to an end about the time that many of his colleagues, such as Lawrence Hafstad and Robert B. Roberts, were quietly moving into another part of the building to engage in war work, following Tuve's call to switch over. Tuve knew that the British were trying to perfect a radio device that could sense the proximity of a reflective target and decided that his DTM staff could help. Under the aegis of the newly formed Office of Scientific Research and Development (OSRD)—which was headed by Vannevar Bush, the Carnegie Institution of Washington's president—Tuve formed Section T (for Tuve) that would work on radio proximity fuses. Van Allen did not join at once, partly because Tuve felt he should complete his research fellowship, and by the end of 1941, Van Allen was part of the war effort.

Van Allen worked first on an optical or photoelectric design that was eventually given over to the National Bureau of Standards, and then joined the main DTM effort directed to the radio technique led by Roberts. The radio proximity device had to be designed to be sensitive to its local environment, just opposite what one would want for any normal transmitter, but not so different than a simple motion detector in a common burglar alarm. But it also had to be small, storable, and extremely rugged, capable of withstanding accelerations from 14,000 to 20,000 times the acceleration due to gravity, and here is where Van Allen made his contribution. His task was to work with Raytheon engineers to make hearing aid vacuum tubes as rugged as possible. He set up a small prototype shop soon after Tuve moved his entire enterprise out of DTM to an abandoned Chevrolet showroom in Silver Spring, Maryland, a few miles away, and called it the Applied Physics Laboratory (APL) in March 1942. His basic testing technique was to place the tubes inside 5-inch artillery shells and fire them vertically from navy grounds on the Potomac. They would then retrieve the shells and examine the tubes to see what components failed. Van Allen designed a potting procedure and a miniature spring-loaded support system to reduce mechanical stress, which worked. He received a congratulatory plaque from Tuve, and a $10 bonus for the issued patent. Millions of these tubes were manufactured by Raytheon and Sylvania.

In November, Van Allen and two other young APL staffers were commissioned as junior grade lieutenants in order to accompany the first shipment to the Pacific theater to put the shells into operation. Van Allen's assignment was to deliver the shells to various ships carrying 5-inch, 38 caliber Mark 12 guns, and instruct the gunnery teams in their use. He was designated assistant staff gunnery officer to Admiral Willis A. Lee, Commander of Battleships, Pacific during his eight months of active duty with the Pacific Fleet, taking the VT (variable time) fuses to destroyers, cruisers, and battleships. He was also involved in evaluating the new shells, finding that they more than met their promise. He saw combat on two occasions.

After his first tour of duty, Van Allen was reassigned the Bureau of Ordnance in Washington to expedite improvements to the VT fuse, working between navy offices in Washington and the APL. After about eight months of this bureaucratic frustration he elected for another tour of duty in the Pacific, this time to establish re-fusing depots on Tulaghi in the Solomon Islands and elsewhere.

Van Allen's wartime experiences facilitated his "coming of age" not only professionally, but personally. He not only gained critical skills at building and perfecting miniaturized electronic devices and making them work under unbelievably harsh conditions, but he also developed the means for improving the flight stability of these projectiles using a rapid spin-up mechanism that also reduced spin-down during flight. Additionally, he acquired many new human skills, such as managing a broad range of workers and working effectively with varied interests and capabilities. He was proud of becoming an "officer and a gentleman." More than ever he appreciated the values of, as he recalled in his oral history, "absolute honesty, absolute integrity, meaning what you say, doing what you say you'll do" (OHI, 1981, p. 104).

His wartime experiences also gave him invaluable training in how to make decisions, using what he called "the method of prudential choices": faced with having to make a decision but not possessing all possible information, you "must use your best judgment based on the validity and trustworthiness of the evidence you have." Van Allen had learned, on his own initiative, how one could work through a logical set of branching decisions to reach a conclusion. "I consider that of very basic importance to all kinds of exploratory scientific work" (OHI, 1981, p 105).

Another major watershed event at this time was marriage. Van Allen met Abigail Halsey when he returned from his second tour in the spring of 1945. She was a mathematician and computer at APL; although trained at Mount Holyoke in English literature, Abby was adept at analysis using calculating machines to compute trajectories. They were married in October 1945, and they rented an apartment in Silver Spring. Their first child, Cynthia, was born in January 1947, and they eventually raised five children.

The Applied Physics Laboratory (1946–1950). Van Allen remained in uniform throughout 1945, acting as liaison between the Bureau of Ordnance and the APL, and eagerly accepted an offer from Tuve to rejoin APL as a civilian employee once his military obligations were met. Tuve felt that the DTM owed Van Allen something for ending his fellowship prematurely, and said he could come back and engage in pure research of his choice.

One of Tuve's senior staff, Henry Porter, kept close contact with trends in the Pentagon and knew about Operation Paperclip and the fact that Army Ordnance was bringing captured German V-2 rockets and rocket parts to the White Sands Proving Grounds to test them and learn from them. Van Allen learned of this program late in 1945 and expressed an interest to Tuve, who accordingly sent Van Allen to a planning meeting at the Naval Research Laboratory (NRL) in January 1946 to see what the army offer entailed. This meeting outlined all the possible scientific experiments that could be done with instruments sent aloft on V-2 flights. Van Allen came away very enthusiastic about conducting cosmic ray research, and Tuve approved his plan to build a new group at APL of about fifteen people who would both instrument V-2 missiles and develop a small rocket that could perform the same function, to sound the uppermost regions of the atmosphere and touch space, performing physical observations of its environment along the way.

Van Allen's team worked fast and had a cosmic-ray detector ready for the first flights of the V-2 in the spring of 1946. As one of the larger groups preparing instruments for the V-2s, the group was also working on solar spectrographs, gas sampling devices, and diagnostic temperature monitors, as well as developing wire-recorders for in-flight data storage, parachute recovery systems, and, through an APL subcontractor, multi-channel radio data transmitters. By June 1946 his group had grown to sixteen people divided into research and engineering sections.

Over the next several years the APL group proved that it was one of the most capable of the various scientific groups. Van Allen's cosmic-ray experiments in particular began to return important data on the variation of incident flux with altitude. By 1948 they had established the existence and intensity of a cosmic-ray plateau, a region above 50 kilometers where the flux remained constant and represented an estimate of the nature of the primary flux beyond the atmosphere. Both APL and NRL initially constructed complex cosmic-ray igloos, conical stacks of coincidence and anti-coincidence counters, but soon found that cross-talk and secondary showers confused the results, and overall taxed the telemetry beyond its capabilities. Even though this finding produced useful diagnostic experience for the command and control aspects of missile technologies, it did not contribute to answering questions about the nature of cosmic rays. Van Allen's team therefore turned to simpler systems that were easier to shield and to assess through telemetered information. Flights in 1947 through 1948 resulted in a refined understanding of the meaning of the plateau.

In 1948, responding to criticisms from physicists about the physical meaning of the plateau, Van Allen and his team launched cosmic-ray payloads aboard their own small sounding rocket, called the Aerobee (a contraction of *Aerojet,* the prime contractor, and *bumblebee*), from shipboard at geomagnetic latitudes far different than White Sands. This new phase of their work was in consonance with the Bureau of Ordnance's interest in developing expertise in shipboard firings of missiles. Although the payload capacity of the Aerobee was far smaller than the V-2, there was enough capability to add other small instruments; Van Allen, prompted by Ernest Harry Vestine and others from DTM, directed his staff to prepare small total field magnetometers to explore the existence of postulated current sheets in the E layer of the ionosphere. From a series of flights at the geomagnetic equator, they discovered what was later called the Equatorial Electrojet. Studies such as these, which were initially mounted to better understand cosmic rays, ultimately led Van Allen and his group into geophysical studies.

Return to Iowa as Physics Department Head (1951–1985). Van Allen always knew that he and his group were not central to APL's mission, nor were they, at the working level, fully welcomed by others who were doing the bulk of the bread-and-butter work on missile development. They were called, somewhat sarcastically, Tuve's "5 percenters," existing mainly on outside contracts and discretionary funds. After Tuve had moved back to DTM as director in 1946, the atmosphere for basic research at APL deteriorated, and by 1949, his successor Ralph Gibson asked Van Allen to resume supervision of the proximity fuse group. This Van Allen definitely did not want to do, and so he began looking for another job, winning a Guggenheim Fellowship in 1950 that he delayed taking until he knew where he would land.

Van Allen had decided to leave APL by the summer of 1950 when he accepted an invitation from his alma mater, the University of Iowa, to become the chairman of the Physics Department. His fears about continued support from APL were realized after he left: Gibson dissolved his group and reassigned its members to other sections of the laboratory. But Van Allen also did not have any bold promises from Iowa other than the satisfaction of going home and striking out in new territory with the sympathies of the university president for his ambitions to strengthen physics.

Once back in Iowa in January 1951, Van Allen spent the spring and summer using his Guggenheim support to be in residence at Brookhaven National Laboratories, in New York State near his wife's family. Van Allen was still oscillating between high-energy studies and geophysics, but once back at Iowa in the fall, with research corporation support, he continued high-altitude observations using balloon-launched detectors. He also put into action an idea that he and his APL colleagues had to combine the economy of balloons with the altitude capabilities of rockets, creating the innovative "Rockoon" system of small balloon-launched rocket sondes that could send his small counters to between 80 and 100 kilometers. Van Allen secured enough support from the Office of Naval Research as well as the Atomic Energy Commission, and with navy logistical support mounted an ambitious high-altitude latitude survey of cosmic ray phenomena. Still searching out the elusive nature of primary cosmic rays, Van Allen also gathered critically useful geomagnetic information.

By the time he had moved back to Iowa, Van Allen had assumed the chairmanship of the Upper Atmosphere Rocket Research Panel (UARRP), a small but significant body of activists who represented both military and academic institutions using rocket flights with V-2s, Vikings, and Aerobees to study the upper atmosphere and celestial phenomena. He had also become active in broadly based efforts to explore geophysical realms, even though he was still focused on cosmic rays. A key event took place in 1950 during a visit by Sydney Chapman to the DTM. Chapman, one of the most influential geophysicists alive, was very interested in mounting a coordinated global study of a wide range of geophysical phenomena. During his DTM visit, Van Allen invited him to APL to lecture and hosted an evening dinner party at his Silver Spring home. Chapman wanted to meet various people, including Lloyd Berkner, and Van Allen was happy to accommodate. Out of that dinner party grew plans for what was to become the third International Polar Year but expanded in scope as the International Geophysical Year (IGY). Van Allen would remain a leader in this landmark campaign, and it would ultimately propel him to world prominence.

Pioneering Space Research. It was no accident that Van Allen and his Iowa graduate students were the first to build a satellite payload that returned important scientific information about the Earth's environment from an orbiting satellite. In the mid-1950s both the United States and the Soviet Union had announced plans to launch satellites; the American contribution was to be a series called Vanguard launched by a multistage navy vehicle that used modified Viking and Aerobee components. Van Allen and his graduate student George Ludwig were literally the first to propose a flight instrument to the chairman of the U.S. National Committee of the IGY. Their September 1955 document, "A Proposal for Cosmic Ray Observations in Earth Satellites," was not specific about the sizes, weights, or geometries, because the navy had not yet even decided those factors.

Van Allen was clear about what he wanted to do, and campaigned intensively to be granted an early berth. By November he knew that his cosmic-ray detector package was scheduled to fly on an early fully instrumented Vanguard, what eventually became a 20-inch spherical craft. But as he watched the development of the navy program, in his various advisory capacities as the chairman of the Working Group on Internal Instrumentation for IGY satellites of the U.S. National Committee, and as a member of the overall IGY Advisory Committee, Van Allen felt that the probability of Vanguard successfully working was slim. Too many components were new and untested or were upgraded but unproven versions of known technology. He therefore maintained contact with the Army Ballistic Missile Agency (ABMA), mainly with Ernst Stuhlinger, one of Wernher Von Braun's Huntsville Germans who was particularly interested in the scientific application of space vehicles, to be sure that the payload he and his students were designing would also fit in the "shell" of an ABMA missile (OHI, 1981, p. 219.) If Vanguard fizzled, Van Allen would be ready to fly with the army.

Sputnik launched in October 1957 when Van Allen was "out of town and out of touch" (OHI, 1981, p. 253) on the USS *Glacier*, roaming south in the central Pacific heading toward Antarctica as part of the IGY's Operation Deep Freeze, where he and his team launched some three dozen Rockoons. On board ship, Van Allen eagerly devoured the telemetry from Sputnik, convincing himself very reluctantly that its Doppler shifted signal could only come from something in Earth orbit. His diary notes reveal considerable apprehension at being "dealt out" of the action, especially after the launch of Sputnik II and spectacular failure in December of the U.S. answer to Sputnik, a 6.4-inch Vanguard test vehicle carrying only a transmitter. In the wake of the success of Sputnik II in early November, a thousand-pound craft carrying the dog Laika, the Pentagon gave the army a green light to launch its own satellite. After hasty telegrams back and forth with William Pickering at Jet Propulsion Laboratory (JPL), reflecting earlier quiet plans between Stuhlinger and Van Allen, Van Allen's Vanguard payload was modified by his graduate student George Ludwig to fit into the army's Explorer satellite even before the Vanguard failure.

This process highlights Van Allen's centrality to the nation's nascent space program. As chairman of the UARRP, recently renamed as the Rocket and Satellite Research Panel, and as a leading spokesman for instrumenting satellites during the IGY, Van Allen had both the connections and the track record to be best positioned as the lead instrument provider. The original full-sized Vanguard would have flown a complement of navy high-energy sensors with Van Allen's cosmic-ray detector, but the Explorer was exclusively Van Allen's—although it did contain a micrometeoroid detector.

The momentum and public equity Van Allen gained as the instrument provider for the first successful American satellite cannot be underestimated. He had a virtual monopoly on the first four Explorers, sending up a succession of cosmic-ray counters. Because of the high spin rate, Explorer I did not carry a data recorder and had no onboard data storage, so it provided data only when in sight of a receiving station. Explorer III, the next successful launch, had data storage and so synoptics could be collected, revealing a fuller picture of the nature of the high-energy particle environment in the highest regions of the Earth's atmosphere. What Van Allen and his team found was truly astounding: a wholly new component of the Earth's magnetosphere: a nested set of shells of trapped particle radiation that were soon called the "Van Allen Radiation Belts." Only after data returned from Explorer IV provided both high-altitude and wide latitude data did the full geometry of the belts emerge.

It is characteristic of Van Allen's research style that the architecture of the belts emerged gradually. In fact, the team was in such a rush to get the instruments ready that they had no fully worked out methods for data analysis, or even a clear view of what they were really looking for.

Among several factors leading Van Allen to his conclusions was his intrinsic faith in his instruments. Van Allen always prided himself as being a highly successful instrument builder. His overarching design philosophy was simplicity. As various commentators on the high failure rate of space hardware have remarked, the success rate seemed to be an inverse function of the complexity of the instrumentation. Both the NRL and APL groups began with highly complex systems, but once at Iowa Van Allen focused on the simplest devices possible to get the job done. He was also quick to take advantage of newly proven technologies: his Rockoon-based detectors utilized miniature vacuum tube electronics, but when transistors came along, Ludwig used them to reduce the weight of the Vanguard/Explorer payloads by a factor of four. These combined traits of opportunism and simplicity remained with Van Allen throughout much of his subsequent career in the post-Sputnik satellite era, and his successes promoted great faith in his hardware. For instance, when the signals dropped from his counter on Explorer I, he was sure that it was not instrument failure, but was due to something the instruments were experiencing.

Operational Space Research. From the early 1960s through the 1980s Van Allen was principal investigator for a wide range of instrumentation launched aboard Earth satellites as well as planetary and interplanetary missions. He and his Iowa colleagues and a continuing flow of students produced instrumentation for the first Pioneers and Mariners, continuing through to exploring the magnetospheres of the outer planets with Pioneers 10 and 11 to Jupiter and Saturn. He also remained an ardent spokesperson for space research, principally for the importance of unmanned missions in an era when manned spaceflight dominated the public imagination and purse. He always remained keenly aware of the extreme costs involved not only in terms of complexity and infrastructure but in terms of priorities, whether they be for national security, national prestige, or the pursuit of pure knowledge.

Van Allen's career personified the role of the enlightened scientist in military and government programs and bureaucracies. During his preparations for the first series of Explorers, Van Allen became a key player in high-altitude atomic and nuclear tests involving the remnant directorate of the U.S. National Committee for the IGY, the National Academy and the National Science Foundation, and the Department of Defense. In May 1958, in conjunction with his continued preparations for Explorer leading to a fourth instrumented flight, Van Allen also

worked with a wide range of physicists preparing for what was called Project Argus, a military experiment to produce an intense shell of trapped radiation from atomic fission processes that would effectively hinder use of the region for military operations as well as cause a severe disruption in radio communications. The test required high-altitude monitoring, which was the contribution of the Van Allen team. Van Allen undertook this work at the invitation of William Pickering; although his priorities were not identical to those of the Department of Defense and he was not fully aware of the goals of Argus, still he viewed it as useful and another means to assess the nature of the primary component of cosmic radiation as a function of geomagnetic latitude. Argus also provided him the chance to experiment with more complex detector arrays offering improved ways to obtain the cosmic-ray spectrum, identify specific components in the flux, and improve dynamic range.

Van Allen was also part of a small circle of prominent scientists asked to testify during congressional hearings on the establishment of a space agency. He had worked with an Iowa congressman to draft a bill for consideration leading to the creation of a national establishment for space research. He felt that the old National Advisory Committee for Aeronautics (NACA) was a good framework to start with but that the NACA itself had not been distinguished in the scientific use of rockets. Something in the way of a completely new agency was needed, and Van Allen made his views known to Congress and the Executive Branch, pushing for some sort of agency structured like the Atomic Energy Commission with a mixed governing body. The National Aeronautics and Space Administration (NASA) plan that emerged, with a single administrator, was sufficiently close to Van Allen's views that he heartily endorsed it to President Lyndon Johnson. He was less interested in a military model, an organization associated with the Advanced Research Projects Agency (ARPA), because of the problem with classification.

Van Allen also lobbied to place particles and fields sensors on the early Pioneer probes originally under ARPA/Air Force sponsorship. He wanted to make a vertical cut through the radiation belt system, and with JPL collaboration built the first four payloads. Pioneer IV reached 658,000 kilometers altitude and pierced the belts in both directions. Meanwhile, Explorer instrument payloads continued to stream out of the Iowa laboratories finding their way into space, such as aboard the last in the IGY series, Explorer 7, launched in October 1959 by an ABMA Juno 2. This was one of the first of the "heavy payload" satellites with multiple experiments and transmitters arrayed in a thick flat cylinder with conical ends and over seventy pounds of instruments from several institutions in addition to Iowa.

Into Deep Space. The Mariner series gave Van Allen a chance to try out his techniques on the other planets. He was one of a half dozen instrument providers for the first Mariners bound for Venus. Mariner 2, launched in August 1962, recorded the character of interplanetary dust and high-energy particles in its three-and-a-half month voyage. In these and other flights Van Allen's team continued to utilize collimated and directionally sensitive Geiger tubes to sense proton and electron fluxes and to search for trapped particle fields surrounding Venus, but the instruments failed to detect any noticeable belts. Van Allen keenly realized that what he had discovered surrounding the Earth needed to be searched for around the planets to gain a fuller appreciation of the phenomenon, and had earlier speculated that Venus might harbor trapped radiation belts. Not finding them was an important clue to the differences between the two planets. In 1965 a suite of Van Allen instruments accompanied Mariner 5 back to Venus, this time recording solar x-ray flare phenomena along the way and correlating these with particle fluxes. The Iowa group had sent similar instruments to Mars aboard Mariner 4 and, as in the case of Venus, found only very weak evidence of trapped radiation.

Van Allen was also one of a group of scientists in the mid-1960s interested in sending Mariners to Jupiter, and then using Jupiter's gravitational field to slingshot them to Saturn and beyond, making a reconnaissance of as many planetary bodies as feasible in the outer Solar System. His own proposal was for a single Jupiter-Saturn encounter, and NASA, the administration, and Congress approved this more modest program. The Mariner Jupiter/Saturn (MJS) was renamed Voyager a few months before their launches in August and September 1977.

Prior to his involvement in MJS, Van Allen was also a principal investigator on Pioneers 10 and 11, the first probes of the outer Solar System. The concept grew out of deliberations he led as chair of the Outer Planets Panel of the Lunar and Planetary Missions Board in the mid-1960s, which led to an initial announcement of opportunity in 1968. Originally intended to go through the asteroid belt and to encounter Jupiter, they were first envisioned as solar powered, but soon were adapted to radioisotope thermoelectric generators (RTGs) used in the Nimbus program. These long-lived power sources made it possible for scientists such as Van Allen and their NASA counterparts to begin thinking of longer-term ventures into deep space, and after launch in March 1972 and April 1973, respectively, Pioneers 10 and 11 visited most of the outer planets.

Iowa instruments measuring particle fluxes and magnetic fields have now flown throughout much of the planetary Solar System, encountering every planet thus far. The Pioneers and Voyagers continued to send back infor-

mation even beyond the known planetary orbits and throughout the remainder of Van Allen's career and life. Among many other goals, he harbored the hope that his instruments would detect the shock front between the Sun's magnetic field and the galaxy, the heliopause, and he lived long enough to witness the first actual evidence of the encounter.

Space Advocacy. In his lifetime, Van Allen did far more than build instruments to probe space. He was a constant advocate for the space sciences since he assumed the chairmanship of the V-2 Panel in September 1947. He saw this body through its many changes until it became the Rocket and Satellite Research Panel and finally became absorbed into the Space Science Board. Van Allen remained external to NASA as a member of a wide range of boards, panels, oversight and review committees, constantly urging policy-making and advice that would maximize scientific return. He hosted a landmark 1962 Iowa conference on goals and priorities for space science, and in 1967 spoke out passionately on how the United States needed to provide greater support for planetary missions. He was a vigorous critic of the space shuttle program, providing congressional testimony during the years 1971 through 1975. He conducted much of this as a member of study panels for the Space Science Board through the decades; one of his later accomplishments was his advocacy, as chair of the Science Working Group, of what became the Galileo mission. His penchant was to remind Congress that despite the focus on high-profile programs fostered by NASA, such as Apollo, the shuttle, or the Space Station, there were important reasons not to abandon robotic missions to the planets, such as Viking or Voyager.

As an advocate, Van Allen keenly knew he was responsible for a burgeoning team at his Iowa home base. He was always careful to align the training of graduate students with his research interests, even as the projects became large-scale and complex enterprises. He was most comfortable with his graduate students in a workshop or laboratory setting, supervising design, fabrication, testing, and then data reduction and publication. Many of the instruments arising from these collaborations became PhD dissertations for his students, like Ludwig, who moved later into NASA. Many of his students remained with him as Iowa colleagues. He also carefully orchestrated the transition his team needed to take when the projects required trained and experienced engineers and administrators. He found a formula that insured that his graduate students would never be far from the data and close enough to the equipment to know how to read the results with the physical intuition he had gained over the years. He remained head of the Physics Department (renamed Physics and Astronomy in 1959) until 1985. He never stopped teaching, including courses in general physics and astronomy as well as specialized courses in solar-terrestrial physics and electromagnetic theory and technique. He greatly enjoyed his introductory lectures in general astronomy that centered upon Solar System topics in a laboratory setting.

Van Allen was survived by his wife of sixty years, Abigail Fithian Halsey, and by their five children, Cynthia, Margot, Sarah, Thomas, and Peter. Except for Cynthia, they were all born and raised in Iowa City. After retirement Van Allen was named Carver Professor of Physics, Emeritus, and in 1990 he became Regent Distinguished Professor. He was a member of the editorial boards of several major journals, and in 1982 became president of the American Geophysical Union. Among literally dozens of honors, in 1987 he was recognized with the National Medal of Science, which was followed by the Crafoord Prize, Royal Swedish Academy of Sciences in 1989, and, in the year of his death, by the National Air and Space Museum Trophy.

BIBLIOGRAPHY

James Van Allen's papers, comprising more than 200 linear feet of materials, are housed in several collections at the University of Iowa, including his personal papers, "The James A. Van Allen Papers," and separated administrative and project collections: "The Physics Department Papers Under James A. Van Allen (1951–1985)," "Project Manager Mission Papers," and "Mission Engineering Papers." Materials relating to his life and career are also housed at the Carnegie Institution of Washington, the Johns Hopkins University Applied Physics Laboratory, and the National Air and Space Museum, which holds a series of oral histories taken with Van Allen in 1981 totaling some eighteen hours that were central to the writing of this essay.

WORKS BY VAN ALLEN

"Absolute Cross-Section for the Nuclear Disintegration Deuteron Plus Deuteron Decaying to (Proton, Triton) and its Dependence on Bombarding Energy." PhD diss., University of Iowa, 1939.

"Cosmic-Ray Observations at High Altitudes by Means of Rockets." *Sky and Telescope* 7 (1948): 171–175.

With Howard E. Tatel. "The Cosmic-Ray Counting Rate of a Single Geiger Counter for Ground Level to 161 Kilometers Altitude." *Physical Review* 73 (1948): 245–251.

With A. V. Gangnes and J. F. Jenkins. "The Cosmic-Ray Intensity above the Atmosphere." *Physical Review* 75 (1949): 57–69.

With S. F. Singer. "On the Primary Cosmic-Ray Spectrum." *Physical Review* 78 (6, 1950): 819.

With Melvin B. Gottlieb. "The Inexpensive Attainment of High Altitudes with Balloon-Launched Rockets." In *Rocket Exploration of the Upper Atmosphere,* edited by R. L. F. Boyd and Michael J. Seaton, in consultation with Harrie S. W. Massey. London: Pergamon Press, 1954.

With Leslie H. Meredith and Melvin B. Gottlieb. "Direct Detection of Soft Radiation above 50 Kilometers in the Auroral Zone." *Physical Review* 97 (1955): 201–205.

As editor. *Scientific Uses of Earth Satellites.* Ann Arbor: University of Michigan Press, 1956. See Chapter 20, "Cosmic Ray Observations in Earth Satellites," and Chapter 21, "Study of Auroral Radiations."

With George H. Ludwig, Ernest C. Ray, and Carl McIlwain. "Observations of High Intensity Radiation by Satellites 1958 Alpha and Gamma." *Jet Propulsion* 28 (1958): 588–592.

With Louis A. Frank. "Survey of Radiation Around the Earth to a Radial Distance of 107,400 Kilometers." *Nature* 183 (430, 1959): 219–224.

With Carl McIlwain and George H. Ludwig. "Radiation Observations with Satellite 1958 Epsilon." *Journal of Geophysical Research* 64 (1959): 271.

With Carl McIlwain and George H. Ludwig. "Satellite Observations of Electrons Artificially Injected into the Geomagnetic Field." *Proceedings of the National Academy of Sciences* 45 (1959): 1152–1170.

Dynamics, Composition and Origin of the Geomagnetically-Trapped Corpuscular Radiation. Iowa City: State University of Iowa, Department of Physics and Astronomy, 1961.

With Louis A. Frank, Stamatios M. Krimigis, and H. Kent Hills. "Absence of Martian Radiation Belts and Implications Thereof." *Science* 149 (3689, 1965): 1228–1233.

With Louis A. Frank, Bernt Maehlum, and Loren W. Acton. "Solar X-Ray Observations by Injun I." *Journal of Geophysical Research* 70 (1965): 1639–1645.

With Stamatios M. Krimigis. "Impulsive Emission of 40-kev Electrons from the Sun." *Journal of Geophysical Research* 70 (1965): 5737.

With Norman F. Ness. "Observed Particle Effects of an Interplanetary Shock Wave on July 8, 1966." *Journal of Geophysical Research* 72 (1967): 935–942.

Oral History Interviews. Washington, DC: National Air and Space Museum, 1981.

"Findings on Rings and Inner Satellites of Saturn." *Icarus* 51 (1982): 509–527.

"NASA and the Planetary Imperative." *Sky and Telescope* 64 (1982): 320–322.

"Absorption of Energetic Protons by Saturn's Ring G." *Journal of Geophysical Research* 88 (1983): 6911–6918.

"Myths and Realities of Space Flight." *Science* 232 , no. 4754 (1986): 1075–1076.

"Space Science, Space Technology, and the Space Station." *Scientific American* 254 (1986): 32.

"What is a Space Scientist? An Autobiographical Example." *Annual Review of Earth and Planetary Sciences* 18 (1990): 1–26.

"Eulogy for the Iowa Shooting Victims." *Eos, Transactions American Geophysical Union* 72 (50, 1991): 563–563.

"The Modern Saga of Planetary Exploration." Iowa City: University of Iowa, 1992. Presidential lecture.

With R. Walker Fillius. "Propagation of a Large Forbush Decrease in Cosmic-Ray Intensity Past the Earth, Pioneer 11 at 34 AU and Pioneer 10 at 53 AU." *Geophysical Research Letters* 19 (14, 1992): 1423–1426.

"Where Is the Cosmic-Ray Modulation Boundary of the Heliosphere?" In *Currents in Astrophysics and Cosmology: Papers in Honor of Maurice M. Shapiro*, edited by Giovanni G. Fazio and Rein Silberberg. New York: Cambridge University Press, 1993.

As editor. *Cosmic Rays, the Sun, and Geomagnetism: The Works of Scott E. Forbush.* Washington, DC: American Geophysical Union, 1993.

"Twenty-five Milliamperes: A Tale of Two Spacecraft." *Journal of Geophysical Research* 101 (A5, 1996): 10479–10496.

Origins of Magnetospheric Physics, expanded edition. Iowa City: University of Iowa Press, 2004.

With Bruce A. Randall. "Projected Disappearance of the 11-year Cyclic Minimum of Galactic Cosmic Ray Intensity in the Antapex Direction within the Outer Heliosphere." *Geophysical Research Letters* 32 (7, 2005): L07102.

"Inference of Magnetospheric Currents from Multipoint Magnetic Field Measurements." *American Journal of Physics* 74 (9, 2006): 809–814.

OTHER SOURCES

Dawson, Jim. "Van Allen, at 90, Sifting Data, Writing Papers, and Enjoying Icon Status." *Physics Today* 57 (12, 2004): 32–33.

Dejaiffe, René. "James A. Van Allen 1914– 2006." *Ciel et Terre. Bulletin de la Société Royale belge d'Astronomie, de Météorologie et de Physique du Globe* 122 (5, 2006): 151.

DeVorkin, David H. *Science with a Vengeance.* New York: Springer-Verlag, 1992.

Foerstner, Abigail. *James Van Allen: The First Eight Billion Miles.* Iowa City: University of Iowa Press, 2007.

Gurnett, Donald A. "Obituary: James A. Van Allen (1914–2006)." *Nature* 443 (7108, 2006): 158.

Thomas, Shirley. *Men of Space: Profiles of the Leaders in Space Research, Development, and Exploration.* Philadelphia: Chilton, 1960.

Van Allen, James. "Craford Prize to James Van Allen." *Eos, Transactions American Geophysical Union* 70 (12, 1989): 180.

David DeVorkin

VAN DE HULST, HENDRIK CHRISTOFFEL (*b.* Utrecht, Netherlands, 19 November 1918; *d.* Leiden, Netherlands, 31 July 2000), *astrophysics, physical optics, radio astronomy, space research.*

Van de Hulst was an astrophysicist with a wide range of interests, who did outstanding work in very diverse fields. As a student, he predicted that interstellar hydrogen must emit a spectral line at the 21-centimeter wavelength, a discovery that revolutionized the study of the Milky Way and of external galaxies. He also made fundamental con-

tributions to the theory of light scattering by small particles, culminating in two books that were—and still are—widely used in various fields of science and technology. For more than twenty years he played a leading role in space research, in Europe and worldwide. He was a member of the Royal Netherlands Academy of Sciences, the American Academy of Arts and Sciences, the U.S. National Academy of Sciences, and the Royal Society. He received prestigious medals from the Royal Astronomical Society, the U.S. National Academy of Sciences, the Royal Society, the Astronomical Society of the Pacific, and the Astronomische Gesellschaft.

Early Life and Study. H. C. (Henk) van de Hulst was a son of Willem G. van de Hulst and Jeannette Maan. He had three sisters and two brothers. Together they formed a warm, balanced family. Van de Hulst's mother was a cheerful, hospitable woman. His father was headmaster of a primary school and an excellent storyteller; he had written a large number of good children's books with a religious slant, including a children's bible and a book of bible stories for youngsters. In Van de Hulst's own, often witty, scientific writings one can trace some of his father's talent and style.

Van de Hulst was a bright youngster, with broad interests; a love for nature, books, and puzzles; and an exceptional ability in mathematics. He entered Utrecht University in 1936 as a student of physics, where he was fascinated by Leonard Salomon Ornstein's lectures on physical optics. But soon the newly appointed astronomy professor, Marcel Gilles Jozef Minnaert, caught Van de Hulst's interest with his brilliant lectures and his novel scheme of practical exercises, including observations with naked eye and telescopes, and mental and slide rule calculations; so Van de Hulst chose astronomy for his major. In 1939 Minnaert completed his monumental *Photometric Atlas of the Solar Spectrum*, with Jakob Houtgast and Gerardus Franciscus Wilhelmus Mulders as coauthors; astronomy students were asked to analyze various aspects of the spectrum. Minnaert invited Van de Hulst to measure the profiles of terrestrial atmospheric lines and derive the instrumental profile of the *Solar Atlas*. Van de Hulst solved this tricky deconvolution problem, and fifteen years later returned to a similar problem in the analysis of 21-centimeter line profiles.

On the roof of the observatory Van de Hulst met a younger fellow student, Wilhelmina Mengerink; the 1943 Easter full moon played a role in their courtship, and they were married in 1946; they had two sons and two daughters.

Van de Hulst was an excellent student and completed the work for his master's degree early in 1943. But in the spring of 1942, Minnaert had been taken hostage by the

126

German occupying forces. Van de Hulst then delayed his master's exam till after the war (September 1945), and continued his work as an assistant at the observatory. However, in 1941 Minnaert had drawn his attention to a prize contest about interstellar particles, announced by Leiden University. Thus, Van de Hulst's research turned away from the Sun to interstellar physics.

Interstellar Dust and the 21-centimeter Line. In 1930 Robert Trumpler of Lick Observatory in California had demonstrated that light suffers a strong general extinction in interstellar space, but the nature of the absorbing particles remained unknown. The prize essay contest announced by Leiden University asked for a discussion of the origin and growth of solid particles in interstellar space. Van de Hulst decided to meet the challenge. He made a thorough study of the physical and chemical aspects of the problem, scanned dozens of books in chemical libraries, and picked up a variety of details on nucleation and coagulation. The jury did not award a prize, but the essay submitted by Van de Hulst in 1942 received "honorable mention," because of its excellent review of the literature, displaying a "mature scientific spirit." Van de Hulst presented his work at a colloquium organized by the Nederlandse Astronomen Club (NAC) on 9 January 1943; the other speakers were the other two competitors: Dirk ter Haar and Adrianus Jan Jasper van Woerkom, plus the two key members of the jury, professors Hendrik Anthony Kramers (theoretical physics) and Jan Hendrik Oort (astronomy).

Oort and Van de Hulst extended the study presented by the latter in his prize essay, and in 1946 published it as a paper on "Gas and Smoke in Interstellar Space." Van de Hulst had used the word "smoke" rather than "dust" for the interstellar solid particles, because it appeared likely that these particles formed in a similar manner as smoke.

Following the NAC colloquium, Oort invited Van de Hulst to spend a few months at Leiden Observatory. The visit took place in January–April 1944. Oort, the leading expert in Galactic structure, had read with great interest Grote Reber's 1940 paper "Cosmic Static" (*Astrophys. J.* 91, 621), which showed radio radiation emitted by the Milky Way at a 1.87-meter wavelength, with a maximum in the region of the Galactic center; Reber's work was the first study of Galactic radio emission after the initial discovery by Karl Jansky in 1931. Oort realized that radio waves would not be absorbed by the micrometer-sized interstellar particles. In January 1944 he asked Van de Hulst to investigate whether there might be any measurable spectral lines at radio wavelengths. If so, Doppler shifts of the lines might betray the motions of the emitters, allow measurements of Galactic rotation and hence determination of the structure of the Galactic System.

Henk Van de Hulst. COURTESY OF WILEY-VCH VERLAG GMBH & CO.

Oort had, in 1927, demonstrated the effects of differential Galactic rotation in the relative motions of stars in the solar neighborhood, but the interstellar extinction of light had limited his studies to distances of a few kpc, whereas the distribution of globular clusters indicated a system size of twenty or thirty kpc; hence, the structure of the Galactic System remained essentially unknown.

At a colloquium of the NAC on 15 April 1944, Van de Hulst reviewed the measurements of Reber, discussed the possible nature of the radio radiation, and presented the results of his search for radio spectral lines. From an analysis of the literature on atomic physics, he had found that the ground state of the hydrogen atom must show hyperfine splitting; the upper and lower sublevels correspond to, respectively, parallel and antiparallel orientations of the proton spin and electron spin. The minute energy difference corresponds to a wavelength of 21.1 centimeters. The importance of this result was very great indeed: The most abundant element in interstellar space, in its dominant ground state, would emit or absorb a spectral line at a radio wavelength to which both the Earth's atmosphere and the interstellar medium would be transparent. Hydrogen emission had so far only been observed from regions where the gas is predominantly ionized (now called HII regions), at optical wavelengths susceptible to interstellar extinction. Although the expected 21-centimeter line strength remained uncertain, the prospects for unraveling Galactic structure appeared bright.

Detection of the hydrogen-line radiation would require a large radio telescope and a sensitive receiver. Oort immediately started attempts to obtain these, but even after the end of World War II in 1945, lack of money, equipment, and experience led to many years of delay. The first detections of the 21-centimeter line occurred in March and May 1951, and soon the hopes held since 1944 were fulfilled (see below).

Meanwhile, Van de Hulst had continued working on his doctor's thesis, which was planned to compare observational data on the wavelength dependence of interstellar extinction with calculations made by Jesse Greenstein and Carl Schalen from Gustav Mie's theory of light scattering. At Oort's suggestion, Van de Hulst decided to study the Mie theory in detail, and in the end the thesis became an extensive development of scattering theory. Van de Hulst presented his thesis at Utrecht on 17 June 1946 and received the rare distinction "cum laude." Within two weeks, he married Wil Mengerink and together they sailed for America.

Postdoc at Yerkes. In June 1945, a month after the liberation of the Netherlands, Gerard P. Kuiper from Yerkes Observatory (University of Chicago), who had obtained a PhD at Leiden in 1933, visited the Dutch astronomical institutes as an officer in the U.S. Army. This visit resulted in an offer to Van de Hulst of a postdoctoral position at Yerkes, at the time one of the world's best astronomical institutes; the faculty included, among others, Subrahmanyan Chandrasekhar, Jesse Greenstein, Louis Henyey, Gerhard Herzberg, William Wilson Morgan, Bengt Strömgren, Otto Struve, and Kuiper himself.

The two postdoc years (1946–1948) proved extremely stimulating and fruitful. Van de Hulst demonstrated a link between the outer parts of the Corona, the hot outer atmosphere of the Sun, and the zodiacal light, the light scattered by a cloud of particles extending from the Sun to beyond the Earth's orbit. This study evolved into an authoritative chapter, "The Chromosphere and the Corona," in Kuiper's book *The Sun* (1953). At the request of Kuiper, who was working on infrared spectra of planets, Van de Hulst also made a study of multiple light scattering in planetary atmospheres, a subject recurring in his later work. In this research, Van de Hulst crossed paths with Chandrasekhar, who was an authority on radiative

transfer. Van de Hulst was able to strike a fruitful balance between Chandra's rigorous mathematical analysis and the physical intuition that he had inherited from Minnaert. When his postdoc position ended in 1948, Van de Hulst accepted an offer by Oort of a faculty position at Leiden, in spite of various attractive possibilities in the United States.

Professor at Leiden. In 1948 Van de Hulst was appointed associate professor ("lector") for theoretical astronomy at Leiden; in 1952 he was promoted to professor. He held this position till his retirement in 1984 but he remained active in research until the end of his life. During his tenure at Leiden, he held visiting appointments at Harvard (1951), at the California Institute of Technology (Caltech, 1954), and at Columbia University and the Goddard Institute of Space Science in New York (1962–1963). Over the years, he received many enticing offers, but he remained at Leiden. Even after his highly stimulating stay at Yerkes, he found the "presence of many different challenges at Leiden invigorating" (1998, p. 9), and he worked on a great variety of subjects: interstellar physics and gas dynamics, radio astronomy and Galactic structure, light scattering, and dynamics of the Solar System and of galaxies, indeed "Roaming through Astrophysics" (1998, p. 1). The following sections discuss some of these subjects in detail. Throughout his work, Van de Hulst emphasized fundamental issues, and he often developed new methods.

Interstellar Physics. In his first year at Leiden, Van de Hulst became involved in the organization, by Oort and Johannes Martinus Burgers, of a conference on cosmical aerodynamics (Paris, 1949), which brought together top specialists from a variety of fields. The 1948 discovery of interstellar polarization by William Albert Hiltner and John S. Hall had demonstrated the importance of interstellar magnetic fields. Van de Hulst reviewed this subject, and together with Burgers he edited the proceedings of the conference. Related conferences (IAU Symposia 2 and 8) were held in 1953 (Cambridge, U.K.) and 1957 (Cambridge, Massachusetts), again with major involvement of Van de Hulst, so that in those years he came to consider gas dynamics his chief field of specialization. In this period he also served as president of Commission 34 (Interstellar Matter) of the International Astronomical Union (1952–1958).

Major progress in surveys of the polarization of radio radiation led in 1967 to reviews by Van de Hulst of the Galactic magnetic field. In the 1970s he was instrumental in the formation of an institute for laboratory astrophysics at Leiden, with J. Mayo Greenberg as director; its aims included simulations and studies of interstellar processes under laboratory conditions.

Radio Astronomy. The 21-centimeter line emitted by interstellar hydrogen atoms, predicted by Van de Hulst in 1944, was first observed at Harvard in March 1951 by Harold I. "Doc" Ewen and Edward Mills Purcell, and at Kootwijk (Netherlands) by Christiaan Alexander Muller and Oort in May 1951. At the time, Van de Hulst was spending a few months at Harvard, where he gave a lecture course on radio astronomy, a course given in Leiden in the fall of 1950, and written up in mimeographed form as the first-ever book on the subject. Frequent correspondence between Van de Hulst at Harvard and Oort at Leiden provided strong liaison between the two groups searching for the 21-centimeter line, which fostered rapid progress. After the detection, this fruitful exchange of information culminated in the simultaneous publication in *Nature* of the first 21-centimeter line observations by Ewen and Purcell and by Muller and Oort.

The first major survey of neutral hydrogen along the Galactic equator was started by Muller at Kootwijk in May 1952. In the spring of 1953, the line profiles (intensity versus line-of-sight velocity), which had been obtained at fifty-three positions, were measured and reduced by a large team of students and observatory personnel working under Van de Hulst's guidance. With a preliminary estimate of the Galactic rotation law, locations of hydrogen concentrations could be derived from the velocities measured, and a first map of the hydrogen distribution over part of the Galactic plane derived. Van de Hulst presented this map in his Halley Lecture for the Royal Astronomical Society, held at Oxford on 13 May 1953; the lecture (1953) included a thorough introduction about the differences between optical and radio astronomy, and showed a clear spiral pattern in the Galaxy. (Short sections of spiral arms had been found already in 1951 by Morgan, Stewart Sharpless, and Donald Osterbrock, from the positions and distances of regions of ionized hydrogen.) A thorough discussion of this first survey by Van de Hulst, Muller, and Oort appeared in 1954.

A second survey, by Muller, Gart Westerhout, and Maarten Schmidt, was carried out in 1953–1955, and yielded the distribution of hydrogen in three dimensions, for those parts of the Galaxy accessible from the Netherlands. (Observations by Frank J. Kerr and associates at Sydney, Australia, filled in the missing parts, and led to a paper "The Galactic System as a Spiral Nebula" by Oort, Kerr, and Westerhout [1958] in the *Monthly Notices* of the Royal Astronomical Society.) For the analysis of these surveys, Alexander Ollongren and Van de Hulst (1957) had developed a method to correct the line profiles for the

smearing effects of limited spectral resolution—a sequel to Van de Hulst's early work on the solar spectrum. Van de Hulst reviewed these groundbreaking results at various international conferences; in fact, he gave major papers at six of the first nine IAU symposia.

When the 25-meter (82-foot) radio telescope at Dwingeloo became available, Van de Hulst took part in the first makeshift observations in November 1955 of the occultation of the Crab Nebula by the Moon, and after an observing night walked 15 kilometers (9 miles) to Hoogeveen railway station, to catch the early morning train to Leiden.

In October 1956, a 21-centimeter line receiver built by Muller became available at Dwingeloo. Van de Hulst had calculated that interstellar hydrogen in the Andromeda Nebula (M31) should be measurable with this instrument. Early attempts by Westerhout and Ernst Raimond failed, because the receiver noise varied too strongly with frequency. But Van de Hulst came for a visit and invented the "on-off" method, in which at each frequency the signal from the Nebula was compared to that several degrees away. With this method, later called the "sky reference," the distribution of hydrogen in M31 could be determined—the first study of neutral hydrogen outside the Galaxy and its satellites. Van de Hulst again developed the methods to derive the distribution from the observations; the angular resolution (0.6 degrees) was a significant fraction of the diameter of M31 (only 3 degrees on photographs).

After 1957, Van de Hulst had to drop his radioastronomical research; he became too heavily occupied in other parts of the spectrum. The work at Kootwijk and Dwingeloo, and later (after 1970) that with the Synthesis Radio Telescope at Westerbork, was done under the aegis of the Stichting Radiostraling van Zon en Melkweg (Netherlands Foundation for Radio Astronomy). For forty years (1948–1988), longer than anyone else, Van de Hulst served on the executive committee of this foundation; he chaired it from 1970 to 1975.

Light Scattering. After his 1946 doctoral thesis "Optics of Spherical Particles," Van de Hulst continued and extended his work on the scattering of light. In 1957 he published a monograph on *Light Scattering by Small Particles*. This book soon became a classic, and was republished by Dover Publications in 1981. The obituaries by Harm Habing and by Joop Hovenier describe in some detail the great merits of this book: It starts with a general solution of a simple problem, and proceeds to problems of greater complexity; its illustrations are clear and efficient; the style is lucid, and it combines arguments based on physical intuition with mathematical derivations. The book was widely consulted, also outside astrophysical contexts. As Van de

Hulst stated in his Karl Schwarzschild Lecture about scaling laws in multiple light scattering, "it gave me peculiar satisfaction when one day … I learned that the computations, which I had initiated for the Milky Way, were now being applied to real milk [in the optical process to monitor the homogenization]" (1996, p. 4). It is striking that this book was completed at a time (1957) when its author was heavily involved in problems of interstellar physics and gas dynamics, and in groundbreaking radio-astronomical work.

A second monograph, *Multiple Light Scattering: Tables, Formulas, and Applications*, was published in 1980. The book deals mainly with scattering in plane-parallel atmospheres. The basis for this book was laid in work with Kenneth Grossman, at the Goddard Institute for Space Physics in 1962–1963, and even already at Yerkes in 1948, in a study of scattering in planetary atmospheres.

Space Research. Van de Hulst's life took a totally unexpected turn in the fall of 1958, as described in his 1998 autobiography (pp. 10–11). At the daily observatory morning coffee on 15 November, Oort told him: "The IAU has asked me to be their representative at a meeting in London. But I have little time. Would you like to go?" Van de Hulst asked what it would involve; and Oort replied: "Not much, unless, of course, you would become a member of the Board." When Van de Hulst returned after ten days, he had missed his daughter's fourth birthday, and his own fortieth, and he had become president of COSPAR, the Committee on Space Research. The International Council of Scientific Unions (ICSU) had established COSPAR to promote international cooperation in space research. At the time, the United Nations was considering proposals to form a new specialized agency dealing with all space matters. ICSU feared that space would become subject to the full hassle of the Cold War, and that research efforts would be pushed into second place. Several international scientific unions had managed to maintain cooperation between Western countries and the Eastern bloc. ICSU hoped to prove through COSPAR that they could foster East-West cooperation in space research informally and efficiently.

As Reimar Lüst mentioned at a memorial symposium held at Noordwijk in the Netherlands on 6 November 2000, Van de Hulst brought several merits to his new job: he had a very strong international reputation as a scientist; he belonged to a younger generation; he came from a small European country, rather than one of the big powers; and he could convince people that he was serving peaceful, scientific interests only. In his Karl Schwarzschild Lecture, Van de Hulst (1996, p. 4) mentions a highlight of his COSPAR years: "the first meeting of a Russian cosmonaut, Titov, with an American cosmonaut,

Glenn. At that occasion I delivered the shortest official speech I ever made. I gave each of the two gentlemen one of a pair of wooden shoes, which I had bought in my home town, adding that these were cut from the same tree and were meant to be used together." The deep meaning of this speech was not lost on anyone.

Van de Hulst's autobiography mentions many examples of the diplomatic work involved in his three years (1959–1962) as COSPAR president. Thereafter, although returning to science, he remained active in European and national space research organizations. He fulfilled several key functions in the European Space Research Organization (ESRO) in 1960–1975, and in its successor, the European Space Agency (ESA), in 1975–1986; he was chairman of the ESRO council during the critical years 1968–1970. Lüst recalls that he was an excellent moderator, free of the suspicion of serving national interests; patient and stubborn, and often able to resolve difficult discussions by the use of a simple metaphor. Also at the Noordwijk memorial symposium, Hermann Bondi cited his honesty and calming influence, based on knowledge and insight and a good judgment of the moods of people. Livio Scarsi emphasized his role in the realization of the gamma-ray satellite COS-B, the first ESA satellite, launched in 1975. Van de Hulst also played a major role in the establishment of ESTEC, the European Space Research and Technology Center, at Noordwijk, a village on the seashore close to Leiden.

When ESA joined NASA with a 15 percent share in the preparation of the Hubble Space Telescope, a weighty contribution was needed in dealing with the major partner. ESA undertook to build the Faint Object Camera (FOC), the most sensitive instrument for the Space Telescope; and with his keen insight and wide influence, Van de Hulst was appointed to the chair of the FOC Instrument Definition Team. As Malcolm Longair recalled at the Noordwijk memorial, Van de Hulst played a diplomatic role in the Space Telescope Institute Council. He also served on ESA's Space Telescope Working Group (STWG), and in 1981 chaired the STWG selection panel for the Space Telescope European Coordinating Facility, which eventually was formed by ESA together with the European Southern Observatory at ESO's headquarters near Munich.

In 1959 the Royal Netherlands Academy of Sciences formed a Committee for Geophysics and Space Research (GROC). Van de Hulst held the chair of GROC from 1959 to 1984, when GROC was succeeded by a new foundation, the Space Research Organization of the Netherlands (SRON), supported by NWO, the Netherlands Organization for Scientific Research. Through GROC, the Netherlands succeeded in making major contributions to space research, including the Astronomical

Netherlands Satellite (ANS); a large (42.5-percent) share in the Infrared Astronomical Satellite (IRAS); and an important share in the gamma-ray satellite COS-B, for which Van de Hulst led a large team of brilliant engineers recruited from Delft Technical University. As emphasized by several speakers at the Noordwijk memorial symposium, Van de Hulst demonstrated and personified the notion that scientific quality is vital to success in space research.

Religion and Philosophy. As mentioned earlier, Van de Hulst grew up in a strongly religious family. As students, he and his later wife Wil were active members of the Nederlandse Christen-Studenten Vereniging (NCSV), the Student Christian Movement in the Netherlands affiliated with the World's Student Christian Federation (WSCF) based in Geneva; Willem "Wim" Visser't Hooft, in 1948 the founder of the World Council of Churches, had earlier been a member of the NCSV, and president of the WSCF. Van de Hulst's strong religious belief is obvious from several sentences in the preface of his 1946 doctor's thesis, including: "May God give me strength and insight to follow the right path. My wife will be at my side in this. In Thee, Lord, we have trusted; never let us be shamed!"

In 1951 the largest Protestant church in the Netherlands, the Nederlandse Hervormde Kerk, through its Council for the Affairs of Church and Theology, formed a Study Committee on Faith and Physical Science, to discuss problems occurring in this area. Several prominent scientists, philosophers, and theologians joined this committee. Van de Hulst was a member from the start; he became its chairman in 1955 and kept the Committee on track, and steered it toward completion of its work in 1963. The final report of the committee took the form of a book *Geloof en Natuurwetenschap* (Faith and Physical Science) in two volumes. Together with the physicist Jan Volger, Van de Hulst contributed a chapter to this book.

In 1953, together with Cornelis Anthonie (Kees) van Peursen, professor of philosophy at Leiden, Van de Hulst published a book *Phaenomenologie en Natuurwetenschap*, in which the relationships of philosophy and the sciences are discussed. Habing writes in his obituary (2001): "about the same time Henk dissociated himself from his earlier religious beliefs." My personal impressions, from close contacts with Van de Hulst in astronomy and in the committee just mentioned, and with his family, do not confirm this, but the dissociation may well have occurred in later years.

After her marriage to Henk, Wil van de Hulst did not continue her astronomical studies. Instead, she moved to a study of psychology, and later started practicing psychotherapy. Habing notes that, after about 1980, Van de Hulst and his wife visited annual psychotherapy work-

shops, and he found great satisfaction in these. And undoubtedly, these shared events further strengthened their happy, stable marriage.

Although often ill in his childhood, Van de Hulst had developed into a strong and healthy man. But around 1995 his health weakened, and in 1999 an inoperable lung cancer was discovered. He lived through his final months with great mental strength, aware that his life had been richly blessed.

Teacher, Guide and Colleague. Van de Hulst served as thesis adviser on twenty-eight PhD projects, covering a wide range of subjects, from Cepheid atmospheres to space research, radio sources and Galactic dynamics. He was an outstanding counsellor: accessible and sensitive, open and direct, and rich in practical advice. In his courses and research, he concentrated on fundamental matters. He emphasized insight rather than facts. Throughout his life, he gave many excellent review talks. The "look-back" papers which he wrote in his last few years make fascinating reading; they are enlightening and full of wit.

After Van de Hulst's appointment at Leiden in 1948, he stayed there forever. Several prominent Leiden graduates, having returned after a foreign postdoc period, left after a few years and made their career elsewhere. Not so Van de Hulst. What then was his relationship with Jan Oort, the powerful, world-renowned Leiden Observatory director?

Oort had put him on the search for a radio spectral line, which resulted in the 1944 prediction of the 21-cm line. Oort had suggested that he make a detailed study of the Mie theory of scattering, which led to his 1946 doctoral thesis. In 1948 Oort offered him a position at Leiden and involved him in cosmical aerodynamics. In 1951, during his stay at Harvard, they exchanged many letters—about the 21-cm line and about general Observatory affairs. In 1952-1954, Van de Hulst was responsible for the reduction and analysis of the first Galactic hydrogen-line survey, and first author on the paper presenting the results. In 1958 Oort asked him to go to London, and Van de Hulst was (as he later put it) "launched into a space career"; Oort of course understood the critical importance of the COSPAR job, but he knew he could not take it on himself.

They worked closely together for many years, but they published few joint papers; both had their separate areas and responsibilities. To quote Blaauw's obituary, "The outstanding but ambitious directorship of Oort left little room for competing initiatives from his—devoted—staff. Van de Hulst's many talents, however, enabled him to stake out his special prominent place beside Oort at Leiden Observatory." I concur with Harm Habing's analysis: that Van de Hulst "had been raised in a religious tradition that emphasizes humility.... He had a strong sense of the relativity of all things. He was a man of great talents, but without a mission. He labored where he considered himself able to contribute, but had no explicit need to achieve great things. In that respect his personality was different from that of Jan Oort, his immediate colleague and paragon." Hovenier writes: "Henk … seemed to consider his fame more like a burden than something of which to be proud. He considered other things far more important, such as authenticity, sincerity and simplicity."

Van de Hulst himself wrote (1998, p. 15): "What I enjoyed most in my research were not the big successes, but rather the little discoveries when a sudden insight revealed a surprising connection between bits of information that had seemed to be far apart." Though modest indeed, he clearly was a leader, who took decisions where required, after listening carefully to everyone concerned; but he acted as a guide rather than a chief.

BIBLIOGRAPHY

A fairly (but not fully) complete bibliography is available from http://adsabs.harvard.edu/abstract_service.html.

WORKS BY VAN DE HULST

"Radiostraling uit het wereldruim. II. Herkomst der radiogolven." *Nederlandsch Tijdschrift voor Natuurkunde* 11 (1945): 210–221. The 1944 NAC presentation predicting the existence of the 21-cm line of neutral atomic hydrogen. Translated as "Paper 34" in *Classics in Radio Astronomy*, edited by Woodruff Turner Sullivan III, pp. 302–316. Dordrecht: Reidel, 1982.

"Optics of Spherical Particles." PhD thesis, University of Utrecht, 1946.

With Jan Hendrik Oort. "Gas and Smoke in Interstellar Space." *Bulletin of the Astronomical Institutes of The Netherlands* 10 (1946): 187–204. Based on the 1942 prize essay by Van de Hulst.

With Johannes Martinus Burgers, eds. *Problems of Cosmical Aerodynamics: Proceedings of the Symposium on the Motion of Gaseous Masses of Cosmical Dimensions Held at Paris, August 16–19, 1949.* Dayton, OH: Central Air Documents Office, 1951.

"The Chromosphere and the Corona." In *The Solar System: 1, The Sun*, edited by Gerard P. Kuiper, pp. 207–321. Chicago: University of Chicago Press, 1953. Standard reference.

With Cornelis Anthonie van Peursen. *Phaenomenologie en Natuurwetenschap: Bezinning op het wereldbeeld.* Utrecht: Erven J. Bijleveld, 1953. Discussion of relationships between philosophy and the sciences.

"The Galaxy Explored by Radio Waves." *The Observatory* 73 (1953): 129–139. The Halley Lecture for 1953, written for nonspecialists. First map of the Galaxy's spiral pattern.

With Christiaan Alexander Muller and Jan Hendrik Oort. "The Spiral Structure of the Outer Part of the Galactic System Derived from the Hydrogen Emission at 21 cm Wavelength."
Bulletin of the Astronomical Institutes of The Netherlands 12 (1954): 117–149. First survey of Galactic atomic hydrogen: full discussion of instrument, observations, analysis, and interpretation.

Light Scattering by Small Particles. New York: Wiley, 1957. Reprint, New York: Dover, 1981. A classic text, with wide applications.

With Ernst Raimond and Hugo van Woerden. "Rotation and Density Distribution of the Andromeda Nebula Derived from Observations of the 21-cm Line." *Bulletin of the Astronomical Institutes of The Netherlands* 14 (1957): 1–16. First hydrogen-line study of an external galaxy beyond the Magellanic Clouds.

Multiple Light Scattering: Tables, Formulas, and Applications. 2 vols. New York: Academic, 1980. Major sequel to 1957 text.

"Space Science beyond the Solar System." *Space Science Reviews* 65 (1993): 201–219. "Distinguished Lecture" presented to the World Space Congress, Washington, DC, on 1 September 1992. Fascinating.

"Scaling Laws in Multiple Light Scattering under Very Small Angles." *Reviews in Modern Astronomy* 9 (1996): 1–16. The Karl Schwarzschild Lecture for the Astronomische Gesellschaft, delivered at Bonn, 19 September 1995. Very readable.

"Roaming through Astrophysics." *Annual Review of Astronomy and Astrophysics* 36 (1998): 1–16. Invited autobiography, giving valuable insight into life and work.

OTHER SOURCES

Blaauw, Adriaan. "Hendrik Christoffel van de Hulst." *Proceedings of the American Philosophical Society* 146 (2002): 420–423. Biography by a long-time colleague. Detailed mention of many honors and distinctions.

Habing, Harm J. "Obituaries: Hendrik Christoffel van de Hulst, 1918–2000." *Astronomy and Geophysics* 42 (2001): 1.33–1.37. Excellent obituary by a close, younger colleague. Appeared first in August 2000 on Leiden Observatory Web page.

Hovenier, Joop W. "Obituary H. C. van de Hulst (19 November 1918–31 July 2000)." *Journal of Quantitative Spectroscopy and Radiative Transfer* 68 (2001): iii–v; reprinted, vol. 27 (2007): e1–e3. Written by one of Van de Hulst's former students, a specialist in scattering in planetary atmospheres.

Hugo van Woerden

VAN GOORLE, DAVID

SEE **Gorlaeus, David**.

VAN KREVELEN, DIRK WILLEM (*b.*
Rotterdam, Netherlands, 8 November 1914; *d.* Arnhem,

Netherlands, 27 October 2001), *chemical engineering, coal science, polymer science.*

Van Krevelen was a prominent industrial chemist who successfully combined a career in the management of research and industry with a scientific career in three different fields. He was among a small number of scientists who introduced the American chemical engineering approach to Europe, and he was one of the first scientists who emphasized that "unit operations" could better be understood in terms of the transfer of mass, momentum, and energy. His research on chemical gas absorption led to an improved understanding of the combined effects of physical transport and chemical reactions. Van Krevelen was a founder of an entirely new branch of chemical engineering: chemical reaction engineering. He was also an important contributor to coal science; he applied the graphical-statistical method of his former supervisor Hein Waterman to coal, obtaining results that were relevant both for geology and the coal industries. His handbook on coal went through several widely used editions. Van Krevelen published extensively on polymer science as well. He developed an additive method of (atomic) group contributions that was used worldwide, and he wrote an important handbook that was reprinted several times. His name lives on in several of his results and methods, in all of these fields: the "Van Krevelen–Hoftyzer diagram" (on chemical gas absorption); the "Mars–Van Krevelen mechanism" (on catalytic oxidation); the "Van Krevelen–Chermin method" (on the estimation of the free energy of organic compounds); the "Van Krevelen diagram" (on coal and coal processes); the "Van Krevelen method" (on additive properties of polymers); and the "Van Krevelen–Hoftyzer relationship" (on the viscosity of polymer fluids).

Childhood and Education. Dirk van Krevelen (known to his friends as Dick) was born in Rotterdam on 8 November 1914, the son of Dirk Willem van Krevelen, Sr., a bookkeeper in the stevedore firm of A. A. Hoogerwerff, and Huberta van Krevelen (née Regoort). From 1927 to 1933 he attended the Marnix Gymnasium at Rotterdam, where he developed a strong interest in both the sciences and the humanities. His decision to study chemistry was inspired by the example of Jacobus Hendricus van 't Hoff and was also influenced by his father, who argued that there were good employment opportunities in that field, even in times of economic crisis. In October 1933 Van Krevelen was enrolled at Leiden University. Though he was quite disappointed by the courses in chemistry during his first year, the academic environment changed significantly with the appointment of Anton E. van Arkel as professor of inorganic chemistry at Leiden in 1934. Van Arkel was an inspiring teacher, and his book *De chemische binding als electrostatisch verschijnsel,* written with Jan de Boer, was a revelation to Van Krevelen, as it demonstrated

an ingenious synthesis of theoretical insights, systematic classification, and presentation of empirical facts. After his *kandidaats* examination (bachelor's degree) in 1935, Van Krevelen decided to study physical and inorganic chemistry with Van Arkel, who asked him to work on the cohesive forces in liquid mixtures.

With an industrial career in mind, Van Krevelen in April 1937 also started with a minor in chemical technology, at the laboratory of professor Hein Waterman at the Technological University of Delft. This step had a decisive influence on his future career. Waterman helped him to find a job in industry, and, more importantly, Waterman's scientific approach—the use of graphical-statistical methods—would become the paradigm that Van Krevelen followed, and perfected, in most of his scientific work.

Since 1927 Waterman had been a scientific advisor to the oil company Royal Dutch/Shell, which provided funds for the employment of three private assistants, who did fundamental research on oil products and processes. Waterman, who wrote dozens of reports every year for Shell (more than 300 in total between 1927 and 1940), also engaged some of his students in research on oil. Van Krevelen was given the task of synthesizing model substances, related to oil components, and of measuring their physical parameters. From November 1937 Waterman employed Van Krevelen as one of his private assistants. Until the end of 1939 Van Krevelen worked for Shell on three topics: the chemical thermodynamics of oil hydrocarbons, related to Waterman's graphical-statistical enterprise; the polymerization of ethylene, as part of attempts to improve the anti-knock properties of gasoline; and the induced pyrolysis of methane, which would become the topic of Van Krevelen's dissertation. Meanwhile, in March 1938, he did his *doktoraal* examination (master's degree) at Leiden University—only four and a half years after his enrollment. At the time, most Dutch chemistry students took six or seven years to achieve the master's degree.

As with all previous private assistants to Waterman, a career at Shell was an almost certain prospect for Van Krevelen. By the time he received his doctorate, though, in December 1939, at the age of twenty-five, the situation had changed dramatically. In September 1939 World War II had broken out and Shell stopped employing new researchers. Moreover, Waterman, who was Jewish, decided to resign as scientific advisor by the end of 1939. He helped Van Krevelen to obtain a position, starting 1 January 1940, within the research organization of DSM (Dutch State Mines), which was just building its new Central Laboratory. Meanwhile, in July 1939, Van Krevelen had married Frieda Kreisel. They had three sons and one daughter.

Research Leader at DSM. When Van Krevelen in January 1940 entered the service of DSM, Frits van Iterson and Daan Ross van Lennep (manager of DSM's chemical division) had just founded DSM's Central Laboratory (under the leadership of the chemist Gé Berkhoff), modeled after the example of the Physics Laboratory of Philips, which was headed by Gilles Holst. Van Iterson and Ross van Lennep wanted to establish a research laboratory that, like the lab at Philips, would create an academic atmosphere in which high-level research was conducted. Initially, though, the differences between the laboratories were great. Whereas the Philips Laboratory in 1940 had a staff of about 520 employees, the staff of the Central Laboratory of DSM was about 80, 20 percent of whom were academics. In the following years the DSM laboratory would grow considerably. By 1941 there was a staff of about 200, including 29 academic scientists and engineers. When Van Krevelen left the laboratory in 1959, there were almost 100 academic scientists and engineers and about 650 employees in lower ranks.

In 1940 Van Krevelen began his research activities in DSM's physical chemistry department, which was headed by Henk de Bruijn. In 1943 Van Krevelen became a department manager himself, as head of the newly created research department on chemical engineering. In early 1948 Berkhoff decided that he would concentrate on the overall supervision of research and development at DSM, which, next to the Central Laboratory, included various chemical pilot plants and a research laboratory on mining technologies, as well as on technology transfer and licensing. Therefore a new position was created for someone who would directly supervise the research at the Central Laboratory. At that time the future course of the DSM research organization was hotly debated. Henk de Bruijn, who had visited the IG Farben laboratories at Ludwigshafen as part of a military mission in June 1947, advocated transforming the Central Laboratory into a laboratory of basic research, and erecting additional applied research laboratories, in close contact with the production departments. Van Krevelen had a far more pragmatic view. He was in favor of a mix of fundamental and applied research at the Central Laboratory, in permanent close contacts with the chemical plants. Van Krevelen won the battle, and in August 1948 he was promoted to the position of research leader of the Central Laboratory of DSM. In early 1955 he became head of the Central Laboratory, directing not only research, but also personnel and administration, which since 1948 had been supervised by his colleague Jan Selman.

During his years as research leader at DSM, Van Krevelen maintained a balance between fundamental high-level research and research with direct economic relevance to the company. He created an academic atmosphere at the Central Laboratory, with colloquia and study groups, and decided that all researchers could spend 20 percent of their time on topics of their own choice. In his yearly reports he eloquently defended the relevance of research against the conservative board of directors, who in general did not support purely scientific work. At the same time, Van Krevelen initiated research projects with direct relevance to the production departments. The fact that research and production at DSM were located quite close to each other played a great role in collaboration between departments. Van Krevelen was in frequent exchange with chemists and engineers working in the production plants.

One of the most striking features of Van Krevelen's career is that, even as a manager, he continued to engage in high-level research himself. He had a few assistants doing the laboratory work for him, but he was active in writing publications and books and in giving numerous lectures. Moreover, Van Krevelen did important work in three large, but very different, fields: chemical engineering, coal science, and polymer science.

Although Van Krevelen's work was highly valued at DSM, there was no chance that he would be promoted to the board of directors. The conservative majority of the DSM board thought that one scientist on the board—chemist Jan van Aken—was enough. They were not willing to add Berkhoff to the board, let alone his deputy Van Krevelen. Therefore, when in March 1959 Van Krevelen was asked to become a member of the board of directors of the Algemene Kunstzijde Unie (AKU; General Rayon Union), a far larger company than DSM, he accepted the offer. In September 1959 Van Krevelen joined the board of directors of AKU with the special task of supervising the research and development activities of the company. Surprisingly, in his new and demanding managerial role, he continued to be actively engaged in research.

Chemical Engineering. In June 1940, soon after he had entered the services of DSM, Van Krevelen was given the task of studying the removal of carbon dioxide (CO_2), hydrogen sulfide (H_2S), and other gases from coal gas with the help of an ammonia (NH_3)–water mixture. This was necessary because coal gas had to be purified before it could be used for lighting purposes by the households in the region, but also because DSM had planned to use CO_2 as a feedstock for the production of soda and urea. The problem was quite new to Van Krevelen. It involved the study of chemical engineering problems such as mass transfer (diffusion) in combination with chemical reactions. Waterman had been one of the first professors of chemical technology on the Continent who had used the American approach to chemical engineering in his lectures, following a visit to the United States in the 1920s; he introduced the concepts of "unit operations" and "unit processes" to the Netherlands. Van Krevelen had of course heard these lectures, but he was not really familiar with the study of unit operations, or of other chemical engineering topics.

Consequently, Van Krevelen started to study books on chemical engineering, such as William H. Walker, Warren K. Lewis, and William H. McAdams's *Principles of Chemical Engineering* (3rd ed., 1937), Walter L. Badger and Warren L. McCabe's *Elements of Chemical Engineering* (1931), and Thomas K. Sherwood's *Absorption and Extraction* (1937). Together with his research assistant Jan Hoftijzer (called Hoftyzer in English sources), he successfully solved the problems concerning the purification of coal gas in 1941; in the following years they worked on improving their theoretical understanding of the process. In 1946 Van Krevelen and his colleague Honoré A. J. Pieters published a book on the new process of coal gas purification developed at DSM. Two years later Van Krevelen and Hoftijzer published their theoretical views on the combined effects of mass transfer and chemical reactions. This represented a great breakthrough in chemical engineering, and their publication was one of the first papers on that particular topic. Their paper became a classic, and the "Van Krevelen-Hoftyzer diagram" on chemical gas absorption (1948), informally called the "shunting yard" by chemical engineers, was often quoted in the literature.

The reason that the Van Krevelen–Hoftijzer paper became a classic had to do with the improved theoretical understanding of chemical engineering that Van Krevelen had acquired during World War II. In 1942 Van Iterson, who was on the supervisory board of the Middelbare Technische School (Polytechnic School) at Heerlen, near DSM, asked Van Krevelen to introduce a course on chemical engineering at that school. Until that time chemical engineering had only been taught in the Netherlands at the Technological University at Delft (by Waterman, until the Nazis forced him to resign in October 1940, and by Willem J. D. van Dijck, a part-time professor who worked at Royal Dutch/Shell), and at the Polytechnic School at Dordrecht. Van Krevelen was thus among the first in the Netherlands who taught about unit operations and unit processes. In 1943 Adriaan Klinkenberg and Herman Mooy of the development group within the engineering department of Royal Dutch/Shell at The Hague published a paper in which they argued that there were strong analogies between the transfer processes of momentum, energy (heat), and matter. They rewrote the fundamental conservation laws of momentum, energy, and matter in such a way that similar equations resulted, with four different terms: changes as a function of time; changes by convection; changes by diffusion; and changes by production (for instance, as a result of an external forces, in the case of momentum, or by a chemical reaction, in the case of the production of heat and matter). They studied these equa-

tions, and their boundary conditions, by introducing dimensionless groups, such as the Reynolds number or the Nusselt number, thus combining in a creative way the study of transport phenomena with P. W. Bridgman's "dimensional analysis" and M. Weber's "theory of similitude," which was crucial for the scaling-up of laboratory experiments to the level of production plants. By so doing, they succeeded in providing a well-structured and rather complete picture of the different dimensionless groups that played important roles in chemical engineering.

Van Krevelen was delighted by the paper of Klinkenberg and Mooy, and he completely restructured his chemical engineering course at the Heerlen Polytechnic School. In his lecture notes, called *Een nieuw ordenend beginsel bij de studie der technologische bewerkingen* (A New Ordering Principle in the Study of Technological Operations), he systematically extended the approach of Klinkenberg and Mooy as a basis for the understanding of unit operations. In Van Krevelen's view, all unit operations—such as distillation, ion exchange, crystallization, filtration, mixing, and gas absorption—could be understood in terms of four fundamental processes: transfer of mass, transfer of momentum, transfer of energy, and transfer of electric charge (which he had added). And, even more systematically than Klinkenberg and Mooy, Van Krevelen developed a complete overview of all possible dimensionless groups, introducing a uniform notation for them. This systematic approach would also characterize much of Van Krevelen's later work.

After 1948 this new, more fundamental understanding of unit operations was introduced at Delft Technological University by Hans Kramers, the successor to Van Dijck as professor of chemical engineering. His course on "transport phenomena" of momentum, energy, and mass followed the classification systems introduced by Klinkenberg, Mooy, and, probably, Van Krevelen, but went into far greater detail with respect to the quantitative empirical study of the transfer processes. R. Byron Bird, who in 1956 worked in Kramers's laboratory as a Fullbright lecturer, followed Kramers's example in his very successful textbook on *Transport Phenomena* (1960), which he wrote with Warren E. Stewart and Edwin N. Lightfoot. Through the use of that text, the approach pioneered by Klinkenberg, Mooy, and Van Krevelen became a standard ingredient of all chemical engineering curricula in the United States and Europe.

Theoretical studies such as the one done by Klinkenberg and Mooy, and by Van Krevelen, were typical of much of the research work done during World War II in the Netherlands. Because of the war, the construction of new installations slowed down, or even came to a halt, as in the case of Royal Dutch/Shell. Without projects with tight deadlines, several industrial scientists and engineers embarked on theoretical studies. Indirectly, these studies had great practical relevance. The theory of gas-liquid reactions and the improved processes for gas absorption developed by Van Krevelen and Hoftijzer clearly built on Van Krevelen's new approach to unit operations with the help of dimensionless parameters. His well-organized "shunting yard" graph was the result of an intelligent choice of three dimensionless parameters that provided insight into the relative importance of the physical diffusion and of the rate of the chemical reaction of the components. Van Krevelen coined the term "Sherwood number" for one of these parameters, named after his American colleague Thomas K. Sherwood.

In 1941 and 1942 Van Krevelen also started a thorough empirical and theoretical study of nitric acid manufacture, one of the key products of the chemical plants of DSM. Absorption of gases by liquids played a significant role in that chemical process. Van Krevelen developed a mathematical model of nitric acid production, which greatly improved the process control of the existing nitric acid plants of DSM, and which also led to the design of a completely new plant, which was built between 1947 and 1951. The new process was a success, and several licenses were sold to chemical companies in England, Germany, Portugal, South Africa, Egypt, and India.

In 1946 and 1947 Van Krevelen made a three-month study tour through the United States to learn about the latest developments in chemical engineering. He met most of the leading figures in the field—such as T. K. Sherwood, W. K. Lewis, W. H. Walker, W. L. McCabe, T. H. Chilton, A. P. Colburn, O. A. Hougen, and K. M. Watson—and was elected as an active member of the American Institute of Chemical Engineers in 1947. Between 1947 and 1951 Van Krevelen published about thirty papers on gas absorption and on many other aspects of chemical engineering, such as the dissolution of solids, the drying of solids, fluidization, and the principles of chemical reaction engineering. In 1951 Van Krevelen was one of the founding editors of the journal *Chemical Engineering Science*. Two years later, the European Federation of Chemical Engineering (EFCE) was established, and Van Krevelen took an active part in organizing its first congress, the First Congress on Chemical Reaction Engineering, which was held in Amsterdam in 1957. At that congress the EFCE Working Party on Chemical Reaction Engineering was formally established, and Van Krevelen became its first chairman; the term *chemical reaction engineering*, which refers to the interplay of chemical engineering and the study of reaction kinetics, had been coined by Van Krevelen himself.

In addition to his other fields of research (see below), Van Krevelen continued to contribute to chemical engineering during the 1950s and 1960s. Between 1951 and 1971 he published more than fifty papers. One important (and still cited) paper was a study with his colleague Pieter Mars of the mechanism of oxidation reactions over oxidic catalysts, such as vanadium oxide (which plays a role, for instance, in sulfuric acid manufacture). Mars and Van Krevelen discovered that oxidation takes place via a two-step mechanism: first, the absorbed reactant is oxidized by the oxygen present in the crystal lattice of the catalyst, followed by desorption of the product; in a second step, the reduced catalyst is oxidized by oxygen from the gas phase. This so-called "Mars–Van Krevelen mechanism" appeared to have a quite universal significance, as it plays a role in numerous catalytic reactions. In 1958 Mars, who worked at the Central Laboratory of DSM, received his PhD from the Technological University at Delft on the basis of his research on the mechanism of oxidation reactions, with the chemist Jan de Boer and Van Krevelen as his supervisors.

Another often-cited publication by Van Krevelen with great relevance to industrial chemical reactions was his work on the "estimation of the free enthalpy (Gibbs free energy) of formation of organic compounds from group contributions," published in 1951, together with his assistant Huub Chermin. Building on Waterman's graphical-statistical method, Van Krevelen showed that the group contributions were additive—a fact that greatly helped to predict the course of new industrial processes. Later, in his work on polymers, Van Krevelen would extend this "atomic group approach" to other physical parameters.

After Van Krevelen left DSM for AKU, he introduced his expertise in chemical engineering to that company. Although a member of the board of directors, he supervised research by Rob Vroom on the chemical reaction engineering aspects of the viscose rayon spinning process, and coauthored several papers on polymer processing. For his "fundamental research on chemical reaction engineering" Van Krevelen was awarded an honorary doctorate by the Technische Hochschule Darmstadt in 1966.

Coal Science. After Van Krevelen had been promoted to research manager of the Central Laboratory of DSM, Berkhoff asked him, at the end of 1948, to become the Dutch representative to the European Working Party on Coal Classification. As a result, Van Krevelen decided to embark on a second large field of research, namely the scientific study of coal. Apart from the direct relevance to the work of the Working Party, this was also a strategic choice because Dutch State Mines primarily was a mining company, though it had a large chemical component, and the mining operations of the company were the primary concern of the board of directors. By taking coal as his topic of research, Van Krevelen was able to show the relevance of chemical research to the mining engineers and coal merchants of the board of DSM, a factor that facilitated the expansion of the Central Laboratory during the 1950s.

The cornerstone of Van Krevelen's coal research was the fruitful application to coal of the graphical-statistical method that his former supervisor Waterman had applied to oil products. Traditionally the properties of crude oil and of oil fractions had been characterized by fractional distillation and by measuring its specific density. For the higher boiling fractions of oil, these methods were far too rough. Before the introduction to the oil industry, in the 1950s, of gas chromatography, mass spectroscopy and NMR, other methods therefore had to be developed to characterize oil fractions. Of these, Waterman's method was one of the most successful.

In 1932 Waterman had published the idea that it was not necessary to characterize oil fractions by identifying all their dozens of components, but that it was sufficient to determine the statistical averages of the three most important structural characteristics of molecules in oil: the percentage of carbon in the aliphatic parts of the molecules (alkanes; paraffines); the percentage of carbon in the cycloalkane (naphtenic) parts of the molecules; and the percentage of carbon in the aromatic parts of the molecules. Together with his students Jozef C. Vlugter and Hendrik A. van Westen, Waterman presented his results in graphs in which the hydrogen percentage was plotted against the average molecular weight for different "ring indices," that is, the average number of naphtenic rings per molecule. It appeared that with the help of these three parameters, crude oils and oil fractions could be characterized quite accurately. Between 1932 and 1942 Waterman and his students also showed that by measuring physical parameters—such as the refraction (n), the density (d), and the average molecular weight (M) (the so-called n-d-M method)—and several other parameters such as the viscosity (ν)—the hydrogen percentages and ring indices could be calculated, so that oil fractions could be characterized with sufficient precision by physical measurements alone. Later in his career Waterman also applied these methods to the characterization of chemical processes such as hydrogenation and aromatization.

Van Krevelen transferred Waterman's methodology to the investigation of coal. As early as 1950 he published a seminal paper in the British journal *Fuel* that would influence the entire field of coal research for decades. With the help of two seemingly simple, dimensionless ratios—the atomic hydrogen to carbon (H/C) ratio, and the atomic oxygen to carbon (O/C) ratio—Van Krevelen constructed a diagram that summarized numerous publications as well as the extensive empirical investigations done by his assistants. On the one hand, the diagram permitted the

rational classification of pre-stages of coal formation and different types of coal, such as wood, cellulose, lignin, peat, brown coal, different grades of bituminous coal, and anthracite. On the other hand, the diagram showed different reaction paths, such as decarboxylation, dehydration, and demethanation, which played a role both during natural coal formation (coalification) and in the industrial processes of coal gas production and coke manufacture (carbonization), hydrogenation, and oxidation.

With the help of the "Van Krevelen diagram," important new insights on coalification and on industrial processes could be gained, and many of these new insights were already in Van Krevelen's 1950 publication. That work accelerated Van Krevelen's very productive research trajectory in coal science. Between 1948 and 1965 he would publish over a hundred papers on coal and coal products. As a result, the "Van Krevelen diagram" found its way into geology and geochemistry, where it is applied today also to the study of the formation of oil and natural gas, and to the study of coal products such as coke, gas, and artificial gasoline. It helped manufacturers to understand which type of coal was best suited for the production of a particular final product.

In 1957 Van Krevelen summarized his research in the book-length monograph *Coal Science: Aspects of Coal Constitution*, which he published with his assistant Jan Schuijer. The book became a great success. In 1961 Van Krevelen published a thoroughly revised edition under the title *Coal: Typology, Chemistry, Physics, Constitution*. The graphical-statistical method and the "Van Krevelen diagram" played a key role in these books. After his retirement from industry in 1976, Van Krevelen again published a revised edition, in 1981. The book had to be reprinted in 1982, and again in 1984. In 1993, at the age of seventy-nine, Van Krevelen published a fourth, updated edition of *Coal: Typology, Chemistry, Physics, Constitution*. Through these books and his numerous papers Van Krevelen dominated the field of coal science for over thirty years. In 1954 he was awarded the medal of the University of Liège for his work on coal, and in the same year he was awarded the Coal Science Medal of the British Coal Utilisation Research Association. In 1959 he was elected a Fellow of the Institute of Fuel. In a generalized form, the H/C and O/C "Van Krevelen diagrams" are today also used in mass spectrometry.

Professor of Fuel Technology and Polymerization Processes at Delft. In 1952 Gerard A. Brender à Brandis, the part-time professor of fuel technology at the Technological University of Delft, retired, and Van Krevelen was invited to succeed him. After the board of directors of DSM gave him permission to teach two days a months at Delft, Van Krevelen in October 1952 was formally appointed as professor of chemical technology, with the special task of teaching about the technology of solid and liquid fuels and the associated production of energy. He held this professorship until his retirement from the Technological University of Delft in 1980.

During his professorship Van Krevelen lectured on all three scientific fields to which he made major contributions: from 1953 to 1957, and in 1959 and 1961, he lectured on fuel technology; in 1958, 1960, and 1963 he gave courses on chemical reaction engineering; and he taught on the process technology of polymers in 1962 and from 1964 to 1980. After his move to AKU, in 1959, the subject of his professorship at Delft was formally changed to the process technology of polymers. For the supervisory board of AKU this had been a pre-condition for granting permission to Van Krevelen to combine his membership on the board of directors with a part-time professorship at Delft.

Although a part-time professor, Van Krevelen supervised the considerable number of twenty-three dissertations. In most cases these PhD students were staff members of the research organizations of DSM (and, later, AKU), who did their research in industry, supervised by Van Krevelen, and who were awarded the doctorate at Delft when their results had enough substance and coherence. Between 1952 and 1966 Van Krevelen supervised nine PhD students in coal research, between about 1955 and 1960 four PhD students in chemical engineering, and between about 1961 and 1977 ten PhD students in polymer production and processing. Several of his PhD students and research assistants later became university professors themselves: Rinus Groenewegen and Jaap Smidt in molecular spectroscopy (which they had applied at DSM to the study of coal); Jan Schuijer and Leen Struik in the technology of polymers; Piet Mars in catalysis; and Rob Deelder in analytical chemistry.

Member of the Board of Directors of AKU and AKZO. When, on 1 September 1959, Van Krevelen succeeded Jan Weeldenburg, who had just died, as board member of AKU with the overall responsibility for research, he entered a company that differed from DSM in many respects. In contrast to DSM, AKU had been a multinational company for many decades. Founded in 1929 as a holding company that united the activities of the Dutch rayon firm Enka and the German Vereinigte Glanzstoff Fabriken, AKU in 1959 had plants for fiber production in Germany, Austria, Britain, Spain, Italy, the United States, Mexico, and the Netherlands. Even before World War II, AKU was one of the leading synthetic fiber producers, together with companies such as Du Pont and IG Farben. Around 1960 its major fiber was still rayon, but nylon-6 (Enkalon®), produced from caprolactam made by DSM,

had been produced since the early 1950s, and the company was constructing plants for glass fibers (together with Pittsburgh Plate Glass) and polyesters (Terlenka®) based on dimethyl terephtalate (together with Amoco). In 1960 the central research and development laboratories near the AKU headquarters at Arnhem had a staff of 1,075 employees. There were also large research laboratories in Germany and the United States. Van Krevelen now had responsibility for a research and development organization that was about four times as large as the Central Laboratory of DSM.

The 1960s were a period of vigorous expansion of the chemical and synthetic fibers industries. Through huge investment programs and mergers, companies tried to improve their economies of scale. Against that background Van Krevelen was a strong advocate of a merger between AKU and DSM. He had the vision that the backward integration of AKU into the domain of organic chemistry and fiber intermediates would strengthen the technological and economic basis of the company. There was a strong synergy, because DSM made growing amounts of caprolactam for AKU's nylon production. At least three times during the 1960s Van Krevelen and his colleagues negotiated seriously with Van Krevelen's former boss Jan van Aken and the other board members of DSM. Although both Van Krevelen and Van Aken were strongly in favor of the merger, members of DSM's advisory board were against the integration of the state-owned DSM into a private corporation, in view of the social responsibility for the miners at a time when all Dutch coal mines were closing their gates. To Van Krevelen's great disappointment, the negotiations between AKU and DSM came to a final end in early 1969.

Only a few months later, AKU merged with Koninklijke Zout Organon (KZO), a company that was a conglomerate of pharmaceutical (Organon and Noury van der Lande), coatings (Sikkens), and chemical (Ketjen and Koninklijke Zout) companies. The result of the merger was incorporated as AKZO (since 1994, Akzo Nobel). Van Krevelen remained a member of the board of directors, and he was, as a result of the divisional structure introduced shortly after the merger, at the same time president of AKZO Research and Engineering. In that role he had the difficult task of integrating the research and development laboratories of the different companies that were now part of AKZO. When Van Krevelen retired from AKZO in 1976, the integration process was still incomplete. He was succeeded by Hans Kramers, his former colleague as professor of chemical engineering at Delft.

Polymer Science. As leading manager and scientist at AKU, Van Krevelen decided to focus his scientific activities on polymer science. This field was not completely new to him. At DSM he had been involved in the supervision of research on the fiber intermediates caprolactam and nylon salt, and on the polymerization of these intermediates. He also had been involved in the acquisition of the technology of the production of high-density and low-density polyethylene, from the German chemist Karl Ziegler and the British company Imperial Chemical Industries (ICI), as well as in organizing the research activities that went hand in hand with those acquisitions.

He again formed a small group of private assistants (including his long-time assistant Jan Hoftijzer, who had followed him from DSM to AKU); he was in close contact with other research scientists at AKU, and he lectured at Delft on polymer science and technology. As the combined result of these activities, Van Krevelen succeeded for the third time in mastering a new field. Between 1960 and 1978 he published about forty papers on polymers and polymer processing. In 1972 he summarized his results, and numerous papers by others, in a handbook written in collaboration with Hoftijzer, called *Properties of Polymers: Correlations with Chemical Structure*. Again, he built on Waterman's graphical-statistical method, on his own approach developed in his book on *Coal*, and on the seminal publication that he wrote with Chermin on the group contributions to the Gibbs free energy of molecules. Van Krevelen and Hoftijzer showed that many physical properties of polymer molecules could be estimated by summing the contributions made by the various structural groups in the polymer repeat unit. The correlations were semi-empirical in nature. In cases of strong interatomic and intermolecular interaction between the groups, or between the molecules, the physical properties are not additive. But in those cases, Van Krevelen showed, the deviations from the additive rule again followed certain regularities.

His book *Properties of Polymers* was considered groundbreaking by organic chemists and chemical engineers working in industry, because it brought order to a large and rapidly developing new field. Van Krevelen realized that the book was not for the polymer scientist proper, "its design being too empirical for him and too much directed to practice" (Van Krevelen and Hoftyzer, 2nd ed., 1976, p. v). The group additive method used in the book is known as the "Van Krevelen method" (or "Van Krevelen–Hoftyzer method"). Because his method was easy to use and covered a wide range of properties, it was quickly accepted by many scientists working in industry. In 1976 Van Krevelen had already published a second edition, reprinted in 1980 and 1986, and in 1990 a third edition came out, which was reprinted in 1997. His work clearly went beyond the skillful summarizing of known results. Many original empirical studies were included in his books. In 1975 Van Krevelen and Hoftijzer published new work on the viscosity of so-called non-Newtonian

(polymer) fluids. The relationship they found between the temperature, the chemical structure of the polymer unit, and the viscosity is known as the "Van Krevelen–Hoftyzer relationship."

Retirement and Awards. After his retirement from AKZO in 1976, Van Krevelen remained active for many years. From 1980 to 1983 he was international research advisor to the oil company Shell, and from 1980 to 1986 he also was research advisor and president of the advisory board of Norit, a company active in the production of adsorbents. In his spare time Van Krevelen studied the history of Egypt and other ancient civilizations.

In 1977 he was awarded the Chemistry Prize of the Society of the Dutch Chemical Industry for his great contributions to the development of that industry in the Netherlands. In 1984 he received the honorary doctorate of the Technological University Delft, in view of his achievements in coal technology, polymer technology, and the fundamentals of chemical engineering. Seven years later, in 1991, he became an honorary member of the Royal Dutch Chemical Society. Dick van Krevelen died on 27 October 2001 after a short period of illness following a stroke.

BIBLIOGRAPHY

The Regionaal Historisch Centrum Limburg, Maastricht, the Netherlands, houses the archive of the DSM company, including the personal files of D. W. van Krevelen (until 1959). For a bibliography of van Krevelen's publications (up to 1980), see his In Retrospect: Een keuze uit de voordrachten, *(Amsterdam: Meulenhoff, 1980), pp. 281–321. A copy of the typescript D. W. van Krevelen,* Een nieuw ordenend beginsel bij de studie der technologische bewerkingen *(n.d., n.p. [ca. 1946–1950]) is in the possession of the author. Together with James Small, the author interviewed Dick van Krevelen on 4 March 1997.*

WORKS BY VAN KREVELEN

"De geïnduceerde pyrolyse van methaan." Dissertation, Technological University of Delft, 19 December 1939.

With H. A. J. Pieters. *The Wet Purification of Coal Gas and Similar Gases by the Staatsmijnen-Otto-Process*. New York: Elsevier, 1946.

With P. J. Hoftijzer. "Kinetics of Gas-Liquid Reactions. Part I: General Theory." *Recueil des Travaux Chimiques des Pays-Bas* 67 (1948): 563–568.

"Graphical-statistical Method for the Study of Structure and Reaction Processes of Coal." *Fuel* 29 (1950): 269–283.

With H. A. G. Chermin. "Estimation of the Free Enthalpy (Gibbs Free Energy) of Formation of Organic Compounds from Group Contributions." *Chemical Engineering Science* 1 (1951): 66–80, 238.

With P. Mars. "Oxidations Carried Out by Means of Vanadium Oxide Catalysts." *Proceedings of the Conference on Oxidation*

Processes, Held in Amsterdam, 6–8 May 1954. Special Supplement to Chemical Engineering Science 3 (1954): 41–57.

Coal: Typology, Chemistry, Physics, Constitution. Amsterdam: Elsevier, 1961. [First edition, 1957, published (with Jan Schuijer) as *Coal Science: Aspects of Coal Constitution.*] 3rd ed., 1981; 4th ed., 1993.

"Waterman en de steenkoolchemie." In *De Oogst: een overzicht van het wetenschappelijk werk van Prof. dr. ir. H. I. Waterman, te zamen gebracht ter gelegenheid van zijn aftreden als hoogleraar in de chemische technologie aan de Technische Hogeschool te Delft,* pp. 24–29, n.p., n.d. [Delft, 1959].

Werdegang und Weg in der chemischen Technologie: Arbeitserinnerungen und Ausblick. Darmstadt: Technische Hochschule, 1966. Lecture given on the occasion of receiving the honorary doctorate.

With P. J. Hoftyzer. *Properties of Polymers: Correlations with Chemical Structure.* Amsterdam: Elsevier, 1972; 2nd ed., 1976; 3rd ed., 1990.

Selected Papers on Chemical Engineering Science. Amsterdam: Elsevier, 1976.

In Retrospect: Een keuze uit de voordrachten. Amsterdam: Meulenhoff, 1980. With a comprehensive bibliography of his over 250 publications up to 1980.

Sleutelwoorden in de proefondervindelijke wijsbegeerte. Rotterdam: Bataafsch Genootschap, 1987.

"Professor Hein Israel Waterman, 1889–1961: Onderzoeker—Vernieuwer—Leermeester." In *Waterman Symposium: Aula TU Delft, 28 April 1989, voordrachtenbundel,* 72–84. Delft: Technische Universiteit Delft, 1989.

"Vijftig jaar activiteit in de Chemische Technologie." In *Werken aan scheikunde. 24 memoires van hen die de Nederlandse chemie deze eeuw groot hebben gemaakt,* 243–263. Delft: Delft University Press, 1993. His autobiography.

OTHER SOURCES

Boelhouwer, C. "De Waterman ringanalyse." In *Chemie achter de dijken: Uitvindingen en uitvinders in de eeuw na Van't Hoff,* edited by Herman van Bekkum and Jan Reedijk, 44–45. Amsterdam: Edita KNAW, 2001.

———. "Hein Israël Waterman: kringen van hoge druk." In *Delfts goud: Leven en werken van achttien markante hoogleraren,* edited by K. F. Wakker et al., 64–79. Delft: Technische Universiteit Delft, 2002.

Challa, Ger. "Polymeren." In *De geschiedenis van de scheikunde in Nederland 3: De ontwikkeling van de chemie van 1945 tot het begin van de jaren tachtig,* edited by Ernst Homburg and Lodewijk Palm, 231–241. Delft: Delft University Press, 2004.

Fortuin, Jan M. H. "Procestechnologie en chemische industrie." In *De geschiedenis van de scheikunde in Nederland 3: De ontwikkeling van de chemie van 1945 tot het begin van de jaren tachtig,* edited by Ernst Homburg and Lodewijk Palm, 61–83. Delft: Delft University Press, 2004.

Homburg, Ernst. *Speuren op de tast: Een historische kijk op industriële en universitaire research.* Maastricht: Universiteit Maastricht, 2003. A history of research and development in the Netherlands.

Klinkenberg, A., and H. H. Mooy. "Overzicht der dimensielooze kengrootheden, die optreden bij het transport van impuls, warme en stof." *Nederlandsch Tijdschrift voor Natuurkunde* 10 (1943): 29–50.

———, and H. H. Mooy. "Dimensionless Groups in Fluid Friction, Heat, and Material Transfer." *Chemical Engineering Progress* 44 (1948): 17–36. An enlarged translation of their 1943 pubication.

Lintsen, Harry W., ed. *Research tussen vetkool en zoetstof: Zestig jaar DSM Research 1940–2000.* Zutphen: Walburg Pers, 2000.

Mars, Pieter. "De kinetica van oxydatiereacties op vanadiumhoudende katalysatoren." PhD diss., Technological University of Delft, 12 March 1958.

Moulijn, J. A., and H. van Bekkum. "De alleskunner. Van Krevelen: Recordhouder chemische vernoemingen." In *Chemie achter de dijken. Uitvindingen en uitvinders in de eeuw na Van 't Hoff,* edited by Herman van Bekkum and Jan Reedijk, 46–47. Amsterdam: Edita KNAW, 2001.

Mijs, Wim. "In Memoriam Prof. Dr. D. W. van Krevelen (1914–2001)." *Chemisch 2 Weekblad* (17 November 2001): 11.

Rooij, Arjan van, *The Company That Changed Itself: R&D and the Transformations of DSM.* Amsterdam: Amsterdam University Press, 2007.

Snelders, Harry A. M. *De geschiedenis van de scheikunde in Nederland 2: De ontwikkeling van chemie en chemische technologie in de eerste helft van de twintigste eeuw.* Delft: Delft University Press, 1997. On the history of Dutch chemistry, 1900–1950.

Valkema, Fridus. "De grondige aanpak van prof. D. W. van Krevelen." *Chemisch Weekblad* (24 January 1991): 37. Interview.

Vermaas, D., ed. *Research bij AKU.* n.p., n.d. [Arnhem, 1968].

Vlugter, J. C., H. A. van Westen, and J. J. Leendertse. "Grafisch-statistische identificatiemethoden." In *De Oogst: Een overzicht van het wetenschappelijk werk van Prof. dr. ir. H. I. Waterman, te zamen gebracht ter gelegenheid van zijn aftreden als hoogleraar in de chemische technologie aan de Technische Hogeschool te Delft,* 45–60. n.p., n.d. [Delft, 1959].

Waterman, H. I., with the collaboration of C. Boelhouwer and J. Cornelissen. *Correlation between Physical Constants and Chemical Structure: Graphical Statistical Methods of Identification of Mineral and Fatty Oils, Glass, Silicones, and Catalysts.* Amsterdam: Elsevier, 1958.

Ernst Homburg

VAN STRAATEN, LAMBERTUS MARIUS JOANNES URSINUS (*b.* Rotterdam, Netherlands, 2 April 1920; *d.* 6 May 2004), *geology, sedimentology, petrology.*

Van Straaten is one of the best known of a famous group of Dutch geologists who were active in the develop-

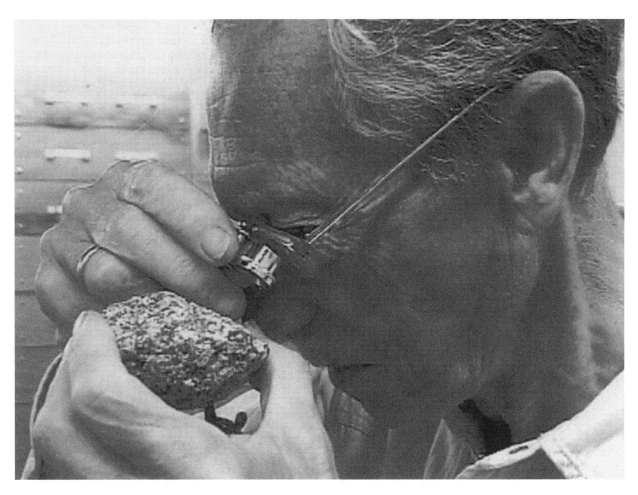

Lambertus Van Straaten. COURTESY OF DR. HEMMO JAN VEENSTRA.

ment of sedimentology in the twentieth century. He published a series of highly original papers on recent marine sediments after he started research on the tidal flats of the Dutch Wadden Sea in 1950.

Youth and University Studies. Van Straaten was born in Rotterdam, but spent most of his youth in Voorburg near The Hague. His father was a bacteriologist, his mother an apothecary. As a boy he was already interested in shells and fossils; he bought a canoe to study freshwater life near his home. Similar to many of his contemporaries, he was stimulated by the highly influential Dutch popular natural history books by Eli Heimans and Jac. P. Thijsse, in particular *Het Geologieboekje* (*Booklet on Geology*), written by Heimans in 1913 (2nd ed. 1923). Later in life Van Straaten himself became an excellent lecturer and popularizer of geology.

After graduating from the Gymnasium (grammar-school) in The Hague, Van Straaten started his studies in geology at Leiden University in 1938. Because of a vigorous protest of the university against the forced dismissal of

Jewish professors in the autumn of 1940, the Nazi occupation of the Netherlands closed Leiden University and Van Straaten went to Utrecht University to continue his studies there.

As unemployed men, including students, were in danger of being sent to Germany for forced labor, Van Straaten welcomed geological work in the province of Limburg organized by the States Collieries. This work was considered to be of economic importance and at first the participants did not have to fear being sent to Germany. In this period Van Straaten collected numerous gravel samples from the Meuse terraces, deposited by an Early Quaternary Rhine from Germany. However, Van Straaten also had to face deteriorating Nazi measures and went underground for two years, from May 1943 until the end of the war in May 1945. He resumed his studies in Leiden after the reopening of the university there. He became research assistant to Professor B.G. Escher, the writer of well-known Dutch textbooks on mineralogy and geology, and received his M.Sc. degree on 12 March 1946. On 10 July 1946 he defended his PhD thesis on the gravels he had collected from the Meuse terraces during the war. Thereafter he worked for a short period with the famous mineralogist Professor Paul Niggli at the E.T.H. Zürich (Switzerland) and started on 1 April 1947 as a co-worker of Professor Philip H. Kuenen, a well-known Dutch geologist, at the Geological Institute of Groningen University.

Studies of Tidal Flat Sediments. In Groningen Van Straaten's main object of study became the holocene sediments of the nearby Wadden Sea, in particular their transport and sedimentation. This resulted in a range of original papers starting in 1950. In 1951 he presented a benchmark paper on texture and genesis of Dutch Wadden Sea sediments at the Third International Sedimentological Congress, held in Groningen. He extended his research area to recent sediments to tidal flats in the province of Zeeland, the Bay of Arcachon, and the Rhone delta in France, and compared these with the Devonian Psammites du Condroz (1954).

Van Straaten was visiting professor of Marine Geology at Texas A&M College from 1954 to 1955. In 1958 he was invited to take part in the Salt Marsh Conference held at the Marine Institute of the University of Georgia at Sapelo Island, where he gave a paper on Dutch tidal flat formations. These visits to the United States and his contributions to congresses made him well known abroad, in addition to his renown in the Netherlands.

A large excavation near Velsen for a tunnel under the North Sea Canal, which connects Amsterdam with the North Sea, enabled detailed studies by a team of geologists and archeologists of recent sediments in this large but temporary exposure. The results were combined in a special publication edited by Van Straaten and Jan D. de Jong (1956).

Henk Postma (1954) described in his PhD thesis, "Hydrography of the Dutch Wadden Sea," a trapping mechanism and transport of small particles from the North Sea toward the shallower parts of the Wadden Sea. This stimulated Van Straaten to work with Philip H. Kuenen to publish on the mechanisms of this accumulation of fine-grained sediments (1957, 1958). They concluded that such processes must also have existed in the past. An increase in mud content may not always indicate increase in depth but sometimes closer approach to the coast.

In 1962 Van Straaten obtained grants from, among others, Royal Dutch Shell; the National Science Foundation (NSF) in Washington, D.C.; and its Dutch counterpart ZWO for an expedition in the Adriatic Sea to solve a dispute among sedimentologists on how troughs were filled with sediment: sideways or lengthwise by turbidity currents, as advocated by his colleague Kuenen. Van Straaten proved that the deeper beds were graded, indicating that turbidity currents, following the length of the

trough, played an important part in filling the basin. Mollusks of the sediment samples were also studied. Since his youth Van Straaten collected shells and was a member of the Dutch Malacological Society since 1953.

Another research topic of Van Straaten's became the building up of the western North Sea coast of Holland (1961, 1965, continuing his earlier studies at the excavation near Velsen). The Holocene history of the Dutch west coast formed by successive beach barriers was elucidated using drillings and numerous grab samples taken in the coastal part of the North Sea.

At Groningen University. In 1962 Van Straaten was appointed extraordinary professor of marine geology and petrology; in 1972 he succeeded Kuenen as ordinary professor, which position he held until his retirement in 1985. Among the eleven students who wrote their PhD theses under Van Straaten's supervision were five French geologists from the University of Strasbourg who had studied Ordivician glacial deposits in the Sahara. After 1970 Van Straaten devoted most of his time to his students: He not only lectured for geology students but also for the much larger group of biology students who had geology in their curriculum. He was an excellent lecturer and his field excursions with students were highly popular. He added four chapters to the first edition of a long-used Dutch textbook, *Algemene Geologie* (*General Geology*, edited by A.J. Pannekoek and the successor of Escher's Dutch textbook on geology of 1920 mentioned above, of which the ninth and last edition appeared in 1954). In 1973 Van Straaten became one of the editors of the book's later editions.

A new research project for Van Straaten became the origin of the famous Jurassic Solnhofen lithographic limestone. Most textbooks following Othenio Abel's (1922) *Lebensbilder aus der Tierwelt der Vorzeit* interpreted these limestones as beach deposits. Van Straaten (1971) discovered fine grading and scour marks indicating transport of carbonate particles in suspension to the Solnhofen basins, which probably were anoxic and without life. He suggested rapid sedimentation (storm events) of the successive layers in probably only a few days, enabling excellent preservation of the animals trapped in the basins. These well-preserved fossils—including *Archaeopterix*—made Solnhofen well known worldwide. Van Straaten also studied the formation of the numerous iron and manganese dendrites occurring in the lithographic limestones.

Besides his vast knowledge of sedimentological structures, Van Straaten possessed a phenomenal knowledge of rocks gained during his PhD studies and his work with Paul Niggli in Zürich. He lectured for more than thirty years on petrology and most of his publications after his retirement dealt with petrology, especially with porphyries.

In 2002 he published his last paper, on porphyries from the Rhine river basin. Up until his death he studied radiolarites and jasper, but unfortunately he could not finish these studies for publication.

As a result of reorganizations of the geological education at university level in the Netherlands, the Geological Institute in Groningen was closed in 1983. Van Straaten saw to it that the geological collection went to the university museum and that the library was made part of the library of the university. As an emeritus without commitments he could dedicate himself to traveling to geologically interesting areas. He visited Siberia, Svalbard, Patagonia, Oman, India, Costa Rica, Australia, and the Philippines. On part of these travels (Svalbard) he functioned as guide, where his wide interest in nature was well appreciated.

Van Straaten was a member of the editorial board of *Marine Geology* from 1964 to 1982. He was elected member of the KNAW, the Royal Dutch Academy of Arts and Sciences, in 1971 and received the Francis Shepard Award of the American Association of Petroleum Geologists in 1972. He was honored with the Van Waterschoot van der Gracht Medal by the KNGMG (Royal Dutch Geology and Mining Society) in 1972, and elected honorary fellow of the Geological Society, London in 1974. He married Johanna Struijk in 1956 and it was a severe blow to him that his beloved and artistic wife died in 1978, only forty-seven years old. They had two sons, Floris and Hans.

BIBLIOGRAPHY

WORKS BY VAN STRAATEN

"Grindonderzoek in Zuid-Limburg." *Mededeelingen van de Geologische Stichting.* C-VI, No. 2 (1946): 1–146. (Gravel Research in S.-Limburg, PhD thesis, in Dutch with a French résumé of 13 p).

"Texture and Genesis of Dutch Wadden Sea Sediments." *Proceedings of the Third International Congress of Sedimentology Groningen.* Wageningen, the Netherlands. 1951.

"Biogene Textures and the Formation of Shell Beds in the Dutch Wadden Sea." *Proceedings Koninklijke Nederlandse Akademie van Wetenschappen Series B*, 55 (1952): 500–516.

"Megaripples in the Dutch Wadden Sea and the Basin of Arcachon (France)." *Geologie en Mijnbouw (New Series)* 15 (1953): 1–11.

"Composition and Structure of Recent Marine Sediments in the Netherlands." *Leidse Geologische Mededelingen* 19 (1954): 1–110.

"Sedimenology of Recent Tidal Flat Deposits and the Psammites du Condroz (Devonian)." *Geologie en Mijnbouw (New Series)* 16 (1954): 25–47.

With Jan D. de Jong, eds. "The Excavation at Velsen" *Verhandelingen van het Koninklijk Nederlands Geologisch-Mijnbouwkundig Genootschap, Geological Series* 17 (1956): 87–218.

With Ph. H. Kuenen. "Tidal Action as a Cause of Clay Accumulation." *Journal of Sedimentary Petrology* 28 (1958): 406–413.

"Directional Effects of Winds, Waves and Currents along the Dutch North Sea Coast." *Geologie en Mijnbouw* 40 (1961): 333–346 and 363–391.

"Deltaic and Shallow Marine Deposits." *Developments in Sedimentology* I. Amsterdam: Elsevier, 1964.

"Coastal Barrier Deposits in South- and North-Holland." *Mededelingen van de Geologische Stichting, Nieuwe Serie* 17 (1965): 41–75.

"Sedimentation in the North-Western Part of the Adriatic Sea." *Colston Papers, Being the Proceedings 17th Symposium of the Colston Research Society, Bristol.* 1965.

"Micro-malacological Investigation of Cores from the Southeastern Adriatic Sea." *Proceedings van de Koninklijke Nederlandse Akademie van Wetenschappen—Amsterdam, Series B.* 69 (1966): 429–445.

"Origin of Solnhofen limestone." *Geologie en Mijnbouw* 50 (1971): 3–8.

"Turbidite Sediments in the Southeastern Adriatic Sea." In *Turbidites. Developments in Sedimentology* 3, edited by A. H. Bouma and A. Brouwer. Amsterdam: Elsevier, 1964.

"Zuidelijke porfieren." *Grondboor en Hamer* 56 (2002): 155–156.

OTHER SOURCES

Cadée, Gerhard C., and Hemmo J. Veenstra. *Levensberichten en herdenkingen.* Koninklijke: Nederlandse Akademie van Wetenschappen, forthcoming in 2007.

Veenstra, Hemmo J. "In memoriam." *Geological Society (London) Annual Report* (2004): 44–45.

———. *Nieuwsbrief Koninklijk Nederlands Geologisch Mijnbouwkundig Genootschap* (June 2004): 12–13.

Gerhard C. Cadée
Hemmo J. Veenstra

VENKATARAMAN, KRISHNASAMI

(*b*. Madras [later Chennai], India, 7 June 1901; *d*. Delhi, India, 12 May 1981), *organic chemistry, flavones, synthetic dyes.*

Widely regarded as the "father of the Indian dyestuff industry," Venkataraman was an author of the Baker-Venkataraman rearrangement of flavones. An institution builder, he nurtured first the University Department of Chemical Technology at Mumbai and then the National Chemical Laboratory at Pune into cutting-edge research centers. His own work, on the analytical chemistry of synthetic dyes, is among the definitive texts on the subject in the twentieth century.

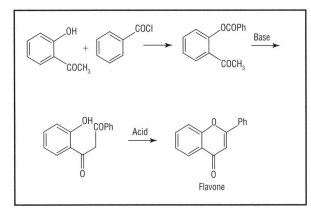

Figure 1. Baker-Venkataraman Rearrangement.

Early Years. Born in south India, Krishnasami Venkataraman—KV to his friends—was the third child in a family whose members were noted for their impish, often mordant, sense of humor and their distinctive, husky voices. His father, Pudukottai Krishnamsami, was a civil engineer and a Sanskrit scholar. His mother, Dharmambal, was frail and constantly unwell. Both parents were strict and the children were brought up in the knowledge that they would be expected to earn their livings as soon as they graduated from university; at the same time they were taught to choose professions that exercised their minds and served the public good. This early training imbued the three brothers with a drive that led them to excel in their chosen fields. Venkataraman's older brother, Krishnasami Swaminathan, was a celebrated teacher and authorized editor of the *Collected Works of Mahatma Gandhi*; a project that he began in 1960 and relinquished thirty years later, shortly before the publication of the 100th volume in 1994. His younger brother, Krishnasami Sanjivi, was a legendary doctor and founder of the Voluntary Health Service of Tamil Nadu, the state where Madras was the capital.

Educated at Presidency College Madras and Madras University, where he received his bachelor's and master's degrees, Venkataraman went to Manchester University in England on a Madras government scholarship in 1923. There he was awarded the MSc (Technology), PhD, and DSc degrees. His research guide was a major figure in modern organic chemistry, the Nobel laureate Robert Robinson.

On his return to India in 1927, Venkataraman held a one-year research fellowship at the Indian Institute of Science in Bangalore. He then moved to northern India in 1928, taking the post of lecturer in Forman Christian College in Lahore (now in Pakistan). It was here that he made one of his most significant contributions to the field of organic chemistry in an article titled "A Synthesis of

Flavones at Room Temperature," published in *Current Science* in 1933. By one of those fortunate conjunctures in science, Wilson Baker published a similar synthesis of flavones and 3-acylchromones ("Molecular Rearrangement of Some O-Acyloxyacetophenones and the Mechanism of the Production of 3-Acylchromones") in the *Journal of the Chemical Society* at about the same time. The reaction that they both described came to be known as the Baker-Venkataraman rearrangement (see Figure 1), and it had immediate application to biologically active compounds.

Flavones are naturally occurring oxygen heterocycles. Their propensity to show biological activity has led to the development of many synthetic flavonoid drugs to treat or inhibit medical ailments. The Baker-Venkataraman rearrangement is a simple, two-step reaction through which substituted flavones can be formed. In the first step, 2-hydroxyacetophenone, or a derivative, is treated with an aromatic acid chloride to form an aryl ester. In the second step, the aryl ester is reacted with a base and transformed into a diaryl 1,3-diketone through an intramolecular rearrangement. When the intramolecular rearrangement product is treated with an acid, the reaction leads to the corresponding flavone.

A range of 2-hydroxyaryl alkyl ketones and aromatic acid chlorides can be deployed through a simple synthetic procedure in order to make a large number of substituted flavones accessible for medical use, especially as preventive mechanisms or disease inhibitors. Moreover, as Venkataraman showed, chalcones and flavanones can further be oxidized by selenium dioxide, and benzyl *o*-hydroxyphenyl ketones can be cyclized to isoflavones by ethyl formate, thus widening the range of available medicinal applications.

The Baker-Venkataraman rearrangement continues to be one of the most effective and widely used methods of creating substituted flavones for medicinal purposes; it was, for example, applied in the early 1990s to the synthesis of styrylchromones, some of which are cytotoxic to specific leukemia cells, selectively inhibiting RNA synthesis.

Move to Bombay. In 1934, as the Indian movement for independence from British rule gathered momentum and the first rifts appeared between Muslims and Hindus in Lahore, Venkataraman left Forman Christian College to join the University of Bombay (later Mumbai) as reader in dyeing and printing in the new Department of Chemical Technology, which was then headed by the British chemist Robert B. Forster. In 1938 Venkataraman succeeded Forster as professor and director of the Department of Chemical Technology and served as its director until 1957. His commitment to institution building made it the foremost center of chemical technology in India during those years.

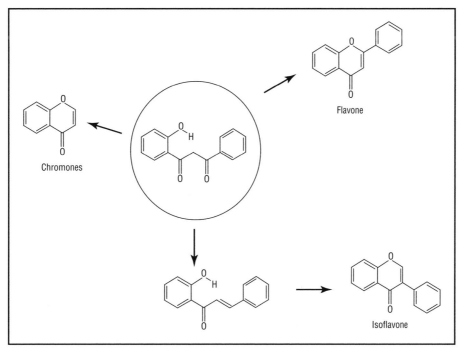

Figure 2. *Some important applications of 1,3-Diketones.*

Venkataraman's approach was unusual in India at the time. He developed a teaching program that encouraged original research, at the same time placing an emphasis on the practical application of research findings. He believed ardently in the potential as well as the need to develop Indian science and technology through private-sector collaboration, and he believed equally that the private sector had an important role to play in contributing towards health and safety in the country at large. His own research on the medical applications of his work on flavones was partly stimulated by conversations with his younger brother, a doctor with whom he was extremely close; the same commitment to health and safety led him to collaborate with Indian pharmaceutical industries, and later the Indian textile industry, on related issues. The cutting edge Ranbaxy Laboratories Ltd. and Bombay Dyeing were among the companies that he advised.

During his tenure as director of the Department of Chemical Technology, Venkataraman pursued, in addition to his work on flavonoids, original research on dyes, dyeing and related textile processing, and mechanistic studies. Color had always fascinated him, and he was able to enlist the support of the Indian textile industries concentrated in and around Mumbai to fund research at the department on the chemistry of natural and synthetic coloring matters, especially textile auxiliaries and naturally occurring anthraquinones and flavones. The new research programs he introduced earned him the nickname of "the

father of dyestuff research in India" and led a group of his students to found the Indian Dyestuffs Industries, Ltd., in Mumbai. The company was the first of its kind in India.

A gifted and inspiring teacher—though his family considered him to be a distant second to his older brother in that profession—Venkataraman was happier among his students than at meetings of administrative or government committees and always favored the former when there was a conflict of schedules. He was a dedicated mentor and a hard task master who demanded undivided attention from his students towards their research. His training placed equal emphasis on research in the laboratory and honing skills in presentations and writing.

Venkataraman's devotion to bringing out the best in his students drew lasting and rueful affection. They joked that though he expected to see them from 8 a.m. to 12 noon in the laboratories and from 4 p.m. to 8 p.m. in his room, he reserved the afternoon for administrative work, so they could use that time to escape to the movies, where they were often joined by Mrs. Venkataraman.

Research on Dyes. Venkataraman's own research now focused on the synthesis of colorants, the determination of structures by degradative and spectroscopic methods, and procedures for the analysis and estimation of dyes. In the course of this research, he developed several new

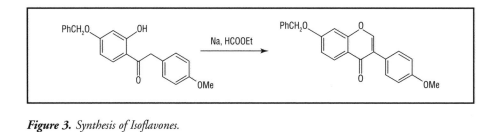

Figure 3. *Synthesis of Isoflavones.*

synthetic procedures and chromatographic separation techniques and invented simple practical methods for the characterization and estimation of dyes.

Amongst Venkataraman's more important contributions in these areas of the chemistry of synthetic dyes were novel applications of Raney nickel reductions for the desulphurization of dyes; exploration of structure-property relationships in insoluble azoic dyes to improve their production directly onto or within the fiber; experiments with temperature to concentrate disperse dyes; and reductions to induce solubility of vat dyes. Among the techniques he used were paper chromatography for separating and identifying mixtures of dyes that are substantive to cotton in their dyeing behavior; and applications of nuclear magnetic resonance (NMR) spectroscopy to solve dye-fiber interaction problems concerning azoic, disperse, reactive, cationic, and vat dyes. His correlation of applications of NMR spectroscopy and mass spectrometry to azophenol-quinone hydrazone tautomerism provided insights into the improved bonding of dyes and fibers. And his studies of structure-property relationships in the surface-active agents that are used in textile processing were of immediate use to the Indian textile industry.

Venkataraman used Raney nickel catalyzed hydrogenation in the synthesis and determination of the structures of dyes and flavones. The method led to the clean desulphurization of sulphonic acid dyes and the production of tosylate derivatives of phenolic compounds and other sulphur-containing compounds, making the dyes more evenly spread and longer lasting on a variety of textiles. The products that were formed by the hydrogenation process were more amenable to analysis by NMR and mass spectral techniques than had been possible earlier. Therefore, many anthraquinone dyes that are used as food as well as textile colorants could be and were analyzed using this procedure, as were violanthrones that act as sensitizers. Additionally, his thiobenzimidazole reagent became the basis for reductive alkylation of amines using alcohols.

Additionally, Venkataraman developed a method for the facile hydrolysis of anilides of *o*-hydroxyphenylcarboxylic acids. Anilides are difficult to hydrolyse; he treated these anilides *o*-hydroxyphenyl carboxylic acids with 2,4-dinitrochlorobenzene, and the resultant N-2,4-dini-trophenyl derivatives underwent hydrolysis under mild conditions.

For the textile industry, Venkataraman's most important research programs were on the synthesis of azo and alizarin dyes, reactive dyes, and lac dyes. He made modifications in the diazotization procedure of specific amines and used the modified procedure not only for the synthesis of several new azo dyes, but also to alter the shades of dyes and improve the durability of natural dyes such as those used in Kutch dyeing and calico printing. The other dyes whose chemistry he researched included naphthol derivatives, indanthrones, and benzanthrones.

Reactive dyes contain the β-sulphatoethyl sulphone functional group that is responsible for bonding with fabric in the presence of alkali. Venkataraman provided direct physical evidence, in particular through the use of NMR data, for the formation of an ether bond between the reactive dye and cellulose and proposed a mechanism for how this bond could be formed, which involved the intervention of allylic carbon to facilitate S_N2 displacement by the cellulosic –OH group (see Figure 5).

In a separate study he showed that only those oxycelluloses containing β-ketonic acid or aldehyde groups would couple with diazonium salts. He investigated the factors that influence the azo-hydroxy tautomerism in *o*-hydroxyazo dyes and demonstrated the deshielding effect of the azo group of dyes in their NMR spectra. Venkataraman also used the diazo coupling of phenolic compounds to introduce a hydroxy group in a specific position and to elucidate structures. In addition, he isolated and characterized a number of natural pigments belonging to the anthraquinonoid group, such as laccaic acids A and B, which are present in lac dye.

Venkataraman's work on textile auxiliary agents proved equally significant to the development of the Indian textile industry. Textile auxiliary agents help in the dispersion of dyes and level dyeing, and they are used for wetting fibers, detergency, emulsifying power, and protective colloidal action during the dyeing process. Yenkataraman developed new textile auxiliary agents for use by industry by experimenting with soaps, Turkey red oil, Monopole oils, and the products obtained from castor oil on its reaction with sulphuric acid.

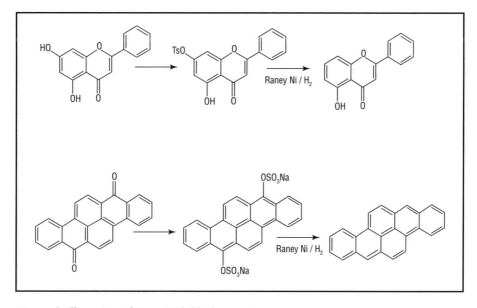

Figure 4. *Illustrations of Raney Nickel hydrogenation.*

Director of the NCL. Having moved from the far south of India to the far north, Venkataraman had by the mid-1950s settled in western India. In 1957 he accepted an invitation to become the first Indian director of the National Chemical Laboratory (NCL) in Pune (97 kilometers from Mumbai), taking over from Professor George I. Finch. The National Chemical Laboratory was not new to him. The first and only Indian institution to be devoted purely to chemical research, it was set up and f___ ' by the Indian government. Venkataraman had been associated with the laboratory from its inception in 1950, first as a member of its Planning Committee and then as a member of its Site Acquisition Committee. When the laboratory was established, he was also on its Executive Council and chaired its Chemical Research Committee.

As director of the NCL, Venkataraman reorganized several departments, adding divisions for Organic Intermediates and Dyes and Essential Oils, and expanded its research activities to include a Fine Chemicals Project. To keep the laboratory at the cutting edge of Indian chemical research, he went on an active recruitment drive to attract new talent and continued it during the ten years that he directed the laboratory. His staff and students were encouraged to publish internationally, and the laboratory soon became the hub of chemical research in the country, particularly in the areas of natural products and synthetic organic chemistry. Also, the laboratory became an essential stop on the itinerary of international scientists visiting India.

Despite the move from Mumbai to Pune, Venkataraman continued to pursue his research on the separation, purification, and analysis of dyes. He developed the use of column chromatography under hot conditions (100–150° C [212°–302° F]) and used highly polar, unconventional solvents in order to resolve difficulties in the solubility and elution of dyes. He applied paper chromatography to the analysis of aminoanthraquinones and used adsorption on cellulose powder for the separation of vat dyes, using such unusual solvents as aqueous tetraethylene pentamine containing hydrosulphite. He studied the influence of the –OH group in azo dyes on their adsorption properties on alumina.

Although he retired in 1966, Venkataraman continued to take PhD students at the National Chemical Laboratory and remained associated with its research activities until 1980. More than eighty students received their doctorates under him, several of them going on to become famous in their own right. His students treated him like an affectionate uncle, and he for his part nagged and fussed over their work while his wife tried to cheer them up with slapdash and loving meals. One of his happiest days was when a former student, Bal Dattatreya Tilak, took over from him as director of the National Chemical Laboratory.

Publications, Honors, and Awards. Retirement allowed him time for his own writing, and between 1970 and 1978 he edited the third through sixth volumes of the monumental six-volume *The Chemistry of Synthetic Dyes* for which he was to become famous. The volumes were an expansion on his two-volume treatise on *The Chemistry of Synthetic Dyes*, which was published in 1952 and was the first definitive twentieth-century work on synthetic dyes; it was subsequently translated into Russian and Chinese.

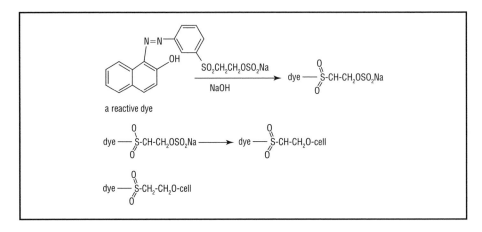

Figure 5. *Mechanism of action (or reaction) of a vinylsulphone reactive dye with cellulose.*

While Venkataraman was working on *The Chemistry of Synthetic Dyes*, the range of detail that he was forced to absorb convinced him of the need for a new, single volume, analytical text. This he later edited as a collection of pieces by international chemists, titled *The Analytical Chemistry of Synthetic Dyes* (1977); repetition was clearly not a concern of his when it came to scientific titles.

In his almost sixty years of scholarly work, Venkataraman wrote 271 published papers. His first, "Notes on Bixin," was published in the *Journal of the Indian Institute of Science* in 1924, and his last, "Cyanuric Chloride, a Useful Reagent for Macrocyclic Lactonization," was published in *Tetrahedron Letters* in 1980.

Venkataraman was on the editorial advisory board of *Tetrahedron, Tetrahedron Letters, Organic Preparations and Procedures International,* and the *Indian Journal of Chemistry*; a member of the USSR Academy of Sciences; and a fellow of the Deutsche Akademie der Naturforscher Leopoldina, the Polish Chemical Society, the Indian Academy of Sciences, and the Indian National Science Academy and an honorary fellow of the Society of Dyers and Colourists (UK). The Mendeleev Institute of Chemical Technology in Moscow conferred an honorary doctorate of science upon him, and in 1961 the government of India awarded him one of its highest honors, the Padma Bhushan. He was president of the Indian Chemical Society in 1959–1960 and received the K. D. Naik and T. R. Seshadri Seventieth Birthday Commemoration Medals.

Personal Life. No scientist is without eccentricities, and Venkataraman's was an excessive, almost faddish, attention to health and hygiene. An asthmatic from birth, he battled his debilitating ailment through a rigorous routine of exercise and diet as well as, in his own words, "segregating potential sources of germs." He carried four handkerchiefs—one for his spectacles, one for his nose, one for his

forehead, and one for his hands. It was this discipline, he always said, that kept his asthma in check and permitted him to work so productively. Tall for an Indian and spindly, he looked frail beside his energetic wife, whom he chided gently for her untidiness; however, he cherished until his dying day the tomboy quality in her that he had fallen in love with when she was fourteen.

Though his home was austere and the food of nursery-like blandness, it was a beacon for family friends and students. Twenty-five years after his death, and almost fifty years after he had left the Department of Chemical Technology, its governing board honored him by naming the lecture theater in which he had taught after him. In 2006, at UICT's Sesquecentennial Celebration, the department—now an institute in its own right—formally inaugurated the Venkataraman Lecture Hall; the ceremony was attended by a large number of his former students, some in their seventies, who had traveled from all over India to attend.

Venkataraman died at the age of seventy-five years. His wife survived him only briefly. His daughter, Dharma Kumar, was a well-known economic historian and founder-editor of the later prestigious *Indian Economic and Social History Review*; she died in 2001, leaving behind her only daughter, Radha Kumar.

BIBLIOGRAPHY

WORKS BY VENKATARAMAN

"Notes on Bixin." *Journal of the Indian Institute Science* 7 (1924): 225–234.

With Wilson Baker. "Molecular Rearrangement of Some O-Acyloxyacetophenones and the Mechanism of the Production of 3-Acylchromones." *Journal of the Chemical Society* (1933): 1381–1389.

With H. S. Mahal. "A Synthesis of Flavones at Room Temperature." *Current Science* 2 (1933): 214–215.

The Chemistry of Synthetic Dyes. 8 vols. Vols. 1–2 edited by Louis F. Fieser and Mary Fieser, vols. 3–8 edited by Krishnasami Venkataraman. New York: Academic Press, 1952–1978.

Editor. *The Analytical Chemistry of Synthetic Dyes.* New York: Wiley, 1977.

With D. R. Wagle. "Cyanuric Chloride, a Useful Reagent for Macrocyclic Lactonization." *Tetrahedron Letters* 21, no. 19 (1980): 1893–1896.

P. K. Ingle
S. Sivaram
Radha Kumar

VERATI, LAURA BASSI

SEE **Bassi Verati (Veratti), Laura Maria Caterina**.

VICKREY WILLIAM SPENCER (*b.* Victoria, British Columbia, Canada, 21 June 1914; *d.* Hastings-on-Hudson, New York, 11 October 1996), *microeconomics, public economics, taxation, efficient pricing structures, incentives and private information, game theory, financial economics, macroeconomic policy.*

Vickrey was among the broadest and most strikingly original economists of the twentieth century, changing the way economists thought about designing markets to provide proper incentives, imperfectly competitive markets, public and congestible goods, efficient provision of public utilities, and taxation and its incentive effects. In so doing, he introduced the notion that relevant information is privately held, by individuals and firms who may respond strategically to requests for their information (or observations of their behavior to glean their information), and he developed many of the mathematical tools used to analyze such situations.

Vickrey earned a BS in mathematics from Yale University in 1935, and was associated with Columbia University's Economics Department for nearly all the remaining sixty-one years of his life. He received an MA in 1937 and first taught at Columbia that year. The next six years he worked on taxation and public utility pricing, and was a prolific contributor to major economics journals. World War II interrupted his academic career: Vickrey was a conscientious objector, and two years' public service included designing an inheritance tax system for Puerto Rico (he would later design Japan's postwar tax system). Back in economics at Columbia, he became a lecturer in 1946, was awarded his PhD in 1947, and became assistant professor in 1948, associate professor in 1950, professor in 1958, and McVickar Professor of Political Economy in 1971.

William Spencer Vickrey. *William Spencer Vickrey prepares for a news conference at Columbia in New York, October 1996.* JON LEVY/AFP/GETTY IMAGES.

Professor emeritus from 1982, he continued to teach occasional courses and interact with students and colleagues at seminars and conferences right up to his death.

Vickrey was ahead of his time in many areas of economics, and it took years, sometimes dozens, for the discipline to catch up. His most lauded works were produced by 1961, but not widely cited at first, sometimes not for decades. He was elected a Fellow of the Econometric Society in 1967, received a University of Chicago honorary degree in 1979, and was elected Distinguished Fellow of the American Economic Association in 1978 and its president in 1992. The year 1996 was particularly eventful: election to the National Academy of Sciences in April, award of the Nobel Prize in Economic Science announced 8 October, and then his death following three hectic days in the resulting spotlight.

An enormous fraction of the theoretical research in microeconomics since the mid-1960s can be characterized as working out details of large ideas that, as his writings make clear, were well understood by Vickrey in the 1940s or 1950s. For one, Vickrey is the father of the vast literature on the "economics of asymmetric information." The Nobel Committee called him the first scholar to focus explicitly on the feature that key information is privately held by individuals (pursuing their informed self-interest), when exploring issues of incentives and the performance of markets, of taxation, and of other public regulations.

The Nobel announcement focused on Vickrey's 1961 paper about auctions, which realizes a principal reason for conducting an auction is that critical information about the value of an auctioned asset lies in privately held knowledge of or estimates of its value to each bidder. Among many seminal contributions in a full and thoughtful paper, the simplest and most noted was introducing the second-price auction, often called the Vickrey auction. In it each bidder privately submits a bid, knowing the rules: the highest bidder will be awarded the asset at a price set by the highest *losing* bid, that is, the "second price." Switching from "pay-your-bid" or first-price auction rules to second-price rules has startling consequences. Suppose you know the asset's worth to you; in a first-price auction, you optimally bid below that by an amount that maximizes a complicated tradeoff between the probability of winning and the profitability should you win. Vickrey's rules induce you simply to bid your value: If a rival bids higher, winning would mean unprofitably overbidding; if all rivals bid less, you want to win, and would gain nothing from bidding lower. Second-price rules are thus "incentive-compatible" in that bidders do not have to be presumed public spirited: Each is given an incentive to truthfully reveal that price at which he or she is indifferent between obtaining the asset and forgoing its purchase. Information thus learned from a second-price auction can be both critical for follow-up decisions (e.g., airwaves auctions yield information about the value of making further slices of the electromagnetic spectrum available for commercial usages) and otherwise unattainable.

In the model he presented, Vickrey also originated the issue of market design—how does a seller or public agency set market rules so as to maximize expected revenue, or some other goal?—and established that a seller on average earns identical revenues from first- and second-price auctions. Later work has found that, in a wide variety of settings with approximately risk-neutral actors, a revenue-seeking seller will prefer a second-price auction, and an efficiency-seeking seller (a governmental agency or other seller motivated to attain the maximal gains from trade for the entire economy, not just its own gains) will more often sell to the highest-valuing bidder via a second-price auction.

Vickrey's 1961 paper also considered allocation of bundles of goods and services (or public projects), and of cost shares, to individuals. He proposed charging an individual the cost to the rest of the economy that resulted from their usage of an endeavor, the basis for what is now called the Vickrey-Clarke-Groves mechanism and the

extensive literature on design of allocation mechanisms for public-good and interrelated-goods problems.

In proposing a framework for understanding auctions and transacting mechanisms, and a simple rule that could improve such markets, Vickrey's insight that the analyst must account for self-interested individuals acting on the basis of private information presaged developments that have dominated game theory since the 1970s. John Harsanyi characterized "games of incomplete information" in the late 1960s, and was a 1994 Nobel laureate for developing techniques that had been correctly used by Vickrey in the 1940s and 1950s. Pathbreaking studies of situations where individuals seek to credibly reveal private information about their own abilities to potential transacting partners ("signaling games") and where firms seek to sort out individuals who are privately aware of their own high intellectual or entrepreneurial abilities from those without the same skills who nonetheless seek the same opportunities ("screening games") were the subject of the 2001 Nobel Prize to George Akerlof, Michael Spence, and Joseph Stiglitz; Vickrey demonstrated his understanding of the key insights in their work nearly a half-century prior to that award.

The 1947 book *Agenda for Progressive Taxation* is essentially Vickrey's doctoral dissertation; to this day it contains frontier research in taxation, and its twenty-one specific recommendations remain sound. It is strikingly original in its conception that taxes distort incentives to engage in taxed transactions, primarily earning income, and that individuals' responses to taxes are based on information (about their abilities in alternative occupations and willingness to undertake efforts) unknowable to government. It is this original idea that James Mirrlees (*b.* 1936) carried to an explicit characterization a quarter century later, in work that led the Nobel Committee to make him the colaureate with Vickrey in 1996.

Concern for human welfare was Vickrey's driving force. In his 1945 paper, "Measuring Marginal Utility by Reactions to Risk," and his 1947 *Agenda*, Vickrey develops a basis for relating social preferences over alternatives to individuals' preferences. In so doing, he lays a part of the foundation for Kenneth Arrow's dissertation, "Social Choice and Individual Values," which Vickrey supervised, and which was the focal work in the Nobel announcement of the 1972 laureate to Arrow. The Nobel award in 1998 to Amartya Sen also cited work elaborating ideas initiated in these writings by Vickrey.

For all the research in theoretical economics that has elaborated on his original ideas, Vickrey himself was totally focused on practical applications, interested in theoretical models solely for the crucial reason of resting practical solutions on an underlying logic. In the late 1930s he proposed the principle that taxation should attempt to be neutral with respect to decisions as to when to realize a gain in income, and published a full-fledged system for doing so in 1939, "Averaging of Income for Income-Tax Purposes."

His most extensive involvement, though, was in suggesting principles for efficient provision of public utilities, and in coming up with inventive, practical mechanisms to fulfill these principles. The theoretical side involved reaching a subtle understanding of the correct marginal cost to attribute to usage of utilities: What is society's economic cost to have one more car traveling that roadway at that hour, or of one more subway rider ten minutes ahead of peak demand? In 1948 Vickrey suggested that seats on airplanes should be purchased on a futures market where prices fluctuated depending on the forecast between demand for seats and supply of seats as the date of the flight approached. Four decades later airlines began to develop yield management software that quotes prices essentially in imitation of such a market. A big difference is that the airlines choose to sell nontransferable and largely nonrefundable tickets; Vickrey proposed resellable tickets with a penalty to discourage speculation.

Two years' study of patterns of subway ridership led to the 1952 monograph, *The Revision of the Rapid Transit Fare Structure of the City of New York*. Vickrey found that marginal-cost pricing implied prices at the very peak of demand five times the off-peak minimum, with substantial savings available if a regular commuter adjusted his schedule as little as fifteen minutes away from peak. Serious savings in the cost of rolling stock could result from aggregate commuter responses. In the first of classic examples of how far he went to demonstrate the practicality of his recommendations, Vickrey constructed a prototype of an electromechanical turnstile that automatically implemented shifting prices. Similar turnstiles came into widespread use three dozen years later, but only small steps in the direction of Vickrey's suggested wide variations in price about peak load times have yet arrived.

His 1959 study of road use around Washington, D.C., led to the congressional report, "Statement on the Pricing of Urban Street Use." Again he found that careful calculation of social marginal costs led to highly differentiated road tariffs according to traffic congestion. Vickrey, though, was appalled at the notion of adding to traffic congestion to collect tolls, and railed against tollbooths, urging the development of a system where small radio transmitters would transmit vehicle or driver identifiers over a distance of a few feet, and a computerized system connected to roadbed receivers would calculate liabilities and bill drivers periodically. A few years afterward, Vickrey was challenged that the system he proposed was infeasible. He responded in typical fashion: in the mid-1960s he first built a rudimentary computer in his home and

connected it to a radio receiver, then limited himself to a three-dollar budget for parts with which he built a small radio transmitter placed under the hood of his car. He could then show anyone who asked a printout of the times his own car went up or down his driveway. As someone who practiced the concern for efficiency in transportation that he preached, Vickrey rarely used his car: For a third of a century, he almost always took the train into Manhattan, then "commuted" the blocks from the station and across Columbia's campus to his office on rollerskates.

Vickrey's 1963 "Pricing in Urban and Suburban Transport" is to this day regarded as the most important paper in the history of urban transport economics. Departure times of commuters are endogenous variables in the model, reacting to personal tastes, plans, and predicted commuting tie-ups. The Belgian economist Jacques Drèze evaluates "That model has received strong empirical support from detailed traffic flow studies, and has changed the way traffic engineers think about the problem" (1998, p. 416), and notes, remarkably, that Vickrey's system of tolls varying with traffic densities "leaves commuters at least as well off as before, so that the toll revenues come free" (pp. 416–417). Vickrey applied similar reasoning to develop efficient pricing structures for telephone services, electricity, water supply, fire protection, parks and recreational services, and education.

For the last decade of his life Vickrey's attention returned to macroeconomic policy, a subject he had analyzed in a 1964 book, *Metastatics and Macroeconomics*. Like his other pursuits, that book broke new ground by expecting that macroeconomic policy ought to be derived from an understanding of the economy grounded in equilibrium models of microeconomic behavior. Indeed, some of the real business cycle modeling honored in the 2004 Nobel award to Finn Kydland (*b.* 1943) and Edward Prescott (*b.* 1940) has its first musings in Vickrey's early analyses. Vickrey's macroeconomics theme reflected his overriding concern for human welfare: He considered inflation minor relative to unemployment, because the burden of above-minimal unemployment fell on the poor. He argued (in his 1964 book and in eleven papers 1986 and later) that over a considerable range of levels of employment, lower unemployment did not create higher inflation, hence both fiscal and monetary policy should address unemployment, with subsidiary policies addressing inflation. As always, he had inventive recommendations for such policies.

The acclaim Vickrey's work eventually attained was to him secondary; he was more concerned with whether practical recommendations of more efficient methods were adopted. On a half-dozen occasions in the 1990s, most notably his 1993 Presidential Address to the Atlantic Economic Society, Bill Vickrey, somewhat jovially but with some melancholy, pronounced himself a failed innovator.

Scores of economists (this writer included) have presented a seminar while Bill Vickrey was to all appearances asleep, only to have him suddenly ask a more penetrating question than any seemingly more attentive audience member can muster. Then, too, I join those described in the American Economic Association's 1978 Distinguished Fellow citation:

> Many of us have had the experience of thinking we were the first to show the neutrality of a particular tax scheme, to prove the incentive characteristics of a particular bidding institution, to deduce the redistributive implications of the expected utility hypothesis, to invent a demand revealing process, and so on, only to find that William S. Vickrey had done it earlier—sometimes much earlier—and whereas our original contribution may have contained a minor or even a substantive error, Vickrey had done it correctly.

BIBLIOGRAPHY

A bibliography of Vickrey's nine books, 166 other publications, and 61 unpublished articles is in the 1994 book listed below.

WORKS BY VICKREY

"Averaging of Income for Income-Tax Purposes." *Journal of Political Economy* 47 (1939): 379–397.

"Measuring Marginal Utility by Reactions to Risks." *Econometrica* 13 (1945): 319–333.

Agenda for Progressive Taxation. New York: Ronald Press Company, 1947.

"Some Objections to Marginal-Cost Pricing." *Journal of Political Economy* 56 (1948): 218–238.

The Revision of the Rapid Transit Fare Structure of the City of New York. New York Mayor's Committee on Management Survey, Finance Project, Technical Monograph no. 3. 1952.

"The Economizing of Curb Parking Space." *Traffic Engineering* 25 (November 1954): 62–67.

"A Proposal for Revising New York's Subway Fare Structure." *Journal of the Operations Research Society of America* 3 (1955): 38–68.

"Reaching a Balance between Mass Transit and Provision for Individual Automobile Traffic," testimony before U.S. Congress, Joint Committee on Washington Metropolitan Problems. *Transportation Plan for the National Capital Region. Hearings, Nov. 9–14, 1959.* Washington, DC: Government Printing Office, 1959.

"Statement on the Pricing of Urban Street Use," to U.S. Congress, Joint Committee on Washington Metropolitan Problems. 11 November 1959. *Transportation Plan for the National Capital Region. Hearings, Nov. 9–14, 1959.* Washington, DC: Government Printing Office, 1959.

"Counterspeculation, Auctions, and Competitive Sealed Tenders." *Journal of Finance* 16 (1961): 8–37.

"General and Specific Financing of Urban Services." In *Public Expenditure Decisions in the Urban Community*, edited by Howard G. Schaller. Washington, DC: Resources for the Future, 1963.

"Pricing in Urban and Suburban Transport." *American Economic Review* 53, no. 2 (1963): 452–465.

Metastatics and Macroeconomics. New York: Harcourt, Brace & World, 1964.

"Responsive Pricing of Public Utility Services." *Bell Journal of Economics and Management Science* 2 (1971): 337–346.

"The City as a Firm." In *The Economics of Public Services,* edited by Martin S. Feldstein and Robert P. Inman. New York: Halsted Press, 1977.

"My Innovative Failures in Economics." *Atlantic Economic Journal* 21 (March 1993): 1–9.

"Today's Task for Economists." *American Economic Review* 83, no. 1 (1993): 1–10.

Public Economics: Selected Papers by William Vickrey. Edited by Richard Arnott, Kenneth Arrow, Anthony Atkinson, and Jacques Drèze. Cambridge, U.K.: Cambridge University Press, 1994.

OTHER SOURCES

American Economic Association. "William S. Vickrey: Distinguished Fellow 1978." *American Economic Review* 69 (September 1979): Two unnumbered pages preceding p. 492.

Arrow, Kenneth J. "Social Choice and Individual Values." PhD diss., Columbia University, 1951.

Clarke, Edward H. "Multipart Pricing of Public Goods." *Public Choice* 11 (1971): 17–33.

Drèze, Jacques. "William S. Vickrey June 21, 1914–October 11, 1996." In *Biographical Memoirs,* vol. 75. Washington, DC: National Academy of Sciences, 1998. Also available from http://www.nap.edu/html/biomems/. A biography by a noted economist.

Groves, Theodore. "Incentives in Teams." *Econometrica* 41 (1973): 617–631. Both Clarke and Groves articles are later contributions developing the Vickrey-Clarke-Groves mechanism.

Ronald M. Harstad

VILLANOVA, ARNALD OF

SEE **Arnald of Villanova**.

VIÑES MARTORELL, CARLOS BENITO JOSÉ (*b.* Poboleda, Spain, 19 September 1837;

d. Havana, Cuba, 23 July 1893), *meteorology, hurricane prediction, colonial science.*

This Jesuit scientist was widely recognized as the world's foremost authority on tropical cyclones at the end of the nineteenth century. Beginning in 1870, Benito Viñes gradually converted a small teaching observatory in Spanish-ruled Havana into the central node of a hurricane forecasting network spanning the Caribbean basin. He attracted an enormous public following in Cuba and directly inspired a similar system dedicated to typhoon prediction for East Asia. Viñes's contribution to tropical meteorology exemplifies the importance of Jesuits to the geophysical sciences during this era, even as it underscores the significance of meteorology to colonial rule.

Colonial Science and the Jesuit Order. As a form of "practical astronomy," meteorology played an important role in imperial expansion during the age of empire. The United States, for example, made a name for itself in the scientific realm not only with its expanding continental empire connected by telegraphic weather stations, but also for theoretical descriptions of severe storms. As a central facet of the regeneration of the Society of Jesus after its suppression (1773–1814), highly trained Jesuits scattered to the ends of the earth, "God-willing," in the words of Viñes, "to provide a service to my brothers and contribute something to the advancement of science and the well-being of humanity" (quoted in Ramos & Enrique, 1996, p. 1). They gave particular attention to scientific education, solar astronomy, terrestrial magnetism, seismology, and meteorology—particularly, in the latter cases, where their studies might protect locals from natural hazards. They established lasting outposts of scientific excellence in the tropics, most notably at Manila (Philippines, est. 1865), Zikawei (China, est. 1872), and Tananarive (now Antananarivo, Madagascar, est. 1889). Even though most Jesuit scientists stayed aloof from colonial politics, they served as powerful agents of Western cultural imperialism.

The Magnetic and Meteorological Observatory established at the Colegio de Belén in Havana in 1857 started small, as an ancillary to the Colegio's preparatory school curriculum. Meanwhile, Andrés Poey y Aguirre, the son of Cuba's foremost naturalist, convinced Havana's colonial elite to bankroll a trip to France with the goal of establishing a competing "physico-meteorological observatory" in Havana capable of acquiring "all the scientific data that can enrich the sciences in the Spanish possessions of America" (quoted in Pyenson, 1993, pp. 271–272). In 1869, in the wake of the 1868 Revolution in Spain, Cuba's governor-general abruptly closed this state-supported observatory after a decade of irregular operation, as Cuba plunged into a ten-year anticolonial war. Poey spent the rest of his life in exile in France, long

his preferred venue for publishing research into the use of clouds as tools for weather prediction and into the history of tropical cyclones. By default, high-level meteorological investigations in Havana were left in Jesuit hands.

Birth of a Hurricane Forecaster. Carlos Benito José Viñes Martorell was born to Carlos Viñes and María Teresa Martorell in a small town in the mountains west of Tarragona in Catalonia. He entered seminary in 1856 and completed his novice training to become a Jesuit in Majorca. He reputedly taught physics at the University of Salamanca during the 1860s while completing the second, advanced phase of his training. Like much of the Jesuit order in Spain after the Liberal Revolution of 1868, he fled to France, and he was ordained in Toulouse. In March 1870, he was sent to join the faculty at the Colegio de Belén and quickly took over directorship of its observatory.

Because of Cuba's size, geographical orientation, and location in the heart of the Caribbean basin, it is extremely vulnerable to violent tropical storms during hurricane season (early June to late November)—and an excellent base for a storm scientist. October 1870 provided a rough introduction to Cuba: a hurricane ripped the zinc roof off the observatory, not long after Viñes had left his post for safer shelter. This was the first and most destructive of three storms passing near Havana that month. At this time, Viñes initiated several practices that eventually made him the world's most celebrated hurricane forecaster. He kept a storm scrapbook recording cloud and instrument observations, conversations with ship captains, telegraph reports, and newspaper clippings useful for tracking storms—a practice his assistants and successors maintained for eighty-seven consecutive years. Viñes also published his observations in Havana newspapers to educate the public.

But no tropical cyclone of comparable intensity passed near Havana for several years. In the meantime, Viñes dedicated himself to the relationship between magnetic and meteorological phenomena, and he threw himself into scientific life in the colonial capital. The Colegio de Belén's staff physician, Carlos Finlay, became a close friend. In 1883, Finlay successfully inoculated a student and demonstrated that mosquitoes serve as vectors for spreading yellow fever. Thus, the Colegio de Belén provided the locus—and dozens of test subjects—for two celebrated programs of tropical research.

In September 1875, Viñes finally had the chance to test his method for tracking storms. On the basis of telegraph reports from Puerto Rico passed on by the Spanish navy, he issued a public hurricane warning on the eleventh, advising ships to avoid sailing east or north from Havana. The eye passed northeast of Havana along its predicted path two days later before heading for Texas. Only one U.S. steamship, the *Liberty*, dared to sail into the Strait of Florida ahead of the storm. All hands were lost—but not a single paying passenger took the risk of embarking from Havana, thanks to Viñes's advisory. On 17 October 1876, based purely on his own cloud and barometric observations, Viñes issued a warning forty-eight hours before a major hurricane made landfall south of Havana.

This success turned Viñes into a scientific celebrity. He used his notoriety to obtain support for three extended tours of damaged areas in Cuba, Hispaniola, and Puerto Rico during the winter of 1876–1877. He used physical evidence and oral reports collected during these trips to produce his first major statement of the laws of hurricane circulation and movement (1877). At least in Havana, his authority as a forecaster became so great that he had the power to cause panic. This made him very protective of his reputation; on more than one occasion, he withheld storm advisories from local newspapers in retaliation for criticizing his forecasts, the Colegio, or the Jesuit order.

International Networks. Even before the 1876 season reached its conclusion, Viñes began exploring ways to establish a telegraphic network of storm observers in the Caribbean. This led the Spanish navy to organize an irregular association reporting storm observations to the Colegio de Belén from Cuban railway operators, Spanish and British consular officials, and U.S. Army Signal Corps observers scattered throughout the region. Meanwhile, Viñes began corresponding with Federico Faura, a Spanish Jesuit administering the Manila Observatory. Based on Viñes's ideas, Faura issued his first storm warning for the Philippines in July 1879. He and his successor, José Algué, greatly extended the methods pioneered by Viñes and organized an international typhoon warning network far more elaborate, respected, and lasting than the one Viñes eventually organized.

In 1882, Viñes journeyed across the Atlantic to purchase instruments in Europe. Stephen Perry, the celebrated director of the Jesuit Observatory of Stonyhurst College in England, was in the midst of preparing for an expedition to Madagascar to observe the transit of Venus across the Sun—the signature event in solar astronomy of this era. Perry personally trained Viñes to use the new, high-precision instruments he purchased for the Colegio de Belén and oversaw their calibration at Kew Observatory, the geophysical center of the British Empire. Back in Havana, Viñes not only observed the transit of Venus in December 1882, he also reported magnetic observations from the tropics as part of the First International Polar Year (1882–1883). These contacts helped cement Viñes's reputation as a trustworthy colonial scientist.

Viñes's vision for a trans-Caribbean storm-warning network finally came to fruition in the wake of an exceptional hurricane season. Seven storms affected Cuba in 1886, including a catastrophic hurricane that destroyed Indianola, Texas, three days after passing over Cuba. In 1887, Havana's Chamber of Commerce inaugurated a telegraphic network incorporating Spanish, British, French, Danish, Dutch, Dominican, and Venezuelan dominions—all reporting to Viñes at the Colegio de Belén. He dutifully passed on his advisories to Washington, D.C. During the hurricane season of 1888, the United States' foremost expert on tropical storms, Everett Hayden, made a pilgrimage to Havana to learn from Viñes. Hayden's Coast Pilot charts from this era strongly urged mariners to heed Viñes's warnings.

The Laws of Hurricane Circulation and Movement. During the twenty-three years Viñes spent as director of the Colegio de Belén observatory, he published two major books, fourteen scientific articles, several observatory yearbooks, and innumerable newspaper articles. He prepared his last and most influential work for presentation at the 1893 Columbian Exposition—and died of cerebral hemorrhage only two days after completing the final manuscript. (Faura and Algué presented it posthumously in Chicago as representatives for science in the Spanish Empire.) This treatise presented two general laws of tropical cyclonic circulation and six laws of hurricane movement applicable to the West Indies, all inspired by midcentury international debates concerning the "law of storms." Viñes modeled these empirical laws, ultimately, on the geometric laws of planetary motion of Johannes Kepler.

Viñes's most valuable discovery, by far, stemmed from his realization that the thin veil of cirrostratus clouds visible on the outer edges of a tropical cyclone was caused by the outflow of winds at high altitudes. These clouds not only provided one of the earliest indications of an approaching storm, the orientation of elongated "plumiform cirrus" clouds at a hurricane's leading edge seemed to indicate the direction of its deadly eye. He developed a landmark, three-dimensional model of hurricane circulation based on careful observation of cloud types formed at different altitudes. From his compilation of historical storm tracks, Viñes also proposed a set of rules indicating the most likely geographical routes taken by storms during different phases of the hurricane season.

These rules were controversial, particularly his laws of "recurvature": the tendency of West Indian hurricanes at some point to reverse their westward movement and curve back toward the northeast. Viñes and Hayden engaged in a vigorous debate regarding why so many storms failed to follow these rules. This debate ultimately weakened the faith of U.S. meteorologists in Cuban forecasts.

Another Spanish Jesuit, Lorenzo Gangoiti, took over for Viñes one month into the 1893 hurricane season. At least in Havana, the public breathed a huge sigh of relief when Gangoiti precisely predicted the next major storm to strike Cuba. In September 1900, during the U.S. occupation, Gangoiti warned that a tropical storm passing over Cuba posed a threat to the Texas coast—just like the September 1875 and August 1886 storms that had done so much to establish Viñes's reputation. But Gangoiti could not transmit an advisory because U.S. Weather Bureau forecasters now controlled the Caribbean network Viñes had established and prohibited anyone from issuing a competing forecast. Unfortunately, this storm followed Viñes's laws almost to the letter and took several thousand lives when it again made landfall in Galveston on 8 September 1900 as the deadliest hurricane in U.S. history.

BIBLIOGRAPHY

Storm notebooks, correspondence, and other archival materials are at the Centro de Estudio de Historia de la Ciencia y la Tecnología and the Instituto de Meteorología, Ministerio de Ciencia, Tecnología y Medio Ambiente, both in Havana, Cuba.

WORKS BY VIÑES

Apuntes relativos a los huracanes de las Antillas en setiembre y octubre de 1875 y 76. Havana: Tipografía y Papelería El Iris, 1877. His first major work; based on three field expeditions. Translated by George L. Dyer under the title *Practical Hints in Regard to West Indian Hurricanes.* Washington, DC: Government Printing Office, 1887.

Investigaciones relativas a la circulación y traslación ciclónica en los huracanes de las Antillas. Havana: Imprenta del Avisador Comercial de Pulido y Diaz, 1895. His capstone work; widely extracted by the international scientific press. Translated under the title *Investigation of the Cyclonic Circulation and the Translatory Movement of West Indian Hurricanes.* Washington, DC: Weather Bureau, 1898.

OTHER SOURCES

Album conmemorativo del quincuagésimo aniversario de la fundación en la Habana del Colegio de Belén de la Compañía de Jesus. Havana: Imprenta Avisador Comercial, 1904. Institutional history of the Colegio de Belén and its observatory.

Hidalgo, Angel. *El P. Federico Faura, S.J. y el Observatorio de Manila.* Manila: Observatorio de Manila, 1974.

———. *El P. José Algué, S.J.: Científico, inventor y pacifista (1856–1930).* Manila: Observatorio de Manila, 1974. Biographies of two Spanish Jesuits who followed Viñes's lead and transformed typhoon prediction in the western Pacific.

Larson, Erik. *Isaac's Storm: A Man, a Time, and the Deadliest Hurricane in History.* New York: Vintage, 2000. Blames colonialist hubris for failed forecast of the 1900 Galveston hurricane.

Pyenson, Lewis. *Civilizing Mission: Exact Sciences and French Overseas Expansion, 1830–1940.* Baltimore, MD: Johns Hopkins University Press, 1993. Explores the uses of meteorology as a tool of cultural imperialism, particularly by French Jesuits.

Ramos, Guadalupe, and Luis Enrique. *Benito Viñes S.J.: Estudio biográfico.* Havana: Editorial Academia, 1996. Uses Cuban archival materials.

Udías, Agustín. "Jesuits' Contribution to Meteorology." *Bulletin of the American Meteorological Society* 77, no. 10 (October 1996): 2307–2315. Global historical overview with focus on tropical-storm prediction; extensive bibliography.

Gregory T. Cushman

VINOGRADOV, IVAN MATVEE-VICH (*b.* Milolyub, Velikie Luki, Russia, 14 September 1891; *d.* Moscow, USSR, 20 March 1983), *analytic number theory, science administration.*

Vinogradov was one of the most prominent mathematicians who worked in analytical number theory. His methods (first of all the method of trigonometric sums) permitted him to make progress with some of the most important and difficult problems in the subject including Goldbach's conjecture and the estimate of Weyl sums.

Education and Early Results. Vinogradov's father, Matvei Avraamievich, was a priest in Milolyub, a village in the Velikie Luki district (now of the Pskov province), and his mother, Mariya Aleksandrovna, was a teacher. Ivan was educated in a high school in Velikie Luki, and in 1910 he entered the Faculty of Mathematics and Physics at St. Petersburg University. Professors Andrei A. Markov and Yakov V. Uspenskii exercised a powerful influence on him, and he became interested in number theory. He graduated in 1914 with the degree candidate of mathematical sciences, and for his outstanding work on the distribution of quadratic residues and nonresidues, supervised by Uspenskii, he was awarded a scholarship in 1915. The scientific degrees were abolished after the revolution of 1917 by the Soviet government and were restored only in 1933. After that, Vinogradov was awarded the degree doctor of mathematical and physical sciences. Between 1914 and 1918 he obtained important results in number theory on the distribution of power nonresidues, he elaborated an elementary method that permitted him to find a general theorem on the number of integral points in plain domains, and he proposed a general analytical method for a solution of the problem of the number of integral points in the domains in the plane and in space, and so forth.

But these were the years of World War I and the Russian Revolution. Many of his results were published very late, and others that were published at the time remained unknown in the West because of wartime difficulties. For the same reason, little information reached Russia about results obtained in the West in those years. For example Hermann Weyl's work on estimates of trigonometric sums and Godfrey Hardy and John Littlewood's results on the Waring problem did not became known in good time.

Disorganization and hunger in postrevolutionary Petrograd (the new name for St. Petersburg) forced the scientists to flee to safety. Some of the young mathematicians (including Abram S. Besicovitch, Yakov D. Tamarkin, and Aleksandr A. Friedman) went to Perm: there in 1916 a branch of Petrograd University was opened that in 1917 became an independent university. I. M. Vinogradov was among them. From 1918 to 1920 he worked in the Perm State University (from 1920 as professor) and at the end of 1920 he returned to Petrograd, where he became a professor at Petrograd University (from 1925 he held the chair of number theory) and at the Polytechnic Institute. At the Polytechnic Institute he elaborated an original course of mathematics for engineers (described in his handbook *Elementy vysshei matematiki* [1932, 1933; Elements of higher mathematics]).

In the university he lectured on number theory, on the basis of which he wrote a famous textbook *Osnovy teorii chisel* (1936; Elements of number theory). Rather concise, this book introduced the elements of theory, beginning with divisibility theory and proceeding via problems with hints for their solutions to problems in the modern theory. This textbook was revised many times—the last (tenth) edition appeared in 2004—and was translated into many languages.

Trigonometric Sums. Vinogradov combined teaching with very intensive research activity. In 1924 he began to study additive problems in number theory. In 1927 he published a new solution of Waring's problem. This was the beginning of his famous method of trigonometric sums. At first he utilized Weyl's method, but already in 1934 he proposed a new and more accurate method for estimating trigonometric sums. With the aid of this method he could significantly improve the available results for the problem of the distribution of fractional parts of the values of a polynomial, for Waring's problem, and for others. Vinogradov's method was elaborated and applied with success to many different problems in number theory (the theory of the Riemann zeta function, Hilbert-Kamke's problem, etc.) by a series of scientists: I. Johannes G. Van der Corput, Nikolai G. Chudakov, Hua Loo-Keng, Yurii V. Linnik, Anatolii A. Karatsuba, and others.

In 1937 Vinogradov developed the method of estimates of trigonometric sums over primes, that is to say of trigonometric sums in which the summation is taken over prime numbers. With this method he solved a series of problems in additive prime number theory. In the same year he demonstrated the asymptotic formula for the number of representations of an odd number as the sum of three primes (Godfrey H. Hardy and John E. Littlewood's 1923 demonstration of this result was based on a certain hypothesis in the theory of *L*-series). One of the consequences of this formula became a solution of Goldbach's problem for odd numbers: every sufficiently large odd integer is representable as a sum of three primes.

In the following years Vinogradov improved his method of trigonometric sums and consequently he found new results for a series of the problems in number theory: an improved estimate for the sum of nontrivial characters in the sequence of shifted primes (1953), a new bound for zeroes of the Riemann zeta function (1957), a new remainder term in the asymptotic expression for the number of integral points in a sphere (1963), and new general theorems on the estimates of Weyl sums (1958–1971). Many of these results were included in his classic monograph *Metod trigonometricheskikh summ v teorii chisel* (1947; *The Method of Trigonometrical Sums in the Theory of Numbers*) and also in his book *Osobye varianty metoda trigonometricheskikh summ* (Special variants of the method of trigonometric sums). His methods were developed widely by others and found application in different parts of mathematics: in mathematical analysis, in the calculus of approximations, in the theory of probability, and in the discrete mathematics.

Vinogradov's results quickly brought him universal acknowledgment. A section titled "Vinogradov's Method" appeared in Edmund Landau's famous *Vorlesungen über Zahlentheorie* (Lectures on number theory) published in 1927. In 1929 Vinogradov became an effective member of the Academy of Sciences of the USSR. Later he was elected to several foreign academies of sciences and scientific societies, and received honorary doctorates from many universities.

Leadership. Very early in his career he became involved with scientific administration. In 1932 he became the head of the Mathematical Department of the Physics and Mathematics Institute of the USSR Academy of Sciences, from which Steklov Mathematical Institute was reorganized as separate institution in 1934. Vinogradov became its director. In the same year the presidium of the Academy of Sciences moved from Leningrad (formerly Petrograd) to Moscow. Together with the presidium several institutes of the academy (including the Steklov Institute) moved to Moscow.

As a result of these moves, the two main Russian mathematical schools—the St. Petersburg–Leningrad and the Moscow schools, which had hitherto been in confrontation—were forced to live together. On the basis of a synthesis of these schools the core of the new organism was born: the Soviet mathematical school, one of the most influential in the twentieth century. The edifice of Soviet science, constructed in the 1930s according to Joseph Stalin's plans, was crowned by its general staff, that is, by the Academy of Sciences of the USSR. Consequently the Steklov Mathematical Institute held the paramount position in the Soviet mathematical community, and the director of this institute became one of the most influential persons in this community. For more than forty-five years this post was occupied (until his death) by Vinogradov (except 1941–1943, when Sergei L. Sobolev was its director).

Under Vinogradov's leadership the Steklov Mathematical Institute—which was comparatively small (by Soviet standards) and whose members were, with rare exceptions, prominent specialists in the main directions of the contemporary mathematics—became one of the most important mathematical institutes of the twentieth century. However, it must be said that Vinogradov's tough line in the selection of the personnel was characterized (especially during the last years of his life) by a remarkable willfulness.

For many years Vinogradov was the president of the bureau of the National Committee of the Soviet Mathematicians and the editor of the mathematical series of the *Izvestiya Akademii nauk SSSR* (Proceedings of the Academy of Sciences of the USSR). Despite the fact that he was not a member of the Communist Party, the Soviet state always supported him. He received many Soviet honors such as: Hero of the Socialist Labor, on two occasions; Order of Lenin, on five occasions; and the Order of the October Revolution. For his mathematical achievements he received the Stalin Prize, the Lenin Prize, and the Lomonosov Gold Medal of the USSR Academy of Sciences.

BIBLIOGRAPHY

WORKS BY VINOGRADOV

Elementy vysshei matematiki [Elements of higher mathematics]. Vol. 1, *Analiticheskaya geometriya* [Analytical geometry]. Leningrad: Kubuch, 1932.

Elementy vysshei matematiki [Elements of higher mathematics]. Vol. 2, *Differentsial'noe ischislenie* [Differential calculus]. Leningrad: Kubuch, 1933.

Osnovy teorii chisel [Elements of number theory]. Moscow: ONTI, 1936. Translated from the 6th Russian ed. by Helen Popova as *An Introduction to the Theory of Numbers*. London: Pergamon, 1955.

Metod trigonometricheskikh summ v teorii chisel. Moscow: Academy of Science of the USSR, 1947 (also Moscow:

Nauka, 1971). Translated as *The Method of Trigonometrical Sums in the Theory of Numbers*. New York: Interscience, 1954 (also Mineola, NY: Dover, 2004).

Izbrannye trudy [Selected works]. Edited by Yu. V. Linnik. Moscow: Izd-vo Akademii nauk SSSR [Editorial house of the Academy of Sciences of the USSR], 1952.

Osobye varianty metoda trigonometricheskikh summ [Special variants of the method of trigonometric sums]. Moscow: Nauka, 1976.

Selected Works. Edited by L. D. Faddeev, R. V. Gamkrelidze, A. A. Karacuba, et al. Berlin: Springer-Verlag, 1985. Pages 393–401 give a chronological list of Vinogradov's works.

OTHER SOURCES

Karacuba, A. A. "Ivan Matveevich Vinogradov (k 90-letiyu so dnya rozhdeniya)." *Uspekhi Matematicheskikh Nauk* 36, no. 6 (1981): 3–15.

Mardzhanishvili, K. K. "Ivan Matveevič Vinogradov." In *Selected Works*, edited by L. D. Faddeev, R. V. Gamkrelidze, A. A. Karacuba, et al. Berlin: Springer-Verlag, 1985.

S. Demidov

VIRCHOW, RUDOLF CARL (*b.* Schivelbein, Pomerania, Germany, 13 October 1821; *d.* Berlin, Germany, 5 September 1902), *pathology, social medicine, public health, anthropology.* For the original article on Virchow see *DSB,* vol. 14.

In the 1990s and early 2000s, Virchow was the object of new historical assessments, which were mostly due to changing perspectives on science and society in the nineteenth century. While previously Virchow was primarily a subject for historians of medicine, he increasingly also became an object of interest in the history of science and in general history. Furthermore, while more traditional historical approaches to Virchow still played an important role, there emerged an important trend to consider him no longer primarily as the "great doctor" but rather as a prototype of the modern scientist and also as a forerunner of scientific expertise in politics. Subsequent historical understandings of Virchow mostly focus on four aspects:

1. medicine;

2. anthropology;

3. science and politics; and

4. science and the public.

Medicine. Virchow's importance in the realm of pathology and physiology but also of social medicine has remained a focus of scholarly interest. He has been an important source of professional identity for the medical

Rudolf Carl Virchow. © BETTMANN/CORBIS

inate his ideas and to exert control over the dissemination of the ideas of others. Virchow can be seen as a forerunner of the modern market-oriented scientist who lived under the terms of "publish or perish" and who was highly effective in organizing material resources—ranging from subjects for dissections to the funding of institutes in Wuerzburg and Berlin—to promote his research. And one might add that he also was highly effective in squeezing academic rivals such as Robert Remak out of the market.

With the establishment of his Pathological Institute in Berlin in 1856, Virchow also participated in the "institutional revolution" (Cahan,) which adapted scientific institutes to the needs of a rising industrial nation. At the Pathological Institute, where Virchow ruled for about forty-five years, a specific scientific culture emerged that molded generations of German medical students who received their professional training there. In particular, Virchow's dissection techniques can be considered both as medical and cultural techniques. His students were trained for Accurate Observation and exact description by help of a variety of means ranging from a "microscopical Railway" where preparations were circling among them around to glasses filled with colored beans. "Learning to see," which formed the core of Virchow's medical educational program, was both essential to his allegedly inductive epistemology and to his liberal worldview.

Anthropology. Recent interest has grown especially in Virchow's anthropological activities, which had moved to the center of his scientific activities in the late 1860s. Again, his role in constructing a new discipline has found special interest, since anthropology had not become a university-based science in Germany before the late nineteenth century. The decisive tool for the institutionalization of anthropology was the Berlin Anthropological Society, over which Virchow presided for decades and which provided the core of the nationwide German Anthropological Society. As in other countries, scientific amateurs were pivotal for the establishment of the new discipline of anthropology in Germany. The membership of amateurs in scientific voluntary associations served both the construction of the disciplinary identity of anthropology and the reinvigoration of a bourgeois identity.

The main interest for Virchow's anthropological activities, however, results from the debate on the origins of modern scientific racism. For a long time, Virchow has been considered as a rock in the racist tide of his time. This point of view has been reinforced by some authors who consider that the illiberal break of anthropology could only have taken place in the generations following Virchow. Others, however, suggest that Virchow himself paved the way if not to racist ideas then to racist practices,

community, which tries to benefit from his heritage. Under such a perspective, Virchow has been described as a harbinger of modern medicine and also of modern medical ethics.

Virchow's role in nineteenth-century medicine, however, may also be considered an important example of modern market dynamics in science, of construction of disciplines, and also as part of state attempts to modernize Germany with the help of science. This might also help to explain why the Prussian state bureaucracy was much more reluctant to chastise the promising young scientist at the end of the revolution in 1848 than in other cases of rebellious scholars. And it also helps to explain the further steps of his astonishing career, which for some time made him to the symbol of modern German science.

In such a critical perspective, which is less interested in the "genius" and more in the institutional and social framework that made the emergence of a scientific star possible, there is also less emphasis on the originality of Virchow's ideas, and more on the techniques he used to strengthen both the disciplinary power of pathology and physiology and his authority within these fields. Especially important in this respect are his numerous publications in scientific journals, which provided him opportunity both to dissem-

notably by his famous anthropological examinations of hair, eye, and skin colors of German schoolchildren which he undertook in 1876. By making anthropological distinctions popular, he might have spread a racist "tacit knowledge" among ordinary Germans.

In this manner, Virchow has become a symbol of the inherent contradictions of the liberal defense against racism and anti-Semitism in the German Empire. He represents the dilemma of liberal anthropology at the fin de siècle: While anthropology finally had achieved academic recognition, it had lost all scientific criteria to define race. At the same time, however, it was not able to get rid of the stereotype of primordial races. So, on the one hand, Virchow strongly disapproved racial anti-Semitism as superstition and atavism. On the other hand, however, he stuck to a intuitive notion of race and to the stereotype of the primordial Teuton.

Science and Politics. A great deal of the interest in Virchow toward the end of the twentieth century was devoted to his political activities, which previously often had been considered a rather ephemeral aspect of his life and work. His political activities, however, should not be considered only as a time-consuming distraction from his scientific work. Rather, they were closely linked not only to his scientific self-understanding, but also to a liberal and bourgeois model of citizenship that contributed highly to the ultimate core of his personality. Therefore, Virchow is also an example for the changing feasibility in combining science and political activities as aspects of a civic lifestyle in the nineteenth century: He might be considered as a prototype of the "scientist as citizen."

While during the revolution of 1848 Virchow had successfully claimed the identity of science and politics, in later years he became more skeptical about the compatibility of the roles of scientist and politician. Nevertheless, he remained extremely active in both fields until the end of his life, and thus he resisted the secular trend toward the "pure" scientist. Virchow never fully agreed to the autonomy of science and politics, because he believed in the validity of the laws of progress in both nature and society. So he can be considered as an outstanding exponent of "progressivism" in Germany, which during much of the nineteenth century was based on a close alliance of science and liberalism.

Virchow's political engagement shifted from radical democratic ideas during the revolution of 1848 to a more moderate liberal stance since his political revival at the end of the 1850s. As a left liberal member of the Berlin City Council, of the Prussian Diet, and for some time also the Reichstag, he was mainly active in fields where he could make use of his scientific authority. Among them, matters of public health and education were most prominent. Also

of special importance, however, was his engagement during the cultural war with the Catholic Church during the 1870s. During that conflict Virchow even became an ally of his archenemy, the conservative Prussian minister-president Otto von Bismarck, against whom he had fiercely fought during the constitutional struggle in Prussia of the early 1860s. But there exists a common element between these two struggles: In both cases Virchow fought for the authority of a scientific model of truth for which he claimed universal validity. So while Bismarck tied his assertion of "Truth" and "Trust" to an aristocratic code of honor, Virchow referred to the praxis of modern science by claiming that "truth" and "trust" in the political realm also should be based on empirical examination of facts and observing the laws of logic.

As Virchow tried to extend his scientific authority to the political field, so his political ideas influenced his scientific work. Especially important for the circulation of ideas between the scientific and political field was his use of metaphors. A classical object for the examination of the reciprocal transfer of meanings between biology and society has been Virchow's cellular pathology. The latter generated a central metaphorical field that encompassed the notions of "cell," "individual," and "state." While in his early days Virchow had defined disease as "life under modified circumstances," at the end of his career he had adopted the growing militarization of public discourse, and now he tended to define disease as a war, where the body was a beleaguered cell state threatened by external forces.

Science and the Public. Virchow was always eager to disseminate his scientific ideas as elements of political reform. Already in his famous report on the typhus epidemic in Upper Silesia in 1848, Virchow had articulated a paternalistic scientific education program as a means for the development of a bourgeois society. While at that time he still considered the state as a close ally for the education of illiterate "masses," later he estimated scientific education as a tool to reform the state itself. Virchow aimed at bringing society in accordance with the laws of nature, which should result from "scientific thinking"—which for him in the first instance meant an opposition to "philosophical," deductive thinking —and "unprejudiced observation." Thus, he considered scientific knowledge and scientific thinking as important tools for liberal reform of state and society.

As a result, after the 1860s, Virchow more and more stepped into the field of popularization of science. He became one of the most important activists of liberal national education of his time in Germany. Virchow participated in voluntary associations devoted to the education of craftsmen, he published numerous books and series devoted to national education, and he also founded several museums, ranging from the Berlin Ethnological Museum established in 1886 to the Pathological Museum at the Charité, which was opened to the public in 1901. Behind all these publication and museum projects stood the idea of "enlightenment," which aimed at both destroying "superstition" and strengthening belief in the authority of science. And after the unification of the German Empire in 1871, Virchow even considered the popularization of German science as a device for national homogenization. Therefore, both his later attacks on Catholicism and Darwinism may be explained as consequences of his quest for national unity and scientific authority. While Catholicism in Virchow's eyes posed a threat of division between national-oriented Protestants and Catholics devoted to a supranational power, the popularization of Darwinism in school curricula meant for him the distribution of still hypothetical knowledge—with all risk of later refutation and consequential concussion of popular trust in science.

Outlook. From the 1880s, Virchow increasingly became a public monument as a symbol of German science. However, he was also more and more criticized both for his growing authoritarianism in the field of science and for his conception of the unity of science and liberalism: The latter no longer fitted either the growing social democratic or the conservative mood in the German Empire. The gap between Virchow's aspirations—to organize a national liberal consensus by way of the popularization of a scientific style of thought—and the real situation in the German Empire was very much widening. Consequently, already before his death, his public image became more and more defined by his role as the great doctor, while his manifold political activities for a long time came to be considered as a kind of intellectual teething troubles. However, Virchow cannot be properly understood if one does not take into account his peculiar position in the center of a "culture of progress" that for many decades played a decisive role in nineteenth-century Germany.

SUPPLEMENTARY BIBLIOGRAPHY

While the major share of the literary remains of Rudolf Virchow belongs to the Archiv der Berlin-Brandenburgischen Akademie der Wissenschaften, Berlin, an additional part can be found at the Pommersches Landesmuseum, Greifswald, Sammlung Rabl-Virchow. Significant segments of Virchow's publications and literary remains have become available by editions. Most important is the gargantuan project of Christian Andree, an edition of Virchow's complete writings, which is anticipated to span seventy-one volumes: Rudolf Virchow, Sämtliche Werke, edited by Christian Andree. As of 2007, fifteen volumes had been published (and publishing houses had changed twice).

WORKS BY VIRCHOW

Die Korrespondenz zwischen Heinrich Schliemann und Rudolf Virchow 1876–1890, bearb. u. hrsg. von Joachim Herrmann und Evelin Maaß in Zusammenarbeit mit Christian Andree und Luise Hallof (Arranged and edited by Joachim Herrmann and Evelin Maaß in cooperation with Christian Andree and Luise Hallof). Berlin: Akademie, 1990.

Anton Dohrn und Rudolf Virchow: Briefwechsel; 1864–1902. Bearb. und mit einer wissenschaftshistorischen Einleitung versehen von Christiane Groeben und Klaus Wenig (Arranged and provided with an introduction by Christiane Groeben and Klaus Wenig). Berlin: Akademie, 1992.

Beiträge zur wissenschaftlichen Medizin aus den Jahren 1846–1850. Vol. 4 of *Sämtliche Werke.* Edited by Christian Andree. Bern: Lang, 1992.

Politische Tätigkeit im Preußischen Abgeordnetenhaus (1861–1893). Vols. 30–37 of *Sämtliche Werke.* Edited by Christian Andree. Bern: Lang, resp. Berlin: Blackwell, 1992 ff.

Rudolf Virchow und Emil du Bois-Reymond. Briefe 1864–1894. Edited by Klaus Wenig. Marburg/Lahn: Basiliken, 1995.

Vorlesungs- und Kursnachschriften aus Würzburg. Wintersemester 1852/53 bis Sommersemester 1854. Vol. 21 of *Sämtliche Werke.* Edited by Christian Andree. Berlin: Blackwell, 2000.

Briefwechsel mit den Eltern und der Familie. Vol. 59 of *Sämtliche Werke.* Edited by Christian Andree. Berlin: Blackwell, 2001.

Zur Kraniologie Amerikas. Vol. 52 of *Sämtliche Werke.* Edited by Christian Andree. Berlin: Blackwell, 2002.

Specielle pathologische Anatomie des Menschen. In der Nachschrift von Friedrich Goll, Sommersemester 1851 in Würzburg. Vol. 20 of *Sämtliche Werke.* Edited by Christian Andree. Berlin: Blackwell, 2003.

OTHER SOURCES

Andree, Christian. *Rudolf Virchow als Prähistoriker.* 3 vols. Cologne, Germany: Böhlau, 1976–1986.

———. *Rudolf Virchow: Leben und Ethos eines großen Arztes.* Munich: Langen Müller, 2002. Hero worship at its best.

Boyd, Byron A. *Rudolf Virchow: The Scientist as Citizen.* New York: Garland, 1991. An excellent description of Virchow's political career.

Cahan, David. "The Institutional Revolution in German Physics, 1865–1914." *Historical Studies in the Physical Sciences* 15, no. 2 (1984): 1–65.

David, Heinz. *Rudolf Virchow und die Medizin des 20. Jahrhunderts.* Munich: Quintessenz, 1993. Mostly a collection of Virchow quotations.

Goschler, Constantin. *Rudolf Virchow: Mediziner, Anthropologe, Politiker.* Cologne, Germany: Boehlau, 2002. A modern biography that focuses on the interrelation of science and politics.

Inspirationen der Medizin durch Virchow: Symposion am 19, Oktober 2002 in Erlangen. Ausgerichtet vom Institut für Geschichte und Ethik der Medizin und vom Pathologisch-Anatomischen Institut der Friedrich-Alexander-Universität Erlangen-Nürnberg. Erlangen and Jena: Palm und Enke, 2003.

Massin, Benoit. "From Virchow to Fischer: Physical Anthropology and 'Modern Race Theories' in Wilhelmine Germany." In *Volksgeist as Method and Ethic: Essays on Boasian Ethnography and the German Anthropological Tradition*, edited by George W. Stocking. Madison: University of Wisconsin Press, 1996.

Matyssek, Angela. *Rudolf Virchow, das Pathologische Museum: Geschichte einer wissenschaftlichen Sammlung um 1900*. Darmstadt: Steinkopff, 2002. A pioneer study on Virchow's role as collector and displayer.

Mazzolini, Renato G. *Stato e organismo, individui e cellule nell'opera di Rudolf Virchow negli anni 1845–1860*. Published in the journal *Annali dell'Istituto storico italo-germanico in Trento* 9 (1983): 153–293. A superb study on the role of metaphors in Virchow's scientific and political thinking.

McNeely, Ian Farrell. *Medicine on a Grand Scale: Rudolf Virchow, Health Politics, and Liberal Social Reform in Nineteenth-Century Germany*. London: The Wellcome Trust Centre for the History of Medicine at University College London, 2002. A brilliant analysis of Virchow's role as medical and social reformer.

Schipperges, Heinrich. *Rudolf Virchow*. Reinbek bei Hamburg, Germany: Rowohlt Taschenbuch Verlag, 1994. A good overview for the general reader.

Smith, Woodruff D. *Politics and the Sciences of Culture in Germany, 1840–1920*. New York: Oxford University Press, 1991.

Trautmann-Waller, Céline, ed. *Quand Berlin pensait les peuples: Anthropologie, ethnologie et psychologie, 1850–1890*. Paris: CNRS, 2004.

Vasold, Manfred. *Rudolf Virchow: Der grosse Arzt und Politiker*. Stuttgart: Deutsche Verlags-Anstalt, 1988. Hero worship meets social history.

Weindling, Paul. "Theories of the Cell State in Imperial Germany." In *Biology, Medicine, and Society, 1840–1940*, edited by Charles Webster. Cambridge, U.K.: Cambridge University Press, 1981.

Wirth, Ingo. *Zur Sektionstätigkeit im Pathologischen Institut der Friedrich-Wilhelms-Universität zu Berlin von 1856 bis 1902: Ein Beitrag zur Virchow-Forschung*. Berlin: Logos, 2005.

Zimmerman, Andrew. *Anthropology and Antihumanism in Imperial Germany*. Chicago: University of Chicago Press, 2001.

Constantin Goschler

VOGT, CÉCILE AUGUSTINE MARIE (NÉE MUGNIER)

(*b.* Annecy, Haute-Savoie, France, 27 March 1875; *d.* Cambridge, England, 4 May 1962) *neurology, brain research, brain maps, psychotherapy, genetics.*

VOGT, OSKAR GEORG DIECKMANN

(*b.* Husum, Prussia, 6 April 1870; *d.* Freiburg im Breisgau, West Germany, 31 July 1959) *neurology, brain research, brain maps, psychotherapy, genetics.*

Cécile and Oskar Vogt made a crucial contribution to twentieth-century brain research as a married couple. Their project was to relate mental, intellectual, emotional, and behavioral capacity to the cellular structures of the brain. They correlated structural difference in brain tissue to mental functions, thus localizing these functions at specific sites, the "architectonic areas" of the cortex or respective fine structures of subcortical gangliae. They established an extensive collection of brains, brain slices, and connected clinical data. To develop functional brain maps, they used a wide range of methodological approaches, including functional and comparative neuroanatomy, clinical neuroanatomy, electrophysiology, and neuropharmacology. Working in the paradigm of evolutionary and developmental biology, they integrated genetics and zoological systematics into their research. In their early years they used hypnosis and psychotherapy and became strong opponents of Sigmund Freud's psychoanalysis. They founded several research institutes, the most prominent being the Kaiser Wilhelm Institute for Brain Research in Berlin, and edited various scientific journals.

Early Years. Cécile Mugnier's father, Pierre Louis Mugnier, had been an army brigadier officer; he died when she was two years old. Her mother, who was not married to Pierre Mugnier, was a freethinker who supported her daughter's private education and her sitting for university entrance exams, which was quite unusual at the time. Cécile Mugnier went to Paris as one of the early female students of medicine and specialized in neurology. She aimed to pursue a scientific career and became "externe" at the men's clinic Bicêtre, led by Pierre Marie, who had been a student of Paul Broca and Jean Martin Charcot. In 1898–1899 she took her medical exams; she earned her doctoral degree based on a study in neuroanatomy and gained her doctor's license for France in 1900. She obtained the German licence in 1920 because of her scientific merits. In 1898 she became engaged to Oskar Vogt. They were married in 1899 in Berlin, where they settled down and started a lifelong scientific collaboration.

Oskar Vogt was the eldest son of the Protestant minister Hans Friedrich Vogt and his wife Maria Vogt. The father died early, leaving his widow with five small children. However, Oskar was able to attend the humanist gymnasium and go to university. A mentor and friend for life was Ferdinand Tönnies from his hometown; Tönnies was later the cofounder of the German society for sociology. Oskar Vogt studied medicine and biology in Kiel and

Jena, where his teachers included Walter Flemming, Ernst Haeckel, Max Fürbringer, and Otto Binswanger. He qualified in medicine in 1893 and obtained his medical doctoral degree in neuroanatomy. At that time he worked as an assistant both to Binswanger at the psychiatric clinic in Jena and to Otto Binswanger's brother Robert at the Sanatorium Bellevue in Kreutzlingen. A short stay with August Forel (at the Burghölzli Hospital in Zürich) established a firm friendship between the two men, subsequently including Cécile Vogt. Forel taught Oskar Vogt the technique of hypnosis and delegated to him the editorship of the *Zeitschrift für Hypnotismus, Psychotherapie sowie andere psychophysiologische und psychopathologische Forschungen.* The journal was continued after 1902 as *Journal für Psychologie und Neurologie* with Forel and Oskar Vogt as coeditors and after 1928 with Cécile Vogt as well.

A short time as an assistant to Paul Flechsig at the Psychiatrische und Nervenklinik in Leipzig in 1894–1895 ended in conflict; Oskar Vogt continued to earn his living as a psychotherapist using hypnosis in private practice. By good fortune he met the steel magnate Friedrich Alfred Krupp and his wife Margarethe and became their personal physician. The Krupp family, and especially the son-in-law, Gustav Krupp von Bohlen und Halbach, later became the most powerful supporters of Oskar and Cécile Vogt—financially and politically. Without the Krupps, their scientific career would have been impossible. In 1897 and 1898 Oskar Vogt went to Paris to work as a psychotherapist and study neuroanatomy in the laboratory of Joseph J. Dejerine and Augusta Dejerine-Klumpke at the women's clinic Salpêtrière. In Paris he met Cécile Mugnier, and soon they began a scientific partnership, in which, with few exceptions, they published all their work together. Their two daughters became famous scientists: Marthe Louise Vogt (1903–2003), a neuropharmacologist, who emigrated to Britain in 1933–1934, and Marguerite Vogt, (b. 1913), a geneticist, who emigrated to the United States in 1952.

Founding of the Research Institutes. Beginning with the private Neurologische Centralstation, founded in 1898 in Berlin, Cécile and Oskar Vogt developed an institute for brain research, which became the world's leading institution in the late 1920s and the precursor of the Max Planck Institutes for Brain Research in West Germany. Named Neurobiologisches Laboratorium, the Centralstation became part of the Friedrich Wilhelm University of Berlin in 1902. In 1914 it was incorporated into the newly founded Kaiser Wilhelm Institute for Brain Research (KWI-B), headed by Oskar Vogt, who had been given the title of professor in 1913. This institutional situation enabled Cécile Vogt to work as a scientist at a time when women were officially not allowed to study in Prussia. In 1920 she got a position as Vorsteher der neuroanatomis-

chen Abteilung at the KWI-B, which was comparable to an associate professorship at university. Oskar Vogt headed the newly established State Institute for Brain Research in Moscow from 1925 to the early 1930s, starting with the spectacular cytoarchitectonical investigation of Vladimir Ilich Lenin's brain. He played a crucial role in German-Soviet scientific relations. He used his political influence and the support of Krupp and the Rockefeller Foundation in the late 1920s to build a new institute in Berlin-Buch with a neurological clinic dedicated to research and eleven departments with different disciplines to support brain research. One of them, the genetic department founded in 1925 and headed by Elena and Nikolai Timoféeff-Ressovsky from Moscow, became famous for its mutation research, for population genetics, and evolutionary synthesis.

Brain Research and Psychotherapy. Between 1902 and 1911 Cécile and Oskar Vogt and their coworker Korbinian Brodmann developed new brain maps, defining different regions of the mammalian and human cortex of the cerebrum according to their differences in the "architectonics," that is the distribution of neuronal cell bodies (Brodmann's cytoarchitectonic areas) or connecting fibers (myeloarchitectonics). In 1907 Cécile and Oskar Vogt presented the results of their experiments, using electrical stimuli applied at these areas to create specific differences in the motor reactions of anesthetized animals, showing for the first time the functional and anatomical difference between the sensory and motor cortices. Cécile Vogt investigated the substructure of the thalamus and subcortical grisea. In 1911 she identified certain movement disorders (ataxias) as caused by anatomical changes in the subcortical area corpus striatum (*Vogtsche Krankheit*). She also investigated the anatomical basis of Huntington's Chorea.

In their work as psychotherapists, with Oskar Vogt using the cathartic method and hypnosis in the years before World War I, the Vogts became strongly critical of Sigmund Freud's psychoanalysis. Cécile Vogt coined the term *disamnesia* for the pathogenic inability to forget traumatic experiences, thus challenging Freud's interpretation of repression as pathogenic. Oskar Vogt experimented with hypnosis and paved the way for the development of autogenic training. However, from World War I on, the Vogts increasingly saw somatic reasons for all psychic disorders—even criminality—as resided in the constitution or structure of the brain tissue. The cellular structures of the cerebellar cortex were represented as maps, and the collection and investigation of brains of people with different mental abilities aimed at a localization of these capacities in certain brain areas (elite brains). From the beginnings, the material basis of the research became the manufactory-like production of very thin slices of brains

Brain slicing machine. *Cécile and Oskar Vogt, ca. 1905, standing at their brain slicing machine in front of the brain slice filing cabinets.* CECILE UND OSKAR VOGT-INSTITUT FÜR HIRNFORSCHUNG GMBH, DUESSELDORF, GERMANY. REPRODUCED BY PERMISSION.

embedded in paraffin wax, the staining of different structures, and their microscopic analysis. The published photographs of the structures seen in the brain slices are of a superb quality.

After World War I the Vogts developed a concept of *pathoclisis,* based on developmental genetics. Small functional units of brain tissue were supposed to have a specific vulnerability to external factors, thus leading to specific lesions and diseases. Using principles of zoological systematics and the intraspecific variations of the coloring of bumblebees as a model, the Vogts created a new way of classifying psychotic disorders, based on specific changes

in brain tissue. Sharing eugenic convictions to "breed better brains" from neo-Lamarckian perspective until the 1940s, Cécile and Oskar Vogt in their later years aimed at specific intervention into certain brain areas at the molecular level, anticipating concepts of somatic gene therapy. In other words they hoped to change human behavior on the somatic level at their will.

Controversial at first, Cécile and Oskar Vogt came to be held in high scientific esteem, both being nominated members of the Kaiser-Wilhelm-Gesellschaft in 1927 and of the Deutsche Akademie der Naturforscher Leopoldina Halle in 1932. In 1950 they received the Nationalpreis erster Klasse of East Germany. West Germany honored Oskar Vogt with the Bundesverdienstkreuz in 1959.

The Vogts' huge collection of brain slices, human and vertebrate, is at the C. u. O. Vogt Institute for Brain Research of the Heinrich-Heine-University, Düsseldorf; Oskar Vogt's collection of bumblebees and beetles (approximately seven hundred thousand specimens) is housed at the Zoological Museum, Amsterdam.

Having been pacifists during World War I, and close to the leftist-liberal political camp, Cécile and Oskar Vogt came under attack in 1933. Forced to leave the KWI-B, but protected by Krupp, they continued their work together at their new private Institut für Hirnforschung und Allgemeine Biologie in Neustadt, Black Forest. During the Nazi period they protected and hid Jewish people, some of them close friends. In 1950 they started the new *Journal für Hirnforschung*, published in Berlin, East Germany. After Oskar Vogt's death in 1959 Cécile Vogt moved to Cambridge, United Kingdom. Until her death in 1962 she lived there with her daughter Marthe.

BIBLIOGRAPHY

WORKS BY CÉCILE AND OSKAR VOGT

"Zur Kenntnis der elektrisch erregbaren Hirnrindengebiete bei den Säugetieren." *Journal für Psychologie und Neurologie* 8, supp. (1907): 277–456.

"Allgemeinere Ergebnisse unserer Hirnforschung." *Journal für Psychologie und Neurologie* 25, supp. 1 (1919): 277–461.

"Zur Lehre der Erkrankungen des striären Systems." *Journal für Psychologie und Neurologie* 25, supp. 3 (1920): 631–846.

"Sitz und Wesen der Krankheiten im Lichte der topistischen Hirnforschung und des Variierens der Tiere." Part 1, *Journal für Psychologie und Neurologie* 47 (1937): 237–457; Part 2, *Journal für Psychologie und Neurologie* 48 (1938): 169–324.

"Morphologische Gestaltungen unter normalen und pathogenen Bedingungen. Ein hirnanatomischer Beitrag zu ihrer Kenntnis." *Journal für Psychologie und Neurologie* 50 (1941–1942): 161–524.

"Thalamusstudien I–III." *Journal für Psychologie und Neurologie* 50 (1941–1942): 32–154.

WORKS BY CÉCILE VOGT

"Quelques considerations générales à propos du syndrome du corps strié." *Journal für Psychologie und Neurologie* 18 (1911): 479–488.

"Einige Ergebnisse unserer Neurosenforschung." *Die Naturwissenschaften* 9, no. 18 (1921): 346–350.

JOURNALS EDITED BY CECILE AND OSKAR VOGT

Zeitschrift für Hypnotismus, Psychotherapie sowie andere psychophysiologische und psychopathologische Forschungen. Edited by Oskar Vogt, 1896–1902. Leipzig: Ambrosius Barth.

Denkschriften der medicinisch-naturwissenschaftlichen Gesellschaft zu Jena. Vols. 9, 10, 12: *Neurobiologische Arbeiten.* Edited by Oskar Vogt, 1902–1904. Jena: Gustav Fischer.

Journal für Psychologie und Neurologie. 51 volumes. 1902–1942. Leipzig: Ambrosius Barth. Published with the subtitles *Zugleich Zeitschrift für Hypnotismus* (1902–1910), and *Mitteilungen aus den Gesamtgebiet der Anatomie, Physiologie und Pathologie des Zentralnervensystems sowie der medizinischen Pschychologie* (1928–1942). Edited by August Forel and Oskar Vogt (1902–1928); by August Forel, CécileVogt, and Oskar Vogt (1924–1931); and by Cécile Vogt and Oskar Vogt (1931–1942).

Journal für Hirnforschung. Internationales Journal für Neurobiologie. Organ des Instituts für Hirnforschung und Allgemeine Biologie in Neustadt (Schwarzwald). Edited by Cécile Vogt and Oskar Vogt, 1954–1960. Berlin-DDR: Akademie Verlag.

OTHER SOURCES

Klatzo, Igor, in collaboration with Gabriele Zu Rhein. *Cécile and Oskar Vogt: The Visionaries of Modern Neuroscience.* Acta Neurochirurgica 80. Vienna: Springer, 2002. A very personal account.

Richter, Jochen. "Das Kaiser-Wilhelm-Institut für Hirnforschung und die Topographie der Grosshirnhemisphären." In *Die Kaiser-Wilhelm-/Max-Planck-Gesellschaft und ihre Institute: Studien zu ihrer Geschichte; Das Harnack-Prinzip,* edited by Bernhard Vom Brocke and Hubert Laitko. Berlin: Walter de Gruyter, 1996.

Satzinger, Helga. *Die Geschichte der genetisch orientierten Hirnforschung von Cécile und Oskar Vogt (1875–1962, 1870–1959) in der Zeit von 1895 bis ca. 1927.* Stuttgart: Deutscher Apotheker Verlag, 1998. Includes a full bibliography of works by Cécile Vogt and Oskar Vogt.

Helga Satzinger

VOIGT, WOLDEMAR (*b.* Leipzig, Saxony, 2 September 1850; *d.* Göttingen, Germany, 13 December 1919), *physics*. For the original article on Voigt see *DSB*, vol. 14.

Voigt's major contributions to physics were in the study of crystals, in which he elaborated the use of symmetry consideration, cultivated phenomenological theories and applied complicated mathematics in analysis of experiments and phenomena. His interests, approaches, and achievements made him a prominent member of Franz Neumann's school. Voigt was a full-fledged theoretician when theoretical physics was formed as a subdiscipline in Germany, but still devoted time for laboratory study. By age and character he was a member of the last generation of classical physicists. His research was almost untouched by the relativity revolution and the early quantum mechanics, despite his precedence in formulating what was later called Lorentz transformation (see the original DSB article). By contrast, changes within classical physics during Voigt's career, especially in electrodynamics, are well reflected in his works. The present article complements the original *DSB* article by discussing these issues in light of subsequent scholarship.

Role of Symmetry Considerations. In his first major research, Voigt supported the so-called multi-constants elastic theory through painstaking precise measurements on rock-salt. In a series of experiments during 1887–1889 on crystals of different systems he practically ended the controversy over the number of elastic constants by refuting the rari constants alternative, which follows from Navier-Poisson molecular theory. Voigt preferred a continuum phenomenological theory, aimed at describing the phenomena and their relations as found empirically on a minimal number of laws, without explaining their origin. Such an elastic theory and approach, which refrained from assumptions about a hidden mechanism, were especially suitable for the application of what he later called the "Neumann Principle," according to which the physical properties of crystals must possess at least the symmetry of their form. Voigt extended Neumann's and Kirchhoff's previous employment of such considerations to all crystal systems, applying symmetry considerations more rigorously and completely.

Symmetry was a guiding principle in Voigt's formulation of a general phenomenological theory of pyroelectricity and piezoelectricity in 1890. That the latter effect of mechanical strain on electric polarization is more complicated than that of stress on strain in elasticity, required from Voigt a more refined use of symmetry conditions. On that and the linearity of the effect, he developed a theory for all crystals that accounted for all observations, including those that were not explained by former (molecular) theories. It continued to be the ground for theory of the field in the early twenty-first century. In many subsequent experimental and theoretical works Voigt made himself the world's expert on piezoelectricity.

Voigt's successful use of symmetry probably stimulated Pierre Curie, the co-discoverer of the piezoelectric effect, in his study and formulation of a more general rule of symmetry in physics, which also relate two abstract magnitudes such as electricity and magnetism. Curie's formulation might have contributed to Voigt's introduction of the term tensor (originally in 1897 lectures) as a pedagogical means to display the relation between symmetry and physical properties. Thereby, he relied on the mathematical tradition in elasticity since Cauchy, and the employment of tensor-like formulas in the physics of crystals.

Theoretical and Experimental Methodology In his theory of the Zeeman effect (the splitting of spectral lines by magnetic field), Voigt's demonstrated the power of his phenomenological approach. Assuming two sets of coupled linear differential equations such as those of a damped harmonic oscillator, Voigt accounted (by experimentally determining coefficients) for the complicated phenomena, including the asymmetric splitting of the line to more than triplets, which Lorentz's electron theory failed to explain. However, Voigt himself regretted the lack of physical visualizability [*Anschaulichkeit*] in the theory. Following Voigt's method, his student Walther Ritz "raised Rydberg constant to a universal one, and identified the quantity whose derivation became the show piece of Bohr's atomic theory" (Heilbron, 1994, p. 181).

Voigt usually preferred phenomenological theory, but his choice depended on the specific scientific problem and on his particular goal. So although he showed the inadequacy of the molecular explanations of piezoelectricity and elasticity and advanced phenomenological theories in these fields, he suggested in each case more complicated molecular theories that yielded the equations of the phenomenological accounts. Voigt claimed that, as in these cases, often explanatory theories are based on phenomenological descriptions. At the beginning of the twentieth century Voigt regarded the existence of atoms and electrons as proved, yet he considered phenomenological theories as indispensable because one cannot account for the observations only by these entities. This methodological position was connected to his work on crystal physics, where the limits of molecular assumptions were evident. Like his contemporaries, Voigt acknowledged the freedom of theoretical physicists in choosing their approach and assumptions, and the fertility of such mixed approaches.

Voigt's ordinary chair for theoretical physics was one of the two of this kind in Germany, whereas others positions for teaching theoretical physics were of the inferior status and often regarded as temporary stages in the way for a chair of experimental physics. "Unlike his predecessor Listing, Voigt was trained in theoretical physics and regarded it as his field, so that his appointment at Göttingen was an important step in the establishment of theoretical physics in Germany" (Jungnickel and McCormmach, 1986, p. 115). Voigt's institute for theoretical physics also included a laboratory, in which its head was expected (as a theoretician) and was very willing to carry out experiments. These were measurements, carried out to obtain precise quantitative data of various coefficients, which contemporaries differentiated from experiments, which did not always involve quantitative information.

Precision was central in this kind of laboratory activity. Voigt devoted much energy to the exactness of his results. Like others in Neumann's school, he preferred theoretical-mathematical elimination of errors, after recording the data. Voigt's measurements were used for confirmation of theories (e.g. piezoelectricity), more often to determine values of constants (e.g. elastic), but also for detecting the existence of genuine effects (e.g. direct pyro-electricity, and direct electro-optics, by Friedrich Pockels his former student) and to decide between two theories (e.g. rari *versus* multi constants in elasticity).

Although the atomic structure of crystal was revealed only at the eve of Voigt's career, and despite the revolutionary changes that physics underwent at the time, parts of his work continued to be relevant in fields of complex matter physics, such as elasticity and piezoelectricity. His 1910 textbook on crystal physics was reprinted in 1946 and it is still occasionally cited. That suggests the durability of his phenomenological accounts, which are independent of fundamental theories, and the continuity in the study of a few physical subfields despite the quantum revolution.

SUPPLEMENTARY BIBLIOGRAPHY

WORKS BY VOIGT

"Bestimmung der Elasticitätsconstante des Steinsalzes." *Annalen der Physik und Chemie* suppl. vol. 7 (1876): 1–53, 177–214. Elaboration of his dissertation.

"Theoretische Studien über die Elasticitätverhältnisse der Krystalle." *Abhandlungen der Königlichen Gesellschaft der Wissenschaften zu Göttingen* 34 (1887): 1–52. Molecular theory of elasticity.

"Allgemeine Theorie der piëzo- und pyroelectrischen Erscheinungen an Krystallen." *Abhandlungen der Königlichen Gesellschaft der Wissenschaften zu Göttingen* 36 (1890): 1–99.

With E. Riecke. "Die Piëzoelectrischen Constanten des Quarzes und Turmalines." *Annalen der Physik und Chemie* 45 (1892): 523–552.

"Ueber Arbeitshypothesen." *Nachrichten von der Königlichen Gesellschaft der Wissenschaften zu Göttingen, Geschäftliche Mitteilungen* (1905): 98–116.

"Phänomenologische und atomistische Betrachtungsweise." In *Physik*, edited by Emil Warburg. Die Kultur der Gegenwart, Tl. 3, Abt. 3,1. Berlin: Teubner, 1915.

OTHER SOURCES

Försterling, K. "Woldemar Voigt zum hundertsten Geburtstage." *Die Naturwissenschaften* 38 (1951): 217–221.

Heilbron, John L. "The Virtual Oscillator as a Guide to Physics Students Lost in Plato's Cave." *Science and Education* 3 (1994): 177–188. On Voigt's view of theories and the Zeeman effect.

Jungnickel, Christa, and Russell McCormmach. "Göttingen Institute for Theoretical Physics." In *Intellectual Mastery of Nature: Theoretical Physics from Ohm to Einstein,* vol. 2. Chicago: University of Chicago Press, 1986. On Voigt's role as a theoretical physicist.

Katzir, Shaul. "The Emergence of the Principle of Symmetry in Physics." *Historical Studies in the Physical and Biological Sciences* 35 (2004): 35–65.

———. *The Beginnings of Piezoelectricity: A Study in Mundane Physics.* Dordrecht, Netherlands: Springer, 2006.

Olesko, Kathryn M. *Physics as a Calling: Discipline and Practice in the Königsberg Seminar for Physics.* Ithaca, NY: Cornell University Press, 1991. On Voigt's early works with Franz Neumann and the latter school, especially pp. 288–296, 434–439.

Reich, Karin. *Die Entwicklung des Tensorkalküls: von absoluten Differentialkalkül zur Relativitätstheorie.* Basel, Switzerland and Boston: Birkhäuser Verlag, 1994. See pp. 111–129.

Wolff, Stefan L. "Woldemar Voigt (1850–1919) und Pieter Zeeman (1865–1943): eine wissenschaftliche Freundschaft." In *The Emergence of Modern Physics: Proceedings of a Conference Commemorating a Century of Physics, Berlin, 22–24 March 1995,* edited by Dieter Hoffmann, Fabio Bevilacqua, and Roger Stuewer. Pavia, Italy: Università degli Studi di Pavia, 1996.

———. "Woldemar Voigt (1850–1919) und seine Untersuchungen der Kristalle." In *Toward a History of Mineralogy, Petrology, and Geochemistry,* edited by Bernhard Fritscher and Fergus Henderson. Munich, Germany: Institut für Geschichte der Naturwissenschaften, 1998.

Shaul Katzir

VOLTA, ALESSANDRO GIUSEPPE ANTONIO ANASTASIO

(*b.* Como, duchy of Milan, Italy, 18 February 1745; *d.* Como, 5 March 1827), *natural philosophy, physics, electricity, chemistry, animal electricity, electrophysiology.* For the original article on Volta see *DSB,* vol. 14.

Alessandro Volta has been studied extensively, and many aspects of his science clarified, but scholars still lack a comprehensive and integrated account of his science. The only general attempt so far, a monograph published by Giovanni Polvani in 1942, is limited by increasingly evident inadequacies. This essay adopts a disciplinary approach, focusing on new perspectives in the three main areas of voltaic science: static electricity, chemistry, and animal electricity and the related invention of the battery.

Static Electricity. Volta's work in the area of static electricity is traditionally divided into two stages. In 1966 Mario Gliozzi introduced the expressions "first manner" and "second manner" to define Volta's differing approaches to electricity in the years 1763–1777 and from 1778 on. Two of Volta's writings, the Latin paper *De Vi Attractiva Ignis Electrici ac Phaenomenis inde Pendentibus* (On the Attractive Force of the Electrical Fire and on the Phenomena Depending Thereon) (*Opere,* vol. 3, pp. 21–52) and an open letter on the capacity of electrical conductors he addressed in 1778 to the Swiss naturalist Horace-Bénédict de Saussure (*Opere*, vol. 3, pp. 199–229), are commonly taken as the manifestos of the two different electrical approaches.

In the "first manner" stage Volta is commonly presented as having tried a general theory, which set itself the high goal of reducing the whole of electricity to the minimum number of fundamental interactions. He is accordingly said to have renounced the idea of mutual repulsion among the particles of the electrical fluid and to have kept only a multipurpose force of attraction, acting at a distance, between the microscopic elements of matter and those of the electrical fluid. The general view is that Volta was not able to fulfill such an ambitious task and that his system remained vague.

The standard view is that Volta started to make real progress only when he finally adopted his "second manner" approach, inspired by other authors and characterized by qualitative similarities with the modern conceptualization of electrostatic phenomena. In his 1778 letter to de Saussure, Volta based his elaborations on two new concepts, "capacity" and "tension," and measured the latter with a device he named "electrometer." These three terms have exact synonyms in modern electrostatics, and this correspondence was the main criterion used to infer that he somehow shifted to conceptual schemes akin to those now used to interpret electrostatic phenomena. At first, Volta's notion of electrical tension was assumed to correspond directly to the modern concept of electrical tension. Henry Cavendish's now-famous 1771 paper on electricity was considered a source for Volta's concepts of capacity and tension, and Franz Ulrich Theodosius Aepinus's 1759 *Tentamen Theoria Electricitatis et Magnetismi* was considered the source that made Volta abandon the old idea that electrical actions are mediated by "atmospheres" of electrical matter diffused around excited bodies, and adopt a system of electrostatic forces qualitatively similar to that employed in modern electrostatics: "repulsions between accumulations of homologous charges, attractions between those of contrary charges" (Heilbron, 1979, p. 422).

More recently, Volta's electrophorus, invented in 1775, with the second manner advancements still to come, has been interpreted as a nearly exclusive outcome of trial and error manipulations to obtain stronger sparks from a device Aepinus used to study the electricity of melted dielectrics. Theory is conceded to have played a more fruitful role in the second manner stage, but not beyond the level of simple "midrange concepts—like capacity, tension, actuation—that stemmed directly from laboratory practice" (Pancaldi, 2003, p. 142).

New analysis of Volta's *De Vi Attractiva* suggests a different picture. The paper, written when Volta was a young man, was a remarkable piece of theoretical physics. Its goal was a unified interpretation of the entire field of electricity, which Volta divided into five areas:

1. attractions and repulsions between electrified bodies;

2. frictional electricity;

3. Leyden jar;

4. electrical atmospheres; and

5. *electricitas vindex.*

Two neglected passages of *De Vi Attractiva* contradict the usual assumption that attraction between matter and the electrical fluid was the only fundamental interaction of Volta's electrical physics. He admitted that strong "elasticity," attributed to the electrical fluid, was a second fundamental property, but chose for the moment to leave it aside, because it was mainly by developing the hypothesis of attraction that he expected to advance theory (see *Opere*, vol. 3, pp. 26, 38).

Volta's later notion of electrical tension can be related to this early conception of the elasticity of the electrical fluid. His development of the hypothesis of attraction produced interesting results, and those on the electrical atmospheres and *electricitas vindex* had a key role in his subsequent inventions of the electrophorus and the *condensatore.*

Parallels can be naturally established between Volta's two-component theory and the "pneumatic-attractive" conceptualization of electricity sketched by Benjamin Franklin in 1751 in one of the pieces appearing in his famous *Experiments and Observations on Electricity.* Franklin's electrical theory was pneumatic in the sense that it established close physical analogies between the electrical fluid and common air. Like air, the electrical fluid was for him elastic and expansive, which, subscribing to Newtonian doctrines of air and elastic fluids, he ascribed to repulsive forces acting among its constituent particles. Franklin's theory was also attractive in the sense that it required an additional force of attraction between the matter and the electrical fluid naturally contained in bodies. This was an action Franklin introduced to keep the electrical fluid in place, counteracting the force of its own self-repulsion.

Franklin's pneumatic-attractive modeling of electricity was extended significantly by the Jesuit Ruggiero Giuseppe Boscovich in his masterpiece *Theoria Philosophiae Naturalis,* and this was the main source to which Volta turned to attempt his own developments in *De Vi Attractiva,* with attention temporarily focused on attraction.

Volta's elastic pneumatic-like conception of the electrical fluid emerged fully in 1778, occasioned by discussions he had with de Saussure in the fall of 1777 on the accumulation of electricity on conductors. In the open letter addressed the following year to his Swiss friend, Volta described the "tension" of electricity accumulated on a conductor as an "effort to thrust itself out" (*Opere*, vol. 3, p. 213), which naturally brings to mind the outward-directed push of compressed air. Echoing Franklin's pneumatic-like modeling, Volta later stated that the electrical fluid has "expansibility," generated presumably by "mutual repulsion among its parts" (*Opere*, vol. 3, p. 236ff.). With the electrical fluid accumulated on a conductor likened to compressed air, the notion of electrical "capacity" is easily formulated by analogy to the volume of the vessel in which the corresponding quantity of compressed air is contained. In the following years, the pneumatic analogy turned up repeatedly in Volta's electrical physics. In 1784 he formulated the complete proportionality $Q = CT$ among charge, capacity, and tension (*Opere*, vol. 4, p. 419). This can be seen as the electrical version of Boyle's pneumatic law $Q = VP$, linking the quantity, volume, and pressure of compressed air contained in a vessel.

The details of how Volta put attraction forces at work in *De Vi Attractiva* in the five electrical areas he identified are complex. The following sketches of *electricitas vindex* and the "electrical atmospheres" will give an idea of their relationship with the electrophorus and the *condensatore*.

In 1767 Giambatista Beccaria introduced the notion of *electricitas vindex* to explain the quiescent union of two mutually touching surfaces (both insulating or one insulating and the other conducting) and the subsequent appearance of electrical signs when the surfaces are separated. Beccaria maintained that the inactive union results from the actual annihilation of any electricity on both the surfaces and that the electrical activity observed at separation occurs because each surface "claims back" (*vindicat*) the electricity it had before union. Volta countered that there is no actual electrical annihilation when the surfaces touch each other. Contrary electricities—positive on one surface and negative on the other—keep separate, enduring existence, despite being in mutual contact. The electrical fluid feels stronger attraction on the positive than on the negative surface and this is why it does not flow from the first to the second. With the surfaces united, the lack of electrical signs proceeds from perfect equilibrium of electrical forces, not from Beccaria's pretended total electrical annihilation. Separation of the surfaces breaks the equilibrium and the contrary electricities manifest themselves.

Under the heading "electrical atmospheres" Volta considered what is now called "electrostatic induction." The effect consists in the appearance of contrary electricities on an insulated neutral body brought close to an electrified body. If, for instance, the electrified body is positive, positive and negative electricities appear respectively on the furthest and closest parts of the neutral body. Volta held that the redundant fluid of the inductor affects the neutral body via "application," that is, by means of attraction forces acting at a distance, not by contact or transfusion (*Opere*, vol. 3, p. 39). The application of the redundant fluid *weakens* the attraction between the matter and the fluid of the induced body, with consequent freeing of part of its natural fluid and appearance of its induced positive electricity. Volta's scheme is different from that of modern electrostatics but to some extent works as effectively and affords a good conceptual handling of electrostatic induction.

In the functioning of the electrophorus electrostatic induction plays an essential part and there are also close connections with Volta's interpretation of *electricitas vindex*. The instrument is composed of an insulating "cake" and a round metal "shield," which can be laid on and lifted from the cake by means of an insulating handle. If the cake's top surface is electrified, for instance positively, and the shield laid on it, positive electricity is induced on the shield's top surface. If this surface is now touched, all electrical signs disappear. In Volta's interpretation, the touch discharges the positive electricity induced on the shield, which becomes then negative. The absence of electrical signs proceeds, as for *electricitas vindex*, from equilibrium between neighboring contrary electricities, plus on the cake's top surface and minus on the shield's bottom surface. If the shield is lifted, the contrary electricities manifest their individual existences. The shield can at this point be used as a source of negative electricity and the process repeated many times to obtain great amounts of it.

Volta invented the *condensatore* in 1780 and produced it in various forms, consisting basically of a conducting disk laid on and lifted from a plane of poor conducting material. Electrostatic induction and survival of contrary electricities touching each other play as in the electrophorus: electricity contrary to that of the disk is induced on the closest parts of the underlying plane and both electricities survive despite being in mutual contact. Volta conceived that the capacity of the disk diminishes when it is lifted from the plane and that the value of tension increases accordingly on it (*Opere*, vol. 3, p. 346). He used this property to turn the arrangement into a sensitive detector of weak electricities.

In two letters on electrical meteorology, addressed to Georg Christoph. Lichtenberg in 1788, Volta presented a general electrometric program for intercomparable standardized measurements of electrical tension (*Opere*, vol. 5, pp. 33–57, 75–85). Direct gauging of electrical tension was impossible at the time, because theory was unable to calculate the relationship between tension and the

Alessandro Volta. *Portrait of Alessandro Volta in old age, probably commissioned by Volta himself. He can be interpreted as stressing close connection between his theoretical conceptions (represented by the book) and his electrical instruments (in particular the* condensatore, *right, and the battery, left).*
COURTESY OF COUNTESS PIERA VOLTA.

observed divergence of "electrometers." Volta dealt with the problem in the opposite way, that is calibrating electrometers on the basis of his fundamental law $Q = CT$ and using them to evaluate tension. He found that the link between the divergence of electrometers and the value of tension was in general not linear and constructed special linearization tables to overcome this difficulty. His newly devised "straw electrometer" responded linearly over its whole measuring scale and was not affected by the trouble. He referred all measurements to a fixed and easily reproducible unit of tension obtained with a standard disk-attraction electrostatic balance.

This shift from viewing Volta in relationship to Aepinus and Cavendish, from the perspective of modern electrostatics, to an emphasis on the influence of the pneumatic-attractive representation of electricity started by Franklin and developed by Boscovich appears in conclusion to provide a more appropriate basis from which to interpret Volta's static electricity. In essence Volta took Franklin's traditional approach to its extreme consequences. Intersections with Aepinus and Cavendish were

scarce and were neutralized by reinterpretations within his own pneumatic-attractive conceptualization of electricity.

Chemistry. In 1784 Volta was among the very first Italian scholars who became "aware of the revolutionary and subversive features of [Antoine-Laurent] Lavoisier's chemical theory" (Abbri, p. 10). Yet, he found no decisive reasons to follow the new approach, and it was only in 1798 that he acknowledged Lavoisier's accomplishment.

Three different phases can be usefully distinguished in Volta's chemistry, the first two (1776–1782, 1783–1784) fully phlogistic and the third (1784–1801) characterized by long critical evaluation of Lavoisier's antiphlogistic alternative (*Nuova Voltiana*, vol. 2).

Joseph Priestley's *Experiments and Observations on Different Kinds of Airs* (1774–1777) provided the general framework for Volta's initial contributions in the new booming field of "airs." Two central points Volta took from Priestley were the definition of "phlogistication" as a general process in chemical change and the qualitative inference of the composition of airs on the basis of the ingredients and preparation methods used to obtain them.

Nevertheless, Volta was able to dissent from Priestley and rework his views on airs taking into account results of his own and of other authors. In 1778, on the basis of his own measurements of phlogiston content in the airs, Volta objected to Priestley that "inflammable air" (hydrogen), not "nitrous air" (nitrous oxide), was the richest of all in phlogiston. This episode shows Volta's adherence to the values of accurate quantification and suggests that he was capable of a balance-sheet way of reasoning closer in spirit to Lavoisier than to Priestley.

Volta's later phlogistic views are found especially in the notes he added, between 1783 and 1784, to the Italian translation of Pierre-Joseph Macquer's *Dictionnaire de chymie* (*Opere*, vol. 6, pp. 345–436; vol. 7, pp. 3–105). To a good extent, his chemical research emerged at this stage as a continuation of Richard Kirwan's views on the composition and roles of "fixed air" (carbon dioxide) in the "reduction" of metal calxes and in various natural processes. Volta's central assumption was that fixed air is the only air naturally contained in bodies. "Dephlogisticated air" (oxygen) is obtained from fixed air by subtraction of a certain amount of phlogiston. Combination of fixed air with phlogiston yields phlogisticated air. Dephlogisticated and phlogisticated air can combine with natural bodies only if they are transformed into fixed air. Volta considered inflammable air to be a combination of phlogiston with an unknown base and thought of its combustion with dephlogisticated air as a phlogistication process accompanied by possible precipitation of material ingredients. His conceptual framework pointed to earthy, salty, and acid precipitates, not to the formation of water. Volta missed the discovery of the synthesis of water, despite having observed the "appearance of vapor" many times (*Opere*, vol. 6, p. 411), because of his enduring reliance on traditional phlogistic chemistry. Theory determined importantly not only his achievements but also his failures.

In 1784 Volta proposed a phlogistic reinterpretation of Lavoisier's synthesis of water that saved its traditional elementary nature and could stand Lavoisier's weight testing methods (*Opere*, vol. 7, p. 101). The luminous phenomena associated with chemical reactions seem to have played a major part in Volta's hesitation to adopt Lavoisier's chemistry. In 1795 he accorded preference to the phlogistic theory of the German chemist Johann Friedrich August Göttling on the grounds that it gave due importance to light, unlike Lavoisier's theory, which appeared "nearly not to take it into account" (Seligardi, p. 95). Similar considerations guided his positive judgment, in 1798, on the phlogistic "correction or addition" to Lavoisier proposed by the German chemists Rüther and Friedrich Albrecht Carl Gren. The official motivation was to give students the possibility to know both approaches. His lack of conviction and scientific conservatism were no doubt deeper causes.

Volta's work on eudiometry emerged as a particular chapter of a general study on combustion he started in 1776 after discovering the "inflammable air native to marshes" (methane). In 1777 he invented the "electrophlogopneumatic pistol," as he called it, and devised an eudiometric method different from that initially proposed by Priestley to test the "goodness" of atmospheric air. Volta's new system was based on the volume diminution that takes place when a mixture of inflammable air and atmospheric air is ignited with an electrical spark. Volta refined this different technique in various separate stages between 1777 and 1790, with increasing quantitative performance of his eudiometric devices. Unlike Marsilio Landriani and Lavoisier, Volta sharply distinguished "salubrity" from "respirability": an air could be highly breathable but have unhealthy effects.

Volta's work on airs and eudiometry produced a positive climate for chemistry in Italy and this contributed to its establishment as an autonomous science, both methodologically and institutionally.

Animal Electricity and Invention of the Battery. The view that Volta's debate with Luigi Galvani and its outcomes resulted mainly from "a conflict between an electro-biological *Gestalt* and an electro-physical *Gestalt* over the same observational domain" (Pera, p. xviii), with Galvani and Volta somehow leading the biological and the physical parties, faces major difficulties. In the Italian setting, physicians, physicists, chemists, and others shifted from one side to the other with complex motivations (see

Bernardi, 1992). Galvani and Volta themselves escape the biology-physics division, and joint focus is needed on both their physical and physiological conceptions.

In a period of hectic and extremely fertile research, conducted between March and June 1792, Volta changed his views on Galvani's animal electricity radically and came out with the unprecedented idea that mere contact between metals and moist conductors suffices to put electricity in motion. Generalization of this hypothesis to the contact between all conductors was to lead him to his epoch-making invention of the battery.

Toward the end of 1791 Galvani had announced the new, surprising phenomenon that muscular contraction is obtained in a frog's leg when a metal arc closes the circuit between the crural nerve and the muscles of the leg. He suggested that the contraction was caused by discharge, through the arc, of "animal electricity" in a state of imbalance, plus on the nerve, minus on the external side of the muscles.

On 5 May 1792, Volta credited Galvani with the "great and stupendous discovery" that animal electricity is the "primary operator of muscular motions" (*Opere*, vol. 1, p. 23–24). By 14 May, he had changed his mind completely and conceded to animal electricity only a remote role in a three-step causal chain, with consecutive activation of two physiological faculties, whose cause he chose not to specify: the "sensibility of nerves" and "muscular force." According to Volta, animal electricity stimulates first the sensibility of nerves, which only at a second stage excites the muscular force truly responsible for the contraction (*Opere*, vol. 1, pp. 56–57). Experiments on the sensations induced by bimetallic arcs on his own tongue and comparison with the sensations excited by artificial electricity played importantly in Volta's formulation of the new idea of electromotion between a metallic and a moist conductor. The effects of bimetallic arcs had to be investigated because Galvani himself had reported that muscular contraction was in general stronger with these than with monometallic arcs. Trying with arcs made of a less noble metal applied on the tip of the tongue and a more noble metal laid further back, Volta discovered an acid taste on the tip, similar to that he experienced with the latter presented to the "fresh breeze" emitted by the points of an electrified body. Inversion of the sequence changed the taste from acid to alkaline (*Opere*, vol. 1, pp. 62, 73–74). Analogy suggested that the bimetallic arcs applied to the tongue or to the frog's leg were not discharging any proper animal electricity, but exciting a weak artificial current, which awakened taste sensation or muscular contraction through stimulation of the nerves. In June Volta put this idea in explicit form by stating that metals "must no longer be considered as simple conductors, but as true motors of electricity" (*Epistolario*, vol. 3, p. 172).

Laboratory workbench. *Picture showing Alessandro Volta's workbench at the University of Pavia, with various original instruments. The batteries (left corner) are modern copies of the originals lost during a fire in 1899.* COURTESY OF MUSEO PER LA STORIA DELL'UNIVERSITA DI PAVIA (UNIVERSITY OF PAVIA, ITALY).

Between 1792 and 1793, Volta investigated how involuntary muscles, various kinds of animals, and the senses different from taste reacted to the bimetallic arcs (*Opere*, vol. 1, pp. 125–126, 207–208, 245). In the following years he returned to these matters and studied later on various physiological effects obtained with the stronger currents his battery made available. The phenomena involved in these enquiries are complex and were disentangled by electrophysiology over a long period of time.

In 1795 Volta extended the hypothesis of electromotion to the contact between dissimilar moist conductors (*a*, *b*, ...), or "second class" conductors and in 1796 to the contact between dry conductors (*A*, *B*, ...), or "first class" conductors. In 1796 he displayed the existence of electromotion in both cases with purely physical tools and this was a fundamental step because electromotion was thus finally demonstrated with no animal elements as detectors. His experimental techniques evolved from those he was employing at the time to reveal the very weak electricities he expected to be formed during the evaporation of fluids (see Pancaldi, 2003). Quantitative evaluation convinced him that contacts *AB* between first class conductors were in general more effective than contacts *Ab*

between a first class and a second class conductor (*Opere*, vol. 1, pp. 418–419, 428–431).

Volta chose not to reveal how he came to assemble the battery in its final form (*ABcABc* ...) of bimetallic couples with a moist conductor between one and the other. Three main factors can nevertheless be indicated, which he saw how to put all together probably in December 1799. The first was psychological: He felt deeply upset by the Galvanists' refusal to admit contact electricity even after his direct demonstration of it (*Opere*, vol. 1, p. 525). Second, his conviction about the relative strengths of electromotion evidently played a role: Electricity is impelled more effectively in the contacts *AB* and in practice the moist layers work as simple conductors conveying electricity from one couple to the other. Against the Galvanists, Volta could now claim that the current of the battery was a direct proof of electromotion. The third factor was the debates stimulated by works published in 1797 by Galvani and William Nicholson on the functioning of the electrical organ of the torpedo fish. It was known that this organ consists of many little vertical columns, composed in their turn of numerous horizontal layers of dissimilar moist tissues. Nicholson likened this laminar sequence to a series of electrophori operating simultaneously during the animal's discharge. Galvani saw the sequence as an array of Franklin squares similarly giving their shocks all at once. Volta considered these analogies inconsistent and too complicated. In the battery, or "artificial electrical organ" (*Opere*, vol. 1, p. 566), Volta reproduced the column and layer structure of the animal organ from the point of view of his theory of electromotion. His hypothesis of electromotion between dissimilar moist conductors allowed him to claim that the physiology of the animal discharge was reducible to the new physical theory of contact electricity.

In the following years of scientific activity Volta had no hesitation in defending his contact interpretation of animal electricity, galvanic phenomena, and functioning of the battery. Once more he remained loyal to his initial way of conceptualizing phenomena and was resistant to different schemes.

SUPPLEMENTARY BIBLIOGRAPHY

A number of the essays below are published in Nuova Voltiana: Studies on Volta and His Times *(see above).*

WORKS BY VOLTA

Bellodi, Giuliano, et al., eds. *Gli strumenti di Alessandro Volta: Il Gabinetto di Fisica dell'Università di Pavia.* Milan: Hoepli, 2002. Contains the catalog of the surviving instruments belonged to Volta's physics cabinet at the University of Pavia and various studies on the instruments and the history of the collection.

Bevilacqua, Fabio, and Lucio Fregonese, eds. *Nuova Voltiana: Studies on Volta and His Times.* 5 vols. Milano: Hoepli, 2000–2003. Available from http://ppp.unipv.it ("Saggi e Studi"). A series of thirty-seven articles by specialized scholars, covering ample areas of Volta's science, context, and subsequent impact. A substantial basis for further studies.

OTHER SOURCES

Abbri, Ferdinando. "Volta's Chemical Theories: The First Two Phases." In *Nuova Voltiana*, vol. 2, pp. 1–14.

Bensaude-Vincent, Bernadette. "Pneumatic Chemistry Viewed from Pavia." In *Nuova Voltiana*, vol. 2, pp. 15–31.

Beretta, Marco. "Pneumatics vs. 'Aerial Medicine': Salubrity and Respirability of Air at the End of the Eighteenth Century." In *Nuova Voltiana*, vol. 2, pp. 49–71.

Bernardi, Walter. *I fluidi della vita: Alle origini della controversia sull'elettricità animale.* Firenze: Olschki, 1992.

———. "The Controversy on Animal Electricity." In *Nuova Voltiana*, vol. 1, pp. 101–114.

Ciardi, Marco. "La chimica pavese e la rivoluzione lavoisieriana." In *Esortazioni alle storie*, edited by Angelo Stella and Gianfranca Lavezzi, pp. 703–718. Milano: Cisalpino, 2001.

Fregonese, Lucio. "Le invenzioni di Volta tra teorie ed esperimenti." In *Gli strumenti di Alessandro Volta: Il Gabinetto di Fisica dell'Università di Pavia*, edited by Giuliano Bellodi et al., pp. 39–132. Milano: Hoepli, 2002.

———. "Volta's Electrical Programme." PhD dissertation, University of Cambridge, 1999.

———. "Volta: Teorie ed esperimenti di un filosofo naturale." *Le Scienze: I grandi della scienza* 11 (1999).

Gliozzi, Mario. "Il Volta della seconda maniera." *Cultura e Scuola* 5 (1966): 235–239.

Heilbron, John L. *Electricity in the 17th and 18th Centuries: A Study of Early Modern Physics.* Berkeley: University of California Press, 1979. Reprint (with new preface), Mineola, NY: Dover, 1999.

Holmes, Frederic L. "Phlogiston in the Air." In *Nuova Voltiana*, vol. 2, pp. 73–113.

Massardi, Francesco. "Concordanza di risultati e formule emergenti da manoscritti inediti del Volta con quelli ricavati dalla fisico-matematica nella risoluzione del problema generale dell'elettrostatica." *Rendiconti dell'Istituto Lombardo* 56 (1923): 293–308.

———. "Sull'importanza dei concetti fondamentali esposti dal Volta nel 1769 nella sua prima memoria scientifica *De vi attractiva ignis electrici*." *Rendiconti dell'Istituto Lombardo* 59 (1926): 373–381.

Pancaldi, Giuliano. *Volta: Science and Culture in the Age of Enlightenment.* Princeton, NJ: Princeton University Press, 2003.

Pera, Marcello. *La rana ambigua: La controversia sull'elettricità animale tra Galvani e Volta.* Torino: Einaudi, 1986. Translated by Jonathan Mandelbaum as *The Ambiguous Frog: The Galvani-Volta Controversy on Animal Electricity* (Princeton, NJ: Princeton University Press, 1992).

Piccolino, Marco, and Marco Bresadola. *Rane, torpedini e scintille: Galvani, Volta e l'elettricità animale.* Torino: Boringhieri, 2003.

Polvani, Giovanni. *Alessandro Volta.* Pisa: Domus galilæeana, 1942.

Seligardi, Raffaella. "Alessandro Volta e la nuova chimica (1783–1800): Atti dell'VIII Convegno Nazionale di Storia e Fondamenti della Chimica." *Memorie di Scienze Fisiche e Naturali, "Rendiconti della Accademia Nazionale delle Scienze detta dei XL,"* ser. 5, vol. 23, book 2 (1999): 87–98.

———. "Volta and the Synthesis of Water: Some Reasons for a Missed Discovery." In *Nuova Voltiana*, vol. 2, pp. 33–48.

———. *Lavoisier in Italia: La comunità scientifica italiana e la rivoluzione chimica.* Firenze: Olschki, 2002. See pages 87–96.

Stella, Angelo, and Gianfranca Lavezzi, eds. *Esortazioni alle storie: Atti del convegno "Parlano un suon che attenta Europa ascolta"; Poeti, scienziati, cittadini nell'Ateneo pavese tra riforme e rivoluzione, Università di Pavia, 13–15 dicembre 2000.* Milano: Cisalpino, 2001.

Lucio Fregonese

VON BRAUN, WERNHER MAGNUS MAXIMILIAN FREIHERR (*b.*
Wirsitz, East Prussia, Germany [now Poland], 23 March

1912; *d.* Alexandria, Virginia, 16 June 1977), *rocket engineering, spaceflight promotion.*

Although his doctorate was in physics, von Braun was one of the most important rocket engineers of the twentieth century. He played a leading role in four achievements: (1) the development of the A-4/V-2 ballistic missile, the world's first large rocket, in Nazi Germany; (2) a 1950s campaign for spaceflight in the United States, which changed public attitudes in America and the West; (3) the launching of the first U.S. satellite, *Explorer 1,* in early 1958; and (4) the development of the gigantic Saturn V launch vehicle that sent the first human landing expedition, *Apollo 11,* to the Moon. But in recent years he is increasingly remembered as well for his compromises with the Nazis, in particular his SS (Schutzstaffel) membership and his participation in the exploitation of concentration-camp labor in V-2 production.

Childhood and Career in Germany. Wernher was the second son of the Prussian civil servant, banker, and right-wing cabinet minister Magnus Freiherr (Baron) von Braun, and his wife Emmy von Quistorp. From 1920 to 1934 the family resided primarily in Berlin. Wernher, although very bright, was sent to boarding school in fall 1925 because of poor grades and lack of motivation. Soon thereafter, through his enthusiasm for amateur astronomy, he discovered the seminal work of German-Romanian spaceflight theorist Hermann Oberth, *Die Rakete zu den Planetenräumen* (The rocket into interplanetary space, 1923), and became a fervent believer in space travel. As a result, he also found his talent for mathematics and science. He graduated in spring 1930 and enrolled in mechanical engineering at the Technische Hochschule Berlin-Charlottenburg; he spent one semester, summer 1931, in Zürich.

After the founding of the Verein für Raumschiffahrt (Society for Space Travel) in 1927, von Braun became a member, and in 1930 he helped found the Raketenflugplatz (Rocketport) Berlin, an amateur rocket group. In June 1932, as a result of a failed Raketenflugplatz demonstration for Army Ordnance, he met Colonel Karl Becker, who arranged his transfer to the University of Berlin. He matriculated in physics, and completed his doctorate in July 1934 under the direction of Erich Schumann, based on secret rocket work at the Kummersdorf army proving ground. His dissertation had a theoretical section on the physics of rocket motor combustion, but it was primarily an engineering report on his liquid-fuel rocket development.

After he successfully launched two A–2 (*Aggregat* 2) rockets in December 1934, Army Ordnance increased its investment in liquid-fuel rocketry as a propulsion system for long-range missiles; in mid-1935, the new Luftwaffe also became intrigued with his work. The result was a joint agreement to fund a secret rocket development center at Peenemünde on the Baltic-coast island of Usedom; it opened in 1937. The two services soon went their separate ways, but funding had dramatically increased.

Although only twenty-five years old, von Braun was named technical director of the army side of Peenemünde; his chief and mentor was Major, later General, Walter Dornberger. In late 1937 the Nazi Party pushed von Braun into joining; previously he had briefly been a member of an SS horse cavalry unit in 1933 and 1934, but showed no particular ideological commitment to National Socialism. In 1940 the SS pressured him to become an officer, and in order to avoid political troubles for his career and the rocket program, he accepted the rank of *Untersturmführer* (second lieutenant); by 1943 he reached *Sturmbannführer* (major).

Despite technical setbacks, including the failure of four A-3 test rockets in 1937, von Braun's charismatic leadership enabled the army center to develop the revolutionary A-4 ballistic missile, with a range of 270 kilometers; the first successful launch took place on 3 October 1942. Although he made contributions to rocket-engine and guidance development in the early years, his true importance lay in the management of huge and complex missile projects. The organizational tools of systems and project management that would be developed in the United States in the 1950s did not yet exist. A-4 systems integration depended on von Braun's personal leadership and mastery of detail in all subsystems and structures, and his ability to inspire large groups of engineers, scientists, and skilled workers to work together for a common goal.

As Adolf Hitler began to take more interest in the A-4, leading to his late-1942 decision to mass produce it as a weapon against Britain, political intervention by Albert Speer's Armaments Ministry and Heinrich Himmler's SS became a greater and greater problem for von Braun and Dornberger. In spring 1943 the first SS concentration-camp workers were deployed on the program; after Allied air raids, A-4 assembly was moved to an underground, slave-labor plant outside Nordhausen. As a result of a conspiracy by Himmler to try to install SS construction chief Hans Kammler as the chief of the program, the Gestapo arrested von Braun in March 1944 for drunken remarks doubting the war's outcome and stating his preference for spaceships over weapons. He was released only after the strenuous lobbying of Dornberger and Speer, who argued his indispensability for the program.

After further technical problems and delays, and the deaths of thousands of camp prisoners from disease, starvation, and beatings in the underground rocket factory, the A-4 was finally launched against Allied cities in September 1944. The Propaganda Ministry dubbed it Vengeance

Weapon 2 (V-2), as it followed the Luftwaffe's cruise missile, the V-1. Ultimately, the A-4/V-2 was a military failure because of its inaccuracy. Vast resources were wasted on an ineffective weapon. Nevertheless, it was a remarkable technological achievement of great potential for the arms race and space exploration.

Early American Career and Space Advocacy in the 1950s. Seeing that the war was lost, von Braun prepared in the winter 1944–1945 to bring his rocket group over to the Americans if possible, but in the end luck as much as anything led to that result. Kammler sent the Peenemünde group to the Nordhausen area in February and March 1945, and then in April further ordered von Braun and 500 top engineers to evacuate to southern Bavaria. On 2 May, von Braun, Dornberger, and several others surrendered to the U.S. Army in the Alps. They were able to convince American officers and scientists of the value of transferring the core of the Peenemünde group to America for further guided-missile development. This project became the heart of Operation Overcast, soon renamed Project Paperclip, which brought hundreds of German scientists and engineers to the United States. Von Braun arrived in September, and over the winter about 120 Peenemünders followed him to Fort Bliss, Texas, outside El Paso, and next to the new White Sands, New Mexico, test range. In 1947 he returned briefly to Germany to marry his first cousin, Maria von Quistorp, with whom he subsequently had three children: Iris Careen, Margrit Cecile, and Peter Constantine. During the late 1940s von Braun's group worked at Fort Bliss for U.S. Army Ordnance, but only on an experimental cruise missile. No priority was placed on ballistic-missile development by an American military riven by interservice rivalries.

The intensification of America's Cold War with the U.S.S.R. eventually permitted the army to found a new rocket center at the Redstone Arsenal in Huntsville, Alabama, in spring 1950, with the Germans as the core leadership. As technical director, von Braun led the development of the 320-kilometer-range Redstone missile, essentially an enlarged, nuclear-armed V-2. In 1955 and 1956, a further escalation of the arms race resulted in an order to develop a 2,500-kilometer-range nuclear missile, the Jupiter. Wernher von Braun's missile development group became the heart of the new Army Ballistic Missile Agency (ABMA). Several months earlier, on 14 April 1955, he had been sworn in as an American citizen.

Meanwhile, von Braun had become famous as a popularizer of spaceflight through a series of articles, books, and television appearances. While one might not normally equate his space propaganda with his technical accomplishments, his publications, speeches, and television appearances laid the groundwork for public support of space exploration and also set the agenda for future American space planners. Frustrated in the late 1940s by the slow pace of rocket development, von Braun had returned to his old enthusiasm for spaceflight. In his spare time he began writing a science-fiction novel, *The Mars Project,* with a detailed mathematical appendix laying out the feasibility of a Mars expedition based on contemporary liquid-fuel rocket technology. His novel was a flop, but the appendix was published in German in 1952, and in English in 1953. That was not the public breakthrough, however. In late 1951 he met a *Collier's* magazine editor and convinced him that spaceflight was feasible. The result was the spectacularly illustrated 22 March 1952 issue, with articles from prominent pro-spaceflight scientists, notably Fred Whipple and Joseph Kaplan. Featured was von Braun's space station, promoted as a nuclear-armed battle station for dominating the Soviet Union through "space superiority." The station would also serve as a stepping-stone to the Moon and Mars. Von Braun's hypothetical expeditions to those places were featured in later issues through 1954. The *Collier's* articles were enlarged into a series of books, and led directly to three Walt Disney television specials in 1955 through 1957 that further spread von Braun's fame and influence.

Polling data show that this campaign was influential in making the American public believe in space travel's feasibility, something most had dismissed as a distant dream in 1950. In popularizing a certain "logical" path for space exploration—reusable rocket planes, a space station, Moon expeditions, Moon bases, and Mars expeditions—von Braun also set the agenda for future U.S. spaceflight advocates. The history of the National Aeronautics and Space Administration (NASA) shows its leading engineers and managers repeatedly attempting to return to what one historian has called the "von Braun paradigm," in spite of political diversions like the Apollo program—hence the later space shuttle and space station. This fixation on an expensive human spaceflight program and a certain "logical" path has not necessarily been a wise use of the American taxpayers' money, but it certainly shows the lasting influence of von Braun's space advocacy of the 1950s.

From Orbiter to Explorer. While selling space travel made him famous, von Braun's job was to lead the development of nuclear-armed ballistic missiles for the army, in competition with the much-better-funded air force. The only significant U.S. space project of the mid-1950s was a scientific satellite for the International Geophysical Year of 1957–1958, which President Dwight D. Eisenhower approved in mid-1955. In one of the greatest disappointments of von Braun's career, his Orbiter proposal for a Redstone topped by small, solid-fuel rockets lost out to the navy Vanguard. That more ambitious project quickly fell behind schedule, but ABMA's appeals to Washington

174

to beat the Soviets into space by reviving Orbiter were rebuffed several times.

During these two years the ABMA carefully preserved its satellite-launching capability by diverting the Redstone-based design into reentry testing for the Jupiter program; the rocket was designated the Jupiter C to take advantage of the larger missile's priority. At the same time, Huntsville's research into ablative reentry heat shields of fiberglass composites was of great importance for ballistic missile warheads, and was much more cost-effective than the air force approach. Von Braun made specific suggestions that contributed to these developments, but as in Peenemünde, his real importance was his virtuoso engineering management in an environment of largely inhouse development.

The Soviet Union's successful launch of *Sputnik* changed everything on 4 October 1957. The public outcry in America broke down the barriers to a parallel project to Vanguard. After *Sputnik 2* was launched a month later carrying a dog, the Eisenhower administration could no longer resist. Following the spectacular failure of the first Vanguard satellite attempt on 6 December, von Braun's group succeeded on 31 January 1958; the army dubbed the satellite *Explorer 1*. Though the second *Explorer* failed to orbit, *Explorer 3* in March 1958 put another cosmic-ray instrument devised by James Van Allen into space, and together the two satellites made the epochal discovery of the radiation belts around Earth.

Saturn, Apollo, and Aftermath. The *Sputnik* shock only magnified interservice battles over missile and space policy. It took two years for the Eisenhower administration and Congress to create a coherent space program, with the new NASA dominating civilian space exploration, and the U.S. Air Force taking the lead role in national security space activities. With ABMA having no future in long-range missiles after Jupiter, Huntsville increasingly pinned its hopes on Saturn, a new, very large launch vehicle. In fall 1958 von Braun rebuffed NASA's first attempt to take over his team, however, because the agency could afford to take only half of his 5,000 workers. A year later, however, the army was finished in the space business, and the administration was willing to give NASA the money to fully support Saturn as a way to catch up with the Soviet Union's lead in large boosters. President Eisenhower approved the transfer in October 1959. On 1 July 1960 von Braun became director of the NASA George C. Marshall Space Flight Center (MSFC), which remained at Redstone Arsenal in Huntsville.

Von Braun's group became the main rocket development center for the agency, and Saturn a launch vehicle for the Apollo Moon program. President John F. Kennedy's decision in May 1961 to make landing a man on the

Wernher von Braun. *Wernher von Braun with two model rockets.* **AP IMAGES.**

Moon "before this decade is out" the central goal of Apollo then gave MSFC its overriding purpose: the development of the gigantic, 110-meter-tall Saturn V launch vehicle needed for this mission, along with the original vehicle, now called Saturn I, and a derivative, the Saturn IB, for launching manned Apollo spacecraft into Earth orbit.

Three of von Braun's management and leadership contributions to Apollo can be singled out as critical. First, in 1961 and 1962 NASA and its various centers were divided as to what method should be chosen to reach the Moon. MSFC studied Earth Orbit Rendezvous (EOR), whereby the lunar landing vehicle would be assembled or fueled near Earth. In June 1962 von Braun surprised his subordinates by supporting Lunar Orbit Rendezvous (LOR), which required only a single Saturn V, instead of two. A small, separate lander would descend to the Moon from lunar orbit. Without LOR, the United States would never have achieved Kennedy's goal. Von Braun's decision was essential to settling the issue.

Secondly, in November 1963 von Braun led his German-dominated MSFC leadership to accept "all-up testing" of the Saturn V, an idea pushed by the new chief of the NASA manned space program, Dr. George Mueller. MSFC's original, cautious schedule required multiple launches to test all three stages, which threatened to derail landing by 1969. Instead, astronauts would fly the vehicle as soon as the third launch attempt. Mueller's idea appalled von Braun's subordinates, and his charismatic leadership was again needed to get them to accept the necessity of this somewhat risky approach.

Finally, von Braun was instrumental in revamping the management structure of MSFC to master the challenges of Apollo-Saturn. In-house development could not cope with a project so large; much more contracting out to aerospace firms was needed, as well as the further adaptation of the air-force- and navy-developed tools of systems management. Although credit for Apollo's success in 1969 must be distributed widely among NASA centers and aerospace corporations, there is little doubt that the excellence of von Braun's engineering management was one of the program's foundations. The ultimate sign of MSFC's competence is this remarkable fact: not one Saturn I, IB, or V failed catastrophically in all their launches from 1961 to 1975—in marked contrast to 1950s rocket programs.

During the late 1960s von Braun fought to bring a greater diversity to the engineering projects of MSFC, as Saturn development passed its peak. He succeeded in winning a place in astronomy programs and a prototype space station that later became the *Skylab* of 1973 and 1974. Yet the post-Apollo decline of MSFC already began in 1966, and accelerated after he left for Washington, D.C., in March 1970. He accepted the job of deputy associate administrator of NASA for advanced planning, a position created in the short-lived optimism following the first Moon landings. Cutbacks in the civilian space program soon completely undercut his position. In mid-1972 he quit to become a vice president at Fairchild Aircraft Corporation in nearby Germantown, Maryland. He was responsible for Fairchild's engineering planning and space endeavors, but his last years were marred not only by his loss of a central position in American space programs, but above all by cancer. After an operation in 1973 the disease went into remission, only to return in 1975. He retired at the end of 1976 and died in June 1977 at the age of 65. He will be remembered for his profound impact on rocketry and spaceflight in the middle decades of the twentieth century, but also for his compromises with the Nazi regime.

BIBLIOGRAPHY

The Wernher von Braun Papers are split between the Library of Congress Manuscript Division, Washington, DC, and the U.S. Space and Rocket Center in Huntsville, Alabama.

WORKS BY VON BRAUN

With Joseph Kaplan, Heinz Haber, Willy Ley, et al. *Across the Space Frontier.* Edited by Cornelius Ryan. New York: Viking, 1952.

Das Marsprojekt [The Mars project]. Frankfurt am Main: Umschau-Verlag, 1952. Translated by Henry J. White. Urbana: University of Illinois Press, 1953.

With Fred L. Whipple and Willy Ley. *Conquest of the Moon.* Edited by Cornelius Ryan. New York: Viking, 1953.

With Willy Ley. *The Exploration of Mars.* New York: Viking, 1956.

"Reminiscences of German Rocketry." *Journal of the British Interplanetary Society* 15 (1956): 125–145.

OTHER SOURCES

Bilstein, Roger E. *Stages to Saturn.* Washington, DC: NASA, 1980.

Eisfeld, Rainer. *Mondsüchtig: Werner von Braun und die Geburt der Raumfahrt aus dem Geist der Barbarei.* Reinbek bei Hamburg, Germany: Rowohlt, 1996.

McCurdy, Howard E. *Space and the American Imagination.* Washington, DC: Smithsonian Institution Press, 1997.

Neufeld, Michael J. *The Rocket and the Reich.* New York: Free Press, 1995.

———. "Wernher von Braun, the SS, and Concentration Camp Labor: Questions of Moral, Political, and Criminal Responsibility." *German Studies Review* 25 (2002): 57–78.

Oberth, Hermann. *Die Rakete zu den Planetenräumen* [The rocket into interplanetary space]. Munich: R. Oldenbourg, 1923.

Stuhlinger, Ernst, and Frederick I. Ordway III. *Wernher von Braun.* Malabar, FL: Krieger, 1994.

Weyer, Johannes. *Wernher von Braun.* Reinbek bei Hamburg, Germany: Rowohlt, 1999.

Wilford, John Noble. "Wernher von Braun, Rocket Pioneer, Dies." *New York Times,* 18 June 1977. A celebratory obituary.

Michael J. Neufeld

VON EULER, ULF SVANTE (*b.* Stockholm, Sweden, 7 February 1905; *d.* 10 March 1983), *pharmacology, physiology, mechanisms of neural transmission, structure and function of noradrenaline.*

Von Euler discovered the structure and function of numerous biologically important substances. His most important discovery, and the one for which he shared the 1970 Nobel Prize in Physiology or Medicine, was the role of noradrenaline as the principal neurotransmitter substance in sympathetic nervous systems. His initial work on the mechanisms of its storage and release blossomed into the current understanding of synaptic vesicles and the reuptake of neurotransmitter substances back into the pre-

Ulf von Euler. *Ulf von Euler, October 19, 1970.* **HULTON ARCHIVE/GETTY IMAGES.**

synaptic neuron. Over a scientific career that spanned six decades, literally up until the time of his death from complications of open heart surgery, von Euler published one book and more than 450 scientific papers. Toward the end of his career he was also an important scientific administrator, serving as a member of the Nobel Committee for Physiology or Medicine beginning in 1953, and as president of the Nobel Foundation beginning in 1965.

Family Background, Scientific Training, and Initial Discoveries. Von Euler's career as a scientist was virtually preordained. His father was Hans von Euler-Chelpin, professor of chemistry in Stockholm and recipient of the Nobel Prize for Chemistry in 1929 (and distantly related to Swiss mathematician Leonhard Euler). His mother, the source of his Swedish heritage, was Astrid Cleve, professor of botany and geology, and daughter of Per Tender Cleve, professor of chemistry at Uppsala University and discoverer of the chemical elements erbium, thulium, and holmium. From his childhood, von Euler enjoyed a lifetime personal link to a northern European cultural and academic tradition.

Von Euler earned his doctorate from the Karolinska Institute in Stockholm in 1930 and immediately began his career there as an assistant professor of pharmacology. He was appointed full professor of physiology in 1939, a position he held until 1971. He spent considerable time abroad, especially early in his career, working with top scientists in Britain, continental Europe, and South America. Four of his international collaborators also won Nobel Prizes: Sir Henry Dale (London), Corneille Heymans (Ghent, Belgium), Archibald Vivian Hill (London), and Bernardo Houssay (Buenos Aires). In his personal life, von Euler married his first wife, the former Jane Sodenstierna, on 12 April 1930. They were divorced in 1957. He later married Dagmar Cronstedt on 20 August 1958. He was the father of four children: two sons, Leo and Christopher; and two daughters, Ursula and Marie.

From the start of his professional career, von Euler established a reputation as a premier research scientist. He quickly amassed important and varied biological discoveries. At age twenty-five, working with John H. Gaddum in Dale's laboratory in London, von Euler discovered an active biological factor in intestinal extracts. He found that this atropine-resistant "substance P" contracted gut muscle and lowered blood pressure in anesthetized rabbits. Over the next few years von Euler described its polypeptide structure, developed methods for its purification and assay, studied its general distribution in the body, and explored many aspects of its biological actions. More than seven decades after his initial investigations, substance P is recognized as the first-discovered member of the class of brain/gut neuropeptides, present in high concentrations in hippocampus and neocortex. It is also released from C-fiber afferents in peripheral nerves that convey information about pain and temperature to the central nervous system.

Upon his return to the Karolinska Institute in Sweden in 1935, von Euler applied the same patience and discipline to his next discovery of another atropine-resistant biological factor, which he dubbed *prostaglandin*. (He coined the term because he first discovered the substance in human seminal fluid and sheep vesicular glands, and he thought that it was secreted by the prostrate gland.) Again he described its basic chemical nature (an unsaturated, lipid-soluble, nitrogen-free organic acid) and its tissue sources, its methods of extraction and purification, and its basic pharmacological properties. In the early twenty-first century the prostaglandins are known as a group of chemically distinct lipids that exert potent actions on blood and fat cells, smooth muscles, and nervous tissue. Prostaglandins are released by cells in damaged tissues; their release induces hyperalgesia (enhanced sensitivity and responsiveness to stimulation) in cells near the damaged area. Aspirin appears to exert its analgesic effects by inhibiting cyclooxygenase, an enzyme important in the biosynthesis of prostaglandins.

Noradrenaline as the "Neurohumoral Transmitter" in Sympathetic Nervous Systems. Von Euler's early discoveries and systematic investigations were the first indicators of his enduring scientific legacy. He had an eye for the potential biological importance of newly discovered substances and the patience to lay the experimental groundwork for many later scientific and clinical advances. However, it was his identification of the sympathetic ("adrenergic") neurotransmitter, noradrenaline, in 1946, and his subsequent research on it, for which von Euler is most remembered. This discovery won him a share of the Nobel Prize in Physiology or Medicine in 1970, with Sir Bernard Katz and Julius Axelrod. The prize was awarded for their discoveries concerning "the humoral transmitters in the nerve terminals and the mechanisms for their storage, release and inactivation." In the press release from October 1970 announcing the awards, von Euler was noted for having discovered that the substance noradrenaline (also known as norepinephrine) serves as a chemical neurotransmitter at synapses in the sympathetic nervous system, and for showing how noradrenaline is stored in "small nerve granules within the nerve fibers of this system." The release further noted that von Euler's (and Axelrod's) discoveries "form the basis for the understanding of the transmission in the central nervous system and its pharmacology"—the basic science of how messages are mediated between nerve cells.

In his presentation speech for the 1970 Nobel Prize, Professor Börje Uvnäs noted the earlier "prize winning" work upon which Katz's, von Euler's, and Axelrod's work built. The theory of chemical neurotransmission had been verified experimentally in the 1920s by Henry Dale, Otto Loewi, and others. But these initial discoveries raised a host of difficult questions. How were these transmitter substances synthesized, stored, and released? How, within a fraction of a second, could they appear in synapses, exert their effects, and be inactivated and removed? What substances served as neurotransmitters? Von Euler addressed and answered some of these questions in the sympathetic nervous system, whose components were more difficult to access experimentally than neuromuscular junctions or parasympathetic components. And his work with Nils-Åke Hillarp provided the first scientific investigation into the "nerve granules" that bind transmitter substances in presynaptic terminals.

Noradrenaline (NA) was the second substance discovered to meet the classic criteria on being a neurotransmitter. (Acetylcholine, owing to the original work of Loewi and Dale, was the first.) It later became known that it is one of the three major brain catecholamines, along with adrenaline (AD) or epinephrine (NA's N-methylated derivative) and dopamine. NA has important effects in both peripheral and central nervous systems. In peripheral neurons NA is an excitatory neurotransmitter; in the central nervous system it appears primarily to be inhibitory. Like many neurotransmitters, NA is packaged in axon terminals in synaptic vesicles, membrane-bound granules that fuse with the presynaptic membrane to release the neurotransmitter substance into the synapse. It is removed from the synaptic cleft primarily by active (energy-dependent) presynaptic reuptake mechanisms. NA released from synaptic terminals binds to adrenoreceptors, all types of which are "slow" (metabotropic) receptors coupled to intracellular G-protein complexes that in turn act directly on ion channels or activate second-messenger systems inside the target cell. The majority of central NA innervations originate in the locus coruleus in the pons central gray region. Several tracts project to targets throughout the brain, including the midbrain tectum, thalamus, hippocampus, neocortex, and olfactory bulb. Decreased activity at particular central noradrenergic synapses has been linked to behavioral depression. There is also evidence that NA plays a role in learning and memory, arousal, and mood.

Of course, in the early 1940s, none of these details was known. In fact, the popular assumption was that AD was the "neurohumoral transmitter" in the sympathetic nervous system. At the turn of the twentieth century Thomas Renton Elliott had emphasized the similarity between the action of AD and stimulation of sympathetic nerves. In 1921 Loewi first demonstrated experimentally the effect of a chemical produced by sympathetic nerve stimulation, which he named *Acceleraransstoff* (accelerating substance). Using the same technique he first used to demonstrate chemical transmission in parasympathetic nerve synapses, Loewi showed that perfusing this substance into beating frog hearts not only accelerated heartbeat at the same rate as directly stimulating sympathetic nerve afferents, but also that this effect was very similar to direct AD perfusion. It turned out that *Acceleraransstoff* in this specific species and tissue was AD, but this was an exception in sympathetic nervous systems. Using the careful and systematic methods that led to his discoveries of substance P and prostaglandin, von Euler perfected techniques for extracting substances from adrenergic nerves and their target organs. His pharmacological studies of these extracts revealed certain key differences between their active compound and AD. Further investigations in von Euler's lab using pharmacological and chemical tools available in the 1940s revealed that this active compound was NA.

Systematic studies by von Euler and colleagues revealed NA to be present in almost all innervated organs and tissues. They demonstrated that its occurrence in organs depended on the presence of nerves by sectioning adrenergic projections to tissues, which led to nerve degeneration. This caused NA concentrations in the tissues to drop to low levels or disappear. Upon nerve projection regeneration to the tissue, NA levels rose back to near-normal values. Von Euler's lab confirmed the general role of NA in sympathetic nervous system activity by measuring the relative amounts of NA found in various organs, all shown eventually to be innervated differentially by sympathetic nerve projections. Sheep spleen, heart, and submaxillary glands, and bull vas deferens and vesicular gland contained considerable amounts, while sheep lungs and striated muscle tissue and bull testicles contained very little.

Subsequent Work on Noradrenaline (NA). Armed with a picture of the overall distribution of NA in biological tis-

sues, von Euler turned to studying its release. Because the amount of both noradrenaline and adrenaline excreted in urine after intravenous injection was relatively constant, von Euler and his colleagues began measuring NA urinary excretion under a number of physiological and pathological conditions. They used this as a measure of adrenergic nervous activity. They discovered that increased NA excretion was tied to blood pressure mechanisms, for example, low excretion during night hours, a sudden rise with the shift from horizontal to vertical body postures, high levels during the day, and an increase in NA excretion with muscular work. Stressful situations also increased NA excretion. Von Euler and his colleagues discovered that NA (and AD) excretion rose significantly during an activity period that included parachute jumps by military officers and trainees, compared to a similar time period that included only ground activities. Exposure to cold temperatures in a laboratory setting likewise led to increased NA excretion in a number of animal models. This work solidified the conclusion that NA was the principal chemical neurotransmitter in sympathetic nervous systems.

In collaboration with Hillarp, von Euler next turned to the method by which NA was stored in sympathetic nerve endings. Hillarp had already shown that microscopic observations of terminal bulbs in adrenergic nerve endings had a beaded appearance. He dubbed these structures "varicosities." Because both Hillarp and von Euler assumed that these varicosities contained high concentrations of NA, they concluded that the NA must be bound up in some way to a specific structure (otherwise the molecules would diffuse away or become inactivated). By homogenizing a variety of adrenergic nerves and their target organs, they isolated a small particle fraction containing a high concentration of NA. Using the electron microscope, von Euler and Hillarp showed that these particles appeared as "granular bodies" with diameters of 300–1500Å and a 70Å covering membrane. Numerous researchers noticed connections between von Euler and Hillarp's work on these "granular bodies" and Julius Axelrod's work on the mechanisms of adrenergic neurotransmission. Their "granular bodies" have since been recognized as membrane-bound synaptic vesicles, each containing small amounts (quanta) of transmitter substances in presynaptic neurons.

Von Euler and his colleagues also demonstrated that the rapid synthesis of noradrenaline following fast and considerable release resulted from both increased synthesis of the transmitter substance in presynaptic neurons and its active reuptake from the synapse. They discovered that NA release rate from the storage particles depended on pH, temperature, and NA concentration. Increased release rate at higher temperatures (within biological limits) suggested metabolic regulation, a conclusion they further established using metabolic inhibitors. Employing yet again the careful, systematic approach that characterized his entire

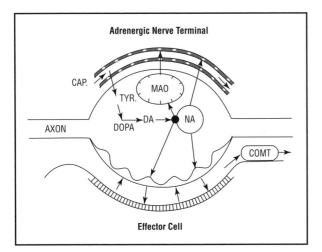

Figure 1. *Representation of Von Euler's (1970) sketch of nerve terminal NA activity.*

scientific career, von Euler (along with his colleague Fjodor Lishajko) showed that a large number and variety of drugs interfered with both NA reuptake and release, including adrenergic antagonists, sympathomimetic amines, and psychoactive compounds. This work was greatly enhanced by their use of then novel radioactively labeled NA.

By the time of his 1970 Nobel address, von Euler had pieced together a "tentative scheme" of the adrenergic nerve terminal (see Figure 1). By current standards it is remarkably simplistic. Yet his sketch already contained key steps in the synthesis of NA from tyrosine, its binding in "storage granules," its oxidization by monoamine oxidase, its release into the synaptic cleft, its synaptic inactivation by catechol-O-methyltransferase (COMT) methylation, and its reuptake back into the presynaptic axon terminal. Progress on neurotransmission and synaptic mechanisms has been enormous since 1970, but it rests on the shoulders of the initial experimental and theoretical work on Ulf von Euler on adrenergic neurons in the sympathetic nervous system.

The Scientist and the Person. Although his deliberate and systematic approach to research might lead one to picture von Euler as obsessively tied to his laboratory bench, he was known to be aristocratic and cosmopolitan. His scientific temperament was nondogmatic. He had the reputation of being an outstanding teacher and mentor, and he encouraged young scientists to try out novel ideas. His well-cited "Editorial" in the journal *Circulation* from 1962 sketches his distinction between "discoveries" and "observations"—from someone who demonstrated an eye for the former throughout his career. He concluded with the maxim that "we must always guard the liberties of the mind and remember that some degree of heresy is often a

sign of health in spiritual life." His friends and professional colleagues knew that he lived by that dictate. Many remarked in print that one could discuss any subject with him, from science to arts to politics to philosophy. Before his death, he was fortunate to witness the scientific and clinical fruition of many of his discoveries, and he enjoyed the international status of a "grand old man" of chemical information transfer and signaling. He died in Stockholm following complications from open heart surgery.

BIBLIOGRAPHY

WORKS BY VON EULER

Noradrenaline. Springfield, IL: Charles C. Thomas, 1956. The definitive work at the time of its publication.

"Editorial." *Circulation* 26 (1962): 1233–1234. An excellent brief introduction to von Euler's philosophy of science and scientific practice.

With Hans Heller, eds. *Comparative Endocrinology.* New York: Academic Press, 1963.

With Rune Eliasson. *Prostaglandins.* New York: Academic Press, 1967.

"Adrenergic Neurotransmitter Functions." Nobel Lecture, 12 December 1970. Available from http://nobelprize.org/medicine/laureates/1970/euler-lecture.html. The best short introduction to von Euler's systematic investigation of NA, from its basic pharmacology through chemical applications.

OTHER SOURCES

Nobel Foundation. "Ulf von Euler: Biography." Available from http://nobelprize.org/medicine/laureates/1970/euler-bio.html.

Sabbatini, Renato M. E. "Neurons and Synapses: The History of Its Discovery IV. Chemical Transmission." *Brain and Mind* (2004). Available from http://www.cerebromente.org.br/n17/history/neurons5_i.htm.

Wolstenholme, Gordon E. W., and Maeve O'Connor, eds. *Adrenergic Neurotransmission: Ciba Foundation Study Group No. 33, in Honour of U. S. von Euler.* Boston: Little, Brown, 1968.

John Bickle

VON HOLST, ERICH (*b.* Riga, Latvia, 28 November 1908; *d.* Herrsching, Bavaria, Germany, 26 May 1962), *experimental zoology, ethology, physiology, musical instruments.*

Von Holst is remembered for his outstanding experimental studies of the central nervous system, the flight of birds, and many other physiological problems. He was one of the founders of behavioral physiology and helped establish ethology as a scientific discipline. He was also a gifted musician and contributed to a scientific understanding of musical instruments.

Life and Passion. Von Holst, son of psychiatrist Dr. Walther von Holst and Dorothea von Holst, was born in Riga, Latvia, but attended school in Danzig (now Gdańsk, Poland). Serious health problems (articular rheumatism) in his childhood led to an incurable cardiac defect and thus negatively affected his life expectancy. He was constantly aware that his life might be rather short. However, early in his youth he discovered both his passion for animals and his enthusiasm for engineering. While recovering in a hospital, he read Alfred Brehm's popular *Tierleben*—a comprehensive (in many aspects anthropomorphic) description of animal life—and was fascinated. Later he combined zoological phenomena with engineering to arrive at highly original solutions of physiological problems. Also, he developed a passion for music and musical instruments, particularly the viola. He was concerned with the construction of this instrument and the generation of its sound pattern.

His former students and colleagues describe von Holst as an outstanding personality with high moral standards, at the same time generous and helpful. He was an indefatigable and keen worker, eager to solve scientific problems. Neither in his professional nor in his private life was he willing to make—or to accept—a compromise. He lived very intensively, due to his early recognition of his heart disease. Worry about death was combined in him with an enormous energy and a tremendous drive to live and to work. The well-known philosophy of "live for today, for there may be no tomorrow" could very well apply to him. This can also help explain the variety of his interests and the remarkable scientific work that he accomplished within just a few decades. His students were allowed to contact him and ask for help at almost any hour of the day (or night), yet he was rigorous when it came to scientific work and did not accept any indolence. Passionate students with original ideas found in him a benevolent supporter. But he could be also merciless in his criticism. In discussions after a lecture it frequently happened that he sharply attacked and discouraged the lecturer. Needless to say, in the eyes of some people he was a difficult man.

Early Scientific Work. Von Holst studied in Kiel, Vienna, and Berlin. Already in his doctoral thesis, which dealt with the function of the nervous system in earthworms (and was published in 1932 in a well-recognized zoological yearbook), he found arguments against the doctrine according to which the behavior of organisms is governed by reflexes. In many experiments he found out that the locomotion of earthworms is not caused by a chain of reflexes stimulating one segment after the other, but that excitations in the head autonomously—without any further stimuli—affect the other parts of the animal.

To appreciate this achievement, one has to remember the philosophical view guiding the study of behavior at that time. In the 1930s the majority of physiologists and behavior scientists were convinced that any organism's activity is mainly a reflex action and that the organism is initially a clean slate or tabula rasa (behaviorism). They followed the tradition of the Russian physiologist Ivan P. Pavlov and defined behavior essentially as the response of living beings to some kind of (external) stimulus (empty-organism doctrine). Thus, they disregarded any notion of innate or instinctive behavior and accepted only those behavioral traits as relevant that could be studied and manipulated in experiments. On the other side, there was a smaller faction of biologists and psychologists holding that some "inner mechanisms" were the very driving forces of animal behavior (purposive psychology, *Zweckpsychologie*).

The opposition between these two schools reflected pretty well the old battle between mechanists and vitalists, which had been ignited by the venerable question how, after all, living beings and their properties are to be explained: as mere machines or complex systems exhibiting some "inner" forces and purposes qualitatively different from physical laws. The question is now obsolete for it is known that any living system is not just a machine but that its specific properties can be sufficiently explained without resort to cryptic vital forces and the like (which, anyway, have no explanatory power). In the early 1930s, however, the methodological stance of biology was different from its status in the early twenty-first century.

Thus, when von Holst entered the scene, the situation in the behavior sciences was somewhat confusing. Von Holst was not at all inclined to vitalism, at the same time he did not embrace the doctrine that the study behavior is to be reduced to the study of reflexes. His own studies were pathbreaking and gave behavioral physiology a new direction. As a neurophysiologist he regarded nervous actions as somehow autonomous and became

> particularly interested in the *spontaneous* action of the central nervous system in addition to the aspect previously so widely studied: the relationship between stimulus and response. He was able to demonstrate that the central system does not passively link stimuli to responses but is highly active in itself, producing "internalstimuli" and incorporating numerous functional systems. (Thorpe, 1979, p. 110)

Von Holst's early scientific work already gave some impetus to the emerging field of ethology, the comparative study of behavior from a biological perspective. Other leading figures in the history of this field are, above all, Oskar Heinroth, Karl von Frisch, Konrad Lorenz, and Nikolaas Tinbergen. Later, due to his many outstanding experimental studies, von Holst would be regarded as one of the founders of behavioral physiology, the discipline concerned with the physiological basis of all kinds of animal (and human) behavior. He introduced the cybernetic approach to ethology and showed that behavioral phenomena are not simply caused by outer stimuli but are rather to be understood on the basis of complex feedback and regulatory principles. In other words: A living being does not simply react to its surroundings, it is not—as the empty-organism doctrine of the behaviorists suggested— "molded" by its environment, but is an active system searching for its possibilities to live and survive.

Professional Career. After he had obtained his PhD, von Holst worked as a fellow in Frankfurt am Main, where he was attracted by the approach of the physiologist Albrecht Bethe, whose conception of plasticity (*Plastizitätslehre*) clearly contrasted with the doctrine of reflexes. In Bethe he found the ideal of an experimental biologist. He combined Bethe's methodology with his own findings from his doctoral thesis. In 1934 and 1935 von Holst took the position of an assistant at the Zoological Station in Naples (Stazione Zoologica di Napoli). From 1936 to 1938 he worked in Berlin and finished his *Habilitation*, a physiological study on the spinal cord. After that, he worked for some years as an academic teacher without salary (privatdozent) in Göttingen, and in 1946 he was appointed full professor of zoology at the University of Heidelberg. Immediately after World War II, von Holst became cofounder and coeditor of the *Göttinger Universitätszeitung*, a journal that expressed the new intellectual freedom after the Nazi regime.

From 1948 on he was head (*Abteilungsleiter*) at the Max Planck Institute for Marine Sciences in Wilhelmshaven (Lower Saxony), where, in 1950, he organized a workshop in ethology that was the prelude, so to speak, to many other regularly organized ethological symposia in the following years. One of the participants of the workshop, W. H. Thorpe, described the conditions in Wilhelmshaven as "curious and inconvenient." The institute was housed in an unfinished naval barracks building; the quarters were cramped, and the staff and students lived closely packed. Nevertheless, in retrospect, this was the important beginning of "institutionalized ethology." Von Holst was eager to establish his discipline, behavioral physiology—and he was very successful. His idea of a research group combining different approaches to the study of behavior was realized in the 1950s when the Max Planck Society approved an institute in Seewiesen (Bavaria) that soon became one of the world's leading institutes in the field.

The Max-Planck-Institut für Verhaltensphysiologie (behavioral physiology) was inaugurated in 1958. Von Holst was appointed director of the institute, Lorenz his codirector. The name of the institute paid tribute to von Holst's work. In fact, his reputation at the Max Planck Society was most remarkable, his scientific integrity undisputed. Already in 1950 he was given a special role in one of the (still) leading scientific journals in Germany, *Die Naturwissenschaften* (the official organ of the Max Planck Society for the Advancement of Science). He became a kind of "super editor" and was asked to shape the direction of this periodical. Also von Holst was, for some decades, coeditor of the *Zeitschrift für vergleichende Physiologie* (Journal of comparative physiology).

The name of the institute in Bavaria (Verhaltensphysiologie) was somehow misleading. Lorenz with his research group was doing mainly descriptive and comparative ethology. Behavioral physiology was only one of the disciplines united in Seewiesen. After von Holst's early death in 1962 the institute's leading figure was definitely Lorenz. But by that time the physiological approach to the study of behavior was already well established. This is not to say that Lorenz's and von Holst's approaches contradicted each other. As Lorenz and von Holst had very different personalities, they advocated different views of the "philosophy" of behavior sciences. But each of them was needed. Brought together, they formed the whole corpus of ethology as a comprehensive study of behavior in animals as well as humans.

Further Scientific Work. In 1933, after his doctoral dissertation, von Holst dedicated his work to a variety of physiological problems and their solution. During his stay in Naples, he observed that some fish—under particular experimental constraints—do not coordinate their fins in an absolute manner, so to speak, although they do not move them separately, one independent from the other. He called this phenomenon "relative coordination" and— in a long series of experiments—found a relation between two centers in the central nervous system: an autonomous and a dependent one. Relative coordination produces a harmony between individual rhythms (e.g., in the fins of a fish). The better this can be achieved, the more stable is the end result: the coordination of the rhythms.

In other studies, von Holst was concerned with—if not obsessed by—the flight of animals, particularly birds. In the search to understand this phenomenon, he built flying objects and constantly rebuilt them so that, in the end, the results were models of flying animals exhibiting a certain autonomy. The intuition of a talented engineer and experimentalist also enabled him, for example, to construct a model of the flying Mesozoic reptile, *Rhamphorhynchus*. The participants of a paleontological meeting were impressed when his artificial pterosaur was flying in the conference room.

The physiology of the nervous system offered von Holst further topics for study. In 1950 his seminal paper "Das Reafferenzprinzip" was published (coauthored by his student Horst Mittelstaedt). The principle of reafference contradicts the stimulus-response conception of the behaviorists and describes mechanisms that check and recheck any newly acquired motor patterns. It is a regulatory principle in the nervous system to control the external stimulus.

In the following years von Holst published many other papers, most of them reporting the results of his own experimental studies that he always carried out with passion. He constantly devised new—and improved old—experimental methods to answer physiological questions. He offered most convincing evidence of the physiological autonomy (*Eigenaktivität*) of the central nervous system. This can be regarded his greatest achievement. Generally, his work clearly demonstrates the complex functionality of organisms and their activities that are not governed by external stimuli and reflexes. Von Holst contributed to a better understanding of the concept of instinct, a previously somewhat confusing and obscure concept.

In his experimental work he was dedicated to analytical thinking; however, he did not neglect the importance of synthesis and the "holistic" approach. In many of his writings, one can find general statements concerning the methodology and philosophy of science. He considered mere counting and measurement insufficient and claimed that truly scientific progress is achieved only through qualitatively new insight. Also, he argued that at the beginning of any physiological investigation the investigator should try to find him- or herself in the situation of the constructor of the respective animal. This is an interesting methodological proposition that at least in von Holst's case led to remarkable and astonishing results.

It may also be noted that von Holst was a brilliant speaker. He did not read a manuscript, but gave in his talks the impression that he was developing his ideas just then. He always encouraged his students to give their presentations the same way. Because of his early death, many of his projects remained unfinished, yet his pioneering work and his meaning for the development of ethology as a particular branch of biology (with essential implications for other sciences, especially psychology) are appreciated by all students working in this field.

Finally, von Holst has to be remembered as an artist. He was a gifted musician. As a violist he could attract and fascinate his listeners for many hours. In earlier years, he used to say that the scientist and the artist are different aspects of his personality. Later, however, he successfully combined his enthusiasm for science with his passion for music and started to study musical instruments in a way similar to his studies of living beings. Several of his publications give evidence of his systematic inquiry into the construction, function, and sound pattern of the viola. In the history of music there are certainly not many people who combined their deep knowledge of physiological processes so successfully with an understanding of the architecture and function of musical instruments. Von Holst started to write a book, *Geigenkunde für Liebhaber* (Violin science for amateurs), which remained unfinished.

BIBLIOGRAPHY

WORKS BY VON HOLST

"Untersuchungen über die Funktion des Zentralnervensystems beim Regenwurm." *Zoologische Jahrbücher, Allgemeine Zoologie* 51 (1932): 547–588; 53 (1932): 67–100.

"Studien über die Reflexe und Rhythmen beim Goldfisch (*Carassius auratus*)." *Zeitschrift für vergleichende Physiologie* 20 (1934): 582–599.

"Über den Prozess der zentralen Koordination." *Pflügers Archiv* 236 (1935): 149–158.

"Versuche zur Theorie der relativen Koordination." *Pflügers Archiv* 237 (1936): 93–121.

"Vom Wesen der Ordnung im Zentralnervensystem." *Naturwissenschaften* 25 (1937): 625–631, 641–647.

"Über die nervöse Funktionsstruktur des rhythmisch tätigen Fischrückenmarks." *Pflügers Archiv* 241 (1939): 569–611.

"Über die relative Koordination bei Arthropoden." *Pflügers Archiv* 246 (1943): 847–865.

"Über 'künstliche Vögel' als Mittel zum Studium des Vogelflugs." *Journal für Ornithologie* 91 (1943): 406–447.

"Vom Flug der Tiere und vom Menschenflug der Zukunft." *Schriften der Universität Heidelberg* 3 (1948): 95–112.

"Von der Mathematik der nervösen Ordnungsleistungen." *Experientia* 4 (1948): 374–381.

"Die Tätigkeit des Statolithenapparates der Wirbeltiere." *Naturwissenschaften* 37 (1950): 265–272.

With H. Mittelstaedt. "Das Reafferenzprinzip." *Naturwissenschaften* 37 (1950): 464–476.

"Ein neuer Vorschlag zur Lösung des Bratschenproblems." *Instrumentenbau-Zeitschrift* 8 (1953): 46–48.

"Physiologie und Verhalten." *Mitteilungen der Max-Planck-Gesellschaft* 5 (1954): 270–275.

"Relations between the Central Nervous System and the Peripheral Organs." *British Journal of Animal Behaviour* 2 (1954): 89–94.

"Zentralnervensystem (Das Muskelspindelsystem der Säuger)." *Fortschritte der Zoologie* 10 (1956): 381–390.

"Aktive Leistungen der menschlichen Gesichtswahrnehmung." *Studium Generale* 10 (1957): 231–243.

"Der Saurierflug." *Paläontologische Zeitschrift* 31 (1957): 15–22.

"Wie flog *Rhamphorhynchus*?" *Natur und Volk* 87 (1957): 81–87.

With U. von Saint Paul. "Vom Wirkungsgefüge der Triebe." *Naturwissenschaften* 47 (1960): 409–422.

Zur Verhaltensphysiologie bei Tieren und Menschen Edited by B. Hassenstein. 2 vols. Munich: Piper, 1969–1970. A collection of von Holst's papers on behavioral physiology. Contains a list of obituaries.

OTHER SOURCES

Burkhardt, Richard W. *Patterns of Behavior: Konrad Lorenz, Niko Tinbergen, and the Founding of Ethology.* Chicago: University of Chicago Press, 2005.

Hassenstein, Bernhard. "Erich von Holst (1908–1962)." In *Darwin & Co.: Eine Geschichte der Biologie in Portraits*, vol. 2, edited by Ilse Jahn and Michael Schmitt. Munich: C. H. Beck, 2001.

Lorenz, Konrad. "Erich von Holst zum Todestag." *Die Naturwissenschaften* 49 (1962): 385–386.

———. "Erich von Holst, Seher und Forscher." *4. Biologisches Jahresheft des Verbandes deutscher Biologen* (1964): 19–24.

Thorpe, W. H. *The Origins and Rise of Ethology.* London: Heinemann, 1979.

Wuketits, Franz M. *Die Entdeckung des Verhaltens: Eine Geschichte der Verhaltensforschung.* Darmstadt, Germany: Wissenschaftliche Buchgesellschaft, 1995.

Franz M. Wuketits

VON KOENIGSWALD, GUSTAV HEINRICH RALPH

(*b.* Berlin, Germany, 13 November 1902; *d.* Bad Homburg, Germany, 10 July 1982), *paleontology, paleoanthropology, human evolution, mammal evolution, geology, ethnology.*

Between 1937 and 1941 von Koenigswald discovered hominid fossils at Sangiran in Java, which is among the most prolific hominid sites on a worldwide scale. He discovered three fragmented skulls, five jaw fragments, and numerous teeth of the Pleistocene hominid *Pithecanthropus* (now *Homo erectus*). Von Koenigswald's finds underlined the central role of *Pithecanthropus* in human evolution and corroborated earlier findings by Eugène Dubois. Von Koenigswald left Java in 1945 and took over the chair of paleontology at Rijksuniversiteit at Utrecht in the Netherlands. There he continued his research on fossil hominids and their geology and paleontology in the Pleistocene of southeast Java.

The Road to Java. Von Koenigswald was born in Berlin and raised in Germany. He studied geology and paleontology at the universities in Berlin, Tübingen, Cologne, and Munich. He completed his doctoral studies in Munich in 1928 under the direction of Erich Kaiser, on the Permian Red Beds of the Weidener Bucht.

As an assistant to the Bavarian State Collection in Munich he was approached by Ferdinand Broili who asked him whether he would be interested in working as a mammal paleontologist at the Netherlands Geological Survey in Java. Since he was interested in fossil hominids, von Koenigswald accepted the opportunity and went to Bandung in 1930, forty years after the Dutch anatomist Eugène Dubois had made his important discovery of *Pithecanthropus erectus* on the island of Java. Von Koenigswald's primary task at the Geological Survey was to work out a fossil mammal stratigraphy for the Javanese Pleistocene in close cooperation with colleagues from geology who were carrying out mapping campaigns thereby elaborating the lithostratigraphy. Soon after his arrival he got involved in the excavation campaign the Geological Survey carried out at Ngandong in East Java. Eleven hominid skulls were found in Pleistocene river sediments, but von Koenigswald was not directly involved in their discovery. The excavations were led by Carel ter Haar and the hominids went to Batavia (now Jakarta) for description and comparison. Von Koenigswald continued to describe mammal species and elaborated his stratigraphy, but because of severe financial cutbacks the Geological Survey was forced to dismiss von Koenigswald in 1934.

Von Koenigswald decided not to return to Europe but to stay in Java and continue with his work. He was allowed to make use of the equipment and library at Bandung and, supplied with funds from Dutch foundations, he was able to resume his studies. He went into the field and discovered stone tools, which attracted the attention of the French Jesuit paleontologist Pierre Teilhard de Chardin, who had participated in the search for hominids at Zhoukoudian in China. Teilhard de Chardin visited von Koenigswald early in 1936, encouraging him to proceed with his studies in Javanese prehistory.

This visit emerged as a decisive turning point for von Koenigswald's career. Teilhard de Chardin realized that the continuation of von Koenigswald's work was permanently endangered due to funding limitations. He approached the Carnegie Foundation and through his mediation von Koenigswald successfully applied for a grant.

Soon after Teilhard de Chardin left Java a new hominid fossil was discovered in East Java, north of Mojokerto, in 1936. This time von Koenigswald did not let the opportunity pass and—supported by Franz Weidenreich, the German anatomist in charge of the Zhoukoudian excavations at Beijing—he published a description of the Mojokerto hominid. It was the cranium of a young child removed from stratigraphically old deposits and von Koenigswald quickly realized the importance of this find. He went on a presentation journey through the United States and Europe in the fall of 1936 and when he returned to Java in spring 1937, he had acquired sufficient funding to conduct exploration and collection at a new site in Central Java called Sangiran. In fact, von Koenigswald

Gustav Heinrich von Koenigswald. *Gustav Heinrich Ralph von Koenigswald examining the upper jaw of Pithecanthropus robustus.* © **BETTMANN/CORBIS.**

was able to ask his collector to begin collecting right away, while he was still traveling. As a result a new hominid specimen already awaited him upon his return.

The Conflict with Dubois. Although von Koenigswald's primary task at the Geological Survey did not involve human paleontology, he knew, of course, about the famous finds made by Dubois in the last decade of the nineteenth century and he hoped to find more. The opportunity came with the discovery of a child's skull in East Java in February 1936. The find itself was made during a mapping campaign by a *mantri,* a local employee of the Geological Survey, who sent the specimen to von Koenigswald at Bandung. Von Koenigswald sent pictures to Dubois to seek his opinion on the fossil. The new discovery was published in the *Proceedings of the Royal Academy of Sciences* in Amsterdam.

The interpretation of the find was nevertheless difficult because von Koenigswald had no training in human

anatomy. From a geological viewpoint, the cranium seemed to be quite old. The only fossil human form with a comparable age from the Pleistocene of Java was *Pithecanthropus,* but nothing was known about the anatomy of *Pithecanthropus* children. Due to its extraordinary age, however, von Koenigswald was convinced that the cranium represented a *Pithecanthropus* child. But since he was unable to find convincing proof, he proposed the name *Homo modjokertensis,* a careless challenge to Dubois, who was convinced that *Pithecanthropus* represented an intermediate form between humans and primates and thus could not be regarded as a member of the genus *Homo.* In his reply, Dubois pointed to the fact that the skull showed an unexpected height whereas the *Pithecanthropus* skull from Trinil is characterized by its extreme lowness. From an anatomical viewpoint, it was far more plausible to assume that the child belonged to the Ngandong group and not to *Pithecanthropus.*

Upon his return to Java, von Koenigswald learned that a new hominid fossil had been found at a site west of Trinil, at Sangiran. It was a fragmented right mandibular ramus. This time, von Koenigswald immediately reported the find to Dubois and promised to send pictures, a promise that was forgotten due to another exciting find at Sangiran, a fragmented cranium. The description of the mandible was published in November 1937. Von Koenigswald attributed the mandible to *Pithecanthropus* and added an extensive discussion of the human nature of *Pithecanthropus.*

The first pictures to reach Dubois were those in the publication, and he started to compare the mandibular fragment with his own find from Kedung Brubus. Dubois stressed a number of anatomical differences between the Kedung Brubus fragment and the mandible from Sangiran. He noticed, moreover, a striking size difference between both of the specimens. Unfortunately, von Koenigswald's publication contained a small but decisive printing error concerning the total length of the fragment. In fact the specimen is 1 centimeter shorter than the published length. Dubois took the given value as correct and assuming that the pictures showed reduced representations, he enlarged von Koenigswald's plates correspondingly. As a result, the Kedung Brubus fragment looked tiny side by side with the Sangiran mandible. Anyone could notice at first glance that both of the fragments could never be attributed to the same form. It is thus not surprising that Dubois again concluded that the new mandible was erroneously attributed to *Pithecanthropus* by von Koenigswald and belonged to the only fossil human known from Java, the Ngandong group. Von Koenigswald corrected that error only in 1940 in his comprehensive publication on all the early hominid specimens from Sangiran.

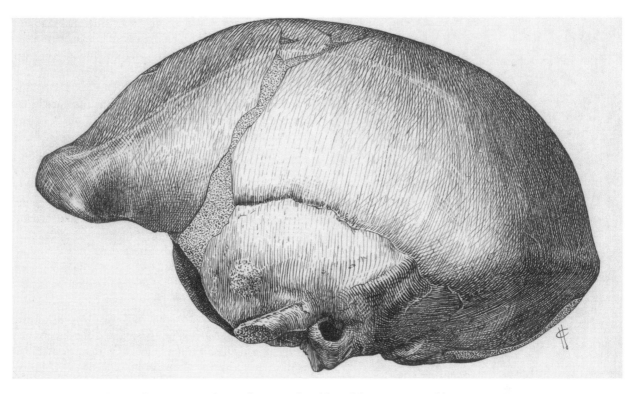

Sangiran 2. *Lateral view of Sangiran 2, a hominid cranium found by Ralph von Koenigswald in 1937 at Sangiran site, Java. Drawing made by Hu Chengzi at the Cenzoic Research Laboratory in Beijing.* **SENCKENBERG INSTITUTE. REPRODUCED BY PERMISSION.**

From spring 1938 onward their correspondence reflects an advancing discordance in their relationship. Von Koenigswald did not publish comparisons of his material with the Ngandong finds as Dubois demanded and Dubois in turn quoted in his publications from von Koenigswald's letters without asking for permission.

Meanwhile, von Koenigswald's initial announcement of the Sangiran cranium appeared in December 1937. Several pictures were printed along with the announcement, in particular a plate showing the thirty fragments of which the skull initially consisted. Again Dubois applied the measuring method that in his eyes already proved useful with the Sangiran mandible. He measured the fragments on the photos and compared their length with the corresponding distances on the picture of the reconstructed skull. On this basis he concluded that the reconstruction had not been properly done. The cranial fragment from Sangiran was damaged by the collectors during the collection process. However, a fossil specimen with fresh breaks is quite easy to reconstruct. Mistakes would either indicate malicious forgery or sheer incompetence.

Von Koenigswald was beside himself with rage, all the more since Dubois again quoted from his letters without asking. With his initial discoveries von Koenigswald wrote to Dubois seeking advice from an elder colleague. Three

discoveries and two years later their relationship had deteriorated into distrust, jealousy, and mutual accusations. Most of their dispute was conducted in publications under the eyes of a scientific audience. Von Koenigswald was worried that this conflict could tarnish his scientific reputation because Dubois was very influential in the Netherlands. However, these fears were unfounded. Von Koenigswald was deeply hurt by Dubois's continued breaches of confidence culminating in the accusation of having falsified a fossil reconstruction. Decades after Dubois's death in 1940 von Koenigswald was still angry. However, a continued lack of diligence in his publications as well as undiplomatic and imprecise arguments certainly enhanced Dubois criticisms about von Koenigswald's expertise.

Fieldwork at Sangiran. Supported by the Carnegie Foundation von Koenigswald was able to proceed with the excavations at Sangiran and several hominid fossils were discovered in quick succession. The first mandible was discovered in late 1936 and the second hominid specimen, a partial cranium, was found in August 1937. Sangiran 2 (or *Pithecanthropus* II) is quite similar to the famous Trinil skullcap. Dubois's suspicions were unsubstantiated in this case and so it was accepted that a second *Pithecanthropus* had been found.

In September 1938 during a visit, Franz Weidenreich identified a third specimen from the Sangiran dome, fragments of a new skull. Weidenreich and von Koenigswald were later able to collect further fragments on site. In order to provide better descriptions and a reconstruction of the *Pithecanthropus* skull, both researchers decided that von Koenigswald should visit Weidenreich's laboratory in Beijing as soon as possible. Von Koenigswald left Bandung for Beijing in the first days of January 1938.

Prior to his departure he received another important hominid find from Sangiran. It was a maxillary, a part of the *Pithecanthropus* skeleton that had not yet been found. With excitement the two scientists recognized fresh breaks on the posterior part of the maxilla. Von Koenigswald urged his collectors to return to the site and search for further pieces. The search was successful and a few weeks later, a package arrived in Beijing containing seven large fragments of an almost complete cranium. The larger part of the skull base was preserved, but unfortunately there was no connection with the maxilla.

Both parts of Sangiran 4 (or *Pithecanthropus* IV) were prepared in Beijing. Careful drawings and casts were made by Hu Chengzi, an assistant of Weidenreich at the Cenozoic Research Laboratory. Von Koenigswald returned to Bandung in April 1938 with drawings, casts, and anatomical descriptions made under the advice of an experienced human anatomist. The anatomical descriptions made up the larger part of the manuscript of one of von Koenigswald's most important publications, a summary of the early discoveries at Sangiran, which was completed and submitted in September 1939.

Upon his return von Koenigswald resumed his work at Sangiran. Late in 1939 another mandible was found, Sangiran 5 (or *Pithecanthropus* C). The specimen possessed a rather strange anatomy, but due to deteriorating working conditions, von Koenigswald was unable to announce the find appropriately. In April 1941 another mandibular fragment was discovered at Sangiran that was by far the largest of all mandibular remains from Sangiran. Its huge dimensions led von Koenigswald to create a new species, *Meganthropus palaeojavanicus*. He completed a publication on both of the specimens in spring 1942 but the manuscript got lost and has never been published.

Von Koenigswald and his family spent World War II as prisoners in various camps in Java. Upon their release late in 1945 the whole family was ill and weak. In the summer of 1946 the von Koenigswald family left Java for New York. Von Koenigswald was allowed to take the precious hominid collection from Java along. All fossil specimens survived the war undamaged because they were hidden by friends and colleagues and only casts were kept

at the Geological Survey. Only one of the Ngandong skulls was seized by the Japanese military and brought to the Imperial collection in Tokyo. However, that skull was discovered soon after the war and returned to von Koenigswald in December 1946.

In 1946 von Koenigswald brought the fossil specimens from Java to Weidenreich at a completely unexpected though highly welcome site, the American Museum of Natural History in New York. Von Koenigswald had recovered from his ordeal and both of the scientists resumed their joint work on human evolution in Southeast Asia, now better equipped with hominids than ever before. Their concepts on human evolution in Southeast Asia had developed in different, although complementary directions. Weidenreich promulgated his idea of giant ancestors in human evolution, a view supported by von Koenigswald's stratigraphic approach.

Based on geology, von Koenigswald divided the Pleistocene in Java into two deposits of different ages, the lower Pleistocene Pucangan formation with the Jetis fauna and the middle Pleistocene Kabuh formation containing the Trinil fauna. Both of the formations were hominid bearing and the deposits ranged from the Sangiran dome in Central Java to Mojokerto in East Java. The classical *Pithecanthropus,* to which von Koenigswald attributed Dubois's initial finds in Trinil and Kedung Brubus as well as the first two skulls from Sangiran, was found in the younger Kabuh formation. According to von Koenigswald the Mojokerto child skull originated from the older Pucangan formation. The first Sangiran mandible, the Sangiran 4 cranium, and the huge *Meganthropus* mandible were collected from these layers. At Sangiran these two beds are lithologically separated by a third layer, the "Grenzbank" (or boundary layer). This Grenzbank layer also contained hominid fossils, for instance, the enigmatic Sangiran 5 mandible.

From this stratigraphic distribution von Koenigswald derived the following picture. The huge *Meganthropus* as well as the robust Sangiran 4 skull represent the oldest fossil humans in Java. The smaller, although still large, form represented by the Sangiran 5 mandible was found in the Grenzbank layer. The fossil humans originating from the Kabuh formation possess a more gracile anatomy and represent the classic *Pithecanthropus* in Java. The Ngandong skulls are stratigraphically younger and represent an enlarged and thus advanced form. Von Koenigswald considered them to be tropical Neanderthals, but he never devoted much attention to them.

This view corresponded to Weidenreich's anatomical view of human evolution, although it was mainly rooted in stratigraphy. Von Koenigswald used anatomical comparisons and taxonomic descriptions to reflect the stratigraphic arrangement. In his mind, the chronological sequence of anatomies provided a direct representation of evolutionary pathways. Von Koenigswald was not primarily concerned with the mechanisms of evolution.

A New Home in the Netherlands. In spring 1948 von Koenigswald took over the professorship of paleontology at the Rijksuniversiteit in Utrecht in the Netherlands. All the hominid fossils moved along with him, thereby finding a new home at the institute's collections. Now based in Utrecht, von Koenigswald enlarged the scope of his studies, in space as well as in time.

In the early 1950s he went to South Africa in order to compare the collection of Sangiran hominids with *Australopithecus*. He carried out his studies jointly with John Robinson. Since *Australopithecus* represented another potential candidate as a human ancestor with a very robust dentition, it was an important question whether there was a particular relation between *Pithecanthropus* from Java and South African australopithecines. The relation between the African and Javanese hominids kept him busy until 1964. Together with the South African paleoanthropologist Phillip V. Tobias, he carried out a comparison of his Sangiran material with the hominid collection from Olduvai. They concluded that the most basal hominid known from Java, *Meganthropus*, represents an advanced form compared to *Australopithecus* and that it corresponds to early hominids like *Homo habilis* from Olduvai. Although the samples differ in some respects, Tobias and von Koenigswald noticed remarkable parallels between the Asian and African sequences.

For two decades von Koenigswald's work focused upon the question of early human ancestry and our primate relatives. The latter topic was particularly relevant for him since he described a new giant primate from South China, *Gigantopithecus blacki*, which was only known from a few teeth. Von Koenigswald considered it to be a huge anthropoid, a view that has recently gained support by in situ discoveries.

He visited Southeast Asia a number of times, including on the occasion of the Indo-Pacific Congress held in Manila in 1953. His studies at Sangiran dome were resumed by Pieter Marks, Teuku Jacob, and Sartono, who themselves made important hominid finds. Taking advantage of his professorship, von Koenigswald tried to enable and encourage Indonesian scholars to acquire scientific training and create an infrastructure on their own. He supported research in Indonesia rather than carrying out research projects himself and carefully followed its progress without getting too personally involved. This was certainly a result of his experiences with Dubois. Forming a sound scientific infrastructure was, moreover, a motivation for von Koenigswald's decision to return the Mojok-

erto skull and the Ngandong hominid collection to Indonesia in 1979.

He now devoted his attention to studies of mammal migrations into the Sunda archipelago. Two regions provide potential candidates for Pleistocene mammal faunas in the Sunda Islands, northern India and Pakistan on one hand, and south China on the other. Together with colleagues from the Natural History Museum in Leiden, Netherlands, von Koenigswald tried to identify potential routes and the chronology of migration events. In 1966 he carried out an excursion to the Siwalik formation in Pakistan. The primate fossils collected during this occasion remained a focus of his studies.

Since chronology was such a critical question for his views on human evolution, improving the dating of hominid sites in Southeast Asia was another important issue. He recognized distinctive layers of tektites in the Sangiran profile. These glass meteorites are the result of a geologically instantaneous event, namely the impact of a meteorite. They result from melting rocks in the course of the impact event and are distributed over a vast area. Determining the number of tektite layers in Southeast Asian deposits and identifying single impact events thus provides distinctive time signals. Von Koenigswald meticulously described his tektite collection.

A Lively Retirement at Frankfurt. After his retirement from the professorship at Utrecht's Rijksuniversiteit in 1968, von Koenigswald turned his attention to one last task. He made plans to set up a center for research on human evolution. At the instigation of Helmut de Terra, a new department for paleoanthropology was established at the Senckenberg research institute in Frankfurt with the support of the Reimers Foundation. Von Koenigswald and his fossil collection moved for one last time, and for a period of fifteen years he continued his studies of fossil primates and explored yet new research fields, such as ethnology and prehistory. He remained deeply involved in research on human evolution in Indonesia and Europe alike.

BIBLIOGRAPHY

WORKS BY VON KOENIGSWALD

"Erste Mitteilung ueber einen fossilen Hominiden aus dem Altpleistocaen Ostjavas." *Proceedings of the Section of Sciences Nederlandse Koninkelijke Akademie van Wetenschapen* 39 (1936): 1000–1009.

"Ein Unterkieferfragment des *Pithecanthropus* aus den Trinilschichten Mitteljavas." *Proceedings of the Koninkelijke Akademie van Wetenschapen* 40 (1937): 883–893.

"Pithecanthropus Received into the Human Family." *Illustrated London News,* 11 December 1937.

"Neue *Pithecanthropus*-Funde 1936–1938." *Wetenschappelijke Mededeelingen van den Dienst van den Mijnbouw* 28 (1940): 1–232.

"*Pithecanthropus, Meganthropus* and the Australopithecinae." *Nature* 173 (1954): 795–797.

Meeting Prehistoric Man. London: Scientific Book Club, 1956.

With Phillip V. Tobias. "A Comparison between the Olduvai Hominines and Those of Java and Some Implications for Hominid Phylogeny." *Nature* 204 (1964): 515–518.

OTHER SOURCES

Franzen, Jens Lorenz. "In Memoriam Gustav Heinrich Ralph von Koenigswald 1902–1982." *Senckenbergiana lethaea* 64 (1983): 381–402. An obituary in German including a complete bibliography.

Huffman, O. Frank, Pat Shipman, Christine Hertler, et al. "Historical Evidence of the 1936 Mojokerto Skull Discovery, East Java." *Journal of Human Evolution* 48 (2005): 321–363. Detailed historical account on the Mojokerto find.

Leinders, J. J., Fachroel Aziz, Paul Y. Sondaar, et al. "The Age of the Hominid-Bearing Deposits of Java: State of the Art." *Geologie en Mijnbouw* 64 (1985): 167–173. Revision of von Koenigswald's stratigraphy of the Pleistocene in Java.

Tobias, Phillip V. "The Life and Work of Professor Dr. G. H. R. von Koenigswald." In *Aufsaetze und Reden der Senckenbergischen Naturforschenden Gesellschaft* 34 (1984): 25–96. A thorough account of his life and work.

Watanabe, Naotune, and Darwin Kadir, eds. *Quaternary Geology of the Hominid Fossil Bearing Formations in Java.* Special Publications of the Geological Research and Development Centre 4. Jakarta: Republic of Indonesia, Ministry of Mines and Energy, Directorate General of Geology and Mineral Resources, 1985. Comprehensive account of the geology and paleontology of the Sangiran dome.

Christine Hertler

VON MUELLER, FERDINAND JAKOB HEINRICH

SEE **Mueller, Ferdinand Jakob Heinrich von**.

VRIES, HUGO DE

(*b.* Haarlem, Netherlands, 16 February 1848; *d.* Lunteren, Netherlands, 21 May 1935), *plant physiology, genetics, mutation theory.* For the original article on de Vries see *DSB*, vol. 14.

After the appearance of the entry on Hugo de Vries in the *DSB*, scholars mainly focused on de Vries's work and ideas on heredity. His role in the rediscovery of the Mendelian laws in 1900 was the topic of various publica-

tions. Newly discovered letters showed that de Vries considered these laws unimportant. Because of the difference between the Mendelian laws and de Vries's ideas and experimental work in the 1890s, various scholars argued that, notwithstanding de Vries's assertion, it is improbable that he rediscovered the Mendelian laws independently. However, from a research note by de Vries from 1896 one could conclude that de Vries had already formulated those statistical laws in that year, although in the framework of his own theory of heredity. In other publications his motivations for his different research topics have been discussed and related to opinions on the significance of his mutation theory for evolution and his broader ideas on the role of science for society. A scholarly biography is still lacking.

Research Topics and Relevance for Society. Looking at de Vries's topics of research, his change from plant physiology to heredity and evolution in the 1880s is striking. Can a thread be discerned in his scientific development? An answer is that this ambitious young man, who from his early youth showed a focused interest in botany, was from the very beginning of his career not only interested in plant physiology, but also in heredity and evolution. He chose to work in physiology because a research program in plant physiology was more easily attainable for him. He was, however, also steeped in Charles Darwin's publications on evolution and heredity. When it became clearer to him how to approach the problems of heredity and when the circumstances became favorable, he did not hesitate and started to work in that field. The reason that de Vries probably wanted to leave the field of plant physiology was his collaboration with his colleague at the University of Amsterdam, the physical chemist Jacobus Hendricus van't Hoff. Aided by de Vries's work on osmosis, van't Hoff was able to formulate his theory of dilute solutions for which he and the Swede Svante Arrhenius would later receive a Nobel Prize. De Vries subsequently felt that he had to redefine the demarcation between their spheres of activity. De Vries then chose to focus on hereditary questions, because of his early interest in this field and its relevance for evolution. At first de Vries's work in heredity was mainly theoretical, but later he started a sizable experimental program, first in variability and heredity but later—through his work on mutations—also in evolution. De Vries always argued that his ideas were in accordance with the essence of Darwin's evolutionary theory.

Another explanation for the choice of his research topics is to point to their possible relevance. At that time Dutch scientists thought that science could have a civilizing influence. It could help to solve problems of society, both social and economic. According to de Vries, botany could very well serve that goal. Moreover, de Vries's

Hugo de Vries. SPL/PHOTO RESEARCHERS, INC.

ultimate aim, to be able to control mutations, was in accordance with Dutch scientists' more general idea of the "improvability" of society with the help of science.

Ideas about Heredity. In 1889 Hugo de Vries published *Intracellulare Pangenesis,* in which he formulated his ideas on heredity. From Darwin he had adopted the idea of independent hereditary particles, termed *gemmules,* which represented individual characters instead of the whole organism, and he agreed with the argument by the German zoologist August Weismann, based on his sharp distinction between germplasm and somatoplasm, that acquired characters were not hereditary.

According to de Vries's theory the visible characters of organisms depended on the properties of small invisible particles in all cells, which he called "pangenes." They were either inactive or active, and they were able to grow and multiply in both states. Their activity depended on the type of cells in which they were located. De Vries claimed that pangenes were usually inactive or latent in the germ lines, and developed their greatest activity in the

somatic lines. Differentiation of organs was because individual pangenes, or groups of pangenes, developed more strongly than others. In the nuclei of all cells all types of pangenes of the individual were present; in each organ only those pangenes that had to carry out their function would go to the cytoplasm and become active. Pangenes multiplied in the nucleus, partly in preparation for the division of the cell nucleus, and partly in order to be transported to the cytoplasm later on. Pangenes represented specific individual characters. De Vries stressed the independence of hereditary properties. Fluctuating variability resulted from varying numbers of pangenes of one kind. During successive divisions, pangenes might change their nature slightly, or even considerably. These changes were the starting points of the emergence of new varieties and species.

De Vries's high expectations of the impression these ideas would make were not fulfilled. From the reactions of his Dutch colleagues and the discussion with Weismann it was clear that the assertion that each cell contains all hereditary material was controversial, and even more the claim that characters are inherited independently of each other. De Vries felt that he had to convince his colleagues of the validity of his theory by providing experimental evidence. He felt compelled to set up an extensive research program, which resulted in the rediscovery of the Mendelian laws and the publication of the *Mutationstheorie* (1901). According to William Bateson, in the third edition of *Mendel's Principles of Heredity* of 1913, the Mendelian laws rescued de Vries's ideas on heredity. Bateson commented upon *Intracellulare Pangenesis* that "this essay is remarkable as a clear foreshadowing of that conception of unit-characters which is destined to play so large a part in the development of genetics" and so de Vries became regarded as a scientist with ideas ahead of his time.

The Rediscovery and Statistics. De Vries's work in the 1890s can be characterized as an attempt to defend his pangene theory, especially the fundamental and controversial idea that different characters have different material hereditary carriers. He started a research program that included the study of variability and hybridizations. In both cases a statistical approach began to play an important role.

In the second half of the 1880s de Vries had probably become accustomed to a statistical interpretation of the results of botanical experiments. From 1894 he regularly applied statistical methods in his publications. He argued that the Belgian statistician Adolphe Quételet and the English scientist Francis Galton had demonstrated that, when a specific trait of a group of individuals was studied, its values are distributed symmetrically around a center and that the distribution can be described by Newton's binomial or Galtonian curve. De Vries showed that this result was not only valid for human and animal traits, but also for plants. In that way such a study of fluctuating variability demonstrated that the value of a character can vary, independently of the value of other characters. The study of variability therefore supports the idea of the independence of characters. The statistical approach also proved applicable to the study of specific variability. During his investigations de Vries had observed variability which had the form of the symmetric half of a Galtonian curve. According to de Vries this phenomenon was the result of a novel "specific variability." The distribution of a character distributed according to such a curve, which he called a "half Galtonian curve," might gradually adopt the form of a symmetrical Galtonian curve and ultimately begin to display the normal fluctuating variability. His conclusion was that such a curve indicated the initial stage of the occurrence of a new character.

In 1894 de Vries started to publish about hybridization experiments. Because by hybridization a property can be transferred from one variety to another, these kinds of experiments could support the view that characters are independent and mixable. From research notes it can be concluded that already in 1896, while unaware of Gregor Mendel's work, de Vries used the laws of dominance and recessiveness of hereditary factors, their segregation in the germ cells, and their independent assortment, to explain the 75 percent–25 percent ratio in the second generation. He had discovered them by applying the "1:2:1 law," as he called it, which law he knew through Quételet. This was the already longer known law of the probabilities to draw two white balls (¼), two black balls (¼), or one white and one black ball (½) from an urn containing equal numbers of black and white balls.

It is obvious from the correspondence between de Vries and his colleague and friend Jan Willem Moll that during the period of the "rediscovery" he did not pay much attention to Mendel, because he was engaged in the composition of *Die Mutationstheorie*. Only eight months after the "rediscovery" did de Vries refer to Mendel for the first time. By then the Mendelian laws were generally recognized as important. In the early part of 1900, de Vries felt that the Mendelian laws were a rather unimportant sideline of his work. He never seemed impressed by Mendel's theory at all.

In *Die Mutationstheorie*, in his attempts to describe Mendelian crossings in terms of pangenes and mutations, de Vries became entangled in a number of contradictions. He tried to identify a pair of Mendelian factors, one recessive and one dominant, with a pair of identical pangenes, one in the latent and one in the active state (see the picture of the lecture plate). Because the pair of concepts

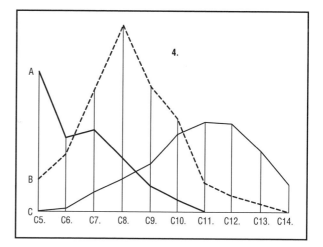

Figure 1. Curves of the number of flower petals of specimens of *Ranunculus bulbosus*, raised in 1891 after three years of selection of the plants with the greatest number of petals. A. Half Galtonian curve of the number of petals of all 126 plants. Most flowers still have five petals, as in the original situation. B. Symmetrical Galtonian curve of the number of flower petals of the offspring of twelve specimens with nine or more petals. C. Symmetrical Galtonian curve of the number of flower petals the offspring of the single specimen with the most petals.

dominant-recessive denotes a relation while the pair active-latent does not, the two pairs of properties of hereditary characters can not, however, be identified with each other. De Vries did not, however, admit that. Some of his remarks convey the impression that he was aware that the Mendelian laws on the one hand and his theories of pangenes and mutations on the other hand could not be brought in line.

SUPPLEMENTARY BIBLIOGRAPHY

WORKS BY DE VRIES

Intracellulare Pangenesis. Jena, Germany: G. Fischer, 1889. Translated by C. Stuart Gager as *Intracellular Pangenesis: Including a Paper on Fertilization and Hybridization.* Chicago: Open Court, 1910.

Die Mutationstheorie: Versuche und Beobachtungen über die Entstehung von Arten im Pflanzenreich. Leipzig, Germany: Veit, 1901. Translated by J. B. Farmer and A. D. Darbishire as *The Mutation Theory: Experiments and Observations on the Origin of Species in the Vegetable Kingdom.* 2 vols. Chicago: Open Court, 1909–1910.

OTHER SOURCES

Bateson, William. *Mendel's Principles of Heredity.* Cambridge, U.K.: Cambridge University Press, 1913.

Bowler, Peter J. "Hugo de Vries and Thomas Hunt Morgan: The Mutation Theory and the Spirit of Darwinism." *Annals of Science* 35 (1978): 55–73.

Campbell, Margaret. "Did de Vries Discover the Law of Segregation Independently?" *Annals of Science* 37 (1980): 639–655.

Darden, Lindley. "Reasoning in Scientific Change: Charles Darwin, Hugo de Vries, and the Discovery of Segregation." *Studies in the History and Philosophy of Science* 7 (1976): 127–169.

————. "Hugo de Vries's Lecture Plates and the Discovery of Segregation." *Annals of Science* 42 (1985): 233–242.

"Hugo de Vries 1848–1998." Special Issue, *Acta Botanica Neerlandica* 47 (1998): 405–507. In English.

Kottler, Malcolm J. "Hugo de Vries and the Rediscovery of Mendel's Laws." *Annals of Science* 36 (1979): 517–538.

Meijer, Onno G. "Hugo de Vries No Mendelian?" *Annals of Science* 42 (1985): 189–232.

Pas, Peter W. van der. "Hugo de Vries and Gregor Mendel." *Folia Mendeliana* 11 (1976): 3–16.

Stamhuis, Ida H. "The 'Rediscovery' of Mendel's Laws Was Not Important to Hugo de Vries (1849–1935): Evidence from His Letters to Jan Willem Moll (1851–1933)." *Folia Mendeliana* 30 (1997): 13–30.

————. "The Reactions on Hugo de Vries's *Intracellular Pangenesis;* The Discussion with August Weismann." *Journal of the History of Biology* 36 (2003): 119–152.

————. "Hugo de Vries's Transitions in Research Interest and Method." In *A Cultural History of Heredity III: 19th and Early 20th Centuries.* Preprint 294 of the Max Planck Institute for the History of Science, 2005. Available from http://www.mpiwg-berlin.mpg.de/en/research/preprints.html.

Stamhuis, Ida H., Onno G. Meijer, and Erik J. A. Zevenhuizen. "Hugo de Vries on Heredity, 1889–1903: Statistics, Mendelian Laws, Pangenes, Mutations." *Isis* 90 (1999): 238–267.

Theunissen, Bert. "Closing the Door on Hugo de Vries' Mendelism." *Annals of Science* 51 (1994): 225–248.

————. "Knowledge Is Power: Hugo de Vries on Science, Heredity and Social Progress." *British Journal for the History of Science* 27 (1994): 291–311.

Visser, Rob P. W. "Hugo de Vries (1848–1935): Het begin van de experimentele botanie in Nederland." In *Een brandpunt van geleerdheid in de hoofdstad: De Universiteit van Amsterdam rond 1900 in vijftien portretten,* edited by J. C. H. Blom. Amsterdam: Amsterdam University Press, 1992.

Zevenhuizen, Erik J. A. *De Wereld van Hugo de Vries.* Amsterdam: University of Amsterdam, 1996. The inventory of the archive of Hugo de Vries. In Dutch with English summary.

————. "Keeping and Scrapping: The Story of a Mendelian Lecture Plate of Hugo de Vries." *Annals of Science* 57 (2000): 329–352.

Ida H. Stamhuis

VYGOTSKY, LEV SEMYONOVICH

(*b.* Orsha, Russia, 5 November 1896, *d.* Moscow, Soviet Union, 11 June 1934), *psychology, education, psycholinguistics, psychoneurology.*

Vygotsky was virtually unknown in the Western world until the first translations of his writings appeared in English (e.g., Vygotsky, 1961, 1962, 1963). He then quickly gained recognition as an original thinker whose views were important for psychology and education. His so-called cultural-historical theory was influential in the creation of the new field of cultural psychology. His views on mental testing led to the new field of dynamic assessment, and his views on the relationship between education and mental development were implemented in many instructional programs and theories. His ideas about the development and function of inner speech found their way into psycholinguistics. Finally, his criticism of existing theories about the localization of mental functions in the brain was used to create the new discipline of psychoneurology.

Biography. Vygotsky grew up in pre-revolutionary Russia in Gomel, Belorussia, as the second child in a Jewish family of eight children. His parents stimulated the children's interest in the belles-lettres, and prose, poetry, and theater remained Vygotsky's passion throughout his life. Having finished the gymnasium in Gomel, Vygotsky moved to Moscow to study law at Moscow State University. At the same time, he studied a broad curriculum of courses in the humanities, plus psychology, at the unofficial Shanyavsky University. During his university years Vygotsky missed no opportunity to attend the performances at Alexander Tairov's Chamber Theater and Konstantin Stanislavsky's Art Theater. Stanislavsky's and Edward Gordon Craig's staging of Shakespeare's *Hamlet* (December 1911–March 1914) deeply impressed Vygotsky and influenced his own analysis of *Hamlet,* which was accepted as a master's thesis at Shanyavsky University in the summer of 1917. As a student Vygotsky also wrote literary reviews for newspapers, a practice that he continued when he returned to Gomel after the October Revolution.

During the civil war, when Gomel was intermittently occupied by German, White, and Red troops, Vygotsky earned his living by giving private lessons. In 1920, he secured a job as an official responsible for the cultural life of the town. In that capacity, he contracted theater groups, delivered popular talks, organized poetry readings, and so on. He also began teaching literature and other subjects at various schools. Around this time Vygotsky became interested in the way the formal properties of a text evoke aesthetic experiences in the reader. This led him to renew his study of psychology and to conduct some empirical investigations.

In 1924, Vygotsky received an invitation to work as a psychologist at Moscow University under the Marxist Konstantin Kornilov. Vygotsky's doctoral dissertation, "The Psychology of Art" (1925), was based on a reworking of his master's thesis on *Hamlet* and on his thinking about literary form, but he soon demonstrated that his interests were much broader. Vygotsky began working at various clinics as a clinical psychologist with mentally disturbed and physically handicapped children; he taught at various institutes and universities, worked for publishing houses, became the editor of scientific journals, supervised doctoral dissertations, and wrote hundreds of papers and books. He quickly became a prominent figure in Soviet psychology—one of the new young professors committed to the Marxist cause—and was acquainted with such high officials as the minister of education, Anatoliy Lunacharsky, and Lenin's wife, Nadezhda Krupskaya, deputy to Lunacharsky.

In the spring of 1934, after ten years of frenetic activity as a psychologist, Vygotsky suffered a major attack of tuberculosis, the disease that had haunted him for the better part of his adult life, and he died at the age of thirty-seven, leaving a wife and two daughters. For reasons that defy rational explanation, his theories soon fell into political disgrace, and for decades it was impossible to refer to his writings. It was only with the republication in the late 1950s of some of his writings that his work became available once again. Still later these were translated from Russian into English, which unexpectedly led to Vygotsky's sudden popularity in the Western world.

Cultural Psychology. In the late 1920s, Vygotsky developed his cultural-historical theory of the higher mental functions. In this theory he made a distinction between lower mental functions, which are innate and which humans share with kindred animals, and higher mental functions, which are based on the mastery of cultural tools. For example, both chimpanzees and human beings have memory for locations, objects, and so on. This is a lower mental function. But only humans have memory based on the cultural tools of language and literacy. In order to remember things, they can categorize them, write down a list, and form an intention—all acts that are heavily language-based. The same holds true for other mental functions such as vision.

What Vygotsky claimed, then, was that the specifically human mental processes are based upon the acquisition of cultural tools that were invented in the history of humankind. This viewpoint led him to explore how children's cognitive functioning changes as they master the cultural tools of their culture. Vygotsky also drew the logical conclusion from his theory that the cognition of people from different cultures may be fundamentally different, and he was among the first to investigate the

thinking of non-Western people. His finding that the people living in Uzbekistan categorized and thought in a different way (Luria, 1976) has been repeatedly confirmed in subsequent investigations with other populations (Scribner and Cole, 1981). Vygotsky drew the conclusion that it may be misleading to investigate the mental functioning of people from other (sub)cultures with tests that have been validated for a certain (i.e., affluent, Western) population.

In the late twentieth century, an increasing number of psychologists came to accept Vygotsky's ideas, and the new field of cultural psychology, the study of the culture's role in the mental life of human beings, emerged (Cole, 1996). For example, researchers may investigate whether the invention of the personal computer and word processing programs (both examples of modern cultural tools) changed the style of writing, or whether becoming literate makes one better at reasoning tasks (Scribner and Cole, 1981). One of the outcomes of such research is that modern psychological literature, previously largely based on data found in experiments with Western adolescents, with the assumption that they were universal, has come to pay much more attention to cultural variations in behavior and cognitive processes.

Dynamic Assessment. Although Vygotsky was skeptical about the use of mental tests, he thought they could be of diagnostic value if used in a proper way. In the early 1930s, he linked up with existing international research and advocated the dual testing of intelligence. In his view, the traditional IQ measurement does not yield enough information. A traditional IQ test measures what a child can do independently, the skills and knowledge the child has mastered. However, it is more revealing to test the child another time, to give him or her prompts and hints, and then to see to what extent he or she is able to profit from this assistance. Vygotsky predicted that some children would be able to profit from help much more than others and that these children would develop faster in the near future. The difference between independent test scores and assisted test scores indicates what Vygotsky called the child's *zone of proximal development*.

Vygotsky saw the dual-testing procedure as a means to fine-tune school instruction to the individual child's abilities, but in the Soviet Union the massive use of mental tests in schools proved rather short-lived; on the basis of their test scores, too many children from various minorities were referred to special schools. The authorities decided not to improve the tests but to prohibit their use. When Vygotsky's writings became available in the West, the idea of dual testing struck a cord with psychologists working with learning-disabled children. Various researchers began developing dual tests, taking into

Lev Semenovich Vygotsky. ARCHIVES OF THE HISTORY OF
AMERICAN PSYCHOLOGY - THE UNIVERSITY OF AKRON.
REPRODUCED BY PERMISSION.

account contemporary demands for standardization and
methodological rigor.

These investigations led to the new subdiscipline of
dynamic testing (Sternberg and Grigorenko, 2002).
Although in the early 2000s much remained to be done to
improve the quality of research, a few preliminary conclusions could be drawn. First, Vygotsky's hunch that a dual-
testing procedure may be more informative than the
traditional single-testing procedure seems valid. Children
who score approximately the same on traditional IQ tests
differ in their ability to profit from assistance. In different
investigations the researchers have distinguished those
who gain much from help and those who gain little. It is
thought that the first group may be simply culturally
deprived, whereas the second group may have organic
problems. There is also evidence that school results can be
predicted better on the basis of the dual-testing procedure
than on the basis of the old static IQ test. Second, if the
above proves true, the dual-testing procedure may be
fairer to the individual child. For example, children who
are able to profit from assistance may be offered enrichment programs that may enable them to attend regular
schools rather than special ones (Van der Veer, 2007).

Education. One reason why Vygotsky insisted that children should be tested twice was that he believed that
instruction co-determines cognitive development. In his
opinion, teachers should offer a level of instruction that is
slightly beyond the child's level of individual performance
but still lies within his or her zone of proximal development. That is, teachers should not wait until the child is
supposedly ready for certain tasks but should offer problems that the child can solve only in cooperation with a
more able peer or adult. Stimulated by these problems and
the assistance offered, the child will realize the next phase
in his or her cognitive development.

Vygotsky believed that instruction in elementary
school leads the child to reflect on his or her own mental
operations and to use them deliberately and efficiently.
His favorite example was that of learning to write a letter.
Letter writing requires the child to spell out information
that the recipient may not have. One cannot write "When
I stood there he laughed at me," because the words "there"
and "he" have no specific meaning outside the context—
hence the need to carefully consider what the recipient
needs to know. The writing of a letter also requires a conscious plan. In these respects letter writing is different
from oral speech, but Vygotsky believed that training in
letter writing led children to speak more deliberately and
efficiently as well. Just like learning mathematical rules
ideally makes one a more deliberate and efficient calculator, exercise in letter writing should make one a more
deliberate and efficient speaker.

At secondary school Vygotsky recommended the
teaching of what he called *scientific concepts*. Scientific
concepts form a system that covers the essential relationships in a certain domain of knowledge. Scientific concepts should be distinguished from the *everyday concepts*
that the child acquires independently or in interaction
with peers and parents. For example, the child's everyday
concept of a king may focus on the king's clothes and his
supposed power. Likewise, the child's everyday concept of
a farmer may concern his appearance and the fact that he
has cute animals. The scientific concept of a king would
involve knowledge about different monarchies and other
forms of government. The scientific concept of a farmer
would involve such interconnected notions as turnover,
demand, supply, costs, profit, and market. Characteristic
of scientific concepts is not only that they cover the non-
accidental, genuine aspects of reality, but also that they
form a systemic, interconnected whole. Vygotsky believed
that everyday and scientific concepts should enrich each
other (the everyday concepts giving body and flesh to the
abstract scientific concepts), but he attached a leading role
to the scientific concepts. Ideally, the mastery of scientific
concepts should lead to a scientific way of thinking that
spreads to the child's everyday thinking.

Vygotsky's global ideas have inspired many researchers to develop new instructional programs. A typical approach is to introduce children to the core concepts (*scientific concepts*) and essential relationships within a knowledge domain with the help of graphs and symbols that graphically depict them. The children are then taught to use these graphs and symbols independently as cultural tools that guide their thinking process. Often, the researchers link up to Vygotsky's idea that cognitive development relies to a considerable extent on the child's interaction with more able peers and adults, stressing the importance of extensive classroom discussion. However, it is difficult to give general characterizations, because current Vygotsky-inspired educational investigations may differ widely (Kozulin, 2003; Moll, 1990).

Psycholinguistics. Strange as it may sound, Vygotsky considered language (or "speech," in his terminology) to be the most fundamental cultural tool. The original function of speech is communication between persons, but fairly soon speech begins to serve intrapersonal goals. Take the example of a toddler who must learn to cross the street safely. In a first stage, the parent will tell the child to watch to the right and to the left, and the child will just follow these instructions. In other words, the child's behavior is regulated or guided by the speech of the social other. In the next stage, the child will tell himself aloud to watch the left and the right and thus will effectively instruct himself how to behave properly. This may be termed a form of external self-regulation of one's behavior (Wertsch, 1985). In the last stage, the child will merely think the instructions. In other words, the child has shifted to internal self-regulation of his behavior. It is important to note that in this development may be distinguished two transitions, so to speak: the transition from social behavior to individual behavior, and the transition from outer to inner behavior. One can speak of a transition from social behavior to individual behavior, because a process that was originally shared between two persons, an interpsychological process, has turned into an individual, intrapsychological process. The child is applying to himself what first was applied to him by others and has thereby mastered his own behavior through the use of speech. One can speak of a transition from outer to inner behavior, because gradually external, audible speech is replaced by inner speech or thinking. Vygotsky's claim that speech develops in an interpersonal situation and subsequently is used to steer the self received additional support through his discussion of the phenomenon of *egocentric speech*. Jean Piaget first described the phenomenon of children who during play speak to themselves in a way that is often not intelligible to others. Piaget hypothesized that such speech is unintelligible because young children are unable to take the other's point of view, that is, they

are egocentric. Only gradually do children learn to replace their egocentric speech by social speech.

Vygotsky criticized Piaget's contention and carried out several little experiments to refute Piaget's views. Vygotsky noted, for example, that egocentric speech is absent or greatly reduced when the child is alone or surrounded by deaf children. This suggests that egocentric speech is meant as social communication. Vygotsky observed that the incidence of egocentric speech rises when the child is confronted with unexpected problems. This suggests that egocentric speech has some function in the solution of problems. Finally, Vygotsky noticed that egocentric speech becomes *less* intelligible as children grow older. From these results Vygotsky drew the conclusion that so-called egocentric speech originates in normal, communicative speech and branches off at a later stage; has as its function to steer the child's behavior when the need arises; and becomes less and less intelligible for the outsider until it has become proper inner speech. According to Vygotsky, then, egocentric speech is an intermediary stage between normal, communicative speech and inner speech. Like communicative speech, it is audible, and like inner speech, it serves to guide the child's thinking. Vygotsky's arguments have inspired an enormous and still growing amount of research that cannot be summarized here. A useful overview of some trends can be found in Zivin (1979).

Psychoneurology. Throughout his scientific career, Vygotsky worked as a clinical psychologist with patients with mental disabilities and physical handicaps. Over the years, he and his collaborator Alexander Luria became increasingly interested in the brain organization of mental processes. To deepen their insight, both Vygotsky and Luria (being professors of psychology) began studying medicine at the Medical Faculty of the Psychoneurological Institute in Kharkov in 1931. At the time, the brain was considered a static structure, but Vygotsky came to believe that the brain is a flexible, dynamic system. In the words of Oliver Sacks, one of the elaborators of Vygotsky's ideas: "We need a new view of the brain, a sense of it not as programmed and static, but rather as dynamic and active, a supremely efficient adaptive system geared for evolution and change, ceaselessly adapting to the needs of the organism" (1995, p. xvii).

The outlines of such a dynamic and systemic view were sketched by Vygotsky in the early 1930s. He argued that the brain organization of mental processes must be different in children and adults, and that mental processes are handled not by strictly localized centers but by brain systems. Take the case of an infant handling a doll. The handling will simultaneously stimulate the brain centers for smell, touch, and vision. Because of this simultaneous stimulation, these different parts will grow connections and form a circuit or system. As the child grows older, he will also learn the word "doll," which means that the system will grow an additional link to the brain parts responsible for language. Thus, one and the same activity will lead to different activation patterns in the brain, depending on the age of the subject. This is the dynamic part of Vygotsky's view. But the brain parts also hang together as a system, which often makes compensation possible. For example, when vision is damaged and the subject cannot produce the name of an object by looking, smell or touch can often do the work. Hence, different trajectories or connections within a system can compensate for each other. Vygotsky discussed the case of patients suffering from Parkinson's disease (1997, p. 105). Such patients may no longer be able to initiate voluntary movements such as walking. But they can walk by stepping on pieces of paper laid on the floor. Sacks (1982, p. 316) describes another Parkinson patient who could only begin walking by shouting "Now!" at herself. In Vygotsky's analysis, the point is that walking again becomes possible, because the patients use external signs to influence their own behavior. The patient as it were influences himself from the outside when some inner connection has gone awry. "The Parkinsonian patient establishes a connection between different parts of his brain through a sign, influencing himself from the periphery," said Vygotsky (1997, p. 106). In a way, then, the patient may be resorting to an ontogenetically prior *modus operandi*, that of external self-regulation.

Such intriguing observations and insights were elaborated after Vygotsky's death by Luria. He and his collaborators investigated countless patients with brain lesions and devised compensatory means for patients with severe disturbances. Together they developed the new discipline of neuropsychology of which Sacks became one of the main proponents. Vygotsky's original ideas may have been rather global and oversimplified, but he was one of the first to see that the brain is a flexible, dynamic system that is crucially influenced by the cultural tools one masters, notably language (Luria, 1961).

Boring (1950) observed that historical recognition of the importance of a thinker depends in part on the successors of that thinker who defend and elaborate his or her theory. In the early 2000s Vygotsky acquired such successors in the West. An early 2000s' inventory ranked him among the one hundred most eminent psychologists of the twentieth century (Haggbloom et al., 2002). Such an assessment must mean that twenty-first century researchers felt inspired by Vygotsky's approach and believed that the issues Vygotsky addressed remain topical. In other words, Vygotsky belonged to the small group of researchers in the history of psychology who really mattered.

BIBLIOGRAPHY

In English, the most complete bibliography of Vygotsky's writings can be found in Van der Veer and Valsiner, 1991, cited below. The six volumes of The Collected Works of L.S. Vygotsky, *published by Plenum Publishers, provide a good idea of Vygotsky's theories but are not complete. Omitted are, among other things, the early writings on literature and art and several psychological monographs.*

WORKS BY VYGOTSKY

"Thought and Speech." In *Psycholinguistics*, edited by Sol Saporta. New York: Holt, Rinehart & Winston, 1961.

With Alexander R. Luria *The Role of Speech in the Regulation of Normal and Abnormal Behavior*. Oxford: Pergamon Press, 1961.

Thought and Language. Cambridge, MA: MIT Press, 1962.

"The Problem of Learning and Mental Development at School Age." In *Educational Psychology in the USSR*, edited by Brian Simon and Joan Simon. London: Routledge & Kegan Paul, 1963.

With Alexander R. Luria. *Cognitive Development: Its Cultural and Social Foundations*. Cambridge, MA: Harvard University Press, 1976.

Rieber, Robert W., ed. *The Collected Works of L. S. Vygotsky*. 6 vols. New York: Plenum Press, 1987–1999.

"On Psychological Systems." In *The Collected Works of L. S. Vygotsky*. Vol. 3: *Problems of the Theory and History of Psychology*, edited by Robert W. Rieber and Jeffrey Wollock. New York: Plenum Press, 1997.

OTHER SOURCES

Boring, Edwin G. A *History of Experimental Psychology*. New York: Appleton-Century-Crofts, 1950.

Cole, Michael. *Cultural Psychology: A Once and Future Discipline*, Cambridge, MA: The Belknap Press of Harvard University Press, 1996. Interesting overview of the field of cultural psychology.

Haggbloom, Steven J., Renee Warnick, Jason E Warnick, et al. "The 100 Most Eminent Psychologists of the 20th Century." *Review of General Psychology* 6 (2002): 139–152.

Kozulin, Alex. *Vygotsky's Psychology: A Biography of Ideas*. New York: Harvester Wheatsheaf, 1990. Excellent presentation and interpretation of Vygotsky's major ideas.

Kozulin, Alex, Boris Gindis, Vladimir S. Ageyev, and Suzanne M. Miller, eds. *Vygotsky's Educational Theory in Cultural Context*. Cambridge, U.K.: Cambridge University Press, 2003.

Lloyd, Peter, and Charles Fernyhough, eds. *Lev Vygotsky: Critical Assessments*. 4 vols. London: Routledge, 1999.

Moll, Luis, ed. *Vygotsky and Education: Instructional Implications of Sociohistorical Psychology*. New York: Cambridge University Press, 1990.

Sacks, Oliver. *Awakenings*. London: Picador, 1982.

———. *An Anthropologist on Mars: Seven Paradoxical Tales*. New York: Alfred A. Knopf, 1995.

Scribner, Sylvia, and Michael Cole. *The Psychology of Literacy*. Cambridge, MA: Harvard University Press, 1981.

Sternberg, Robert J., and Elena L. Grigorenko. *Dynamic Testing.* New York: Cambridge Unversity Press, 2002.

Van der Veer, René. "Vygotsky's Educational Thinking." In *Biographical Encyclopedia of Educational Thought.* Vol. X, edited by Richard Bailey. London and New York: Continuum Publishers, 2007.

Van der Veer, René, and Jaan Valsiner. *Understanding Vygotsky: A Quest for Synthesis.* Oxford, U.K.: Blackwell, 1991. The most comprehensive historical analysis of the development of Vygotsky's theories.

Wertsch, James V. *Vygotsky and the Social Formation of Mind.* Cambridge, MA: Harvard University Press, 1985. In-depth analysis of Vygotsky's work with the focus on his psycholinguistic ideas.

Zivin, Gail, ed. *The Development of Self-Regulation through Private Speech.* New York: John Wiley, 1979.

René van der Veer

W

■

WADATI, KIYOO (*b.* Nagoya, Japan, 8 September 1902; *d.* Tokyo, Japan, 5 January 1995), *seismology, Wadati-Benioff zone, ground subsidence.*

Wadati is known as a seismologist who presented convincing evidence of the occurrence of earthquakes deeper than 300 kilometers (186 miles). He identified the intermediate and deep earthquake zone dipping away from oceanic trenches, now known as the Wadati-Benioff zone, thus establishing the basis of the plate tectonics hypothesis.

Early Life. Wadati's grandfather was the fifth mayor of Sendai City, and president of local banks in the Tohoku district. His father died when Wadati was twenty years old and his brother died at the age of twenty-six. His wife predeceased him by several decades. In 1925 Wadati graduated from the Institute of Physics, Imperial University of Tokyo. After graduation, he was engaged in the observation of earthquakes at the Central Meteorological Observatory, where he discovered deep earthquakes.

Presentation of Convincing Evidence of Deep Earthquakes. In seismology, P waves are the primary, compressional waves, which travel fastest through the earth; S waves are the secondary, transverse waves. Shock waves are measured in at least three different locations to accurately determine the hypocenter of an earthquake. Arrival time refers to the arrival of the waves at the measuring stations. In 1928, in central Honshū (the largest of Japan's four main islands), Wadati compared the consecutive curves of supposedly equal "S minus P" waves (showing the difference between the arrival time of S and P waves) and equal arrival time of P waves for the North Tazima earthquake, which occurred on 23 May 1925, and for the earthquake of 15 January 1927. The centers of the curves for both earthquakes were close to one another, so their epicenters must have been close. However, for the former earthquake the distances to the consecutive curves were less than those for the latter earthquake, while "S minus P" at the epicenter was about 10 seconds for the former and nearly 35 seconds for the latter. Based on the travel-time curves of a hypothetical (S-P) curve, he showed that the former earthquake took place at a depth of 30 kilometers (19 miles) and the latter was at a depth greater than 300 kilometers (186 miles).

The distribution of seismic intensity was different for the 1925 and 1927 earthquakes. For the former it was greatest near the epicenter and decreased gradually outward. For the latter, intensity II in the scale of the Central Meteorological Observatory (corresponding to IV on the Medvedev-Sponheuer-Karnik, or MSK scale) was noted not only near the epicenter, but also in the areas of northeast Honshū facing the Pacific Ocean.

A seismogram of the latter showed distinct P and S wave arrivals, and very short durations of pulsation, compared with that of the former. The period of the latter seismic waves was comparatively short, showing very rapid oscillations even when the distance from the epicenter was great. The usual dominant coda of surface waves following the P and S arrivals was not observed,

Wadati determined the hypocenters of twelve earthquakes deeper than 300 kilometers (186 miles) between 1924 and 1927, and showed that they occurred in a deep earthquake zone traversing central Honshū. In addition to that, he insisted that the destructive earthquakes in 1891, 1909, 1923, 1925, and 1927 took place in the same zone.

Discovery of the Wadati-Benioff Zone. Wadati compiled the data for these deep earthquakes and showed their geographical distribution in 1929 and 1931, and summarized them in 1935, demonstrating that most of the deep earthquakes occurred along the Traversing and Soya deep-focus earthquake zones. The former zone extended more than 2,000 kilometers (1,243 miles) from Vladivostok to the Bonin Islands, traversing central Honshū. The latter one ran northeastward along the Kuril Islands (Chishima Retto), extending from the northern part of the Sea of Japan through the Strait of Soya. In addition to those zones, the Kyūshū deep-focus earthquake zone was revealed near the Ryukyu Islands, extending to northern Kyūshū (the southernmost of the four main islands of Japan).

Based on the depth of the hypocenters of those earthquakes, Wadati drew the lines of equal focal depth for intermediate and deep earthquakes, and showed the inclined intermediate and deep earthquake zone dipping away from the oceanic trench toward the Asiatic continent northwestward and the Philippine Sea westward. A similar zone was suggested under Kyūshū and its southern extension. Similar intermediate-deep earthquake zones were found in South America by S. W. Visser in 1936, and in the Philippines and Indonesian archipelagoes by Hendrik Petrus Berlage (1937). (Victor) Hugo Benioff (1954) showed the inclined intermediate-deep earthquake zone from the trench toward the surrounding continent in each area in the circum-Pacific region, based on the data presented by Beno Gutenberg and Charles Francis Richter (1953). He supposed the plane to be reverse faults, following Eduard Suess's idea. Thus the intermediate-deep earthquake zone has been called the Wadati-Benioff zone after its discoverers.

Prehistory of the Discovery of Deep Earthquakes. Prior to the 1920s, earthquakes were supposed to occur at a depth shallower than 30 to 40 kilometers (19 to 25 miles), and the earth was supposed to be statically stable below a depth of 120 kilometers (75 miles) or so, based on the isostasy hypothesis. In 1922, while editing the International Seismological Summary, Herbert Hall Turner recognized an earthquake with a wave that arrived at the distant stations one minute or more earlier than the expected time calculated from the arrival time at nearby stations. He insisted that it must be due to a deep earthquake, but the occurrence of deep earthquakes was not accepted, and he had no proof from actual seismograms.

Turner published a paper regarding Wadati's previously mentioned results, checking his hypocenters by the records of distant stations in 1929. Meanwhile, F. J. Scrase

(1931) and V. C. Stechshulte (1932) examined seismograms of Turner's supposed deep earthquake, and showed that his result was correct. Thus the discovery of deep earthquakes was attributed to Turner.

In Japan, Toshi Shida studied a strong earthquake that occurred on 21 January 1906, which shook seismograms over the whole globe. He concluded that the earthquake must have taken place deep in the earth, as the difference of arrival times in the Japanese islands was very small, and the arrival time was 10 seconds or more earlier, compared with those of ordinary earthquakes for observatories in foreign countries, according to the data in the International Seismological Summary. He traced the epicenter to central Honshū, but he did not publish the result, worrying about the isostasy hypothesis. A strong earthquake shook the Kansai area, in central Honshū, on 27 July 1926. Shida fixed the hypocenter near Lake Biwa, at a depth of 260 kilometers (162 miles). He read a paper on the discovery of deep earthquakes at the opening ceremony of the Beppu Geophysical Laboratory, the Imperial University of Kyoto on 28 October 1926, and the abstract was distributed to the guests and reprinted posthumously in *Geophysics,* the Japanese-language journal of geophysics of the university in 1937.

Estimation of the Magnitude of Earthquakes. In the paper describing deep earthquakes published in 1931, Wadati showed the relation between maximum amplitude and epicentral distance for thirty-one shallow earthquakes. He plotted the maximum ground motion at each station as ordinate (using a logarithmic scale) with the corresponding epicentral distances as abscissa. He pointed out that all the curves were concave upward, and their curvatures were more acute according to the size of the earthquakes. Seismograms of the shallow earthquakes showed the predominance of surface waves, and the maximum amplitudes were interpreted as being due to those waves, except at the areas near epicenters. He sought to apply this diagram to the estimation of the scale of destructive earthquakes. Richter adopted this diagram to define his magnitude scale in 1935.

Study of Ground Subsidence. Wadati was promoted to director of Osaka District Meteorological Observatory in and studied ground subsidence in Osaka. Two wells were drilled to observe ground subsidence. He pointed out the intimate relation between the subsidence and the level of ground water, and insisted that the subsidence was due to the shrinkage of mudstone in 1939 and 1940. Wadati and Takuzo Hirono (1942) developed the theory of subsidence due to consolidation of mudstone. Those studies were highly appreciated after World War II, when ground subsidence was a serious problem caused by the recovery of industries in Japan.

Education, Major Career, Honors, and Awards. Though he was seriously ill with tuberculosis while at the Central Meteorological Observatory and was placed on the retired list from 1929 to 1931, Wadati published many papers and several books on seismology from 1925 to 1935. He was promoted to director of the Central Meteorological Observatory in 1947, and to director-general of the Japan Meteorological Agency in 1956. He retired from the position because of the age limit in 1963.

Wadati was president of Saitama University from 1966 to 1972, of the Japan Academy from 1974 to 1980, and of the Japan Science Council from 1960 to 1962. He received an academy prize with an imperial gift for the discovery of deep earthquakes in 1932. He received an Order of Cultural Merits in 1985. He was an honorary member of the Seismological Society of America and the Royal Astronomical Society.

He died at age ninety-two of old age.

BIBLIOGRAPHY

WORKS BY WADATI

"On the Mohorovicic Wave Observed in Japan." *Geophysical Magazine* 1 (1927): 87–96.

"Shallow and Deep Earthquakes." *Geophysical Magazine* 1 (1928): 162–202.

With Masuda Kunimo. "On the Travel Time of Earthquake Waves (Part VI)." *Geophysical Magazine* 8 (1934): 187–194.

"On the Activity of Deep-Focus Earthquakes in the Japan Islands and Neighbourhoods." *Geophysical Magazine* 8 (1935): 305–325.

With Hirono Takuzo. "On Ground Subsidence in West Osaka (Third Report)" [in Japanese]. *Report of the Institute of Disaster Science* 6 (1942): 1–33.

OTHER SOURCES

Benioff, Hugo. "Orogenesis and Deep Crustal Structure: Additional Evidence from Seismology." *Bulletin of the Geological Society of America* 65, no. 5 (1954): 385–400.

Gutenberg, Beno, and Charles F. Richter. *Seismicity of the Earth and Associated Phenomena.* Princeton, NJ: Princeton University Press, 1949.

Hirono Takuzo. "A Tribute to the Memory of Wadati Kiyoo." *Newsletter of the Seismological Society of Japan* 6, no. 6 (1995): 35–36.

Yasumoto Suzuki

WADDINGTON, CONRAD HAL (*b.* Evesham, United Kingdom, 8 November 1905; *d.* Edinburgh, United Kingdom, 26 September 1975), *embryology, developmental biology, evolutionary biology, genetic assimilation, canalization, epigenetics, epigenetic landscape.*

The discovery in 1900 of Mendel's experiments on genetics, coupled with a burst of research on genes and genetics in the ensuing several decades revolutionized the understanding of heredity but at the cost of divorcing embryos from genetics and from heredity. Conrad Hal Waddington was one of the first scientists to integrate genetics with embryology and evolution. He performed this remarkable feat (1) by formulating and providing experimental evidence for the mechanisms of genetic assimilation and canalization; and (2) by fostering—through direct experimentation and publication of seminal textbooks—an epigenetic (multi-process) rather than a genes-only basis of embryonic development and of evolutionary change in development and adult form. Waddington coined the term epigenetics for the causal analysis of embryonic development, by which he meant all the factors acting on a cell or embryo to allow it to develop, including genetic, and internal and external environmental factors. He saw phenotype as processes, not static structures and behaviors. A foundational member of the Theoretical Biology Club, Waddington was a pioneering theoretical biologist, especially in the application of the philosophy espoused by the philosopher and metaphysician Alfred North Whitehead: "Thus my particular slant on evolution—a most unfashionable emphasis on the importance of the developing phenotype—is a fairly direct derivative from Whiteheadian-type metaphysics" (Waddington, 1975, p. 597). Epigenetic and hierarchical approaches, which Waddington saw as metaphysical, stand in contrast to the reductionist approaches typical of most geneticists.

Origins and Early Interests. Waddington had the early life typical of so many of the children of British citizens who made their living in what were then the colonies. The first three years of his life were spent on a tea plantation in India with his parents Hal and Mary Ellen before being sent back to England to live with Quaker relatives, initially an uncle and aunt on a farm in Sedgeberrow, Worcestershire. Waddington did not see his father between his fifth and fifteenth birthday and was not reunited with his parents until he was a twenty-three-year-old married Cambridge graduate. As told by Barton Worthington to Alan Robertson, both undergraduate friends—"Waddington … became remarkably bald at about the age of twenty-one and in the early part of his career this, coupled with his erudition, caused many people to think that he was much older than he actually was" (Robertson, 1977, p. 578). He was known as Con to his relatives and childhood friends, Conway to his undergraduate friends, and as Wad to his wife and professional friends.

His early fascination, acquired in Sedgeberrow, was with fossils, especially ammonites (a subclass of extinct cephalopods), which he collected from the gravel used to make paths and studied with a passion; he thought he could understand ammonite development by studying records of that development left in the forming and formed shell. His museum, a collection of biological, geological, and archaeological specimens, set the stage for a scholarship to Clifton, Sidney Sussex College, Cambridge, and a First Class Honours degree in geology. He married in the same year (1926), a marriage that produced a son, Jake, but which ended in divorce in 1936.

A well-rounded individual, Waddington was a capable runner, an enthusiastic walker and climber, and squire of the Cambridge Morris Men, which group he led on tours throughout the south and southwest of England, and for whom he collected Morris dances and folk tunes. Also a poet, he recalled,

> More interested in poetry than in science as an undergraduate, I edited and printed a magazine of poetry that had the distinction of being the first vehicle in which Christopher Isherwood, the English novelist, appeared in print. (quoted in Robertson, 1977, p. 579)

Waddington's scientific breadth and interests went beyond geology and natural history; he held an 1851 exhibition studentship in paleontology and an Arnold Gerstenberg studentship in philosophy, the latter won for an essay on the "Vitalist-Mechanist Controversy" that permeated much of the experimental embryology of the latter part of the nineteenth and first third of the twentieth centuries.

Waddington began graduate studies on the systematics of his boyhood passion, ammonites, with the intention of becoming an oil exploration geologist. However, he was diverted from paleontology into evolution and genetics, in part through a friendship with Gregory Bateson, the man who introduced genetics to England in 1900. Waddington never did finish his thesis, nor did he obtain any graduate degree, although he was awarded a Cambridge ScD in 1936 on the basis of his published work. His first four published papers illustrate the breadth of his interests as he sought a subject to devote himself to. In 1929, he published a method for recording the sizes of fossil ammonites and a paper on the genetics of germination in stocks of the genus *Matthiola*. His third paper (1930), a letter to *Nature*, was on the experimental embryology of avian embryos, and the fourth (1931)—coauthored with the polymath J. B. S. Haldane—was on genetic linkage.

Subsequently, Waddington became one of the great synthesizers of biology, although his prescience was only fully realized in the early 2000s. The British Society for Developmental Biology established the Waddington medal and Waddington Medal Lecture as its most prestigious award and the only national award in developmental biology within the United Kingdom. Most appropriately the obverse of the medal depicts an ammonite drawn by Waddington in his days as a budding paleontologist, and whose development he inferred from the fossilized remains of their shells.

Overview of His Career. Waddington spent six months of 1931 in Germany with Hans Spemann learning the techniques of experimental embryology, especially transplantation of small regions between amphibian embryos; a region of the early embryo named the organizer by Spemann and his student Hilda Mangold had been shown by them in 1924 to be responsible for inducing the formation of the nervous system and around it the entire embryonic axis. This seminal discovery demonstrated that a single region of frog embryos (the organizer) was responsible for "organizing" the entire embryo. Many of the worlds embryologists devoted themselves understanding the organizer, just as embryologists of the early twenty-first century (developmental biologists) pursue the genetic control of development. So, in the 1930s, genetics and experimental embryology replaced paleontology as Waddington began intensive investigation and experimental studies on the chemical nature of the primary organizer using amphibian embryos; Waddington received the first Albert Brachet Prize by the Royal Academy of Belgium, awarded for the best embryological research published in that year. Waddington extended his research to pioneering studies with avian and mammalian embryos at the Strangeways Research Laboratories in Cambridge, supporting himself, his first wife, and young family as a demonstrator in zoology at Cambridge and (from 1933 on) as a Fellow of Christ's College. He was the first to use organ culture methods to culture whole chick embryos, which he used to study induction of the nervous system, the first to demonstrate the presence of an organizer in mammalian embryos, and the first to use radioactive tracers to analyze development.

A fruitful collaboration with Joseph and Dorothy Needham, development of the concepts central to embryonic induction, and of the founding of The Theoretical Biology Club (whose members included the Needhams, the biologist turned philosopher Joseph Woodger, the physicist John D. Bernal, cell biologist E. Neville Willmer, and future Nobel Laureate Peter B. Medawar) characterized this period of Waddington's career.

During the 1930s, Waddington also began his close association with such emerging avant-garde painters, sculptors, and architects as Henry Moore, Barbara Hepworth, Ben Nicholson, John Piper, Sandy Calder, and Walter Gropius. Waddington's knowledge and appreciation of art was considerable; more than thirty years later he wrote his enormously ambitious analysis *Behind Appearance: A Study of the Relations between Painting and the Natural Sciences in This Century* (1969). In 1936, he married painter and architect Justin Blanco White. The two daughters from this marriage (Dusa and Caroline) and his son from his first marriage, all became academics, in mathematics, social anthropology, and physics respectively.

During World War II Waddington served in the Coastal Command. Thirty years later, based on his experience with anti-U-boat operations, he wrote *Operational Research in World War II: O. R. against the U-boat* (1973). In 1947, the year he was elected a Fellow of the Royal Society, Waddington extended his influence in genetics as chief geneticist and deputy director of an Agricultural Research Council Unit on Animal Breeding and Genetics Research, based in Edinburgh, coupled with his election to the Buchanan Chair of Genetics in the University of Edinburgh. By his fiftieth birthday in November 1955, Waddington had built the Edinburgh unit into the largest and strongest Genetics Department in the United Kingdom and one of the largest and strongest anywhere in the world.

During his career, Waddington was preoccupied with the integration of genetics, embryology (developmental biology), and evolution into an approach he called *epigenetics*. Unlike reductionism, which seeks all explanations at lower (often regarded as more fundamental) level, epigenetics takes a multi-causal approach to explanations of biological phenomena. Indeed, this is what distinguished biology from physics and chemistry— properties emerge at higher levels that could not be predicted from the properties of the lower level. Embryonic induction so long studied by Waddington is a classic example of emergent properties—the inductive influence of one region of an embryo on another region can neither be predicted from the properties of the inductive region nor from the properties of the responding region. Waddington's epigenetic approach and philosophical/mathematical background provided a natural link to his efforts to seek a theoretical foundation for biology that went beyond reductionism. Epigenetics is Waddington's most lasting legacy to development and evolution (see below). He also administered worldwide scientific activities through the International Biological Programme (IBP), as president of the International Union of Biological Sciences (IUBS), as a founding member of the Club of Rome, and by playing an instrumental role in starting journals such as *Genetical Research*. Waddington's search for a theoretical biology, fostered in the Theoretical Biology Club, were manifested in his editorship of a four-volume series entitled *Towards a Theoretical Biology* (1968–1972), the proceedings of four IUBS meetings he organized in the late 1960s and early 1970s at the Villa Serbelloni in Bellagio, Italy; a chance attendance at the IUBS general assembly in Amsterdam in July

1961 resulted in Waddington being asked by the internationally renowned developmental biologist Paul Weiss to stand for president. Waddington saw an opportunity to further his aims for theoretical and integrative biology and so accepted the invitation, and proposed a series of IUBS symposia titled "Towards a Theoretical Biology." The first biological application of catastrophe theory by René Thom appeared in this series. In all, Waddington wrote eighteen and edited nine books, published over a forty-two-year period, the last appearing posthumously in 1977. Robertson's summary of these books is that "On the whole, his books are too stimulating, too wide-ranging and too speculative to be ideal textbooks" (1977, p. 595).

The combination of embryology and genetics provided a logical outlet for Waddington's philosophical interests—embryology was emerging from the vitalist-mechanist controversies of the late 1800s—and for which Waddington had received a studentship at Cambridge. The study of embryos embodied the search for causal links between ontogeny and phylogeny; genetics provided the basis through which development was manifest. In 1965, he established an epigenetics research group in Edinburgh funded by the Medical Research Council and then an Epigenetics Laboratory with its own building, funded by the Wellcome Foundation and the Distillers Company. Waddington now had the resources to investigate development within the broad context provided by his epigenetic approach. However, the time was not ripe for launching a major thrust into epigenetics; the mood of the biological world was molecular and reductionist, not developmental and integrative. In the service of promoting a synthesis of genetics, development, and evolution, Waddington wrote no fewer than eleven books, beginning with *How Animals Develop* (1935) and ending with *New Patterns in Genetics and Development* (1962). In addition there were books on theoretical biology and other matters.

Named a Commander of the British Empire (CBE) in 1958, Waddington was elected to foreign membership in the American Academy of Arts and Sciences and the Finnish Academy, to fellowship in the Deutsche Akademie der Naturforscher Leopoldina and received honorary degrees from Université de Montreal and from universities in Prague, Geneva, Cincinnati, Aberdeen, and Trinity College Dublin. Waddington spent the year 1970–1971 in an Albert Einstein Chair in Science at the State University of New York in Buffalo, where the first signs appeared of the heart condition that would kill him on 26 September 1975, two months short of his seventieth birthday.

Development and Evolution. In 1924, the German embryologists Hans Spemann and Hilda Mangold published their seminal paper on the initiation of the nervous system by interaction between two regions of the early amphibian embryo. The early 1930s saw Waddington pursuing the chemical nature of embryonic inducers in which he made the distinctions between induction and individuation, the latter as the formation of interdependent, spatially organized units such as tissues or organs, evoked by developmental processes such as induction and individuation, which he defined as the organizing effect of the organizer, the consequence of induction. His interests during this phase were virtually entirely developmental as he sought the chemical nature of induction.

Throughout his career, Waddington was concerned with integrating embryology (development) and genetics and with linking these two subfields of biology to evolution. His developmental studies were performed on the premise that gene activity lies at the heart of embryonic development. He came to this conclusion while a Rockefeller Fellow in Thomas Hunt Morgan's laboratory at Columbia University in New York, where he initiated the first studies on organ formation in the fruit fly *Drosophila* using developmental mutants. His sensitivity to the genetic basis of development, coupled with the realization of the dynamic, organized, integrated, and channeled nature of embryonic development, led Waddington to develop the twin concepts of epigenetics and canalization, the latter being that development proceeds along channels, which once entered, are difficult to exit; cells stay on their path of differentiation. Spemann remained with experimental embryology for the rest of his career. Morgan switched from embryology to genetics and only returned to experimental embryology in post-retirement, Spemann was not concerned with evolution, Morgan placed his emphasis on the genes as the hereditary unit. Of the three only Waddington sought to integrate genes, development, and evolution.

Waddington's position was initially articulated in *Organisers and Genes* (1940) and illustrated by the later well-known analogy of the epigenetic landscape, which was depicted initially as a bifurcating valley (representing channels of development) drawn by his friend, the artist John Piper, at Waddington's fiftieth birthday party at the Genetics Institute in Edinburgh. The epigenetic landscape was represented as a pinball machine, with the ball running down valleys to produce wild type or mutant phenotypes.

His conviction that development was more than the working out of gene action led Waddington into evolutionary studies; the evolution of organisms reflects the evolution of developmental systems. Much of the motivation for Waddington's approach to evolutionary studies lay in his persistent criticism of the adequacy of population genetics to provide a realistic model of how genes really operate in development and evolution; population geneticists treated gene frequencies in populations and ignoring

any role for the embryos in which those genes nestled; they saw evolution as a property of populations; Waddington saw evolution as the working out of altered embryonic development, which only later would be reflected in changing gene frequencies in populations. The dual concepts of canalization and genetic assimilation were the platform from which Waddington launched his attacks on evolution as population genetics (Waddington, 1942).

Much of his boundless energies throughout the 1950s were devoted to documenting evidence for these two phenomena. Early twenty-first century conception of embryonic development as a highly integrated series of canalized pathways owes much to Waddington's development of the concepts that embryos could buffer themselves against environmental influences, that development followed well-defined paths, and that genetic and nongenetic factors influenced development.

Waddington was a prodigious coiner of terms and neologisms. The metaphorical epigenetic landscape became the way that most developmental biologists "saw" the organization of embryonic development. As Thom (1989) noted, a person can never be considered as the owner of an idea but words that he creates follow him through life and hopefully outlive him. Some of the terms and concepts coined by Waddington—epigenetics, epigenetic landscape, genetic assimilation, canalization—have entered general usage in development, especially in analyses of development in relation to evolution. Others, such as epigenotype, individuation, chreod, evocation, and homeorhesis (the regular and regulatory pathways of development that canalization allows) have survived the test of time less well. The concept embryonic development as controlled by heritable and epigenetic factors is Waddington's lasting legacy.

The Epigenetic Landscape and the Epigenotype. Waddington repeatedly stressed the role of the organization that links the genotype to the phenotype. With the term *epigenotype* Waddington (1939) sought to capture that linkage as the series of interrelated developmental pathways through which the genotype is manifest in the phenotype. The epigenotype encompasses all the interactions among genes and between genetic and environmental signals that produce the final phenotype, or epiphenotype. Interaction, integration, and heritability of these stable interactions are the essential elements of the epigenotype. Epigenetics and epigenotype are often used interchangeably in the early twenty-first century.

The *epigenetic landscape* is a visual analogy of the embryo, embryonic regions, or groups of cells progressing through ontogeny. In the epigenetic landscape, development is treated as a terrain with valleys serving as the developmental paths traversed by cells, which, moving through development down the valleys, may be moved up the slopes of the valley wall by potentially perturbing genetic or environmental influences but will, because of canalization, roll back down the valley wall to remain on the same developmental path or trajectory. If the influences are such that the zygote or embryonic region is pushed over the valley wall, it will come to lie within a new valley and develop along a new canalized path. Inductive and tissue interactions, altered timing of development or perturbations of growth take cells from one valley to another.

Epigenetics, by contrast, is a term and a concept that has been elusive and difficult to incorporate into models of evolutionary change, despite the perception of many that epigenetics represents an important missing element in evolutionary analyses. Waddington thought of epigenetics as the causal analysis of development and defined it as such in *The Epigenetics of Birds* (1952). While others were seeking developmental programmes based in instructions in the genome, Waddington developed a more multifactorial approach, and one of the few that attempted to provide a mechanism for how environmentally induced responses could be inherited. After that, biologists found more practical value in defining epigenetics as the sum of the genetic and non-genetic factors acting upon cells to control selectively the gene expression that produces increasing phenotypic complexity during development and evolution.

Canalization and Genetic Assimilation. Canalization was central to Waddington's thinking; the collective action of groups of genes can isolate a developmental event from perturbations arising from the action of single or small numbers of genes. Such supragenomic organizational thinking is typically Waddington. Essentially similar concepts were developed by I. Michael Lerner (1954) as genetic homeostasis and Sewall Wright (1968) as universal pleiotropy.

Canalization produces canalized characters, i.e., phenotypes whose expression is restricted within narrow boundaries. Canalizing selection eliminates genotypes that would expose the organism to environmental fluctuations or genetic variability, i.e., there is selection for some independence from destabilizing influences. Canalization has resurfaced in evolutionary studies in the concept of developmental stability (Maynard Smith et al., 1985). Canalization allows the build-up of genetic variability within the genotype, even though that variability is not expressed phenotypically. Such hidden genetic variability can be brought to light and subjected to selection through genetic assimilation.

The essence of Waddington's concept of genetic assimilation is that embryos possess the genetic capability

to respond to environmental perturbations. By means of genetic assimilation, a phenotypic character initially produced only in response to some environmental influence, by responding to the operation of selection in subsequent generation is taken over by the genotype. The character then can form even in the absence of the environmental influence that evoked it in the initial generation. In a series of papers published between 1956 and 1961, Waddington provided experimental evidence for genetic assimilation by inducing phenotypic changes (crossveinless and bithorax) in *Drosophila* exposed to a heat or ether shock and then selected for the phenotype in the absence of the environmental stimulus (see Rendel (1968) and Hall (1992) for discussions).

Often, the features produced by genetic assimilation are an environmentally-evoked copy (a phenocopy) of a suite of features known to result following a mutation, evidence used by Waddington to argue for the genetic basis of assimilated phenotypes. The time of action of an environmental agent leading to assimilation often coincides with the known time of action of the mutant gene that results in the equivalent phenotype. But genetically assimilated phenotypes are not based on a mutation. They have a polygenic basis, often involving genes on several chromosomes (Waddington, 1957). The three processes—phenocopies, genetic assimilation, and canalization—demonstrate the considerable unexpressed genetic variability that can be evoked by selection following either a mutation or an environmental stimulus.

Waddington argued that genetic assimilation could produce adaptive change in nature (1956a), citing the experiments by Piaget on the European snail *Limnaea* as a prime example (Waddington, 1975), but had to argue strenuously that there is nothing Lamarckian about genetic assimilation. Its genetic basis lies in the genetic capability of organisms to respond to environmental changes, unexpressed genetic variability, and the ability of selection to increase the frequency of individuals expressing the previously hidden genetic potential. While the initial stimulus is environmental and the initial response is phenotypic, the transgenerational result is genetic. The identification of types of epigenetic interactions and their integration with zygotic and parental genomic control in producing phenotypic change in development and evolution (phenotypes as process and pattern) are the lasting legacy of Waddington's conceptualization of the integration of genetics, development, and evolution through epigenetics.

BIBLIOGRAPHY

WORKS BY WADDINGTON

With Joseph Needham and Dorothy M. Needham. "Physico-Chemical Experiments on the Amphibian Organizer."

Proceedings of the Royal Society of London, Series B, 114 (1934): 393–422. An early study on the chemical nature of embryonic induction.

How Animals Develop. London: Allen and Unwin, 1935.

With Dorothy M. Needham. "Studies on the Nature of Amphibian Organization Centre. II. Induction by Synthetic Polycyclic Hydrocarbons." *Proceedings of the Royal Society of London,* Series B, 117 (1935): 310–317. The chemical nature of induction.

An Introduction to Modern Genetics. London: Allen and Unwin, 1939.

Organisers and Genes. Cambridge, U.K.: Cambridge University Press, 1940. The book in which the concept of epigenetics was first outlined.

"Canalization of Development and the Inheritance of Acquired Characters. "*Nature (London)* 150 (1942): 563.

The Epigenetics of Birds. New York: Cambridge University Press, 1952.

"Genetic Assimilation of the bithorax Phenotype." *Evolution* 10 (1956a): 1–13. Pioneering study on genetic assimilation.

"The Genetic Basis of the 'assimilated bithorax' Stock." *Journal of Genetics* 55 (1956b): 240–245.

The Strategy of the Genes. London: Allen and Unwin, 1957. The most complete development of Waddington's ideas.

"Inheritance of Acquired Characters." *Proceedings of the Linnaean Society of London* 169 (1958): 41–62.

"Canalisation of Development and Genetic Assimilation of Acquired Characters." *Nature (London)* 183 (1959): 1654–1655.

"Genetic Assimilation." *Advances in Genetics* 10 (1961): 257–293.

New Patterns in Genetics and Development. New York: Columbia University Press, 1962. A textbook that unified genetics and developmental biology.

ed. *Towards a Theoretical Biology,* vols. 1-4. Edinburgh: Edinburgh University Press, 1968–1972. An ambitious search for a theory for all of biology.

Behind Appearance: A Study of the Relations between Painting and the Natural Sciences in This Century. Edinburgh: Edinburgh University Press, 1969. Perhaps the best book on art by any scientist.

Operational Research in World War II: O. R. against the U-Boat. London: Elek Books, 1973. Autobiographical.

The Evolution of an Evolutionist. Ithaca and New York: Cornell University Press, 1975. What Waddington referred to as "an exposition with some autobiographical background."

OTHER SOURCES

Bard, Jonathan "Waddington's Legacy to Developmental and Theoretical Biology." In *Arriving at a Theoretical Biology: The Waddington Centennial,* edited by Manfred Laubichler, Brian K. Hall, and Gerhard B. Müller. Cambridge, MA: MIT Press (forthcoming). An expert assessment by one who knew Waddington.

Gilbert, Scott F. "Diachronic Biology Meets Evo-Devo: C. H. Waddington's Approach to Evolutionary Developmental Biology." *American Zoologist* 40 (2000): 729–737.

Hall, Brian K. "Waddington's Legacy in Development and Evolution." *American Zoologist* 32 (1992): 113–122. An overview of Waddington's contributions.

———. *Evolutionary Developmental Biology.* London: Chapman and Hall, 1992. 2nd ed., Dordrecht: Kluwer, 1999. Contains an analysis of Waddington's views in the context of epigenetics and of interactions between development and evolution.

"Baldwin and Beyond: Organic Selection and Genetic Assimilation." In *Evolution and Learning: The Baldwin Effect Reconsidered,* edited by Bruce H. Weber and David J. Depew. Cambridge, MA: MIT Press, 2003. An evaluation of genetic assimilation and the Baldwin Effect. Evaluates Waddington's position on genetic assimilation in relation to organic selection.

Lerner, I. Michael. *Genetic Homeostasis.* Edinburgh: Oliver and Boyd, Edinburgh, 1954.

Maynard Smith, John; Richard Burian; Stuart Kauffman; et al. "Developmental Constraints and Evolution." *Quarterly Review of Biology* 60 (1985): 265–287.

Palmer, A. Richard. "Symmetry Breaking and the Evolution of Development." *Science* 306 (2004): 828–833. A ground breaking paper on how to identify genetic assimilation in nature.

Polikoff, D. "C. H. Waddington and Modern Evolutionary Theory." *Evolutionary Theory* 5 (1981): 143–168. A clear and authoritative analysis.

Rendel, J. M. "Genetic Control of Developmental Processes." In *Population Biology and Evolution,* edited by Richard C. Lewontin. Syracuse: Syracuse University Press, 1968. A comprehensive review of Waddington's work.

Robertson, Alan. "Conrad Hal Waddington." *Biographical Memoirs of Fellows of the Royal Society* 23 (1977): 575–622. A detailed biography, including a list of Waddington's publications.

Saunders, P. T. "The Epigenetic Landscape and Evolution." *Biological Journal of the Linnaean Society* 39 (1990): 125–134. An overview of the impact of Waddington's metaphor on evolutionary theory.

Slack, Jonathan M. W. "C. H. Waddington—The Last Renaissance Biologist." *Nature Reviews Genetics* 3 (2002): 889–895.

Spemann, Hans. *Embryonic Development and Induction.* New Haven, CT: Yale University Press, 1938. Reprinted New York: Hafner Publishing, 1962; and New York: Garland Publishing Inc., 1988.

Spemann, Hans, and Hilde P. Mangold. "Über Induktion von Embryonalanlagen durch Implantation artfremder Organisatoren." *Wilhelm Roux Archiv für Entwicklungsmechanik* 100 (1924): 599–638.

Stern, Claudio D. "Conrad H. Waddington's Contributions to Avian and Mammalian Development, 1930–1940." In "Developmental Biology in Britain," edited by James C. Smith. Special Issue, *International Journal of Developmental Biology* 44, no. 1 (2000): 15–22. Evaluation of Waddington's experimental embryology by a leading authority.

Thom, R. "An Inventory of Waddingtonian Concepts." In *Theoretical Biology. Epigenetic and Evolutionary Order from*

Complex Systems, edited by Brian Goodwin and Peter Saunders. Edinburgh: Edinburgh University Press, 1969. A thoughtful commentary from the then leading theoretical biologist.

Van Speybroeck, Linda. "From Epigenesis to Epigenetics: The Case of C. H. Waddington." *Annals of the New York Academy of Sciences* 981 (2002): 61–81.

Wilkins, Adam S. "Canalization: A Molecular Genetic Perspective." *BioEssays* 19 (1997): 257–262. An in-depth analysis of Waddington's concept of canalization from the genetic point of view.

Wright, Sewall. *Evolution and the Genetics of Populations,* vol. 1. Chicago: The University of Chicago Press, 1968.

Yoxen, Edward. "Form and Strategy in Biology: Reflections on the Career of C. H. Waddington." In *A History of Embryology*, edited by Tim J. Horder, Jan A. Witkowski, and Christopher C. Wylie. Cambridge, U.K.: Cambridge University Press, 1986.

Brian K. Hall

WADIA, DARASHAW NOSHER-WAN

(*b.* Surat, Bombay State, India, 23 October 1883; *d.* New Delhi, India, 15 June 1969), *geology (stratigraphy, tectonics, paleontology, economic geology).*

Wadia is regarded as India's most important geologist. He made major contributions to the understanding of Himalayan tectonics and to the administration of science and technology in India. His range extended from immensely strenuous field mapping, to stratigraphy, paleontology and soil science, and to problems in economic and engineering geology. He was an important administrator for the identification and exploitation of India's mineral resources, including petroleum and uranium. He was also involved in geophysics and oceanography and wrote on Pleistocene geology. His influence as a teacher and author was very considerable.

Early Life. The future geologist was born to Nosherwan and Cooverbai Wadia, the fourth child of a family of nine. Their Parsee family had commercial, engineering, and industrial interests in Bombay and Surat that went back to the shipbuilding days of the East India Company in the eighteenth century. His father was a stationmaster for the Bombay, Baroda, and Central Indian Railway.

Wadia was educated at schools in Surat and then at Baroda High School, whence he proceeded at sixteen to Baroda College, where he studied botany, zoology, and geology. He became a fellow of the college upon graduation and in 1907 was appointed a geology professor at the Prince of Wales College in Jammu. In his fourteen years there, he explored the geology of the Himalayan foothills,

collecting materials for teaching and finding the elephant-like fossil *Stegodon ganesa* in the Siwalik beds near Jammu. Lacking a suitable textbook, he wrote *Geology of India for Students* (1919). It was later revised and expanded as *Geology of India* (1939), which became a standard text on Indian geology until the 1960s.

Career. In 1921 Wadia joined the Geological Survey of India and began his arduous systematic mapping of Kashmir and Punjab, especially around Nanga Parbat. This led to his basic publications on Himalayan geology in the late 1920s and early 1930s and lectures on the results of his mapping at the Survey headquarters in Calcutta (now Kolkata) and at Calcutta University. He was a founder of the Geological Society of India (founded 1958), later serving as president. Having reached the survey's retirement age in 1938 without the promotions that might have been his due (it was still British India), Wadia was appointed government mineralogist in Ceylon (now Sri Lanka). There he promoted a systematic geological survey of the island, with emphasis on its economic resources. In 1942 he was president of the Indian Science Congress's meeting in Baroda and urged the establishment of the Indian Academy of Social Sciences; and he was again president in 1943. He was also active in founding the Ceylon Association of Science in 1944.

Returning to India in 1945, Wadia served as minerals advisor to the Indian government and on the Board of Scientific and Industrial Research. He urged that the country should, after independence, support science and technology rather than turn away from them in Gandhian fashion. He advised on the need for a proper assessment of India's mineral resources and in 1947 was appointed first director of the Indian Bureau of Mines. In that post he drafted legislation to regulate the mineral and mining industries. From 1949 he worked for the Atomic Minerals Commission, overseeing searches for radioactive minerals; several uranium deposits were discovered and exploited as a result of these efforts. He also supported the more general expansion of Indian mining and metallurgy and became chief Indian representative at various international meetings such as the Commonwealth Mineral Conferences (1946 and 1948), the Empire Mining and Metallurgical Congress (1953), a United Nations Conference on Atomic Energy (1955), and several international geological congresses, including the ill-fated one of 1968 in Prague, where he performed the opening ceremony before the meeting that had to be terminated due to political/military disturbances. Besides his industrial interests, Wadia contributed to studies in soil science, the study of arid regions, glaciation, geophysical research, and oceanography. In addition, he worked to encourage scientific and technical education and founded the Indian

Institute of Himalayan Geology (now the Wadia Institute of Himalayan Geology) in 1968.

In his later career Wadia became the international leader for India in a wide range of matters to do with Earth sciences. He held important positions in Indian learned societies and presided at the Twenty-second International Geological Congress in New Delhi in 1964. His awards, both national and international, were numerous and included the Geological Society's Lyell Medal (1943) and a Fellowship of the Royal Society (1957). A commemorative postage stamp, bearing his portrait, was issued in 1984.

Survey of the Himalayas. When Wadia started work in the western Himalayas (chiefly in what is now Pakistan), pioneering surveying had already been done there for the Indian Survey by the English stratigrapher Charles Middlemiss. Wadia greatly extended this work, and published his initial results in 1928. On the basis of his examination of areas around the Kashmir Valley and the valleys of the upper reaches of the Indus River and its tributaries, he proposed a stratigraphic succession for the region, from Precambrian (Purana Group) to Pleistocene. It appeared that in northwestern Kashmir there was a major thrust fault (the Panjal Thrust) underlying the Pir Panjal Mountains between Srinagar and Jammu, with the Kashmir Nappe, containing rocks from Precambrian to Triassic, overlying. A second major thrust fault (the Murree Thrust, dipping more steeply than the almost-horizontal Panjal Thrust) was also revealed farther south, below which lay the Murree Series (Miocene), which mantled the underlying foreland rocks. Between the two faults was a belt of folded "autochthonous" rocks (Carboniferous to Eocene). Thus it appeared that the Himalayas had been thrust over the lower-lying rocks to the south, because older rocks lay over the younger ones as a result of thrust faulting.

Wadia then turned his attention to the region around the great mountain of Nanga Parbat and northward, in western Jammu Province, publishing his findings in 1931. He had not been able to ascend the mountain and had to prepare his own topographic maps but he was able to report that the Nanga Parbat massif consisted of gneisses intruded by granite. To the south were Precambrian metamorphics of the Salkhala series and an intermediate zone where these two main units were intermingled in a zone of great tectonic complexity. Also there were intruded basic igneous rocks that had eroded out to form the upper Indus Valley. The form of the main ranges was remarkable: to the west of Nanga Parbat the mountains ranged northwest to southeast; to the north they ranged east to west; and to the west they trended north-northeast to south-southwest. It was as if Nanga Parbat were a kind of knot in the structure. That is, the Himalayas formed a knee bend (or *syntaxis* in the terminology of Eduard Suess) around the "peg," as Wadia called it, of Nanga Parbat.

Previously, Suess had envisaged that this syntaxis was the result of the formation of two separate mountain systems (the Himalayas and the Hindu Kush), which converged north of Nanga Parbat. But Wadia showed that the aforementioned thrust planes, folds, and analogous stratigraphic successions all looped round the mountain's massif, so that the structure must somehow have formed as a whole. He hypothesized that the rising and south-thrusting Himalayan chain had encountered an obstacle in the form of the Nanga Parbat, which was an outlying bloc of the Archean Shield rocks of Peninsula India. Later, in 1936, he proposed an analogous structure for the curve of the eastern Himalayas around the mountain of Namcha Barwa (Namuchabawashan), Tibet, near the great bend in the Brahmaputra River, and their extension into Yunnan and Burma (now Myanmar).

There could, however, be two explanations of such phenomena (or perhaps a combination of the two): the younger rocks of the Himalayas could have been thrust over the resistant foreland of Peninsula India; or (if one were a "continental drifter") one could envisage Peninsula India breaking away from the supercontinent Gondwanaland and drifting northeastward, eventually colliding with the main mass of Asia and penetrating into and under it. The latter interpretation was preferred by "drifters" such as Frank B. Taylor and Alex L. du Toit, and was eventually adopted. Wadia's fieldwork provided du Toit with the necessary supporting evidence. Thus, Wadia's heroic efforts, in extremely difficult country, with his mapmaking based on modern lithological and paleontological criteria, provided crucial evidence in favor of the major breakthrough in geological theory of the twentieth century: the hypothesis of continental drift, leading on to plate tectonics.

Wadia has been described as wiry, healthy, and able to accomplish 20-mile traverses on foot over trackless and mountainous terrain, taking lunch as his first meal of the day. He was austere, quiet, and genial, did not have hobbies other than reading, and in the early twenty-first century would have been called a workaholic. He was one of the great contributors to independent India and is appropriately revered by his compatriots.

BIBLIOGRAPHY

Wadia's scientific bibliography is provided by Cyril J. Stubblefield, "Darashaw Nosherwan Wadia, 1883–1969," in Biographical Memoirs of Fellows of the Royal Society *16 (1970): 543–562.*

WORKS BY WADIA

Geology of India for Students. London: Macmillan, 1919. Revised as *Geology of India* (London: Macmillan, 1939).

"Geology of the Poonch State (Kashmir) and Adjacent Portions of the Punjab." *Records of the Geological Survey of India* 51 (1928): 185–370.

"The Syntaxis of the North-West Himalaya: Its Rocks, Tectonics, and Orogeny." *Records of the Geological Survey of India* 65 (1931): 189–220.

"Notes on the Geology of Nanga Parbat (Mt. Diamir) and Adjoining Portions of Chilas, Gilgit District, Kashmir." *Records of the Geological Survey of India* 66 (1932): 212–234.

"The Trend-Line of the Himalaya—Its North-West and South-East Limits." *Himalayan Journal* 8 (1936): 63–69.

OTHER SOURCES

"D. N. Wadia: A Biographical Sketch." *Journal of the Palaeontological Society of India* 2 (1957): 2–8.

Mahanti, Subodh. "Darashaw Nosherwan Wadia: Pioneer of Geological Investigations in India." Available from http://www.vigyanprasar.gov.in/scientists/DNWadia.html.

Stubblefield, Cyril J. "Darashaw Nosherwan Wadia, 1883–1969." *Biographical Memoirs of Fellows of the Royal Society* 16 (1970): 543–562.

Thakur, Vikram C. "Research Contributions of D. N. Wadia." *Resonance: Journal of Science Education* 8 (2003): 65–75.

West, William D. "D. N. Wadia—An Appreciation." In *Dr. D. N. Wadia Commemorative Volume,* edited by A. G. Jhingran. Calcutta, India: Geological and Metallurgical Institute of India, 1965.

David Oldroyd

WAGNER, MORITZ

WAGNER, MORITZ (*b.* Bayreuth, Bavaria, 3 October 1813, *d.* Munich, Germany, 30 May 1887), *geography, natural history, biogeography, evolution.*

Wagner is best known for his "law of migration," which he introduced in 1868 as a complement to Darwin's theory of natural selection and then developed increasingly as an alternative to it. A long-time travel writer and geographer and the first curator of the Bavarian state ethnography collection, Wagner formed a bridge between the early-nineteenth-century geographical style of Alexander von Humboldt and the "modern" German geography developed in the last quarter of the century by Friedrich Ratzel and Ferdinand Freiherr von Richthofen.

Early Years and Natural History Travel. Moritz Wagner was the second son among six children of an impoverished but independent-minded secondary school (gymnasium) professor, Lorenz Heinrich Wagner. He left school at the age of fifteen to work in trade. His early interests in botany and zoology were encouraged by his older brother Rudolf, the professor of zoology at the University of Erlangen (later at Göttingen), with whom he studied.

Without receiving a degree, Moritz Wagner turned to journalism, a profession that allowed him to study natural history while traveling. From 1836 to 1838 he reported on the French wars in Algeria as a correspondent to several German periodicals owned by Cotta, a major German publishing house; concurrently he studied Algerian natural history and collected specimens. His observations resulted in his first book, *Reisen in der Regentschaft Algier in den Jahren 1836, 1837, und 1838* (1841). The scientific part of this work earned Wagner an honorary degree at the University of Erlangen (probably through the intervention of his brother)—the only university degree he would ever receive.

Wagner continued working as a travel writer, reporting to Cotta's magazines from southern Russia, the Caucasus, Armenia, and Persia in the early 1840s and publishing travel writings that included both political and natural historical observations. In the later 1840s he worked in his homeland, reporting on German revolutionary activities as a newspaper correspondent. Disappointed by the failure of the revolutions, he spent the 1852–1855 period traveling across North and Central America with a Viennese friend, Karl Scherzer (later an Austrian diplomat), returning with a massive natural history collection. For their coauthored book on Costa Rica, Wagner wrote mainly on natural history and the possibility of colonization; the work became the leading source of knowledge about this country in Germany. Between 1857 and 1859 Wagner undertook a second trip to Central America, this time under the aegis of the Bavarian government.

The results of these trips, published as magazine articles and then as travel books, combined observations about people, politics, land (including both geological and geographical features), botany, and zoology, in the style made popular by Alexander von Humboldt. Wagner also published in the more scholarly geographical journal *Petermanns Mittheilungen.* His works contained important observations: For example, he was the first European to report on the source of the western Euphrates River in Armenia and to offer a detailed map of the Isthmus of Panama, speculating in 1861 on the possibility of building a canal there. His observations about the lands, resources, and native peoples he encountered were generally made with an eye to possible German emigration, in line with the concerns of the Bavarian king Maximilian II about Bavaria's overpopulation.

First Curator of Ethnography in Bavaria. Wagner expected his travel experiences and collections to net him an academic position in Bavaria upon his return in 1859, but he was disappointed. A Protestant in a Catholic land, a traveler and collector whose style of natural history seemed antiquated to scientists seeking to modernize academia, and a scholar whose only university degree was honorary, Wagner had credentials that were unsuited to a university professorship (despite his election to the Leopoldina, a leading scientific society, in 1860). Instead, in 1862 he became the founding curator of the state ethnography collections and received the title of honorary professor at the University of Munich and extraordinary membership in the Bavarian Academy of Sciences—positions he would hold for the rest of his life. As curator, he organized previously scattered ethnographic collections and newly collected material into a unified collection, separate from other areas of natural history. But his chief research interest remained the geographical distribution of plants, animals, and humans, on which subject he gave regular university lectures.

Biogeographical Theory. The appearance of Darwin's *On the Origin of Species* in 1859 led Wagner to view his many accumulated biogeographical observations in a new way. On 3 March 1868 Wagner introduced his "law of migration" in a lecture to the Bavarian Academy of Sciences, expanding it into a pamphlet soon thereafter. Wagner accepted evolution, but in his view, Darwin's theory was incomplete, for natural selection required two causal elements underappreciated by Darwin: migration and geographical isolation. Wagner argued that natural selection could not operate within a species' primary distribution area. Organisms pressed the outer edges of their range to avoid competition; if a small group of pioneers migrated beyond the limits of the original population area, they were subjected to a changed environment that would increase their variability and provide the material upon which selection could work. If the "emigrant" population was geographically continuous with the original population, its new variations would be swamped by those of the larger group. But if the emigrants became geographically isolated from the original one, Wagner thought, they could found a new stable variety, and eventually a new species. Wagner came to call this his "separation theory" of evolution.

As he developed his theory over the 1870s and 1880s, Wagner grew increasingly hostile to Darwin's theory, soon according selection itself a relatively minor role in the process of evolution and giving a much more prominent role to Lamarckian factors attendant on migration and isolation. This drew the ire of both species fixists, who disagreed with his evolutionism, and adherents to Darwinian selectionism such as August Weismann, with whom he exchanged polemics in the 1870s. By the time Wagner took his own life in 1889, despondent over his poor health and the unfriendly reception of his life's work, his separation theory had little stock among his contemporaries. He could hardly have imagined that his ideas would be revived by evolutionary biogeographers such as David

Starr Jordan in the early twentieth century and would yet again become a central topic of controversy among the architects of the evolutionary synthesis (especially Ernst Mayr and Theodosius Dobzhansky) in the 1930s, 1940s, and 1950s.

Despite the general opposition of German Darwinists, Wagner's ideas about migration gained a powerful adherent in his student Friedrich Ratzel, who developed Wagner's primary concept of the need for space as the cause of migration into the doctrine of the "Lebensraum," which claimed that every species, including humans, naturally sought to expand its territory to reduce competition. This doctrine, which Ratzel placed at the base of his "anthropogeography," was essential to Ratzel's influential revival of geography in the context of German colonialism. It would eventually be employed by Nazi ideologues as a "natural" justification for the imperial expansion of the German "race." Wagner, a democrat who theorized (1886) that racial mixing was a natural consequence of migration and the human incest taboo, limited only in recent human history by cultural selection based on factors such as class and religion, would have been appalled.

BIBLIOGRAPHY

As of 2007, no unified archive of Wagner's papers exists. The largest publicly available extant collection of letters is at the Deutsches Literaturarchiv, Marbach, which mainly comprises his correspondence with the Cotta Publishing House. Wagner wrote many articles for magazines and newspapers, some of which are listed in Smolka (below). A complete bibliography is not available.

WORKS BY WAGNER

Reisen in der Regentschaft Algier in den Jahren 1836, 1837, und 1838. 3 vols. Leipzig, Germany: Voss, 1841.

Der Kaukasus und das Land der Kosaken in den Jahren 1843–1846. 2 vols. Dresden and Leipzig, Germany: Arnoldi, 1848; 2nd ed., 1850.

Reise nach dem Ararat und dem Hochland Armenien. Stuttgart, Germany: Tübingen, 1848.

Reise nach Kolchis und nach den deutschen Colonien jenseits des Kaukasus: Mit Beiträgen zur Völkerkunde und Naturgeschichte Transkaukasiens. Leipzig, Germany: Arnoldi, 1850.

Reise nach Persien und dem Lande der Kurden. Leipzig: Arnoldi, 1852.

With Karl Scherzer. *Reisen in Nordamerika in 1852 und 1853.* Leipzig, Germany: Arnoldi, 1854.

With Karl Scherzer. *Die Republik Costa Rica in Central-Amerika mit besonderer Berücksichtigung der Naturverhältnisse und der Frage der deutschen Auswanderung und Colonisation: Reisestudien und Skizzen aus den Jahren 1853 und 1854.* Leipzig, Germany: Arnoldi, 1856.

Travels in Persia, Georgia, and Koordistan: With sketches of the Cossacks and the Caucasus. London: Hurst and Blackett, 1856.

Beiträge zu einer physisch-geographischehen Skizze des Isthmus von Panama. Petermanns Geographische Mitteilung, Ergänzungsheft 1, H. 5. Gotha, Germany: Perthes, 1861.

Die Darwinsche Theorie und das Migrationsgesetz der Organismen. Leipzig, Germany: Duncker & Humblot, 1868.

"Über die hydrographischen Verhältnisse und das Vorkommen der Süßwasserfische in den Staaten Panama und Ecuador: Ein Beitrag zur Zoogeographie Amerika's." *Abhandlungen der königlich bayerischen Akademie der Wissenschaften, Mathematisch-Physikalische Classe* 10 (1870): 63–113.

"Die Kulturzüchtung des Menschen gegenüber der Naturzüchtung im Tierreich." *Kosmos* 10, Heft 18 (1886): 19–34; reprinted in *Die Entstehung der Arten durch räumliche Sonderung* (see below), pp. 519–539.

Die Enstehung der Arten durch räumliche Sonderung: Gesammelte Aufsätze von Moriz Wagner, edited by Moriz Wagner. Basel: Benno Schwabe, 1889. Contains Wagner's most important theoretical essays on migration and geographical isolation, beginning with his 1868 "Migrationsgesetz," as well as a biographical sketch and commentary by the editor, the biogeographer's nephew who shared his name.

OTHER SOURCES

Mayr, Ernst. "Darwin and Isolation." In his *Idem, Evolution and the Diversity of Life: Selected Essays.* Cambridge, MA: Harvard/Belknap, 1976. As much about Wagner as about Darwin.

Ratzel, Friedrich. "Moritz Wagner." In his *Allgemeine Deutsche Biographie,* vol. 40. Leipzig, Germany: Duncker & Humblot, 1896.

Scherzer, Karl von. "Biographische Skizze." In *Die Entstehung der Arten durch räumliche Sonderung: Gesammelte Aufsätze von Moriz Wagner,* edited by Moriz Wagner. Basel: Benno Schwabe, 1889.

Smolka, Wolfgang J. *Völkerkunde in München. Voraussetzungen, Möglichkeiten und Entwicklungslinien ihrer Institutionalisierung (ca. 1850–1933).* Berlin: Duncker & Humblot, 1994. The leading modern source on Wagner, emphasizing his relationship to the development of ethnology. Includes a full bibliography of older secondary sources and archival materials.

Sulloway, Frank J. "Geographic Isolation in Darwin's Thinking: The Vicissitudes of a Crucial Idea." *Studies in History of Biology* 3 (1979): 23–65. Addresses Wagner's debate with Darwin.

Lynn K. Nyhart

WALD, GEORGE

WALD, GEORGE (*b.* New York, New York, 18 November 1906; *d.* Cambridge, Massachusetts, 12 April 1997), *biochemistry of vision, photoreception, retinol (vitamin A), color vision.*

Wald made crucial contributions to the study of vision and, in so doing, provided a molecular basis for photoreception research in the twentieth century. In the early 1930s, Wald found a derivative of vitamin A in the retina of the eye. This allowed him to assign, for the first time, a functional role in the body for a fat-soluble vitamin. Wald went on to biochemically analyze the light-sensitive pigments that reside in the rods and cones of the eye. By the 1950s Wald and his colleagues had described, in molecular terms, how a visual pigment reacts to light. It is this light reaction that "triggers" the molecular events that lead to photoreceptor excitation and vision. In recognition of these fundamental discoveries, Wald was awarded the Nobel Prize in Physiology or Medicine in 1967.

Wald was a highly regarded teacher at Harvard University for forty-three years, retiring in 1977 as Higgins Professor of Biology. He taught biochemistry, photobiology, and an introductory biology course that earned him a 1966 citation in *Time* magazine as "one of the ten best teachers in the country" (unsigned article, 6 May 1966). A scientist of broad intellectual interests, Wald wrote and taught on topics ranging from the origin of life to the evolution of consciousness. From the mid-1960s until the time of his death, Wald devoted much of his time to social activism. He traveled widely and spoke out eloquently against the U.S. war in Vietnam, nuclear power and weaponry, and violations of human rights.

Early Years and Education. George Wald was the youngest of three children of immigrant parents. His father, Isaac Wald, a tailor, was from a village near Przemyśl in what was then Austrian Poland. His mother, Ernestine Rosenmann, came from a village near Munich, Bavaria. Wald grew up in Brooklyn, New York, and attended Manual Training High School (now Brooklyn Technical High School). He showed aptitude and interest in mechanical things and science, especially electricity, from an early age. Wald also had a lively wit and flair for the dramatic, and he created a vaudeville act that he and a friend performed at local Jewish community centers.

The first member of his family to attend college, Wald received a bachelor of science degree from Washington Square College of New York University (NYU) in 1927. He had started at NYU as a prelaw student, but eventually decided "law was an artificial, manmade thing and I needed to be able to get into something more substantial, more organic" (Hubbard and Wald, 1999, p. 6). Wald switched to premed studies, but became disenchanted with the idea of caring for patients and attracted to the pursuit of scientific research after reading Sinclair Lewis's *Arrowsmith.* After NYU, Wald entered Columbia University as a graduate student in zoology.

In his first year at Columbia, Wald took a genetics course with Thomas H. Morgan, whose work to establish chromosomes as the carriers of genetic material would win him a Nobel Prize in 1932. But Wald was more taken with the biophysics professor he met his first year: Selig Hecht, a leader in the field of visual physiology and a man of vigorous personality and considerable culture. Wald joined Hecht's laboratory as his graduate student and research assistant, and Hecht became for him a mentor, father figure, and lifelong role model. Hecht's laboratory was, for Wald, a stimulating place where conversation was devoted each day not just to science but to topics in art, literature, music, and politics. Wald, when he later joined the faculty of Harvard University, would foster such an intellectually lively atmosphere in his own laboratory.

Hecht was engaged in analyzing photoreception (the detection, absorption, and use of light) in organisms ranging from the relatively simple *Ciona* (sea squirt) and *Mya* (soft-shell clam) to humans. Hecht investigated dark adaptation, brightness discrimination, the visual threshold, and other physiological aspects of vision. For his doctoral research, Wald studied visual acuity in the fruit fly *Drosophila*. To do so, Wald glued two microscope slides together to make a narrow glass track for the fly to walk in. He then projected stripes of various widths along the track and measured the limits of visual acuity in the dark-adapted fly, because when a fly saw two stripes merge into a continuum, it would stop dead. Wald enjoyed conceptualizing and even building his experimental apparatus, an interest that did not wane throughout his scientific career.

Hecht's generalized theory of photoreception would guide Wald toward his postgraduate studies. Hecht in 1920 had postulated that a photosensitive substance S in the retina is decomposed by light into the precursor products P and A (light adaptation). In the dark, P and A combine to reform S (dark adaptation) (Hecht, 1920, p. 112). After completing his graduate work in 1932, Wald left Hecht's laboratory "with a great desire to lay hands on the molecules for which these were symbols" (Wald, 1967a, p. 292). This desire led him to the laboratories of three different past or future Nobel Prize winners within the space of several months, supported by a fellowship from the U.S. National Research Council. Wald was accompanied by his wife, Frances Kingsley Wald, whom he married in 1931.

The Role of Vitamin A in the Retina. The first laboratory he went to visit was that of biochemist Otto Warburg in Berlin. Since the mid-1920s, Warburg had been using spectrophotometry to identify an enzyme (now called cytochrome oxidase) involved in cellular respiration. In spectrophotometry, light is passed through a solution of interest in order to differentiate the solution's components by their characteristic pattern of absorbing some wavelengths and transmitting others. For this work, Warburg had received the Nobel Prize the year before Wald joined his laboratory.

Wald learned how to extract retinas in Warburg's laboratory, and initially tried experiments on retinal respiration both in the dark and the light. But he was more interested in Hecht's "S" substance. A light-sensitive pigment had been discovered in frog retinas in 1876 by Franz Boll. Boll and Willy Kühne, a professor of physiology at Heidelberg, soon after showed that the visual pigment is reddish-purple in dark-adapted retinas (visual purple) but when exposed to light it "bleaches" to a yellowish-orange color (visual yellow) and then fades over time to a colorless substance (visual white). Kühne also extracted visual purple (which Boll had named rhodopsin) into aqueous solution with bile salts and showed it was a protein.

In Warburg's laboratory, Wald hypothesized that rhodopsin was a carotenoid pigment, akin to the pigments responsible for phototropism in plants (the tendency to be attracted to light). Reading the literature, Wald found that the carotenoids, when mixed with antimony chloride, turn bright blue. So Wald isolated some frog retinas, shook them with chloroform, and mixed the extract with an antimony chloride solution. The extracts turned blue and, when analyzed spectrophotometrically, showed an absorption band characteristic of vitamin A (at wavelength 320 nanometers). The "vitamins were still deeply mysterious, and at that time one hardly expected them to participate directly in physiological processes" (Wald, 1967a, p. 293). Yet when Wald read further, he found literature linking vitamin A deprivation to night blindness, an abnormal insensitivity to light. This condition could be cured by administering cod-liver oil, which was known to contain vitamin A.

After Wald found vitamin A in the eye, Warburg suggested he go to the laboratory of Paul Karrer, an organic chemist in Zürich, to confirm his result. Karrer had just described in 1930 and 1931 the structural formulas of β-carotene, a carotenoid found in plants that animals can convert to vitamin A, and of vitamin A itself. By showing that vitamin A is one-half of a carotene molecule with a hydrogen and a hydroxyl (OH) attached to the broken end, Karrer had given the first description of the chemical structure of any provitamin or vitamin. Wald and his wife collected thousands of eyes from sheep, pigs, and cattle at slaughterhouses. They then isolated the retinas and extracted them with fat solvents. With Karrer, they confirmed that the retinas yielded vitamin A (Wald, 1935).

The Discovery of Retinal. Wald then went to Heidelberg and the laboratory of Otto Meyerhof, a distinguished physiologist and an expert in muscle biochemistry. While there, Wald extracted three hundred frog retinas and analyzed them. It was then that he discovered a previously unknown yellow carotenoid, similar to vitamin A but with a different absorption spectrum, present in dark-adapted

George Wald. *George Wald receives the 1967 Nobel Prize in Medicine from King Gustav Adolf of Sweden at the Stockholm Concert Hall, 10 December 1967.* HULTON ARCHIVE/GETTY IMAGES.

retinas and in retinas bleached to the visual yellow stage. He named this substance retinene (now called retinal). As the visual yellow continued to fade to the visual white stage, the retinal disappeared and in its place, Wald found vitamin A. Wald had here succeeded in identifying some of the molecules in Hecht's conception of the visual process. The visual pigment rhodopsin (S), which contains retinal bound to a protein, is decomposed by light into products P (a protein) and A (retinal). Retinal is then converted to vitamin A, and vitamin A somehow reconstitutes rhodopsin. (Retinal itself can also combine with protein to form rhodopsin.) Because some vitamin A is lost during this cycle, it must be replenished through dietary consumption of plant carotenoids (Wald, 1936a).

By that time, the summer of 1933, the Nazis had come to power in Germany and the National Research Council insisted that Wald, who was Jewish, must return to the United States. Wald continued his fellowship at the University of Chicago and, in 1934, he accepted a position as tutor in biochemical sciences at Harvard University. Wald would remain at Harvard for the rest of his academic career, becoming professor of biology in 1948

and retiring in 1977. Wald, also in 1934, began a long association with the Marine Biological Laboratory (MBL) in Woods Hole, Massachusetts, where Selig Hecht had carried out his *Mya* and *Ciona* studies and had brought Wald as his student in 1929. Wald returned to Woods Hole almost every summer for the rest of his life, becoming an instructor in the MBL's famous Physiology Course in 1947 and serving as a trustee of the laboratory for thirty-four years during the period 1948 to 1997.

In Woods Hole, Wald confirmed in several marine fishes the cycle of rhodopsin–retinal–vitamin A–rhodopsin that he had observed in the frog (Wald, 1936b). However, he was puzzled by an 1896 finding by two German biologists, Else Köttgen and Georg Abelsdorff, that the visual pigment of fishes was a darker purple than the rhodopsin of frogs and mammals. Looking into that, he discovered in freshwater fishes a new visual pigment, which he called porphyropsin, that engaged in a cycle like rhodopsin but in which different carotenoids took the place of retinal and vitamin A (Wald, 1939). Saltwater fishes, on the other hand, had rhodopsin. That raised the question: What visual pigment would be found in euryhaline fishes, which migrate back and forth between freshwater and saltwater? Wald determined that they possess either the visual system that goes with the fish's spawning environment, or a mixture of both systems, with the one that goes with its spawning environment predominating (Wald, 1941). This intriguing result led Wald to larger questions on biochemical changes during vertebrate metamorphosis, the evolution of visual systems, and the origin of life. He took special pleasure in exploring these kinds of relationships for the rest of his life (Wald, 1957, 1958b, 1964b).

Thus far, Wald had studied the visual pigments found in the rods of the eye, which mediate vision in dim light. In the mid-1930s he set out to find a visual pigment in the cones, which are the receptors of daylight vision and color vision. From chicken retinas, which contain primarily cones, Wald extracted two photosensitive pigments: rhodopsin and a new, more violet one, which he called iodopsin (Wald, 1937). He was unable to separate the two pigments, though, so could not confirm whether iodopsin, like rhodopsin, yields retinal and vitamin A when bleached by light. Nor was he able to differentiate the proteins present in each pigment, as protein chemistry at this time was in its infancy. It was not until the mid-1950s that Wald and his coworkers were able to synthesize visual pigments and thereby show that iodopsin does, in fact, bleach to retinene and vitamin A. This implied that the rod and cone pigments differ only in the proteins—by then called opsins—with which the carotenoid combines (Wald, Brown, and Smith, 1955).

The Trigger of Vision. World War II interrupted Wald's work on the chemistry of visual pigments, which distressed him. "Those who think that war stimulates scientific research are not scientists," he wrote in a 1953 review article. War

> may stimulate technology. All the organized projects, the money and material poured into them, the committees and conferences, succeed mainly in obscuring the fact that little of scientific importance is being accomplished. One of our problems is to keep these conditions from continuing throughout the peace. (Wald, 1953, p. 497)

During the war, Wald worked at Harvard under contract for the U.S. Army Board of Engineers and the Office of Naval Research, studying the limits of human vision in the infrared range as well as chromatic aberration of the human lens.

After the war, he resumed his study of visual pigments with a new group of graduate students. One was Ruth Hubbard, who would perform distinguished research and in 1973 become a tenured biology professor at Harvard. Wald's first marriage ended in divorce, and he and Hubbard married in 1958. Another person who played an important role in the laboratory was Paul K. Brown, who became Wald's research assistant in 1946 and remained for more than forty years. Brown never finished college, but he had exceptional scientific skill and insight. He designed and built equipment for the laboratory, coauthored numerous papers, and lectured on vision in Harvard's graduate course in photobiology.

Wald's laboratory leaped forward in analyzing visual pigments after R. A. Morton and his colleagues in Liverpool, in 1946, showed that retinal is the aldehyde form of vitamin A. This enabled Wald's group to obtain ample amounts of retinal by purchasing and oxidizing vitamin A. A few years later, Hubbard and Wald described the enzymatic interconversion of retinal and vitamin A, and the following year Brown synthesized rhodopsin by simply mixing retinal and the opsin protein in the dark (Wald and Hubbard, 1949; Wald and Brown, 1950).

For Wald, the central question of his research was how the visual pigment acts in photoreception: how it interacts with light to trigger the neural excitation that leads to vision. Wald's group was aware of a 1944 result by Leonard Zechmeister showing that light, along with an iodine catalyst, can induce carotenoid molecules to assume different geometrical shapes, called *cis-trans* isomers. In the *cis* form of the isomer, the carotenoid molecule is bent around one or more of its carbon double bonds, while in the *trans* form, it is straight.

Hubbard showed that, when illuminated, retinal yielded rhodopsin when mixed with opsin, and it did so

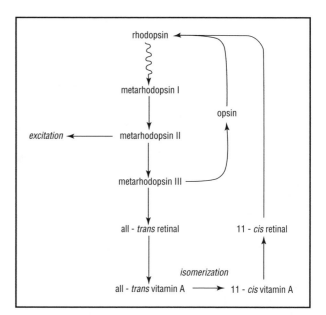

Figure 1. *Scheme of the sequence of events that occurs following the absorption of a quantum of light by the rod visual pigment, rhodopsin. Light initiates the conversion of rhodopsin to retinal and opsin through a series of metarhodopsin intermediates. Metarhodopsin II is the active intermediate leading to excitation of the photorecrptor cell. Eventually, the chromophore of rhodopsin, retinal, separates from the protein opsin and is reduced to vitamin A (retinol). For the resynthesis of rhodopsin, the vitamin A must be isomerized from the all-trans to the 11-cis from, and this isomerization takes place in the pigment epithelium overlying the receptors. Vitamin A is replenished in the eye from the blood.*

with or without an iodine catalyst. This led Hubbard and Wald to express the rhodopsin visual cycle in terms of a *cis-trans* isomerization cycle. Rhodopsin, in the dark-adapted eye, contains retinal in a bent, *cis* form plus opsin. Upon the absorption of light, the *cis*-retinal straightens out to the all-*trans* form, which is then reduced to all-*trans* vitamin A. In order for rhodopsin to be resynthesized, as a first step the vitamin A must be re-isomerized from the all-*trans* form back to the bent, *cis* form (Wald and Hubbard, 1952).

Working with several organic chemists, Wald, Hubbard, and Brown then showed that only one *cis* shape of retinal—the 11-*cis* isomer—combines with opsin to form rhodopsin. This shape, the 11-*cis* isomer, is the precursor to all visual pigments. (They found that another isomer, the 9-*cis* isomer, can form a photosensitive pigment with opsin, which they called isorhodopsin, but this pigment is less light sensitive than rhodopsin and is not ordinarily found in the eye.)

By 1958, Hubbard and Allen Kropf had shown in Wald's laboratory that the only action of light in vision is to isomerize the retinal from the 11-*cis* to the all-*trans* configuration. All other changes are "dark" consequences of this one light reaction. The 11-*cis*-retinal thus is the chromophore in visual pigments: it is the molecule that absorbs light, which results in the molecular changes that eventually cause excitation of the photoreceptor cells (Hubbard and Kropf, 1958). This trigger of vision is found in all animals.

But exactly when and how does visual excitation occur? Wald's group made important contributions to answering these questions. By bringing rhodopsin to very low temperatures and then warming it slowly in the dark, Wald and Tōru Yoshizawa were able to identify several intermediate stages between the time the rhodopsin chromophore absorbs light and the time it is released as all-*trans*-retinal (Yoshizawa and Wald, 1963a). These intermediate stages represent conformational changes in the opsin, and one of these stages, metarhodopsin II, leads to excitation of the photoreceptor.

Wald also provided a prescient conceptual framework for how visual excitation might occur. Selig Hecht and coworkers had shown in the late 1930s that absorption of a single photon is enough to stimulate a rod, which implies that just one molecule of rhodopsin needs to be activated. How could this one isomerization trigger such a large response as light perception? Wald, in 1965, proposed that when a molecule of rhodopsin absorbs light, it sets off a cascade of enzymatic reactions, similar to what happens in blood clotting, that lead to excitation of the photoreceptor cells (Wald, 1965). As was shown by several laboratories in the mid-1980s, this is indeed what happens in the cyclic-GMP cascade of vision, as reported in Lubert Stryer's 1986 article.

Color Vision and Social Activism. In the 1960s, Wald's research focused on human color vision, a topic that had long intrigued him. It had been known for more than a century that normal color vision involves three independent variables. So, presumably, there would be three types of cones. Wald and Brown determined that there are, indeed, three types of cones in human and monkey retinas, with each type absorbing light predominantly in the red, blue, or green parts of the visible spectrum. Crucial to this work was the design of a microspectrophotometer, which Brown built, that allowed them to measure the difference spectra (the changes in absorbance) of the visual pigment in single rods and cones. Brown and Wald went on to show that each of the three cone pigments has an 11-*cis*-retinal chromophore, and thus it must be differences in their opsins that tune the pigments to absorb different wavelengths of light (Wald and Brown, 1963b; Wald and Brown, 1964a; Wald, 1964b).

Wald's laboratory made another contribution with the discovery, by John Dowling, that retinoic acid (an acid corresponding to vitamin A) can substitute for all functions of vitamin A in the body except as precursor to visual pigments (Wald and Dowling, 1960). Retinoic acid is now believed to play an important role in the development of many tissues.

Wald was elected to the National Academy of Sciences in 1950 and to the American Philosophical Society in 1958. In 1967 Wald was awarded the Nobel Prize for Physiology or Medicine in Stockholm, sharing the prize with two other vision researchers, Ragnar Granit and Keffer Hartline. The three had worked independently, although Hartline, too, had been active at the Marine Biological Laboratory in Woods Hole for nearly three decades.

Two years later, Wald's life changed dramatically after he delivered a speech at the Massachusetts Institute of Technology called "A Generation in Search of a Future" (Wald, 1969). This speech, which criticized the U.S. war in Vietnam and the nation's buildup of nuclear weapons, was published in periodicals around the world, and it propelled Wald into the limelight of social activism. Over the next twenty-five years he traveled extensively, using his great skill as a teacher to speak out on these issues as well as on human rights and the misuse of genetic engineering. Wald continued to teach his highly regarded introductory biology course, Natural Sciences 5: The Nature of Living Things, at Harvard until his retirement in 1977. But he largely stopped doing research after 1969, except for summer investigations in Woods Hole on lobster photoreception.

At age ninety, Wald died at his home of natural causes. He was survived by his wife, Ruth Hubbard, their two children, Elijah and Deborah, two children from his first marriage, Michael and David, nine grandchildren, and three great-grandchildren.

BIBLIOGRAPHY

The George Wald papers, 1927–1996, Harvard University archives, Harvard Depository hugfp143, Hollis no. 008421916, in 145 boxes, document the public life of George Wald, including his work as a scientist and his efforts as a prominent social activist. As such, the papers document the field of vision science and liberal American politics, especially the era of the late 1960s to early 1970s. Also included are materials relating to Wald's varied interests in the arts, sciences, and other aspects of culture. Chronologically, the papers cover Wald's adult life; the earliest material dates from his college years. Material consists of many formats: correspondence, manuscripts, publications, notebooks, note cards, photographs, video, and audio tapes.

WORKS BY WALD

"Vitamin A in Eye Tissues." *Journal of General Physiology* 18 (1935): 905–915.

"Carotenoids and the Visual Cycle." *Journal of General Physiology* 19 (1936a): 351–371.

"Pigments of the Retina: II. Sea Robin, Sea Bass and Scup." *Journal of General Physiology* 20 (1936b): 45–56.

"Photo-labile Pigments of the Chicken Retina." *Nature* 140 (1937): 545–546.

"The Porphyropsin Visual System." *Journal of General Physiology* 22 (1939): 775–794.

"The Visual Systems of Euryhaline Fishes." *Journal of General Physiology* 25 (1941): 235–245.

"Human Vision and the Spectrum." *Science* 101 (1945): 653–658.

With Ruth Hubbard. "The Reduction of Retinene$_1$ to Vitamin A$_1$ *in Vitro*." *Journal of General Physiology* 32 (1949): 367–390.

With Paul K. Brown. "The Synthesis of Rhodopsin from Retinene$_1$." *Proceedings of the National Academy of Sciences of the United States of America* 36 (1950): 84–92.

With Ruth Hubbard. "The Mechanism of Rhodopsin Synthesis." *Proceedings of the National Academy of Sciences of the United States of America* 37 (1951): 69–79.

———. "*Cis-trans* Isomers of Vitamin A and Retinene in the Rhodopsin System." *Journal of General Physiology* 36 (1952): 269–315.

"The Biochemistry of Vision." *Annual Review of Biochemistry* 22 (1953): 497–526.

With Paul K. Brown and Patricia H. Smith. "Iodopsin." *Journal of General Physiology* 38 (1955): 623–681.

"The Metamorphosis of Visual Systems in the Sea Lamprey." *Journal of General Physiology* 40 (1957): 901–914.

With Paul K. Brown. "Human Rhodopsin." *Science* 127 (1958a): 222–227.

"The Significance of Vertebrate Metamorphosis." *Science* 128 (1958b): 1481–1490.

"Light and Life." *Scientific American* 201 (October 1959): 92–108.

With John E. Dowling. "The Biological Function of Vitamin A Acid." *Proceedings of the National Academy of Sciences of the United States of America* 46 (1960): 587–608.

With Tōru Yoshizawa. "Pre-lumirhodopsin and the Bleaching of Visual Pigment." *Nature* 197 (1963a): 1279–1286.

With Paul K. Brown. "Visual Pigments in Human and Monkey Retinas." *Nature* 200 (1963b): 37–43.

———. "Visual Pigments in Single Rods and Cones of the Human Retina." *Science* 144 (1964a): 45–52.

"The Receptors of Human Color Vision." *Science* 145 (1964b): 1007–1017.

"The Origins of Life." *Proceedings of the National Academy of Sciences of the United States of America* 52 (1964c): 595–611.

"Visual Excitation and Blood Clotting." *Science* 150 (1965): 1028–1030.

"The Molecular Basis of Visual Excitation." Nobel Lecture, 12 December 1967a. Available from http://www.nobelprize.org.

With Tōru Yoshizawa. "Photochemistry of Iodopsin." *Nature* 214 (1967b): 566.

"A Generation in Search of a Future." Speech given at the Massachusetts Institute of Technology, 1969. Available from http://www.elijahwald.com/generation.html.

"Life and Mind in the Universe." *International Journal of Quantum Chemistry* 11 (1984): 1–15.

OTHER SOURCES

Dowling, John E. "George Wald." *Biographical Memoirs,* vol. 78. Washington, DC: National Academy of Sciences, 2000. Available from http://www.nasonline.org. Dowling's memoir, and the memorial talk by Ruth Hubbard and Elijah Wald cited below, are the two most complete and accurate accounts of Wald's life and scientific contributions.

Hecht, Selig. "Human Retinal Adaptation." *Proceedings of the National Academy of Sciences of the United States of America* 6 (1920): 112–115.

Hubbard, Ruth, and Allen Kropf. "The Action of Light on Rhodopsin." *Proceedings of the National Academy of Sciences of the United States of America* 44 (1958): 130–139.

Hubbard, Ruth, and Elijah Wald. "George Wald Memorial Talk." In *Rhodopsins and Phototransduction.* Novartis Foundation Symposium 224. Chichester, U.K.: Wiley, 1999.

Stryer, Lubert. "Cyclic-GMP Cascade of Vision." *Annual Review of Neuroscience* 9 (1986): 87–119.

Diana E. Kenney

WALKER, GILBERT THOMAS (*b.* Rochdale, Lancashire, United Kingdom, 14 June 1868, *d.* Surrey, United Kingdom, 4 November 1958), *statistics, electrodynamics, meteorology.*

The Walker Circulation was named after the man who systematically studied, identified, and named the "Southern Oscillation." Credit also goes to him for linking the monsoon with other global meteorological features. Swings of the Southern Oscillation were later linked by Jacob Bjerknes with the El Niño phenomenon in the equatorial Pacific Ocean. Bjerknes coined the term "Walker Circulation" describing the east-west vertical circulation in the equatorial plane. Walker's name is also part of the statistical "Yule-Walker equations," where his contribution arose in conjunction with an attempt to develop a model for the Southern Oscillation phenomenon. His success in his work concerning the Southern Oscillation and teleconnections can be explained to some extent by his climatological expertise, but to a larger extent was a result of his expertise in mathematics and statistics, coupled with a dedicated effort to solve the problem of climate forecasting. Walker was elected a Fellow of the Royal Meteorological Society, Royal Astronomical Society, Royal Aeronautical Society, an Honorary Fellow of Imperial College, and a corresponding member of most of the meteorological societies of Europe.

Walker's Background. The eldest son and fourth child of a family of seven (some sources indicate that there were eight), Walker was born in Rochdale, Lancashire. Soon after, the family moved to Croydon in London, where his father Thomas, a civil engineer, became the borough's chief engineer. Thomas Walker was a pioneer of the use of concrete in the construction of dams. Gilbert was admitted to Whitgift School in 1876 and won a scholarship to St. Paul's School in 1881. At St. Paul's School, a famous nursery of university scholars, he showed his gift for mathematics and command of subjects in both the arts and sciences. He excelled in pure and applied mathematics and at the age of seventeen was awarded a prize for an essay on the dynamics of gyroscopes. In 1885 he gained an Exhibition Scholarship in mathematics at Trinity College, Cambridge University, and in 1899 graduated as Senior Wrangler as first man in the Mathematical Tripos. Two years later Walker was elected to a fellowship at Trinity College and was appointed a lecturer in mathematics in 1895.

At the turn of the twentieth century, Walker was awarded the Adams Prize for a paper on electromagnetic fields, receiving a personal commendation from Lord Kelvin. Walker was a "mathematician to his finger-tips" (Simpson, 1959) and was elected Fellow of the Royal Society in 1904 on the strength of his research in pure and applied mathematics, including "original work in dynamics and electromagnetism before ever he turned his thoughts to meteorology" (Normand, 1958). He also received the degree of ScD from Cambridge University the same year. Among his first papers (published in 1895) was one that dealt with the purely mathematical subject of the properties of Bessel functions (solutions to specific differential equations). Walker was recognized in London and Cambridge scholarly circles as a mathematician of high ability who had achieved high academic honors.

In addition to being a mathematician, Walker was also a painter of watercolors and an accomplished flutist, making changes to the instrument that are still retained in its modern form. He published several papers on the flight of birds, having made observations of them with a telescope at Simla in India. Walker was intrigued by the dynamics of projectiles and spinning tops, and his fascination with the throwing sticks of indigenous peoples led him to have a special interest in boomerangs. He was adroit in the practical throwing and worked out the mathematics of the flight of the boomerang, writing a book titled *Boomerangs* in 1902. As a result of these activities, his nickname at Cambridge was "Boomerang Walker." In addition, he was an expert ice skater, a mountaineer, and a naturalist.

Director of the Indian Meteorological Service and Research on World Weather. In 1903 Sir John Eliot, the second director of the India Meteorological Service who was about to retire, returned to England in search of a successor as chief meteorological reporter to the government of India and director-general of Indian observatories. Eliot

proposed to the government of India that the Service should be reorganized with a small staff of trained British scientists at its headquarters. The government agreed and established a new meteorological department with a director-general of observatories and three imperial meteorologists. Walker seemed an unlikely candidate in 1904, at age thirty-six, to head India's growing meteorological service since he had no formal meteorological training, but he had many qualities that were suitable for this position. Eliot chose Walker because he saw the need for his successor to be someone with strong mathematical abilities. In 1903 Walker left academia, preparing for his new post by visiting meteorological services in Europe and the United States, and he became the director of the Indian Meteorological Department the next year. Eliot retired on the last day of 1903 and Walker took charge on the following day. Like Eliot before him, he pressed for the appointment of scientific assistants. Walker chose J. Patterson, J. H. Field, and G. C. Simpson for the first three imperial meteorologist positions. They all proved to be first-class meteorologists and they subsequently became directors of meteorological services in Canada, India, and United Kingdom, respectively.

The situation in India after the famines of 1877 and 1899 was desperate. Millions had died as a result of droughts that were caused by the failure of the monsoons. There was an urgent need to try to better understand the monsoon and the seasonal rains associated with this event. By the last decade of the nineteenth century, the forecasts were often completely incorrect, partly as a result of a lack of rigorous meteorological or statistical basis but also because of a change in the climate system that Eliot had documented in his 1904 paper. The scientific merit of any kind of weather forecasting was still a subject of great debate in Europe at the turn of the twentieth century, and the idea of the long-range forecasting of monsoons was thought by many to be an unachievable task. Scientific attempts to forecast the monsoon rains had started approximately twenty-five years before Walker's arrival in India, with official forecasts being issued beginning in 1886.

These efforts led to the tentative identification of predictor variables for the monsoon, including Himalayan snow cover and atmospheric pressure at other locations such as Australia and southern Africa. Other prior meteorological research also indicated that connections existed between the variations in atmospheric pressure at distant locations. Walker faced a situation in which no quantitative theory for forecasting the Indian monsoon was available with any agreed explanation of the general circulation. Using some of the earlier studies, Walker began his investigation to improve Indian monsoon forecasts using statistical techniques, having realized that the mathematical and dynamical meteorological theories of the time were insufficiently developed for the task.

Walker noticed the connection between statistics and the forecasting of the monsoon, and he became the first to apply statistical methods to the problem. He became a pioneer in the use of correlations and their statistical significance testing in meteorology (Normand, 1953). Walker made use of the techniques of correlation, regression, and harmonic analysis. The first of his many meteorological papers appeared in 1909, titled "Correlation in Seasonal Variation of Climate," and was published in the *Indian Meteorological Memoirs*. He realized that he could not tackle monsoon forecasting by means of mathematical analysis based upon established techniques, and he chose to use empirical techniques. Building on the works of Henry Blanford (the first director of the Indian Meteorological Department), Sir Norman Lockyer and his son William, H. H. Hildebrandsson, John Eliot, and others, he calculated statistical lag correlations between antecedent meteorological events within and outside India and the subsequent behavior of the Indian monsoon.

Walker obtained pressure, temperature, and rainfall records for the previous forty-year period. He also sought out time series of other parameters such as river flood stages, mountain snow pack depths, lake levels, and sunspot activity in an effort to identify the key relationships. Each weather record was averaged by season within each year and then grouped by season to form four time series for each variable at each station. He began extensive statistical studies of correlations with worldwide meteorological data to find a way of forecasting the yearly changes in the monsoon, which, he was convinced, were in some way tied to global weather. It was during this time, when World War I had taken away Walker's European staff and had drained him of most departmental resources for routine work, that he created a "human computer," using his Indian clerical staff to compile numerous tables of global correlation coefficients—numerical measures of the closeness of the relationship between any two variables.

Walker's mathematical talents were fundamental in these efforts. Where a method did not exist to handle a particular statistical problem, Walker invented one to suit the situation. Some of these methods were innovative for the time, and to statisticians, the name "Walker" is applied to the Yule-Walker recursion, a set of equations used to discern periods in time-series analysis. Walker employed Yule's modern notation for correlation, introduced in 1907, and attached probable error to statistics such as the correlations coefficient. Even though the network of meteorological observations was sparse, especially over the Pacific Ocean, Walker tried to decompose the variations in large-scale weather into a few dominant centers of action.

As he sorted through world weather records, he recognized some patterns of rainfall in South America and the associated changes in ocean temperatures. He also found a connection between barometric pressure readings at stations on the eastern and western sides of the Pacific (Tahiti and Darwin, Australia). Based on statistical techniques and through careful interpretation of correlation tables, Walker was able to identify three pressure oscillations. Walker noticed that when pressure rises in the east, it usually falls in the west, and vice versa, and he used the term "Southern Oscillation" to explain this changing pattern. Besides Southern Oscillation, he named the seesaw in pressure between the Icelandic Low and Azores High the "North Atlantic Oscillation" (NAO), and the seesaw in the Pacific, the "North Pacific Oscillation" (NPO). Walker also stated that the Southern Oscillation is the predominant oscillation. He noted a tendency of the Southern Oscillation to persist for at least one or two seasons using his correlation tables, suggesting the potential for using the Southern Oscillation in forecasting world weather. These findings were all published in a series of papers titled "World Weather" in the mid-1920s to 1930s, when Walker had returned to England from his tenure at the Indian Meteorological Department. Thus, when Jacob Bjerknes later identified the atmospheric circulation related to the Southern Oscillation, he named it after Walker, stating that it "must be part of the larger 'Southern Oscillation' statistically defined by Sir Gilbert Walker" (Bjerknes, 1969).

Walker also realized that Asian monsoon seasons under certain barometric conditions were linked to drought in Australia, Indonesia, India, and parts of Africa, and mild winters in western Canada. He noted the relationship between oscillations of air pressure in the eastern and western Pacific and the monsoons in India, in addition to the rainfall in Africa. At this point, he was becoming convinced that all these events were part of the same phenomenon. Walker found that the random failure of the monsoon in India often coincides with low pressure over Tahiti, high pressure over Darwin, and calmer winds over the Pacific.

However, during and immediately following Walker's research career, the general reaction within the meteorological community to statistical methods was extreme skepticism. As a result, Walker was publicly criticized for suggesting that climatic conditions over such widely separated regions of the globe could be possibly linked. Others in the field questioned his writings, since they were skeptical of theories that gave a simple explanation of global weather patterns. The main conclusion that Walker presented in 1928 to the Royal Meteorological Society "is that there are three big swayings or surgings: a) The North Atlantic oscillation of pressure between Azores or Vienna on one hand and Iceland or Greenland on the other; b)

The North Pacific oscillation between the high pressure belt and the winter depression near the Aleutian Islands; and c) The southern oscillation, mainly between the South Pacific and the land areas round the Indian Ocean." He later added, "The southern oscillation is more far-reaching than the two oscillations just described, and as the effect of an abnormal season is propagated slowly, it may not appear at the other side of the earth until after an interval of six months or more." He thought this was the key to forecasting the monsoon and seasonal weather. "Examination by statistical methods has brought to light many relationships between seasonal conditions in different parts of the world, usually contemporary but often three months or more apart, and in the latter case knowledge of the earlier conditions in one region may give a rough idea of what will occur later on in the other." With this data he pointed to the possibility of long-range forecasting. Walker's studies held the promise of the prediction of events in regions other than India during a time when important and critical pieces of data were not available. For example, no data were available on the upper air or sea-surface temperatures. Under his directorship, the observatories issued several publications, including *Tables for the Reduction of Meteorological Observations* and *Meteorological Atlas of the Indian Seas and North Indian Ocean.*

Walker was unable, however, to translate his findings into a method that predicts the nature of the monsoons. He conceded that he could not prove his theory, but he predicted that whatever was causing the connection in weather patterns would become known once global meteorological data above ground level, which were not routinely observed at that time, were used in this study. Walker was right in his prediction, but his results were not utilized until 1960, when Jacob Bjerknes expressed an interest in studying the El Niño phenomenon. Bjerknes connected what Walker had found to what others were finding in the ocean and explained the global effects of the El Niño/Southern Oscillation, or ENSO.

Imperial College of Science and Technology. Walker was knighted by the king of England on his retirement in 1924 and became Sir Gilbert Walker, primarily for his accomplishments in directing the Indian Meteorological Department. He then became a professor of meteorology at the Imperial College of Science and Technology, University of London, succeeding Sir Napier Shaw. He not only continued his studies of world weather but also was involved in experimental physics, turning his attention to laboratory studies of convection in unstable fluids, with particular reference to the formation of clouds. Walker, along with his students, studied turbulence and focused on the cellular structure of an unstable fluid. In laboratory experiments, they were able to obtain an array of cellular forms such as polygons and transverse and longitudinal vorticities.

Walker retired from Imperial College in 1934, was involved in classified work on meteorological correlations over the Atlantic Ocean region during World War II, and lived in Cambridge until 1950. Thereafter, he did not settle in any one place but lived mostly in Surrey and Sussex.

Walker remained an active researcher after his retirement and continued to write papers on meteorological topics. He served as the editor of the *Quarterly Journal of the Royal Meteorological Society* from 1935 to 1941 and published several papers in this journal, the last in 1947. He became a Fellow of the Royal Society of London in 1905 and served as the president of the Royal Meteorological Society in 1926 and 1927. An Honorary Fellow of Imperial College and a Fellow of the Royal Astronomical Society, he was a corresponding member of most of the meteorological societies of Europe.

Walker married May Constance Carter in 1908 and they had a son and a daughter. May died in 1955. He died at the age of ninety at Coulsdon, Surrey, on 4 November 1958.

In 2001 the Indian Meteorological Society instituted the Sir Gilbert Walker Gold Medal to be presented biennially to an eminent Indian or international scientist recognized in the field of monsoon studies. On 2 November 2006, the University of Reading in the United Kingdom launched the Walker Institute, named in memory of Sir Gilbert Thomas Walker.

BIBLIOGRAPHY

WORKS BY WALKER

Outlines of the Theory of Electromagnetism. London: Cambridge University Press, 1910.

"Tables for the Reduction of Meteorological Observations." Prepared by G. C. Simpson, Imperial Meteorologist under the Direction of Gilbert T. Walker, Director-General of Observatories, 1910.

"Correlation in Seasonal Variations of Weather." *Quarterly Journal of theRoy al Meteorological Society* 44 (1918): 223–224.

"On Periodicity (with Discussion)." *Quarterly Journal of the Royal Meteorological Society* 51 (1925): 337–346.

With E. W. Bliss. "On Correlation Coefficients, Their Calculation Use (with Discussion)." *Quarterly Journal of the Royal Meteorological Society* 52 (1926): 73–84.

———. "Seasonal Weather and Its Prediction." *Smithsonian Annual Report for 1935* (1936): 117–138.

OTHER SOURCES

Bjerknes, J. "Atmospheric Teleconnections from the Equatorial Pacific." *Monthly Weather Review* 97 (1969): 163–172.

Cox, John D. *Storm Watchers.* New York: John Wiley & Sons, 2002.

Katz, R. W. "Sir Gilbert Walker and a Connection between El Niño and Statistics." *Statistical Science* 17 (2002): 97–112.

Montgomery, R. B. "Report on the Work of G. T. Walker. Reports on Critical Studies of Methods of Long-Range Weather Forecasting." *Monthly Weather Review* Supplement no. 39 (Apr. 1940): 1–22.

Normand, C. "Sir Gilbert Walker, C.S.J., F.R.S." *Nature* 182 (1958): 1706.

Simpson, G. C. "Sir Gilbert Walker, C.S.J., F.R.S." *Weather* 14 (1959): 67–68.

Taylor, G. I. "Gilbert Thomas Walker, 1868–1958." *Biographical Memoirs of Fellows of the Royal Society* 8 (1962): 166–174.

Walker, J. M. "Pen Portrait of Sir Gilbert Walker, CSI, MA, ScD, FRS." *Weather* 52 (1997): 217–220.

Sepideh Yalda

WALKER, JOHN

WALKER, JOHN (*b.* Edinburgh, Scotland, United Kingdom, 1731, *d.* Edinburgh, 31 December 1803), *chemistry, botany, mineralogy, geology, anthropology.* For the original article on Walker see *DSB,* vol. 14.

Walker was one of the most influential natural historians in late enlightenment Edinburgh. After a career as a traveler and a parson naturalist, he went on to become professor of natural history at the University of Edinburgh in 1779. In this capacity he served as the secretary of the Royal Society of Edinburgh's physical section and as curator for the city's museum of natural history. Though marginalized by nineteenth- and early twentieth-century historians of science, research from the 1960s onward revealed that Walker made original contributions to the biological and physical sciences. In addition to identifying and classifying new botanical and mineralogical specimens, he diligently campaigned for the Linnaean nomenclature to be adopted in Scotland. By the end of his career, he had amassed one of the largest natural history collections in Europe and had taught more than one thousand students, many of whom would go on to have a substantial impact on nineteenth-century biological and physical sciences as practiced in the British Empire and the United States.

Education and Training. Rev. Dr. John Walker received his secondary education at Canongate High School, Edinburgh. There he was taught to read Latin and Greek and in 1746 he matriculated as a divinity student in the University of Edinburgh. While reading for his degree, he also attended the lectures of Robert Steuart (natural philosophy), Andrew Plummer (chemistry), and, most probably, Charles Alston (materia medica). He graduated in 1749 and he spent the next few years preparing for a career in the Church of Scotland. He was ordained as a minister in

Glencorse in 1758 and he was then transferred to a church in Moffat in 1762.

Throughout the 1750s and 1760s Walker worked hard to develop close relationships with members of the Philosophical Society of Edinburgh, especially the Judge Advocate Lord Kames and the physician William Cullen. Under Cullen's guidance, Walker perfected his knowledge of chemistry and began to conduct his own experiments on marls and mineral wells. In particular, Cullen taught Walker how to track chemical reactions gravimetrically, especially those which involved minerals that were important to mining, agriculture, and materia medica. In 1757 Walker published an article on the chemical composition of mineral water in the *Philosophical Transactions*, and for the next two decades he split his time between his parish duties in Moffat and his scientific and political interests in Edinburgh. In 1764 his politicking paid off and he was appointed to make an official report on the economic and educational resources of the Highlands and Hebrides. His journey was supported by the church (the General Assembly and Scotland's Society for the Propagation of Christian Knowledge) and the state (the Board of Annexed Estates). This endeavor involved more than 3,000 miles of travel and resulted in him being appointed to make several more journeys over the next fifteen years, including another substantial northern trip in 1771.

Professorial Career. After returning from his 1764 travels, Walker made an unsuccessful bid for the professorship of natural and civil history at the University of St. Andrews. This left him demoralized and he considered emigrating to the North American colonies. Through the encouragement of Cullen and Lord and Lady Kames, he stayed and continued to gather academic and political patrons. During the mid-1770s Robert Ramsay, Edinburgh's first professor of natural history, became terminally ill, and Walker mounted a full-scale political battle against William Smellie for the post. In the end, Walker was appointed to the chair in 1779. Keeping with the subject's long ties to materia medica, the post was attached to the medical school. During his tenure he taught around one thousand medical, arts, divinity, and law students, many of whom came from mainland Europe, the British colonies, and the newly established United States. He divided his lectures into two sections. The first detailed the classification systems that he had constructed for mineralogy, botany, and zoology, that is, the three kingdoms of nature. The second covered meteorology, hydrology, and geology. Walker called these the "Hippocratean" lectures because they addressed environmental factors that the classical physician Hippocrates had linked to health. The course covered a staggering amount of information, and copies of the syllabus were sold by local printers. A book-length version of the lecture heads, *Institutes of Natural History,* appeared in

Burrum chundalle. *Two-page drawing of the Scottish flower by John Walker.* UNIVERSITY OF EDINBURGH SPECIAL COLLECTIONS.

1792. Students attended class twice per week; at the end of the year some handed their notes over to a stenographer to be copied and then bound into manuscript volumes that served as reference "books" for the rest of their careers. More than twenty sets of these have been preserved, many of which are housed at the University of Edinburgh.

During the late 1790s, Walker's eyesight began to fail and he asked one of his former students, Robert Jameson, to help him with the lectures. Jameson obliged and eventually was appointed to the post after Walker died in 1803. In addition to lectures, Walker organized field trips, held tutorials in the university's Natural History Museum, and actively supported his students when they founded the Natural History Society (1782) and a Chemical Society (1785). Indeed, several of his students also went on to found the Highland Society of Scotland and the Agricultural Society (1792). He was a long-standing member of the city's Philosophical Society, and he was instrumental in transforming it into the Royal Society of Edinburgh in

1783. In 1794 he was made a Fellow of the Royal Society of London.

Botany. Throughout his entire career, Walker remained interested in botany and agriculture. His early thoughts on the subject were influenced by the work of John Ray and Charles Alston, and as early as 1750 he was collecting and cultivating specimens from Canon Mill Bog near Edinburgh. Over the next three decades he assembled an herbarium, planted gardens, and amassed a sizable collection of field notes. In addition to identifying new species, he was especially interested in botanical hydrostatics and he made one of the earliest known attempts to identify the different genera of aquatic algae. To arrange his specimens, he turned to Carolus Linnaeus's binomial nomenclature. During the 1760s, Walker exchanged letters with Linnaeus and then successfully nominated the Swede to membership in the Philosophical Society. This nomination, combined with Walker's superior knowledge of Scottish peat moss, grasses, grains, lichens, willows, and various materia medica simples, established him as a notable British botanist.

For the rest of the century Walker's advice was sought by leading naturalists, including Thomas Pennant, Sir Richard Pultney, Lord Bute, and Sir Joseph Banks. By the time he started lecturing in the university, he had created a unique classification of Scottish plants from which his botanical lectures drew freely. Thus, though he did not publish a systematic botanical text, his ideas were bequeathed orally to his students. In particular, he developed a close relationship with James Edward Smith, future founder of the Linnaean Society of London. They shared an interest in willows (*salix*) and they took field trips around the Lowlands. Likewise, Walker encouraged Robert Brown's early research, which eventually led Brown to write a highly influential work on the movement of particles through botanical fluids (Brownian motion). After Walker died, Charles Stewart (another former student) gathered together several of his botanical manuscripts and edited them into two books titled *An Economical History of the Hebrides* (1808) and *Essays on Natural History and Rural Economy* (1812). These essays were recommended as important reference books by several Scottish university professors during the first three decades of the nineteenth century.

Although Walker was an avid botanist, he was an even more enthusiastic mineralogist. As a child he had collected minerals in the Pentland Hills and on the Firth of Forth. As a young cleric he busied himself by assaying soil samples. Unlike his botanical system, he forsook Linnaeus's use of natural characters (based on color and shape) and turned to chemical characters. In following this path, he aligned himself with the work of Cullen,

Joseph Black, and other medical school chemists, and with the mineralogical research tradition led by J. G. Wallerius, Axel Cronstedt, and Torbern Bergman in Sweden. From the 1760s to the 1780s, Cullen, Lord Kames, and Lord Bute helped him acquire specimens for his collection and mineralogy books for his library. During this period he also served as a scientific advisor in the mines of Lords Hopetoun and Cathcart.

Chemical Mineralogy. By the time that Walker started lecturing, he had created his own mineralogical system, which consisted of eighteen classes that were based on chemical characters. Over the next twenty years he added, removed, and renamed species, genera, orders, and classes based upon his own experiments, those conducted by colleagues in the medical school, or those related in recent books, articles, or museum catalogs. The research that he pursued during the 1780s can be traced via the classificatory headings listed in the syllabi that he had printed for the mineralogy sections of his lectures: *Schediasma fossilium* (1781), *Delineatio fossilium* (1782), and *Classes fossilium* (1787). His work during the 1790s is evinced in the *Institutes* and his *Systema fossilium* (c. 1795); the former being the enormous manuscript catalog that he created for the mineralogy collection in the Natural History Museum. The collection contained minerals from all over the world and was one of the largest in Britain. His 1795 system contained nineteen classes and references to hundreds of sources printed in Europe and the Americas. Walker's expertise on the subject was readily acknowledged in Scotland and abroad. Joseph Black regularly recommended Walker's course to his own chemistry students, and James Hutton and John Playfair, two of Edinburgh's geological theorists, also attended his lectures. Other students included Sir James Hall, Thomas Beddoes, Robert Jameson, and Samuel Latham Mitchell. Like his work on botany, the specifics of Walker's mineralogical system were given to his students orally.

Geology. Walker's chemical approach to minerals strongly influenced how he viewed the form and structure of the globe. In his geological lectures, he taught that the surface of Earth consisted of three different types of strata: primary, secondary, and tertiary. The minerals of primary strata were indurated and exhibited strong bonds of chemical affinity similar to those formed by the cement used by Edinburgh's farmers and masons. Secondary strata contained softer minerals with weaker bonds of affinity. Tertiary strata consisted of organic remains (such as peat moss) and sedimentary formations, either from river silt or mountain debris. As such, they exhibited little to no affinity. Interacting with the strata of the globe were aerial and aqueous fluids, and Walker addressed these substances in his hydrology and meteorology lectures. In

particular, like many medically trained naturalists of his time (including Hutton), he held that water both percolated through and flowed over the earth in a fashion analogous to circulation. As much of the chemistry in Edinburgh's medical school utilized humid analysis, this created a direct link between material transformations that took place on Earth's surface and those within the human body. Thus, many of the mineralogical terms that Walker introduced into geology were imported from the medically orientated chemistry of Cullen and Black. This connection was by no means unique, and it was practiced by many of the authors listed in Walker's reading lists, including Wallerius, Cronstedt, and Bergman. Such an overriding commitment to humid analysis also led Walker (as well as Black) to conclude that primary strata had originally formed from some sort of prehistoric aqueous solution that had subsequently hardened. This solution was not equated with the biblical Flood and, as it occurred before written history, it was hard to determine its temporal framework. As a general rule, most Scottish naturalists of Walker's generation treated any theory that sought to postulate the pre-primary strata composition of the globe as conjecture, as no empirical evidence existed to support it. Walker advanced this cosmological agnosticism in his lectures. In his private papers, however, he entertained the possibility that causal irregularities may have affected Earth's form and composition before recorded history.

Anthropology. Walker also maintained a strong interest in what later would be called anthropology. For the Lowland Scots at this time, the language and customs of the Highland and Hebrides clans were sometimes just as foreign as those of Native Americans or East Asians. When Walker traveled through these areas in 1764 and 1771, he took detailed notes not only on the flora and fauna, but also on local rituals, culinary traditions, farming practices, and variations in dialect. He submitted reports on these subjects to the General Assembly and the Board of Annexed Estates. In recognition of his medically relevant observations, the University of Glasgow awarded him an MD in February 1765. Because Walker's reports also addressed religious literacy and history, the University of Edinburgh gave him a DD the next month. The following year he published some of his travel observations as articles in the gentlemanly *Scots Magazine*. This strengthened his status as an expert in natural history, and soon Lord Kames engaged him as an advisor in a debate that he was having with Edinburgh's Lord Monboddo over the classification of human beings and "orang-outangs" (chimpanzees).

During the Enlightenment, many naturalists held that the ability to speak categorically separated humans from other animals. Walker accepted this view, but his connections with the medical school also meant that he was respectably familiar with anatomy and physiology. As a result, he rejected Linnaeus's use of external morphological characters in favor of internal anatomical characteristics. To counter Monboddo, Kames asked Walker to comment on Monboddo's belief that it was civilized society, not language or morphology, that separated humans from simians—the difference being of degree and not of kind. Walker advised Kames via consultations and correspondence. He provided counterexamples taken from natural history, medicine, and philosophy to undermine the claim that humans and simians should be classified under the same genus. This nomenclatural separation, however, did not extend any further. Although he acknowledged different races, Walker firmly believed that there was only one human species—an assumption that was no doubt linked to the monogenism promoted in the Bible and other texts from antiquity. This commitment is significant, as Walker did in fact accept that variations could occur in other plant and animal species. The name that he gave to this type of change was *evolution*. As he promoted this term in his natural history lectures, it should perhaps be noted that he taught Robert Waring Darwin, father of Charles Darwin, and Mungo Park, the famed traveler whose works on Africa were read widely in Britain, Europe, and America.

Later Career. After settling himself into his natural history chair, Walker married Jane Wauchope of Niddrie in 1789. Throughout his entire career, he actively participated in the Republic of Letters. His correspondence increased during the 1780s on account of his professorship and his secretaryship of the physical section of the Royal Society of Edinburgh (1784–1803). From the 1780s to about 1800, he corresponded with Britain's leading politicians and educators and continued to maintain close ties with the church. In 1782 Lord Lauderdale appointed him minister to Colinton, and from 1790 to 1791 he served as moderator of the Church of Scotland.

At the time of Walker's moderatorship, the church and the state were jointly collaborating to produce the *Statistical Account of Scotland* (20 vols., 1791–1799). Local ministers were asked to write articles on the natural history, civil history, and economic (statistic) viability of their own parish. The result was one of the largest scientific publications of late-eighteenth-century Britain. To prepare future ministers for such projects, Walker campaigned for measures that would require divinity students to take a natural history course as part of their degree. He also supported the *Statistical Account* by writing articles on the parishes of Glencorse and Colinton.

As his eyesight started to fade later in his life, Walker began to write down his reflections about various scientific and artistic matters that had guided or stimulated his thoughts about the natural world. These notes, along with the bulk of his manuscripts, are housed in the University of Edinburgh. After his death on 31 December 1803, he was buried in Canongate Graveyard and his library was auctioned. To accompany the sale, Cornelius Elliot published a list of Walker's books as *A Catalogue of the Books in Natural History with a Few Others, Which Belonged to the Late Rev. Dr. Walker* in 1804. Notably, many of the books in the catalog are the very same editions as those cited in Walker's lectures. In accordance with his will, the proceeds of the sale were divided between his widow and the university.

SUPPLEMENTARY BIBLIOGRAPHY

Most of Walker's manuscripts are housed in the University of Edinburgh's Special Collections Department. Adversaria, *his personal diary from the 1760s, and* Systema fossilium *(c. 1795), the catalog of the University of Edinburgh's mineralogy collection, are housed in the Special Collections Department of the University of Glasgow. Throughout his career, Walker composed many manuscript essays that addressed the natural history of the Highlands and the Hebrides. A good number of these were published posthumously as articles in* Prize Essays *and* Transactions of the Highland Society of Scotland *and as chapters in* An Economical History of the Hebrides and Highlands of Scotland, *C. Stewart, ed. (Edinburgh: University Press, 1808) and in* Essays on Natural History and Rural Economy, *Charles Stewart, ed. (Edinburgh, 1808). Many of Walker's published works are listed in a table at the end of* Lectures on Geology: Including Hydrology, Mineralogy, and Meteorology with an Introduction to Biology *by John Walker, Harold W. Scott, ed. (Chicago: University of Chicago Press, 1966). This list, however, is far from complete and excludes several significant publications, cited below.*

WORKS BY WALKER

"Dr. John Walker's Report to the Assembly 1–65 concerning the State of the Highlands and the Islands." *Scots Magazine* 28 (1766): 680–689.

The Rev. Dr. John Walker's Report on the Hebrides of 1764 and 1771, edited by Margaret M. McKay. Edinburgh: John Donald, 1980.

"Dr. Walker's Report concerning the State of the Highlands and Islands." *Scots Magazin* 34 (1772): 288–293.

Schediasma fossilium. Edinburgh, n.p., 1781.

Delineatio fossilium. Edinburgh, n.p., 1782.

Classes fossilium. Edinburgh, n.p., 1787.

Institutes of Natural History: Containing the Heads of Lectures in Natural History. Edinburgh: Steward, Ruthven & Co., 1792.

"A Memorandum Given … to a Young Gentleman Going to India." *Bee* 17 (1793): 330–333.

With W. Torrence. "Number XXI. Parish of Glenncross." In *A Statistical Account of Scotland. Drawn up from the Communications of the Ministers of the Different Parishes.* Vol. 15, edited by John Sinclair, pp. 435–446. Edinburgh: W. Creech, 1799.

"Number XXVII. Parish of Colington." In *A Statistical Account of Scotland. Drawn up from the Communications of the*

Ministers of the Different Parishes. Vol. 19, edited by John Sinclair, pp. 579–591. Edinburgh: W. Creech, 1799.

Letter to Colonel Dirom, Quarter Master General of Scotland, on the Discovery of Coal. Edinburgh: 1800.

OTHER SOURCES

Eddy, Matthew D. "Geology, Mineralogy and Time in John Walker's University of Edinburgh Natural History Lectures." *History of Science* 39 (2001): 95–119.

———. "Scottish Chemistry, Classification and the Early Mineralogical Career of the 'Ingenious' Rev. Dr. John Walker." *British Journal for the History of Science* 35 (2002): 382–422.

———. "Scottish Chemistry, Classification and the Late Mineralogical Career of the 'Ingenious' Professor John Walker (1779–1803)." *British Journal for the History of Science* 37 (2004): 373–399.

———. "The University of Edinburgh Natural History Class Lists." *Archives of Natural History* 30 (2003): 97–117.

Shapin, Steven. "Property, Patronage, and the Politics of Science: The Founding of the Royal Society of Edinburgh." *British Journal for the History of Science* 7 (1974): 1–41.

Taylor, G. "John Walker, D.D., F.R.S.E. 1731–1803: Notable Scottish Naturalist." *Transactions of the Botanical Society of Edinburgh* 38 (1959): 180–203.

Withers, Charles W. J. "'Both Useful and Ornamental': John Walker's Keepership of Edinburgh University's Natural History Museum, 1779–1803." *Journal of the History of Collections* 5 (1993): 65–77.

Matthew D. Eddy

WALLACE, ALFRED RUSSEL (*b.* Usk, Monmouthshire, Wales, 8 January 1823; *d.* Broadstone, Dorset, England, 7 November 1913), *evolutionary biology, biogeography, physical geography, social theory, astrobiology.* For the original article on Wallace see *DSB,* vol. 14.

Considering the fact he was nearly forgotten after his death for some fifty years, the "rediscovery" of Wallace since the 1960s, at an ever-accelerating pace, is a remarkable story. By the end of the 1970s his fundamental contributions to evolutionary theory (including, of course, his independent discovery of the principle of natural selection), biogeography, anthropology, and physical geography had been revealed, but in the years following scholars have recognized his significance to a number of other individual subjects as well. Further, significant progress has been made since the mid-1980s in clarifying the weave of his idiosyncratic worldview. Many observers now rate Wallace as the single most outstanding field biologist and tropical regions naturalist in history; he can also be credited as one of the founders of astrobiology studies (and in turn as one of the first modern proponents of the anthropic principle in cosmology), a pioneer in the use of statistics in epidemiology, and an influential humanitarian many of whose ideas for social improvement later flourished as elements of the liberal agenda of the twentieth century.

A major reason for Wallace's "return" has been the birth and growth of the biodiversity studies movement since the late 1980s. At that time the individual species–focused thinking of classical Darwinism increasingly came under fire as researchers strove for new understandings of the diversity and interrelatedness of life and its implications for one's own well-being. Biogeographical studies suddenly became fashionable again, and in turn many biologists and conservationists rediscovered Wallace's ideas and writings. Among those Wallace-associated biogeography models under renewed consideration are the so-called riverine barriers theory (that diversity patterns in Amazonia might be related to the isolating effect of the river's main tributaries), his observations on the history of Wallace's Line in Indonesia, his explanations for the origin of planet-level latitudinal species diversity gradients, and his suggestion that rapid climatic changes might account for accelerated species change.

Another reason for Wallace's reemergence has been the increased attention given to his full bibliography, including the clarifications that hundreds of rediscovered works (and even passages) have provided. The additional material has not only made it possible to develop a better model of his overall worldview (as discussed below), but to improve time lines and correct misappreciations of many of his more specific positions. For example, it turns out that his first public statement expressing a divergence of view from Charles Darwin on human evolution appeared not in the famous *Quarterly Review* article of April 1869, but instead at a British Association for the Advancement of Science meeting eight months earlier; similarly, his first public embrace of socialism came in a short published letter in November 1889, not in the well-known essay "Human Selection" that came out ten months later. As to one factual correction, Wallace has frequently been cited as stating that life could only have evolved on Earth, whereas in an interview printed in 1903 he specifically states he only intended his words to mean "intelligent beings" akin to humans, and not all life forms. Again, Wallace has typically been cast as one of those adhering to a gradualistic, Darwinian model of organic change, whereas it is apparent from passages in several of his lesser known writings that this was not the case and that he instead had embraced something akin to what in the early twenty-first century would be termed a punctuated equilibrium model: that is, change occurring in spurts and separated by long periods of relative stasis.

Further, the portrayal of Wallace as a dispersalist has come under attack by Bernard Michaux, Charles H. Smith, and Bruce S. Lieberman, who point out that his earliest efforts at understanding evolutionary histories (as in the "Sarawak law" essay) actually anticipate vicariance biogeography. Also generally overlooked by pre-1980 sources were the clear indications that prior to 1858 he opposed the very same principle of necessary utility of adaptations that he rigorously supported after that date. In another misconception, his opposition to smallpox vaccination has often been taken as indicating his belief that vaccination was, and always had been, absolutely ineffective—despite the existence of an 1895 publication that directly states his real appreciation that the practice had only in recent years become as dangerous as the likelihood of incidence of the disease, and should therefore be abandoned. Another recently rediscovered article somewhat surprisingly exposes him, despite his spiritualist beliefs, as a sharp critic of theosophy, and in particular reincarnation, which he terms a "grotesque nightmare."

Views on Social Issues. Indeed, one might reasonably suggest that in the thirty-plus years since the first *DSB* article, the main progress that has been made in Wallace studies overall has been a realization that earlier ad hoc associations of his name with a variety of positions—including some seemingly, but incorrectly, explained by period social trends and institutions—has had a crippling effect on dispassionate analysis of his actual mindset. Both individual investigators and the recent domination of externalist research agendas must bear some responsibility for this state of affairs, as the evidence was always there.

Another such assumption that does not stand up to close examination pertains to his many forays into social criticism and planning—that these were the rabble-rousing efforts of a crank. Wallace took his social theorizing and involvements very seriously, actually, and the degree to which they presaged later eventualities remains only lightly investigated. As founder and president of the Land Nationalization Society, for example, he led a movement to retrieve ownership of the land from Britain's relatively few large holders; along the way he devised ingenious compensation schemes that might well have relevance to the way natural lands are now being set aside for purposes of nature conservancy. The system as described in *Land Nationalisation* was in part based on his recognition of the relationships among (inherent) locational values, value added to the land during its periods of custodianship, and the setting of rents, anticipating elements of twentieth-century economic geography. The same work included suggestions for setting aside land for historic memorials and as greenbelts, another distinctly twentieth-century trend. He was also an early champion of the "new town" planning efforts of Ebenezer Howard.

Alfred Russel Wallace. HULTON ARCHIVE/GETTY IMAGES.

Wallace also entered into period discussions on economics, addressing those forces he believed were damaging to both national and individual interests. Some of these complaints were predictable (for example, emotional tirades against war expenses and the profligate vices of the wealthy), but some were better thought out and influenced later thinkers: for example, his thoughts on the development of a paper money standard, which were taken seriously by the American economist Irving Fisher and later by members of the Chicago School. One of Wallace's main pleas in the economics arena was that the "old" ideas invested in political economy should be replaced by more soundly relevant principles contributing to what he termed a "social economy." Among these new principles was the startling idea that the state should not legally recognize wills and trusts bearing on far-future events—a concept that is actually beginning to find its place in the world of early twenty-first century philanthropic practices.

To understand how such interests followed from Wallace's investment in the general subject of evolution, one requires a passably good picture of his overall operating cosmology, and in this realm the availability of the rediscovered sources and an alertness to avoid a priori assumptions sustained considerable progress. Wallace was represented in the *DSB* essay of 1976 as a man who had adopted a general—actually rather modern—evolutionary perspective around 1845 with his reading of the anonymously penned *Vestiges of the Natural History of Creation*, made a rather slow but steady kind of progress in unraveling the change-invoking influences involved, and had a revelation as to an exact mechanism (natural selection) in 1858, but then several years later had second thoughts about the universality of that mechanism and began to backslide on the theory accordingly. Supposedly, his defection from his original view (in 1858) came about as a result of his adoption of spiritualism, his waning respect for natural selection as a positive force in evolution, disillusioned Owenite leanings, or some combination of the three. This theory, the "change of mind" interpretation of his intellectual development, was as of 2007 in the process of being overturned by a new "no change of mind" model that better fits the known facts, and does not rely so heavily on negative evidence.

Route to Ideas about Selection. The "change of mind" model derives most centrally from the notion that in the "Ternate Essay" of 1858 Wallace had accepted that natural selection pertained to humans as it did to other living things, and secondarily (and implicitly) on the idea that his route to the discovery of natural selection was a relatively linear, if not very speedy one. But humankind is not referred to in the essay (nor did he ever later say they were meant to be included in the argument), which nevertheless does contain seeds of his later-used argument that humans *are* different, based on the analogy of domesticated animals (that is, both humans and domesticated animals are changed in a manner distinct from the operation of a rote natural selection process). Further, it is apparent that Wallace's route to 1858 was not a linear one. As alluded to earlier, he clearly believed prior to 1858 that adaptive structures were not necessarily utilitarian, and very probably believed that after coming into being through unknown means they were then secondarily shaped (developed further, or went away through disuse or extinction) by gradual, large-scale environmental forces that somehow provided overriding direction—a model invoking implied final causes. Along these lines it is significant that the 1858 natural selection paper contains no mention of any of the thoughts on evolution introduced in the 1855 "Sarawak [a state of Malaysia, on northwest side of the island of Borneo] Law" essay, nor to the several papers between 1855 and 1858 that represented developments of it, and thus that a new direction is suggested.

As of mid-1858, therefore, it looks as though Wallace was in possession of a model that accounted for the adaptive shaping of lower life forms, but not, considering his many years of experience observing native peoples with abilities they seemed to have no need for, people. In analogy with the domestication process and in continuation of

his final causes-centered approach, Wallace began to look for mechanisms that might serve to help human beings evolve in spite of themselves; that is, without their being aware of it.

Distracted on returning to England in 1862 by the success of Darwin's materialist approach and the writings of the English philosopher Herbert Spencer, Wallace at first laid off "big picture" thinking and concentrated on the disposal/description of his natural history specimens. His misgivings about the range of applicability of natural selection soon resurfaced obliquely, however, in a series of papers and discussions beginning in September 1864 dealing with the means of civilizing savages. Around the time the last of these appeared, he was introduced to the writings of spiritualism, perhaps by his sister. On investigating he discovered that these preached a philosophy of acting on intelligent conviction, exactly the kind of mechanism that in theory might serve a societal final cause. He began attending séances in the hope that these would prove the existence of a domain of spirits contributing to that final cause. Eventually he was convinced by what he saw, and by the beginning of 1867 was not only advocating objective analysis of spiritualism, but had become a full believer besides. His final public break on the evolution of humankind with Darwin in 1868–1869 was delayed by his writing *The Malay Archipelago* in the interim, but when it did take place it signaled not a change of mind, but instead the completion of a teleological model of evolution: that is, as enacted through final causes.

What of the remaining threads used to defend the old "change of mind" hypothesis? It should first be pointed out that there is nothing in Wallace's writings at this time (or later) to suggest that he was a "disillusioned socialist" during this period; in fact, just about all of his writings on socialism and the social reformer Robert Owen date from 1889 on, because before that point he simply had not felt that socialism was practicable. Further, while it has often been posed that Wallace's adoption of spiritualism caused him to alter his position on humankind's evolution, he is on record himself (in the preface to his book *On Miracles and Modern Spiritualism*) as saying this was not the case. The changes that he made in his 1864 essay "The Origin of Human Races and the Antiquity of Man" when it was included in the collection *Contributions of the Theory of Natural Selection* in 1870 have sometimes been offered as evidence of a change of mind, but were this the case, why in the preface of the latter work would he specifically say "I had intended to have considerably extended this essay, but on attempting it I found that I should probably weaken the effect without adding much to the argument. I have therefore preferred to leave it as it was first written, with the exception of a few ill-considered passages which never fully expressed my meaning" (p. viii)? Again, there is no real evidence here or in the adjusted passages of owning up to a "change of mind" of the sort accused. Finally, there is Wallace's 18 April 1869 letter to Darwin, in which he states:

> I can quite comprehend your feelings with regard to my 'unscientific' opinions as to Man, because a few years back I should myself have looked at them as equally wild and uncalled for … My opinions on the subject have been modified solely by the consideration of a series of remarkable phenomena, physical and mental, which I have now had every opportunity of fully testing. (in Marchant, pp. 199–200)

Here Wallace simply states a fact: that his opinions have been "modified"—not changed (that is, reversed)—by this new source of information. The interpretation that this modification constituted a full-blown reversal of position has for many years been fed by the assumption that Wallace intended his ideas as expressed in 1858 to apply to humankind, which as shown above is an unlikely stretch.

To summarize, in his early years Wallace held a Bauplan-like view of nature and society, which featured a utilitarian role for productive belief in the social milieu but rejected necessary utility of adaptations at the biological level (that is, both bad ideas and bad biological structures were eventually weeded out by more remote, weighty forces). In 1858 he realized how a "necessary utility" model not related to first causes thinking—natural selection—could operate. This however still left him unable to explain how the turnover process might operate at the level of higher consciousness. In late 1865, while already investigating séance phenomena, he began attending a series of public soirees, given by the spiritualist lecturer Emma Hardinge, that linked spiritualist teachings to natural science. Wallace was obviously impressed, soon after beginning to compose his *Scientific Aspect of the Supernatural*, published in a magazine in the summer of 1866 and soon thereafter as a pamphlet (this contains many quotations from Hardinge's writings). There had been no "change of mind," just the finalization of an evolutionary model in which natural selection and spiritualism stood side by side. (Further development of the "no change of mind" model appears in this author's *Alfred Russel Wallace: Evolution of an Evolutionist*, an online monograph hosted by *The Alfred Russel Wallace Page*).

The "no change of mind" model leaves the scholar in a much better position to understand Wallace's later work, and indeed to contrast his approach to evolutionary studies with Darwin's. As one example, the anthropologist Gregory Bateson recognized as early as 1972 that Wallacean natural selection, describing as it does a mechanism for removal of the unfit (and hence a net return toward

the norm), represents a negative feedback process that of itself does not capture the entire "push-pull" character of irreversible biological change. Understanding this, one can in turn recognize that Wallace was not the hyperselectionist many (especially the late Stephen Jay Gould) have accused him of being: Wallace never argued that natural selection necessarily created the variation on which it acted (and indeed in several instances pointed out that we were entirely ignorant of its origin), merely that all such variation, *once existing*, was subject to its action. One next naturally wonders how exactly to contextualize the remaining positive feedback part of the process, a question central to biogeographic and evolutionary studies alike.

Despite the many advances that have been made in appreciating Wallace on his own terms since 1976, one cannot end here without mentioning the ongoing (more than thirty-year) discussion as to whether Darwin might possibly have stolen ideas from Wallace's 1858 paper "On the Tendency of Varieties to Depart Indefinitely from the Original Type" to help him complete what would become *On the Origin of Species* in 1859. This theory, especially as developed by Arnold C. Brackman in 1980 and John L. Brooks in 1983, is based on real, though by no means overwhelming, evidence. In any case, little new evidence of a kind that could either silence or markedly encourage conspiracy theorists has surfaced for many years.

The complete Wallace is still emerging. In early 2006 this author discovered an unpublished paper that Wallace wrote in 1843 at the age of twenty. This short work, explaining a possible mercury-based technology for preparing lenses in telescopy, was sent to William Henry Fox Talbot, one of the inventors of photography, for comment. There is no evidence Talbot ever responded, but it is intriguing that in 1850 a friend of one of Talbot's colleagues (the prominent astronomer Giovanni Amici, who actually visited Talbot in England in 1844), read a paper in Italy laying out principles fundamental to what in the early twenty-first century is known as spinning mirror telescopy, a related mercury-based technology.

SUPPLEMENTARY BIBLIOGRAPHY

A thorough bibliography of secondary sources, including period reviews of Wallace's books, an iconography, and a list of obituaries, is provided at the Alfred Russel Wallace Page *Web site. The most complete listing of archival resources is in Shermer. A Wallace correspondence project was as of 2007 underway under the direction of the historian James Moore.*

WORKS BY WALLACE

The Alfred Russel Wallace Reader: A Selection of Writings from the Field. Edited by Jane R. Camerini. Baltimore: Johns Hopkins University Press, 2002.

Infinite Tropics: An Alfred Russel Wallace Anthology. Edited by Andrew Berry. London and New York: Verso, 2002.

Alfred Russel Wallace: Writings on Evolution, 1843–1912. Edited by Charles H. Smith. 3 vols. Bristol, U.K.: Thoemmes Continuum, 2004.

OTHER SOURCES

Bateson, Gregory. *Steps to an Ecology of Mind: Collected Essays in Anthropology, Psychiatry, Evolution, and Epistemology.* London: Intertext, 1972.

Brackman, Arnold C. *A Delicate Arrangement: The Strange Case of Charles Darwin and Alfred Russel Wallace.* New York: Times Books, 1980.

Brooks, John L. *Just before the Origin: Alfred Russel Wallace's Theory of Evolution.* New York: Columbia University Press, 1984.

Fichman, Martin. *An Elusive Victorian: The Evolution of Alfred Russel Wallace.* Chicago and London: University of Chicago Press, 2003.

Lieberman, Bruce S. "Geobiology and Paleobiogeography: Tracking the Coevolution of the Earth and Its Biota." *Palaeogeography, Palaeoclimatology, Palaeoecology* 219 (2005): 23–33.

Marchant, James, ed. *Alfred Russel Wallace: Letters and Reminiscences.* New York: Arno, 1975. Reprint of 1916 edition published by Cassell.

Michaux, Bernard. "Distributional Patterns and Tectonic Development in Indonesia: Wallace Reinterpreted." *Australian Systematic Botany* 4 (September 1991): 25–36.

———. "Island Life." *Journal of Biogeography* 27 (2000): 219–222.

Raby, Peter. *Alfred Russel Wallace: A Life.* Princeton, NJ: Princeton University Press, 2001.

Shermer, Michael. *In Darwin's Shadow: The Life and Science of Alfred Russel Wallace: A Biographical Study on the Psychology of History.* New York: Oxford University Press, 2002.

Slotten, Ross A. *The Heretic in Darwin's Court: The Life of Alfred Russel Wallace.* New York: Columbia University Press, 2004.

Smith, Charles H. "Alfred Russel Wallace, Past and Future." *Journal of Biogeography* 32 (2005): 1509–1515.

———. "Wallace's Unfinished Business." *Complexity* 10 (November–December 2004): 25–32.

Charles H. Smith

WALLIS, SARAH EGLONTON

SEE **Lee, Sarah Eglonton Wallis Bowdich**.

WALSH, ALAN (*b.* Hoddlesten, England, 19 December 1916; *d.* Melbourne, Australia, 3 August 1998), *physics, chemical analysis, atomic absorption spectroscopy.*

Walsh originated and developed the atomic absorption method that revolutionized chemical analysis in the 1960s. Atomic absorption spectroscopy provided for the first time a rapid, easy, accurate, and highly sensitive method of determining the concentrations of nearly all the elements in the periodic table. In the early twenty-first century the method is used worldwide in many fields, including medicine, agriculture, mineral exploration, metallurgy, food analysis, and environmental control.

Early Years. Alan Walsh grew up in Hoddlesden, a small moorland village in Lancashire, England. He was the eldest son of Thomas Haworth Walsh, who managed a small cotton mill, and Betsy Alice Walsh. He attended the local grammar school in the nearby town of Darwen, and in 1935 he entered the honors school of physics at the University of Manchester. He went on to do postgraduate research in x-ray crystallography in the Physics Department at the Manchester College of Technology—later to become the University of Manchester Institute of Science and Technology (UMIST)—where he was awarded an MSc (Tech).

Walsh's postgraduate research was interrupted by the outbreak of World War II. In September 1939 he started work with the British Non-Ferrous Metals Research Association (BNF) in London to determine the composition of alloys being used in enemy bombers that had been shot down. The procedure he used was to make the alloy sample an electrode of an electric arc or spark discharge and to analyze the wavelengths of the emitted atomic spectral lines in a spectrograph. During his time at the BNF he devised and built a prototype of the General Purpose Source Unit (Walsh, 1946), which was a versatile but simple electrical source unit that could generate arc-like and spark-like discharges for use in spectrographic emission analysis. The source unit was subsequently manufactured by Hilger and Watts Ltd., London, as the BNF Spectrographic Source Unit FS 130.

CSIR/CSIRO Years. After World War II, Walsh accepted a position as research officer in the Division of Industrial Chemistry at the Council for Scientific and Industrial Research (CSIR)—now the Commonwealth Scientific and Industrial Research Organization (CSIRO)—in Melbourne, Australia. Shortly after arriving in Melbourne he met an English-born nurse, Audrey Dale Hutchinson, whom he married on 25 June 1949. They had two sons, Thomas Haworth and David Alan.

At CSIR Walsh established the first infrared spectrometer in Australia—a Perkin-Elmer Model 12B—which was used for research in infrared molecular spectroscopy and was also available for use by various chemists around Australia. Walsh soon realized, however, that the resolution of the infrared spectrometer was inadequate for resolving the rotational structure of all but the lightest molecules. To improve the resolution he devised a simple and elegant modification of the infrared prism monochromator by placing a pair of right-angle mirrors at the exit slit to reflect the radiation back through the prism (Walsh, 1951). To isolate the desired multiple-pass beam from the other beams, he placed a rotating "chopper" in front of the additional mirrors to modulate only the multiple-pass beam and fed the output of the detector to an amplifier tuned to the frequency of the chopper. Perkin-Elmer secured an exclusive license for the double-pass monochromator and in 1953 began manufacturing a kit of Walsh Mirrors to allow their standard infrared spectrometer to be converted to a double-pass system.

After arriving at CSIR Walsh also initiated a project to investigate the fundamental processes occurring in spectrographic atomic emission sources similar to the General Purpose Source Unit he developed at the BNF in London. Although such source units were by then well established in laboratories in England, the CSIR unit proved to be rather unreliable and Walsh became disillusioned with it.

Atomic Absorption Method. One Sunday morning in March 1952, while gardening at his home, Walsh had a flash of thought, something that stemmed from his previous experiences in atomic emission spectroscopy and infrared molecular absorption spectroscopy. He had been wondering why it was that molecular spectra were usually obtained in absorption while atomic spectra were obtained in emission. He could see that atomic absorption spectra offered many important advantages over atomic emission spectra as far as spectrochemical analysis was concerned. Early next morning he set up a simple experiment consisting of a standard sodium vapor lamp as a source of the sodium yellow D lines and an air-coal gas flame as the sampling medium. The sodium vapor lamp was operated from a 50 Hz mains electric supply to provide an alternating source of light, and the D lines were isolated, but not resolved from each other, by means of a simple low-resolution spectrometer. The combined intensity of the D lines transmitted by the flame was recorded by a photomultiplier at the exit slit of the monochromator, and the output signal fed to the AC input of a cathode ray oscillograph. When a solution containing a few milligrams of sodium chloride was sprayed into the air supply of the flame, the cathode spot on the oscillograph deflected to zero, thus establishing the principle of the atomic absorption method of spectrochemical analysis.

Apparently, while reading Samuel Tolansky's book *High Resolution Spectroscopy* (1947), Walsh learned that a hollow-cathode discharge can provide a source of sharp

spectral lines for a very wide range of elements. In early 1953 he and a colleague, John Shelton, set out to construct hollow-cathode lamps of the type described by Tolansky, in which the rare gas was pumped continuously through traps in a closed circulating system to remove molecular impurities liberated by the cathode and the walls of the tube. During a visit to the United States in mid-1953, Walsh became aware of the work of Gerhard Dieke and H. Milton Crosswhite (Letter to the editor, *Journal of the Optical Society of America* 42, 1952, p. 433) who were using compact sealed-off hollow-cathode lamps in which the gaseous impurities were removed by a "getter" of activated uranium. Walsh and Shelton then abandoned the complex gas circulating system and began the development of sealed-off hollow-cathode lamps with zirconium getters for all the elements that could be determined by atomic absorption. The first satisfactory sealed-off hollow-cathode lamps were constructed and tested towards the end of 1953.

Walsh had now arrived at a satisfactory method for making the atomic absorption measurements and a basic experimental arrangement that had all the essential components of a modern commercial atomic absorption spectrophotometer: a sealed-off hollow-cathode lamp as the source, a flame as the sampling absorber, and a "chopper" and synchronously tuned amplifier to separate the emission of the source from the luminous emission of the flame absorber. A provisional patent application was lodged on 17 November 1953. Soon after filing the final patent specification (Australian Patent Specification 163,586, Oct. 21, 1954), Walsh submitted his landmark paper "The Application of Atomic Absorption Spectra to Chemical Analysis" (Walsh 1955). At virtually the same time, a paper titled "A Double-Beam Method of Spectral Selection with Flames" was published by Kees Alkemade and Jan Milatz (*Applied Science Research* B4, 1955, pp. 289–299), who had arrived independently at the concept of atomic absorption spectroscopy. Alkemade and Milatz, however, did not pursue their work further.

The first working atomic absorption spectrophotometer was exhibited in March 1954 at an exhibition of scientific instruments held by the Victorian Division of the (British) Institute of Physics at the University of Melbourne (see Figure 1). The instrument demonstrated the analysis of copper samples, using a copper hollow-cathode source. However, there was also provision for a sodium vapor lamp, and viewers were invited to dip their (salty) finger into a beaker of water, and this would register a deflection on the strip chart recorder.

Commercialization of Atomic Absorption. During 1953 Walsh had toured England and the United States and discussed the possible commercial exploitation of atomic

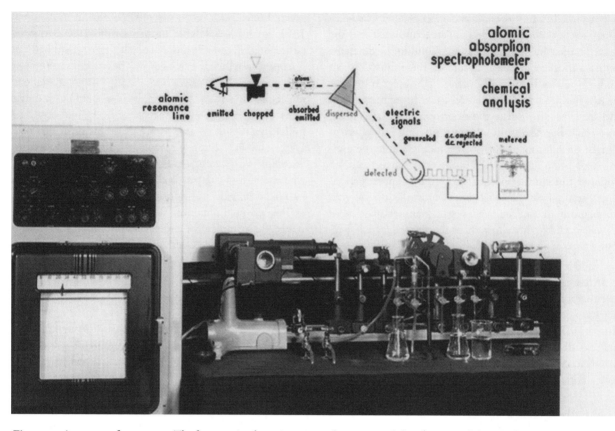

First atomic spectrophotometer. *The first atomic absorption spectrophotometer, exhibited at an Exhibition of Scientific Instruments, Victorian Branch of the (British) Institute of Physics, Melbourne, in March 1954. This instrument is located at the Science Works Museum, Melbourne.* **SCIENCE PHOTO LIBRARY/PHOTO RESEARCHERS, INC.**

absorption with a number of instrument manufacturers. The only person to show any enthusiasm in commercializing atomic absorption equipment was Alexander Menzies, a physicist and director of research for Hilger and Watts Ltd., with whom Walsh had previously had dealings through the manufacture of the BNF General Purpose Source Unit. CSIRO arrived at an exclusive license agreement with Hilger and Watts, based on the provisional patent application. During the period Hilger and Watts held an exclusive license (1953–1957), progress was slowed by technical difficulties, including the development of satisfactory hollow-cathode lamps. They had decided to manufacture the atomic absorption equipment as an attachment to an existing Hilger and Watts Uvispek spectrophotometer and there was no provision in the attachment for modulating the light from the source, and thus for discriminating the emission of the source from the emission of the luminous flame absorber. Although Hilger and Watts recognized the limitations of the Uvispek attachment, it was decided to continue with the manufacture of the simple attachment. The first atomic absorption instrument, the Model H 909, was sold in

early 1958, and sales continued at about thirty to sixty instruments a year for several years.

By 1958 there was still no instrument company prepared to produce the type of atomic absorption instrument Walsh considered necessary. He then decided to produce a list of instructions on how to put together a do-it-yourself kit. Fred Box of CSIRO designed and built the prototype electronics, which included a broadband AC amplifier—the "Working Man's Amplifier"—and a power supply to run the hollow-cathode lamps; George Jones and later John Sullivan of CSIRO developed and provided the expertise and hands-on skills for producing the hollow-cathode lamps; and a simple commercially available monochromator such as the Zeiss quartz-prism monochromator was recommended for isolating the relevant atomic absorption lines.

Walsh then went in search of businesses that were prepared to manufacture components that were not available commercially. The electronics part of the equipment was perfectly conventional, so he put out a tender for manufacturing six amplifiers and power packs. A small firm, Techtron Appliances, put in the lowest bid and got the business. He also toured the backyards of Melbourne and found a small machine shop, run by Stuart R. Skinner, to make various mechanical components. He then tried various glass-blowing people to make the lamps and found a small firm, Ransley Glass Instruments—later to become Atomic Spectral Lamps—that was willing to try. By mid-1962 more than thirty of these do-it-yourself kits had been supplied to Australian laboratories and about ten to other parts of the world, including New Zealand and South Africa.

In July 1962 Walsh and his CSIRO Chief, Lloyd Rees, arranged a symposium on atomic absorption spectroscopy, which was attended by about eighty potential users and CSIRO staff. At the end of the symposium the chairman of Techtron Appliances Pty. Ltd., Geoffrey Frew, declared his intention to manufacture a "complete" atomic absorption spectrophotometer. By early 1964 Techtron had produced the first all-Australian atomic absorption instrument, the Model AA-3, which incorporated a "Sirospec" grating monochromator designed by John McNeill at CSIRO, diffraction gratings ruled on a ruling engine designed and constructed at CSIRO, and an AC amplifier unit designed by Fred Box at CSIRO. The AA-3 was exhibited publicly for the first time at the Pittsburgh Conference on Analytical Chemistry in March 1964.

During his lecture tour to the United States in 1958, Walsh visited the Perkin-Elmer Corporation, with whom he had previously had dealings with regard to the double-pass infrared monochromator. A Perkin-Elmer representative indicated to him that the company would be interested in becoming a licensed manufacturer of atomic absorption equipment if it could be shown capable of determining calcium in blood serum. In March 1959 a colleague of Walsh's, John Willis, submitted a report of his atomic absorption work on calcium and magnesium in blood serum to Perkin-Elmer. In November 1959 Perkin-Elmer was granted a license from CSIRO to manufacture atomic absorption equipment and, in 1960, a group headed by Walter Slavin was established to develop an atomic absorption instrument. In March 1962 Perkin-Elmer began building a completely new atomic absorption instrument, the Model 303, which was released on the market in April 1963, at about the same time as the first Techtron atomic absorption instrument, the AA-2, which used an imported monochromator. By 1965 the Model 303 had already overtaken infrared spectroscopy as Perkin-Elmer's largest product line and had captured the bulk of the atomic absorption market.

In August 1965 Techtron Appliances merged with Atomic Spectral Lamps to form Techtron Pty. Ltd., which manufactured the Techtron Model AA-4 with a synchronously tuned amplifier and a nitrous oxide-acelylene burner. This was followed by a period of rapid growth in the company. In October 1967 Techtron was approached with an offer of acquisition by Varian Associates, thus becoming Varian Techtron Pty. Ltd., and later Varian Australia Pty. Ltd. As of 2007 Varian Australia in Melbourne, with a staff of around 400, had the second-largest share of the atomic absorption market after the Perkin-Elmer Corporation, while GBC Scientific Equipment Pty. Ltd. in Melbourne, with a staff of around 180, was the third largest.

In 1966 Max Amos from Sulphide Corporation in Australia and John Willis from CSIRO published a paper on the use of the high-temperature nitrous oxide-acetylene flame, which extended the applicability of the atomic absorption method to more than sixty-five elements. From that stage onward there was a dramatic increase in interest in the atomic absorption method and it rapidly gained worldwide acceptance.

In 1968 A. W. Brown, a scientist with qualifications in business administration, was approached by CSIRO to conduct a cost-benefit analysis of the atomic absorption project. Brown's study conservatively assessed the value of the net benefits to the Australian economy at around $22 million (in 1968 Australian dollars), compared with $1.3 million originally spent on the research (Brown, 1969). Later estimates gave the accumulated benefit to Australia by the year 1977 as in excess of $200 million, including overseas royalties, the setting up of new industry, and the productivity increases in a wide range of enterprises. Surprisingly, Brown found that the major benefits to the Australian economy were not through the manufacture of atomic absorption equipment but rather through benefits to the end user, that is, benefits associated with productivity gains, especially the ability to perform large numbers of assays very rapidly and with high accuracy. This component far outweighed the benefits of manufacture and royalties.

After development the atomic absorption method, Walsh's research was directed toward developing novel instruments and techniques to simplify and improve atomic absorption equipment. In particular, he believed it should be possible to replace the monochromator, which was rather fragile, bulky, and expensive, with a simpler, more rugged device suitable for use in working environments where the samples were actually being taken. In 1965 he and John Sullivan developed the so-called resonance detector which consisted of a vapor cell of the appropriate element to selectively absorb the resonance lines from the source and a photomultiplier to detect the atomic fluorescence emitted by the vapor cell. The resonance detector was followed by the development of the ingenious technique of "selective modulation" for isolating atomic resonance lines (Walsh and Sullivan, 1966). With this technique, radiation from a sharp-line source such as a hollow-cathode lamp is passed through a pulsating vapor of absorbing atoms, and the resonance lines are detected using a synchronous amplifier tuned to the frequency of modulation of the atomic vapor.

For applications involving resonance detectors or the detection of the fluorescence radiation, light intensities higher than those available from standard hollow-cathode lamps were needed. In 1965 Walsh and John Sullivan developed the "high-intensity" hollow-cathode lamp (Walsh and Sullivan, 1965), which has two discharges—a hollow-cathode discharge to generate an atomic vapor by cathodic sputtering and a high electron-current discharge to excite the atoms. The Sullivan-Walsh high-intensity lamp allows the intensity of the resonance lines to be increased up to a hundredfold without significant increase in atom density, and hence line width, and it also allows most of the light output to be concentrated in the strongest resonance line. Such lamps are manufactured by Varian Australia Pty. Ltd., by the Perkin-Elmer Corporation, and by Photron Pty. Ltd. in Melbourne.

Walsh was particularly conscious of the limitations of the flame as an atomizer, such as incomplete atomization of most elements (giving rise to low sensitivity and possible "chemical interferences"); the necessity of having an oxidant in the flame rendering vacuum UV wavelengths inaccessible; the need for prior dissolution of the sample; the presence of various molecular species that can introduce unwanted background absorption signals; and the need for an explosive gas such as acetylene, which is undesirable in certain working environments such as hospitals. In 1959 Walsh and Barbara Russell reported that a hollow-cathode discharge can provide a simple and convenient means of generating an atomic vapor of essentially any solid element. With the sputtering method, energetic rare-gas ions formed in the hollow-cathode discharge bombard the surface of the cathode and eject atoms to produce an atomic vapor, thus providing a means BY which metals and alloys can be atomized directly without prior dissolution. Furthermore, the method should, in principle, not be subject to any of the above limitations of the flame. In 1973 Walsh, together with David Gough and Peter Hannaford, reported the first results, on the determination of a range of elements in solid samples of iron-base. An atomic absorption system based on the sputtering method of vaporization was later manufactured by the Analyte Corporation, United States, in 1988.

Later Career. In January 1977, just after his sixtieth birthday and after thirty years of service, Walsh retired from CSIRO. About a year later he became a formal consultant to Perkin-Elmer. He had earlier participated with Perkin-Elmer in some major commercial decisions, including decisions to construct their own hollow-cathode lamps, to

manufacture a Zeeman attachment to correct for background absorption, and to manufacture the inductively coupled plasma (ICP) source. Between 1978 and 1982 he and his wife, Audrey, spent several European summers beside the Bodensee near Überlingen, Germany, where he made frequent visits to Perkin-Elmer's Bodenseewerk. At that time the main research interest at Bodenseewerk was the hydride generation technique for atomic absorption. Walsh suggested that it might be interesting to combine the hydride work with a solar-blind photomultiplier to provide a simple non-dispersive atomic fluorescence spectrometer for the determination of arsenic and selenium. The engineers build a prototype that worked nicely. Some years later the Chinese built a highly successful hydride instrument.

During the early 1980s Walsh initiated a project to investigate a new type of spectrochemical analysis based on coherent forward scattering (Walsh 1984), which had been pioneered as a spectroscopic technique in the mid-1960s by George Series in Oxford. The technique relies on the fact that the light emitted by atoms in the forward direction is phase-coherent, and so the signal intensity is proportional to the square of the number of atoms rather than to the number of atoms, thus offering the prospect of much higher sensitivity than atomic absorption spectroscopy. The technique also has the advantage that the signal is insensitive to any background light scattered from particles in the atomic vapor. With Walsh's help, Perkin-Elmer conducted AN extensive development program on coherent forward scattering and built a system derived from their Zeeman background correction instrument. The program was later abandoned when it was considered not to be commercially attractive. In 1982 Walsh was invited back to CSIRO as a senior research fellow, where he remained until shortly before his death in August 1998.

Honors and Awards. Walsh's scientific contributions were recognized by a number of prestigious honors and awards. He was elected a fellow of the Australian Academy of Science in 1958, a fellow of the Royal Society of London in 1969, and a foreign member of the Royal Swedish Academy of Sciences in 1969. His list of awards includes the Britannica Australia Award for Science (1966), Talanta Gold Medal (1969), Maurice Hasler Award of the Society of Applied Spectroscopy USA (1975), Kronland Medal of the Czechoslovak Spectroscopy Society (1975), Royal Medal of the Royal Society of London (1976), Torbern Bergman Medal of the Swedish Chemical Society (1976), and Robert Boyle Medal of the Royal Society of Chemistry (1982). He was created a knight bachelor in 1977 for his services to science.

BIBLIOGRAPHY

A complete bibliography of Alan Walsh's works can be found in Historical Records of Australian Science *13 (2000): 179–206. His personal papers are kept in the Basser Library at the Australian Academy of Science in Canberra, Australia.*

WORKS BY WALSH

"A General-Purpose Source Unit for the Spectrographic Analysis of Metals and Alloys." *Bulletin of the British Non-Ferrous Metals Research Association* 201 (1946): 60–80.

"Design of Multiple Monochromators." *Nature* 167 (1951): 810–811.

"The Application of Atomic Absorption Spectra to Chemical Analysis." *Spectrochimica Acta* 7 (1955): 108–117; erratum, 252.

With Barbara J. Russell and John P. Shelton. "An Atomic Absorption Spectrophotometer and Its Application to the Analysis of Solutions." *Spectrochimica Acta* 8 (1957): 317–328.

With Barbara J. Russell. "Resonance Radiation from a Hollow Cathode." *Spectrochimica Acta* 15 (1959): 883–885.

With B. M. Gatehouse. "Analysis of Metal Samples by Atomic Absorption Spectroscopy." *Spectrochimica Acta* 16 (1960): 602–604.

With W. Goerge Jones. "Hollow-Cathode Discharges: The Construction and Characteristics of Sealed-off Tubes for Use as Spectroscopic Light Sources." *Spectrochimica Acta* 16 (1960): 249–254.

With G. Fred Box. "A Simple Atomic Absorption Spectrophotometer." *Spectrochimica Acta* 16 (1960): 255–258.

With John V. Sullivan. "High Intensity Hollow-Cathode Lamps." *Spectrochimica Acta* 21 (1965): 721–726.

With Judith A. Bowman and John V. Sullivan. "Isolation of Atomic Resonance Lines by Selective Modulation." *Spectrochimica Acta* 22 (1966): 205–210.

With David S. Gough and Peter Hannaford. "The Application of Cathodic Sputtering to the Production of Atomic Vapours in Atomic Fluorescence Spectroscopy." *Spectrochimica Acta B,* 28 (1973), 197–210.

"Atomic Absorption Spectroscopy—Stagnant or Pregnant?" *Analytical Chemistry* 46 (1974): 689A–708A.

"The Application of Atomic Absorption Spectrometry to Chemical Analysis." Matthews Flinders Lecture of the Australian Academy of Science. *Historical Records of Australian Science* 5 (1980): 129–162.

"Atomic Absorption Spectroscopy—Some Personal Recollections and Speculations." *Spectrochimica Acta Part B* 35 (1980): 639–642.

With J. M. Ottaway, Walter Slavin, and Sydney S. Greenfield. "Atomic Absorption Symposium." *Analytical Proceedings,* 21 (1984): 54–55.

"The Development of Atomic Absorption Methods of Elemental Analysis 1952–1962." *Analytical Chemistry* 63 (1991): 933A–941A.

OTHER SOURCES

Alan Walsh Memorial Issue. *Spectrochimica Acta Part B* 54 (1999): 1933–2194.

Amos, Max, and John B. Willis. "The Use of High-Temperature Pre-Mixed Flames in Atomic Absorption Spectroscopy." *Spectrochimica Acta* 22 (1966): 1325–1343.

"Atomic Absorption Spectroscopy: Past, Present, and Future: To Commemorate the 25th Anniversary of Alan Walsh's Landmark Paper in *Spectrochimica Acta.*" *Spectrochimica Acta Part B* 35 (1980): 637–993.

Brown, A. W. "The Economic Benefits to Australia from Atomic Absorption Spectroscopy." *Economic Record* (June 1969): 158–180.

Carseldine, M. L. "The Development of Atomic Absorption Spectroscopy and Subsequent Instrument Manufacturing Industry that Has Arisen in Australia." MSc thesis. Griffith University, Brisbane, 1984.

Hannaford, Peter. "Alan Walsh 1916–1998." *Historical Records of Australian Science* 13 (2000): 179–206.

———. "Sir Alan Walsh." *Biographical Memoirs of Fellows of the Royal Society of London* 46 (2000): 533–564.

Larkins, P. L. "Sir Alan Walsh: The Scientist and the Man." *Analyst* 117 (1992): 231–233.

Willis, H. A. "Sir Alan Walsh, the Inventor of Atomic Absorption Spectrometry." *ESN Interviews, European Spectroscopy News* 24 (1979): 18–23.

Willis, J. B. "Spectroscopic Research in the CSIRO Division of Chemical Physics 1944–1986." *Historical Records of Australian Science* 8 (1989): 151–182.

Peter Hannaford

WASHBURN, SHERWOOD LAR-NED (*b.* Cambridge, Massachusetts, 16 November 1911; *d.* Berkeley, California, 16 April 2000), *physical anthropology, primatology, human evolution.*

Washburn is regarded as the most influential North American physical anthropologist of the postwar decades. A sharp and incisive thinker who transcended narrow disciplinary boundaries, he reshaped physical anthropology from a formerly race-ridden discipline to a modern field of evolutionary research. Fascinated by what the behavior of monkeys and apes might reveal about human origins, he was also instrumental in the emergence of American primatology. Though he never wrote a book, did little primary research, and was not a specialist in any particular field, his forty years of teaching at Columbia, Chicago, and Berkeley left their mark on generations of students. The hunting hypothesis, his principal theory of human evolution, however, has been largely discarded.

Sherwood Larned Washburn. *Sherwood Washburn in his office at University of California at Berkeley.* © TED STRESHINSKY/CORBIS.

Upbringing and Education (1911–1940). The second son of a well-to-do New England family, Sherwood ("Sherry") Washburn grew up in an intellectually privileged environment. His father, Henry Bradford Washburn, a minister and former professor of church history, was dean of the Episcopal Theological School in Cambridge. Young Washburn was impressed by his father's oratory qualities, but felt little urge to follow in his religious footsteps. As a boy, he was fascinated by natural history and kept captive hawks and three great horned owls. Weekends and school holidays were spent at the Harvard Museum of Comparative Zoology where he helped to prepare birds and small mammals. He was sent to private schools at Belmont Hill and Groton and went on to Harvard, the university also attended by his brother, father, and uncles. Family connections helped in this early stage: the anthropologist Alfred Tozzer, Washburn's freshman advisor, was an old family friend. His appealing mixture of biological evolution, cultural anthropology, and prehistoric archaeology steered Washburn's interest from zoology and medicine to anthropology.

Completing his BA in 1935 summa cum laude, Washburn enrolled for graduate school at Harvard with Earnest A. Hooton and attended courses on comparative anatomy and vertebrate paleontology. At the end of his first year, an opportunity arose to participate in the legendary Asiatic Primate Expedition of 1937. The Sheldon fellowship granted by the university allowed him first to travel to the University of Michigan where Wilfrid Taylor Dempster introduced him to the functional anatomy of joints and bones, and then to Oxford where the great morphologist Wilfrid E. Le Gros Clark taught him a more systemic, pattern-based approach to primate anatomy. These perspectives were to become crucial in Washburn's work.

The expedition took him to Sri Lanka, Singapore, Thailand, and Borneo and has been described as "one of the last of the nineteenth-century-style colonial collecting ventures and the first of the new primate behavior field trips" (Haraway, 1989, p. 205). The expedition was led by the zoologist and conservationist Harold J. Coolidge. Washburn worked most closely together with Adolph H. Schultz, the Swiss primate morphologist for whom he dissected and prepared fresh kills. Schultz focused on biometrical aspects of growth and variation with proboscis monkeys, gibbons, and orangutans, while he let Washburn study the smaller monkeys. For a couple of weeks Washburn helped the primate behaviorist Clarence Ray Carpenter with his groundbreaking observational study of gibbons—one of the first successful studies of primate behavior in the wild—but he later recalled that "it was just the wrong time to expect me to shift gears from anatomy to behaviour" (DeVore, 1992, p. 415).

Upon his return to Harvard, he used the material from the expedition for his doctoral dissertation, which he completed in 1940 under the title "A Preliminary Metrical Study of the Skeleton of Langurs and Macaques," the first in anthropology on nonhuman primates. Paraphrased in a twenty-eight-page article two years later, it was the longest of all the single-authored papers he would write throughout his life. His supervisor Hooton was the most influential and popular physical anthropologist of his generation. Hooton was generous to Washburn, Washburn was loyal to Hooton, but the intellectual differences between them were frankly enormous. The guiding principle of Hooton's work, as witnessed in his witty, if race-based classic *Up from the Ape* (1931), was the validation of existing racial typologies through metrical and statistical procedures. That races were not fixed and clearly delineated biological entities, but at best fluid populations that only differ in gene frequencies, was something Washburn could not get across to him. Washburn thought in terms of adaptations, Hooton in terms of traits. Nonetheless, Washburn could "appreciate his undergraduate teaching, his support of evolutionary studies, and his interest in behavior, but repudiate[d] his concept of race, research methods, and his applications of physical anthropology" (Washburn, 1983, p. 2).

Experimental Research at Columbia University (1939–1947). After an early teaching experience at Harvard, Washburn was hired in 1939 by Samuel Detwiler as an assistant professor at Columbia University's College of Physicians and Surgeons. The move to New York proved important in several respects. As an experimental embryologist, Detwiler helped Washburn with a series of laboratory experiments with live animals. In one of them, the eye of a large amphibian embryo was put into the developing eye socket of a smaller species. Washburn observed how the bony structure of the socket could grow by 140 percent. On other occasions, the cheekbone, parietal bone, or temporal muscle of rats were removed, so that the skull growth could be studied.

These "Frankensteinian" experiments demonstrated that the skull's bony structure—the very basis on which many racial typologies had been based—was not determined by genetic design, but was something highly malleable. Muscles were the form-determining element in bone growth, while "bone was, next to the blood, the most plastic tissue in the body" (Washburn, 1983, p. 7). For many physical anthropologists, experiments on rats and amphibians seemed like a long way from home. But Washburn's surprising results showed that the scalpel could be as useful to anthropology as the calipers.

This research would eventually cumulate in a forceful theoretical reorientation of the field, which found its apogee in the 1951 article "The New Physical Anthropology." While the old school of Hooton was descriptive, speculative, and impressionistic, Washburn pleaded for a new physical anthropology that was explanatory, experimental, and theoretical. An integrated approach was needed:

> Bones, ligaments, muscles have to be discussed together, not as separate entities, and I argued that this was equivalent to the kind of change that Malinowski brought to ethnology. The goal is to look for functional patterns, trying to see how the thing works as a system. It isn't as though one is going to do a distribution of paddles around the Pacific and talk about the reconstruction of history only from paddles. (DeVore, 1992, p. 418)

Much like Bronisław Malinowski believed that societies should be understood as functional wholes rather than as poorly conceptualized trait lists, Washburn argued for a physical anthropology that considered the organism as a functional whole rather than as a series of anatomic features. If Malinowski provided a metaphor (paddles were to society what cranial indices were to the body, i.e.,

observations with little explanatory power), the modern evolutionary synthesis the substance. This synthesis of Darwinian evolution with Mendelian genetics evolved in the 1930s and 1940s and became the twentieth century's leading paradigm in biology. Instead of considering species as abstract entities with distinct traits, it focused on populations with their dynamic adaptations. Almost single-handedly, Washburn introduced this neo-Darwinist synthesis into physical anthropology which, for a while, he preferred to label "biological anthropology." Once the organism is no longer understood as a set of fixed features, but as a dynamic and functional whole, the unit of analysis no longer becomes the individual organism but the population with all its variability. For Hooton, this variability was a nuisance, for Washburn it was the essence of a more dynamic view of biology.

Next to Columbia's laboratory facilities, New York in the 1940s also offered numerous encounters with intellectuals from all over the world. The city was teeming with exiled scholars from Europe. At the American Museum of Natural History, Washburn repeatedly discussed fossils with Franz Weidenreich, a German paleontologist who had earned worldwide recognition for his excavation of Peking Man but who, as a Jew, had fled Germany in 1934. He equally befriended Theodosius Dobzhansky, the Ukrainian-born geneticist who had come to the United States in 1927 and whose work on the fruit fly was essential for the modern evolutionary synthesis. Two other architects of that synthesis, the German-born Ernst Mayr (who settled in the United States in 1932) and George Gaylord Simpson, were at the Museum of Natural History and Washburn became well acquainted with the latter. At Columbia's Department of Zoology, he discussed ideas with the great comparative anatomist and paleontologist William King Gregory, whose emphasis on function left a lasting impression. Gabriel W. Lasker, one of the founders of a more modern physical anthropology, became a close friend. Washburn was never immediately involved with the war, but these contacts made him sharply aware of the role science had played in paving the way for political racism.

Most importantly in the light of his further career, Washburn encountered Paul Fejos, the flamboyant Hungarian American film director and anthropologist who was the first director of the Viking Fund, later called the Wenner-Gren Foundation for Anthropological Research. Benefiting from an important endowment by the Swedish industrialist Alex Wenner-Gren, the Viking Fund was to become a major force shaping North American anthropology. Washburn called its director "one of the most imaginative and creative people I have ever known" (1983, p. 20). Fejos invited Washburn to his monthly supper conferences, supported Washburn's summer schools on physical anthropology, and invited him on travels to Africa. In

1948 Washburn flew to Uganda to collect cercopithecine monkeys and then to South Africa to study the first australopithecine fossils discovered by Raymond Dart and Robert Broom.

At the crossroads of this new physical anthropology, the modern evolutionary synthesis, the Viking Fund, and the former British colonies in East and South Africa, during the following decades a research program would unfold in which australopithecine fossils, savanna baboons, the Kalahari Bushmen, and the hunting hypothesis provided a new, inclusive, antiracial story of human origins (Haraway, 1989, p. 187). In line with the UNESCO declarations on race and the "unity of mankind" and the sense of "universal brotherhood" that emanated from Edward Steichen's contemporary monumental photograph exhibition *The Family of Man*, Washburn's research program stressed that all of humanity shared the same deep ancestry in which hunting was the quintessential adaptation. Ironically, the prime financier of this program, the multimillionaire home-appliance patriarch and fridge patriarch Alex Wenner-Gren, one of the world's wealthiest men in the 1940s, was accused of affinities with the Nazis and friendship with Hermann Goering.

Behavioral Research at the University of Chicago (1947–1958). In 1947 Washburn moved from Columbia to Chicago to replace Wilton Krogman at a joint appointment in anthropology and anatomy. When the anatomy department withdrew its support, Washburn was deprived of access to a laboratory. It was in Chicago, however, that Washburn achieved his apex as a theoretician for the radically new physical anthropology. With Dobzhansky he organized the landmark symposium Origin and Evolution of Man at Cold Spring Harbor in 1950. One year later, the publication of his essay "The New Physical Anthropology" confirmed his stature as the leading physical anthropologist of his generation. That year he was elected president of the American Association of Physical Anthropologists. He was forty and full of ideas.

Chicago was an extraordinary place. "The people there were very active, very imaginative, very widely read, completely different and yet they got along marvelously" (DeVore, 1992, p. 418). The anthropology department—the famous "Chicago school" with Sol Tax, Fred Eggan, and Robert Redfield—was strongly influenced by the British functionalism of Malinowski and Alfred Radcliffe-Brown, while the rest of the country was still largely Boasian. Functionalist anthropology believed that society is a dynamic system of functional elements in which social phenomena act as adaptations, pretty much as Washburn regarded an organism and its features.

In 1955 Washburn participated at the Pan-African Congress in Livingstone, Northern Rhodesia (now Zambia), organized by the British archaeologist J. Desmond Clark. While the 1937 expedition to Asia had been critical to his anatomical work, the 1955 trip in Africa would steer his research toward behavior.

> After the Congress [...] I arranged for a small collection of baboons. But much more importantly, as it turned out, there were troops of baboons close to the Victoria Falls Hotel where I was staying. The supply of baboons was irregular, and I spent any extra time watching the local troops. This was so much more rewarding that I closed out the collecting and spent my time watching the tame baboons. [...] Almost at once the animals ceased to be just baboons; they became personalities. (Washburn, 1983, p. 16)

Imbued with British functionalist anthropology, Washburn observed locomotion, group structure, and dominance hierarchies, and soon came to believe that "Malinowski's functional theory probably works more usefully for monkey than for human beings" (Washburn, 1983, p. 17). Back home, he urged graduate student Irven DeVore to join him on a more extensive fieldwork project with olive baboons in the Nairobi and Amboseli National Parks in Kenya. DeVore, who was trained as an anthropologist, recalls Washburn's instructions: "My marching orders were very straight-forward. 'DeVore, you've absorbed Murdock, Radcliffe-Brown, and Malinowski. Go out and tell us what it's like with the baboons'" (Haraway, 1989, p. 219). Phyllis Jay (later Dolhinow), another of Washburn's first graduate students, started to study hanuman langurs in India.

Primatology was still in its infancy then. Apart from Carpenter's work on howler monkeys and gibbons and Stuart and Jeanne Altmanns' work on baboons, little naturalistic observations on wild primates had been done. Jane Goodall and Dian Fossey had not yet begun their research; Hans Kummer, Thelma Rowell, Adriaan Kortlandt, and George Schaller were only starting; and Eugène Marais was forgotten. Family reasons prevented Washburn from undertaking much fieldwork himself, but his style of primatology was explicitly organized from the perspective of human evolution. "The greatest contribution of the study of the nonhuman primates," he later wrote, "might be to free us from some of the traditional limitations and points of view" (Washburn, 1973, p. 178). In a series of papers around 1960, he successively explored how the behavior of baboons could help to understand the primeval stock from which humanity had sprung. As the enormous variation of primate social life was still unclear, for Washburn the baboon simply embodied a generic primate pattern.

Teaching at University of California, Berkeley (1958–1979). Having revolutionized physical anthropology with a few critical papers and having stimulated primatology with a handful of graduate students, Washburn had become a cardinal figure in American science. After a year as a fellow at the Institute for Advanced Study in Behavioral Sciences in Palo Alto, he was offered a professorship at Berkeley in 1958. He served as president of the American Anthropological Association (AAA) in 1962 and became a member of the National Academy of Sciences in 1963. He was awarded the Viking Fund Medal by the Wenner-Gren Foundation in 1960, the CIBA foundation Annual Lectureship Medal in 1965, and the Huxley Medal from the Royal Anthropological Institute in 1967. In 1972, the Fourth International Congress of Primatology was dedicated in his honor, and a year later the *American Journal of Physical Anthropology*, which he had edited from 1955 to 1957, dedicated an issue to him. From 1956 to 1960, he had also been the editor of the *Viking Publications in Anthropology*.

During the last two decades of his professional career, he undertook little primary research, though his influence continued to grow. His presidential address on race with which he opened the AAA's annual meeting of 1962 made a profound impact. Fiercely attacking Carleton Coon's *The Origin of Races* (1962) while praising Dobzhansky's *Mankind Evolving* (1962), he set the record straight by telling a packed auditorium with more than one thousand delegates in his typically unadorned prose: "Races are products of the past. They are relics of times and conditions which have long ceased to exist. [...] Racism is based on a profound misunderstanding of culture, of learning, and of the biology of the human species" (Washburn, 1963a, pp. 528, 531). He received a standing ovation that lasted several minutes. Thirty years later, he drew a clear line between his scientific stance and the postwar context:

> An attack on typological race was in a way an attack on physical anthropology itself, and specifically on the way a lot of people were teaching it then. If I had it to do again, I would handle it the same way, despite the negative impact on some. The amazing thing to me was that here were people living that close to Hitler and that close to the war who really hadn't changed their teaching. That was the shocking thing to me, and I think it has been very bad for anthropology. (DeVore, 1992, p. 422)

His statement was courageous, but by stressing the biological basis of humanity while dismissing cultural differences, it did not equal the subtlety of Claude Lévi-Strauss's contemporary argument on race and culture. For Washburn, humanity was universal and unique. Universal, because of the very old shared biological descent. Unique, because hunting and language set us apart from the other primates. He was as infuriated by the older racial theories as by the new sociobiological doctrine that belittled, in his view, the uniqueness of humans.

Conferences proved an important tool for developing the discipline. Between the closed gatherings of nineteenth-century-style learned societies and the mass meetings of contemporary academia, in the middle of the twentieth century small specialist conferences were often milestones of scholarship. In 1959, Washburn organized a Wenner-Gren Conference on "The Social Life of Early Man" at Burg Wartenstein in Austria, followed by another on "Classification and Human Evolution" in 1961. These were true international and interdisciplinary encounters. The latter, in particular, was revolutionary as it was the first time that the relevance of immunology and molecular biology to human evolution studies was realized. Washburn had never been a fossil fetishist and realized that genetics was to become essential. The Primate Project, which he established in 1962 and 1963 with psychiatrist and close friend David Hamburg at the Center for Advanced Study in Behavioral Sciences in Stanford resulted in a state-of-the-art appraisal of knowledge of primate behavior.

Washburn also enthusiastically supported Irven DeVore and Richard Lee with their "Man the Hunter" conference in Chicago in 1966, where he developed the full-fledged version of his hunting hypothesis for human origins. Hunting, in that view, was what had made us human; it was the total adaptation responsible for anything human: "The biology, psychology, and customs that separate us from the apes—all these we owe to the hunters of time past" (Washburn and Lancaster, 1968, p. 303). In the 1980s, this influential theory was discarded as the archaeological and ethnographic evidence on which it rested was eroded. Ironically, Washburn, the champion of antiracism, was associated with a man-the-hunter hypothesis deemed by some to be sexist.

At Berkeley, Washburn was charged with teaching an introductory course on human evolution that became extremely popular, sometimes attracting more than twelve hundred students. In 1975 he was given the prestigious title of university professor at the nine-campus system of the University of California. Securing extramural money from the Ford Foundation and National Institutes of Health, he assembled a very successful, truly interdisciplinary research group on human evolution in Berkeley. In addition to some of his former Chicago graduates (primatologists Irven DeVore and Phyllis Dolhinow, primate morphologist F. Clark Howell), it consisted of two Paleolithic archaeologists, J. Desmond Clark and Glynn Isaac, the Bushmen ethnographer Richard Lee, as well as the molecular anthropologist Vincent Sarich. There was even a facility for studying nonhuman primates.

His graduate students were numerous, his impact enormous. Of the first nineteen doctorates in primatological anthropology in the United States, fifteen were supervised by Washburn. And twenty out of forty-seven anthropological doctorates on primate behavior before 1979 were completed in Berkeley (Haraway, 1989, p. 218). Among his graduates were people such as Russell Tuttle, Ralph Halloway, Adrienne Zihlman, Ted Grand, Jane Lancaster, and Shirley Strum. Washburn was an inspiring supervisor, full of ideas and always interested in new tendencies, but "his shoot-from-the-hip approach to alternative ideas and his toughly competitive spirit frustrated and angered protégés" (Tuttle, 2000, p. 867). Always the son of a preacher, he was never quite freed from proselytism in his arguments with colleagues. Nonetheless, Washburn's intellectual progeny populated American physical anthropology and primatology until well into the twenty-first century.

Impact (1979–2000). After his retirement in 1979, Washburn received numerous awards, such as the Berkeley Citation for meritorious service, the American Anthropological Association's Distinguished Service Award, the American Association of Physical Anthropologists' Charles Darwin Lifetime Achievement Award, and an honorary doctorate from Witwatersrand University, Johannesburg, in 1985. He was honorary Fellow of the Royal Anthropological Institute of Great Britain and Ireland and a founding member of the L. S. B. Leakey Foundation. In 1989, Ann and Gordon Getty donated 15 million dollars to the University of California, the largest gift ever received at that time, in honor of Washburn, for the refurbishment of the biology facilities. After his death, the American Association of Physical Anthropology created the Sherwood Washburn Prize.

Epitomizing the generation that had come to intellectual maturity during World War II, Washburn's long career was motivated by a disavowal of racial thought. He proposed a universal narrative for human origins in which cultural differences were just a very thin icing on the cake of our shared biology. Yet unlike Stephen J. Gould or E. O. Wilson, he never was a public intellectual who spoke out in defense of particular issues. When he saw the student riots on the Berkeley campus in 1964, he preferred to observe the crowd in the street as if it was a troop of baboons rather than to overtly sympathize. A positivist by default and a postwar scholar by accident, his hopes were not with the past: "The less we trust the past, the more likely we are to be useful in the present" (Washburn, 1973, p. 182). Ironically, that useful present had to contain a better understanding of our remote past.

BIBLIOGRAPHY

Washburn donated his archive (1932–1996) to The Bancroft Library, University of California, Berkeley. Its online inventory can be accessed at the Online Archive of California, http://www.oac.cdlib.org.

WORKS BY WASHBURN

"The New Physical Anthropology." *Transactions of the New York Academy of Sciences,* series 2, 13 (1951): 298–305. Landmark paper.

With Irven DeVore. "Social Behavior of Baboons and Early Man." In *Social Life of Early Man,* edited by S. L. Washburn. New York: Wenner-Gren Foundation for Anthropological Research, 1961. First exploration of baboons as models for human evolution; the book publishes proceedings of a conference.

"The Study of Race." *American Anthropologist,* n.s., 65 (1963a): 521–531. His most forceful statement on race.

Ed. *Classification and Human Evolution.* Viking Fund Publications in Anthropology, no. 37. Chicago: Aldine, 1963b. Conference proceedings that Washburn edited.

With C. S. Lancaster. "The Evolution of Hunting." In *Man the Hunter,* edited by Richard B. Lee and Irven DeVore. Chicago: Aldine, 1968. The hunting hypothesis in a nutshell. Washburn's most cited paper.

With P. Dolhinow, eds. *Perspectives on Human Evolution.* New York: Holt, Rinehart and Winston, 1968.

"The Promise of Primatology." *American Journal of Physical Anthropology* 38, no. 2 (1973): 177–182.

With R. Moore. *Ape into Man: A Study of Human Evolution.* Boston: Little, Brown, 1974. A popular textbook.

With E. R. McCown, eds. *Human Evolution: Biosocial Perspectives.* Menlo Park, CA: Benjamin Cummings, 1978.

"Evolution of a Teacher." *Annual Review of Anthropology* 21 (1983): 1–24. A good autobiography.

The New Physical Anthropology: Science, Humanism, and Critical Reflection, edited by Shirley Strum, Donald G. Lindburg, and David Hamburg. Upper Saddle River, NJ: Prentice Hall, 1999. Contains all the classic papers by Washburn and some of his students, as well as the complete bibliography (pp. 277–285).

OTHER SOURCES

Coon, Carleton Stevens. *The Origin of Races.* New York: Knopf, 1962.

DeVore, Irven. "An Interview with Sherwood Washburn." *Current Anthropology* 33 (1992): 411–423. Illuminating and personal.

Dobzhansky, Theodosius Grigorievich. *Mankind Evolving: The Evolution of the Human Species.* New Haven, CT: Yale University Press, 1962.

Gilmore, H. A. "From Radcliffe-Brown to Sociobiology: Some Aspects of the Rise of Primatology within Physical Anthropology." *American Journal of Physical Anthropology* 56 (1981): 387–392.

Haraway, Donna. *Primate Visions: Gender, Race, and Nature in the World of Modern Science.* London: Verso, 1989. Chapter

8, "Remodelling the Human Way of Life: Sherwood Washburn and the New Physical Anthropology, 1950–1980," offers a valuable if poorly written deconstructivist perspective, placing Washburn in the context of international, colonial, economic, and gender politics.

Howell, F. Clark. "Sherwood Larned Washburn 1911–2000." *Biographical Memoirs,* vol. 84. Washington, DC: National Academy of Sciences, 2003. Available from http://www. nap.edu/readingroom/books/biomems/. A useful introduction.

Marks, J. "Sherwood Washburn, 1911–2000." *Evolutionary Anthropology* 9 (2000): 225–226.

Tuttle, R. H. "Sherwood Larned Washburn (1911–2000)." *American Anthropologist* 102 (2000): 865–869.

Zihlman, A. L. "In Memoriam: Sherwood Washburn, 1911–2000." *American Journal of Physical Anthropology* 116 (2001): 181–183.

David Van Reybrouck

WATSON, JOHN BROADUS (*b.* Travelers Rest, South Carolina, 9 January 1878; *d.* New York, New York, 25 September 1958), *psychology, theory and practice of behaviorism, emotional conditioning, comparative psychology.*

Watson was one the most visible and notable psychologists of the twentieth century. He is matched only by the psychoanalyst Sigmund Freud in terms of being written about, both during their careers and after their deaths. In 1915 Watson became the youngest elected president of the American Psychological Association. Despite leaving the discipline only a few years later, the interest in him and his work continues, with publications and controversies devoted to whether and to what degree his writings on behaviorism, research methods, and infant development and emotions affected psychology.

Background. Watson is described in some reports as being born to a poor farm family (his parents were Emma Kesiah Roe Watson and Pickens Butler Watson); however, in a lengthy obituary by a senior psychologist who knew him well, Robert S. Woodworth (1959), he is described as "… the second of five children of a well-to-do farmer"; still another reports puts him as the fourth child. Be that as it may, in his 1936 "Autobiography" (Watson, 1961), in which he never discusses his parents or siblings, Watson describes with evident pride the many manual skills he acquired as a farm child, which persisted into construction projects in his fifties (p. 271). These same skills likely helped him in field and laboratory research projects and were reflected in his readiness to take advantage of technology; he was a tinkerer and experimenter. Watson's par-

ents separated when he was twelve years old and he and his mother moved to nearby Greenville, South Carolina, where he describes himself as having done poorly in grammar and high school and being a troublemaker: "I was lazy, somewhat insubordinate, and, so far as I know, I never made above a passing grade" (p. 271).

Academic Career. Despite a purported poor high school record, Watson persuaded Furman University in Greenville to admit him at the age of sixteen in 1894. He writes disparagingly about his college performance and most of his experiences there except for one professor, Gordon B. Moore in philosophy, under whom he earned an MA in 1899. He entered graduate school in 1900 at the University of Chicago and three years later, in 1903, was awarded the PhD. He wrote that he believed he was the "youngest PhD turned out by that institution," which was, one should understand, relatively new, having been founded in 1891. Sadly, in his eyes, the degree was blemished. On his receiving the degree magna cum laude, he was told by John Dewey and James Rowland Angell that his "… exam was much inferior to that of Miss Helen Thomson who had graduated two years before with a summa cum laude. I wondered then if anybody could ever equal her record. That jealousy existed for years" (Watson, 1936, p. 274). And well it might, as Helen B. Thompson Woolley went on to a notable career in research—on psychometrics and gender differences—and in academic administration; she founded the Experimental Laboratory at Mt. Holyoke College in 1902 and served as dean at the University of New Hampshire.

Watson planned to major in philosophy. He took courses and readings in philosophy with some of the university's luminaries: Dewey, Angell, George Herbert Mead, and James Hayden Tufts. His interest in philosophy palled, however, and under Angell's guidance he switched to psychology as a major, with neurology as a second minor. As his advisor, Angell made sure that Watson acquired the knowledge and skills necessary to be an experimental psychologist by arranging for him to work with the controversial biologist Jacques Loeb and the neurologist Henry H. Donaldson. Under Loeb he took biology and physiology, and under Donaldson neurology, both programs fitting in with an early plan of obtaining a medical degree. While he was too poor to continue along that line, Watson's subsequent research and writing revealed that Loeb and Donaldson had done their job well and had produced a scientist extremely knowledgeable in neurology and general physiology. Watson writes, "Loeb wanted me to do my research under him on the physiology of the dog's brain. Neither Angell nor Donaldson in those days felt that Loeb was a very 'safe' man for a green PhD candidate so I took my research jointly under Donaldson and Angell on the correlation between increasing complexity of the behavior of the white rat and the growth of medullation in the central nervous system" (Watson, 1936, p. 271).

One wonders what his career might have been like had he worked with Loeb instead of his less controversial advisors, although Loeb's influence is clearly to be seen later in Watson's advocacy of behaviorism. Watson's ambitiousness is made clear early on; he published the dissertation as a separate monograph (Watson, 1903), borrowing $350 from Donaldson that took him years to repay. Despite the self-deprecating tone of the early autobiography, it is clear that Watson was recognized as a gifted scholar and researcher by the faculty and fellow students at Chicago and he reciprocated their esteem. He writes warmly and appreciatively of all of them, particularly Mead, Angell, Donaldson, Harvey Carr, and C. S. Yoakum; as will be seen below, such generous amiability did not characterize all of his personal and professional relationships later in life.

Professional Career. Watson's academic career was meteoric: brightly visible and brief. In a profession that measures careers in decades, his lasted less than twenty years, from 1903 to 1921, ending spectacularly in a public divorce and a forced resignation from The Johns Hopkins University. In between, he became the youngest president of the American Psychological Association in 1915; headed two major journals, as editor of *Psychological Review* and founding editor of the *Journal of Experimental Psychology* (1916); wrote two famous papers on behaviorism (1913 and 1915) that staked out his version of psychology as a purely objective science; and proposed how behaviorism's principles could lead to the betterment of society and peoples' individual lives. Watson also served in several different capacities as a psychologist in World War I: on the Committee on Classification of Personnel in the Army, and in the Signal Corps and the Aviation Medical Corps, before being (he asserted) punitively transferred to the General Staff to be trained for overseas military intelligence work in Europe; he wrote that this work was designed, ultimately, so that "…I was sure to be killed" (p. 278). By his own account, his military career was one of fractiousness and disagreements with superiors on research methods and results.

At war's end in 1918, he returned to Johns Hopkins and the Phipps Clinic, wrote *Psychology from the Standpoint of a Behaviorist* (1919) and began some experimental studies of infants. Soon he was romantically entangled with his research assistant, Rosalie Rayner. Watson subsequently divorced his first wife and was remarried to Rayner. The circumstances of his divorce led to his dismissal from Johns Hopkins in 1920. With help from friends and his characteristic energy, Watson then

obtained a position with one of America's premier advertising agencies, J. Walter Thompson Advertising Company, at a salary of $25,000, more than four times his academic salary. At the same time, he declined the offer of a position with the newly-created New School for Social Research in New York City.

This career choice was quite compatible with his often-stated belief that psychology had a duty to influence and better the lives of people and the functioning of society. Given that he was newly married, needed employment, and had led a relatively impecunious life since childhood, the attraction of a significant executive position and large salary makes perfect sense. He later moved to another similar firm, William Esty & Company, and remained in the advertising business until his retirement in 1945.

Despite his new career, however, he did not desert psychology: He wrote, "Leaving Hopkins did not mean a complete giving up of intellectual activity" (Watson, 1961, p. 280), and he remained a member of the American Psychological Association until his death (Holsopple, 1958, p. 559). For the following decade and a half he wrote a number of articles for the scientific journal *Psychological Review* and embarked on a writing career that interpreted psychology and behaviorism for popular audiences. He wrote several popular books and many articles for popular magazines, including the *New Republic*, *Harper's Magazine*, *Colliers*, and *Cosmopolitan*—for all of which, he points out, he was paid generously. He gave lectures at the Cooper Institute and at the New School in New York City, and even on a street corner on one occasion. In 1924, Watson and William McDougall engaged in a public debate at the Psychology Club of Washington about behaviorism (Watson and McDougall, 1928). These talks and writing kept him in public circulation until the mid 1930s and his 1936 autobiography seems to have been a final statement. Thereafter, his time was devoted to what he had become: an important executive in the world of applied psychology—advertising and publicity.

Research: Fields and Publications. Watson's research and writings may be divided into four groups that correspond roughly with different stages of his career: comparative-animal psychology; behaviorism; emotional conditioning; and miscellaneous topics in vision, learning, and general psychological matters. He was an extremely energetic researcher in several fields and a prolific publisher. Watson was a good writer, lucid and uncomplicated, qualities he generously attributes to Angell, who worked on his thesis with him daily. His writings include articles, monographs, book reviews, regular journal surveys on selected psychological topics, published lectures, and nine books. In addition, there are numerous writings on non-psychological

John Watson. THE LIBRARY OF CONGRESS.

topics; these are poorly documented and will not be taken up here.

Comparative-Animal Psychology. Watson's first publication was his thesis, "Animal Education: An Experimental Study on the Psychical Development of the White Rat, Correlated with the Growth of its Nervous System," in which he sought to correlate growth of the central nervous system and the development of learning ability (1903). Note the term "psychic" in the title, a term that, among others, Watson was soon to anathematize. The research displayed two features present in almost all of Watson's work: first, his preoccupation with the role of learning in the development of all animals—which led some, mistakenly, to charge him with rejecting the role of instincts in animal life; second, his preoccupation with research methods and what might be called "proper science" as basic to understanding the results of science and communicating them meaningfully to students and the public.

The two themes were fused in his book *Behavior: An Introduction to Comparative Psychology* (1914). In Chapter One, the arguments for behaviorism—already advanced in earlier writings and preceded by the notorious proclamation paper (Watson, 1913)—are gone over. The several

chapters are detailed examinations of basic problems in different kinds of studies, including field versus laboratory studies, and measuring vision, hearing, organic and other senses, learning, and perception. Chapter Three, "Apparatus and Methods," considers how to avoid or get around problems discussed in previous chapters, such as animal control boxes for studying hearing, devices for motor habits or serial learning. Chapter Four is "Observational and Experimental Studies upon Instinct," which should put to rest some discussions about Watson and instincts. The book was a manual of the problems and strategies facing every scientist studying animals in the wild or in a laboratory. It is clearly informed by Watson's own laboratory and fieldwork experiences. A contemporary student could probably profit greatly from this book, despite its age.

Interestingly, Watson does not refer to the very similar book published some five years earlier by Margaret Floy Washburn, *The Animal Mind: A Text-book of Comparative Psychology* (1908), which covered much the same territory at the same technical level but from a different perspective. One has to wonder why he did not do so directly in the first chapter, which dealt with the same fundamental problems that she too had addressed. In any case, she got redress in the second edition of her book (Washburn, 1917) with criticism of behaviorism and of Watson's explanations for various research findings on habit and, especially, his frequency theory of learning.

In the latter part of the nineteenth century, the ancient device of the maze became an important tool for psychologists and zoologists trying to understand how people and animals learned. How mazes, locations, and other serial habits are acquired, it should be noted, is a question that is by no means settled. Watson asked, what were the specific cues rats used to learn a maze? They might be sensory, such as visual, auditory, olfactory, cutaneous, somaesthetic, and so on. Adopting the most basic procedure of scientific research, Watson decided to eliminate each possible factor successively until left with only one remaining possibility. He did this by depriving each rat of sensory cues in sequence, one by one. He blinded, deafened, anaesthetized paws, cut off whiskers, and otherwise removed or damaged the organs that transmitted particular sensory cues. When his rat subjects learned mazes even though deprived of major sensory abilities or, as others had shown earlier, different views of the maze's orientation in a room, he concluded that the remaining sense that he could not remove, kinesthesia, was the mechanism by which rats learned the maze (Watson, 1907). It was not until many years later that Watson's most prominent student, Karl Lashley, would show that even this residual, spared sense could not be the sole basis for serial learning (Lashley and Ball, 1929). In any case, Watson generalized this conclusion to other serial and motor habits, and for the next ten years carried out a number of experiments with Harvey Carr and Lashley studying kinesthetic factors in human learning—for example, archery.

Critics were quick to point out, however, that this did not mean that normal animals didn't ordinarily use vision or olfaction when learning a maze, an obvious point. By the same token, however, it did not exclude the likelihood that kinesthesia could be a joint factor in serial motor actions. Objections and discussions about Watson's argument for kinesthesia—that is, that learning the maze occurred by learning motor movement sensory cues in traversing the maze—had a long life and lasted well beyond 1907. It led ultimately to the "place versus response" debate that the behaviorist Edward Chase Tolman triggered, and which occupied behaviorist and cognitive learning theorists until well into the 1970s. It cannot be said to have been satisfactorily resolved even then, and the emergence of brain research on movement-memory areas of the hippocampus reopens the issue, though, of course, at a more profound physiological level. Nevertheless, the research was a tour de force, a demonstration of Watson's technical competence in sensory psychology and neurology and his persistence in pursuing a problem. At this point, his first exposure to public notoriety occurred: He was attacked in a *New York Times* article for animal cruelty because of his techniques to deprive subjects of sensory information.

Behaviorism. There can be little doubt that Watson's early claim to fame and notoriety was his advocacy of the objectivist psychology he called behaviorism. It was offered in contrast to what he regarded as the dominant psychology of his day, which he described as a subjectivist discipline devoted mainly to the study of consciousness by introspection. Watson, as an animal psychologist, believed that man "… is an animal different from other animals only in the types of behavior he displays" (Watson, 1930, p. ix), whereas the psychology he attacked appeared to posit an absolute, qualitative gulf between humans and all other animals. Do animals have experiences that are like the ones humans have? Can animals actually have ideas? Do they have consciousness? Do they have feelings, emotions, images? Is there any reason to think that these are not the essence of human experience? Aren't they what we have discovered from studying peoples' minds and emotions by introspective methods since ancient times? In any case, even if animals had minds and experiences such as humans have, how could we know? Even were they capable of introspection, how would we know what their consciousness, their experiences consisted of? As they don't have language, they cannot tell us anything about their experiences. Why, then, attribute to them what they cannot possible convey to us? This interesting paradox, a positivist argument against behaviorism, presented an impasse. This is the problem that Watson confronted:

how to show that humans and animals, in principle, were not different.

He undertook a multipronged approach that has engaged psychologists of all varieties, pro and con, into the twenty-first century. Some of the negative literature was extremely immoderate and even unrelenting (see, for example, Roback, 1923, 1937). Stung by much of it, Watson describes it as a "… literature of criticism. Some of this has been personal, even vituperative. I have never replied to a criticism. Only rarely has any one taken up the cudgels for behaviorism. Each behaviorist has been too busy presenting his experimental results or his generalizations to concern himself with answering criticisms" (Watson, 1930, p. x). It has to be said, however, that the evidence points to Watson's being thin-skinned and provocative. The vocabulary of his writings and lectures was forceful, occasionally extreme, and invited equally strong reactions. But such is the polemics of serious advocacy and rejection of deep, unsettling proposals about the basics of a science; see, for example, the strong emotions displayed by early opponents of relativity theory (Crelinsten, 2006). From the very start, behaviorism touched on basic beliefs about humanity and it is no surprise that vigorous opposition resulted.

Watson's behaviorism rested on the following themes:

- psychology is a natural science;

- behavior is the fundamental biological mode of all living creatures;

- there are native ways of behavior in reaction to the environment as a result of evolution;

- organisms accommodate and adjust to the impact of the environment upon them by changes in behavior according to specific principles of development and learning, for example, reflex conditioning;

- insofar as consciousness and its introspection is held to be uniquely human, it should be seen, even in 1913, as at best a limited area of psychological research compared with such basic aspects of psychology as: instincts, learning and habit formation, sensations, perception, attention, emotions, personality and social behavior, psychopathology, and the many behavioral methods available for studying and changing them;

- insofar as conscious experience is a unique property of humans, its study is as much the province of the physicist and chemist in their research as it is of psychologists;

- while there are no such *entities* as mental states—images, ideas, or thoughts—what people say is a response and should be regarded as such. If they say they see or hear something we accept it as such; what its theoretical status is, is another matter.

Here is found what is in effect a doctrine of phenomenology. Watson was not unsophisticated philosophically, if one takes seriously the listing of classes in philosophy that he took at Chicago, but it is unlikely that he would have identified with the variety of phenomenology propounded by Edmund Husserl, though it too rejected introspectionism.

The proposal that the study of behavior and measurable responses is the main task of psychology, combined with the rejection of mental states and of introspection as a significant or verifiable method, are the two proposals that led to the persistent objections and controversies. Nevertheless, the introspective study of psychological events is but a fraction of the research devoted to studying the responses of people, verbal and otherwise, in all areas of psychology, including perception and sensation in the twenty-first century. Watson's rejection of introspection was not a perverse whim; it mirrored serious debates among psychologists at the time he was writing about imageless thought. The imageless thought controversy was about whether there could be thoughts without images and revolved around the legitimacy of introspective claims. As a replacement for introspective analysis, Watson proposed that the rigorous application of standard experimental methods would reveal in humans, as they did in animals, the causes and interrelationships between stimuli and responses in all the domains of psychology. There was no longer a need to depend on unverifiable accounts by people of their experiences. As a result, psychology would finally have the ability to predict and control behavior. Needless to say, Watson's vision about the prediction and control of behavior, especially of people, sparked a new controversy about his views and led to another body of criticism (see, for example, Samelson, 1994, pp. 3–18).

Watson's attack on introspection and images went far beyond the psychological disputes of his colleagues. They argued about such questions as where images were or how evanescent they were. Watson, on the other hand, said that introspection and mental images or ideas were impossible. The way the brain worked made them impossible; stable or enduring mental things could not exist. He is very explicit about it, as can be seen in the following, which was correct for its time but, sadly for his argument, no longer holds true:

The tendency to make the brain itself something more than a mechanism for coordinating incoming and outgoing impulses has been very strong among psychologists, and even among psychologically inclined neurologists. A still wilder hypothesis is held in regard to the neural impulse.

According to many psychologists we are taught that an incoming impulse may be held *in statu quo* for long periods of time, or at least that it may ramble around in the nervous system for an indefinite period of time, until it can "obtain possession of the motor field," at which time it exerts its effects. So far as we know no such thing occurs. The nervous system functions in complete arcs. An incoming impulse exerts its effect relatively immediately upon one system of effectors or another, as shown by inhibition, reinforcement, summation, phenomena in the muscle in operation or by inciting wholly new effectors to action. (1914, p. 20).

Does one detect some influence from Dewey's famous paper on the reflex arc? In any event, being unusually well informed on brain matters in Watson's case made him a victim of history.

Although Watson relied on physiology for his argument about introspection, he was very firm about psychology as a separate discipline with its own phenomena and tasks. To be sure, psychology was a biological discipline for him, but he writes, "Our task begins only when the physiologist puts the separate organs together again, and turns the whole (man) over to us. The physiologist qua physiologist knows nothing of the total situations in the daily life of an individual that shape his action and conduct" (1919, p. 22). This is a distinction that he reiterated ever more forcefully in later writings; as he became increasingly convinced about the role of experience and learning in the behavior of humans, his interest in them supplanted his interest in animals.

Emotional Conditioning and Child Development. The last phase of Watson's academic and research career may be dated from his presidential address to the American Psychological Association in December 1915, "The Place of the Conditioned-Reflex in Psychology" (Watson, 1916, pp. 89–116). In it, he proposed that the conditioned reflex can serve in the place of introspective procedures with people. Further, it could reveal information about the experiences of persons who are non-verbal or handicapped, such as children, psychiatric patients, and neurologically damaged. He discussed a variety of conditioning research that he and Lashley were conducting with animals and humans, distinguishing between the Pavlovian secretory response and the motor response studied by Vladimir M. Bekhterev. After outlining many of the technical features and problems of each, Watson stated that he favored a motor response, particularly the conditioned finger reaction on which he had done some research. The research program was clearly preliminary, and ended with the entry of the United States into World War I in 1917.

Watson and Lashley enrolled in military activities, and their program was not resumed when the war was over.

Watson's presidential address looked backward; it was an answer to those who had regarded Watson's criticism of introspection as empty because he didn't offer a viable alternative. It explored the many ways in which, by conditioning, fundamental psychological processes in sensory and motor realms—for example, habits—could be explored. However, in several places in the address one finds premonitions of Watson's postwar interests. In a footnote he writes: "I wish I had the time to develop the view that the concept of the conditioned reflex can be used as an explanatory principle in the psychopathology of hysteria and the various 'tics' which appear in so-called normal individuals. It seems to me that hysterical motor manifestations may be looked on as conditioned reflexes (1916, p. 95)." In fact, aside from continuing to write about them later in connection with behaviorism and the truncated program with Lashley, his research with animals was ended. On his return from the military, his work and thinking centered on the plasticity of emotions by conditioning, infant development, and the implications for people and society.

Early in his writing, Watson described emotions as instinctive, universal, natural reactions. Whereas he ultimately rejected the notion of instinct as superfluous (see Watson, 1930, for a detailed examination of instinct vis a vis emotions), he assumed that fear, rage, and love were primary emotional responses and undertook to investigate their modifiability in children. He had already shown an interest in emotional modifiability in a paper with John J. B. Morgan (Watson and Morgan, 1917) about the effect of emotional disruption on work and attention and the return of control. However, Watson and Rosalie Rayner prepared two reports in which they revealed work that would become central to this area of study (Watson and Rayner, 1920; Watson and Watson, 1921). They reviewed experiments and tests in which children were exposed to a variety of stimuli such as objects, sounds, and noises (for example, rabbits, strange human faces, furry objects, and clanging sounds; see photograph in Drunen and Jansz, 2004, p. 69) to determine their "natural" reactions. Then, in their most famous and notorious experiment, they claimed that they had successfully conditioned a child, known forever after as "Little Albert," to fear a rat by pairing its exposure with the loud striking of an iron bar, and that the fear had generalized to other furry objects. Generalization is the gold standard test of conditioning, so the results were compelling, generally believed, widely reported, and published in both popular magazines and such professional psychological literature as textbooks (see Todd, 1994). It is now generally agreed that the tests and experiments were poorly conceived and executed, and inadequately and incorrectly reported (Harris, 1979), but

the damage had been done and Little Albert became a symbol of behaviorism's possibilities and dangers.

The Watsons were thoroughly convinced that they had shown how malleable children were and how early parental actions could affect emotional behavior and learning. As Watson developed the implications of the work, he became increasingly critical and polemical about literature that took for granted the inheritance of traits and dispositions. The most formal presentation of his arguments appeared as early as the 1924 edition of *Behaviorism,* but the implications for instincts and emotions became explicit in his chapter in Carl Murchison's *Psychologies of 1925* (Watson, 1926). Again, Watson became the target of a critical literature around a presumed extreme environmentalist position that denied hereditary factors in psychology. In any event, his assertion that early learned experience was responsible for personality, social behavior, and pathology fit in with a number of social trends at the time: the mental hygiene movement, expansion of child laws, increased employment of women, and a growing feminist movement, all of which concerned themselves with the management of children from infancy on. Watson's argument that children's emotional behavior could be trained provided an answer to questions about discipline; his own stated preferences for dutiful children, appearing in popular venues such as *Parents Magazine,* appealed to many young parents (Watson and Watson, 1928). A counter-literature quickly arose to oppose the strict childrearing program he advocated (See Drunen and Jansz, 2004). In general, it seems fair to say that his views appealed to some peoples' predilections, but that the majority of mothers favored less strictness, especially in the early years. (For a bittersweet commentary, see Rosalie Watson's article in *Parents Magazine,* 1930).

With the publication of *Psychological Care of the Infant and Child* in 1928, Watson's work in psychology was truly finished. He had started out as an experimental animal psychologist and finished with an exclusive concern with human children. Along the way, he generated attention by novel research and radical proposals that often put him at odds with colleagues. He was a productive researcher but didn't follow up on much of what he did. His behaviorist proposals are generally acknowledged to be schematic, at best. Yet much of his work sparked others to pursue the issues, either pro or con, and so, long after his career had ended, something Watsonian was, and still is, present in the activities of psychologists.

BIBLIOGRAPHY

WORKS BY WATSON

Animal Education: An Experimental Study on the Psychical Development of the White Rat, Correlated with the Growth of the Nervous System. Chicago: University Of Chicago Press, 1903.

"Kinaesthetic and Organic Sensations: Their Role in the Reactions of the White Rat to the Maze." *Psychological Review Monograph Supplement* 8, no. 33 (1907): 1–100.

"Psychology as the Behaviorist Views It." *Psychological Review* 20 (1913): 158–177.

Behavior: An Introduction to Comparative Psychology. New York: Henry Holt, 1914.

"The Place of the Conditioned Reflex in Psychology." *Psychological Review* 23 (1916): 89–117.

With John J. B. Morgan. "Emotional Reactions and Psychological Experimentation." American Journal of Psychology 11 (1917): 163–177.

Psychology, from the Standpoint of a Behaviorist. Philadelphia: J. B. Lippincott, 1919.

With Rosalie Rayner. "Conditioned Emotional Reactions." *Journal of Experimental Psychology* 3 (1920): 1–14.

With Rosalie Rayner Watson. "Studies in Infant Psychology." *Scientific Monthly* 13 (1921): 493–515.

"What the Nursery Has to Say about Instincts: Experimental Studies on the Growth of Emotions, Recent Experiments on How We Lose and Change Our Emotional Equipment." In *Psychologies of 1925,* edited by Carl Murchison. Worcester, MA: Clark University Press, 1928.

With William McDougall. *The Battle of Behaviorism: An Exposition and an Exposure.* London: Kegan Paul, Trench, Trubner & Co., 1928.

With Rosalie Rayner Watson. *Psychological Care of Infant and Child.* New York: Norton, 1928. Usually cited with John B. Watson as sole author.

Behaviorism, revised ed. New York: W. W. Norton, 1930.

"John Broadus Watson." In *A History of Psychology in Autobiography, Volume III,* edited by Carl Murchison. New York: Russell & Russell, 1961 [1936].

OTHER SOURCES

Buckley, Kerry W. *Mechanical Man: John Broadus Watson and the Beginnings of Behaviorism.* New York: Guilford Press, 1989.

Cohen, David. *J. B. Watson, the Founder of Behaviorism: A Biography.* London: Routledge & Kegan Paul, 1979. Useful general references and sources.

Crelinsten, Jeffrey. *Einstein's Jury: The Race to Test Relativity.* Princeton, NJ: Princeton University Press, 2006.

Drunen, Peter van, and Jeroen Jansz. "Child-rearing and Education." In *A Social History of Psychology,* edited by Jeroen Jansz and Peter van Drunen. Malden, MA: Blackwell, 2004.

Harris, Benjamin. "Whatever Happened to Little Albert." *American Psychologist* 34 (1979): 151–160.

Holsopple, John. Q. Jr., ed. *American Psychological Association 1958 Directory.* Washington, DC: The American Psychological Association, 1958.

Lashley, Karl S., and Josephine Ball. "Spinal Conduction and Kinesthetic Sensitivity in the Maze Habit." *Journal of Comparative Psychology* 9 (1929): 71–105.

Paicheler, Geneviève. *L'Invention de la Psychologie Moderne.* Paris: L'Harmattan, 1992. A discerning and European perspective on American psychology and on Watson.

Roback, Abraham A. *Behaviorism and Psychology.* Cambridge, MA: Sci-Art Publishers, 1923.

———. *Behaviorism at Twenty-Five.* Cambridge, MA: Sci-Art Publishers, 1937.

Samelson, Franz. "Struggle for Scientific Authority: The Reception of Watson's Behaviorism, 1913–1920." *Journal of the History of the Behavioral Sciences* 18 (1981): 399–425.

———. "John B. Watson in 1913: Rhetoric and Practice." In *Modern Perspectives on John B. Watson and Classical Behaviorism,* edited by James T. Todd and Edward K. Morris. Westport, CT: Greenwood Press, 1994.

Todd, James T. "What Psychology Has to Say about John B. Watson: Classical Behaviorism in Psychology Textbooks, 1920–1989." In *Modern Perspectives on Classical Behaviorism,* edited by James T. Todd and Edward K. Morris. Westport, CT: Greenwood Press, 1994.

———, and Edward K. Morris, eds. *Modern Perspectives on John B. Watson and Classical Behaviorism.* Westport, CT: Greenwood Press, 1994. Includes extensive references.

———, and Edward K. Morris, eds. *Modern Perspectives on B. F. Skinner and Contemporary Behaviorism.* Westport, CT: Greenwood Press, 1995. Includes extensive references.

Washburn, Margaret Floy. *The Animal Mind: A Text-book of Comparative Psychology,* 2nd ed. New York: Macmillan, 1917.

Watson, Rosalie Rayner. "I Am the Mother of a Behaviorist's Sons." *Parents Magazine* 67 (1930): 16–18.

Woodworth, Robert S. "John Broadus Watson: 1878–1958." *American Journal of Psychology* 72 (2, 1959): 301–310.

Richard A. Littman

WEGENER, ALFRED LOTHAR (*b.* Berlin, Germany, 1 November 1880; *d.* West Greenland, November 1930), *atmospheric physics, geophysics.* For the original article on Wegener see *DSB,* vol. 14.

Alfred Wegener was selected for inclusion in the first edition of the *Dictionary of Scientific Biography* because of the renewed interest in the early 1970s in his theory of continental displacements. It is therefore not surprising that the entry by Keith Bullen characterized Wegener as a scientist with a strong interest in geology and geophysics and passed over his considerable career in meteorology and atmospheric physics. Yet it was precisely this work in atmospheric physics that prepared Wegener to develop a slender intuition concerning the outlines of continents on a map of the Atlantic Ocean into a well-argued geophysical theory of continental displacements.

Early Training. Wegener was born and raised in Berlin and lived there until the completion of his PhD in 1905.

He began his graduate career in physics and mathematics and attended Planck's lectures in thermodynamics and thermochemistry. Wegener adopted Planck's phenomenological approach, his indifference to hypothetical causal mechanisms, and his concentration on the bulk properties of matter—temperature, pressure, mass, and volume. Wegener heeded Planck's injunction to think of good theory simply as that mode of treating phenomena that corresponded to the state of empirical research at the moment.

These physical and mathematical studies were pursued in the context of a PhD in astronomy. Berlin astronomy leaned strongly toward planetary astronomy and particularly toward the use of astronomical data to study the Earth. One of Wegener's instructors had been a leading observer in a program to measure the amount and direction of that slight oscillation of the Earth's axis of rotation later known as *Chandler Wobble*. Another instructor concentrated on demonstrating the reality of latitude displacements, and those displacements of the Earth's axis commonly called *pole wander*.

After 1903 Wegener began to pursue studies in meteorology with Wilhelm von Bezold, including atmospheric thermodynamics. Bezold, then near the end of his career, spoke of the wonderful new opportunities in atmospheric physics for aspiring scientists and Wegener resolved to pursue atmospheric physics as a career.

In the year following his degree, Wegener worked at the German Aeronautical Observatory at Lindenberg, sending up kites and balloons to study the structure and properties of the atmosphere at altitudes up to five kilometers. He had a minor role in confirming the existence of the stratosphere and with his brother set a world record for time aloft in a balloon—fifty-two hours. From 1906 to 1908, he took part in a Danish expedition to Northeast Greenland. There he conducted a full program of atmospheric investigations with kites and balloons and gained many other necessary skills for polar life and travel, including experience in driving sled dogs.

In 1909 he began his university career at the Physical Institute in Marburg, where he pursued a systematic study of surfaces of discontinuity in the atmosphere: characteristic global levels at which sudden sharp temperature and pressure differences appeared both in cloud layers and in clear air. He wrote to a colleague that his interest in surfaces of discontinuity had the character of an obsession. Between 1909 and 1912, Wegener published almost forty scientific papers, many of which were devoted to this topic. He collected these into a textbook entitled *Thermodynamik der Atmosphäre*, published in 1911 and in print until it was replaced by his own *Physik der Atmosphäre*, edited posthumously by Wegener's brother Kurt in 1935. Wegener's 1911 textbook contained, among many other

Alfred Wegener. *Alfred Wegener, circa 1920.* HULTON ARCHIVE/GETTY IMAGES.

novelties, a full theory of atmospheric discontinuities, including a hypothetical geocoronium layer (later identified as the ionosphere) and a novel theory of the formation of precipitation in cold clouds that continued to be generally accepted under the name of the Wegener-Bergeron theory.

Path Toward Continental Drift. It was at this time, 1910 to 1911, that Wegener had the first intuitions that led to the theory of continental displacements. Returning from the Christmas holidays in late 1910 to his office at the Physical Institute in Marburg, he was invited by his officemate to peruse a new edition of Richard Andree's *Allgemeine Handatlas*. This was among the first atlases in Germany to show pictures of the Atlantic continental margins of South America and Africa with the bathymetry data from the Challenger Expedition. Wegener noticed immediately that the outlines of the continents at sea level were repeated at the two-hundred meter depth contour. This meant (to him) that the matching of the east coast of South America and the west coast of Africa was not an artifact of sea level, but something that reflected the structure of the planet as a whole.

Louis Pasteur remarked in an 1854 lecture that "in the field of observation, chance favors only the prepared mind." What is of interest in this story of Wegener noting the parallelism of the coastlines, observed many times before him, is the way his mind was prepared to see this geophysically significant datum from the standpoint of his work on surfaces of discontinuity in the atmosphere. He immediately hypothesized that the continental surfaces were one earth layer, and the ocean floor was another layer beneath them. By Wegener's own account, this intuition lay dormant until later in the year 1911, when he came upon a summary of paleontological correlations between Africa and South America of species that could not themselves have crossed an abyssal ocean.

Wegener undertook a more systematic study of geology, geophysics, paleontology, and oceanography in order to get a sense of the theoretical organization tying together these disparate fields. His rapid traverse through these disciplines in late 1911 taught him two things. The first was that there was massive and incontrovertible evidence—stratigraphical, structural, and paleontological—of former continuity across the Atlantic, and between south hemispheric continents now widely separated by deep oceans. The second was that all the current geophysical explanations of how this former continuity had been broken were impossibly flawed. All were versions of the contraction theory, the nineteenth-century notion that the Earth was continually cooling from an original incandescent state. All versions of the theory implied that the current floors of the ocean were former continental surfaces that had somehow sunk there. Wegener knew this was impossible—the theory of isostasy had established that the continents floated and the discovery of radioactivity indicated that the Earth was not cooling. It occurred to Wegener that the only reasonable explanation, which honored the geological and paleontological evidence of former continuity in the context of some sort of geophysical plausibility, was that the continents had split apart and drifted away from one another. In later 1911 and early 1912 he wrote two papers, both entitled "Die Entstehung der Kontinente" (The origin of continents), defending this position.

Immediately after publishing this hypothesis in 1912 Wegener left for Greenland where he spent the next eighteen months crossing the Greenland ice cap. Most of the scientific work was classical glaciology, though Wegener hoped that the geodesy could support his ideas about continental movement. Upon his return in 1913 he married Else Köppen, daughter of the distinguished climatologist Wladimir Köppen: The latter had already aided him considerably in his meteorological work and would later become his closest collaborator.

Mobilized at the outbreak of World War I (he was a lieutenant and later a captain of infantry) he was wounded twice and remained on convalescent leave through 1915,

when he was remobilized into the Army Weather Service. In 1915 he published a book-length extension of his work on continental displacements now entitled *Die Entstehung der Kontinente und Ozeane.* Near the end of the war he published a catalog of occurrences of tornadoes and water spouts in Europe: This was his reentry into the boundary-layer meteorology which was his principal area of research at this time. Returning to Marburg at the end of the war, he published some interesting simulations on the origins of lunar craters and in 1920 published an extended edition of his book on continental displacements.

As hope evaporated for a professorship at Marburg, Wegener moved his family to Hamburg and merged households with his in-laws. He took up a government job at the German Marine Observatory and directed the geophysical colloquium at the new University of Hamburg.

The period between 1920 and 1924 marked Wegener's deepest involvement with the theory of continental displacements. A third edition of his book on the subject appeared in 1922 and was translated into English, French, Russian, Italian, Spanish, and Japanese. The theory was widely discussed and seems to have been favored more by geographers and paleoclimatologists than by geologists and geophysicists. It appealed to geologists whose fieldwork took place in the southern hemisphere much more than to those who worked in the northern hemisphere.

In 1924, in combination with his father-in-law, Wegener published a book: *Die Klimate der geologischen Vorzeit* (Climates of the geological past). The book mapped systematic displacements of the equator and the poles of the Earth by plotting glacial deposits, coal deposits, evaporates, and reef limestones through geologic time. In Wegener's theory of continental displacement, in contradistinction to modern plate tectonics, the motions of continents were interpreted as the results both of mobility of continental fragments and of true polar wander.

In 1924 Wegener finally obtained a professorship of meteorology and geophysics at the University of Graz in Austria. In these years he was principally concerned with atmospheric optics and acoustics, on which he was the leading expert in the world and on which he wrote a long treatise as part of the encyclopedic *Physik der Erde* (Geophysic). He was also the general editor of this text, which appeared in 1928. Notably, he declined to write on the mechanics and thermodynamics of the solid Earth and assigned this section to the young seismologist Beno Gutenberg.

In 1928 Wegener was offered a chance to return to Greenland as the head of his own polar expedition: the first overseas scientific work conducted by Germans since the end of World War I. In 1928 he made a reconnaissance expedition to west Greenland to pick out a landing site and base camp. In 1929 he departed for Greenland with a full shipload of equipment and a team of eager but inexperienced young scientists whom he planned to train as the next generation of German polar scientists. Part of the plan for this expedition was to establish and occupy a base that would overwinter in the middle of the Greenland ice cap, and produce the first complete set of meteorological data from this region. The expedition would also use seismic reflection profiling to determine the extent of the downed flexure of the rock beneath the Greenland ice cap by the weight of the ice itself. Nothing in the expedition plans mentions the theory of continental displacements. Indeed, it was entirely intended to support Wegener's plan to lead a German expedition to Antarctica in the International Polar Year 1933.

Severe weather and difficulties of supply in the fall of 1929 put the Greenland expedition far behind schedule, and in October Wegener undertook a very dangerous attempt to supply the incomplete base at the center of the ice cap. He left the mid-ice station on his fiftieth birthday, 1 November 1930, planning to return to the west coast base. He died a week later, either of heart failure or of asphyxiation by carbon monoxide from his stove. His body was recovered the following spring. He was found sewn into a sleeping bag next to a cairn marked by his crossed skis. His companion Rasmus Willemsen perished on the return to the coast after marking Wegener's grave. His body, and Wegener's final diary which he carried, have never been found. The discovery of Wegener's body in May 1931 was headline news around the world. In 1931 Leni Riefenstahl starred in an action film entitled *SOS Eisberg*, which had as its premise an attempt to find Wegener's lost scientific notes.

In 1929, shortly before his departure for Greenland, Wegener published a fourth and, according to him, final edition of his work on the origin of continents and oceans. Unlike the previous three editions, it is not a work of advocacy, but a catalog of contributions to a growing field of research, which, as Wegener noted, was now so large that one person could no longer master it. In response to his many critics who lamented the lack of a mechanism for continental drift, Wegener proposed six candidate mechanisms, and noted laconically that one or more of them might be the case. His studied indifference to plausible but untestable mechanisms persisted to end of his life.

Wegener's collected works would fill many volumes, most of them connected not with continental displacement or paleoclimatology, but with atmospheric optics, atmospheric acoustics, and atmospheric layering and thermodynamics. Contrary to the notion that he was an outsider and a maverick, he was an extremely influential and well-connected scientist throughout his career. Wegener

was known at home and abroad for his work on the complex layering and thermodynamic behavior of the troposphere. This work was the source of his inspiration concerning displacement of continents and put his work squarely in the mainstream of German geophysical speculation during his lifetime. That Germany's principal scientific institution for polar and marine research should be named the Alfred Wegener Institute is an accurate reflection of his scientific interest and accomplishments.

SUPPLEMENTARY BIBLIOGRAPHY

Wegener's manuscripts and papers were lost and/or destroyed in 1945. A few hundred surviving letters are in the Deutsches Museum in Munich. Photographs and slim documentary resources are also available in the Heimatsmuseum, Neuruppin, and the Wegener Gedankstätte in Zechlinerhütte bei Reinsberg—both in Germany. Abundant material pertaining to his Greenland work resides in the Dansk Polarcenter in Copenhagen. Scant additional resources lie in the university archives of Graz, Austria, and Marburg and Hamburg, Germany. A complete and annotated checklist of Wegener's papers and letters became available in 1998 through the labors of Ulrich Wutzke: "Alfred Wegener. Kommentiertes Verzeichnis der schriftlichen Dokumente seines Lebens und Wirkens," Berichte zur Polarforschung *288 (1998). This supersedes the list (still useful) in Hans Benndorf, "Verzeichnis der Veröffentlichungen von Alfred Wegener,"* Gerlands Beiträge zur Geophysik *31 (1931).*

WORKS BY WEGENER

"Drachen- und Fesselballonaufsteige ausgeführt auf der Danmark-Expedition 1906–1908." *Meddelelser om Grønland* XLII, no. 1 (1909): 5–75.

Thermodynamik der Atmosphäre. Leipzig: J. A. Barth, 1911.

"Die Entstehung der Kontinente." *Petermann's Mitteilungen* 58 (1912): 185–195, 253–256, 305–309.

Wind-und Wasserhosen in Europa, Sammlung Wissenschaft Bd. 60. Braunschweig, Germany: Friedrich Vieweg & Son, 1917.

Die Entstehung der Mondkrater. Braunschweig, Germany: Friedrich Vieweg & Son, 1921.

Die Entstehung der Kontinente und Ozeane. 3rd (completely revised) ed. Braunschweig, Germany: Friedrich Vieweg & Sohn, 1922.

Köppen, Wladimir, and Alfred Wegener. *Die Klimate der geologischen Vorzeit.* Berlin: Gebrüder Bornträger, 1924.

OTHER SOURCES

Wegener, Else. *Alfred Wegener: Tagebücher, Briefe, Erinnerungen.* Wiesbaden, Germany: F. A. Brockhaus, 1960.

Wutzke, Ulrich. *Durch die weiße Wüste: Leben und Leistungen des Grönlandforschers und Entdeckers der Kontinentaldrift Alfred Wegener, Edition Petermann.* Gotha, Germany: Justus Perthes Verlag, 1997.

Mott T. Greene

WEIDENREICH, FRANZ (*b.* Edenkoben, Germany, 7 June 1873; *d.* New York, New York, 11 June 1948), *human anatomy, paleoanthropology, human evolution, physical anthropology, histology.*

Weidenreich discovered and described the initial finds of *Sinanthropus*, now classified as *Homo erectus.* He went to China in the midthirties and resumed the work of Davidson Black at Zhoukoudian. Because the *Sinanthropus* originals disappeared during World War II, Weidenreich's descriptions and the casts prepared under his advice provide the only traces left of these famous hominid fossils. Prior to the stay in China, Weidenreich studied histology and comparative anatomy of primates at several German universities, among them Strasbourg, Heidelberg, and Frankfurt am Main.

Early Career as Histologist in Strasbourg. Franz Weidenreich was born the youngest of four children in Edenkoben in the Palatinate. In 1893 he began to study medicine at universities in Munich, Kiel, Berlin, and Strasbourg. In his early career, Weidenreich was interested primarily in cell and tissue biology, in histology. Weidenreich completed his studies in Strasbourg under the direction of Gustav Schwalbe. When Weidenreich arrived in Strasbourg, Schwalbe was studying the Neanderthal skeleton. This first fossil encounter did not, however, lead Weidenreich to change his subject of study. In his doctoral thesis in 1899 he described the anatomy of central nuclei in the mammalian cerebellum. In July 1901 he habilitated with a thesis on the vascular system of the human spleen. After a brief stay at Paul Ehrlich's institute of experimental therapy in Frankfurt am Main he returned to Strasbourg where he was finally appointed as associate professor of anatomy in 1902. While his research interests focused on the cellular composition of blood, a list of his classes reveals a wider scope of interests. Besides histology and cellular correlates of the immune system, he taught classes in developmental biology, comparative anatomy, anthropology, the locomotor system, and the peripheral nervous system. Due to his passion for the composition of the blood and the structure of blood cells he was labeled with the nickname "bloody Weidenreich."

Although his professional interests focused in histological studies of the blood, he occasionally touched problems of the morphology of the human skeleton. In 1904 he entered into a dispute with the physicist Otto Walkhoff on the interpretation of x-ray scans of the human chin—then a brand-new technique.

A decade later Weidenreich published the results of another study in human anatomy. He had investigated the anatomy of the human pelvis and its relation to an upright posture. In this study Weidenreich was able to demonstrate that the human pelvis compared to that of apes underwent specific transformations. The geometry and arrangement of pelvic elements had changed corresponding to the increased load in upright posture. Simultaneously muscular attachments controlling the posture in the hip joint and the movement of the legs had changed. In order to fully understand the structure of the human pelvis, it was therefore necessary to relate the locomotory apparatus with functional requirements. There is thus a particular and close relation between form and function of the skeleton and its elements. In order to explain the structure of skeletal elements, it is necessary to determine their functions, if possible, on a mechanical basis. Weidenreich considered comparative anatomy to be an important method in this context. Comparing the pelvis of apes and monkeys with that of humans reveals the structural changes developing in response to the specific mode of locomotion.

The years he spent in Strasbourg were the quietest ones in Weidenreich's life. In 1904 he married Mathilde Neuberger and three daughters were born to them. The quiet years ended in 1914 with the political catastrophe of World War I and a severe interruption in Weidenreich's academic career. Weidenreich had been a member of the Democratic Party in Alsace-Lorraine for which he held a seat in the Strasbourg parliament. When war broke out he focused on his political duties. His decision resulted in a six-year gap in his publications between 1915 and 1921.

Back to the Lectern at Heidelberg. Upon the end of the war the territory of Alsace-Lorraine fell to France. Weidenreich and his family were forced to leave Strasbourg early in 1919. He went to Heidelberg and started teaching anatomy classes for hospital staff. In winter 1919 he endeavored to refresh his biological knowledge and visited classes in zoology and botany at Heidelberg University, and in winter 1921 he was appointed professor of anatomy on the medical faculty at Heidelberg.

After a six-year gap he published two substantial papers, on which he must have been working for a longer period due to their sheer length. He devoted two hundred pages to an anatomical description and comparative study of the structure of the human foot. The other paper was a study of general problems of evolutionary theory. Weidenreich reorganized his research focus and addressed general problems in evolutionary theory, the comparative anatomy of the skeleton as well as the growth and development of osseous and dental tissues. He dropped the histological studies of blood components that made up a major part of his work prior to the first world war. In his studies of the human skeleton he focused on changes correlated with an upright posture and a bipedal mode of locomotion. Following his initial studies of the pelvis and foot he turned to structural transformations of the human skull. These studies culminated fifteen years later in the publication of his widely acknowledged paper on the brain and its role in the phylogenetic transformation of the human skull.

Weidenreich regarded skeletal transformations as a response to specific functional requirements, themselves being determined by a specific mode of usage. Initially, the skeletons of apes and humans were quite similar, but in the course of their evolutionary history their respective structures had been adjusted to specific modes of locomotion. In the case of humans, this transformation can be observed regularly in individual development. Young children are crouching at first, before they learn to walk upright. Pathologies preventing a normal use of the skeleton do not allow characteristic transformations. The function of walking upright thus represents in some sense a stimulus that calls forth specific reactions by the organism, leading to the production of adjusted structures. Of course, organisms are not completely independent in the selection of the responses stimuli. They do not produce arbitrary structures, but reproduce an inherited type. However, depending on individually different factors imposed during individual growth and development, the general form is adjusted corresponding to individual requirements. In his paper on evolutionary theory in 1921, he tried to introduce the illustrated stimulus-response relationship into an evolutionary context. He took a stand in a debate raging in the early twenties on the mechanisms of evolution.

Weidenreich's professorship at Heidelberg University turned out to be rather ephemeral. Already in 1924 the institute for cancer research at the medical faculty was closed and Weidenreich was forced to retire at the age of fifty-two. However, he was able to continue his studies. The Portheim Foundation at Mannheim took over parts of the institute and appointed Weidenreich as head of the biomechanics laboratory. Weidenreich realized that his studies of the human skeleton and his conclusions about anatomical changes in evolution might contribute to the interpretation of human fossils. He was asked to provide the anatomic description and morphological reconstruction of a skull found in September 1925 in a quarry in the suburbs of Weimar. Weidenreich published the full description in a monograph in 1928, covering in separate papers also the geological and archaeological context of the find. This careful study was Weidenreich's ticket to paleoanthropology.

Human Variability and Human Races. Meanwhile, events on the public stage demanded Weidenreich's attention. Human variability had been put on the agenda by the National Socialist Party (NSDAP, or Nazis) from 1924 onward. By then the NSDAP gained growing influence on public opinion. The Nazi party supported biological race ideology and anti-Semitism. Weidenreich, who was of Jewish descent, recognized a threat in the political rise of the Nazi party and the increasing public presence of its supporters, which he intended to counter by the means available to him as a scientist. As an anatomist he was bothered by the irrational up- and downgrading of certain races, promulgated by the National Socialists.

He thus started to study race concepts from a scientific perspective. In evolution, races were thought to represent one of several sources of variation among humans. According to Weidenreich's approach races can be regarded as evolutionarily relevant only if they correspond to individual and functional differentiations. These differentiations should be related to geographic distribution. Besides, the term *race* was scientifically discredited by its political instrumentalization.

Weidenreich explored the advantages and disadvantages of race concepts in a book *Rasse und Körperbau* (Race and constitution) published in 1927. Already in its initial pages he discarded the use of the term *race* in a scientific context, instead proposing to make use of the medical concept of constitution. The present use of this term in medicine was too restricted though. Constitution concepts were mainly used to characterize pathologies occurring in correspondence with a certain constitutional type, for example, in the sense of a weak constitution making its bearer susceptible to particular diseases. Weidenreich proposed to extend its meaning beyond the restrictions of pathological phenomena, thereby including other sources of individual variability such as functional, developmental, or even geographical factors. His concept delimited two extreme constitutional types and included a continuum of forms linking the extremes.

With this book he attracted the attention of the rector of the Johann Wolfgang Goethe University in Frankfurt, Fritz Ernst Drevermann. Drevermann had decided to widen the scope of disciplines taught at Frankfurt University by including physical anthropology. Weidenreich accepted the chair at Frankfurt University and started teaching classes in winter 1928. The facilities of the newly installed professorship were not luxurious, however. It was, for instance, difficult to find adequate space in the university's compound. Drevermann, by then also director of the nearby Forschungsinstitut und Natur-Museum Senckenberg (Senckenberg Research Institute and Nature Museum), housed Weidenreich's new institute there. A glance at Weidenreich's publication list reveals that he did not restrict himself to academic teaching duties. He made use of the opportunities offered to him at Senckenberg and prepared an exhibition on human evolution at the museum. He started to publish for regional newspapers and for the magazine of the Senckenberg Research

Franz Weidenreich. *Franz Weidenreich with two 500,000-year-old skulls.* AP IMAGES.

Society. Weidenreich continued to study fossil hominids, in particular the Broken Hill skull, the australopithecine fossils discovered in South Africa and—in close detail—the new *Sinanthropus* fossils from Zhoukoudian in China. Chinese paleontologists Yang Zhongjian and Weng Wenhao sent casts to Senckenberg; among them was a cast of the skull found in Zhoukoudian in 1929.

Chicago Interlude. Weidenreich was not allowed to stay at Frankfurt University for long. After five brief years he was forced to leave the university in 1933. Already at the beginning of the year, an association of National Socialist lecturers prepared reports on unwanted colleagues. Weidenreich did not make friends among them by his discussion of race concepts. The new rector at Frankfurt University reshaped the university according to National Socialist principles. Following the Nazi takeover in April professors and lecturers of non-Aryan descent were subsequently dismissed. Weidenreich was forced to go on unpaid leave in 1934. But fortunately he was offered a guest professorship at the University of Chicago. Banned from his job and any opportunity to work, Weidenreich accepted and went to Chicago later that year. In the United States he met a scientific community that was openly organized. Nevertheless, he had to struggle with a

new language at the age of sixty-five. The professorship at Chicago was moreover limited to nine months.

By mid-1934 he was approached by colleagues asking him to apply for the chair held by Canadian anatomist Davidson Black at Beijing. Black, who died unexpectedly of a heart attack in 1934, held a professorship of anatomy at the Peiping Union Medical College (PUMC) in Beijing, an institution operated by the American Rockefeller Foundation. Weidenreich, who had already become interested in the *Sinanthropus* fossils while at Frankfurt, accepted immediately. By the end of 1934 Weidenreich returned to Germany to await the decision from the Rockefeller Foundation, which arrived soon after.

Describing *Sinanthropus*. Early in 1935 Weidenreich traveled to Beijing, where he arrived in April. Weidenreich was now professor of anatomy at the PUMC. The PUMC was meant to represent a center of cultural exchange. The Cenozoic Research Laboratory, to which Weidenreich was appointed as one of the directors, coordinated research at Zhoukoudian.

Franz Weidenreich initially had to cope with practical difficulties. He could neither speak nor read or write Chinese. Moreover his knowledge of English was also quite limited. Until he moved to Beijing he had published only a single paper in English, a summary of his publication on the human foot from 1921. Now he needed to adapt, and he would not have succeeded without the support of his secretary, Olga Hempel-Gowen. Olga Gowen had been born and raised in China and was fluent in English and Chinese. She translated his manuscripts and corrected them, so that Weidenreich was able to publish predominantly in English from 1935 onward.

Fossil remains of Peking Man, or *Sinanthropus*, had been discovered at Zhoukoudian since 1921. The site was exceptionally prolific. Unlike other hominid sites, Zhoukoudian provided a large number of individuals. It was thus possible to study the variability among a *Sinanthropus* population, instead of dealing with more or less artificial compositions of single fragments. Franz Weidenreich started with detailed descriptions of the finds already made by Davidson Black and published in rapid succession a general overview of the finds (1935), a study of the endocranial casts and a reconstruction of the mandible (both in 1936).

He left the direction of the excavations to the able hands of paleontologist Pei Wenzhong and the young geologist Jia Lanpo, who were involved in the excavations already since the beginning of the thirties. In November 1936 their enduring efforts were rewarded with the unearthing of three *Sinanthropus* skulls within eleven days. The finds permitted a complete reconstruction of the *Sinanthropus* skull. In addition, Weidenreich provided a study of *Sinanthropus* teeth and dentition in 1937. In 1936 fragments of limb bones were also found. It was thus possible to reconstruct the figure and posture of *Sinanthropus*.

Japanese troops put a sudden end to the excavations at Zhoukoudian when late in 1937 three workers were shot at the site. Under these circumstances it was impossible to continue with the excavations. When it became evident that the excavations could not be resumed in 1938, Weidenreich accepted an invitation to an anthropological congress in Denmark. He took the opportunity to visit friends and colleagues in the United States and a number of other European countries. He left in March 1938 for the United States and introduced the *Sinanthropus* fossils and reconstructions at numerous American universities, research institutes, and scientific societies. On the basis of his descriptions and detailed comparisons he was able to draw inferences about human evolution. Weidenreich used the Zhoukoudian hominids as empirical evidence for his concepts on human evolution developed earlier. In the first days of August, Weidenreich presented the fossils and reconstructions at the congress in Copenhagen. He then proceeded to the Netherlands, visiting the discoverer of the first fossils of *Pithecanthropus* in Java, Eugène Dubois.

Dubois had carried out excavations in the last decade of the nineteenth century and discovered hominid fossils at Trinil and Kedung Brubus. More Pleistocene hominids were excavated in Java after 1936, in particular by the young geologist Ralph von Koenigswald. Initially having been delighted by these new finds, Dubois started to doubt their value.

Weidenreich, knowing about von Koenigswald's discoveries, was determined to form his own picture of the fossils. He studied Dubois's finds and headed on to Bandung in Java, where he met with von Koenigswald in September. He inspected von Koenigswald's finds and identified another *Pithecanthropus* fragment from Sangiran, which he found in a basket containing fossils from Sangiran. Weidenreich and von Koenigswald announced the new find in a joint publication.

They decided that von Koenigswald should come to Beijing as soon as possible in order to compare *Sinanthropus* and *Pithecanthropus*. In February 1939 von Koenigswald arrived in Beijing, bringing along another surprise from Sangiran, a fossil maxilla, which was soon followed by a package with further cranial fragments belonging to the same individual. Weidenreich and von Koenigswald announced the new discovery and provided careful comparisons between *Pithecanthropus* and *Sinanthropus*. Before Weidenreich left Beijing in the first days of April for the United States, they completed a paper introducing the results of their comparisons. The comparison

led the researchers to conclude that *Sinanthropus* and *Pithecanthropus* represent geographical variants of hominids at a similar stage of evolution. Weidenreich took the casts of the specimens from Java along to the United States. He reconstructed the cranial vault of Sangiran 4 from the seven fragments that had initially been collected. In the course of this reconstruction he studied while in the United States the morphological relations and the growth conditions of the human skull. Resuming his studies from 1924 he published a monograph in 1941 on the transformations of the human skull in evolution.

In this paper Weidenreich developed two important conclusions on human evolution. According to the comparisons executed at Beijing, *Sinanthropus* and *Pithecanthropus* represented two geographically different forms of hominid at the same evolutionary stage. Since there are modern humans in both areas and since modern humans differ in a corresponding way from each other as the Pleistocene fossils do, this indicates a continuous evolutionary process going on from the Pleistocene until the present running in parallel in China as well as in Java. The development of *Pithecanthropus* and *Sinanthropus* followed a parallel track. An underlying general evolutionary trend thus seems to lead to corresponding results, even in case the actual steps in evolution happen in geographically different places. Such a model is called polycentric, because corresponding evolutionary stages are independently passed in different places. Weidenreich's theory of polycentric evolution is rooted in this observation. At that point Weidenreich merely suggested an interpretation of the observed parallelism. It was not before 1946 in his book on *Apes, Giants, And Man,* where he introduced his well-known network chart on human evolution, that he offered a mechanism for his earlier observations. Vertical connections in this graphical depiction indicate ancestry, horizontal lines represent distribution and specialization, and diagonal lines finally suggest interchange. Later, the rather general expression interchange was replaced by crossing or cross breeding.

Furthermore, Pleistocene and modern humans characteristically differ in some respects, first of all in size and robusticity. The proportion of the skull also differs. Compared with modern humans the cranial capacity of Pleistocene humans is generally smaller, the skull is not as highly vaulted, and the teeth and jaw are comparatively large. These characteristic changes in the organization of the skull correspond to those occurring in dwarf forms of dogs. The modern human skull may thus be regarded as the pygmy form of a larger Pleistocene human. Earlier forms thus must have been robust giants. Based on this idea Weidenreich later developed the concept of giants as human ancestors.

After spending a year in the United States as required for naturalization, Weidenreich returned to Beijing in August 1940. The political situation still did not allow excavations to resume at Zhoukoudian. In fact it got even worse, so that the Rockefeller Foundation decided in spring 1941 to close their facilities in China and bring all foreign scientists to the United States. In April 1941, only eight months after his return, Weidenreich was urged to leave Beijing again and return to the American Museum of Natural History at New York.

Concluding Six Eventful Years. Weidenreich was unable to take the precious *Sinanthropus* fossils along, but a concerted effort was made to protect the hominid fossils and if possible to bring them out of the country. The fossil collection was packed in boxes in order to transport them to the United States. However, somewhere along the route from Beijing to the coast the fossils were lost. Since then the original fossils of *Sinanthropus* and other treasures from Zhoukoudian have been lost—a terrible and irretrievable loss.

Weidenreich continued his studies on the skull of *Sinanthropus* with the casts he brought along to America and published his results in 1943. Meanwhile, he also lost contact with von Koenigswald in Java. The fate of the Zhoukoudian hominids raised similar apprehensions about von Koenigswald himself and his precious collections. In 1941 Weidenreich received casts from the fossils von Koenigswald found after they met in Beijing, but no one knew whether von Koenigswald was still alive. Facing this desperate situation Weidenreich decided to describe the fossils not yet published by von Koenigswald on the basis of the casts at his disposal. Weidenreich provided an anatomical interpretation of the finds and fitted them into his evolutionary scheme. Shortly before the publication von Koenigswald reemerged on the scene to Weidenreich's delight and pleasure. Von Koenigswald had survived the war in a prison camp.

The anatomical descriptions provided by Weidenreich were welcome, although von Koenigswald did not agree with all the details of Weidenreich's systematic and evolutionary conclusions. Later, he corrected Weidenreich's taxonomic attributions. Von Koenigswald brought along the whole collection of Javanese hominids, including the specimens from Ngandong. Although they had been found fifteen years earlier, the specimens had not yet been carefully described so Weidenreich immediately started working on the fossils. According to Weidenreich the hominid finds from Ngandong represented the Neanderthal stage in human evolution. Weidenreich did not manage to complete more than the bare anatomical description. He died 11 June 1948, a few days after his seventy-fifth birthday in New York. Death overtook him in the midst of his work, and something else is hard to imagine for such an agile and vivid personality.

BIBLIOGRAPHY

WORKS BY WEIDENREICH

"Der Menschenfuss." *Zeitschrift für Morphologie und Anthropologie* 22 (1921): 51–282. Weidenreich's exhaustive study on the comparative anatomy of the primate foot.

"Das Evolutionsproblem und der individuelle Gestaltungsanteil am Entwicklungsgeschehen." *Roux' Vorträge und Aufsätze über Entwicklungsmechanik der Organismen* 27 (1921): 1–120. Weidenreich's key paper on his ideas on evolution.

"Evolution of the Human Foot." *American Journal of Physical Anthropology* 6 (1923): 1–10. English summary of "Der Menschenfuss."

Rasse und Körperbau. Berlin: Springer, 1927. Introducing the concept of constitution.

Der Schädelfund von Weimar-Ehringsdorf. Jena, Germany: Fischer, 1928. Weidenreich's first fossil description.

"The *Sinanthropus* Population of Choukoutien (Locality 1) with a Preliminary Report on New Discoveries." *Bulletin of the Geological Society of China B* 14 (1935): 427–461.

"Observations on the Form and Proportions of the Endocranial Casts of *Sinanthropus* Pekinensis, Other Hominids and the Great Apes: A Comparative Study of Brain Size." *Palaeontologia Sinica,* Series D, 3 (1936): 1–50.

"The Mandibles of *Sinanthropus pekinensis:* A Comparative Study." *Palaeontologia Sinica,* Series D, 7. (1936): 1–162.

"The Dentition of *Sinanthropus pekinensis:* A Comparative Odontography of the Hominids." 2 *Palaeontologia Sinica,* n.s. D, no. 1 (1937).

"The Brain and Its Role in the Phylogenetic Transformation of the Human Skull." *Transactions of the American Philosophical Society* 31 (1941): 321–442.

Apes, Giants and Man. Chicago: University of Chicago Press, 1946.

The Shorter Anthropological Papers of Franz Weidenreich Published in the Period 1939–1948: A Memorial Volume. Edited by Sherwood Larned Washburn and Davida Wolffson. New York: Viking Fund, 1949. Includes a complete bibliography of Weidenreich.

OTHER SOURCES

Gregory, William K. "Franz Weidenreich, 1873–1948." *American Anthropologist* 51 (1948): 85–90.

Jia Lanpo and Huang Weiwen. *The Story of Peking Man: From Archaeology to Mystery.* Translated by Yin Zhiqi. Hong Kong: Foreign Languages Press, 1990. Historical account of the excavations at Zhoukoudian site.

Teilhard de Chardin, Pierre. "Franz Weidenreich." *L'Anthropologie* 52 (1948): 328–330.

Wolpoff, Milford, and Rachel Caspari. *Race and Human Evolution.* New York: Simon & Schuster, 1997. Contains a reconstruction of Weidenreich's views on human variability and evolution.

Christine Hertler

WEIL, ANDRÉ

(*b.* Paris, France, 6 May 1906; *d.* Princeton, New Jersey, 6 August 1998), *number theory, algebra, analysis, geometry.*

Weil was an arithmetician in the broadest possible sense. His work on Diophantine equations drew on all the fields of pure mathematics and developed methods so deep and elegant as to influence each of those fields in turn. He was a founder of the Bourbaki group and its strongest mathematician, the most prominent mathematician at the University of Chicago when it was arguably the world's leading mathematics department, and a member of the Institute for Advanced Study. He decisively shaped the style and direction of all post–World War II mathematics.

Childhood. The Alsatian Jewish medical doctor Bernard Weil and Russian-Austrian Jewish Salomea (Selma) Reinherz Weil were very comfortably established in Paris when their first child, André, was born, and three years later their daughter Simone, who became known as a philosopher. The children, raised especially by their mother, were precocious and accomplished. The parents had seen bitter anti-Semitism in eastern Europe and in the Dreyfus affair in France. They raised their children so thoroughly assimilated that André was around thirteen before he learned that Jewish descent could matter in any way. At age eight, as a gift to their father, André taught his five-year-old sister to read the newspaper aloud to the family. By age twelve he worked on university-level mathematics, played the violin, taught himself to read Homer and Plato in Greek, and to read Sanskrit. The family often conversed in English or German.

At age fourteen, three years below the minimum age, he took the state baccalaureate exam by special permission and got the highest scores in the nation. He began preparing for the exam to enter the École Normale Supérieur (ENS), which generally takes two years and not rarely more. He took one. During that year with advice from Jacques Hadamard he began to study analysis and differential geometry.

He entered the ENS with the highest exam scores in the nation. He felt he became a mathematician in Hadamard's nearby seminar at the Collège de France, where he presented at least once: on domains of convergence of power series in several complex variables. He took courses with Henri-Léon Lebesgue and Charles-Émile Picard, which did not prevent his also studying Sanskrit at the Sorbonne and reading the *Bhagavad Gita* in the original, which he would carry with him for the rest of his life both for its poetic beauty and its philosophy.

Beginning a Career. During his time at ENS he lived at home as did many students with family in Paris. The family was extremely close, and brother and sister were devoted to each other. He graduated from the ENS at nineteen, too young for military service, and so had time for what he later regarded as his gift for traveling. A summer with his family in the French Alps left him with notebooks full of Diophantine equations plus a plan to always write so as to draw the reader beyond the manifest content toward yet more distant perspectives.

A scholarship from the Sorbonne took him to Rome for six months of mathematics and study of Italian painting up through the modernists. He heard Francesco Severi on algebraic surfaces and encountered Solomon Lefschetz. He read a paper containing a theorem and a conjecture by Louis Mordell (1922) without guessing how important they would soon be to him. Support from the Rockefeller Foundation let him spend much of 1927 in Göttingen, Germany. He describes encounters with Richard Courant, Emmy Noether, and others in his autobiography (1991). Over this time and the next year he crystallized a thesis topic based on the Mordell paper.

Weil was steeped in the long-prestigious subject, from Niels Abel and Carl Jacobi at the beginning of the nineteenth century to Karl Weierstrass and Jules-Henri Poincaré at the end, of integrals of multiple-valued complex functions or in modern terms integration on Riemann surfaces. His teachers Hadamard and Picard were personally involved in it. An *elliptic curve*, or genus one Riemann surface C, is topologically a torus and algebraically is defined by a nice cubic polynomial $P(X,Y)$ in two variables. Integration along paths on C produces a natural Abelian group structure on the points of C. Any points p,q of C have a kind of geometrical sum $p+q$ and this addition law is associative, commutative, and has a zero point and additive inverses. This group structure efficiently organizes the theory of integration on C. Higher degree polynomials $P(X,Y)$ define Riemann surfaces of higher genus, which topologically are surfaces with more than one torus-handle.

The number of handles g is called the *genus* of the surface. Jacobi already knew in effect that integration on a genus g surface C is organized by a group structure on a space $J(C)$ of complex dimension g, called the *Jacobian* of C. A genus one Riemann surface is its own Jacobian. A higher genus Riemann surface C maps as a complex 1-dimensional subspace into its complex g-dimensional Jacobian $C{\rightarrow}J(C)$.

Poincaré drew arithmetic conclusions from the trivial observation that if a cubic polynomial $P(X,Y)$ has rational coefficients then any geometrical sum $p+q$ of rational points on its curve C is again rational. He conjectured that the group of rational points is finitely generated: a finite number of rational solutions to the cubic $P(X,Y)$ suffices to generate all the rational solutions by the addition law. Mordell proved this and gave his own conjecture: in genus higher than one a Riemann surface *C* has at most finitely many rational points. Weil set out to generalize Mordell's proof, prove Mordell's conjecture, and introduce systematically useful tools to do it. He succeeded at the first goal and the last.

In place of rational points Weil proved the theorem for points in any *algebraic number field k*, that is: Fix any finite list of irrational numbers, and take solutions using those irrationals along with the rational numbers. And he proved it for the Jacobian of any Riemann surface: For any Riemann surface of any genus, defined over any algebraic number field *k*, the group of *k*-valued points of the Jacobian is finitely generated. Weil's clear organization of the proof made the more general conclusion natural. His proof presaged the arithmetic theory of *heights*, where rational numbers are ordered by increasing complexity so that there are only finitely many below any fixed level of complexity. This allows inductive proofs on the complexity of rational points. And he made elegant use of Galois groups, presaging *Galois cohomology* bringing methods of algebraic topology into arithmetic. Typical of Weil's work, it is a tough, elegant argument and inspired much further progress.

Hadamard encouraged Weil to prove the Mordell conjecture in his thesis so as not to leave the work half done. Weil's result on Jacobians suggested a strategy: The rational points (or *k*-valued points) of *J*(*C*) are finitely generated and so are sparse in *J*(*C*). For genus *g* greater than one, the surface *C* forms a 1-dimensional subspace of its higher dimensional Jacobian *J*(*C*), thus also sparse. Two sparse subsets should meet only rarely—and the right details might show these meet only finitely many times. A proof would have to be much more sophisticated and no one has yet made it work. The theorem was proved fifty-five years later by Gerd Faltings (1983), by quite other means descended from the *Weil conjectures*, described below. Weil liked to say he had done well to reject Hadamard's advice and submit his dissertation as it was.

Weil lived with his family as he wrote the dissertation and indeed during his following year of military service. Because of his age he missed the military training usual at the ENS. So he was placed in the infantry rather than the traditional artillery, and officials secured him an easy station in Paris. He got leave time to correct the printer's proofs of his dissertation.

Having made clear his desire to see India, Weil was offered a job at Aligarh Muslim University near Delhi. He agreed to teach French civilization but then the university could not create a position for it. He would have to teach mathematics. He did so from 1930 to 1932. Back in France he was highly esteemed by top mathematicians, but arithmetic was an odd specialty there at the time. Few

could read his dissertation. He found a good position at the University of Strasbourg and held it until 1939.

During these years he worked in analysis, especially integration on topological groups, and on algebraic and arithmetic topics derived from his dissertation. His most widely used innovation was in point set topology, namely the idea of *uniform spaces*. Such a space has no metric giving a distance between points, yet it makes sense to talk of different sequences "converging at the same rate" to different points. In particular there is a well-defined notion of uniform convergence of a series of functions from one uniform space to another.

Bourbaki. France could claim to lead nineteenth-century mathematics. Germany had a decisive lead by the 1930s in part because, unlike France, Germany had a policy of protecting promising academics through World War I. Weil happily visited Germany but was ambitious for his own country. Many young mathematicians in France were unhappy with their outdated curriculum. And classmates from the ENS by design looked to each other as an elite destined precisely to assure French greatness in all things. In 1934 Weil assembled a handful of his friends, all admitted to the ENS between 1922 and 1926, to write a definitive new analysis textbook. He met with Henri Cartan, Claude Chevalley, Jean Delsarte, Jean Dieudonné, and René de Possel at the now-vanished Café Capoulade near the ENS on Monday 10 December 1934. The textbook project expanded into a series of books covering the basics of all pure mathematics, none of which would make any references except to earlier books in the series. The group published under the name Nicolas Bourbaki and kept enough secrecy that for decades many mathematicians were unsure just who this Bourbaki was.

These mathematicians had closely similar backgrounds, tastes, and goals. The work was intensely collaborative and cannot be divided into parts attributable to each separate member. But nothing came out of Bourbaki against Weil's wishes. Indeed nothing came out at all for several years. Weil spent much of 1937 at the Institute for Advanced Study in Princeton, New Jersey. He returned to France via New Orleans and Mexico. Soon after that the book series was named the *Elements of Mathematics*. The French title *Éléments de mathématique* expresses the unity of mathematics by using a made-up singular noun *mathématique* rather than the standard plural form *mathématiques*.

The first volume appeared in 1939. It was a preliminary treatment of set theory and the basic idea of *structure*. By the 1950s Bourbaki produced books on algebra, topology, functions of one real variable, topological vector spaces, and integration—very close to Weil's range of research topics. Other volumes came later and the

Elements of Mathematics were never actually completed, but the series had a huge influence on worldwide standards for rigor and style of argument. Bourbaki became the standard reference fixing the definitions of modern terminology in most fields of mathematics. Perhaps the main influence was to reorganize all of pure mathematics around recent abstract techniques instead of traditional subject areas. Weil was the leading member of Bourbaki until, following a rule that he had introduced at the beginning, he retired from the group at age fifty.

World War II and America. During the early Bourbaki years Weil met Évelyne (Eveline) de Possel, then wife of René de Possel, who divorced Possel and in October of 1937 married Weil. They would have two children, daughters, Sylvie born 12 September 1942 and Nicolette born 6 December 1946, after they left Europe for the United States.

As World War II approached, Weil thought of the philosophy of the *Bhagavad Gita* and of the loss France suffered in World War I by not protecting her scientists. He rejected the general pacifism of his sister—as she would also during the war—but resolved that if war came he had a duty to keep himself out of it by going to the United States. When it came he was in Finland with that plan in mind. He stayed there until he was arrested as a suspicious foreigner. The story that he was nearly shot as a spy seems to be exaggerated (Pekonen, 1992). He was shipped to jails in Sweden, England, and finally France, where he was arrested for failing to report for military duty. Convicted in May 1940, he asked to be sent to the front rather than jail, and this was granted. The front collapsed before he reached it. In January 1941 he, Eveline, and his parents left for the United States.

The Rockefeller Foundation helped him get teaching work briefly at Haverford College. There he began influential work in geometry with all of his hallmarks: a classical problem with many easily visualized cases is elegantly solved and generalized by using the latest reputedly abstract tools. Karl Friedrich Gauss showed that the sum of the angles of a triangle on a hyperbolic (constant negative curvature) plane is less than 180°, while the angle sum on an elliptic plane (constant positive curvature) is greater than 180°. Much more, on either kind of plane, the difference from 180° is directly proportional to the area of the triangle. The Gauss-Bonnet theorem generalized this to any region P surrounded by a curve C on a surface S of variable curvature, where P itself may have some complicated topology. The integral of the surface curvature over P replaces the area of the triangle, while the integral of the geodesic curvature along C replaces the angle sum. The sum of the two integrals equals 2π times the *Euler number* of P which measures how many "holes" and "handles"

the region P has. In particular the integral of the curvature over an entire surface S is always 2π times some integer uniquely determined by the topology of S. Carl Allendoerfer at Haverford generalized this latter result to n-dimensional manifolds M embedded in some Euclidean space R^m. Allendoerfer and Weil (1943) together generalized the whole Gauss-Bonnet theorem to n-dimensional regions P in Riemannian manifolds and mistakenly thought they had eliminated the need for a Euclidean space.

The next year Shiing-Shen Chern, visiting the Institute for Advanced Study in Princeton from China, sharply simplified the Allendoerfer-Weil proof and did eliminate the Euclidean embeddings. He used a very pretty geometric construction with a *fibre bundle* over the manifold M, that is a map of manifolds $B \longrightarrow M$ which in Chern's case bundles together one $n-1$ dimensional sphere for each point x of M and depicts each as the sphere of unit tangent vectors at x. Fibre bundle techniques were new and growing quickly at Princeton. A series of private letters by Weil used all of the tools of integration on manifolds, and topological groups, and *cohomology* to streamline Chern's construction. Typical of his best work, Weil showed how a quick and natural treatment of that construction led seamlessly to a vast generalization. The *Chern-Weil homomorphism* gives an analogue of Gauss-Bonnet for any fibre bundle with a *connection*, that is with an abstract analogue of differentiation along tangent vectors. The abstract concept has geometric uses far remote from the original motivation. The result and the means used to prove it became cornerstones of the theory of *characteristic classes* on fibre bundles.

Weil next worked at Lehigh University in Pennsylvania. Depressed by the heavy teaching load and uninterested students, in 1944 he resolved to quit and do anything else. The structural anthropologist Claude Lévi-Strauss got him a position at the Universidade de São Paulo in Brazil, a center for algebraic geometry. With a visit to Paris in 1945 he stayed at São Paulo until 1947, when he was appointed professor at the University of Chicago. He had a leave in Paris for 1957–1958 and then became a professor at the Institute for Advanced Study starting in 1958 and retiring in 1976. He traveled back to India in 1967, and made several trips to Japan.

Simone joined Charles De Gaulle's Free French movement in England. She had adopted a passionate Christian asceticism and self-denial, she requested to be sent on hopelessly dangerous missions in France, and ate less and less, purportedly to express solidarity with the suffering in France. Stricken with tuberculosis, she refused food and medical care. She died 24 August 1943. André was devastated by the loss and by her role in it. He helped produce her posthumous publications and never got over the pain though he lived another fifty-five years. In his own words he lived less than that. His life "or at least what of it deserves the name" ended when his wife died 24 May 1986 (1991, p. 11).

The Weil Conjectures. Nineteenth-century number theorists already saw deep analogies between the ordinary integers Z on one hand and polynomials in one variable with complex coefficients $C(z)$ on the other. The square root of 2 is an *algebraic number* because it satisfies an integer polynomial equation namely $X^2-2=0$ so that $X=\sqrt{2}$. The complex square root function is an *algebraic function* since it satisfies a similar equation $X^2-z=0$ so that $X=\sqrt{z}$ where z is not a number but a variable over the complex numbers. Theorems on algebraic numbers often had analogues for complex algebraic functions although the proofs might be quite different. Sometimes the proof was easier for algebraic numbers and sometimes for algebraic functions. No general, routine way of turning proofs for one case into proofs for the other is known as of 2007.

Weil wrote to his sister about this, saying, "we would be badly blocked" if we could find no good link between the cases, but "God beats the devil" because there is a promising intermediary: replace the complex numbers by any *finite field* (Letter of 26 March 1940, in Weil, 1979, vol. 1, p. 252). One simple finite field is the integers modulo 5, which is a five-element set {0,1,2,3,4} with addition and multiplication defined by casting out 5s. So 1+2=3 as usual, but 3+4=2 modulo 5. This is obviously like the ordinary integers, but also like the complex numbers in the key respect that each integer has an inverse modulo 5: $1\times1 = 2\times3 = 4\times4 = 1$ modulo 5.

Weil proved an analogue to no small theorem for this case, but to the deepest most sought-after theorem in number theory: the Riemann hypothesis. In 1940–1941 he proved a Riemann hypothesis for curves over any finite field.

These curves have genus in the same algebraic sense as Riemann surfaces although they are not continuous curves or surfaces in any way, so their genus has no evident topological meaning. The "coordinates" of points on such a curve lie in finite fields rather than in the continuous complex plane. Yet Weil saw that great results would fall out if he could generalize topological ideas related to the genus of continuous curves.

During Weil's time in Göttingen he heard of Heinz Hopf's work on the *Lefschetz fixed point theorem* using topology to count the solutions to suitable equations without actually solving them. Weil made pioneering use of the theorem in 1935 in an elegant new proof of a known theorem on Lie groups. By the late 1930s the relevant topological tools were embodied in *cohomology* theory. He found an often-useful method of showing when

different cohomology theories will agree on specified cases. But the known cohomology theories all relied on the continuity of the real numbers. They had no contact with finite fields or in other words with *finite characteristic*. Yet Weil conjectured that an analogue in finite characteristic could give stunningly simple proofs of some powerful arithmetic claims.

The conjectures became famous as the *Weil conjectures*. They are concise, harmonious, penetrating, and surprising. The known special cases were already impressive. They were too beautiful not to be true. Yet it was nearly inconceivable that they could even be stated precisely. Weil himself would not affirm that such a cohomology theory could exist. Perhaps he did not believe it could. Jean-Pierre Serre did, and convinced Alexander Grothendieck, and took part with him and Pierre Deligne in creating it: "This truly revolutionary idea thrilled the mathematicians of the time, as I can testify at first hand; it has been the origin of a major part of the progress in algebraic geometry since that date. The objective was reached only after about twenty-five years, and then not by Weil himself but (principally) by Grothendieck and Deligne" (Serre, 1999, p. 525).

It is typical of Weil that his sweeping vision of unity among the great branches of mathematics produced specific insights and proved hard theorems in specific branches. In this case the impact began with algebraic geometry and number theory. It required a thorough reconception of topological tools in explicit algebraic terms and these fed back into algebra and topology. It affected the related parts of complex analysis and differential geometry. It had eventual repercussions for more or less all of mathematics. These conjectures were Weil's single most influential and ultimately most productive contribution. No doubt he hoped and intended to prove them as well, but the conjectures as such were a work of transcendent genius, and he knew it.

Weil also contributed to the so-called Taniyama-Shimura-Weil conjecture that all elliptic curves are modular. But this might better have been called a question than a conjecture. None of the three felt strongly that it was true. Weil never claimed he originated it. He worked on it and encouraged work on it. The key advance on it came when Andrew Wiles, using tools descended from the Weil conjectures proper, proved nearly the entire Taniyama-Shimura-Weil conjecture as the last step in the proof of Fermat's Last Theorem.

He kept residence in Princeton after retiring in 1976. But he spent each spring in Paris in his parents' apartment overlooking the Jardin du Luxembourg. He spent each summer in the Mayenne where Brittany meets Normandy and the Loire Valley. He wrote history of mathematics in a way that affected current research in number theory, especially his 1976 book on Eisenstein and Kronecker. His wife's death led him to write his autobiography (1991). By age eighty he suffered poor eyesight and failing health and he died of old age while his formidable and sometimes mocking personality left him feeling isolated from colleagues. Despite his attachment to the *Bhagavad Gita* he expected no personal survival after death. He was confident that the work of Bourbaki would endure. In the early twenty-first century that work is less in fashion. Yet it remains a decisive influence on mathematics.

Honors. Weil became an honorary member of the London Mathematical Society in 1959, a Foreign Member of the Royal Society of London in 1966, a member of the U.S. National Academy of Sciences in 1977, and of the French Académie des Sciences in 1982. He received the Wolf Prize in Mathematics for 1979 jointly with Jean Leray, and was presented the Barnard Medal by Columbia University in 1980, the AMS Steele Prize of 1980 for lifetime achievement, and the Kyoto Prize in 1994.

BIBLIOGRAPHY

WORKS BY WEIL

Arithmétique et géométrie sur les variétés algébriques. Paris: Hermann, 1935.

Sur les espaces à structure uniforme et sur la topologie générale. Paris: Hermann, 1938.

With Carl Allendoerfer. "The Gauss-Bonnet Theorem for Riemannian Polyhedra." *Transactions of the American Mathematical Society* 53 (1943): 101–129.

Foundations of Algebraic Geometry. New York: American Mathematical Society, 1946.

L'intégration dans les groupes topologiques et ses applications. 2nd ed. Paris: Hermann, 1953.

Elliptic Functions According to Eisenstein and Kronecker. Berlin: Springer-Verlag, 1976.

Oeuvres Scientifiques, Collected Works. 3 vols. New York: Springer-Verlag, 1979.

Number Theory: An Approach through History from Hammurapi to Legendre. Boston: Birkhäuser, 1984.

Souvenirs d'apprentissage. Boston: Birkhäuser, 1991. Translated as *The Apprenticeship of a Mathematician.* Boston: Birkhäuser Verlag, 1992.

OTHER SOURCES

Beaulieu, Liliane. "A Parisian Café and Ten Proto-Bourbaki Meetings (1934–1935)." *The Mathematical Intelligencer* 15 (1993): 27–35.

Borel, Armand. "André Weil and Algebraic Topology." *Notices of the American Mathematical Society* 46 (1999): 422–427.

Borel, Armand, Pierre Cartier, Komaravolu Chandrasekharan, et al. "André Weil (1906–1998)." *Notices of the American Mathematical Society* 46 (1999): 440–447.

Dieudonné, Jean. "On the History of the Weil Conjectures." In *Étale Cohomology and the Weil Conjecture*, edited by Eberhard Freitag and Reinhardt Kiehl. New York: Springer-Verlag, 1988.

Faltings, Gerd. "Endlichkeitssätze für abelscheVarietäten über Zahlkörpern." *Inventiones Mathematicae* 73 (1983): 349–366.

Mashaal, Maurice. *Bourbaki: Une société secrète de mathématiciens.* Paris: Pour la Science, 2000.

Mordell, Louis. "On the Rational Solutions of the Indeterminate Equations of the Third and Fourth Degrees." *Proceedings of the Cambridge Philosophical Society* 21 (1922): 179–192.

Pekonen, Osmo. "L'affaire Weil à Helsinki en 1939." *Gazette des Mathématiciens* 52 (1992): 13–20. With an afterword by Weil.

Pétrement, Simone. *Simone Weil: A Life.* New York: Pantheon, 1976. Contains much from André Weil on his sister and their childhood.

Serre, Jean-Pierre. "André Weil. 6 May 1906–6 August 1998." *Biographical Memoirs of Fellows of the Royal Society* 45 (1999): 520–529. This survey approaches Weil's own elegant and widely knowledgeable style motivating specific hard mathematical results by a sweeping vision of their place in the unity of mathematics.

Shimura, Goro. "André Weil as I Knew Him." *Notices of the American Mathematical Society* 46 (1999): 428–433.

Wiles, Andrew. "Modular Curves and Fermat's Last Theorem." *Annals of Mathematics* 141 (1995): 443–551.

Colin McLarty

WEISMANN, AUGUST FRIEDRICH LEOPOLD

(*b.* Frankfurt am Main, Germany, 17 January 1834; *d.* Freiburg im Breisgau, Germany, 5 November 1914), *zoology, heredity, evolution.* For the original article on Weismann, see *DSB*, vol. 14.

The necessary starting point for evaluating Weismann's career remains his zoological writings. This is not a large corpus in comparison to those of some of his contemporaries, say, Charles Darwin or Ernst Haeckel. It consists, however, of professionally solid and challenging monographs and books, including *Das Keimplasma* (1892), that were influential in their own day and still referred to in the early twenty-first century. It also consists of many elegant essays and monographs on evolution and heredity. Finally, there exist three editions of Weismann's comprehensive advanced textbook, *Vorträge über Descendenztheorie* (1902, 1904, 1913) devoted to a neo-Darwinian view of evolution. This comprised the first such modern textbook that framed an elaborate mechanistic model for evolution, heredity, and development. Most, but not all, of this literature was translated into English during Weismann's lifetime.

The primary account of Weismann's work remains the biography written by the Freiburg anatomist, Ernst Gaupp (1917). As a younger colleague of Weismann, Gaupp knew Weismann's family and after Weismann's death in 1914 had access to some of Weismann's papers. World War I, dramatic changes in the heredity and developmental sciences during these and subsequent years, the emergence of biometrics and endocrinology, and a disciplinary shift from German universities, marine laboratories, and independent museums to American biology, which was fostered not only by the same kind of institutions but supported by agricultural programs and philanthropic foundations dramatically diminished the need of revisiting Weismann's work. Not until the second half of the twentieth century were serious historical efforts begun to review Weismann on his own terms.

Since the publication of Gloria Robinson's informative and judicious assessment of August Weismann in the *DSB* (1976) and her more ample discussion of 1979, new material and new scientific concerns have emerged that indicate how important it is to again reevaluate Weismann's entire career. This is reflected not only by the collection of Weismann's *Selected Letters and Documents* assembled by the author and his colleague Helmut Risler (1999) but by analytical essays about Weismann's career by Ernst Mayr (1985), Rasmus Winther (2001), Ida Stamhuis (2003), and the author. Above all, a conference held in Freiburg in 1984 (Sander, 1985) with contributions by eighteen European and American scholars has demonstrated how complex and multifaceted Weismann's zoology had been at a time when general zoology was coming into its own as an independent field of research at German universities. It is also clear that Weismann's contributions continue to be invoked by twenty-first century biologists in multiple ways to justify or denigrate positions that have not been in keeping with the spirit of Weismann's work and ideas. (See Berrill and Liu [1948], Blacher [1971], Gould [1977], Buss [1987], and Griesemer and Wimsatt [1989].) This entry does not attempt to duplicate or replace what Robinson has already presented in her original article, but surveys some of the historiographical advances that have been made since that was written.

Relationship to Haeckel. One important question that is much clearer now is Weismann's relationship with Ernst Haeckel. The publication of what appears to remain of the Haeckel-Weismann correspondence, cited but not closely examined by Robinson, has made this possible (Uschmann and Hassenstein, 1965; see bibliography in original article for citation.). Born only a month apart in early 1834, the two zoologists became identified toward the end of their careers as the foremost evolutionists of the immediate post-*Origin* generations. Both read and were captivated by Darwin's *Origin* when it appeared in the Heinrich Georg Bronn translation. Both shared a belief that the evolution of life must be explained in mechanical terms. Both soon sensed the importance of the germ-layer theory for providing a mechanism for explaining development and phylogeny.

Weismann encouraged Haeckel in his early publications, especially his study of calcareous sponges and the development of his biogenetic law. Haeckel sympathized with Weismann's devastating retinal affliction, which for the ten years between 1864–1874 and again after 1884 curtailed his microscopic research. Furthermore, Haeckel assisted his friend, as the latter returned to study and write major monographs on cladocerans and hydroids. Both spent their entire careers at small universities at the periphery of German academic life, and both founded and turned their zoological institutes into major research and teaching centers for developmental and evolutionary biology. They shared information about and specimens of organisms and about the details of the construction of their respective new institutes. They celebrated each other's birthdays and the birth of children; they consoled the other when each lost his first wife.

Notwithstanding the warm scientific and personal ties, the research and commitments of these two Darwinian warhorses diverged. Never a proponent of the Lamarckian mechanism of the inheritance of acquired characters, Weismann found by the early 1880s in his demonstration of a continuity of germplasm in hydroids and in its conjectured segregation from the differentiating cells of the soma an a priori argument against such inheritance. As a consequence natural selection appeared to him the "all sufficient" mechanism for evolution. Haeckel to the contrary became ever more supportive of the inheritance of acquired traits, a process that he had redesignated *progressive inheritance*.

Added to this fundamental theoretical difference was a divergence in research styles. At first both zoologists had approached evolution as natural historians and descriptive embryologists. Continuing within this framework, Haeckel constructed further taxonomies and proposed ever more phylogenies. He occasionally supported his conclusions with the microscopy of germ-layer formation.

During the 1870s and 1880s, however, morphology was undergoing fundamental changes. By tracing the formation and lineages of germ cells, Weismann refocused his attention on questions of fertilization and germ-cell maturation. He was soon swept up by the new wave of nuclear cytology promoted by the Hertwig brothers, Otto Bütschli, Walther Flemming, Eduard Strasburger, Edouard van Beneden, and many more, most of them younger biologists. From the early 1880s till the end of the century, and with the assistance of advanced students,

August Weismann. © BETTMANN/CORBIS.

such as Eugen Korscheldt, Ernst Ziegler, Chiyomatsu Ishikawa, and Valentin Haecker, Weismann expanded his institute to include the descriptive study of polar bodies and their chromosomes. These latter structures, mobile and complex, provided an empirical foundation upon which Weismann constructed his germ plasm theory.

Haeckel could not tolerate either this plunge into the mysteries of cellular mechanics or a provisional explanation for evolution that seemed to undercut the central causal role of his biogenetic law and the need for progressive inheritance. He publicly attacked Weismann's germplasm theory, but shortly thereafter sent Weismann a letter of reconciliation. The two continued to exchange birthday greetings for the rest of Weismann's life, and agreed to disagree on fundamental principles. When in 1908 Haeckel was attacked by the conservative Protestant Keplerbund for misrepresenting many of his illustrations, Weismann, along with other biologists, signed the so-called Leipzig Declaration supporting his friend.

Importance of Experiment. Another side of Weismann's science to receive increased attention concerns his use of experimentation to explore and explain natural phenomena. This is particularly evident in his study of seasonal and geographical dimorphism in butterflies where there is often a dramatic difference in the color and patterns in the wings of spring and summer broods. These phenomena could plausibly be explained by differences in the temperature of the seasons and locations, and the Austrian naturalist Georg Dorfmeister had already published an account of exposing butterfly larvae and pupae to abnormal temperatures in the effort to induce variations. His concerns, however, were simply taxonomic.

Weismann began his experiments in 1866, before learning of Dorfmeister's results, and it is clear from the outset that he was concerned about the evolutionary implication of temperature-induced changes. He carried out his first set of experiments at a time when he could not use the microscope because of his eye illness. Instead he used ice chests and cold rooms and traveled to Sardinia to study southern populations. The work enabled him to explore the value of natural cyclical patterns in alternating generations. In the end he recognized that the spring broods were more stable than the summer, and this in turn led him to assume that they expressed an older and more stable constitution. Newer colors and patterns, he explained, reflected warmer temperatures associated with a general warming after the last ice age.

He picked up temperature experiments again at a time when he was developing his germplasm theory. They helped him find ways of confirming what became known as parallel induction of soma and germplasm without resorting to a Lamarckian-type inheritance. In both of these periods of experimentation Weismann showed an awareness of the importance of a large number of tested organisms and of sets of controls taken from the same brood, but his statistical analysis remained simply a comparison of averages. Similar designs characterized Weismann and Marie von Chauvin's experiments on axolotl and the three years of studies he and his students carried out in collaboration with the apiarist Ferdinand Dickel in 1897 to 1900 to determine whether drone eggs did, in fact, develop parthenogenetically.

Concept of Germplasm. When Weismann introduced the term *amphimixis* in 1891, he was building on two decades of research in nuclear cytology that demonstrated that the process of fertilization in metazoans and plants and of conjugation in protozoans and other protists, "has no significance except the union in the single offspring of the hereditary substance from two individuals" (1891 [1892, vol. 2, p. 113]). It is this "union" of the chromosomal constitutions of the *germ cells* of two individuals that inspired Weismann to fashion his notion of the germplasm into a complex model of nested units. These, in turn, accounted for reduction division, transmission, parental and ancestral inheritance, differentiation, expression of sexual traits, and regeneration, and, in his opinion, provided the grist for natural selection. It was his model of the germplasm that undergirded this first of neo-Darwinian "syntheses."

With the rise of classical genetics after Weismann's death there was a tendency on the part of historians and biologists to assume that Weismann interpreted somatic variations as simply a product of recombinations within the germplasm. More recent research has pointed out that from the start Weismann considered the changing composition of the germplasm to be a response to nutritional and external conditions. It must be emphasized that such variations were not adaptive responses on the part of the organism, but the result of nonadaptive molecular reactions.

Throughout his career Weismann held a nominalistic view of the nature of species and remained committed to what later would be called sympatric speciation. Whether he was examining the paleontological records of the snail *Planorbis,* determining the phylogenetic relationship of saturniid moths, or responding to Moritz Wagner's migration theory of evolution, he never felt the species category was unique in contrast to the variety, on the one hand, and genus, on the other.

At the end of the century, partially in response to criticisms by George John Romanes and Herbert Spencer, Weismann resorted to what he called a germinal selection between different homologous determinants to explain the results of intra- and interspecific hybridizations and the decline and disappearance of morphological traits in phylogeny. Moreover, germinal selection became for him a Darwinian-like mechanism for effecting additional change in the germplasm itself. Influenced by the physical anthropologist Otto Ammon, Weismann also attempted to describe evolution in terms of a changing biometrical curve of somatic traits. The bottom line, however, in his understanding of evolution remained the continual change in the germplasm of a species wrought by germinal and natural selection, possible asymmetries in the mating process, and the perceived randomness in the maturation divisions of gametes. When Paul and Fritz Sarasin detailed "Formenketten" or chains of forms in populations of land snails of the island of Celebes, Weismann found in their descriptions further documentation of the arbitrariness of the species category.

Given his model of the germplasm, Weismann had a difficult time adjusting to the discovery of Mendel's laws, the increasing recognition that chromosomes possessed individuality, and the demonstrations by Theodor Boveri and Walter Sutton that Mendelian factors correlated with chromosomal segregation at meiosis. With the help of his assistant, Waldemar Schleip, Weismann attempted to make appropriate adjustments in the second and third editions of his *Vorträge.* By the last edition, however, Weismann was seventy-nine years old and nearly blind. The task of reconstructing the germplasm model was beyond him, or for that matter, anyone else.

SUPPLEMENTARY BIBLIOGRAPHY

A comprehensive bibliography of Weismann's publications may be found in Gaupp (1917) and an updated version in Churchill and Risler (1999).

WORKS BY WEISMANN

"Amphimixis or the Essential Meaning of Conjugation and Sexual Reproduction" (1891). In Weismann's *Essays upon Heredity and Kindred Biological Problems.* 2 vols. Edited and translated by Edward B. Poulton and Arthur E. Shipley. Oxford: Clarendon Press, 1892.

Das Keimplasma: Eine Theorie der Vererbung. Jena, Germany: Fischer, 1892.

Vorträge über Descendenztheorie. 2 vols. Jena, Germany: Gustav Fischer, 1902. Revised 1904 and 1913.

"Der Briefwechsel zwischen Ernst Haeckel und August Weismann." In *Kleine Festgabe aus Anlass der hundertjährigen Wiederkehr der Gründung des Zoologischen Institutes der Friedrich-Schiller-Universität Jena im Jahre 1865 durch Ernst Haeckel,* edited by Manfred Gersch. Jena, East Germany: Friedrich Schiller Universität, 1965. Cited but not discussed in Robinson's *DSB* entry on Weismann.

August Weismann: Ausgewählte Briefe und Dokumente, Selected Letters and Documents. Edited by Frederick B. Churchill and Helmut Risler. 2 vols. Schriften der Universitätsbibliothek, Freiburg im Breisgau, vol. 24, parts 1 and 2. Freiburg im Breisgau, Germany: Universitätsbibliothek, 1999. Volume 2 includes the essay by Churchill, "August Weismann: A Developmental Evolutionist."

OTHER SOURCES

Berrill, N. John, and C. K. Liu. "Germplasm, Weismann, and Hydrozoa." *Quarterly Review of Biology* 23 (1948): 124–132.

Blacher, Leonid I. *The Problem of the Inheritance of Acquired Characters: A History of a Priori and Empirical Methods Used to Find a Solution.* Edited by Frederick B. Churchill. Translated by Noel Hess. New Delhi: Published for the Smithsonian Institution Libraries and the National Science Foundation, by Amerind Publishing Co., 1982. Originally published Moscow: Nauka, 1971.

Buss, Leo W. *The Evolution of Individuality.* Princeton, NJ: Princeton University Press, 1987.

Churchill, Frederick B. "Rudolf Virchow and the Pathologist's Criteria for the Inheritance of Acquired Characteristics." *Journal of the History of Medicine* 31 (1976): 117–148.

———. "The Weismann-Spencer Controversy over the Inheritance of Acquired Characters." In *Human Implications of Scientific Advance: Proceedings of the XV International Congress of the History of Science, Edinburgh, 10–15 August*

1977, edited by Eric G. Forbes. Edinburgh: Edinburgh University Press, 1978.

———. "Weismann, Hydromedusae, and the Biogenetic Imperative: A Reconsideration." In *A History of Embryology*, edited by Thomas J. Horder, Jan A. Witkowski, and C. C. Wylie. Cambridge, U.K.: Cambridge University Press, 1986.

———. "From Heredity Theory to Vererbung: The Transmission Problem, 1850–1915." *Isis* 78 (1987): 337–364.

———. "Life before Model Systems: General Zoology at August Weismann's Institute." *American Zoologist* 37 (1997): 260–268.

———. "August Weismann and Ferdinand Dickel: Testing the Dzierzon System." In *Science, History, and Social Activism: A Tribute to Everett Mendelsohn*, edited by Garland Allen and Roy MacLeod. Dordrecht, Netherlands: Kluwer Academic, 2001.

Gaupp, Ernst Wilhelm Theodor. *August Weismann: Sein Leben und sein Werke.* Jena, Germany: G. Fischer, 1917.

Gould, Stephen Jay. *Ontogeny and Phylogeny.* Cambridge, MA: Harvard University Press, 1977.

Griesemer, James, and William Wimsatt. "Picturing Weismannism: A Case Study of Conceptual Evolution." In *What the Philosophy of Biology Is: Essays for David Hull*, edited by Michael Ruse. Dordrecht, Netherlands: Kluwer Academic, 1989.

Mayr, Ernst. "Weismann and Evolution." *Journal of the History of Biology* 18 (1985): 295–329.

Robinson, Gloria. *A Prelude to Genetics: Theories of a Material Substance of Heredity, Darwin to Weismann.* Lawrence, KS: Coronado Press, 1979.

Sander, Klaus, ed. *August Weismann (1834–1914) und die theoretische Biologie des 19. Jahrhunderts.* Freiburger Universitätsblätter, Hefte 87/88, Jha. 27 (1985). This contains essays on Weismann and his school by Sander, Risler, Schwoerbel, Mayr, Robinson, Sitte, Cremer, Churchill, Danailow, Jahn, Schott, Uschmann, Groeben, Sorensen, Müller, Lücke, Regelmann, and Harwood.

Stamhuis, Ida H. "The Reactions on Hugo de Vries's *Intracellular Pangenesis:* The Discussion with August Weismann." *Journal of the History of Biology* 36 (2003): 119–152.

Winther, Rasmus. "August Weismann on Germ-Plasm Variation." *Journal of the History of Biology* 34 (2001): 517–555.

Frederick B. Churchill

WEISSKOPF, VICTOR FREDERICK

(*b.* Vienna, Austria-Hungary [now Austria], 19 September 1908; *d.* Newton, Massachusetts, 22 April 2002), *physics, quantum electrodynamics, nuclear theory.*

Weisskopf, known by students and colleagues alike as "Viki," was among the most accomplished and admired physicists of the twentieth century. He made lasting contributions to the study of quantum fields and to nuclear physics. He also assumed leadership roles in science administration and science policy. A beloved teacher, he developed a sought-after style that emphasized conceptual understanding and qualitative description above rigorous mathematical derivation. Over his long career, he published nearly four hundred scientific articles, technical reports, textbooks, and popular books about science.

A Physicist's Grand Tour. Weisskopf was born into a cultured, upper-middle-class family of assimilated Jews in Vienna. His father, Emil, originally from Czechoslovakia, was trained in law. His mother, Martha, hailed from one of the leading families of fin-de-siècle Vienna. They instilled in Viki and his siblings—an older brother named Walter and a younger sister named Edith—a strong appreciation for music and the arts, often taking the children to concerts, plays, and museums. Viki began studying music at an early age and quickly developed into an accomplished pianist; he performed chamber music with friends and colleagues throughout his life. His family also supported his budding interest in socialism and political activism. He joined a socialist student group in high school, worked with the Social Democratic Party, and took part in the general progressive movement often dubbed "Red Vienna," which aimed to improve education and housing for workers.

From his earliest days, Weisskopf also harbored a deep interest in science and nature. As a fifteen-year-old, he conducted a detailed astronomical study with a boyhood friend, staying up all night to catalog the shooting stars during the peak of the annual Perseid meteor showers. Their work appeared in the leading astronomical journal, the *Astronomische Nachrichten* (Astronomical notices), in 1924. He followed upon this success with avid studies of physics at the University of Vienna, where he quickly impressed the physicist Hans Thirring. Thirring encouraged young Viki to continue his education beyond the confines of Austria. And so, at the age of twenty, Weisskopf moved to Göttingen, Germany, to study with the great Max Born. He completed his PhD under Born's direction in 1931, working on the application of quantum theory to the breadth of spectral lines, the thin beams of light emitted by atoms when excited by an outside source of energy.

Next came a string of postdoctoral fellowships. Weisskopf hit every major stop along the way, studying with all the principal inventors of the new theory of quantum mechanics, physicists' description of matter and forces at the atomic scale. These leaders had only just finished cobbling together quantum mechanics—rife with bizarre departures from ordinary experience—during the mid-1920s, a few years before Weisskopf embarked on his tour. The new material, and the enduring sense that physics had undergone a major revolution, was still fresh.

Weisskopf's first destination was Leipzig, Germany, to study with Werner Heisenberg in the fall of 1931 before moving to Berlin to work with Erwin Schrödinger in the spring of 1932. A Rockefeller Foundation Fellowship allowed Weisskopf to spend the 1932–1933 academic year studying with Niels Bohr in Copenhagen, Denmark, and Paul Dirac in Cambridge, England. Wolfgang Pauli hired Weisskopf as his assistant in Zurich, Switzerland, beginning in the autumn of 1933, where he remained until the spring of 1936. Then it was back to Copenhagen for more work with Bohr. The novelist Henry James could scarcely have invented a more spectacular grand tour for a young physicist of Weisskopf's generation. In 1932, during his first stay in Copenhagen, Viki met and fell in love with a young Danish woman, Ellen Tvede. They married in 1934 and spent the next fifty-five years together, until her death in 1989.

Quantum Electrodynamics. Weisskopf had been surprised when Pauli offered him the assistantship position in 1933; Viki always harbored a certain lack of self-confidence when it came to his work. This was hardly helped when he arrived in Zurich and the imposing, acerbic Pauli asked who he was. Flummoxed, Weisskopf stammered something about the job offer. Pauli looked up from his desk and explained that he had really wanted to hire Hans Bethe, but Bethe's interests had already shifted to solid-

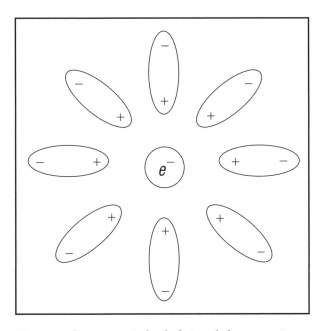

Vacuum polarization. A cloud of virtual electron-positron pairs surrounds an electron.

state physics (a topic Pauli famously dismissed as "squalid-state" physics), and so Weisskopf would have to do.

Despite the inauspicious beginning, Weisskopf's stay in Zurich proved to be remarkably productive. With Pauli, he delved into quantum electrodynamics (QED), a topic recently spearheaded by Pauli, Heisenberg, Dirac, and others. The goal was to describe electromagnetic phenomena—the motion of charged particles, the behavior of electric and magnetic fields—in a manner consistent with the still-new quantum mechanics. Only a few years old, the subject was already mired in difficulties, but Weisskopf would soon produce several major breakthroughs.

In Dirac's earliest efforts with QED in the late 1920s and early 1930s, he had found unexpected solutions to his equations. Though baffling at first, in time physicists came to interpret these solutions to mean that every type of ordinary particle has an antimatter cousin carrying the same mass but opposite electric charge. Electrons, for example, should have companion particles (dubbed "positrons") that each carry one unit of positive electric charge. As will be seen below, Dirac developed an elaborate physical picture to explain why antiparticles had never been seen before. His explanation remained quite controversial, even after the first experimental evidence for positrons was found in 1932.

Further conceptual problems marred QED. As the early architects of QED had found to their dismay, straightforward application of their new equations yielded nonsensical results. Whenever they posed simple questions, such as the probability for two electrons to scatter, their formalism returned "infinity" rather than some finite number. Electrons might have a high probability to scatter (say, 75 percent) or a low one (10 percent), but whatever it was, it simply could not be infinite. Yet try as they might, none of these physicists had found any way to complete meaningful calculations in QED.

Weisskopf reanalyzed one of these stubborn calculations, regarding how an electron would interact with its own electric field. Charged objects serve as the source for electric and magnetic fields, and their behavior is affected, in turn, by the presence of electric and magnetic fields. So how would an electron behave in its own self-field? The problem seemed intractable because the strength of an object's electric field grows the closer one approaches that object. This is rarely a problem for macroscopic objects, which always have some finite spatial extension. But physicists believed that electrons were pointlike objects, with virtually no spatial extension at all. Indeed, the first attempts to calculate an electron's self-energy found it to diverge—that is, blow up to infinity—as $1/r_e^2$, where r_e was the radius of the electron. A point particle, with $r_e = 0$, would have an infinite self-energy.

These early calculations had ignored possible effects from the still-controversial positrons. By the time Weisskopf took up the problem, however, early evidence seemed to indicate that positrons might really exist after all. He reworked the self-energy calculation, taking into account the behavior of both electrons and positrons. At first he found the divergence to be even worse, rising more quickly than $1/r_e^2$. Soon after publishing this result, he received a letter from Wendell Furry, a postdoctoral fellow studying with J. Robert Oppenheimer at the University of California at Berkeley. Furry found that Weisskopf had made a sign error in the midst of his calculation: two different terms had appeared to add up instead of canceling each other out. When the error was corrected, Weisskopf's calculation showed a much more gradual breakdown of the equations than anyone had found previously: The electron's self-energy diverged as the logarithm of the electron radius. Such a function would still become infinite in the limit of a genuine point particle (with $r_e = 0$), but this gentle divergence seemed far less threatening to the entire QED edifice than the earlier results. Indeed, Weisskopf's revised calculation, published in 1934, gave many physicists hope that the problems of QED might be conquered after all. (Weisskopf offered to include Furry as a coauthor on the follow-up article, but Furry demurred, suggesting only that he be thanked in the acknowledgments.)

That same year, Weisskopf teamed up with Pauli to scrutinize the behavior of antiparticles. Central to Dirac's interpretation of antimatter was the behavior of particles with half-integer "spin." Just a few years before, various physicists had found that many elementary particles carry an intrinsic angular momentum, or "spin"—that is, a tendency to continue spinning around a given direction. The amount of spin carried by a given type of particle was quantized. Every electron carried one-half unit of spin (when measured in units of Planck's constant, h, divided by 2π); every photon, the particle-like quanta of light, carried one unit of spin, and so on. Pauli had found that particles carrying half-integer spin obeyed an "exclusion principle": no two particles could occupy the same state at the same time. (Particles with integer spin, on the other hand, could be readily clumped together, which is why many photons can add up to a coherent, macroscopic light wave.)

Dirac had found that his relativistic equation governing the electron contained four pieces: two describing electrons with positive energy and two describing electrons with negative energy. (In either energy state, the electron could have spin "up" or spin "down" along a given direction, making four states in total.) Rather than toss out the strange-looking negative-energy states—what would it mean, after all, for an object to have negative energy?—Dirac retained them in his solutions. He pictured a vast, infinite sea of electrons filling these negative-

energy states. Thanks to Pauli's exclusion principle, if an electron already occupied one of these negative-energy states, then no additional electrons could be added to that same state. If the sea were all filled up, little further activity would be possible. In effect, the observer would be blind to this vast sea of particles—it would blend into the background—because they would so rarely change their state.

But, Dirac continued, if some outside source of energy, such as a powerful cosmic ray, collided with one of these negative-energy electrons, the electron could absorb energy, rise into a positive-energy state, and leave a "hole" behind in the negative-energy sea. To an observer, this "hole" would behave as if it had the same mass as an electron but the opposite charge: The effect of removing one unit of negative charge from the sea would be the same as adding in one unit of positive charge. Thus, Dirac eventually concluded that antimatter such as positrons could exist, even if under ordinary circumstances—absent the powerful source of outside energy that would knock an electron out of the negative-energy sea—we remained unaware of their presence.

Pauli found the notion of an infinite sea of negative-energy electrons too clever by half. He and Weisskopf showed that even charged particles with zero spin—as yet entirely hypothetical, because no such spinless particles were known—would necessarily have antiparticle partners. Their conclusion, published in 1934, followed from the mathematical structure of quantized fields, sidestepping entirely Dirac's reliance on half-spin particles and the exclusion principle. Antiparticles were in; Dirac's unobserved sea was out. Pauli dubbed this influential paper with Weisskopf their "anti-Dirac" paper.

In 1936 Weisskopf completed another major article on QED. He returned to the behavior of an electron's self-field. As many physicists knew by that time, the self-field was complicated because of Heisenberg's uncertainty principle and the presence of "virtual" particles. In 1927, capping off years of work on quantum mechanics, Heisenberg had deduced that certain pairs of quantities, such as a particle's position and its simultaneous momentum, could no longer be specified with unlimited precision in the quantum realm. The same held for the energy involved in a physical process, E, and the time over which the process unfolded, t: residual uncertainties, ΔE and Δt, would remain, subject to $\Delta E \Delta t \ r \ h$, where h was Planck's constant. In the context of QED, Heisenberg and others realized, the uncertainty relation meant that even empty space would not be truly empty. Particles could "borrow" energy all the time, popping into existence, as long as they paid that energy back sufficiently quickly. Physicists dubbed these strange, ghostlike particles "virtual particles."

Quantum-mechanically, the electron's self-field thus could be pictured as a cloud of virtual pairs of electrons and positrons. Because opposite charges attract while like charges repel, Weisskopf realized that these virtual particles would arrange themselves like the petals of a daisy around the original electron. (See Figure 2.) The effect would be to polarize the vacuum—that is, even "empty" space would have a definite electrical directionality or orientation. Moreover, the virtual pairs would screen the original electron's charge, so that an observer would only measure the combined charge of the original electron plus the cloud. Because the virtual particles could borrow any amount of energy whatsoever—even infinite energy—so long as they paid it back quickly enough, the quantum-mechanical contribution to the electron's charge would be infinitely large. It appeared as if one more infinity had marred QED.

Weisskopf turned this particular infinity into a triumph. He reminded his colleagues that there was no way to turn off the uncertainty principle; virtual particles would always be popping into and out of existence. Thus, physicists could never measure the "bare" charge of an electron apart from this virtual cloud. Because the total charge of an electron was small, the effect of the virtual cloud was ultimately unobservable: The "bare" charge of the electron—never measurable even in principle—was offset by the (infinite) contribution from the virtual particles, leaving a finite overall charge. The virtual cloud "renormalized" the electron's charge but did not affect any other properties of the electron's behavior.

Weisskopf completed this last work in Copenhagen rather than Zurich. Although Viki and his wife Ellen had enjoyed their time in Zurich, dangerous reminders about the changing state of Europe intruded. The city's rich cultural life had been infused by a steady flow of German refugees fleeing Adolf Hitler, including many avant-garde artists and actors. Weisskopf himself was hauled before the Swiss *Fremdenpolizei* (special police force in charge of foreigners) in 1935 and told he would have to leave Switzerland, never to return, as soon as his fellowship with Pauli was over. As far as the authorities were concerned, Weisskopf had too many Communist and otherwise suspicious acquaintances. When his appointment ended, he and Ellen returned to Niels Bohr's institute in Copenhagen. (Twenty-five years later, Weisskopf moved back to Switzerland as a leading scientific statesman; by that time the earlier, frightening run-in with the authorities could be laughed off.)

War Work. Weisskopf had difficulty finding work in the 1930s because of the worldwide economic depression; his Jewish background only made things harder once the Nazis assumed power. Weisskopf visited the Soviet Union late in 1936 and considered job offers in both Kiev and Moscow, but decided against moving there; the purge trials that would unleash Joseph Stalin's great terror had already begun. The possibility of a position in the United States seemed much more enticing. Knowing of the budding interest in nuclear physics that many American physics departments harbored—galvanized by Ernest Lawrence's famous work with cyclotrons at Berkeley—Weisskopf began shifting his research focus while in Copenhagen. He turned his attention to nuclear physics and began publishing, for the first time in English, in the American journal *Physical Review*. This strategy, combined with Bohr's active lobbying on his behalf, led to an offer of a low-level instructorship at the University of Rochester in upstate New York. Weisskopf accepted the job and moved there in 1937.

While at Rochester, Weisskopf continued to pursue his interest in QED, while also spending more and more time on nuclear theory. By the time World War II broke out, he was already recognized as one of the most accomplished theorists working in the United States. Not surprisingly, Oppenheimer tapped him to join the budding laboratory at Los Alamos, New Mexico, part of the fast-growing Manhattan Project to design and build nuclear weapons. Weisskopf was among the first to arrive at the laboratory in the spring of 1943; he became second-in-command of the theoretical physics division, serving as deputy division leader under Hans Bethe.

Part of Weisskopf's task was trying to understand the basic physics of nuclear fission, the process by which certain large nuclei break apart into smaller pieces, releasing energy. Weisskopf focused on how neutrons—tiny nuclear particles that carry no electric charge but interact strongly with other nuclear matter—would behave in and around fissionable material. He developed a keen intuitive sense for these interactions. At one point early in the project, he guessed that the fission cross section (that is, the probability that a neutron would cause a large nucleus to split in two) would rise sharply for neutrons in a particular energy range, even though data for a nearby energy range seemed to indicate otherwise. When newer experimental data vindicated Weisskopf's hunch, his office was nicknamed the seat of "the oracle"; others teased that it was the "cave of hot air."

Weisskopf's other main tasks were decidedly more of an applied nature. He aimed to calculate the effects of a nuclear bomb's detonation: the explosive yield (that is, the force of the bomb's blast as compared to so many tons of conventional explosives); the shape and force of the shock wave; the extent of radioactivity; and so on. Like his work on fission cross sections, Weisskopf's approach belied a characteristic trait: He aimed for qualitative description rather than formal mathematical derivation. Meanwhile, he served for several terms on the Los Alamos town council, including one term as chair. Even in the midst of the world's largest military-technical project, Weisskopf remained true to his roots. Just as in his Red Vienna days, he championed the cause of the low-paid workers and technicians at the laboratory, negotiating on their behalf with the military authorities to improve housing and other features of daily life.

Because of his work on blast effects, Weisskopf was one of the first scientists to relocate late in the war from Los Alamos to the Trinity test site at Alamagordo, New Mexico, 200 miles south of Los Alamos. (Oppenheimer had dubbed the first test of a nuclear bomb the "Trinity" test, taking the name from a John Donne poem.) For weeks in advance of the 16 July 1945 test, Weisskopf helped set up measuring devices and diagnostic tools at various checkpoints. He was among the handful of theoretical physicists who witnessed the explosion, seeing the characteristic mushroom cloud rise above the desert.

Weisskopf and some colleagues had calculated that thirty-six hours after the detonation, residual levels of radioactivity at ground zero should fall low enough to allow brief inspections. And so Hans Bethe, Enrico Fermi, and he strapped on radiation-measuring tags and drove a Jeep down to the blast site a day and a half after the test. What they saw amazed them. Not only had the scaffolding and other equipment in the immediate vicinity of the bomb been vaporized, but the force and heat of the blast had even fused the desert's sand into glass (later dubbed "trinitite"). This physical transformation gave Weisskopf a visceral sense of the bomb's power. To his chagrin, the presence of trinitite seemed to hold little special meaning for the military officials, including General Leslie Groves, the overseer of the entire Manhattan Project.

Postwar Research. Immediately after the war, Jerrold Zacharias recruited Weisskopf to move to the Massachusetts Institute of Technology (MIT) in Cambridge, Massachusetts. (Zacharias himself had been recruited to MIT only a few months before.) Weisskopf found several features of the offer alluring: the establishment of a research laboratory for electronics, incorporating MIT's wartime Radiation Laboratory, epicenter of Allied efforts to design radar; the new Laboratory for Nuclear Science; and the broader intellectual and cultural attractions of Cambridge. By 1946, Weisskopf had joined MIT's physics department.

Soon he was back into the thickets of QED. He began working with MIT graduate student Bruce French to calculate the energy levels within hydrogen, taking into account effects from virtual particles. They received extra impetus to plow through their laborious calculation in 1947 when Columbia University's Willis Lamb

Victor Frederick Weisskopf. © CORBIS.

announced that he had measured a miniscule—but nonzero—energy difference between two particular states of hydrogen, even though quantum mechanics predicted they should have precisely the same energy. Weisskopf compared his calculated value for the Lamb shift with both Richard Feynman and Julian Schwinger—two young guns of theoretical physics who had separately worked out new ways to calculate the effects of virtual particles in QED. To Weisskopf's disappointment, Feynman's and Schwinger's calculations matched each other but differed from that of Weisskopf and French. Congenitally unsure of himself, Weisskopf held his paper back until he and French could find their error. In the meantime, Lamb himself published a theoretical study of the energy-level shift, along with his graduate student Norman Kroll. Lamb and Kroll had arrived (independently) at the same result as Weisskopf and French. Six months later, Feynman sheepishly called Weisskopf to apologize: He and Schwinger had been the ones in error, and Weisskopf and French had been correct all along.

The mix-up marked one of Weisskopf's last active encounters with QED. Beyond this tragicomic snafu, however, several of Weisskopf's earlier insights finally bore fruit. Building on Weisskopf's work on self-energy, vacuum polarization, and charge renormalization, Schwinger, Feynman, Sin-itiro Tomonaga, and Freeman Dyson pieced together a successful renormalization program from 1947 to 1949. At long last, the infinities that had long plagued QED had been banished, leaving behind finite numbers that stood in remarkably good agreement with the latest experimental results.

By this time, Weisskopf's own interests had turned squarely to nuclear theory. Working closely with fellow MIT theorist Herman Feshbach, as well as several graduate students (especially David Peaslee and Charles Porter), Weisskopf developed a string of successful models of nuclear behavior. Like the best of his wartime work, these models featured intuitive approaches and clever rules of thumb rather than mathematical rigor. Weisskopf's particular brand of nuclear theory also infused his major textbook, *Theoretical Nuclear Physics* (1952), written with MIT postdoctoral fellow John Blatt. Quickly considered the "bible" for the subject, this influential textbook had the distinction for several years of being the most frequently stolen book from the MIT libraries.

Emblematic of Weisskopf's approach was the "clouded crystal ball" model, developed in 1954. As physicists knew well by then, the nucleus was a complicated collection of many nuclear particles—protons and neutrons—held together by a strong nuclear force. All efforts to date to calculate nuclear properties from first principles, by considering each nuclear particle separately and trying to sum over each of its effects on all of its neighbors, had run aground: There were too many distinct arrangements to consider and the nuclear force was too strong to allow the kinds of iterative, perturbative approximations that had worked so well for weaker forces like electromagnetism. Instead, Weisskopf and colleagues treated the interaction between a neutron and a nucleus as if the neutron were an incoming light beam and the nucleus a translucent object (such as a clouded crystal ball). Sometimes the neutron would be absorbed by the nucleus, other times it would pass through as if the nucleus were transparent. Both of these qualitative behaviors could be captured surprisingly well by an appropriately course-grained approximation inspired by the optical analogy. With this intuitive simplification, theorists at once could begin to make contact with the latest experiments.

During this period, Weisskopf trained twenty-one PhD students at MIT, including such accomplished theorists as J. David Jackson, Kurt Gottfried, Kerson Huang, J. Dirk Walecka, and the Nobel laureate Murray Gell-Mann. He also stepped up his activities beyond the classroom. He was among the original eight members of the Emergency Committee of Atomic Scientists, founded in 1946. The brainchild of Leo Szilard and chaired by Albert Einstein, the Emergency Committee sought to educate the public and politicians about the dangers of a runaway nuclear arms race. At the same time, Weisskopf also helped to found the Federation of Atomic Scientists (FAS, later changed to Federation of American Scientists), which likewise lobbied for civilian rather than military control of atomic energy. Soon FAS's mandate widened to combat the excesses of McCarthyism. Weisskopf served for many years on the FAS executive council and also chaired its committee on visas. During the late 1940s and early 1950s, the U.S. State Department frequently denied visas to foreign scientists deemed to be politically suspect; Weisskopf testified before the U.S. Congress in 1952 to argue for a reform of the system. He later joined the budding Pugwash movement, founded in 1957, which was devoted to halting the nuclear arms race.

Leading CERN. Fifteen years after moving to MIT, Weisskopf took an extended leave of absence. He had been invited to serve as director general for the European Organization for Nuclear Research (CERN), a new multinational laboratory for high-energy physics in Geneva, Switzerland. First proposed in 1950, the laboratory was operating by 1954. It achieved its first beam of accelerated protons in 1959. Weisskopf became director general in 1961.

Part of the attraction for Weisskopf was the opportunity to learn more about particle physics, which by this time had separated into a distinct specialty from nuclear physics. In addition to immersing himself in the day-to-day activities at the laboratory—he took inspiration from Oppenheimer's leadership style at wartime Los Alamos—Weisskopf also began to deliver popular lectures on the state of the field for students and new arrivals at the laboratory. The lectures became a long-running tradition, featuring (as usual by now) Weisskopf's famously conceptual, intuitive approach. He later wrote up the lectures with his former graduate student, Kurt Gottfried, as the two-volume textbook, *Concepts of Particle Physics* (1984–1986).

Weisskopf served as director general for nearly four and a half years (August 1961—December 1965), and left two principal legacies. First was his strong backing of the controversial decision that the next major accelerator at the laboratory should be a colliding beam machine rather than a fixed-target accelerator. Until that time, particle accelerators worked by speeding up a beam of particles and smashing them into a stationary target so that physicists could study the debris that came out. Weisskopf insisted instead on forging ahead with an intersecting storage ring (ISR) design, in which two beams of protons were separately accelerated and then made to collide head-on. Although more difficult to build, the interaction energies achieved by such a machine promised to rise much higher than conventional accelerators had achieved, and in high-energy physics, higher energies was the name of the game. (The interaction energy in a colliding beam machine scaled roughly as the square of the energy of an ordinary fixed-target device.) Plans took shape during Weisskopf's tenure, and the ISR came online in 1971.

Second, Weisskopf concluded negotiations with the French government to expand the laboratory beyond Swiss soil. The new real estate proved crucial to the ISR and to later developments at the laboratory. Thanks to Weisskopf's diplomacy, protons now cross the Swiss-French border billions of times each second as they get whipped around to higher and higher energies.

Later Work. Weisskopf returned to MIT early in 1966. He continued to work with younger theorists on nuclear and particle theory. His role increasingly became that of wise sounding board, offering counsel to graduate students, postdoctoral fellows, and young faculty alike. He excelled in this role, for example, in the mid-1970s as he and several younger colleagues developed a new model for the structure of nuclear particles. Dubbed the "MIT bag model," their work built upon the latest discoveries in particle theory. The paper appeared in 1974.

Just a few months earlier, theorists at Harvard University in Cambridge, Massachusetts (H. David Politzer), and at Princeton University in New Jersey (David Gross and Frank Wilczek) separately found that the strength of the strong nuclear force becomes weaker the closer one approaches the subnuclear particles, or quarks, within protons and neutrons. Conversely, the strong force becomes stronger with increasing distance. This is exactly the opposite of how more familiar forces such as electromagnetism behave, which led to the self-energy divergences that Weisskopf first tackled in the 1930s.

Until the mid-1970s, no one had made much progress in trying to calculate the effects of the strong nuclear force from first principles, precisely because its strength ruled out perturbative approaches. (The same stumbling block had led Weisskopf, Feshbach, and their students to try phenomenological approaches, such as the "clouded crystal ball" model, twenty years earlier.) Armed with the news that the strong force actually became weak at short distances, several young MIT theorists—Alan Chodos, Robert Jaffe, Kenneth Johnson, and Charles Thorn—together with Weisskopf, introduced a new way to study the behavior of neutrons and protons. In a typical Weisskopfian move, they simplified the problem, honing in on the essentials without getting bogged down in mathematical details.

They pictured protons, neutrons, and similar nuclear particles as bags filled with quarks. Because the strong force grew in strength with increasing distance, they simply hypothesized that the quarks remain rigidly contained within some volume (the bag); but at shorter distances (within the bag), the force between quarks fell rapidly, and so it could essentially be ignored altogether. Treating protons and neutrons as bags filled with free (that is, noninteracting) quarks sidestepped most of the horrendously complicated dynamics, allowing the theorists to make rapid progress in estimating how real nuclear particles behave. Although Weisskopf often joked that all he had contributed to the study was the "don't-know-how," his younger colleagues insisted that his name appear with theirs as an author. In fact, explained Jaffe, Weisskopf had supplied some of the crucial statistical arguments that the group employed, hearkening back to some of Weisskopf's own work from the 1930s and 1940s.

Weisskopf reached the mandatory retirement age in 1974, after which he spent even more time in leadership roles around the world. He was elected to the Pontifical Academy of Science in 1976, which allowed him to continue his decades-long work on nuclear policy. He encouraged Pope John Paul II to speak out about the horrors of nuclear war and to work toward arms control and reduction, a topic that the pope championed during the early 1980s. He also built upon his earlier success as an author of popular science, publishing *The Privilege of Being a Physicist* (1989) and his scientific autobiography, *The Joy of Insight* (1991), to complement his acclaimed *Knowledge and Wonder* (1962) and *Physics in the Twentieth Century* (1972).

Weisskopf died in 2002 at the age of ninety-three. He often remarked that he had "lived a happy life in a dreadful century." He was survived by his second wife, Duscha Scott; his two children, Thomas and Karen; and several grandchildren.

BIBLIOGRAPHY

Weisskopf's papers at the Institute Archives of the Massachusetts Institute of Technology in Cambridge, Massachusetts, contain unpublished correspondence and lecture notes. A complete list of Weisskopf's publications is in Physics and Society: Essays in Honor of Victor Frederick Weisskopf by the International Community of Physicists *(1998), edited by V. Stefan.*

WORKS BY WEISSKOPF

With John M. Blatt. *Theoretical Nuclear Physics.* New York: John Wiley, 1952.

With H. Feshbach and Charles E. Porter. "Model for Nuclear Reactions with Neutrons." *Physical Review* 96 (1954):

448–464. The paper introducing the "clouded crystal ball" model of nuclear reactions.

Knowledge and Wonder: The Natural World as Man Knows It. Garden City, NJ: Doubleday, 1962.

Physics in the Twentieth Century: Selected Essays. Cambridge, MA: MIT Press, 1972.

With Alan Chodos, Robert L. Jaffe, Kenneth Johnson, et al. "New Extended Model of Hadrons." *Physical Review D* 9 (1974): 3471–3495. The paper introducing the MIT bag model of nuclear particles.

With Kurt Gottfried. *Concepts of Particle Physics.* 2 vols. New York: Oxford University Press, 1984–1986.

The Privilege of Being a Physicist. New York: W. H. Freeman, 1989.

The Joy of Insight: Passions of a Physicist. New York: Basic Books, 1991. Weisskopf's autobiography.

Early Quantum Electrodynamics: A Source Book. Edited by Arthur I. Miller. Translated by Walter Grant. New York: Cambridge University Press, 1994. Contains English translations of Weisskopf's most important papers on quantum electrodynamics from the 1930s.

OTHER SOURCES

Jackson, J. David, and Kurt Gottfried. "Victor Frederick Weisskopf, 1908–2002." *Biographical Memoirs of Fellows of the National Academy of Sciences* 84 (2003): 3–27.

Miller, Arthur I. "Frame-Setting Essay." In *Early Quantum Electrodynamics: A Source Book,* by Arthur I. Miller. Translated by Walter Grant. New York: Cambridge University Press, 1994. Describes Weisskopf's and others' work on quantum electrodynamics during the 1930s.

Schweber, Silvan S. *QED and the Men Who Made It: Dyson, Feynman, Schwinger, and Tomonaga.* Princeton, NJ: Princeton University Press, 1994. Describes Weisskopf's and others' work on quantum electrodynamics, including the successful postwar renormalization program.

Stefan, Vladislav, ed. *Physics and Society: Essays in Honor of Victor Frederick Weisskopf by the International Community of Physicists.* New York: Springer, 1998. Collection of reminiscences by students and colleagues.

David Kaiser

WESTPHAL, JAMES A. (*b.* Dubuque, Iowa, 13 June 1930; *d.* Pasadena, California, 8 September 2004), *astronomy, petroleum geology, instrument design and development.*

James Westphal had careers in the petroleum industry and science, eventually becoming professor at the California Institute of Technology (Caltech) as a leader in scientific instrument design and development in geophysics and astronomy. He was the principal investigator of the instrument team that built the Wide Field/

Planetary Camera for the Hubble Space Telescope and later became the director of Palomar Observatory.

Early Years. Born in Dubuque, Iowa, but raised in Tulsa, Oklahoma, until age twelve, Westphal moved with his parents, Henry Westphal and the former Katharyn Wise, to the Westphal ancestral home in a mountaintop community in central Arkansas affiliated with the Lutheran Church, Missouri Synod. The community was named Petit Jean and was located near the town of Morrilton, where his paternal grandparents lived. He was an only son and his father had been an accountant who was moved around by his company until retirement in 1940, when he ran a service station in Tulsa and ultimately settled on Petit Jean to take up family ranching. Westphal enjoyed odd jobs around the service station and learned both metal and woodwork from his father and grandfather, who he recalled was a respected local "jack-leg mechanic, or a shade-tree mechanic" (1982a, p. 2).

He attended a local one-room schoolhouse in Petit Jean for a year, but his unrest after his exposure to the larger Tulsa system led his parents to send him to Morrilton, even though it meant a difficult daily commute by bicycle, car, and bus. By the ninth grade, Westphal was sent to live with a recently widowed family friend so he could attend the better junior and high schools in Little Rock. He earned his keep by yard work and taking care of chickens.

Westphal haunted the Carnegie Library in Morrilton and gained local notice after he read all the books available there on aviation. He continued this trait in Little Rock, but after finding Albert G. Ingalls's *Amateur Telescope Making* became a devoted astronomy enthusiast. He also joined the science club at Little Rock High School and fell in with a small group that decided to build a telescope for the school. By the time of high school graduation in May 1948, the group had built several reflecting telescopes and mounted the largest in a tower on the campus bandstand, making it available to the school almost every clear night. Although most of the fun was reading license plates in a nightclub parking lot a few miles away, Westphal also became an ardent member of the national amateur Association of Lunar and Planetary Observers. He was also an avid science fiction reader and dabbled with friends in model rocketry.

After high school graduation Westphal decided to move back to Tulsa, a town he preferred for its good family memories. He stayed with another family friend and landed a job in a filling station while he looked for something better. His uncle had connections in a local Tulsa firm, the Seismograph Service Corporation (SSC), where Westphal was hired to join a geophysical exploration crew near Spearman, in the Texas Panhandle. He started as a "jug hustler" who placed the geophones and portable seismometers and then became a rodman for the crew surveyor. This experience convinced him to try to go to college, and the money he had saved that year made it possible.

His work experience exposed him to the value of geophysical training, so he entered the University of Tulsa in engineering physics with a geophysics option in the fall of 1949. Westphal worked through school, partly out of necessity, and in the summers did field work for SSC, becoming exposed to electronics when he was given the job of "junior observer," assisting the leader of the seismic field crews who managed data collection using electronics in the recording truck. The company soon asked him to work throughout the year, assembling electronics at their home plant. As he worked through school, he worked up the company ladder, eventually leading seismic teams in the field all over the Midwest in the summers and acting as an acceptance-testing engineer during the school year. Westphal's goal at graduation was to become part of the company's research section, so he continued to hone his skills using ham radio as a medium. He recalled characteristically, "I wasn't so interested in gabbing with somebody with a radio as I was with making the stuff work" (1982a, p. 15).

Upon graduation, however, with a considerable amount of petroleum geology training under his belt, Westphal returned to the field rising to become a "party chief" responsible for planning out, executing, and then analyzing field observations. He was soon "farmed out" by SSC to a subsidiary, Wells Site International Services Inc., to develop expertise in radioactive well logging, using gamma ray and neutron penetration techniques. He quickly rose from party chief to project manager in SSC, leading teams throughout southern Mexico.

Petroleum Industry. In late 1954 Westphal accepted a more lucrative and better growth position with Sinclair Oil Research Laboratories, which also brought him back to the United States. His responsibility and research focus became exploration geology, and his specialty was recognized as instrument development and the problems of performing practical field work. He was delighted to be responsible for finding ways to build better amplifiers and craft more effective and sensitive exploration techniques, and soon drew around him an informal group of experimenters using an IBM 604 to refine techniques in gravity-field sensing.

During this time Westphal remained active in both ham radio and amateur telescope-making groups in Tulsa, finding in both of them a wide range of technical expertise that could cross-fertilize his growing interests. He also became familiar and comfortable working with more the-

oretically oriented PhD-trained specialists, both in Sinclair and in his club activities, sensing how his background and training could be an invaluable complement to their capabilities. Most of all he flourished in what he perceived as an open-ended laissez-faire research and development atmosphere maintained at Sinclair. Westphal remained at Sinclair from 1955 to 1961, ending up running a team whose task was to search out and test nonconventional techniques for finding oil. Among the myriad avenues of exploration, his team applied techniques in geochemistry, gamma ray spectroscopy, gravity detection, radio surface propagation, and aerial photography through colored filters, and even searched out and examined folk-methods of oil and mineral exploration. The gravity work brought him eventually to Caltech on a leave of absence to refine data reduction methods.

The problem Westphal addressed was how to refine techniques for determining the character of the vertical gravity field in a potential oil field. This was central to finding regions where oil was likely to be. Westphal devised a method of measuring variations in the gravitational field by sending sensors down a well shaft. As the shaft was dug out, the sensor would be sent to rest on the bottom to take measurements. It would then be removed and the shaft deepened to take the next measurement. In so doing, they always had a stable platform from which highly sensitive measurements could be taken. He discussed his ideas with C. Hewitt Dix, professor of geophysics at Caltech and a major name in the field of exploration seismology. He had been able to attract Dix to Sinclair after he organized a team to track large quarry blasts to see if they could detect the Mohorovicic discontinuity (the boundary between Earth's crust and its mantle) in the earth. They sent their data to Dix, who became very enthusiastic about this clever technique and spent the summer consulting for Sinclair. With Dix at hand, Westphal began thinking about better ways to do seismic data processing using cross-correlation and Fourier analysis. Westphal devised a way, using film-strip data and photomultipliers, to digitize data to make it amenable to processing on an IBM 650. In consequence, Dix invited him to refine his analysis methods and to use Caltech facilities to build what was effectively an analog-to-digital data converter. Westphal took a leave of absence from Sinclair, and arrived in January 1961 to build his device, as well as to audit an applied mechanics course, again inspired and enabled by Dix.

As Westphal worked away at his device, geophysicists and other Caltech staff would stop by and discuss their interests. He became acquainted with Bruce Murray, who was working with Harrison Brown and was interested in thermal infrared techniques for doing lunar surface geology using ground-based telescopes. This interaction became something of a blueprint for a long and fruitful association for Westphal, who stayed at Caltech for the rest of his life, collaborating with a wide array of geophysicists and astronomers. As he recalled "Everybody in this division was starved for instrumentation types" (1982a, p. 72).

Caltech. Indeed, Westphal found himself in a place that keenly recognized his potential value. Although he returned briefly to Sinclair in the summer, he soon accepted employment at Caltech and returned in August 1961, accompanied by his wife and their newborn first child. "We settled in and I dug right in to all the nifty things that were laying around to do, again, mainly working with Bruce Murray by then." Indelible in his memory were the words of the division chairman who hired him, Robert Sharp, "Anything that you do that decreases the resistance to accomplishing research by anybody at Caltech, and I don't even care if it's in this division … I will support it entirely. I don't care what area it's in, who it is, or anything else" (1982a, p. 76).

Westphal worked half-time on a National Aeronautics and Space Administration (NASA) grant Murray had secured, and the balance of his time was supported by grants awarded to Dix as well as to a group of marine biologists who found his underwater photography techniques, another hobby, of great value. He performed a wide variety of functions centered on conceiving, designing, building, testing, and operating new tools and techniques for research. He sensed a greater freedom of action at Caltech, and was drawn to the academic environment there, including the astrophysics colloquia.

He worked with Murray to develop thermal-infrared systems for use at a variety of telescopes including the venerable 152-centimeter (60-inch) reflector at Mount Wilson. Although he was generally aware of how these different projects were funded, knowing that there were in effect unlimited resources available, he preferred to work frugally and creatively, employing his knowledge and expertise gathered from his amateur days and scrounging in the field. Westphal contributed to a wide variety of projects and programs ranging from monitoring volcanic activity and glacial ice flows to building special aquaria for sustained and systematic studies of deep-sea life for the paleoecologist Heinz Lowenstam, who used isotope chemistry to understand the environmental conditions under which shellfish thrived or starved. This was of critical interest to Lowenstam's Office of Naval Research (ONR) sponsors, who hoped to find ways to keep their deep-sea operations free from fouling, or incrustation. Westphal worked for Lowenstam quarter-time for many years, helping devise both a means of capturing deep-sea life, using the bathysphere *Trieste* to bring samples back to the laboratory, and high-pressure aquaria for extended studies.

But his major contributions came in the field of astronomy, where he became both a source and a conduit for new infrared detector technologies and electronic imaging techniques, performing the latter function partly through contact with classified navy programs at the Naval Ordnance Test Station (NOTS) at Inyokern, and partly developing detector systems in his own laboratory on campus. His first association with NOTS in the early 1960s, working with Murray, was to design a mechanical interface for NOTS detectors that they could use on telescopes. As he recalled, the NOTS people were anxious for a critical evaluation of this technology, and so told Westphal that "We could stick it on a telescope and see what happens, without telling you what is in it, or how it works, or anything about it, because it is still classified" (1982a, p. 76). This kind of relationship continued for some time, but eventually Westphal began experimenting with new designs adapted from television technologies.

Starting in the 1960s, Westphal joined others who were keenly interested in developing electronic imaging devices for astronomical application. Increases in sensitivity were a primary goal, but also the ability to return images by telemetry from space-borne telescopes. He worked first with Murray and then with Gerry Neugebauer, Robert Leighton, and others building a survey instrument for assessing the amount and distribution of infrared sources in the sky. He contributed an amplifier design and assisted Dowell Martz to improve thermal-insulating vacuum bottles called "Dewars" for the instrument. In the early 1970s he teamed up with Thomas McCord and others to adapt a small Bellcom device from an experimental picture phone into what he called an integrating two-dimensional Silicon Vidicon photometer, or "SIVIT." His goal was to couple the two-dimensional imaging capabilities of conventional photography with the high sensitivity and linearity of photoelectric photomultipliers, especially for the red region, which was an important spectral range for planetary studies and studies of star-forming regions in external galaxies.

In what would be a signature style, Westphal parlayed expertise from Bell Laboratories, the Massachusetts Institute of Technology (MIT) and the Jet Propulsion Laboratory (JPL) as well as Caltech to develop the SIVIT. He also experimented with another variant of silicon-diode technology, the Silicon Intensified Target or "SIT" detectors, which he found more amenable to use in imaging spectrographs. Westphal and McCord tried these new devices on at the 508-centimeter (200-inch) telescope, achieving sensitivity gains for the SIT thousands of times more than photography. Naturally these new detectors created a great deal of excitement, but by the end of the 1970s it was clear that their magnetic sensitivity gave them limited "flat field" capabilities. As two-dimensional photometers they could not do better than about 1 percent accuracy over the entire field. Never fully wedded to any specific technology, Westphal was quick to appreciate the potential of another newly developed Bell Laboratories product, the charge-coupled device (CCD). By the late 1970s he and his colleagues were testing both SITs and CCDs in various instrumentation at the 508-centimeter (200-inch) telescope.

Westphal saw all sorts of applications for the CCD, none more so than in space astronomy. His entry into space astronomy proved to be the most dramatic of them all. In the 1970s Westphal had been approached on a number of occasions to participate in developing instrumentation for airborne and space-borne craft, but declined, preferring to remain working at a personal level, seeking out expertise wherever he found it. But after Gerry Wasserburg pushed to make him a member of a subcommittee of the National Research Council (NRC) Space Science Board in the mid-1970s, and he agreed because, as he recalled, it would put him in contact with real heroes such as James A. Van Allen, Westphal was drawn into space astronomy. His membership on the committee provided early access to knowledge of the CCD, ironically after he read through a JPL proposal for a new orbiter and probe to Jupiter, what became Galileo. Westphal tracked down the JPL staff who had made the proposal, to learn about the CCD, and soon realized it offered an enormous new potential for astronomical imaging. He and Jim Gunn at Caltech teamed up to adapt it to use at the 508-centimeter (200-inch) telescope, and with Maarten Schmidt put the CCD through trials on ultrafaint extended sources.

Instruments for the Hubble. Sometime in the summer of 1976, Gunn convinced Westphal to join in a proposal to NASA to build what came to be known as the wide field/planetary camera (WF/PC) for the Hubble Space Telescope (HST). Westphal recalls that he resisted for some time, because it meant working at a level that was not his style. He wanted always to be "very personally involved in the design, the construction, the checkout and the use of the hardware. When I'm building hardware, I am often in the machine shop, and I very often do the electronics, the wiring. It depends on the timing and who's around to help and so forth; but I am very intimately involved in it at every level" (1982a, p. 147). He knew this would not be possible for any prime instrument that was to fly on HST. And indeed, it was not.

In the course of developing WF/PC, Westphal, Gunn, and Schmidt built a device for the 508-centimeter (200-inch) telescope; dubbed the "4-shooter," the device demonstrated how one could take four small CCDs and combine their fields electronically into one wide field. Thus they overcame what was the one lingering concern about the new technology's limitations, and with it proposed successfully for the HST instrument itself. When

HST was launched in 1990, even though WF/PC was fully successful, its productivity and impact were severely compromised by the famous flaw in the HST primary mirror. A slightly redesigned WF/PC II, still closely based on the original but corrected for the flaws in the mirror, replaced the original in 1993, and began producing the images that made HST a popular revolution in astronomical imaging capability. Westphal also played a major role in many aspects of the development of the HST and was influential far beyond the construction of the WF/PC.

Westphal reluctantly agreed to assume the directorship of Palomar in 1994, at a difficult time in the observatory's history, when its domain and operation were in a state of turbulent flux. Abruptly replacing his friend Neugebauer, Westphal was faced with a daunting task that included the management of the new multi-institutional Keck Observatory, a task he was grateful to share with Joseph Miller, the capable and unflappable Lick Observatory director. In the end, Westphal's infectious enthusiasm, creativity, mechanical insights, and drive endeared him to an ever-widening circle of Caltech faculty and staff, and to the extent he was able to apply these virtues to his three-year directorship of Palomar, he managed to survive and, in terms of Keck instrumentation, to flourish. He agreed to undertake the challenge on the basis it would be a three-year tenure, and that he could write his own job description. When he stepped down in 1997 he retired a few months later, fully intending to keep working. One of his last projects was to devise a detector system that could penetrate the depths of the Old Faithful vent in Yellowstone National Park, yet another project that lingering revenue from an earlier MacArthur Fellowship had made possible.

Many awards and honors came to Westphal. Beyond the usual NASA encomia, the American Institute of Aeronautics and Astronautics recognized him for introducing the CCD into space astronomy. He was also a member of the American Academy of Arts and Sciences. His first marriage to Jean Wimbish ended in divorce. They had one son, Andrew Westphal. In October 1967 Westphal was remarried to Barbara Jean Webster, a programmer at Caltech working in chemistry. He thereby gained two stepdaughters, Robin and Susan Stroll. He died at home after suffering a long illness and complications from a neurological disorder.

BIBLIOGRAPHY

This essay draws extensively from two oral histories taken in 1982 and 2002, cited below, as well as from a third series conducted at Caltech by Shirley Cohen in 1998, and from the cited published works.

WORKS BY WESTPHAL

With Gerry Neugebauer. "Infrared Observations of Eta Carinae." *Astrophysical Journal* 152 (1968): L89.

With Allan Sandage and Jerome Kristian. "Rapid Changes in the Optical Intensity and Radial Velocities of the X-Ray Source SCO X-1." *Astrophysical Journal* 154 (1968): 139–156.

With Jerome Kristian, Natarajan Visvanathan, and Grant H. Snellen. "Optical Polarization and Intensity of the Pulsar in the Crab Nebula." *Astrophysical Journal* 162 (1970): 475.

With Thomas B. McCord. "Mars: Narrow-Band Photometry, from 0.3 to 2.5 Microns, of Surface Regions during the 1969 Apparition." *Astrophysical Journal* 168 (1971): 141.

"Application of Silicon Image Tubes (SIVIT and SIT) to Ground-Based Astronomy." *NASA SP-338* (1973): 93–106.

With Jerome Kristian and Allan Sandage. "Absorption-Line Redshifts of Galaxies in Remote Clusters Obtained with a Sky-Subtraction Spectrograph Using an SIT Television Detector." *Astrophysical Journal,* pt. 2, 197 (1 May 1975): L95–L98.

With Allan Sandage and Jerome Kristian. "The Extension of the Hubble Diagram. I. New Redshifts and BVR Photometry of Remote Cluster Galaxies, and an Improved Richness Correction." *Astrophysical Journal* 205 (1976): 688–695.

With Peter J. Young, Jerome Kristian, et al. "Evidence for a Supermassive Object in the Nucleus of the Galaxy M87 from SIT and CCD Area Photometry." *Astrophysical Journal,* pt. 1, 221 (1 May 1978): 721–730.

With Peter J. Young, James E. Gunn, et al. "The Double Quasar Q0957 + 561 A, B - A Gravitational Lens Image Formed by a Galaxy at Z = 0.39." *Astrophysical Journal,* pt. 1, 241 (15 October 1980): 507–520.

With James E. Gunn. "Care, Feeding, and Use of Charge-Coupled Device (CCD) Imagers at Palomar Observatory," *Solid State Imagers for Astronomy* SPIE 290 (1981): 16.

With William A. Baum, Tobias Kreidl, et al. "Saturn's E Ring." *Icarus* 47 (July 1981): 84–96.

Interview with James A. Westphal. Space Astronomy Oral History Project, National Air and Space Museum, Smithsonian Institution, Washington, DC, 1982a.

"The Wide Field/Planetary Camera." *Space Telescope Observatory, Space Telescope Science Institute* (1982b): 28–39.

With William A. Baum, Tod R. Lauer, et al. "Hubble Space Telescope Wide-Field/Planetary Camera Images of Saturn." *Astrophysical Journal,* pt. 2-Letters, 369 (10 March 1991): L51–L53.

With James E. Gunn. "Care, Feeding, and Use of Charge-Coupled Device Imagers at Palomar Observatory (in Solid State Imagers for Astronomy 1981)." In *Selected Papers on Instrumentation in Astronomy,* edited by William Livingston and Brian J. Thompson, 506. SPIE Milestone Series MS 87. Bellingham, WA: SPIE Optical Engineering Press, 1993.

With John T. Trauger, Gilda E. Ballester, et al. "The On-Orbit Performance of WFPC2." *Astrophysical Journal,* pt. 2-Letters, 435, no. 1 (1994): L3–L6.

With Roderick A. Hutchinson and Susan W. Kieffer. "In Situ Observations of Old Faithful Geyser." *Geology* 25, no. 10 (1997): 875–878.

Interview with James A. Westphal. Oral History Project, California Institute of Technology Archives, Pasadena, California, 2002.

With Eric E. Bloemhof. "Design Considerations for a Novel Phase-Contrast Adaptive-Optic Wavefront Sensor." In *Adaptive Optics Systems and Technology II,* edited by Robert K. Tyson, Domenico Bonaccini, and Michael C. Roggemann. *SPIE Proceedings* 4494 (2002): 363–370.

OTHER SOURCES

California Institute of Technology Press Office. "Maverick Scientist and Instrument Builder James Westphal Dies." Press release of Wednesday, 15 September 2004. Available from http://www.spaceref.com/news/viewpr.html?pid=15042.

Danielson, G. Edward. "James Adolph Westphal, 1930–2004." *Bulletin of the American Astronomical Society* 36, no. 5 (2004): 1687–1688.

Preston, Richard. *First Light: The Search for the Edge of the Universe.* New York: Atlantic Monthly Press, 1987.

Smith, Robert W., with contributions by Paul A. Hanle, Robert H. Kargon, and Joseph N. Tatarewicz. *The Space Telescope: A Study of NASA, Science, Technology, and Politics.* Cambridge, U.K.: Cambridge University Press, 1989.

David DeVorkin

WEXLER, HARRY

WEXLER, HARRY (*b.* Fall River, Massachusetts, 15 March 1911; *d.* Woods Hole, Massachusetts, 11 August 1962), *meteorology.*

Wexler was one of the most influential meteorologists of the twentieth century. Mentored by Carl-Gustaf Rossby and Hurd C. Willet, Wexler held research and teaching positions in meteorology with the Massachusetts Institute of Technology (MIT), the U.S. Weather Bureau, the University of Chicago, and the U.S. Air Force. As chief of research for the Weather Bureau, he was involved in the development of a number of new technologies, including airborne observations of hurricanes, sounding rockets, radar, the use of electronic computers for numerical weather prediction, and satellite meteorology. As chief scientist for the U.S. expedition to the Antarctic for the International Geophysical Year, he kept a journal for the years 1955–1959 that is a detailed record of the organization and the conduct of the mission.

Early Years. Harry Wexler was the third son of Russian immigrants Samuel and Mamie (Hornstein) Wexler. He was interested in science at an early age and enjoyed "mathematical recreations" with his brothers and friends. His scientific interests were stimulated by his physics teacher, Leslie W. Orcutt, who was also his baseball coach. Wexler claimed his interest in meteorology developed while delivering newspapers through fair weather and foul. He shared a common interest in meteorology with his childhood friend and future brother-in-law, Jerome Namias.

After graduating from Dunfee High School in 1928, Wexler attended Harvard University, where he majored in mathematics, graduating in 1932 magna cum laude. From 1932 to 1934 Wexler attended MIT, where he studied meteorology under the mentorship of Rossby, Willet, and Bernhard Haurwitz. He also worked for Charles Franklin Brooks as a part-time research assistant at Blue Hill Observatory. During this period he published several papers on atmospheric turbidity, air mass formation, and the behavior of frontal surfaces.

U.S. Weather Bureau. Wexler began his lifelong affiliation with the Weather Bureau in 1934, working as an assistant meteorologist in Chicago and Washington, D.C. He was assigned to develop operational techniques of "air mass or frontal analysis," a system developed in Norway by the Bergen School. He also helped develop "isentropic analysis," which was a favorite technique of Rossby. During this time he published papers on atmospheric turbidity, warm-type occluded weather fronts, lower atmospheric cooling, and the structure of polar continental air. Wexler married Hannah Paipert on 3 December 1934 in Chicago.

The Weather Bureau sent him back to MIT in 1937–1938 for further study. There he conducted research, funded by the Weather Bureau and the U.S. Department of Agriculture, on the general circulation of the atmosphere and developed techniques useful in extended or long-range forecasting. In 1938 he was promoted to associate meteorologist in the Weather Bureau. MIT awarded him the ScD degree in 1939; his dissertation was titled, "Observed Transverse Circulations in the Atmosphere and Their Climatological Implications." From June to September 1940, Wexler served as supervisor of forecasting at LaGuardia Field, New York.

Following the outbreak of war in Europe, the U.S. military began a program to train weather forecasters. Wexler took a leave of absence from the Weather Bureau in 1940 to teach in this program at the University of Chicago as an assistant professor of meteorology. In 1941 he returned to the Weather Bureau in Washington as senior meteorologist in charge of training and research, working to assist in defense preparations related to meteorology. In 1942 he accepted a commission as captain in the U.S. Army and served as the senior instructor of meteorology to the Army Air Force (AAF) Aviation Cadet School at Grand Rapids, Michigan. While in this position, he joined the University Meteorological Committee established to assist the military services in matters related to meteorological services. Following his promotion to

Harry Wexler. AP IMAGES.

major in 1943, Wexler worked in the Pentagon as research executive, Weather Division, AAF Headquarters, in charge of research and development. The task at hand was to utilize meteorology more effectively in aerial navigation, bombing ballistics, and weather forecasts for military operations.

First Hurricane Flight. On 14 September 1944 Major Harry Wexler participated in what may be called the first research reconnaissance flight into a hurricane, with pilot Colonel Floyd Wood in a Douglas A-20 "Havoc." In his published account of the mission, he described the data collected, concluding, "that the major portion of this hurricane cloud was caused by a strong but narrow area of ascending air near the center of the storm and that outside this area, descending air was found" (Wexler, 1945b in Rigby and Keehn, 1963).

Chief of Scientific Services Division. Following his honorable discharge from the military in January 1946 with the rank of lieutenant colonel, Wexler returned to the U.S. Weather Bureau, becoming the chief of the Special Scientific Services division. As head of research at the Weather Bureau, Wexler encouraged the development of new technologies, including weather radar, digital computing, and sounding rockets, and sponsored a study of the atmospheres of planets other than Earth. He served on numerous panels and committees, including the military's Research and Development Board and the National Advisory Committee for Aeronautics (NACA) Subcommittee on Meteorological Problems. He was a liaison to the Institute for Advanced Study's meteorology program, a delegate to the Toronto meetings of the International Meteorological Organization, and he chaired the U.S. delegation on aerology. He was a member of the Advisory Committee on Reactor Safeguards for the Atomic Energy Committee and served as a U.S. delegate to the "Atoms-for-Peace" Conference in Geneva, Switzerland, in 1955. He was the vice president of the American Meteorological Society, and the chairman of the Upper-Atmosphere Committee of the American Geophysical Union. He also chaired the NACA Special Committee for the Upper Atmosphere; the Geophysical Research Panel of the Scientific Advisory Board to the Chief of Staff, U.S. Air Force; and a study group on Meteorological Aspects of the Effects of Atomic Radiation for the National Academy of Science. He served on the National Research Council Space Science Board as well as its Committee on Arctic and Antarctic Research.

Wexler was an enthusiastic promoter of the idea of a World Weather Watch, which became a reality in 1963. According to Jerome Namias, "As the coverage of meteorological data over the world reaches the stage recommended in the report detailing the World Weather Watch in which Wexler played a major role, meteorologists may reinstitute the search for interactions with the help of synoptic as well as statistical tools, thereby providing more concrete evidence to assist in the formulation of physical theories" (Namias et al., 1963, p. 482).

Mauna Loa Observatory. Wexler was closely associated with the Weather Bureau Research Station, Mauna Loa Observatory. The observatory staff directly reported to Wexler and he gave it a special measure of his interest and attention. He visited the observatory often and took intense pleasure in the ecology of the lush rain forest. A number of atmospheric baseline and other measurements were conducted there, including, significantly, the ongo-

ing series of carbon dioxide measurements begun by Charles David Keeling in 1958.

International Geophysical Year and Satellite Meteorology. During the International Geophysical Year (IGY) of 1957–1958, Wexler served in a number of positions for the U.S. National Committee (USNC), including as a member of the Technical Panel on Meteorology, deputy to chief of the Weather Bureau F. W. Reichelderfer on the USNC/IGY and its Executive Committee, chief scientist of the USNC/IGY Antarctic Programs and consultant to the Antarctic Committee, member of the ad hoc Arctic and Equatorial Committee, and member of the ad hoc Panel for Radioactivity of the Air. In 1957 Wexler wrote a classic paper on "Meteorology in the International Geophysical Year" that highlighted some of the fundamental issues in the understanding of the atmosphere, meteorology's relationship to other geophysical sciences, and the importance of Antarctic science, climate science, and weather satellites. This was a timely paper, as Wexler states "the answers to many of these problems will have to wait for the digestion of data obtained during the 1957–58 International Geophysical Year and probably also for the obtaining of additional data from future International Geophysical Years. The world's geophysicists bear a heavy responsibility to future generations in insuring that basic environmental measurements are carefully recorded and that new ones are initiated" (Wexler, 1957b, in Rigby and Keehn, 1963).

Wexler was a big promoter of the use of satellites in meteorology and was actively involved in the Joint Meteorological Satellite Advisory Committee (JMSAC) in 1959; he commented at the First National Conference on Peaceful Uses of Space: "A system of satellites of two types would be ideal for charting the world's weather. One system would circle the earth over the poles; the other would circle around the equator. Both types of satellites could send their observations into a central office. They could also pick up and transmit information from automatic weather stations located in uninhabited areas" (Wexler, 1957a, in Rigby and Keehn, 1963). He believed that information gathered from satellites on the international scale would be of great value to everyone in the world for warning of severe weather and other weather changes. In 1961 he served as the lead negotiator for the United States in talks with the Soviet Union concerning the joint use of meteorological satellites.

Wexler was the author of over fifty published papers on various subjects, including radiative cooling of the air, polar anticyclones, atmospheric turbidity, structure of hurricanes, and upper atmosphere temperatures and dynamic connections with the lower atmosphere (Rigby and Keehn, 1963). He died suddenly of a heart attack while vacationing in Woods Hole, Massachusetts. He was survived by his wife and daughters, Susan Carol and Libby. His wife donated his papers to the Library of Congress in 1963, with additional papers received in 1971 from the Department of Commerce. Wexler's breadth of knowledge and wide-ranging interests are evident in the memorial issue of the *Monthly Weather Review* in December 1963, which contained thirty contributions by leading meteorologists. The number of contributions was so large that the memorial issue was expanded from an originally planned single issue to the combined issue of three numbers.

Awards and Honors. Wexler was the recipient of numerous awards and honors. He received medals from three branches of the military: the U.S. Army Air Medal for his 1944 flight into the "Great Atlantic Hurricane," the U.S. Air Force Award for Exceptional Service in 1956 for his work as a member of the Scientific Advisory Board to the Chief Staff, and the U.S. Navy Distinguished Public Service Award in 1959 for contributions to the USNC/IGY Antarctic Programs. He earned the Robert M. Losey Award in 1946 from the Institute of Aeronautical Sciences in recognition of outstanding contributions to the science of meteorology as applied to aeronautics, and the Department of Commerce awarded him an Exceptional Service Medal in 1958 for contributions to the science of meteorology and for outstanding leadership in the 1957–1958 IGY Program. In 1961 he received the Career Service Award of the National Civil Service League. Wexler was elected a Fellow of the American Academy of Arts and Sciences in 1956, a Fellow of the American Astronautical Society in 1960, and a member of the Cosmos Club in 1961. Wexler Crater on the Moon was named after him, and in 1977, the University of Wisconsin–Madison established the Harry Wexler Professorship of Meteorology.

Wexler was a dedicated scientist and hands-on administrator who found time to do his own research, encourage the work of others, and communicate the excitement of scientific research to school groups and the general public. An admirer of Benjamin Franklin's scientific work, he practiced what Franklin had advised: "He who would master nature must obey her laws. He must learn her laws and then obey them."

BIBLIOGRAPHY

The Harry Wexler Papers, Manuscript Division, Library of Congress, 13,200 items, cover the years 1929–1962 and contain information relating to all the major areas of his career. For a comprehensive bibliography, see Malcolm Rigby and Pauline A. Keehn, "Bibliography of the Publications of Harry Wexler," Monthly Weather Review *91 (December 1963): 477–481.*

WORKS BY WEXLER

"Turbidities of American Air Masses and Conclusions Regarding the Seasonal Variation in Atmospheric Dust Content." *Monthly Weather Review* 62 (1934): 397–402.

"Analysis of a Warm-Front-Type Occlsuion." *Monthly Weather Review* 63 (1935): 213–221.

"Cooling in the Lower Atmosphere and the Structure of Polar Continental Air." *Monthly Weather Review* 17 (1936): 122–136.

"The Structure of the September 1944 Hurricane When off Cape Henry, Virginia." *Bulletin of the American Meteorological Society* 26 (1945): 156–159.

"Meteorology in the International Geophysical Year." *Scientific Monthly* 84 (1957): 141–145.

"TIROS I." *Monthly Weather Review* 88 (1960): 79–87.

OTHER SOURCES

Belanger, Dian Olson. *Deep Freeze: The United States, the International Geophysical Year, and the Origins of Antarctica's Age of Science.* Boulder: University Press of Colorado, 2006.

Namias, Jerome, et al. "Contributions in Memory of Harry Wexler." *Monthly Weather Review* 91 (1963): 477–748.

Price, Saul, and Jack C. Pales. "Mauna Loa Observatory: The First Five Years." *Monthly Weather Review* 91 (1963): 665–680.

U.S. Weather Bureau. *Weather Bureau Topics* 10, no. 12 (1951).

Sepideh Yalda

WEYL, HERMANN CLAUS HUGO

(*b.* Elmshorn, Germany, 9 November 1885; *d.* Zürich, Switzerland, 8 December 1955), *mathematics, mathematical physics, philosophy.* For the original article on Weyl, see *DSB* vol. 14.

The original *DSB* article focuses on Weyl's contributions to analysis, analytical number theory, and the representation theory of Lie groups. Other fields of study are mentioned only in passing. This appendix presents some aspects of Weyl's ideas in the foundations of mathematics, differential geometry, and mathematical physics.

It was already mentioned in the main article that Weyl changed his research orientation under the impact of the experience of World War I and the crisis in its aftermath. As Weyl later said, he looked for safeness in his main fields of research. He turned toward the foundations of analysis and to the newly founded theory of general relativity with its strong appeal to philosophically intriguing interrelations of mathematics and physics. In 1918 Weyl published two books on these two rather distinct topics: *The Continuum* and *Space, Time, Matter.*

Constructivist Sympathies and Transitional Turn to Intuitionism. In *The Continuum* Weyl proposed a constructivist arithmetical foundation of analysis or, more properly, for a part of analysis. This began his public intervention into the foundations of mathematics, in clear opposition to David Hilbert's program of a purely formalistic axiomatic foundation. He sketched how a reduced part of real analysis could be secured by constructions in a semiformalized arithmetical language, respecting the restrictions of predicativity, although the constructivist (reduced) continuum stood in stark contrast to the intuitive continuum and physical ideas of space-time. That seems to have contributed to his change of mind already a year after the publication of the book. He started to support Luitzen Egbertus Jan Brouwer's more radical intuitionistic program and attacked Hilbert's foundational views even more strongly in a programmatic article on the recent foundational crisis of mathematics (1921). But his initial hopes of a unified intuitionist foundation of mathematics, which would also serve the purpose of a deeper understanding of the physical space-time were not fulfilled.

Weyl soon realized that the intuitionist foundation of mathematics led to undesirable technical complications and relied too much on a kind of evidence that was difficult to reconcile with his interests in mathematical physics. Hilbert's foundational program seemed to be better adapted to providing the symbolical tools needed in most advanced contemporary mathematical physics, in particular the rising quantum mechanics. In the late 1920s Weyl showed more sympathy with Hilbert's foundational view, but could not avoid being irritated by Kurt Gödel's negative result of 1930 for Hilbert's strategy of founding modern analysis on a finitistic consistency proof. He even returned after World War II to a weak preference of his arithmetical constructive approach of 1918.

Linking Geometry and Physics. Parallel to the work on the foundations of analysis and the concept of the continuum, Weyl started to analyze and to deepen the links between differential geometry and the newly established general theory of relativity. *Space, Time, Matter* was one of the first text books on the subject and among the most influential ones over decades to come. It was revised in five successive editions until 1923. In the first part of this book, Weyl gave an up-to-date introduction to Riemannian and Lorentzian geometry, which made it an important introductory monograph to modern differential geometry. At the time when the book first went to print, Weyl developed a generalization of Riemannian geometry, which was more firmly built on what he called a "purely infinitesimal" point of view. He avoided a direct comparison of lengths and other quantities at different points of the manifold and introduced the seminal concept of

point-dependent gauges and a *gauge field* (a scale connection) to allow the transfer of metrical concepts from one point to another. The scale connection had formal properties that made it appear as an appropriate mathematical expression for the potential of the electromagnetic field. It became the embryonic core of a tradition of physical field theories which—in a more general form—became important in high energy physics of the last third of the twentieth century.

The gauge geometry of 1918 served Weyl as a starting point for an attempt at unifying electromagnetism and gravity. In this respect Weyl took up and tried to improve Hilbert's program to derive the basic matter structures from purely field theoretical considerations (extending an approach of Gustav Mie; see Weyl, "Gravitation und Elektrizität"). For about two years he believed he had found a clue to the problem of understanding matter by such a classical field theoretical approach. In the third edition of *Space, Time, Matter* he added a passage on a gauge geometric generalization of semi-Riemannian geometry and his unified field theory. But already a year later he realized that the derivation of matter structures from pure field theory had no chance for success.

Space, Time, Matter was only a small part of the contributions to the interchange between differential geometry and general relativity. Weyl pursued it in his own peculiar way based on a broad conceptual and philosophical view. He studied the interrelation of conformal and projective differential geometric structure and realized that both together specify a (Weylian) metric uniquely. An even deeper conceptual approach was contained in his *Mathematische Analyse des Raumproblems* (1923; Analysis of the Problem of Space), in which the older space problem of the nineteenth century was transplanted into the context of purely infinitesimal geometry. Here Weyl (sketchily) introduced concepts of infinitesimal group operations and connections. Independently developed by Élie Cartan in 1922, they were later turned into the language of fiber bundles and led to the study of geometries characterized by gauge structures.

Group Theory and Physics. The study of differential geometry and the problem of space led Weyl to studying the representation theory of Lie groups. In the mid-1920s he delved into what became his most influential contributions to pure mathematics, the study of the representations of semisimple Lie groups (1925–1926). Extended and refined, this work formed the core of his later book *The Classical Groups* (1939), written as a harvest of his work and his lecturing activities on this topic during his Princeton years.

During his work on the representation theory of Lie groups, Weyl actively followed the turn toward the new

Hermann Weyl. AP IMAGES.

quantum mechanics of Werner Heisenberg, Max Born, and Pascual Jordan and started to explore the possibilities opened up by the interplay of infinitesimal and finite group operations in quantum mechanics. In 1927–1928 he gave a lecture at Zürich Eidgenössische Technische Hochschule (ETH) on the topic, which gave rise to his second, again very influential, book on mathematical physics, *The Theory of Groups and Quantum Mechanics* (1928; Engl. trans. 1931). Here he emphasized the conceptual role of group methods in the symbolic representation of quantum structures, in particular the intriguing interplay of representations of the special linear group and permutations groups. In this interplay he also saw the mathematical clue to understanding the phenomenon of spin coupling, studied at the time by some of the young physicists turning toward quantum chemistry (Fritz London, Walter Heitler, and others). Moreover, Weyl explored the central role of the discrete symmetries (parity, charge conjugation, and time inversion) in the first steps toward a quantized version of electrodynamics, thus anticipating structural elements that turned into important questions for physics three decades later.

Not covered in the book, but published separately, was a second step for his gauge theory of the electromagnetic field. Quantum theorists had proposed reconsidering the gauge idea for the phase of wave functions rather than for scale gauge as in Weyl's original idea of 1918. Weyl (1929) took up the proposal and explored it after

the rise of Paul Dirac's spinor fields for the electron (as was done similarly and independently by Vladimir Fock). He came to the conclusion that the new context demanded considering symmetry extension of the Lorentz group by unitary transformations in $U(1)$. That gave rise to a modified gauge theory of electromagnetism, which was endorsed by leading theoretical physicists (among them Wolfgang Pauli, Erwin Schrödinger, and Fock) and served as a starting point for the next generation of physicists, who molded the symbolic frame of gauge field theories in the 1950s and 1960s.

Weyl's Philosophical Writings. Hermann Weyl was not only a philosophically interested researcher in mathematics and physics. He had close, but changing relations to philosophers such as Edmund Husserl, Fritz Medicus, and later to the existential philosophies of Karl Jaspers and Martin Heidegger. He gave active literary expression to his philosophical reflections of scientific activity in many of his publications. Most influential was his philosophical handbook *Philosophy of Mathematics and Natural Science*, originally published in German in 1927, and translated into English in 1949. It became a classic in the philosophy of science. A central topic of his thought was the mode and the role of symbolic construction in scientific knowledge of the world. It reappeared in his later reflections on twentieth-century science (1953). Like others of his generation, Weyl was shocked not only by the atrocities of the Nazi regime but also by the destructiveness of the nuclear weapons developed during the war. He considered it as a kind of hubris of modern techno-scientific culture, which had started to step beyond the circle of activities that can be accounted for. He hesitatingly hoped that it might perhaps be contained, if at all, by a slow rise of moral awareness of users and producers of scientific knowledge.

SUPPLEMENTARY BIBLIOGRAPHY

WORKS BY WEYL

The Concept of a Riemann Surface. Translated by Gerald R. MacLane. Reading: MA: Addison-Wesley, 1964. Originally published 1913.

The Continuum: A Critical Examination of the Foundation of Analysis. Translated by Stephen Pollard and Thomas Bole. Kirksville, MO: Thomas Jefferson University Press, 1987. Corrected republication, New York: Dover, 1994. First published 1918.

"Gravitation und Elektrizität." In *The Dawning of Gauge Theory,* by Lochlainn O'Raifeartaigh. Princeton, NJ: Princeton University Press, 1997. First published 1918.

Space, Time, Matter. Translated by Henry L. Brose (from the 1921 German 4th edition). London: Methuen, 1922. First published 1918.

"Theorie der Darstellung kontinuierlicher halbeinfacher Gruppen durch lineare Transformationen. I, II, III und

Nachtrag." *Mathematische Zeitschrift* 23 (1925): 271–309; 24 (1926): 328–395, 789–791.

Philosophie der Mathematik und Naturwissenschaft. Handbuch der Philosophie, Abt. 2, Beitr. A. Munich: Oldenbourg, 1927.

"Elektron und Gravitation." *Zeitschrift für Physik* 56 (1929): 330–352. In English in O'Raifeartaigh, 1997, pp. 121–144.

Mathematische Analyse des Raumproblems: Vorlesungen gehalten in Barcelona und Madrid; Was ist Materie?; zwei Aufsätze zur Naturphilosophie.. Darmstadt: Wissenschaftliche Buchgesellschaft, 1963. First published 1923.

The Theory of Groups and Quantum Mechanics. Translated by H. P. Robertson (from the German 2nd edition). New York: Dutton, 1931. First German edition 1928.

The Classical Groups: Their Invariants and Representations. Princeton, NJ: Princeton University Press, 1939.

Philosophy of Mathematics [blank included] *and Natural Science.* Revised and augmented English edition, based on a translation of Olaf Helmer. Princeton, NJ: Princeton University Press, 1949.

Wissenschaft als symbolische Konstruktion des Menschen. Eranos-Jahrbuch Zürich: Rhein-Verlag, 1949.

"Über den Symbolismus der Mathematik und mathematischen Physik." *Studium generale* 6 (1953): 219–228.

OTHER SOURCES

Borel, Armand. *Essays in the History of Lie Groups and Algebraic Groups.* Providence, RI: AMS; London: Mathematical Society, 2001.

Chandrasekharan, Komaravolu, ed. *Hermann Weyl: 1885–1985: Centenary Lectures Delivered by C. N. Yang, R. Penrose, and A. Borel at the ETH.* Zürich; Berlin: Springer, 1986.

Chevalley, Claude, and André Weil. "Hermann Weyl (1885–1955)." *L'Enseignement Mathématique* 2, no. 3 (1957): 157–187.

Coleman, Robert, and Herbert Korté. "Hermann Weyl: Mathematician, Physicist, Philosopher." In *Hermann Weyl's Raum-Zeit-Materie and a General Introduction to His Scientific Work,* edited by Erhard Scholz. Basel: Birkhauser Verlag, 2001.

Frei, Günther, and Urs Stammbach. *Hermann Weyl und die Mathematik an der ETH Zürich, 1913–1930.* Basel: Birkhäuser, 1992.

Hawkins, Thomas. *Emergence of the Theory of Lie Groups: An Essay in the History of Mathematics, 1869–1926.* Berlin: Springer, 2000.

Hendricks, Vincent F., Stig Andur Pedersen; and Klaus F. Jørgensen, eds. *Proof Theory: History and Philosophical Significance.* Dordrecht: Kluwer, 2000. Includes chapters on Weyl by Solomon Feferman, Erhard Scholz, and Dirk van Dalen.

Mackey, George. "Hermann Weyl and the Application of Group Theory to Quantum Mechanics." In *Exact Sciences and Their Philosophical Foundations,* edited by Werner Deppert et al. Frankfurt am Main and New York: Lang, 1988.

Mancosu, Paolo. *From Brouwer to Hilbert: The Debate on the Foundations of Mathematics in the 1920s.* Oxford: Oxford University Press, 1998.

———, and Thomas Ryckman. "The Correspondence between O. Becker and H. Weyl." *Philosophia Mathematica* 10 (2002): 130–202.

Newman, M. H. A. "Hermann Weyl, 1885–1955." *Biographical Memoirs of Fellows of the Royal Society London* 3 (1957): 305–328.

O'Raifeartaigh, Lochlainn. *The Dawning of Gauge Theory.* Princeton, NJ: Princeton University Press, 1997.

———, and Norbert Straumann. "Gauge Theory: Historical Origins and some Modern Developments." *Reviews of Modern Physics* 72 (2000): 1–23.

Scholz, Erhard. "Hermann Weyl's Analysis of the 'Problem of Space' and the Origin of Gauge Structures." *Science in Context* 17 (2004): 165–197.

———. "Local Spinor Structures in V. Fock's and H. Weyl's Work on the Dirac Equation (1929)." In *Géométrie au XXième siècle,* edited by D. Flament, C. Houzel, et al. Paris: Hermann, 2005.

Sieroka, Norman. "Weyl's 'Agens Theory' of Matter and the Zurich Fichte." *Studies in History and Philosophy of Science* 38 (2007): 84–107.

Sigurdsson, Skúli. "Hermann Weyl, Mathematics and Physics, 1900–1927." PhD diss., Harvard University, 1991.

———. "Physics, Life, and Contingency: Born, Schrödinger, and Weyl in Exile." In *Forced Migration and Scientific Change: Emigré German Speaking Scientists and Scholars after 1933,* edited by Mitchell G. Ash and Alfons Söllner. Washington, DC: German Historical Institute; Cambridge, U.K.: Cambridge University Press, 1996.

Slodowy, Peter. "The Early Development of the Representation Theory of Semisimple Lie Groups: A. Hurwitz, I. Schur, H. Weyl." *Jahresbericht der Deutschen Mathematiker-Vereinigung* 101 (1999): 97–115.

Van Atten, Mark, Dirk van Dalen, and Richard Tieszen. "Brouwer and Weyl: The Phenomenology and Mathematics of the Intuitive Continuum." *Philosophia Mathematica* 10 (2002): 203–226.

Wells, Raymond O., ed. *The Mathematical Heritage of Hermann Weyl.* Providence, RI: American Mathematical Society, 1988.

Erhard Scholz

WHEWELL, WILLIAM (*b.* Lancaster, England, 24 May 1794; *d.* Cambridge, England, 6 March 1866), *theology, history and philosophy of science, physical astronomy, mineralogy, tidal theory, science education, political economy, architectural history, moral philosophy.* For the original article on Whewell see *DSB,* vol. 14.

An avalanche of research on William Whewell since the 1970s added considerably to an understanding of him and his nineteenth-century context. Scholars always recognized Whewell as a religious man, for example, but have come to better see exactly how his religion mixed with other areas of thought—especially his philosophy of science, itself better understood in the early twenty-first century. Publications have examined his collaboration with Richard Jones in developing political economic theory, including their debates with other political economists. Much scholarship has addressed the institutional and social contexts of Whewell's life, such as the nature of education at Cambridge University and the creation of scientific societies in Britain. Whewell's conceptual controversies included his rejection of Darwinian evolution, that with David Brewster on the extent of life in the universe, and those with John Stuart Mill involving philosophy, moral theory, and economics.

Cambridge University immersed the young would-be carpenter Whewell in a network of like-minded intellectuals who would collectively contemplate many subjects. He was one of the poor scholarship students (sizars) at Trinity College, all of whom received contributions from better-off students. He took his BA degree in 1816 as second wrangler and second Smith's prizeman, that is, with the second-highest honors in his class. Succeeding the next year in the highly competitive fellowship examination at Trinity College, he virtually guaranteed himself a lifelong Cambridge career, which is what came to pass. He held professorships in two quite different subjects, mineralogy from 1828 to 1832 and moral philosophy from 1838 to 1855. Surely spurred significantly by his own example, he praised the socially transforming power of English universities to enable sons of peasants to become country clergymen. Physically as well as intellectually vigorous, Whewell died when thrown from the horse he was riding near Cambridge when he was nearly seventy-three years old. He outlived two wives, the second dying in 1865. He had no children.

Religion and Science. Theology provided Whewell his deepest knowledge. He wrote religious letters of comfort to his mortally ill sister, who died in 1821. He assured his colleague Hugh James Rose that science would not undermine religion, and in his Cambridge sermons of 1827 he explained that revelation provided more secure theological insights than did natural theology, as valuable as the latter was. In a Cambridge sermon of 1828 Whewell underscored the point he had made to Rose by citing the religion of the likes of Isaac Newton. Natural theology's value appeared strikingly in Whewell's Bridgewater Treatise, *Astronomy and General Physics, Considered with Reference to Natural Theology*, published in 1833 and many times thereafter. Design in the physical world certainly disclosed the existence of a designing God, but it revealed more than that. God also designed man's morality and intellect, for instance. Though decidedly inferior to God's mind, man's mind mirrored God's. Hence, man's degree of pleasure in contemplating a particular scientific theory was a measure of God's own pleasure in creating the world with

William Whewell. SCIENCE PHOTO LIBRARY

that theory in mind. That is, such pleasure suggested, but did not guarantee, the theory's truth. Whewell's theology would provide a context for his philosophy of science, and as master of Trinity he delivered sermons into the 1860s.

Geology was the current science most responsible for disagreements involving science and religion. The conflict, however, was not simply between religion and geology but, even more, between competing views of scripture. Whewell had been reading works by leading geologists as early as 1818, and he went on geological field trips in the 1820s with Cambridge's new professor of geology, Adam Sedgwick. Sedgwick and Whewell established a Cambridge approach to geology that emphasized probing the geometrical form of geological strata and comprehending their configuration in dynamical terms, that is, in terms of the laws of motion. In the early 1830s Whewell praised Charles Lyell's contribution to geological dynamics, but he disagreed with Lyell's "uniformitarian" (Whewell's word) conclusions that the Earth had remained essentially the same, experiencing only nonprogressive and rather gradual changes. Both Lyell and the "catastrophist" (Whewell's word) geologists concluded that the Earth had a vast age, and Whewell agreed. That is, Whewell was not one of the young-Earth, scriptural geologists of the day but one who valued scripture primarily for its revelation of such as God, Christ, and the afterlife. Earth's changing life and the fossil record's discontinuities, however, did bespeak miraculous interventions to Whewell, scripture and geology essentially agreeing in this regard.

Political Economy. Whewell's partner in the study of political economy was Richard Jones, another Trinity man who had taken his degree in 1816. David Ricardo's recent books on economic theory roused their inductivist ire. Compared to mechanics and astronomy, political economy was far too immature a science for Ricardo to make the assumptions and deductions that he did, they argued. Though claiming universal conclusions, Ricardo actually ignored agricultural economic arrangements for most of the world. Contrary to Ricardo, they asserted, there was no perpetual equilibrium, as was disclosed by other sciences. Whewell rejected Ricardo's conclusion that landowners' interests conflicted with those of others in society. Whewell endorsed the English class system as a judicious social control. Jones inductively amassed the evidence that Whewell could draw upon in his mathematical demonstration of Ricardo's errors. Whewell presented papers on political economy to the Cambridge Philosophical Society in 1829 and 1831. Also in 1831 appeared Jones's long-awaited *Essay on the Distribution of Wealth and on the Sources of Taxation.*

Natural Science. In addition to his significant research on mineralogy and the tides, Whewell kept careful track of other physical sciences within an increasingly institutional scientific context. In the early 1820s he was reading French works in physics and taking detailed notes on Michael Faraday's earliest research concerning connections between electricity and magnetism. A few years later Whewell contributed the extensive mathematical portion of Francis Lunn's article on "Electricity" in the *Encyclopaedia Metropolitana.* A Cambridge graduate of 1818, Lunn became a fellow of the Royal Society of London the next year and helped sponsor Whewell's successful application for membership in 1820. Whewell presented his paper on mineralogy to the Royal Society in 1824 and others on the subject to the Cambridge Philosophical Society, which he had helped found in 1819. By around 1830 Whewell strongly advocated the new undulatory theory of light with its concept of a luminiferous ether. The British Association for the Advancement of Science was established in 1831, and Whewell presented to it long reports on the current state of mineralogy in 1832 and on the current state of mathematical theories of electricity, magnetism, and heat in 1835. He became president of the Geological Society of London in 1837, the next year inducing Charles Darwin to assume the burdens of secretary. Though the word *scientist* gained currency only well after

Whewell's lifetime, his invention of it in the 1830s symbolized the increasing professionalization of science.

Education. Whewell helped change Cambridge education in important ways. In 1816, instruction within colleges prepared pupils for the university's Senate House examination upon which a Cambridge honors degree depended. Lectures by university professors could be interesting but were generally not relevant to Senate House examination subjects, which were classics, moral philosophy, and especially mathematics. The last included pure mathematics (with Isaac Newton's fluxional notation for the calculus) and mixed mathematics—that is, those successfully mathematized areas of science: mechanics, observational astronomy, gravitational theory, hydrostatics, and geometrical optics. During the previous century French savants using the Continental version of the calculus had dramatically developed Newton's gravitational theory. That was excellent motivation for John Herschel, Charles Babbage, and George Peacock to form their Analytical Society and to try to alter the Cambridge curriculum. Whewell joined their cause with his *Elementary Treatise on Mechanics* (1819) and *Treatise on Dynamics* (1823), both of which employed the Continental calculus. In addition, Whewell essentially separated statics from dynamics, rewriting Newton's laws of motion in the process. More fundamental, he declared those laws to be necessary truths—a conclusion that would eventually provide a basis for his philosophy of science.

Whewell continued to influence Cambridge studies into mid-century. He departed somewhat from the Analytical Society's exuberance for the calculus, arguing that students must first master more elementary mathematics in preparation for logical thinking in other—and ultimately more significant—areas of thought. In his *Principles of English University Education* (1837), he emphasized the university's role in converting undergraduates into Englishmen during that crisis period when youth became man. England was something like a present-day Greece or Rome, and the university bore much of the duty to maintain that reality. He identified permanent knowledge as classics and mathematics, which at Cambridge were the preserve of college instruction. Progressive knowledge included not-yet-mathematized areas of science, which at Cambridge were part of professorial instruction. With both the fate of the nation and his own success in mastering many subjects undoubtedly in mind, Whewell pursued his convictions. He succeeded in getting some questions on heat, electricity, and magnetism included in the mathematical tripos (as the Senate House examination came to be called). As master of Trinity he was one of the examiners for the Smith's prize examination, and his questions included a few on heat, electricity, and magnetism as well as engineering. As chair of key committees in the

1840s he was instrumental in establishing the natural sciences tripos and the moral sciences tripos at mid-century, thus making professorial lectures (including his own) directly relevant to Cambridge education.

Philosophy. Whewell's philosophy of science combined primarily the philosophies of Francis Bacon and Immanuel Kant. Bacon was one of the most famous of Trinity men, and his legacy would have been ever present to the young Whewell. Whewell's diaries reveal his awareness of Kant by spring 1820 and of Kant's nonutilitarian moral philosophy by February 1821, evidently from reading Madame de Staël's advocacy of Kant in her *Germany* (1813). Though the mature philosophy that Whewell formulated in the 1830s would have totally pleased neither Bacon nor Kant, it did explain how an empirical study of nature had led to necessary truths. Not merely a random gathering of information, induction required an active mind, seeking patterns and forming explanations—though without jumping to conclusions or pursuing wild hypotheses. Whewell termed resultant successes the "colligation" of facts and the "consilience" of inductions. Colligation involved one idea explaining different but similar observations. The more powerful consilience required an idea to explain quite different phenomena, the classic example being Newton's gravitational theory, which united the celestial and terrestrial worlds. Moreover, such successful theories could disclose "true causes"—causes known actually to exist in nature, even though unobservable. The luminiferous ether was a prime example. No Kantian-like doubt of a real, external world arose. God had created both humans and nature, designing them for each other.

Whewell's Kantian-like "fundamental ideas" provided necessary truths. The history of science showed that knowledge of such fundamental ideas emerged through long and careful empirical studies of nature. Because of colligation and consilience, laws of motion would appear first as powerful inductive truths that were still subject to refutation. Eventually, though, one recognized their necessity, that their truth depended not upon experience but upon their logical connection to the fundamental idea of cause. Gravitational theory, then, *must* accord with the laws of motion, but not the reverse. That is, gravitational theory was not a necessary truth because, in principle, contrary evidence could disprove it. Whewell identified several fundamental ideas, such as that of affinity for chemical knowledge. However, the existence of necessary truths did not preclude change in scientific understanding. The future could bring additional fundamental ideas, for example, including more inclusive ones that could effect something like a consilience of already known fundamental ideas. Fundamental ideas allowed the human mind glimpses of God's.

Such glimpses of course were relevant to Whewell's moral philosophy. Indeed, he articulated such a view in his *Foundation of Morals*, the published version of four sermons he delivered in Cambridge in 1837. As with the Ten Commandments, revelation provided moral guidance, but scriptural passages such as Romans 2:14 also signaled the presence of innate moral ideas in man's mind. Whewell's prime opponent here was utilitarianism, especially that of William Paley, whose *Principles of Moral and Political Philosophy* (1785) argued that when scripture was not specific enough, the happiness produced by proper behavior indicated the morality of that behavior. Because Paley's book was required reading at Cambridge, Whewell once more confronted the Cambridge curriculum. As professor of moral philosophy and in later publications, Whewell pursued his anti-utilitarian theme. For Whewell, the history of innate ideas in moral philosophy resembled that of fundamental ideas in science.

Controversies. Controversies were not confined to Cambridge. John Stuart Mill disagreed with Whewell not only about utilitarianism but about political economy and induction as well. Whewell's *Of Induction* (1849) responded at length to Mill. The eminent Scottish scientist David Brewster engaged Whewell in acrimonious and entangled debate on the plurality of worlds—that is, on whether the rest of the universe was also inhabited. Supporting the widely held plurality view, Brewster declared, for example, that God would not create wasted worlds, that is, worlds absent life. Geology, Whewell countered, demonstrated that the Earth itself had existed for eons with no life, indicating by analogy that God could create such worlds. In his *Origin of Species* (1859), Darwin quoted from Whewell's Bridgewater Treatise regarding God's law-governed universe. Darwin may have called upon Whewell's formulation of scientific knowledge in defending his theory of evolution, but he was also obviously rejecting Whewell's published opposition to any such theory. Whewell added a preface to the 1864 edition of his Bridgewater Treatise confirming that opposition.

Thus, at an Anglican university where competing theologies vied, William Whewell endorsed a theology that supported a philosophy of human knowledge. It in turn provided what he regarded as the proper understanding of the true science that had emerged historically in the epoch of Isaac Newton. The man who invented the word *scientist* was not himself a scientist in exactly the modern sense of the word. Indeed, he was more interesting than that.

SUPPLEMENTARY BIBLIOGRAPHY

The bibliography in Fisch and Schaffer 1991 (see Other Sources) lists some 130 works by Whewell. The bibliography that follows here includes none of those works nor any in the original DSB bibliography.

WORKS BY WHEWELL

Sermons Preached in the Chapel of Trinity College, Cambridge. London: John W. Parker; Cambridge, U.K.: J. & J. J. Deighton, 1847.

Collected Works of William Whewell. 16 vols. Edited with an introduction by Richard Yeo. Bristol, U.K.: Thoemmes Press, 2001. Includes one edition or another of most of Whewell's major works as well as the two-volume biography of him by Isaac Todhunter published in 1876.

Of the Plurality of Worlds: A Facsimile of the First Edition of 1853; Plus Previously Unpublished Material Excised by the Author Just before the Book Went to Press; and Whewell's Dialogue Rebutting His Critics, Reprinted from the Second Edition. Edited with new introductory material by Michael Ruse. Chicago: University of Chicago Press, 2001.

OTHER SOURCES

Becher, Harvey W. "William Whewell and Cambridge Mathematics." *Historical Studies in the Physical Sciences* 11 (1980): 1–48.

Brooke, John H. "Natural Theology and the Plurality of Worlds: Observations on the Brewster-Whewell Debate." *Annals of Science* 34 (1977): 221–286.

———. "Indications of a Creator: Whewell as Apologist and Priest." In *William Whewell: A Composite Portrait*, edited by Menachim Fisch and Simon Schaffer. Oxford: Clarendon Press, 1991. Explores the complexities for Whewell of the empirical argument from design, including the superiority of revelation as a way of knowing God's existence.

Butts, Robert E. *Historical Pragmatics: Philosophical Essays.* Dordrecht and Boston: Kluwer, 1993. Reprints thirteen articles by Butts, five dealing with Whewell.

Fisch, Menachim. *William Whewell: Philosopher of Science.* Oxford: Clarendon Press, 1991.

———, and Simon Schaffer, eds. *William Whewell: A Composite Portrait.* Oxford: Clarendon Press, 1991. Contains thirteen chapters by thirteen authors.

Henderson, James P. *Early Mathematical Economics: William Whewell and the British Case.* Lanham, MD: Rowman & Littlefield, 1996.

Marsden, Ben. "'The Progeny of These Two "Fellows"': Robert Willis, William Whewell, and the Sciences of Mechanism, Mechanics, and Machinery in Early Victorian Britain." *British Journal for the History of Science* 37 (2004): 401–434.

Reidy, Michael. *Tides of History: Ocean Science and Her Majesty's Navy.* Chicago: University of Chicago Press, forthcoming 2008. Places Whewell's tidal research thoroughly within its practical and social contexts.

Ross, Sydney. "'Scientist': The Story of a Word." *Annals of Science* 18 (1962): 65–85.

Ruse, Michael. "William Whewell and the Argument from Design." *Monist* 60 (1977): 244–268.

Schneewind, Jerome B. "Whewell's Ethics." *American Philosophical Quarterly Monograph Series 1* (1968): 108–141.

Smith, Crosbie. "Geologists and Mathematicians: The Rise of Physical Geology." In *Wranglers and Physicists: Studies on Cambridge Physics in the Nineteenth Century*, edited by

Peter M. Harman. Manchester, U.K.: Manchester University Press, 1985.

Snyder, Laura J. "William Whewell." In *The Stanford Encyclopedia of Philosophy*, edited by Edward N. Zalta. Spring 2004. Available from http://plato.stanford.edu/archives. Discusses and evaluates previous interpretations of Whewell's philosophy of science.

———. *Reforming Philosophy: A Victorian Debate on Science and Society.* Chicago: University of Chicago Press, 2006. Examines the many aspects of the Whewell-Mill debate.

Wettersten, John R. *Whewell's Critics: Have They Prevented Him from Doing Good?* Edited by James A. Bell. Amsterdam: Rodopi, 2005.

Wilson, David B. "Herschel and Whewell's Version of Newtonianism." *Journal of the History of Ideas* 35 (1974): 79–97.

———. "Convergence: Metaphysical Pleasure versus Physical Constraint." In *William Whewell: A Composite Portrait*, edited by Menachim Fisch and Simon Schaffer. Oxford: Clarendon Press, 1991.

———. "Arbiters of Victorian Science: George Gabriel Stokes and Joshua King." In *From Newton to Hawking: A History of Cambridge University's Lucasian Professors of Mathematics*, edited by Kevin C. Knox and Richard Noakes. Cambridge, U.K.: Cambridge University Press, 2003. Indicates various ways in which Whewell's ideas and committees helped shape the context of two of Cambridge's Lucasian professors.

Wise, M. Norton, and Crosbie Smith. "Work and Waste: Political Economy and Natural Philosophy in Nineteenth Century Britain (II)." *History of Science* 27 (1989): 391–449. Discusses Whewell at length.

Yanni, Carla. "On Nature and Nomenclature: William Whewell and the Production of Architectural Knowledge in Early Victorian Britain." *Architectural History* 40 (1997): 204–221.

Yeo, Richard. *Defining Science: William Whewell, Natural Knowledge, and Public Debate in Early Victorian Britain.* Cambridge, U.K.: Cambridge University Press, 1993.

David B. Wilson

WHIPPLE, FRED LAWRENCE (*b.* 5 November 1906, Red Oak, Montgomery, Iowa; *d.* 30 August 2004, Cambridge, Massachusetts), *astronomy, meteoritics, orbit calculations, upper atmosphere studies, space research.*

Whipple was a leading planetary astronomer in the mid to late twentieth century who contributed to a wide array of problems that involved the minor bodies of the Solar System, meteors and comets, and the nature of the Earth's upper atmosphere. He will be popularly remembered for his model of a comet nucleus, but his impact was largely through his institution building and leadership in the astronomical profession.

Early Life. Born on a farm near Red Oak, Iowa, Fred Whipple was the only surviving son of Harry Lawrence Whipple and Celestia (MacFarland) Whipple of English and Scotch-Irish descent. He survived polio at age five after experiencing the trauma of his younger brother's death a year earlier. Education began in a rural one-room schoolhouse, and Whipple became a habitué of the Red Oak Library some ten miles away. As a youngster, Whipple engrossed himself in solitary and escapist activities, reading mainly fairy tales and adventure science fiction, enjoying everything from Edgar Allan Poe through H. G. Wells. He also read the *Electrical Experimenter*. In high school Whipple distinguished himself in spelling and ciphering bees. Exposed to farm life, he became fascinated with machinery and its functional aspects, occupying himself with Meccano and Erector sets as well as some chemistry experiments. Another fascination was radio, based upon watching one of his friends build and operate a ham set. At age fifteen, in his junior year of high school, he moved with his family to Long Beach, California, where his father became a commercial grocer. Whipple's father had been an elder in the local Presbyterian church in Red Oak, and the family took religion very seriously. Whipple broke away when he left home for college, but continued as a member of the Christian Endeavor Society for some time.

College Years. Whipple was bound for a college education. His precocity and the death of his brother focused his parents on his success. Los Angeles was a major change of life for Whipple, who enjoyed the climate and wider opportunities for recreation. He made friends, played tennis and started building radio sets when his family sent him to Occidental College, a small Presbyterian school in Eagle Rock, east of Los Angeles. He found Occidental wanting and so lobbied his parents to allow him to switch to UCLA, which he did, though he was required to come home on the weekends to work in the grocery store.

Whipple's parents hoped he would take up medicine, but he resisted, opting for mathematics, in which he excelled. At UCLA, however, he found astronomy intriguing as it was then taught by Frederick C. Leonard. Through Leonard, Whipple secured a graduate fellowship to Berkeley in 1927. Whipple did not attribute his later interests to Leonard, and in fact dated his exposure to orbit theory to his graduate years, when he studied mainly under Armin Otto Leuschner. Throughout the 1920s and 1930s he was still an avid reader of science fiction, devouring issues of Hugo Gernsback's *Amazing Stories* and other pulp fiction series.

At Berkeley Whipple was supported mainly by graduate teaching fellowships (1927–1929), summer work at home and then, in 1929, by summer teaching at Stanford.

In 1930–1931 he was awarded a Lick Fellowship. He married Dorothy Woods of Los Angeles in 1928 and they had one son, Earle Raymond, born in 1930.

Whipple excelled in orbit theory under Leuschner, but he was also exposed to astrophysics under Donald Menzel from Lick Observatory, and to stellar astronomy under Robert Trumpler and C. Donald Shane. There was a competitive spirit among the graduate students performing orbit computations, seeing who could compute the fastest. Whipple's orbit for newly discovered Pluto, cogenerated with Ernest Clare Bower and two other students working under Leuschner's direction, was published in 1930. It was his second publication, and gained some notoriety in the initial excitement over the question of whether Pluto was in fact the planet predicted by Percival Lowell in 1915.

Despite his passion for orbit theory, Whipple knew that an astrophysics thesis would put him in the mainstream. So he worked under Menzel at Lick to conduct spectroscopic observations, and in 1931 completed his thesis, a spectrophotometric study of two Cepheid variables in which he attempted to describe the variations in line profiles for Cepheids based upon a pulsation model. He did not succeed in this, although his thesis was accepted. This experience, and subsequent attempts at Harvard to engage in mainstream astrophysics, proved elusive, so he concentrated in the more tractable realm of mathematical astronomy and orbit theory.

Even so, Whipple worked better with Menzel than with any of the more traditional Lick astronomers. Menzel recommended Whipple to Harlow Shapley, director of the Harvard College Observatory, for a junior observer position. There were other openings, but Whipple opted for the "big puddle" (Whipple oral history, 29 April 1977, p. 35).

Harvard College Observatory. One of Whipple's first tasks as an instructor at Harvard was to transfer a set of photographic patrol cameras and other instruments some twenty-six miles to the west, to the Agassiz Observing Station in Harvard, Massachusetts. He also engaged in a range of observational studies that centered on Shapley's galaxy programs, studied Nova Herculis with Cecilia Payne-Gaposchkin, designed prismatic instruments for the Agassiz Station, discovered new comets, computed asteroid orbits from observations by the Harvard patrol cameras, collaborated with Jesse Greenstein on an attempt to interpret radio noise from the Milky Way as thermal radiation, pondered the ages of planetary nebulae, and in 1939 began to take an interest in the use of meteors to study the upper atmosphere of the Earth.

Whipple's main line of work, however, emerged from contact with the Estonian astronomer Ernst Öpik, who was the stimulus for the Harvard Meteor Expedition to Arizona in the years 1931–1933, where widely spaced cameras stereoscopically captured photographic records of meteor trails to improve knowledge of their orbits, specifically to confirm that a large portion had hyperbolic orbits and therefore came from deep space. Öpik held firmly to a vision of a vast reservoir of comet nuclei, asteroids, and meteors centered on the Sun but at nearly interstellar distances. Using Öpik's statistical methods, Whipple began studying meteor radiants in 1933, and then started improving Harvard's observational techniques using new reliable synchronous motors to drive image choppers that provided rate information for the trails. He set up cameras on campus and at Agassiz, and was soon rewarded with sets of trail plates that promised improved orbits. Expecting to confirm Öpik's hyperbolic orbits, Whipple soon realized that all the orbits were elliptical. His conclusions drew Öpik's enmity initially, but it led Whipple to refine his techniques of analysis and to improve knowledge of meteor orbits to the point where he realized that their velocities and deceleration rates could reveal valuable information about the earth's uppermost atmosphere. He was promoted to lecturer in 1938.

The War Years. In January 1943, Whipple entered war work at Harvard's Office of Scientific Research and Development (OSRD) facility, the Radio Research Laboratory, focusing on radar countermeasures. The previous several years, however, had not been easy for him. At Shapley's behest, he wrote one of the Harvard Books on Astronomy, *Earth, Moon and Planets,* which appeared in 1941. But personal pressures had been building, evidently since childhood, and were probably deepened by his divorce from his first wife in 1935. He suffered a complete breakdown in the spring of 1942, from which he did not recover fully until the end of the year. He was confined to a sanitarium in Milwaukee till September.

Once back at Harvard in the late fall, Whipple saw to the publication of a paper that he had planned to give in Chicago, where he had taken ill. It appeared the next year as a major contribution, "Meteors and the Earth's Upper Atmosphere." By then he was deeply involved with airborne radar countermeasures, applying theory developed by an antennae expert at the RRL to design an airborne chaff generating system that possessed the best ratio of radar reflection to weight. Throughout his civilian service he supervised five technicians and two research associates, and evidently the experience gave him seminal training in how to operate effectively within a large-scale government and military infrastructure. It was a watershed period during which Whipple gained deep insight into ways of securing research support and becoming a player in setting guidelines and boundaries for the military support of research in postwar America.

Postwar Research and Planning. Meteor research continued to be Whipple's focus after the war, but the scale of the enterprise changed significantly. Supported first by the Navy Bureau of Ordnance and the Office of Naval Research and then by the U. S. Air Force's Air Research and Development Command and the Air Materiel Command, and later by the Office of Ordnance Research, by 1950 Whipple had replaced the small cameras at Harvard's observing stations with wholly new and radical designs based upon James G. Baker's adaptation of the fast Schmidt reflector dubbed the "Super-Schmidt," with 12-inch aperture, 8-inch focal length, and 55-degree photographic field. Whipple wanted to reach magnitude limits where radio meteors were now being routinely recorded, so that correlation studies could be made that would yield critical information on the ionosphere as well as on the meteor trails themselves.

Whipple's postwar career took on a very different flavor from his solitary work prior to the war. Emerging from war work, he reorganized his programmatic research interests under subordinates at Harvard, and in the late 1940s devoted himself to becoming active in a wide range of committees and panels centered upon the organization of scientific research by the military. He worked in various capacities for the Joint Research and Development Board, later the RDB, after the establishment of the Department of Defense. In January 1946 he became a charter member of the V-2 Panel, later called the Rocket and Satellite Research Panel, under the auspices of Army Ordnance. He was a subcommittee member for the National Advisory Committee on Aeronautics from 1946, and chaired numerous study panels and review boards dealing with the conduct of the atmospheric sciences. All of this activity greatly facilitated his ability to work within government and military research and development circles, seeking ways to build up his various research interests. As an elite academic, Whipple was often sought out and encouraged by these Washington institutions; his membership lent authority and prestige.

Whatever the causes for his breakdown in 1942, the experience of the war, his steady rise in the ranks at Harvard and in the astronomical profession, and his extremely adept networking style in Washington, attest to a man who became more than fully functional, though how satisfied that made him remains unknown. He was promoted to associate professor in 1945 and in 1947 became chairman of the Committee on Concentration in the Physical Sciences at Harvard. By the late 1940s he was lecturing some six hours per week, supervising upward of fifteen graduate students, and in 1949 was asked to assume the responsibility of chairman of the Department of Astronomy, the teaching arm of Harvard College Observatory. He administered the academic affairs of the observatory, supervising four lecturers and five research assistants. He may not have been too happy with this responsibility, a chore Menzel himself had earlier rejected, because in July 1949 he applied for the position of superintendent of the Optics Division at the Naval Research Laboratory, claiming this would increase his chances of performing scientific research. He made his intentions known to his superiors, and soon Harvard provost Paul Buck promised him a promotion to full professor not later than July 1951. Although still carrying the chore of the chairmanship, Whipple stayed at Harvard.

Whipple was remarried in 1946. He and his second wife Babette Frances Samelson had two daughters, Dorothy Sandra Whipple and Laura Whipple.

Harvard Astronomy at a Crossroads. The late 1940s and early 1950s were turbulent years for the astronomical staff at Harvard. Shapley's outspoken public persona had made him a pariah to the Harvard administration, which considered the state of astronomy to be in a shambles. His scheduled retirement in September 1952 gave the administration the chance to appoint an external review committee, headed by J. Robert Oppenheimer. They duly found Harvard astronomy seriously deficient, mainly in facilities, but also in staff. No one on the present staff was deemed worthy to be the new director. Divisive factions on the staff, split along lines created during the war over war research, were making the place dysfunctional. Of all the senior staff, Whipple tried to keep the lowest profile until Menzel emerged as acting director, whereupon Whipple backed him vigorously. He aligned with Menzel as both saw the value of parlaying Washington contacts to establish new lines of patronage that weakened the traditional autocracy of the observatory director, Shapley. Bart Bok, who aligned with Shapley, bitterly accused Whipple of chiding his righteous refusal to court military funding and suggesting that he modify his research programs to be amenable to military support.

In one of his first actions, Menzel managed to get Bok and Whipple to shake hands and agree to work together to manage observatory responsibilities. Menzel also campaigned for equitable pay for Cecilia Payne-Gaposchkin, and as a result garnered support from the majority of the senior staff. Drastic steps he took to bring fiscal controls to observatory operations earned him the enmity of some staff, but convinced the Harvard administration that Menzel would be an effective director if no truly outstanding external candidate came forth. Menzel was designated Shapley's successor in January 1954.

Whipple's Growing Research Empire. Menzel was Whipple's strongest ally at Harvard and under his direction Whipple flourished. Baker's Super-Schmidt design had improved knowledge of meteor orbits by two orders of

Fred L. Whipple. Whipple holding a 20 pound chunk of metal believed to be part of Sputnik IV, the Russian satellite. © BETTMAN/CORBIS.

magnitude, making it possible to explore the physics of meteor ablation caused by frictional heating from atmospheric drag. He and his assistants also studied the "jet action" on heated rotating solid bodies, which he soon found he could apply to the behavior of cometary nuclei encountering solar heating in the inner Solar System. Whipple and others had long suspected that a comet nucleus had to carry a reservoir of gaseous material in the solid state that would sublime into jets of gas when heated by solar radiation. But Whipple also realized that jets from a spinning nucleus would produce an acceleration different from the direction of solar gravitational forces, and hence there would be non-gravitational forces perturbing the comet's motion around the sun. This, he realized, could explain the peculiar motions plotted for some comets that oddly deviated from simple elliptical motion. Whipple parlayed this brilliant interpretation into a series of studies of non-gravitational effects on long-period comets including an analysis of the orbit of the famous Comet Encke, showing it to be a very old comet associated with the Taurid meteoroid streams.

Of even greater value was Whipple's development of a theory of cometary structure, his "icy conglomerate model" that emerged as he was exploring deviations from purely gravitational influences. In December 1949 he proposed a series of tests of his model, both orbital tests and spectroscopic tests for suspected emission characteristics of the jets, and in subsequent years, brought many of them to fruition, firmly establishing the model.

Among American astronomers of that day, Whipple was the strongest advocate of space flight. He remained with the interservice V-2 Panel from its inception through every stage of its evolution until it suspended operation in the early 1960s. His passion for science fiction and his pursuit of upper atmosphere studies placed him not only at the center of the actual activities, but among those advocating a future in space.

After participating in a 1951 Symposium on Spaceflight held at the Hayden Planetarium, Whipple became part of a group of writers for *Collier's* that produced a popular book titled *Across the Space Frontier*, published in 1952. He wrote about the exploration of the Moon, the kinds of astronomical observations possible from a space station, the use of robotic telescopes free-flying around a manned space station, and means of securing spectroscopic and photometric observations in the far-UV and x-ray regions of the spectrum. He wrote avidly for *Saturday Review* and for *Sky & Telescope*, and in June 1954 joined the Project Orbiter committee, supported first by the Air Branch of the Office of Naval Research and soon joined by Wernher von Braun's team at the Army Ballistic Missile Agency. In early 1955, as Whipple became the new director of the Smithsonian's Astrophysical Observatory, he participated in an Army-Navy proposal to the Department of Defense to launch the first artificial satellite, a proposal that lost out to the competing Navy proposal, Project Vanguard.

Whipple's advocacy of the infrastructure for space flight in most all of its forms became his public face over the next decade, as he sought to parlay his new Smithsonian Astrophysical Observatory affiliation with its new Harvard base into a major institutional center for government and military-supported space research. The steps he took in the following several years reflect this ambition. As he continued his own high-profile activities, issuing public statements and participating in advisory panels and committees, he enlarged his meteor tracking capabilities with new technologies and expertise capable of high-precision optical satellite tracking. The new Smithsonian connection made that possible.

Creation of the Smithsonian Astrophysical Observatory. One of the most significant transformations of Harvard astronomy since Edward C. Pickering was installed as director in 1877 came when the Smithsonian moved its Astrophysical Observatory to Cambridge. In 1953, the new Smithsonian secretary Leonard Carmichael pondered options for its venerable, but moribund, Astrophysical Observatory. Realizing that he could not attract a first-rate astronomer to the National Mall for solar work, he settled on an academic setting and liaison with a major teaching and research center. Among others, Carmichael consulted Donald Menzel, and by the end of 1954, Menzel proposed that the Smithsonian move to Harvard. Menzel was, of course, a major figure in solar research and so the association made good sense. He initially had a younger theorist in mind to head the Smithsonian unit at Harvard, but when its enormous potential became evident, he focused on Whipple. By mid-1955 a plan was in place. There would be shared facilities and joint appointments between the Smithsonian and Harvard, with the opportunity to build major new projects that would attract government and private patronage. The Smithsonian would fund the construction of new buildings and would act as a means for accepting a wide range of government and military contracts. Acquired Smithsonian expertise would complement Harvard strengths in solar astrophysics and in meteors, drawing to it problems of the upper atmosphere and a cross-over area envisioned as "astronomical geophysics." Advanced training for astronomers, use of new technologies such as radio and radar, and Whipple's theoretical studies in aerodynamics were also identified as ingredients in a mix that would find application in fields as diverse as astrophysics, the design of airplanes, the study of explosive shockwaves, and the pursuit of climatology models from a fuller reconnaissance of the upper atmosphere.

Dean of the faculty McGeorge Bundy endorsed this plan with Whipple as the director. Bundy saw Whipple as a man of broad vision and great dreams, most of all as someone who knew Washington and who could manage classified research projects as well as those in the open civilian sector. Whipple recalled that he saw this post as his best opportunity to realize his goal of creating a worldwide photographic satellite observing program as a first step toward building an infrastructure for managing space research. It is not difficult to imagine his vision extending seamlessly from the practical necessity of satellite tracking to the capability of a space station.

With Whipple's energies rekindled by this new administrative challenge, combined with his prudent but remarkably agile strategy and extensive Washington connections, the new Smithsonian Astrophysical Observatory (SAO) was not a mere appendage of Harvard astronomy, but a full partner and soon a vigorous competitor.

Growth of the SAO. Under Whipple, the growth of SAO was meteoric. In 1956 his division organization included solar astrophysics, meteor studies, and a satellite program supported by the National Science Foundation, the Army

Ballistic Missile Agency, the Air Force and the Smithsonian. In 1957, the same divisions remained, but staffing was tripled to several dozens of professionals. The satellite program, by far the largest in manpower and funding, was split into two divisions: a worldwide photographic network using a vastly enhanced Super-Schmidt system—the Baker-Nunn network—and a volunteer visual tracking network, Project Moonwatch, that became a burgeoning data collecting and public relations entity that, for all intents and purposes, provided public access to the Space Age. At the center of all this was a large computational analysis group.

By 1958 SAO was contracting to provide orbital analysis services for the army, and beginning to propose preliminary studies leading to launching scientific earth satellites for geodesy and astronomy. A greatly enlarged computation and analysis group now included satellite tracking, orbit prediction and analysis, and studies of the earth's albedo. A new Upper Atmosphere division pursued air density studies, stellar scintillation, lunar dust studies, and planning for x-ray and ultraviolet space telescopes. Through 1959 and into the early 1960s there was explosive growth of all these divisions save for solar astrophysics; from an original staff of less than one dozen personnel in 1955 (none who actually physically transferred from Washington), Whipple commanded a staff of more than 300 in 1961. By 1965 the roster had grown to 468 people, organized into nine bureaus and 73 identified programs, projects, problem areas, and missions. In addition to the large Astrophysical Observing Stations and the Meteors Bureaus, which included atmospheric studies, ablation experimentation and ballistics analysis, there was now a multifaceted laboratory astrophysics division for meteoritic sampling and assaying techniques, electron-beam studies and comet nuclei problems, as well as facilities to explore prebiotic organic chemistry experiments on macromolecular structure and mineral studies relevant for Martian surface evaluation.

Flight Operations managed an early SAO initiative to build and fly an ultraviolet mapping satellite, which rapidly grew as Project Celescope, initially to include facilities for tracking, data acquisition, and data analysis that would eventually serve as a model national facility. By 1965, Celescope had suffered technical delays and cutbacks, but was scheduled for launch in 1968 on the second Orbiting Astronomical Observatory. Celescope, however, also was part of a Stellar Observations division at the SAO that included a new Stellar Theory section responsible for the theoretical and observational analysis of stellar atmospheres. This section prospered and grew into a full-blown theoretical analysis group. SAO also participated with Harvard in instrumenting the Orbiting Solar Observatory series, as well as numerous experiments for balloons and rockets. A Stellar and Planetary Observation Bureau included both technical innovation and traditional astronomical studies of planets, stars and galaxies, and a large Theoretical Astrophysics Bureau explored a wide range of problems in planetary, solar and stellar atmospheres, cosmic rays, and cosmology. Smaller bureaus studied astronomical history and chronology, and there were two Central Bureaus for the dissemination of astronomical telegrams, late breaking alerts about celestial phenomena, and satellite geodesy.

SAO grew into a truly large-scale complex of systems that informed Whipple's long-term interests in the nature of the upper atmosphere, in both the physical and celestial dynamics of meteorites as probes of the history of the solar system, and in the highly critical area of geodesy, which simultaneously added to the scientific understanding of Earth and to ballistic orbit prediction and place-finding (target acquisition) on Earth. Indeed, Whipple's geodetic interests, combined with his work on the upper atmosphere, were the two most significant geophysical variables affecting the determination of satellite and ballistic trajectories.

Widening Influence. Whipple engaged in the debate over the shape of the nation's space program. He was one of a few elite scientists called to testify in April 1958 before the House Select Committee on Astronautics and Space Exploration. He urged Congress to make space a high-priority government activity, but to keep management away from the military, and, most of all, to put the control of all space research in the hands of civilian, university-based scientists. The government and military certainly had to play a role, but it would be as coordinator and launch facilitator, not as controller, in what he envisioned had to be a competitive peer-reviewed government contracting process.

Whipple's early orchestration of SAO programs reflected his view of a national space policy, but as the world changed, so did Whipple. SAO structure through the early 1960s was marked by constantly-shifting bureau and division titles, boundaries, staffing, and emphasis as the staff grew into the multiple hundreds. By the mid-1960s, the International Geophysical Year (IGY) and military-inspired divisions were no longer defined or justified in terms of a centralized capability for national purpose. Now they were organized in terms of traditional problem areas familiar to astronomers. More than an institutional retreat from early ambitions, this was a strategy Whipple adapted to strengthen the SAO's position in the American astronomical community as well as at Harvard.

Whipple was a fervent practitioner of what one of his colleagues called "organizational independence" (Lundquist, 2005, p. 5) which neatly describes how he interacted with his two institutional overseers. He pushed for institutional and professional equity for SAO within Harvard, and vigorously defended SAO's independence of action within the Smithsonian's hierarchy. Whipple's biggest challenge had been the recruitment of staff to perform the tasks he envisioned, and still satisfy the requirements of a joint appointment with Harvard. Although he attracted first-class talent, he had less success satisfying stringent Harvard standards. In time, some of the senior members of the SAO staff did gain faculty status and engaged in a substantial amount of teaching and graduate instruction. Possibly the most visible and important synergistic activity, however, was the expansion of computing facilities and square-footage available to Harvard as a result of Smithsonian growth.

Though SAO staff numbers peaked in the mid-1960s, by then Whipple began thinking about a far larger project more in line with traditional astronomical interests. His efforts to manage space research had been only partially successful at the levels he sought out, so now he turned back to ground-based astronomy, pushing for a large optical observatory in the southwest again appealing to new technologies and strategies. Aligning with visionary tool-builders at the University of Arizona, notably Frank Low and Aden Meinel, Whipple formed a multi-institutional consortium to build the first multi-mirror telescope on a scale large enough not only to demonstrate a new radical design option for obtaining huge optical collecting areas, but to compete with the largest telescopes in the world. What came to be called the MMT, or Multi-Mirror Telescope, was dedicated on Mount Hopkins, Arizona, in 1979, six years after Whipple's retirement from the directorship. Its six 72-inch mirrors were equivalent to a 4.5 meter collecting area, then second only to the Hale Telescope on Mount Palomar in the continental United States.

Whipple created his empire, building programs, staff, and facilities through what he described as a "brinksmanship principle" (Whipple Oral History, June 1976, pp. 32–33). He attracted competent scientific staff protected by Federal Civil Service guidelines. He then leveraged administrative and technical support from Congress saying his staff needed proper support as he campaigned with private benefactors pleading for a place to house all these people and facilities, and then used the facilities to attract top notch researchers. Whipple continued this style of entrepreneurship with his advocacy of the Smithsonian's observatory facility on Mount Hopkins in southern Arizona, a project he described as "a case of opportunism, making use of the Satellite Tracking Program to get the real observatory going" (Whipple Oral History, June 1976, p. 67).

A Change in Focus. At times, Whipple felt seriously hampered by Smithsonian oversight, as well as NASA oversight and Harvard constraints. The more voluble members of his staff sometimes reflected his disdain for bureaucracy. When Leo Goldberg succeeded Donald Menzel as the director of Harvard College Observatory in 1966, adjustments were not forthcoming between the two old friends and colleagues. Goldberg had been attracted to Harvard in 1960 by Menzel, his old professor, and had established a vigorous program in space solar astrophysics. By the mid-1960s, in parallel with Whipple's ambitions, Goldberg wanted to build a large telescope for Harvard in some suitable climate, but the two were never able to settle on a single vision.

The end of the 1960s was a time for retrenchment and refocus on ground-based activities. In a spring 1970 meeting of the Harvard College Observatory Visiting Committee, which included the new Smithsonian secretary S. Dillon Ripley and other high officials (the SAO had no corollary oversight committee), Goldberg was bluntly asked what he was doing about long-range planning and stability, in case agencies such as NASA were to disappear and NSF were to be downsized. Goldberg responded strongly that no plan could be created without the full participation (and consequently, oversight of) the Smithsonian Astrophysical Observatory. Whipple, in spite of Ripley's query, feared that such oversight would weaken his autonomy and so he strongly resisted the suggestion, hoping to keep the Smithsonian free of, and hence not subject to, Harvard's planning. Indeed, it would be particularly difficult to continue to execute his successful brinksmanship style, shifting back and forth deftly playing off parallel funding sources against one another.

Goldberg announced that he was resigning in July 1971, partly in protest to difficulties working with Whipple. This created a crisis that led to the full merging of the two observatories under one director. Whipple also stepped down from the directorship in 1972, and retired a year later, maintaining many of his personal research interests in cometary phenomena, meteoritics, and the upper atmosphere.

Although Whipple was encouraged to retire from the directorship, no one contested the fact that he had built up one of the greatest astronomical institutions on the planet. But more than that, and beyond his science, Whipple should be remembered as an innovator, both of new tools and of new forms of institutional arrangements. He acted as a catalyst, directing attention to new technologies associated with rocketry, space flight, optical and non-optical astronomy. He was also an inspiration, keeping planetary astronomy very much alive.

Fred Whipple died at a hospital near Boston at age ninety-seven after a long illness. His personal papers are housed in various collections in the Harvard University Archives, at the Smithsonian Institution Archives, and at the American Philosophical Society. For a man who has an asteroid, various comets, and an observatory named in his honor, citations are too numerous to mention, but he probably would have listed at the top the Distinguished Federal Civilian Service award he received from President John F. Kennedy in 1963.

BIBLIOGRAPHY

PRIMARY SOURCES

American Philosophical Society Archives.

Harvard University Archives, various collections.

Records of the Radio Research Laboratory, 1942–1946, Harvard University Archives, Pusey Library. Cambridge, MA 02138.

Smithsonian Institution Archives, various collections.

With Pamela Hension Oral History, June 1976. RU 9520. SIA.

With David DeVorkin. Oral History, 29 April 1977. SHMA AIP.

With Owen Gingerich. Oral History, 12 February 1981. AIP AV C-81-6 z.

WORKS BY WHIPPLE

With Louis Berman. "Elements and Ephemeris of Comet j 1927 Schwassmann-Wachmann." *Lick Observatory Bulletin,* no. 394 (1928): 117–119.

With Ernest C. Bower. "Elements and Ephemeris of the Lowell Observatory Object (Pluto) second paper," *Lick Observatory Bulletin,* no. 427 (1930): 35–42.

With Ernest C. Bower. "The Orbit of Pluto." *Publications of the Astronomical Society of the Pacific* 42 (1930): 236.

With Ernest C. Bower, William F. Meyer and Ferdinand J. Neubauer, "Preliminary Elements and Ephemeris of the Lowell Observatory Object," *Lick Observatory Bulletin,* no. 421 (1930): 189–192.

"A Spectrophotometric Study of the Cepheid Variables Eta Aquilae and Delta Cephei." Ph.D. diss., University of California, 1931. Reprinted, *Lick Observatory Bulletin,* no. 442 (1932).

"The Colors and Spectra of External Galaxies." *Harvard College Observatory Circular* 404 (1935): 1–21.

"Photographic Meteor Studies II. Non-Linear Trails." *Proceedings of the American Philosophical Society* 82 (1940): 275–290.

Earth, Moon and Planets. Philadelphia: Blakiston, 1941. Rev. 1958, 1963, 1968.

"Meteors and the Earth's Upper Atmosphere." *Reviews of Modern Physics* 15 (1943): 246–264.

With Joseph L. Gossner, "An Upper Limit to the Electron Density Near the Earth's Orbit." *Astrophysical Journal* 109 (1949): 380.

"A Comet Model. I. The Acceleration of Comet Encke." *Astrophysical Journal* 111 (1950): 375–394.

With S. P. Wyatt, "The Poynting-Robertson Effect on Meteor Orbits." *Astrophyical Journal* 111 (1950): 134–141.

"A Comet Model. II. Physical Relations for Comets and Meteors." *Astrophysical Journal,* vol. 113 (1951): 464–474.

With Richard N. Thomas, "The Physical Theory of Meteors. II. Astroballistic Heat Transfer." *Astrophysical Journal* 114 (1951): 448.

"On Meteor Masses and Densities," *Astronomical Journal* 57 (1952): 28.

"Photographic Meteor Orbits and their Distribution in Space." *Astronomical Journal* 59 (1954): 201.

"A Comet Model. III. The Zodiacal Light." *Astrophysical Journal* 121 (1955): 750.

With J. Allen Hynek and Karl G. Henize. "Report on the Precision Optical Tracking Program for Artificial Earth-Satellites." *Astronomical Journal* 64 (1959): 52.

"Evidence for a Comet Belt beyond Neptune." *Proceedings of the National Academy of Sciences* 51 (1964): 711–718.

With Richard B. Southworth and Carl S. Nilsson, "Studies in Interplanetary Particles." SAO Special Report #239, 1967.

The Collected Contributions of Fred L. Whipple. Cambridge, MA: Smithsonian Astrophysical Observatory, 1972.

"Incentive of a Bold Hypothesis: Hyperbolic Meteors and Comets." In *Education in and History of Modern Astronomy,* edited by Richard Berendzen. New York: New York Academy of Sciences, 1972.

With Walter F. Huebner. "Physical Processes in Comets." *Annual Review of Astronomy and Astrophysics* 14 (1976): 143–172.

"Rotation and Outbursts of Comet P/Schwassmann-Wachmann 1." *Astronomical Journal* 85 (1980): 305–313.

"The Cometary Nucleus—Current Concepts." *Astronomy and Astrophysics* 187 (1987): 852–858.

"Comets in the Space Age." *Astrophysical Journal* 341 (1989): 1–15.

"The Black Heart of Comet Halley," *Sky and Telescope* 73 (March 1987): 242–245.

OTHER SOURCES

Aguirre, Edwin L. "Fred L. Whipple (1906–2004)." *Sky & Telescope* 108, no. 6 (2004): 130.

DeVorkin, David. *Science with a Vengeance: How the Military Created the US Space Sciences after World War II.* New York: Springer-Verlag, 1992. Reprinted, 1993, paperback study edition.

———. "Who Speaks for Astronomy? How Astronomers Responded to Government Funding after World War II." *Historical Studies in the Physical and Biological Sciences* 31, part 1 (2000): 55–92.

———. "SAO during the Whipple Years: The Origins of Project Celescope." In *The New Astronomy: Opening the Electromagnetic Window and Expanding our View of Planet Earth,* edited by Wayne Orchiston. New York: Springer, 2005.

Doel, Ronald E. "Redefining a Mission: The Smithsonian Astrophysical Observatory on the Move." *Journal for the History of Astronomy* 21 (1990): 137–153.

———. *Solar System Astronomy in America.* Cambridge, U.K. and New York: Cambridge University Press, 1996.

Lundquist, Charles A. "Fred L. Whipple, Pioneer in the Space Program." *Papers of the International Astronautical Congress,* 17–21 October 2005. IAC-05-E4.1.04.

Marsden, Brian. "Fred Lawrence Whipple (1906–2004)." *Publications of the Astronomical Society of the Pacific* 117 (2005): 1452–1458.

Thomas, Shirley. "Fred L. Whipple." In *Men of Space,* vol. 2, Philadelphia, PA: Chilton, 1961.

Yeomans, Donald Keith, "Fred Lawrence Whipple, 1906–2004." *Bulletin of the American Astronomical Society* 36 (2004): 1688–1690.

David DeVorkin

WHITNEY, HASSLER (*b.* New York, New York, 23 March 1907; *d.* Princeton, New Jersey, 10 May 1989), *mathematician, topology, geometry.*

One of the most creative mathematicians of the twentieth century, Whitney contributed fundamental notions and results to several areas of mathematics. His impact was most forcefully felt in topology, where he founded the field of differential topology.

Hassler Whitney was born to an accomplished family; his father, Edward Baldwin Whitney, was a state supreme court judge and his mother, Josepha Newcomb, an artist, was active in politics. His grandfathers were William D. Whitney, a noted Sanskrit scholar, and Simon Newcomb, a renowned astronomer and political economist. While young, Whitney spent two years in Switzerland, where he took up mountaineering, a lifelong passion. Among climbers, he is known for the first ascent of the Whitney-Gilman ridge on Cannon cliff in New Hampshire, which he made with his cousin in 1929. He is considered a pioneer in the fast and light style of climbing. His passion of mountaineering was shared by some of his colleagues in topology with whom he climbed in Switzerland.

Whitney went to Yale University, where he graduated in 1928 with a degree in physics. He stayed on a year longer to earn a degree in music in 1929; he was an accomplished player of the violin and the viola, and a member of local orchestras during his life. He earned a PhD in mathematics at Harvard University in 1932, under the direction of George Birkhoff, on the subject of graph coloring. By 1930 he was already an instructor at Harvard, and he remained there until 1952, a full professor from 1946. He became a permanent member of the faculty at the Institute for Advanced Study in Princeton in 1952, where he stayed until retirement in 1977.

Whitney's thesis on graph theory was motivated by the four-color conjecture, that every planar map of con-

nected countries may be colored using four colors; he became interested in this famous problem as an undergraduate and remained so throughout his career. The problem of coloring a map may be studied by assigning to a planar map its dual graph constructed as follows: place a point, a vertex, in each country; then join two points together with a line, an edge, if there is a border shared by two countries. This set of vertices, edges, and adjacency data form the dual graph. If you can color the vertices of this graph in such a way that no edge joins vertices of the same color, then you have colored the original map. Whitney studied the number of colorings of a graph as a function of the number of colors used. This function is a polynomial, now called the chromatic polynomial of the graph. He derived formulas for the coefficients of this polynomial using what he called a "logical expansion," which is a version of the principle of inclusion-exclusion for which he gave several other applications. Borrowing from the apparatus of combinatorial topology, he introduced in 1932 a combinatorial generalization of the dual of a planar graph, now called the Whitney dual. He proved that the existence of this dual is equivalent to a graph being planar.

During the years 1931–1933, Whitney was named a National Research Council Fellow, and he spent the academic year 1931–1932 in Princeton. He finished his thesis while there, and began to shift his research to topology, a subject being developed actively at Princeton. Whitney was attracted to problems that presented an immediate and usually elementary challenge. For example, he noticed common features in the descriptions of the edge-sets of graphs and of the linear independence of columns of a matrix. His abstraction of these ideas, which he named matroids, developed into a central idea in combinatorics.

While at Yale he got interested in the Whyburn problem on the existence of nonconstant differentiable functions with a prescribed set of critical points. In a series of papers in the early 1930s, he developed the analysis of differentiable functions on Euclidean space, proving results about when a given function could be extended from a given domain to all of space with a given degree of differentiability. Around this time the notion of a manifold was given a working, abstract definition in the 1932 work of Oswald Veblen and J. H. C. Whitehead. Their abstract definition provided a foundation to differential geometry by unifying the many competing definitions of manifold. Equipped with his results on extensions of functions, Whitney proved that the abstract manifolds of Veblen and Whitehead can always be identified with a subset of Euclidean space. This theorem provided many concrete properties that could be used to study manifolds; for example, distances make sense inside a Euclidean space, and so a manifold inherits a notion of distance from its embedding. This shows that abstract manifolds always have a Riemannian structure. Any particular embedding of a manifold determines a set of directions at each point of the manifold that are either tangent to it, or perpendicular to the tangent directions. This decomposition into tangent directions and normal directions played a key role in Whitney's later research.

In another work of his time in Princeton, Whitney studied the curves that solve a differential equation as a topological and geometric object, introducing functions that allow cross sections and tubes to be defined. These ideas were current in the study of certain manifolds of three dimensions introduced by Karl Johannes Herbert Seifert. Whitney greatly generalized this class of manifolds with the introduction of his sphere-spaces in 1935. A sphere-space consists of a base space and a total space, where the base space is a parameter space for a family of spheres whose union makes up the total space. In this context, the embedding of a manifold gave rise to two sphere-spaces with base space the manifold, one from the tangent directions and the other from the normal directions. He also introduced invariants of a sphere-space, defined by mapping simplices of the base space to collections of unit orthogonal directions in a sphere identifiable with the sphere at a given point. The set of all such collections of unit orthogonal directions in Euclidean space was being studied independently in Switzerland by Heinz Hopf and Eduard Stiefel; the manifold of such collections became known as a Stiefel manifold. The invariants were identified with classes in the homology of the base space with coefficients in the homology of the Stiefel manifolds, and these elements are called the characteristic classes of the sphere-space. Whitney's work on the embeddings of manifolds implied that the characteristic classes of the tangent sphere-space and normal sphere-space were related by what is now called Whitney duality.

Whitney traveled to Moscow in 1935 to participate in the International Conference in Topology organized by P. S. Alexandroff. The conference brought together an international community of researchers for whom common problems and newly found methods could be shared. Here Whitney presented his work on embeddings and on sphere-spaces, and he learned of Stiefel's parallel work from Hopf. He also learned of the independent discoveries by James W. Alexander and A. N. Kolmogoroff of a product structure in a simplicial complex. However, their definitions were flawed. Eduard Čech and Whitney in the coming months independently figured out how to rectify the definition. Whitney's paper established the terminology of *cohomology, coboundary, cocycle, cup product,* and *cap product* now used in topology. He was also able to apply the new structures to give proofs of Hopf's foundational results on the classification of continuous functions from an n-dimensional complex to an n-dimensional sphere.

In the years leading up to World War II, Whitney extended his results on embeddings, proving that an n-dimensional manifold can be embedded in $2n$-dimensional Euclidean space. To reduce this dimension further is not possible, but it is possible to immerse the manifold in $(2n\text{-}1)$-dimensional Euclidean space, that is, to find a mapping that is locally nice, but might cross itself in places where the crossing is well-behaved. In proving the result on immersions, Whitney began forging the foundations for the study of singularities of differentiable mappings, a subject he developed further after the war.

During the war, Whitney became involved in the war effort through the Applied Mathematics Panel, for which he served as a consultant. He worked with the group at Columbia University on problems of fire control, that is, weapons guidance on airplanes, boats, and on the ground. A coworker, Mina Rees, commented that Whitney "turned out to have an absolute genius for airplane problems from guidance studies." His involvement was deep and, though he was naturally shy, he brought his findings before military officials in an effort to change policy, and he was successful.

After the war, Whitney turned his research from topology to focus on singularities of differentiable mappings, integration theory, and complex algebraic geometry. After joining the permanent faculty at the Institute for Advanced Study in Princeton, he wrote two books, on geometric integration theory and on complex analytic varieties, which are unique in their geometric approach to these subjects. Late in his career, he returned to the four-color conjecture when one of the first attempts at a computer proof suggested a simpler argument. With William T. Tutte, Whitney analyzed the work of Y. Shimamoto and disagreed with the outcome of the computer results. Tutte and Whitney were correct, and this approach to a proof of the four-color theorem was abandoned.

By the time of his retirement from the institute, Whitney had turned his energies to mathematics education. His writings on education emphasized the need to let young learners explore "naturally, … finding one's way through problems of new sorts, and taking responsibility for the results." He involved himself thoroughly in this research, visiting schools, and talking with teachers. He also served as president of the International Commission on Mathematical Instruction, 1979–1982. For his pioneering work in mathematics, Whitney was honored with the National Medal of Science in 1976, the Wolf Foundation Prize in 1982, and the Steele Prize from the American Mathematical Society for his seminal work in 1985.

BIBLIOGRAPHY

The mathematical works of Whitney can be found in Collected Papers, *Vols. I and II. Edited and with a preface by James Eells and Domingo Toledo. Boston: Birkhäuser, 1992.*

WORKS BY WHITNEY

"The Coloring of Graphs." *Annals of Mathematics* 33 (1932): 688–718.

"Analytic Extensions of Differentiable Functions Defined in Closed Sets." *Transactions of the American Mathematical Society* 36 (1934): 63–89.

"On the Abstract Properties of Linear Dependence." *American Journal of Mathematics* 57 (1935): 509–533.

"Differentiable Manifolds." *Annals of Mathematics* 37 (1936): 645–680.

"Sphere-Spaces." *Proceedings of the National Academy of Science of the United States of America* 21 (1936): 787–791.

"On Products in a Complex." *Annals of Mathematics* 39 (1938): 397–432.

"The Self-Intersections of a Smooth *n*-Manifold in 2*n*-Space." *Annals of Mathematics* 45 (1944): 220–246.

"On the Singularities of Mappings of Euclidean Spaces I. Mappings of the Plane into the Plane." *Annals of Mathematics* 62 (1955): 374–410.

Geometric Integration Theory. Princeton, NJ: Princeton University Press, 1957.

Complex Analytic Varieties. Reading, MA: Addison-Wesley, 1972.

"Coming Alive in School Math and Beyond." *Journal of Mathematical Behavior* 5 (1986): 129–140.

OTHER SOURCES

Chern, Shing-Shen. "Hassler Whitney, 1907–1989." *Proceedings of the American Philosophical Society* 138 (1994): 465–467. Biographical sketch.

Rees, Mina. "The Mathematical Sciences and World War II." *American Mathematical Monthly* 87 (1980): 607–621. A description of Whitney's war work.

John McCleary

WIGNER, EUGENE PAUL (JENÓ PÁL) (*b.* Budapest, Hungary, 17 November 1902; *d.* Princeton, New Jersey, 1 January 1995), *quantum physics and chemistry, mathematics, nuclear engineering.*

Wigner lived a long and productive life. Born in Hungary, Wigner received most of his formal university training in chemistry in Germany, at the same time training himself in physics and mathematics. From this beginning Wigner made numerous important cross-disciplinary contributions, first in Europe and later in the United States, where he spent most of his adult life. Wigner demonstrated the importance of symmetry principles in quantum mechanics, an accomplishment that led to the Nobel Prize in Physics for 1963. Wigner made numerous other contributions to a wide variety of fields. In particular, he was one of the first to apply quantum mechanics to the theory of solids and chemical kinetics, led the World

War II effort to design the first high-powered reactors and made numerous other contributions to reactor engineering, and pioneered work in the quantum theory of chaos. Throughout his long career, Wigner trained more than forty doctoral students in theoretical physics as a Princeton University professor and acted as a statesman, lobbying in particular for civil defense. Later in life, even as he continued his scientific and political work, he also turned his talents to the philosophy of science.

The Early Years. Wigner was born on 17 November 1902 to an upper-middle-class, mostly Jewish family in Budapest, Hungary. Eugene was one of three children born to Erzsébet and Antal Wigner; Antal managed a leather tanning factory and Erzsébet was a devoted housewife and mother. Eugene's tranquil childhood in Budapest was interrupted by World War I, and his managerial-class family was subsequently compelled to flee to Austria for most of 1919, when Hungary fell to communist control.

Although both parents were Jewish, Judaism was not practiced strictly in the home. As an adolescent Wigner received religious education from a local rabbi as well as a priest. Although he prepared for his bar mitzvah at thirteen, later in his teens his family converted to Lutheranism.

Wigner attended a Lutheran high school, where he received solid training in Hungarian literature and language, Latin, history, mathematics, and religion; he received less rigorous training in physics and chemistry. During these years, as his love of mathematics and physics took root, he was known as an excellent but not brilliant student. He also got to know a student in the class one year behind his, Jancsi (Johnny) von Neumann, who would later become a close friend.

Beginning in Europe. When Wigner graduated from high school as a top student in 1920, he was well read in mathematics and physics and wanted a career in the latter field. However, prospects for obtaining a physics professorship in Hungary were poor; Hungary had only three such positions at the time, and Wigner was at a competitive disadvantage in pursuing any sort of academic position due to his Jewish descent. At the same time, Wigner's father argued that the only practical course was to take chemical engineering as preparation to join the family tanning business. Thus, Wigner began his university career in chemistry, enrolling for one year at the Technical Institute in Budapest and then, in 1921, transferring to Technische Hochschule in Berlin.

Alongside his chemistry course work, Wigner studied physics and mathematics on his own during the next three years. It was an exciting time in physics, and Wigner was in a position to see firsthand the transformation that came with the emerging understanding of quantum mechanics. The University of Berlin attracted many who were making history. Wigner particularly enjoyed a Thursday afternoon colloquium. Regular attendants included Max Planck, Albert Einstein, Max von Laue, and Walther Nernst; Wolfgang Pauli and Werner Heisenberg sometimes joined the discussion. It was at this colloquium that Wigner met other, younger men, including fellow Hungarians Edward Teller and Leo Szilard.

During his third year in Berlin, Wigner began working at the Kaiser Wilhelm Institute in the suburb of Dahlem. It was there that he met Michael Polanyi, a physical chemist who was also a native of Budapest. Polanyi agreed to be Wigner's thesis advisor for a doctoral dissertation in chemical engineering that contained the first theory of rates of disassociation and association of molecules.

After receiving his doctoral degree in 1925, the twenty-two-year-old Wigner dutifully returned home to Budapest to help his father at the tannery. Not satisfied with the work, however, after a year he happily accepted an assistantship set up by Polanyi with the x-ray crystallographer Karl Weissenberg at the University of Berlin.

Recognizing Wigner's fine command of mathematics, Weissenberg assigned him a problem that required an exploration of the elementary aspects of group or symmetry theory. Since he was also well-versed in the new physics of the time, Wigner soon realized the vast potential of applying symmetry theory to quantum mechanics. Using the tools of group theory, Wigner was able to derive many rules for atomic spectra following from the existence of rotational symmetry.

After a few months, Weissenberg made arrangements for Wigner to work with Richard Becker, who had recently been given a chair at the university in theoretical physics. In 1927 Becker, in turn, suggested that Wigner work with David Hilbert, a highly distinguished mathematician at the University of Göttingen. Hilbert became ill and retreated from professional work, leaving Wigner without formal responsibilities. Wigner's time in Göttingen was hardly unproductive, however. He formed friendly ties with James Franck and collaborated with Victor Weisskopf, who was then a student, on a paper on spectral line shape. In addition, at the suggestion of Szilard, Wigner began a book, *Group Theory and Its Application to Quantum Mechanics* (1931), which became famous. By the time he left Göttingen, Wigner had firmly launched a career in science. Not only had he begun the book that would make his name, but he had started the line of research that would later lead to the Nobel Prize.

The Young American Professor. Wigner returned to Berlin in 1928 to work on his book, which was published in 1931, and continue his research. While there he

Eugene Wigner. © CORBIS.

received a letter from Princeton University in New Jersey that opened a new chapter in his life. Princeton offered a lectureship in mathematical physics. Although the position was half-time and temporary, the salary was relatively enormous—at seven hundred dollars per month, the pay was more than eight times what Wigner had received in Germany. The unusual offer came because John von Neumann had been offered a full-time tenured faculty position at Princeton but was reluctant to cut his ties in Europe, despite the growing wave of anti-Semitism. To get his foot in the U.S. door while preserving an exit strategy, he asked the Princeton administration to allow himself and Wigner to share an appointment. Princeton agreed, with the proviso that Wigner would not have tenure.

The end result was that in 1930, both von Neumann and Wigner joined the Princeton faculty. For the next three years both young scientists split their time between Europe and Princeton, until the rising tide of Nazism ended their transatlantic crisscrossings. The half-time Princeton arrangement was extended until 1936; von Neumann subsequently joined the faculty of the newly created Institute of Advanced Study at Princeton.

Wigner decided to emigrate permanently and on 8 January 1937 became a U.S. citizen. The previous fall Wigner, disappointed that he had not been given tenure and a promotion, took a leave of absence from Princeton and accepted an acting professorship arranged by Gregory Breit at the University of Wisconsin–Madison.

In his first eight years in America, Wigner conducted research in a wide range of topics in physics and chemistry. During this intensely productive period he made advances in three subfields of physics.

Wigner's contribution to solid-state physics began at Princeton and continued at Madison. Working with Frederick Seitz, his first graduate student, he found ways to connect aspects of solid-state physics to quantum mechanics. A prime example was the development of a wave function for metallic sodium's ground state. When the results of this work were combined with calculations made by Wigner on a gas of free electrons, quantum mechanics could be used to derive the binding energy (or energy of sublimation) of the metal from fundamentals. This line of inquiry was expanded upon by Wigner and various students, including John Bardeen.

Wigner also made major contributions to theoretical nuclear physics at its earliest stage. Shortly after the discovery of the neutron in 1932 and the subsequent understanding that atomic nuclei are built from protons and neutrons, he investigated a number of related topics, including early measurements of deuteron properties, neutron-proton scattering, and the internucleon force and its symmetry properties. His work with nuclear forces led to the conclusion that there were four types of such forces, depending on whether they allow for exchange of electric charge and/or spin between neutrons and protons. The force that allows neither exchange came to be known as the Wigner force. Later in the decade Wigner and others, including Eugene Feenberg, developed supermultiplet theory, which employed spatial symmetry to help describe nuclear states. In addition, while at Wisconsin, Wigner worked with Breit to develop a tool still standard in nuclear theory: the Breit-Wigner formula for the reaction cross section in terms of nuclear parameters.

Wigner also made important contributions to the development of relativistic quantum mechanics. In a 1939 paper, "On Unitary Representations of the Inhomogeneous Lorentz Group," he set his sights on the homogeneous Lorentz group, a group involving time-dependent symmetries (or symmetry groups) that also include time-translation invariance. In his analysis of its irreducible representations, he was able to provide a complete classification of all the elementary particles that were then known.

In Madison, Wigner met and married a young physics student, Amelia Frank. Tragically, she died of cancer less than a year after their December 1936 wedding. Despite the many close relationships he had developed in Wisconsin and his highly productive years there, Wigner in his grief longed for a change of scene. Therefore, he was receptive when Princeton made him an offer. In the autumn of 1938, Wigner arrived at Princeton with the promotion he had previously craved: he was now Thomas D. Jones Professor of Mathematical Physics.

War Takes Center Stage. After returning to Princeton, Wigner became so concerned with the rising power of Adolf Hitler and the growing threat of world war that he brought his parents to the United States. Shortly thereafter came the announcement that fission had been discovered. Like others who knew subatomic physics, Wigner immediately realized that fission opened the possibility of a weapon of unprecedented power.

Although Wigner continued to pursue his multifaceted basic research program, he was increasingly drawn to war-related applied projects. His first worry was that a fission weapon was feasible and the Germans might develop it. He discussed the issue with Szilard and Teller, cohorts from his early Berlin days who had by then also emigrated to the United States. They agreed that Wigner and Szilard should enlist Einstein's help in warning the U.S. government of the potential threat. The result was the famous letter from Einstein to President Franklin D. Roosevelt delivered by economist Alexander Sachs, who acted as the president's unofficial advisor.

Wigner and others wondered whether, given subsequent bureaucratic sluggishness, the letter actually speeded the formation of the U.S. atomic bomb project. In any case, the letter did provide six thousand dollars from the U.S. government to Enrico Fermi to further his efforts to create a nuclear chain reaction in a system of natural uranium and pure graphite. Alongside these efforts Wigner and others—including Werner Heisenberg in Germany—made the necessary theoretical calculations, so that by 1942 much of the basic theory for reactor physics had been developed.

In April 1942 Wigner took a formal leave of absence from Princeton and joined the University of Chicago's Metallurgical Laboratory, where nuclear chain reaction studies were consolidated. He came with his second wife, Mary Wheeler; they had been married a little more than a year. The couple would eventually have two children, Martha and David.

From 1942 to 1945 Wigner supervised twenty theoretical physicists in office space at the University of Chicago. About half a year after his transfer to the Midwest, he was one of fifty people to witness Fermi's demonstration of the first self-sustaining chain reaction underneath the university's Stagg Field Stadium.

Wigner and his group studied chain reactions, the effect of neutrons and (γ-rays on matter; they also helped plan and evaluate experimental work. Their main task, however, was a job of enormous proportions: they designed the first full-scale plutonium producing reactors that were later build at Hanford, Washington.

The job drew on Wigner's knowledge of chemical engineering as well his background in theoretical physics. From the beginning, the general outlines of the Hanford reactors were specified: They would have a lattice made of natural uranium fuel rods that were embedded in a graphite moderator. This left open a number of major decisions, however, including the choice of coolant and how it would be used; the dimensions of the reactor and fuel rods; the design of the fuel rods; and the exact placement of cladding, tube materials, and control rods. All of these decisions required detailed analysis of such issues as heat transfer and pressure drops. Wigner was intimately involved in the smallest design decisions; when DuPont later built the reactors, he personally double-checked every blueprint.

The choice of coolant was particularly key. The original idea was that the reactors would be helium cooled. Thanks to his chemical engineering background, however, Wigner saw a problem, noting that helium-cooled reactors would have to be operated at excessively high temperatures, causing tremendous materials problems. He suggested that, instead, ordinary water be used, a brave suggestion because it had not yet been proven that such a system could sustain a chain reaction. Wigner acknowledged that reactivity would be a bit less if water were used rather than helium, but he insisted that his calculations and Fermi's experiments showed that a workable water-cooled reactor could be built. As he noted, such a reactor could also be constructed more quickly than a reactor with helium cooling. The head of the Metallurgical Laboratory, Arthur Compton, was convinced by Wigner's arguments and approved the design of a massive, water-cooled reactor.

Wigner's group completed a design report for the reactors in January 1943. For the most part, DuPont adopted the design and began construction of the reactors. The start-up of the first reactor in 1944 was marred by crisis: Xenon-135, an unexpected fission product, absorbed so many neutrons that the chain reaction stalled before going to full design power. A team that included Fermi and John Wheeler diagnosed the problem, and DuPont engineers found a way to add extra uranium to the reactor to counteract the xenon poisoning. The Hanford reactors went on successfully to complete their mission: they produced sufficient plutonium for the second atomic weapon, which was dropped on Nagasaki in August 1945.

Further Contributions to Reactors. Wigner returned to Princeton in 1947. As he resumed his research career, he

and his group went on to make numerous other contributions to reactor engineering after they turned the Hanford reactors over to DuPont for routine operation. During this period Wigner invented techniques later taught in reactor-design textbooks. In addition, he anticipated what later came to be known as the Wigner disease, that is, the swelling of a reactor's crystal lattice that occludes the fuel elements, a condition resulting from the intense bombardment of graphite by neutrons. During the war, Wigner's name was on thirty-seven engineering patents for various types of reactors.

In 1945 Wigner proposed that Clinton Laboratories in Tennessee (which during World War II housed pilot plutonium-producing reactors and enriched uranium for the uranium bomb) should be converted into a postwar reactor facility. In 1948 Clinton became such a facility, known as the Oak Ridge National Laboratory.

In 1947, before the conversion, Wigner served as Clinton's research director. In this capacity he formed that same year the Oak Ridge School of Reactor Technology, which became an important training facility for the new field of reactor engineering. The most famous graduate of the school was Hyman Rickover, who went on to develop nuclear submarines. As research director, Wigner also laid the groundwork for the Materials Testing Reactor at Oak Ridge, the first enriched-uranium high-powered reactor that was cooled and moderated with water.

After a short time in Tennessee, Wigner decided that he was not well-suited to be a manager in the highly politicized environment of the emerging U.S. reactor program. Therefore, he returned to Princeton at the end of summer in 1947 to do basic research. Wigner continued to be a consultant to Oak Ridge under the management of his successor, Alvin Weinberg. Wigner also served as a consultant to DuPont for the company's Savannah River heavy-water reactors.

Postwar Academic and Statesman. For the next quarter of a century, Wigner would serve as a Princeton professor, rounding out an academic career that would, in all, span four decades. In addition to pursuing his own research, Wigner supervised a large number of PhD students; most of his more than forty graduate students got their degrees during the postwar period.

Wigner's scientific interests continued to be broad. He undertook topics in nuclear physics, investigated the foundations of quantum mechanics, and worked in relativistic wave equations. Although his interest in nuclear structure waned, he became increasingly involved in the study of nuclear reactions, a line of inquiry that resulted in more articles than in any other of his subjects of interest.

Wigner also started and fully developed R-matrix theory for nuclear reactions. His work with R-functions and R-matrices extended beyond direct application to resonance reactions. One result of his continuing fascination with mathematics was work on random matrix elements that led to the founding of quantum chaos theory.

Wigner retained a passionate interest in civil defense issues alongside his academic pursuits. Through the 1960s he vociferously argued against the idea of countering the threat of nuclear war by building weapons arsenals capable of mutual assured destruction. In 1963, the year he won the Nobel Prize in Physics for his work on symmetry principles in quantum mechanics, he also directed the Harbor Project, a six-week National Academy of Sciences study of civil defense that included sixty-two scientists, statesmen, and engineers. Wigner's work as a statesman of science also included participation in international Pugwash Conferences on Science and World Affairs dedicated to reducing the use of atomic weapons. In addition, he edited and contributed to a 1969 volume on civil defense, again warning about the danger of atomic weaponry.

Retirement. Wigner retired from Princeton University as a physics professor in 1971. This milestone did not, however, mark the end of his career as an intellectual and statesman. In the scientific arena he continued pursuing his lifelong fascination with the mathematical foundations of quantum mechanics, in particular the use of techniques derived from group theory. He also continued teaching, accepting a variety of visiting professorships at, for example, Louisiana State University at Baton Rouge and the Erice summer school in Sicily.

Wigner's interest in civil defense and statesmanship also persisted. He continued as an adviser to Oak Ridge, particularly focusing on research aimed at finding ways to protect civilians from nuclear war. As part of this effort he devoted considerable attention to work with the Federal Emergency Management Agency. Because the Soviets had loosened political control of his native Hungary by this time of his retirement, Wigner also became active in fostering cultural and scientific ties between Hungarians and the rest of the free world and furthering Hungarian freedom.

At this stage in his life Wigner also turned to philosophical queries. He participated in a broad range of meetings with a philosophical bent, from the annual meetings of Nobel laureates to groups associated with the Unification Church of the Reverend Sun Myung Moon. He also published a series of philosophical essays, *Symmetries and Reflections* (1967).

Mary, Wigner's wife of forty years, died of cancer in 1977. In 1979 he married Edith Hamilton. With Edith as his close companion, he continued a vigorous schedule until he was well over eighty. Wigner died on 1 January 1995 in Princeton, New Jersey.

BIBLIOGRAPHY

Wigner's papers are located at the Manuscript Division, Department of Rare Books and Special Collections, Princeton University Library, Princeton, New Jersey. A complete bibliography of Wigner's published works is in the Collected Works volumes, listed below.

WORKS BY WIGNER

"On Unitary Representations of the Inhomogeneous Lorentz Group." *Annals of Mathematics* 40 (1939): 149–204.

With Leonard Eisenbud. "Higher Angular Momenta and Long Range Interaction in Resonance Reactions." *Physical Review* 72 (1947): 29–41.

"On the Distribution of the Roots of Certain Symmetric Matrices." *Annals of Mathematics* 67 (1958): 325–328.

With Alvin M. Weinberg. *The Physical Theory of Neutron Chain Reactors.* Chicago: University of Chicago Press, 1958.

Group Theory and Its Application to the Quantum Mechanics of Atomic Spectra. Translated by J. J. Griffin. New York: Academic Press, 1959. Originally published as *Gruppentheorie und Ihre Anwendung auf die Quantenmechanik der Atomspektren* (Brunswick, Germany: F. Vieweg und Sohn, 1931).

"Events, Laws of Nature, and Invariance Principles." Nobel Lecture, 1963. Available from http://nobelprize.org/physics.

Symmetries and Reflections: Scientific Essays by Eugene P. Wigner. Bloomington: Indiana University Press, 1967.

The Collected Works of Eugene Paul Wigner. Edited by Arthur S. Wightman and Jagdish Mehra. Berlin, and New York: Springer-Verlag, 1992–1998.

OTHER SOURCES

Pais, Abraham. "Eugene Wigner." In *The Scientific Genius: A Portrait Gallery of Twentieth-Century Physicists.* Oxford: Oxford University Press, 2000.

Seitz, Frederick, Erich Vogt, and Alvin M. Weinberg, "Eugene Paul Wigner." Available from http://www.nap.edu.

Szanton, Andrew. *The Recollections of Eugene P. Wigner as Told to Andrew Szanton.* New York: Plenum Press, 1992.

Weinberg, Alvin. "Eugene Wigner, Nuclear Engineer." *Physics Today* 55 (October 2002): 42–47. Available from http://www.aip.org/pt/vol-55/iss-10/p42.html.

Catherine Westfall

WIGNER, JENÓ PÁL

SEE **Wigner, Eugene**.

WILKINS, MAURICE HUGH FRE-DERICK (*b.* Pongaroa, New Zealand, 15 December 1916; *d.*, London, United Kingdom, 5 October 2004), *physics, Manhattan Project, biophysics, molecular biology.*

Originally trained as a physicist, Wilkins was one of the participants in the Manhattan Project who moved into the nascent field of molecular biology in the immediate post–World War II era. Working at King's College, London, he used x-ray diffraction of the DNA molecule in order to discern its structure. His preparations were used by Rosalind Franklin to take x-ray photographs of DNA in crystalline form. Those photographs helped James Watson and Francis Crick to elucidate the double-helical structure of DNA. Wilkins shared the 1962 Nobel Prize in Physiology or Medicine with Watson and Crick and was active in the British Society for Social Responsibility in Science. He is perhaps best known in the history of science for his conflict with Franklin, which was scientifically and personally damaging to both.

Early Life. Maurice Hugh Frederick Wilkins was born in New Zealand to Irish parents. His father Edgar was a physician who had a strong interest in public health and the family moved to London in 1922 so that he could pursue a diploma of public health. When he finished, the family moved to Birmingham, where Edgar was a school doctor. In his autobiography, Maurice Wilkins recalled how as a boy he developed a love of science and sense of pride in British achievements in technology by reading the *Modern Boy* magazine. His childhood hobby of building models of flying machines matured into the study of astronomy and physics at Cambridge University.

Physics Career. Wilkins thrived intellectually and socially at Cambridge. He became active in several student organizations, including the Cambridge Scientists' Anti-War Group and the Natural Sciences Club. His talk for the club was a presentation on J. D. Bernal's work on x-ray crystallography. Wilkins's first mentor in physics at Cambridge was Marcus Oliphant, and after graduating in 1938, he followed his professor back to Birmingham to study thermoluminescence under John T. Randall. Luminescence allowed Wilkins to combine his interests in crystalline structure and x-ray diffraction. After World War II began, nearly the entire Department of Physics was involved in defense research on radar. Wilkins completed the requirements for his PhD in 1940, and soon joined Oliphant's atomic bomb research team and investigated how to evaporate uranium metal.

In 1944, the Birmingham Bomb Lab relocated to Berkeley, California, to join forces with the Manhattan Project. When the war ended, Wilkins was not interested in continuing nuclear research. Randall was starting a new

Maurice Hugh Frederick Wilkins. *Maurice Hugh Frederick Wilkins at work in his laboratory.* SPL/PHOTO RESEARCHERS, INC.

project exploring the links between physics and biology and offered Wilkins a spot in his laboratory. After reading Erwin Schrödinger's *What Is Life?*, he was inspired to join Randall and investigate Schrödinger's proposal that the gene was an aperiodic crystal. After spending a year at St Andrews in Scotland, Randall's biophysics group moved to King's College, London, with funding from the Medical Research Council early in 1947.

Biophysics to the Double Helix of DNA. Wilkins cast about for an appropriate research subject within the complex structure of the cell. While he was searching, he met a physics graduate student named Francis Crick, who was interested in interdisciplinary approaches to biology. Although Randall did not offer Crick a position in the biophysics unit, Wilkins and Crick socialized often.

By 1950, Wilkins had settled on macromolecules as a way to combine his physics skills and biology interests. The question of macromolecular structure was tantalizing, and evidence was accumulating from biochemistry, genetics, and x-ray crystallography. In 1944, Oswald Avery had shown that genes were made of DNA, and his work was slowly disseminated through the genetics community. In the mid-1940s, a team of researchers in Leeds had determined that DNA fibers repeated their structure every 3.4 angstroms (Å) along their backbone. Wilkins began to collect specimens of nucleic acids, proteins, and viruses to x-ray and examine using ultraviolet microscopes, and soon narrowed his focus to DNA.

In a stroke of luck, he attended a seminar on 12 May 1950 by the Austrian researcher Rudolf Signer, who distributed samples of his high-quality calf thymus DNA. While preparing the samples for x-raying, Wilkins noticed that when he touched a glass rod to the moist DNA gel, he was able to draw out a thin filament of the molecule. As he recalled in his Nobel lecture, "the perfection and uniformity of the fibres suggested that the molecules in them were regularly arranged" and would be "excellent objects to study by X-ray diffraction analysis" (p. 756). Wilkins applied this technique to extracted DNA as well as to DNA in cells, but the Signer DNA gave the clearest pictures. Along with a graduate student, Raymond Gosling, Wilkins obtained clear diffraction patterns of wet DNA and noted that when the fibers were stretched and then constricted, they made patterns that appeared to be crystals. If DNA were a crystal, then it would be possible to analyze the x-ray images and draw conclusions about its structure. The correct model would have to account for the biochemical, genetic, and physical data on DNA, but the images could provide a direct method for determining its molecular structure.

Earlier that spring, Randall had endorsed the application of a talented x-ray crystallographer named Rosalind Franklin for a fellowship to join the biophysics unit at King's. Franklin was scheduled to begin her fellowship in January 1951, and in November 1950, Randall sent her a letter describing her future research project on "certain biological fibres in which we are interested." It was a small group, Randall noted, and so "as far as the experimental X-ray effort is concerned there will be at the moment only yourself and Gosling" (cited in Maddox, 2002, p. 114, and Olby, 1994, p. 346). Apparently, he intended for Franklin and Gosling to study extracted DNA while Wilkins focused on cellular samples. Nevertheless, it is unclear why he excluded Wilkins from the description of DNA research at King's, and Wilkins was unaware of this letter.

The ensuing misunderstandings and acrimony led Franklin's biographer Brenda Maddox to call this letter "the biggest mistake" of Randall's life (p. 116). When Franklin first arrived at King's, she and Wilkins had cordial interactions, and even had meals together at the lab-

oratory. They soon clashed over scientific questions, and by the summer of 1951, their working relationship had degenerated and they had little direct communication. Franklin was committed to a fine analysis of the x-ray diffraction patterns and was not interested in Wilkins's more free-flowing approach. They rarely shared data, and Wilkins often disparaged her to Crick and Watson. In his frustration, Wilkins referred to Franklin as "Rosy," or "the dark lady." To the chagrin of many who knew her, James Watson used the same disrespectful nickname in *The Double Helix* (1980).

In May 1951, Wilkins traveled to Naples, Italy, to report on his research to a meeting on "Submicroscopical Structure of Protoplasm." His images of a crystalline DNA pattern caught the attention of James Watson, who was in his first year of his European postdoctoral research. Wilkins's presentation was part of the reason Watson decided to move to Cambridge to study the structure of nucleic acids under Lawrence Bragg. Wilkins went to the United States that summer to attend the Gordon Conference and meet Erwin Chargaff, the Columbia biochemist whose research on DNA had established the 1:1 ratio of its base pairs, adenine to thymine and guanine to cytosine.

Stimulated by his encounter with Chargaff, Wilkins returned to London only to discover that Franklin was not interested in biochemical data. She had recently noticed that DNA actually formed two patterns, labeled A and B, depending on how wet the samples were. The B, or "wet," form yielded a clear crystalline pattern, but Franklin was focusing on doing a Patterson analysis of the more complicated A form. Although Randall told Wilkins to concentrate on the B form, he was soon inspired by Linus Pauling's publication on the protein α-helix to search in his experimental data for evidence that DNA was also helical. He spent the rest of that year taking more x-ray photographs of different living samples of DNA, and trying to reconcile the diffraction and biochemical data. Wilkins contacted Signer in Vienna to try to get more samples of his high-quality DNA, since he had given all of his to Franklin, but Signer had none left.

Despite his lack of progress, Wilkins was heartened when he, Franklin, and several other colleagues were invited to Cambridge in late November 1951 to see a three-chain model of the DNA molecule that Watson and Crick had built. One look from Franklin was all it took to tell them that their model did not fit the diffraction data or rules of chemistry. When Bragg and Randall heard about the incorrect model, they agreed that Watson and Crick should leave the DNA problem to the team at King's.

However, Wilkins and Franklin made little noticeable progress on DNA in 1952. In May, Franklin took a clear photograph of the B form, which she labeled 51, but put it aside because she was intently focused on a mathematical analysis of the A form. Wilkins spent most of the summer at a scientific conference in Brazil, and he brought back more cellular specimens to analyze as he perfected his x-ray equipment.

January 1953 brought renewed energy to the DNA project at King's. Wilkins saw Franklin's clear Photograph 51 from May 1952, and understood that it showed a helical structure. He also began thinking seriously about the implications of Chargaff's base-pair ratios. Franklin had decided to leave King's and DNA research in favor of virus research at Birkbeck College, but as she was finishing up her research, she began to consider the possibility that the B form was evidence of a two-chain helix. However, because the relationship between them was so hostile, they did not consult each other on how to combine these ideas with the experimental evidence.

The King's College researchers were unaware that Watson and Crick had once again begun working on DNA after hearing that Pauling was interested in its structure. When Wilkins showed Watson a copy of Photograph 51 in early February 1953, he had no idea that it would be the catalyst for Watson's building of a correct model. Soon thereafter, Watson and Crick invited Wilkins to Cambridge to show him Pauling's incorrect structure and to ask if they could once again tackle the DNA problem. He agreed, not knowing how close they were to a complete model. When they finished it in early March, Wilkins was the first person outside of Cambridge to see the double helix. After an afternoon of difficult conversation about how much the King's work had helped Watson and Crick, he agreed that Wilkins and his colleagues would publish their data jointly with Watson and Crick's announcement in *Nature*. Gosling and Franklin added a short note describing the helical evidence in the B photographs, and the three papers appeared on 25 April 1953.

Life after the Double Helix. The validity and importance of the double helix was quickly accepted by the scientific community, and its discoverers were given numerous awards. Wilkins was elected to the Royal Society in 1959, and he shared the 1960 Albert Lasker Award with Watson and Crick. Two years later, they were awarded the Nobel Prize in Physiology or Medicine for "discoveries concerning the molecular structure of nucleic acids and its significance for information transfer in living material." (Nobel citation). In 1962, Wilkins was also honored as a Companion of the British Empire. Wilkins married Patricia Chidgey in 1958; they had four children.

Horace Freeland Judson describes Wilkins as "one who came early to X-ray studies of DNA and stayed late" (1979, p. 25). Wilkins spent many years using x-ray techniques to confirm and expand the double helix model of

DNA and RNA, and officially stopped his DNA research in 1967. With colleagues at King's College, he then turned to neurobiology and used diffraction techniques to examine cellular structures such as nucleohistone, lipids, photoreceptors, and different types of membranes.

Wilkins was dogged by historical accounts of his relationship with Franklin. He was outraged by the manuscript of Watson's *The Double Helix* in part because of the portrayal of his relationship with Franklin. Wilkins was cast as a villain in Anne Sayre's 1975 biography of Franklin, intended to be a balance to the story told in *The Double Helix*. He deeply resented Judson's implication that he deliberately took Photograph 51 out of Franklin's drawer to show Watson and defended himself on several occasions. Maddox's 2002 biography of Franklin places part of the blame for her unhappiness at King's on Randall, but provides evidence from Franklin's letters that Wilkins's behavior was a large factor in her decision to move to Birkbeck. In 2003, Wilkins published *The Third Man of the Double Helix* as an attempt to clarify his interactions with Franklin. In his account, he and Franklin both behaved in ways that prevented them from collaborating on DNA, and he regretted that their personal clash had a role in their losing the race to the double helix.

Science and Society. Since his student days at Cambridge, Wilkins was interested in the social implications of science and technology. Starting in the 1960s, he was involved with various antinuclear groups, including Pugwash, Food and Disarmament International, and the Campaign for Nuclear Disarmament. Wilkins was particularly proud of his role as president of the British Society for Social Responsibility in Science (BSSRS) from 1969 to 1991. In 1970, with support from the Salk Institute in San Diego, BSSRS organized a three-day public meeting to discuss "the social impact of modern biology." Wilkins served as the chair of the discussions, and offered introductory and closing remarks to the eight hundred attendees. In an atmosphere of intense antiscience sentiment, Wilkins argued for the value of scientific research to modern society and noted that scientists had an obligation to ensure that the public had a thorough understanding of the content and applications of their work.

In 1984, Wilkins expounded on the same theme in an address on "The Nobility of the Scientific Enterprise," delivered at the thirty-fourth meeting of medical Nobel laureates. Unabashedly optimistic, he praised scientists for their love of nature and dedication to knowledge, and urged them to consider the advancement of science as a way to further human ideals. Science and technology had done harm to the world in the twentieth century, but with a moral approach, scientists could simultaneously "save the world from war and restore dignity and nobility to science" (1985, p. 90).

Wilkins retired from teaching at King's College in 1981, having spent virtually his entire career there, as professor of molecular biology from 1963 to 1970, professor of biophysics from 1970 to 1981, and director of the MRC Cell Biophysics Unit from 1974 to 1980. In March 2000, King's named a major new building for Franklin and Wilkins. He continued to attend seminars on scientific and social issues until shortly before his death on 5 October 2004.

BIBLIOGRAPHY

A complete list of Wilkins's scientific publications is available through the Web of Science database. Archival collections with correspondence from Wilkins include the Francis Crick Papers, the Wellcome Library for the History and Understanding of Medicine; the James D. Watson Papers, the Cold Spring Harbor Laboratory; and the Linus and Ava Helen Pauling Papers, Oregon State University.

WORKS BY WILKINS

With Raymond Gosling and William E. Seeds. "Physical Studies of Nucleic Acid: An Extensible Molecule." *Nature* 167 (1951): 759–760.

"Engineering, Biophysics and Physics at King's College, London." *Nature* 170 (1952): 261–263.

With Alec R. Stokes and Herbert R. Wilson. "Molecular Structure of Deoxypentose Nucleic Acids." *Nature* 171 (1953): 738–740.

With William E. Seeds, Alec R. Stokes, and Herbert R. Wilson. "Helical Structure of Crystalline Deoxypentose Nucleic Acid." *Nature* 172 (1953): 759–762.

"Physical Studies of the Molecular Structure of Deoxyribose Nucleic Acid and Nucleoprotein." In *Genetic Mechanisms: Structure and Function.* Cold Spring Harbor Symposia on Quantitative Biology 21. Cold Spring Harbor, NY: Biological Laboratory, 1956.

"Structure of DNA and Nucleoprotein." *Transactions of the Faraday Society* 53 (1957): 249.

"The Molecular Structure of Nucleic Acids." In *Nobel Lectures, Physiology or Medicine, 1942–1962.* Amsterdam: Elsevier Publishing Company, 1964. Also available from http://nobelprize.org/.

With J. F. Pardon and B. M. Richards. "Super-Helical Model for Nucleohistone." *Nature* 215 (1967): 509.

With Max Perutz and James D. Watson. "DNA Helix." *Science* 164 (1969): 1537–1539.

"Introduction" and "Possible Ways to Rebuild Science." In *The Social Impact of Modern Biology,* edited by Watson Fuller. London: Routledge and Kegan Paul, 1971.

"The Nobility of the Scientific Enterprise." *Interdisciplinary Science Reviews* 10 (1985): 86–90.

"John Turton Randall, 23 March 1905–16 June 1984." *Biographical Memoirs of the Fellows of the Royal Society* 33 (1987): 491–535.

"DNA at King's College, London." In *DNA: The Double Helix. Perspective and Prospective at Forty Years,* edited by Donald A. Chambers. *Annals of the New York Academy of Sciences* 758 (1995): 200–204.

The Third Man of the Double Helix: The Autobiography of Maurice Wilkins. Oxford: Oxford University Press, 2003.

OTHER SOURCES

Crick, Francis. *What Mad Pursuit? A Personal View of Scientific Discovery.* New York: Basic Books, 1988.

De Chadarevian, Soraya. *Designs for Life: Molecular Biology after World War II.* Cambridge, U.K.: Cambridge University Press, 2002.

Franklin, Rosalind E., and R. G. Gosling. "Molecular Configuration in Sodium Thymonucleate" *Nature* 171 (1953): 740–741.

Gratzer, Walter. "Obituary: Maurice Wilkins (1916–2004)." *Nature* 431 (2004): 922.

Judson, Horace Freeland. *The Eighth Day of Creation: Makers of the Revolution in Biology.* New York: Simon and Schuster, 1979.

Maddox, Brenda. *Rosalind Franklin: The Dark Lady of DNA.* New York: HarperCollins, 2002.

Morange, Michel. *A History of Molecular Biology.* Cambridge, MA: Harvard University Press, 1998.

"Nobel Prize in Physiology or Medicine, 1962." Nobel Prize. Available from http://www.nobelprize.org/nobelprizes/medicine. Includes the Nobel citation and text of Nobel speeches.

Olby, Robert. *The Path to the Double Helix: The Discovery of DNA.* Seattle: University of Washington Press, 1974. 2nd ed. 1994.

Sayre, Anne. *Rosalind Franklin and DNA.* New York: Norton, 1975.

Stent, Gunther S. "That Was the Molecular Biology That Was." *Science* 160 (26 April 1968): 390–395.

Watson, J. D. and F. H. C. Crick. "A Structure for Deoxyribose Nucleic Acid." *Nature* 171 (1953): 737–738.

Watson, James D. *The Double Helix: A Personal Account of the Discovery of the Structure of DNA.* Norton Critical Edition, edited by Gunther Stent. New York: W. W. Norton Company, 1980.

Rena Selya

WILKINSON, DAVID TODD (*b.* Hillsdale, Michigan, 13 May 1935; *d.* Princeton, New Jersey, 5 September 2002), *experimental physics, observational astrophysics, observational cosmology, studies of the cosmic background radiation.*

Wilkinson was one of the most respected and beloved physicists of the past half century. He was the acknowledged leader of research in the cosmic microwave background (CMB) and an exceptional teacher of professional physicists, as well as a successful expositor of science to the general public. He was a model for experimental physicists in both his style of research and his genuine lack of pretense and ability to focus colleagues on the job that needed to be done to get to the science. A testimony to his modesty lies in his curriculum vitae, which contains the minimum information required and, certainly, no reference to the honors and awards that he received during his professional life. We now know that he was awarded an honorary doctorate from the University of Chicago in 1996 and in 2001 received the James Craig Watson Medal for astronomy of the National Academy of Sciences (of which he was a member) for his and his student's elegant experiments to measure the spectrum of the cosmic background radiation.

Beginnings with Atomic Physics. Wilkinson—known to all as "Dave"—was a product of his Midwest rural background in Michigan. He attended the University of Michigan at Ann Arbor, beginning in engineering physics as an undergraduate. As a graduate student he received a master's degree in nuclear engineering and then moved into atomic physics to gain a PhD in 1962 with H. Richard Crane in a second iteration of the electron g-2 experiment. At the time precise experiments to measure the consequences of quantum electrodynamics (QED) were at the forefront of fundamental physics research. The key element of the g-2 experiment was that it provided a direct observation of the quantum corrections to the electron magnetic moment.

Moreover, the observation was made in a free-particle system with no need to estimate corrections derived from messy calculations of the many-body problem in atoms. Wilkinson, as he wrote in a review paper (1967), believed that a fundamental result would be best understood (and believed) in a system which was pristine and for which one could directly measure the systematic terms that influenced the result. He achieved a result precise to a part in 10^8, good enough to show the quantum corrections at the level of the square of the fine structure constant to a part in ten thousand. The result confirmed the then-current theory. A prescient comment at the end of the g-2 paper (1963) states that the next-order corrections would be too difficult to measure by the technique used; a new idea would be needed.

The experience with the g-2 experiment carried forward to much of his research later. The experiments he would consider had to be fundamental, they had to be understood at the most basic level, and the systematic problems had to be measured and eliminated or at worst modeled. He recognized that developing technology to achieve a result was part of experimental physics. Finally,

David Wilkinson. *David Wilkinson at the blackboard.*
COURTESY OF PRINCETON UNIVERSITY PHYSICS DEPARTMENT.

there was a time to quit and go on to imagine and invent a new idea or technique to get at the science.

Early Princeton Times. In 1963 Wilkinson was drawn to the brilliance and elegance of the experiments of Robert H. Dicke at Princeton University. Dicke was exploring the gravitational interaction as a branch of physics and not merely mathematics. He was attempting to establish the experimental basis for the general theory of relativity and knew enough of the rapid developments in technology to apply them to new measurements and observations. Princeton had become the world center for experimental relativity. The Dicke gravitation group was an intellectually exciting environment for a young physicist interested in fundamental experiments.

Precision measurement of the Moon's orbit around Earth using laser ranging was one idea being considered. Wilkinson became part of a group that designed the array of corner reflectors placed on the Moon by the Apollo project. The corner reflectors have been one of the most enduring legacies of the Apollo program. With centimeter ranging precision using ground-based telescopes as laser transmitters and receivers, the ranging program established that the gravitational self-energy of Earth satisfies the weak principle of equivalence (Nordtvedt effect) and set stringent limits on the amplitude of the scalar part of the scalar-tensor theory.

As part of the investigations of the consequences of a scalar-tensor theory, Dicke began to think about the influence of the scalar component on cosmic evolution. At the time Dicke favored an oscillating universe and reasoned that, since the universe was not primarily made of iron (the nucleus with maximal binding energy per nucleon), there had to be heat to dissociate the nuclei remaining from prior cycles. In one of the evening meetings of the group, he suggested that one ought to think about making an observation of the radiation left from this hot epoch. Jim Peebles began to look into this theoretically and Dave Wilkinson and Peter Roll began to design an experiment. This was the beginning of cosmic microwave background research at Princeton, which in the hands of Wilkinson and his students and colleagues resulted in a revolution in our understanding of cosmology.

Initial CMB Spectrum Measurements. The story that led to the Nobel Prize–winning but accidental discovery of the 3 K background by Arno Penzias and Robert W. Wilson at Bell Labs is described in many cosmology books. The critical paper authored by Dicke, Peebles, Roll, and Wilkinson (1965) gave the rationale for the 3 K measurement at 7 centimeters wavelength made at Bell Labs. At the time of the discovery the Princeton group was well on the way to making their own measurements at X-band (3.2 cm).

By the end of 1968 Wilkinson, with his student Robert Stokes and colleagues Paul Boynton and R. Bruce Partridge, had made measurements of the cosmic background spectrum at 3.2, 1.58, 0.86, and 0.33 centimeters. The data, combined with the longer wavelength Bell Labs measurement, showed a spectrum that was closely thermal in the Rayleigh-Jeans part of the Planck blackbody curve of 2.7 K and also gave hints of a rollover at short wavelengths, the real telltale for a blackbody. The observations were all made from the ground using the type of differential radiometer Dicke had invented in his early work at the end of World War II.

The observations were not easy. They were absolute measurements in which one had to account for all the radiation entering the receiving system. The incoming radiation was ultimately compared with that from a source with known emission properties at a known calibration temperature. It was relatively easy to establish the properties of the calibration source using Kirchhoff's laws of radiation but it was not easy to account for every scrap of radiation entering the observation port.

Any hot surface at 300 K (about room temperature) radiated more than the universe, it was very important not to "look" at any hot surface even with the wings of the antenna beam. The atmosphere itself emitted and this needed to be accounted for by measuring the amount of atmospheric radiation at different zenith angles. Finally, it was critical to account for the emission by foreground astrophysical processes in our own galaxy such as synchrotron, free-free, and dust emission. The relative importance of these foregrounds depends on the frequency of observation.

By the early 1970s Wilkinson realized that the point of diminishing returns of spectrum observations from the ground was approaching and that new ideas were needed. Some other groups had begun to use balloonborne observations to at least eliminate the atmospheric emission and to allow explorations of the spectrum in the region embracing the 3 K blackbody peak. Although he eventually also began to use balloon platforms for spectral measurements, Wilkinson's attention turned to measurements of the angular distribution of the cosmic radiation.

Anisotropy of CMB Angular Distribution. Wilkinson and Peebles had the realization that the cosmic microwave background should not be the same in every direction. Instead it should exhibit a dipole anisotropy due to Earth's motion relative to the average rest frame of the universe (or expressed another way, relative to the last scatterers of the radiation, which in effect form a plasma wall around us at a red shift of ɪ1000). The major part of the velocity was expected to be due to the rotation of our galaxy (there is also a component from a galactic translation relative to the Hubble flow). The estimates for the dipole anisotropy were a fractional change of temperature of about a part in a thousand, a few millikelvin. In addition to this kinematic anisotropy, an intrinsic anisotropy due to gravitationally induced density fluctuations was expected. These fluctuations would in later epochs grow to become the large-scale structure of the universe. The amplitude and the angular scale of the fluctuations depend on the constituents of the primeval universe and were initially not well bounded by theoretical considerations.

The detection of the anisotropy became a new frontier in studies of the CMB and a new probe of the processes at work in the cosmic explosion. During this time it also was realized that the evolution of the universe was a giant physics laboratory sampling energies unattainable in particle accelerators and that the relics from the various epochs of the evolution of the universe may be still around for us to observe and measure. The synthesis of fundamental particle physics and cosmology had begun.

Wilkinson embarked on both large- and small-scale anisotropy measurements from the ground with the aim of measuring the dipole on large scales and intrinsic anisotropies on the smaller scales. The experiments carried different challenges than the absolute experiments to measure the spectrum. Now, sensitivity became important. The temperature differences expected were 100 microkelvin or smaller. There were many systematic effects which could produce false anisotropies: anisotropically distributed near radiators, lumpiness in the atmosphere, and structure in the galactic foregrounds. For large angular-scale measurements, it became important to reduce the atmospheric noise and to be able to operate at multiple wavelengths to understand and be able to remove the galactic foregrounds. Balloon experiments, even with their additional complexity and inconvenience, became the method of choice.

By the end of the 1970s both the Princeton group (Paul Henry, Paul Boynton, Edward Cheng, Peter Saulson, Stephen Boughn, and Brian Corey), using balloons, and a group at Lawrence Berkeley (Luis Alvarez, George Smoot, Mark Gorenstein, and Richard Muller), using the U2 airplane as an observing platform, had established the dipole anisotropy. The intrinsic anisotropy remained elusive. In the early 1980s Wilkinson made a major technical advance with Boughn, Dale Fixsen, and Cheng to apply a cryogenic low-noise MASER amplifier to a differential radiometer at 24.5 gigahertz to improve the sensitivity in a search for the intrinsic anisotropy.

COBE and WMAP: Satellite Measurements of the CMB. In 1972 NASA solicited proposals (Announcement of Opportunity AO6 and AO7) from a wide range of disciplines. John Mather, who had just received his PhD with Paul Richards at Berkeley, pulled together a team of scientists to propose a new satellite called the Cosmic Background Explorer (COBE). Mather conceived of a constellation of three mutually interdependent experiments to study the cosmic background spectrum and anisotropy with precision. A liquid helium dewar contained a Fourier Transform Infrared Absolute Spectrometer (FIRAS) to measure the spectrum between 3 to 20 cm^{-1} and 20 to 50 cm^{-1} as well as a radiometer to measure the Diffuse Infrared Background Radiation (DIRBE) in ten bands between 300 microns and 1 micron. Outside the dewar the satellite carried three Differential Microwave Radiometers (DMR) operating at 30, 50, and 90 gigahertz. The intent of the mission was to determine the spectrum and anisotropy of the cosmic background to a precision limited only by the ability to measure and model the foreground emission, and to search for an infrared background thought to arise from the formation of the first stars.

Wilkinson was part of the initial scientific group that proposed the COBE mission, which eventually grew to include twenty-one members who worked together for about twenty-five years. Although Wilkinson did not want an in-line position in this group, he played a key role

in the project. His wisdom derived from prior experience and his continuous attention to the systematics and their potential effect on the science were critical to the mission success.

COBE measured the cosmic background spectrum with unprecedented precision, showing no deviations from a blackbody to a part in 10^4 in the 3 to 20 cm^{-1} band, the region embracing the peak. The universe was truly in thermal equilibrium at the time of decoupling. The blackbody temperature is 2.725 ± 0.002 K, (1994a) a value consistent with those measured by Wilkinson in the early days of the field.

The intrinsic anisotropies of the CMB were finally observed, extending from the largest angular scale (the quadrupole moment) down to the COBE DMR beam size of 7 degrees (1994b). The root-mean-square amplitudes were in the 100 microkelvin region and the spatial spectrum followed a Harrison-Zel'dovich power law with amplitude independent of scale. The observations supported inflation theories of the universe's origin and strikingly demonstrated the need for cold dark matter as the source of the density perturbations that lead to the large-scale anisotropy. The observation gave strong support to the idea that the structure seen in the surface of last scattering was due to quantum fluctuations of the much earlier universe preserved by the dark matter, which does not diffuse or respond to buffeting from the photons during the expansion.

Once the COBE mission was functioning, Wilkinson began planning the next step. He had experienced the significant advantages offered by space observations in these fussy experiments. In particular, he noted the ability to observe for years from a platform with a benign (unchanging) environment and, if the instrument was designed properly, the ability to measure and control the systematic errors that plagued both ground-based and balloonborne observations. The advantages and the elegance of the science one could do outweighed the painful prospects of the many meetings and conference calls as well as the politics of big science.

He jumped in with both feet and organized the collaboration between the NASA Goddard Space Flight Center and Princeton to design, build, and fly the Microwave Anisotropy Probe (MAP). The mission measures the CMB anisotropy in five bands between 23 and 96 gigahertz on angular scales extending from 0.2 (96 GHz) to 0.9 (23 GHz) degrees. Multifrequency observations were used to separate foregrounds from the CMB. Wilkinson insisted that the mission use differential radiometers, which had been found to exhibit low systematic errors, and, furthermore, that the satellite be placed at the L2 Lagrange point of the Earth-Sun system, where the solar illumination is invariant over the year (1999). At Goddard

Charles Bennett, who had been the deputy principal investigator on the COBE DMR experiment, led the effort, while at Princeton Lyman Page and Norman Jarosik took the leads in the development.

The MAP mission was renamed the Wilkinson Microwave Anisotropy Probe (WMAP) in honor of his critical role. The publication of the first results from this mission (2003) was indeed a major step in precision cosmology and the best testimony to his unrelenting attention to performing a good and trustworthy experiment. WMAP results show structure in the last scattering surface due to acoustic oscillations in the plasma (one of these acoustic peaks had been observed from the ground earlier by Page and his students and confirmed by other groups). The angular scale of the acoustic peaks gives a standard length at a known distance and allows for the determination of a large set of cosmological parameters. The data show the universe to have a flat geometry; to be composed of specific proportions of baryons, dark matter, and dark energy; to have a well-determined age; and (besides the acoustic peaks) to have an approximately scale-invariant power spectrum of density fluctuations. In addition, WMAP, through its ability to measure the polarization of the radiation, has found when the universe was reionized at a later epoch when the first stars were formed.

On the larger angular scales, the WMAP and COBE results are consistent. More WMAP results are still to come at the time of this writing. The measurements of the CMB polarization (which Wilkinson began in the early 1970s with George Nanos, a student) is expected to start a new branch of cosmological investigations into processes during the very earliest moments of universal expansion, which may have generated gravitational waves that subsequently polarized the cosmic background through Thomson scattering. Suzanne Staggs, once Wilkinson's student who worked on a spectrum measurement at 1.4 gigahertz, has concentrated her research on the measurement of the polarization patterns in the cosmic background.

Other Significant Astrophysical Research. Although studies of the primeval cosmic explosion are the major theme in Wilkinson's scientific life, he had other interests in observational astrophysics. In 1968 it was discovered that the Crab Nebula pulsar (NP 0532) emitted optical pulses in addition to the radio pulses by which the pulsar was initially discovered. Sensing that there would be an interesting experiment using pulsars as clocks in different gravitational potentials, Wilkinson joined with Partridge, Boynton, and Edward Groth, then a graduate student, to measure the long-term frequency stability of the Crab pulsar. They developed a rapid transient photometer with high quantum efficiency to observe the pulses with high timing precision. The instrument was versatile and could

be used effectively on a small telescope; hence it was portable and one did not have to compete for precious telescope time.

To their amazement and (possibly horror) they discovered that the Crab pulsar was an irregular clock. The clock experiment they had contemplated was a failure but they had discovered that the moment of inertia of the pulsar changed discontinuously; the pulsar seemed to have a solid surface which experienced star quakes. Much later in his life Wilkinson returned to this type of transient detector in his search (with Paul Horowitz, who by the way had also observed the optical pulses from the Crab) for extraterrestrial civilizations that might make themselves known by emitting optical pulses—OSETI.

Early on Jim Peebles and Dave Wilkinson began thinking about the other consequences and observable relics of the evolving cosmology that was being discovered. The various epochs in the cosmic explosion would have left fossils. An epoch of particular interest to the Princeton group was the time when the first stars and galaxies formed. How did the first luminous objects form in the large-scale structure set by the distribution of density fluctuations that originated in the prior plasma? An observational program was contemplated to look for the infrared light from redshifted ultraviolet light of the nuclear burning from the first aggregations—the so-called second ignition in the universe.

This program was part of the motivation for Wilkinson to investigate the use of charge-coupled devices (CCD) as array detectors in astrophysical measurements. The devices at the time had been developed for the military surveillance program from space. Wilkinson recognized that they also could have properties useful to astronomy and could even be a substitute for film if the arrays were made with sufficiently large formats. They could be used in the low light levels associated with astrophysical measurements and, in distinction to film, would be linear over a large dynamic range. Furthermore, one could accumulate charge in the pixels over time without loss and thereby integrate, especially if the CCD were operated at low temperatures. Finally, they should have much larger quantum efficiency than film and could be effective in the silicon band extending to wavelengths as long as 1.1 microns.

Wilkinson and his group learned how to convert CCDs to astronomical observations and devised methods to deal with their flaws. In the early 1980s a set of students including Stephan Meyer, Mark Bautz, and Edward Loh used the CCD detectors to measure the emission by low-brightness red early galaxies and other low luminosity/mass ratio objects.

Teaching and Public Service. Wilkinson was the Cyrus Fogg Brackett Professor of Physics (a position that does not require teaching) and onetime head of the Physics Department at Princeton. He performed his departmental duties with care and excellence. He also performed a large number of public service functions for science by chairing numerous committees and studies for the National Science Foundation, NASA, and the National Academy of Sciences. His abiding interest was in teaching. Throughout his life as a scientist Wilkinson held the conviction that the most valuable thing he could do for others was to have them experience his joy in observing nature and understanding how it worked. Research was a medium for human interactions and a means of transmitting the pleasure of learning. There was never a dichotomy between research and teaching; they were part of the same process.

This approach applied not only to his graduate students but to his interaction with undergraduates and his own children. The interest in helping people understand science and the pleasure of knowing brought him into the Princeton Science and Technology Council, which was addressing the problems of bringing rational and quantitative reasoning to the average student, not just those interested in science and technology. As related by several of his colleagues, Wilkinson was one of the most influential and successful educational reformers at the university. In 1996, the year of Princeton's 250th anniversary, he was given the Outstanding Teacher Award. His style of leading by example but from behind was not intimidating and drew people in as though they were the initiators.

In the process of organizing lectures and seminars for this program he invited Paul Horowitz to talk about the search for extraterrestrial intelligence (SETI). Horowitz explained that he was seeing a few optical pulses per day at the Harvard Observatory that could be candidates from an extraterrestrial intelligence. Wilkinson saw that it would be useful to make coincident measurements at Princeton to confirm that the pulses were coming from outside the atmosphere. This was the origin of OSETI at Princeton, which became a communal, university-wide science project to refurbish an existing telescope and to operate it with amateur observers. It turned out to be a marvelous way to get many people, not necessarily scientists, into the action.

Dave Wilkinson balanced a life in science with one rich in enjoying family and the pleasures of exploring nature in the laboratory and in the wild. He dealt with the cancer that afflicted him for the last fourteen years of his life with dignity and grace. He was active to the end.

BIBLIOGRAPHY

A list of Wilkinson's publications can be found at http://www. physics.princeton.edu/www/jh/history/wilkinson_david.html.

WORKS BY WILKINSON

With H. R. Crane. "Precision Measurement of the *g* Factor of the Free Electron." *Physical Review* 130 (1963): 852–863. One of Wilkinson's earliest but also seminal papers was the subject of his PhD thesis.

With R. H. Dicke, P. J. E. Peebles, and P. G. Roll. "Cosmic Black Body Radiation." *Astrophysical Journal* 142 (1965): 414–419. His most quoted paper, which interpreted the measurements by Penzias and Wilson.

"Properties of Free Electrons and Positrons." In *Methods of Experimental Physics 4. Atomic and Electron Physics, Part B: Free Atoms,* edited by Vernon W. Hughes and Howard L. Schultz. New York: Academic Press, 1967.

With J. C. Mather, et al. "Measurement of the Cosmic Microwave Background Spectrum by the COBE FIRAS." *Astrophysical Journal* 420 (1994a): 439–444. The spectrum measurement made by COBE.

With C. L. Bennett, et al. "Cosmic Temperature Fluctuations from Two Years of COBE DMR Observations." *Astrophysical Journal* 436 (1994b): 423–442. The paper announcing the discovery of intrinsic cosmic anisotropy.

With L. Page. "Cosmic Microwave Background Radiation." *Reviews of Modern Physics* 71, no. 2 (1999): S173–S179. A summary of the observational state of the CMB.

With C. L. Bennett, et al. "First-Year Wilkinson Microwave Anisotropy Probe (WMAP) Observations: Preliminary Maps and Basic Results." *Astrophysical Journal Supplement Series* 148 (2003): 1–27. The first WMAP results opening the epoch of precision cosmology.

OTHER SOURCES

Chang, Kenneth. "Dr. David T. Wilkinson, 67, a Physicist Who Searched for Big Bang's Echoes, Is Dead." *New York Times,* 8 September 2002.

Rainer Weiss

WILKINSON, GEOFFREY (*b.* Springside, near Todmorden, Yorkshire, United Kingdom, 14 July 1921; *d.* London, United Kingdom, 26 September 1996), *inorganic chemistry, radiochemistry, coordination chemistry, organometallic chemistry, and catalysis chemistry.*

Wilkinson was one of the most influential inorganic chemists in the last half of the twentieth century. The extraordinary insight that he gained into the chemistry of most of the elements of the periodic table stemmed largely from his early work on radiochemistry. His subsequent work at Harvard University and the Massachusetts Institute of Technology (MIT), both in Cambridge, Massachusetts, before returning to his native Britain in 1956, introduced him to the relatively new science of organometallic chemistry, to which he made fundamental advances in metallocene chemistry (in particular his early recognition of the true nature of ferrocene), which was

Geoffrey Wilkinson. *Wilkinson receiving the Nobel Prize from Swedish King Carl XVI Gustaf.* AP IMAGES.

justly recognized by his Nobel Prize in Chemistry, awarded in 1973.

Later his work in transition metal chemistry was wide-ranging and led to applications of coordination complexes to organic catalysis. Two particularly significant milestones were the development of key catalysts: the eponymous "Wilkinson's catalyst" $RhCl(PPh_3)_3$, effective in olefin hydrogenation, and the industrially important olefin hydroformylation catalyst $RhH(CO)(PPh_3)_3$. He also worked extensively on metal alkyl and aryl chemistry.

Wilkinson was one of the first to apply a wide range of physical methods to elucidate the structures of his complexes. With other distinguished chemists, he was a prime contributor to the renaissance of inorganic chemistry, and with F. Albert Cotton, a former student of his, to the dissemination of knowledge of coordination and organometallic chemistry in a series of influential textbooks.

Childhood and Education. Wilkinson was the eldest of the three children of Henry Wilkinson, a master painter and decorator, and Ruth Crowther, a weaver. His interest in chemistry was aroused at the early age of six by his uncle, who had a small manufacturing laboratory in Todmorden. He attended the local primary school and then, at the age of ten, won a scholarship to Todmorden's secondary school. In 1939, he was awarded a Royal Scholarship to Imperial College (then part of the University of London) and studied chemistry. In 1941, Wilkinson was awarded the BS degree with top first-class honors, receiving an overall mark of 80 percent. He then joined Henry Vincent Aird Briscoe to work on the vapor-phase hydrolysis of halides, including that of phosgene, which was probably, in part, research for the wartime effort.

First Work on Radiochemistry. In late 1942, Wilkinson was recruited by Friedrich Adolf Paneth to work as a scientific officer on Canada's atomic energy project, first at the University of Montreal starting in 1943 and then at the project's Chalk River site in Ontario beginning in 1944. Here he met many people who were or would become celebrated scientists—his old schoolmate John Cockroft, Alfred Maddocks, Bertrand Goldschmidt, Pierre Auger, Jules Guéron, and many others, including two later exposed as Soviet spies, Alan Nunn May and Bruno Pontecorvo.

His work at this time was classified, and so he was unable to publish much of it, but he was one of the first to handle plutonium in the laboratory and to use heavy water, D_2O, for radiochemical purposes. He witnessed two spectacular incidents involving these materials: one was the accidental dropping by a colleague on the floor of the first litre of heavy water (i.e., D_2O), the second was a spillage involving plutonium nitrate. His first publication, "The Fission Yields of Ba^{139} and Ba^{140}," was on the formation of lanthanum-140 from barium-140, although because of declassification delays, it was not published until 1947. The work of which he was most proud from this early period, however, was that on the double-humped curve for the products of the slow fission of U^{235} ("Fission Products of U^{235}," 1946), in which yields of the fission products of this material were plotted against their atomic numbers. After declassification he was to write in all some twenty papers on his radiochemical work.

Final Radiochemical Work. In 1946, Wilkinson returned briefly to Britain to be examined for his PhD but went back to North America the same year, this time to the Lawrence Livermore Laboratory at the University of California at Berkeley. He was the first non-American to be cleared by the U.S. Atomic Energy Commission for work at the laboratory. There he worked with Glenn T. Seaborg (a 1951 Nobel Prize winner) on nuclear taxonomy—the study of the neutron-deficient isotopes of the transition metals and lanthanides—using the cyclotron at the Radiation Laboratory at Berkeley. It was said by Seaborg that there, Wilkinson made more new artificial isotopes—eighty-nine—than anyone else had ever done. He was particularly proud of his transmutation of platinum to gold—published in "Radioactive Isotopes of Platinum and Gold" in 1949—a feat that caught the public imagination at that time. With hindsight it is clear that this was a seminal point for Wilkinson: Working with these diverse elements gave him an unrivalled knowledge of their properties, which was essential in order to separate the elements' isotopes. This gave him a very special feel for these elements—in particular the transition metals—which he would put to good use for the rest of his scientific career. He also possessed, and developed further in subsequent years, a profound knowledge of organic chemistry, essential for a good organometallic chemist, and assimilated the physico-chemical techniques needed to characterize and make full use of these compounds.

Coordination and Organometallic Chemistry. In 1949, Wilkinson returned to Britain for a radiochemical conference and met his old mentors Paneth (who offered him a job in Durham) and Briscoe. The latter advised him against continuing his career in radiochemistry, largely because of the dependence on the availability of a cyclotron that this would entail. Taking this good advice to heart, Wilkinson decided that a new and exciting area was the branch of coordination chemistry dealing with transition elements to which are attached, or "coordinated," a variety of electron donor groups called ligands. He returned to MIT, collaborating with Charles Coryell in 1950 and 1951, and did some useful work in the area,

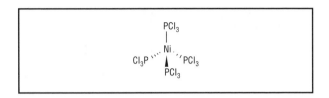

Figure 2. *Structure of $Ni(PCl_3)_4$*

making for example the novel zerovalent tetrahedral nickel complex $Ni(PCl_3)_4$ (see Figure 2).

In 1951, Wilkinson became an associate professor in the Chemistry Department at Harvard and started his classic work in organometallic chemistry, the study of compounds in which there are one or more metal-to-carbon bonds in the molecule. In the same year he married Dr. Lise Sølver Schou, a Danish plant physiologist whom he had met at Berkeley; they had two daughters in their long and happy marriage.

He was fortunate to meet Robert Burns Woodward, a Nobel Prize winner in 1965 for outstanding achievements in organic synthesis. Together they grappled with the problem of the unusual molecule ferrocene. Although it had been prepared previously, its structure and the nature of the chemical bonding involved in it was not understood. Wilkinson and Woodward, apparently independently, conceived of a revolutionary structure in which the iron atom lay between two negatively charged parallel cyclopentadiene ($C_5H_5^-$, often abbreviated as Cp) rings. In a classic one-page paper, "The Structure of Iron Bis-Cyclopentadienyl" (1952), they and two coauthors argued that the diamagnetism of the compound and the presence of only one carbon-hydrogen stretching vibration in the infrared spectrum could only mean that the bonding between the rings and the metal was "delocalized"—a well-known concept in organic but not in inorganic chemistry. They also proposed a structure for the compound in Figure 3(a), and subsequent x-ray work by others was to show that their proposal was correct (see Figures 3[a] and 3[b]). The essential point, that the iron atom lay between two parallel Cp rings, was their main achievement. They further realized that this compound obeyed the eighteen-electron rule, in which the 3d orbitals of the iron are filled by the π electrons of the delocalized rings. Woodward was later to name the compound "ferrocene." Wilkinson later published a recollection of his part of the work in "The Iron Sandwich, a Recollection of the First Four Months" (1975).

The molecule is illustrated in Figure 3(a) as the authors first envisaged it. Subsequently, it would be drawn as in Figure 3(b), but the essential idea of the structure is the same.

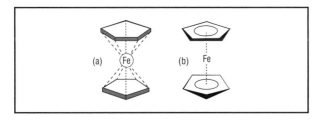

Figures 3 (a) and 3 (b). *Structure of Ferrocene.*

A lesser chemist might well have simply tinkered with that one molecule, making small changes to the groups attached to it. However, after one other paper, "The Heat of Formation of Ferrocene" (1952), in which he and F. Albert Cotton measured the heat of combustion of ferrocene, Wilkinson—drawing on his extensive knowledge of the transition and rare earth (lanthanide) elements—made analogous molecules using a variety of different metals. These included titanium, chromium, manganese, cobalt, nickel, and the later transition metals: zirconium, niobium, tantalum, molybdenum, tungsten, rhodium, iridium, and ruthenium; and several members of the lanthanide elements and of the actinides thorium and uranium. He also found it possible to attach other ligands to these metallocenes, usually by replacing one of the rings. It was this and later work on the metallocenes, as they were to be later called, which was to form the basis for the award of his Nobel Prize.

On a short sabbatical trip to Copenhagen, he made another metallocene, Cp_2ReH (see Figure 4), in which, he postulated, there was a direct metal-hydrogen bond, for its time a very novel discovery. On his return to Harvard in 1951, he was able to demonstrate that such a bond was indeed present, using the then-novel technique of NMR, or nuclear magnetic resonance spectroscopy, at that time a very recently developed technique. The use of NMR spectroscopy was to serve him well in the following years.

Return to Britain. In 1955, he was offered the chair of inorganic chemistry at his old alma mater Imperial College; almost certainly his old supervisor, Henry V. A. Briscoe, was the moving force behind the offer, recogniz-

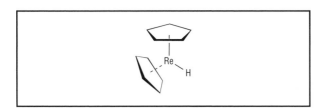

Figure 4. *Structure of Cp_2ReH.*

ing with considerable prescience the value of the metallocene work and Wilkinson's potential for initiating and doing innovative chemistry. At that time it was the only established chair in inorganic chemistry in the country, and Wilkinson accepted with alacrity. For what was then a rather old-fashioned department, it was an astonishingly bold move to appoint a thirty-four-year-old chemist who, at that time, had only some fifty publications to his credit, mostly in what might then have been considered a rather obscure area of organometallic chemistry. It was a decision that would pay off handsomely.

One of his first moves at Imperial College was to cajole twenty thousand pounds—a very large sum in those days—from government authorities to buy one of the first NMR instruments in Britain, invaluable for the study of organometallic species. Not only did it help him greatly in his research, but the acquisition stimulated other academic departments in the country to acquire and use NMR for a variety of applications.

Wilkinson spent the rest of his career at Imperial, becoming a Fellow of the Royal Society (FRS) in 1965 and receiving his Nobel Prize in 1973. The prize, awarded jointly with Ernst Otto Fischer of Munich, was "for their pioneering work, performed independently, on the chemistry of the organometallic, so called sandwich compounds." He was knighted for contributions to chemistry in 1976, and many other honors came to him. He became head of the Chemistry Department in 1976. In 1978 his chair was named the "Sir Edward Frankland chair of inorganic chemistry'" (Frankland, the "father of organometallic chemistry" [*vide infra*] had been at the Royal College of Chemistry—the precursor of Imperial College—from 1865 to 1885.) Wilkinson's formal retirement from the department came in 1988, but until the day before he died, of coronary thrombosis, he continued doing innovative research with a group of dedicated postgraduate and postdoctoral collaborators.

Wilkinson's main achievements at Imperial College can be grouped under organometallic, coordination, and catalytic chemistry, although these areas overlap considerably. These three areas are discussed below in roughly chronological order.

Organometallic Chemistry. This is the study of compounds containing a metal-carbon bond. The "father" of the subject is generally acknowledged to be Sir Edward Frankland (1825–1899), who made zinc and tin dialkyls and was responsible for fundamental advances in valency theory. Victor Grignard (1871–1935, Nobel laureate 1912) discovered the eponymous magnesium alkyl halides that continued to be used for many organic syntheses. Another key early worker was Ludwig Mond (1839–1909) who synthesised nickel carbonyl, $Ni(CO)_4$.

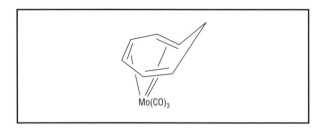

Figure 5. *Structure of Mo(η-C₇H₈)(CO)₃*

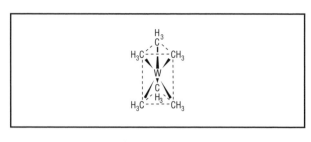

Figure 6. *Structure of W(CH₃)₆*

Prior to, during, and after World War II, Walter Hieber in Germany made many useful advances in transition metal carbonyls, and his later student E. O. Fischer (b. 1918, co-Nobel laureate with Wilkinson in 1973) also made fundamental advances, e.g., in the discovery of dibenzene chromium, (π-C_6H_6)$_2$Cr. In Britain Joseph Chatt and others elucidated that nature of metal-alkene bonding. It was however Wilkinson and Woodward's demonstration of the sandwich structure of ferrocene in 1952 that revolutionized and rejuvenated the subject.

It is typical of Wilkinson that he often changed fields, anxious to move on to new areas and his organometallic research in Britain entered new areas for him.

A significant early discovery in his Imperial College career was that of Mo(η-C_7H_8)(CO)$_3$, in which a delocalized seven-membered cycloheptatrienyl ring was bonded to molybdenum (see Figure 5). Amongst other work in this area by Wilkinson was the preparation of some unusual metallocenes with tantalum, molybdenum, and tungsten, some being hydridic species.

In 1970, he took another fundamental step in organometallic chemistry: the preparation of the first homoleptic alkyl and aryl complexes of the transition metals. (Homoleptic complexes are those in which all the ligands coordinated to the metal are identical; alkyl ligands contain no aromatic rings, while aryls do contain such rings.) This had been preceded by his isolation of transition-metal alkyl complexes containing the bulky and relatively unreactive trimethylsilylmethyl ligand, namely, $[Cr\{(CH_2Si(CH_3)_3\}_4]^-$ and $Cr\{(CH_2Si(CH_3)_3\}_4$. The most dramatic example, though, was his synthesis in 1972 and 1973 of tungsten hexamethyl, $W(CH_3)_6$, whose existence overturned the widely held supposition then that such species not only did not, but could not, exist. Later work by others was to show that it did not have the octahedral structure that might have been expected, but the more unusual trigonal pyramidal configuration (see Figure 6).

Preparation of the rhenium analogue $Re(CH_3)_6$ followed, and the rich reaction chemistry of these and other such species was studied. These two (i.e., $M(CH_3)_6$ (M = W, Re) were the only uncharged hexamethyl complexes known to exist as of the early 2000s, but he also made a number of tetra-aryls, namely, MR_4 (M = niobium, tantalum, chromium, molybdenum, tungsten, rhenium, osmium, iridium; R represents a variety of bulky aryl ligands). His Nobel Prize speech in 1973 characteristically did not dwell on metallocene complexes at all, but instead was a review of such alkyls. In 1991, he coauthored a review, "Homoleptic and Related Aryls of Transition Metals," on transition-metal aryls. He made and studied the structures and reactivities of many more alkyl and aryl complexes that were not homoleptic, and indeed this was a major theme of his organometallic work, particularly in later years.

Coordination Chemistry. Coordination complexes have been known since the eighteenth century, but it was Alfred Werner (1866–1919, Nobel laureate 1913) who from 1894 to 1910 clarified the nature of these compounds, defining the coordination number and oxidation state of the central metal atom and rationalising their geometrical and optical isomerism. Advances in the understanding of the bonding in complexes were made by Linus Pauling in the United States and William Penney in Britain in the 1930s, while later influential figures were Nevil V. Sidgwick, Leslie Orgel, and Joseph Chatt in Britain (bonding), and Francis Patrick Dwyer and Ronald Sydney Nyholm in Australia (synthesis of novel coordination complexes); in Britain Nyholm also used magnetochemistry and spectroscopy to study these materials, while in the United States Fred Basolo and coworkers carried out pioneering work on mechanisms of reactions of coordination complexes. Wilkinson's main contribution was to synthesis further novel, complexes, often with very unusual ligands, and to use some of them in homogeneous catalysis.

Good accounts of the history of coordination chemistry, by George B. Kauffman and by Fred Basolo, are given in the first two chapters of *Comprehensive Coordination Chemistry* (1987), referred to below—Wilkinson was one of the editors.

Much of Wilkinson's major work after his return to Britain in 1956 was in the area of coordination chemistry. In his early work at Imperial College, he carried out a great deal of work on rhodium, although he was fond of all six platinum-group metals (ruthenium, which he called an "element for the connoisseur," osmium, rhodium, iridium, palladium, and platinum). He used NMR spectroscopy to investigate some remarkably stable hydrido and alkyl complexes of rhodium, such as sulfates or chlorides of the cation $[RhR(NH_3)_5]^{2+}$ (see Figure 7). Wilkinson also started, with Jack Lewis, a systematic study of metal-nitric oxide (nitrosyl) complexes

In 1966, Wilkinson discovered the famous complex $RhCl(PPh_3)_3$, known as Wilkinson's catalyst, in which a chloride and three triphenylphosphine ligands surround the rhodium center in a plane (see Figure 8). Its function as a catalyst will be discussed below, but this was a turning point in his career, probably more significant than the ferrocene episode, and although not mentioned as such in the Nobel citation of his work, it must have contributed substantially to the case for the prize being given to him. "The Preparation and Properties of Tris(triphenylphosphine)halogenorhodium(I) and Some Reactions Thereof" (1966), the paper describing its discovery and the realization that it would—with molecular hydrogen—catalyze the hydrogenation of alkenes, is a classic, despite its uncharacteristically overlong and completely unpunctuated title. Another major result from this very productive period was his realization that the known complex $RhH(CO)(PPh_3)_3$, easily obtainable from Wilkinson's catalyst, is an effective hydroformylation catalyst (see below and Figure 9).

He carried out much coordination chemistry with all the transition elements, and in this respect his wide-ranging studies on rhenium are particularly prominent. Although he carried out much more coordination chemistry, the work in his later years on transition metal imido complexes (species containing the [=NR] ligand, bound to the metal from nitrogen via a double bond), was particularly significant, and his isolation and characterization by x-ray crystal structure analysis of the tertiary butylimido complex $Os(N^tBu)_4$ was a major triumph (see Figure 10). The chemistry of these complexes and their analogues were explored subsequently by many other chemists.

Catalysis Chemistry. Catalysis is the process whereby the rate of a reaction is increased by the catalyst, which is not itself consumed during the reaction. Countless industrial processes depend on it—petroleum refining, plastics production, synthesis of drugs, and so on. There are two principal classes: heterogeneous, in which the catalyst is normally a solid and functions at an interface; and homogeneous, in which the catalyst functions in one phase. It was to the latter area that Wilkinson contributed.

Homogeneous catalysis refers to reactions in one medium (usually the solution phase), while heterogeneous

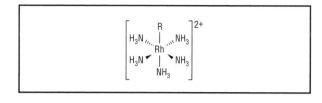

Figure 7. *Structure of $[RhR(NH_3)_5]^{2+}$*

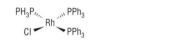

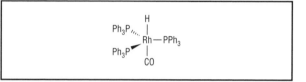

Figure 8. *Structure of $RhCl(PPh_3)_3$*

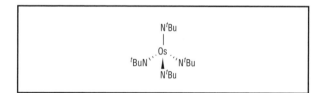

Figure 9. *Structure of $RhH(CO)(PPh_3)_3$*

Figure 10. *Structure of $Os(N^tBu)_4$*

catalysis, which in general has a longer history and greater industrial usage, involves two or more phases. Two good examples of earlier but still used homogeneous transition metal catalytic reactions are the Wacker process (1959) for aerobic conversion of ethylene to acetaldehyde catalysed by palladium and copper dichlorides, and the Monsanto process (1966) for carbonylation of methanol to acetic acid, which uses rhodium catalysts. Again, there was an explosion of interest in the area, much of it occasioned by Wilkinson's paper of 1966.

In 1965, Wilkinson found that a previously known compound, $RhCl_3(PPh_3)_3$, would catalyze the hydroformylation of hex-1-ene to n-heptaldehyde:

$$\eta\text{-}CH_3(CH_2)_3CH=CH_2 + CO + H_2 \rightarrow CH_3(CH_2)_3CH_2CHO$$

He reported this in a brief note, "Mild Hydroformylation of Olefins Using Rhodium Catalysts" (1965). The complex is difficult to make, however, and during attempts to improve the process the new complex $RhCl(PPh_3)_3$—Wilkinson's catalyst, as it was afterwards called—was found to be a much more effective catalyst for such reactions and also to effect hydrogenation reactions of alkenes and alkynes (see Figure 8). This ubiquitous catalyst effects the hydrogenation of alkenes, hydrogen transfer reactions, hydrosilations, hydroacylations, decarbonylations, hydroformylation, hydroboration, oxidations, and alkene cleavage.

In 1968, Wilkinson showed that a complex already known, $RhH(CO)(PPh_3)_3$ (see Figure 9), would effect hydroformylation—the reaction of alkenes with carbon monoxide and hydrogen to give aldehydes—and that indeed this was the active intermediate in the hydroformylation reactions of $RhCl(PPh_3)_3$, for example, for the industrially important conversion of propene to n-butyraldehyde:

$$CH_3CH=CH_2 + CO + H_2 \rightarrow CH_3CH_2CH_2CHO$$

At that time such reactions were effected industrially, through the "oxo" process, by using cobalt catalysts. But with $RhH(CO)(PPh_3)_3$ (see Figure 9), the reaction is much more stereospecific than with cobalt catalysts and works under much milder conditions. This was Wilkinson's major contribution to industrial chemistry, and after some disputes with interested industrial parties, he patented it.

Use of Physical Methods. One of the more easily overlooked contributions that Wilkinson made to chemistry in general is his integrated approach to the use of physical methods for studying the structures of the complexes that he made. Although one cannot claim him as the only pioneer in any single method, it is probably fair to say that he was the first major inorganic chemist to have assimilated and used a variety of physical techniques for the study of any one complex. Thus, by 1965, he was using NMR, infrared, Raman and electronic spectroscopy, polarography, thermochemistry, and single-crystal x-ray studies, often employing a number of these together. The use of x-ray crystallography subsequently became commonplace but was rare in the 1960s. His first paper using the technique, "A Cyclic Acetylene Complex of Hecacarbonyldicobalt," coauthored with distinguished co-workers, appeared in 1964 to establish the structure of a cyclic perfluoroacetylene cobalt complex, $(CO)_3Co(C_6F_6)Co(CO)_3$. Rather than obtaining an intimate knowledge of the techniques themselves, he was able to attract people to Imperial College who were experts in these particular areas, notably Denis Evans and Leslie

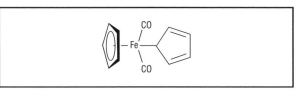

Figure 11. Structure of $Fe(\pi\text{-}C_5H_5)$ $(\sigma\text{-}C_5H_5)(CO)_2$

Pratt for NMR and Ronald Mason for x-ray crystallography.

A good though early example of his multi-technique approach, used back in his Harvard days, is one in which he showed, by the careful, combined use of infrared and NMR, that in the compound $Fe(C_5H_5)_2(CO)_2$, made originally by Peter Pauson in Britain, that there was both a delocalized (π–bonded) and a σ-bonded cyclopentadiene ring, that is, Fe ($\pi\text{-}C_5H_5$) ($\sigma\text{-}C_5H_5)(CO)_2$, and that this had a fluxional structure (later called a "ring-whizzing" structure) (see Figure 11).

Contributions to Industrial Chemistry. In the twenty-first century era of industry-related grant applications, a potential contribution to industrial chemistry is often expected from research in academic chemistry. Wilkinson, in contrast, was a surprisingly scholastic chemist, interested in the fundamental rather than the applied aspects of his work. However, as pointed out above, his work on homogeneous rhodium-catalyzed work in particular was to become industrially important, and indeed, the hydroformylation work was eventually to earn him some significant monetary reward from patents. That is because most of the butyraldehyde used for the synthesis of bis(2-ethylhexyl)phthalate, a plasticizer for preparation of PVC, uses his hydroformylation catalyst $RhH(CO)(PPh_3)_3$ for its preparation.

Although it was not realized at the time when he worked in the area, metallocene chemistry was to become very important industrially. That is particularly true in regard to polymerization catalysis and in the production of materials having interesting nonlinear optical properties.

Publications. Wilkinson published 557 research papers in his life. He believed that all scientists should make their work known to the scientific world, and a vital part of the training that he gave his students was to have their results published with minimal delay. He had virtually all his papers after 1956 published in British journals (mostly those of the Royal Society of Chemistry), believing that such national journals needed support.

In 1962, he published, with his ex-student F. Albert Cotton, a textbook called *Advanced Inorganic Chemistry: A Comprehensive Text* that eventually ran to no less than six editions. (The sixth edition, appearing in 1999, bore the names of two more authors, Carlos A. Murillo and Manfred Bochmann.) This was for its time a new kind of book, and for a whole generation of students and chemists it was a very novel approach to the teaching of inorganic chemistry. The one volume, for the first time, gave up-to-date descriptions of main-group and coordination chemistry with appropriate key literature references, together with a modern and comprehensible description of the bonding within the compounds. It remains a revered and much-used work into the early 2000s.

In 1976, a more elementary but still compendious book, *Basic Inorganic Chemistry, by Wilkinson and Cotton*, appeared; two more editions followed, the latter (1995) with Paul Gaus as coauthor. Wilkinson also co-edited two massive reference texts: *Comprehensive Organometallic Chemistry* (1982), in nine volumes (reissued in 1995 as a second edition of fourteen volumes); and *Comprehensive Coordination Chemistry* (1987), in seven volumes.

BIBLIOGRAPHY

The archives of Imperial College London hold eleven boxes of photographs, papers, correspondence, memorabilia, and other materials relating to Wilkinson, at reference code GB0098 B/WILKINSON. Lectures given by Wilkinson are at British Library Sound Archive Catalogue in London catalogue no. H7931–7932. The audio lectures are not yet available online as of early 2007 though there are plans to do this. A full list of Wilkinson's 557 papers is in Martin A. Bennett, Andreas A. Danopoulos, William P. Griffith, and Malcolm L. H. Green, "The Contributions to Original Research in Chemistry by Professor Sir Geoffrey Wilkinson FRS 1921–1996," Journal of the Chemical Society, Dalton Transactions *(1997): 3049–3060.*

WORKS BY WILKINSON

With W. E. Grummitt. "Fission Products of U²³⁵." *Nature* 158 (3 August 1946): 163.

With W. E. Grummitt, J. Guéron, and L. Yaffe. "The Fission Yields of Ba¹³⁹ and Ba¹⁴⁰ in Neutron Fission of U²³⁵ and U²³⁸." *Canadian Journal of Research*, Section B, 25 (1947): 364–370.

"Radioactive Isotopes of Platinum and Gold." *Physical Review* 75 (7) (1949): 1019–1029.

With F. Albert Cotton. "The Heat of Formation of Ferrocene." *Journal of the American Chemical Society* 74 (1952): 5764–5765.

With M. Rosenblum, Mark C. Whiting, and Robert Burns Woodward. "The Structure of Iron Bis-Cyclopentadienyl." *Journal of the American Chemical Society* 74 (1952): 2125. Wilkinson's most important early chemical paper.

With J. M. Birmingham. "Bis-cyclopentadienylrhenium Hydride—A New Type of Hydride." *Journal of the American Chemical Society* 77 (1955): 3421–3422.

With T. S. Piper. "Alkyl and Aryl Derivatives of π-Cyclopentadienyl Compounds of Chromium, Molybdenum, Tungsten, and Iron." *Journal of Inorganic Nuclear Chemistry* 3 (1956): 104–124.

With E. W. Abel and M. A. Bennett. "cycloHeptatriene Metal Complexes." *Proceedings of the Chemical Society* (May 1958): 152.

With F. Albert Cotton. *Advanced Inorganic Chemistry: A Comprehensive Text.* New York and London: Interscience 1962. Subsequent editions appeared in 1966, 1972, 1980, 1999, the last with Carlos A. Murillo and Manfred Bochmann as additional authors.

With N. A. Bailey, M. R. Churchill, R. Hunt, et al. "A Cyclic Acetylene Complex of Hecacarbonyldicobalt, (CO)₃Co(C₆F₆)Co(CO)₃." *Proceedings of the Chemical Society* (Dec. 1964): 401.

With J. A. Osborn and J. F. Young. "Mild Hydroformylation of Olefins Using Rhodium Catalysts." *Chemical Communications* (1965): 17.

With J. A. Osborn, F. H. Jardine, and J. F. Young. "The Preparation and Properties of Tris(triphenylphosphine)halogenorhodium(I) and Some Reactions Thereof Including Catalytic Homogeneous Hydrogenation of Olefins and Acetylenes and Their Derivatives." *Journal of the Chemical Society* (A) (1966): 1711–1732. One of the twentieth century's classic papers on inorganic chemistry.

With D. Evans and G. Yagupsky. "Reaction of Hydridocarbonyltris(triphenylphosphine)rhodium with Carbon Monoxide, and of the Reaction Products, Hydridocarbonylbis-(triphenylphsphine)rhodium and Dimeric Species, with Hydrogen." *Journal of the Chemical Society* (A) (1968): 2660–2665.

With Anthony J. Shortland. "Preparation and Properties of Hexamethyltungsten." *Journal of the Chemical Society, Dalton Transactions* (1973): 872–876.

"The Long Search for Stable Transition Metal Alkyls." Les Prix Nobel en 1973 (The Nobel Foundation) (1974): 147–157.

"The Iron Sandwich, a Recollection of the First Four Months." *Journal of Organometallic Chemistry* 100 (1975): 273–278.

With F. Albert Cotton. *Basic Inorganic Chemistry.* Chichester, U.K.: John Wiley, 1976. Subsequent editions appeared in 1987 and 1995.

With E. W. Abel and Gordon A. Stone, eds. *Comprehensive Organometallic Chemistry: The Synthesis, Reactions, and Structures of Organometallic Compounds.* 9 vols. Oxford and New York: Pergamon, 1982. A revised, fourteen-volume edition was published in 1995.

Comprehensive Coordination Chemistry. 7 vols. Oxford and New York: Pergamon, 1987.

With S. U. Koschmieder. "Homoleptic and Related Aryls of Transition Metals." *Polyhedron* 10 (1991): 135–173.

With D. W. H. Rankin, H. E. Robertson, A. A. Danopoulos, et al. "Molecular Structure of Tetrakis(tertbutylimido)osmium(VIII), Determined in the Gas Phase by Electron Diffraction." *Journal of the Chemical Society, Dalton Transactions* (1994): 1563–1569.

OTHER SOURCES

Bennett, Martin A., Andreas A. Danopoulos, and William P. Griffith, et al. "The Contributions to Original Research in Chemistry by Professor Sir Geoffrey Wilkinson FRS 1921–1996." *Journal of the Chemical Society, Dalton Transactions* (1997): 3049–3060. This biography is in a commemorative issue of the journal dedicated to Wilkinson, which has a frontispiece that is the National Portrait Gallery's picture of him.

Cotton, F. Albert. "Geoffrey Wilkinson as a Research Mentor." *Polyhedron* 16 (1997): 3877–3878. A recollection by one of his early and most prominent students, with a brief "genealogy" of Wilkinson's past students.

Green, M. L. H., and W. P. Griffith. "Sir Geoffrey Wilkinson 14 July 1921–26 September 1996." *Biographical Memoirs of Fellows of the Royal Society* 46 (2000): 594–606. A general account, with one photograph, listing many of his honors, especially those connected with the Royal Society.

———. "Geoffrey Wilkinson and Platinum Metals Chemistry." *Platinum Metals Review* 42 (1998): 168–173. Focuses on his contribution to the chemistry of the platinum-group metals.

Griffith, W. P. "Wilkinson, Sir Geoffrey (1921–1996)." In *Oxford Dictionary of National Biography*, vol. 58, edited by H. C. F. Matthew and Brian Harrison, pp. 999–1002. Oxford, U.K.: Oxford University Press, 2004. A general biography containing relatively little scientific detail but with more anecdotal material.

William P. Griffith

WILKINSON, JAMES HARDY (*b.* Strood, England, 27 September 1919, *d.* Teddington, England, 5 October 1986), *mathematics, numerical analysis, computing, linear algebra.*

Wilkinson was responsible for leading the team that constructed the Pilot ACE computer at the National Physical Laboratory in Teddington, England, in 1950, following a short period of work with Alan Turing on its design. He went on to become a leading authority on computer-based numerical analysis. He is best known for his work on backward error analysis (which had both practical and theoretical value) and linear algebra, but his work in numerical analysis was wide ranging, and he authored well over one hundred published papers, three influential books, and several unpublished reports. In 1962, George Forsythe, a numerical analyst based at Stanford University, wrote:

> In my opinion Wilkinson is single-handedly responsible for the creation of almost all the current body of scientific knowledge about the computer solution of the problems of numerical algebra. He has devised many of the best algorithms himself. Far from that he has personally tested most of the algorithms proposed all over the world, has found their weak and strong points, has published variations that work better, has exposed numerous fallacies about them, has analyzed their errors and tried them on hundreds of matrices.
>
> In order to give error bounds Wilkinson had to create a theory of error analysis for floating-point computation, something that has never been achieved but often attempted. … His unique genius has been to balance mathematical analysis so intimately with practical computing. (quoted in Fox, 1987, p. 689)

Early Life and Career. Wilkinson was born on 27 September 1919 into a large happy family of modest means in Strood in Kent, England. He showed early mathematical ability and won a scholarship to Sir Joseph Williamson's Mathematical School in Rochester. Encouraged by his headmaster, Wilkinson later won a scholarship place to Trinity College, Cambridge, at the age of seventeen. At Cambridge he studied classical analysis with Godfrey Harold Hardy and John Edensor Littlewood, graduating first class in 1939.

Like many of his British mathematical and scientific contemporaries, during World War II Wilkinson was drafted into scientific work rather than being sent directly to fight with the armed forces. He initially worked for the Ordnance Board of the Ministry of Supply. Because of its very wide range of calculating equipment, the Ordnance Board had requisitioned the Cambridge Mathematical Laboratory for the duration of the war. At that time the Cambridge Mathematical Laboratory was one of only two places in England to possess a full-sized differential analyzer—an analogue computing device made up of interconnected disk and wheel integrators designed to solve differential equations. In addition, the laboratory was equipped with a model differential analyzer, the Mallock Machine (a unique analogue device for solving simultaneous equations), and several desk calculating machines. At the Cambridge Mathematical Laboratory, Wilkinson worked on ballistics problems, mainly calculating trajectories using hand-cranked desk calculating machines. He found the work very dull, with each member of the staff being required to compute a set number of trajectory calculations each day. In 1943 Wilkinson was transferred to the Military of Supply Armament Research Laboratory at Fort Halstead and began working on problems associated with the thermodynamics of explosions. Again, the work involved routine computations.

In late 1945, Wilkinson moved to the newly created Mathematics Division of the National Physical Laboratory (NPL) at Teddington in Middlesex. The move was to shape the rest of his career. He had intended to return to

James Wilkinson. COURTESY OF NPL © CROWN COPYRIGHT 1979.

academic life in Cambridge, but as a result of the research opportunities offered to him at the NPL, he remained in the British Scientific Civil Service for the rest of his distinguished career. The NPL Mathematics Division had been created by the U.K. Department of Scientific and Industrial Research to act as a national center of expertise in numerical computation. It had a twofold role: to provide a computing service to government and industry; and to carry out numerical and computational research. Over the next thirty-five years Wilkinson contributed to all these aspects of the NPL Mathematics Division's work.

Turing and the Pilot ACE. On his appointment to the NPL, Wilkinson was assigned part-time to the General Computing Section and part-time to the ACE section. The General Computing Section consisted of a strong team of mathematicians concentrating mainly on numerical research and a team of well-trained and well-equipped desk calculating machine operators who did computing work from both inside and outside the NPL. Wilkinson was involved in devising algorithms for solving a range of problems, many of which involved the solution of linear simultaneous equations using both desk calculating machines and the NPL Hollerith punched card installation. However, it was the opportunity to work with Alan

Turing in the ACE section that really excited Wilkinson, and he commented (1971) that it was the experience of working with Turing that finally convinced him that a career working on numerical analysis with computers was more interesting than returning to Cambridge for a career in classical analysis.

Turing had been appointed to the NPL in 1945 and was given the opportunity to design an electronic stored program computer. In the postwar period, ideas about the concept of the stored program computer were emerging from the ENIAC project at the University of Pennsylvania, and it was a natural step for the NPL, in its role as a national computing center, to take a lead in developing the new technology. Turing had had wartime experience with the Colossus machine at Bletchley Park and had contributed theoretically to the field. When Wilkinson arrived at the NPL, Turing was working on a highly original design for a computer called ACE (Automatic Computing Engine). Most other early computers were heavily based on the EDVAC design by John Mauchley, John Presper Eckert, John von Neumann, and others. Turing's design was influenced by this work but had a different architecture and electronic timings that allowed the programmer to creatively use the mercury delay line memory to place both machine instructions and numbers so that significant computational speed could be acheived. Wilkinson worked very closely with Turing on the logical design of the machine and on programming numerical algorithms. Turing proved occasionally difficult to work for, and, as he described in 1971, Wilkinson chose his moments to work with the General Computing Section carefully. The dual role proved fruitful, as it gave Wilkinson valuable practical experience in solving difficult problems using desk calculating machines, coupled with an understanding of the logical and physical design of the ACE. Both experiences gave him a strong foundation for his later work on computer-based numerical analysis.

Despite a great deal of work on the design of the ACE, there was initially little progress made on actually building the machine. The original intention had been to subcontract out the construction work, but this proved untenable, as groups with the relevant expertise, such as those at Manchester and Cambridge Universities or the Post Office, were interested in other projects or in building computers to their own design and thus were not interested in constructing the ACE for NPL. In early 1947, Harry Huskey, who had worked on the ENIAC project in the United States, joined the small ACE team for a sabbatical year, and he immediately suggested that the NPL build a Test Assembly to test the feasibility of Turing's design. Turing was discouraged; he was not interested in building a small machine but wanted to make progress with the larger machine. He took sabbatical leave back to Cambridge, leaving the relatively inexperienced

Wilkinson as leader of the ACE section. It had been decided that the electronic hardware work for the Test Assembly was to be carried out in collaboration with the NPL Electronics Division, but at that time there was little enthusiasm for the ACE project within the Electronics Division, and the Test Assembly project floundered. By the end of the year, Huskey had returned to the United States, and Turing had moved permanently to Manchester University, where computer developments under Frederic ("Freddie") Williams and Tom Kilburn had proceeded more quickly.

In 1948, Wilkinson was invited by the new head of the NPL Electronics Division to build a pilot version of ACE as a collaborative venture based on Turing's design. The ACE section, now consisting of four staff members including Wilkinson, gladly accepted the offer; the team, led by Wilkinson, began in seriousness to build what became known as the Pilot ACE. While Wilkinson's expertise was in the logical design and programming of the machine, he nonetheless contributed to the physical construction in order to speed up the project. In May 1950, the machine ran its first simple program and was demonstrated to the press in November of that year. It was the third electronic stored program computer to be operational in the United Kingdom. Although originally the machine was intended to be experimental, Wilkinson soon found the section under considerable pressure to use the machine for useful work, and the Pilot ACE went into regular service in 1952. NPL users such as the Royal Aircraft Establishment and the Atomic Weapons Research Establishment began requesting solutions to large, complex problems using the Pilot ACE—requests that both challenged and stimulated Wilkinson and his staff. The Pilot ACE was actually a small machine with limited memory, a fact that forced Wilkinson and his NPL colleagues to produce very efficient algorithms. Efficiency and reliability became the key elements of Wilkinson's later extensive contributions in the application of computers to numerical problems.

Numerical Analysis. Although Wilkinson has no algorithms named after him, he contributed very significantly to the development of computer-based numerical analysis and especially in comparing different methods and establishing their good and bad points. His experience of working with Turing on developing theoretical algorithms for problems using floating point arithmetic before he had a machine to run them on proved invaluable and meant that Wilkinson was theoretically well ahead of his contemporaries when computers using floating point arithmetic became more freely available.

Computers allowed large numbers of repeated arithmetical operations to be carried out during a solution to a problem, but they also stored numerical data in a limited form. This introduced the very real possibility of cumulative rounding errors sometimes negating the usefulness of a solution to some problems. The study of how and why seemingly effective algorithms produce incorrect results is called error analysis; it is for his contributions to this field that Wilkinson became well known. In the late 1940s and early 1950s, there was great pessimism about the effect of rounding errors in the analysis, of problems by electronic computers as well as by more traditional computational methods. Wilkinson's great achievement was to bring insight and understanding into the way algorithms running on electronic computers performed in detail.

Drawing on work by both John von Neumann and Turing, Wilkinson explored and further developed the method of backward error analysis. Backward error analysis was not new, but Wilkinson showed how it could be used in practice to good effect. Traditionally forward error analysis examines what errors are produced by each intermediate stage of the solution of a problem with a view to understanding the error in the final result. In backward error analysis, the aim is to find the modified data set for which the computed solution is exact and then compare the modified data with the original data. The great value of backward error analysis was that it offered insight into how the numerical processes of various algorithms actually influence the data. This in turn indicated the numerical stability and/or computer efficiency of a given algorithm, and this information could be used to select a particular algorithm or to show the way toward developing new algorithms. The technique could also be used to examine the effect of small changes to the original data. If the small changes led to large errors in the final result, this method could ascertain whether the problem being considered was itself unstable (or ill conditioned), or whether the algorithm being used to solve it was the cause of the instability. In a great part of his numerical analysis work, Wilkinson was able to use error analysis to illustrate how each stage of an algorithm operated and the effect it had on the data, therefore proving the stability of the algorithm in question.

Wilkinson published the results of his work in *Rounding Errors in Algebraic Processes* in 1963, a book that proved influential to an entire generation of numerical analysts. A very large proportion of Wilkinson's published works concentrated on the algebraic eigenvalue problem and its many associated subproblems. (The eigenvalue problem refers to finding a set of characteristic values associated with a matrix or matrices and can take several forms. It is used in a variety of theoretical and applied mathematical contexts.) His work was published in *The Algebraic Eigenvalue Problem* in 1965 and, like *Rounding Errors,* this book became a classic in the field. The algebraic eigenvalue problem occurs in many branches of physics in which real world systems are described by a large matrix. Wilkinson's early work in the field was based on finding the characteristic polynomial associated with the matrix, and he built on his work on backward error analysis to closely examine a whole range of algorithms in this field, testing them both theoretically and practically. He was able to present the way that each algorithm worked in detail and to use that information to go from describing an algorithm to synthesizing new algorithms. Using this knowledge, Wilkinson could identify which parts of an algorithm were most sensitive and needed additional accuracy for their solution. To provide this additional accuracy Wilkinson developed inverse iterative methods for finding eigenvalues and eigenvectors.

Wilkinson also developed transformation methods that first produce simplified matrices for which the solution of the eigenvalue is easier using one of a number of tried and tested algorithms. In addition he worked extensively on methods for the computation of eigenvectors in a condensed form when an eigenvalue had already been found by one of his stable methods.

Another important contribution by Wilkinson was his work on the QR algorithm for computing eigenvalues. The QR algorithm had been developed by J. G. F. Francis and has become known as one of the most stable algorithms for solving eigenvalue problems. In 1968, Wilkinson published a shift within the algorithm that accelerated the convergence of the solution and made it more efficient in terms of computing time. He also proved a proof for the convergence of the method. In 1976, Wilkinson and Gene Golub published a major article on the Jordan canonical form of a block matrix and showed how matrices could be transformed into this form. The paper also considered where this technique could be used for practical calculations and where its use was limited.

Another aspect of Wilkinson's numerical analysis work involved computations with polynomials, and here too he used backward error analysis to investigate different algorithms for their solution. His initial work had been conducted as test runs for the Pilot ACE, but the results surprised Wilkinson and led him to investigate more deeply. His work in this area is consolidated in Chapter 2 of *Rounding Errors*, but he was still thinking about polynomials toward the end of his career. In 1984, he published "The Perfidious Polynomial" to sum up his experiences for the general reader. Wilkinson was posthumously awarded the Chauvenet Prize from the Mathematical Association of America for the essay's clarity of mathematical exposition.

Algorithm Sharing, Lecturing, and International Recognition. In the 1950s and 1960s, computers were often very differently and individually designed, and it was not possible to run software developed for one machine on any other computer. By the late 1960s, high level programming languages, such as ALGOL and FORTRAN, had been developed to enable programs to be transferable from one machine to another. The increasing availability of generic rather than machine-specific programs and algorithms allowed Wilkinson's work to be increasingly influential. There was an atmosphere of mutual help and cooperation in the field of numerical analysis, and his dominance in the field meant that Wilkinson was invited to both lecture and collaborate internationally.

In the late 1960s, Wilkinson was invited to contribute to an international project designed to provide the scientific community with a series of well-tested algorithms for common numerical problems. The result of this work was the *Handbook for Automatic Computation: Linear Algebra*, published in 1971 by Wilkinson and Christian Reinsch. The volume was part of an edited collection of internationally developed algorithms based on papers published in the journal *Numerische Mathematik*, but Wilkinson's dominance of the field was such that over half of the contributions are by Wilkinson himself.

Wilkinson was also involved in the creation of the Numerical Algorithms Group (NAG), which has become the main numerical software organization in the United Kingdom and whose published algorithms underpin many academic and industrial applications. The Nottingham Algorithms Group (later changed to Numerical Algorithms Group) officially began in 1970 when Brian Ford collaborated with Wilkinson to translate some of the ALGOL routines developed at NPL and for the *Handbook* into FORTRAN in order to make them more widely available. The work linked several workers in different institutions in an open spirit of collaboration. Wilkinson continued to collaborate with the Numerical Algorithms Group right up until his death.

Wilkinson was a frequent visitor and consultant to both Stanford University and the Applied Mathematics Division of the Argonne National Laboratory in the United States. At Argonne he served as an advisor on the Eispack project, a library of FORTRAN subroutines for computing matrix eigenvalues and eigenvectors. The project had some parallels with the Numerical Algorithms Group in the United Kingdom and had its basis in the 1971 *Handbook*.

While Wilkinson's position at the NPL made research, rather than teaching, the focus of his work, he did lecture widely. As early as 1954, Wilkinson was invited to Oak Ridge National Laboratory in the United States to speak on matrix computations, from which evolved the regular Gatlinburg conferences on linear algebra for which Wilkinson sat on the organizing committee. He regularly contributed to conferences and meetings in the United States and for more than ten years gave a regular series of lectures every summer at the University of Michigan. From the mid-1960s onward, Wilkinson regularly visited the Argonne National Laboratory to lecture as well as to collaborate and consult. Following his death, Argonne created the J. H. Wilkinson Fellowship in Computational Mathematics. From 1974 to 1986, Wilkinson held a part-time professorship with Stanford University.

Outside the United States and Britain, Wilkinson collaborated with numerical analysts working in Europe and in Russia. In 1968, he visited Russia under an exchange agreement between the Royal Society and the U.S.S.R. Academy of Sciences. He was a corresponding member of the Bavarian Academy of Sciences and served on the editorial advisory board of the U.S.S.R. *Computational Mathematics and Mathematical Physics* and the French *R.A.I.R.O. Analyse Numérique.*

In 1969, Wilkinson was elected a Fellow of the Royal Society in recognition of his contributions to numerical analysis and his leadership of the Pilot ACE project. From 1974 to 1977, he served on the Council of the Royal Society and was also for a time secretary of the physical sciences section.

At the NPL Wilkinson's services to numerical analysis were recognized in the form of personal promotions not linked to his role at the NPL but to the internationally recognized research he undertook. In 1974, he was promoted to Chief Scientific Officer on individual merit, which Yates (1997) and Goodwin (1987), both NPL insiders, claim to have been a very rare distinction. In addition, Wilkinson was awarded numerous fellowships and prizes, including the A. M. Turing Award of the Association for Computing Machinery and the J. von Neumann Award of the Society for Industrial and Applied Mathematics. He was a founding member of the British Computer Society and the Institute of Mathematics and its Applications. Fox (1987) gives a complete list of awards and honors received by Wilkinson.

Wilkinson died on 5 October 1986 from a heart attack. He was survived by his wife Heather and his son David; his daughter Jenny predeceased him.

BIBLIOGRAPHY

A complete list of Wilkinson's publications is given in L. Fox, "James Hardy Wilkinson," Biographical Memoirs of Fellows of the Royal Society *33 (1987): 669–708. There is a recorded interview with Wilkinson that is commercially available from SIAM (Society for Industrial and Applied Mathematics).*

WORKS BY WILKINSON

Rounding Errors in Algebraic Processes. London: HMSO, 1963; New York: Prentice-Hall, 1964.

The Algebraic Eigenvalue Problem. Oxford: Clarendon Press, 1965.

"Global Convergence of Tridiagonal QR Algorithm with Origin Shifts." *Linear Algebra Applications* 1 (1968): 409–420.

With Christian Reinsch. *Handbook for Automatic Computation: Linear Algebra.* Vol. 2. New York: Springer-Verlag, 1971.

"Some Comments from a Numerical Analyst." *Journal of the Association for Computing Machinery* 18 (1971): 137–147.

"The Pilot ACE at the National Physical Laboratory." *The Radio and Electronic Engineer* 45 (1975): 336–340.

With Gene Golub. "Ill-Conditioned Eigensystems and the Computation of the Jordan Canonical Form." *SIAM Review* 18 (1976): 548–568.

"The Perfidious Polynomial." In *Studies in Numerical Analysis,* edited by Gene Golub, pp. 1–28. Washington, DC: Mathematical Association of America, 1984.

OTHER SOURCES

Albasiny, Ernie. "Dr. James Hardy Wilkinson, FRS, 1919–1986." *Utilitas Mathematica* 31 (1987): 7–12.

Copeland, B. Jack, ed. *Alan Turing's Automatic Computing Engine: The Master Codebreaker's Struggle to Build the Modern Computer.* Oxford: Oxford University Press, 2005.

Croarken, Mary. *Early Scientific Computing in Britain.* Oxford: Clarendon Press, 1990.

Fox, Leslie. "James Hardy Wilkinson." *Biographical Memoirs of Fellows of the Royal Society* 33 (1987): 669–708.

Goodwin, Eric Thomson. "Dr James Hardy Wilkinson, FRS FIMA." *Bulletin of the Institute of Mathematics and Its Applications* 23 (1987): 76–77.

Parlett, Beresford N. "The Contribution of J. H. Wilkinson to Numerical Analysis." In *A History of Scientific Computing,* edited by Stephen G. Nash. New York: ACM Press, 1990.

Yates, David M. *Turing's Legacy: A History of Computing at the National Physical Laboratory, 1945–1955.* London: Science Museum, 1997.

Mary Croarken

WILSON, ALAN HERRIES (*b.* Wallasey, Cheshire, United Kingdom, 2 July 1906; *d.* Brent, United Kingdom, 30 September 1995), *solid-state physics, semiconductor physics, nuclear fission, chemical engineering, pharmaceuticals, computers, science education, public service.*

Wilson had two successful careers, the first from 1926 to 1945 in physics, the second from 1945 in industry. In physics he developed the first quantum-mechanical picture of semiconductors, and in particular his work was seminal in our understanding of semiconductors. He explained the difference between metals, insulators, and semiconductors in terms of a simple band theory of solids accessible to both experimental and theoretical researchers. Partly as a result of his war work, he moved into industry, serving as a director and chairman with the Courtaulds company and later with Glaxo and International Computers and Tabulators. He was active in promoting scientific research in the industrial sector.

Education. Wilson's forebears were tenant farmers, blacksmiths, and small builders. His father, Herries Wilson (born in 1868), was a marine engineer who left the sea on marriage and then worked as the chief maintenance engineer for the Wallasey Corporation Ferries in the north of England. In 1901 Herries Wilson married Annie Bridges (born in 1865), and in 1904 a daughter, Elizabeth, was born.

Alan Wilson's education was not unusual for a clever boy. From primary school at the age of nine, he gained a scholarship to attend his local grammar school. For a boy from his background, full-time education would normally end by age sixteen at the latest and be followed by employment in local industries. In preparation for a commercial career, Wilson had followed evening courses in bookkeeping and shorthand. During the end of World War I however, changes had been wrought in secondary education in England and Wales, in particular with the introduction of the Higher School Certificate. As Wilson was successful in the Oxford Senior Local Examinations, at sixteen he was able to remain in school studying for a higher certificate without any clear view of the future. His headmaster introduced him to a scholarship with a value of £150 per annum awarded to any boy from Wallasey who was accepted by Emmanuel College, Cambridge. Taking courses in mathematics, physics, and chemistry, Wilson passed the entrance examination and was awarded the scholarship. His success in the Northern Universities Higher School Certificate was rewarded by a second scholarship.

To avoid having to reread materials that he had already studied, Wilson changed his route from a degree in natural sciences to a degree in mathematics. During the final years of this study, he followed courses in applied mathematics. He encountered Werner Heisenberg's matrix theory of quantum mechanics (1925), which Wilson found extremely interesting. He graduated in the summer of 1926 with a first-class degree, sharing the Mayhew Prize awarded to the best candidate in applied mathematics.

In 1926, even a first-class degree in mathematics from Cambridge did not necessarily result in a job. Wilson was, however, awarded a research studentship with a grant of £250 per annum offered by the Goldsmiths' Company. This allowed him to become a research student working with the theoretical physicist Ralph H. Fowler. According to one of Wilson's students, Ernst Sondheimer,

Alan Wilson. COURTESY OF THE PRESS AND COMMUNICATIONS OFFICE, UNIVERSITY OF LEEDS.

Fowler was somewhat elusive. Wilson was rather surprised when his supervisor told him "he could now forget all that he had learned in Fowler's lectures on quantum mechanics" (Sondheimer, 1999, p. 550), because that year Erwin Schrödinger published his wave-mechanical version of quantum mechanics, a new approach that theoretical physicists found far less cumbersome to work with than Heisenberg's formulation. Fowler suggested that Wilson use Schrödinger's mechanics to calculate the energy levels of the ionized hydrogen molecule. With his excellent command of mathematics, Wilson managed to tease out this problem, which had been previously intractable to the Bohr-Sommerfeld approach to quantum mechanics. The result was Wilson's first two papers in 1928, the first of which provided solutions to a generalized spheroidal wave equation, which were then applied to the problem of an ionized hydrogen molecule in the second paper. In order to progress in research in Cambridge, Wilson now had to obtain funding. By obtaining a Smith's Prize for 1928 and a research fellowship in 1928, he was able to stay at Emmanuel College.

An Academic in Cambridge. At Cambridge Wilson produced a few papers relating to the development of quantum mechanics: two concerned with perturbation theory, and one with tunneling in alpha-particle emission. But, under the influence of Ernest Rutherford, experimental work on the nucleus dominated physics in Cambridge. Mathematical physics was but an adjunct to mathematics; until the end of the 1930s theoretical physics was considered applied mathematics.

Pyotr Leonidovich Kapitza's recent experimental results on the magnetoresistance in bismuth crystals catalyzed Wilson's interest in the problems of solids, but he found little success in his efforts to understand this property of bismuth. Wilson had become a member of the Kapitza club, an informal group of mathematicians whose membership was by invitation only. The club brought the European idea of theoretical physics to Cambridge, which Wilson accepted. Nevertheless, he found theoretical physics in Cambridge uninterested in problems of the solid state, which by the end of the 1920s Wilson considered his research interest. Thus Wilson considered himself very fortunate to receive a Rockefeller Traveling Fellowship, which in the first nine months of 1931 allowed him to work in Leipzig with Heisenberg and to visit Niels Bohr and his colleagues in Copenhagen. It was during Wilson's sojourn in Leipzig that he had the insights that led to his pathbreaking theory of semiconductors and to his two seminal papers on this subject in 1931; these could be taken as a paradigm of a discovery being a fortunate conjunction of the place and the person. In Leipzig Wilson joined a number of theoreticians who were both skilled in quantum mechanics and interested, as he was, in the properties of solids. Among the researchers then working with Heisenberg were Felix Bloch, Edward Teller, and Peter Debye.

According to Wilson (1973), a presentation he gave during a colloquium in Leipzig led to his theory of semiconductors. The research workers at Leipzig were expected to read seminar papers and Heisenberg asked Wilson to present an appreciation of Rudolf Peierls's recent work on the effects of magnetic fields in metals. Peierls had arrived at puzzling results concerned with the motion of electrons within certain types of solid; they appeared to move in the wrong direction. Wilson was concerned to understand Peierls's papers fully for, "to give a seminar in German at which I would be cross-examined back and forth would be a bit of an ordeal, and therefore one had to understand someone else's work more thoroughly than if one was talking about one's own" (1973, p. 5). This effort, and Heisenberg's demand that explanations should be made

physically intuitive, led Wilson to his band theory of semiconductors. Wilson realized that if bound electrons and the gaps between energy bands were used as the starting point of the explanation, then the anomalous results could be explained in terms of vacancies in the valence bands of crystals and elements. This physical picture led to his insights into holes and electrons in semiconductors. It is interesting to note that positively charged holes in full valence bands could have been considered as negative mass electrons. As Wilson stated, however, "It's much easier physically to consider a positive charge rather than a negative mass" (1973, p. 5).

Wilson's first discussion of his theory of semiconductors was followed by other meetings in which he expanded his ideas. One of the meetings was attended by a group of experimentalists from Erlangen headed by Bernhard Gudden. Gudden had been interested in semiconductors from the early 1920s, when he was a colleague of Robert Pohl of Göttingen, whose group in the 1920s were pioneers in the modern study of semiconductors. Gudden had been trying to sort out the confusion that in 1931 surrounded the understanding of metals, semiconductors, and insulators. Wilson's two papers on semiconductors in 1931 outlined a simple model of semiconductors in which he introduced the concept of donor impurities and calculated many properties of the materials.

In 1932 Wilson decided to submit an enlarged version of his Leipzig work for the Adams Prize, the most prestigious mathematics prize awarded by the University of Cambridge. Founded in the memory of the nineteenth-century astronomer John Couch Adams, this prize was awarded for an essay on a defined topic. For the years 1931–1932 the subject was "the quantum-mechanical theory of aperiodic phenomena." Though "aperiodic phenomena" does not immediately relate to semiconductors, Wilson's work won the 1932 Adams Prize.

Between 1932 and 1938 Wilson continued his work on solids. In 1932 two papers considered rectification (the process of converting alternating to direct current), in metal-semiconductor junctions and electrolytic rectifiers. These properties had been used in industrial applications since the end of the nineteenth century but no plausible theoretical pictures had been developed. A paper pointed at the theory of metals proved to be a blind alley. Wilson had expected this work to be a critique of an electron-lattice interactions theory developed by Peierls and others, but it was wrong. In the same year a paper discussing the internal photoelectric effect in crystals presaged Wilson's interest in the optical properties of metals. And in 1935 his "The Optical Properties of Solids" exhaustively examined the visible and ultraviolet optical properties of metals. In 1936 Wilson detailed the state of the knowledge of metals, semiconductors, and insulators in his important and widely read text, *The Theory of Metals,* one of a series of important books on the theory of solids that appeared between 1933 and 1936, making the study of the electronic structure of solids into a well-established subfield of modern physics.

It was evident that Wilson's theory of semiconductors was intuitively attractive, but there remained many areas of disagreement between experimentalists. There was a need for new experiments and for the confirmation or denial of earlier knowledge. Wilson found it almost impossible to persuade any of his Cambridge contemporaries to carry out the necessary work and recognized that it would be difficult, perhaps impossible, to progress in his research on solids without colleagues with whom he could discuss his ideas. Thus from about 1936 he moved his interest to nuclear physics.

Before that occurred, Wilson had been appointed a university lecturer in mathematics and had become a fellow and lecturer of Trinity, a post previously held by Fowler, who in the meantime had become the first Plummer Professor of Mathematical Physics in 1932. Since 1929 Wilson had presented a course of advanced lectures on the quantum theory of spectra based on wave mechanics, and joined Fowler teaching thermodynamics. By all accounts he was a good lecturer (Sondheimer, 1999, p. 553). Expecting to remain in academia and become a professor, Wilson worked on two or three papers in the area of nuclear physics but World War II interrupted academic work before he could complete these projects.

The Second World War. World War II changed the course of Wilson's career. As early as 1938 he had offered his services to the government in case of war, but in the autumn of 1939 he was told his skills were valueless to the war machine. He remained, therefore, in Cambridge continuing lecturing and finishing off some of the research he had begun before the war, as well as carrying out some (part-time) defense research for the government. Since many of his colleagues had been drafted into war work, his workload was enormous.

In early 1941 he was recruited into an organization called the Inter Services Research Bureau (ISRB), which was the public face of the Special Operations Executive (SOE). Wilson found himself attached to a secret establishment known as Station IX near Welwyn, Hertfordshire, U.K. Station IX had been founded in July 1940 on the instigation of Winston Churchill as a mechanism for conducting warfare by means other than direct military engagement; much of this was related to agents in occupied Europe. The work in the station dealt largely with wireless telegraphy and radio and had no resemblance to anything that Wilson ever had done. But after some persuasion he accepted the appointment. Many of the personnel were from the military, but Wilson remained a civilian. After a short time Wilson came to the conclusion that his head of department was not suitable to the demands of the work, a fact he brought delicately to his superiors. He then discovered that this had been the real reason that he was brought to Station IX—the work of the section required "gingering up." After Wilson's intervention the section head was moved to less urgent work and within a few weeks Wilson was promoted to be in charge of research and development.

Wilson discovered that he had a talent for running a research and development organization and that he had a special aptitude for managing political situations. Having achieved his purposes at the SOE, Wilson was asked to join Tube Alloys, the British operation related to the atomic bomb, and went to Birmingham where he joined Peierls and Klaus Fuchs, who were then studying the gaseous separation of uranium isotopes. In 1944, when many of the scientists and the bulk of the work of Tube Alloys was transferred to America, Wilson volunteered to remain in Britain. Nineteen forty-four saw his return to Cambridge where he resumed academic work, dividing his time half and half between the atomic bomb and academic research.

Industry. In 1944, responding to the events that had occurred during the war, Wilson left academia to forge a new career in industry. In the course of his war work he impressed some significant men with his organizational talents. One of these, the industrialist Samuel Courtauld of the Courtaulds textile company, realized that after the war scientific research would be vital to industry. Wilson was surprised to be invited in 1944 to join the board of Courtaulds company and serve as its director of research and development.

Wilson was aware that he had no knowledge of the chemistry of artificial fibers with which the Courtaulds' business dealt, and it seemed at first that joining Courtaulds would be a mistake. But he then came under considerable pressure from those who thought that university men should go into industry. According to Wilson, Sir Edward Appleton, the head of the Department of Scientific and Industrial Research, considered that while there are lots of good scientists in the universities and industry, good organizers who also know anything about science are very rare (Wilson, 1974). In the end Wilson accepted Courtauld's offer and gave up his hope of succeeding Fowler as the Plummer Professor of Mathematical Physics at Cambridge. He proved very successful in introducing a research stream in the company. By 1961 he became the company's chairman-designate. Within a year, however, Wilson became unhappy at Courtaulds, because of its involvement with Imperial Chemical Industries in a takeover battle. While this battle was won by Courtaulds, the victory was Pyrrhic and Wilson resigned from the company in 1962.

In January 1963, he joined Glaxo, a leading British pharmaceutical company, and was elected chairman of the board in July 1963. Under Wilson's leadership Glaxo's efforts were redirected from the British Commonwealth to European markets and research was restructured with one group dominated by organic chemists, another by biologists. Eventually both groups found major marketable products. When Wilson retired in 1973, the United States was the only noncommunist country in which Glaxo did not have a place. From 1962 Wilson was also a director of International Computer and Tabulators, and for ten years he was active as well in the British computer industry.

From Science and Industry. Wilson received many honors during his life, among them: Fellow of the Royal Society in 1942; a knighthood in 1961; various honorary fellowships, including of Emmanuel College, Cambridge, of St. Catherine's College, Oxford, and of the University of Manchester Institute of Science and Technology (now part of the University of Manchester); honorary doctorates from Edinburgh and Oxford universities; honorary fellowships of the Institute of Physics, Institution of Chemical Engineers, and the Institute of Mathematics and Its Applications (from which he received a Gold Medal in 1984).

Wilson also played a considerable part in public life, serving as: president of the Institute of Physics and the Physical Society from 1962 to 1964; prime warden of the Goldsmiths' Company 1969 to 1970; University Grants Committee from 1964 to 1966; the Electricity Council (deputy chairman 1973–1976); Scientific Advisory Committee of the National Gallery from 1955 to 1960; and Board of Governors of the Bethlem Royal and Maudsley Hospitals, chairman, 1973–1980.

According to his former student Sondheimer, Wilson had outstanding intellectual gifts. His understanding of situations was so fast that his conclusions could seem intuitive. His disdain for ruthless maneuverings in business was perhaps a weakness in that domain, for he was a kindly man. Away from work and physics he was interested in art and literature, and mountain walking (see Sondheimer, 1999, p. 561). Wilson married Margaret Monks in 1934, and sons were born in 1939 and 1944. His marriage was very happy, and his wife became a confidante, particularly during his industrial career. Sir Alan remained active for most of his retirement and died peacefully on 30 September 1995.

BIBLIOGRAPHY

Documentary material on Alan Wilson can be found in the Archives of the Royal Society; the London School of Economics; Emmanuel College, Cambridge; the American Institute of Physics; and Cambridge University.

WORKS BY WILSON

"The Theory of Electronic Semi-Conductors." *Proceedings of the Royal Society,* Series A, 133 (1931): 458–491.

"The Theory of Electronic Semi-Conductors. II." *Proceedings of the Royal Society,* Series A, 134 (1931): 277–287.

"The Optical Properties of Solids." *Proceedings of the Royal Society,* Series A 151 (1935): 274–295.

The Theory of Metals: Based on an Essay Awarded the Adams Prize in the University of Cambridge, 1931–1932. Cambridge, U.K.: Cambridge University Press, 1936.

Semi-conductors and Metals: An Introduction to the Electron Theory of Metals. Cambridge, U.K.: Cambridge University Press, 1939.

"Theory and Experiment in Solid State Physics." *Bulletin, Institute of Physics and the Physical Society* 14 (1963): 173–180.

"Conversation with A. H. Wilson." Oral history interview of Sir Alan Herries Wilson by Colin A. Hempstead. Recording and transcript. November 1973. Copies in Niels Bohr Library, American Institute of Physics, College Park, MD, and in London School of Economics and Political Science Archive. This interview demonstrated Wilson's character, and that his memory of his seminal work was sharp and accurate.

"My Turbulent Years in Industry" (unpublished manuscript). 1974. London School of Economics and Political Science Archives, COLL MISC 1034.

"Solid State Physics 1925–33: Opportunities Missed and Opportunities Seized." In *The Beginnings of Solid State Physics: A Symposium Held 30 April–2 May 1979,* edited by Nevill Mott. London: Royal Society, 1980. Symposium first published in *Proceedings of the Royal Society of London,* Series A, 371 (1980): 1–177.

OTHER SOURCES

Hendry, J. *Cambridge Physics in the Thirties.* Bristol, U.K.: Adam Hilger, 1984. Contains essays written by physicists working in Cambridge in the thirties. These, and the introductions, include comments on Wilson's work, the relationships between mathematics, theoretical and experimental physics, and the institutional contexts in Cambridge.

Hoddeson, Lillian, Gordon Baym, and Michael Eckert. "The Development of the Quantum Mechanical Electron Theory of Metals." In *Out of the Crystal Maze: Chapters from the History of Solid-State Physics,* edited by Lillian Hoddeson, Ernest Braun, Jürgen Teichmann, and Spencer Weart. New York: Oxford University Press, 1991.

Sondheimer, Ernst H. "Sir Alan Herries Wilson." *Biographical Memoirs of Fellows of the Royal Society* 45 (1999): 548–562. Includes a fuller account of Wilson's life and work by a coauthor and research student of Wilson's. The memoir includes a bibliography of Wilson's published works. I am indebted to Professor Sondheimer for letting me use his memoir as a guide for this entry.

Colin Hempstead

WILSON, JOHN TUZO (*b.* Ottawa, Canada, 24 October 1908; *d.* Toronto, Canada, 15 April 1993), *geophysics, geology, plate tectonics, transform faults, hot spots.*

Wilson's most significant work involved finding support for continental drift and seafloor spreading, especially with the development of the transform fault concept. He also proposed that groups of linear volcanic islands were caused by mantle plumes, foreshadowing W. Jason Morgan's idea of hotspots. Wilson led an enormously rich life, as a student traveler attempting to learn geophysics, as a member of the Geological Survey of Canada, as an active researcher at the University of Toronto, as the first principal of the Erindale College, and as director general of the Ontario Science Centre. To avoid confusion with another J. T. Wilson, he used his middle name, and became known professionally as J. Tuzo Wilson or simply Tuzo Wilson.

Education and Early Career. The eldest child of three children of John Armistead and Henrietta Wilson (née Tuzo), Wilson was born in 1908 in Ottawa, Canada. His Scottish father, just sixteen when his own father died, was forced to learn engineering as an apprentice. After contracting malaria in India, he sought a colder climate, settling in Alberta, Canada. Spending most of his professional career working for the Canadian government, he helped develop civil aviation in Canada. Thus, Wilson met many aviators while growing up; he later attributed his love of travel to their influence. Wilson's mother was born in British Columbia, Canada. Her father, trained as a physician at McGill University in Montreal, joined the Hudson Bay Company in 1853 and traveled with fur traders by canoe to Manitoba, on horseback through the mountains of Alberta, and down the Columbia River by longboat to the Pacific. He died while Wilson's mother was in medical school, and she had to leave before getting her degree to take care of her own mother. An avid mountain climber, she and her Swiss guide Christian Bohren were the first to climb "Peak Seven" in the Valley of the Ten Peaks, Alberta, Canada. In honor of the accomplishment, the mountain was named Mount Tuzo.

Although Tuzo's family was not rich, they still traveled, and Tuzo obtained an excellent education. He and his siblings were expected to study, work in the garden, and walk four miles to and from school. Their weekends

were filled with swimming, canoeing, and skiing, and, like his mother, he developed a love for the outdoors. He excelled academically at a private school in Ottawa. Often alone, he became accustomed to following his own path, and developed a distrust of orthodoxy. At seventeen, he became a field assistant for Noel Odell, the English geologist and mountaineer, who introduced him to geology.

Wilson majored in honors mathematics and physics his first year at the University of Toronto (1926). However, in part because of his encounter with Odell, he switched to geology, much to the dismay of his physics teachers. Even though he appreciated the elegance of physics, he preferred working in the field to the laboratory. His geology professor told him that he would have to repeat his first year because he needed introductory geology and biology courses. However, Professor Lachlan Gilchrist, a classical physicist who realized the promise of geophysics for prospecting, proposed a double major for Wilson in physics and geology. Wilson graduated in 1930 as the first Canadian to obtain a geophysics degree. Awarded a Massey Fellowship to study at Cambridge University, he decided to pursue a second BA degree in geophysics. Edward Bullard was to be his tutor, but was delayed in East Africa doing gravity work. Wilson took Harold Jeffreys's course of lectures in geophysics but failed to understand them. Jeffreys told him not to worry. Tuzo spent much of his time learning how to fly, rowing, and traveling throughout Europe. Nonetheless, he was influenced by Jeffreys, and later adopted his contractionist account of mountain building.

Wilson returned to Canada with his BA from Cambridge, and spent a year working under William Henry Collins, director of the Geological Survey of Canada. Although Collins recognized the need for geologists to work with geophysicists, he was unable to secure Wilson a position, and suggested that he get a PhD in geology and return to Canada once the economy improved. Tuzo chose Princeton University over Harvard University and the Massachusetts Institute of Technology (MIT) because Princeton offered him more money, and Professor Richard M. Field told him that Princeton was going to begin teaching geophysics. Although Field failed to recruit a geophysicist to Princeton, he obtained funding from the U.S. Coast and Geodetic Survey to support Maurice Ewing's seismic study of the New Jersey coastal plain, and Wilson occasionally worked with Ewing at nearby Lehigh University. Wilson also became friends with Harry Hess, who joined the Princeton faculty in 1934, a year after Wilson arrived. Wilson's dissertation advisor was the structural geologist Professor Taylor Thom, an expert on the Beartooth Mountains of Montana. Thom gave Wilson $180, told him to buy a car for $50 and spend the summer mapping a section of the Beartooth Mountains.

Wilson's assigned area included the 3,749-meter (12,300-foot) Mount Hague, which he was the first to ascend.

Obtaining his PhD from Princeton in 1936, he spent three years at the Geological Survey of Canada before joining the Royal Canadian Engineers during World War II. In the field for most of his time with the survey, he worked in the Maritime Provinces, Quebec, and the Northwest Territories. Once short of food in the Northwest, Wilson found an ancient Indian birch-bark canoe, paddled up to a moose in a large lake, and killed it with a blow to the head with his ax. It was during this time with the survey, that he learned the value of surveying by air, and showed his skeptical colleagues in the survey that major trends could be spotted and mapped more successfully from the air than on foot. His appreciation of flight, learned from his father, proved professionally helpful. It also gave him a way to look at huge areas in ways accenting large structures, a theme that he would later exploit. Wilson married Isabel Dickson of Ottawa in 1938, a year before he joined the war effort. She accompanied him to England during the war.

In 1946, a year after his return to Canada, Wilson had three career choices: stay in the army, where he had reached the rank of colonel; return to the survey, where he was promised the directorship; or accept a position as professor of geophysics in the Department of Physics at the University of Toronto in 1946. He followed the advice of Chalmers Jack Mackenzie, then president of the National Research Council of Canada, who told him to return to university life and spend twenty years doing basic research. Indeed, he remained at the University of Toronto until 1967, becoming one of the most creative Earth scientists of his generation.

Research on Earth's Crust. Wilson began making a name for himself as a researcher in 1949/1950 when several of his papers, one coauthored with the applied mathematician Adrian E. Scheidegger, appeared, defending and expanding Jeffreys's contractionism to explain the origin of continents, their growth, and the origin of mountains and island arcs. Wilson proposed that Earth first solidified without a sialic (continental) outer crust; that its outer crust repeatedly fractured as Earth contracted by cooling; that uprising sial reached the surface through fractures and first formed volcanic islands; that eroded sediments from the islands combined with repeated rising sial through old and new fractures and formed mountain ranges surrounding the original volcanic islands; that these new structures combined to become continental shields; and that the repetition of such processes led to continental growth by addition of peripheral island arcs and mountain ranges. He paid particular attention to the geometry of groups of island arcs (1949a, 1950b); extend-

ing the British geologist Philip Lake's (1931) suggestion that such groups typically form circular or spiral arcs, he proposed that similarly shaped fractures would occur in Earth's outer layer as it contracted. Wilson argued that his updated contractionism was superior to mantle convection, which he considered to be the only alternative worth serious consideration. He discarded continental drift in a single paragraph arguing that there are no physical forces strong enough to break apart a supercontinent, that it could account only for formation of recent orogenic belts, and that there was no reason, as Alfred Wegener had proposed, that continental drift should have occurred only once and, in geological terms, so recently (1949b, p. 173).

Wilson espoused the same view throughout most, if not all, of the 1950s, as witnessed by the 1959 publication of his 1957–1958 Sigma Xi National lecture. He incorporated the new discovery by Bruce Heezen, Marie Tharp, and Ewing of the mid-ocean ridge system into his contractionist theory, claiming that it should be viewed as a gigantic fracture system rivaling the terrestrial one formed by mountain belts and island arcs, and arguing that it was caused by uprising basalt that reached the surface through a continuous fracture zone that formed early in Earth's history (1959). He made no mention of developments in paleomagnetism that suggested continental drift and polar wandering, and again effortlessly dismissed continental drift: "Continental drift is without a cause or a physical theory. It has never been applied to any but the last part of geological time" (1959, p. 23)—Wilson, apparently, had never read Émile Argand, who spoke of a proto-Atlantic and formation of Wegener's supercontinent, and he either thought little of Arthur Holmes's mantle-convection mechanism of continental drift or did not know of it. Wilson did, however, acknowledge the possibility of polar wandering, and noted that it could be included within his contractionist theory.

Wilson had yet to waver from contraction theory. Within a few years, however, he became inclined toward continental drift. Wilson retrospectively claimed that he "was too stupid to accept, until I was fifty, the explanation which Frank Taylor and Alfred Wegener had advanced in the year I was born" (1982). The "too stupid" was likely said in good humor; he was wrong in claiming that Taylor *and* Wegener advanced their views in 1908; Wilson probably misremembered how old he was when he accepted continental drift. He favored Earth expansion in 1960 without drifting continents when he was already fifty-one, and did not "welcome" continental drift in print until October 1961, when approaching his fifty-third birthday. Regardless of his age, once Wilson let go of contractionism, he began to apply his fertile mind to the consequences of continental drift, and developed a series of interesting, often original, hypotheses.

Wilson entertained Earth expansion but explicitly rejected its use as an explanation for continental drift (1960). After noting Paul A. M. Dirac's suggestion that the gravitational constant G may be decreasing over time and Heezen's hypothesis that Earth expansion not only explains the formation of the system of mid-ocean ridges but causes the widening of ocean basins and drifting continents, Wilson argued that the rate of Earth expansion needed to cause continental drift was unreasonably high (1960). He suggested that a much slower and reasonable rate of expansion could explain formation of ridges, and, just as with Earth contraction, formation of arcuate fracture zones where island arcs and mountains form. He argued that his view, unlike mantle contraction, avoided the difficulty of continental flooding by ocean waters with the shrinking of ocean basins.

Wilson came out in favor of continental drift and seafloor spreading, approximately a year and a half after entertaining slow expansion (1961). He favorably reviewed both Hess's and Robert Dietz's versions of seafloor spreading. Instead of analyzing seafloor spreading per se, he acknowledged the paleomagnetic support of continental drift put forth by Kenneth Creer, Edward Irving, Keith Runcorn, Patrick Blackett, John A. Clegg, and Peter H. S. Stubbs. He also removed a difficulty facing seafloor spreading, and in so doing was the first to suggest that ridges themselves may migrate (1961, p. 126). Given that ridges entirely surround Antarctica, if new seafloor flows toward Antarctica from all directions, it seemed that Earth would have to expand because Antarctica lacks sinks where seafloor is destroyed. To avoid the difficulty, he proposed that the surrounding ridges themselves migrate northward.

Once committed to seafloor spreading and continental drift, Wilson applied them to a nest of problems. Turning his attention back to his homeland, he suggested that previous pre-Pangea breakups and collisions of drifting continents could explain ancient mountain systems and differently aged provinces of the Canadian Shield (1962a). He then argued that Cabot fault, which he claimed extends through New England and the Canadian Maritime Provinces, and the Great Glen fault in Scotland once formed a single fault before the continents separated (1962b, 1962c). Turning to the rest of the world, Wilson wondered about the origin of the Hawaiian Islands and other such parallel, linear chains of volcanic islands and seamounts found in the Pacific (1963). Most claimed that such island chains formed as lava reached the surface along large linear faults. Invoking seafloor spreading, he argued that the upwelling basalt comes from "a deep source" below the mass of moving sea floor and upper mantle (1963). As the spreading seafloor went over the plume, islands were created when the basalt reached the surface. He noted that this solution explained, unlike the received view, why the age of islands within such island chains increases the further the islands are from the East Pacific Rise (1963). His "deep source" was the precursor for W. Jason Morgan's (1968) hotspots. Wilson first sent the paper to the *Journal of Geophysical Research* where it was rejected; he then sent it to the *Canadian Journal of Physics*.

Transform Faults. His next major contribution, and his most important, was his concept of transform faults. Wilson (1965) was impressed by the fact that movements of Earth's crust appeared to be concentrated in three types of tectonic features, mid-ocean ridges, mountain ranges (including island arcs and trenches), and major faults with large horizontal displacements. These features seemed to end abruptly, and up to the middle 1960s were generally viewed as unconnected. He proposed that they were connected, not isolated features. Although the features end abruptly, he claimed that they actually are transformed into one of the other features. A ridge, for example, could be transformed into a horizontal fault, which could be transformed into a trench. Wilson named these horizontal faults transform faults. These horizontal faults had been viewed previously as transcurrent faults. Wilson further applied his transform fault concept to fracture zones that connect segments of oceanic ridges. Mid-ocean ridges are not continuous, but are made up of ridge segments that are offset from each other by fracture zones. He reasoned that if seafloor spreading occurs, the fracture zones connecting ridge segments should be transform not transcurrent faults. He further explained how seismological data could be used test his idea. If the fracture zones were transform faults, then movement along them should be in the opposite sense to that of transcurrent faults. He also noted that current seismicity should be confined to the segment of the fault between ridge segments, whereas it should extend along the whole of the fracture zone, if transcurrent faulting occurs. When Wilson proposed his idea the relevant seismological data were missing to determine if the faults between ridge segments were transform or transcurrent. Lynn Sykes (1967) presented the missing data, and confirmation of Wilson's transform fault concept and the Fred J. Vine–Drummond H. Matthews hypothesis (1963) led to the acceptance of seafloor spreading and continental drift by many who had vehemently argued against them. Indeed, Vine and Wilson (1965) coauthored a paper that explained generation of seafloor from the Juan de Fuca and Gorda ridges south of Vancouver Island in terms of seafloor spreading, the Vine-Mathews hypothesis, and transform faults. Wilson's transform fault concept became a crucial element of plate tectonics. Morgan, coinventor of plate tectonics, went so far as to characterize plate tectonics as "an extension of the transform fault hypothesis [Wilson, 1965] to a spherical surface"(1968, p. 1959).

Later Career and Honors. Wilson recalled that by 1967 his "research had reached an impasse" and that he was unsure as to whether he had enough "will and strength" to continue (1990, p. 281). Moreover, he had spent about twenty years doing research, as his old mentor Mackenzie had advised. So, with strong encouragement by his wife, he accepted the offer to become the principal of Erindale College, a suburban campus of the University of Toronto. In just seven years, when he was forced to take mandatory retirement at age sixty-five, he turned 300 acres of land with just one building into a thriving campus.

With his impending retirement, Wilson was asked by the premier of Ontario to become director general of the Ontario Science Centre. With usual enthusiasm he directed the Science Centre from 1974 until 1985. During his directorship, the Science Centre expanded its "hands-on approach," which allows visitors to "do experiments" and see science as a creative and fun activity. He also organized traveling exhibits to remote places in Ontario, and with his support, a northern extension of Science Centre, Science North, was built in Sudbury, Ontario.

Recognized as one of the most imaginative Earth scientists of his generation, and a leader among Canadian scientists, Wilson received many honors and awards. He was Officer, Order of the British Empire (1946); Order of Canada, Officer (1970); Order of Canada, Companion (1974). He was elected Fellow of the Royal Society of London (1968). His awards and medals include the R. M. Johnston Medal, Royal Society of Tasmania (1950); the Willet G. Miller Medal, Royal Society of Canada (1958); the S. G. Blaylock Medal, Canadian Institute of Mining and Metallurgy (1959); the Logan Medal, Geological Association of Canada (1968); the Bancroft Award, Royal Society of Canada (1968); the Bucher Medal, American Geophysical Union (1968); the Penrose Medal, Geological Society of America; the J. J. Carty Medal, U.S. National Academy of Sciences (1974); the Gold Medal, Royal Canadian Geographical Society (1978); the Wollaston Medal, Geological Society of London (1978); the Vetlesen Prize, Columbia University (1978); the J. Tuzo Wilson Medal, Canadian Geophysical Union (1978); the Ewing Medal, American Geophysical Union (1980); the M. Ewing Medal, Society of Exploration Geophysics (1980); the Albatross Award, American Miscellaneous Society (1980); the Huntsman Award, Bedford Institute of Oceanography (1981); the Alfred Wegener Medal, European Union of Geosciences (1989); and the Killam Award, Canada Council (1989). Wilson died on 15 April

1993. He was eighty-four and was survived by his wife, two daughters, and three grandchildren.

Tuzo Wilson was a remarkable scientist. An antidrifter until his fifties, he, unlike many of his peers, was able to change his mind relatively late in his career and embrace continental drift. He also was able to transcend the regionalism that he shared with most Earth scientists, and begin to take a more global approach. The permanence of the Canadian Shield spoke against continental drift. But once he began to appreciate continental drift's paleomagnetic support, and realized the explanatory promise of seafloor spreading, he changed his mind, and then, through hard thinking and voracious reading of the literature relevant to a mobilistic Earth in fields beyond those in which he was trained, he drew out unsuspected consequences of continental drift and seafloor spreading, culminating in his transform fault concept.

BIBLIOGRAPHY

WORKS BY WILSON

"An Extension of Lake's Hypothesis concerning Mountain and Island Arcs." *Nature* 164 (1949a): 147–148.

"The Origin of Continents and Precambrian History." *Transactions of the Royal Society of Canada* 43 (1949b): 157–184.

With Adrian E. Scheidegger. "An Investigation into Possible Methods of Failure of the Earth." *Proceedings Geological Association of Canada* 3 (1949c): 167–190.

"Recent Applications of Geophysical Methods to the Study of the Canadian Shield." *Transactions-American Geophysical Union* 31 (1950a): 101–114.

"An Analysis of the Pattern and Possible Cause of Young Mountain Ranges and Island Arcs." *Proceedings Geological Association of Canada* 3 (1950b): 141–166.

"Geophysics and Continental Growth." *American Scientist* 47 (1959): 1–24.

"Some Consequences of Expansion of the Earth." *Nature* 185 (1960): 880–882.

"Continental and Oceanic Differentiation." *Nature* 192 (1961): 125–128.

"The Effect of New Orogenetic Theories upon Ideas of the Tectonics of the Canadian Shield." In *The Tectonics of the Canadian Shield*, edited by John S. Stevenson, 174–180. Royal Society of Canada, Special Publications, no. 4. Toronto: University of Toronto Press, 1962a.

"Some Further Evidence in Support of the Cabot Fault, a Great Palaeozoic Transcurrent Fault Zone in the Atlantic Provinces and New England." *Transactions of the Royal Society of Canada* 56 (1962b): 31–36.

"Cabot Fault, an Appalachian Equivalent of the San Andreas and Great Glen Faults and Some Implications for Continental Displacement." *Nature* 195 (1962c): 135–138.

"A Possible Origin of the Hawaiian Islands." *Canadian Journal of Physics* 41 (1963): 863–870.

"A New Class of Faults and Their Bearing on Continental Drift." *Nature* 207 (1965): 343–347.

With Fred J. Vine. "Magnetic Anomalies over a Young Oceanic Ridge off Vancouver Island." *Science* 150 (1965): 485–489.

"Early Days in University Geophysics." *Annual Review of Earth and Planetary Sciences* 10 (1982): 1–14.

"J. Tuzo Wilson, Killam Laureate, 1989." In *In Celebration of Canadian Scientists: A Decade of Killam Laureates,* edited by Geraldine A. Kenney Wallace, Mel G. MacLeod, and Ralph G. Stanton, 266–286. Winnipeg, Canada: Charles Babbage Research Centre, 1990.

OTHER SOURCES

Garland, George D. "John Tuzo Wilson." *Biographical Memoirs of Fellows of the Royal Society* 41 (1995): 535–552.

Glen, William. *The Road to Jaramillo: Critical Years of the Revolution in Earth Science.* Stanford, CA: Stanford University Press, 1982.

Lake, Philip. "Island Arcs and Mountain Building." *Geographical Journal* 78 (1931): 149–160.

Morgan, W. Jason. "Rises, Trenches, Great Faults, and Crustal Blocks." *Journal of Geophysical Research* 73 (1968): 1959–1982.

Sykes, Lynn R. "Mechanism of Earthquakes and Nature of Faulting on the Mid-Oceanic Ridge." *Journal of Geophysical Research* 72 (1967): 2131–2153.

Vine, Fred J., and Drummond H. Matthews. "Magnetic Anomalies over Ocean Ridges." *Nature* 199 (1963): 947–949.

Henry Frankel

Robert Rathbun Wilson. AP IMAGES.

WILSON, ROBERT RATHBUN (*b.* Frontier, Wyoming, 4 March 1914; *d.* Ithaca, New York, 16 January 2000), *high-energy physics, particle physics, particle accelerators, Fermi National Accelerator Laboratory.*

Wilson is remembered for his bold and imaginative designs of particle accelerators, for his leadership of experimental physics research at Los Alamos, New Mexico, during the period of the Manhattan Project, and for building the Fermi National Accelerator Laboratory, which for more than thirty years offered the international particle physics community the world's highest-energy protons for fundamental research in an aesthetically designed environment.

Early Years. Wilson's father, Platt Wilson, the son of an Iowa preacher, was a civil engineer who worked in both the coal mining and automobile industries. Platt subsequently entered politics, became chairman of the Democratic Party in Wyoming, and was later elected a state senator. Robert Wilson's mother, Edith Rathbun, came from a family of ranchers who had moved to Wyoming after the California gold rush. The Rathbun family's high regard for learning had a formative influence on Robert Wilson.

Spending much of his young years on his family's cattle ranches in Wyoming, Wilson became a skilled horseman who could throw a lariat and ride after cattle. He initially aspired to become a cowboy. The experience of spending long periods alone riding great distances with a pack horse, reading the sky for weather, and generally pitted against nature, nurtured Wilson's resourcefulness and helped him develop a sense of closeness with nature, as well as the belief that he was "unique in the world." He felt that his early experiences of fixing tools and apparatus in the blacksmith's shop helped him build "the confidence that with your own hands you could build large contraptions and make them work" (Weart, 2000). Experimenting in his mother's attic, Wilson taught himself practical skills, such as blowing glass, which he drew on in building a mercury vacuum pump and a Crooke's tube. He also read insatiably in his local library, where he found role models in works of literature that proved more formative than any of the schools he attended, a different school each year after his parents separated while he was still in grade school. The hero of Sinclair Lewis's novel *Arrowsmith* exemplified for Wilson the noble scientist seeking practical solutions in the service of humanity. Going back and forth between his parents, he was often in the care of his maternal grandmother, Nellie Rathbun, the grand-daughter of the abolitionist John G. Fee, who founded Berea College, a racially integrated school, in pre–Civil War Kentucky. Nellie helped to instill strong social and educational values into Robert. Although he remained shy and withdrawn through high school and college, rarely speaking up in class, he readily learned from his father the value and skill of rhetoric and storytelling (Weart, 2000, pp. 151–154).

Physics Training under Lawrence. Following in the tradition of his maternal family, Wilson pursued a college education, gaining admission in 1932 to the University of California at Berkeley, despite his undistinguished high school record. Like many physicists who began their studies during the Great Depression, he enrolled in an electrical engineering program, which offered the promise of future employment. But beyond his love for nature and philosophy he discovered his passion for physics, which he proceeded to teach himself as a freshman. A particular attraction was the nuclear physics research pursued at the Radiation Laboratory directed by Ernest Orlando Lawrence, who had recently invented the cyclotron in 1930. One day during Wilson's freshman year, he stood in the rain peering through a window into the Rad Lab. When he was invited inside, he was shown the cyclotron and he decided on the spot that working with such machines was what he would do in life (Weart, 2000, p. 157). Within several years he would join Lawrence's "boys," the group of graduate students, including M. Stanley Livingston, Edwin McMillan, Philip Abelson, Luis Alvarez, and Milton White, who worked around Lawrence and his cyclotrons.

During his junior year, Wilson nervously asked Lawrence whether he would be willing to sponsor his independent project. Lawrence directed the shy young man to Harry White, under whom Wilson invented a vacuum switch. By the time he entered his senior year, Wilson was conducting original research on the lag time of the spark discharge. Staying on for graduate study under Lawrence, Wilson took up a range of physics problems, including the theory of the cyclotron. An invention resulted: the waxless cyclotron vacuum seal, which became known as the "Wilson seal."

Wilson experienced Lawrence's laboratory as an adventuresome, special place, without hierarchy, but with Lawrence, affectionately known as "the Maestro," very much in charge. Wilson regretted the subtle change he noticed over his five years there, as Lawrence gradually withdrew from working alongside his "boys" into his office to deal with administrative matters, leaving a microphone hanging in his place. Wilson nevertheless came away from his training under Lawrence with many valu-

able lessons, such as: "If you want something to come true, you can make it come true just by pushing like hell." or "There are many ways of getting to a result." or "If you tried, it was a question of being optimistic or pessimistic." Wilson's thesis experiment on proton-proton scattering failed because he could not make the cyclotron work well enough. But as Wilson could not delay moving to Princeton University to begin his appointment there as an instructor in physics, he wrote his thesis in 1940 on the theory of the cyclotron. He did until the last possible moment try to make the cyclotron work, arriving late for his wedding to Jane Inez Scheyer in August 1940 (Weart, 2000, pp. 175–185). Jane and Bob Wilson were to enjoy a long and happy marriage of fifty-nine years. They had three sons, Daniel, Jonathan, and Rand.

Princeton, Los Alamos, Cornell. At Princeton, Wilson continued to pursue proton-proton scattering, and he used the Princeton cyclotron to aid the experimental work at Columbia University of Enrico Fermi and Herbert Anderson leading to their successful demonstration of the first nuclear chain reaction at the University of Chicago. In subsequent work, Wilson showed that a resonant mode of fission occurs. He also invented the electromagnetic isotope separation method known as the "Isotron method," a project canceled early in 1943. At that time, his group's members and its apparatus were shipped to Los Alamos, the secret laboratory in New Mexico under the direction of J. Robert Oppenheimer, organized in 1942 to build the atomic bomb. As a pacifist, Wilson initially felt that he could not be involved in the war. But as Nazism took hold, he "grew more and more uneasy." As he later explained, "If Hitler indeed conquered the world, could I bear to stand by and watch it happen, could I bear to think what life in such a world might be like?" (Wilson, 1970a, p. 30). Reversing his position on the war, he accepted an invitation to work on radar at the Massachusetts Institute of Technology "Radiation Lab," which Lawrence was then helping to organize. Soon Wilson decided that he would be more helpful to his country if he worked on problems of nuclear physics. He moved to New Mexico.

Wilson flourished in the austere environment of Los Alamos, where military deadlines brought physicists and chemists to employ practical methodologies to compensate for their incomplete theories and limited experimental knowledge of nuclear physics. Following in his father's footsteps, Wilson dabbled in Los Alamos politics, serving on the Town Council and later as the council's leader. When the laboratory decided that the Harvard cyclotron was the accelerator best suited for its nuclear physics research, the military sent to Harvard a team, including Wilson, instructed to purchase the cyclotron under the pretext that the accelerator was needed for medical work in Saint Louis. The Harvard physicists suspected the team's underlying motive and told its members that it could have the cyclotron without payment if the accelerator were used in the fission project. But despite Wilson's embarrassment, the army personnel obeyed orders and stuck with their story, paying Harvard a large sum for the Los Alamos cyclotron (Hoddeson et al., 1993, pp. 63–65). As the leader of the cyclotron group, Wilson then proceeded to study a number of critical issues essential to building an atomic bomb, among them, how many neutrons emerge on average per fission of an atom of uranium or plutonium, and whether neutrons are emitted from uranium instantaneously or with some delay.

The discovery in April 1944 that pile-produced plutonium contains a spontaneously fissioning isotope caused a massive reorganization at Los Alamos aimed at building a plutonium implosion bomb in time to be useful in the war. Wilson succeeded Robert Bacher as head of the Experimental Physics Division when Bacher was asked to lead the new implosion gadget division. In July 1945, Wilson experienced the Trinity test of the implosion bomb as a "re-awakening from being completely technically-oriented" (Wilson, 1970a, p. 33). He subsequently criticized the decision to drop atomic bombs on Hiroshima and Nagasaki and became a founding member of the Federation of Atomic Scientists, an organization created explicitly to "promote humanitarian uses of science and technology." Wilson served as chairman in 1946. He resolved to work henceforth on nuclear energy only as "a positive factor for humanity" (Wilson, 1970a, p. 33). In 1946 he left Los Alamos to join the physics faculty at Harvard University as an associate professor. There he designed a 150 MeV cyclotron and explored using it in cancer therapy.

In February 1947, Wilson moved to Cornell University as a full professor, once again succeeding Bacher, this time as the director of Cornell's Laboratory of Nuclear Studies. He made one of the first applications of the Monte Carlo method, a procedure that grew out of calculations made at Los Alamos in developing the atomic bomb, which provides approximate solutions to problems by performing statistical sampling experiments on a computer. Using this method, Wilson developed a way to produce very high temperatures in plasmas by producing an imploding shock wave in an ionized gas, and separated the nucleon's electromagnetic form factors through elastic, electron-nucleon scattering experiments. Over his twenty years at Cornell, Wilson built four electron synchrotrons, each more powerful than the previous one, culminating in Cornell's 10 GeV synchrotron. The 1.5 GeV synchrotron in this series, later upgraded to 2.2 GeV, was the first accelerator to use the strong-focusing principle invented in 1952 by Ernest Courant, Stanley Livingston, and Hartland Snyder. All four synchrotrons reflected Wilson's

emerging philosophy of frugal design from both a technological and economic point of view, a philosophy based on the approaches to physics he had experienced working under Lawrence and Oppenheimer. A consequence of Wilson's philosophy was that "something that works right away is over-designed and consequently will have taken too long to build" (Wilson, 1966, p. 235).

Wilson was happy at Cornell, but a part of him yearned to express his emerging artistic sensibility. An opportunity arose in the fall of 1965 during an instrumentation conference he attended in Frascati, Italy. There, hearing a group of Berkeley colleagues present their plans for a proton synchrotron with the unprecedented energy of 200 GeV, Wilson was offended by the machine's unimaginative design and high cost. After the meeting, while taking classes in drawing at La Grande Chaumière in Paris, he found himself "consumed with a passion for designing machines." In this romantic setting he drew images of magnets, rather than of the nude models, as he worked out frugal designs for synchrotrons. Considering Gothic cathedrals and accelerators in the same terms, he asked how could both "express the aspirations and spirituality of their age?" (Wilson, interview by Lillian Hoddeson, 12 January, and 8, 10, and 12 May 1978.) He then sent a critical note to Edwin McMillan, Lawrence's successor at Berkeley, explaining why he considered Berkeley's design "much too conservative," "lacking in imagination," and "without enough regard for economic factors." Wilson said he feared the Berkeley machine's high cost would kill the exciting 200 GeV project and endanger a future 600–1000 GeV machine (Wilson, 1965). He included with his note several alternative designs of his own, including one for a 200 GeV machine, priced at roughly $100 million with completion in three years, offering a striking contrast to Berkeley's design estimated at $348 million with completion in seven years. In December 1966, the Atomic Energy Commission (AEC) selected a site for the new machine in Weston, Illinois, a suburb of Chicago. Early in the following year Wilson accepted the challenge of building the world's most powerful accelerator in the American Midwest.

Fermi National Accelerator Laboratory. The Illinois site, 6,800 acres, consisting mainly of farmland in DuPage County, became a blank canvas for Wilson to express his aesthetic and noble ideals for the new laboratory, which he named the National Accelerator Laboratory (NAL) to indicate that it would offer democratic access to anyone whose work had sufficient merit. He called for frugal and functional components, combined harmoniously into a design which would contribute to society "not only in a technical but also in an esthetic, social, and philosophical sense" (Wilson, 1968, p. 490). Wilson would continue to express his artistic sensibility in his dream laboratory, and

Fermilab. *Exterior photograph of Fermi National Accelerator Laboratory, or Fermilab. Batavia, Illinois.* © MICHAEL S. YAMASHITA/CORBIS.

throughout the rest of his life, in the form of sculptures, drawings, and architecture. With his politically skilled deputy director, Edwin Goldwasser, Wilson planned a physics community reflecting great beauty, based on civil rights and diversity—a laboratory that would inspire solutions to a broad range of social, economic, and cultural, as well as physics, problems. Into his holistic design of the laboratory, Wilson projected his respect for nature and the environment.

To help lobby against racial discrimination in Du Page County, Illinois, Wilson and Goldwasser designed NAL's official human rights policy "to seek the achievement of its scientific goals within a framework of equal employment opportunity and of a deep dedication to the fundamental tenets of human rights and dignity" (NAL, 1968b). At the laboratory's Congressional authorization hearings in 1969, Wilson responded to Senator John Pastore's question about what the laboratory would offer for national defense:

It only has to do with the respect with which we regard one another, the dignity of men, our love of culture … it has to do with: Are we good painters, good sculptors, great poets? I mean all the things that we really venerate and honor in our country and are patriotic about…. it has nothing to do directly with defending our country except to help make it worth defending. (Wilson, 1970a, p. 113)

By taking risks on some twenty aspects of the design of the new accelerator, Wilson saved about $5 million on each and found ways to stretch the performance of the components so that he could raise the energy of the accelerator to 500 GeV, yet stay within his limited budget. One of his riskiest gambles was to design the accelerator's tunnel so it "floated" on the glacial till beneath the topsoil, thus avoiding the need to anchor the tunnel in bedrock using pylons. He further economized by accelerating the building schedule to reduce personnel costs. Advancing the deadline for installing the Main Ring of the accelerator by six months (from 1 January 1972 to 1 July 1971) had the effect of moving the schedule for completion of the accelerator by an entire year. "We knew something would fail," Harvard's Norman Ramsey noted, "but we figured it would be much less expensive to fix the failure than to play it safe with all twenty items" (interview by Lillian Hoddeson, 26 and 27 February 1980).

Yet as Wilson's ambitious mid-1971 deadline for completing the Main Ring's installation approached, no one was prepared for the traumatic events that dashed his dream of completing the accelerator a year ahead of schedule. Magnets began to fail at an alarming rate as the weather grew warmer. There is still disagreement about exactly what caused these failures. The crisis caused considerable trouble for experimenters who had arranged their sabbatical leaves based on Wilson's optimistic projections. Wilson coped with the crisis in his own way. One day in January 1972, he entered the control room and pulled out a small book from which he read in French from the *Song of Roland,* an eleventh-century chanson de geste (epic ballad) whose original intent had been to inspire Charlemagne's soldiers during the Crusades. In time many of the Main Ring magnets were replaced with reconditioned or newly built magnets. The milestone energy of 200 GeV was finally achieved on the afternoon of 1 March 1972, surpassing the 76 GeV record at the Serpukov machine in the USSR, and recapturing the energy lead for the United States. While many of the risky elements of the accelerator had failed, more had succeeded, so that much money was saved on the whole project. Wilson triumphantly announced to the AEC that the project had come in under budget and ahead of schedule (even if not as far ahead as he had hoped).

By the time NAL was renamed Fermi National Accelerator Laboratory (Fermilab) in 1974, in line with a 1969 AEC decision to honor Enrico Fermi, experimental research areas were in operation. The application of Wilson's philosophy of frugality to the experimental program meant that most of the experimental areas were "rough-and-ready places," as Wilson later described them (Wilson and Kolb, 1997, p. 356). The discomforts of experimenting at Fermilab in its early years bred widespread criticism from experimenters who did not agree with Wilson that a laboratory was better off providing minimal facilities because expensive ones "may tend to paralyze better developments later on," as Wilson had already cautioned McMillan in 1965 (Wilson, 1965).

These "better developments" included a new accelerator of higher energy than the Main Ring. Wilson began working on this upgrade, which he called the Energy Doubler (it was referred to during the nation's "energy crisis" as the Energy Saver, and later as the Tevatron), even before completing the Main Ring. His imaginative plan, revealed in March 1971, called for doubling the energy to a trillion electron volts (1 TeV), saving power as well, using the phenomenon of superconductivity as an "elixir to rejuvenate old accelerators and open new vistas for the future" (U.S. Congress, 1971; Wilson, 1977, p. 23). The in-house magnet factory that Wilson had built to help create the Main Ring's magnets, served as a research tool in developing the innovative superconducting magnets: by building hundreds of small-scale (and sometimes full-scale) prototypes, it was possible to observe their behavior and use the results in designing better magnets. Wilson estimated that this Energy Doubler would cost less than $20 million, roughly the amount left over from building the Main Ring, but the Washington-based AEC rejected Wilson's request to use this money for building the Doubler.

The funding prospects for the Doubler continued to worsen. Wilson had dealt comfortably with the Congressional Joint Committee on Atomic Energy (JCAE) and the AEC itself throughout the 1960s and early 1970s. His Berkeley and Los Alamos connections gave him an insider's conduit to the leadership of these funding sources. But when President Gerald Ford's administration transformed the AEC into two new bodies, the Energy Research Development Agency (ERDA) and the Nuclear Regulatory Commission (NRC), Wilson's advantage disappeared. Moreover, when Wilson turned to ERDA in early 1976 to request construction funds for the Doubler, he found the agency committed to ISABELLE, Brookhaven National Laboratory's superconducting colliding beams accelerator. The reorganization in October 1977 that produced a new Department of Energy (DOE), replacing ERDA, further crippled Wilson's ability to secure funding for his laboratory. By this time, Wilson was

painfully aware of the multiple tensions inherent in his vision for Fermilab, for example, between the notion of a large collaborative venture and the lone, self-reliant frontiersman scientist, pursuing his individual initiatives. That his laboratory had become a vehicle for the rise of what he considered bureaucratic megascience was a great disappointment to Wilson. On 9 February 1978 he submitted his resignation as the director of Fermilab.

Last Years. Wilson continued to work on Fermilab's programs, especially the Doubler, after his retirement from the laboratory. He also continued to lecture and consult on many topics ranging from magnet design to architectural and artistic design. He held a joint appointment in the Department of Physics and the College of the University of Chicago from 1967 to 1980 and became the Peter B. Ritzma Professor there in 1978. He was appointed the I. I. Rabi Visiting Professor of Science and Human Values at Columbia University in the fall of 1979 and the Michael Pupin Professor of Physics in 1980. In 1982 he returned to Cornell as a professor emeritus. He passed away in Ithaca on 16 January 2000, having suffered a stroke three years earlier, from which he never recovered. His ashes were buried on 28 April 2000 in the nineteenth-century Pioneer Cemetery on Fermilab's site.

Wilson received many honors during his life. He was elected to the National Academy of Sciences in 1957, awarded the National Medal of Science in 1973, and the Enrico Fermi Award in 1984. In 1985 he became president of the American Physical Society.

BIBLIOGRAPHY

WORKS BY WILSON

"Radiological Use of Fast Protons." *Radiology* 47 (November 1946): 487–491.

Letter to Edwin McMillan, 27 September 1965.

"An Anecdotal Account of Accelerators at Cornell." In *Perspectives in Modern Physics: Essays in Honor of Hans A. Bethe,* edited by Robert Marshak. New York: Interscience Publishers, 1966.

"The Richtmyer Memorial Lecture—Particles, Accelerators and Society." *American Journal of Physics* 36 (June 1968): 490–495.

"Conscience of a Physicist." *Bulletin of the Atomic Scientists* 26 (June 1970a): 30–34.

"My Fight against Team Research." *Daedalus* 99 (Fall 1970b): 1076–1087.

"The Tevatron." *Physics Today* 30 (October 1977): 23–30.

With Adrienne W. Kolb. "Building Fermilab: A User's Paradise." In *The Rise of the Standard Model: Particle Physics in the 1960s and 1970s,* edited by Lillian Hoddeson, L. Brown, M. Riordan, et al. New York: Cambridge University Press, 1997, pp. 338–363.

OTHER SOURCES

Crease, Robert P. "Quenched! The ISABELLE Saga." *Physics in Perspective* 7:3 I (December 2006) 330–376, II (December 2006) 404–452.

Goldwasser, Edwin L. "Robert R. Wilson: A Man for All Seasons." American Physical Society. Long Beach, CA. 1 May 2000.

Heilbron, John, and Robert Seidel. *Lawrence and His Laboratory,* vol. 1, *A History of the Lawrence Berkeley Laboratory.* Berkeley: University of California Press, 1989.

Hoddeson, Lillian. "Establishing KEK in Japan and Fermilab in the US: Internationalism, Nationalism and High Energy Accelerator Physics during the 1960s." *Social Studies of Science* 13 (1983): 1–48.

Hoddeson, Lillian, Laurie Brown, Michael Riordan, et al., eds. *The Rise of the Standard Model: Particle Physics in the 1960s and 1970s.* New York: Cambridge University Press, 1997.

Hoddeson, Lillian, Paul W. Henriksen, Roger A. Meade, et al. *Critical Assembly: A Technical History of Los Alamos during the Oppenheimer Years, 1943–1945.* New York: Cambridge University Press, 1993.

Leposky, George. "What's the Best Way to Build a $250 Million Atom Smasher?" *Inland Architect* (August/September 1960), p. 24.

McDaniel, Boyce, and Albert Silverman. Obituary. *Physics Today* 53 (April 2000): 82–83.

National Accelerator Laboratory (NAL). "Design Report." January 1968a.

———. "Policy Statement on Human Rights." 15 March 1968b.

Sokolov, Raymond. "Fermilab: Utopia on the Prairie." *Wall Street Journal,* 11 February 1983.

U.S. Congress. *AEC Authorizing Legislation Fiscal Year 1970: Hearings before the Joint Committee on Atomic Energy.* 91st Cong., 1st sess., on *General, Physical Research Program, Space Nuclear Program, and Plowshare.* April 17–18, 1969, part 1. Washington, DC: U.S. Government Printing Office, 1969. See pp. 112–118.

———. *AEC Authorizing Legislation Fiscal Year 1972: Hearings before the Joint Committee on Atomic Energy.* 92nd Cong., 1st sess., on *Physical Research, Space Nuclear, and Nuclear Waste Management Programs.* March 9, 16, 17, 1971, part 3. Washington, DC: U.S. Government Printing Office, 1971. See pp. 1191–1247.

Weart, Spencer. "From Frontiersman to Fermilab: Robert R. Wilson." *Physics in Perspective* 2 (June 2000): 141–203. Based on interview of Wilson by Weart, 19 May 1977.

Lillian Hoddeson
Adrienne Kolb

WINCKELMANN, MARIA MARGARETHA

SEE **Winkelmann, Maria Margaretha**.

WINKELMANN, MARIA MARGARETHA

(*b.* Panitzsch, Germany, 25 February 1670; *d.* Berlin, Germany, 29 December 1720), *astronomy, astrology, calendar making.*

Winkelmann petitioned the Academy of Sciences in Berlin (founded as the Societas regia scientiarum) for the position of academy astronomer to replace her husband, the celebrated Gottfried Kirch, when he died in 1710. In so doing, she invoked a principle well established within the organized guilds that recognized the right of a widow to carry on the family business. Despite the ardent support of academy president, Gottfried Wilhelm Leibniz, her request was denied. Academy officials did not question Winkelmann's qualifications but complained that already during her husband's lifetime the society was burdened with ridicule because its calendar was prepared by a woman. Although the Berlin Academy extended honorary membership to several women of high rank in the eighteenth century, no woman scientist was elected until 1949, when the physicist Lise Meitner became a corresponding member.

European universities were closed to women until the late-nineteenth century. Maria Margaretha Winkelmann, the daughter of a Lutheran minister, was educated privately by her father and, after his death, by her uncle. She received advanced training in astronomy in the home of the peasant and self-taught astronomer Christoph Arnold. Here she met Gottfried Kirch, Germany's leading astronomer. By marrying Kirch—a man some thirty years her senior—in 1692 Winkelmann secured a career in astronomy. Knowing she would have no opportunity to practice astronomy as an independent woman, she moved, in typical guild fashion, from assisting Arnold to assisting Kirch.

Kirch was called to Berlin as academy astronomer in 1700. Winkelmann assisted her husband in observation, and in this capacity made the academy's first discovery— the sighting of a previously unknown comet in 1702. Although the report published in the *Acta eruditorum,* then Germany's leading scientific journal, bore his name and not hers, Kirch's notebooks and a report published eight years later in the academy's *Miscellanea Berolinensia* make clear that Winkelmann discovered the comet (while he slept).

In addition to daily observation, Winkelmann assisted in the preparation of the academy's calendars. Each calendar fixed the days and months, predicted the position of the Sun, Moon, and planets (calculated using the Rudolphine tables), the phases of the Moon, eclipses of the Sun or Moon to the hour, and the rising and setting of the Sun within a quarter of an hour for each day. The monopoly on the sale of calendars was one of two monopolies granted to the academy by the king (the revenues helped support the academy). Between 1709 and 1712, Winkelmann also published three astronomical/astrological pamphlets under her own name. Different members of the Kirch/Winkelmann family kept a daily record of the weather from 1697 to 1774 with the aid of a "weatherglass."

In 1709 Leibniz presented Winkelmann to the Prussian court, where she explained her sighting of sunspots. In a letter of introduction Leibniz wrote:

> There is [in Berlin] a most learned woman who could pass as a rarity. Her achievement is not in literature or rhetoric but in the most profound doctrines of astronomy…. I do not believe that this woman easily finds her equal in the science in which she excels…. She favors the Copernican system (the idea that the sun is at rest) like all the learned astronomers of our time. And it is a pleasure to hear her defend that system through the Holy Scripture in which she is also very learned. She observes with the best observers, she knows how to handle marvelously the quadrant and the telescope. (Letter to Sophie Charlotte, January 1709)

Winkelmann's work was widely celebrated, and in 1711 she received an academy medal.

When Winkelmann lost her bid to become academy astronomer, she moved with her son and two daughters—each of whom she and her husband had trained as astronomers—to Baron von Krosigk's private observatory in Berlin. Here she served as "master" astronomer with two students to assist her. When Krosigk died in 1714, Winkelmann took a position in Danzig as assistant to a professor of mathematics. She and her son were subsequently invited by Johannes Hevelius's family to reorganize the deceased astronomer's observatory for the Winkelmann-Kirch family's own use. In 1716 the Winkelmann-Kirch family received an invitation from Peter the Great of Russia to become astronomers in Moscow, but they returned instead to Berlin where Winkelmann's son, Christfried, was appointed observer for the academy. Winkelmann and her two daughters, Christine and Margaretha, worked as his assistants. In 1717 Winkelmann was reprimanded by the academy council for taking too public a role at the observatory and was finally forced to leave. She died of fever in 1720.

Winkelmann was not the only woman astronomer in Germany in this period. Between 1650 and 1710 some 14 percent of all German astronomers were women. These included Maria Cunitz, Elisabetha Koopman Hevelius, Maria Eimmart, Christine Kirch, and Margaretha Kirch. Reflecting on their achievement, Alphonse des Vignoles, vice president of the academy in Berlin, wrote in 1721, "If one considers the reputations of Madame Kirch [Winkel-

mann] and Mlle Cunitz, one must admit that there is no branch of science … in which women are not capable of achievement, and that in astronomy, in particular, Germany takes the prize above all other states in Europe."

BIBLIOGRAPHY

WORKS BY WINKELMANN

With Gottfried Kirch. *Das älteste Berliner Wetter-Buch: 1700–1701.* Edited by G. Hellmann. Berlin, 1893.

Vorstellung des Himmels bey der Zusammenkunfft dreyer Grossmächtigsten Könige. Potsdam, 1709.

Vorbereitung, zur grossen Opposition, oder merckwürdige Himmels-Gestalt im 1712. Cölln an der Spree, 1711.

Ob vielleicht in diesem Jahre ein neuer Comet erscheinen möchte. Cölln an der Spree, 1712.

OTHER SOURCES

Aufgebauer, P. "Die Astronomenfamilie Kirch." *Die Sterne* 47 (1971): 241–247.

Jöcher, Christian G. "Kirchin (Maria Margaretha)." In *Allgemeines Gelehrten-Lexicon.* Leipzig, 1750.

Leibniz, G. W. G. W. Leibniz to Sophie Charlotte, January 1709. *Die Werke von Leibniz*, 1864–1884. Edited by Onno Klopp. Hanover. Vol. 9, pp. 295–296.

Schiebinger, Londa. "Maria Winkelmann at the Berlin Academy: A Turning Point for Women in Science." *Isis* 78 (1987): 174–200.

———. *The Mind Has No Sex? Women in the Origins of Modern Science.* Cambridge, MA: Harvard University Press, 1989.

Vignoles, Alphonse des. "Eloge de Madame Kirch à l'occasion de laquelle on parle de quelques autres femmes & d'un paison astronomes." *Bibliothèque germanique* 3 (1721): 115–183.

Londa Schiebinger

WINTHROP, JOHN, JR. (*b.* Groton, Suffolk, England, 12 February 1606; *d.* Boston, Massachusetts, 5 April 1676), *alchemy, iatrochemistry, natural philosophy.* For the original article on Winthrop see *DSB*, vol. 14.

The degree to which alchemy influenced John Winthrop's activities as a New England colonial leader has been significantly reevaluated. Alchemical knowledge and related philosophies, formerly considered avocations, have come to be seen as central to Winthrop's plans and his successes as a political leader, industrial entrepreneur, town founder, physician, and transatlantic diplomat.

Pursuing Alchemical Knowledge. From the time Winthrop began alchemical experimentation as a student at London's Inner Temple from 1625 to 1627, his interest

John Winthrop. THE LIBRARY OF CONGRESS.

in alchemical arts was purposeful and expansive. He was especially attracted to the pansophic Christian alchemical philosophies of Paracelsus, John Dee, and the supposed secret order of the Rosicrucians. Pansophism was the belief that humankind could systematically acquire total knowledge of the natural world, and that this knowledge was to be used to improve both the everyday world and human society. These improvements were seen as prerequisites to Christ's return and the onset of the millennium. Alchemy was an essential part of this quest. Winthrop pursued pansophic alchemical reforms on a number of levels throughout his life.

In 1627 he sailed with the Duke of Buckingham's fleet to help defend the Protestants at La Rochelle, on which voyage he began a lifelong friendship with the German alchemist Abraham Kuffler, son-in-law of the Dutch alchemical authority Cornelius Drebbel. A year later, to acquire the alchemical knowledge of the Middle East, Winthrop sailed to Venice and Constantinople, further extending his abilities and chemical contacts.

The Alchemy of Colonization. In 1631 Winthrop joined his father and namesake, the governor of the Massachusetts Bay Colony, in New England. Welcomed immedi-

ately into the governing elite, the younger Winthrop hastened to put his chymical—a modern term often used to describe the utilitarian aspects of alchemical research—skills to work for the fledgling Puritan colony. He surveyed the country assaying ores, while conducting alchemical experiments and building up his already prodigious library of alchemical and iatrochemical, that is, alchemical-medical, texts. In 1633 he founded the town of Agawam (now Ipswich, Massachusetts), and in 1635, after a brief return to England, he founded Sayebrook (now Saybrook) at the mouth of the Connecticut River for a group of Puritan grandees led by William Fiennes, first Viscount Saye and Sele, and Robert Greville, second Lord Brooke.

Winthrop's English connections to the Reverend John Everard, a Christian alchemist with marked antinomian beliefs, have led some scholars to speculate that Winthrop, too, was a religious antinomian, that is, a believer in the direct infusion of grace from God, independent of preaching or pious effort. They cite in support of this view Winthrop's notable absence as a judge from the trial of the Massachusetts antinomian Anne Hutchinson. Winthrop's interest in Everard, however, was focused on determining whether the minister was a member of the Rosicrucians, a question that Winthrop ultimately concluded in the negative. Winthrop's absence from Hutchinson's trial more likely rose from his pansophic tolerance of sectarian differences, an ecumenism advocated by many English Puritan grandees such as first Viscount Saye and Sele and Lord Brooke. To the more conservative of New England's Puritans, however, such tolerance of radicals verged on apostasy. As a result, Winthrop's and his associates' pansophic alchemy was always held in suspicion by some, and was sometimes held in suspicion by many.

Creating a New London. Following the collapse of New England's economy at the outbreak of the English civil war, Winthrop returned to Europe from 1641 to 1643. While there, he was influenced by Samuel Hartlib and members of his circle, including Gabriel Plattes, Johann Moriaen, and Jan Comenius. Winthrop secured investors and capital for New England's first industrial ironworks. Simultaneously, he privately promoted investment in a second venture: the creation of an alchemical research center in southern Connecticut that would be funded by the proceeds from a silver mine Winthrop believed he had found in southern Massachusetts. Ore samples from the mine brought to England repeatedly assayed with relatively high concentrations of silver, and Winthrop offered partial interest in the venture to alchemical friends such as Robert Child, who planned to emigrate to New England. He promoted the venture to alchemical associates on the continent, several of whom found Winthrop's plan to create a "New London" along Long Island sound appealing enough to commit to join Winthrop in America.

Establishing the research center, however, proved difficult. Mining the silver ore (actually graphite) proved extremely laborious, and Indians effectively resisted Winthrop's plan to transport ore through their lands. Moderating tensions in Europe also caused several men who had signed on to the project to rethink their commitment. One alchemist who did come, Robert Child, got in deep trouble with authorities almost immediately by demanding that the Puritan leaders liberalize their restrictive political and religious enfranchisement policies.

Child's confrontation generated a backlash that cast a cloud over alchemy in New England in the late 1640s. Winthrop's new town was repeatedly harassed by local Mohegan Indians with the tacit approval of Connecticut's Puritan leaders. Child was placed under house arrest and ultimately fined heavily and deported. George Starkey, a young alchemist whom Winthrop helped train, reported to Hartlib that he was held under arrest in Massachusetts for two years under suspicion of being a Jesuit or a spy. Starkey emigrated to England, where he gained a significant reputation as an adept and influenced the alchemical research of both Robert Boyle and Isaac Newton.

Winthrop persevered in his effort to establish the alchemical research center. He attracted and developed a cadre of New England alchemists, such as Jonathan Brewster, near New London, and he continued to promote the benefits that alchemy could provide a colonial society—through advances in mining, metallurgy, agriculture, and medicine. He focused much attention on alchemical medicine. While seeking knowledge of the weapon salve—an alchemical balm that could heal diseases from a distance—he made New London a hospital town, to which the afflicted came from all across New England to receive treatment. He developed proprietary alchemical medicines and distributed them through a network of elite women healers in many New England towns. Winthrop became the most sought after physician in New England. At his death, he was eulogized as Hermes Christianus, and was praised as one who had mastered the ultimate alchemical secret of transmuting lead to gold. From his beginnings as a suspect newcomer to Connecticut when he laid out his alchemical town in 1645, Winthrop became Connecticut's governor in 1657, and he was reelected to the position from 1659 until his death in 1676.

The Charter and the Society. Winthrop's greatest service to Connecticut came through his securing of the Royal Charter of 1662, which incorporated the colony of New Haven into Connecticut and gave the new, larger entity virtual political autonomy. Winthrop's ability to secure such favorable terms from a monarch with little reason to favor Puritan causes was due in part to his international reputation as an alchemist and the court connections he had gained through membership in the Royal Philosophical Society. Winthrop, already well known in England as an accomplished colonial natural philosopher, was also reputed to be Eirenaeus Philalethes, a pseudonymous author whose widely praised texts were then circulating in English alchemical circles. These works have been conclusively identified by William Newman as the productions of George Starkey, who, in an effort to obscure his own authorship, had claimed they were penned by an anonymous American adept. This reputation had helped Winthrop gain immediate acceptance into the group founding the Royal Philosophical Society. Well-connected members of the Society such as Boyle, Lord William Brouncker, and Sir Robert Murray helped Winthrop gain both access to the king's court and a remarkably favorable charter, which speedily received the Great Seal on 10 May 1662.

In return for their support of his charter efforts, the society imposed a series of expectations upon Winthrop—that as colonial correspondent he would furnish useful information about New England back to the society. This quid pro quo is revealed through the repeated and insistent demands made by society secretary Henry Oldenburg, Boyle, Murray, and others that Winthrop compile a natural history of New England, a study useful not just for natural philosophers but for royal agents intent on gaining greater control of New England's people and resources. The arrival of Royal Commissioners to New England in 1664 made the Crown's imperial ambitions over the region unmistakable. Winthrop thereafter fended off the Royal Society's demands for intelligence with a steady stream of polite excuses, usually delivered with shipments of colonial curiosities—items that inspired wonder about New England without revealing information of strategic or utilitarian value. Winthrop continued this benign resistance to society pressure until his death in Boston on 5 April 1676.

Although Winthrop cannot be said to have made significant scientific advances, his commitment to and use of alchemical knowledge exemplified the many ways in which alchemy could embody the political, utilitarian, spiritual, scientific, and cultural aspirations of the early modern era, even in a place as remote as seventeenth-century New England.

SUPPLEMENTARY BIBLIOGRAPHY

The primary repository for the papers of John Winthrop Jr. is the Massachusetts Historical Society in Boston, Massachusetts, Winthrop Family Papers II, 1587–1977. Many of the manuscripts have been printed in Winthrop Papers, *6 vols. (Boston, Massachusetts, Historical Society, 1929–).*

OTHER SOURCES

Canup, John. *Out of the Wilderness: The Emergence of an American Identity in Colonial New England.* Middletown, CT: Wesleyan University Press, 1990.

Como, David R. *Blown by the Spirit: Puritanism and the Emergence of an Antinomian Underground in Pre-Civil-War England.* Stanford, CA: Stanford University Press, 2004. Discusses Winthrop's links to antinomians.

Dunn, Richard S. *Puritans and Yankees: The Winthrop Dynasty of New England, 1630–1717.* Princeton, NJ: Princeton University Press, 1962. Good biography, but dismissive of alchemy.

Kamil, Neil. *Fortress of the Soul: Violence, Metaphysics, and Material Life in the Huguenots' New World, 1517–1751.* Baltimore, MD: Johns Hopkins University Press, 2005.

Newman, William Royall. *Gehennical Fire: The Lives of George Starkey, an American Alchemist in the Scientific Revolution.* Chicago: University of Chicago Press, 2003.

Woodward, Walter William. "Prospero's America: John Winthrop, Jr., Alchemy and the Creation of New England Culture, 1606–1676." PhD diss., University of Connecticut, Storrs, 2001.

Walter W. Woodward

Georg Wittig. AP IMAGES.

WITTIG, GEORG (*b.* Berlin, Germany, 16 June 1897; *d.* Heidelberg, Germany, 26 August 1987), *organic chemistry.*

Wittig's work was guided by the general idea of establishing the field of carbanion chemistry as equal in importance to the fields of free radical and carbonium ion chemistry. His studies led him to a great variety of new structures. Best known is his work on phosphorus ylides, which condense with carbonyl compounds to form alkenes. This concept, the Wittig reaction, opened the door to important classes of substances, such as vitamins and hormones, which are nowadays synthesized on an industrial scale. In 1979 he was awarded the Nobel Prize in Chemistry.

Early Life and Career. Wittig was born in Berlin, Germany, and grew up in Kassel, where his father was a professor of applied arts. Strongly encouraged by his mother, he learned to play the piano with enthusiasm. Nevertheless, he decided to study chemistry in Tübingen after having finished school in 1916. His academic career was interrupted by World War I, when Wittig was drafted into the army. He became a prisoner of war in 1918. After his return to Germany in 1919, Wittig found it difficult to get into a German university because the universities were overcrowded at that time. Following several rejections, he finally was accepted by the director of the Chemical Insti-

tute in Marburg, Karl von Auwers. Because of this experience, he later supported students who came back after World War II as former prisoners of war.

After Wittig completed his doctoral thesis in 1923, von Auwers encouraged him to pursue an academic career. In 1926 Wittig was appointed lecturer at the University of Marburg after the completion of his *Habilitation* (permission to lecture in a university). In his early days in Marburg, he and Karl Ziegler (a 1963 Nobel laureate in chemistry) became lifelong friends. Both chemists were not only extraordinary scientists but enthusiastic rock climbers in the Alps. Another friend and colleague of Wittig's who accompanied him on his hikes and climbing tours was Walter Hückel, a professor of chemistry in Breslau and later in Tübingen.

When Hans Meerwein succeeded von Auwers as director of the Chemical Institute, he renewed Wittig's contract and employed him as a senior research assistant, having been deeply impressed by his textbook, *Stereochemie* (1930). In Marburg, Wittig married Waltraud Ernst, who also worked in von Auwers's group. They had three daughters. Waltraud Wittig, who also had a doctoral degree, took great interest in the scientific work of her husband until her early death in 1978. She also regularly invited the members of Wittig's research group to social events.

In 1932 Wittig received his first permanent position with an appointment as *Außerplanmäßiger Professor* (a title awarded to lecturers who are neither full nor associate professors) at the Technische Hochschule in Braunschweig. However, his time in Braunschweig proved to be a problematic period in Wittig's academic career. The director of the institute, Karl Fries, who was well-known for the discovery of the Fries rearrangement, strongly opposed the Nazi regime. Eventually, the Nazi government forced him to retire. Wittig, who had always supported Fries, feared that he, too, would lose his academic position.

Fortunately, he was invited by Hermann Staudinger, the director of the Chemical Institute at the University of Freiburg in Breisgau, to become an associate professor at that institution in 1937. (In Braunschweig there was a strong Nazi among the lecturers at that time. Staudinger also refused the Nazi regime and had to suffer under political pressure. Fortunately he could hold his position in this difficult period because of his very high scientific reputation.) Wittig presumably was chosen for this position because he had supported Staudinger's concept of high polymers in his *Stereochemie* in the face of much scientific opposition to the latter's fundamental work. (Staudinger eventually was awarded the Nobel Prize in Chemistry in 1953.)

Many of Wittig's important contributions were planned and begun at the University of Freiburg. Examples are the formulation of dehydrobenzene; the Wittig rearrangement of ethers; and the discovery of the new class of ammonium ylides. However, because this work was started during World War II, these concepts were not examined thoroughly until later, in the postwar period.

At Tübingen and Heidelberg. In 1943 Wilhelm Schlenk, a very capable organometallic chemist, died in Tübingen. The faculty of the University of Tübingen nominated Wittig as his successor there, and he was appointed full professor and director of the university's Chemical Institute. Finally, at the age of forty-seven years, Wittig reached a position where he would have the facilities and equipment that he needed.

After the end of the war, the number of students increased and Wittig was able to establish a very active research group. It was characteristic of him that he took care of each graduate student personally, even later in Heidelberg, when he had a large group. Often, he made sure to be present when an important experiment was started, maintaining that "four eyes see more than two." Wittig particularly wanted to see whether color changes occurred during a reaction, being one of those chemists who were interested in the relationship between the constitution and color of a substance. The purity of the reagents and solvents that were used was an important consideration for Wittig. The practical abilities of a graduate student were to be supervised through his personal control of all elemental analyses of new compounds isolated in his group. This procedure prevented him from drawing false conclusions.

Wittig set high standards regarding his students' qualifications and enthusiasm and demanded careful experiments performed at a clean laboratory space. On the other hand, he acknowledged the contributions and merits of each graduate student in his lectures.

Wittig gave strong attention to his academic duties. In Tübingen he chose promising younger colleagues—Walter Theilacker, Karl Dimroth, Rolf Huisgen, Friedrich Weygand—as associate professors; all got appointments as full professors from other universities in short order.

In 1956 Wittig moved once more. The director of the Chemical Institute at the University of Heidelberg, Karl Freudenberg, famous for his work in the field of natural products, retired, and the faculty nominated Wittig as his successor. Wittig accepted this prestigious appointment at the age of fifty-nine, although he had had great success during his time in Tübingen.

Heidelberg offered several advantages to Wittig. He could move into a large new building and establish a group of from thirty to forty members. The BASF company, where the Wittig reaction was being run on an industrial scale, was nearby in Ludwigshafen am Rhine. Two institutes, one for organic chemistry and a second one for inorganic chemistry, had recently been founded in Heidelberg. This made it possible to appoint three additional full professors for organic chemistry: Heinz A. Staab, Hermann Schildknecht, and Hans Plieninger. As a result, up to fourteen different research groups were active in the organic chemistry institute. The appeal of this institute is documented by the list of its distinguished visiting professors, including Donald J. Cram, Herbert C. Brown, Gerhard M. J. Schmidt, and Arthur G. Anderson Jr.

Wittig also had a great success as mentor. In Heidelberg, he encouraged many young scientists to start an academic career. The first one was Ulrich Schöllkopf, who demonstrated the value of the Wittig reaction as a graduate student. Other former students of Wittig had the same opportunity at other universities. Nearly all of them were appointed professors in Germany, the Netherlands, Switzerland, and the United States.

In 1979 Georg Wittig, together with Herbert C. Brown, was awarded the Nobel Prize in Chemistry. The Royal Swedish Academy of Science honored Brown and Wittig "for their development of the use of boron- and phosphorus-containing compounds, respectively, into important reagents in organic synthesis."

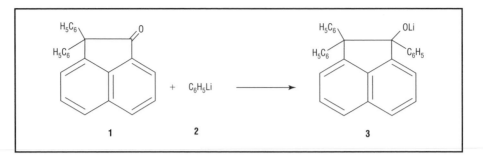

Figure 1. *Discovery of the Superiority of Phenyllithium (2) over against Phenylmagnesium Bromide.*

Between 1953 and 1979, Wittig received many awards, honorary doctorates, and other forms of recognition. He was the first German after World War II to receive an honorary doctorate from the Sorbonne, in Paris, in 1957. This was an acknowledgment of his meritoriousness for reestablishing the reputation of German science after the war.

Wittig's last years in Heidelberg were dominated by the sudden death of his wife and his own physical weakness. Wittig died a few weeks after his ninetieth birthday.

During his long career, more than three hundred graduate students and postdoctoral colleagues were associated with Wittig. The more than three hundred scientific papers that were published between 1924 and 1980 demonstrate the fruitfulness of his career. With his demise, the international community of organic chemists lost one of its greatest representatives in the twentieth century.

From Arenes to Organometallics. The first independent work of Wittig in Marburg followed from the chemistry of his academic teacher, von Auwers. He synthesized aromatic compounds with oxygen functionality and related heterocycles. However, Wittig soon entered new fields. His aim was to find highly strained three- and four-membered ring systems with a tendency to form diradicals. Physical methods to detect radicals were not available to Wittig at that time, so his efforts could not be brought to completion.

Nevertheless, Wittig's interest in radicals had a great impact on his further scientific work because it led him to organometallic chemistry. He needed sterically hindered compounds with phenyl groups as starting material. These substances were usually synthesized by the addition of organomagnesium derivatives, the Grignard compounds, to ketones. This classical reaction failed in the case of the ketone **1** in Figure 1. Therefore, Wittig used phenyllithium (**2**), the preparation of which had just been reported by his friend Ziegler. Indeed, phenyllithium proved to be superior to phenylmagnesium bromide and formed the desired product **3** in high yield.

This success led Wittig to a new orientation of his research interests. He now wanted to study the chemistry of the new reagent **2** in detail. In this way he entered the field of "carbanion chemistry," as he called it. Later, *organometallic chemistry* or *carbanionoid chemistry* became the preferred terms.

Discoveries with Phenyllithium. The most important discoveries of Wittig fall into the period between 1937 and 1956. In 1942 his review, "Phenyl-lithium, der Schlüssel zu einer neuen Chemie metallorganischer Verbindungen" (Phenyllithium, the key to a new chemistry of organometallic compounds), was published. In the course of his investigations, he observed the exchange of hydrogen for lithium and the exchange of bromine against lithium, the metalation and the halogen-metal exchange reactions. Simultaneously and independently, Henry Gilman, at Iowa State University in Ames, Iowa, observed the same behavior upon treating aryl halides with n-butyllithium. At that time, both exchanges were considered very unusual, but since then, they have become among the most widely used reactions in organometallic chemistry.

The treatment of fluorobenzene with phenyllithium gave surprising products again, which led Wittig in 1942 to propose dehydrobenzene C_6H_4 (benzyne **4**) as a reactive intermediate (see Figure 2). At first he hesitated to publish this adventurous hypothesis because he feared for his scientific reputation. Fortunately, John D. Roberts, at the California Institute of Technology (Caltech) at Pasadena, and Rolf Huisgen at the University of Munich found evidence to support the concept of dehydroaromatic compounds (arynes) in independent studies. Wittig himself succeeded in trapping the reactive intermediate **4** with furan (**5**) by means of a Diels-Alder reaction that proceeded to give **6** proceeded in high yield (see Figure 2).

The arynes and strained cycloalkynes that were generated in Heidelberg were later developed as valuable building blocks in organic synthesis because they undergo

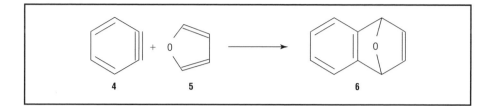

Figure 2. *The First Diels-Alder Reaction with Dehydrobenzene (Benzyne).*

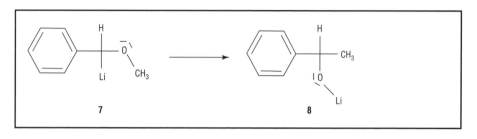

Figure 3. *The Wittig Rearrangement.*

manifold additions and cycloadditions. Reinhard W. Hoffmann, later professor at Marburg, published a comprehensive monograph, *Dehydrobenzene and Cycloalkynes*, in 1967. The diversity of reactions of organolithium derivatives was also demonstrated by the metalation of benzyl ethers. As in Figure 3, the lithiated ethers like **7** rearrange to carbinolates 8. The Wittig rearrangement of the type **7→8** has an interesting mechanism and a broad scope of application that is discussed in modern textbooks of organic chemistry.

Encouraged by the success with phenyllithium, Wittig began another bold research project in Freiburg. A dogma was often a challenge for him. Therefore, he sought to overthrow the octet rule for nitrogen compounds. To that end, he tried to prepare the pentacovalent compounds, tetramethylphenyl- and pentamethylnitrogen. As a result of his efforts, he discovered the new class of ammonium ylides.

Other authors later showed that derivatives containing a lithium salt should be considered as lithiated ammonium salts rather than as ylides. The ammonium ylides undergo various rearrangements and elimination reactions. In the course of this work Wittig always used benzophenone to determine the position of lithiation. This principle of obtaining crystalline derivatives for characterization sounds trivial, but it was just this procedure, using benzophenone, that led him in 1953 to the discovery of the Wittig reaction.

New Topics at Tübingen. Wittig's time in Tübingen was characterized by further successful research topics. The first organic ate-complexes with the structure **10** in Figure 4 were synthesized. The role of these complexes as reaction-determining intermediates was outlined and later found broad acceptance in the field of organometallic chemistry. In this context Wittig repeatedly pointed to the work of Hans Meerwein on onium-complexes **9** in cation chemistry. He was able to demonstrate that the basic concept of anionic activation of ligands in ate-complexes **10** as a counterpart to cationic activation in onium-complexes **9** is a useful one. A well-known representative is sodium tetraphenylborate (**11**), which was introduced in analytical chemistry as an excellent reagent for the quantitative determination of potassium and ammonium ions in aqueous solution.

Continuing the work on hypervalent compounds of the elements in the main groups 5–7 of the periodic table, Wittig was able to synthesize pentaphenyl phosphorane. Its higher homologues, tetraphenyltellurium and triphenyliodine, followed later.

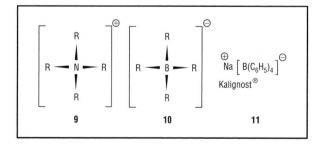

Figure 4. *Onium- and Ate-complexes.*

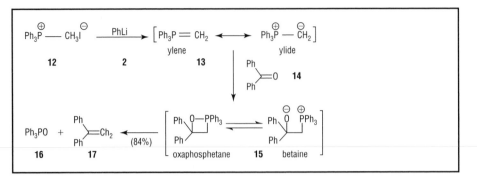

Figure 5. *The First Wittg Reaction (1953).*

In the course of these investigations, methyltriphenylphosphonium iodide (**12**) in Figure 5 was treated with phenylllithium (**2**). By analogy to the behavior of related ammonium salts, **2** did not add to the central atom but yielded triphenylphosphonium methylide (**13**) by proton abstraction. The use of the above-mentioned benzophenone (**14**) for the determination of the deprotonated position gave surprising products. Triphenylposphine oxide (**16**) and 1.1-diphenylethylene (**17**) were formed in high yield via the intermediate (**15**).

Wittig immediately recognized the need to examine the significance of this experiment. This was done by Ulrich Schöllkopf, later professor at Göttingen, in his doctoral thesis. Only one year later, Wittig and Schöllkopf published a pioneering paper, "Über Triphenyl-phosphin-methylene als olefinbildende Reagenzien (I. Mitteil)" (1954; Triphenyl phosphine methylene derivatives as reagents for the formation of olefins), in *Chemische Berichte* in which they demonstrated the broad scope of the reaction of **13** and higher homologues with ketones and aldehydes. In all cases, the new carbon-carbon double bond was formed in the original position of the former carbon-oxygen double bond. Such a regioselective carbonyl olefination under mild conditions without use of acids was not known at that time. Now, many unsolved problems could be overcome. For some fields, such as the synthesis of polyenes, this method was a revolution. Well-known examples are vitamin A and ß-carotene, for which syntheses on a large scale were developed by the chemical industry. Horst Pommer at BASF converted the Wittig reaction to industrial practice.

The Wittig reaction is one of the very important reactions in organic chemistry for industrial applications as well as academic research. This principle, modified and improved by many groups throughout the world, turned out to be highly reliable in numerous cases. The formation of the carbon-carbon double bond in the original position of the former carbon-oxygen bond was a prerequisite for the total synthesis of natural products performed with the aim of proving a proposed structure. In Germany, Leopold Horner at the University of Mainz developed related valuable olefination reactions.

The Wittig reaction was not designed—real novelties are seldom planned. It was, rather, the result of a theoretical quest, the search for pentacovalent compounds. In this context, Wittig possessed the ability to interpret an unexpected observation and to perceive at once its potential for the future.

Accomplishments at Heidelberg. The efforts of his many co-workers and the excellent equipment in Heidelberg made it possible for Wittig to fulfill his lifework. About 150 of his papers appeared in print between 1958 and 1980. The last one was Wittig's Nobel lecture. It is noteworthy that only eleven publications deal with the carbonyl olefination, the Wittig reaction. A new aldehyde synthesis was presented in one of these contributions. It was typical for Wittig not to accumulate analogous examples of a known method but, rather, to enter new territory. However he promoted the work of Manfred Schlosser, later a professor at the University of Lausanne in Switzerland, who found methods for performing the Wittig reaction in a stereoselective manner.

In Heidelberg, much effort was made to examine the generation of the highly strained lower cycloalkynes (cycloheptyne, cyclohexyne, and cyclopentyne) with a bent carbon-carbon triple bond as reactive intermediates. The alkyne synthesis from 1,2-diketones via 1,2-bis-hydrazones, developed by Theodor Curtius in 1891, proved to be especially suitable for this project. New approaches to the related arynes were also elaborated. A nonorganometallic route started with a heterocycle (1,2,3-benzothiadiazole-1,1-dioxide) that could be cleaved to give dehydrobenzene, nitrogen, and sulfur dioxide. Using different precursors for dehydrobenzene, Huisgen proved the existence of the intermediate C_6H_4 in cycloadditions.

The development of the directed aldol condensation was one of the new topics at that time. This method leads to ß-unsaturated carbonyl compounds such as ß-phenyl cinnamic aldehyde. The reaction sequence is a complement of the carbonyl olefination because unsaturated aldehydes and ketones are not available via phosphonium ylides.

The discovery of the directed aldol condensation is an impressive example of Wittig's persistence in his research. In 1942 a graduate student made an observation that could not be understood without the use of spectroscopic methods not available at that time. Later two other graduates were engaged to solve this problem in their doctoral theses. Only twenty years afterward did things become clear when it could be shown that lithium diethylamide, used in the earlier experiment, serves as lithium hydride donor to benzophenone.

This unusual redox reaction, which probably proceeds via an ate-complex, was the key to the solution of the problem and confirmed once more the importance of ate-complexes in organometallic chemistry. Wittig himself used this redox system for the enantioselective reduction of prochiral ketones with chiral amides. Later, other authors could obtain enantioselectivities up to 95 percent by the use of improved chiral lithium amides.

The syntheses of hypervalent phosphorus and arsenic compounds were continued in Heidelberg with the aim of exploring their interesting stereochemistry. Aside from Wittig, his former student, Dieter Hellwinkel, later a professor at Heidelberg, worked successfully in this field. Also, the interest of the Wittig group in strained compounds was shown by the elaboration of new cyclopropane syntheses via ylides and organozinc derivatives.

After his formal retirement Wittig came back to aromatic compounds and diradicals in which he had been interested more than fifty years earlier as a young lecturer. These late studies as professor emeritus opened an elegant way for other authors after his death to a dendrimer, a member of a modern class of macrocycles.

Finally, it should be noted that female graduate students participated in important developments. Utta Pockels found the hydrogen- and bromine-lithium exchange at Braunschweig, Maria-Helene Wetterling obtained trimethylammonium methylide at Freiburg, Lisa Löhmann observed the Wittig rearrangement at the same university, Liselotte Pohmer succeeded in trapping dehydrobenzene with furan at Tübingen, and Hannelore Renner worked out the fundamentals for the directed aldol condensation in Heidelberg.

Outlook. How can great contributions such as Wittig's be summarized briefly? The progress of organic syntheses in the twentieth century may be attributed to the use of derivatives of nearly all elements of the periodic table. Using simple compounds such as triphenylborane,

phenyllithium, and triphenylphosphine, Wittig opened new possibilities of fundamental importance.

On the occasion of the one hundredth anniversary of his birth in 1997, the Chemische Gesellschaft zu Heidelberg organized a special symposium, "The Research of Georg Wittig—Relevance to Chemistry Today." In his published lecture, "The Wittig and Related Reactions in Natural Product Synthesis" (1997), K. C. Nicolaou of the Skaggs Institute for Chemical Biology at La Jolla, California, concluded on pages 1297–1300:

> Having experienced the Wittig and related reactions in total synthesis, one can only attempt to imagine the state of art without them. Very few reactions can claim similar status to the Wittig reaction in revolutionizing organic synthesis. It is to say that, collectively, these discoveries have changed not only the way we do chemistry today, but, most significantly the way we live, through developments in chemistry that have found application in nutrition, cosmetics, agriculture, clothing, dyestuffs, plastics, high-tech materials, and medicine.

In 1999 the Georg Wittig Lectureship was inaugurated at the University of Heidelberg. Reinhard W. Hoffmann of the University of Marburg gave a lecture titled, "Wittig and His Accomplishments—Still Relevant beyond His 100th Birthday." Therein he not only summarized the most significant results but presented also examples of other authors who benefited from Wittig's work after his death. Hoffmann closed his review on page 1416 (2001) with these words: "The many examples provided in this essay show that Wittig's accomplishments become and remain important to chemists in changing contexts far beyond his hundredth birthday. The next generation of chemists has only to realize that Wittig's oeuvre is still a gold mine of facts and concepts to be exploited."

BIBLIOGRAPHY

A comprehensive list of the publications and awards of Georg Wittig can be found in the obituary by Werner Tochtermann in Liebigs Annalen/Recueil *(1997): i–xxi. Additional unpublished documents relating to Wittig can be found in the University Library and in the Library of the Chemical Institute in Heidelberg.*

WORKS BY WITTIG

Stereochemie. Leipzig, Germany: Akademische Verlagsgesellschaft, 1930.

"Phenyl-lithium, der Schlüssel zu einer neuen Chemie metallorganischer Verbindungen." *Naturwissenschaften* 30 (1942): 696–703.

With Ulrich Schöllkopf. "Über Triphenyl-phosphin-methylene als olefinbildende Reagenzien (I. Mitteil)." *Chemische Berichte* 87 (1954): 1318–1330.

"Small Rings with Carbon-Carbon Triple Bonds." *Angewandte Chemie* (International Edition in English) 1 (1962): 415–419.

"1,2-Dehydrobenzene." *Angewandte Chemie* (International Edition in English) 4 (1965): 731–737.

"The Role of Ate Complexes as Reaction-Determining Intermediates." *Quarterly Reviews* (Chemical Society, London) 20 (1966): 191–210.

With Helmut Reiff. "The Directed Aldol Condensations." *Angewandte Chemie* (International Edition in English) 7 (1968): 7–14.

"From Diyls over Ylides to My Idyll." *Accounts of Chemical Research* 7 (1974): 6–14.

OTHER SOURCES

Hoffmann, Reinhard W. *Dehydrobenzene and Cycloalkynes.* New York: Academic Press, 1967.

———. "Wittig and His Accomplishments—Still Relevant beyond His 100th Birthday." *Angewandte Chemie* (International Edition in English) 40 (2001): 1411–1416.

Maercker, Adalbert. "The Wittig Reaction." In *Organic Reactions,* edited by Arthur C. Cope. Vol. 14. New York: Wiley, 1965.

Nicolaou, K. C., Michael W. Härter, Janet L. Gunzner, et al. "The Wittig and Related Reactions in Natural Product Synthesis." *Liebigs Annalen/Recueil* (1997): 1283–1301.

Pommer, Horst. "The Wittig Reaction in Industrial Practice." *Angewandte Chemie* (International Edition in English) 16 (1977): 423–429.

Tochtermann, Werner. "Structures and Reactions of Organic Ate-Complexes." *Angewandte Chemie* (International Edition in English) 5 (1966): 351–371.

Werner Tochtermann

WOLLASTON, WILLIAM HYDE (*b.* East Dereham, Norfolk, England, 6 August 1766; *d.* London, 22 December 1828), *metallurgy, chemistry, optics, instrumentation, physiology.* For the original article on Wollaston see *DSB,* vol. 14.

Research since the 1970s has drawn heavily on the original laboratory notebooks, letters, and documents held by Cambridge University Library to reveal much new information about Wollaston's unhappy career as a physician, his business partnership with Smithson Tennant, and their entrepreneurial activities in the production and marketing of malleable platinum and organic chemicals. In addition, a more complete understanding has been gained of Wollaston's influential role in the development of atomistic thinking, his methods of scientific research,

and his reports of the visual disturbances known as hemianopsia.

Francis Wollaston married Althea Hyde in 1758, and over the years 1760–1778 they had seventeen children, of which fifteen survived into adulthood; William was the seventh child and third son. Francis was made rector of East Dereham, Norfolk, in 1761 but relocated to Chislehurst, Kent, as rector in 1769; the family continued to reside there until his death in 1815. William received his early education at Lewisham and Charterhouse before moving to Caius College, Cambridge, in 1782 to study medicine.

An Unhappy Physician. As described in the main article, Wollaston qualified as a physician and began his practice in Huntington in 1792, but within a few months he relocated to Bury St. Edmunds, where his uncle Charleton had practiced three decades previously. In 1797 he moved his practice to Cecil Street in London, where another uncle, the famed clinician William Heberden, had begun forty years earlier. By the time he left Bury, William had gained the necessary experience and maturity and seemed destined to advance his reputation in the capital. But he was miserable. In a letter to his lifelong Bury friend Henry Hasted, Wollaston wrote that "the practice of physic is not calculated to make me happy … [and] I have fully determined & now declare that *I have done with it.…* even if I turn waiter at a tavern ready to say "Yes Sir" to everyone that calls at any hour of the day or night, I cannot be a greater slave" (29 December 1800, Hasted correspondence, University College Library).

It is now known how Wollaston was able to escape his unhappy profession. His uncle West Hyde had died in 1797 and, without surviving children of his own, willed his considerable estate to his sister Althea's second-oldest son, George. In March 1799 George transferred £8,000 in Bank of England stock to William, who decided that he would use the money to establish a chemical business in secret partnership with an older Cambridge schoolmate and fellow London resident, Smithson Tennant. Tennant was the antithesis of Wollaston in many ways; he was parentless, eccentric, gregarious, and undisciplined but a competent chemist with ideas on how to make a living by converting abundant, low-cost materials into high-value commercial products.

Chemical Business. Tennant and Wollaston began their entrepreneurial activities with the purchase of nearly 6,000 troy ounces of granular alluvial platinum ore in December 1800 at a cost of £794. The two men had decided to keep all aspects of their partnership and research interests secret; not even their closest friends knew of the partnership, and details have only become known by study of the Cambridge notebooks. Evidence in the notebooks suggests that Wollaston assumed responsibility for the research and development side of the business while Tennant was to look after marketing and sales. In November 1800 Wollaston optimized the chemical process for the production of a purified platinum powder that he was able to compact into a solid, malleable mass in April 1801. Then, confident of commercial success, Wollaston purchased a house on the outskirts of London and converted its rear rooms into a large chemical laboratory.

Wollaston and Tennant knew that commercial production of malleable platinum had the potential to be a lucrative business, but only if they could secure access to the crude ore (then available only from the Spanish-controlled viceroyalty of New Granada and legally only through Spain) and protect the chemical and metallurgical details of the production process. They achieved these ends by committing to buy all platinum ore that became available in Kingston, Jamaica, after being smuggled out of New Granada, and by imposing rigorous security on Wollaston's production process (Usselman, 1980, 1989). Over a period of twenty years Wollaston, assisted only by his manservant, processed more than 47,000 troy ounces of crude platinum ore in a series of 16-to-30-ounce batches. Malleable ingots of platinum were sold for seventeen shillings per ounce by the London instrument maker William Carey, who received a 10 percent commission for his role (Chaldecott, 1979). The finest-quality platinum was used primarily for chemical apparatus, but the biggest markets were the gunnery business, where platinum replaced gold in the touchholes of firearms, and the sulfuric acid industry, where platinum boilers were used for the concentration of the corrosive acid. Total profits from the platinum business totaled about £17,000 by the time Wollaston closed down the business in 1820. Wollaston, who did all the processing work and even ended up superintending most of the marketing due to Tennant's increasing lack of focus, received 10 percent of the profits before equal division.

As Wollaston purified thousands of ounces of platinum, he accumulated large amounts of chemical by-products. Wollaston gave the portion of the ore insoluble in aqua regia to Tennant for investigation (the discovery of osmium and iridium followed in 1804), and he himself studied the portion of the ore that remained in solution after platinum had been precipitated from acidic solution. In 1802 he isolated and characterized the new metal palladium, which was present in the original crude ore in amounts of less than 1 percent. Wollaston was credited by his contemporaries as a chemical wizard for discovering an element so scarce in natural ores; they did not know that he was working with large amounts of ore much enriched in palladium, and Wollaston did not correct them. But his need to keep his platinum work secret created a dilemma. He wished to publicize his discovery of a new chemical

William Hyde Wollaston. *William Hyde Wollaston, circa 1810.* HULTON ARCHIVE/ GETTY IMAGES.

element and stake a claim to his priority, but he believed an honest account of the discovery process would draw others into platinum purification while he was slowly and tediously building up a supply of the metal for first sale in 1805. He decided to offer palladium for sale anonymously through a mineralogical shop with the consequences described in the main article (also Usselman, 1978). Chastened by the unfavorable publicity this mode of action occasioned, Wollaston announced his 1804 discovery of a second new element, rhodium, in an article in the *Philosophical Transactions of the Royal Society,* although without clues to the enabling platinum work.

Although Wollaston has been criticized for keeping the details of his platinum purification process secret, the strategy was a sound one. No one else was able to market platinum of Wollaston's quality until his process was published shortly before his death—it had been generally and erroneously believed that some unknown chemistry was the key to success. It is now understood why Wollaston restricted access to the rear of his house, where the furnaces, glass vessels, and chemicals were spread along benches; guests with an interest in chemistry were shown only portable equipment for chemical analysis in an anteroom.

Contributions to the Atomic Hypothesis. Wollaston and Tennant also hoped to convert the dregs left behind by wine production, known as argol (containing a large proportion of tartaric acid salts), into higher-value organic acids. As with the platinum work, Wollaston did all the exploratory chemistry and from 1802 until 1812 converted about 15,000 pounds of crude argol into tartaric acid, oxalic acid, and salt of sorrel (acid potassium hydrogen oxalate), all for subsequent sale. The organic business was even more labor-intensive than the platinum work and, when brought to a halt on Tennant's death in 1815, had netted the partners a profit of only £700. Although not financially lucrative, the work did draw Wollaston into a study of the composition of tartaric and oxalic acid salts and examples of multiple combining proportions. In 1803 and 1804 Wollaston found that potash could form three different salts with oxalic acid, and the amounts of acid relative to a fixed weight of base in the salts were in the ratio of 1:2:4. After reading the account of John Dalton's atomic hypothesis in Thomas Thomson's 1807 edition of *A System of Chemistry,* and learning of Thomson's forthcoming paper in the *Philosophical Transactions* on multiple proportions in two salts of oxalic acid, Wollaston quickly prepared his paper "On Super-Acid and Sub-Acid Salts" to follow Thomson's in early 1808. Wollaston recognized that the law of integral multiple proportions was a logical consequence of atom-to-atom combination, and he accepted Dalton's hypothesis as an adequate explanation. Wollaston's paper gave further examples of multiple proportions in the salts of carbonic and sulfuric acids and procedures for determining the ratios. Near the end of the paper (and confounding the mistaken view of him as a cautious thinker) Wollaston proposed that after the combination of atoms became better understood "we shall be obliged to acquire a geometrical conception of their relative arrangement in all the three dimensions of solid extension" (1808, p. 101). Wollaston's examples (coupled with his reputation for careful and correct analysis) gave atomic theory heightened credibility.

In later papers that involved atomistic ideas Wollaston was consistent in his acceptance of material atoms as the best available explanation for a wide range of chemical phenomena. However, until some mode of investigation could give concrete evidence of the reality of atoms, he believed that experimental results ought not be skewed to fit the hypothesis. Thus although he explained crystal structures by the ordered packing of particulate spheres and oblate spheroids, he admitted that point-centered force fields of similar peripheral extent could yield the same result, and although combining weights were consistent with atom-to-atom combination they were not incontrovertible evidence for material atoms. Wollaston was not so much an early positivist as he was someone willing to entertain multiple hypotheses until the experi-

mental superiority of one of the contenders became compelling. And he believed he provided that evidence for atomic theory with his paper on the finite extent of the atmosphere in 1822.

Wollaston's interest in the visual disturbance known as hemianopsia emanated from his own episodes of visual problems. In 1800 he lost the left half of his visual field in both eyes for several minutes, and in 1822 he temporarily lost the right half of his vision. Wollaston correlated these afflictions with the upset stomachs and headaches suffered by others who reported similar occurrences, a grouping of symptoms now known to be associated with migraine. That Wollaston suffered from migraine is substantiated by an 1828 notebook record of zigzag lines in his visual field, an early record of the "fortification spectra" that George Airy later connected with migraine. Although Wollaston's death from a brain tumor was confirmed by a postmortem examination, his earliest visual problems were likely unrelated to that lesion.

Character. Comments written by his closest friends and associates portray Wollaston as a publicly quiet and austere figure who treasured uninterrupted time to pursue his scientific interests. But when in the frequent company of friends, family, children, and the genuinely and unaffectedly curious, he became sociable, generous, warmhearted, informative, and occasionally even mischievous. Unfortunately the most reliable contemporary portraits were removed from the public record by Henry Warburton, who collected all of Wollaston's notebooks, letters, and memorials after his friend's death, kept them out of others' hands, and died without publishing a planned biography. Until the Warburton material was rediscovered in Cambridge in 1949, Wollaston's historical persona had been shaped by a sprinkling of anecdotes told by a few contemporaries who did not know him well, and his reputation suffered as a result. However, subsequent research has begun to corroborate the opinion of many of his contemporaries, who judged Wollaston to be the leading natural philosopher of his time.

SUPPLEMENTARY BIBLIOGRAPHY

The L. F. Gilbert papers at University College Library, London, contain several original letters to and from Wollaston, together with typed copies of important correspondence between Wollaston and Henry Hasted, and Wollaston and Alexander Marcet. Another valuable series of letters from Wollaston to Edward Daniel Clarke is held in private hands.

WORKS BY WOLLASTON

"Reward of Twenty Pounds for the Artificial Production of Palladium." *Journal of Natural Philosophy, Chemistry and the Arts* 7 (1804): 75.

"On Super-Acid and Sub-Acid Salts." *Philosophical Transactions* 98 (1808): 96–102.

"Extract of a Letter from Dr. Wollaston." *Annals of Philosophy* 2 (1813): 316.

"Letter from W. H. Wollaston … Together with a Report of Mons. Biot. … upon Periscopic Spectacles." *Journal of Natural Philosophy, Chemistry and the Arts* 36 (1813): 316–321; also in *Philosophical Magazine* 42 (1813): 387–390.

"Crimson-Coloured Snow, and Meteoric Iron." Appendix iii in John Ross, *A Voyage of Discovery … for the Purpose of Exploring Baffin's Bay.* London: J. Murray, 1819.

Patents

1804, No. 2752. "Spectacles," for concavo/convex spectacle lenses.

1806, No. 2993. "Drawing Apparatus," for the camera lucida.

OTHER SOURCES

Chaldecott, John A. "William Cary and His Association with William Hyde Wollaston." *Platinum Metals Review* 23, no. 3 (1979): 112–123.

Coatsworth, L. L., B. I. Kronberg, and M. C. Usselman. "The Artifact as Historical Document. Part 2: The Palladium and Rhodium of W. H. Wollaston." *Ambix* 28, no. 1 (1981): 20–35.

Kronberg, B. I., L. L. Coatsworth, and M. C. Usselman. "Mass Spectrometry as an Historical Probe: Quantitative Answers to Historical Questions in Metallurgy." In *Archaeological Chemistry–III,* edited by Joseph B. Lambert, 295–310. ACS Advances in Chemistry Series no. 205. Washington, DC: American Chemical Society, 1984.

McDonald, Donald, and Leslie B. Hunt. *A History of Platinum and Its Allied Metals.* London: Johnson Matthey, 1982.

Usselman, Melvyn C. "The Platinum Notebooks of William Hyde Wollaston." *Platinum Metals Review* 22, no. 3 (1978): 100–106.

———. "The Wollaston/Chenevix Controversy over the Elemental Nature of Palladium: A Curious Episode in the History of Chemistry." *Annals of Science* 35, no. 6 (1978): 551–579.

———. "William Wollaston, John Johnson, and Colombian Alluvial Platina: A Study in Restricted Industrial Enterprise." *Annals of Science* 37, no. 3 (1980): 253–268.

———. "Merchandising Malleable Platinum: The Scientific and Financial Partnership of Smithson Tennant and William Hyde Wollaston." *Platinum Metals Review* 33, no. 3 (1989): 129–136.

———. "William Hyde Wollaston's Platinum Process: The Bicentenary of the Platinum Industry." *Chemistry in Britain* (December 2001): 38–40.

Melvyn C. Usselman

WOOD, HARLAND GOFF (*b.* Delavan, Minnesota, 2 September 1907; *d.* Cleveland, Ohio, 12 September 1991), *biochemistry, enzymology, intermediary metabolism.*

Wood was a major force in biochemistry's twentieth-century disciplinary evolution. His revolutionary work on heterotrophic CO_2-fixation (the ability of nonplants and specialized bacteria to fix CO_2), an investigative pathway that shaped his entire career, challenged existing biological paradigms and was twice nominated for the Nobel Prize. His major biochemical contributions include: demonstrating the biochemical importance of CO_2 (Wood, 1982); using isotopes (especially radioisotopes) as tools to understand metabolic processes (Wood, 1963); elucidating the bacterial propionic acid cycle (Wood, 1976); analyzing the extremely complex structure and mechanism of the enzyme transcarboxylase (Wood, 1979); characterizing the metabolic role of pyrophosphate (PPi) (Wood, 1988); and clarifying the clostridial acetate biosynthesis pathway (Drake, 1993). Completed near his career end, the last project described a totally novel CO_2-fixation mechanism. Wood's biochemical contributions are historically important because, unlike many of his contemporaries, he focused *primarily* on bacterial systems that had no medical significance. Wood also contributed to biochemistry's disciplinary structure as Biochemistry chair at Western Reserve Medical School, where he built the department into one of national distinction. He was also instrumental in organizing and implementing Western Reserve's unique and innovative medical curriculum that led "the way to experimentation and change in almost every medical school in the nation" (Harvey and Abrams, 1986, p. 253). In all of these activities Harland's personal and scientific style was characterized by a potent ability to develop close collaborative relationships.

Early Life and Education. Wood was the third son of six children in a middle-class, Midwestern family. His father, William C. Wood, was a real estate businessman and also operated a small family farm in Mankato, Minnesota. His mother, Inez Goff Wood, "operated the family," no small task considering its size and the economic times. Despite the family's modest means, all six Wood children completed college degrees; several of Wood's siblings completed advanced degrees (his younger brother, Earl, was an early recipient of a combined MD/PhD degree).

Wood's early education was in Mankato's public schools. A high school yearbook suggests that he was a "school hero"; he lettered in several sports, was Honor Society vice president, class leader, and apparent "heartthrob" of several female classmates. Medicine was his high school career goal, but because of difficulty translating Cicero, a Latin teacher diverted him into chemistry.

In 1927 Wood entered Macalester College in St. Paul, Minnesota, where he completed an undergraduate degree in chemistry. His athletic interests continued in varsity football, track, and swimming. He worked in the college dining hall and as an athletic trainer to help pay college expenses. An unusual aspect of his college education was his marriage to Mildred Davis in September 1929. The marriage, which lasted for more than six decades, began a month before the Great Depression and required the college president's approval. In his senior year Wood was unsuccessfully applying to chemistry graduate programs, when his biology professor suggested that he apply to the Iowa State College Bacteriology Department in Ames, Iowa. Shortly thereafter he received a $450 fellowship to study bacteriology in Chester Hamlin Werkman's laboratory.

Iowa State College and Werkman. When Wood joined Werkman's lab, Werkman apparently provided little direction for his research, beyond handing him a copy of Cornelis Bernardus van Niel's doctoral thesis on the propionic acid bacteria metabolism (1928) and telling him to find a problem. Wood began to study the organism's physiology using an analytical technique called a "fermentation balance."

In 1935, as he was completing his PhD thesis, Wood noticed that when the bacteria were grown on glycerol, not all of the carbon balances totaled 100 percent, nor were the O/R (oxidation and reduction) reactions balanced. However, when he assumed the bacteria fixed CO_2, both experimental components balanced. The difficulty with this assumption was that the existing biological dogma stated that heterotrophic organisms, such as the propionic acid bacteria, could not fix CO_2.

Wood wanted to delay his thesis completion in order to further test the heterotrophic CO_2-fixation hypothesis. However, Werkman—apparently not believing the data—resisted, and Wood finished and defended the dissertation (1934). He spent the next year (1935–1936) at the University of Wisconsin working in William Peterson's laboratory with Edward Lawrie Tatum on a National Research Council (NRC) postdoctoral fellowship. During the year he wrote the first papers discussing the notion of heterotrophic CO_2-fixation (Wood and Werkman, 1936 a,b). Because of financial considerations and increasing European political instability, Wood abandoned a planned second NRC year in Germany and returned to Ames as a postdoctoral associate with Werkman.

Whatever initial resistance Werkman had to the idea, his laboratory rapidly became devoted to understanding the biochemistry behind heterotrophic CO_2-fixation, a process referred to as "the Wood-Werkman Reaction." Over the next seven years the lab produced twenty-nine full papers, most of which focused on various aspects of the reaction's biochemistry.

By the early 1940s Wood had helped establish Werkman's laboratory as one of the most productive and creative microbial physiology research centers in the country. The laboratory produced several leading American biochemists and microbiologists; three former students (Wood, Merton Utter, and Lester Krampitz), as well as Werkman, were elected to the National Academy of Sciences. Hugo Theorell and Carl and Gerty Cori nominated both Werkman and Wood for the Nobel Prize in Physiology or Medicine in 1948 and 1949.

Breakup with Werkman. Despite its creative and productive nature, Wood's collaboration with Werkman ended abruptly. In 1942 Wood received the Society of American Bacteriologists' (subsequently American Society for Microbiology) Eli Lilly Award. The award, one of the society's most prestigious honors, came with a $1,000 check that the Wood family intended to use for an Ames home purchase. When Werkman heard about the real estate plan, he asked Wood, "Why did you do that, do you think you can stay here forever?" The comment precipitated a major argument; Wood apparently believed that his position was indeed permanent. Within months Wood left Iowa for the University of Minnesota as associate professor of physiological chemistry.

Utter joined Wood in St. Paul, beginning a lifelong friendship and collaboration. Their research focused on using ^{13}C to study metabolism in poliovirus-infected rats and to trace CO_2 incorporation into glycogen. Their Minnesota sojourn was brief; in 1946 Wood was invited to reorganize and chair the Department of Biochemistry at Western Reserve University School of Medicine (WRU, later Case Western Reserve University or CWRU) in Cleveland, Ohio. Although initially perceived as a "farm bacteriologist," Wood was rapidly recognized as Western Reserve's leading biomedical faculty member (Williams, 1980, p. 489).

Western Reserve University School of Medicine. Up until the mid-twentieth century, biochemistry at Western Reserve was initially dominated by what Robert Kohler describes as "medical chemists" who were then displaced by practitioners of "physiological or pathological chemistry" (1982). In May 1945, Joseph Treloar Wearn was appointed Medical School dean with a charge to "rehabilitate" both the medical school and its curriculum. To rehabilitate the existing biochemistry program, he transferred its faculty to a newly created Clinical Biochemistry Department. Then, in 1946, he recruited Wood to chair the, now empty, Biochemistry Department and gave him free reign to hire new faculty. Over the next ten to fifteen years the department evolved into one of the top-ranked biochemistry departments in the country.

Early Scientific Research at Western Reserve. Wood's Western Reserve career, which spanned more than half his life, was extremely diverse, however the papers that he initially published after his arrival at WRU possibly suggest a lack of focus. He and Utter completed projects on poliovirus started at Minnesota. He also extended experiments using ^{13}C as a tracer to study connections between fatty acids and carbohydrate metabolism in rats. When ^{14}C became commercially available in the late 1940s Wood immediately shifted to using the isotope and rapidly became a master at tracing metabolic pathways by following isotope labeling patterns. While he explored a variety of different metabolic processes during this time, increasingly his work followed two dominant threads: clarifying metabolic pathways of bacterial propionic acid formation and elucidating the mechanism whereby glucose is fermented to acetic acid.

Trailing the Propionic Acid Bacteria. Although Wood viewed himself as an enzymologist throughout his career, much of his research work prior to the mid-1950s involved whole cells or tissue slices. By 1960, however, this practice changed, and his laboratory began to isolate and characterize pure enzymes in a way that Arthur Kornberg described as "brilliant" (Singleton, 1997b, p. 366).

During the period from 1950 to 1960, Wood returned to the work he had begun at Iowa State. His lab purified all of the major enzymes that cyclically produced propionic acid in the propionic acid bacteria; the research resolved the chemical mechanism for the "Wood-Werkman reaction." Wood's research style was critical to this endeavor. The laboratory worked with a sense of unity. Bacteria were grown and harvested, often commercially, in large quantity. Common procedures were used to purify individual enzymes. Enzymatic assays often were performed by coupling reactions with other enzymes under investigation elsewhere in the laboratory. All of these approaches were combined in a single 1964 paper; the Wood lab reported the extensive purification of the major enzymes involved in the cycle, which were combined to achieve a partial reconstitution of the propionate fermentation.

The Role of CO_2 in Acetate Biosynthesis. Shortly after his move to Cleveland, Wood became interested in bacteria that ferment glucose to acetic acid (reaction 1):

$$C_6H_{12}O_6 \rightarrow 3\ CH_3 \cdot COOH \qquad (1)$$

In this reaction, one six-carbon compound is converted into *three* two-carbon compounds, a reaction that posed the following conundrum. When glucose is anaerobically

oxidized to pryuvate via glycolysis, reduced nicotinamide adenine dinucleotide (NADH) accumulates; unless NADH is reoxidized to NAD, glucose oxidation ceases. Over evolutionary history, a variety of biochemical processes have evolved to regenerate NAD. The puzzle was that in most of these pathways, pyruvate was converted to either three-carbon entities or two-carbon compounds and CO_2.

Based on Horace Albert Barker and Martin David Kamen's 1945 work with $^{14}CO_2$ and his own work with $^{13}CO_2$ in 1952, Wood suggested that the fermentation involved two reactions:

$$C_6H_{12}O_6 + 2H_2O \rightarrow$$
$$2\ CH_3 \cdot COOH + 8\ H^+ + 2\ CO_2 \qquad (2)$$

$$8\ H^+ + 2\ CO_2 \rightarrow$$
$$CH_3 \cdot COOH + 2\ H_2O \qquad (3)$$

Wood then embarked on an investigative trail to clarify the nature of reaction (3), which along with work on transcarboxylase dominated the rest of his career.

Numerous individuals collaborated on the acetate biosynthesis problem; however, Lars Ljungdahl was central to the problem's resolution. Ljungdahl joined Wood's lab in the early 1960s, initially as a technician. Wood especially wanted Ljungdahl to be involved in the acetate problem; in a 1962 job offer letter, he stated: "I'd just love to have that problem solved, and I think with more time you could do it. It certainly would be a big feather in your cap if you did and would, I believe, unfold some new things in biochemistry of great importance." Ljungdahl accepted the job, completed a PhD with Wood in 1964, and became heavily involved in the acetate biosynthesis problem. When he moved to a University of Georgia faculty position in 1967, Wood agreed that Ljungdahl could take part of the problem with him.

After Ljungdahl moved to Athens, Georgia, the two men were clear about which problem component was their individual "territory" and did not hesitate to object when someone appeared to cross the "boundary." Nevertheless, students might complete a PhD in Athens and move to Cleveland as a postdoctoral, or vice versa. Ljungdahl occasionally went to Cleveland for a crucial experiment; Wood spent a 1969 sabbatical year in Athens. In the days before faxes and e-mail, copies of lab notebook pages were mailed from one lab to the other; long phone conversations involved sometimes heated arguments over the meaning of data. Manuscript drafts were mailed from Cleveland to Athens and back for commentary and revision.

Wood's 1962 comment to Ljungdahl that the acetate problem might "unfold some new things in biochemistry of great importance" was a significant understatement.

Over the next twenty plus years the two labs collaborated to resolve a complete pathway that confirmed Wood's 1952 proposal outlined in reactions (2) and (3). Part of the pathway [reaction (2)] involved conventional reactions whereby glucose is fermented to acetate and CO_2. The mechanism of CO_2-fixation [reaction (3)], however, was far more complex and novel, involving several newly discovered enzymes and unique cofactors. The research was made more difficult because several key enzymes or intermediates were oxygen or light sensitive, and required anaerobic conditions and absence of light. By 1986 the reaction sequence was referred to in the literature as the "Wood-Ljungdahl pathway" of CO_2 autotrophic fixation (Drake, 1993).

Summary. Arthur Kornberg noted that science is a discipline "that enables *ordinary* people … to go about doing *ordinary* things, which, when assembled, reveal the *extraordinary* intricacies and awesome beauties of nature … [science also] permits them to contribute to grand enterprises" (1987, p. 6891). Wood's career vividly illustrates these themes. His early life on the Midwestern prairie was certainly ordinary. Yet, within a few years he became a major contributor to the "grand enterprise" of biochemistry's twentieth-century disciplinary explosion. Furthermore, there is an aesthetic beauty in the intricacy of the two pathways of CO_2-fixation and the complex structure and chemistry of the enzyme transcarboxylase that he described.

Wood's career is an exemplar of another modern science practice in its illustration of ways that scientific collaboration can alter career patterns. He was, from his earliest days, an accomplished collaborator, who worked with individuals from a variety of disciplines. For example, Wood began as the junior person in his collaboration with Werkman. Within a few years he was virtually running Werkman's laboratory, so that both men were elected to the National Academy of Sciences and twice nominated for the Nobel Prize. Arguably, Werkman would not have accrued this prestige had he not had Wood as a collaborator; his productivity significantly decreased after Wood's departure.

Wood's relationship with Ljungdahl illustrates another aspect of scientific collaboration. Like Wood's encounter with Werkman, Ljungdahl joined the Wood lab in a junior role as technician/student and rapidly evolved to a coequal stature. However, as the work progressed the two men were able to maintain the collaborative effort for more than thirty years. Both of their careers were enhanced by the interaction, and they remained lifelong friends.

Wood served as a presidential science advisor and was on numerous journal editorial boards. In his life's last decades he was active in the International Union of Biochemistry and Molecular Biology. However, the laboratory was Wood's real life passion. Unlike many of his contemporaries, he was active in the lab at the time of his death. Though he had dealt with a form of lymophoma for several years, he died as a result of a fall in a hospital after undergoing chemotherapy. Perhaps much of his life was summarized by his brother Earl, who commented, "Harland and I had three passions in life. Our families were first, science was second, and hunting was third."

BIBLIOGRAPHY

WORKS BY WOOD

The Physiology of the Propionic Acid Bacteria. PhD diss., Iowa State College, Ames, Iowa, 1934.

With Chester H. Werkman. "Mechanism of Glucose Dissimilation by the Propionic Acid Bacteria." *Biochemical Journal* 30 (1936a): 618–623.

———. "The Utilization of CO_2 in the Dissimilation of Glycerol by the Propionic Acid Bacteria." *Biochemical Journal* 30 (1936b): 48–53.

"Letter to Lars Ljungdahl, dated Oct. 30, 1962." Personal communication kindly provided by Professor Ljungdahl.

With Joseph Katz and Bernard Landau. "Estimation of Pathways of Carbohydrate Metabolism." *Biochemische Zeitschrift* 338 (1963): 809–847.

"My Life and Carbon Dioxide Fixation." In *The Molecular Basis of Biological Transport: Proceedings of the Miami Winter Symposia,* vol. 3, edited by Jacob Frederick Woessner Jr. and F. Huijing. New York: Academic Press, 1972.

"Trailing the Propionic Acid Bacteria." In *Reflections on Biochemistry: In Honour of Severo Ochoa,* edited by Arthur Kornberg, Bernard Horecker, L. Cornudella, and Juan Oro. New York: Pergamon, 1976.

"The Anatomy of Transcarboxylase and the Role of Its Subunits." *Critical Reviews of Biochemistry and Molecular Biology* 7 (1979): 143–160.

"The Discovery of the Fixation of CO_2 by Heterotrophic Organisms and Metabolism of the Propionic Acid Bacteria." In *Of Oxygen, Fuels, and Living Matter,* edited by Giorgio Semenza. New York: Wiley, 1982.

"Then and Now." *Annual Review of Biochemistry* 54 (1985): 1–41.

"Squiggle Phosphate of Inorganic Pyrophosphate and Polyphosphates." In *The Roots of Modern Biochemistry: Fritz Lipmann's Squiggle and Its Consequences,* edited by Horst Kleinkauf, Hans von Döhren, and Lothar Jaenicke. Berlin: Walter de Gruyter, 1988.

Interview by J. James Bohning. 19 January 1990 at Case Western Reserve University. Oral History Transcript #0082. Chemical Heritage Foundation. Philadelphia, Pennsylvania.

OTHER SOURCES

Barron, E. S. "Mechanisms of Carbohydrate Metabolism: An Essay on Comparative Biochemistry." In *Advances in Enzymology and Related Subjects of Biochemistry,* vol. 3, edited by Friedrich Franz Nord and Chester H. Werkman. New York: Interscience, 1943.

Cartter, Allan Murray. *An Assessment of Quality in Graduate Education.* Washington, DC: American Council on Education, 1966.

Drake, Harold L. "Co$_2$, Reductant, and the Autotrophic Acetyl-Coa Pathway: Alternative Origins and Destinations." In *Microbial Growth On C$_1$ Compounds,* edited by J. Colin Murrell and Don P. Kelly. Andover: Intercept Ltd.

Harvey, A. McGehee, and Susan L. Abrams. *"For the Welfare of Mankind": The Commonwealth Fund and American Medicine.* Baltimore: Johns Hopkins University Press, 1986.

Kohler, Robert E. *From Medical Chemistry to Biochemistry: The Making of a Biomedical Discipline.* Cambridge, U.K.: Cambridge University Press, 1982.

Kornberg, Arthur. "The Two Cultures: Chemistry and Biology." *Biochemistry* 26 (1987): 6888–6891.

Nier, Alfred O. C. Unpublished interview by Michael A. Grayson and Thomas Krick. 7 and 8 April 1989. Oral History Transcript #0112. Chemical Heritage Foundation, Philadelphia, Pennsylvania.

Ragsdale, Stephen W. "Life with Carbon Monoxide." *Critical Reviews in Biochemistry and Molecular Biology* 39 (2004): 165–195.

Singleton, Rivers, Jr. "Heterotrophic CO$_2$-fixation, Mentors, and Students: The Wood-Werkman Reactions." *Journal of the History of Biology* 30 (1997a): 91–120.

———. "Harland Goff Wood: An American Biochemist." In *Selected Topics in the History of Biochemistry: Personal Recollections,* vol. 5, edited by Giorgio Semenza and Rainer Jaenicke. Amsterdam: Elsevier Science, 1997b.

———. "From Bacteriology to Biochemistry: Albert Jan Kluyver and Chester Werkman at Iowa State." *Journal of the History of Biology* 33 (2000): 141–180.

Van Niel, Cornelis Bernardus. *The Propionic Acid Bacteria.* Haarlem, The Netherlands: Boisevain, 1928.

Williams, Greer, assisted by Margaret Henning. *Western Reserve's Experiment in Medical Education and Its Outcome.* New York: Oxford University Press, 1980.

Wood, Chester W., comp. *The Wood-Goff Family Chronicle.* Leesburg, FL: privately printed, 1976. Photocopy available from Preservation Department, Iowa State University Library, Ames, Iowa. 2003.

Rivers Singleton Jr.

WOODWARD, ROBERT BURNS (*b.* Boston, Massachusetts, 10 April 1917; *d.* Cambridge, Massachusetts, 8 July 1979), *organic chemistry—synthetic organic, reaction mechanisms.*

Woodward was one of the preeminent organic chemists of the twentieth century. Spending most of his career at Harvard University in Cambridge, Massachusetts, he won the 1965 Nobel Prize in Chemistry for his contributions to the science and art of organic chemistry. Woodward was acclaimed for his syntheses of complex organic molecules, including cholesterol and cortisone (1951), strychnine (1954), reserpine (1956), and vitamin B$_{12}$ (1972).

Woodward elegantly reproduced in the laboratory many chemical products of nature. A master at designing these complex syntheses, he was also known for determining the chemical structures of natural products, for his innovative thinking on the theory of organic chemistry, and for his aggressive use of the latest in analytical equipment. He believed instruments could routinely assist the chemist in the characterization of compounds and suggest new generalizations about the relationship of chemical structure to physical properties. Given Woodward's diverse professional attachments and eye for the latest trends in chemistry, his career was emblematic of the growth of synthetic organic chemistry in the middle decades of the twentieth century. Though employed at Harvard from 1937 until his death in 1979, Woodward had extensive ties to commercial firms, especially in the pharmaceutical industry. Woodward was married in 1938 to Irja Pullman, with whom he had two daughters, Siiri and Jean; in 1946, he married Eudoxia Muller, with whom he had a daughter and a son, Crystal and Eric. This second marriage, though longer than the first, also ended in divorce.

Early Life and Career. Woodward's father, Arthur, died in the influenza pandemic of 1918, when Robert was an infant. An only child raised by his mother, Margaret (née Burns), in often tight financial circumstances, Woodward attended public schools in Quincy, Massachusetts, but much of his education did not take place in the classroom. He was an autodidact whose interest in chemistry dated from his early years. At the age of fourteen, Woodward bought a copy of Ludwig Gattermann's *Practical Methods of Organic Chemistry* (1896). In later life he did not discourage persistent rumors that he had performed all the experiments in Gattermann's book. The youthful Woodward also received a number of catalogs and manuals from various chemical supply and laboratory equipment companies, and he requested issues of *Liebigs Annalen der Chemie* [Liebig's Annals of Chemistry] and *Berichte der Deutschen Chemischen Gesellschaft* [Reports of the German Chemical Society] from Verlag Chemie of Berlin. Woodward's interest in organic chemistry remained at the center of his being throughout his life.

Entering the Massachusetts Institute of Technology in 1933 at the age of sixteen, Woodward gained fame in the Boston newspapers as a prodigious youth. However, his narrow focus on chemical pursuits led to some difficulty at MIT. Only the personal intervention of James

Flack Norris, Woodward's organic chemistry professor, saved him from dropping out. Norris provided Woodward and MIT with a solution wherein Woodward satisfied his course requirements by examination without having to attend lectures. At MIT he earned his bachelor's degree in 1936 and his doctorate in 1937. His thesis dealt with the female steroid hormone, estrone. Woodward's estrone research resulted in the publication of several papers in the *Journal of the American Chemical Society* in 1940. By this time Woodward had already formed bonds with industry—industrial collaborators had provided intermediates for his estrone synthesis, free of charge.

After Woodward's MIT graduation, he accepted a position at the University of Illinois, where he had significant difficulties finding his niche. Following an abortive summer there, he was able to return to Harvard when E. P. Kohler hired him as a private research assistant in the fall of 1937. Although the Harvard Society of Fellows turned him down in 1937, Woodward had better luck the next year, becoming a member of the society the following fall. Though he enjoyed the freedom this position allowed, he wanted to pursue a more aggressive research program, and this required collaborators, especially graduate students. In a country headed to war, a responsible teaching position may also have provided greater refuge from the draft. In the fall of 1941, he accepted the position of instructor in chemistry at Harvard, yet 1942 saw him entertaining an offer of a research fellowship at the California Institute of Technology in Pasadena from Linus Pauling and looking at the Chemistry Department at the University of California in Berkeley. The reason was that although he was happy at Harvard, it remained unclear whether there would be a long-term position for him there.

At this juncture, Woodward's industrial connections proved their worth. Edwin Land, founder and head of the Polaroid Corporation, stepped in and offered Woodward some research opportunities. During World War II, Japanese advances in the Pacific in 1942 had cut off Polaroid from its sources of quinine, a key ingredient in the production of its light polarizing sheets and films. In that year, Woodward and his Polaroid collaborators produced a chemically simple, light-polarizing replacement for quinine. He had been interested in quinine itself since he was a child, using approaches to the synthesis of quinine as exercises while teaching himself chemistry. Now he asked Land to support an attempt at quinine's synthesis. After Woodward failed to secure federal support, Polaroid agreed to fund his synthesis. In February 1943, Woodward and coworker William E. Doering began a synthesis of quinine, building on the work of German chemist Paul Rabe, who had determined quinine's structure in 1908. They completed the synthesis of their key intermediate, quinotoxine, on 10 April 1944, Woodward's twenty-sev-

enth birthday. While some have since questioned whether their quinotoxine work constituted a total synthesis of quinine, there is no doubt that the wartime attention that quinine attracted gave Woodward national and even international recognition, including a large photo-news story in *Life* magazine. The excitement generated in the lay press by his approaches to quinine illustrated his keen ability to identify critical and high-profile targets for his chemical research. Also, Land's bridging support for a team effort on quinine boosted Woodward's career at a crucial moment. In 1944, he was appointed assistant professor and began his climb through the ranks of the Harvard faculty.

Synthesis. After World War II, Woodward worked on syntheses of patulin (an antibiotic), morphine, protein, and other materials with industrial potentials. He was promoted to associate professor in 1946, full professor in 1950, and Morris Loeb Professor of Chemistry in 1953. Much as he had before the war, Woodward continued to foster connections within both academe and industry, exchanging materials and findings with a large number of chemists. In 1948, with interest in cortical compounds growing, he again turned his attention to steroids. In the following years, he undertook and completed some of the first total syntheses of the steroids cholesterol and cortisone (1951) and then the related terpene lanosterol (1954). Woodward's steroid work illustrated various strategies of competition or cooperation that he employed for academic as well as industrial research. His work on cortisone was in an intensely competitive field with a number of international groups vying to be the first to create this new "miracle" drug in the laboratory, with Woodward's close industrial collaborations supporting his Harvard-based research efforts. Cortisone work brought Woodward into conflict with such eminent competitors as Oxford University's Robert Robinson, much as Woodward's work on the structure of strychnine did later. One can contrast the cortisone competition with the international cooperation that existed in the synthesis of the steroid lanosterol, on which Woodward and British chemist Derek H. R. Barton cooperated, or the collaboration of Barton and Woodward with the Swiss group of Vladimir Prelog and Oskar Jeger on the structure of cevine. In 1954, Woodward announced syntheses of strychnine and lysergic acid, followed in 1956 by a synthesis of reserpine that became a model of elegant technique and was employed commercially for reserpine production. Subsequent synthetic achievements included chlorophyll (1960), tetracycline (1962), colchicine (1963), and cephalosporin C (1965). With Konrad Bloch, he also first proposed the correct biosynthetic pathway to the steroidal hormones in living organisms. At the time of his death, Woodward was working on the synthesis of erythromycin.

Perhaps Woodward's most highly regarded synthetic efforts were those he directed to reserpine in the mid-1950s. In 1953, the medical application of this natural product as a sedative contributed to a radical change in the treatment of mental illness. Urgency was added to reserpine research in the spring of 1955, when the Indian government, in response to increased western demand, placed an embargo on the export of *Rauwolfia* root, the natural source of the drug. While pharmaceutical firms successfully searched Africa and the Americas for alternative sources of the roots, Woodward completed the synthesis of this antihypertensive and antipsychotic drug in the spring of 1956, less than one year after its structural elucidation. Reserpine was one of his quickest major syntheses, a model of chemical efficiency and one of his most rapid publications of a total synthesis, appearing as a fifty-seven-page paper, "The Total Synthesis of Reserpine," in *Tetrahedron* in 1958. In general, Woodward's syntheses appeared quickly as brief published communications, but the full papers, complete with experimental and spectroscopic details, often appeared years later or not at all, because of his desire for the papers to be flawless. The resperine synthesis, with its highly effective transformations, readily lent itself to rapid publication without a great deal of experimental tinkering to maximize yields. The synthesis of this alkaloid was creative both because it produced a valuable commodity and because of its imaginative design.

In many ways reserpine was a model for the Woodward method of synthesis: coherent, concise, efficient. Woodward exercised precise control over the stereochemical outcome of the reserpine synthesis. Its initial structural solution was a two-dimensional picture, but the molecule existed in three dimensions. Reserpine, with six chiral (asymmetric) carbons, each of which could exist in two distinct configurations, might have sixty-four distinct isomers, all of them subsumed in the flat, two-dimensional drawing. Only one of these isomers was the natural product. To assemble such a complex natural product, one had to think and make representations in three dimensions. Beyond conception and design, Woodward's co-workers had to perform a great deal of chemical manipulation in the laboratory. His synthetic route became the basis for the industrial production of reserpine. As with all of his best work, he was supported by students and collaborators of the highest quality. He also operated in a cooperative community that supported his work: He received authentic samples of reserpine and instrumental assistance from Pfizer; reserpine, reserpine intermediates, and compounds for resolving reserpine from Eli Lilly; compounds related to reserpine, such as yohimbines, from the French group of Maurice-Marie

Janot; and advice and encouragement from the Squibb Institute and Merck.

Woodward patented his reserpine work and assigned the patent to a nonprofit foundation, the Research Corporation. Woodward gave the Swiss pharmaceutical firm Sandoz unpublished procedures and details of his synthesis as early as January 1957. In the next two years, Sandoz developed methods for scaling up and simplifying Woodward's procedures. Sandoz's method paralleled Woodward's in its main points, but the Sandoz workers resolved their material at an earlier stage, thus saving expensive reagents in later steps. Through licensing agreements, commercial exploitation of Woodward's synthesis continued on several fronts, though with less success on Woodward's side of the Atlantic. As with quinine, reserpine brought Woodward to the attention of the general public through popular press reports.

While reserpine was a molecule of great practical importance, Woodward also pursued targets that were much more purely chemists' challenges. In this vein, Woodward's total synthesis of strychnine capped his earlier work on the structure of this deadly alkaloid. The publication in 1963 of this synthesis provided the final confirmation of his structure determination. Woodward was fascinated by this poison, with its exotic origins in the forests of Southeast Asia and its use in "extermination of rodents and other undesirables" (1963a, p. 247). Woodward's strychnine work recalled the traditional relationship between structure determination and synthesis—in which the synthesis is the ultimate and necessary confirmation of structure—at a time when that relationship was changing in the face of new, powerful, analytical instruments. Later in his career Woodward synthesized other high visibility, complex molecules with little direct practical outcome. Vitamin B_{12} and chlorophyll were the two giants in this category. While both were compounds considered vital to life, both were also readily available, cheaply, by means other than long, multistep chemical syntheses. Both chlorophyll and vitamin B_{12} are large molecules with many rings containing heteroatoms (atoms other than the basic carbons fundamental to organic chemistry), particularly nitrogen.

Woodward's synthesis of chlorophyll was begun on the heels of the reserpine work and completed in 1960, in just four years, by the efforts of more than a dozen postdoctoral students. As with other molecules, Woodward immersed himself in the existing literature, much of it in German, going back for decades. And as before, Woodward did not deploy much in the way of new chemistry, but he always used his encyclopedic knowledge of the synthetic chemistry literature and was able to utilize even rather obscure reactions to great and novel effect. In addition, he did bring to bear his structural insights to

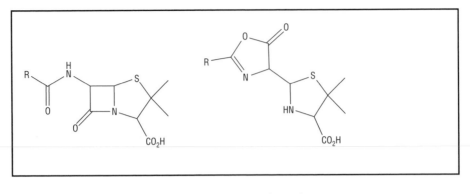

Figure 1. *Penicillin Possibilities:* B-*lactam structure and oxazolone structure.*

assemble the molecule convergently in two pieces and bring it all together with stereochemical control. This synthesis showed Woodward's ability to plan meticulously and still cope brilliantly with unforeseen chemical contingencies. Though he gave lectures on the subject, Woodward never published a full-length article on the chlorophyll synthesis, and therefore much of the technical detail remains unknown.

Following chlorophyll, Woodward approached the B_{12} synthesis that would bring together the best aspects of his reserpine and his chlorophyll work. The coenzyme vitamin B_{12} (cyanocobalamin) was large and complicated enough to merit the collaboration of Woodward's group with that of another world leader in organic chemistry, Albert Eschenmoser of the Swiss Federal Institute of Technology (ETH) in Zürich. While the two men had independently begun work on this structure in the late 1950s and early 1960s, an exchange of information between them evolved into a full-scale collaboration by about 1965. Eschenmoser did the final assembly of the two halves—Woodward's "western" half and his own "eastern" half—in 1972, after some twelve years of work. In 1976, after further refinements, Woodward's group celebrated the completion of totally synthetic B_{12} by a sequence of more than one hundred reactions. As with chlorophyll, controlling the relative positions of numerous substituents during construction was essential to a successful outcome.

Instruments and Structure Determination. Woodward garnered fame and recognition not just from syntheses but also from determining the precise chemical structures of complex natural products. His achievements in the field of structure determination were milestones: penicillin (1945), patulin (1948), strychnine (1947), ferrocene (1952), terramycin (1952), cevine (1954), gliotoxin (1958), ellipticine (1959), calycanthine (1960), oleandomycin (1960), streptonigrin (1963), and tetrodotoxin (1964). He never hesitated in adopting the latest analytical instrumentation, which—during the postwar

decades—removed much that was chemically difficult from the process of structure determination. In Woodward's view, instruments gave rapid access to chemical structure and also fostered new ways of thinking about chemistry. Woodward was an early adopter of ultraviolet and infrared spectroscopy. These instrumental techniques altered the traditional, complementary relationship between synthesis and structural determination and reduced the latter to a relatively commonplace procedure. Instruments increased the productivity of organic chemists by removing some of the painstaking work of isolating every intermediate in a synthesis, and they also provided insight into the reaction mechanisms by revealing by-products. Woodward believed that organic chemists should make use of instruments and interpret spectra as part of their daily practice. With this, Woodward claimed for synthetic organic chemists territory that once had belonged to their physical collaborators. At the same time, he labeled those synthetic organic chemists who disagreed with him inefficient and old-fashioned.

Beyond ultraviolet and infrared spectrometry, Woodward was an early promoter of another instrumental technology that would further the transformation of organic chemical practice, namely nuclear magnetic resonance spectroscopy (NMR). First developed in the late 1940s to investigate the properties of nuclei, NMR moved into mainstream organic chemistry a decade later for quite different purposes. NMR was set to take its place alongside infrared spectrometry as a probe of reaction mixtures and isolated products. Woodward was pleased with the results he obtained from the new method, and he believed NMR to be a method well suited to hands-on, regular, practical use by organic chemists.

For Woodward, the 1940s and 1950s were marked by new concepts of molecular shape and interaction and by instruments that gave new access to the molecular realm. Woodward believed that a revolution was underway in chemistry and actively sought to change the way other chemists thought about their subject. The revolution was embodied in both chemical theory and new physical methods. In the first instance, there was an understanding of how functional groups and molecular structures even within the same molecule interacted, what Woodward called nearest-neighbor relationships. This knowledge gave chemists the ability to predict the outcome, or possible outcomes, of reactions based on chemical mechanisms. He promoted mechanistic thinking, a way of conceptualizing chemistry as the interaction between reactants; as the making and breaking of bonds; and as a dynamic, spatially dependent process. In particular, early work on ultraviolet spectra and Arnold Beckman's introduction in 1941 of a commercial ultraviolet instrument, pushed organic chemists to take note of advances in physical chemistry and instrumentation. Woodward's innovations proved successful both for himself and for organic chemistry as a discipline.

With regard to structural elucidation, Woodward had two early, high-profile successes in competitive arenas: penicillin and strychnine. Both brought him into conflict with one of the twentieth century's other great chemists, Oxford University's Robert Robinson (the 1947 Nobel Prize winner in chemistry). During World War II, Woodward and Robinson had disagreed about the structure of penicillin. By 1945, work on penicillin was well advanced. Based on the data then available, Woodward proposed a structure for penicillin. His position, supporting a B-lactam structure for this antibiotic over Robinson's oxazolone structure, proved correct.

Key to Woodward's correct prediction were new spectroscopic data on the drug, made possible by new instruments. In 1948, Woodward published the structure of strychnine, again beating Robinson in the competition to solve this difficult chemical, again with the help of instrumental data. Indeed, Robinson's relative lack of faith in spectroscopic data marked a generational difference in the chemical community. Though Woodward had correctly deduced the final structure of strychnine, by the time he came to the problem it had been nearly solved, much as in the case of penicillin. In both cases, two serious possibilities remained for the correct structure. Woodward's task was to distinguish between those for strychnine, as he had for the B-lactam and oxazolone structures of penicillin. Woodward was able to absorb and assimilate an enormous amount of information and, through a mixture of deduction and chemical intuition, identify a solution that fit all the data. Conflicts over penicillin and strychnine—as well as competition over steroid syntheses—personally alienated these two men. Furthermore, Woodward's avid adoption of instrumentation separated him from Robinson's generation of chemists.

Woodward's work in the area of structural elucidation did not end with strychnine. During the 1950s, he collab-

orated with Pfizer on the structural analysis of a new series of antibiotics: terramycin, aureomycin, and magnamycin. He also solved other prominent puzzles, including the structure of tetrodotoxin, a neurotoxin chemically interesting primarily for its structural complexity. Tetrodotoxin was infamously known as the poison found in the puffer fish, or *fugu*. While the puffer fish is considered a delicacy, its liver, gonads, and skin contain lethal amounts of tetrodotoxin. This dangerous profile, alongside its structural challenge, made it an appealing target to Woodward. Terramycin, on the other hand, was a medically and commercially important antibiotic whose structure was of great interest for the light it could shed on related compounds; in this regard terramycin was like penicillin. In contrast to penicillin, terramycin research was not sponsored and coordinated by the federal government, but by a pharmaceutical firm. Woodward consulted for Pfizer and worked closely with its team of chemists; the results of their collaboration were published in the *Journal of the American Chemical Society*. Sir Derek Barton described this work as the most brilliant analysis of a structural puzzle ever performed. Provocative structural puzzles such as tetracycline engaged Woodward, but he never wavered from simplifying them by instrumental insights.

Rules and Generalizations. Woodward's use of theory—of generalizations—in organic chemistry underpinned his own success in synthesis and structure determination and revolutionized the entire field. Though often diffused through his practical work, these generalizations took shape as formal rules on at least three occasions during Woodward's career: once in the 1940s with the Woodward rules and twice in the 1960s with the Octant rule and the Woodward-Hoffmann rules. In each instance, Woodward seamlessly mixed physical techniques and data with chemical intuition.

The same analytical instruments that routinely assisted the chemist in the characterization of unknown natural products and synthetic intermediates—compounds made along the way to the final target molecule—also suggested new generalizations about the relationship of structure to physical properties. Woodward's early theoretical pursuits centered on the use of ultraviolet absorption spectra. In the early 1940s, Woodward published a series of papers correlating the ultraviolet spectra of α,B-unsaturated ketones with their structures. Professionally, these were his first major chemical achievements. These correlations of structure and spectra became known as the Woodward rules (or sometimes the Woodward-Fieser rules in acknowledgment of Louis and Mary Fieser's contributions to them). Although the Woodward rules drew nothing like the public attention shown his quinine synthesis, they were well noted in the chemical community. Woodward relied heavily on spectroscopic data in

Robert Burns Woodward. *Robert Woodward in his laboratory.* **AP IMAGES.**

developing his rules for determining the structures of these compounds from their ultraviolet spectra. This was an application for organic chemists, not physicists. Although not unusual for this period, the Woodward rules were among the first of these types of generalizations, and they were quite numerically accurate and comprehensive in scope. They proved very useful in the structural determination of steroids, an important area of research at the time, a coincidence that contributed to the large volume of data already available to Woodward in the literature. Generalizations about chemical structures and physical properties could be expanded as new physical methods were brought into chemical laboratories. Woodward's contributions lay in recognizing the power of these meth-

ods and in interpreting their output—he was not involved in developing the instruments themselves.

Woodward took a keen interest in promoting the method of optical rotatory dispersion (ORD). In 1961, Woodward and four coauthors published their work on the Octant rule, which correlated the ORD spectra of saturated ketones with their structures. (All the experimental data were provided by coauthor Carl Djerassi.)The Octant rule was of wide utility, as many biologically active molecules contained such structures. Thus, with a plot of wavelength—typically in the ultraviolet region of the spectrum—versus angle of rotation, an ORD curve could yield conformational and structural information about a compound that is of interest. Woodward and his collaborators took great pleasure in finding compounds and data that fulfilled all the possible predictions of the Octant rule. The rule proved valuable to the organic chemists in its simple qualitative form. Woodward's network provided him with all the essentials for his work: moral support and appreciation; data and materials; and the most qualified collaborators. The Octant rule was the result of the highly productive crossroads of chemistry that was Harvard in the 1950s. Both the Woodward rule and the Octant rule were useful generalizations about the relationship between spectra and structure and created new uses for routine spectroscopic measurements. Both foreshadowed Woodward's later work with Roald Hoffmann, though the earlier generalizations gave information about structures, while the latter was about the Woodward-Hoffmann rules,—work for which Hoffmann shared the Nobel Prize with Kenichi Fukui in 1981.

Woodward's synthetic work on vitamin B_{12} led to the recognition and formulation, with Hoffmann, of the concept of conservation of orbital symmetry, explicating a broad group of fundamental reactions. The resulting Woodward-Hoffmann rules were probably the most important theoretical advance of the 1960s in organic chemistry. They were first published serially as a number of papers and then in book form as *The Conservation of Orbital Symmetry* (1970). The rules were qualitative but firmly based on quantum mechanical arguments. Woodward and Hoffmann considered the absence of mathematical derivations in their work to be its great strength. By basing their rules on symmetry arguments rather than on the numerical approximations required for quantum mechanical calculations, Woodward and Hoffman believed the calculations to be more authoritative.

By employing these rules, chemists could predict the outcomes of a number of synthetically important reaction types. Notably, Hoffmann and Woodward made a crucial generalization that allowed chemists to distinguish the outcome of thermal as opposed to photochemical reactions. The same compound, when activated by heat, would yield a different product than if activated with light. The Woodward-Hoffmann rules predicted the product in each case. Although based on molecular orbital theory, the rules were readily usable by synthetic organic chemists. Representation and thinking in three dimensions were a defining aspect of theory in organic chemistry.

This conceptualization of the molecular realm in terms of shape and space—instead of equation and number—ran through much of Woodward's work. In a real sense, the Woodward-Hoffmann rules contained much of what made the former's contributions to synthesis transformative. Of course, they also contained a good deal of Hoffmann's own special insight into molecular orbital theory and extended Hückel theory. Once again Woodward had provided himself with the best of collaborators.

Woodward's synthetic work on vitamin B_{12} led to the recognition and formulation, with Roald Hoffmann, of the concept of conservation of orbital symmetry, explicating a broad group of fundamental reactions. The instrumental techniques of structure determination, the readiness of journals to publish representations of three-dimensional chemical structures, and the availability of molecular model sets gave chemists a revolutionary new vision of what molecules looked like and a new conception of chemical reactions might or might not be possible.

Scientific Style. Woodward paid assiduous attention to detail in every publication and every public lecture. In his work as a teacher and promoter of organic chemistry, Woodward's talks and lectures were fastidious and well prepared; they were exhibitions of his chemical prowess that often lasted for hours. Using his famous box of colored chalk, Woodward delivered to his audiences thorough chemical expositions that were carefully rehearsed to appear spontaneous and flawless. Precision marked his chemical work as well. Throughout his career, he demonstrated that understanding nearest-neighbor relationships made possible the planning and successful execution of extended sequences of reactions, building chemically complex compounds from the simplest starting materials. His publications were as perfect as he could make them, in both content and appearance. He took many editors, and even publishers, to task for not properly reproducing his diagrams, or worse, substituting other diagrams for his. Woodward's precision and his successes drew attention from the press and from industry. His career was well documented in the media, and he was much sought after as a chemical consultant. Woodward moved expertly between the realms of academe and industry. During his career, he held consultancies with Lilly, Merck, Mallinckrodt, Monsanto, Polaroid, and Pfizer. In 1963, Ciba, a Swiss drug firm, established the Woodward Research Institute in Basel. Woodward then held dual appointments as Donner Professor of Science at Harvard and director of his institute. Counting both Cambridge and Basel, more than four hundred graduate and postdoctoral students trained in Woodward's laboratories. Woodward promoted his methods through lectures, through the training of graduate and postdoctoral students, and through his publications.

Woodward possessed superb mental organization and a vast capacity for facts. Unlike some of his peers, he only rarely created new reagents for novel molecular transformations; rather, his genius lay in his ability to marshal all available data to solve even the most intricate of puzzles. He strove to out perform all others and to be the best organic chemist in the world. His competitive nature was a burden and a gift. It was a burden in connection with some of Woodward's other passions, such as drinking and smoking, both of which may have contributed to his early death from heart disease. But in combination with his passion for chemistry, it was a marvelous gift. Given the set of data on a structure, or the planning of a synthesis, Woodward brought to bear a most remarkable ability to see the entire problem at once and to solve it systematically. His brilliance lay in the quality and depth of his thought, his painstaking preparations, and his chemical intuition. Woodward's work was central to the chemical thought of the times, and his influence on other organic chemists was arguably greater than that of any of his professional colleagues. Woodward understood molecules as having shapes and reactivities governed by their nearest-neighbor relationships, which enabled chemists to understand the capability of a part of a molecule to undergo a transformation in terms of the properties and locations of the rest of the molecule. This structural understanding allowed the thoughtful practitioner to predict reliably the possible outcomes of chemical reactions. Nevertheless, Woodward's ideal chemist had to be thoughtful without being fanciful. Logic and, whenever possible, physical data were Woodward's tools for giving credence to his mechanistic thinking. Truth was paramount and deduction could reveal how chemical transformations took place. Woodward brought a special creativity to his work, as is suggested by the following words from his 1965 Nobel citation: "for his outstanding achievements in the art of organic chemistry."

BIBLIOGRAPHY

Woodward's extensive papers are held by the Harvard University Archives, Cambridge, Massachusetts. Both the Benfey and Morris collection and Todd and Cornforth article (cited below) contain a complete bibliography of Woodward's published works.

WORKS BY WOODWARD

The Mechanism of the Diels-Alder Reaction." *Journal of the American Chemical Society* 64 (1942): 3058–3059.

With Warren J. Brehm. "The Structure of Strychnine. Formulation of the *Neo* Bases." *Journal of the American Chemical Society* 70 (1948): 2107–2115.

With Gurbakhsh Singh. "The Structure of Patulin." *Experientia* 6 (1950): 238–240.

With Franz Sondheimer, David Taub, Karl Heusler, and W. M. McLamore. "The Total Synthesis of Steroids." *Journal of the American Chemical Society* 74 (1952): 4223–4251.

With F. A. Hochstein, C. R. Stephens, L. H. Conover, et al. "The Structure of Terramycin." *Journal of the American Chemical Society* 75 (1953): 5455–5475.

"The Total Synthesis of Strychnine." *Experientia Supplementum* Supplement 2 (1955): 213–228.

"Synthesis." In *Perspectives in Organic Chemistry*, edited by A. R. Todd. New York: Interscience Publishers, 1956.

With F. E. Bader, H. Bickel, A. J. Frey, et al. "The Total Synthesis of Reserpine." *Tetrahedron* 2 (1958):1–57.

"The Total Synthesis of Chlorophyll." *Pure and Applied Chemistry* 2 (1961): 383–404.

With W. Moffitt, A. Moscowitz, W. Klyne, et al. "Structure and the Optical Rotary Dispersion of Saturated Ketones." *Journal of the American Chemical Society* 83 (1961): 4013–4018.

With M. P. Cava, W. D. Ollis, A. Hunger, et al. "The Total Synthesis of Strychnine." *Tetrahedron* 19 (1963a): 247–288.

"Art and Science in the Synthesis of Organic Compounds: Retrospect and Prospect." In *Pointers and Pathways in Research*, edited by Maeve O'Connor. Bombay: CIBA of India, 1963b, 23–41.

"The Structure of Tetrodotoxin." *Pure and Applied Chemistry* 9 (1964): 49–74.

"Recent Advances in the Chemistry of Natural Products." [Cephalosporin C] *Science* 153 (1966): 487–493.

"Recent Advances in the Chemistry of Natural Products." [Vitamin B_{12}] *Pure and Applied Chemistry* 17 (1968): 519–547.

With Roald Hoffmann. *The Conservation of Orbital Symmetry*. Weinheim, Germany: Verlag Chemie, 1970.

OTHER SOURCES

Benfey, Otto Theodor and Peter J. T. Morris, eds. *Robert Burns Woodward: Architect and Artist of the World of Molecules*. Philadelphia: Chemical Heritage Foundation, 2001. Contains Woodward's major papers with historical annotations.

Blout, Elkan. "Robert Burns Woodward, April 10, 1917–July 8, 1979." *Biographical Memoirs of the National Academy of Sciences* 80 (2001): 3–23.

Slater, Leo B. "Industry and Academy: The Synthesis of Steroids." *Historical Studies in the Physical and Biological Sciences* 30 (2000): 443–480.

———. "Woodward, Robinson, and Strychnine: Chemical Structure and Chemists' Challenge." *Ambix* 48 (2001): 161–189.

———. "Instruments and Rules: R. B. Woodward and the Tools of Twentieth-Century Organic Chemistry." *Studies in History and Philosophy of Science* 33 (2002): 1–33.

Todd, Alexander R., and John Cornforth. "Robert Burns Woodward." *Biographical Memoirs of the Fellows of the Royal Society* 27 (1981): 628–695.

Leo B. Slater

WRIGHT, SEWALL

WRIGHT, SEWALL (*b.* Melrose, Massachusetts, 21 December 1889; *d.* Madison, Wisconsin, 3 March 1988), *population genetics, evolutionary theory.*

Wright, along with John Burdon Sanderson Haldane and Ronald Aylmer Fisher, founded modern evolutionary theory, that is, mathematical population genetics. Wright is probably best known for his general evolutionary theory, the shifting balance theory. But he is also responsible for the mathematical theory of inbreeding and population structure. In mathematics, Wright invented the method of path analysis. For his groundbreaking work in population genetics, he was the recipient of the Elliott and Kimball awards from the National Academy of Sciences, the Lewis Prize from the American Philosophical Society, the Weldon Medal from Oxford University, the Darwin Medal from the Royal Society of London, the National Medal of Science from the United States, and the Balzan Prize from Italy. Wright's life's work is represented by his four-volume *Evolution and the Genetics of Populations* (1968–1978). The authoritative biography of Wright is William Provine's *Sewall Wright and Evolutionary Biology* (1986).

Early Years. Sewall Wright was born in Melrose, Massachusetts, on 21 December 1889, to Elizabeth Quincy Sewall and Philip Green Wright. Wright had two brothers, Quincy and Theodore. Each was well known in his respective field, namely, law and aeronautical engineering. Wright spent his childhood and early adulthood in Galesburg, Illinois, where his father held a teaching post at Lombard College. Wright enrolled at Lombard College, taking his BSc degree in 1911. Wright studied mathematics mainly, but by his last year Wright's interests in biology took center stage because of the mentoring of Wilhelmine Entemann Key (who was one of the first women to earn a PhD at the University of Chicago). Indeed, in the summer of 1911 Key sent Wright to Cold Spring Harbor Laboratory on Long Island, New York, where Wright learned from world-class biologists, including Key's former mentor Charles Benedict Davenport (1866–1944). Wright found his experience at Cold Spring Harbor rewarding, and he returned there during the summer of 1912. In the fall of 1911, Wright entered the graduate program in biology at the University of Illinois at Urbana-Champaign.

By the spring of 1912, Wright completed his master's thesis on the anatomy of the trematode *Microphallus opacus*. Wright completed the thesis in short order on account of a chance meeting after a lecture by the geneticist William Ernest Castle (1867–1962) of Harvard University's Bussey Institute, another student of Davenport. Castle lectured on his selection experiments on hooded rats and on mammalian genetics. Wright was fascinated and approached Castle about working with him. Castle was sufficiently impressed by Wright, and they decided that Wright would quickly finish his master's thesis and enroll at Harvard University in the fall of 1912.

At Harvard, Wright engaged in original experimental research in physiological genetics. Wright's research was directed by Castle, but he was also considerably influenced by the geneticist Edward Murray East. While at Harvard and the Bussey Institute, Wright worked closely with Castle on his hooded rat selection experiments and on the genetics of small mammals. By 1915 Wright completed his doctoral thesis on coat color inheritance in guinea pigs. Wright's research demonstrated the existence of multiple loci and alleles affecting coat color in the animal; it further set out the hypothesis that enzyme pathways and pigment precursors provided the physiological basis for observed patterns of inheritance of coat coloration. Around the time Wright was finishing his thesis, he accepted a position as senior animal husbandman at the U.S. Department of Agriculture (USDA) in Beltsville, Maryland. Wright's work as a physiological geneticist permeated his work in evolutionary theory.

At the USDA. Wright was with the USDA for ten years, from 1915 to 1925. During this period, Wright published widely on physiological genetics, inbreeding and crossbreeding, and statistics, where he created the method of path analysis. In 1921 he married Louise Williams, a member of the faculty of biology at Smith College. The Wrights had three children, Elizabeth Rose, Richard, and Robert.

In 1917–1918, Wright published a ten-paper series on coat color inheritance in mice, rats, rabbits, guinea pigs, cattle, horses, swine, dogs, cats, and humans (1917; 1918a). Wright's work was cutting-edge at the time: He found similarities and purported homologies among genes with similar effects in all these species, some of which were later confirmed; he also interpreted coat colors in terms of contemporaneous knowledge of enzymes and pigment chemistry. In addition, Wright analyzed the inheritance of size factors into components based on correlation of various body parts (1918b). He partitioned the variance in size into components of general size, limb-specific factors, forelimb and hind-limb factors, upper-limb and lower-limb factors, and special factors for each part.

Two publications of Wright's from 1921 stand out. The first, "Correlation and Causation," described Wright's invention of the method of path analysis, that is, the method for estimating the magnitude and significance of hypothesized causal connections between sets of variables (1921a). Wright used partial regression analysis, a standard statistical tool, but his approach was unique. He hypothesized what the causal paths were and then aimed to determine the relative magnitudes of different paths. Wright's procedure was to diagram a series of paths. A path of causal influence was indicated by an arrow, while unanalyzed correlations were indicated by double arrows. Each step in a pathway was associated with a "path coefficient," a partial regression coefficient standardized by being measured in standard deviation units. A path

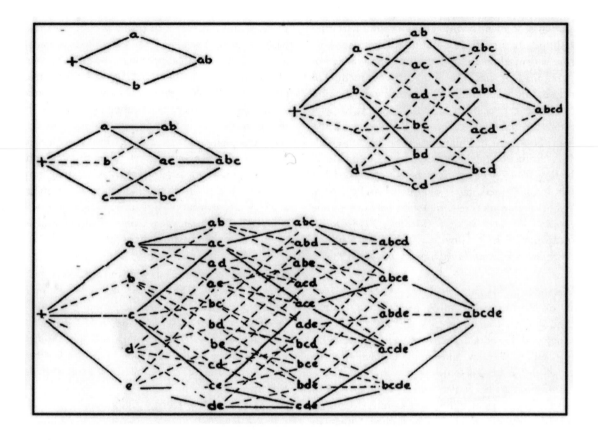

Figure 1. *Wright's representation of two to five allelomorphs in combination.* **COURTESY OF THE GENETICS SOCIETY OF AMERICA.**

coefficient is a measure of the relative contribution of this step in the pathway. Wright devised rules by which the relevant equations may be written from the path diagram. The equations can then be solved for the unknown variables. Wright's method of path analysis was used widely by animal breeders early on, but later was superceded by other methods. But it is common to see path analysis used by social scientists.

The other "stand out" work in 1921 was a series of papers published under the heading "Systems of Mating" (1921b). While a graduate student at Harvard, Wright devised a method for measuring the proportion by which the heterozygosity of an individual is reduced by inbreeding. The method results in what is familiarly known as Wright's "inbreeding coefficient." Wright subsequently analyzed the history of inbreeding in American shorthorn cattle using his method. This work formed the basis of Wright's well-known F-statistics, where F (or f) is the measure of inbreeding, and later helped Wright in elaborating his isolation-by-distance model in the 1940s (1943b; 1951b).

Wright's work on physiological genetics and inbreeding during his tenure at the USDA profoundly affected

the way he understood the genetic basis of evolutionary change and population structure. Indeed, much of his thought had crystallized by 1925, but his results were not published until 1931.

The Shifting Balance Theory. In 1926 Wright joined the faculty of biology at the University of Chicago. There Wright's contribution as an architect of the synthesis of Darwinism and Mendelism was completed. Wright's most famous paper, "Evolution in Mendelian Populations," was published in 1931. Wright demonstrated the mathematical unification of Darwinian natural selection and the principles of Mendelian heredity, and he communicated this synthesis in the form of his famous shifting balance theory of evolution. To be sure, Wright's long 1931 paper is a masterpiece of mathematical population genetics. But the central ideas of Wright's shifting balance theory are inextricably tied to his communication of them through his "adaptive landscape" diagram in 1932.

Wright's aim in the 1931–1932 papers was to determine the ideal conditions for evolution to occur given specific assumptions about the relationship between

Mendelian heredity and the adaptive value of gene complexes (1931, p. 158; 1932, p. 363). Wright's view was that his "shifting-balance" process of evolution described those conditions. Its driving assumptions were part and parcel of Wright's understanding of genetic interaction, mating, and population structures. According to Wright (1932, pp. 361–363), accurately representing the population genetics of the evolutionary process requires thousands of dimensions. This is because the field of possible gene combinations in the field of gene frequencies of a population is vast (approximately 10^{1000}). Indeed, Wright begins the 1932 paper by asking about the nature of this field of possible gene combinations. Figure 1 is Wright's first illustration, in which he depicts the combinations of two to five allelomorphs (see Figure 1). Here, Wright illustrates how quickly the dimensionality of the field expands as the number of combinations expands: for the case of thirty-two combinations, five dimensions are required, plus a sixth to represent adaptive value. In the case of a species, with 10^{1000} combinations, the required dimensions number at nine thousand.

Wright used the two dimensional graphical depiction of an adaptive landscape in Figure 2 as a way of intuitively conveying what he thought can be realistically represented only in thousands of dimensions. The surface of the landscape is typically understood as representing the joint gene frequencies of all genes in a population graded for adaptive value. The surface of the landscape is very "hilly," says Wright, because of epistatic relations between genes, the consequences of which (for Wright) are that genes adaptive in one combination are likely to be maladaptive in another. Given Wright's view of epistasis and the vastness of the field of gene combinations in a field of gene frequencies, Wright estimates the number of adaptive "peaks" separated by adaptive "valleys" at 10^{800}. Peaks are represented by "+"; valleys are represented by "−".

The adaptive landscape diagram sets up Wright's signature problem, namely, the problem of peak shifts. That is, given that the adaptive landscape is hilly, the ideal conditions for evolution to occur must allow a population to shift from peak to peak to find the highest peak. In his 1931 paper Wright demonstrated mathematically the statistical distributions of genes under alternative assumptions of population size, mutation rate, migration rate, selection intensity, and so forth. In the 1932 paper the graphs displaying the results appear, and he uses them in

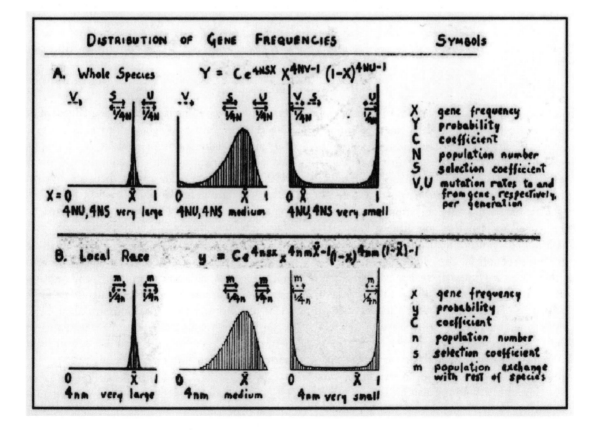

Figure 2. *Wright's adaptive landscape diagram.* **COURTESY OF THE GENETICS SOCIETY OF AMERICA.**

Figure 3. *Wright's results from 1931 on the statistical distribution of genes under varying assumptions.* **COURTESY OF THE GENETICS SOCIETY OF AMERICA.**

combination with the landscape diagram to argue for his three-phase shifting-balance model of the evolutionary process (window F in Figure 4) as the solution to his problem of peak shifts via assessments of alternative models of the process (windows A–E in Figure 4). Evolution on the shifting-balance process occurs in three phases: Phase I—random genetic drift causes subpopulations semi-isolated within the global population to lose fitness; Phase II—selection on complex genetic interaction systems raises the fitness of those subpopulations; Phase III—interdemic selection then raises the fitness of the large or global population. In his 1932 paper Wright used the adaptive landscape diagram to demonstrate why he thought such an apparently complicated process was required for the ideal conditions for evolution to occur. The central assumptions of Wright's shifting balance theory have been challenged since he first published them. In fact, in the early twenty-first century the shifting balance theory is probably less well received than it was during Wright's career.

Controversies and Collaborations. Wright was a key figure in one of the great controversies of evolutionary genet-

ics, that between himself and another architect of population genetics, Fisher. Wright also participated in one of the great collaborations of evolutionary genetics, that between himself and Theodosius Dobzhansky (1900–1975). The controversy between Wright and Fisher was central, fundamental, and very influential. And the collaboration with Dobzhansky popularized Wright's shifting balance theory as it helped refine it.

From 1929 until 1962, Wright and Fisher debated the very fundamentals of adaptive evolution: its ecological context, genetic basis, major processes, and modes of speciation. The debate has persisted long after the involvement of its principals, expanding on old problems and raising news ones. Illustrative of the disagreements between Fisher and Wright is their debate over the importance of genetic drift in evolution.

In 1947 Fisher, with the ecological geneticist Edmund Brisco Ford (1901–1988), published an experimental paper aimed at discrediting Wright's shifting balance theory and substantiating Fisher's panselectionism. Fisher and Ford's paper describes and analyzes data from what was at the time a fairly novel field experimental technique, the capture and release protocol, targeting wing coloration in populations of the moth, *Panaxia dominula* in Oxfordshire, England. Fisher and Ford argued that even in small(ish) populations (between 10^3 and 10^4) Wright's assumed norm, genetic drift—Wright's most important evolutionary factor, according to Fisher and Ford—was evolutionarily inefficacious. Indeed, Fisher and Ford argued further that natural selection, *even in smallish populations,* is the driving factor of evolution.

Fisher and Ford claimed that their data showed that fluctuations in the frequencies of the heterozygous form of the moth (called *medionigra*) were too large from year to year to be due to genetic drift. Their specific argument was that even though population size was sufficiently small for genetic drift to be effective, drift nevertheless was not a factor (because the gene frequency changes were too high to be due merely to chance). For the years Fisher and Ford studied the population, the average population size was in the range of thirty-two hundred to four thousand moths, with approximately 11 percent overall being the *medionigra* form and a total gene frequency change of approximately 6 percent (1947, pp. 150, 164). Fisher and

Ford ultimately inferred that because changes in gene frequencies in the moth populations were not due to genetic drift, they must be due to natural selection.

In 1948 Wright published a critique of Fisher and Ford's study. Wright objected (1) that Fisher and Ford had misinterpreted the role Wright had assumed for random genetic drift—in their reading of Wright's work, they attributed more of a role to drift than Wright himself did—and (2) that their inference that selection must be the cause of the changes in gene frequencies in the populations of the moths was not justified experimentally. Fisher and Ford did not provide any direct evidence that selection is the cause; they only infer it after rejecting drift. Wright's paper drew an acerbic attack from Fisher and Ford published in 1950. Wright again responded in 1951 (1951a). The substance of the disagreement after Wright's 1948 paper is the problem of interpreting Wright's view of the role of genetic drift in evolution.

The field work on *P. dominula* continued long after the 1950s and has come to form one of the longest-running field experiments in ecological genetics. Ironically,

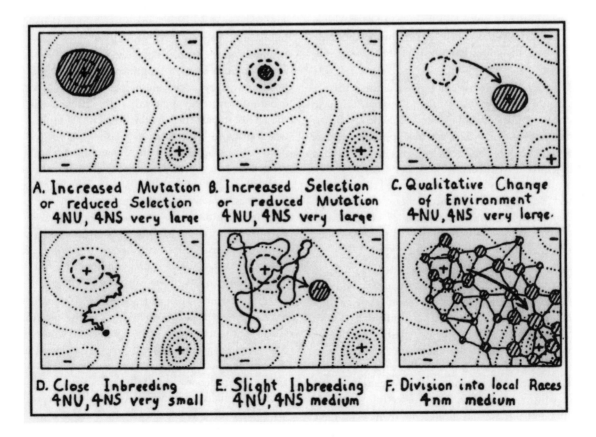

Figure 4. *Evolution occurring on the adaptive landscape under alternative assumptions.* COURTESY OF THE GENETICS SOCIETY OF AMERICA.

however, since the late 1990s it has become clear that the selectionist interpretation that has held sway from the beginning is on shaky ground. But genetic drift is not the right interpretation, either: temperature fluctuations affecting the expression of wing color in the moths explains much of the fluctuation of the *medionigra* form.

Probably more heat than light was generated by the controversy between Fisher and Wright. The opposite may be said about the collaboration between Wright and Dobzhansky. Wright clearly had a major influence on Dobzhansky's important 1937 book, *Genetics and the Origin of Species* and also on the *Genetics of Natural Populations* series published between 1937 and 1975. However, Dobzhansky's influence on Wright and in particular the promulgation of the shifting balance theory cannot be underestimated. Wright's influence on evolutionary biology was powerfully communicated through Dobzhansky's own work and through his collaboration with Wright through the 1950s. *Genetics and the Origin of Species* provided Wright with the empirical underpinning he knew his abstract theoretical work lacked. And naturalists who did not possess Wright's mathematical expertise were finally able, with Dobzhansky's book, to see Wright's particular synthesis of Mendelian heredity and Darwinian natural selection. Moreover, Dobzhansky's tireless work in the field yielded theoretical insights Wright may not have otherwise had, including his model of isolation by distance, published in 1943.

Population structure is central to the shifting balance theory. But it was not until Dobzhansky asked Wright to analyze data on the distribution of the desert flower *Linanthus parryae* that Wright was able to fully articulate the model. Indeed, in the 1930s he had only been able to produce a qualitative theory of isolation by distance. As it happens, Dobzhansky (with Carl Epling [1894–1968]) published "Microgeographic Races in *Linanthus parryae*" in 1942 as part of the *Genetics of Natural Populations* series before Wright was able to develop the quantitative model. Wright published the model in 1943 (1943b).

Wright used his theory of *F*-statistics to partition a series of related inbreeding coefficients that were individually relevant to a particular population structure. Wright invented inbreeding coefficients for an individual relative to its subpopulation, for an individual with respect to the total population, and for the correlation between randomly uniting gametes drawn from the same subpopulation. With these coefficients and derived equations for the gene frequencies of subgroups, their effective population sizes, migration index, and mean gene frequency of the population, Wright was able to develop models that captured the evolutionary effect of isolation by distance. The equations showed that when populations were small ($<10^3$), considerable random differentiation would be expected in population subdivisions. As population size increased ($>10^4$), values for the effect of isolation by distance were essentially what would be expected of a randomly interbreeding population. A companion piece followed Wright's isolation-by-distance paper, in which he applied his models to Dobzhansky's data (Wright, 1943a). Because of the centrality of isolation by distance to Wright's shifting balance theory, the *L. parryae* fieldwork stood as a major illustration of the theory as a whole (Provine, 1986, p. 379).

The controversies and collaborations of which Wright was a part helped refine his evolutionary thought. Just as Fisher forced Wright to clarify his theoretical assumptions, Dobzhansky led him to new theoretical insights that shaped and reshaped his shifting balance theory. More generally, these controversies and collaborations would direct the field of evolutionary biology and have lasting influence.

Retirement to Madison. In 1955 Wright was subject to mandatory retirement from the University of Chicago. He became Leon J. Cole Professor of Genetics at the University of Wisconsin, Madison, where he remained for the rest of his long career. Wright was prolific throughout. And perhaps there is no better testament to that than the publication, between 1968 and 1978, of his four-volume magnum opus, *Evolution and the Genetics of Populations*. These volumes were the culmination of his work in evolutionary theory. Each volume painstakingly reworks the evolutionary problems he originally attacked starting in the 1920s. In particular, he revisits all of the problems that were central to his debates with Fisher and his collaborations with Dobzhansky. Thus, he revisits the problem of the genetic basis of evolutionary change, population structure, and the ecological genetics of *P. dominula* and *L. parryae*, as well as other work not discussed here, including the evolution of the nematode *Cepaea nemoralis*, the statistical distribution of *Drosophila pseudoobscura*, and so on. Wright was ruthless with his examination, reviewing huge amounts of updated literature on these topics. The quantity and quality of the work is staggering.

But Wright's career did not end with *Evolution and the Genetics of Populations*, in spite of the fact that the fourth and final volume was published when he was eighty-eight years old. Indeed, Wright continued reading and writing, publishing his last paper the year he died, in 1988. The paper was a mostly favorable reaction to his biography published by William B. Provine two years earlier. Wright died at the age of ninety-eight, on 3 March 1988, of complications from a broken pelvis after a slip on an icy sidewalk during one of his usual walks.

Wright is remembered as a towering figure among American evolutionary biologists. His adaptive landscape diagram permeates evolutionary thought, and his statistical theory of inbreeding is standard in evolutionary genetics. Wright was the recipient of numerous awards, including the Weldon Medal of the Royal Society of London in 1947, the National Medal of Science in 1966, and the Medal of the Royal Society of London in 1980. And many of those who worked with Wright, including James Crow, Motoo Kimura, Janice Spofford, and Michael Wade, staked out careers that are a testament to his stature. Wright the man was described by his friends and associates as shy, but warm, and unflinching when discussion turned to his interests.

BIBLIOGRAPHY

WORKS BY WRIGHT

"Color Inheritance in Mammals I–VI." *Journal of Heredity* 8 (1917): 224–235, 373–378, 426–430, 473–475, 476–480, 521–527, 561–564.

"Color Inheritance in Mammals VII–XI." *Journal of Heredity* 9 (1918a): 33–38, 89–90, 139–144, 227–240.

"On the Nature of Size Factors." *Genetics* 3 (1918b): 367–374.

"Correlation and Causation." *Journal of Agricultural Research* 20 (1921a): 557–585.

"Systems of Mating." *Genetics* 6 (1921b): 111–178.

"Evolution in Mendelian Populations." *Genetics* 16 (1931): 97–159.

"The Roles of Mutation, Inbreeding, Crossbreeding, and Selection in Evolution." *Proceedings of the Sixth Annual Congress of Genetics* 1 (1932): 356–366.

"An Analysis of Local Variability of Flower Color in *Linanthus parryae*." *Genetics* 28 (1943a): 139–156.

"Isolation by Distance." *Genetics* 28 (1943b): 114–138.

"On the Roles of Directed and Random Changes in Gene Frequency in the Genetics of Populations." *Evolution* 2 (1948): 279–294.

"Fisher and Ford on the 'Sewall Wright Effect.'" *American Scientist* 39 (1951a): 452–458, 479.

"The Genetical Structure of Populations." *Annals of Eugenics* 15 (1951b): 323–354.

Evolution and the Genetics of Populations: A Treatise. 4 vols. Chicago: University of Chicago Press, 1968–1978.

"Surfaces of Selective Value Revisited." *American Naturalist* 131 (1988): 115–123.

OTHER SOURCES

Cook, Laurence M., and David Jones. "The *Medionigra* Gene in the Moth *Panaxia dominula:* The Case for Selection." *Philosophical Transactions of the Royal Society of London* B 351 (1996): 1623–1634.

Coyne, Jerry A., Nicholas H. Barton, and Michael Turelli. "Perspective: A Critique of Sewall Wright's Shifting Balance Theory of Evolution." *Evolution* 51 (1997): 643–671.

Dobzhansky, Theodosius. *Genetics and the Origin of Species.* New York: Columbia University Press, 1937.

———. *Dobzhansky's Genetics of Natural Populations: I–XLIII.* Edited by Richard C. Lewontin, John A. Moore, William B. Provine, et al. New York: Columbia University Press, 2003. First published 1981.

Fisher, Ronald A., and Edmund B. Ford. "The Spread of a Gene in Natural Conditions in a Colony of the Moth, *Panaxia dominula*, L." *Heredity* 1 (1947): 143–174.

———. "The Sewall Wright Effect." *Heredity* 4 (1950): 117–119.

Goulson, David, and Denis Owen. "Long-Term Studies of the *medionigra* Polymorphism in the Moth *Panaxia dominula:* A Critique." *Oikos* 80 (1997): 613–617.

Jones, David. "Temperatures in the Cothill Habitat of *Panaxia (Callimorpha) dominula* L. (the Scarlet Tiger Moth)." *Heredity* 84 (2000): 578–586.

Provine, William B. *Sewall Wright and Evolutionary Biology.* Chicago: University of Chicago Press, 1986.

Skipper, Robert A., Jr. "The Persistence of the R. A. Fisher–Sewall Wright Controversy." *Biology and Philosophy* 17 (2002): 341–367.

Wade, Michael, and Charles J. Goodnight. "Perspective: The Theories of Fisher and Wright in the Context of Metapopulations; When Nature Does Many Small Experiments." *Evolution* 52 (1998): 1537–1548.

Robert A. Skipper Jr.

WU CHIEN-SHIUNG (Wu Jianxiong in pinyin) (*b.* Shanghai, China, 31 May 1912; *d.* New York, New York, 16 February 1997), *nuclear and particle physics.*

Wu was one of the leading experimental physicists of the twentieth century and a recognized authority on the nuclear phenomenon of beta decay whose research helped overturn the notion of parity conservation in weak interactions. As the first female and Chinese American president of the American Physical Society (APS), she fought for equal opportunities for women in science and inspired women and girls in the United States, China, and all over the world to pursue scientific careers.

Early Years and Education. Wu grew up in one of the most turbulent periods in modern Chinese history, but fortunately for her, she enjoyed a happy childhood due primarily to the encouragement and support of an enlightened father, Wu Zhongyi. Among the first Chinese to receive a western-style education, Wu Zhongyi not only acquired technical training but also an understanding and appreciation of democracy, human rights, and equality for women. A passionate Chinese nationalist, he participated in Shanghai in both the Republican revolution in 1911 to overthrow the Qing dynasty and the unsuccessful 1913 revolt against Yuan Shikai, a military strongman who had

Wu Chien-Shiung. © BETTMANN/CORBIS.

seized power and become the first president of the new republic. Thereafter, Wu Zhongyi returned to his family in the town of Liuhe near Shanghai to open Mingde, the first school for girls in the region. To overcome the traditional resistance to educating girls, he enlisted his wife, Fan Fuhua, to visit families and persuade them to allow their daughters to attend the school.

Chien-Shiung, whose name means "a strong hero" in Chinese, went to Mingde for her elementary education up to the fourth grade. She apparently first became fascinated with the wonders of modern learning and technology when her father reportedly built the first radio sets in town. As perhaps the most important influence in her life, Wu Zhongyi instilled in his daughter a pride in Chinese culture, a love of science, and a belief in herself. "Ignore the obstacles … and keep walking forward," he told her (McGrayne, 1993, p. 255).

In 1923, after passing a competitive entrance examination, Chien-Shiung, then eleven years old, left home for the Suzhou Women's Normal School in Suzhou, where she trained to be an elementary school teacher. There she excelled in all her classes but became attracted especially to physics, inspired partly by what she learned about Nobel Prize–winner Marie Curie. Much of the science that she acquired came through self-study late at night, revealing, even at this early stage, a remarkable capacity for passionate and self-disciplined intellectual pursuit that would become her trademark. At the school she also had the chance to hear lectures by well-known Chinese and foreign scholars. Among these, Hu Shi, the Chinese philosopher who had studied in the United States, especially impressed her. As a leader of the May Fourth Movement, Hu sought to reform traditional Chinese culture into what was called a New Culture with the introduction of democracy, science, and an easy-to-learn vernacular Chinese language. Her admiration for Hu deepened when she enrolled in his class on modern Chinese history at a school in Shanghai following her graduation from Suzhou in 1929. On his part, Hu recognized Chien-Shiung's superior intellect and would provide crucial encouragement to her to pursue her scientific ambitions during their lifelong friendship.

In the fall of 1930, Wu entered the National Central University in Nanjing, then the capital of China under Nationalist rule. She majored in mathematics for the first year apparently because she recognized its importance to her chosen field of physics. At the time that she switch to physics as a sophomore, China entered into an era of intensified sense of national crisis triggered by the Japanese invasion of northeastern China on 28 September 1931. Students at the National Central, for example, staged demonstrations urging the government under Jiang Jieshi (Chiang Kai-shek in Wade-Giles) to take stronger actions against Japanese aggression. Wu, not a radical activist, nevertheless harbored a strong sense of Chinese nationalism and was made a leader in some of these agitations. It was said that her excellent academic records and sterling revolutionary family background would afford her protection that other students did not have. Occupying the courtyard of the presidential mansion one snowy night, she and her comrades actually succeeded in gaining an audience with Jiang himself. But physics remained her true love and Curie her role model. In this regard, she especially enjoyed taking classes with Professor Shi Shiyuan, who returned from Curie's lab in Paris in 1933 after receiving his PhD under her direction and who often told stories about Curie's intellectual curiosity and perseverance in a field dominated by men. She completed her senior thesis with Shi concerning crystal structure, investigating nuances of the twenty-year-old Bragg's law on x-ray diffraction.

After graduating in 1934, Wu first worked as an teaching assistant in the Physics Department at Zhejiang University in Hangzhou for a year before taking up a research assistant position in the Academia Sinica's Institute of Physics in Shanghai upon Shi's recommendation. There she worked on x-ray crystallography under Gu Jinghui (Zing Whai Ku), who had received her PhD in physics from the University of Michigan in Ann Arbor in 1931. In August 1936, with Gu's encouragement, financial support from her businessman uncle, and some preparation in English, Wu boarded the ship *President Hoover*, bound for the United States to pursue graduate study at Gu's alma mater.

Graduate Education at Berkeley. Wu changed her mind about Michigan, however, shortly after landing in San Francisco. She decided, instead, to enroll in the University of California at Berkeley, partly because of stories she heard about the discrimination against women students at Michigan, partly due to the attraction of the Physics Department at Berkeley, especially Ernest Lawrence's Radiation Laboratory. In addition, Luke Chia-Liu Yuan

(Yuan Jialiu in pinyin), a fellow Chinese student in physics at Berkeley who preceded Wu by only a couple of weeks, did his best to persuade Wu to stay. Only later did she find out that Yuan was a grandson of Yuan Shikai, whose rule her own father had fought against in the early 1910s. At Berkeley, Wu's fellow students included, besides Yuan, Robert R. Wilson and Willis Lamb. Her main advisor was Lawrence, but she also worked closely with J. Robert Oppenheimer and Emilio Segrè. She quickly impressed them all not only with her intellectual and experimental talent but also her charm and elegance. Despite constant worries about her family and fellow countrymen in a war-torn China, she thrived scientifically at Berkeley.

In 1938–1940 Wu completed two separate experiments in nuclear physics for her PhD thesis. The first one, assigned by Lawrence, was on bremsstrahlung (braking radiation), which refers to the radiation that comes from a charged particle when it decelerates. At the suggestion of Enrico Fermi, the eminent Italian American physicist, Wu chose to focus on a comparative study of the internal and external x-ray radiation excited by electrons shooting out of the nucleus during the process of beta decay. "Internal" here refers to the x-rays produced by the deceleration of electrons when they come out of the nucleus itself and "external" to x-rays caused by electrons' deceleration when they move through the nucleus's electromagnetic field. Using artificially radioactive phosphorus ^{32}P, Wu's experiment offered some of the earliest confirmations of theories regarding these phenomena. When a report from others contradicted her results, she successfully undertook, with characteristic confidence and meticulousness, not only to repeat her own experiment, but also to determine the errors in the one that contradicted hers. This project demonstrated Wu's ability to relate her experimental discoveries to theoretical advances. It also marked her entrance into beta decay, a field that she soon would make her own. The second part of Wu's thesis reported her experiments with Segrè, using Berkeley's 37-inch and 60-inch cyclotrons, on the production of radioactive xenon from iodine as a product of the fission of uranium. The work initiated Wu into the new field of nuclear fission research and would later bring her into the Manhattan Project to make atomic bombs. In four short years, Wu had transformed herself at Berkeley from an ambitious student to a confident and competent young scientist making contributions at the frontier of her field. In June 1940, after Wu received her PhD, she stayed at Lawrence's lab as a research fellow for two years, working on fission. Despite Lawrence's and Segrè's glowing recommendations, she could not find a stable position at a research university; being a woman and a Chinese alien may have been held against her.

On 30 May 1942, the day before her thirtieth birthday, Wu and Yuan were married in the courtyard of Robert Millikan, head of the California Institute of Technology (Caltech) at Pasadena, where Yuan had transferred and received his PhD in 1940. Afterward, they moved to the East Coast, he obtaining a job designing radar at RCA laboratories in Princeton, New Jersey, and she becoming an assistant professor at Smith College in Northampton, Massachusetts. Dissatisfied with the lack of opportunities for research and feeling out of touch with the scientific world at Smith, Wu moved to Princeton University in 1943 as an instructor of physics for naval officers upon Lawrence's recommendation, making her the first woman instructor in the university's history. In March 1944, however, after only a few months at Princeton, she moved once again, recruited by the Division of War Research at Columbia University in New York to develop radiation detectors for the Manhattan Project. Perhaps of equal importance to the success of the atomic bomb, her earlier research at Berkeley on xenon now found unexpected applications in solving the so-called xenon-poisoning problem in the plutonium-producing reactors at Hanford, Washington. (Xenon, as a by-product of uranium fission, was absorbing neutrons and shutting down the chain reactions.)

Recognized Authority in Beta Decay. The end of the war in 1945 brought welcome news from several fronts: Wu heard from her family in China, learning that they had survived the Japanese invasion; Columbia invited her to stay as a senior scientist with a lab of her own; and Yuan found a position designing accelerators at the newly established Brookhaven National Laboratory on Long Island. In 1947 their son, Vincent Wei-chen Yuan, was born (and later followed his parents' footsteps to become a physicist). Meanwhile, their intention to return to China was frustrated first by the civil war between the Nationalists and the Communists and then by the cutoff of Sino-American relations following the Communist victory in 1949 and the outbreak of the Korean War in 1950. Finally, in 1954 they decided to become naturalized U.S. citizens, joining thousands of other Chinese students and scholars who settled in the United States permanently in this period.

Scientifically, Wu focused, in 1946–1952, on the problem of beta decay, an important area of nuclear physics. As one of the three kinds of radiation to come out of a radioactive nucleus (the other two are alpha rays of protons and gamma rays of photons), beta decay was understood to be made up of electrons and neutrinos, but the mechanism for their production was in dispute. According to Fermi's influential theory, for example, electrons should come out of the nucleus with higher energies than what were commonly reported from experiments. In a series of ingeniously designed experiments with Richard David Albert at Columbia in 1948–1949, Wu proved that

the discrepancy derived not from theoretical flaws but from the uneven thickness of the radioactive materials used in earlier experiments by others. Electrons that came out of one nucleus but had to travel through the electromagnetic fields of others would necessarily be slowed down. Thus, she invented an innovative but simple process to prepare an extremely thin and even source that yielded results in remarkable agreement with Fermi's predictions. This and other experiments of Wu's around the same time not only made her a recognized authority in beta decay, but also cemented her reputation for accuracy and technical sophistication. These successes also helped her to overcome resistance to women in Columbia's Physics Department—chiefly by Isidor I. Rabi—and brought her a promotion to associate professor with tenure in 1952.

Triumph: The Parity Experiment. For a few years after 1952, Wu's interest gradually shifted from beta decay to other topics. But a conversation with her Columbia colleague and fellow Chinese American physicist Tsung Dao Lee (Li Zhengdao in pinyin) in the spring of 1956 rekindled her passion for beta decay. At the time, Lee and Chen Ning Yang (Yang Zhenning in pinyin), another Chinese American physicist at Princeton's Institute of Advanced Study, were investigating the possibility that particles involved in weak interactions—beta decay was one example—might not follow the law of parity. Simply stated, the law of parity—or the conservation of parity—meant that nature did not discriminate between right and left; if a process is possible, its mirror imaged counterpart should be equally possible. But in order to explain several mysteries in the behaviors of elementary particles, Lee and Yang were forced to suspect that perhaps the widely accepted law of parity was violated in weak interactions. While most physicists—theoretical and experimental—were highly skeptical of any such speculation, Wu took it seriously. What Lee and Yang found, with Wu's assistance, was that no one had ever tested the law in weak interactions. So Wu reasoned that even if the law held, an experiment to prove it would be significant and worthwhile. Her choice of a reaction for testing parity was the beta decay of radioactive cobalt ^{60}Co.

Wu's idea was to line up the spins of the ^{60}Co nuclei and then detect the direction of the beta particles (electrons) that were emitted from the nuclei. If the law of parity held, electrons should come out in both directions—along and opposite the direction of the spin of the nuclei—in equal numbers. Otherwise, parity would be broken. Conceptually simple, the experiment was technically extremely difficult. A big challenge was to cool the ^{60}Co to 0.01 degree Celsius above absolute zero (-273.14^0C[-459.65^0F]) to reduce background noise. Fortunately, Wu found a group of capable collaborators, headed by Ernest Ambler, with low-temperature facilities at the National Bureau of Standards (NBS) to carry out the experiment, with additional assistance from her graduate student Marion Biavati. Overcoming many obstacles they found, by late 1956 and early 1957, that indeed, as Lee and Yang had suggested, the law of parity was violated in beta decay: more beta particles were emitted in the direction opposite that of the nuclear spin than along it. Two groups of physicists—Richard Garwin, Leon Lederman, and Marcel Weinrich at Columbia and Jerome Friedman and Valentine Telegdi at the University of Chicago—quickly confirmed the breaking of parity in other processes of weak interactions.

The fall of parity came as a shock to many physicists, including Wolfgang Pauli, the sharp-tongued Austrian-Swiss physicist (and Wu's close friend), who could not believe that God was "left-handed" (in weak interactions). As one of the most dramatic episodes in modern physics, the investigation on parity overthrew one of the fundamental laws of nature and heralded, in Wu's own words, a "sudden liberation of our thinking on the very structure of the physical world" (Wu, 1973, p. 118.) It led to new advances in many directions and paved the way, eventually, for the unification of the weak and electromagnetic forces. Columbia's Physics Department called a press conference on 15 January 1957, which was presided over by a proud Rabi, to announce the breakthrough by Wu and her colleagues. The next day the *New York Times* carried the news on its front page and spread it to the rest of the world.

The significance of the research by Lee, Yang, Wu, and her NBS collaborators was immediately recognized by the physics community, but when the Nobel Prize in Physics for 1957 was announced, it went only to Lee and Yang, not Wu. While she felt happy for her friends, who were the first Chinese to ever win the prize, and she never conducted research just to win the prize, she clearly was disappointed by her exclusion, as were many others, including Lee, Yang, and Rabi, who felt that she deserved the honor. Over the years Wu received just about every other award for a scientist, mainly for her parity experiment but also for her other achievements. She was given an honorary doctorate of science by Princeton University, elected a member of the National Academy of Sciences, promoted—finally—to full professorship at Columbia, and named recipient of the Research Corporation Award, all in 1958. From the National Academy she also received the Comstock Award in 1964. In 1972 she was made the first Michael I. Pupin Professor of Physics at Columbia and elected a member of the American Academy of Arts and Sciences. Three years later she became the president of the APS and received the National Medal of Science from President Gerald Ford. Then, in 1978, she received the first Wolf Prize in physics from the Wolf Foundation

of Israel. For many of these awards, she was the first woman or one of the first women so honored.

Later Research and Activities. Wu maintained a strong track record following her parity triumph, as best exemplified by her experiment on the conservation of vector current (CVC) in beta decay in 1963. In the late 1950s, particle theorists Richard Feynman and Murray Gell-Mann at Caltech, whose thinking had been liberated by the breaking of parity, had proposed the CVC theory in a major step toward the unification of two of the four fundamental forces in nature: the electromagnetic and weak forces (the other two are strong and gravitational forces). When initial experiments failed to confirm the CVC hypothesis, Gell-Mann turned to Wu, reportedly pleading: "How long did Yang and Lee pursue you to follow up on their work?"(McGrayne, 1993, p. 278). When she finally did the experiment with two graduate students, the results unequivocally confirmed the theory. Other experiments that Wu conducted with students and collaborators in the 1960s and 1970s upheld her reputation for being both accurate and hard-driving. These included investigations on double-beta decay, carried out half a mile underground in a salt mine near Cleveland, Ohio on the so-called muonic atoms in which muons take the place of electrons in normal atoms; on Mössbauer spectroscopy and its application in the study of sickle-cell anemia; and on Bell's theorem, with results confirming the orthodox interpretation of quantum mechanics.

Taking advantage of her parity celebrity, Wu began to speak out on social and political issues, especially on equality for women in science. At a Massachusetts Institute of Technology symposium in 1964, for example, she lamented the lack of women in science due to both cultural biases and professional discrimination. "I sincerely doubt that any open-minded person really believes in the faulty notion that women have no intellectual capacity for science and technology" (Wu, 1965, p. 45). Counting proudly the achievements of women nuclear physicists such as Marie Curie and Lise Meitner, she declared that "never before have so few contributed so much under such trying circumstances!" (p. 47). In 1975, from the platform of the APS presidency, she urged the federal government to increase funding for education and basic research.

During the later stage of Wu's life, her Chinese heritage and connections began to take on growing importance for her. She had always maintained contact with the scientific community in Taiwan, even though the parity experiment in 1956 prevented her from taking a prearranged around-the-world trip that had included a stop there. In 1962 she finally traveled, with her husband, to Taiwan for a meeting of the Academia Sinica, of which she was elected the first woman member in 1948 and of which her beloved teacher Hu Shi was then president. While apolitical in general, around this time she signed petitions against the arrests of political dissidents and advised Jiang Jieshi against launching a project to make atomic bombs. The reopening of U.S.-China relations in the early 1970s made possible her first return to the mainland, again with her husband, in 1973. On this bittersweet and nostalgic journey, Wu mourned the fact that she never got to see her parents and brothers again before they died in the 1950s and 1960s. She was, however, delighted by a six-hour meeting with Premier Zhou Enlai, whom she admired as a moderate leader pushing for the modernization of China. With the flexibility that came with her retirement from Columbia in 1981, Wu traveled more frequently to both sides of the Taiwan Strait to advise the governments on science policy, promote education and science, and receive many honors and awards. In 1989, when the Chinese government cracked down on students demanding democracy and political reform in Beijing's Tiananmen Square, she voiced her disapproval. Nevertheless, she was elected one of the first foreign academicians of the Chinese Academy of Sciences in 1994. A household name in mainland China, Taiwan, and Hong Kong, Wu, as a "Chinese Curie," became a role model for many Chinese students, especially girls and women, with scientific aspirations. When Wu died, her ashes were buried, according to her will, in the courtyard of her father's Mingde school, joined several years later by that of her husband.

BIBLIOGRAPHY

Many of Wu's unpublished papers are deposited at the Chien-Shiung Wu Memorial Hall at Southeast University in Nanjing, one of two universities that grew out of her alma mater the National Central University. Yuelin Zhu, "Chien-Shiung Wu: An Intellectual Biography" (PhD diss., Harvard University, 2001), has a fairly complete list of Wu's writings.

WORKS BY WU

"Identification of Two Radioactive Xenons from Uranium Fission." *Physical Review* 58 (1940): 926.

With E. Segrè. "Some Fission Products of Uranium." *Physical Review* 57 (1940): 552.

"The Continuous X-Rays Excited by the Beta-Particles of $_{15}P^{32}$." *Physical Review* 59 (1941): 481–488.

With R. D. Albert. "The Beta-Spectrum of S^{35}." *Physical Review* 74 (1948): 847–848.

———. "The Beta-Ray Spectra of Cu^{64}." *Physical Review* 75 (1949): 315–316.

———. "The Beta-Ray Spectra of Cu^{64} and the Ratio of N + /N -." *Physical Review* 75 (1949): 1107–1108.

With E. Ambler, R. W. Hayward, D. D. Hoppes, et al. "Experimental Test of Parity Conservation in Beta Decay." *Physical Review* 105 (1957): 1413–1415.

With Luke C. L. Yuan, eds. *Methods of Experimental Physics: Nuclear Physics.* 2 vols. New York: Academic Press, 1961–1963.

With Y. K. Lee and L. W. Mo. "Experimental Test of the Conserved Vector Current Theory on the Beta Spectra of B^{12} and N^{12}." *Physical Review Letters* 10 (1963): 253–258.

"The Universal Fermi Interaction and the Conserved Vector Current in Beta Decay." *Reviews of Modern Physics* 36 (1964): 618–632.

"Panel Discussion [on] the Commitment Required of a Woman Entering a Scientific Profession." In *Women and the Scientific Professions,* edited by Jacquelyn A. Mattfeld and Carol G. Van Aken. Cambridge, MA: MIT Press, 1965.

With S. A. Moszkowski. *Beta Decay.* New York: Interscience Publishers, 1966.

"One Researcher's Personal Account." *Adventures in Experimental Physics* γ (1973): 101–123.

"The Discovery of Nonconservation of Parity in Beta Decay." In *Thirty Years since Parity Nonconservation: A Symposium for T. D. Lee,* edited by Robert Novick. Boston: Birkhäuser, 1988.

OTHER SOURCES

Jiang, Caijian. *Wu Jianxiong: Wu li ke xue di di yi fu ren* [Chieng-Shiung Wu: The first lady of the physical sciences]. Taipei: Shibao Wenhua, 1996. The first full-length biography of Wu in Chinese, based largely on interviews with Wu and others.

McGrayne, Sharon Bertsch. *Nobel Prize Women in Science: Their Lives, Struggles, and Momentous Discoveries.* Secaucus, NJ: Carol Publishing Group, 1993. Chapter 11 is on Wu.

Zhu, Yuelin. "Chien-Shiung Wu: An Intellectual Biography." PhD diss., Harvard University, 2001.

Zuoyue Wang

WU JIANXIONG

SEE **Wu Chien-Shiung**.

WUNDT, WILHELM (*b.* Neckarau, Baden, Germany, 16 August 1832; *d.* Grossbothen, Germany, 31 August 1920), *psychology.* For the original entry on Wundt see *DSB,* vol. 14.

In studies of the history of psychology, nothing could likely be more illustrative of how dynamic, fluid, and changing the study of history can be than the topic of Wilhelm Wundt and his system of psychology. In one generation, scholars such as Edward Titchener and E. G. Boring were caught up in looking through historical filters that created a particular view of that individual and his time. Then in a later generation, those filters began to dissolve as scholars such as Kurt Danziger and Arthur

Blumenthal began critical reexaminations that saw that past in a radically different light.

A Theoretician. Wundt has been consistently described in introductory textbooks as the father of modern experimental psychology because he created the first major laboratory for that enterprise, doing so by adapting instruments from physiology laboratories for use in tests and measurements of mental processes. Because physiology laboratories were the source of instrumentation, experimental psychology in Germany was for that reason originally called "*physiologische Psychologie*" (from the title of Wundt's major work, *Grundzüge der physiologischen Psychologie* [1902–1903]). But the great majority of Wundt's efforts were in theoretical psychology; he devoted relatively little effort to experimenting. His students were the ones who carried experimental psychology forward. And when many of them grew increasingly focused on the design and precision of laboratory instruments, he faulted them for losing sight of the big picture, namely, the major historical questions that confront the explanation of psychological processes.

Wundt's systematic and gradually unfolding psychological theory was his true and distinctive contribution. His theoretical system was logically enough an example of a trend of thought that had been prominent in central Europe and at the end of the nineteenth century was resurfacing under the titles of neo-idealism and neo-Romanticism. But it was about to be overwhelmed by the revitalization of positivism and the parallel development of behaviorist psychology. Those forces were largely responsible for the subsequent obliteration of Wundt's system from the minds of many.

Though Wundtian psychological theory was little mentioned in twentieth-century writings in which Anglo-American influences were superseding the Germanic ones in psychology, his prominence as a founding father of psychology was remembered, so homage of some sort had to be paid to him in textbooks. Since he was the arch mentalist who stood in opposition to the antimentalistic trends of the following era, historical accounts often focused negatively on his personal mannerisms, alleged character flaws, and points of inconsistency, or merely on tangential information about his personal life.

Views on Consciousness. Wundt's psychological system was first and foremost the science of consciousness. It was predicated on the view that consciousness is a natural phenomenon as distinct and real as any other natural phenomenon and that it could in principle be studied scientifically. Wundt studied it because it was there, it was interesting, and a better understanding of it could be beneficial to humanity. This was all proposed in steadfast opposition to Cartesian materialistic dualism that had suggested a separate "mind stuff" distinct from other forms of matter. Wundtian theory starts with the definition of consciousness as a flowing process, not an alternative substance, and as not being understandable by approaching it through neurology or brain chemistry in which it is not observable. The extensive study of emotion at Leipzig in the 1890s, where the investigations of Alfred Lehmann were dominant, concluded that the course, the fluctuations, and the colorations of emotion are not understood by attributing them to those bodily responses that may occur during variations of emotion. Instead, and in the tradition of Fechnerian psychophysics, the Leipzig approach involved early efforts at multidimensional scaling of subjective judgments of feelings, along with techniques for timing and analyzing the course of subjective emotional processes.

American histories of psychology focused on Wundt's earlier studies of selective attention (then called "apperception") that dominated his theorizing during the first years of his Leipzig Psychological Institute as well as his earlier research at Heidelberg. The experimental methodology used in those early studies employed primarily reaction-time measurements, which encouraged a prolific development of a delicate time-measurement technology by Wundt's students. Later American textbooks misleadingly referred to this effort as "research on reaction time." Reaction time, however, was only a research methodology. It was not the subject of the research, which should have been described as "research on central self-controlled mental processes in the analysis of judgment and decision making."

A central control process was the key concept, and it led Wundt's school to be named "voluntarism" (or voluntaristic psychology) in contrast to another school of thought that was later to be associated mistakenly with Wundt. That other school was Edward Titchener's "structuralism." Titchener was an Englishman transplanted to the United States. The greater part of his education was at Oxford University and was based in British associationist mental philosophy, with James Mill's writings on associationism and systematic introspection having the most influence on Titchener. With no graduate program in psychology available in Great Britain, he was forced to go to Leipzig to obtain his doctorate with Wundt. While there, he came under the influence of Wundt's arch opponents, the new positivists, such as Ernst Mach. But later, in the United States, Titchener was to be interpreted erroneously as the representative of Wundtian psychology, which led to major distortions in subsequent historical descriptions of Wundt particularly in the English-speaking world.

Opposition to Mechanistic Approaches. Wundt had consistently opposed the classic Enlightenment mental philosophies (particularly mechanistic associationism), so well rooted in British and French intellectual history. He disputed that tradition of thought in his basic psychological theory as well as in his large body of research on psycholinguistics (then known as *Sprachpsychologie*) and on *Voelkerpsychologie,* which is correctly translated for Wundt's meaning as "cultural psychology." Later American historians translated it as "folk psychology" (as if from *Volkspsychologie*). It seems clear that American historians for most of the twentieth century seldom if ever read Wundt's cultural psychology, except for one relatively shorter speculative work on historical processes: *Elemente der Völkerpsychologie. Grundlinien einer psychologishen Entwicklungsgeschichte der Menschheit* (1912), translated as *Elements of Folk Psychology* (1916). The German subtitle could be rendered as *Outlines of a psychological developmental history of humanity.* That book was quite different in content from his other multivolume *Voelkerpsychologie.*

Beginning in the 1880s, Wundt began to publish a series of diatribes against introspection as a source of psychological data. His own research methodology was named *selbstbeobactung,* in retrospect an unfortunate choice of terminology. Superficial translations easily rendered *selbstbeobachtung* into the English term *introspection.* However, that translation ignores the specialized meaning Wundt gave to his German term. He used his term in opposition to traditional *Introspektion* because his method was to involve publicly replicable objective laboratory procedures for assessing the fluctuations of mental processes. Yet American history texts were later to discredit Wundt as an "introspectionist." Wundt's apparently unnoticed refutations of introspection research methodology were first directed at British mental philosophers, then at Titchener and his school, then at the Würzburg psychologists in their early-twentieth-century introspective studies of thought processes.

Opposition to Herbart. Wundt's psychological system arose in reaction against earlier mechanistic conceptions of mental processes that had been highly influential in the psychological thought of the nineteenth century. The Anglo-American intellectual world had often been receptive to such views but took little notice of their prominent manifestation in the early-nineteenth-century German works of Johann Herbart. In the English literature Herbart is cited primarily as an educational theorist and a speculative mental philosopher who attempted unsuccessfully to apply a discursive mathematics to the description of mental processes. But Herbart's voluminous primary work, *Psychologie als Wissenschaft* (2 vols., 1824, 1825; Psychology as science), was never translated into English.

Wilhelm Wundt. *Painting of Wilhelm Wundt by Dora Arndt-Raschid, circa 1910.* **HULTON ARCHIVE/GETTY IMAGES.**

Its mechanical mental associationism is nothing less than elaborate and exotic. It inspired a century of theorizing in all of the social sciences in the German literature. Wundt rose to prominence at the end of that century by effectively refuting the Herbartian system in the eyes of many of his followers in the German universities.

In Herbart's descriptions, psychological processes are mechanical elements flowing across the stage of consciousness. He described how dominant elements (sensations or impressions) can create a central focus in consciousness. He established thresholds of consciousness, processes of repression, and numerous forms of the association or blendings and fusions of elementary ideas into mental schemas. Emotion in Herbart's view is a secondary factor, a spark, a tension, which occurs as a by-product of other mental events, as when opposed ideas collide. Wundt referred to this picture of mental objects and events as Herbart's billiard-ball-table description of the mind. Wundt found, in contrast to Herbart, that emotion, or urges and feelings, are primary in mental processes, not secondary side effects. Emotional feelings, he argued, form a system that supports what Herbart's theory most basically lacked—a central process of self-control, which came to be the primary process in Wundt's theory. As Wundt reputedly showed, that central process has consistent temporal characteristics and a developmental capacity for creating automatic control schemas that take over the guidance of formerly deliberate or voluntary thoughts and actions. Rules that govern alternations between conscious, self-controlled actions and automatic actions were the focus of considerable Wundtian theorizing.

At the heart of Wundt's system is his seminal principle, from which a set of interlocking principles evolved. It was that of *schöpferishe Synthese,* or "creative synthesis." It states that mental processes are generative, meaning they create qualities not found in the physical sciences nor in other sensory elements in mental processes. That principle first appeared in Wundt's writings in 1862, and it supported the derivation of a branching set of related principles in all of his subsequent writings.

Most of the Wundtian corpus never appeared in the Anglo-American theater of psychological theory owing to the rise of behaviorism, the world wars, tedious terminological barriers, translation problems, and other cultural differences. More space in American textbooks was devoted to describing tangential aspects of Wundt's life, manners, work habits, lecturing style, counts of books published, numbers of pages in those books, and ad hominem polemics against him than was devoted to explaining his research and theories.

SUPPLEMENTARY BIBLIOGRAPHY

Blumenthal, Arthur L. *Language and Psychology: Historical Aspects of Psycholinguistics.* New York: John Wiley, 1970.

———. "A Reappraisal of Wilhelm Wundt." *American Psychologist* 30 (1975): 1081–1088.

———. "Wilhelm Wundt: Psychology as the Propaedeutic Science." In *Points of View in the Modern History of Psychology,* edited by Claude E. Buxton. New York: Academic Press. 1985.

———. "A Wundt Primer: The Operating Characteristics of Consciousness." In *Wilhelm Wundt in History,* edited by Robert W. Rieber and David K. Robinson. New York: Plenum, 2001.

Danziger, Kurt. "The History of Introspection Reconsidered." *Journal of the History of the Behavioral Sciences* 16 (1980): 241–262.

———. "The Unknown Wundt: Drive, Apperception, and Volition." In *Wilhelm Wundt in History,* edited by Robert W. Rieber and David K. Robinson. New York: Plenum, 2001.

Kusch, Martin. *Psychologism: A Case Study in the Sociology of Philosophical Knowledge.* London and New York: Routledge, 1995.

Leahey, Thomas H. *A History of Psychology: Main Currents in Psychological Thought.* 6th ed. Upper Saddle River, NJ: Prentice-Hall, 2004.

Robinson, D. K. "Wilhelm Wundt and the Establishment of Experimental Psychology, 1875–1914: The Context of a New Field of Scientific Research." PhD diss., University of California, Berkeley, 1987.

Arthur L. Blumenthal

WURTZ, ADOLPHE (*b.* Wolfisheim, near Strasbourg, France, 26 November 1817; *d.* Paris, France, 12 May 1884), *chemistry.* For the original article on Wurtz see *DSB,* vol. 14.

Wurtz's research spanned the entire science of chemistry and was notable for its volume, importance, and influence; moreover, from about 1854 until his death he was the principal French advocate of atomic-molecular theory and structural organic chemistry. Taking advantage of scholarship that has appeared subsequent to the original *DSB* article, the author of this postscript intends to provide a fuller assessment of Wurtz's contributions to science, particularly his advocacy for state support of French science and his ardent defense of atomistic ideas.

Early Career. Although Wurtz was French, his development as a scientist was crucially shaped by his association with Justus von Liebig in Giessen, with whom he spent the summer semester of 1842, prior to the award of his MD degree from the Faculty of Medicine in Strasbourg. (Due to his Alsatian roots, Wurtz was fluent in German, unusual for French chemists at this time.) He was equally influenced by his association with Jean-Baptiste Dumas, whom he met when he traveled from Strasbourg to Paris in 1844 and into whose private laboratory (unconnected with Dumas's position in the Paris Faculty of Medicine) he soon was accepted. Wurtz became *agrégé* in the Faculty of Medicine in 1847; he was *suppléant* (substitute lecturer) for Dumas from 1849 and then replaced him as professor of pharmacy and organic chemistry in February 1853. In December 1853 this position was abolished; a new professorship of organic and mineral chemistry was created in the faculty, and Wurtz was given this chair instead. In 1875, following lobbying by Wurtz and his allies, he was appointed to a newly created chair for organic chemistry in the Sorbonne. (Some of the information in this paragraph differs slightly from the material in the original *DSB* article.)

Wurtz's personal relationship with the militant would-be reformer of the science of chemistry, Charles Gerhardt, was always difficult, even though they were fellow Strasbourgeois and almost exact contemporaries. Nonetheless, he converted wholeheartedly to many of Gerhardt's leading ideas shortly before the latter's early

ALMANACH DE L'ILLUSTRATION

M. ADOLPHE WURTZ — Voir page 47.

Adolphe Wurtz. *Adolphe Wurtz, circa 1870.* HULTON
ARCHIVE/GETTY IMAGES.

death in 1856. Wurtz's work was instrumental in the rise
of valence theory and highly influential on August
Kekulé's formulation in 1858 of the principles of what
became known as the theory of chemical structure. Surprisingly, Wurtz strongly championed Kekulé against the
claim by Archibald Scott Couper of having independently
developed structure theory, even though Couper had
worked in his own laboratory.

Educator and Advocate. Couper was one of probably
more than three hundred of Wurtz's laboratory students;
like Couper, most of his students were either foreign or
French-Alsatian. Wurtz's laboratory, attached to the Faculty of Medicine, was the site of a preeminent laboratory-
based teaching/research school and was internationally
recognized as providing the finest training for elite
research chemists. For all that, it was not officially a part
of the faculty at all; Wurtz was forced to run it as a private
venture, while his superiors turned a blind eye to the business. The situation highlighted a deficiency of the French
system of higher education in science during the nineteenth century, the near absence of properly state-supported academic laboratory facilities. Wurtz strove
energetically over his entire career to urge the government

to address the problem, though with only partial success.
For nine years (1866–1875), Wurtz was an effective dean
of the Faculty of Medicine of the University of Paris,
working effectively not only for the welfare of the school,
its students and faculty, but also for principles of academic
freedom and the struggle for women to gain entry into
French academic life.

Leading a laboratory-based school frequented largely
by foreigners and speaking several European languages
fluently, Wurtz became a principal conduit for foreign
theories into French scientific culture. After about 1854
Wurtz was an ardent advocate of the atomic theory and of
a school of organic chemistry founded upon Kekulé's (and
others') molecular-structural ideas; indeed, he was the
acknowledged leader of the atomist/structuralist camp in
France. But he was opposed by those who firmly regarded
atomic and structural theories as insecure and hypothetical, such as Marcellin Berthelot, Henri Sainte-Claire De-
ville, and Louis Troost, and by those who were dogmati-
cally uninterested in taking any position on such questions, such as Dumas, Antoine-Jérome Balard, and
Edmond Frémy. Unfortunately for Wurtz, until 1875 the
six scientists just named controlled instruction in chemistry in all of the important Parisian academic institutions:
the Sorbonne, the Collège de France, the École Polytech-
nique, the École Normale, and the Muséum d'Histoire
Naturelle. Wurtz was well isolated at the Faculty of Medicine, where pure research in a physical science such as
chemistry could never be anything more than an ancillary
study. One consequence was that French chemistry continued to use the so-called equivalent-weight system of
formulas (founded on, e.g., H = 1, C = 6, O = 8, and S =
16) rather than the atomic weight system that had become
standard in most other European countries.

Wurtz's 1875 appointment to the Sorbonne as a new
professor of organic chemistry finally created a forum in
which Parisian students could become familiar with mod-
ernist atomic/structural chemical theory, but this circum-
stance had only a limited immediate influence on the
course of French chemistry. Despite all of Wurtz's efforts,
a powerful anti-atomist current continued until the turn
of the twentieth century, at which time most French
chemists finally adopted atomic weights, the atomic theory, and the theory of chemical structure.

SUPPLEMENTARY BIBLIOGRAPHY

Carneiro, Ana. *The Research School of Chemistry of Adolphe
Wurtz, 1853–1884.* PhD diss., University of Kent,
Canterbury, U.K., 1992.

———. "Adolphe Wurtz and the Atomism Controversy." *Ambix*
40, no. 2 (1993): 75–95.

Carneiro, Ana, and Natalie Pigeard. "Chimistes alsaciens à Paris au 19ème siècle: un réseau, une école?" *Annals of Science* 54, no. 6 (1997): 533–546.

Fox, Robert. *The Culture of Science in France, 1700–1900.* Aldershot, U.K.: Variorum, 1992.

Fox, Robert, and George Weisz, eds. *The Organization of Science and Technology in France, 1808–1914.* Cambridge, U.K.: Cambridge University Press, 1980.

Pigeard, Natalie. "L'oeuvre du chimiste Charles Adolphe Wurtz (1817–1884)." Thèse de maîtrise, Université de Paris X Nanterre, 1993.

———. "Charles Adolphe Wurtz, doyen de L' École de Médecine de Paris (1866–1875)," PhD thesis, Université de Paris X Nanterre, 2007.

Rocke, Alan J. "History and Science, History of Science: Adolphe Wurtz and the Renovation of the Academic Professions in France." *Ambix* 41, no. 11 (1994): 20–32.

———. *Nationalizing Science: Adolphe Wurtz and the Battle for French Chemistry.* Cambridge, MA: MIT Press, 2001.

Alan J. Rocke

WÜST, GEORG (*b.* Posen, Poland, 15 June 1890; *d.* Erlangen, Germany, 8 November 1977), *physical oceanography.*

Wüst's standing as one of the most prominent German physical oceanographers is based on his participation in the famous German South Atlantic Expedition onboard the research vessel *Meteor* (1925–1927) and his many detailed publications on the Atlantic bottom water sphere. Furthermore, he was interested in the Gulf Stream and other western boundary current systems in the world ocean and the influence of bottom topography on the general vertical and horizontal circulation patterns of the world ocean, as well as in specific problems of regional seas such as the Mediterranean, the Baltic, and the Caribbean. Academically Wüst was associated with the famous Museum und Institut für Meereskunde (Museum and Institute for Oceanography) in Berlin and, after World War II, with the Kiel Institut für Meereskunde. After his retirement he spent five very productive years in the United States, mainly at Columbia University. Wüst had many friends and students in Germany and worldwide. He was the leading figure in physical oceanography in Germany for many decades. His ideas and publications remained in the early 2000s important for modern international marine research projects.

Early Life and Career in Berlin. Wüst was born on 15 June 1890 in Posen (later Poznan, Poland), the son of a Prussian official. Shortly after Georg's birth his parents moved to Berlin, where Wüst spent his childhood. He went to Charlottenburg Gymnasium and in 1910 entered the Friedrich-Wilhelms University in Berlin, where he studied geography, oceanography, meteorology, mathematics, and physics. From the beginning of his career his main academic focus was geography and oceanography. The Berlin Museum und Institut für Meereskunde, established by Ferdinand Freiherr von Richthofen in 1900, was closely linked to the university's Department of Geography, and Albrecht Penck, a noted geographer, was director of both departments (since 1905). Penck was succeeded at the Berlin Museum und Institut in 1910 by Alfred Merz, an Austrian hydrographer who had conducted research in the Adriatic Sea; Merz's work fascinated the young student Wüst.

In 1920 Merz became the first director of the Berlin Institut für Meereskunde, now a separate and independent institution, serving in that capacity until his tragic death in Buenos Aires in 1925. Albert Defant was subsequently appointed director. Both were Wüst's superiors during this first long phase of scientific development in Berlin, which lasted until the end of World War II.

Merz, who planned to study an entire ocean systematically, sent Wüst to work with Björn Helland-Hansen in Bergen in Norway in 1912 to gain acquaintance with modern Scandinavian methods in oceanography. In addition, Wüst took an active role in the observational program onboard the lightships off the German coast and joined a summer class in oceanography organized at Rovigno, the shore station of the Berlin Institute in the northern Adriatic Sea. Under the guidance of Merz, Wüst prepared his doctoral thesis about evaporation above the sea surface. The date of his promotion was 28 August 1914, but officially his PhD was awarded on 30 June 1919. During the war Wüst served as a meteorologist and was wounded in action near Verdun on 1 October 1917. In June 1919 Wüst was appointed as Merz's assistant and joined a number of shorter research cruises in the North Sea and the Baltic. Theirs was also a close personal relationship, and Wüst became Merz's son-in-law in 1921.

Onboard R.V. *Meteor* (1925–1927). The German *Meteor* expedition was a major accomplishment for the German science community after the war and a highlight in the history of oceanography. Merz proposed to study one ocean systematically in detail, according to a strict plan. Altogether there were 310 hydrographic stations arranged on fourteen more or less latitudinal sections across the South Atlantic Ocean between 20° north to 65° south. In 1924 Merz's proposal to the German Society for the Advancement of Science (Notgemeinschaft der Deutschen Wissenschaft) was approved, and a navy survey vessel was put at his disposal. From the beginning Wüst was involved in this pioneering approach to studying the horizontal and vertical circulation patterns of water masses in an ocean. Wüst and Merz coauthored a number of papers on the vertical circulation in the Atlantic Ocean before the cruise started in April 1925.

Merz fell ill onboard the *Meteor* during the initial leg of the expedition, which began in Buenos Aires; he had to be taken back and died there on 13 June 1925. After this tragic event, Wüst took over most of Merz's responsibilities, according to the last wish of his mentor. As supervisor of the oceanographic task, Wüst's mission was to bring the *Meteor* expedition to a successful end, to evaluate the rich harvest of oceanographic data, and to publish the main results. In retrospect Wüst was an excellent caretaker of Merz's legacy. In addition to its main focus, which was physical oceanography and the identification and movements of different water masses, the *Meteor* expedition had interdisciplinary aspects as well. A number of well-known oceanographers were onboard, such as Günther Böhnecke, Arnold Schuhmacher, and Hermann Wattenberg. Moreover, a biologist (E. Hentschel), geologists (O. Pratje and C. W. Correns), and meteorologists (J. Reger and E. Kuhlbrodt) were part of the scientific staff of the German Atlantic Expedition. Albert Defant joined for the last three transects as principal investigator; he was appointed director of the Berlin Institute in 1927, taking over Merz's position. Defant officially was in charge of the complicated editing and publishing process of the numerous expedition reports of this *Meteor* expedition, which inaugurated a new chapter in the development of ocean sciences. Wüst accepted Defant as his superior, and Defant trusted Wüst and delegated much of the publishing work.

Wüst made very substantial contributions to the *Meteor* reports, especially on deep sea and bottom circulation. His study of the deep water sphere of the Atlantic Ocean, originally published as part of Volume VI in 1935, became a classical text; it was translated into English in 1978 for the National Science Foundation in Washington, DC, as a late tribute. To study the spread of bottom water Wüst relied on bathymetric information. He used the 33,000 echo soundings obtained during the cruise. Theodor Stocks, cartographer of the Berlin Institute since 1930, evaluated this voluminous data set and produced a more or less reliable picture of the sea floor morphology. This bathymetric chart of the Atlantic Ocean was a standard for decades.

Kustos and Professor. The vessel *Meteor* returned home in July 1927, and Wüst was appointed Kustos (custodian or provost) of the Berlin Institute on 1 April 1928. This function involved administrative and organizational duties as well, and Wüst was responsible for the library, the public lecture series, and other public outreach activi-

ties of the museum and the Institut für Meereskunde in Berlin. He was editor of a very popular book series (*Das Meer in volkstümlichen Darstellungen*). Wüst arranged a special exhibition room for the *Meteor* cruise in the museum.

Wüst was a descriptive oceanographer with a strong background in geography. From 1922 until 1929 he was president of the Berlin Geographical Society (Gesellschaft für Erdkunde zu Berlin). In 1928 Wüst arranged an international oceanographic conference in Berlin on occasion of the Society's centenary, one of the highlights in Wüst's long career. He received the Carl Ritter Award for his effective help in managing and publishing the *Meteor* observations according to the plan of A. Merz in 1928. Wüst was an honorary member of the geographical societies of Frankfurt and Amsterdam. The Netherlands asked him to be an advisor for the *Willebrord Snellius* Expedition in Indonesian waters in 1929–1930.

In July 1929 Wüst finished his postdoctoral qualification process with a thesis on the Florida Current, in which he showed that the dynamical method allowed calculations of currents from the density field in the ocean. On 1 April 1934 he was appointed kustos and honorary professor; two years later he was appointed extraordinary professor. His longtime interest in the Gulf Stream system brought him back to sea again onboard the vessel *Altair* in 1938 for the first quasi-synoptic study of the highly variable branching area of the Gulf Stream northwest of the Azores. This was an international endeavor involving vessels from Germany, Denmark, Norway, Scotland, Iceland, and France.

During World War II, Wüst served with the Navy. He continued to stay in Berlin and was transferred to the nautical-scientific division of the supreme naval command. In 1943 he was appointed full professor and head of a department at the institute and museum in Berlin. At the admiralty Wüst and other colleagues were engaged in preparing charts of temperature and salinity, which were not unimportant for submarine warfare. During the war Wüst obviously had a double function and continued to look after the institute. However, the well-known building in the university campus area of central Berlin was completely destroyed in a number of bomb raids in 1944.

Wüst had two daughters, Ilse and Louise, with his first wife, who died in 1941. The last day of 1944 Wüst married Marie Vollmer, called Mimi. Shortly before the end of the war Wüst had to leave Berlin with the staff of the Navy Command and came to Schleswig-Holstein. Here he was able to start a new phase of his life after a productive thirty-five years in the German capital.

Director of the Institut für Meereskunde. From 1945 until his retirement in 1959 Wüst remained in Kiel. He was transferred to the directorship of the Institut für Meereskunde of Christian Albrecht University at Kiel. The Kiel Institute was established only in 1937, although marine research in this city on the Baltic Sea is much older. Otto Krümmel had been working there from 1884 to 1911 at the Department of Geography. The Kiel Institute on the east shore of Kiel fjord had been completely destroyed in an air raid on a nearby navy installation on 24 July 1944. Hermann Wattenberg, former *Meteor* staff member and then director of the institute, died, along with all staff members.

Perhaps the Royal Air Force had the institute on the target list, as oceanographic research was considered militarily important. Kiel was in the British occupation zone, and Wüst, who was living near Kiel with his family after the end of the war, was asked to continue his Berlin career by reestablishing the Department of Oceanography in cooperation with some biologists who had survived the war. Some British navy officers and members of the military government, who were aware of Wüst's merits, helped to arrange his appointment, which officially began on 1 February 1946. One of Wüst's British friends at that time was James N. Carruthers. Wüst, who was on good terms with the local state government and the university administrators, succeeded in getting a new extensive laboratory annex built near the west shore of Kiel fjord in 1956. New departments and positions were created, and Kiel gradually acquired the leading German position in ocean sciences that was formerly held by Berlin. Wüst managed to get the scientific part of the library of the Museum and Institute of Oceanography in Berlin and succeeded in taking over a small patrol vessel of the former navy, refitting it as a research craft (*Südfall*). Certainly Wüst's international reputation was valuable in many ways. In Kiel he shifted his interest to special Baltic Sea problems and started to study other semi-enclosed seas such as the Mediterranean. He went to conferences in Genua (1951), Helsinki, and elsewhere. Many of his publications of these years were printed in *Kieler Meeresforschungen*, the institute's journal. Some of Wüst's doctoral students at Kiel, such as Willi Brogmus, Klaus Wyrtki, Selim Morcos, Hartwig Weidemann, and Lorenz Magaard, became important figures in the international marine community in later years. Wüst's official retirement date was 30 September 1958, but he stayed in office until 30 March 1959.

Emeritus Years. Immediately after retirement Wüst left Kiel and his beloved golf course and house on the east shore. Rather unexpectedly, he accepted the invitation of Maurice Ewing to come to the Lamont-Doherty Geological Observatory of Columbia University in Palisades, New York. He stayed there five years as a visiting professor. In spring 1962 Wüst was at the University of Washington in Seattle, filling the Walter Ames Chair for Oceanography. In the United States, Wüst transferred much of his rich knowledge and experience to students at a time of increasing interest in ocean sciences and a new era of instrumentation. He lectured in his unique "Wüstian English," but his American colleagues and students understood and liked him. Wüst became interested in the water masses and circulation of the Caribbean Sea. One of his coworkers at Lamont-Doherty was Arnold L. Gordon, who arranged a two-volume tribute to Wüst on his eightieth birthday in 1972, containing twenty-four contributions by friends of Wüst. Furthermore, Gordon initiated an English translation of Wüst's famous study of the Atlantic deep ocean sphere (1978). So there was a certain revival of Wüst's descriptive oceanography at a time when the legacy of Wüst somehow faded away in Germany. But it should be emphasized that most of the international or national physical marine research projects of the late twentieth and early twenty-first centuries—such as the WOCE effort (World Ocean Circulation Experiment) and the modern concept of a global ocean conveyor belt driven by deep convection cells—had a relation to Wüst's pioneering studies.

In 1965 Wüst returned to Germany and stayed at the Department of Meteorology of Bonn University for two more years as visiting professor. From there he went to Erlangen, where he lived to the end of his long life in a residence for well-to-do senior citizens. He liked to receive friends and visitors and talk of the good old days. He enjoyed his last years in rather good health and in the familiar presence of his wife Mimi and his dog Whiskey.

When Georg Wüst died at the age of eighty-eight on 8 November 1977, an epoch in the history of marine sciences came to an end. His successor in Kiel, Günter Dietrich, listed all 112 scientific publications Wüst had produced over six decades. In 1972 he identified seven main areas of research interests in Wüst's career:

1. Evaporation and water budget of the world ocean;

2. Vertical circulation of the Atlantic Ocean as the central topic of the *Meteor* Expedition (1925–1927);

3. Geostrophic movement in the Gulf Stream and Kuroshio systems;

4. Bottom circulation in the world ocean and its dependence on sea floor topography;

5. Atlantic deep-sea convection and typical water masses;

6. Circulation and water masses in the Mediterranean; and

7. History of oceanography and deep-sea research.

In the early twenty-first century Wüst's prominent role in the history of oceanography in Germany is well established, though less known by students and young scientists. Studying the life and letters of Wüst means covering the development of oceanographic institutions and three generations of German marine scientists of all disciplines, who had the pleasure and honor of knowing him personally.

BIBLIOGRAPHY

WORKS BY WÜST

"Die Verdunstung über dem Meere." Berlin: Veröffentl. Inst. f. Meereskunde, N. F., Reihe A, H. 6, 1920.

"Florida- und Antillenstrom. Eine hydrodynamische Untersuchung." Berlin: Veröff. Inst. F. Meerreskunde, N. F., Reihe A, H. 12, 1924.

"Ozeanographische Methoden und Instrumente der Deutschen Atlantischen Expedition." *Ergänzugs-Heft III, Zeitschrift der Gesellschaft für Erdkunde Berlin* (1928): 66–83.

"Die Stratosphäre des Atlantischen Ozeans." In *Wissenschaftliche Ergebnisse der Deutschen Atlantischen Expedition "Meteor" 1925–1927* VI, pp. 1–144, 253–288. Berlin and Leipzig: Notgemeinschaft der Deutschen Wissenschaft,1935. Atlas attached.

"Bodentempßeratur und Bodenstrom in der atlantischen, indischen und pazifischen Tiefsee." *Gerlands Beiträge zur Geophysik* 54 (1938): 1–8.

"Blockdiagramme der atlantischen Zirkulation auf Grund der *Meteor*-Ergebnisse." *Kieler Meeresforschungen* 7 (1950): 24–34.

With W. Brogmus. "Ozeanographische Ergebnisse einer Untersuchungsfahrt mit Forschungskutter "Südfall" durch die Ostsee Juni–Juli 1954." *Kieler Meeresforschungen* 11 (1955): 3–21.

With C. Hoffmann, C. Schlieper, R. Kändler, et al. "Das Institut für Meereskunde der Universität Kiel nach seinem Wiederaufbau." *Kieler Meeresforschungen* 12 (1956): 127–153.

"Die Tiefenzirkulation des Mittelländischen Meeres in den Kernschichten des Zwischen- und Tiefenwassers." *Deutsche Hydrographische Zeitschrift* 13 (1960): 105–133.

"On the Stratification and Circulation of the Cold Water Sphere of the Caribbean-Antillan Basins." *Deep Sea Research* 10 (1960): 163–167.

"The Major Deep-Sea Expeditions and Research Vessels, 1873–1960: A Contribution to the History of Oceanography." *Progress in Oceanography* 2 (1964): 1–52.

"The Stratosphere of the Atlantic Ocean." *Scientific Results of the German Atlantic Expedition of the Research Vessel Meteor 1925–1927*, Vol. VI, sec. 1. English translation edited by William J. Emery. New Delhi: Al-Ahram Center for Scientific Translations, 1978.

OTHER SOURCES

Dietrich, Günter. "Georg Wüst's Scientific Work. Dedication to His Eightieth Birthday." In *Studies in Physical Oceanography: A Tribute to Georg Wüst on his 80th Birthday*, edited by Arnold L. Gordon. 2 vols. New York, London, and Paris: Gordon and Breach Science, 1972. Vol. 1, XI–XX (with full list of Wüst's publications).

Roll, Hans Ulrich. "Georg Wüst, 1890–1977." *Deutsche Gesellschaft für Meeresforschung-Mitteilungen* (1987): 25–28.

Schott, Wolfgang. *Early German Oceanographic Institutions, Expeditions and Oceanographers.* Compiled for the Fourth International Congress on the History of Oceanography. Hamburg: Deutsches Hydrographisches Institut, 1987.

Stocks, Theodor. "Georg Wüst und seine Stellung in der neueren Ozeanographie." *Petermanns Geographische Mitteilungen* 104 (1960): 292–205. Includes a list of Wüst's publications up to 1960.

Weidemann, Hartwig. "Georg Wüst und das Kieler Institut für Meereskunde (zum 100. Geburtstag am 15. 6. 1990)." *Deutsche Gesellschaft für Meeresfgorschung-Mitteilungen* (1990): 10–11.

Gerhard Kortum

WYNNE-EDWARDS, VERO COPNER

(*b.* Leeds, United Kingdom, 4 July 1906; *d.* Banchory, Aberdeenshire, United Kingdom, 5 January 1997), *ecology, evolution, social behavior, population biology.*

As a pioneer in the study of social behavior, Wynne-Edwards focused debate on the question of the level at which natural selection acted. Contrary to the increasingly reductionist focus of evolutionary biology on individual organisms and subsequently genes, Wynne-Edwards argued that an explanation of the evolution of social behavior required the mechanism of natural selection acting on groups of organisms rather than individuals or genes. This theory, most comprehensively described in his 1962 book *Animal Dispersion in Relation to Social Behavior,* became the target of sharp critique and generated an extended response from the community of evolutionary theorists. Although Wynne-Edwards's formulation of the theory of group selection was never accepted into the mainstream of evolutionary biology, later models of group selection have continued the debate about the levels of selection that was crystallized by Wynne-Edwards's work.

Early Life and Education. Wynne-Edwards was born in Leeds, the fifth of six children of the Reverend Canon John Rosindale Wynne-Edwards, headmaster of the Leeds grammar school, and his wife Lillian Agnes, née Streatfield. As a young boy growing up in the Yorkshire Dales, Wynne-Edwards developed a deep fondness for natural history. His early exposure to natural history was not much different from the experience of young English naturalists a century before; he was an avid collector and list maker. His first success as a young naturalist was the 1918 junior botany prize from Leeds for his collection of named wildflowers and ferns. He received a copy of Gilbert

White's eighteenth-century classic *The Natural History of Selbourne* (1789), which led Wynne-Edwards to his next project, "The Flora of Austwick," which he completed that summer.

In January 1920, at age thirteen, Wynne-Edwards was sent to boarding school at Rugby. It was here he became interested in astronomy and further developed his love of natural history in the school's museum, herbarium, and natural history society. At Rugby, Wynne-Edwards attended lectures by august visitors such as Sir Ernest Shackleton on the eve of his final Antarctic expedition and Julian Huxley, a renowned biologist, that inspired him with visions of the adventurous scientific life. In 1924 he prepared to leave Rugby with visions of Himalayan expeditions to study alpine flora and fauna; his father, however, had more traditional plans for him. In the end, Wynne-Edwards entered New College, Oxford, in 1925 to read zoology with the hope of having Huxley as tutor.

Although Huxley was to leave for the chair of zoology at King's College London after Wynne-Edwards's his first year, Oxford remained a propitious choice. The comparative anatomist Edwin S. Goodrich was Linacre Professor and head of the zoology department and had assembled at Oxford an unrivaled collection of biologists. Wynne-Edwards read comparative anatomy with Goodrich, embryology and experimental zoology with Gavin de Beer, genetics with Edmund B. Ford, and ecology with Charles Elton. Reflecting on his experience at Oxford in 1985 Wynne-Edwards wrote,

> Looking back fifty-five years later, I know how often I have been glad to have studied every phylum of the animal kingdom in detail, and thus acquired enormously more straight zoological knowledge than comes the way of students nowadays…. The apparent narrowness of the Oxford degree never seemed a handicap in my career in university teaching and research. The biological revolution has of course been running at flood level all my life, and we have never stopped having to study new subjects, often in widely diverse fields, just to keep up with our work. (pp. 489–490)

Given the scope of Wynne-Edwards's later theorizing, this breadth of training was indeed fortunate. It was, however, the ecologist Elton who had the most significant and long-lasting influence on Wynne-Edwards's scientific career. It was during Wynne-Edwards's first year as a student that Elton had begun his studies on periodic rodent population cycles in Bagley wood. These studies, along with a consulting position as biologist for the Hudson's Bay Company, set the foundation for the establishment of the Bureau of Animal Population at Oxford (Elton's institutional home for the rest of his career) and fired an inter-

est in animal populations that would dominate Wynne-Edwards's career and lead to the development of his most significant and controversial contribution to science, his theory of group selection.

Wynne-Edwards completed his studies at Oxford in 1927 with first-class honors. Initially, he took a position at the Marine Biological Laboratory at Plymouth, studying the distinct male morphs of the marine crustacean *Jassa falcata*. Although this project foundered, Wynne-Edwards was simultaneously pursuing an interest in the roosting behavior of starlings. The starling study marked the beginning of a lifelong fascination with birds and their social behavior and dispersion patterns.

After two years at Plymouth, he took a job as assistant lecturer at Bristol University and married his Oxford classmate Jeannie Morris. The position at Bristol was short lived; within months of his arrival he received an offer for a position as assistant professor at McGill University in Montreal. In September 1930, Jeannie and Wynne-Edwards emigrated to Canada.

Professional Life: Canada. For Wynne-Edwards the voyage from England to Canada was not merely a mode of transport to his new position; rather, it was an opportunity for research. Through the course of the transit, he kept numerical logs of the various species of birds he saw. As he later reported: "The data threw new light for me on seabird ecology" (1985, p. 494). He decided to make several more transatlantic data collection trips and ultimately published an article describing the basic pattern of inshore (coastal), offshore (to the edge of the continental shelf), and pelagic (deep-water) zones of seabird distribution. The resulting article, "On the Habits and Distribution of Birds on the North Atlantic" (1935), won the Walker Prize of the Boston Society of Natural History and established the arrival of a sharp new zoologist at McGill.

Wynne-Edwards remained at McGill through the end of World War II. During his fifteen years in Canada he became deeply familiar with Canadian natural history. He participated in multiple field expeditions to Newfoundland, Labrador, and the Arctic. He conducted faunal surveys of the St. Lawrence River and its tributaries for the Canadian Fishery Research Board, and in 1944 and 1945 he surveyed the Mackenzie and Yukon rivers in the Yukon Territory. The results of these expeditions tended initially to be of greater interest to government agencies than to research scientists. Ultimately, however, Wynne-Edwards would put his survey results to use in developing his theory of group selection.

At the end of the war, Wynne-Edwards was presented another fortuitous opportunity; the Regius Chair for Natural History at Aberdeen University in Northern Scotland had become available. After his return from the Yukon,

Wynne-Edwards applied and ultimately was appointed to the chair in 1946.

Professional Life: Scotland. The move to Aberdeen University allowed Wynne-Edwards to continue his interest in population ecology; pursue his love of skiing, hiking, and birding; and to develop the Zoology Department at Aberdeen into a center for ecological research. He also continued to serve as a scientific member of various government advisory committees, such as the Nature Conservancy, and the Natural Environment Research Council (NERC), which he chaired from 1968 to 1971. As he pointed out in his autobiographical memoir, these administrative duties "kept me in close contact with scientists working at sea and at the bench, and added very opportunely to my intellectual stock in trade in the important decade of 1952–62" (1985, p. 501). Indeed, it was during that decade that Wynne-Edwards developed the theory of group selection that would make him famous (or infamous as the case may be).

The seeds of the theory were sown in an offer he received to review Oxford ornithologist David Lack's 1954 book *The Natural Regulation of Animal Numbers*. In his review, Wynne-Edwards praised the value of this broad ranging work but took Lack to task for some of the hypothetical assertions. He pointed out that on Lack's view natality is the independent variable and that mortality adjusts itself (through density-dependent effects) to match it. Wynne-Edwards quoted Lack asserting, "Natural selection cannot favour smaller egg-number as such" (Wynne-Edwards, 1955a, p. 433). This, in particular, is one of the hypothetical assertions that Wynne-Edwards questioned. He countered that Lack had mistaken fecundity for fitness and that this was deeply problematic. If indeed the most fecund are not the most fit, then over time the "stock will very likely fall on evil days" (Wynne-Edwards, 1955a, p. 434).

Further, according to Wynne-Edwards, selection could just as readily favor a lower as a higher reproductive rate, differentially permitting survival of those populations that continue to live in harmony with their environments. Wynne-Edwards's claim that selection could favor lower reproductive rates was a restatement of the controversial theory he had introduced the previous summer at the eleventh International Ornithological Congress in Basel, Switzerland. In the paper, Wynne-Edwards argued for a "collective response" by a social group to general conditions of food productivity rather than the individual response of a male bird claiming territory as suggested by Lack. In the concluding paragraph Wynne-Edwards wrote:

> The theory that slowly breeding birds have evolved a series of interrelated adaptations, giving

them a great measure of autonomic control of their numbers, permits, at any rate, a rational explanation to be offered of many hitherto unconsidered features of their breeding biology. It shows that if they were adapted to impose their own limit on the number and size of their breeding colonies (as an alternative to limiting the minimum size of individual breeding territories) they could combine optimum feeding conditions with maximum numbers. (1955b, p. 547)

This paper described the theory that Wynne-Edwards would elaborate in his 1962 book and would spend the rest of his career defending. Between 1955 and 1962 Wynne-Edwards did not publish a great deal, rather, he continued to collect evidence for his theory and work on the book.

A Life's Work. *Animal Dispersion in Relation to Social Behavior* was published in 1962 and vaulted Wynne-Edwards to the forefront of evolutionary biology and ecology. The book synthesized his years of field experience in Canada and the United Kingdom, his knowledge of population management policies of various environmental agencies, and his love of natural history into a theory of group selection that challenged a growing consensus among biologists that Darwin's mechanism of natural selection worked exclusively at the level of the individual organism or below (i.e., on the gene). The book was born of the interest that Elton had sparked almost forty years earlier in population biology and provoked by the elegant work of Lack that Wynne-Edwards sought to challenge.

For example, Wynne-Edwards and Lack were at odds over the evolutionary explanation of brook size. Lack argued the individual breeding pairs were selected to raise as many offspring as the food supply would allow. Wynne-Edwards argued that selection acted on groups of breeding pairs (i.e., colonies) and maintained the breeding level below the threshold of available food. Wynne-Edwards argued that Lack's explanation would lead to overexploitation of the food resource by the individual pairs ending in the extinction of that population. While on his model, groups of breeding pairs were selected to maintain their population at a level that would ensure long-term success of the population.

The realization of the theory of group selection was consistent with Wynne-Edwards's earliest work on starling roosts, as well as his work in the late 1930s on nonbreeding behavior in sexually mature fulmars (sea birds). In *Animal Dispersion* he offered explanations of these phenomena that were significantly different from the prevailing individual-level explanations at the beginning of Charles Darwin's second century. According to Wynne-Edwards, the proper understanding of these, among many other social behaviors, required his theory of group selection. He was careful at the outset of the book to distinguish his theory from the traditional "Darwinian heritage" (read neo-Darwinism). He cited the standard interpretation of natural selection, which occurs at two levels, the individual (intraspecific) and the species (interspecific) levels, and argued that neither of these covered the social adaptations of interest.

On his account, it takes a group of individuals to maintain social conventions. He cited the work of geneticists Theodosius Dobzhansky and Sewall Wright as supportive of the notion that social grouping is of the utmost importance to evolution and the distribution of populations. In the first chapter Wynne-Edwards laid out the theory in no uncertain terms.

> Evolution at this level can be ascribed, therefore, to what is here termed group-selection—still an intra-specific process, and, for everything concerning population dynamics, much more important than selection at the individual level. The latter is concerned with the physiology and attainments of the individual as such, the former with the viability of the stock or race as a whole. Where the two conflict, as they do when the short-term advantage of the individual undermines the future safety of the race, group selection is bound to win, because the race will suffer and decline, and be supplanted by another in which antisocial advancement of the individual is more rigidly inhibited. (1962, p. 20)

This unequivocal statement of Wynne-Edwards's theory, which was expanded upon at length in the 650 pages of the book, led to a quick and ultimately devastating response from the community of evolutionary biologists. Among the most influential of these critics were William Hamilton, John Maynard Smith, George C. Williams, and David Lack. By the mid-1960s with the development of Hamilton's kin-selection model and the theory of inclusive fitness, the focus of selection had shifted to the level of the gene and Wynne-Edwards's theory of group selection was largely rejected.

In 1966, Williams published the now classic *Adaptation and Natural Selection* where he argued convincingly that although group selection might be theoretically possible it was practically unimportant. Individual level selection was more efficient, quicker, and would always undermine group selection except in extremely limited circumstances. The influence of Williams's book on evolutionary theory would be difficult to exaggerate and its effect on Wynne-Edwards was telling. Although Wynne-Edwards continued to publish in support of his theory throughout the 1960s and early 1970s, by the mid-1970s he was ready to capitulate. After his retirement from Aberdeen in 1974 Wynne-Edwards nearly gave up

on group selection. At a 1977 conference on Population Control by Social Behavior Wynne-Edwards gave the opening paper and said:

> In the past 15 years many theoreticians have wrestled with it, and in particular with the specific problem of the evolution of altruism. The general consensus of theoretical biologists at present is that credible models cannot be devised, by which the slow march of group selection could overtake the much faster spread of selfish genes that bring gains in individual fitness. I therefore accept their opinion. (1978, p. 19)

This recantation was short lived. Soon thereafter Wynne-Edwards began work on a second book that he claimed would answer the criticisms that had been leveled against his theory.

Wynne-Edwards's second book, *Evolution through Group Selection* (1986), was met largely with silence. Many of the reviews dismissed the book as one of advocacy rather than science. What is not generally recognized is that Wynne-Edwards had modified his position to some degree (Pollock, 1989). He had become convinced that his theory was consistent with the early models of Sewall Wright, and most importantly that group selection and individual-level selection did not necessarily work in opposite directions. Into his late eighties, Wynne-Edwards continued to publish and advocate for the importance of group selection to evolution. Moreover, he continued to emphasize the connection of his own work to Wright's. In a 1991 article in the *Ecologist* he cited Wright's review of George Gaylord Simpson's *Tempo and Mode in Evolution*, writing:

> Neo-Darwinian evolutionists, however, hold firmly to the belief that natural selection can operate only on individual organisms, and that all the adaptations and advances which evolution has witnessed must have arisen by that process alone.... Theoretical defects on this scale again point to the existence of a second, slower process of innovation and natural selection, with self-perpetuating groups or sub-populations as the separate units on which selection works. The theoretical conditions required to make group selection work have been well understood for many years. [(i.e., Wright, 1945)]. (Wynne-Edwards, 1991, p. 138)

Wynne-Edwards had also begun to incorporate some of the more recent research on group selection that had been conducted by Michael Wade and David Sloan Wilson.

Wynne-Edwards published his last article, "A Rationale for Group Selection," in the *Journal of Theoretical Biology* in 1993, at the age of eighty-six. Perhaps not surprisingly, he reiterated his support for the importance of group selection theory. Interestingly, the response to the review article was generally positive. Although the theory of group selection remains outside the mainstream of evolutionary biology, Wynne-Edwards's contribution should not be underestimated. The debate over group selection has outlived its most prominent proponent. Evolutionary biology has benefited from the focus on the question of the level at which natural selection occurs, which was precipitated by Wynne-Edwards's formulation of the theory of group selection. Wynne-Edwards's advocacy of group selection theory ought not to be his only legacy; he was also influential in the synthesis between ecology, evolution, and animal behavior that occurred in the latter half of the twentieth century.

In the course of his career Wynne-Edwards received many awards and honorary degrees. He was elected a Fellow of the Royal Society in 1970 and appointed Commander of the British Empire in 1973. Wynne-Edwards spent his retirement in Banchory, Aberdeenshire, where he lived with his wife Jeannie until his death in 1997. His family attests that he had his binoculars and his bird logs at the ready to the end.

BIBLIOGRAPHY

The Wynne-Edwards collection is stored in the Queen's University Archive, Kingston, Ontario, Canada.

WORKS BY WYNNE-EDWARDS

"On the Habits and Distribution of Birds on the North Atlantic." *Proceedings of the Boston Society of Natural History* 40, no. 4 (1935): 233–346.

"The Dynamics of Animal Populations." *Discovery: A Monthly Popular Journal of Knowledge* (October 1955a): 433–436.

"Low Reproductive Rates in Birds, Especially Sea-Birds." *Acta of the XI International Congress of Ornithology* (1955b): 540–547.

Animal Dispersion in Relation to Social Behavior. Edinburgh: Oliver and Boyd, 1962.

"Intrinsic Population Control: An Introduction." In *Population Control by Social Behaviour,* edited by F. J. Ebling and D. M. Stoddart. London: Institute of Biology, 1978.

"Backstage and Upstage with 'Animal Dispersion.'" In *Leaders in the Study of Animal Behavior: Autobiographical Perspectives,* edited by Donald Dewsbury. London and Toronto: Associated University Presses, 1985.

Evolution through Group Selection. Oxford: Blackwell Scientific Publications, 1986.

"Ecology Denies Neo-Darwinism." *Ecologist* 21 (1991): 136–141.

"A Rationale for Group Selection." *Journal of Theoretical Biology* 162 (1993): 1–22.

OTHER SOURCES

Borrello, Mark E. "Synthesis and Selection: Wynne-Edwards' Challenge to David Lack." *Journal of the History of Biology* 36 (2003): 531–566.

———. "Mutual Aid and Animal Dispersion: An Historical Analysis of Alternatives to Darwin." *Perspectives in Biology and Medicine* 47, no. 1 (2004): 15–31.

———. "Dogma, Heresy and Conversion: Wynne-Edwards's Crusade and the Levels of Selection Debate." In *Rebels of Life: Iconoclastic Biologists of the Twentieth Century,* edited by Oren Harman and Michael Dietrich. New Haven, CT: Yale University Press, (in press).

———. "Shifting Balance and Balancing Selection: A Group Selectionist's Interpretation of Wright and Dobzhansky." In *Descended from Darwin: Insights into American Evolutionary Studies 1925–1950,* edited by Joseph Cain. Philadelphia: American Philosophical Society Press, (in press).

Pollock, Gregory B. "Suspending Disbelief—Of Wynne-Edwards and His Reception." *Journal of Evolutionary Biology* 2 (1989): 205–221.

Sober, Elliott, and David S. Wilson. *Unto Others: The Evolution and Psychology of Unselfish Behavior.* Cambridge, MA: Harvard University Press, 1998.

Wade, Michael J. "Experimental Study of Group Selection." *Evolution* 31 (1977): 134–153.

———. "A Critical Review of the Models of Group Selection." *Quarterly Review of Biology* 53 (1978): 101–114.

———. "Soft Selection, Hard Selection, Kin Selection and Group Selection." *American Naturalist* 125 (1985): 61–73.

Wilson, David S. "A Theory of Group Selection." *Proceedings of the National Academy of Sciences of the United States of America* 72 (1975): 143–146.

———. "The Group Selection Controversy: History and Current Status." *Annual Review of Ecology and Systematics* 14 (1983): 159–187.

Wright, Sewall. "Tempo and Mode in Evolution: A Critical Review." *Ecology* 26 (1945): 415–419.

Mark E. Borrello

X

XENARCHUS (*fl.* Seleucia, Cilicia, first century BCE), *celestial physics, Aristotelian tradition.*

Xenarchus wrote a book against Aristotle's thesis that the celestial bodies are made of a special simple body, unique to them: the so-called fifth substance (also known as the fifth body, the fifth element, *quinta essentia,* or aether). The book is not extant and only a few citations are preserved by Simplicius in his commentary on the *De caelo.* Xenarchus is often presented as an unorthodox Peripatetic philosopher or even an early commentator. These descriptions are misleading. They obscure the fact that there is no orthodoxy in the Aristotelian tradition at this early stage. The revival of interest in the philosophy of Aristotle that took place in the first century BCE did not involve either the acceptance of the views stated by Aristotle or their codification in the form of commentary.

Strabo asserted that Xenarchus was originally from Seleucia in Cilicia, but that he spent most of his life away from home teaching philosophy first in Alexandria, then in Athens, and finally in Rome (*Geo.* XIV 5,4,670). Strabo attended his lectures. On the basis of this information, Xenarchus's activity as a teacher and a philosopher took place in the second half of the first century BCE.

Xenarchus wrote a book against Aristotle's thesis that the heavens are made of a celestial simple body, unique to them. Simplicius said that this book was titled *Against the Fifth Substance.* There is no evidence that this title goes back to Xenarchus. Yet, the transmitted title is a significant testimony about the way Aristotle's thesis was received in antiquity. It was considered a controversial doctrine about the existence of an additional body whose theoretical necessity was dubious at best.

The decidedly polemical nature of the book cannot be disputed. The target was the thesis that the heavens are made of a celestial simple body distinct from and not reducible to earth, water, air, and fire. Xenarchus advanced objections with the intent to refute Aristotle's thesis. It is also clear that Xenarchus focused on the arguments offered in the *De caelo.* Since Simplicius is the only source of information about Xenarchus's book, it must be accepted that a reconstructed text independent of Simplicius's citations is impossible. In other words, it is impossible for us to evaluate just how many liberties Simplicius took in reporting Xenarchus's objections.

Xenarchus was not content with demolishing Aristotle's arguments. He developed a theory of natural motion that was a revision of Aristotle's doctrine of natural motion. It is possible to reconstruct this theory to some extent.

It was a substantial claim of Aristotle's that a simple body naturally performs a simple rectilinear motion. If unimpeded, a simple body naturally moves upward or downward until it has reached its natural place. But, at least for Aristotle, the nature of a simple body is such that it stops moving when it has reached its natural place. Xenarchus consciously departed from this crucial tenet by claiming that a simple body in its natural place either is at rest or moves in a circle. This revision can lead to a crucial revision of Aristotle's physics. If one of the bodies encountered on Earth can move in a circle once it has reached it natural place, there is no need to introduce a special body that naturally performs circular motion in order to account for celestial motion. Consider the case of fire. Nobody in antiquity disputed that mobility is a conspicuous feature of fire. If unimpeded, fire regularly moves upward. But what happens to fire when it has reached its natural place? According to Aristotle, this fire loses its mobility. Xenarchus developed a theory of natural motion that allows one to say that fire does not lose its mobility once it has reached its natural place. Quite the contrary: this mobility manifests itself in a different and more perfect form: circular motion. There is evidence that this theory was successful. Simplicius credits Plotinus and Plolemy with a version of Xenarchus's doctrine of natural motion (*In cael.* 20. 10–25). This testimony is confirmed by Proclus in his commentary on Plato's *Timaeus* (in *Tim.* III 11. 24–12; III 11. 104 26–105. 12). In the case of Ptolemy, this doctrine was reconciled with the acceptance of Aristotle's fifth body.

Xenarchus's critique was well known and highly regarded in antiquity. At the time when Simplicius wrote his commentary on the *De caelo,* a more recent criticism was moved against Aristotle's doctrine by Philoponus in the treatise that is traditionally known by the title *De aeternitate mundi: contra Aristotelem.* According to Simplicius, the objections of Philoponus depended heavily on those of Xenarchus. Simplicius and Philoponus were only the last link of a long and complicated chain that goes back, ultimately, to Alexander of Aphrodisias and his (lost) commentary on the *De caelo.* Thanks to Simplicius, Xenarchus's objections were passed on to the Middle Ages and the Renaissance. Galileo Galilei makes use of these objections in his *Discorso sopra i due massimi sistemi del mondo,* though he never named Xenarchus and knows of this objection only in a derivative way.

BIBLIOGRAPHY

Falcon, Andrea. *Corpi e Movimenti. Il* De caelo *di Aristotele e la sua fortuna nel mondo antico.* Naples, Italy: Bibliopolis Press, 2001, pp. 80–118, 144–174.

———. *Aristotle and the Science of Nature: Unity without Uniformity.* Cambridge, U.K.: Cambridge University Press, 2005, pp. 62–71.

Hankinson, Robert James. "Xenarchus, Alexander and Simplicus on Simple Motion, Bodies and Magnitudes." *Bulletin of the Institute of Classical Studies* 46 (2002–2003): 19–42.

Moraux, Paul. "Xenarchos von Seleukia." *Paulys Realencyclopädie der classischen Altertumswissenschaft.* Revised by G. Wissowa. Edited by Konrat Ziegler, Walther Sontheimer, and Hans Gärtner. Stuttgart, Germany: Druckenmüller, 1964. Vol. 9 A2, 1420–1435.

———. *Der Aristotelismus bei den Griechen.* Vol. I: *Die Renaissance des Aristotelismus im I. Jh. v. Chr.* I. Berlin: De Gruyter, 1973, pp. 192–214.

Samburky, Samuel. *The Physical World of Late Antiquity.* London: Routledge and Kegan Paul, 1962, pp. 125–132.

Simplicius. *In De caelo.* Edited by Johan Ludvig Heiberg. Berlin: Commentaria in Aristotelem Graeca 7, 1894.

———. *On Aristotle's On the Heavens 1.1.1–4.* Edited by Robert James Hankinson. Ancient Commentators on Aristotle series. London: Duckworth, 2002.

Andrea Falcon

Y

YANG ZHONGJIAN (*b.* Hauxian, Shaanxi Province, China, 1897; *d.* Beijing, 1979), *vertebrate paleontology.*

Yang Zhongjian—anglicized as Chung Chien Young and more commonly recognized in scientific circles as C. C. Young—was undoubtedly the most famous and important student of Chinese vertebrate paleontology of the twentieth century. Almost single-handedly responsible for generating research in the field of vertebrate paleontology through the century's central decades, Yang also named many of the most iconic dinosaurs from the Mesozoic formations of China. His enduring intellectual legacy is represented by the renowned IVPP (Institute of Vertebrate Paleontology and Paleoanthropology) in Beijing.

Early Life. Yang graduated from the Geological Sciences Department of Beijing University in 1923. He received a doctorate degree at Munich University in 1927, and during his stay in Germany he established contacts with many leading European paleontologists. Yang returned to China in 1928 to join the China Geological Survey and almost single-handedly built the reputation of Chinese vertebrate paleontological research. His industry and originality were quickly recognized, and he established a Laboratory of Vertebrate Paleontology in the Geological Survey. As his authority grew, he rose to hold a number of key positions, including professorships at the Geological Survey of China, Beijing University, and Northwest University of Xi'an, and the directorships of both the Institute of Vertebrate Paleontology and Paleoanthropology (Beijing) and the Beijing Natural History Museum. His publication record began in 1929 and continued until the year of his death in 1979 and even then a number of his manuscripts were completed and published posthumously in 1982.

Era of Great Dinosaur Discoveries. Yang's life and career fits neatly into the worldwide development of vertebrate fossil research (and a notable resurgence in interest in dinosaur research) that occurred during the 1920s. Following a relative lull in the intellectual "hostilities" associated with the period of the "bone wars" in the American Midwest, perpetrated by Othniel Charles Marsh and Edward Drinker Cope in the latter half of the nineteenth century, new discoveries began to be made in other parts of the world. In the first decade of the twentieth century, German East Africa (now Tanzania) witnessed the discovery of some colossal dinosaur remains at Tendaguru. The 1920s (following World War I) was especially important with respect to Yang and his burgeoning career. It was a period of spectacular discoveries in the form of new dinosaurs at Trossingen in southern Germany and those made by the remarkable Central Asiatic Expeditions (1922–1925) launched by the American Museum of Natural History in New York. The latter expeditions revealed that rather than barren wastelands, as they were often portrayed, Mongolia and Chinese Inner Mongolia were richly fossiliferous, with an abundance of new and fascinating dinosaurs as part of a rich and varied fossil fauna.

These exciting discoveries were being published and widely promoted during the mid- and late 1920s, just at the time when Yang Zhongjian was learning his trade in geology in Beijing and Munich. Following the problems generated by the auctioning of a dinosaur egg collected from Mongolia by the American museum expedition, relations between the Americans and the Chinese,

Mongolians, and Russians deteriorated badly, and further expeditions were curtailed. However, throughout this period various Swedish scientists had been involved in expeditions and geological survey work in China on a more cooperative basis. From 1927 onward, expeditions were organized jointly by Chinese and Swedish scientists, and some of the scientific research of these later expeditions was published by Yang. One of his earliest papers concerned discoveries of a rich fossil fauna at the "Peking Man" site at Zhoukoudian (formerly Choukoutien) in collaboration with the natural historian and Jesuit missionary Pierre Teilhard de Chardin (who was himself at this time also acting as a geological advisor to the Beijing government). Yang was also able to describe some of the dinosaurs collected during the Sino-Swedish expeditions led by the Austrian paleontologist Otto Zdansky.

Geological Expeditions. From the time of Yang's return to China, and given the intensity of interest in the fossil history of China, his primary research focus became fossil vertebrates. As part of his role in the geological survey he was involved in a series of exploratory expeditions and excavations in Sichuan, Yunnan, Xinjiang, and Gansu provinces. This work identified new vertebrate fossil faunas (including dinosaurs) and led most spectacularly, in 1938, to excavations that focused on a site near the city of Lufeng in Yunnan Province. This site revealed abundant remains of the prosauropod dinosaur *Lufengosaurus*, and rich associated fauna of dinosaurs and other reptiles, particularly early mammal-like synapsids. The most dramatic and public product of these discoveries was the first Chinese-mounted dinosaur skeleton (*Lufengosaurus huenei*), which was put on display in Beipei, Chongqing, Sichuan Province in 1941. This discovery echoed, to a remarkable degree, the important discovery of a collection of closely related prosauropod dinosaurs in a quarry at Trossingen in the Neckar Valley of southern Germany in the 1920s: *Plateosaurus*. The fame of the German discovery and its detailed description by the most eminent of German vertebrate paleontologists, Friedrich Freiherr von Huene, would have been very familiar to Yang from his time as a doctoral student. Hence, Yang named the new but relatively closely related prosauropod from China *Lufengosaurus huenei*, in honor of von Huene.

Political Harassment. From the fieldwork and descriptive papers that he generated in the 1930s, Yang firmly established himself as one of the foremost researchers in China. His productivity increased with a series of substantial and important monographs on new dinosaurs during the 1940s. At the time of the Communist Revolution (1949) he was the most eminent researcher in his field in China. Out of that social and political upheaval, he emerged at the forefront of the development of the Institute of Verte-

brate Paleontology, which was sponsored by Academia Sinica. This institute became China's first research center devoted to the study of vertebrate fossils. Yang became its founding director, and in 1958 the laboratory was renamed as the later renowned Institute of Vertebrate Paleontology and Paleoanthropology (IVPP). He established it as the leading training institute for the development of fossil preparation skills and as an intellectual breeding ground for future Chinese paleontologists. According to John W. Olsen, under Yang the institute was known for its promotion of openness and free exchange of ideas, including with non-Chinese paleontologists. During the Cultural Revolution of the late 1960s, Yang was forced to wear a dunce cap in public, and to accept the assertion that Teilhard de Chardin was his father.

Nonetheless, he returned to research and until his death in 1979 Yang produced a steady and consistent stream of publications on the fossil vertebrate fauna of China. In addition to important monographs describing some of the striking new dinosaurs such as *Psittacosaurus*, *Yunnanosaurus*, *Mamenchisaurus*, and *Tsintaosaurus*, he also published on a bewildering variety of other forms: early mammal-like reptiles (synapsids), early true mammals, fossil footprints, dinosaur eggs, pterosaurs (flying reptiles), marine reptiles, and crocodiles, and produced numerous descriptive reviews of entire faunas that had been newly discovered right across China.

In many ways Yang occupies a unique position as one of the "greats" involved in the birth of the field of vertebrate paleontology in China. He may well have come into the field at a propitious time, given the undoubted excitement of discoveries in Europe and Asia in the 1920s, but his intellect and personal drive allowed this branch of science to flourish in China (where it had previously languished, largely unrecognized). In helping to found the IVPP in Beijing, he established a lasting center of academic excellence in this field and established the careers of a stream of students and younger colleagues who rose to prominence in their own right, including Pei Wenzhong (or W. C. P'ei, 1904–1982) and Jia Lanpo (or Yusheng Jia, 1908–2001).

BIBLIOGRAPHY

Universally reported as C. C. Young in the literature.

WORKS BY YANG ZHONGJIAN

With P. Teilhard de Chardin. "On Some Traces of Vertebrate Life in the Jurassic and Triassic Beds of Shansi and Shensi." *Bulletin of the Geological Society of China* 8 (1929): 131–133.

"On Some New Dinosaurs from Western Suiyan, Inner Mongolia." *Bulletin of the Geological Society of China* 2 (1931): 259–266.

"On a New Nodosaurid Dinosaur from Ningshia." *Palaeontologia Sinica Series C,* 11 (1935): 1–33.

"A New Dinosaurian from Sinkiang." *Palaeontologia Sinica Series C,* 105 (1937): 1–23.

"A Complete Osteology of *Lufengosaurus huenei* Young (gen. et sp. nov.)." *Palaeontologia Sinica Series C,* 7 (1941a): 1–53.

"*Gyposaurus sinensis* (sp. nov.), a New Prosauropoda from the Upper Triassic Beds at Lufeng, Yunnan." *Bulletin of the Geological Society of China* 21 (1941b): 205–252.

"*Yunnanosaurus huangi* Young (gen. et sp. nov.), a new Prosauropoda from the Red Beds of Lufeng, Yunnan." *Bulletin of the Geological Society of China* 22 (1942): 63–104.

With Min-chen. Chow. "New Fossil Reptiles from Szechuan, China." *Acta Scientia Sinica* 2 (1953): 216–243.

With A. L. Sun. "Note on a Fragmentary Carnosaurian Mandible from Turfan, Sinkiang." *Vertebrata Palasiatica* 1 (1957): 159–162.

"The Dinosaurian Remains of Laiyang, Shantung." *Palaeontologia Sinica Series C,* 16 (1958): 1–138.

"Fossil Eggs from Nanhsiung, Kwangtung, and Kanchou, Kiangsi." *Vertebrata Palasiatica* 9 (1965): 141–170.

With Xijing Zhao. "*Mamenchisaurus hochuanensis.*" *Memoires of the Institute of Vertebrate Paleontology and Paleoanthropology, Academia Sinica* 8 (1972): 1–30.

Selected Works of Yang Zhongjiang (C. C. Young). Beijing: Science Press, 1982.

OTHER SOURCES

Etler, Dennis A. "Jia Lanpo (1908–2001)." *American Anthropologist* 104, no. 1 (2002): 297–299.

Jia Lanpo and Huang Weiwen. *The Story of Peking Man: From Archaeology to Mystery.* Translated by Yin Zhiqi. Beijing: Foreign Languages Press; Hong Kong: Oxford University Press, 1990.

Olsen, John W. "A Tribute to Jia Lanpo (1908–2001)." *Asian Perspectives: The Journal of Archeology for Asia and the Pacific* 43, no. 2 (Fall 2004): 191–196.

David Norman

YIN TSAN-HSUN

SEE **Yin Zanxun**.

YIN ZANXUN (Yin Tsan Hsun) (*b.* Dashi Village, Pingxiang, Hebei Province, China, 2 February 1902; *d.* Beijing, China, 27 January 1984), *geology, stratigraphy, and paleontology; educator in geology.*

Yin Zanxun was one of the most conspicuous among the outstanding geologists who initiated modern geological studies in China in the 1920s and 1930s. A veteran stratigrapher and paleontologist, he took an interest in a broad range of earth sciences. He contributed greatly to China's geological undertakings, both in academic research and administration. Yin was director of the Geological Survey of China (地质调查所; dizhi diaochasuo) and chaired the section of Earth Science of the Chinese Academy of Sciences (中国科学院地学部; zhongguo kexueyuan dixue) for many years. He was always at the leading edge of Earth science, focusing on its fundamental aspects. He worked assiduously to promote the drafting and improvement of the Chinese stratigraphic code in order to regulate and standardize stratigraphical work in China. He introduced plate tectonics theory to China in the 1970s.

Yin Zanxun grew up in an intellectual family. His father was a middle school teacher and had once been a county magistrate in Hebei Province; his mother was a housewife taking care of three children, Yin being the youngest. As a boy he was first educated in a private school and then entered the Yude middle school in Baoding, Hebei Province. After graduation he studied at Peking University from 1919 to 1923, majoring first in Chinese literature and then in philosophy. In 1923 he went to France and studied geology at the University of Lyon. He received his doctorate in geology there in 1931.

Soon after his return to China in the 1930s, Yin began his work on the Geological Survey of China in Peiping (now Beijing). He published altogether more than 150 papers and monographs, covering many disciplines in geology. His main interests were in stratigraphy and paleontology, especially in the Paleozoic, Triassic, and Quaternary eras and in graptolites and mollusk faunas. But most of his research concentrated on the Silurian period of China, including biostratigraphy, lithostratigraphy, paleogeography, tectonic frame, and worldwide correlation of the stratigraphic system in China. During the years from 1931 to 1935, he published several monographs and many papers on the Permo-Carboniferous and Triassic mollusks and the Late Paleozoic ammonoids (ammonites). He was also the first geologist to report on the icnogenus *Cruziana* and coprolites in China.

Yin was a leading member of the Chinese Commission on Quaternary studies. In that capacity he contributed much to the excavation of Quaternary fossil mammals in northeastern China, the study of Quaternary volcanoes in Shanxi, and the examination of the Yunshui caves near Peiping in the early 1930s.

In 1936 Yin took the post as director of the Geological Survey of Jiangxi Province and in 1940 became the acting director of the Geological Survey of China. Under extremely difficult conditions during the war years (1937–1945) he was able to organize and complete seven sheets of the 1:200,000 series of geological maps of China's extensive and remote regions in the northwest and southwest.

After the founding of People's Republic of China in 1949, Yin was appointed first deputy chairman of the

All-China Planning and Guiding Commission of Geological Undertakings (中国地质工作计划指导委员会; zhongguo dizhigongzuo jihuazhidao weiyuanhui), in charge of geological education. As the main organizer, he became vice president of the Beijing College of Geology, one of the mono-disciplinary colleges established in imitation of the Soviet system. During the four years of his tenure from 1952 and 1956, Yin did his best to set up and improve the overall administration and teaching staff of the college and made great contributions in providing tens of thousands of graduates in geology that were urgently needed for the economic development of the country.

Yin was always concerned with the fundamental problems and documents of stratigraphy. His *Zhongguo quyu dicengbiao cao'an* (1956; Regional stratigraphic tables of China) was awarded National Natural Science Prize by the Chinese Academy of Sciences. As vice president of the All-China Stratigraphic Commission, he organized the compilation of regional stratigraphic correlation charts and *Zhongguo dicengdian:VII shitanxi* (1966; Stratigraphic lexicon of China: VII Carboniferous system) in the 1950s and 1960s. He was the leading organizer of the First and Second All-China Stratigraphic Congresses in 1959 and 1979, after which his *Zhongguo diceng guifan (cao'an)* (1961; Stratigraphic code of China) and *Zhongguo diceng zhinan ji diceng zhinan shuomingshu* (1981; Stratigraphic Guide of China) were published. The *Stratigraphic Code* mainly followed the Soviet code, and the *Stratigraphic Guide* adopted the multiple stratigraphical classification of Heidelberg (1976). Both were successful in standardizing and enhancing the overall efficiency of stratigraphical work in China. Furthermore, after both congresses, he helped issue systematic summaries consisting of serial publications of fossil faunas in different classes and stratigraphy in different periods.

In the meantime, Yin had also contributed much by introducing and promoting new geological ideas. These included the new global tectonics—the plate tectonics theory and the idea of paleontologic clock. These ideas advanced the overall modernization and progress of geological science in China.

As a result of his great effort over the preceding twenty years in geological undertakings and his great attainments in stratigraphy and paleontology, he was awarded the fourth Ding Wenjiang Prize from the Geological Society of China in 1946. The Chinese Academy of Sciences elected Yin a member in 1955. He became director of the Earth Sciences Division in 1957, a post he held for over twenty-five years. He was elected president of the Geological Society of China and of the Paleontological Society of China (中国古生物学会; zhongguo gushengwu xuehui) several times.

Yin was married and had two daughters and one son. The elder daughter, Professor Yin Wenying an entomolo-gist, is a member of Chinese Academy of Science. She works for the Institute of Entomology in Shanghai. Yin died of leukemia on 27 January 1984, six days before his eighty-second birthday.

BIBLIOGRAPHY

WORKS BY YIN

"Étude de la faune du Tithonique coralligene du Gard et de e'Herault" (The research on the fauna of Tithonian stage from Gard and Herault provinces). In *Travaux du Laboratorire de geologie Université Lyon*. Fascicule 17. 1931.

"Gastropoda of the Penchi and Taiyuan Series of North China." *Paleontologia Sinica,* series B, 11, no. 2 (1932): 1–53.

"Upper Paleozoic Ammonoids of China." *Paleontologia Sinica,* series B, 11, no. 4 (1935): 1–49.

"Brief Description of the Ordovician and Silurian Fossils from Shitien." *Bulletin of the Geological Society of China* 16 (1937): 281–302.

"A New Staurea from Kueichou." *Bulletin of the Geological Society of China* 24 (1944): 15–20.

With A. T. Mu. "Lower Silurian Graptolites from Tongzi." *Bulletin of Geological Society of China* 25 (1945): 211–219.

"Tentative Classification and Correlation of Silurian Rocks of South China." *Bulletin of the Geological Society of China* 29 (1949): 1–61.

Zhongguo quyu dicengbiao cao'an (Regional stratigraphic tables of China). Beijing: Science Press, 1956.

"Diceng guifan cao'an shuomingshu" (Explanatory notes on stratigraphic code of China). In *Zhonguo diceng guifan (cao'an)ji zhongguo diceng guifan* (cao'an) *shuomingshu* (Stratigraphic code and its explanation). Beijing: Science Press, 1960.

With Chow Min-Chen and Hsu Jen. "Progress of Paleontology in China." *Nature* 205 (1965): 646–649.

"China in the Silurian Period." *Journal of Geological Society of Australia* 13 (1966): 277–297.

With Chen Jingshi, Zhang Shouxin, Luo Jinding, et al. "The Stratigraphic lexicon of China. VII. Carboniferous system." (zhongguo dicengdian: VII shitanxi.) Beijing: Science Press, 1966.

OTHER SOURCES

Shangfeng, Yi. "Yin Zanxun." In *Zhongguo dabaikequanshu: Dizhixue juan* (Chinese encyclopedia: Geology volume). Beijing: Chinese Encyclopedia Press, 1993.

Tungsheng, Liu. "Yin Zanxun jiaoshou yu zhongguo de disiji yanjiu" (Professor Yin Zanxun and the Quaternary research in China). *Quaternary Sciences* no. 2 (1994): 106–112.

You Zhendong

YOUNG, CHUNG CHIEN (C. C.)

SEE **Yang Zhongjian.**

Z

ZABARELLA, JACOPO (GIACOMO)

(*b.* Padua, Italy, 5 September 1533; *d.* Padua, 15 October 1589), *natural philosophy, scientific method, classification of the sciences.* For the original article on Zabarella see *DSB,* vol. 14.

Zabarella is considered the prime representative of Italian Renaissance Aristotelianism. His use of Aristotle and other authorities was both eclectic and critical, and his style of writing decidedly systematic. Zabarella sought to build a coherent body of Aristotelian logic and natural philosophy, which generated his interest in the classification of the disciplines and the relationships between various areas of academic learning. He was an orthodox Aristotelian who defended the scientific status of theoretical natural philosophy against the pressures emanating from the practical disciplines, that is, the art of medicine and anatomy. The debate goes on about his influence on Galileo Galilei and the birth of modern science.

Arts and Sciences. The hierarchical ordering of different disciplines was a widely debated topic in Renaissance philosophy. The hierarchical nature of the division between different disciplines was also emphasized by Zabarella. The continual discussion of the methodology of arts and sciences in the sixteenth century may be seen as an attempt to defend the scientific status either of the recently discovered autonomous sciences, such as natural philosophy, or of the empirically based productive arts. The methodological writings are, therefore, not merely further elaborations of an old Aristotelian tradition, but also expressions of opinion in a lively argumentation on the changing relationships between various arts and sciences in sixteenth-century Italian universities.

The Aristotelian distinction between arts (*artes*) and sciences (*scientiae*) serves as the starting point for Zabarella's philosophical system. In the opening of his *Opera logica*, Zabarella draws a distinction between the eternal world of nature and the contingent human world. From this distinction he proceeds to two corresponding kinds of knowledge and to two distinct methods of defining them. Zabarella maintained that sciences are concerned with the eternal world of nature and are thus contemplative disciplines, whereas the arts refer to the contingent world of human beings and are thus productive and noncontemplative. In the proper sense of the term, the sciences, as pertaining to demonstrative knowledge, are limited to those disciplines that deal with the necessary and eternal or with what can be deduced from necessary principles. In productive disciplines (i.e., arts) it is not necessary to define the objects under production as strictly as in the contemplative sciences, because the productive arts do not aim at knowledge. The ultimate purpose of the contemplative science is the pursuit of knowledge for its own sake, while in the productive arts the end result is an actual product.

Zabarella also analyzed the relationships and hierarchy among the theoretical sciences themselves. To him, the contemplative or speculative sciences in an Aristotelian manner were only three in number: divine science, also called metaphysics; mathematics; and natural philosophy. Zabarella presents these contemplative sciences as the only defenders of true knowledge. He emphasized in many instances that each speculative science should demonstrate its own principles and not borrow them from metaphysics.

Zabarella's approach to the study of nature remained causal and qualitative in the traditional Aristotelian vein rather than mathematical. Therefore, he gave little attention to the possible uses of mathematics as a tool for understanding the physical world.

Logic and Methods. As Charles B. Schmitt remarked in his article, "Zabarella, Jacopo" in the *Dictionary of Scientific Biography* (vol. 14, 1970), most interpreters have pinpointed Zabarella's lasting contribution to his work on logic and the scientific method. As an instrumental discipline, logic makes for a useful tool of inquiry for all the arts and sciences. Logic is a rational discipline that is not philosophy in itself, but springs from philosophy and is devoted to philosophical ends. For Zabarella, methods also served to differentiate the sciences from the arts. The term can be understood in two ways, either in a wide sense as a method of presenting existing knowledge, which he prefers to call an order (*ordo*) of presentation, or in a narrow sense as a method of discovering knowledge, for which he reserves the word *method* (*methodus*) in its proper understanding. According to Zabarella, *ordo* is an instrumental *habitus* that prepares teachers to lay out the parts of each discipline in such a way that the discipline may be taught as well and easily as possible. There are two demonstrative methods in the narrow sense of the word, composition and resolution, which have argumentative force instead of arranging the contents of a whole discipline. For Zabarella the so-called *regressus* method used in natural philosophy is a model for combining the methods of composition and resolution. The idea of this combinatory process is found in the Aristotelian tradition from Averroes on, and it was revived among the Italian Aristotelians and medical authors.

It is this very distinction between the method of inquiry and the order of teaching that led Zabarella to a bitter controversy with his Paduan colleague, Francesco Piccolomini. They agreed that ethical inquiry must proceed by deduction from an understanding of the end. In Zabarella's view, however, all the disciplines whose end is action should be explained in this same way. While Piccolomini admitted that this order of teaching applied to ethics and other practical disciplines, he excluded theoretical subjects from such an order of understanding. The fundamental question embedded in this dispute is the following: Is the order of teaching a particular discipline necessary or contingent? Zabarella argued for the former. Both in discovery and in teaching, one should follow the synthetic order in the sciences and the analytic order in the arts. By making a sharp distinction between the method of discovery and the order of teaching, however, Piccolomini instead embraced a contingent view of the pedagogical method. Hoping to teach others, Piccolomini saw his duty as that of starting out from first princi-

ples. In such a case it is better to begin with the simpler matters and progress toward the end or goal.

Through their rival claims about the orders of presentation, Zabarella and Piccolomini also revealed very different perceptions of academic and civil order and very different ways of conceiving and pursuing the office of philosopher within that order. Zabarella wholeheartedly endorsed the purely contemplative nature of philosophy and the superiority of the contemplative life. He was also frequently dismissive of the disciplines he regarded as active or operative, such as law, medicine, ethics, politics, and mechanics. Piccolomini's position was sharply opposed. For him, philosophy is, indeed, crucial for the spiritual perfection of man. However, in the form of *scientia civilis* (i.e., *the theoretical part of ethics and politics*), it is also the key to the this-wordly perfection that could be attained in the just administration of the Venetian republic.

The Perfection of Philosophy. In the Aristotelian tradition, which addresses the relationship between the theoretical or speculative sciences, the most influential section is the beginning of Aristotle's treatise *On the Soul* (*De anima*). In Zabarella's view it is obvious that the science of the soul is the most noble part of natural philosophy, because it shows the first cause and the sum of everything that is in animals and in plants. The science of the soul is more exquisite and certain than any other part of natural philosophy. Zabarella's position can be interpreted as an attempt to raise the status of an independent natural philosophy by emphasizing the nobility of the science of the soul. What in the Middle Ages had perhaps been considered to be part of metaphysics was now the most valuable part of natural philosophy. Zabarella himself left the question of the immortality of the soul to the theologians, since Aristotle, as a natural philosopher, had not been explicit about it.

In *De naturalis scientiae constitutione,* the first treatise in his collected works on natural philosophy (*De rebus naturalibus,* 1590), Zabarella deals in detail with the questions of the order and perfection of the natural sciences. He claims, for example, that the book on minerals is necessary because natural philosophy would otherwise be incomplete. In the Aristotelian corpus on natural philosophy, the book on minerals follows the book *On Meteorology*. Whether Aristotle himself wrote on minerals is questionable, but at least he recognized the importance of the subject. However, both Theophrastus and Albertus Magnus later wrote on this significant subject. Thus, Zabarella did not consider Aristotle's works as a complete corpus to which nothing could be added. In *De methodis,* Zabarella states that Aristotle wrote on subjects of his own choice, but that it would be an exaggeration to claim he was incapable of making mistakes. Aristotle was not infallible, and it would be erroneous to insist he knew the truth of everything he wrote. However, he remained an outstanding scholar for Zabarella, who would turn the study of logic into a discipline.

In the last chapter of *De naturalis scientiae constitutione*, Zabarella discusses the question of the perfection of the natural sciences. He states that whereas Aristotle's philosophy of nature may be perfect in structure and form, it is incomplete in terms of its reference to natural beings. There is much Aristotle did not discuss at all and, indeed, much that was outside his cognizance. Zabarella therefore emphasizes that Aristotle's philosophy of nature is complete at least in theory, comparing Aristotle's works on natural philosophy to the geometry and arithmetic of Euclid. There are many theorems that can be demonstrated from his works, even if he did not himself actually write the theorems. For Zabarella, this is no reason to judge Euclid's geometry or arithmetic defective or incomplete. If Euclid had wished, he could have demonstrated all the particular cases, but his book would have become so enormous that it surely would have daunted the reader. Zabarella suggests that this is exactly why Euclid titled his book *The Elements:* From this foundation all the other theorems can be demonstrated. Similarly, Zabarella finds that Aristotle's natural philosophy can be called perfect, because it deals with all the knowledge that is possible for human intellect to obtain, either in practice or at least in theory.

Natural Philosophy and Medicine. Among the Paduan Aristotelians, Zabarella probably wrote most thoroughly about the relationship between the philosophy of nature and medical art. While in subject matter these disciplines were close to one another, in their essence and methodology they were far apart. In spite of medicine's prominent place among the arts, Zabarella sharply denied its scientific status. Neither the art of medicine nor its singular parts can be regarded as science. For him it was enough to admit that it is the noblest of all arts. No matter how valuable and precise medicine may be, it could never be a science because it is practiced not for the sake of knowledge, but for an end product: that is, the maintenance or restoration of health.

Zabarella recognizes two different ways in which a physician can know the parts of a human body. First, he may learn them through perceptive knowledge and anatomical observations, thereby assimilating the matter of his discipline without understanding its rationale. A physician can also become familiar with parts of the human body through the philosophy of nature: He may learn the reasons that lie behind what he actually sees. In *De rebus naturalibus*, Zabarella points out that the art of medicine adopts the physiological part from the philoso-phy of nature. What a natural philosopher writes about animals, a medical writer should apply to human beings.

Zabarella's conclusion about the relationship between the art of medicine and natural philosophy is that the latter must consider the universal qualities of health and sickness, while the former concentrates on finding remedies for particular diseases. Where the philosopher ends, the physician begins (*ubi desinit philosophus, ibi incipit medicus*). From the universal consideration of sickness and health, the physician descends to the treatment of all particular diseases and to the knowledge of their causes. While discussing the principles of medical art, Zabarella compares anatomical principles with principles derived from natural philosophy. In his view, only the philosophy of nature, not anatomy, can provide a solid basis for medical practitioners.

Aftermath. After the 1960s Zabarella's name was linked to modern science. As early as 1940 in "The Development of Scientific Method at the School of Fatima" (and again in 1961 in *The School of Padua and the Emergence of Modern Science*), John Herman Randall published his famous idea on "the School of Padua" as the precursor of modern science. Following Ernst Cassirer, Randall referred to the Renaissance discussions of the *regressus* method up to Zabarella as a preparation for Galileo Galilei's new method of natural science. However, the Aristotelian terminology and doctrines shared by Zabarella and Galileo seem for the most part to have been commonplace in late medieval and Renaissance thought. Galileo may have known Zabarella's writings, but a far more important source for Galileo were the Jesuit scholars, above all Paolo della Valle, working at the Collegio Romano at Rome.

Moreover, the scientific ideal that Zabarella presents is profoundly different from the modern view of a scientist making new discoveries. According to Zabarella, science can be new only in a restricted sense; the work of a scientist is more like correcting the mistakes and filling the gaps in a ready-made Aristotelian world system. Therefore, Zabarella cannot be considered a precursor of modern experimental science. In spite of its empirical basis, Zabarella's natural philosophy is not concerned with anything akin to experiment. Indeed, if experiments were to be developed, they would find their place in the productive arts rather than in natural philosophy. Zabarella did not use experiments in order to verify or falsify theories in the modern sense. He did make observations of natural things, but just to exemplify and illustrate the demonstrative reasoning used in theoretical natural philosophy.

Instead of overemphasizing the connection between Zabarella and Galileo, it should be noted that Zabarella's thought had a lasting impact on Protestant Aristotelians in Germany and the Low Countries during the late six-teenth century and the first part of the seventeenth century. His clear and systematic interpretation of Aristotle's logic and natural philosophy was used as a basis for numerous Aristotelian textbooks printed in Germany. Also, in the British Isles the Scholastic revival of the early seventeenth century owed much to Zabarella's writings. His commentaries have been consulted with profit by even some modern scholars of Aristotle.

SUPPLEMENTARY BIBLIOGRAPHY

The author knows of no publication as of 2007 that has a complete bibliography of Zabarella's work. One could perhaps refer to Charles H. Lohr (1988): Latin Aristotle Commentaries II: Renaissance Authors, *Florence: Leo S. Olschki. On Zabarella's publications and manuscripts, see pages 497–503.*

WORKS BY ZABARELLA

De methodis liber quatuor; Liber de regressu. Edited by Cesare Vasoli. Bologna, Italy: Clueb, 1985.

OTHER SOURCES

Berti, Enrico. "Metafisica e diallectica nel 'Commento' di Giacomo Zabarella agli 'Analitici posteriori.'" *Giornale di metafisica,* new series, 14 (1992): 225–244.

Bouillon, Dominique. "Un discours inédit de Iacopo Zabarella préliminaire à l'exposition de la 'Physique' d'Aristote (Padoue 1568)." *Atti e Memorie dell'Accadema Galileiana di Scienze, Lettere ed Arti in Padova* 111, part 3 (1998–1999): 119–127.

Copenhaver, Brian P., and Charles B. Schmitt. *Renaissance Philosophy.* Oxford; New York: Oxford University Press, 1992.

Grendler, Paul F. *The Universities of the Italian Renaissance.* Baltimore, MD, and London: Johns Hopkins University Press, 2002.

Jardine, Nicholas. "Epistemology of the Sciences." In *The Cambridge History of Renaissance Philosophy,* edited by Charles B. Schmitt. Cambridge, U.K., and New York: Cambridge University Press, 1988.

———. "Keeping Order in the School of Padua: Jacopo Zabarella and Francesco Piccolomini on the Offices of Philosophy." In *Method and Order in Renaissance Philosophy of Nature: The Aristotle Commentary Tradition,* edited by Daniel DiLiscia, Eckhard Kessler, and Charlotte Methuen. Aldershot, U.K.: Ashgate, 1997.

Kessler, Eckhard. "The Intellective Soul." In *The Cambridge History of Renaissance Philosophy,* edited by C. B. Schmitt. Cambridge, U.K.: Cambridge University Press, 1988.

———. "Zabarella, Jacopo (1533–1589)." In *Routledge Encyclopedia of Philosophy,* edited by Edward Craig. Vol. 9. London and New York: Routledge, 1998.

Laird, W. R. *The "Scientiae Mediae" in Medieval Commentaries on Aristotle's "Posterior Analytics."* PhD diss., University of Toronto, 1983.

———. "Zabarella, Jacopo (1533–1589)." In *Encyclopedia of the Scientific Revolution: From Copernicus to Newton,* edited by Wilbur Applebaum. New York and London: Garland, 2000.

Lines, David A. *Aristotle's Ethics in the Italian Renaissance (ca. 1300–1650): The Universities and the Problem of Moral Education.* Leiden, The Netherlands, and Boston: Brill, 2002.

Michael, Emily. "The Nature and Influence of Late Renaissance Paduan Psychology." *History of Universities* 12 (1993): 65–94.

Mikkeli, Heikki. *An Aristotelian Response to Renaissance Humanism: Jacopo Zabarella on the Nature of Arts and Sciences.* Helsinki: Finnish Historical Society, 1992.

———. "The Foundation of an Autonomous Natural Philosophy: Zabarella on the Classification of Arts and Sciences." In *Method and Order in Renaissance Philosophy of Nature: The Aristotle Commentary Tradition,* edited by Daniel DiLiscia, Eckhard Kessler, and Charlotte Methuen. Aldershot, U.K.: Ashgate, 1997.

———. "Jacopo Zabarella (1533–1589): Ordnung und Methode der wissenschaftlichen Erkenntnis." In *Philosophen der Renaissance,* edited by Paul Richard Blum. Darmstadt, Germany: Primus Verlag, 1999.

———. "Giacomo Zabarella." *Stanford Encyclopedia of Philosophy.* Available from http://plato.stanford.edu/entries/zabarella.

Poppi, Antonino. "La struttura del discorso morale nell'opera di Iacopo Zabarella." In *L'etica del rinascimento tra Platone e Aristotele,* by Antonino Poppi. Naples, Italy: La Città del Sole, 1997.

———. *Ricerche sulla teologia e la scienza nella Scuola padovana del Cinque e Seicento.* Soveria Mannelli, Italy: Rubbettino Editore, 2001.

Randall, John H., Jr. "The Development of the Scientific Method at the School of Padua." *Journal of the History of Ideas* 1 (1940): 177–206.

———. *The School of Padua and the Emergence of Modern Science.* Padua, Italy: Editrice Antenore, 1961.

Risse, Wilhelm. "Zabarellas Methodenlehre." In *Aristotelismo veneto e scienza moderna,* edited by Luigi Oliveri. Padua, Italy: Editrice Antenore, 1983.

Rossi, Paolo. "Aristotelici e 'moderni': Le ipotesi e la natura." In *Aristotelismo veneto e scienza moderna,* edited by Luigi Olivieri. Padua, Italy: Editrice Antenore, 1983.

Schmitt, Charles B. "Zabarella, Jacopo." In *Dictionary of Scientific Biography,* edited by Charles Coulston Gillispie. Vol. 14. New York: Scribner, 1970.

———. *Aristotle and the Renaissance.* Cambridge, MA, and London: Harvard University Press, 1983.

South, James B. "Zabarella and the Intentionality of Sensation." *Rivista di storia della filosofia* 57 (2002): 5–25.

Wallace, William A. *Galileo's Logic of Discovery and Proof: The Background, Content, and Use of His Appropriated Treatises on Aristotle's Posterior Analytics.* Dordrecht, The Netherlands; Boston: Kluwer, 1992.

———. "Zabarella, Jacopo." In *Encyclopedia of the Renaissance,* edited by Paul F. Grendler. Vol. 6. New York: Scribner's, 1999.

Heikki Mikkeli

ZELDOVICH, YAKOV BORISO-VICH

(*b*. Minsk, Russia [later Belarus], 8 March 1914; *d*. Moscow, USSR, December 2, 1987), *theoretical physics, astrophysics, cosmology.*

Zeldovich was one of the leading physicists of the twentieth century. He made fundamental contributions to the physics of chemical catalysis and kinetics, physics of combustion and hydrodynamics of explosive phenomena, nuclear energy physics, astrophysics and cosmology, and physics of elementary particles.

Early Work. The son of Boris Naumovich Zeldovich, a lawyer, and the former Anna Petrovna Kiveliovich, a translator, Yakov Zeldovich spent his younger years in Petrograd (later named Leningrad, USSR), entered elementary school in 1924 directly into the third grade, and graduated from high school in 1930. Immediately after that he enrolled in a training program for laboratory assistants run by the Leningrad Institute of Mechanical Processing of Mineral Resources. In 1931 Zeldovich began his work as a laboratory assistant at the Institute of Chemical Physics (ICP) of the Academy of Sciences of the USSR. Zeldovich came to the ICP in 1931 right after high school and worked there until 1948, many years after becoming a Doctor of Sciences. He studied adsorption, catalysis, phase transitions, hydrodynamics, theory of combustion and detonation with application to rocket ballistics, and nuclear chain reactions.

Remarkably, he started his scientific research work without having any college degree, graduate or undergraduate. The theorists of the ICP spotted the very talented youth right away and helped him to comprehend the foundations of theoretical physics, outside the formal setting of a college classroom. Thus Zeldovich received an undergraduate education without formally enrolling in an undergraduate college program. (He did attend some classes at Leningrad University from 1932 to 1934, but did not graduate.) In 1936 Zeldovich proceeded straight to receiving his PhD in physics and mathematics, and three years later he obtained the highest scientific degree of the USSR—Doctor of Sciences (equivalent to the German *Habilitation*)—in physics and mathematics.

During the period from 1939 to 1943, Zeldovich wrote several papers on the mechanism of fission of heavy nuclei and especially on a theory of the chain fission reaction of uranium. Especially important were four of these papers, written in collaboration with Yuli B. Khariton (1904–1996). All the papers of this series form the foundation of the modern physics of nuclear reactors and nuclear power. Zeldovich was a theoretical physicist; however, he was equally at home in laboratory discussions of experimental techniques or in technology-oriented studies of shock waves and explosive phenomena. As a specialist

in combustion and detonation, he was involved in the efforts of assuring the survival of the USSR as a nation in the Second World War. His role in the creation of new weapons for the country was invaluable. He worked on the burning of solid fuel in the special legendary Katyusha launchers, and on other projects with important technological and defense applications. From 1943 to 1963 Zeldovich participated in the development and building of atomic (and later hydrogen) weapons.

His contributions to science and technology in the USSR during the war and immediately after it were noticed by the government: He became one of the most decorated of Soviet scientists. His awards included three Gold Stars, the Lenin Prize, four State Prizes, and several orders.

In addition to his work in other fields of physics, from 1947 to 1963 Zeldovich kept working in the area of nuclear physics and the physics of elementary particles. In the early 1960s Zeldovich began turning his attention to astrophysics and cosmology. He devoted almost the last twenty-five years of his life (1963–1987) to these branches of science.

Chemical Physics and Hydrodynamics. Zeldovich began his scientific work in the Catalysis Laboratory of the ICP. His first scientific research was devoted to adsorption and catalysis. Some of the ideas in his publications were far ahead of their time. Only many years later were analogous ideas rediscovered and used. Such rediscoveries involved his ideas of absorption and catalysis, among others.

In the mid-1930s Zeldovich began his research in hydrodynamics, heat transfer, and turbulence. He introduced the notion of the rate of decay of temperature inhomogeneities, which plays the same role in the distribution of temperature in matter as does the rate of energy dissipation in the velocity field in a viscous fluid. Twelve years later Aleksandr Mikhailovch Obukhov independently introduced this quantity as a governing characteristic of the local temperature field in developed turbulent flows. Obukhov's theory proved to be of exceptional practical importance because temperature fluctuations determine the dispersion of light in the atmosphere. Another important result in this period is the similarity laws in the development of ascending convective. These ideas were later developed by other authors; in the early twenty-first century, they were widely used by geophysicists in studies of atmospheric and oceanic convection.

Starting in the mid-1930s, Zeldovich turned his attention to hydrodynamics and thermal processes in shock waves, and to magnetohydrodynamics (magnetic field generation in the motion of a conducting fluid). In 1942 Zeldovich published a fundamental theoretical study which played an enormous role in the development of physical and chemical kinetics. This paper was devoted to calculations of the rate of formation and subsequent growth of vapor bubbles in a fluid which is in a metastable (superheated) state. It turned out that the technique developed in this paper may be transferred almost without change to a large number of kinetic problems in which the slow decay of nonequilibrium states is considered.

Zeldovich was one of the founders of the Soviet school of specialists on combustion and detonation. This school received worldwide recognition. His own studies in this field were diverse and multidirectional. They included many purely theoretical aspects and also such applied topics as combustion of gases and solid rocket fuels, condensed liquid explosives and powders, combustion of premixed fuel compounds, and diffusive combustion. In particular, together with David Al'bertovich Frank-Kamenetskii (1910–1970), Zeldovich found the structure of a laminar flame: the authors separated the flame into a narrow zone of chemical transformation situated near the region of maximum temperature, and a wider zone of heating. In this last zone, the chemical reactions can be ignored. They also found the temperature and concentration distributions in the flame. Finally they found the simple analytical formula for the velocity of flame propagation. This formula is known as the Zeldovich-Frank-Kamenetskii formula. The simple theory of flame propagation was generalized by Zeldovich and other scientists to complex chemical transformations with chain reactions, with many stages and many separate reaction zones.

Particles and Nuclei. In 1939 Zeldovich began his very fruitful studies of nuclear fission of uranium. Four important papers of this series were written in collaboration with Khariton. It was shown in the first two papers (published in 1939 and 1940) that chain fission reactions by fast neutrons in pure metallic natural uranium, as well as self-sustained chain reactions in a homogeneous natural uranium light water system, are impossible. The third paper (1940) was devoted to the role of the delayed neutrons in a chain reaction and the need to account for them. The theory of nuclear reactor control uses the significant conclusions outlined in this paper. The fourth paper (1941) deals with the problem of the critical size of a sample of uranium-235 in the fission of nuclei by fast neutrons. It was shown that for the self-sustained chain fission reaction in a sample of uranium-235 surrounded by a neutron reflector, the critical mass is about ten kilograms. The theory developed in the paper allows calculations of the critical mass of uranium-235 dissolved in light water. This and other works by Zeldovich had very important practical applications.

At the same time, this was the beginning of his work in the theory of nuclei and in the physics of elementary particles. One of the most significant contributions of Zeldovich to the theory of nuclei was the indication of the possibility of existence of nuclei at the threshold of stability, due to the large numbers of neutrons. In 1960 Zeldovich predicted the existence of a new helium isotope, helium-8, with an excessive number of neutrons. This helium-8 isotope was soon discovered experimentally.

In the early 1950s Zeldovich began his research into the theory of elementary particles. The most important contribution to this field was one idea proposed by Zeldovich in 1955, in collaboration with Simon Solomonovich Gershtein (*b.* 1929). The idea consisted of the following statement: if there is a so-called vector current in β-decay, then it can be made a conserved one. Subsequent experiments confirmed this prediction. In the paper published in 1955, Zeldovich and G. M. Gandelman pointed out that the very precise measurement of the magnetic moment of an electron can be considered as a method for determining the limits of applicability of quantum electrodynamics at small distances. After that, the idea was developed and became the classical method for finding the limits of applicability of quantum electrodynamics.

In 1966 Zeldovich and Gershtein estimated the upper limit for the rest mass of a muonic neutrino. This limit is of the order of 100 eV. It was obtained from cosmological considerations: if the rest mass is greater than this limit, then the total mass of all relic neutrinos which survived after the big bang would be more than the mass of all forms of matter in the universe, which is incompatible with the astronomical observations. This and Zeldovich's other works from that period marked the beginning of the modern physics of cosmological elementary particles. Also Zeldovich's pioneering ideas in the theory of the physics of vacuum were very important for the development of modern cosmology.

Astrophysics and Cosmology. During the last twenty-five years of Zeldovich's life, his main scientific interests were astrophysics and cosmology. Zeldovich himself emphasized that his first scientific love was the theory of combustion. Astrophysics and cosmology were his last loves. His work in these new fields was very successful. The beginning of the time when Zeldovich concentrated on astrophysics and cosmology corresponded to the time of the second revolution in astrophysics, the epoch of Sturm und Drang, when the habitual fixed conceptions were broken and replaced by new ones. Many wonderful discoveries were made at that period, and many revolutionary ideas were proposed. Zeldovich himself participated in this revolution very actively; he was one of its leaders and creators.

Astronomy became an "all-wavelength" science, which meant that astronomers started to obtain information from all spectral bands of electromagnetic radiation from the universe: radio, infrared, optical, ultraviolet, and high energy. Astronomers began using satellites and spacecraft, new technology, and fast computers. It became clear that the observable universe was born in the grand quantum explosion (big bang) that occurred about 13.5 billion years ago. The Cosmic Microwave Background (CMB) electromagnetic radiation had been discovered. This radiation was born in the hot epoch of the early universe. The radiation cooled down because of the expansion of the universe, to its current temperature of 2.7 K. Observations of CMB are able to probe directly into the very early universe. Very unusual celestial objects were discovered during the epoch of the second astronomical revolution: radio stars, radio galaxies, quasars, infrared sources, radio pulsars, x-ray sources, and others. The question "What is this?" became central for theoreticians. Zeldovich played a leading role in constructing proper models in attempts to understand the nature of various objects. He was one of the founders of relativistic astrophysics, which addresses phenomena where relativistic effects in gravitational fields are crucial, and the release of energy in stormy processes is often enormous.

Zeldovich studied the properties of black holes in detail, including the amazing physical processes that occur in their vicinity. These unusual celestial bodies were predicted by the general theory of relativity. They emerge when the mass of an object is compressed so much that the gravitational field becomes enormous. Light itself cannot escape from this region, nor can anything else. Zeldovich and his collaborators demonstrated that the compression of a (nonrotating), nonsymmetrical body produces a black hole, which very rapidly becomes perfectly symmetrical. Any deviation from sphericity in the gravitational field must be radiated outward (by gravitational waves) during the formation of the black hole. This radiation creates gravitational waves. The emerging boundary of a black hole, the event horizon, is spherical and only spherical. By contrast, the collapse of a rotating mass leads to a rotating black hole. Thus the gravitational field of a (uncharged) black hole is completely determined by its mass and angular momentum. This seminal work had enormous influence on experts within the field. Another important contribution to black hole physics was Zeldovich's theoretical discovery of the possibility of quantum radiation of waves (for example, electromagnetic ones) by a rotating black hole. This work stimulated many subsequent studies.

In 1964 Zeldovich put forward the idea of observing black holes using the radiation from gas moving in their gravitational fields. Independently, an analogous idea was proposed by Edwin E. Salpeter (*b.* 1924). In 1964, just after quasars had been discovered, Zeldovich and his coworkers conjectured that the main engine of a quasar can be a supermassive (millions and billions of solar masses) black hole with gas accretion onto it. Quasars, located at the centers of big galaxies, are among the most powerful sources of energy in the contemporary universe. On the basis of data from one of the quasars, 3C273, the authors gave the first estimates of the mass of the central black hole: a hundred million solar masses.

In 1966, Zeldovich, and his collaborators, predicted that black holes (as well as neutron stars) could act as extremely powerful sources of x-radiation because of the physical processes in their vicinity. This situation occurs if there is an ordinary (normal) star quite close to the black hole in a binary system, and the matter from the upper layers of the normal star comes to the very vicinity of the black hole. The x-ray emission of such matter, which heats up, makes the black hole visible. The first black holes of stellar mass were discovered a few years later as x-ray sources in binary stellar systems.

Also in 1966, Zeldovich and his coworkers predicted the possibility of the generation of primordial small black holes in the early stages of the evolution of the universe. The same hypothesis was independently proposed by English physicist Stephen Hawking (*b.* 1942).

Despite his having made many discoveries in other areas of astrophysics, Zeldovich's major field of study in astrophysics was cosmology. In the 1940s George Gamow and his coauthors had hypothesized that the beginning of the evolution of the universe was hot. At the beginning of his work in cosmology in the 1960s Zeldovich proposed an alternative to the hot model, called the cold model. He always supported the search for observational methods of testing cosmological models. In 1964 collaborators of Zeldovich showed that weak Cosmic Microwave Background electromagnetic radiation (a relic of the hot universe) could be observed in the centimeter and millimeter region of the spectrum. This radiation was discovered in 1965 by Arno Penzias (*b.* 1933) and Robert Wilson (*b.* 1936). Zeldovich was one of the first who proposed to use this CMB radiation as a powerful tool for the investigation of the evolution of the universe. In 1968 Zeldovich, with coworkers, solved the problem of hydrogen recombination in the course of the expansion of the hot universe. During this process, the hot plasma of the universe was converted into neutral gas. After this epoch, the formation of the first celestial bodies from initially small fluctuations of matter density in space began. It was the beginning of the formation of galaxies and their clusters, the formation of the large-scale structure of the modern universe. In a series of publications, Zeldovich and his collaborators showed what types of CMB spectrum distortions had been formed at various stages in the evolution of the universe, and specified different types of physical processes that could be responsible for these distortions, among which were the decay of unstable particles, dissipation of rotational and irrotational motions of matter, quantum evaporation of primordial black holes of small masses, and matter/antimatter annihilation.

The study of the formation of the large-scale structure of the universe from the initially small fluctuations of the matter in space is probably Zeldovich's most important achievement of in cosmology. In 1970 he proposed a so-called pancake theory. Before his work was published, cosmologists commonly accepted the picture of the quasi-spherical compression of the protoclusters of galaxies during the last stages of their formation under the action of the self-gravitational forces. Zeldovich showed that, under some conditions, this picture was highly improbable. He proved that compression along only one direction must dominate. As a result flat structures, pancakes, must form.

In the subsequent publications with his collaborators, Zeldovich indicated that pancake formation must lead to shock waves. The gas density must increase in cooling zones, which leads to the formation of separate galaxies. The theory predicted the formation of the characteristic cell structure with gigantic voids, which are free from galaxies. This structure with voids has been discovered in observations, and some details of the theory have been confirmed by numerical simulations.

Another important work was published by Zeldovich with astrophysicist Rashid Alievich Sunyaev (*b.* 1943) in 1972. They showed that relatively cold photons of CMB after scattering by the hot electrons in the intergalactic gas of some galactic clusters must increase their energy and be transmitted into another spectral band. This leads to a decrease in the number of photons of CMB in the typical radio band of the spectrum. As a result of this scattering, the intensity of the CMB radiation in this spectral band must decrease. This theory predicts that the intensity of the CMB radiation in the direction of the galaxy clusters with hot intergalactic gas must decrease. This phenomenon was later observed and named the Zeldovich-Sunyaev effect. This effect, together with observations of hot gas in the cluster of galaxies, allows one to determine the absolute linear size of the galaxy cluster. The analogous effect enables one to find the peculiar velocity of the cluster with respect to the CMB radiation. These phenomena became powerful tools of observational cosmology.

Zeldovich and his collaborators, and later his followers, predicted and analyzed the tiny variations (anisotropy) of the intensity of the CMB radiation at different directions in the sky, which reflect the tiny fluctuations of the primordial hot matter distribution in space in the past epoch before galaxy formation. This anisotropy contains information about the physics of the early universe, as well

as information about the parameters of the modern universe, including information about mysterious invisible "dark energy" and "dark matter"—which (as became clear at the end of the 1990s) is what most of the universe is made of. The CMB anisotropy was discovered in the 1990s, and later on many ground-based telescopes, balloons, and space missions performed such observations.

In his last years Zeldovich published on the problem of the birth of the universe and its early evolution. He emphasized the role of quantum phenomena in enormous dynamic gravitational fields at the very beginning of the universe. He was interested in the physics of the so-called Λ-term in the Einstein equations of general relativity. Later called the problem of dark energy, this exotic form of energy corresponds to a repulsive cosmic force acting at very long distances. At the very beginning of the twenty-first century the problem of dark energy became one of the most important and mysterious problems in physics and cosmology.

Zeldovich's works inspired new projects not only among theoreticians but also among experimental physicists and observational astronomers. Many of his predictions have been confirmed, and thus played a leading role in the development of science. Zeldovich was also an outstanding teacher. He was a professor at the Institute of Engineering Physics in the 1940s and a professor at Moscow State University from 1965 to 1987; he was a founder of a school of world-famous physicists and astrophysicists, and an author of widely read texts at all levels. Zeldovich was elected a corresponding member of the Academy of Sciences of the USSR in 1946 and was elected a full member of the academy in 1958. He was also a member of many other academies and scientific societies.

It should also be mentioned that during almost all periods of his life, he was not able to travel beyond the Iron Curtain, and his personal contacts with foreign scientists were very restricted. This created additional difficulties for him in his scientific work. Such obstacles make his outstanding achievements in many different branches of science even more remarkable. It is hard to believe that a single person did all this research. The famous British physicist Stephen Hawking wrote to Zeldovich after first meeting with him: "Now I know that you are a real person and not a group of scientists like the Bourbaki."

BIBLIOGRAPHY

A detailed scientific bibliography of Zeldovich is in his Selected Works, *vol. 1, number 9 (below).*

WORKS BY ZELDOVICH

With Aleksandr Solomonovich Kompaneetz. *The Theory of Detonation.* New York: Academic Press, 1960.

With M. A. Rivin and David Al'bertovich Frank-Kamenetskii. *Impul's reaktivnoi sily porokhovykh raket.* Moscow, 1963. Translated as *Impulse of Reactive Force of Solid Propellant Rockets.* Ohio: Wright-Patterson Air Force Base, 1966.

With Yurii Petrovich Raizer. *Physics of Shock Waves and High-Temperature Hydrodynamic Phenomena.* Edited by Wallace D. Hayes and Ronald F. Probstein. Translated by Scripta Technica. New York: Academic Press, 1966.

With Yurii Petrovich Raizer. *Elements of Gasdynamics and the Classical Theory of Shock Waves.* New York: Academic Press, 1968.

With Igor Dmitrievich Novikov. *Relativistic Astrophysics,* vol. 1, *Stars and Relativity,* edited by Kip S. Thorne and W. David Arnett. Translated by Eli Arlock. Chicago: University of Chicago Press, 1971.

With Igor Dmitrievich Novikov. *Relativistic Astrophysics,* vol. 2, *The Structure and Evolution of the Universe,* edited by Gary Steigman. Translated by Leslie Fishbone. Chicago: University of Chicago Press, 1983.

With Aleksandr Andreevich Ruzmaikin and D. D. Sokolov. *Magnetic Fields in Astrophysics.* New York: Gordon and Breach, 1983.

With Grigory Barenblatt, V. B. Librovich, and G. M. Makhviladze. *The Mathematical Theory of Combustion and Explosions.* Translated by Donald H. McNeill. New York: Plenum, 1985.

Selected Works of Yakov Borisovich Zeldovich, vol. 1: *Chemical Physics and Hydrodynamics,* edited by J. P. Ostriker, G. I. Barenblatt, and Rashid Alievich Sunyaev. Translated by A. Granik and E. Jackson. Princeton, NJ: Princeton University Press, 1992. This volume and the next include his most essential works.

Selected Works of Yakov Borisovich Zeldovich, vol. 2, *Particles, Nuclei, and the Universe,* edited by J. P. Ostriker, G. I. Barenblatt, and Rashid Alievich Sunyaev. Translated by A. Granik and E. Jackson. Princeton, NJ: Princeton University Press, 1993.

OTHER SOURCE

Sunyaev, Rashid Alievich, ed. *Zeldovich: Reminiscences.* Boca Raton, FL: CRC Press, 2004.

Igor Novikov

ZELINSKIĬ, NIKOLAY DMITRIE-VICH
(*b.* 6 February 1861, Tiraspol, Russia [later Moldavia]; *d.* 31 July 1953, Moscow, Russia), *organic synthesis and catalysis; petrochemistry, biochemistry.* For the original article on Zelinskiĭ, see *DSB* vol. 14.

In post-1970 publications and articles about Zelinskiĭ, especially in those of the post-perestroika period, great attention is placed on shedding light on his private life during his student years, his intense scientific work abroad, and his contacts with colleagues. The archival materials relating to Zelinskiĭ's legacy, published in the early 2000s, allow scholars to place different priorities on his creative output. Nevertheless, it is necessary to supplement this published information with facts relating to the early years of Zelinskiĭ's life and activities (for example, in Soviet times it was unacceptable to make reference to the fact that he was of noble birth). The material below adds significantly to the knowledge of Zelinskiĭ's private life, and to the development of his career. In some respects, it also broadens scholars' knowledge about his creative legacy.

New Biographical Information. Zelinskiĭ's father, Dmitry Osipovich Zelinskiĭ, was descended from hereditary nobility of the Volyn' province. His great-grandfather on his mother's side was a Turk, taken captive as a child by soldiers of A. V. Suvorov in 1790 during the storming of the city of Izmail in the course of the Russo-Turkish war, and given the last name of Vasilev.

Nikolay lost his father and mother at an early age. They died of tuberculosis in 1863 and 1865, respectively. The orphaned boy was raised by his grandmother, Maria Petrovna Vasil'eva and received his initial education at home. Subsequently he studied in a district school in the town of Tiraspol, and then in the famous Richelieu gymnasium in Odessa, which, although it was distinguished by the high level of its instructional staff, provided its graduates with an education predominantly in the arts. The young man's interest in natural sciences was awakened by I. M. Sechenov, whose public lectures on physiology were given in the 1870s at Novorossiysk (later Odessa) University, and which were attended by his grandmother, together with her grandson. Precisely for this reason, having finished the gymnasium, Zelinskiĭ entered the Physics and Mathematics Department at Novorossiysk University. In the 1880s the instructors in the department were such leading lights of Russian natural sciences as the chemist A. A. Verigo, the zoologist Alexander O. Kovalevsky, the microbiologist and immunologist I. I. Mechnikov, the physiologist Ilya M. Sechenov, the physicist Nikolay A. Umov, and others. There is no question that these learned men exerted a powerful influence on the formation of Zelinskiĭ's views and on the breadth of his scientific outlook.

Zelinskiĭ's first trips abroad played a significant role in his subsequent scientific work. During his graduate work in German scientific centers in 1885–1886, Zelinskiĭ worked out an original method of treating acids and their derivatives with *a*-bromine, a method that has entered the history of science as the "Hell-Volhard-Zelinskiĭ reaction." In Victor Meyer's Göttingen laboratory he also worked out a new system of obtaining stereoisomeric dimethyl-succinic acids, which served as the beginning of wide-ranging stereochemical investigations by Zelinskiĭ, and which became the basis of his doctoral thesis.

Zelinskiĭ's second trip to Leipzig also belongs to the Odessa period of his scholarly activity. This time Zelinskiĭ spent the entire summer semester of 1890 with Wilhelm Ostwald. The work in the Leipzig laboratory helped the young scientist to master experimental techniques in the area of electroconductivity (which found its reflection in his doctoral dissertation and publications examining halogenid solutions of alkal metals) and other areas of physical chemistry. As a result, Zelinskiĭ became one of the pioneers in the study of the electrical conductivity of nonaqueous solutions of mineral salts. In the following years, apparently under the influence of Ostwald, Zelinskiĭ developed an interest in working in the area of organic catalysis. It was to Ostwald that his chemistry students in the physics and mathematics faculty of Moscow University went for their graduate training, among them, S. G. Krapivin, A. V. Rakovsky, A. V. Speransky, and N. A. Shilov.

It is also absolutely necessary to supplement the Moscow period of Zelinskiĭ's activities with new biographical information. At Moscow University he took it upon himself to give a basic course in organic chemistry for students of natural sciences in the physics and mathematics department, and he took general charge of their practical training in organic and analytical chemistry. For a number of years (1899–1904) Zelinskiĭ gave a course on organic chemistry for students of the medical faculty. In addition, he was actively engaged in public life. In 1900 higher education courses for women, established originally in 1872 by V. I. Ger'e of Moscow University, were reopened. In conjunction with these courses, Zelinskiĭ organized a chair of organic chemistry, took charge of it, and brought in his followers to teach the courses. In 1908 he took part in founding the public A. L. Shaniavsky University. Through his efforts the Moscow laboratory of the Ministry of Finance was organized (1903) and headed by Zelinskiĭ. He also took an active part in the work of natural science societies, such as the Society of Lovers of the Natural Sciences, Anthropology, and Ethnography; the Kh. S. Ledentsov Society for the welfare of experimental sciences and their practical application (starting in 1909); the Russian Physical and Chemical Society (the RFKhO, of which he was a member from 1887), which in 1932 became the All-Union D. I. Mendeleev Chemical Society (VKhO), and in which he was a member of the presidium from its inception, the chairman of the Moscow branch from 1933 to 1945, and, from 1946, the honorary chairman of this branch. For sixty years, Zelinskiĭ was connected to the Moscow Society of Natural Studies, a member from 1893, and president from 1933 to 1953.

In 1937 the public University of Physical Chemistry and Chemical Technology, named after Zelinskiĭ, entered the All-Union Chemical Society. Its aim was to raise the qualifications of the society members and of the workers in the field of technical engineering. At the same time sci-

entific research for industry took place here. During World War II (1941–1945) the university carried on work relating to the defense of the country. Zelinskiĭ, as the honorary chairman of the academic council of the university, took active part in the university's activities.

The brief St. Petersburg period of Zelinskiĭ's career also deserves some clarification. In 1911 the presidium of the Moscow University council was dismissed *in corpore* by order of the Ministry of Public Education. To protest such a violent act against the autonomy of the university, more than one hundred of its professors resigned. Zelinskiĭ also left, as a sign of his solidarity with his colleagues. He taught for a few months at Shaniavsky University, and then left for St. Petersburg at the invitation of the minister of finance Vladimir N. Kokovtsov, who offered him the position of chair of commodity research in the Economics Department of the St. Petersburg Polytechnic Institute. Within the bounds of the central laboratory of the Ministry of Finances he was able to continue his experimental investigations.

Research on Practical Problems. The range of scientific problems undertaken by Zelinskiĭ in the course of his entire life was unusually broad. In this context one should also mention his work connected to the exploitation of the country's natural resources, including the exploration of the rich reserves of Glauber's salt in the Kara-Bogaz Gol; his study of sapropel in the Balkhash region (1913), and other sapropels as a means of obtaining light and heavy oil (1925–1933); and his work in the area of shale oil, in particular on the removal of sulfur.

An important area of investigation was to solve the problem of synthesizing Soviet rubber. In 1933 a specialized laboratory was created in the Chemistry Department of Moscow University. Under the direct leadership of Zelinskiĭ the synthesis of chloroprene rubber from acetylene was achieved, thiokol was derived, and so forth. In future years this work was continued under the auspices of the Institute of Organic Chemistry (such as the working out of methods deriving synthetic rubber from nonconsumable raw materials). Of special interest are the collaborative works by Zelinskiĭ directed at clarifying the chemical nature of India-rubber, the aim of which was to shed light on the question of the genesis of rubber in natural conditions.

Zelinskiĭ's published investigations with a practical application are closely tied to works of a predominantly theoretical character. "The boundary between living and non-living matter and their organic interaction" (1981, p. 43) is one of the leitmotifs in the scientific work of this scientist during the entire course of his life. This is the source of his interest in problems associated with the origins of petroleum, in questions of fermentative catalysis, and his study of sapropels, proteins, and amino acids.

Zelinskiĭ first encountered the study of the influence of living matter on the formation of nonliving forms after he took part in a scientific expedition, undertaken in 1981 on the initiative of the academician A. O. Kovalevsky, to study the Black Sea. Its primary aim was to establish the reason for the formation of hydrogen-sulfide in deep waters (the absence of life in the sea at great depths was considered to be connected to this). On the basis of the analysis of the gathered specimens in the Black Sea silt, Zelinskiĭ proposed a new theory—which ran counter to the theory of professor Nikolai I. Andrusov—positing a bacterial origin of hydrogen-sulfide. As a result, it seems only logical that he would subsequently turn his attention to the study of sapropels, the basic materials for the formation of which in water reservoirs are microflora and microfauna, which exist in a symbiotic relationship with one another and, in the course of the biochemical process, transform into a sediment saturated with microorganisms. Ultimately this led to study of fermenting catalysis in protein bodies, since it is precisely the latter which play a decisive role in all natural processes of an organism.

The multifaceted nature of Zelinskiĭ's investigations has earned this scientist deserved recognition. Zelinskiĭ's achievements were highly valued both by the scientific community and by the state. He was accepted as a member to the French Chemistry Society and elected honorary member of the London Chemistry Society. In 1924 the Russian Chemistry and Physics Society awarded him the important A. M. Butlerov Prize. In 1926 he was awarded the title of honored scientist. He was a winner of the State Prize of the USSR three times (1942, 1946, and 1948), and he was named Hero of Socialist Labor (1945). He was awarded the Lenin Order four times (l940, 1945, 1946, and 1951), and the Red Banner of Labor twice (1941 and 1943).

Zelinskiĭ was married three times. His first wife, Raisa Ivanovna (née Drokova, b. 1850) died in 1908 after a difficult, long illness. His son, Alexandr is from this marriage. In 1909 he married Evgeniia Pavlovna Kuz'mina-Karavaeva (b. 1881). From this marriage he had a daughter, Raisa (married to A. F. Platě). His wife died after a brief illness in 1934. Zelinskiĭ was married for the third time to Nina Evgenievna Bok (née Zhukovskaia), with whom he had two sons, Andreĭ and Nikolay.

SUPPLEMENTARY BIBLIOGRAPHY

The Moscow branch of the Russian Academy of Sciences Archive (Fund 629) contains the following materials relating to the legacy of Zelinskii (1888–1942): his participation in various organizations and institutions (1902–1939); patents and certificates of authorship (from the 1920s and 1930s); and correspondence (1911–1939). Archival material can also be found in the collections of the N. D. Zelinskii Memorial Office and Library in Moscow.

OTHER SOURCES

Akademija Nauk SSSR. Zelinskiĭ, Andreĭ. *Akademik N. D. Zelinskiĭ* [The academician N. D. Zelinskiĭ]. Moscow: Znanie, 1981.

Andrusev, M. M., and A. M. Taber. *N. D. Zelinskiĭ: Kniga dlia uchashchikhsia* [N. D. Zelinskiĭ: A book for students]. Moscow: Prosveshchenie, 1984.

Bogatskiĭ, Alekseĭ V., Georgiĭ V. Lazur'evskiĭ, and A. Nirka Evgeniĭ. *N. D. Zelinskiĭ (1861–1953): Stranitsy zhizni i tvorchestva* [N. D. Zelinskiĭ (1861–1953): Pages from his life and writing]. Kishinev: Shtiintsa, 1976.

Institut Organicheskoĭ Khimii imeni N. D. Zelinskogo (1934–1984) [The N. D. Zelinskiĭ Institute of Organic Chemistry]. Moscow: Nauka, 1983.

Nikogosian, Nikolaĭ B. "Vstrechi s Zelinskim" [Encounters with Zelinskiĭ]. *Khimiia i zhizn'* [Chemistry and life] 2 (1986): 91–93.

Sterligov, Oleg D. "K 125-letiiu so dnia rozhdeniia akademika N. D. Zelinskogo" [In Honor of the 125th anniversary of the academician N. D. Zelinskiĭ's birth]. *Vestnik AN SSSR* [Bulletin of the Academy of Sciences, USSR] 10 (1986): 129–132.

Solov'ev, Iuriĭ I., and Oleg D. Sterligov. "Nauka sblizhaet liudeĭ naibolee prochno: Iz arkhiva akademika N. D. Zelinskogo" [Science brings people together most closely: From the archive of N. D. Zelinskiĭ]. *Vestnik RAN* [Bulletin of the Russian Academy of Sciences] 8 (1992): 111–128.

Solov'ev, Iuriĭ I., ed. *Khimiki o sebe* [Chemists about themselves]. Moscow: Vladmo, Graff-Press, 2001. See pp. 96–98.

Lunin, Valeriĭ V., ed. *Khimicheskiĭ fakul'tet MGU. Put' v tri chetverti veka* [The chemistry department at MGU: Its three-quarter-century path]. Moscow: Terra-Kalender, 2005. See pp. 17–20, 159–161, and passim.

Elena Zaitseva

ZHAO ZHONGYAO

ZHAO ZHONGYAO (Chung-Yao Chao in Wade-Giles; *b.* Zhuji County, Zhejiang Province, China, 27 June 1902; *d.* Beijing, China, 28 May 1998), *nuclear physics.*

Zhao was a Chinese experimental nuclear physicist whose research on light-nuclei interactions in the 1930s helped inspire the discovery of the positron and pave the way for the acceptance of quantum electrodynamics. He also helped to found the field of nuclear physics in China and to train generations of Chinese nuclear physicists in the twentieth century.

Early Years and Education. Zhao's remarkably long life began at the turn of the twentieth century in an area of southern China known for its strong scholarly tradition. Ironically for a man who would make his reputation as an experimental physicist, Zhao—as the overprotected youngest child and the only son in the family—was forbidden by his elderly parents from engaging in any kind of physical activity. His father, Zhao Jihe, earned a meager living as a schoolteacher and a practitioner of traditional Chinese medicine in the countryside. He did, however, inspire a strong sense of Chinese nationalism in his son and encouraged him to pursue an academic career.

Taking advantages of the educational reform that had commenced during the last days of the Qing dynasty, Zhao went to Zhuji middle school to receive a western-style education in the late 1910s. He excelled in both the sciences and humanities but eventually decided to pursue the former when he went to the Advanced Normal School of Nanjing in 1920. The college, soon renamed the Southeastern University, attracted Zhao because of its free tuition and the high reputation of the faculty, many of whom had recently returned from studying abroad. Finally on his own, Zhao enjoyed hands-on laboratory experiments and decided to major in chemistry, even though he also maintained a strong interest in mathematics and physics. Indeed, he chose to work as an assistant in the Department of Physics even before graduation.

At Southeastern, Zhao came under the influence of Ye Qisun (Chi-Sun Yeh in Wade-Giles), an experimental physicist who had studied at the University of Chicago and received a PhD from Harvard University in 1923 after conducting research on the measurement of the Planck constant and on magnetism with William Duane and Percy Bridgeman. When Ye was offered the chairmanship of the Department of Physics at the newly reconstituted Qinghua University in Beijing in 1925, he brought Zhao with him. Zhao first served as an assistant but soon was promoted to be an instructor, supervising laboratory sessions and making physics instruments. Under Ye's leadership, the department developed into perhaps the best program in the field in China. Following Ye's example, Zhao decided to further his education in the United States. In 1927, after scraping together enough funds by tapping into his own savings, borrowing from relatives and friends, and getting a small grant from the university, he set sail for the California Institute of Technology (Caltech) in Pasadena, leaving behind his newlywed bride, Zheng Yuying, to care for his mother in Zhuji.

What drew Zhao to Caltech was Robert Millikan, the Nobel laureate in physics for 1923 who had taught Ye at Chicago. With quiet determination, Zhao worked hard and made great progress, publishing a theoretical paper on the problem of the ionized hydrogen molecule in the *Pro-*

ceedings of the National Academy of Sciences less than two years after his arrival. His performance in the preliminary examinations so impressed Millikan that the latter persuaded the China Foundation for the Promotion of Education and Culture to grant Zhao a three-year fellowship. It was Millikan's practice to assign a thesis topic to each of his students, and to Zhao he prescribed a project related to the use of the optical interferometer. To Millikan's surprise, Zhao demurred, regarding it as too easy. Millikan then suggested the study of the absorption of hard (high energy) gamma rays in matter. When Zhao, still not satisfied, hesitated, Millikan blew up. He said, according to Zhao, that "This is a very interesting and important topic. We have looked at your records and believe that you will be the appropriate person to carry it out. If you don't want to do it, just tell me now. There is no need to put off a decision" (Zhao, 1992, p. 199). Zhao quickly accepted the topic and would realize only later what an excellent choice it was.

Major Discoveries, 1929–1932. By the late 1920s, after the triumph of quantum mechanics, physicists increasingly turned their attention to nuclear physics and quantum electrodynamics (QED). The latter, most prominently developed by Paul Dirac, aimed to combine quantum mechanics and relativity in explaining interactions between light (photons) and electrons. When Zhao started his experiment, a major step in QED had just been undertaken in 1929 by two physicists, Oscar Klein of Sweden and Yoshio Nishina of Japan, who—building on Arthur Compton's work—derived a formula on the scattering of photons by electrons. Millikan, sensing the importance of the subject, wanted Zhao to check experimentally the validity of the new theory.

Zhao's experiment proceeded smoothly. Using thorium C" (Thallium-208), a powerful radioactive source, he obtained gamma rays of the highest energy available at that time, 2.65 MeV. Directing the gamma rays through different absorbers in an ionization chamber, he obtained their respective absorption coefficients by measuring the ionic currents caused by the rays with and without the absorbers. To accomplish the latter, he used two measuring instruments: an electroscope devised by Millikan for cosmic ray research and the vacuum electrometer newly invented by the German physicist Gerhard Hoffmann. To his and Millikan's surprise, Zhao found that while the absorption ratios for lighter elements corresponded to the Klein-Nishina formula, there was an abnormally large absorption, by about 40 percent more than the predicted values, of gamma rays by heavy elements such as lead. Puzzled by these results, it was now Millikan's turn to hesitate, in this case about whether to allow Zhao to publish his paper, which he had completed by the end of 1929. Finally, Ira Bowen, a physics professor who was familiar with Zhao's experiment, came to Zhao's rescue as he vouched to Millikan for the accuracy of Zhao's data. The paper, titled "The Absorption Coefficient of Hard γ-Rays," was then published in the 15 June 1930 issue of *Proceedings of the National Academy of Sciences* with Millikan's recommendation. It turned out to be one of three simultaneous but independent reports—the other two were by scientists working in Britain and Germany, respectively—on the abnormal absorption of gamma rays by heavy elements.

What caused the abnormal absorption of the gamma rays by heavy elements? In his paper, Zhao made several speculations, including the possibility that there might be electrons inside the nucleus that produced additional scattering of the gamma rays. Millikan had earlier suggested the existence of nuclear electrons in connection with his investigation of the scattering of cosmic rays. In any case, Zhao now believed that scattering was the key to understanding the abnormal absorption of the gamma rays. With the approval of Bowen and Millikan, Zhao designed a new experiment to measure the scattering of gamma rays by aluminum and lead, as representatives of light and heavy elements, respectively, at various angles using the Hoffmann vacuum electrometer. The scattering experiment turned out to be much more difficult than the absorption one, demanding great care, patience, and technical ingenuity, which Zhao had acquired partly from his earlier experiment and partly by working on a used car that he had bought for twenty-five dollars. Once again, Zhao made a startling finding: there seemed to be extra "anomalous scattering" of gamma rays by lead, especially in the region behind the scatterer, with energy estimated at about 0.5 MeV, that could not be explained by the Klein-Nishina theory or other existing mechanisms. As the first physicist to record this remarkable phenomenon, Zhao again speculated that, like the abnormal absorption, the anomalous scattering of gamma rays was a nuclear phenomenon.

Naturally, these anomalous phenomena intrigued Zhao and other physicists. He continued to conduct experiments in this area during a tour in Europe after receiving his PhD at Caltech in late 1930. He spent a year with Hoffmann at the University of Halle in Germany and then paid a short visit to the Cavendish Laboratory at Cambridge University in England. There he met the great nuclear physicist, Ernest Rutherford, who encouraged him to continue his research once he returned to China. News of the Japanese invasion and occupation of northeastern China in September 1931 caused Zhao to cut his trip short and quickly return to China. Finding that there was little he could do to contribute directly to national defense, he resumed his teaching and his experiments on hard gamma rays and on neutrons at Qinghua University.

Meanwhile, Zhao's experiments at Caltech had triggered an unexpected sequence of developments that quickly helped to solve the puzzle presented therein. In 1929–1930 Carl D. Anderson, a fellow graduate student, had watched Zhao's experiment with great interest. At one point, he discussed informally with Zhao the possibility of using a cloud chamber, instead of the electroscope, to get a better picture of what happened when the gamma rays were scattered by lead, but nothing apparently was accomplished along this line before Zhao's departure. Afterward, Anderson inherited Zhao's thorium C'' and started to design a cloud chamber for this purpose. Millikan, however, persuaded him at this point to use the cloud chamber to study the scattering of cosmic rays, not gamma rays. As he took pictures of the particle tracks in the cloud chamber, Anderson discovered the presence of positively charged electrons—positrons. Subsequent experiments and studies in 1933 by Patrick M. S. Blackett and Giuseppe P. S. Occhialini as well as J. Robert Oppenheimer and others led to the recognition that Anderson's positrons were produced as a result of pair-production: a high energy photon would be transformed into an electron and positron when it entered the coulomb field of a heavy nucleus. Shortly after their creation, however, the electron-positrons would "annihilate" each other while giving off two photons. This interpretation, which corresponded to Dirac's QED theory, also explained the excess absorption and scattering of gamma rays by heavy elements that Zhao was the first or among the first to observe: the former was caused by pair-production and the latter by annihilation.

In retrospect, Zhao's well-designed and beautifully executed gamma ray experiments helped to inspire the discovery of the positron and pave the way for the acceptance of QED. They represented one of the earliest and most significant achievements by a Chinese physicist in the twentieth century. In the exciting and somewhat chaotic atmosphere of nuclear physics in the early 1930s, however, Zhao's contributions were overshadowed by other, more striking discoveries such as the neutron, the positron, and artificial radioactivity. Anderson won his much-deserved Nobel Prize in Physics in 1936, partly upon Millikan's strong recommendation, but it was not until the 1980s when participants such as Anderson and Occhialini more publicly acknowledged the impact of Zhao's work and when historical research by the Chinese and Chinese American physicists Bing An Li and Chen Ning Yang (Yang Zhenning in pinyin), Nobel laureate in physics in 1957 and former student of Zhao's, brought the spotlight to Zhao's accomplishments.

Experience during the Anti-Japanese War. When Zhao returned to Qinghua in late 1932, he was an internationally recognized authority in experimental nuclear physics and the founder of the field in China. As a professor and, for a while, the chairman of the Department of Physics, he quickly organized the first nuclear physics laboratory in China. He assembled a small team of assistants and students, including a skilled technician he hired from Germany, to make instruments, including small cloud chambers and Geiger counters, and conduct research, under primitive conditions, on gamma rays, the resonance levels of neutrons in silver nuclei, and artificial radioactivity, resulting in publications in Chinese physics journals as well as in *Nature*. His colleagues included, besides Ye, other pioneers of modern physics in China such as Wu Youxun (Yui Hsun Woo in Wade-Giles), who had made major contributions to the elucidation of the Compton effects when he studied with Arthur Compton in Chicago in the 1920s, and Zhou Peiyuan (Pei Yuan Chou in Wade-Giles), who had received his PhD at Caltech two years ahead of Zhao. Together they helped train a large number of the leading Chinese nuclear physicists of the twentieth century, including many of those who would become leaders of the Chinese atomic bomb project in the 1960s. Alarmed by the gathering Japanese threat in the 1930s, Zhao was increasingly filled with a sense of national crisis and sought to do something to help strengthen China. Not a revolutionary by temperament, Zhao joined many Chinese intellectuals in advocating the "saving of China" through science, education, and industry. As an example of the latter, he and his colleagues from the Physics Department started a factory to manufacture pencils, first in Beijing and then in Shanghai.

Following the full-scale Japanese invasion of China in July 1937, the Zhaos embarked with the rest of the university on a journey of southward exile. In 1937–1938 he taught at Yunnan University in Kunming in southwestern China but returned to Qinghua when it joined with Beijing University and Nankai University to form the Southwestern Associated University (SAU) in Kunming. Pooling the faculty and resources of the three top universities in China, the SAU became an intellectual powerhouse, producing, among others, Yang and Tsung Dao Lee (Li Zhengdao in pinyin), who went on to receive their PhDs in the United States and to become the first ethnic Chinese to share the Nobel Prize in Physics in 1957. During the eight-year stay in Kunming, Zhao collaborated with another physicist, Zhang Wenyu, to conduct research on cosmic rays. After the end of World War II in 1945, Zhao moved to Chongqing to take up the chairmanship of the Physics Department at the National Central University.

Second Sojourn in America. Zhao did not stay in Chongqing long before America beckoned again in the summer of 1946. The U.S. government invited its Chinese ally to send two observers to witness its nuclear test-ing at Bikini Atoll in the Pacific. Recommended by Sa Bendong (Adam Pen-Tung Sah in Wade-Giles), a former Qinghua colleague who was then serving as executive director of the Academia Sinica, headquartered in Nanjing, Zhao was chosen to be the scientific representative. The first test, conducted in the atmosphere, took place on 1 July 1946, and the second, underwater, went off on 25 July. Following the tests, Zhao did not return to China immediately; he had a special task. Before his departure Sa had given him fifty thousand dollars to purchase instruments in the United States for nuclear physics research at the Academia Sinica. Subsequently, he was entrusted with another seventy thousand dollars to buy instruments for other scientific fields.

With characteristic thoroughness and persistence, Zhao set out to accomplish his mission despite meager resources. The first choice in nuclear physics instrumentation at the time was an accelerator, but even the least expensive of them, the electrostatic generator, invented by and named after the American physicist Robert J. Van de Graaff, would cost more than $400,000. Zhao decided to design a Van de Graaff of his own, with some of the key components purchased but the rest made by himself in the United States or in China after his return. He spent half a year at the Massachusetts Institute of Technology (MIT), where he learned to design the machine with the help of John G. Trump, a professor of electrical engineering who had teamed up with Van de Graaff to form the High Voltage Engineering Company to commercialize the accelerator. Zhao spent another half year at the Carnegie Institution of Washington, which had two Van de Graaffs and one cyclotron, to continue his design work. He then returned to MIT to work on cosmic rays in Bruno Rossi's laboratory and to purchase the various components for his accelerator as well as the other instruments on his shopping list.

In late 1948 Zhao finished his mission for the Academia Sinica, but amidst the chaos of the Chinese Civil War between the Nationalist government under Jiang Jieshi (Chiang Kai-shek) and the Communist forces under Mao Zedong, Zhao decided to stay in the United States for the time being, both to wait for the political situation to settle and to acquire more experience in using accelerators. Zhao returned to California, where he worked with Thomas Lauritsen and others on nuclear physics at Caltech's Kellogg Laboratory. By late 1949 the Chinese Communists had won the civil war and had driven the Nationalists to Taiwan.

With his wife and three children still in Nanjing, Zhao decided to return to China in early 1950 after first sending his instruments home. In the atmosphere of the cold war and McCarthyism, the journey turned into a saga, with Zhao at the center of an international political dispute. The Federal Bureau of Investigation (FBI), clearly aware of Zhao's background in nuclear physics, opened and searched Zhao's shipment of instruments. Most of them were released shortly afterward, when Jesse DuMond, a professor of physics at Caltech, told agents that they were not related to nuclear weapons. Thus, except for four sets of electronic circuitry for nuclear physics that Rossi's lab had made for Zhao and which the FBI confiscated (but later returned them to Caltech after Zhao's departure), most of his instruments, packaged into more than thirty cases, made it back to China. Remarkably, for a short period following the Communist takeover in mainland China, it was still possible for shipments and Chinese expatriates to move from the United States to China, often via Hong Kong, despite the lack of diplomatic relations between the two countries. Hundreds of Chinese students and scientists in the United States took advantage of the opportunity to return home. The outbreak of the Korean War in June 1950, however, greatly heightened the tension between the two countries. Unfortunately for Zhao, he did not board the boat *President Wilson* for China via Hong Kong until late August, so FBI agents searched his checked luggage and confiscated some books and journals. More sensationally, they prevented the boarding of his fellow Chinese scientist Qian Xuesen (Hsue-Shen Tsien in Wade-Giles). Qian, the Guggenheim professor of aerodynamics at Caltech, had just lost his security clearance on suspicion of his being a Communist Party member, and the FBI agents detained him on a charge of violating export control. Zhao and other Chinese returnees were alarmed by Qian's arrest but were also relieved that they were allowed to depart on schedule.

It was not, however, smooth sailing all the way for Zhao. When the boat stopped at the port city of Yokohama in Japan, he and two other Chinese from Caltech—Shen Shanjiong, a biologist who had just received his PhD there, and Luo Shijun, an aerodynamic scientist who had completed his PhD under Qian—were hauled off the ship by the U.S. military authorities stationed in the city. Apparently, their connections with Qian had aroused American suspicion. They were led to a Central Intelligence Agency (CIA) office onshore for questioning and were stripped so their clothes could be searched. Inside the CIA office, Zhao, Shen, and Luo demanded a justification for their detention and were told that their checked-in luggage needed to be examined. As the U.S. government flew their luggage to San Francisco for examination, the three were detained in a U.S. Army jail near Tokyo. The Nationalist government in Taiwan tried to convince the trio to go to Taiwan or return to the United States, but they refused, citing the fact that they had families in China. Meanwhile, the news of their detention galvanized a huge outcry by many Chinese and several western scientists in protest of the American action. Finally, on 31 October 1950, they were told that an examination had

found that several items in their luggage violated American export control rules but none was related to national security, and therefore they were to be released. Finally, they boarded *President Wilson* in mid-November and arrived in Hong Kong on 20 November, and then enjoyed a hero's welcome in China.

Later Years. In 1951 Zhao joined the newly established Chinese Academy of Sciences, which had been built on the former Academia Sinica but headquartered in Beijing, as director of nuclear physics at its Institute of Modern Physics in Beijing. His colleagues included many of his former students and colleagues from Qinghua, such as Wang Ganchang (Kan Chang Wang in Wade-Giles) who, after graduating from Qinghua, had gone to study with Lise Meitner in Berlin in the 1930s and would later become one of the chief designers of the Chinese nuclear weapons program in the 1960s. In his new position Zhao conducted some research but devoted most of his energy in the 1950s and the first half of the 1960s to building accelerators and training young scientists. When two cyclotrons arrived from the Soviet Union in the late 1950s, Zhao used one of them to study the elastic scattering of neutrons and nuclear reactions involving deuterons. In 1958 he took on the additional responsibility as chairman of the Department of Modern Physics at the newly established University of Science and Technology of China in Beijing, helping make it quickly one of the top programs in China. Yet, despite his patriotic actions, Zhao failed to gain complete political trust by the Communist Party, partly due to his extensive sojourns in the West. He held many honorific positions, but wielded limited influence in science policy and saw few of his proposals for advancing nuclear physics realized. He was only tangentially involved in the Chinese nuclear weapons projects, even though a large number of his colleagues and former students were active participants.

Like most Chinese scientists, the worst for Zhao came during the radical Cultural Revolution (1966–1976). Accused, ironically, of being an American agent (due to his observation of the atomic bomb tests and his detention in Japan) and a capitalist (due to his role in starting the pencil factory), he was detained for a time by the Maoist Red Guards in the Chinese Academy of Sciences. Zhao's conditions improved, as did those of many other senior Chinese scientists, in the early 1970s, when American scientists, especially Chinese American scientists, visited China following President Richard Nixon's groundbreaking trip in 1972. In 1973 Zhao became deputy director of the newly established Institute of High Energy Physics (IHEP) of the Chinese Academy of Sciences. When Mao's death in 1976 led to an end of the Cultural Revolution, Zhao reemerged as a senior Chinese nuclear physicist and was much honored by the post-Mao government and the scientific community. Before his death in 1998 due to an illness, he was especially delighted to see the building and successful operation of the Beijing Electron-Positron Collider in the IHEP in the 1980s and 1990s, the result of a collaboration between the United States and China in high-energy physics.

BIBLIOGRAPHY

There is no known depository of Zhao's correspondence or unpublished papers but presumably some of them are contained in the archives at the Chinese Academy of Sciences and its Institute of High Energy Physics in Beijing. A fairly complete list of his scientific publications are included in Zhao Zhongyao lunwen xuanji *(Selected papers of Zhao Zhongyao), 1992.*

WORKS BY ZHAO

"The Problem of the Ionized Hydrogen Molecule." *Proceedings of the National Academy of Sciences of the United States of America* 15, no. 7 (15 July 1929): 558–565.

"The Absorption Coefficient of Hard γ-Rays." *Proceedings of the National Academy of Sciences of the United States of America* 16, no. 6 (15 June 1930): 431–433.

"Scattering of Hard γ-Rays." *Physical Review* 36, no. 10 (15 November 1930): 1519–1522.

"The Abnormal Absorption of Heavy Elements for Hard γ-Rays." *Proceedings of the Royal Society of London* 135 [A], no. 826 (1 February 1932): 206–213.

With He Zehui and Yang Chengzong, eds. *Yuanzineng de yuanli he yingyong* [Principles and applications of atomic energy]. Beijing: Science Press, 1956.

Zhao Zhongyao lunwen xuanji [Selected papers of Zhao Zhongyao]. Beijing: Science Press, 1992. Includes most of Zhao's scientific publications and an autobiographical account by Zhao.

OTHER SOURCES

Cao, Cong. "Chinese Science and the 'Nobel Prize Complex.'" *Minerva* 42 (2004): 151–172.

Li, Bing An, and C. N. Yang. "C. Y. Chao, Pair Creation and Pair Annihilation." *International Journal of Modern Physics A* 4 (1989): 4325–4335. The first careful historical examination of the process and significance of Zhao's work in the 1930s.

Wang, Xueying, and Zheng Linsheng. "Zhao Zhongyao." In *Zhongguo xiandai kexuejia zhuanji* [Biographies of modern Chinese scientists], 6 vols., edited by Lu Jiaxi, vol. 4, 85–93. Beijing: Science Press, 1993.

Zuoyue Wang

ZHU KEZHEN (Chu Coching, Chu Co-ching, or Chu K'o-chen in Wade-Giles; *b.* Shaoxing County [now Shangyu County], Zhejiang Province, China, 7 March 1890; *d.* Beijing, China, 7 February 1974), *meteorology, climatology, geography, education, science policy.*

Zhu was a founder of modern meteorology and geography in China who made significant contributions to the studies of typhoons, rainfall patterns, phenology, geographic regions, and, especially, historical climate change of China. He also played a prominent role in science policy, higher education, natural resources surveys, the history of science, and popularization of science in China in the twentieth century.

Early Years and Education. Zhu's father, Zhu Jiaxian, was a rice merchant in Shaoxing and his mother Gu Jinniang, a devout Buddhist, ran a busy household with six children. Kezhen was the youngest in the family. Like many of the prominent figures in Chinese history who originated in the region, Zhu was reared in an environment that valued scholarship and a sense of Chinese nationalism. There he received his elementary education in Chinese classics before entering a western-style middle school in Shanghai in 1905. Four years later he enrolled in the Tangshan School of Railroads and Mines in Tangshan, Hebei Province, to study civil engineering. In 1910, he became one of about seventy students from all over China who passed a set of competitive examinations and were selected for study in the United States with the support of the so-called Boxer fellowships, which derived from the returned surplus from the indemnity that China had agreed to pay the United States following the Boxer unrest in 1900.

Arriving at the University of Illinois at Urbana-Champaign, in 1911, Zhu chose to study agriculture due to its importance to China. But he soon realized that the American way of farming—what he perceived to be large-scale and employing African Americans as slavelike plantation workers—would not work back home. Thus he shifted to meteorology as his field of graduate study at Harvard University in 1913, after graduating from Illinois. Working with Robert DeCourcy Ward and Alexander G. McAdie, Zhu quickly demonstrated both his scientific talent and capacity for careful scholarship in the new field. While still a graduate student, he published several papers on Chinese rainfall, typhoons, and Chinese contributions to meteorology. His abiding interest in the history of science in China was in part stimulated by his interactions with the historian of science George Sarton, then at Harvard. Zhu also became a leader in the newly established Science Society of China, with its headquarters first at Cornell University and then at Harvard. He wrote several articles on Chinese meteorology in the society's journal *Kexue* (Science), which was published in Chinese in China as a way to spread scientific knowledge. In 1918, Zhu received his PhD with a dissertation on "A

New Classification of Typhoons of the Far East" and soon thereafter set sail for home.

Pioneering Meteorology and Geography in China. Back in China, Zhu started his teaching career in fall 1918 at Wuchang Advanced Normal School (now Wuhan University) in Wuhan, Hubei Province, where he taught meteorology and geography. In early 1920 he married Zhang Xiahun, a schoolteacher, and together they would have three sons and two daughters. In fall 1920, Zhu moved to Nanjing Advanced Normal School in Nanjing, which was expanded and renamed the National Southeastern University a year later. With the arrival of Zhu and several other leaders of the Science Society, Southeastern soon boasted some of the best science faculty in the nation. They helped reestablish the Science Society in China as the largest and most important Chinese scientific organization as well as a symbol of their pursuit to "save China through science" and through an expansion of autonomous civil society institutions. Zhu became one of *Kexue*'s most prolific authors, writing more than fifty articles from 1916 to 1950, and would later serve as its editor and the president of the society. In his writings, Zhu not only sought to popularize science but also to critique government policy and promote scientific research and education.

Meanwhile, at Southeastern, where he became professor and the founding chairman of the Department of Geosciences in 1921, Zhu trained modern China's first generation of meteorologists and geographers. Prominent alumni included the agricultural climatologist Lü Jiong and the human geographers Hu Huanyong and Zhang Qiyun. In this connection, Zhu wrote some of the earliest textbooks in meteorology and geography in China. In 1924, Zhu helped found the Chinese Meteorological Society. His own research on reconstructing Chinese climatic changes from the abundant historical and phenological records also gained momentum, resulting in several publications, including one on "Climatic Pulsations during Historic Time in China" in *Geographical Review* in 1926.

Zhu's career went into a transitional phase in the late 1920s as China came near the end of the chaotic warlord period. In 1925, disgusted by a political fight over the presidency of Southeastern, Zhu left the university for the Commercial Press in Shanghai to work on its *International Encyclopedia*. The next year, he went north to Nankai University in Tianjin as a professor of geography before returning, a year later, to Southeastern, which was now expanded and renamed, first the Fourth Zhongshan University in 1927 and then the National Central University in 1928. As the Nationalist government brought a measure of national unity to the country, it established the Academia Sinica in 1927 to centralize Chinese scientific

resources. The academy's first president, Cai Yuanpei, had long been the president of Beijing University and a strong supporter of the Science Society; he immediately recruited leaders of the society, including Zhu, to head many institutes of the academy.

In 1928, Zhu became director of the Institute of Meteorology in Nanjing while retaining his positions at Southeastern. He quickly built the institute up as an important site for meteorological research. Viewing weather forecasting as an important part of reasserting China's sovereignty, he pushed for the establishment of a national network of dozens of standardized weather stations, including one in Tibet, trained a large number of observers to staff them, and gradually took over the function from foreign-controlled stations in the country. In 1929, he left Southeastern to focus his energy on the new institute but continued to give some lectures there. In this period Zhu also expanded his research into Chinese monsoons, floods in the Tianjin area, weather in Nanjing, the division of China into climatic regions, and aridity of North China.

President of Zhejiang University. Zhu's career and life took a sharp turn in 1936 when Jiang Jieshi (Chiang Kaishek), leader of the Nationalist government, personally recruited him to take the helm at Zhejiang University (Zheda for short in Chinese) at Hangzhou, Zhejiang, the native province for both men. Under his leadership, the university, despite difficult conditions, greatly strengthened its faculty not only in meteorology and geography, but also in other fields, such as mathematics, physics, biology, and the humanities.

The year after his arrival, the Japanese invasion forced him to lead the university on a perilous long march inland, settling eventually at a mountainous site in Zunyi, Guizhou. Zhu's integrity and devotion won him deeply felt respect and loyalty from all members of the university community. In turn, Zhu saw to it that research and teaching continued unabatedly in the face of overwhelming adversities. Indeed, by the end of the war, Zheda emerged as one of the best universities in China, impressing visitors such as Joseph Needham, who worked as a scientific liaison for the British Mission in China.

These remarkable achievements came at a great personal sacrifice to Zhu: his second son, Zhu Heng, and his wife fell ill and died within days of each other in 1938, delivering one of the worst blows of his life. His own scientific research also took a back seat to his wartime administrative duties even though he continued to head the Meteorology Institute. The only area of scholarship in which he remained active was the history of Chinese science, with two classic papers on ancient Chinese astronomy and on why ancient China did not produce a systematic natural science; he believed that overtly utilitarian values of the Chinese agricultural society suppressed the curiosity-driven pursuit of science. Learning of Needham's budding interest in ancient Chinese science, Zhu helped him with materials, knowledge, and contacts. He remarried in 1940, to Chen Ji, and together they would have one daughter.

The end of World War II brought welcome relief to Zhu and his university, which returned to Hangzhou, but not the peaceful, stable political environment everyone had hoped for. A civil war soon broke out between the Nationalists under Jiang and the Communists under Mao Zedong. A majority of students and professors in many universities, including Zheda, had long resented the corruption and political repression of the Nationalist regime; many of them now began to view the Communists' cause with sympathy. Zhu Kezhen, who considered himself a liberal, not a communist, often found himself caught between the government that became increasingly oppressive and the radical students whom he tried to protect. Eventually, like many other leaders of the Science Society, Zhu became disillusioned with the Nationalists and cast his lot with the Communists, hoping that they would focus on national reconstruction once victorious.

Thus in May 1949, when Jiang sent for Zhu to retreat with him to Taiwan as the Communist forces advanced toward Hangzhou, Zhu declined. Instead, he resigned the presidency of Zheda and went into hiding in Shanghai to avoid possible assassination by Nationalist agents. Soon he was invited by leaders of the new government to participate in science policy making in Beijing, including the establishment of the Chinese Academy of Sciences (CAS), which was based on the institutes of the Academia Sinica and of the Peking Academy that did not move with the Nationalists to Taiwan.

Vice President of the Chinese Academy of Sciences. In late 1949, Zhu was appointed vice president of the CAS in charge of geosciences and biosciences. In this position, he played a leading role in both the development and utilization of these scientific disciplines in the 1950s and early 1960s. For Zhu, the key to a successful science and technology policy was balance and integration—between basic and applied research, between advancing disciplinary development and serving national needs, between different disciplines, and between economic development and environmental protection. The latter was most clearly revealed in his shaping of national surveys of natural resources, on the basis of which he cautioned the government against focusing on "conquering nature" without first understanding the potential ecological consequences of such actions.

In this period, he also supervised the founding of the Institute of Oceanology in Qingdao under the leadership of marine zoologist Tong Dizhou (T. C. Tung) and the marine botanist Zeng Chengkui (C. K. Tseng), the Office of the History of Natural Sciences in Beijing, as well as a number of institutions in geosciences. He coauthored a well-received book on phenology (the study of the relationship between climate and periodic biological phenomena) and a major article on agricultural climatology. His call for closer ties between climatology and agriculture earned him an audience with Mao himself in 1964, the same year he was admitted to the Communist Party.

Zhu consistently advocated China's participation in international scientific communication, both within and without the Soviet bloc. In the mid-1950s, Zhu chaired the Chinese National Committee on the International Geophysical Year (IGY) and negotiated China's participation in the global cooperative project. When the International Council of Scientific Unions, sponsor for the IGY, admitted Taiwan as a separate member in the project, however, Zhu had to withdraw China's participation in the IGY to avoid a "two Chinas" situation. Nevertheless, the National Committee continued to operate under Zhu's leadership to collect geophysical data and to carry out a limited exchange of information with the Soviet Union. Zhu also advocated China's eventual participation in research and exploration at the Arctic and Antarctica, partly because of their impact on the climate in China. The dream was finally realized by the end of the twentieth century.

Never an outspoken political activist, Zhu survived the various political purges under Mao relatively unscathed. His eldest son, Zhu Jin, a schoolteacher, however, was persecuted during the "Anti-Rightist" campaign in 1957 and died four years later at a labor camp. During the Cultural Revolution from 1966 to 1976, Zhu and most other senior scientists in the CAS were "sidelined" by radical Maoist Red Guards; he avoided further harm due to protection by Premier Zhou Enlai. In turn Zhu was able to help some of his former associates and students by offering them supporting evidence from a diary he had meticulously kept for much of his adult life when they came under suspicion. When the worst phase of the Cultural Revolution passed in 1970, Zhu and other scientist-leaders of the CAS made a push for the revitalization of scientific research and education that had been almost completely halted earlier. In this they received crucial backing from Zhou. The reopening of China-U.S. relations during President Richard Nixon's visit in 1972 provided further momentum to Zhu's efforts, as did the visits of prominent Chinese American scientists in this period, many of whom had been Zhu's students in the 1930s and 1940s.

It was in this context that Zhu completed his last major scientific work, titled "A Preliminary Study on the Climatic Fluctuations during the Last 5000 Years in China," published in 1972. Drawing on his lifelong examination of China's uniquely rich archaeological, historical, and phenological records, Zhu made a graph of fluctuation of the mean annual temperature in China from 3000 BCE to the 1970s. To his surprise, it corresponded remarkably well with those derived from studies of the heights of the snow line in Norway and from the oxygen isotope profile of the Greenland ice sheet, leading him to speculate that the variation was global in nature and that the cold wave moved east (Pacific coast of Asia) to west while the warming trend moved west to east. In this and several earlier studies he also noted a warming trend in the twentieth century.

Zhu was elected an academician of Academis Sinica in 1948 and a divisional member of the Chinese Academy of Sciences in 1955—highest academic honors in China. He was also elected president of the Chinese Geographical Society and the Chinese Meteorological Society.

On the evening of 6 February 1974, Zhu made, as he had done every day for the last sixty years, an entry in his diary about the day's weather. A few hours later he died of pneumonia.

BIBLIOGRAPHY

Zhu's papers are stored in the history office of the Chinese Academy of Sciences, Beijing, China.

WORKS BY ZHU

"Rainfall in China, 1900–1911." *Monthly Weather Review* 44, no. 5 (1916): 276–281.

"A New Classification of Typhoons of the Far East." *Monthly Weather Review* 52, no. 12 (1924): 570–579.

"The Place of Origin and Recurvature of Typhoons." *Monthly Weather Review* 53, no. 1 (1925): 1–5.

"Climatic Pulsations during Historic Time in China." *Geographical Review* 16, no. 2 (1926): 274–282.

"A Preliminary Study of Weather Types of Eastern Asia." *Bulletin of the American Meteorological Society* 8 (1927): 164–167.

Climatic Provinces of China. Memoirs of the Institute of Meteorology, no. 1. Nanking, China: Institute of Meteorology, 1929.

With Wan Minwei. *Wu hou xue* [Phenology]. Beijing: Science Popularization Press, 1963. 2nd ed. Beijing: Science Press, 1973.

"A Preliminary Study on the Climatic Fluctuations during the Last 5000 Years in China." *Acta Archaeologica Sinica,* no. 1 (1972): 226–256.

Zhu Kezhen wen ji [Collected papers of Zhu Kezhen]. Beijing: Science Press, 1979. Contains most of Zhu's publications, including Chinese translations of his papers in English, and a bibliography of both his Chinese and English publications.

Zhu Kezhen ri ji [Diaries of Zhu Kezhen]. Vols. 1–2, covering 1936–1949. Beijing: People's Press, 1984. Vols. 3–5, covering 1950–1974. Beijing: Science Press, 1989–1990.

Zhu Kezhen quan ji [The complete works of Zhu Kezhen]. 20 vols. (projected). Shanghai: Shanghai Science, Technology, and Educational Press, 2004–. This set is the most comprehensive compilation of Zhu's writings, including papers, books, correspondence, autobiographical pieces, and diaries.

OTHER SOURCES

Hsieh Chiao-Min. "Chu K'o-chen and China's Climatic Changes." *Geographical Journal* 141, no. 2 (July 1976): 248–256.

Shen Wenxiong. "Zhu Kezhen." In *Zhongguo xiandai kexuejia zhuanji* [Biographies of modern Chinese scientists], edited by Lu Jiaxi et al., vol. 5. Beijing: Science Press, 1994.

Wang, Zuoyue. "Saving China through Science: The Science Society of China, Scientific Nationalism, and Civil Society in Republican China." *Osiris*, 2nd series, 17 (2002): 291–322.

Zhu Kezhen zhuan bianjizu (editorial group of biography of Zhu Kezhen). *Zhu Kezhen zhuan* [Biography of Zhu Kezhen]. Beijing: Science Press, 1990.

Zuoyue Wang

ZOSIMOS OF PANOPOLIS (*b.* Panopolis [now Akhmīm], Egypt; fl. c. 300 CE), *alchemy.* For the original article on Zosimos see *DSB*, vol. 14.

Unanimously recognized as the greatest of the Graeco-Egyptian alchemists, Zosimos was a prolific author whose texts have survived only in tiny scraps. His very complex manuscript tradition raises many questions that remained unresolved as of 2007. Imbued with gnosticism and hermetism, Zosimos may be said to have raised alchemy to the most sophisticated level that it attained in antiquity by impregnating technical preoccupations with mysticism for the sake of spiritual salvation.

Biographical Data. With the exception of the *Suda*, where Zosimos is said to be Alexandrian, all sources call him Panopolitan or Theban (i.e., born in the Thebaid). This discrepancy has puzzled modern scholars who, following Johannes Albertus Fabricius, consider that Zosimos, born in Panopolis, lived in Alexandria. Actually, nothing prevents scholars from assuming that Zosimos may have spent at least part of his life in his native city.

Zosimos is thought to have been active around 300 CE, for he quoted Julius Africanus, who died after 240, and mentioned the Serapeum in Alexandria, which was destroyed in 391. Furthermore, Zosimos perhaps alluded to the presence of Manichaeism in Egypt, which points to a date around 300 CE.

Zosimos may be considered as representing Graeco-Egyptian alchemy in its heyday because he came after the so-called old authors (between the first and third centuries CE), to whom belong the *Physika and Mystika* of a pseudo-Demokritos as well as the citations or short treatises attributed to legendary or celebrated figures, and because he preceded the times of the commentators, which began at the end of the fourth century with Synesios.

Manuscript Tradition. Zosimos undoubtedly wrote a vast number of texts in Greek, of which only a fragmentary part has come down to the present in the corpus of the Greek alchemists. Put together during the Byzantine period in what in the early 2000s remained unclear circumstances, this corpus loosely gathers writings of extremely varied periods ranging from the beginning of this era to the fifteenth century. The three principal witnesses, out of a large number of medieval manuscripts, are the Marcianus graecus 299 (= M; tenth or eleventh century), the Parisinus graecus 2325 (= B; thirteenth century), and the Parisinus graecus 2327 (= A; fifteenth century). They differ from one another by the number of texts they contain, by the organization of those texts, and by their state of preservation. The relations between those three manuscripts have as of 2007 not yet been conclusively clarified.

In contrast to most ancient texts, Zosimos's works have not been preserved separately but have been disseminated among other Greek alchemists' texts. Locating and identifying his works remain difficult tasks, because the corpus is made of inextricably assembled pieces of work, more or less complete. The manuscripts do not make much distinction between headings and subheadings, so that it is extremely difficult, in this hodgepodge of texts, to understand where a text begins and where it ends. Last but not least, manuscript M underwent various material accidents, which make the matter worse. However, a thorough examination of the manuscripts permits grouping the *membra disjecta* (scattered fragments) of Zosimos's works into four bodies of texts:

1. The *Authentic Memoirs* (also titled *On Apparatus and Furnaces*) consists of a series of thirteen opuscules that open with the famous treatise *On the Letter Omega*. Several sections deal with the technical apparatus and are illustrated with remarkable drawings of alchemical instruments; these sketches raise their own specific problems; for instance, when they coincide only partially with their descriptions. Others are expositions about a puzzling substance called "divine water." Three of the thirteen opuscules are titled *On Excellence*

(or *On the Composition of Waters*) and are known as Zosimos's "Visions."

2. The *Chapters to Eusebia,* as they are called according to the title that is found in the table of contents of the *Marcianus* (this title, however, is problematic), appears as a series of extracts on various subjects collected by a Byzantine compiler.

3. The *Chapters to Theodore* appears as a series of short paragraphs, summaries of summaries.

4. The *Final Count* forms a group with the two extracts of the *Book of Sophe,* between which it is enclosed.

Each group raises specific questions, and the attribution of certain passages to Zosimos sometimes remains problematic. It is evident that most of the texts have suffered badly from the transmission. To these four groups of writings, one must add a number of fragments of Zosimos disseminated among later alchemists.

Moreover, Zosimos himself and some commentators alluded to several writings that have not been preserved in the direct tradition, such as *Cheirokmēta (Things Wrought by Hand), According to Action, Letter Kappa, Letter Sigma, On the Intensity of Fire*, and *The Book of Keys*. Scholars also have the nonalchemical testimonies of George the Synkellos, who referred to a book *Imouth*, and of the *Suda*, which credits Zosimos with twenty-eight books "designated by letters of the alphabet."

The problem, therefore, is that if one starts from the remaining opuscules and from the other available pieces of evidence, it is extremely difficult to imagine Zosimos's work as a whole. It is likely that the treatise *On the Letter Omega*, which has been preserved, constituted the introduction to the *Book Omega*, one of the twenty-eight books to which the *Suda* refers; the same applies to the books entitled *Letter Kappa* and *Letter Sigma*. As for the other titles preserved, it is impossible to situate them in Zosimos's work. What seems to be certain is that what has come down from Zosimos cuts a sorry figure compared with what must have been a very wide production. The complexity of this manuscript tradition no doubt explains why the sole general edition of the Greek texts as of 2007 remains the *Collection des anciens alchimistes grecs* (1888) of Berthelot-Ruelle, which is rather mediocre.

Writings under Zosimos's name have also been preserved in Syriac, Arabic, and Latin. The Syriac tradition remains largely inaccessible: Rubens Duval has given a partial and not too reliable translation of it in the second volume of *La chimie au Moyen Âge* (1893), but it seems sufficient to ascertain that these texts are undeniably somehow related to the Greek ones. A critical edition of the Syriac tradition would be most welcome and would procure a deeper insight into the general structure of the

Panopolitan's work. Our principal witness, the Cambridge manuscript Mm 6,29 (fifteenth century), has been the subject of partial studies by Alberto Camplani in "Procedimenti magico-alchemici" (2000), Alessandra Giumlia-Mair in "Zosimos the Alchemist" (2002), and Erica C. D. Hunter in "Beautiful Black Bronzes" (2002).

In the Arabic tradition, Zosimos had a great influence upon later alchemists, particularly Ibn Umail. His name is variously transcribed as Zūsimūs, Rīsamūs, Rūsim, and Arsīmūn, among other names. This tradition is as of 2007 an almost uncharted territory, but a study of the figure of Zosimos in Arabic writings, which will contain editions and translations of most of the Arabic Zosimos texts, was as of 2007 being prepared by Bink Hallum, whose research already allowed scholars to distinguish three groups of writings under the name of the Panopolitan: (1) genuine translations from the Greek tradition; (2) original works based on a knowledge of, at least, some aspects of the Greek tradition; and (3) Arabic forgeries passed off under the name of Zosimos.

In the Latin tradition, Zosimos appears under the names of Rosinus, Datin, or Reson, names that bring out its affiliation with the Arabic tradition. A few manuscripts have been located so far. But since they have been neither edited nor translated as of this writing, there is no indication available as to the content of these texts.

Practices and Ideas. Although fragmentary, the Greek tradition, as it stands, enables scholars to make some general reflections on Zosimos's practices and ideas. It is not easy to assess how far he was original in his practices, because he is most probably indebted to Mary the Jewess, whose work is lost. The main apparatuses described by Zosimos are as follows: (1) multi-piped alembics for the distillation of liquids; (2) the so-called kerotakis, a kind of closed vessel, heated from under, inside which sheets of metal were exposed to tinctorial vapors; and (3) sublimation equipment. One must here single out the role of the divine water or sulphur water (*theion hydōr*), which is mentioned in several texts: it can be the liquid obtained by distillation in order to color metals, and it can also be "the one and the whole," that is, the undifferentiated original matter, perhaps mercury, that was considered as the basic substance for transmutation.

Zosimos's ideas were clearly influenced by hermetism and gnosticism; his writings contain some references to the Hermetic Corpus, and many parallels can be drawn between Zosimos and the gnostic texts from Hag Hammadi. (If one accepts that Zosimos could be influenced by a Christian gnosis, it is not necessary to expel from his work passages in which Christ is mentioned.) For instance, Zosimos not infrequently liked to establish symbolic correspondences between alchemical operations and the alchemist's spiritual elevation. Playing on the notion of "pneuma," which designates the spiritual part of man and the volatile part of a substance or of a metal, obtained by distillation or sublimation, Zosimos brought out a parallelism between the liberation of the divine spark of humans and the transformation of substances or the transmutation of metals. In the "Visions," this liberation of the pneuma is ritualized under the form of torture, death, and resurrection; the alchemical utensils become temples and altars, whereas the vile metals are figured as human beings that must be sacrificed before they are raised in the shape of noble metals.

In short, Zosimos may be credited with endowing alchemy with a real mystical dimension. With him, alchemy appears to have become a way of life that demanded from its followers a preliminary work of mental purification and that would give them access to spiritual salvation.

SUPPLEMENTARY BIBLIOGRAPHY

The Greek texts by Zosimos contained in the Marcianus graecus 299 (Venice) and in the Parisini graeci 2325 & 2327 (Paris) have been edited by Berthelot and Ruelle in their Collection des anciens alchimistes grecs *(1888), and partly reedited by the author of this article (1995). The Syriac manuscripts of Zosimos (Cambridge Mm 6,29 and British Museum Egerton 709 and Oriental 1593) have been at least partially translated or edited by R. Duval (1893). There are Arabic manuscripts containing texts under the name of Zosimos in Teheran, Cairo, Istanbul, Dublin, Gotha and Rampur, among other places, but whether they contain significant quantities of documents is not known. As far as the Latin tradition is concerned, there are manuscripts in Glasgow, Brussels, Palermo, Cambridge, Naples, Rome, Venice, Florence, and London (this list is certainly not exhaustive), but as they have been neither edited nor translated; scholars are not even sure that the texts they contain are really translations from Zosimos.*

WORK BY ZOSIMOS

Collection des anciens alchimistes grecs. Edited and translated by M. Berthelot and C. E. Ruelle. 3 vols. Paris: G. Steinheil, 1888. The only complete edition of the Greek text of Zosimos.

Zosimos of Panopolis, On the Letter Omega. Edited and translated by Howard M. Jackson. Missoula, MT: Scholars Press, 1978.

Zosime de Panopolis, Mémoires authentiques. Texte établi et traduit par [Text edited and translated by] Michèle Mertens. Les alchimistes grecs, vol. 4, pt. 1. Paris: Les belles lettres, 1995. An edition of the *Authentic Memoirs*, with a survey of the whole manuscript tradition and a study of the technical apparatus, includes indexes and illustrations.

OTHER SOURCES

Berthelot, M. *La chimie au Moyen Âge.* 3 vols. Paris: Imprimerie Nationale, 1893. Repr. Amsterdam: Philo Press, 1967.

Camplani, Alberto. "Procedimenti magico-alchemici e discorso filosofico ermetico." In *Il tardoantico alle soglie del Duemila—Diritto, religione, società: Atti del quinto Convegno nazionale dell'Associazione di studi tardoantichi,* edited by Giuliana Lanata. Pisa, Italy: ETS, 2000.

Carusi, Paola. "Filosofia greca e letteratura nel Mā' al-waraqī di Ibn Umail al-Tamīmī (X secolo)." In *Aristotele e Alessandro di Afrodisia nella tradizione araba: Atti del Colloquio La ricezione araba ed ebraica della filosofia e della scienza greche,* edited by Cristina D'Ancona and Giuseppe Serra. Padua, Italy: Il poligrafo, 2002.

Charron, Régine. "The *Apocryphon of John* (NHC II, 1) and the Graeco-Egyptian Alchemical Literature." *Vigiliae Christianae* 59, no. 4 (2005): 438–456.

Edwards, M. J. "The Vessel of Zosimus the Alchemist." *Zeitschrift für Papyrologie und Epigraphik* 90 (1992): 55–64.

Elkhadem, Hossam S. "A Translation of a Zosimos' Text in an Arabic Alchemy Book." *Journal of the Washington Academy of Sciences* 84, no. 3 (1996): 168–178.

Fowden, Garth. *The Egyptian Hermes: A Historical Approach to the Late Pagan Mind.* Cambridge, U.K.: Cambridge University Press, 1986. See in particular pp. 120–126. For an updated version in French, see *Hermès l'Egyptien: Une approche historique de l'esprit du paganisme tardif* (Paris: Les Belles Lettres, 2000), translated by Jean-Marc Mandosio, especially pp. 182–191.

Fraser, Kyle A. "Zosimos of Panopolis and the Book of Enoch: Alchemy as Forbidden Knowledge." *Aries* 4, no. 2 (2004): 125–147.

Giumlia-Mair, Alessandra. "Zosimos the Alchemist—Manuscript 6.29, Cambridge, Metallurgical Interpretation." In *I bronzi antichi—Produzione e tecnologia: Atti del XV Congresso internazionale sui bronzi antichi (Grado-Aquileia, 22–26 maggio 2001),* edited by Alessandra Giumlia-Mair. Monagraphies instrumentum 21. Montagnac, France: Monique Mergoil, 2002.

Halleux, Robert. *Les textes alchimiques.* Typologie des sources du moyen âge occidental 32. Turnhout, Belgium: Brepols, 1979. See, in particular, pp. 60–64.

———. "Alchemy." In *The Oxford Classical Dictionary,* edited by Simon Hornblower and Antony Spawforth. 3rd ed. Oxford; New York: Oxford University Press, 2003.

Hallum, Bink. "Zosimos of Panopolis." In *The Biographical Encyclopedia of Ancient Natural Sciences,* edited by Paul T. Keyser and Georgia L. Irby-Massie. London; New York: Routledge, 2007.

Hunter, Erica C. D. "Beautiful Black Bronzes: Zosimos' Treatises in Cam. Mm.6.29." In *I bronzi antichi—Produzione e tecnologia: Atti del XV Congresso internazionale sui bronzi antichi (Grado-Aquileia, 22–26 maggio 2001),* edited by Alessandra Giumlia-Mair. Monagraphies instrumentum 21. Montagnac, France: Monique Mergoil, 2002.

Jong, Albert F. de. "Zosimus of Panopolis." In *Dictionary of Gnosis and Western Esotericism,* edited by Wouter J. Hanegraaff. Leiden, The Netherlands: Brill, 2005.

Letrouit, Jean. "Chronologie des alchimistes grecs." In *Alchimie—Art, histoire, et mythes: Actes du 1er colloque international de la Société d'Étude de l'Histoire de l'Alchimie (Paris, Collège de France, 14–15–16 mars 1991),* edited by Didier Kahn and Sylvain Matton. Paris: S.É.H.A.; Milan: Archè, 1995.

———. "Hermetism and Alchemy: Contribution to the Study of *Marcianus Graecus* 299 (= M)." In *Magia, alchimia, scienza dal '400 al '700: L'influso di Ermete Trismegisto,* edited by Carlos Gilly and Cis van Heertum. Vol. 1. Florence, Italy: Centro Di, 2002. An edition of *On the Letter Omega.*

Mertens, Michèle. "Alchemy, Hermetism, and Gnosticism at Panopolis c. 300 A.D.: The Evidence of Zosimus." In *Perspectives on Panopolis—An Egyptian Town from Alexander the Great to the Arab Conquest: Acts from an International Symposium Held in Leiden on 16, 17, and 18 December 1998,* edited by A. Egberts, Brian P. Muhs, and Jacques van der Vliet. Papyrologica Lugduno-Batava 31. Leiden, The Netherlands: Brill, 2002.

———. "Graeco-Egyptian Alchemy in Byzantium." In *The Occult Sciences in Byzantium,* edited by Paul Magdalino and Maria Mavroudi. Geneva, Switzerland: La pomme d'or, 2006.

Saffrey, Henri Dominique. "Historique et description du manuscrit alchimique de Venise *Marcianus Graecus* 299." In *Alchimie—Art, histoire, et mythes: Actes du 1er colloque international de la Société d'Étude de l'Histoire de l'Alchimie (Paris, Collège de France, 14–15–16 mars 1991),* edited by Didier Kahn and Sylvain Matton. Paris: S.É.H.A.; Milan: Archè, 1995.

———. "Mort et transformation de la matière: À propos d'un *locus desperatus* des *Mémoires authentiques* de Zosime de Panopolis (X 6.130)." In *L'alchimie et ses racines philosophiques: La tradition grecque et la tradition arabe,* edited by Cristina Viano. Paris: Vrin, 2005.

Stolzenberg, Daniel. "Unpropitious Tinctures: Alchemy, Astrology, and Gnosis according to Zosimos of Panopolis." *Archives internationales d'histoire des sciences* 49 (1999): 3–31.

Viano, Cristina. "Alchimie gréco-alexandrine." In *Dictionnaire critique de l'ésotérisme,* edited by Jean Servier. Paris: Presses universitaires de France, 1998.

Michèle Mertens

ZUSE, KONRAD

(*b.* Berlin, Germany, 22 June 1910; *d.* Hünfeld, Germany, 18 December 1995), *logic, computers, programming, computer industry.*

Zuse is popularly recognized in Germany as the "father of the computer," having built the world's first programmable computing machine in 1941. Zuse is less well known in other countries because most of his early computers were built during World War II and became famous in and outside Germany only several years after the war.

Early Years. Konrad Zuse was born in Berlin to Emil and Maria Crohn Zuse. His father was a Prussian civil servant working for the postal service who relocated the family to

Braunsberg (now Braniewo in Poland) when Konrad was still a child. Konrad attended elementary school in that town and began studying at the local Gymnasium Hosianum. The family moved again in 1923 to Hoyerswerda (a town in Germany near what is now the border with Poland). In Hoyerswerda, Zuse was registered at the *Realschule*, a school that allowed pupils to continue studying at any of the several technical universities established in Germany. The family eventually moved back to Berlin and Konrad Zuse began his studies at the Technische Hochschule Charlottenburg (renamed Technical University of Berlin after World War II). Zuse started studying mechanical engineering, changed to architecture, thought for some time of becoming a commercial graphic designer, and settled finally on civil engineering. Years later Zuse wrote in his autobiography that he eventually discovered civil engineering to be the ideal field for him because he could combine his artistic interests with his technical prowess, especially regarding mechanical constructions. The young Konrad Zuse was an inventor and a tinkerer, often withdrawing to work with his "Stabil" mechanical set (a German version of the Meccano or Erector Set). As a student he won several prizes for his constructions, which he enjoyed showing off.

As part of his civil engineering studies at the Technische Hochschule, Zuse learned to perform repetitive static calculations like those needed to determine the stress on materials of structures such as bridges or cranes. Static calculations were performed completely by hand or with the help of desk calculators. Spreadsheets, on which all necessary formulas had been preprinted, were laboriously filled row by row. It was tedious and repetitive work that led Zuse to consider the possibility of automating the task. If engineers simply had to fill in data and follow a fixed computational path, then a machine could take over.

The Mechanical Programmable Machine. After his graduation in 1935 Zuse started working as a stress analyzer for the airplane manufacturer Henschel Flugzeugwerke. He kept this position for less than a year, resigning with the purpose of starting his own company. He wanted to build automatic calculating machines and had already made contact with Kurt Pannke, a constructor of mechanical desk calculators. However, Zuse's short-lived employment at Henschel would prove crucial for him in later years: Twice in his life his superiors at Henschel would help him secure a deferment from the army, both times arguing that he was needed as an engineer and not as a soldier on the battlefield.

In 1936, with his parents' financial support, Zuse began to build the automaton that so far had only existed in his imagination. Some friends at the university assisted by working for him while others offered small monetary

contributions so that he could finish what would become the machine V1 (Versuchsmodell 1, "experimental model one"). Perhaps the most important difference between Zuse and other computer inventors working in the late 1930s was that Zuse was designing his machine essentially alone, whereas in the United States scientists such as John Atanasoff and Howard Aiken had the resources of universities or important companies at their disposal. The entire mechanical conception of the V1 (later renamed to Z1) was his brainchild.

Zuse, ignorant of the internal structure of any type of calculator built at the time, started from scratch and developed an entirely new kind of mechanical assembly. Whereas contemporary desktop calculators were based on the decimal system and used rotating mechanical components, Zuse decided to use the binary system and metallic shafts that could move only in one direction. That is, the shafts could only slide from position 0 to position 1, and vice versa. Such shafts were all that was needed for a binary machine, but important obstacles had yet to be surmounted. It was necessary to design the complete logical description of the machine and then "wire" it accordingly. The mechanical components, however, posed a formidable challenge because every movement of one logical gate had to be mechanically coupled with the movement of the other gates. Horizontal displacements of the components had to be transformed into sliding displacements across different layers of the machine, or even into vertical displacements. From an early twenty-first century perspective, the mechanical design of the machine was much harder than conceiving the pure logical structure. It is fair to say that none of Zuse's friends understood exactly how the machine worked, although they spent weeks manufacturing the hundreds of metallic shafts needed for the apparatus.

The Z1 was operational in 1938. It was shown to several people who saw it rattle and compute the determinant of a three-by-three matrix. The machine, however, was not reliable enough. The mechanical components, all machined at home, had a tendency to get stuck. Nevertheless, the mechanical Z1 proved that the logical design was sound. Therefore, an electrical realization, using telephone relays, could be contemplated as the next step. Helmut Schreyer, an electronics engineer and college friend of Zuse, suggested the use of vacuum tubes. Schreyer, in fact, adopted this as his PhD project and developed some vacuum tube circuits for an electronic machine. Zuse, however, was not convinced that vacuum tubes should be used, although they promised extremely fast calculations. He doubted that in the long run vacuum-tube machines could be made to perform as reliably as relays or even mechanical components. Zuse had already been contemplating possible uses for his machine: His goal was the development of a programmable replacement for

Konrad Zuse. *Zuse with an original part of his Z1 computer.*
AP IMAGES.

mechanical desktop calculators for deployment in large or medium-size companies. This was to be a "computing machine for the engineer," eventually so small that it could be placed on top of a desk.

In 1938 Schreyer and Zuse explained some of the electronic circuits to a small group at the Technische Hochschule. When asked how many vacuum tubes would be needed for a computing machine, they replied that two thousand tubes and several thousand other components would be enough. The academic audience was in disbelief: The most complex vacuum circuits at the time contained no more than some hundred tubes, and the electric power necessary to keep such a machine working would be prohibitive. Just six years later the ENIAC, built at the Moore School of Electrical Engineering in Philadelphia, would show the world that vacuum-tube machines were indeed expensive but entirely feasible.

The start of World War II had immediate consequences for Zuse; he was called to serve in the army, and was for six months deployed on the Eastern front. With the help of Kurt Pannke, Zuse tried to obtain a transfer to Berlin in order to continue his work on the next comput-

ing machine. Helmut Schreyer, who worked as an engineer at the university, also tried to obtain Zuse's discharge by offering to build the military an automatic air-defense machine that could be operational in two years. His offer was met with the sardonic reply that the war would be over by then. Finally Zuse's previous superiors at Henschel were able to obtain his transfer to the Henschel airplane factory in Berlin-Adlershof, where he was hired to make the calculations necessary to correct the wings of the "flying bombs" (now called cruise missiles) being built in Berlin.

In 1940 Zuse started working for the Special Section F at the Henschel factory. During the next five years he developed the machines S1 and S2. The latter could automatically measure some parameters of missile wings, transform the analog measurement into a digital number, and compute a correction to the wing based on these values. The earlier model, the S1, needed such numbers to be typed on a decimal keyboard. The S1 and S2 were probably the first digital computing machines used for factory process control. The measurement instrument used in the S2 was also almost certainly the first industrial analog-to-digital converter, although it was never used in real production. Both machines were, from the computational point of view, subsets of the machines described below. Their existence remained unknown to the public at large for many years after the war.

In 1940 Zuse put together the machine Z2, an experimental model that used an integer processor built out of relays and a mechanical memory cannibalized from the Z1. This machine helped Zuse convince the German Airspace Research Office (DLV in German) to partially finance the development of the successor to the Z1, the Z3, which would be built using only relays. The Z3 became operational in 1941. It had the same logical design of the Z1 but was built with electrical telephone relays.

Structure and Capabilities of the Z1 and Z3. The Z1 and Z3 worked with floating-point numbers (that is, numbers such as, for example, +12.654 with an integer and a fractional part). Zuse developed an internal numerical representation that strongly resembles the internal number format used in modern computers. Each number was stored separated in three parts: the sign of the number, the exponent of the number in twos complement notation, and the mantissa of the number. In order to handle each part, the processor of the Z1 and Z3 consisted of two main blocks, one for processing the exponents of numbers and one for processing the mantissas.

The two machines, Z1 and Z3, shared a common architecture. Their main components were:

1. the memory for storing numbers (sixty-four in total);

2. the processor for computing;

3. A punched tape for storing the sequence of program instructions; and

4. an input-output console.

The instructions were read from the tape and were executed one by one by the processor. The console allowed the user to enter decimal numbers with a decimal keyboard (similar to the keyboard of a cash register) while the results were shown in a panel with digits illuminated by lamps.

The instruction set of the Z1 and Z3 consisted of the four arithmetical operations (addition, subtraction, multiplication, and division) as well as the square root operation. There were four additional operations for reading and displaying results and for moving numbers between processor and memory. The Z3 was very much like an early electronic calculator of the 1970s but much slower; a multiplication required eighteen machine cycles and was executed in three seconds.

Using the instruction set mentioned above, it was possible to process any arithmetical formula of the kind used in engineering applications. However, the instruction set did not provide a conditional branching instruction, so that it was relatively difficult, although not unfeasible, to perform more complex computations. Also, the two ends of the punched tape could be bound to form a loop, so that repeated execution of the same program was possible.

Zuse avoided the use of an excessive number of logical gates for the processor by relying on control units that worked as microsequencers, one for each command in the instruction set. A microsequencer consisted of a rotating arm that advanced one step in each cycle of the machine like a rotary dial. A clock (a rotating motor) provided the clock cycles needed to synchronize the machine. In the case of the Z3, the operating frequency was set at five cycles per second. Five times per second the rotating arm in a microsequencer activated the next step of the operation at hand. For example, in the case of multiplication, repeated addition and shifting of numbers were needed (as happens when two numbers are multiplied by hand). The eighteen partial operations needed were all started by a microsequencer with eighteen contacts for the rotary dial. The microsequencer can thus be thought of as a kind of hardwired program that reduced very complex instructions to a sequence of simple operations. Therefore, modifying the complete internal operation of the machine consisted only of rewiring the microsequencers without having to modify the rest of the processor. This resulted in a very efficient and flexible architecture, explaining how Konrad Zuse was able to build a machine that rivaled the British or American computers built during the same period, even with only a hundredth of the resources at his disposal.

During World War II, Zuse worked continuously for the Henschel factory but was able to start his own business in 1941. The Zuse Ingenieurbüro und Apparatebau, Berlin, was the first company founded with the sole purpose of developing computers. The Z3's successful demonstration brought Zuse a contract with the German aircraft research unit (DLV) to develop a still larger computer, the Z4. This machine had a very similar design to the Z3 but would have 1,024 memory words instead of only 64. The machine was built and was almost operational by early 1945, when Russian troops approached Berlin.

War's Aftermath and the Plankalkül. Zuse fled with the Z4 before Berlin fell to the victorious Soviet army. One of his collaborators was able to obtain train transport for the machine, somehow managing to smuggle it as a valuable military asset. The Z1 and Z3 had already been destroyed by air raids during the war, so that the Z4 constituted the only asset of Zuse's company. After several detours Zuse established himself in Bavaria, where he would survive the following years by painting, consulting, and attempting to restart his company. During this period of forced inactivity, he finished his manuscript on the Plankalkül, a remarkable document first published in the 1970s.

The Plankalkül (calculus of programs) was the first high-level programming language conceived in the world. It was designed by Zuse between 1943 and 1945, that is, at a time when the first computers were being built in the United States, United Kingdom, and Germany. It represents one of the major achievements in the history of ideas in the computer field, although it was first implemented in 1999 by a team of researchers in Berlin.

The Plankalkül corresponded to Zuse's mature conception of how to build a computer and how to allocate the total computing work to the hardware and software of a machine. Zuse called the first computers he constructed "algebraic machines" in contrast to "logistic machines." The former were specially built to handle scientific computations while the latter could deal with both scientific and symbolic processing. Zuse's "logistic machine" was never built, but its design called for a one-bit word memory and a processor that could compute only the basic logic operations (conjunction, disjunction, and negation). It was a minimalistic computer in which the memory consisted of a long chain of bits, which could be grouped in any desired form to represent numbers, characters, arrays, and so on. In some ways the logistic machine resembles Alan Turing's proposal of 1936, later known as the Turing Machine.

The Plankalkül was the software counterpart of the logistic machine. Complex structures could be built from elementary ones, the simplest being a single bit. Also, sequences of instructions could be grouped into subroutines and functions so that the user dealt only with a powerful high-level instruction set that masked the complexity of the underlying hardware. The Plankalkül heavily exploited the concept of modularity, which later became so important in computer science: Several layers of software made the hardware invisible for the programmer. The hardware itself was to be simple and only able to execute the minimal instruction set.

In Plankalkül the programmer uses variables to perform computations. There are no separate variable declarations: Any variable can be used in any part of the program, and its type is written together with the name. Variable assignment is done as in modern programming languages where a new value overwrites the old value. Many operations are those used in modern programming languages (addition, subtraction, and so on).

Plankalkül is universal. It can deal with conditional instructions of the "if then else" type and makes available an iteration operator W that repeats the execution of a sequence of instructions until a loop-breaking condition is met. Using these constructs, any kind of computation can be coded with Plankalkül.

Although Zuse published some minor papers about the Plankalkül and tried to make it known in Germany, the language fell into oblivion. The main problems were its ambitious scope, the large variety of instructions that it contained, a modular architecture that called for incremental compilation, and the presence of dynamical structures and functionals. Some aspects of the definition were not quite clean, and the absence of type checking would have made it extremely difficult to debug. A practical implementation of the Plankalkül certainly requires a major revision of Zuse's draft of 1945. However, Plankalkül was very much ahead of its time considering that many of the concepts on which it was based were rediscovered much later. It would take many more years for programming languages to achieve Plankalkül's level of sophistication.

Rebirth of Zuse's Company. After World War II, Zuse's company was revitalized when Professor Eduard Stiefel, from the Technical University of Zurich (ETH), drove to Bavaria to see the refurbished Z4 in operation. He decided to rent the machine for his university. The Z4 was installed in Zurich in 1950, several months before the first UNIVAC was delivered in the United States, and was therefore the first commercial computer in operation in the world. For several years the Z4 was the only computer operating in continental Europe. The machine had the same logical structure as the Z3 but contained more memory and an expanded instruction set. It was used for many years at the ETH and is now part of the history of computing exhibition of Deutsches Museum in Munich. It is

the sole Zuse machine built before 1945 that has been preserved.

Zuse's company (with the new name Zuse KG) flourished after the war, and many other machines were built. They were all numbered progressively (e.g., Z5, Z11) according to their introduction. For some years Zuse continued building relay computers and even argued in favor of micromechanical elements. Gradually, however, the electronic components were miniaturized, their reliability increased, and with the dominance of American companies in this field, Zuse KG had no choice but to develop vacuum-tube and transistor-based machines. The first Zuse KG transistorized computer was the Z23, a commercial success: Eighty machines were delivered in Germany and eighteen to other countries. The German Research Foundation actively promoted the machine and subsidized its introduction in universities, where it was used to jump-start most of the computer science education in universities.

The Z23 and the Z22 (built with vacuum tubes) were remarkable in that they constituted the first radical departure from the architecture of all previous Zuse machines. Their internal structure consisted of serial registers, which allowed the use of fewer components. The number of instructions was kept to a minimum. A compiler allowed programmers to write code with a syntax that was in between assembly code and a high-level programming language. After the Z22 and Z23, Zuse would often confide that the new machines were being designed not by him but by his engineers.

Another important development, and Zuse's last encore, was the introduction of the Graphomat in 1961, a plotter that could be used by architects and geologists to generate diagrams and drawings. The Graphomat could be connected to the Zuse computers and used gears that provided smooth, continuous movement in each direction. The gears were designed by Zuse himself.

The Z23 and the Graphomat were successful, but the development of the next line of computers proved too costly. Eventually the dominance of the U.S. computer industry in Europe, as well as the late adoption of a fully electronic design, brought financial difficulties to Zuse KG. The company was sold first to Brown Boveri and Company in 1962 and later to Siemens. Production of the Zuse series of computers was eventually stopped. Zuse retired after the Siemens takeover and received retirement benefits. In the ensuing years he continued writing, applying for patents, and making a case for his place in the history of computing.

In retrospect it can be said that Konrad Zuse's greatest achievement was the development of a family of fully digital, floating-point, programmable machines that were built in almost total intellectual isolation from 1936 to 1945. His dream was to create the small computer for business and scientific applications. He worked single-mindedly during many years to achieve this objective. His 1941 patent application for the computing machine Z3 was refused in 1967 by a German judge as it was deemed to lack "inventiveness." The decision on the application was delayed so long, firstly, because of the war, and secondly, because a number of major computer companies battled against Zuse in court. Zuse, however, always considered himself the one and true inventor of the computer, and his public statements on this subject demonstrated some bitterness about his lack of recognition in other countries.

Epilogue. Konrad Zuse married Gisela Brandes on 6 January 1945. Gisela gave birth to their first son a few months later, and four more children followed in the ensuing years. But Konrad Zuse was not a family man: Over the years his sole obsession was starting and leading his company. After his retirement he was much decorated in Germany, receiving, among other distinctions, the Federal Cross of Merit and the Siemens Ring. He was named a fellow of the Computer History Museum in California in 1999. Several honorary doctorates, as well as a professorship, were bestowed on him. Furthermore, the most important prize in Germany in the field of computer science bears Konrad Zuse's name. Zuse died on 18 December 1995, at the age of eighty-five.

His early machines have been reconstructed: A model of the Z1 was built in the 1980s by Zuse himself and is on display at the German Technology Museum in Berlin. The Z3 was reconstructed by Zuse's engineers in the 1960s and is on display at Deutsches Museum in Munich. A new functional replica of the Z3 was built in Berlin and is on display at the Zuse Museum in Hünfeld, Germany, where several of Zuse KG's computers are also housed.

It has been frequently said and written that the computer is a by-product of World War II, or at least that its birth was catalyzed by the events surrounding that conflagration. In the case of Konrad Zuse this is only partially true. The inspiration for his first computing machine, the Z1, predates the war. The six months that Zuse spent on the Eastern front in 1939–1940 were certainly an interruption of the project he already had been working on for almost three years. If the war had not started, the Z3 computing machine would have been built sooner. But once hostilities broke out, Zuse at least was able to convince the military establishment that computing machines were useful for aerodynamical numerical calculations. The successful demonstration of the Z2 prototype led to a contract with the German Airspace Research Office (DLV), which financed most of the construction of the Z3. Once the Z3 was operational Zuse built the special-purpose machine S1 and also started building the more powerful computing

machine he had being dreaming about all those years, the Z4. The construction of the Z4 was done under a war contract financed by the German military until 1945.

Although almost no one in Germany fully understood the importance of Zuse's work, at least the people in charge of the strategic management of aeronautic research and development recognized the relevance of fast computations. It is noteworthy that Zuse could leave the Eastern front and be freed of day-to-day responsibilities at the Henschel Werke in order to attend to his own company. This would not have happened if the military experts had not thought that his company was useful and necessary for the war effort.

Konrad Zuse was no resistance hero, but he certainly never tried to gain office or position himself in academic politics. While professors and researchers at German universities, especially at the Technische Hochschule Charlottenburg, flocked to the Nazi party in order to advance in their professions, Zuse's own career was cut short by the war. Unfortunately, not much is known about his political views at the time. In his memoirs Zuse deals with the regime and politics during the war in just a few paragraphs. Ideologically he was very much impressed by Oswald Spengler's theory of the decline of Western civilization. He continued to mention Spengler in his late years.

It was probably Konrad Zuse's personal tragedy that he conceived all the elements of the computer sooner and more elegantly than any other computer pioneer but was living in Germany when the country was on the path to self-destruction. Outside of Germany, and outside a very small circle for that matter, nobody took notice of the Z1, Z2, Z3, and Z4. The S1 and S2 were secret machines. Zuse's work was not rediscovered until the late 1940s, and by then it was too late for his machines to have had any serious impact on the design and construction of modern computers. Zuse's work was worth a footnote, at most, in early scholarly books about the history of computing. This has changed since the 1990s, as more has become known about the life and work of this most remarkable computer pioneer.

BIBLIOGRAPHY

Konrad Zuse's notebooks and documents were sold by his widow in 2006 to the Deutsches Museum in Munich, where they are stored in the archives.

WORKS BY ZUSE

Der Plankalkül. Technical Report 63. Bonn: Gesellschaft für Mathematik und Datenverarbeitung, 1972.

Ansätze einer Theorie des Netzautomaten. Leipzig: Barth, 1975.

Petri-Netze aus der Sicht des Ingenieurs. Braunschweig; Wiesbaden: Vieweg, 1980.

The Computer: My Life. Berlin: Springer-Verlag, 1993.

OTHER WORKS

Peters, Arno. *Was ist und wie verwirklicht sich: Computer-Sozialismus: Gespräche mit Konrad Zuse.* Berlin: Neues Leben, 2000.

Rojas, Raul. "Konrad Zuse's Legacy: The Architecture of the Z1 and Z3." *IEEE Annals of the History of Computing* 19, no. 2 (1997): 5–16.

Raul Rojas

ZYGMUND, ANTONI

ZYGMUND, ANTONI (*b.* Warsaw, Poland, 26 December 1900; *d.* Chicago, Illinois, 30 May 1992), *mathematics, harmonic analysis, trigonometric series, singular integrals.*

The mathematician Zygmund was one of the twentieth century's leading exponents of Fourier analysis. He was a major figure in taking the subject from one to several variables and in the creation of a theory of singular integrals.

Early Life and Career. Zygmund's schooling was interrupted by World War I when the family moved from Poland to Ukraine. On his return to Warsaw he found there was no opportunity to study astronomy, his first interest, so he switched to mathematics at the University of Warsaw. There he became attached to Aleksander Rajchman and Stanislaw Saks. He learned Riemann's theory of trigonometric series from Rajchman and Saks and, after taking his doctorate in 1923, wrote several research papers with them. A Rockefeller Fellowship enabled him to spend the academic year 1929–1930 in England with Godfrey H. Hardy at Oxford University and John E. Littlewood at Cambridge University; he also met and worked with Raymond E. A. C. Paley that year. Zygmund found the visit to England was a tremendous stimulus. He went on to write five papers with Paley and a joint paper with Paley and Norbert Wiener on lacunary and random series. On his return to Poland he became a professor of mathematics at Stefan Batory University in Wilno. There he met Jozef Marcinkiewicz, who was then a student but soon became a collaborator with Zygmund.

Even in the early 1930s, Zygmund showed his distaste for manifestations of anti-Semitism, which eventually cost him his job in a politically motivated purge of the university in 1931. Hardy, Littlewood, Henri Lebesgue in France, and other eminent mathematicians wrote in protest, and Zygmund was reinstated. It was during his time at Wilno that Zygmund wrote the first edition of his book *Trigonometric Series* (1935). This volume was so complete in its treatment that it was revised and reprinted by Cambridge University Press in 1959 and was reprinted

six times, to become the standard work in its subject. The 1930s were productive for Zygmund in many ways, but they ended in tragedy. Zygmund and Marcinkiewicz joined the Polish army, but the partition of Poland between the Nazis and the Soviets saw Wilno fall in the Russian zone. Many of the Polish Officer Corps were rounded up by the Russians and massacred at Katyn in Poland, and most likely Marcinkiewicz was among them. Saks and Rajchman were murdered by the Nazis, and so in a brief and surely terrifying period of time, Zygmund lost most of his collaborators and close friends.

Given Zygmund's international reputation and the efforts of the mathematicians Jerzy Neyman and Norbert Wiener, Zygmund was able to get out of Europe, and starting in 1940 he survived the war teaching at Mount Holyoke College in South Hadley, Massachusetts. In 1945 he transferred to the University of Pennsylvania in Philadelphia, and two years later he moved to the University of Chicago, where he stayed for the rest of his career. There he joined a remarkably strong Mathematics Department put together by Marshall Stone, and the result was a golden period for Zygmund, marked most famously by his collaboration with Alberto Calderón. It was in the 1950s that he and Calderón formulated the theory of singular integrals that now carries their names. A few years later, Elias Stein came to Chicago as a doctoral student of Zygmund's and began another remarkable collaboration. All told, Zygmund had thirty-five students, many of whom went on to have distinguished careers. Robert Fefferman described Zygmund's own career as being characterized by "his tremendous desire to work with people of the greatest mathematical ability, and his absolute devotion to those people."

Zygmund received many honors in his lifetime. They included the National Medal of Science in 1986, the highest honor awarded by the U.S. government for work in science, and membership in the U.S. National Academy of Sciences (1961) and other national science academies, including those of Poland, Argentina, and Spain.

Trigonometric Series. Zygmund's early work was on trigonometric series. These had been introduced by Bernhard Riemann in 1854 as a significant generalization of the usual Fourier series. As Zygmund learned from Rajchman, the key questions here concern the uniqueness of the series and its local properties (such as continuity at a point). Uniqueness requires the nontrivial result that a trigonometric series that converges to zero everywhere has all of its coefficients zero (and is therefore the trivial series). This leads to the study of sets E such that any trigonometric series that converges to zero outside E is necessarily the trivial series. Such sets have measure zero, so their study requires new analytic tools, and Zygmund made a profound investigation of these sets.

The book *Trigonometric Series* owes much to the influences of Saks and Marcinkiewicz. Integrable functions of one variable have an averaging property that is easy to generalize to functions of n variables. However, Zygmund showed in 1927, by using a construction of Otton Nikodym, that the generalization is false in dimensions higher than 1, and Saks then showed that even modest generalizations will fail. Zygmund was able to show, however, that the generalization can be made to work for functions of several variables that are in the class L^p for some p. In later work with Marcinkiewicz, the class of functions for which the generalization holds was widened considerably.

This work undoubtedly stimulated Zygmund's interest in extending the results of classical one variable harmonic function theory to several variables, but there was a major obstacle. Single variable harmonic function theory is almost interchangeable with single variable complex function theory; indeed, that was the key insight of Riemann. To create a deep theory of harmonic functions in several variables required building up the theory of functions of several real variables, and this was to be the theme of Zygmund's work with Calderón.

Calderón and Zygmund embarked on the task of producing a n-real variable version of the Hilbert transform. Their paper, "On the Existence of Singular Integrals," published in *Acta Mathematica* in 1956, was described by Stein in these terms: "There is probably no paper in the last fifty years which has had such widespread influence in analysis" (1998, p. 1133). They used ideas of Marcinkiewicz (as Zygmund was later to acknowledge) and a number of powerful original ideas to establish the existence of the relevant singular integrals. Both the techniques and the results of this paper exerted a considerable influence on the future direction of work in this field.

Singular Integrals. The integral operators in which they were interested have their roots in the classical theory of partial differential equations. In pursuing this connection, Calderón and Zygmund were led to a theory of symbols, with implications for the theory of linear partial differential operators. Calderón pushed for a version of the theory of singular integrals that applied to manifolds, and the breakthrough came with his student Robert Seeley's discovery that the symbol is actually a function on the cotangent space of the manifold. This allowed their theory to merge with the ideas of Russian mathematician Israel M. Gelfand about elliptic operators on manifolds, and Seeley's calculus was very useful in the first proof of the Atiyah-Singer index theorem, undoubtedly one of the major mathematical events of the century. A profusion of

work by many authors in many countries saw the theory of singular integrals become a major part of a much broader theory of what are called pseudo-differential operators. Singular integrals, however, remain central to the study of real functions of several variables, and the work of Zygmund and his collaborators in the Chicago school of analysis decisively deepened that whole branch of mathematics.

Trigonometric Series was first published in 1935 and in a third edition in 2002. The book is remarkable for both its thoroughness and its many highlights, among which is the Marcinkiewicz interpolation theorem, which was to play an important part in the creation of the theory of singular integrals. It applies to operators of weak type, and singular integrals on the space L^1 are of weak type. The Marcinkiewicz integral is another highlight, and here it illuminates the L^p theory of the Hilbert transform, which is a preview of the Calderón-Zygmund theory. Zygmund also drew on his time with Hardy, Littlewood, and Paley in writing the book, and the Hardy-Littlewood maximal theorem is central to it. Indeed, it is Zygmund, Calderón, and Stein who gave the theorem its central role in analysis. It led Zygmund to deepen the approach to Fourier series of a single variable by using complex variable methods, and it has implications for the study of the Hardy spaces H^p, all of which are described in the book. Zygmund himself had a particular liking for the material on the Littelwood-Paley functional, which applied to a function produces a new function with an L^p norm comparable in size with the L^p norm of the original function. This makes it very useful, and Zygmund used it to study Hardy spaces. Later it was given a simple conceptual proof using the theory of singular integrals, an important moment in the generalization of the single variable theory to the several variables theory that was one of Zygmund's most profound achievements.

BIBLIOGRAPHY

Selected Papers of Antoni Zygmund, *cited below, contains a complete bibliography of Zygmund's published works.*

WORKS BY ZYGMUND

With Alberto Calderón. "On the Existence of Certain Singular Integrals." *Acta Mathematica* 78 (1956): 289–309.

Selected Papers of Antoni Zygmund. Edited by Andrzej Hulanicki, Przemyslav Wojtaszczyk, and Wieslaw Zelazko. 3 vols. Dordrecht, Netherlands; Boston: Kluwer Academic, 1989. Includes a complete bibliography of Zygmund's published works.

Trigonometric Series, 3rd ed. Cambridge, U.K.; New York: Cambridge University Press, 2002.